MANAGEMENT
PRINCIPLES AND PRACTICES

ELEVENTH EDITION

RICKY W. GRIFFIN

Texas A&M University

 SOUTH-WESTERN
CENGAGE Learning·

Australia • Brazil • Japan • Korea • Mexico • Singapore • Spain • United Kingdom • United States

SOUTH-WESTERN
CENGAGE Learning·

Management: Principles and Practices, Eleventh International Edition
Ricky W. Griffin

Vice President of Editorial/Business: Jack W. Calhoun

Publisher: Erin Joyner

Executive Editor: Scott Person

Senior Developmental Editor: Julia Chase

Senior Editorial Assistant: Ruth Belanger

Marketing Manager: Jonathan Monahan

Senior Marketing Communications Manager: Jim Overly

Marketing Coordinator: Julia Tucker

Production Manager: Jean Buttrom

Media Editor: Rob Ellington

Rights Acquisition Director: Audrey Pettengill

Rights Acquisition Specialist, Text and Image: John Hill

Manufacturing Planner: Ron Montgomery

Senior Art Director: Tippy McIntosh

Cover Designer: Patti Hudepohl

Internal Designer: PreMediaGlobal

Cover Photo Credits:

   B/W Image: iStockphoto

   Color Image: Shutterstock Images/Andresr

Library of Congress Control Number: 2011942164

International Edition:

ISBN-13: 978-1-111-96972-1

ISBN-10: 1-111-96972-8

Cengage Learning International Offices

Asia
www.cengageasia.com
tel: (65) 6410 1200

Australia/New Zealand
www.cengage.com.au
tel: (61) 3 9685 4111

Brazil
www.cengage.com.br
tel: (55) 11 3665 9900

India
www.cengage.co.in
tel: (91) 11 4364 1111

Latin America
www.cengage.com.mx
tel: (52) 55 1500 6000

UK/Europe/Middle East/Africa
www.cengage.co.uk
tel: (44) 0 1264 332 424

Represented in Canada by Nelson Education, Ltd.
www.nelson.com
tel: (416) 752 9100 / (800) 668 0671

Cengage Learning is a leading provider of customized learning solutions with office locations around the globe, including Singapore, the United Kingdom, Australia, Mexico, Brazil, and Japan. Locate your local office at: **www.cengage.com/global**

For product information: **www.cengage.com/international**
Visit your local office: **www.cengage.com/global**
Visit our corporate website: **www. cengage.com**

Printed in Canada
1 2 3 4 5 6 7 16 15 14 13 12

Brief Contents

Contents

Preface

Since the publication of its first edition in 1984, around two million students have used *Management: Principles and Practices* in preparation for their careers in business. *Management: Principles and Practices* continues to be used in hundreds of universities, graduate programs, community colleges, and management development programs throughout the world today. Indeed, the last edition of the book was used in over 40 countries and translated into several foreign languages.

I'm extremely proud that the book has grown in popularity every year since its initial publication. In this eleventh edition, I have retained all the elements that have contributed to the book's success in the past while also taking a clear look toward the future—the future of business, of management, and of textbooks.

Writing a survey book poses a number of challenges. First, because it is a survey, it has to be comprehensive. Second, it has to be accurate and objective. Third, because management is a real activity, the book has to be relevant. Fourth, it has to be timely and up-to-date. And fifth, it must be as interesting and as engaging as possible. Feedback on previous editions of the text has always suggested that I have done an effective job of meeting these goals. In this edition, I think these goals have been met even more effectively.

I believe that current and previous users of *Management: Principles and Practices* will be pleased with how we have retained the essential ingredients of a comprehensive management textbook while adding a variety of new elements and perspectives. I also believe that those new to this edition will be drawn to the solid foundations of management theory and practice combined with new and exciting material.

HIGHLIGHTS AND IMPROVEMENTS IN THE ELEVENTH EDITION

The eleventh edition of *Management: Principles and Practices* is a substantive revision of the earlier work. Rather than simply adding the "hot topics" of the moment, I continue to thoroughly revise this book with the long-term view in mind. There are significant revisions of key chapters; an increased emphasis on the service sector, ethics, global management, and information technology; and an integrated organization of chapters. These changes reflect what I believe, and what reviewers and employers have confirmed, students will need to know as they enter a brand new world of management. In addition, several integrated pedagogical features such as "Concept Check" will also prove to be invaluable.

Revisions in the Eleventh Edition

While the eleventh edition represents a comprehensive revision of the previous edition, there are also a number of specific changes that have been made. These include:

1. The text has been revised in numerous places to reflect and discuss the slow and sluggish recovery from the recent recession.
2. The text covers the unrest in the Middle East and its implications for business.
3. There is also coverage of the Japanese earthquake and tsunami and their impact on global business operations.

4. All data and statistics related to small business, international business, unionization, executive compensation, and other areas of business have been updated to the most current information available.

5. Over half of the chapter opening cases ("Management in Action") are new; the others have all been revised and updated.

6. Over half of the end-of-book cases ("Management at Work") are new; the others have all been revised and updated.

7. The eleventh edition includes a total of 44 boxed inserts (two per chapter). Thirty of these boxes are all new, and the others have been revised and updated.

8. There are over 150 new examples in the eleventh edition. In addition, those examples retained from the previous edition have all been checked for currency and continued applicability.

9. The latest research on international business, entrepreneurship, strategic management, decision making, organization design, organization change, individual behavior, leadership, teams, motivation, control, information technology, productivity, and quality management has been cited and integrated throughout the text.

10. All supplements have been updated to match these text changes, including the CourseMate website.

To get access, visit CengageBrain.com

Integrated Coverage

Many textbooks set certain material off from the rest of the text in a separate section at the end of the book or a website called "Emerging Trends," "Special Challenges," or something similar. New and emerging topics, and other material that doesn't easily fit anywhere else, are covered in such a section. Unfortunately, by setting those topics apart in this way, the material often gets ignored or receives low-priority treatment.

But I decided several editions back that if this material was really worth having in the book at all, it needed to be fully merged with the core material. Thus, all material—both traditional and contemporary—is integrated throughout the text in order to provide more uniform and cohesive coverage of the entire field of management. This framework also helps to streamline the book's overall organization into six logical and symmetrical parts. Because reviewers and students have responded so favorably to this approach, it has been retained in the eleventh edition. Furthermore, cross-referencing strengthens the integrated coverage throughout the text.

Logical Chapter Organization

This integrated approach to management also results in a logical and very effective chapter organization. Part 1 introduces the field of management, while Part 2 focuses on the environment of management. The remaining four parts cover the basic managerial functions of planning and decision making, controlling, organizing, and leading.

FEATURES OF THE BOOK
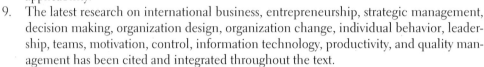

Basic Themes

Several key themes are prominent in this edition of *Management: Principles and Practices*. One critical theme is the ethical scrutiny under which managers work today. While the book has always included substantial coverage of ethics and social responsibility, even more attention has been devoted this time to topics such as corporate governance, ethical leadership, and the proper role of auditing. Another continuing theme is the global character of the field of management, which is reinforced throughout the book by examples and cases. A third key theme, information technology, is covered in detail in Chapter 13. Still another theme is the balance of theory and practice: Managers need to have a sound basis for their decisions, but the theories that provide that basis must be grounded in reality. Throughout the book I explain the theoretical frameworks that guide managerial activities, and provide illustrations and examples of how and when those theories do and do not work. A fifth theme is that management is a generic activity not confined to large businesses. I use examples and discuss management in both small and large businesses as well as in not-for-profit organizations.

A Pedagogical System That Works

The pedagogical elements built into *Management: Principles and Practices*, Eleventh Edition continue to be effective learning and teaching aids for students and instructors.

- Learning objectives preview key themes at the start of every chapter. Key terms and concepts are highlighted in red type, and most terms are defined in the margin near where they are discussed. Effective figures, tables, and photographs with their own detailed captions help bring the material to life.

- Another popular feature is called "Concept Check." Each major section in every chapter concludes with two questions tied back to that section. The first question tests recall of a basic fact, definition, or concept. The second is more thought provoking and analytical in nature. These questions allow students to continuously assess their mastery of the subject as they are reading and studying the material.

- Three kinds of questions at the end of every chapter are designed to test different levels of student understanding. "Questions for Review" ask students to recall specific information, "Questions for Analysis" ask students to integrate and synthesize material, and "Questions for Application" ask students to apply what they've learned to their own experiences.

- Each chapter also includes useful skill-development exercises, which can be found at the end of the book. These exercises give students insight into how they approach various management situations and how they can work to improve their management skills in the future. The exercises are derived from the overall managerial skills framework developed in Chapter 1. For this edition, many of the exercises were replaced or substantially revised.

Applications That Keep Students Engaged

To fully appreciate the role and scope of management in contemporary society, it is important to see examples and illustrations of how concepts work in the real world. I rely heavily on fully researched examples to illustrate real-world applications. They vary in length, and all were carefully reviewed for their timeliness. To give the broadest view possible, I include examples of both traditional management roles and nontraditional roles; profit-seeking businesses and nonprofits; large corporations and small businesses; manufacturers and services; and international and U.S. situations.

Furthermore, in this edition I have developed a better balance of large and established businesses (such as Home Depot, Coca-Cola, Boeing, Intel, and General Electric) and new, emerging businesses (such as Google, Starbucks, Video Game Corporation, Facebook, Urban Outfitters, and Abercrombie & Fitch).

Other applications include:

- Opening incidents at the beginning of every chapter. These brief vignettes, titled "Management in Action," draw the student into the chapter with a real-world scenario that introduces a particular management theme. Companies highlighted include Netflix, Bigfoot Entertainment, Abercrombie & Fitch, Wegmans, and many more.

- A companion end-of-book feature called "You Make the Call." This feature is tied back to each chapter-opening incident; it requires the student to play the role of a consultant, a manager, or other stakeholder in the organization featured earlier. Students are asked to comment, critique, or make suggestions about how well the business is doing and/or what it needs to do differently.

- Call-out quotations. Spread throughout each chapter, these quotations provide real insights into how managers and other experts see the world of business as it relates to the topic at hand.

- Boxed features. Each chapter includes two boxed features. These boxes are intended to depart briefly from the flow of the chapter to highlight or extend especially interesting or emerging points and issues. There are five types of featured boxes represented throughout the text:

 *Ethically Speaking* (the increasing importance of ethics in management)

 *A World of Difference* (the role of diversity in organizations)

 *The More Things Change* (a variety of current topics, including current economic challenges, the energy crisis, and workplace security issues post-9/11)

 Technically Speaking (the role and impact of technology in business)

 Greening the Business Environment (the impact of sustainable, eco-friendly approaches to business)

- End-of-book cases. Each chapter has a detailed case study at the end of the book, called "Management at Work," written especially for the context of this book. These cases represent companies familiar to students, including Facebook, IKEA, Intel, Amazon, Wikipedia, and many more.

I would also like to invite your feedback on this book. If you have any questions, suggestions, or issues to discuss, please feel free to contact me. The most efficient way to reach me is through e-mail at *rgriffin@tamu.edu.*

Ricky W. Griffin

Acknowledgments

I am frequently asked by my colleagues why I write textbooks, and my answer is always, "Because I enjoy it." I've never enjoyed writing a book more than this one. For me, writing a textbook is a challenging and stimulating activity that brings with it a variety of rewards. My greatest reward continues to be the feedback I get from students and instructors about how much they like this book.

I owe an enormous debt to many different people for helping me create *Managment: Principles and Practices*. My colleagues at Texas A&M University have helped create a wonderful academic climate. The rich and varied culture at Texas A&M makes it a pleasure to go to the office every day.

The fine team of professionals at Cengage Learning has also been instrumental in the success of this book. Erin Joyner, Scott Person, Julia Chase, Jennifer Ziegler, Karunakaran Gunasekaran, Christina Ciaramella, Tippy McIntosh, Jonathan Monahan, and Jim Overly were instrumental in the production of this edition. Ron Librach also provided valuable assistance with his work on the cases and boxed inserts in this edition. Many reviewers have played a critical role in the continuous evolution and improvement of this project. They examined my work in detail and with a critical eye. I would like to tip my hat to the following reviewers, whose imprint can be found throughout this text:

Pamela Acuff
University of Nebraska–Omaha

Ramon J. Aldag
University of Wisconsin

Dr. Raymond E. Alie
Western Michigan University

Roanne Angiello
Bergen Community College

William P. Anthony
Florida State University

Jeanne Aurelio
Stonehill College

Jay B. Barney
Ohio State University

Richard Bartlett
Muskingum Area Technical College

Michael Bento
Owens Community College

John D. Bigelow
Boise State University

Bruce Bloom
DeVry University–Chicago

Allen Bluedorn
University of Missouri

Thomas M. Bock
The DeVry Institute of Technology

Henry C. Bohleke
Tarrant County College

Marv Borglett
University of Maryland

Gunther S. Boroschek
University of Massachusetts–Boston Harbor Campus

Jennifer Bott
Ball State University

John Brady
Indiana Tech

Paula Brown
Northern Illinois University

Dean Bruce
Northwest College

Gerald E. Calvasina
University of North Carolina–Charlotte

Joseph Cantrell
DeAnza College

George R. Carnahan
Northern Michigan University

Bruce Charnov
Hofstra University

Ron Cheek
University of New Orleans

Anwar Chowdhury
DeVry University

Thomas G. Christoph
Clemson University

Charles W. Cole
University of Oregon

Elizabeth Cooper
University of Rhode Island

C. Brad Cox
Midlands Technical College

Carol Cumber
South Dakota State University

Joan Dahl
California State University–Northridge

Carol Danehower
University of Memphis

Roger Dean
Washington and Lee University

Satish Deshpande
Western Michigan University

Gregory G. Dess
University of Kentucky

Ron DiBattista
Johnson & Wales University

Gary N. Dicer
University of Tennessee

Nicholas Dietz
State University of New York—Farmingdale

Thomas J. Dougherty
University of Missouri

Shad Dowlatshahi
University of Wisconsin—Platteville

John Drexler Jr.
Oregon State University

Joe Eassa
Palm Beach Atlantic University

Stan Elsea
Kansas State University

Douglas A. Elvers
University of South Carolina

Jim Fairbank
West Virginia University

Dan Farrell
Western Michigan University

Gerald L. Finch
Universidad Internacional del Ecuador and Universidad San Francisco de Quito

Charles Flaherty
University of Minnesota

Marcy Fusilier
Northwestern State University

Ari Ginsberg
New York University Graduate School of Business

Norma N. Givens
Fort Valley State University

David Glew
University of North Carolina–Wilmington

George Goerner
Mohawk Valley Community College

Carl Gooding
Georgia Southern College

George J. Gore
University of Cincinnati

Bill Gray
San Diego City College

Jonathan Gueverra
Lesley College

Stanley D. Guzell Jr.
Youngstown State University

John Hall
University of Florida

Mark A. Hammer
Washington State University

Barry Hand
Indiana State University

Paul Harmon
University of Utah

Roxanne Helm
Azusa Pacific University

Stephanie Henagan
Louisiana State University

Nathan Himelstein
Essex County College; New Jersey Institute of Technology

John Hughes
Texas Tech University

J. G. Hunt
Texas Tech University

John H. Jackson
University of Wyoming

Neil W. Jacobs
University of Denver

Arthur G. Jago
University of Missouri

Madge Jenkins
Lima Technical College

Kathy Jones
University of North Dakota

Gopol Joshi
Central Missouri State University

Norman F. Kallaus
University of Iowa

Ben L. Kedia
University of Memphis

Joan Keeley
Washington State University

Thomas L. Keon
University of Central Florida

Charles C. Kitzmiller
Indian River Community College

Barbara Kovach
Rutgers University

William R. LaFollete
Ball State University

Kenneth Lawrence
New Jersey Institute of Technology

Cynthia Lengnick-Hall
University of Texas–San Antonio

Clayton G. Lifto
Kirkwood Community College

John E. Mack
Salem State University

Elaine Madden
Anne Arundel Community College

Myrna P. Mandell
California State University–Northridge

Patricia M. Manninen
North Shore Community College

Thomas Martin
University of Nebraska–Omaha

Barbara J. Marting
University of Southern Indiana

Lisa McConnell
Oklahoma State University

Melvin McKnight
Northern Arizona University

Wayne A. Meinhart
Oklahoma State University

Sandy Miles
Murray State University

Aratchige Molligoda
Drexel University

Behnam Nakhai
Millersville University of Pennsylvania

Robert Nale
Coastal Carolina University

Linda L. Neider
University of Miami

Mary Lippitt Nichols
University of Minnesota

Winston Oberg
Michigan State University

David Oliver
Edison College

Michael Olivette
Syracuse University

Eugene Owens
Western Washington University

Daewoo Park
Xavier University

Sheila Pechinski
University of Maine

Monique Pelletier
San Francisco State University

E. Leroy Plumlee
Western Washington University

Raymond F. Polchow
Muskingum Area Technical College

Boris Porkovich
San Francisco State University

Paul Preston
University of Texas–San Antonio

John M. Purcell
State University of New York–Farmingdale

James C. Quick
University of Texas–Arlington

Clint Relyea
Arkansas State University

Ralph Roberts
University of West Florida

Christopher Roe
DeVry University

Nick Sarantakas
Austin Community College

Khaled Sartawi
Fort Valley State University

Gene Schneider
Austin Community College

H. Schollhammer
University of California–Los Angeles

Diane R. Scott
Wichita State University

Mike Shaner
St. Louis University

Harvey Shore
University of Connecticut

Marc Siegall
California State University–Chico

Nicholas Siropolis
Cuyahoga Community College

Michael J. Stahl
University of Tennessee

Diane Stone
Ivy Technical State College

Marc Street
University of Tulsa

Charlotte D. Sutton
Auburn University

Kambiz Tabibzadeh
Eastern Kentucky University

Robert L. Taylor
University of Louisville

Mary Thibodeaux
University of North Texas

Joe Thomas
Middle Tennessee State University

Leslie User
Concordia University St. Paul

Sean Valentine
University of Wyoming

Robert D. Van Auken
University of Oklahoma

Billy Ward
The University of West Alabama

Richard Warner
Lehigh Carbon Community College

Liesl Wesson
Texas A&M University

Fred Williams
University of North Texas

Mary Williams
Community College of Southern Nevada

James Wilson
University of Texas–Pan American

Carl P. Zeithaml
University of Virginia

I would also like to make a few personal acknowledgments. The fine work of Rob Thomas, Roy Orbison, Lyle Lovett, Johnny Rivers, and the Nylons helped me make it through many late evenings and early mornings of work on the manuscript that became the book you hold in your hands. And Stephen King, Lee Child, James Lee Burke, Peter Straub, and Carl Barks provided me with a respite from my writings with their own.

Finally, there is the most important acknowledgment of all—my feelings for and gratitude to my family. My wife, Glenda, and our children, Dustin, Ashley, and Matt, are the foundation of my professional and personal life. They help me keep work and play in perspective and give meaning to everything I do. It is with all my love that I dedicate this book to them.

R.W.G.

For Glenda, my island, my rock, and the center of my universe
RWG

CHAPTER

Managing and the Manager's Job

LEARNING OBJECTIVES

After studying this chapter, you should be able to:

1. Describe the nature of management, define management and managers, and characterize their importance to contemporary organizations.

2. Identify and briefly explain the four basic management functions in organizations.

3. Describe the kinds of managers found at different levels and in different areas of the organization.

4. Identify the basic managerial roles played by managers and the skills they need to be successful.

5. Discuss the science and the art of management, describe how people become managers, and summarize the scope of management in organizations.

6. Characterize the new workplace that is emerging in organizations today.

MANAGEMENT IN ACTION   What Reed Hastings Has to Say for Himself

Back in 1997, Reed Hastings, a California entrepreneur between startup ventures, incurred a $40 late fee at Blockbuster. "It was six weeks late," he admits. "I had misplaced the cassette [and] I didn't want to tell my wife. . . . I was embarrassed about it." The next day he dropped off the VHS cassette and paid the late fee on his way to the gym. As it turns out, his itinerary for the day was quite opportune: In the middle of his workout, he recalls, "I realized [the gym] had a much better business model. You could pay $30 or $40 a month and work out as little or as much as you wanted."

Thus was born the idea for Netflix, although Hastings' immediate inspiration—the idea of signing up customers on a subscription basis—wasn't actually part of his original business plan. When Netflix launched in April 1998, its only innovations involved the convenience of ordering movies over the Internet and receiving and returning them by mail: Netflix merely rented movies for $4 apiece plus $2 for postage (and, yes, it charged late fees). Basically, the customer base consisted of people who wanted to watch movies without having to leave the house.[1]

The rental-by-mail model, admits Hastings, who's been Netflix's CEO since its inception, "worked more like Blockbuster. Some people liked it, but it wasn't very popular," and in 1999, Hastings and cofounder Marc Randolph decided to test a subscription-based model—unlimited

"Don't be afraid to change the model."

—NETFLIX CEO REED HASTINGS, 2009

rentals by mail for a flat fee and, perhaps most importantly, no due dates (and thus no late fees). Current customers were first offered the opportunity to shift from their pay-per-rental plans to subscription plans on a free-trial basis and then given the chance to renew the subscription plan on a paid basis. "We knew it wouldn't be terrible," says Hastings, "but we didn't know if it would be great." In the first month, however, 80 percent of Netflix users who'd tried the no-cost subscription plan had renewed on a paid basis.

"Having unlimited due dates and no late fees," said Hastings back in 2003, "has worked in a powerful way and now seems obvious, but at that time, we had no idea if customers would even build and use an online queue." The "queue," as any Netflix user will tell you, is the list of movies that the customer wants to watch. Netflix maintains your queue, follows your online directions in keeping it up to date, and automatically sends you the next movie you want each time you send one back.

The essence of queuing—and of the Netflix business model—is clearly convenience, and although the ability to enhance customer convenience, even when combined with cost savings, often gives a company a competitive advantage in its industry, it doesn't always

Reed Hastings, founder and CEO of Netflix, has done a great job of launching and managing his business. But like most managers, he has also made his share of mistakes as well.

REUTERS/Mike Cassese

have the industrywide effect that it's had in the case of Netflix. Marketing consultant Sally Aaron reminds us that Netflix "revolutionized how people rent movies," and its impact on the movie-rental industry was that of a *disruptive innovation:* Not only did the Netflix subscriber model improve the service provided by the industry in an unexpected way; ultimately it also weakened the competitive positions of companies already doing business in the industry—notably, Blockbuster. At the beginning of 2011, the onetime industry leader's market capitalization, which had peaked at $5 billion in 2002, was languishing at $35 million. At the same time, Netflix's market cap stood at nearly $10 billion and would reach nearly $15 billion by the middle of the year.

How had Hastings' upstart company managed to put itself in such an enviable position? For one thing, it got off to a fast start. In 1997, for example, when DVDs were just being test-marketed in the United States, Hastings and cofounder Marc Randolph decided that the new medium would eventually overtake videocassettes as the format of choice for both the home-movie industry and the home-movie renter. They were right, of course: By 2002, one in four U.S. households owned a DVD player, and the number today is close to nine in ten. (In any case, it would have cost about $4 to mail a videocassette both ways, compared to the $0.78 that it costs to ship a DVD disc back and forth.)

More importantly, as the first company to rent movies by mail, Netflix was the first to establish a rental-by-mail customer base. At first, says Hastings, "people thought the idea was crazy. But it was precisely because it was a contrarian idea that [it] enabled us to get ahead of our competitors." As Netflix has continued to expand and nurture its subscriber base, it's also generated both brand recognition and brand loyalty. "Netflix has customer loyalty. It's a passion brand," explains Hastings, who hastens to add that keeping customers happy is crucial "because the more someone uses Netflix, the more likely they are to stay with us."

Hastings admits that, back in 1999, "what gave us the courage to switch" from a pay-per-rental plan to a subscription plan "was the necessity to switch." It's not hard to pinpoint that "necessity": Netflix had to provide some form of customer satisfaction greater than the mere convenience of being able to consume movies without budging from the couch, and the switch to a subscription-based business model ultimately did much more than give customers the added benefit of freedom from late fees: It spurred a change in consumer behavior in the movie-rental business. From the outset, says Hastings, the goal at Netflix has been to become "a company like HBO that transforms the entertainment industry. . . . I've always thought [that] trying

to change consumer behavior is scary, and most companies that promote that fail. But when it works, like iPod"—and like Netflix—"it works big."

By 2005, Netflix had emerged from various skirmishes as the leader in the movie-rental industry, but tech analysts were already warning (in the words of Sally Aaron) that "the real battle in the movie-rental business will be in competing with VoD technology." Ironically, she predicted, *video on demand* (VoD)—systems that allow customers to choose both what and when to watch by delivering cinema-quality movies to computers or television sets—promised to be "a disruptive innovation, even to the startup Netflix."

As a rule, disruptive innovations change the conditions of an industry *in unexpected ways*, but it's hardly accurate to say that Hastings did not expect the arrival of VoD. "Movies over the Internet are coming," he said in 2005, "and at some point it will become big business. We started investing 1 percent to 2 percent of revenue every year in downloading [because] . . . we want to be ready when video-on-demand happens. That's why the company," he was quick to point out, "is called Netflix, not DVD-by-Mail." At the same time, however, although Netflix was actively researching VoD technology, Hastings remained reluctant to commit fully to the developing technology: "If I survey my customers and ask, 'Do you want the low-quality Internet offering being downloaded to your computer?' I'll get a response telling me that .001 percent of customers are interested in it. So, by being customer-centric, I would probably say downloading is snake oil."

By mid-2008, however, Netflix had moved quickly and proactively—and with its usual innovative vigor—into the VoD arena. Once again, reported *Advertising Age*, Netflix "is poised to be a major disrupter in the entertainment landscape. . . . It is the rare case of a company that has out-innovated competitors rather than hanging on to an entrenched business model." "What's so impressive to me," added business writer John M. Caddell,

> . . . is that Netflix is investing in technology and partnerships expressly designed to make their old business model obsolete. When I think about how much they have spent, in dollars and time and thought, on the sending-videos-through-the-mail model, I wonder how they were able to make the leap to say, "We have this process optimized, but it's not the future. Time to build a new model."

By 2011, Hastings was apparently ready to get out in front of the industry's latest innovative surge: As one IT expert put it, he made the decision to "destroy a low-margin business in DVDs and grow a high-margin streaming service." The strategy called for separating the company's DVD-by-mail and VoD streaming services. Customers could pick either service for $7.99 or both for $15.98. Eventually, however, the DVD end of the business would be marginalized so that Netflix could emerge as a leader in the streaming-entertainment industry. The DVD business would be branded as *Qwikster* while the Netflix brand would be dedicated to the streaming service.

Customers, however—a *lot* of customers—didn't like the idea. The problem? Among other things, most of Netflix's nearly 24 million subscribers wanted both services, and the price for access to both effectively went up from $9.99 to $15.99. Nor did they care for the idea of separating the two services, calling Qwikster "Qwikstupid" and complaining about the hassle of maintaining two different accounts. In the third quarter of 2011, Netflix lost 810,000 customers, and panic selling caused share prices to fall by 31 percent; market cap plummeted from nearly $15 billion in July to barely $4 billion in October.

Hastings readily admitted his mistake. "We've hurt our hard-earned reputation," he said in a letter to shareholders. "There is a difference between moving quickly—which Netflix has done very well for years—and moving too fast, which is what we did in this case."

Steve Jobs is clearly a manager. So, too, are Phil Knight (chairman of Nike), Ursula Burns (CEO of Xerox), Yorihiko Kojima (chairman of Mitsubishi), Neil MacGregor (director of the British Museum), Richard Hayne (president and chairman of Urban Outfitters), Tim Ruskell (director of player personnel of the Chicago Bears football team), Barack Obama (president of the United States), Benedict XVI (pope of the Roman Catholic Church), and Marilyn Ferguson (owner of Gifts and Gabs in Bryan, Texas). As diverse as they and their organizations are, all of these managers are confronted by many of the same challenges, strive to achieve many of the same goals, and apply many of the same concepts of effective management in their work.

For better or worse, our society is strongly influenced by managers and their organizations. Most people in the United States are born in a hospital (an organization), educated by public or private schools (all organizations), depend on organizations for their income, and buy virtually all of their consumable products and services from businesses (organizations). And much of our behavior is influenced by various government agencies (also organizations). We define an organization as a group of people working together in a structured and coordinated fashion to achieve a set of goals. The goals may include profit (Starbucks Corporation), the discovery of knowledge (University of Missouri), national defense (the U.S. Army), coordination of various local charities (United Way of America), or social satisfaction (a sorority). Because organizations play such major roles in our lives, understanding how they operate and how they are managed is important.

This book is about managers and the work they do. In Chapter 1, we examine the general nature of management, its dimensions, and its challenges. We explain the concepts of management and managers, discuss the management process, present an overview of the book, and identify various kinds of managers. We describe the different roles and skills of managers, discuss the nature of managerial work, and examine the scope of management in contemporary organizations. In Chapter 2, we describe how both the practice and the theory of management have evolved. As a unit, then, these first two chapters provide an introduction to the field by introducing both contemporary and historical perspectives on management.

◆ An Introduction to Management

Although defining the term *organization* is relatively simple, the concept of *management* is a bit more elusive. It is perhaps best understood from a resource-based perspective. As we discuss more completely in Chapter 2, all organizations use four basic kinds of resources from their environment: human, financial, physical, and information. Human resources include managerial talent and labor. Financial resources are the capital used by the organization to finance both ongoing and long-term operations. Physical resources include raw materials, office and production facilities, and equipment. Information resources are usable data needed to make effective decisions. Examples of resources used in four very different kinds of organizations are shown in Table 1.1.

organization
A group of people working together in structured and coordinated fashion to achieve a set of goals

Organization	Human Resources	Financial Resources	Physical Resources	Information Resources
Royal Dutch/Shell Group	Drilling platform workers Corporate executives	Profits Stockholder investments	Refineries Office buildings	Sales forecasts OPEC proclamations
Michigan State University	Faculty Administrative staff	Alumni contributions Government grants	Computers Campus facilities	Research reports Government publications
New York City	Police officers Municipal employees	Tax revenue Government grants	Sanitation equipment Municipal buildings	Economic forecasts Crime statistics
Susan's Corner Grocery Store	Grocery clerks Bookkeeper	Profits Owner investment	Building Display shelving	Price lists from suppliers Newspaper ads for competitors

TABLE 1.1
EXAMPLES OF RESOURCES USED BY ORGANIZATIONS

All organizations, regardless of whether they are large or small, profit-seeking or not-for-profit, domestic or multinational, use some combination of human, financial, physical, and information resources to achieve their goals. These resources are generally obtained from the organization's environment.

© Cengage Learning 2013

Managers are responsible for combining and coordinating these various resources to achieve the organization's goals. A manager at Royal Dutch/Shell Group, for example, uses the talents of executives and drilling platform workers, profits earmarked for reinvestment, existing refineries and office facilities, and sales forecasts to make decisions regarding the amount of petroleum to be refined and distributed during the next quarter. Similarly, the mayor (manager) of New York City might use police officers, a government grant (perhaps supplemented with surplus tax revenues), existing police stations, and detailed crime statistics to launch a major crime prevention program in the city.

How do these and other managers combine and coordinate the various kinds of resources? They do so by carrying out four basic managerial functions or activities: planning and decision making, organizing, leading, and controlling. **Management**, then, as illustrated in Figure 1.1, can be defined as a set of activities (including planning and decision making, organizing, leading, and controlling) directed at an organization's resources (human, financial, physical, and information), with the aim of achieving organizational goals in an efficient and effective manner.

The last phrase in our definition is especially important because it highlights the basic purpose of management—to ensure that an organization's goals are achieved in an efficient and effective manner. By **efficient**, we mean using resources wisely and in a cost-effective way. For example, a firm like Toyota Motor Corporation, which produces high-quality products at relatively low costs, is efficient. By **effective**, we mean making the right decisions and successfully implementing them. Toyota also makes cars with the styling and quality to inspire consumer interest and confidence. A firm could very efficiently produce portable CD players but still not succeed because the market for such devices has largely been supplanted by the iPod and similar MP3 players. A firm that produces products that no one wants is therefore not effective. In general, successful organizations are both efficient and effective.[2]

With this basic understanding of management, defining the term *manager* becomes relatively simple: A **manager** is someone whose primary responsibility is to carry out the management process. In particular, a manager is someone who plans and makes decisions, organizes, leads, and controls human, financial, physical, and information resources. Today's managers face a variety of interesting and challenging situations. The average executive works over 60 hours a week, has enormous demands placed on his or her time, and faces increased complexities posed by globalization, domestic competition, government regulation, shareholder pressure, and Internet-related uncertainties. The job is complicated even

management
A set of activities (including planning and decision making, organizing, leading, and controlling) directed at an organization's resources (human, financial, physical, and information), with the aim of achieving organizational goals in an efficient and effective manner

efficient
Using resources wisely and in a cost-effective way

effective
Making the right decisions and successfully implementing them

manager
Someone whose primary responsibility is to carry out the management process

FIGURE 1.1 MANAGEMENT IN ORGANIZATIONS

Basic managerial activities include planning and decision making, organizing, leading, and controlling. Managers engage in these activities to combine human, financial, physical, and information resources efficiently and effectively and to work toward achieving the goals of the organization.

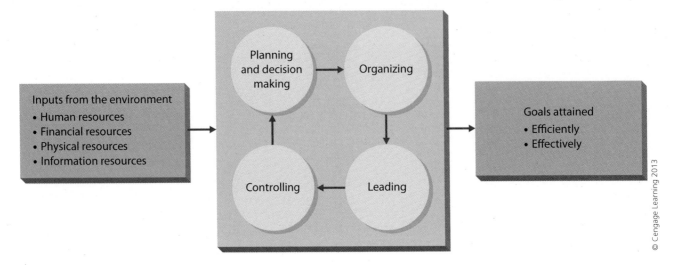

© Cengage Learning 2013

more by rapid changes (such as the recession of 2008–2010), unexpected disruptions, and both minor and major crises. The manager's job is unpredictable and fraught with challenges, but it is also filled with opportunities to make a difference. Good managers can propel an organization into unprecedented realms of success, whereas poor managers can devastate even the strongest of organizations.[3]

Many of the characteristics that contribute to the complexity and uncertainty of management stem from the environment in which organizations function. For example, as shown in Figure 1.1, the resources used by organizations to create products and services all come from the environment. Thus it is critical that managers understand this environment. Part 2 of the text discusses the environmental context of management in detail. Chapter 3 provides a general overview and discussion of the organization's environment, and Chapters 4 through 6 address specific aspects of the environment more fully. In particular, Chapter 4 discusses the ethical and social context of management. Chapter 5 explores the global context of management. Chapter 6 describes the cultural and multicultural environment of management. After reading these chapters, you will be better prepared to study the essential activities that comprise the management process.

The Management Process

We noted earlier that management involves the four basic functions of planning and decision making, organizing, leading, and controlling. Because these functions represent the framework around which this book is organized, we introduce them here and note where they are discussed more fully. Their basic definitions and interrelationships are shown in Figure 1.2. (Note that Figure 1.2 is an expanded version of the central part of Figure 1.1.)

Consider the management process at Google. Sergey Brin and Larry Page, Google's founders and top managers, must first create goals and plans that articulate what they want the company to become. Then they rely on effective organization to help make those goals and plans reality. Brin and Page also pay close attention to the people who work for the company. And they keep a close eye on how well the company is performing. Each of these activities represents one of the four basic managerial functions illustrated in the figure—setting goals is

© Cengage Learning 2013

FIGURE 1.2
THE MANAGEMENT PROCESS

Management involves four basic activities—planning and decision making, organizing, leading, and controlling. Although there is a basic logic for describing these activities in this sequence (as indicated by the solid arrows), most managers engage in more than one activity at a time and often move back and forth between the activities in unpredictable ways (as shown by the dotted arrows).

part of planning, setting up the organization is part of organizing, managing people is part of leading, and monitoring performance is part of controlling.

It is important to note, however, that the functions of management do not usually occur in a tidy, step-by-step fashion. Managers do not plan on Monday, make decisions on Tuesday, organize on Wednesday, lead on Thursday, and control on Friday. At any given time, for example, a manager is likely to be engaged in several different activities simultaneously. Indeed, from one setting to another, managerial tasks are as different as they are similar. The similarities that pervade most settings are the phases in the management process. Important differences include the emphasis, sequencing, and implications of each phase.[4] Thus the solid lines in Figure 1.2 indicate how, in theory, the functions of management are performed. The dotted lines, however, represent the true reality of management. In the sections that follow, we explore each of these activities.

Planning and Decision Making: Determining Courses of Action

In its simplest form, planning means setting an organization's goals and deciding how best to achieve them. Decision making, a part of the planning process, involves selecting a course of action from a set of alternatives. Planning and decision making help maintain managerial effectiveness by serving as guides for future activities. In other words, the organization's goals and plans clearly help managers know how to allocate their time and resources. When Alan Mulally took over the ailing Ford Motor Company a few years ago, he walked into a business that had low cash reserves, an unpopular product line, a confusing strategy, and a culture that was so resistant to change that one insider said it was "calcified." His first agenda was to set performance goals for all of Ford's top executives and clarify the strategic direction that would guide Ford in the future. He also worked to ensure that decision making was transparent.[5] The four chapters making up Part 3 of this text are devoted to planning and decision making. Chapter 7 examines the basic elements of planning and decision making, including the role and importance of organizational goals. Chapter 8 looks at strategy and strategic planning, which provide overall direction and focus for the organization. Chapter 9 explores managerial decision making and problem solving in detail. Finally, Chapter 10 addresses planning and decision making as they relate to the management of new ventures and entrepreneurial activities, increasingly important parts of managerial work.

planning
Setting an organization's goals and deciding how best to achieve them

decision making
Part of the planning process that involves selecting a course of action from a set of alternatives

Controlling: Monitoring and Evaluating Activities

Another phase of the management process is **controlling**, or monitoring the organization's progress toward its goals. As the organization moves toward its goals, managers must monitor progress to ensure that it is performing in such a way as to arrive at its "destination" at the appointed time. A good analogy is that of a space mission to Mars. NASA does not simply shoot a rocket in the general direction of the planet and then look again in four months to see whether the rocket hit its mark. NASA monitors the spacecraft almost continuously and makes whatever course corrections are needed to keep it on track. Controlling similarly helps ensure the effectiveness and efficiency needed for successful management. For example, during a routine quality control inspection of a prototype of Boeing's new 787 Dreamliner aircraft, an inspector discovered that literally thousands of fasteners had been improperly installed. This finding required managers to push the completion schedule for the plane back several months[7] in order to locate and replace all of the questionable fasteners. If control had not worked properly, the subsequent impact could have been disastrous. At Ford, Alan Mulally installed a more rigorous financial reporting system so that he could better assess how various parts of the far-flung Ford empire were performing and get information he needed to make strategic decisions faster and easier than was the case when he first took over.

> "The speed with which [Alan] Mulally has transformed Ford into a more nimble and healthy operation has been one of the most impressive jobs I've seen. It probably would have been game over for Ford but for the changes he has brought."
>
> —JOHN CASESA, HIGHLY RESPECTED AUTOMOBILE INDUSTRY CONSULTANT[6]

The control function is explored in Part 4. First, Chapter 11 explores the basic elements of the control process, including the increasing importance of strategic control. Managing operations, quality, and productivity is explored in Chapter 12. Finally, Chapter 13 addresses the management of information and information technology, which are also important areas of organizational control.

Pixland (RF)/Jupiter Images

Leading is the set of processes used to get members of the organization to work together to further the interests of the organization. Consider this manager, for example, who is explaining a new project to his team. Part of his job is to make sure they understand the project and why it is important. But he must also motivate them to be enthusiastic and excited about the project.

Organizing: Coordinating Activities and Resources

Once a manager has set goals and developed a workable plan, the next management function is to organize people and the other resources necessary to carry out the plan. Specifically, **organizing** involves determining how activities and resources are to be grouped. After Alan Mulally clarified Ford's strategy, he then overhauled the company's bureaucratic structure in order to facilitate coordination across divisions and promote faster decision making. Organizing is the subject of Part 5. Chapter 14 introduces the basic elements of organizing, such as job design, departmentalization, authority relationships, span of control, and line and staff roles. Chapter 15 explains how managers fit these elements and concepts together to form an overall organization design. Organization change and innovation are the focus of Chapter 16. Finally, processes associated with managing the organization's workforce so as to most effectively carry out organizational roles and perform tasks are described in Chapter 17.

Leading: Motivating and Managing People

Another basic managerial function is leading. Some people consider leading to be both the most important and the most challenging of all managerial activities. **Leading** is the set of processes used to get members of the organization to work together to further the interests of the organization. Alan Mulally has taken several steps to change the leadership culture that existed at Ford. In earlier times

controlling
Monitoring organizational progress toward goal attainment

organizing
Determining how activities and resources are to be grouped

leading
The set of processes used to get members of the organization to work together to further the interests of the organization

the firm had used a directive, top-down approach to management. But Mulally decentralized many activities so as to put the responsibility for making decisions in the hands of those best qualified to make them. He also clarified channels of communication and revamped the incentive system used for senior managers. Leading involves a number of different processes and activities, which are discussed in Part 6. The starting point is understanding basic individual and interpersonal processes, which we focus on in Chapter 18. Motivating employees is discussed in Chapter 19, and leadership itself and the leader's efforts to influence others are covered in Chapter 20. Managing interpersonal relations and communication is the subject of Chapter 21. Finally, managing work groups and teams, another important part of leading, is addressed in Chapter 22.

CONCEPT CHECK

What is a manager, and what are the fundamental functions that comprise the management process?

Describe examples of how the management functions might be performed in different sequences.

Kinds of Managers

Not all managers are the same, of course, nor is the work they perform. Among other things, we can classify managers according to their level in the organization and the area in which they work.

Managing at Different Levels of the Organization

levels of management
The differentiation of managers into three basic categories—top, middle, and first-line

Managers can be differentiated according to their level in the organization. Although large organizations typically have a number of levels of management, the most common view considers three basic levels: top, middle, and first-line managers, as shown in Figure 1.3.

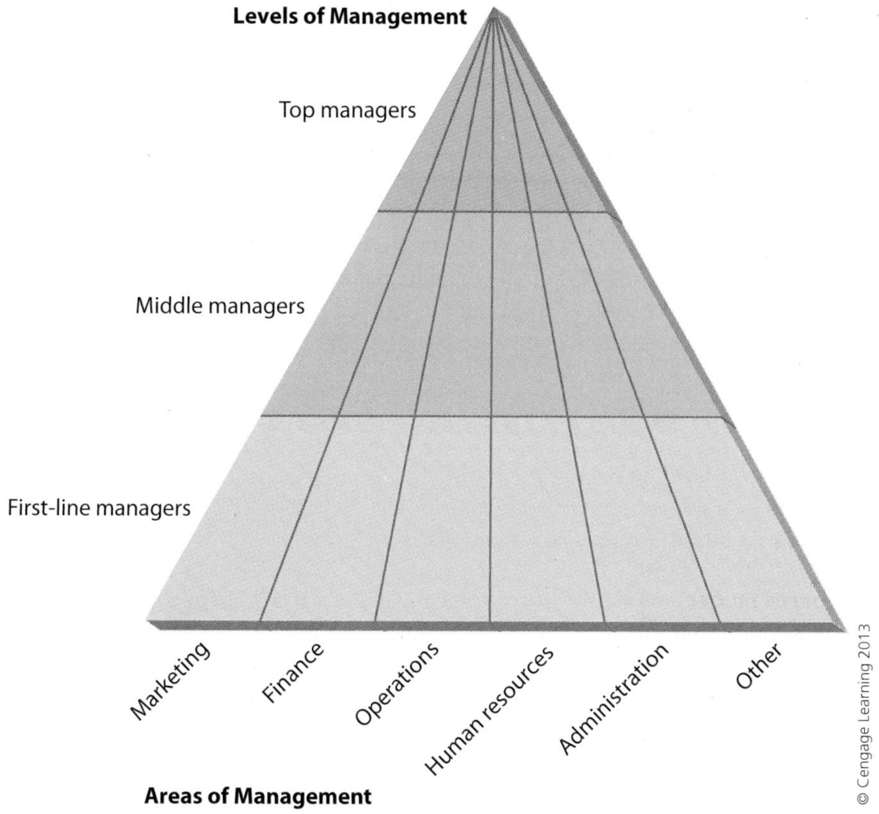

FIGURE 1.3 KINDS OF MANAGERS BY LEVEL AND AREA

Organizations generally have three levels of management, represented by top managers, middle managers, and first-line managers. Regardless of level, managers are also usually associated with a specific area within the organization, such as marketing, finance, operations, human resources, administration, or some other area.

Levels of Management

Top managers

Middle managers

First-line managers

Marketing   Finance   Operations   Human resources   Administration   Other

Areas of Management

© Cengage Learning 2013

Top Managers Top managers make up the relatively small group of executives who manage the overall organization. Titles found in this group include president, vice president, and chief executive officer (CEO). Top managers create the organization's goals, overall strategy, and operating policies. They also officially represent the organization to the external environment by meeting with government officials, executives of other organizations, and so forth.

Howard Schultz, CEO of Starbucks, is a top manager, as is Deidra Wager, the firm's executive vice president. Likewise, Sergey Brin, Larry Page, and Alan Mulally are also top managers. The job of a top manager is likely to be complex and varied. Top managers make decisions about such activities as acquiring other companies, investing in research and development, entering or abandoning various markets, and building new plants and office facilities. They often work long hours and spend much of their time in meetings or on the telephone. In most cases, top managers are also very well paid. In fact, the elite top managers of very large firms sometimes make several million dollars a year in salary, bonuses, and stock.[8] In 2010 Ford paid Alan Mulally $1.4 million in salary. He also earned $127,699 in other compensation and more than $14 million in stock and option awards.[9]

Middle Managers Middle management is probably the largest group of managers in most organizations. Common middle-management titles include plant manager, operations manager, and division head. Middle managers are responsible primarily for implementing the policies and plans developed by top managers and for supervising and coordinating the activities of lower-level managers.[10] Jason Hernandez, a regional manager at Starbucks responsible for the firm's operations in three eastern states, is a middle manager.

Ford plant managers, also middle managers, must meet various production quotas and goals and handle inventory management, quality control, equipment failures, and union problems. They also coordinate the work of supervisors within the plant. In recent years, many organizations have thinned the ranks of middle managers to lower costs and eliminate excess bureaucracy. Still, middle managers are necessary to bridge the upper and lower levels of the organization and to implement the strategies developed at the top. Although many organizations have found that they can indeed survive with fewer middle managers, those who remain play an even more important role in determining how successful the organization will be.

First-Line Managers First-line managers supervise and coordinate the activities of operating employees. Common titles for first-line managers are supervisor, coordinator, and office manager. Positions like these are often the first held by employees who enter management from the ranks of operating personnel. Wayne Maxwell and Jenny Wagner, managers of Starbucks coffee shops in Texas, are first-line managers. They oversee the day-to-day operations of their respective stores, hire operating employees to staff them, and handle other routine administrative duties required of them by the parent corporation. Assembly line supervisors at Ford plants are first-line managers. In contrast to top and middle managers, first-line managers typically spend a large proportion of their time supervising the work of subordinates.

Managing in Different Areas of the Organization

Regardless of their level, managers may work in various areas within an organization. In any given firm, for example, areas of management may include marketing, financial, operations, human resource, administrative, and other areas.

areas of management
Managers can be differentiated into marketing, financial, operations, human resource, administration, and other areas

Marketing Managers Marketing managers work in areas related to the marketing function—getting consumers and clients to buy the organization's products or services (be they Nokia cell phones, Ford automobiles, *Newsweek* magazines, Associated Press news reports, flights on Southwest Airlines, or cups of latte at Starbucks). These areas include new-product development, promotion, and distribution. Given the importance of marketing for virtually all organizations, developing good managers in this area can be critical.

Financial Managers Financial managers deal primarily with an organization's financial resources. They are responsible for such activities as accounting, cash management, and investments. In some businesses, such as banking and insurance, financial managers are found in especially large numbers.

Operations Managers Operations managers are concerned with creating and managing the systems that create an organization's products and services. Typical responsibilities of operations managers include production control, inventory control, quality control, plant layout, and site selection.

Human Resource Managers Human resource managers are responsible for hiring and developing employees. They are typically involved in human resource planning, recruiting and selecting employees, training and development, designing compensation and benefit systems, formulating performance appraisal systems, and discharging low-performing and problem employees.

Administrative Managers Administrative, or general, managers are not associated with any particular management specialty. Probably the best example of an administrative management position is that of a hospital or clinic administrator. Administrative managers tend to be generalists; they have some basic familiarity with all functional areas of management rather than specialized training in any one area.[11]

Other Kinds of Managers Many organizations have specialized management positions in addition to those already described. Public relations managers, for example, deal with the public and media for firms like Philip Morris and the Dow Chemical Company to protect and enhance the image of the organization. Research and development (R&D) managers coordinate the activities of scientists and engineers working on scientific projects in organizations such as Monsanto Company, NASA, and Merck & Company. Internal consultants are used in organizations such as Prudential Insurance to provide specialized expert advice to operating managers. International operations are often coordinated by specialized managers in organizations like Eli Lilly and Rockwell International. The number, nature, and importance of these specialized managers vary tremendously from one organization to another. As contemporary organizations continue to grow in complexity and size, the number and importance of such managers are also likely to increase.

Identify different kinds of an organization's managers by level and area.

How might the importance of different areas of management vary as a function of the firm's business?

CONCEPT CHECK

Basic Managerial Roles and Skills

Regardless of their levels or areas within an organization, all managers must play certain roles and exhibit certain skills if they are to be successful. The concept of a role, in this sense, is similar to the role an actor plays in a theatrical production. A person does certain things, meets certain needs, and has certain responsibilities in the organization. In the sections that follow, we first highlight the basic roles managers play and then discuss the skills they need to be effective.

Managerial Roles

Henry Mintzberg offers a number of interesting insights into the nature of managerial roles.[12] He closely observed the day-to-day activities of a group of CEOs by literally following them around and taking notes on what they did. From his observations, Mintzberg concluded that managers play ten different roles, as summarized in Table 1.2, and that these roles fall into three basic categories: interpersonal, informational, and decisional.

Interpersonal Roles   There are three interpersonal roles inherent in the manager's job. First, the manager is often expected to serve as a *figurehead*—taking visitors to dinner, attending ribbon-cutting ceremonies, and the like. These activities are typically more ceremonial and symbolic than substantive. The manager is also expected to serve as a *leader*—hiring, training, and motivating employees. A manager who formally or informally shows subordinates how to do things and how to perform under pressure is leading. Finally, managers can have a *liaison* role. This role often involves serving as a coordinator or link among people, groups, or organizations. For example, companies in the computer industry may use liaisons to keep other companies informed about their plans. This enables Microsoft, for example, to create software for interfacing with new Hewlett-Packard printers at the same time those printers are being developed. And, at the same time, managers at Hewlett-Packard can incorporate new Microsoft features into the printers they introduce.

Informational Roles   The three informational roles flow naturally from the interpersonal roles just discussed. The process of carrying out the interpersonal roles places the manager at a strategic point to gather and disseminate information. The first informational role is that

interpersonal roles
The roles of figurehead, leader, and liaison, which involve dealing with other people

informational roles
The roles of monitor, disseminator, and spokesperson, which involve the processing of information

TABLE 1.2 TEN BASIC MANAGERIAL ROLES

Pioneering research by Henry Mintzberg suggests that managers play ten basic managerial roles.

Category	Role	Sample Activities
Interpersonal	Figurehead	Attending ribbon-cutting ceremony for new plant
	Leader	Encouraging employees to improve productivity
	Liaison	Coordinating activities of two project groups
Informational	Monitor	Scanning industry reports to stay abreast of developments
	Disseminator	Sending memos outlining new organizational initiatives
	Spokesperson	Making a speech to discuss growth plans
Decisional	Entrepreneur	Developing new ideas for innovation
	Disturbance handler	Resolving conflict between two subordinates
	Resource allocator	Reviewing and revising budget requests
	Negotiator	Reaching agreement with a key supplier or labor union

of *monitor*, one who actively seeks information that may be of value. The manager questions subordinates, is receptive to unsolicited information, and attempts to be as well informed as possible. The manager is also a *disseminator* of information, transmitting relevant information back to others in the workplace. When the roles of monitor and disseminator are viewed together, the manager emerges as a vital link in the organization's chain of communication. The third informational role focuses on external communication. The *spokesperson* formally relays information to people outside the unit or outside the organization. For example, a plant manager at Union Carbide may transmit information to top-level managers so that they will be better informed about the plant's activities. The manager may also represent the organization before a chamber of commerce or consumer group. Although the roles of spokesperson and figurehead are similar, there is one basic difference between them. When a manager acts as a figurehead, the manager's presence as a symbol of the organization is what is of interest. In the spokesperson role, however, the manager carries information and communicates it to others in a formal sense.

Decisional Roles The manager's informational roles typically lead to the decisional roles. The information acquired by the manager as a result of performing the informational roles has a major bearing on important decisions that he or she makes. Mintzberg identified four decisional roles. First, the manager has the role of *entrepreneur*, the voluntary initiator of change. A manager at 3M Company developed the idea for the Post-it note pad but had to "sell" it to other skeptical managers inside the company. A second decisional role is initiated not by the manager but by some other individual or group. The manager responds to her role as *disturbance handler* by handling such problems as strikes, copyright infringements, or problems in public relations or corporate image.

The third decisional role is that of *resource allocator*. As resource allocator, the manager decides how resources are distributed and with whom he or she will work most closely. For example, a manager typically allocates the funds in the unit's operating budget among the unit's members and projects. A fourth decisional role is that of *negotiator*. In this role the manager enters into negotiations with other groups or organizations as a representative of the company. For example, managers may negotiate a union contract, an agreement with a consultant, or a long-term relationship with a supplier. Negotiations may also be internal to the organization. The manager may, for instance, mediate a dispute between two subordinates or negotiate with another department for additional support.

Managerial Skills

In addition to fulfilling numerous roles, managers also need a number of specific skills if they are to succeed. The most fundamental management skills are technical, interpersonal, conceptual, diagnostic, communication, decision-making, and time-management skills.[13]

Technical Skills Technical skills are the skills necessary to accomplish or understand the specific kind of work being done in an organization. Technical skills are especially important for first-line managers. These managers spend much of their time training subordinates and answering questions about work-related problems. They must know how to perform the tasks assigned to those they supervise if they are to be effective managers. Brian Dunn, director and CEO of Best Buy, began his career in 1985 as a store associate when Best Buy consisted of only twelve stores. He continued to work his way up into various positions including store manager, district manager, regional manager, regional VP, senior VP, executive VP, and president of Retail (North America). Hence, he literally learned the technical aspects of retailing from the ground up. While Sergey Brin and Larry Page spend most of their time now dealing with strategic and management issues, they also keep abreast of new and emerging technologies that may affect Google.

Interpersonal Skills Managers spend considerable time interacting with people both inside and outside the organization. For obvious reasons, then, the manager also needs

decisional roles
The roles of entrepreneur, disturbance handler, resource allocator, and negotiator, which relate primarily to making decisions

technical skills
The skills necessary to accomplish or understand the specific kind of work being done in an organization

Bloomberg/Getty Images

It's no secret that Mark Zuckerberg is quiet and introverted. That's one reason that he and Sheryl Sandberg make such a great team at Facebook. Sandberg is charismatic and extroverted, helping her become a frequent public representative for Facebook. Ms. Sandberg is shown here addressing a graduation ceremony at Barnard College in New York.

interpersonal skills—the ability to communicate with, understand, and motivate both individuals and groups. As a manager climbs the organizational ladder, he or she must be able to get along with subordinates, peers, and those at higher levels of the organization. Because of the multitude of roles managers must fulfill, a manager must also be able to work with suppliers, customers, investors, and others outside the organization. Although some managers have succeeded with poor interpersonal skills, a manager who has good interpersonal skills is likely to be more successful. Sheryl Sandberg joined Facebook in 2008 as chief operating officer, following careers at the World Bank, the Treasury Department, and Google. Sandberg is renowned for her interpersonal skills and sharp intellect, balancing CEO Mark Zuckerberg's introversion. These skills have helped to cultivate strong relationships with key advertisers and bring continued growth and stability to Facebook.

Conceptual Skills Conceptual skills depend on the manager's ability to think in the abstract. Managers need the mental capacity to understand the overall workings of the organization and its environment, to grasp how all the parts of the organization fit together, and to view the organization in a holistic manner. This allows them to think strategically, to see the "big picture," and to make broad-based decisions that serve the overall organization.

Diagnostic Skills Successful managers also possess diagnostic skills, or skills that enable a manager to visualize the most appropriate response to a situation. A physician diagnoses a patient's illness by analyzing symptoms and determining their probable cause. Similarly, a manager can diagnose and analyze a problem in the organization by studying its symptoms and then developing a solution.[14] When the original owners of Starbucks failed to make a success of the business, Howard Schultz took over and reoriented the business away from mail order and moved it into retail coffee outlets. His diagnostic skills enabled him to understand both why the current business model was not working and how to construct a better one.

Communication Skills Communication skills refer to the manager's abilities both to effectively convey ideas and information to others and to effectively receive ideas and information from others. These skills enable a manager to transmit ideas to subordinates so that they know what is expected, to coordinate work with peers and colleagues so that they work well together, and to keep higher-level managers informed about what is going on. In addition, communication skills help the manager listen to what others say and to understand the real meaning behind e-mails, letters, reports, and other written communication.

Decision-Making Skills Effective managers also have good decision-making skills. Decision-making skills refer to the manager's ability to correctly recognize and define problems and opportunities and to then select an appropriate course of action to solve problems and capitalize on opportunities. No manager makes the right decision *all* the time. However, effective managers make good decisions *most* of the time. And when they do make a bad decision, they usually recognize their mistake quickly and then make good decisions to recover with as little cost or damage to their organization as possible. After joining Gap Inc. in 2007, CEO Glenn Murphy focused his energy on the Gap brand in an effort to revive growth. However,

interpersonal skills
The ability to communicate with, understand, and motivate both individuals and groups

conceptual skills
The manager's ability to think in the abstract

diagnostic skills
The manager's ability to visualize the most appropriate response to a situation

communication skills
The manager's abilities both to effectively convey ideas and information to others and to effectively receive ideas and information from others

decision-making skills
The manager's ability to correctly recognize and define problems and opportunities and to then select an appropriate course of action to solve problems and capitalize on opportunities

when the company revealed its new logo in 2010, replacing its classic white and navy square logo, customer backlash quickly ensued as its brand identity crumbled. Gap took shoppers' complaints to heart, scrapping the new logo and reverting to its iconic brand. So flawed decision making may have led to the logo change, but more effective decision making quickly allowed the firm to reverse itself.

Time-Management Skills   Finally, effective managers usually have good time-management skills. Time-management skills refer to the manager's ability to prioritize work, to work efficiently, and to delegate appropriately. As already noted, managers face many different pressures and challenges. It is too easy for a manager to get bogged down doing work that can easily be postponed or delegated to others.[15] When this happens, unfortunately, more pressing and higher-priority work may get neglected.[16] Jeff Bezos, CEO of Amazon.com, schedules all his meetings on three days a week but insists on keeping the other two days clear so that he can pursue his own ideas and maintain the flexibility to interact with his employees informally.[17]

List and define the basic managerial skills that contribute to success.

How might the various managerial skills relate to different managerial roles?

CONCEPT CHECK

The Nature of Managerial Work

We have already noted that managerial work does not follow an orderly, systematic progression through the workweek. Indeed, the manager's job is fraught with uncertainty, change, interruption, and fragmented activities. Mintzberg's study, mentioned earlier, and other research suggests that, in a typical day, CEOs are likely to spend their time in both scheduled and unscheduled meetings, doing "desk work," talking on the telephone, reading and responding to e-mail, and responding to various situations requiring them to make decisions. (The time spent on each activity, of course, varies constantly.) Moreover, the nature of managerial work continues to change in complex and often unpredictable ways.[18]

In addition, managers perform a wide variety of tasks. In the course of a single day, for example, a manager might have to make a decision about the design of a new product, settle a dispute between two subordinates, hire a new assistant, write a report for his boss, coordinate a joint venture with an overseas colleague, form a task force to investigate a problem, search for information on the Internet, and deal with a labor grievance. Moreover, the pace of the manager's job can be relentless. She may feel bombarded by mail, telephone calls, and people waiting to see her. Decisions may have to be made quickly and plans formulated with little time for reflection.[19] But, in many ways, these same characteristics of managerial work also contribute to its richness and meaningfulness. Making critical decisions under intense pressure, and making them well, can be a major source of intrinsic satisfaction. And managers are usually well paid for the pressures they bear.

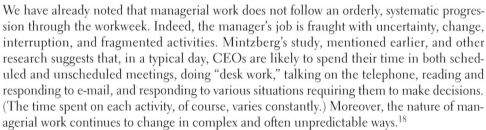

"Business is simple. Management's job is to take care of employees. The employees' job is to take care of the customers. Happy customers take care of the shareholders. It's a virtuous circle."

—JOHN MACKEY, FOUNDER AND CEO OF WHOLE FOODS[20]

time-management skills
The manager's ability to prioritize work, to work efficiently, and to delegate appropriately

The Science and the Art of Management

Given the complexity inherent in the manager's job, a reasonable question relates to whether management is a science or an art. In fact, effective management is a blend of both science and art. And successful executives recognize the importance of combining both the science and the art of management as they practice their craft.[21]

The Science of Management Many management problems and issues can be approached in ways that are rational, logical, objective, and systematic. Managers can gather data, facts, and objective information. They can use quantitative models and decision-making techniques to arrive at "correct" decisions. And they need to take such a scientific approach to solving problems whenever possible, especially when they are dealing with relatively routine and straightforward issues. When Starbucks considers entering a new market, its managers look closely at a wide variety of objective details as they formulate their plans. Technical, diagnostic, and decision-making skills are especially important when approaching a management task or problem from a scientific perspective.

The Art of Management Even though managers may try to be scientific as often as possible, they must frequently make decisions and solve problems on the basis of intuition, experience, instinct, and personal insights. Relying heavily on conceptual, communication, interpersonal, and time-management skills, for example, a manager may have to decide among multiple courses of action that look equally attractive. And even "objective facts" may prove to be wrong. When Starbucks was planning its first store in New York City, market research clearly showed that New Yorkers preferred drip coffee to more exotic espresso-style coffees. After first installing more drip coffee makers and fewer espresso makers than in their other stores, managers had to backtrack when New Yorkers lined up, clamoring for espresso. Starbucks now introduces a standard menu and layout in all its stores, regardless of presumed market differences, and then makes necessary adjustments later. Thus managers must blend an element of intuition and personal insight with hard data and objective facts.[22]

"Business is really an art form. At its best, it's the artistry of how people create things together."

—PETER SENGE, A LEADING BUSINESS EXPERT[23]

Becoming a Manager

How does one acquire the skills necessary to blend the science and art of management and to become a successful manager? Although there are as many variations as there are managers, the most common path involves a combination of education and experience.[24] Figure 1.4 illustrates how this generally happens.

The Role of Education Many of you reading this book right now are doing so because you are enrolled in a management course at a college or university. Thus you are acquiring management skills in an educational setting. When you complete the course (and this book), you will have a foundation for developing your management skills in more advanced courses. A college degree has become almost a requirement for career advancement in business, and virtually all CEOs in the United States have a college degree. MBA degrees are also common among successful executives today. More and more foreign universities, especially in Europe, are also beginning to offer academic programs in management.

FIGURE 1.4 SOURCES OF MANAGEMENT SKILLS

Most managers acquire their skills as a result of education and experience. Though a few CEOs today do not hold college degrees, most students preparing for management careers earn college degrees and go on to enroll in MBA programs.

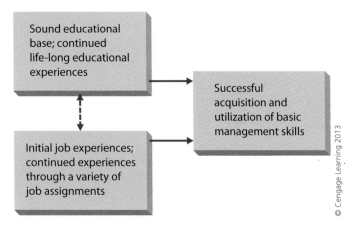

© Cengage Learning 2013

Even after obtaining a degree, most prospective managers have not seen the end of their management education. Many middle and top managers periodically return to campus to participate in executive or management development programs ranging in duration from a few days to several weeks. First-line managers also take advantage of extension and continuing education programs offered by institutions of higher education and/or through online media. A recent innovation in extended management education is the executive MBA program offered by many top business schools, in which middle and top managers with several years of experience complete an accelerated program of study on weekends.[25] Finally, many large companies have in-house training programs for furthering managers' education. Indeed, some firms have even created what are essentially corporate universities to provide the specialized education they feel is required for their managers in order for them to remain successful.[26] McDonald's and Shell Oil are among the leaders in this area. Regardless of the type of training, there is also a distinct trend toward online educational development for managers.[27] The primary advantage of education as a source of management skills is that, as a student, a person can follow a well-developed program of study, becoming familiar with current research and thinking on management. And many college students can devote full-time energy and attention to learning. On the negative side, management education is often very general, to meet the needs of a wide variety of students, and specific know-how may be hard to obtain. Further, many aspects of the manager's job can be discussed in a book but cannot really be appreciated and understood until they are experienced.

The Role of Experience This book will help provide you with a solid foundation for enhancing your management skills. Even if you were to memorize every word in every management book ever written, however, you could not then step into a top management position and immediately be effective. The reason? Management skills must also be learned through experience. Most managers advanced to their present positions from other jobs. Only by experiencing the day-to-day pressures a manager faces and by meeting a variety of managerial challenges can an individual develop insights into the real nature and character of managerial work.

David Woo/Dallas Morning News/Corbis

For this reason, most large companies, and many smaller ones as well, have developed management training programs for their prospective managers. People are hired from college campuses, from other organizations, or from the ranks of the organization's first-line managers and operating employees. These people are systematically assigned to a variety of jobs. Over time, the individual is exposed to most, if not all, of the major aspects of the organization. In this way the manager learns by experience. The training programs at some companies, such as Procter & Gamble, General Mills, and Shell Oil, are so good that other companies try to hire people who have graduated from them.[28] Even without formal training programs, managers can achieve success as they profit from varied experiences. For example, Herb Kelleher was a practicing attorney before he took over at Southwest Airlines and led it to become one of the most successful and admired businesses in the United States. Of course, natural ability, drive, and self-motivation also play roles in acquiring experience and developing management skills.

Most effective managers learn their skills through a combination of education and experience. Some type of college degree, even if it is not in business administration, usually provides a foundation for a management career. The individual then gets his or her first job and subsequently progresses through a variety of

Herb Kelleher is an icon in American business. His leadership helped redefine competition in the airline industry as Southwest Airlines took on established giants like American and United. A combination of education, experience, drive, and motivation all played a role in his success.

management situations. During the manager's rise in the organization, occasional education "updates," such as management development programs, may supplement on-the-job experience. And, increasingly, managers need to acquire international expertise as part of their personal development. As with general managerial skills, international expertise can be acquired through a combination of education and experience.[29]

The Scope of Management

When most people think of managers and management, they think of profit-seeking organizations. Throughout this chapter, we use people like Sergey Brin and Larry Page of Google, Howard Schultz of Starbucks, and Alan Mulally of Ford as examples. But we also provide examples from sports, religion, and other fields in which management is essential. Indeed, any group of two or more persons working together to achieve a goal and having human, material, financial, or informational resources at its disposal requires the practice of management.

Managing in Profit-Seeking Organizations Most of what we know about management comes from large profit-seeking organizations because their survival has long depended on efficiency and effectiveness. Examples of large businesses include industrial firms such as ExxonMobil, Toyota, BMW, Xerox, Unilever, and Levi Strauss; commercial banks such as Citicorp, Fuji Bank, and Wells Fargo; insurance companies such as Prudential, State Farm, and Metropolitan Life; retailers such as Sears, Safeway, and Target; transportation companies such as Continental Airlines and Consolidated Freightways; utilities such as Pacific Gas & Electric and Consolidated Edison of New York; communication companies such as CBS and the New York Times Company; and service organizations such as Kelly Services, KinderCare Learning Centers, and Century 21 Real Estate.

Although many people associate management primarily with large businesses, effective management is also essential for small businesses, which play an important role in the country's economy. In fact, most of this nation's businesses are small. In some respects, effective management is more important in a small business than in a large one. A large firm such as ExxonMobil or Monsanto can recover relatively easily from losing several thousand dollars on an incorrect decision; even losses of millions of dollars would not threaten their long-term survival. But a small business may ill afford even a much smaller loss. Of course, some small businesses become big ones. Dell Computer, for example, was started by one person—Michael Dell—in 1984. By 2010 it had become one of the largest businesses in the United States, with annual sales of almost $53 billion.

In recent years, the importance of international management has increased dramatically. The list of U.S. firms doing business in other countries is staggering. ExxonMobil, for example, derives 70 percent of its revenues from foreign markets, and Coca-Cola derives 85 percent of its sales from foreign markets. Other major U.S. exporters include General Motors, General Electric, Boeing, and Caterpillar. And even numbers like Ford's are deceptive. For example, the automaker has large subsidiaries based in many European countries whose sales are not included as foreign revenue. Moreover, a number of major firms that do business in the United States have their headquarters in other countries. Firms in this category include the Royal Dutch/Shell Group (the Netherlands), Fiat S.p.A. (Italy), Nestlé S.A. (Switzerland), and Massey Ferguson (Canada). International management is not, however, confined to profit-seeking organizations. Several international sports federations (such as Little League Baseball), branches (embassies) of the federal government, and the Roman Catholic Church are established in most countries as well. In some respects, the military was one of the first multinational organizations. International management is covered in depth in Chapter 5.

Managing in Not-for-Profit Organizations Intangible goals such as education, social services, public protection, and recreation are often the primary aim of not-for-profit organizations. Examples include United Way of America, the U.S. Postal Service, Girl

Scouts of the U.S.A., the International Olympic Committee, art galleries, museums, and the Public Broadcasting System (PBS). Although these and similar organizations may not have to be profitable to attract investors, they must still employ sound management practices if they are to survive and work toward their goals.[30] And they must handle money in an efficient and effective way. If the United Way were to begin to spend larger portions of its contributions on salaries and perks for its top managers, contributors would lose confidence in the organization and make their charitable donations elsewhere.

The management of government organizations and agencies is often regarded as a separate specialty: public administration. Government organizations include the Federal Trade Commission (FTC), the Environmental Protection Agency (EPA), the National Science Foundation, all branches of the military, state highway departments, and federal and state prison systems. Tax dollars support government organizations, so politicians and citizens' groups are acutely sensitive to the need for efficiency and effectiveness. For instance, the FTC's annual budget is $256.2 million.

Public and private schools, colleges, and universities all stand to benefit from the efficient use of resources. Growing pressures on state budgets have reduced money available for education. Fewer resources combined with surging costs, in turn, force administrators to make tough decisions about allocating remaining resources.

Managing healthcare facilities such as clinics, hospitals, and HMOs (health maintenance organizations) is now considered a separate field of management. Here, as in other organizations, scarce resources dictate an efficient and effective approach. In recent years some universities have established healthcare administration programs to train managers as specialists in this field.

Good management is also required in nontraditional settings to meet established goals. To one extent or another, management is practiced in religious organizations, terrorist groups, fraternities and sororities, organized crime, street gangs, neighborhood associations, and individual households. In short, as we noted at the beginning of this chapter, management and managers have a profound influence on all of us.

Successful nonprofit organizations are typically very businesslike. Such is certainly the case with Mercy Corps, a provider of humanitarian and development aid on a global scale. To see how Mercy Corps has expanded its operations into the international financial sector, see the *Change* box entitled "Capital Adventures in Microfinance" on page 20.

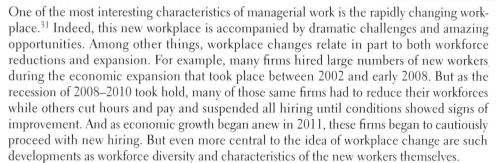

Is management an art or a science?

Identify four very different kinds of organizations and describe the role of management in their success.

CONCEPT CHECK

The New Workplace

One of the most interesting characteristics of managerial work is the rapidly changing workplace.[31] Indeed, this new workplace is accompanied by dramatic challenges and amazing opportunities. Among other things, workplace changes relate in part to both workforce reductions and expansion. For example, many firms hired large numbers of new workers during the economic expansion that took place between 2002 and early 2008. But as the recession of 2008–2010 took hold, many of those same firms had to reduce their workforces while others cut hours and pay and suspended all hiring until conditions showed signs of improvement. And as economic growth began anew in 2011, these firms began to cautiously proceed with new hiring. But even more central to the idea of workplace change are such developments as workforce diversity and characteristics of the new workers themselves.

THE MORE THINGS CHANGE

Capital Adventures in Microfinance

Mercy Corps, a nongovernmental, nonprofit organization that provides humanitarian aid and development assistance around the world, is one of the top *social business enterprises (SBEs)* in the United States. What's an SBE? It's a business formed to pursue social objectives in such areas as health, education, poverty, or the environment. Legally speaking, an SBE is a *non-loss/non-dividend company*. It strives for sustainability in its operations, and investors don't take profits; earnings are used to expand the organization and enhance its efforts to achieve its goals. The idea originated with Muhammad Yunus, a Bangladeshi economist and banker who's also responsible for the concept of *microcredit*—the principle of making small loans (called *microloans*) to entrepreneurs who can't meet the minimum qualifications for credit from traditional sources.

Today, microcredit is actually one form of *microfinance*—providing a broad range of financial services to the same type of underserved borrower. Mercy Corps has long been active in providing immediate-response assistance in times of crisis, such as the aftermath of the earthquake that killed 230,000 people in Haiti in January 2010. Since the mid-1990s, however, Mercy Corps has concentrated more of its resources on sustainable financial assistance as a means of producing lasting change. "Traditional ways of doing things," says CEO Neal Keny-Guyer, "haven't produced the kind of progress we all hoped for. So we're trying to come up with new approaches that are fully transformational." In 2008, for example, Mercy Corps launched Bank Andara in Indonesia to provide financial services and products to reliable microfinance institutions (MFIs), which, in turn, make direct microloans to entrepreneurs and small businesses.

Keny-Guyer likens his organization's financial focus to that of *venture capitalists*—investors who specialize in companies with significant growth potential (see Chapter 10). "You could say we're social VCs," he says, and he hopes to exercise financial strength in the public sphere in much the same way that VCs exercise it in the private sector—"by bringing economic opportunity, through financial services, to low-income businesspeople." In the business world, explains Keny-Guyer, "the infrastructure is aligned to support innovation and entrepreneurship," but "in the public sphere, we haven't had the financial infrastructure to support innovation."

LAN/Corbis

He's convinced, however, that things are changing in the world of SBEs and that "new paradigms for creating social value are emerging." Bank Andara, for example, along with other initiatives in microfinancial outreach, put Mercy Corps on what Keny-Guyer calls "the edge of . . . prudent risk." It's an important step in SBE strategy, he insists, because undeveloped economies don't need more well-funded retail institutions. What's needed is to develop MFI as a real industry that's integrated with the commercial banks, so there will be a seamless web of financial institutions that serve everyone, from the poorest borrower to the richest, with a full range of products and services. That's the real home run.

References: Bija Gutoff, Steve Hamm, "Social Entrepreneurs Turn Business Sense to Good," *BusinessWeek*, November 25, 2008, www.businessweek.com on February 4, 2011; "Neal Keny-Guyer—Social Entrepreneurship at Mercy Corps," *Global Envision*, December 11, 2007, www.mercycorps.org on February 4, 2011; Richard Read, "Mercy Corps Teams Up with Bank, Telecom in New Haiti Program," *Oregon Live*, September 21, 2010, http://blog.oregonlive.com on February 4, 2011; Jennifer Vilaga, "Mercy Corps: The Bank of Banks," Fast Company.com, November 25, 2008, www.fastcompany.com on February 4, 2011; Ipek Kuran, "Microcapital Story: Mercy Corps Buys a Commercial Bank in Bali to Service the Microfinance Sector in Indonesia," *Microcapital*, June 23, 2008, www.microcapital.org on February 4, 2011; "Integrated Marketing Communications for Bank Andara and AndaraLink in Indonesia," *Devex*, January 21, 2011, www.devex.com on February 4, 2011.

The management of diversity continues to be an important organizational opportunity—and challenge—today. The term *diversity* refers to differences among people. Diversity may be reflected along numerous dimensions, but most managers tend to focus on age, gender, ethnicity, and physical abilities and disabilities.[32] For example, the average age of workers in the United States is gradually increasing. This is partly because of declining birthrates and partly because people are living and working longer. Some organizations have found retirees to be excellent part-time and temporary employees. McDonald's has hired hundreds of elderly workers in recent years. Apple Computer has used many retired workers for temporary assignments and projects. By hiring retirees, the organization gets the expertise of skilled workers, and the individuals get extra income and an opportunity to continue to use their skills.

An increasing number of women have also entered the U.S. workforce. Fifty years ago only about one-third of U.S. women worked outside their homes; today, 59.2 percent of women aged 16 and older are in the workforce. Many occupations traditionally dominated by women—nursing, teaching, secretarial work—continue to be popular with females. But women have also moved increasingly into occupations previously dominated by males, becoming lawyers, physicians, and executives. Further, many blue-collar jobs are increasingly being sought by women; and women are increasingly moving into positions as business ownership as entrepreneurs and as senior executives in major corporations. Similarly, more and more men are also entering occupations previously dominated by women. For example, there are more male office assistants and nurses today than ever before.

The ethnic composition of the workplace is also changing. One obvious change has been the increasing number of Hispanics and African Americans entering the workplace. Further, many of these individuals now hold executive positions. In addition, there has been a dramatic influx of immigrant workers in the last few years. Immigrants and refugees from Central America and Asia have entered the U.S. workforce in record numbers.

Some companies, of course, are more successful than others when it comes to embracing demographic changes. The *World of Difference* box entitled "Aetna Ensures Diversity" on page 22 shows how one such company has acted to integrate these changes into both its employment practices and its business strategy.

The passage of the Americans with Disabilities Act also brought to the forefront the importance of providing equal employment opportunities for people with various disabilities. As a result, organizations are attracting qualified employees from groups that they may have once ignored. Clearly, then, along just about any dimension imaginable, the workforce is becoming more diverse. Workforce diversity enhances the effectiveness of most organizations, but it also provides special challenges for managers. We return to these issues in Chapter 6.

Aside from its demographic composition, the workforce today is changing in other ways as well. During the 1980s, many people entering the workforce were what came to be called *yuppies*, slang for "young urban professionals." These individuals were highly motivated by career prospects, sought employment with big corporations, and often were willing to make work their highest priority. Thus, they put in long hours and could be expected to remain loyal to the company, regardless of what happened.

But younger people entering the workforce over the past 20 to 30 years are frequently quite different from their parents and other older workers. Generation X, Generation Y, and the Millennials, as these groups are called, tend to be less devoted to long-term career prospects and less willing to adapt to a corporate mind-set that stresses conformity and uniformity. Instead, they often seek work in smaller, more entrepreneurial firms that allow flexibility and individuality. They also place a premium on lifestyle preferences, often putting location high on their list of priorities when selecting an employer.

Thus managers are increasingly faced with the challenge of first creating an environment that will be attractive to today's worker. Second, managers must address the challenge of providing new and different incentives to keep people motivated and interested in their work. They must build enough flexibility into the organization to accommodate an ever-changing set of lifestyles and preferences. And, of course, as these generations eventually move into top spots of major corporations, there may even be entirely new paradigms for managing that cannot be foreseen today.[33]

A WORLD OF DIFFERENCE

Aetna Ensures Diversity

Did you know that 10 percent of white Americans have no health insurance? Did you know that 18 percent of Asian Americans, 19 percent of African Americans, and 33 percent of Hispanics have no coverage? When you consider the fact that people of color are also less frequently diagnosed with major diseases and less likely to receive prescription medicines, you're looking at the picture of a healthcare system whose colors and contours are decidedly out of balance.

Aetna is one company that's trying to adjust that imbalance. The insurer, which provides coverage for health, life, disability, and long-term care, has created a variety of innovative programs to aid minorities. One program, for example, focuses on the high rate of certain diseases in ethnic populations, such as the prevalence of diabetes among African Americans. While Aetna supplies special educational materials, case managers, health screenings, and online patient support, the Aetna Foundation, the company's independent philanthropic arm, takes the initiative further by funding research into better diagnostic tools and new treatments; in 2010, the Foundation contributed $15.6 million toward this effort.

Aetna's interest in diversity also includes its employment practices. The company's workforce includes 36 percent people of color and 75 percent women, and one-third of its top management team consists of women and members of racial minorities. Aetna chairman and CEO Ronald A. Williams is one of just five African Americans (including one woman) currently serving as CEOs of *Fortune* 500 corporations (and one of just eight ever to attain the position). Every year since 2003, Aetna has received a top rating of 100 percent in the Corporate Equality Index, a survey of diversity-related practices and policies conducted by the Human Rights Campaign Foundation. In 2010, Aetna also made DiversityInc's list of the Top 50 Companies for Diversity® (for the second straight year) and *Black Enterprise* magazine's list of the "40 Best Companies for Diversity" (for the fifth straight year).

Under Williams, a soft-spoken master implementer as well as a forceful leader, Aetna has increased its focus on better and more

Joshua Prezant/Bloomberg /Getty Images

inclusive healthcare coverage, and in the process, the company has both expanded its customer base and driven down costs. "We know," says Chief Diversity Officer Raymond Arroyo, "that culturally competent programs . . . are effective in improving the quality of care of our members, who are people of color." They're also cost effective because the insurer has lower costs when patients enjoy better treatment outcomes and stay healthier. "Quality costs less," says CEO Williams, and it's a policy that's paying off for a company that suffered a net loss of $280 million back in 2001. Net profits hit $1.7 billion in 2007 before leveling off in 2008–2010 because of losses stemming from the recession.

References: "Aetna," *DiversityInc Top 50 Companies for Diversity*, March 9, 2010, www.diversityinc.com on January 25, 2011; "Aetna, Aetna Foundation Awarded $15.6 Billion in 2010," *Philanthropy News Digest*, March 27, 2011, http://foundationcenter.org on May 10, 2011; Andrés Tapia, "Take Five with Raymond Arroyo, CDO at Aetna, Ranked among Top Companies in Diversity," *The Inclusion Paradox*, August 26, 2010, http://inclusionparadox.com on January 25, 2011; Wayne Cascio, *Aetna: Investing in Diversity Case* (Alexandria, VA: Society for Human Resource Management, 2009), www.shrm.org on January 25, 2011; Aetna Inc., "Company Demographics," "Commitment to Diversity," "Racial and Ethnic Health Care Equity," "Serving a Diverse Marketplace," "The Aetna Foundation," www.aetna.com on January 25, 2011.

Managers must also be prepared to address organization change.[34] This has always been a concern, but the rapid, constant environmental change faced by businesses today has made change management even more critical. Simply put, an organization that fails to monitor its environment and to change to keep pace with that environment is doomed to failure. But more and more managers are seeing change as an opportunity, not a cause for alarm. Indeed, some managers think that if things get too calm in an organization and people start to become complacent, managers should shake things up to get everyone energized.

New technology, especially as it relates to information, also poses an increasingly important challenge for managers. Communications advances such as smart phones and other wireless communication networks have made it easier than ever for managers to communicate with one another. At the same time, these innovations have increased the pace of work for managers, cut into their time for thoughtful contemplation of decisions, and increased the amount of information they must process.

A final element of the new workplace we will note here is the complex array of new ways of organizing that managers can consider. Many organizations strive for greater flexibility and the ability to respond more quickly to their environments by adopting flatter structures. These flat structures are characterized by fewer levels of management, wider spans of management, and fewer rules and regulations. The increased use of work teams also goes hand in hand with this new approach to organizing. We will examine these new ways of organizing in Chapters 15 and 22.

CONCEPT CHECK

What are the central components that characterize the new workplace?

What are some even newer issues that managers today confront?

Summary of Learning Objectives and Key Points

1. Describe the nature of management, define management and managers, and characterize their importance to contemporary organizations.

   - Management is a set of activities (including planning and decision making, organizing, leading, and controlling) directed at an organization's resources (human, financial, physical, and information) with the aim of achieving organizational goals in an efficient and effective manner.
   - A manager is someone whose primary responsibility is to carry out the management process within an organization.

2. Identify and briefly explain the four basic management functions in organizations.

   - Planning and decision making (determining courses of action)
   - Organizing (coordinating activities and resources)
   - Leading (motivating and managing people)
   - Controlling (monitoring and evaluating activities)
   - These activities are not performed on a systematic and predictable schedule.

3. Describe the kinds of managers found at different levels and in different areas of the organization.

   - By level, we can identify top, middle, and first-line managers.
   - Kinds of managers by area include marketing, financial, operations, human resource, administrative, and specialized managers.

4. Identify the basic managerial roles that managers play and the skills they need to be successful.

   - Interpersonal roles (figurehead, leader, and liaison)
   - Informational roles (monitor, disseminator, and spokesperson)
   - Decisional roles (entrepreneur, disturbance handler, resource allocator, and negotiator)
   - Key management skills are technical, interpersonal, conceptual, diagnostic, communication, decision-making, and time-management skills.

5. Discuss the science and the art of management, describe how people become managers, and summarize the scope of management in organizations.

   - The effective practice of management requires a synthesis of science and art, that is, a blend of rational objectivity and intuitive insight.
   - Most managers attain their skills and positions through a combination of education and experience.
   - Management processes are applicable in a wide variety of settings, including profit-seeking organizations (large, small, and start-up businesses and international businesses) and not-for-profit organizations (government organizations, educational organizations, health-care facilities, and nontraditional organizations).

6. Characterize the new workplace that is emerging in organizations today.

   - The new workplace is characterized by workforce expansion and reduction.
   - Diversity is also a central component, as is the new worker.
   - Organization change is also more common, as are the effects of information technology and new ways of organizing.

Discussion Questions

Questions for Review

1. Contrast efficiency and effectiveness. Give an example of a time when an organization was effective but not efficient, efficient but not effective, both efficient and effective, and neither efficient nor effective.
2. What are the four basic activities that comprise the management process? How are they related to one another?

3. Briefly describe the ten managerial roles described by Henry Mintzberg. Give an example of each.
4. Describe a typical manager's day. What are some of the expected consequences of this type of daily experience?

Questions for Analysis

5. Recall a recent group project or task in which you have participated. Explain how members of the group displayed each of the managerial skills.
6. The text notes that management is both a science and an art. Recall an interaction you have had with a "superior" (manager, teacher, group leader). In that interaction, how did the superior use science? If he or she did not use science, what could have been done to use science? In that interaction, how did the superior use art? If he or she did not use art, what could have been done to use art?

7. Visit the websites of at least five large corporations and locate a biography of each CEO. What formal management education do these leaders have? In your opinion, what is the appropriate amount of formal education needed to be a corporate CEO? Why?

Questions for Application

8. Interview a manager from a local organization. Learn about how he or she performs each of the functions of management, the roles he or she plays, and the skills necessary to do the job.
9. Find an organization chart. You can find one in the library or by searching online. Locate top, middle, and first-line managers on the chart. What are some of the job titles held by persons at each level?

10. Watch a movie or television program that involves an organization of some type. One of the newer *Harry Potter* or *James Bond* movies would be good choices (or perhaps *Citizen Kane* for classic movie buffs). For television, options like *The Office*, *30 Rock*, or *The Good Wife* would be ideal. Identify as many management activities, skills, and roles as you can.

 CengageNow™ Highlights

Now use your CengageNow™ homework to help you:
- Apply management theories in your life
- Assess your management skills
- Master management terms and concepts
- Apply your knowledge to real-world situations
- Analyze and solve challenging management problems

In order to take advantage of these elements, your instructor will need to have set up a course for your class within CengageNow™. Ask your instructor to contact his/her Cengage sales representative and Digital Solutions Manager to explore testing CengageNow™ in your course this term.

2 CHAPTER

Traditional and Contemporary Issues and Challenges

LEARNING OBJECTIVES

After studying this chapter, you should be able to:

1. Justify the importance of history and theory to management and discuss precursors to modern management theory.

2. Summarize and evaluate the classical perspective on management, including scientific and administrative management, and note its relevance to contemporary managers.

3. Summarize and evaluate the behavioral perspective on management, including the Hawthorne studies, human relations movement, and organizational behavior, and note its relevance to contemporary managers.

4. Summarize and evaluate the quantitative perspective on management, including management science and operations management, and note its relevance to contemporary managers.

5. Discuss the systems and contingency approaches to management and explain their potential for integrating the other areas of management.

6. Identify and describe contemporary management issues and challenges.

MANAGEMENT IN ACTION Some Keys to Making a Steinway

Everybody knows what a grand piano looks like, although it's hard to describe its contour as anything other than "piano shaped." From a bird's-eye view, you might recognize something like a great big holster. The *case*—the curved lateral surface that runs around the whole instrument—appears to be a single continuous piece of wood, but it isn't really. If you look carefully at the case of a piano built by Steinway & Sons, you'll see that you're actually looking at a remarkable composite of raw material, craftsmanship, and technology. The process by which this component is made—like most of the processes for making a Steinway grand—is a prime example of a *technical, or task, subsystem* at work in a highly specialized factory.

The *case* starts out as a *rim*, which is constructed out of separate slats of wood, mostly maple (Eastern rock maple, to be precise). Once raw boards have been cut and planed, they're glued along their lengthwise edges to the width of 12½ inches. These composite pieces are then jointed and glued end-to-end to form slats 22 feet long—the measure of the piano's perimeter. Next, a total of 18 separate slats—14 layers of maple and 4 layers of other types of wood—are glued and stacked together to form a *book*—one (seemingly) continuous "board" 3¼ inches thick. Then comes the process that's a favorite

> "It's a product that in some sense speaks to people. . . . What [Steinway] craftsmen work on today will be here for another 50 or 100 years."
>
> —STEINWAY EXECUTIVE LEO F. SPELLMAN

of visitors on the Steinway factory tour—bending this rim into the shape of a piano. Steinway does it pretty much the same way that it has for more than a century—by hand and all at once. Because the special glue is in the process of drying, a crew of six has just 20 minutes to wrestle the book, with block and tackle and wooden levers and mallets, into a *rim-bending press*—"a giant piano-shaped vise," as Steinway describes it—which will force the wood to "forget" its natural inclination to be straight and assume the familiar contour of a grand piano.

Visitors report the sound of splintering wood, but Steinway artisans assure them that the specially cured wood isn't likely to break or the specially mixed glue to lose its grip. It's a good thing, too, both because the wood is expensive and because the precision Steinway process can't afford much wasted effort. The company needs 12 months, 12,000 parts, 450 craftspeople, and

Creating a Steinway piano is a labor of love that involves many different management techniques and processes.

Craig Ellenwood/Alamy

countless hours of skilled labor to produce a grand piano. Today, the New York factory turns out about 10 pianos in a day or 2,500 a year. (A mass-producer might build 2,000 pianos a week.) The result of this painstaking task system, according to one business journalist with a good ear, is "both impossibly perfect instruments and a scarcity," and that's why Steinways are so expensive—currently, somewhere between $45,000 and $110,000.

But Steinway pianos, the company reminds potential buyers, have always been "built to a standard, not to a price." "It's a product," says company executive Leo F. Spellman, "that in some sense speaks to people and will have a legacy long after we're gone. What [Steinway] craftsmen work on today will be here for another 50 or 100 years." Approximately 90 percent of all concert pianists prefer the sound of a Steinway, and the company's attention to manufacturing detail reflects the fact that when a piano is being played, the entire instrument vibrates—and thus affects its sound. In other words—and not surprisingly—the better the raw materials, design, and construction, the better the sound.

That's one of the reasons why Steinway craftsmen put so much care into the construction of the piano's case: It's a major factor in the way the body of the instrument resonates. The maple wood for the case, for example, arrives at the factory with water content of 80 percent. It's then dried, both in the open air and in kilns, until the water content is reduced to about 10 percent—suitable for both strength and pliability. To ensure that strength and pliability remain stable, the slats must be cut so that they're horizontally grained and arranged, with the "inside" of one slat—the side that grew toward the center of the tree—facing the "outside" of the next one in the book. The case is removed from the press after one day and then stored for ten weeks in a humidity-controlled *rim-bending room*. Afterwards, it's ready to be sawed, planed, and sanded to specification—a process called *frazing*. A black lacquer finish is added, and only then is the case ready to be installed as a component of a grand piano in progress.

The Steinway process also puts a premium on skilled workers. Steinway has always been an employer of immigrant labor, beginning with the German craftsmen and laborers hired by founder Henry Steinway in the 1860s and 1870s. Today, Steinway employees come from much different places—Haitians and Dominicans in the 1980s, exiles from war-torn Yugoslavia in the 1990s—and it still takes time to train them. It takes about a year, for instance, to train a case maker, and "when you lose one of them for a long period of time," says Gino Romano, a senior supervisor hired in 1964, "it has a serious effect on our output." Romano recalls one year in mid-June when a case maker was injured in a car accident and was out for several weeks. His department fell behind schedule, and it was September before Romano could find a suitable replacement (an experienced case maker in Florida who happened to be a relative of another Steinway worker).

The company's employees don't necessarily share Spellman's sense of the company's legacy, but many of them are well aware of the brand recognition commanded by the products they craft. "The payback," says Romano,

is not in [the factory]. The payback is outside, when you get the celebrity treatment for building a Steinway, when you meet somebody for the first time and they ooh and ahh: "You build Steinways? Wow." You're automatically put on a higher level, and you go, "I didn't realize I was that notable."[1]

As Steinway managers are well aware, it's critically important that all managers focus on today's competitive environment and the ways in which that environment will change tomorrow. But as our story indicates, it's also important that they use the past as context. Managers in a wide array of organizations can learn both effective and ineffective practices and strategies by understanding what managers have done in the past. Indeed, history plays an important role in many businesses today, and more and more managers are recognizing that many lessons of the past are important ingredients in future successes.

This chapter provides an overview of traditional management thought, so that you, too, can better appreciate the importance of history in today's business world. We set the stage by establishing the historical context of management. We then discuss the three traditional management perspectives—classical, behavioral, and quantitative. Next we describe the systems and contingency perspectives as approaches that help integrate the three traditional perspectives. Finally, we introduce and discuss a variety of contemporary management issues and challenges.

The Role of Theory and History in Management

Practicing managers are increasingly seeing the value of theory and history in their work. In this section, we first explain why theory and history are important and then identify important precursors to management theory.

The Importance of Theory and History

Some people question the value of history and theory. Their arguments are usually based on the assumptions that history is not relevant to contemporary society and that theory is abstract and of no practical use. In reality, however, both theory and history are important to all managers today.

Why Theory? A theory is simply a conceptual framework for organizing knowledge and providing a blueprint for action.[2] Although some theories seem abstract and irrelevant, others appear very simple and practical. Management theories, used to build organizations and guide them toward their goals, are grounded in reality.[3] Practically any organization that uses assembly lines (such as Daimler AG, Black & Decker, and Maytag) is drawing on what we describe later in this chapter as "scientific management." Many organizations, including Best Buy, Texas Instruments, and Seiko, use concepts developed from the behavioral perspective (also introduced later) to improve employee satisfaction and motivation. And naming a large company that does not use one or more techniques from the quantitative management perspective would be difficult. For example, retailers like Kroger and Target routinely use operations management to determine how many checkout lines they need to have open at any given time.

In addition, most managers develop and refine their own theories of how they should run their organizations and manage the behavior of their employees. For example, James Sinegal, founder and CEO of Costco Wholesale, believes that paying his employees well but otherwise keeping prices as low as possible are the key ingredients in success for his business. This belief is based essentially on his personal theory of competition in the warehouse retailing industry.

Why History? Awareness and understanding of important historical developments are also important to contemporary managers.[4] Understanding the historical context of management provides a sense of heritage and can help managers avoid the mistakes of others. Most courses in U.S. history devote time to business and economic developments in this country, including the Industrial Revolution, the early labor movement, and the Great Depression, and to such captains of U.S. industry as Cornelius Vanderbilt (railroads), John D. Rockefeller (oil), and Andrew Carnegie (steel). The contributions of those and other industrialists left a profound imprint on contemporary culture.[5]

Many managers are also realizing that they can benefit from a greater understanding of history in general. For example, Ian M. Ross of AT&T's Bell Laboratories cites *The Second World War* by Winston Churchill as a major influence on his approach to leadership. Other books often mentioned by managers for their relevance to today's business problems include such classics as Plato's *Republic*, Homer's *Iliad*, and Machiavelli's *The Prince*.[6] And new business history books have also been directed at women managers and the lessons they can learn from the past.[7]

theory
A conceptual framework for organizing knowledge and providing a blueprint for action

Managers at Wells Fargo clearly recognize the value of history. For example, the company maintains an extensive archival library of its old banking documents and records, and even employs a full-time corporate historian. As part of their orientation and training, new managers at Wells Fargo take courses to become acquainted with the bank's history.[8] Similarly, Shell Oil, Levi Strauss, Halliburton, Lloyd's of London, Disney, Honda, and Unilever all maintain significant archives about their pasts and frequently evoke images from those pasts in their orientation and training programs, advertising campaigns, and other public relations activities.

> "Business history lets us look at what we did right and, more important, it can help us be right the next time."
>
> —ALFRED CHANDLER, NOTED BUSINESS HISTORIAN[9]

Precursors to Management Theory

Even though large businesses have been around for only a few hundred years, management has been practiced for thousands of years. By examining management in antiquity and identifying some of the first management pioneers, we set the stage for a more detailed look at the emergence of management theory and practice over the last hundred years.

Management in Antiquity The practice of management can be traced back thousands of years. The Egyptians used the management functions of planning, organizing, and controlling when they constructed the pyramids. Alexander the Great employed a staff organization to coordinate activities during his military campaigns. The Roman Empire developed a well-defined organizational structure that greatly facilitated communication and control. Socrates discussed management practices and concepts in 400 B.C., Plato described job specialization in 350 B.C., and Alfarabi listed several leadership traits in A.D. 900.[10] Figure 2.1 is a simple time line showing a few of the most important management breakthroughs and practices over the last 4,000 years.

Early Management Pioneers In spite of this history, however, management *per se* was not given serious attention for several centuries. Indeed, the study of management did not begin until the nineteenth century. Robert Owen (1771–1858), a British industrialist and

FIGURE 2.1 MANAGEMENT IN ANTIQUITY

Management has been practiced for thousands of years. For example, the ancient Babylonians used management in governing their empire, and the ancient Romans used management to facilitate communication and control throughout their far-flung territories. The Egyptians used planning and controlling techniques in the construction of their pyramids.

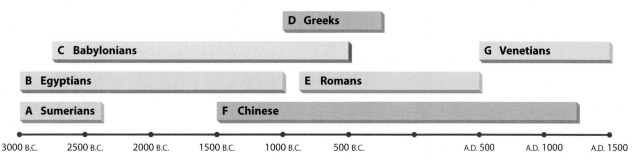

A Used written rules and regulations for governance

B Used management practices to construct pyramids

C Used extensive set of laws and policies for governance

D Used different governing systems for cities and state

E Used organized structure for communication and control

F Used extensive organization structure for government agencies and the arts

G Used organization design and planning concepts to control the seas

© Cengage Learning 2013

reformer, was one of the first managers to recognize the importance of an organization's human resources. Until his era, factory workers were generally viewed in much the same way that machinery and equipment were. A factory owner himself, Owen believed that workers deserved respect and dignity. He implemented better working conditions, a higher minimum working age for children, meals for employees, and reduced work hours. He assumed that giving more attention to workers would pay off in increased output.

Whereas Owen was interested primarily in employee welfare, Charles Babbage (1792–1871), an English mathematician, focused his attention on efficiencies of production. His primary contribution was his book *On the Economy of Machinery and Manufactures*.[11] Babbage placed great faith in the division of labor and advocated the application of mathematics to such problems as the efficient use of facilities and materials. In a sense, his work was a forerunner of both the classical and the quantitative management perspectives. Nor did he overlook the human element. He understood that a harmonious relationship between management and labor could serve to benefit both, and he favored such devices as profit-sharing plans. In many ways, Babbage was an originator of modern management theory and practice.

Why are theory and history each important to managers?

Identify a key historical figure who interests you and then describe that person's contributions from a managerial or an organizational perspective.

CONCEPT CHECK

The Classical Management Perspective

At the dawn of the twentieth century, the preliminary ideas and writings of these and other managers and theorists converged with the emergence and evolution of large-scale businesses and management practices to create interest and focus attention on how businesses should be operated. The first important ideas to emerge are now called the **classical management perspective**. This perspective actually includes two different viewpoints: scientific management and administrative management.

Scientific Management

Productivity emerged as a serious business problem during the first few years of this century. Business was expanding and capital was readily available, but labor was in short supply. Hence, managers began to search for ways to use existing labor more efficiently. In response to this need, experts began to focus on ways to improve the performance of individual workers. Their work led to the development of **scientific management**. Some of the earliest advocates of scientific management included Frederick W. Taylor (1856–1915), Frank Gilbreth (1868–1924), Lillian Gilbreth (1878–1972), Henry Gantt (1861–1919), and Harrington Emerson (1853–1931).[12] Taylor played the dominant role.

One of Taylor's first jobs was as a foreman at the Midvale Steel Company in Philadelphia. It was there that he observed what he called **soldiering**—employees deliberately working at a pace slower than their capabilities. Taylor studied and timed each element of the steelworkers' jobs. He determined what each worker should be producing, and then he designed the most efficient way of doing each part of the overall task. Next he implemented a piecework pay system. Rather than paying all employees the same wage, he began increasing the pay of each worker who met and exceeded the target level of output set for his or her job.

classical management perspective
Consists of two distinct branches—scientific management and administrative management

scientific management
Concerned with improving the performance of individual workers

soldiering
Employees deliberately working at a slow pace

FIGURE 2.2 STEPS IN SCIENTIFIC MANAGEMENT

Frederick Taylor developed this system of scientific management, which he believed would lead to a more efficient and productive workforce. Bethlehem Steel was among the first organizations to profit from scientific management and still practices some parts of it today.

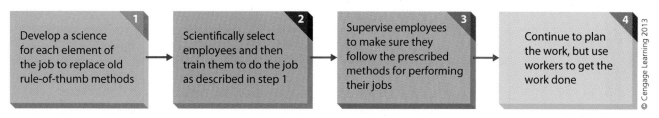

1	2	3	4
Develop a science for each element of the job to replace old rule-of-thumb methods	Scientifically select employees and then train them to do the job as described in step 1	Supervise employees to make sure they follow the prescribed methods for performing their jobs	Continue to plan the work, but use workers to get the work done

© Cengage Learning 2013

After Taylor left Midvale, he worked as a consultant for several companies, including Simonds Rolling Machine Company and Bethlehem Steel. At Simonds he studied and redesigned jobs, introduced rest periods to reduce fatigue, and implemented a piecework pay system. The results were higher quality and quantity of output, and improved morale. At Bethlehem Steel, Taylor studied efficient ways of loading and unloading railcars and applied his conclusions with equally impressive results. During these experiences, he formulated the basic ideas that he called "scientific management." Figure 2.2 illustrates the basic steps Taylor suggested. He believed that managers who followed his guidelines would improve the efficiency of their workers.[13]

Taylor's work had a major impact on U.S. industry. By applying his principles, many organizations achieved major gains in efficiency. Taylor was not without his detractors, however. Labor argued that scientific management was just a device to get more work from each employee and to reduce the total number of workers needed by a firm. There was a congressional investigation into Taylor's ideas, and evidence suggests that he falsified some of his findings.[14] Nevertheless, Taylor's work left a lasting imprint on business.[15]

Frank and Lillian Gilbreth, contemporaries of Taylor, were a husband-and-wife team of industrial engineers. One of Frank Gilbreth's most interesting contributions was to the craft of bricklaying. After studying bricklayers at work, he developed several procedures for doing the job more efficiently. For example, he specified standard materials and techniques, including the positioning of the bricklayer, the bricks, and the mortar at different levels. The results of these changes were a reduction from 18 separate physical movements to five and an increase in output of about 200 percent. Lillian Gilbreth made equally important contributions to several different areas of work, helped shape the field of industrial psychology, and made substantive contributions to the field of personnel management. Working individually and together, the Gilbreths developed numerous techniques and strategies for eliminating inefficiency. They applied many of their ideas to their family and documented their experiences raising 12 children in the book and original 1950 movie *Cheaper by the Dozen.*

Henry Gantt, another contributor to scientific management, was an associate of Taylor at Midvale, Simonds, and Bethlehem Steel. Later, working alone, he developed other techniques for improving worker output. One, called the "Gantt chart," is still used today. A Gantt chart is essentially a means of scheduling work and can be generated for each worker or for a complex project as a whole. Gantt also refined Taylor's ideas about piecework pay systems.

Like Taylor, the Gilbreths, and Gantt, Harrington Emerson was a management consultant. He made quite a stir in 1910 when he appeared before the Interstate Commerce Commission to testify about a rate increase requested by the railroads. As an expert witness, Emerson asserted that the railroads could save $1 million a day by using scientific management. He was also a strong advocate of specialized management roles in organizations, believing that job specialization was as relevant to managerial work as it was to operating jobs.

Administrative Management

Whereas scientific management deals with the jobs of individual employees, administrative management focuses on managing the total organization. The primary contributors to administrative management were Henri Fayol (1841–1925), Lyndall Urwick (1891–1983), Max Weber (1864–1920), and Chester Barnard (1886–1961).

Henri Fayol was administrative management's most articulate spokesperson. A French industrialist, Fayol was unknown to U.S. managers and scholars until his most important work, *General and Industrial Management*, was translated into English in 1930.[16] Drawing on his own managerial experience, he attempted to systematize the practice of management to provide guidance and direction to other managers. Fayol also was the first to identify the specific managerial functions of planning, organizing, leading, and controlling. He believed that these functions accurately reflect the core of the management process. Most contemporary management books (including this one) still use this framework, and practicing managers agree that these functions are a critical part of their jobs.

After a career as a British army officer, Lyndall Urwick became a noted management theorist and consultant. He integrated scientific management with the work of Fayol and other administrative management theorists. He also advanced modern thinking about the functions of planning, organizing, and controlling. Like Fayol, he developed a list of guidelines for improving managerial effectiveness. Urwick is noted not so much for his own contributions as for his synthesis and integration of the work of others.

Although Max Weber lived and worked at the same time as Fayol and Taylor, his contributions were not recognized until some years had passed. Weber was a German sociologist, and his most important work was not translated into English until 1947.[17] Weber's work on bureaucracy laid the foundation for contemporary organization theory, discussed in detail in Chapter 15. The concept of bureaucracy, as we discuss later, is based on a rational set of guidelines for structuring organizations in the most efficient manner.

Chester Barnard, former president of New Jersey Bell Telephone Company, made notable contributions to management in his book *The Functions of the Executive*.[18] The book proposes a major theory about the acceptance of authority. The theory suggests that subordinates weigh the legitimacy of a supervisor's directives and then decide whether to accept them. An order is accepted if the subordinate understands it, is able to comply with it, and views it as appropriate. The importance of Barnard's work is enhanced by his experience as a top manager.

The Classical Management Perspective Today

The contributions and limitations of the classical management perspective are summarized in Table 2.1. The classical perspective is the framework from which later theories evolved, and many of its insights still hold true today. For example, many of the job specialization techniques and scientific methods espoused by Taylor and his contemporaries are still reflected in the way that many industrial jobs are designed today.[19] Moreover, many contemporary organizations still use some of the bureaucratic procedures suggested by Weber. Also, these early theorists were the first to focus attention on management as a meaningful field

administrative management
Focuses on managing the total organization

TABLE 2.1 THE CLASSICAL MANAGEMENT PERSPECTIVE

The limitations of the classical perspective should not be overlooked. These early writers dealt with stable, simple organizations; many organizations today, in contrast, are changing and complex. They also proposed universal guidelines that we now recognize do not fit every organization. A third limitation of the classical management perspective is that it slighted the role of the individual in organizations. This role was much more fully developed by advocates of the behavioral management perspective.

General Summary	The classical management perspective had two primary thrusts. Scientific management focused on employees within organizations and on ways to improve their productivity. Noted pioneers of scientific management were Frederick Taylor, Frank and Lillian Gilbreth, Henry Gantt, and Harrington Emerson. Administrative management focused on the total organization and on ways to make it more efficient and effective. Prominent administrative management theorists were Henri Fayol, Lyndall Urwick, Max Weber, and Chester Barnard.
Contributions	Laid the foundation for later developments in management theory.
	Identified important management processes, functions, and skills that are still recognized today.
	Focused attention on management as a valid subject of scientific inquiry.
Limitations	More appropriate for stable and simple organizations than for today's dynamic and complex organizations.
	Often prescribed universal procedures that are not appropriate in some settings.
	Even though some writers (such as Lillian Gilbreth and Chester Barnard) were concerned with the human element, many viewed employees as tools rather than resources.

of study. Several aspects of the classical perspective are also relevant to our later discussions of planning, organizing, and controlling. And recent advances in areas such as business-to-business (B2B) electronic commerce also have efficiency as their primary goal.

Summarize scientific management and describe the key ideas set forth by Taylor.

Compare and contrast scientific management and administrative management.

CONCEPT CHECK

The Behavioral Management Perspective

Early advocates of the classical management perspective viewed organizations and jobs from an essentially mechanistic point of view; that is, they essentially sought to conceptualize organizations as machines and workers as cogs within those machines. Even though many early writers recognized the role of individuals, their focus tended to be on how managers could control and standardize the behavior of their employees. In contrast, the behavioral management perspective placed much more emphasis on individual attitudes and behaviors and on group processes, and recognized the importance of behavioral processes in the workplace.

The behavioral management perspective was stimulated by a number of writers and theoretical movements. One of those movements was *industrial psychology*, the practice of

behavioral management perspective
Emphasizes individual attitudes and behaviors and group processes

Courtesy of At&T Archives and History Center, Warren, NJ

The Hawthorne studies were a series of early experiments that focused on behavior in the workplace. In one experiment involving this group of workers, for example, researchers monitored how productivity changed as a result of changes in working conditions. The Hawthorne studies and subsequent experiments led scientists to the conclusion that the human element is very important in the workplace.

applying psychological concepts to industrial settings. Hugo Munsterberg (1863–1916), a noted German psychologist, is recognized as the father of industrial psychology. He established a psychological laboratory at Harvard in 1892, and his pioneering book, *Psychology and Industrial Efficiency,* was translated into English in 1913.[20] Munsterberg suggested that psychologists could make valuable contributions to managers in the areas of employee selection and motivation. Industrial psychology is still a major course of study at many colleges and universities. Another early advocate of the behavioral approach to management was Mary Parker Follett (1868–1933).[21] Follett worked during the scientific management era, but quickly came to recognize the human element in the workplace. Indeed, her work clearly anticipated the behavioral management perspective, and she appreciated the need to understand the role of behavior in organizations.

Although Munsterberg and Follett made major contributions to the development of the behavioral approach to management, its primary catalyst was a series of studies conducted near Chicago at Western Electric's Hawthorne plant between 1927 and 1932. The research, originally sponsored by General Electric, was conducted by Elton Mayo and his associates.[22] Mayo was a faculty member and consultant at Harvard. The first study involved manipulating illumination for one group of workers and comparing their subsequent productivity with the productivity of another group whose illumination was not changed. Surprisingly, when illumination was increased for the experimental group, productivity went up in both groups. Productivity continued to increase in both groups, even when the lighting for the experimental group was decreased. Not until the lighting was reduced to the level of moonlight did productivity begin to decline (and General Electric withdrew its sponsorship).

Another experiment established a piecework incentive pay plan for a group of nine men assembling terminal banks for telephone exchanges. Scientific management would have predicted that each man would try to maximize his pay by producing as many units as possible. Mayo and his associates, however, found that the group itself informally established an acceptable level of output for its members. Workers who overproduced were branded "rate busters," and underproducers were labeled "chiselers." To be accepted by the group, workers produced at the accepted level. As they approached this acceptable level of output, workers slacked off to avoid overproducing.

Other studies, including an interview program involving several thousand workers, led Mayo and his associates to conclude that human behavior was much more important in the workplace than had been previously believed. In the lighting experiment, for example, the results were attributed to the fact that both groups received special attention and sympathetic supervision for perhaps the first time. The incentive pay plans did not work because wage incentives were less important to the individual workers than was social acceptance in determining output. In short, individual and social processes played major roles in shaping worker attitudes and behavior.

The Human Relations Movement

human relations movement
Argued that workers respond primarily to the social context of the workplace

The **human relations movement,** which grew from the Hawthorne studies and was a popular approach to management for many years, proposed that workers respond primarily to the social context of the workplace, including social conditioning, group norms,

TABLE 2.2 THEORY X AND THEORY Y

Douglas McGregor developed Theory X and Theory Y. He argued that Theory X best represented the views of scientific management and Theory Y represented the human relations approach. McGregor believed that Theory Y was the best philosophy for all managers.

Theory X Assumptions	1. People do not like work and try to avoid it. 2. People do not like work, so managers have to control, direct, coerce, and threaten employees to get them to work toward organizational goals. 3. People prefer to be directed, to avoid responsibility, and to want security; they have little ambition.
Theory Y Assumptions	1. People do not naturally dislike work; work is a natural part of their lives. 2. People are internally motivated to reach objectives to which they are committed. 3. People are committed to goals to the degree that they receive personal rewards when they reach their objectives. 4. People will both seek and accept responsibility under favorable conditions. 5. People have the capacity to be innovative in solving organizational problems. 6. People are bright, but under most organizational conditions their potential is underutilized.

Source: D. McGregor and W. Bennis, *The Human Side Enterprise: 25th Anniversary Printing*, 1985. Copyright © 1985 The McGraw-Hill Companies, Inc. Reprinted with permission.

and interpersonal dynamics. A basic assumption of the human relations movement was that the manager's concern for workers would lead to increased satisfaction, which would in turn result in improved performance. Two writers who helped advance the human relations movement were Abraham Maslow (1908–1970) and Douglas McGregor (1906–1964).

In 1943 Maslow advanced a theory suggesting that people are motivated by a hierarchy of needs, including monetary incentives and social acceptance.[23] Maslow's hierarchy, perhaps the best-known human relations theory, is described in detail in Chapter 19. Meanwhile, Douglas McGregor's Theory X and Theory Y model best represents the essence of the human relations movement (see Table 2.2).[24] According to McGregor, Theory X and Theory Y reflect two extreme belief sets that different managers have about their workers. Theory X is a relatively pessimistic and negative view of workers and is consistent with the views of scientific management. Theory Y is more positive and represents the assumptions that human relations advocates make. In McGregor's view, Theory Y was a more appropriate philosophy for managers to adhere to. Both Maslow and McGregor notably influenced the thinking of many practicing managers.

The Emergence of Organizational Behavior

Munsterberg, Mayo, Maslow, McGregor, and others have made valuable contributions to management. Contemporary theorists, however, have noted that many assertions of the human relationists were simplistic and provided inadequate descriptions of work behavior. For example, the assumption that worker satisfaction leads to improved performance has been shown to have little, if any, validity. If anything, satisfaction follows good performance rather than precedes it. (These issues are addressed in Chapters 18 and 19.)

Current behavioral perspectives on management, known as **organizational behavior**, acknowledge that human behavior in organizations is much more complex than the human

Theory X
A pessimistic and negative view of workers consistent with the views of scientific management

Theory Y
A positive view of workers; it represents the assumptions that human relations advocates make

organizational behavior
Contemporary field focusing on behavioral perspectives on management

relationists realized. The field of organizational behavior draws from a broad, interdisciplinary base of psychology, sociology, anthropology, economics, and medicine. Organizational behavior takes a holistic view of behavior and addresses individual, group, and organization processes. These processes are major elements in contemporary management theory.[25] Important topics in this field include job satisfaction, stress, motivation, leadership, group dynamics, organizational politics, interpersonal conflict, and the structure and design of organizations.[26] A contingency orientation also characterizes the field (discussed more fully later in this chapter). Our discussions of organizing (Chapters 14–17) and leading (Chapters 18–22) are heavily influenced by organizational behavior. And, finally, managers need a solid understanding of human behavior as they address such diversity-related issues as ethnicity and religion in the workplace. Indeed, all of these topics are useful to help managers better deal with fallout from the consequences of layoffs and job cuts and to motivate today's workers.

The Behavioral Management Perspective Today

Table 2.3 summarizes the behavioral management perspective and lists its contributions and limitations. The primary contributions relate to ways in which this approach has changed managerial thinking. Managers are now more likely to recognize the importance of behavioral processes and to view employees as valuable resources instead of mere tools. On the other hand, organizational behavior is still relatively imprecise in its ability to predict behavior, especially the behavior of a specific individual. It is not always accepted or understood by practicing managers. Hence, the contributions of the behavioral school have yet to be fully realized. The *Ethically Speaking* box on page 37, entitled "Do You Feel Like You Have 'Kick Me' Tattooed on Your Forehead?" discusses just one form of organizational behavior that could use a little more study.

TABLE 2.3 THE BEHAVIORAL MANAGEMENT PERSPECTIVE

General Summary	The behavioral management perspective focuses on employee behavior in an organizational context. Stimulated by the birth of industrial psychology, the human relations movement supplanted scientific management as the dominant approach to management in the 1930s and 1940s. Prominent contributors to this movement were Elton Mayo, Abraham Maslow, and Douglas McGregor. Organizational behavior, the contemporary outgrowth of the behavioral management perspective, draws from an interdisciplinary base and recognizes the complexities of human behavior in organizational settings.
Contributions	Provided important insights into motivation, group dynamics, and other interpersonal processes in organizations.
	Focused managerial attention on these same processes.
	Challenged the view that employees are tools and furthered the belief that employees are valuable resources.
Limitations	The complexity of individual behavior makes prediction of that behavior difficult.
	Many behavioral concepts have not yet been put to use because some managers are reluctant to adopt them.
	Contemporary research findings by behavioral scientists are often not communicated to practicing managers in an understandable form.

© Cengage Learning 2013

ETHICALLY SPEAKING

Do You Feel Like You Have "Kick Me" Tattooed on Your Forehead?

Have you ever encountered a bully? If you've ever worked in an organizational setting, there's a pretty good chance—75 percent, says one study—that you've at least witnessed some form of the unsavory organizational behavior known as *bullying*. In fact, according to the Workplace Bullying Institute, 37 percent of the U.S. labor force—that's 54 million people—have actually been the object of bullying at some point during their work lives. And "anything that affects 37 percent of the public is an epidemic," says Institute director Gary Namie, who adds that, unfortunately, it's a "a silent epidemic" because victims tend to confide their experiences to close friends rather than to the higher-ups who might be expected to take some kind of action.

What is *bullying*? For one thing, it's a form of *aggression*—it's intended to intimidate, offend, or degrade a particular person or group of people. For another, it's a *pattern* of aggression—it involves repeated incidents or instances of certain behavior. And because it works through repetition, it often takes subtle forms and may, according to one expert, "include behaviors that don't appear obvious to others. For instance, how does an employee relate to their boss that they've been excluded from lunch? Or that they're being ignored by a coworker? The insidious nature of these behaviors makes them difficult to deal with and sanction."

Physical abuse or the threat of it are obvious forms of bullying, as are tampering with someone's personal property or workplace equipment and yelling at someone or using profanity. Other less obvious but still fairly subtle examples include:

- Spreading rumors or gossip about someone
- Excluding someone socially
- Undermining or impeding someone's work
- Intruding on someone's privacy by pestering or spying

Work-related bullying may also take the following forms:

- Removing areas of responsibility without cause
- Constantly changing work guidelines
- Establishing impossible deadlines
- Assigning unreasonable duties or workload
- Assigning too little work (to foster a sense of uselessness)

What about the consequences of bullying? How does it affect its victims? They report feeling "beaten," "abused," "broken," "maimed," "eviscerated," and "character assassinated," and many describe the sensation of having been reduced to a level of vulnerability associated with children, prisoners, and slaves. "I feel like I have 'kick me' tattooed on my forehead," admits one victim. According to a psychologist who's studied the effects of workplace bullying, "There's no question that unrelenting, daily hostilities" in the workplace ". . . can be on a par with torture" and that "repeated and severe bullying can cause psychological trauma." Adds another researcher: "Targets of severe workplace bullying are suffering from physical and psychological conditions that would drive even the strongest of us into the ground."

Paula Connelly/iStockphoto.com

References: Steve Opperman, "Workplace Bullying: Psychological Violence?" Workplace Bullying Institute, December 3, 2009, www .workplacebullying.org on March 31, 2011; Jeanna Bryner, "Workplace Bullying 'Epidemic' Worse Than Sexual Harassment," *LiveScience*, March 8, 2008, www.livescience.com on March 31, 2011; Jan Aylsworth, "Sociopaths and Bullying in the Workplace," WorkplaceViolenceNews.com, July 28, 2009, http://workplaceviolencenews.com on March 31, 2011; Teresa A. Daniel, "Tough Boss or Workplace Bully?" *SHRM*, June 1, 2009, www.shrm.org on March 31, 2011.

What were the Hawthorne studies? What was learned from this research?

What are the differences between the human relations movement and organizational behavior?

CONCEPT CHECK

The Quantitative Management Perspective

The third major school of management thought began to emerge during World War II. During the war, government officials and scientists in England and the United States worked to help the military deploy its resources more efficiently and effectively. These groups took some of the mathematical approaches to management developed decades earlier by Taylor and Gantt and applied them to logistical problems during the war.[27] They learned that problems regarding troop, equipment, and submarine deployment, for example, could all be solved through mathematical analysis. After the war, companies such as DuPont and General Electric began to use the same techniques for deploying employees, choosing plant locations, and planning warehouses. Basically, then, this perspective is concerned with applying quantitative techniques to management. More specifically, the **quantitative management perspective** focuses on decision making, economic effectiveness, mathematical models, and the use of computers. There are two branches of the quantitative approach: management science and operations management.

Management Science

Unfortunately, the term *management science* appears to be related to scientific management, the approach developed by Taylor and others early in the twentieth century. But the two have little in common and should not be confused. **Management science** focuses specifically on the development of mathematical models. A mathematical model is a simplified representation of a system, process, or relationship.

At its most basic level, management science focuses on models, equations, and similar representations of reality. For example, managers at Detroit Edison use mathematical models to determine how best to route repair crews during blackouts. Citizens Bank of New England uses models to figure out how many tellers need to be on duty at each location at various times throughout the day. In recent years, paralleling the advent of the personal computer, management science techniques have become increasingly sophisticated. For example, automobile manufacturers Daimler AG and General Motors use realistic computer simulations to study collision damage to cars. These simulations give them precise information and avoid the costs of crashing so many test cars.

Operations Management

Operations management is somewhat less mathematical and statistically sophisticated than management science and can be applied more directly to managerial situations. Indeed, we can think of **operations management** as a form of applied management science. Operations management techniques are generally concerned with helping the organization produce its products or services more efficiently and can be applied to a wide range of problems.

For example, Rubbermaid and Home Depot each use operations management techniques to manage their inventories. (Inventory management is concerned with specific inventory problems, such as balancing carrying costs and ordering costs, and determining the optimal order quantity.) Linear programming (which involves computing simultaneous solutions to a set of linear equations) helps United Airlines plan its flight

quantitative management perspective Applies quantitative techniques to management

management science Focuses specifically on the development of mathematical models

operations management Concerned with helping the organization more efficiently produce its products or services

schedules, Consolidated Freightways develop its shipping routes, and General Instrument Corporation plan what instruments to produce at various times. Other operations management techniques include queuing theory, break-even analysis, and simulation. All of these techniques and procedures apply directly to operations, but they are also helpful in such areas as finance, marketing, and human resource management.[28]

The Quantitative Management Perspective Today

Like the other management perspectives, the quantitative management perspective has made important contributions and has certain limitations. Both are summarized in Table 2.4. It has provided managers with an abundance of decision-making tools and techniques and has increased understanding of overall organizational processes. It has been particularly useful in the areas of planning and controlling. Relatively new management concepts such as supply chain management and new techniques such as enterprise resource planning, both discussed later in this book, also evolved from the quantitative management perspective. Even more recently, mathematicians have been using tools and techniques from the quantitative perspective to develop models that might be helpful in the war against terrorism.[29] On the other hand, mathematical models cannot fully account for individual behaviors and attitudes. Some believe that the time needed to develop competence in quantitative techniques retards the development of other managerial skills. Finally, mathematical models typically require a set of assumptions that may not be realistic.

Operations management, a form of applied management science, helps improve efficiency in the production and distribution of goods and services. This warehouse manager, for example, is showing an employee how to input and retrieve data from the firm's information system that will enable him to more efficiently manage its inventory.

sturti/Istockphoto.com

"Credit cards, bank accounts. Everything is being analyzed 24/7 whether we like it or not. You would be amazed how much data is available."

—SAMER TAKRITI, SENIOR MANAGER OF STOCHASTIC ANALYSIS AT IBM[30]

TABLE 2.4 THE QUANTITATIVE MANAGEMENT PERSPECTIVE

General Summary	The quantitative management perspective focuses on applying mathematical models and processes to management situations. Management science deals specifically with the development of mathematical models to aid in decision making and problem solving. Operations management focuses more directly on the application of management science to organizations. Management information systems are developed to provide information to managers.
Contributions	Developed sophisticated quantitative techniques to assist in decision making. Application of models has increased our awareness and understanding of complex organizational processes and situations. Has been very useful in the planning and controlling processes.
Limitations	Cannot fully explain or predict the behavior of people in organizations. Mathematical sophistication may come at the expense of other important skills. Models may require unrealistic or unfounded assumptions.

© Cengage Learning 2013

What is management science? What is operations management?

What kinds of businesses are most and least likely to be affected by concepts from the quantitative perspective? Why?

Integrating Perspectives for Managers

It is important to recognize that the classical, behavioral, and quantitative approaches to management are not necessarily contradictory or mutually exclusive. Even though each of the three perspectives makes very different assumptions and predictions, each can also complement the others. Indeed, a complete understanding of management requires an appreciation of all three perspectives. The systems and contingency perspectives can help us integrate the earlier approaches and enlarge our understanding of all three.

The Systems Perspective

We briefly introduced the systems perspective in Chapter 1 in our definition of management. A system is an interrelated set of elements functioning as a whole.[31] As shown in Figure 2.3, by viewing an organization as a system, we can identify four basic elements: inputs, transformation processes, outputs, and feedback. First, inputs are the material, human, financial, and information resources the organization gets from its environment. Next, through technological and managerial processes, inputs are transformed into outputs. Outputs include products, services, or both (tangible and intangible); profits, losses, or both (even not-for-profit organizations must operate within their budgets); employee behaviors; and information. Finally, the environment reacts to these outputs and provides feedback to the system.

Thinking of organizations as systems provides us with a variety of important viewpoints on organizations, such as the concepts of open systems, subsystems, synergy, and entropy. Open systems are systems that interact with their environment, whereas closed systems do not interact with their environment. Although organizations are open systems, some make the mistake of ignoring their environment and behaving as though their environment is not important.

FIGURE 2.3 THE SYSTEMS PERSPECTIVE OF ORGANIZATIONS

By viewing organizations as systems, managers can better understand the importance of their environment and the level of interdependence among subsystems within the organization. Managers must also understand how their decisions affect and are affected by other subsystems within the organization.

system
An interrelated set of elements functioning as a whole

open system
A system that interacts with its environment

closed system
A system that does not interact with its environment

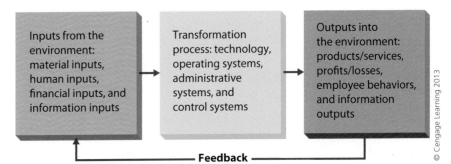

© Cengage Learning 2013

"This isn't like the auto industry, where the combustible engine still exists, or oil, where many parts of the business are the same. We have to let go of what we have invented. We stopped making typewriters, punch-card machines, PCs. We had to move on."

—JON IWATA, IBM EXECUTIVE[32]

The systems perspective also stresses the importance of subsystems—systems within a broader system. For example, the marketing, production, and finance functions within Mattel are systems in their own right but are also subsystems within the overall organization. Because they are interdependent, a change in one subsystem can affect other subsystems as well. If the production department at Mattel lowers the quality of the toys being made (by buying lower-quality materials, for example), the effects are felt in finance (improved cash flow in the short run owing to lower costs) and marketing (decreased sales in the long run because of customer dissatisfaction). Managers must therefore remember that although organizational subsystems can be managed with some degree of autonomy, their interdependence should not be overlooked. For instance, recent research has underscored the interdependence of strategy and operations in businesses.[33]

Synergy suggests that organizational units (or subsystems) may often be more successful working together than working alone. The Walt Disney Company, for example, benefits greatly from synergy. The company's movies, theme parks, television programs, and merchandise-licensing programs all benefit one another. Children who enjoy a Disney movie like *Cars 2* want to go to Disney World, see the *Cars* attractions there, and buy stuffed toys and action figures of the film's characters. Music from the film generates additional revenues for the firm, as do computer games and other licensing arrangements for lunchboxes, clothing, and so forth.

Synergy was also the major objective of the recent merger between United and Continental Airlines. The merger was projected to bring in revenue gains of $800 million to $900 million while also increasing advancement opportunities for employees. The majority of United passengers in 2010 flew in and out of Chicago, Denver, San Francisco, Washington Dulles, and Los Angeles, while Continental's main hubs were Houston, Newark, and Cleveland. Because the two companies had little overlap in their domestic routes and hubs, customers will presumably have more destination options. In terms of international travel, United has long been focused primarily between the United States and Asia and Continental has long offered more European destinations. So the combined airline will have the opportunity to outperform the combined individual airlines that existed previously.[34]

Finally, entropy is a normal process that leads to system decline. When an organization does not monitor feedback from its environment and make appropriate adjustments, it may fail. For example, witness the problems of Studebaker (an automobile manufacturer) and Circuit City (a major retailer). Each of these organizations went bankrupt because it failed to revitalize itself and keep pace with changes in its environment. A primary objective of management, from a systems perspective, is to continually re-energize the organization to avoid entropy.

Allstar Picture Library/Alamy

Disney is a master of synergy. The firm's movies, theme park attractions, and merchandise, for example, are all linked together so that each enhances the others. For instance, the recent Disney movie *Cars 2* was widely promoted at Disney World and Disneyland before the movie ever opened. And long after the movie left theaters people could still buy *Cars* merchandise throughout all Disney retail outlets.

subsystem
A system within another system

synergy
Two or more subsystems working together to produce more than the total of what they might produce working alone

entropy
A normal process leading to system decline

The Contingency Perspective

Another noteworthy recent addition to management thinking is the contingency perspective. The classical, behavioral, and quantitative approaches are considered **universal perspectives** because they try to identify the "one best way" to manage organizations. The contingency perspective, in contrast, suggests that universal theories cannot be applied to organizations because each organization is unique. Instead, the contingency perspective suggests that appropriate managerial behavior in a given situation depends on, or is contingent on, unique elements in that situation.[35]

Stated differently, effective managerial behavior in one situation cannot always be generalized to other situations. Recall, for example, that Frederick Taylor assumed that all workers would generate the highest possible level of output to maximize their own personal economic gain. We can imagine some people being motivated primarily by money—but we can just as easily imagine other people being motivated by the desire for leisure time, status, social acceptance, or any combination of these (as Mayo found at the Hawthorne plant). In 2000 Cisco Systems had the largest market cap in the world and was growing at a rate of 50 percent per year. A recession and the terrorist attacks in September 2001, however, caused the technology sector to crash and Cisco's stock dropped in value by 86 percent. Cisco's CEO, John Chambers, had to downsize the company through layoffs and divestitures and transform it into a smaller company. As he went through this process, he also changed his management style. He had previously been an autocratic manager and led Cisco using a command-and-control hierarchy. As a result of the transformation at Cisco, however, Chambers also decided he needed to change his own management style as well. So he began to adopt a much more democratic approach and to run Cisco using a more democratic organizational structure.[36]

> "Without exception, all of my biggest mistakes occurred because I moved too slowly."
>
> —JOHN CHAMBERS, CISCO CEO[37]

An Integrating Framework

We noted earlier that the classical, behavioral, and quantitative management perspectives can be complementary and that the systems and contingency perspectives can help integrate them. Our framework for integrating the various approaches to management is shown in Figure 2.4. The initial premise of the framework is that before attempting to apply any specific concepts or ideas from the three major perspectives, managers must recognize the interdependence of units within the organization, the effect of environmental influences, and the need to respond to the unique characteristics of each situation. The ideas of subsystem interdependencies and environmental influences are given to us by systems theory, and the situational view of management is derived from a contingency perspective.

With these ideas as basic assumptions, managers can use valid tools, techniques, concepts, and theories of the classical, behavioral, and quantitative management perspectives. For example, managers can still use many of the basic techniques from scientific management. In many contemporary settings, the scientific study of jobs and production techniques can enhance productivity. But managers should not rely solely on these techniques, nor should they ignore the human element. The behavioral perspective is also of use to managers today. By drawing on contemporary ideas of organizational behavior, managers can better appreciate the role of employee needs and behaviors in the workplace. Motivation, leadership, communication, and group processes are especially important. The quantitative perspective provides managers with a set of useful tools and techniques. The development and use of management science models and the application of operations management methods can help managers increase their efficiency and effectiveness.

Consider the new distribution manager of a large wholesale firm whose job is to manage 100 truck drivers and to coordinate standard truck routes in the most efficient fashion.

universal perspective
An attempt to identify the one best way to do something

contingency perspective
Suggests that appropriate managerial behavior in a given situation depends on, or is contingent on, a wide variety of elements

FIGURE 2.4　AN INTEGRATIVE FRAMEWORK OF MANAGEMENT PERSPECTIVES

Each of the major perspectives on management can be useful to modern managers. Before using any of them, however, managers should recognize the situational contexts within which they operate. The systems and contingency perspectives serve to integrate the classical, behavioral, and quantitative management perspectives.

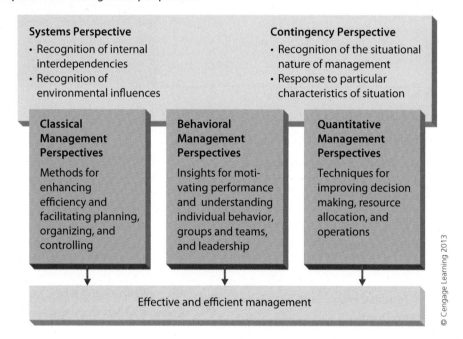

© Cengage Learning 2013

This new manager, with little relevant experience, might attempt to increase productivity by employing strict work specialization and close supervision (as suggested by scientific management). But doing so may decrease employee satisfaction and morale, and increase turnover (as predicted by organizational behavior). The manager might also develop a statistical formula to use route driver time more efficiently (from management science). But this new system could disrupt existing work groups and social patterns (from organizational behavior). The manager might create even more problems by trying to impose programs and practices derived from her previous job. An incentive program welcomed by retail clerks, for example, might not work for truck drivers.

The manager should soon realize that a broader perspective is needed. Systems and contingency perspectives help provide broader solutions. Also, as the integrative framework in Figure 2.4 illustrates, applying techniques from several schools works better than trying to make one approach solve all problems. To solve a problem of declining productivity, the manager might look to scientific management (perhaps jobs are inefficiently designed or workers improperly trained), organizational behavior (worker motivation may be low, or group norms may be limiting output), or operations management (facilities may be improperly laid out, or material shortages may be resulting from poor inventory management). And before implementing any plans for improvement, the manager should try to assess their effect on other areas of the organization.

Now suppose that the same manager is involved in planning a new warehouse. She will probably consider what type of management structure to create (classical management perspective), what kinds of leaders and work-group arrangements to develop (behavioral management perspective), and how to develop a network model for designing and operating the facility itself (quantitative perspective). As a final example, if employee turnover is too high, the manager might consider an incentive system (classical perspective), plan a motivational enhancement program (behavioral perspective), or use a mathematical model (quantitative perspective) to discover that turnover costs may actually be lower than the cost of making any changes at all.

What is the contingency perspective?

Select an organization and diagram its inputs, transformation processes, and outputs, consistent with the systems perspective.

Contemporary Management Issues and Challenges

Interest in management theory and practice has heightened in recent years as new issues and challenges have emerged. No new paradigm has been formulated that replaces the traditional views, but managers continue to strive toward a better understanding of how they can better compete and lead their organizations toward improved effectiveness. Figure 2.5 summarizes the historical development of the major models of management, described in the preceding sections, and puts into historical context the contemporary applied perspectives discussed in the next section.

FIGURE 2.5 THE EMERGENCE OF MODERN MANAGEMENT PERSPECTIVES

Most contemporary management perspectives have emerged and evolved over the last hundred years or so. Beginning with the classical management perspective, first developed toward the end of the nineteenth century, and on through contemporary applied perspectives, managers have an array of useful techniques, methods, and approaches for solving problems and enhancing the effectiveness of their organizations. Of course, managers also need to recognize that not every idea set forth is valid, and that even those that are useful are not applicable in all settings. And new methods and approaches will continue to be developed in the future.

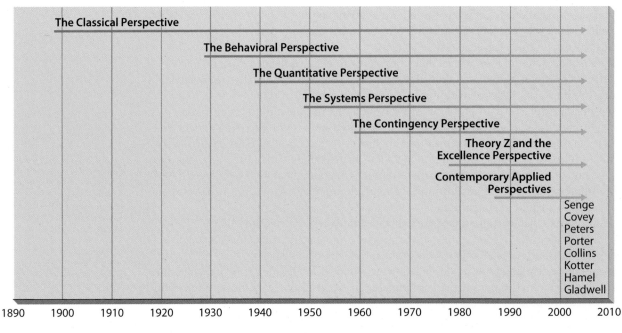

Contemporary Applied Perspectives

In recent years, books written for the popular press have also had a major impact on both the field of organizational behavior and the practice of management. This trend first surfaced in the early 1980s with the success of William Ouchi's *Theory Z* and Thomas Peters and Robert Waterman's *In Search of Excellence*. Each of these books spent time on the *New York Times* best-seller list and was required reading for any manager wanting to at least appear informed. Biographies of executives such as Warren Buffett and Jack Welch also have received widespread attention. For instance, the bidding for the publishing rights to the legendary Jack Welch's memoirs, published when he retired as CEO from General Electric, exceeded $7 million.[38]

"You are what you read."

—MARTHA FINNEY, BUSINESS WRITER[39]

Other authors have greatly influenced management theory and practice. Among the most popular such authors today are Peter Senge, Stephen Covey, Tom Peters, Jim Collins, Michael Porter, John Kotter, and Gary Hamel.[40] Their books highlight the management practices of successful firms such as Shell, Ford, IBM, and others, or outline conceptual or theoretical models or frameworks to guide managers as they formulate strategies or motivate their employees. Malcolm Gladwell's books *The Tipping Point*, *Blink*, and *Outliers* have all the caught the attention of many contemporary managers. Scott Adams, creator of the popular comic strip *Dilbert*, is also immensely popular today. Adams is a former communications industry worker who developed his strip to illustrate some of the absurdities that occasionally afflict contemporary organizational life. The daily strip is routinely posted outside office doors, above copy machines, and beside water coolers in hundreds of offices.

Contemporary Management Challenges

Managers today also face an imposing set of challenges as they guide and direct the fortunes of their companies. Coverage of each of these is thoroughly integrated throughout this book. In addition, many of them are highlighted or given focused coverage in one or more special ways.

One of the most critical challenges facing managers today is a sluggish economy that limits growth. A second important challenge is the management of diversity, as noted in Chapter 1. Another is employee privacy. A related issue has to do with the increased capabilities that technology provides for people to work at places other than their offices. The appropriate role of the Internet in business strategy is also a complex arena for managers.

Globalization is another significant contemporary challenge for managers. Managing in a global economy poses many different challenges and opportunities. For example, at a macro level, property ownership arrangements vary widely. So does the availability of natural resources and components of the infrastructure, as well as the role of government in business. Moreover, behavioral processes vary widely across cultural and national boundaries. For example, values, symbols, and beliefs differ sharply among cultures. Different work norms and the role that work plays in a person's life, for example, influence patterns of both work-related behavior and attitudes toward work. They also affect the nature of supervisory relationships, decision-making styles and processes, and organizational configurations. Group and intergroup processes, responses to stress, and the nature of political behaviors also differ from culture to culture. Chapter 5 is devoted to such global issues.

Another management challenge that has taken on renewed importance is ethics and social responsibility and their relationship to corporate governance. Unfortunately, business scandals involving unethical conduct have become almost commonplace today. From a social responsibility perspective, increasing attention has been focused on pollution and business's obligation to help clean up our environment, business contributions to social causes, and so forth. The proper framework for corporate governance is often at the center of these debates and discussions.[41] Chapter 4 covers ethics and social responsibility in more detail. Meanwhile, the *Change* box on page 46 entitled "Make a Few Pills and Call Me in 13 Years" shows how trying to take advantage of new opportunities in international relations may be a prescription for quality control problems.

THE MORE THINGS CHANGE

Make a Few Pills and Call Me in 13 Years

Generic drugs are produced with the same active ingredients as their patented counterparts; only the formulations are different. They're cheaper, of course (about one-third the price), and although there's some debate on the matter, they've always done pretty much the same thing as brand-name drugs. As recently as 2005, medical FAQ sites on the Internet typically assured concerned consumers that because the Food and Drug Administration (FDA) applies the same standards to all drug-making facilities, there was no truth to rumors that generics often came from factories with subpar quality standards. Today, however, generics are far more likely to be made overseas—a fact that has taken on additional importance in light of government plans to cut prescription-medication costs by importing more generic drugs from developing countries.

A lot of generic drugs now come from China, which is the world's leading supplier of active pharmaceutical ingredients (APIs). Unfortunately, China's reputation for safety and quality isn't exactly impeccable. In 2007, for example, the U.S. Centers for Disease Control (CDC) received reports of extreme allergic reactions to the anticoagulant heparin, which is manufactured by Baxter Healthcare, a U.S. maker of both drugs and medical equipment. In January 2008, Baxter issued 13 different recalls of heparin injections, and the FDA reported 93 deaths and hundreds of adverse reactions between January and March. In December, the CDC confirmed that Baxter's heparin supplies had been tainted by a counterfeit ingredient produced by Changzhou SPL, a Chinese plant partially owned by Scientific Protein Laboratories (SPL), a Wisconsin-based supplier of APIs.

Among other things, reported the FDA, Changzhou "actually went through a screening process, determined a supplier was unacceptable, and then went ahead and used raw material from that supplier anyway. . . . [It's] like a school system screening for sex offenders in its teachers and then hiring a teacher who was a sex offender, anyway." (In 2010, the FDA also cited SPL for lax investigation into a customer complaint about contaminated batches of heparin.)

Fuse/Jupiter Images

The FDA is charged with inspecting pharmaceutical plants both at home and abroad, but with the proliferation of facilities in foreign countries, literally years may elapse between inspections. The process is further hampered in China because of language barriers, record-keeping discrepancies, and confusing company names. In September 2008, the Government Accountability Office (GAO) criticized the FDA's handling of overseas inspections, charging that, between 2002 and 2007, the FDA issued 15 warnings to foreign manufacturers but followed up by re-inspecting only four of the facilities—and then only after lapses of two to five years. Among other recommendations, the GAO suggested that the FDA monitor foreign drug-handling facilities as closely as it does those in the United States, which are inspected every 2.7 years. The GAO admitted, however, that with 10,000 sites scattered around the world, the FDA's present resources would permit the agency to visit each of them only once every 13 years. "Significant challenges remain," concluded the report.

References: "Tainted Baxter Heparin Behind Allergic Reactions, CDC Says" (New York: Parker Waichman Alonso LLP, 2008), www.yourlawyer.com on January 28, 2011; Nick Taylor, "GAO Critical of FDA's Overseas Inspections," In-PharmaTechnologist.com, October 23, 2008, www.in-pharmatechnologist.com on January 28, 2011; U.S Food and Drug Administration, "Information on Heparin," "FDA Public Health Alert: Change in Heparin USP Monograph," "FDA Drug Safety Communication: Update: Follow Up to the Public Health Alert about Changes to the Heparin Sodium USP Monograph," April 7, 2010, www.fda.gov on January 28, 2011; Alicia Mundy, "FDA Finds Heparin Maker Violations," Wall Street Journal, October 14, 2010, http://online.wsj.com on January 28, 2011.

Quality also continues to pose an important management challenge today. Quality is an important issue for several reasons. First, more and more organizations are using quality as a basis for competition. Second, improving quality tends to increase productivity because making higher-quality products generally results in less waste and rework. Third, enhancing quality lowers costs. Managers at Whistler Corporation once realized that the firm was using 100 of its 250 employees to repair defective radar detectors that had been built incorrectly in the first place. Quality is also important because of its relationship to productivity. Quality is highlighted in Chapter 12.

Finally, the shift toward a service economy also continues to be important. Traditionally, most U.S. businesses were manufacturers—using tangible resources like raw materials and machinery to create tangible products like automobiles and steel. And manufacturing is indeed still important in the U.S. economy. The United States remains by far the world's largest manufacturer. Between 1990 and 2009, for example, U.S. manufacturing output grew by nearly $800 billion.[42] And in 2010 U.S. manufacturers produced nearly $1.7 trillion worth of goods.[43]

In the last few decades, however, the service sector of the economy has become much more important. Indeed, services now account for well over half of the gross domestic product in the United States and play a similarly important role in many other industrialized nations. Service technology involves the use of both tangible resources (such as machinery) and intangible resources (such as intellectual property) to create intangible services (such as a haircut, insurance protection, or transportation between two cities). Although there are obviously many similarities between managing in a manufacturing and a service organization, there are also many fundamental differences.

Besides *Dilbert*, what other comic strips routinely reflect contemporary organizational life?

Which contemporary management challenge interests you the most? Why?

CONCEPT CHECK

Summary of Learning Objectives and Key Points

1. Justify the importance of history and theory to management and discuss precursors to modern management theory.

   - Theories are important as organizers of knowledge and as road maps for action.
   - Understanding the historical context and precursors of management and organizations provides a sense of heritage and can also help managers avoid repeating the mistakes of others.
   - Evidence suggests that interest in management dates back thousands of years, but a scientific approach to management has emerged only in the last hundred years.

2. Summarize and evaluate the classical perspective on management, including scientific and administrative management, and note its relevance to contemporary managers.

   - The classical management perspective had two major branches: scientific management and administrative management.
   - Scientific management was concerned with improving efficiency and work methods for individual workers.

   - Administrative management was more concerned with how organizations themselves should be structured and arranged for efficient operations.
   - Both branches paid little attention to the role of the worker as a person.

3. Summarize and evaluate the behavioral perspective on management, including the Hawthorne studies, human relations movement, and organizational behavior, and note its relevance to contemporary managers.

   - The behavioral management perspective, characterized by a concern for individual and group behavior, emerged primarily as a result of the Hawthorne studies.
   - The human relations movement recognized the importance and potential of behavioral processes in organizations but made many overly simplistic assumptions about those processes.
   - Organizational behavior, a more realistic outgrowth of the behavioral perspective, is of interest to many contemporary managers.

4. Summarize and evaluate the quantitative perspective on management, including management science and

operations management, and note its relevance to contemporary managers.

- The quantitative management perspective and its two components, management science and operations management, attempt to apply quantitative techniques to decision making and problem solving.
- Their contributions have been facilitated by the tremendous increase in the use of personal computers and integrated information networks.

5. Discuss the systems and contingency approaches to management and explain their potential for integrating the other areas of management.

- The three major perspectives should be viewed in a complementary, not a contradictory, light. Each has something of value to offer.

- Two relatively recent additions to management theory, the systems and contingency perspectives, appear to have great potential both as approaches to management and as frameworks for integrating the other perspectives.

6. Identify and describe contemporary management issues and challenges.

- A variety of popular applied perspectives influence management practice today.
- Important issues and challenges facing managers include employee retention, diversity, the new workforce, organization change, ethics and social responsibility, the importance of quality, and the continued shift toward a service economy.

Discussion Questions

Questions for Review

1. Briefly describe the principles of scientific management and administrative management. What assumptions are made about workers?
2. What are the differences between the contingency and the universal perspectives on management? How is the contingency perspective useful in the practice of management today?

3. Describe the systems perspective. Why is a business organization considered an open system?
4. For each of the contemporary management challenges, give at least one example, other than the examples found in the text.

Questions for Analysis

5. Young, innovative, or high-tech firms often adopt the strategy of ignoring history or attempting to do something radically new. In what ways might this strategy help them? In what ways might this strategy hinder them?
6. Can a manager use tools and techniques from several different perspectives at the same time? For example, can a manager use both classical and behavioral perspectives? Give an example of a time when a manager did this and explain how it enabled him or her to be effective.

7. Visit the website of Amazon.com. Select the tab that reads "See All 32 Product Categories" and then choose the link for "Books." Next select the link for "Bestsellers" and click on "Business & Investing" from the categories listed down the left side of the screen. Look at Amazon's list of best-selling business books. What ideas or themes do you see in the list? Which business leaders do you see?

Questions for Application

8. Go to the library or go online and locate material about Confucius. Outline his major ideas. Which seem to be applicable to management in the United States today?
9. Find a company that has laid off a significant number of workers in the last year. (*Hint:* Use the word *layoff* as a search term on the Internet.) Investigate that company. Why did the firm make the layoffs? In your opinion, is the company likely to accomplish its

intended goal by laying off so many workers? Why or why not?
10. Read about management pioneer Frederick Taylor at **www.cftech.com/BrainBank/TRIVIABITS/FredWTaylor.html** or another source. Describe Taylor's background and experience. How does an understanding of Taylor's early career help you to better understand his ideas about scientific management?

CengageNow™ Highlights

Now use your CengageNow™ homework to help you:
- Apply management theories in your life
- Assess your management skills
- Master management terms and concepts
- Apply your knowledge to real-world situations
- Analyze and solve challenging management problems

In order to take advantage of these elements, your instructor will need to have set up a course for your class within CengageNow™. Ask your instructor to contact his/her Cengage sales representative and Digital Solutions Manager to explore testing CengageNow™ in your course this term.

3
CHAPTER

The Environment and Culture of Organizations

LEARNING OBJECTIVES

After studying this chapter, you should be able to:

1. Discuss the nature of the organizational environment and identify the environments of interest to most organizations.

2. Describe the components of the general and task environments and discuss their impact on organizations.

3. Identify the components of the internal environment and discuss their impact on organizations.

4. Discuss the importance and determinants of an organization's culture and how the culture can be managed.

5. Identify and describe how the environment affects organizations and how organizations adapt to their environment.

6. Describe the basic models of organizational effectiveness and identify contemporary examples of highly effective firms.

MANAGEMENT IN ACTION   The NetApp Approach to Net Satisfaction

NetApp, a computer storage and data-management company headquartered in Sunnyvale, California, is no stranger to best-places-to-work lists. Since 2005, it's been ranked among the top 15 employers in Europe, Australia, and, India. In 2011, it came in fifth on *Fortune* magazine's list of the "100 Best Companies to Work For" in the United States—a drop from No. 1 in 2009, but the firm's ninth consecutive appearance on the list. *Fortune* also ranked NetApp among the top 10 in Australia, Switzerland, Canada, France, the Netherlands, and the United Kingdom.

NetApp likes to cite employee-survey scores as a key reason for its regular appearance on the annual list compiled by *Fortune* and the Great Place to Work® Institute. According to the company's website, worker surveys reflect "our employees' experiences and opinions about our culture and values, trust in leadership, integrity and fairness, teamwork, and camaraderie." High on the list of things that keep workers satisfied and motivated seems to be a culture that encourages employee input and the sharing of ideas. The "most impressive thing . . . about the company," says one engineer, "is the open-door culture. I can approach any other engineer with technical issues, product marketing with new ideas, and anyone in management with any questions." Also highly satisfying appears to be the collaborative approach to work processes.

"Funny, no one mentions wanting free M&Ms."

—CONSULTANT GEORGE BRYMER ON WHAT NETAPP EMPLOYEES DO AND DON'T WANT

"Cooperation is the . . . actual norm," reports one worker. "This company is unique in my experience for avoiding the politics and empire building typical in growing companies." "The focus is on the issues," adds another employee, "and in most cases, you find that the issues aren't owned by one particular function," such as marketing or operations. "The focus is on team problem solving."

Most of all, NetApp employees seem happy with the level of freedom that they're given in the pursuit of both organizational and personal goals. In particular, says one worker, "I have . . . lots of freedom to implement my ideas to make things better, and [I'm] also able to make decisions in order to get the job done." Another employee thinks that "the most unique thing about NetApp . . . is that they give us a lot of the free stuff—*free* as in *freedom*, not 'free beer.'" Granted, he adds, "there's a lot of 'free beer' here—free gifts, goodies, lunches. But I think giving 'free beer' to keep employees happy works only as long as the company is [riding] high. Freedom lasts forever." Or at least as long as it's embedded in the company culture, according to George Brymer, founder and president of All Square Inc., a provider of

NetApp has worked hard to maintain its reputation as a great place to work.

managerial training programs. Brymer, who's also the author of *Vital Integrities: How Values-Based Leaders Acquire and Preserve Their Credibility*, contrasts the role of "free beer" at NetApp with its more highly publicized counterpart at Google. "Among the perks enjoyed by Google employees," he writes,

> *are onsite haircuts, free laundry facilities, workout and massage rooms, in-house childcare, and car washes. And then there's the free food. The campus has eleven cafeterias serving everything from gourmet meals to M&Ms. . . .*
>
> *Unlike Google, which got to the top [of the Fortune list of "100 Best Companies to Work For" in 2007] largely by providing employees with lots of goodies, NetApp earned [its] spot because of its culture of trust. NetApp's leaders promote an atmosphere of openness and honesty, and they go out of their way to proactively share information with workers. . . .*
>
> *For their part, NetApp employees say they appreciate how easy it is to share ideas, get answers to questions, meet with senior leaders, and find opportunities to take responsibility. Funny, no one mentions wanting free M&Ms.*

In placing NetApp on its lists of the "UK's 50 Best Workplaces" and the "100 Best Workplaces in Europe," the Great Place to Work® Institute cited employees' opinions that company management is approachable and easy to talk to, is forthcoming with straight answers to reasonable questions, and keeps workers informed about important issues and changes.

In addition, the principle of trust at NetApp extends beyond management's confidence in the ability of informed employees to make good operational decisions: It also applies to management's confidence that satisfied employees will live up to item number six on the company's list of "living values"—namely, that they'll "Get Things Done!" "What I appreciate most about NetApp," says one worker,

> *is that I'm respected—to manage my time, my day, my workload. No one's telling me to be at my desk by a certain time or gives me a strange look if I'm leaving the office early. It's expected that you get your work done, and if you do that late at night or early in the morning, that's your choice. . . . No one's watching your movements. It's about performance, achieving goals. . . .*

When things get done—when individuals and teams perform and achieve goals—NetApp has a number of programs in place to recognize them. The SHARE Rewards program, for instance, offers incentives for knowledge sharing; a program called Total Customer Experience Champions offers rewards for enhancing customer views of the company, and the NetApp Patent Award program distributes up to $15,000 to employees involved in projects that produce patents. NetApp is also ranked among *Fortune*'s list of "25 Top-Paying Companies." In order to recruit and retain top talent, it regularly monitors the competitiveness of its pay rates among high-tech companies, and in one recent year, 98 percent of all employees received incentive bonuses totaling $47 million.[1]

The NetApp culture is certainly nurtured by internal forces—by decisions, both conscious and unconscious, that reflect the familiarity of decision makers with organization values and other priorities. At the same time, however, the culture at NetApp reflects—indeed, is in large part a product of—forces at work in its external environment.* As we noted in Chapter 1, managers must have a deep understanding and appreciation of the environments in which they and their organizations function. Without this understanding, they are like rudderless ships—moving along, but with no way of maneuvering or changing direction.

This chapter is the first of four devoted to the environmental context of management. After introducing the nature of the organization's environment, we describe first the general and then the task environment in detail. We next discuss key parts of the internal environment of an organization. We then address organization–environment relationships and, finally, how these relationships determine the effectiveness of the organization.

* The *Change* box in Chapter 19, entitled "The NetApp Approach to Net Jobs," discusses the pressure that certain forces in the company's *economic environment* have recently put on its efforts to apply some of its cultural values.

The Organization's Environments

To illustrate the importance of the environment to an organization, consider the analogy of a swimmer crossing a wide stream. The swimmer must assess the current, obstacles, and distance before setting out. If these elements are properly evaluated, the swimmer will arrive at the expected point on the far bank of the stream. But if they are not properly understood, the swimmer might end up too far upstream or downstream. The organization is like the swimmer, and the environment is like the stream. Thus, just as the swimmer needs to understand conditions in the water, the organization must understand the basic elements of its environment to properly maneuver among them.[2] More specifically, a key element in the effective management of an organization is determining the ideal alignment between the environment and the organization and then working to achieve and maintain that alignment. To do so, therefore, the manager must first thoroughly understand the nature of the organization's environments.[3]

The external environment is everything outside an organization's boundaries that might affect it. As shown in Figure 3.1, there are actually two separate external environments: the general environment and the task environment. An organization's internal environment

FIGURE 3.1 THE ORGANIZATION AND ITS ENVIRONMENTS

Organizations have both an external and an internal environment. The external environment consists of two layers: the general environment and the task environment.

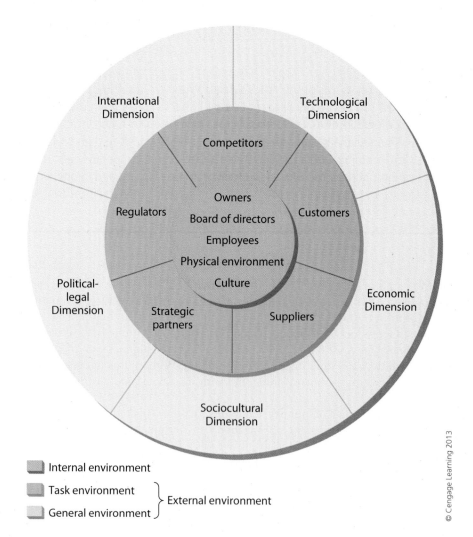

external environment
Everything outside an organization's boundaries that might affect it

internal environment
The conditions and forces within an organization

© Cengage Learning 2013

consists of conditions and forces within the organization. Of course, not all parts of these environments are equally important for all organizations.

A small, two-person partnership does not have a board of directors, for example, whereas a large public corporation is required by law to have one. A private university with a large endowment (like Harvard) may be less concerned about general economic conditions than might a state university (like the University of Missouri), which relies on state funding from tax revenues. Still, organizations need to fully understand which environmental forces are important and how the importance of others might increase.

Define *environment* as it relates to organizations.

How easily differentiated are an organization's external and internal environments?

CONCEPT CHECK

The External Environment

As just noted, an organization's external environment consists of two parts. The **general environment** of an organization is the set of broad dimensions and forces in its surroundings that create its overall context. These dimensions and forces are not necessarily associated with other specific organizations. The general environment of most organizations has economic, technological, sociocultural, political-legal, and international dimensions. The other significant external environment for an organization is its **task environment**. The task environment consists of specific external organizations or groups that influence an organization.

"If you manage the business well throughout the good times, then the bad times are not quite as pronounced or profound. But it's actually more difficult to manage during the good times."

—WILLIAM WELDON, CEO OF JOHNSON & JOHNSON[4]

The General Environment

Each of these dimensions embodies conditions and events that have the potential to influence the organization in important ways. Some examples to illustrate these dimensions as they relate to McDonald's Corporation are shown in Figure 3.2.

The Economic Dimension The **economic dimension** of an organization's general environment is the overall health and vitality of the economic system in which the organization operates.[5] Particularly important economic factors for business are general economic growth, inflation, interest rates, and unemployment. After several strong years of growth, the U.S. economy fell into recession during 2008–2010. During this period energy and related prices jumped, growth slowed dramatically, and unemployment mushroomed as one struggling business after another made workforce cuts.

As noted in Figure 3.2, since late 2008 McDonald's U.S. operation has been functioning in an economy characterized by weak growth, high unemployment, and low inflation. These conditions produce paradoxical problems. High unemployment means that fewer people can eat out, but those who do are looking for inexpensive options—like McDonald's. McDonald's can also pay lower wages to attract new employees, since many people are looking for work and there are fewer opportunities available than was the case a few years ago. Similarly, low inflation means that the prices McDonald's must pay for its supplies remain relatively constant, but it also is somewhat constrained from increasing the prices it charges consumers for a hamburger or milkshake. The economic dimension is also important to nonbusiness organizations. For example, during weak economic conditions, funding for state universities may drop, and charitable organizations like the Salvation Army are asked

general environment
The set of broad dimensions and forces in an organization's surroundings that create its overall context

task environment
Specific organizations or groups that influence an organization

economic dimension
The overall health and vitality of the economic system in which the organization operates

FIGURE 3.2 MCDONALD'S GENERAL ENVIRONMENT

The general environment of an organization consists of economic, technological, sociocultural, political-legal, and international dimensions. This figure clearly illustrates how these dimensions are relevant to managers at McDonald's.

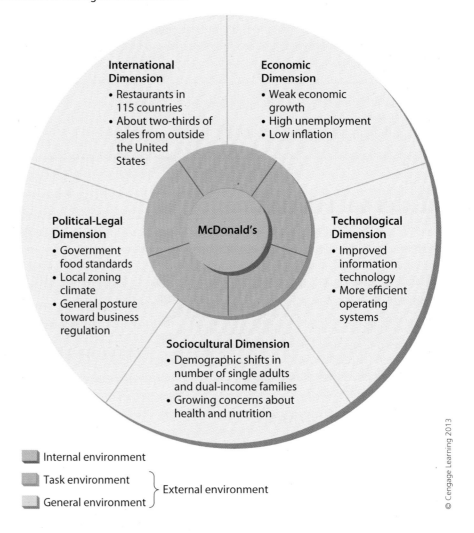

to provide greater assistance at the same time that their incoming contributions dwindle. Similarly, hospitals are affected by the availability of government grants and the number of low-income patients they must treat free of charge.

The Technological Dimension The technological dimension of the general environment refers to the methods available for converting resources into products or services. Although technology is applied within the organization, the forms and availability of that technology come from the general environment. Computer-assisted manufacturing and design techniques, for example, allow Boeing to simulate the more than three miles of hydraulic tubing that run through a 777 aircraft. The results include decreased warehouse needs, higher-quality tube fittings, fewer employees, and major time savings.

In a roundabout way, the resources to be converted can also come from the technological dimension of the general environment. The computer company Hewlett-Packard, for instance, uses advanced technology to recycle technological refuse—in particular, discarded printer cartridges—into profitable new products. See the *Greening the Business Environment* box entitled "HP Keeps Itself in the Recycling Loop" on page 57.

technological dimension
The methods available for converting resources into products or services

GREENING THE BUSINESS ENVIRONMENT

HP Keeps Itself in the Recycling Loop

Starting in 1987, Hewlett-Packard (HP), which offers a comprehensive product line of computer hardware, software, and services, was one of the first companies to recycle computer software and hardware products and components. The project became a matter of sustained companywide policy with the inception of HP Planet Partners in 1991, and today HP proudly announces that it's "committed to providing customers with inventive, high quality products and services that are environmentally sound and to conduct[ing] our operations in an environmentally responsible manner." As "one of [the] guiding principles . . . deeply ingrained in our values," that commitment, says HP, has become a legitimate reflection of the firm's overall culture.

How does Planet Partners work? First of all, HP takes back discarded hardware and cartridges from individual and business users. Cartridge recycling has always been free, and since 2009, HP has offered free recycling for any brand of computer equipment, up to five items per customer. In 2009, HP also expanded the Planet Partners print-cartridge return and recycling program under which users can return HP ink and LaserJet toner cartridges directly to HP or (using special postage-paid envelopes or boxes) to authorized retail and recycling locations such as Staples, the world's largest office-products retailer.

Once they're returned, cartridges enter the HP Closed Loop System for Plastics Recycling—so called because plastic from discarded cartridges goes right back into new cartridges. At facilities in Nashville and Germany, the plastic (about 80 percent of an inkjet cartridge) is separated from electrical circuits, foam, metal, and residual ink and shipped to a plant run by the Lavergne Group, which makes plastic resins from recycled material, in Montreal, Canada. There, it's mixed with other materials (including a lot of plastic-bottle waste), and when the process is complete, the new compound is ready to be used in the manufacture of new cartridges. Since launching the closed-loop system in 2005, HP has produced more than 500 million new cartridges, and at present the company's entire cartridge product line contains 60 percent recycled materials.

Not surprisingly, making cartridges is cheaper with recycled materials than with virgin materials, but its closed-loop recycling operations haven't yet had any positive effect on HP's bottom line. In fact, the Nashville facility operates as a *cost center*—it costs money to run it but it doesn't directly contribute to profits. At the same time, of course, saving the environment is not what HP does for a living, and few people, either outside or inside HP, would argue that its culture is inherently altruistic. HP has been investing money in its recycling infrastructure for decades, and that investment has paid off handsomely in lower production costs and a competitive advantage in the secondary market for computer equipment. HP has even turned "asset management"—the process of protecting the data left on discarded equipment—into a profitable customer-service operation.

Ned Dishman/NBAE via Getty Images

References: Hewlett-Packard, "HP Planet Partners Recycling," "United States—Computer Hardware Recycling," "Product Reuse and Recycling," "Environmental, Health and Safety Policy," 2010, www.hp.com on February 2, 2011; Sarah Meyer, "How HP Does Green: Recycling Facility Tour," PrinterComparison.com, March 23, 2009, www.printercomparison.com on February 2, 2011; Cora Nucci, "Inside HP's Ink Jet Cartridge Recycling Process," *InformationWeek*, March 27, 2009, www.informationweek.com on February 2, 2011; Keith Kmetz, *HP Shows Off Another Phase of Its "Closed Loop" Inkjet Cartridge Recycling Process with a Tour of the Lavergne Group Facility* (Framingham, MA: IDC, April 2010), www.hp.com on February 2, 2011; Jim Motavalli, "See How Printer Cartridges Are Recycled," *The Daily Green*, April 17, 2010, www.thedailygreen.com on February 2, 2011.

Finally, although some people associate technology with manufacturing firms, it is also relevant in the service sector. For example, just as an automobile follows a predetermined path along an assembly line as it is built, a hamburger at McDonald's follows a predefined path as the meat is cooked, the burger assembled, and the finished product wrapped and bagged for a customer. The rapid infusion of the Internet into all areas of business is also a reflection of the technological dimension. Another recent advancement is the rapid growth of integrated business software systems.

The Sociocultural Dimension The sociocultural dimension of the general environment includes the customs, mores, values, and demographic characteristics of the society in which the organization functions. Sociocultural processes are important because they determine the products, services, and standards of conduct that the society is likely to value. In some countries, for example, consumers are willing to pay premium prices for designer clothes, whereas the same clothes have virtually no market in other countries. Consumer tastes also change over time. Preferences for color, style, taste, and so forth change from season to season, for example. Drinking hard liquor and smoking cigarettes are less common in the United States today than they were just a few years ago. And sociocultural factors influence how workers in a society feel about their jobs and organizations.

Appropriate standards of business conduct also vary across cultures. In the United States, accepting bribes and bestowing political favors in return are considered unethical (as well as illegal). In other countries, however, payments to local politicians may be expected in return for a favorable response to such common business transactions as applications for zoning and operating permits. The shape of the market, the ethics of political influence, and attitudes in the workforce are only a few of the many ways in which culture can affect an organization. Figure 3.2 shows that McDonald's is clearly affected by sociocultural factors. For example, in response to concerns about nutrition and health, McDonald's has added salads to its menus and experimented with other low-fat foods. And the firm was among the first fast-food chains to provide customers with information about the ingredients used in its products.

The Political-Legal Dimension The political-legal dimension of the general environment refers to government regulation of business and the relationship between business and government. This dimension is important for three basic reasons. First, the legal system partially defines what an organization can and cannot do. Although the United States is basically a free market economy, there is still major regulation of business activity. McDonald's, for example, is subject to a variety of political and legal forces, including food preparation standards and local zoning requirements.

Second, pro- or antibusiness sentiment in government influences business activity. For example, during periods of probusiness sentiment, firms find it easier to compete and have fewer concerns about antitrust issues. On the other hand, during a period of antibusiness sentiment, firms may find their competitive strategies more restricted and have fewer opportunities for mergers and acquisitions because of antitrust concerns. During the prolonged period of economic growth that ended in 2008, the U.S. government adopted a very "hands off" approach to business, letting market forces determine business successes and failures. However, as the economy ground to a halt in 2008 and first one and then another industry began to stumble, critics began to point to lack of regulation and oversight as contributing factors. As a result, lawmakers began to take a much more pronounced interest in adopting new and stricter regulations for business.[6]

> "We're in for a potentially significant regulatory response. The hope is we won't overreact."
>
> —DAVID GLENN HUBBARD, DEAN OF COLUMBIA UNIVERSITY'S
> BUSINESS SCHOOL AND FORMER CHIEF ECONOMIST
> FOR THE BUSH WHITE HOUSE[7]

Finally, political stability has ramifications for planning. No business wants to set up shop in another country unless trade relationships with that country are relatively well defined and stable. Hence, U.S. firms are more likely to do business with England, Mexico, and Canada than with Haiti and Afghanistan. The political upheavals in the Middle East in 2011 created complications for many businesses with operations in the region. Similar issues are relevant to assessments of local and state governments. A new mayor or governor can affect many organizations, especially small firms that do business in only one location and are susceptible to deed and zoning restrictions, property and school taxes, and the like.

sociocultural dimension
The customs, mores, values, and demographic characteristics of the society in which the organization functions

political-legal dimension
The government regulation of business and the relationship between business and government

The International Dimension Yet another component of the general environment for many organizations is the international dimension, or the extent to which an organization is involved in or affected by businesses in other countries.[8] As we discuss more fully in Chapter 5, multinational firms such as General Electric, Boeing, Nestlé, Sony, Siemens, and Hyundai clearly affect and are affected by international conditions and markets. For example, as noted in Figure 3.2, McDonald's operates restaurants in 118 countries and derives about two-thirds of its total sales from outside the United States. Even firms that do business in only one country may face foreign competition at home, and they may use materials or production equipment imported from abroad. The international dimension also has implications for not-for-profit organizations. For example, the Peace Corps sends representatives to underdeveloped countries. As a result of advances in transportation and information technology in the past century, almost no part of the world is cut off from the rest. As a result, virtually every organization is affected by the international dimension of its general environment.

The Task Environment

Because the impact of the general environment is often vague, imprecise, and long term, most organizations tend to focus their attention on their task environments. These environments include competitors, customers, suppliers, strategic partners, and regulators. Although the task environment is also quite complex, it provides useful information more readily than does the general environment because the manager can identify environmental factors of specific interest to the organization, rather than having to deal with the more abstract dimensions of the general environment.[9] Figure 3.3 depicts the task environment of McDonald's.

FIGURE 3.3 MCDONALD'S TASK ENVIRONMENT

An organization's task environment includes its competitors, customers, suppliers, strategic partners, and regulators. This figure clearly highlights how managers at McDonald's can use this framework to identify and understand their key constituents.

■ Internal environment

■ Task environment

© Cengage Learning 2013

international dimension
The extent to which an organization is involved in or affected by business in other countries

Competitors An organization's competitors are other organizations that compete with it for resources. The most obvious resources that competitors vie for are customer dollars. Reebok, Adidas, and Nike are competitors, as are Albertson's, Safeway, and Kroger. McDonald's competes with other fast-food operations, such as Burger King, Starbucks, Subway, and Dairy Queen. But competition also occurs between substitute products. Thus Ford competes with Yamaha (motorcycles) and Schwinn (bicycles) for your transportation dollars; and Walt Disney World, Marriott Resorts, and Carnival Cruise Lines compete for your vacation dollars. And ironically, sometimes a business suffers because of problems that beset its competition. The economic recession of 2008–2010 hit many retailers just as the holiday season was gearing up. As some retailers such as KB Toys, Circuit City, and Linens 'n Things were closing down, they launched major "going out of business" or "inventory reduction" sales to generate cash. But these same sales hurt other retailers, such as Toys 'R' Us, Best Buy, and Bed, Bath, and Beyond, who were otherwise in a good position to weather the economic storm.[10]

Nor is competition limited to business firms. Universities compete with trade schools, the military, other universities, and the external labor market to attract good students; art galleries and museums compete with each other to attract the best exhibits; and state governments compete for federal grants and tax dollars. Organizations may also compete for different kinds of resources besides consumer dollars. For example, two totally unrelated organizations might compete to acquire a loan from a bank that has only limited funds to lend. Two retailers might compete for the right to purchase a prime piece of real estate in a growing community. In a large city, the police and fire departments might compete for the same tax dollars. And businesses also compete for quality labor, technological breakthroughs and patents, and scarce raw materials.

Customers A second dimension of the task environment is customers, or whoever pays money to acquire an organization's products or services. Most of McDonald's customers are individuals who walk into a restaurant to buy food. But customers need not be individuals. Schools, hospitals, government agencies, wholesalers, retailers, and manufacturers are just a few of the many kinds of organizations that may be major customers of other organizations. Some institutional customers, such as schools, prisons, and hospitals, also buy food in bulk from restaurants like McDonald's.

Dealing with customers has become increasingly complex in recent years. New products and services, new methods of marketing, and more discriminating customers have all added uncertainty to how businesses relate to their customers, as has lower brand loyalty. A few years ago, McDonald's introduced a new sandwich called the Arch Deluxe, intended to appeal to adult customers. Unfortunately, the product failed because most adult customers preferred existing menu choices like the Quarter Pounder.

Companies face especially critical differences among customers as they expand internationally. McDonald's sells beer in its German restaurants, for example, and wine in its French restaurants. Customers in those countries see those particular beverages as normal parts of a meal, much as customers in the United States routinely drink water, tea, or soft drinks with their meals. The firm has even opened restaurants with no beef on the menu! Those restaurants are in India, where beef is not a popular menu option. Instead, the local McDonald's restaurants in that country use lamb in their sandwiches.

Suppliers Suppliers are organizations that provide resources for other organizations. McDonald's buys soft-drink products from Coca-Cola; individually packaged servings of ketchup from Heinz; ingredients from wholesale food processors; and napkins, sacks, and wrappers from packaging manufacturers. Common wisdom in the United States used to be that a business should try to avoid depending exclusively on particular suppliers because a firm that buys all of a certain resource from one supplier may be vulnerable if the supplier raises its prices, goes out of business, or is shut down by a labor strike. This practice can also help maintain a competitive relationship among suppliers, keeping costs down. But firms eager to emulate successful Japanese firms have started changing their approach. Japanese

competitor
An organization that competes with other organizations for resources

customer
Whoever pays money to acquire an organization's products or services

supplier
An organization that provides resources for other organizations

firms have a history of building major ties with only one or two major suppliers. This enables them to work together better for their mutual benefit and makes the supplier more responsive to the customer's needs.

Honda picked Donnelly Corporation to make all the mirrors for its U.S.-manufactured cars. Honda chose Donnelly because it learned enough about the firm to know that it did high-quality work and that its corporate culture and values were consistent with those endorsed by Honda. Recognizing the value of Honda as a customer, Donnelly built an entirely new plant to make the mirrors. And all this was accomplished with only a hand-shake. Motorola goes even further, providing its principal suppliers with access to its own renowned quality training program and evaluating the performance of each supplier as a way of helping that firm boost its own quality. On the other hand, auto manufacturers around the world experienced production interruptions following the earthquake and tsunami that struck Japan in 2011 as parts suppliers in that country were forced to suspend production and shipping for weeks.

Strategic Partners Another dimension of the task environment is strategic partners (also called *strategic allies*)—two or more companies that work together in joint ventures or other partnerships.[11] For instance, Disney and Steven Spielberg's Dreamworks film studio recently formed a partnership that calls for Disney to provide investment capital to Dreamworks and to distribute four to six Dreamworks films each year. In return, Disney gets 10 percent of the box office revenue from each film, as well as additional revenue from the distribution of DVDs.[12] As shown in Figure 3.3, McDonald's has several strategic partners. For example, it has one arrangement with Walmart whereby small McDonald's restaurants are built in many Walmart stores. The firm also has a long-term deal with Disney: McDonald's promotes Disney movies in its stores, and Disney has built McDonald's restaurants and kiosks at some of its resorts and theme parks. And many of the firm's foreign stores are built in collaboration with local investors. Strategic partnerships help companies get from other companies the expertise they lack. They also help spread risk and open new market opportunities. Indeed, most strategic partnerships are actually among international firms. For example, Sony (a Japanese firm) and Samsung (a South Korean company) are fierce competitors in many sectors of the electronics industry but are also co-owners of a $2 billion factory that makes flat panel televisions and computer monitors.[13]

Regulators Regulators are elements of the task environment that have the potential to control, legislate, or otherwise influence an organization's policies and practices. There are two important kinds of regulators. The first, regulatory agencies, are created by the government to protect the public from certain business practices or to protect organizations from one another. The second, interest groups, are organized by their members to attempt to influence organizations.

Powerful federal regulatory agencies include the Environmental Protection Agency (EPA), the Securities and Exchange Commission (SEC), the Food and Drug Administration (FDA), and the Equal Employment Opportunity Commission (EEOC). Many of these agencies play important roles in protecting the rights of individuals. The FDA, for example, helps ensure that the food we eat is free from contaminants and thus is an important regulator for McDonald's. At the same time, many managers complain that there is too much government regulation. Most large companies must dedicate thousands of labor hours and hundreds of thousands of dollars a year to complying with government regulations. To complicate the lives of managers even more, different regulatory agencies sometimes provide inconsistent—even contradictory—mandates.

For example, the *Exxon Valdez* tanker ran aground, spilling 11 million gallons of crude oil off the coast of Alaska. The EPA forced ExxonMobil to cover the costs of the ensuing cleanup. Because an investigation suggested that the ship's captain was drunk at the time, the EPA also mandated that ExxonMobil impose stricter hiring standards for employees in high-risk jobs. To comply with this mandate, ExxonMobil adopted a policy of not assigning

strategic partners (strategic allies)
An organization working together with one or more other organizations in a joint venture or similar arrangement

regulator
A unit that has the potential to control, legislate, or otherwise influence the organization's policies and practices

regulatory agency
An agency created by the government to regulate business activities

interest group
A group organized by its members to attempt to influence business

anyone with a history of alcohol or substance abuse to certain jobs such as tanker captain. However, another regulatory agency, the EEOC, then sued ExxonMobil on the grounds that restricting people who have been rehabilitated from alcohol abuse from any job violates their rights under the Americans with Disabilities Act. ExxonMobil was thus forced to change its policy, but was then again sanctioned by the EPA.

The regulatory environment in other countries, however, is even more stringent. When U.S. retailer Walmart wants to open a new store, its regulatory requirements are actually quite low, and the procedures it must follow are clearly spelled out. In a sense, within reason and general basic ground rules, the firm can open a store just about anywhere it wants and operate it in just about any manner it wants. But conditions in Germany are quite different. That country's largest retailer, Allkauf, tried for over 15 years to open a store in one town—on land that it already owned. But the city government did not allow it because it feared that local competitors would suffer. And, by German law, all retailers—including Allkauf—can only be open between the hours of 6:00 A.M. and 8:00 P.M. Monday through Saturday and must remain closed on Sunday. They can also hold large sales only twice a year and can never discount food items.

The other basic form of regulator is the interest group. Prominent interest groups include the National Organization for Women (NOW), Mothers Against Drunk Drivers (MADD), the National Rifle Association (NRA), the League of Women Voters, the Sierra Club, the Center for the Study of Responsive Law, Consumers Union, and industry self-regulation groups like the Council of Better Business Bureaus. Although interest groups lack the official power of government agencies, they can exert considerable influence by using the media to call attention to their positions. MADD, for example, puts considerable pressure on alcoholic-beverage producers (to put warning labels on their products), automobile companies (to make it more difficult for intoxicated people to start their cars), local governments (to stiffen drinking ordinances), and bars and restaurants (to refuse to sell alcohol to people who are drinking too much). An interesting new interest group is the Basel Action Network (BAN), a three-person environmental nonprofit that serves as a watchdog over the rapidly growing electronics recycling industry. Among other things, BAN keeps an eye on shipments of discarded televisions, computer parts, and so forth to developing nations for dumping. While this practice is legal under narrow and controlled circumstances, there have been many reports of businesses attempting to circumvent both international and local regulations in their efforts to dump electronic components, some containing toxic components, as inexpensively as possible.[14] Similarly, several interest groups have been lobbying the FDA to require soft drink distributors to add a label to their products indicating that the caramel coloring used in colas may cause cancer.[15]

Basel Action Network

The Basel Action Network (BAN) is an interest group devoted to monitoring how computer and other electronics components are disposed of or recycled. This child is sitting on a large pile of old computer parts—junk—that have simply been dumped outside of a village in China. Piles and piles of these old computer parts can be found throughout the region.

"Sometimes, pricing is too good to be true. You can guess where the material is going."

—DOUG SMITH, DIRECTOR OF ENVIRONMENTAL AFFAIRS FOR SONY[16]

List the dimensions of the general and the task environments of a business.

Identify linkages between dimensions of the general environment and dimensions of the task environment.

CONCEPT CHECK

The Internal Environment

As we showed earlier in Figure 3.1, organizations also have internal environments that consist of their owners, boards of directors, employees, physical work environments, and cultures.

Owners

The owners of a business are, of course, the people who have legal property rights to that business. Owners can be a single individual who establishes and runs a small business, partners who jointly own the business, individual investors who buy stock in a corporation, or other organizations. McDonald's has 1.075 billion shares of stock, each of which represents one unit of ownership in the firm. The family of McDonald's founder Ray Kroc stills owns a large block of this stock, as do several large institutional investors. In addition, there are thousands of individuals who own just a few shares each. McDonald's, in turn, owns other businesses. For example, it owns several large regional bakeries that supply its restaurants with buns. Each of these is incorporated as a separate legal entity and managed as a wholly or partially owned subsidiary by the parent company. McDonald's is also a partner in some Russian farms that grow potatoes to supply regional restaurants with french fries.

Board of Directors

A corporate board of directors is a governing body elected by the stockholders and charged with overseeing the general management of the firm to ensure that it is being run in a way that best serves the stockholders' interests. Some boards are relatively passive. They perform a general oversight function but seldom get actively involved in how the company is really being run. But this trend is changing, as more and more boards are carefully scrutinizing the firms they oversee and exerting more influence over how they are being managed. This trend has in part been spurred by numerous recent business scandals. In some cases, board members have been accused of wrongdoing. In other cases, boards have been found negligent for failing to monitor the actions of firm executives.[17] At issue is the concept of corporate governance—who is responsible for governing the actions of a business.

Employees

An organization's employees are also a major element of its internal environment. Of particular interest to managers today is the changing nature of the workforce, as it becomes increasingly diverse in terms of gender, ethnicity, age, and other dimensions. Workers are also calling for more job ownership—either partial ownership in the company or at least more say in how they perform their jobs.[18] Another trend in many firms is increased reliance on temporary workers—individuals hired for short periods of time with no expectation of permanent employment. Employers often prefer to use "temps" because they provide greater flexibility, earn lower wages, and often do not participate in benefits programs. But these managers also have to deal with what often amounts to a two-class workforce and with a growing number of employees who feel no loyalty to the organization where they work because they may be working for a different one tomorrow.[19]

The permanent employees of many organizations are organized into labor unions, representing yet another layer of complexity for managers. The National Labor Relations Act of 1935 requires organizations to recognize and bargain with a union if that union has been legally established by the organization's employees. Presently, around 11.9 percent of the U.S. labor force is represented by unions. Some large firms, such as Ford, Exxon, and General

owner
Whoever can claim property rights to an organization

board of directors
Governing body elected by a corporation's stockholders and charged with overseeing the general management of the firm to ensure that it is being run in a way that best serves the stockholders' interests

Motors, have several different unions. Even when an organization's labor force is not unionized, its managers do not ignore unions. For example, Honda of America, Walmart, and Delta Air Lines all actively work to minimize the presence of unions in their organizations. And even though people think primarily of blue-collar workers as union members, many white-collar workers, such as government employees and teachers, as well as many professional athletes, are also represented by unions.

Physical Work Environment

A final part of the internal environment is the actual physical environment of the organization and the work that people do. Some firms have their facilities in downtown skyscrapers, usually spread across several floors. Others locate in suburban or rural settings and may have facilities more closely resembling a college campus. Some facilities have long halls lined with traditional offices. Others have modular cubicles with partial walls and no doors. The top hundred managers at Mars, makers of Snickers and Milky Way, all work in a single vast room. The president's desk is located in the very center of the room, while others are arrayed in concentric circles around it. Increasingly, newer facilities have an even more open arrangement, where people work in large rooms, moving among different tables to interact with different people on different projects. Freestanding computer workstations are available for those who need them, and a few small rooms might be off to the side for private business.

Identify the main parts of an organization's internal environment.

What is corporate governance, and how is it related to the environment of business?

The Organization's Culture

An especially important part of the internal environment of an organization is its culture. Organization culture is the set of values, beliefs, behaviors, customs, and attitudes that helps the members of the organization understand what it stands for, how it does things, and what it considers important.[20] Culture is an amorphous concept that defies objective measurement or observation. Nevertheless, because it is the foundation of the organization's internal environment, it plays a major role in shaping managerial behavior.

The Importance of Organization Culture

Culture determines the "feel" of the organization. The stereotypic image of Microsoft, for example, is a workplace where people dress very casually and work very long hours. In contrast, the image of Bank of America for some observers is a formal setting with rigid work rules and people dressed in conservative business attire. And Texas Instruments likes to talk about its "shirtsleeve" culture, in which ties are avoided and few managers ever wear jackets. Southwest Airlines maintains a culture that stresses fun and excitement.

Of course, the same culture is not necessarily found throughout an entire organization. For example, the sales and marketing department may have a culture quite different from that of the operations and manufacturing department. Regardless of its nature, however, culture is a powerful force in organizations, one that can shape the firm's overall effectiveness and long-term success. Companies that can develop and maintain a strong culture, such as Hewlett-Packard and Procter & Gamble, tend to be more effective than companies that have trouble developing and maintaining a strong culture, such as Kmart.[21]

organization culture
The set of values, beliefs, behaviors, customs, and attitudes that helps the members of the organization understand what it stands for, how it does things, and what it considers important

Determinants of Organization Culture

Where does an organization's culture come from? Typically, it develops and blossoms over a long period of time. Its starting point is often the organization's founder. For example, James Cash Penney believed in treating employees and customers with respect and dignity. Employees at J. C. Penney are still called "associates" rather than "employees" (to reflect partnership), and customer satisfaction is of paramount importance. The impact of Sam Walton, Ross Perot, and Walt Disney is still felt in the organizations they founded.[22] As an

organization grows, its culture is modified, shaped, and refined by symbols, stories, heroes, slogans, and ceremonies. For example, an important value at Hewlett-Packard is the avoidance of bank debt. A popular story still told at the company involves a new project that was being considered for several years. All objective criteria indicated that HP should borrow money from a bank to finance it, yet Bill Hewlett and David Packard rejected it out of hand simply because "HP avoids bank debt." This story, involving two corporate heroes and based on a slogan, dictates corporate culture today. And many decisions at Walt Disney Company today are still framed by asking, "What would Walt have done?"

Hallmark Cards has a strong and enduring culture. Its employees talk about the "Hallmark family," and many of them spend their entire careers with the greeting card giant.

Corporate success and shared experiences also shape culture. For example, Hallmark Cards has a strong culture derived from its years of success in the greeting card industry. Employees speak of "the Hallmark family" and care deeply about the company; many of them have worked at the company for years. At Kmart, in contrast, the culture is quite weak, the management team changes rapidly, and few people sense any direction or purpose in the company. The differences in culture at Hallmark and Kmart are in part attributable to past successes and shared experiences.

Managing Organization Culture

How can managers deal with culture, given its clear importance but intangible nature? Essentially, the manager must understand the current culture and then decide whether it should be maintained or changed. By understanding the organization's current culture, managers can take appropriate actions. At Hewlett-Packard, the values represented by "the HP way" still exist, guiding and directing most important activities undertaken by the firm. Culture can also be maintained by rewarding and promoting people whose behaviors are consistent with the existing culture and by articulating the culture through slogans, ceremonies, and so forth.

But managers must walk a fine line between maintaining a culture that still works effectively and changing a culture that has become dysfunctional. For example, many of the firms already noted, as well as numerous others, take pride in perpetuating their culture. Shell Oil, for example, has an elaborate display in the lobby of its Houston headquarters that tells the story of the firm's past. But other companies may face situations in which their culture is no longer a strength. For example, some critics feel that General Motors' culture places too much emphasis on product development and internal competition among divisions, and not enough on marketing and competition with other firms. They even argue that this culture was a major contributing factor in the business crisis GM faced in 2009.

Culture problems sometimes arise from mergers or the growth of rival factions within an organization. For example, Continental and United recently merged to form one of the world's largest airlines. Delta recently merged with Northwest Airlines. Combining the two companies led to numerous cases of conflict and operational difficulties because the cultures of the merging firms were so different.[23] To change culture, managers must have a clear idea of what they want to create. While focusing on three key areas for improvement within the company's restaurants, Yum! Brands' CEO Dave Novak realized that its lack of a single corporate culture was standing in his way. In order to provide healthier items and more variety across brands, Novak had to tackle the fact that the various brands and operations across countries had little to do with one another. By adopting an innovative focus and creating specialized courses for employees, the new culture spread down from senior executives to restaurant employees across the world.[24]

One major way to shape culture is by bringing outsiders into important managerial positions. The choice of a new CEO from outside the organization is often a clear signal that things will be changing. Adopting new slogans, telling new stories, staging new ceremonies, and breaking with tradition can also alter culture. Culture can also be changed by methods discussed in Chapter 16.[25]

What is organization culture?

Does your college or university have a culture? How would you describe it to someone?

Organization–Environment Relationships

Our discussion to this point identifies and describes the various dimensions of organizational environments. Because organizations are open systems, they interact with these various dimensions in many different ways. Hence, we will now examine those interactions. First we discuss how environments affect organizations, and then we note a number of ways in which organizations adapt to their environments.

How Environments Affect Organizations

Three basic perspectives can be used to describe how environments affect organizations: environmental change and complexity, competitive forces, and environmental turbulence.[26]

uncertainty
Unpredictability created by environmental change and complexity

Environmental Change and Complexity James D. Thompson was one of the first people to recognize the importance of the organization's environment.[27] Thompson suggested that the environment can be described along two dimensions: its degree of change and its degree of homogeneity. The degree of change is the extent to which the environment is relatively stable or relatively dynamic. The degree of homogeneity is the extent to which the environment is relatively simple (few elements, little segmentation) or relatively complex (many elements, much segmentation). These two dimensions interact to determine the level of uncertainty faced by the organization. Uncertainty, in turn, is a driving force that influences many organizational decisions. Figure 3.4 illustrates a simple view of the four levels of uncertainty defined by different degrees of homogeneity and change.

"The world has changed and so you have to react dramatically and more aggressively, in a less forgiving, harsher way."

—LEE SCOTT, FORMER WALMART CEO[28]

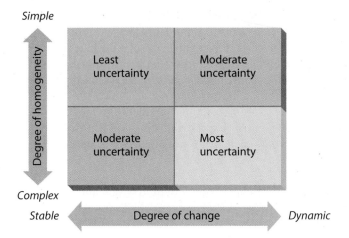

FIGURE 3.4

ENVIRONMENTAL
CHANGE, COMPLEXITY,
AND UNCERTAINTY

The degree of homogeneity
and the degree of change
combine to create uncer-
tainty for organizations.
For example, a simple and
stable environment creates
the least uncertainty, and a
complex and dynamic envi-
ronment creates the most
uncertainty.

Source: From J. D. Thompson,
Organizations in Action, 1967.

The least environmental uncertainty is faced by organizations with stable and simple envi-ronments. Although no environment is totally without uncertainty, some entrenched franchised food operations (such as Subway and Taco Bell) and many container manufacturers (like Ball Corporation and Federal Paper Board) have relatively low levels of uncertainty to contend with. Subway, for example, focuses on a certain segment of the consumer market, produces a limited product line, has a stable network of suppliers, and faces relatively consistent competition.

Organizations with dynamic but simple environments generally face a moderate degree of uncertainty. Examples of organizations functioning in such environments include cloth-ing manufacturers (targeting a certain kind of clothing buyer but sensitive to fashion-induced changes) and music producers (catering to certain kinds of music buyers but alert to changing tastes in music). Levi Strauss faces relatively few competitors (Diesel, Wrangler, and Lee), has few suppliers and few regulators, and uses limited distribution channels. This relatively simple task environment, however, also changes quite rapidly as competitors adjust prices and styles, consumer tastes change, and new fabrics become available.

Another combination of factors is one of stability and complexity. Again, a moderate amount of uncertainty results. Ford, Nissan, and, Daimler AG face these basic conditions. Overall, they must interact with myriad suppliers, regulators, consumer groups, and com-petitors. Change, however, occurs quite slowly in the automobile industry. Despite many stylistic changes, cars of today still have four wheels, a steering wheel, an engine, a glass windshield, and many of the other basic features that have characterized cars for decades.

Finally, very dynamic and complex environmental conditions yield a high degree of uncertainty. The environment has a large number of elements, and the nature of those ele-ments is constantly changing. Intel, Apple, IBM, Sony, and other firms in the electronics field face these conditions because of the rapid rate of technological innovation and change in consumer markets that characterize their industry, their suppliers, and their competitors. Internet-based firms like eBay and Amazon.com face similarly high levels of uncertainty.

Competitive Forces Although Thompson's general classifications are useful and provide some basic insights into organization–environment interactions, in many ways they lack the precision and specificity needed by managers who must deal with their environments on a day-to-day basis. Michael E. Porter, a Harvard professor and expert in strategic management, has proposed a more refined way to assess environments. In particular, he suggests that man-agers view the environments of their organization in terms of **five competitive forces**: the threat of new entrants, competitive rivalry, the threat of substitute products, the power of buyers, and the power of suppliers.[29]

The threat of new entrants is the extent to which new competitors can easily enter a mar-ket or market segment. It takes a relatively small amount of capital to open a dry-cleaning service or a pizza parlor, but it takes a tremendous investment in plant, equipment, and

five competitive forces
The threat of new entrants,
competitive rivalry, the threat of
substitute products, the power
of buyers, and the power of
suppliers

distribution systems to enter the automobile business. Thus the threat of new entrants is fairly high for a local sub shop or pizzeria but fairly low for Ford and Toyota. The advent of the Internet has reduced the costs and other barriers of entry in many market segments, however, so the threat of new entrants has increased for many firms in recent years.

Competitive rivalry is the nature of the competitive relationship between dominant firms in the industry. In the soft-drink industry, Coca-Cola and PepsiCo often engage in intense price wars, comparative advertising, and new-product introductions. Other firms that have intense rivalries include American Express and Visa, and British Airways and Virgin Atlantic. And auto companies continually try to outmaneuver one another with warranty improvements and rebates. Local car-washing establishments or dry cleaners, in contrast, seldom engage in such practices.

The threat of substitute products is the extent to which alternative products or services may supplant or diminish the need for existing products or services. The electronic calculator eliminated the need for slide rules. The advent of personal computers, in turn, reduced the demand for calculators as well as for typewriters and large mainframe computers. And now electronic tablets like the iPad are cutting demand for personal computers. DVD players are rendering VCRs obsolete, but high-definition DVD technology is now replacing today's DVD players. Also on the way out may be mass-market TV programming (or a lot of it, anyway). As you can see from the *Technically Speaking* box entitled "TV Gets Personal" on page 69, today's home-entertainment providers are increasingly target-marketing personal preferences and catering to increasing consumer demand for customized products.

The power of buyers is the extent to which buyers of the products or services in an industry have the ability to influence the suppliers. For example, a Boeing 777 has relatively few potential buyers. Only companies such as Delta, Emirates, and KLM Royal Dutch Airlines can purchase them. Hence, these buyers may have considerable influence over the price they are willing to pay, the delivery date for the order, and so forth. United Airlines attempted to exploit this power recently by requesting that Boeing and Airbus bid on a massive single order of up to 150 new planes. United felt that since the global recession was hurting sales at both manufacturers, and the costs of parts, labor, and credit were dropping, it would be able to get more favorable terms than might otherwise be the case.[30] On the other hand, during times of shortage, individual buyers have little power; if one buyer will not pay the asking price, others are waiting in line. For instance, if global airline traffic is booming and many carriers are buying new planes, manufacturers like Boeing and Airbus can negotiate from strength and make few price concessions.

The power of suppliers is the extent to which suppliers have the ability to influence potential buyers. The local electric company is the only source of electricity in your community. Subject to local or state regulation (or both), it can therefore charge what it wants for its product, provide service at its convenience, and so forth. Likewise, even though Boeing has few potential customers, those same customers have only two suppliers that can sell them a 300-passenger jet (Boeing and Airbus, a European firm). So Boeing and Airbus, too, have power. On the other hand, a small vegetable wholesaler has little power in selling to restaurants because if they do not like the produce, they can easily find an alternative supplier.

Environmental Turbulence   Although always subject to unexpected changes and upheavals, the five competitive forces can nevertheless be studied and assessed systematically, and plans can be developed for dealing with them. At the same time, though, organizations face the possibility of environmental change or turbulence, occasionally with no warning at all. The most common form of organizational turbulence is a crisis of some sort.

The terrorist attacks on September 11, 2001, are, of course, one obvious illustration of environmental turbulence. Beyond the human and social costs, these events profoundly affected myriad businesses ranging from airlines to New York's entertainment industry to those firms with operations in the World Trade Center.[31] Natural disasters like the 2011 earthquake and tsunami in Japan and resultant nuclear power plant crisis, as well as political unrest in the Middle East like the revolt in Libya, all lead to resource shortages and higher levels of uncertainty.[32] Another

TECHNICALLY SPEAKING

TV Gets Personal

Personalized phone service? Tailor-made blue jeans? Coffee concoctions brewed to your personal taste? Just a few years ago, products like these would have been props in a science fiction movie. Today, however, the ability to personalize just about every feature of every product and service on the market has become so important to consumers that virtually every industry worth its customer orientation has been shaken to its mass-market core.

Consider, for example, the distribution of programming for home viewing—which, today, means via TV or computer. About 20 years ago, when the advent of digital cable made 500 TV channels a reality, specialized broadcasters began developing content-specific programming for targeted audiences. If your passion was auto racing, for example, you could subscribe to the Speed Channel; for military buffs, there was the Military Channel, and for animal lovers, there was Animal Planet. It wasn't long before cable and satellite systems were filled up, but newer technology was soon available to handle the overflow of special-interest programming that *Wired* magazine dubbed "the long tail" of the home-viewing market. The key, of course, was the Internet: Along with the ease of digital video production, the Internet provided an impetus for thousands of producers wanting to reach small but dedicated audiences with special-interest programming. The *New York Times* coined the term "slivercasting" to characterize the new sector of the media industry, and today there's slivercasting for vegans (VegTV), sailboat enthusiasts (Sail.tv), lovers of classic TV comedy (Yuks TV), the be-

trothed (The Knot TV), and even surgery buffs (OR Live). Online revenue streams are also beginning to flow more smoothly: In 2009 (the last year for which data are available), TV advertising declined by 21.2 percent, while online ad revenues grew by 8.3 percent—mainly because of online TV.

In 2010, Google entered yet another sector of the emerging industry—delivering programming through Internet-connected TV sets. Partnering with such content providers as HBO, CNBC, Turner Broadcasting, Twitter, and Netflix, Google TV is only the latest (albeit the most prominent) company to announce the proposed marriage of the two media. "One of our goals," says Google TV product manager Ambarish Kenghe, ". . . is to finally open up the living room and enable new innovation from content creators, programmers, [and] developers." And, of course, advertisers: Analysts predict that there will be 43 million Internet-connected TV sets in the United States by 2015.

Perhaps the most popular medium for home viewing, however, is the social website that allows users to distribute videos that they've made themselves. One of the most successful of these sites is YouTube, which was founded in 2005 by three 20-something friends who wanted to share party videos. After just one year of operation, YouTube was screening 30 million videos per day. In October 2006, when that number reached 100 million, its founders sold the company to Google for $1.65 billion. Today it's estimated that users post 24 hours of new videos each minute—more video in a 60-day period than all three major broadcast networks created in the last 60 years. Those videos attract more than 2 billion views a day—about double the combined prime-time audience of all three networks. Boasts YouTube cofounder Chad Hurley, "We're creating a new way to reach audiences in an era where the traditional TV time slot doesn't exist anymore."

References: Heather Green, "Way Beyond Home Videos," *BusinessWeek*, April 10, 2006, www.businessweek.com on February 1, 2011; Saul Hansell, "Much for the Few," *New York Times*, March 12, 2006, http://query.nytimes.com on February 1, 2011; "TV Advertising Revenue Dropping while Online Grows," WorldTVPC.com, April 16, 2010, www.worldtvpc.com on February 1, 2011; Claire Miller and Brian Stelter, "Google TV Announces Its Programming Partners, but the Top Networks Are Absent," *New York Times*, October 4, 2010, www.nytimes.com on February 1, 2011; Marc Metekohy, "YouTube Statistics," *ViralBlog*, May 17, 2010, www.viralblog.com on February 1, 2011.

PSL Images/Alamy

type of crisis that has captured the attention of managers in recent years is workplace violence—situations in which disgruntled workers or former workers assault other employees, often resulting in injury and sometimes in death. The economic downturn that started in 2008 and concerns about the H1N1 (swine) flu virus in 2009 are other recent examples.

Such crises affect organizations in different ways, and some organizations have developed crisis plans and teams.[33] When a US Airways plane recently made an emergency landing in the Hudson River, rescue boats were on their way to the disabled plane within minutes. Their preparedness came from crisis plans developed after the September 11 terrorist attacks. Similarly, a grocery store in Boston once received a threat that someone had poisoned cans of its Campbell's tomato juice. Within six hours, a crisis team from Campbell Soup Company removed two truckloads of juice from all 84 stores in the grocery chain. Still, far too few companies in the United States have a plan for dealing with major crises. For example, during the H1N1 virus scare in 2009, one survey reported that only 27 percent of all U.S. employers had plans for dealing with such a potential health crisis.[34] Similarly, even though General Motors had a contingency plan for disruptions in its supply chain, the firm was still not adequately prepared to deal with parts shortages caused by the Japanese earthquake and tsunami.[35]

How Organizations Adapt to Their Environments

Given the myriad issues, problems, and opportunities in an organization's environments, how should the organization adapt? Obviously, each organization must assess its own unique situation and then adapt according to the wisdom of its senior management.[36] Figure 3.5 illustrates the six basic mechanisms through which organizations adapt to their environments. One of these, social responsibility, is given special consideration in Chapter 4.

FIGURE 3.5   HOW ORGANIZATIONS ADAPT TO THEIR ENVIRONMENTS

Organizations attempt to adapt to their environments. The most common methods are information management; strategic response; mergers, acquisitions, and alliances; organization design and flexibility; direct influence; and social responsibility.

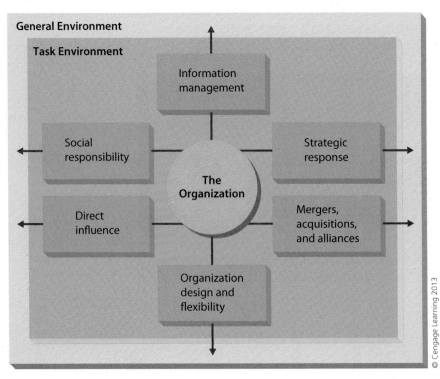

© Cengage Learning 2013

Information Management One way organizations adapt to their environments is through information management. Information management is especially important when forming an initial understanding of the environments and when monitoring the environments for signs of change. One technique for managing information is relying on boundary spanners. A *boundary spanner* is an employee, such as a sales representative or a purchasing agent, who spends much of his or her time in contact with others outside the organization. Such people are in a good position to learn what other organizations are doing. All effective managers engage in *environmental scanning*, the process of actively monitoring the environments through activities such as observation and reading. Within the organization, most firms have also established computer-based *information systems* to gather and organize relevant information for managers and to assist in summarizing that information in the form most pertinent to each manager's needs. (Information systems are covered more fully in Chapter 13.) Enterprise resource planning techniques are also useful methods for improving information management.

Strategic Response Another way that an organization adapts to its environments is through a strategic response. Options include maintaining the status quo (for example, if its management believes that it is doing very well with its current approach), altering strategy a bit, or adopting an entirely new strategy. If the market that a company currently serves is growing rapidly, the firm might decide to invest even more heavily in products and services for that market. Likewise, if a market is shrinking or does not provide reasonable possibilities for growth, the company may decide to cut back. For example, a few years ago managers at Starbucks recognized that the firm's growth opportunities in the United States were slowing simply because there already were so many Starbucks shops. Accordingly, they devised a new plan to expand aggressively into international markets, thus providing an avenue for continued growth.

Mergers, Acquisitions, and Alliances A related strategic approach that some organizations use to adapt to their environments involves mergers, acquisitions, and alliances. A *merger* occurs when two or more firms combine to form a new firm. For example, as noted earlier, Delta merged with Northwest Airlines. Part of the logic behind this merger was that the two firms had strength in different but complementary markets and so by merging a much stronger airline would result. Meanwhile, Continental and United believed that the Delta–Northwest merger threatened their markets, so they subsequently decided to merge as well. An *acquisition* occurs when one firm buys another, sometimes against its will (usually called a "hostile takeover"). The firm taken over may cease to exist and becomes part of the other company. For example, as part of its international expansion, Starbucks bought a British coffee shop chain called the Seattle Coffee Company. Starbucks subsequently changed many Seattle Coffee outlets into Starbucks shops.

In other situations, the acquired firm may continue to operate as a subsidiary of the acquiring company. Royal Caribbean Cruise Lines bought a controlling interest in Celebrity Cruise Lines, but maintains it as a separate cruise line. And, as already discussed, in a *partnership* or *alliance* the firm undertakes a new venture with another firm. A company engages in these kinds of strategies for a variety of reasons, such as easing entry into new markets or expanding its presence in a current market.

In a somewhat unusual case, SBC Communications acquired AT&T. But even though SBC was the acquiring company, it adopted the AT&T name for the combined enterprise. Why? Because its managers felt that AT&T had more national brand recognition and the name would better enable the firm to gain market share. They felt it would be especially helpful in attracting new corporate clients.[37]

Organization Design and Flexibility An organization may also adapt to environmental conditions by incorporating flexibility in its structural design. For example, a firm that operates in an environment with relatively low levels of uncertainty might choose to use a design with many basic rules, regulations, and standard operating procedures. Alternatively, a firm that faces a great deal of uncertainty might choose a design with relatively few standard operating procedures, instead allowing managers considerable discretion and flexibility with decisions. The former type, sometimes called a "mechanistic organization design," is characterized by formal and rigid rules and relationships. The latter, sometimes called an "organic design," is considerably more flexible and permits the organization to respond quickly to environmental change. We learn much more about these and related issues in Chapter 15.

Direct Influence   Organizations are not necessarily helpless in the face of their environments. Indeed, many organizations are able to directly influence their environments in many different ways. For example, firms can influence their suppliers by signing long-term contracts with fixed prices as a hedge against inflation. Or a firm might become its own supplier. Sears, for example, owns some of the firms that produce the goods it sells, and Campbell Soup Company makes its own soup cans. Similarly, almost any major activity in which a firm engages affects its competitors. When Mitsubishi lowers the prices of its DVD players, Sony may be forced to follow suit. Organizations also influence their customers by creating new uses for a product, finding entirely new customers, taking customers away from competitors, and convincing customers that they need something new. Automobile manufacturers use this last strategy in their advertising to convince people that they need a new car every two or three years.

Lobbying involves sending company or industry representatives to Washington in an effort to influence legislators, regulators, and other government agents. Senator Sam Brownback (R-KS) is shown here meeting with lobbyists from the biotechnology industry about pending legislation affecting stem cell research.

Organizations influence their regulators through lobbying and bargaining.[38] Lobbying involves sending a company or industry representative to Washington in an effort to influence relevant agencies, groups, and committees. For example, the U.S. Chamber of Commerce lobby, the nation's largest business lobby, has an annual budget of more than $150 million. The automobile companies have been successful on several occasions in bargaining with the EPA to extend deadlines for compliance with pollution control and mileage standards.

KEVIN DIETSCH/UPI/Landov

How do environments affect organizations? How do organizations affect their environments?

What are some recent high-profile mergers? Why do you think they occurred?

The Environment and Organizational Effectiveness

Earlier in this chapter we noted the vital importance of maintaining proper alignment between the organization and its environments. The various mechanisms through which environments and organizations influence one another can cause this alignment to shift, however, and even the best-managed organizations sometimes slip from their preferred environmental position. But well-managed companies recognize when this happens and take corrective action to get back on track. Recall that we said in Chapter 1 that effectiveness involves doing the right things. Given the interactions between organizations and their environments, it follows that effectiveness is related ultimately to how well an organization understands, reacts to, and influences its environments.[39]

Models of Organizational Effectiveness

Unfortunately, there is no consensus on how to measure effectiveness. For example, an organization can make itself look extremely effective in the short term by ignoring research and development (R&D), buying cheap materials, ignoring quality control, and skimping on wages. Over time, though, the firm will no doubt falter. On the other hand, taking action consistent with a longer view, such as making appropriate investments in R&D, may displease investors who have a short-term outlook. Little wonder, then, that there are many different models of organizational effectiveness.

The *systems resource approach* to organizational effectiveness focuses on the extent to which the organization can acquire the resources it needs.[40] A firm that can get raw materials during a shortage is effective from this perspective. The *internal processes approach* deals with the internal mechanisms of the organization and focuses on minimizing strain, integrating individuals and the organization, and conducting smooth and efficient operations.[41] An organization that focuses primarily on maintaining employee satisfaction and morale and on being efficient subscribes to this view. *The goal approach* focuses on the degree to which an organization reaches its goals. When a firm establishes a goal of increasing sales by 10 percent and then achieves that increase, the goal approach maintains that the organization is effective. Finally, the *strategic constituencies approach* focuses on the groups that have a stake in the organization.[42] In this view, effectiveness is the extent to which the organization satisfies the demands and expectations of all these groups.

Although these four basic models of effectiveness are not necessarily contradictory, they do focus on different things. The systems resource approach focuses on inputs, the internal processes approach focuses on transformation processes, the goal approach focuses on outputs, and the strategic constituencies approach focuses on feedback. Thus, rather than adopting a single approach, one can best understand organizational effectiveness through an integrated perspective like that illustrated in Figure 3.6. At the core of this unifying model is the organizational system, with its inputs, transformations, outputs, and feedback. Surrounding this core are the four basic approaches to effectiveness as well as a combined approach, which incorporates each of the other four. The basic argument is essentially that an organization must satisfy the requirements imposed on it by each of the effectiveness perspectives.

Achieving organizational effectiveness is not an easy task. The key to doing so is understanding the environment in which the organization functions. With this understanding as a foundation, managers can then chart the "correct" path for the organization as it positions itself in that environment. If managers can identify where they want the organization to be relative to other parts of their environment, and how to best get there, they stand a good chance of achieving effectiveness. On the other hand, if they pick the wrong target to aim for, or if they go about achieving their goals in the wrong way, they are less likely to be effective.

Examples of Organizational Effectiveness

Given the various models of and perspectives on organizational effectiveness, it is not surprising that even the experts do not always agree on which companies are most effective. For example, for years *Fortune* has compiled an annual list of the "Most Admired" companies in the United States. Based on a large survey of leading executives, the rankings presumably reflect the organizations' innovativeness, quality of management, value as a long-term investment, community and environmental responsibility, quality of products and services, financial soundness, use of corporate assets, and ability to attract, develop, and keep talented people. The 2011 list of *Fortune*'s ten most admired American firms is shown in Table 3.1.

FIGURE 3.6 A MODEL OF ORGANIZATIONAL EFFECTIVENESS

The systems resource, internal processes, goal, and strategic constituencies approaches all focus on different aspects of organizational effectiveness. Thus they can be combined to create an overall integrative perspective on effectiveness.

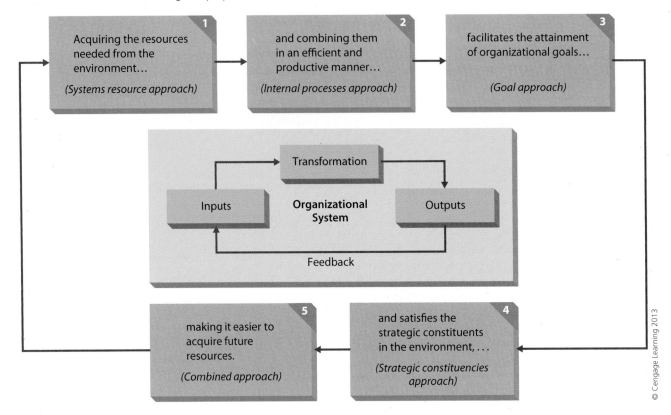

© Cengage Learning 2013

Also illustrated in the table is part of a list published in *BusinessWeek*, also in 2011. This list represents the ten best-performing big companies in the United States as determined by revenue and profit growth, return on investment, net profit margins, and return on equity over periods of one and three years. In some years there are several firms on both lists; in 2011, though, only Apple appears on both lists. Given that both "admiration" and

TABLE 3.1 EXAMPLES OF ADMIRED AND HIGH-PERFORMING FIRMS

Fortune's Most Admired Companies (2011)	*BusinessWeek*'s Best Performing Companies (2011)
1. Apple	1. Priceline.com
2. Google	2. Intuitive Surgical
3. Berkshire Hathaway	3. Southwestern Energy
4. Southwest Airlines	4. Apple
5. Procter & Gamble	5. salesforce.com
6. Coca-Cola	6. Express Scripts
7. Amazon.com	7. Flowserve
8. FedEx	8. FMC Technologies
9. Microsoft	9. Cliff's Natural Resources
10. McDonald's	10. Amazon.com

Source: "The World's Most Admired Companies," *Fortune*, March 21, 2011, p. 110; "The *Bloomberg BusinessWeek* 50 List," businessweek.com, June 12, 2011.

"performance" would seem to be highly related to effectiveness, a stronger correspondence between the two lists might be expected. It is important to note, of course, that different variables and methods are used to develop the two lists, and every firm included on either list is a very well-managed company. But the disparities in the lists also underscore the difficulties and judgment calls that are involved when trying to really evaluate the effectiveness of any given company or organization.

What are the four basic models of organizational effectiveness?

What local businesses do you especially admire? Why?

CONCEPT CHECK

Summary of Learning Objectives and Key Points

1. Discuss the nature of the organizational environment and identify the environments of interest to most organizations.

   - Environmental factors play a major role in determining an organization's success or failure.
   - Managers should strive to maintain the proper alignment between their organization and its environments.
   - All organizations have both external and internal environments.

2. Describe the components of the general and task environments and discuss their impact on organizations.

   - The external environment is composed of general and task environment layers.
   - The general environment consists of five dimensions: economic, technological, sociocultural, political-legal, and international.
   - The task environment consists of five elements: competitors, customers, suppliers, strategic partners, and regulators.

3. Identify the components of the internal environment and discuss their impact on organizations.

   - The internal environment consists of the organization's owners, board of directors, employees, physical environment, and culture.

4. Discuss the importance and determinants of an organization's culture and how the culture can be managed.

   - Organization culture is the set of values, beliefs, behaviors, customs, and attitudes that helps the members of the organization understand what it stands for, how it does things, and what it considers important.
   - Managers must understand that culture is an important determinant of how well their organization will perform.
   - Culture can be determined and managed in a number of different ways.

5. Identify and describe how the environment affects organizations and how organizations adapt to their environment.

   - Environmental influences on the organization can occur through uncertainty, competitive forces, and turbulence.
   - Organizations use information management; strategic response; mergers, acquisitions, and alliances; organization design and flexibility; direct influence; and social responsibility to adapt to their environments.

6. Describe the basic models of organizational effectiveness and provide contemporary examples of highly effective firms.

   - Organizational effectiveness requires that the organization do a good job of acquiring resources, managing resources properly, achieving its goals, and satisfying its constituencies.
   - Because of the complexities associated with meeting these requirements, however, experts may disagree as to the effectiveness of any given organization at any given point in time.

Discussion Questions

Questions for Review

1. Consider the three environments of a firm. Which of the environments has the most direct and immediate impact on the firm? Which of the environments has a more diffuse and delayed impact? Explain.
2. Describe the organization's general environment. For each dimension, give at least one specific example, other than the examples mentioned in your text.

3. What are the major forces that affect organization–environment relationships? Describe those factors.
4. Describe the four approaches to organizational effectiveness. Give a specific example of something that a company should measure in order to evaluate its effectiveness under each approach.

Questions for Analysis

5. Elements from the general environment affect all organizations, but they may not affect all organizations in the same way. Choose an industry and discuss the impact of at least two different elements from the general environment on firms in that industry. Are all firms affected equally? Explain.

6. Which of the firm's environments is most readily changed by the firm? Which of the firm's environments is least amenable to change by the firm? How does this influence the actions that firms take?

Questions for Application

7. Go to Hoover's Online at **www.hoovers.com**. Enter a company name in the Search boxes. When that company's profile is shown, go to "Top Competitors." Here you can learn who the firm's top competitors are. Were you surprised by the list? How do you think Hoover's determines the list?
8. Go to the library or online and research a company. Characterize its level of effectiveness according to each of the four basic models. Share your results with the class.

9. Interview a manager from a local organization about his or her organization's internal environment, including owners, directors, employees, the physical work environment, and the organization culture. How do these various elements interact?
10. Consider an organization with which you are familiar. Outline its environments in detail. Then provide specific examples to illustrate how each dimension affects your organization.

CengageNow™ Highlights

Now use your CengageNow™ homework to help you:
- Apply management theories in your life
- Assess your management skills
- Master management terms and concepts
- Apply your knowledge to real-world situations
- Analyze and solve challenging management problems

In order to take advantage of these elements, your instructor will need to have set up a course for your class within CengageNow™. Ask your instructor to contact his/her Cengage sales representative and Digital Solutions Manager to explore testing CengageNow™ in your course this term.

CHAPTER

The Ethical and Social Environment

LEARNING OBJECTIVES

After studying this chapter, you should be able to:

1. Discuss managerial ethics, three areas of special ethical concern for managers, and how organizations manage ethical behavior.

2. Identify and summarize key emerging ethical issues in organizations today.

3. Discuss the concept of social responsibility, specify to whom or what an organization might be considered responsible, and describe four types of organizational approaches to social responsibility.

4. Explain the relationship between the government and organizations regarding social responsibility.

5. Describe some of the activities organizations may engage in to manage social responsibility.

MANAGEMENT IN ACTION   Is Fair Trade a Fair Trade-Off?

Do you know where chocolate comes from? It comes from cocoa, which is produced by roasting and grinding the almond-sized beans that grow on cacao trees. More than 40 percent of the world's cacao-bean supply comes from small farms scattered throughout the West African nation of Ivory Coast, which may ship as much as 47,000 tons per month to the United States. According to reports issued at the end of the 1990s by the United Nations Children's Fund and the U.S. State Department, much of the labor involved in Ivory Coast cocoa production is performed by children, chiefly boys ranging in age from 12 to 16. Most of them have been tricked or sold into forced labor—slavery—many by destitute parents unable to feed them.

How did enslaving children become business as usual in the Ivory Coast cocoa industry? Because fully one-third of the country's economy is based on cocoa exports, Ivory Coast is heavily dependent on world market prices for cocoa. Unfortunately, cocoa is an extremely unstable commodity—global prices fluctuate significantly. Profitability in the industry, therefore, depends on prices over which farmers have no control. This problem is compounded by

> "Fair-trade programs make a promise that the producers will get a good deal. They do not promise that the consumer will get a good deal."
>
> —TIM HARFORD, ENGLISH ECONOMIST

unpredictable natural conditions, such as drought, over which they also have no control. To improve their chances of making a profit, they look for ways to cut costs, and the use of slave labor is the most effective money-saving measure.

This is where the idea of "fair trade" comes in. *Fair trade* refers to programs designed to ensure that export-dependent farmers in developing countries receive fair prices for their crops. Several such programs are sponsored by Fairtrade Labelling Organizations International (FLO), a global nonprofit network of fair-trade groups headquartered in Germany. Here's how it works: FLO partners with cooperatives representing cocoa producers in Africa and Latin America to establish certain standards, not only for the producers' products but for their operations and socially relevant

Fair trade programs help farmers in developing nations get better prices but it is often others who benefit the most.

Lana Sundman/Alamy

policies (such as enforcing anti–child-labor laws and providing education and healthcare services). In return, FLO guarantees producers a "Fairtrade Minimum Price" for their products. Since 2007, FLO has guaranteed cocoa farmers a price of $1,750 per ton. If the market price falls below that level, FLO guarantees the difference. If the market price tops $1,750, FLO pays producers a premium of $150 per ton.

Where does the money come from? The cost is borne by the importers, manufacturers, and distributors who buy and sell cocoa from FLO-certified producers. These companies are in turn monitored by a network of FLO-owned organizations called TransFair, which ensures that FLO criteria are met and that FLO-certified producers receive the fair prices guaranteed by FLO.

What incentive encourages importers, manufacturers, and distributors not only to adopt FLO-TransFair standards but to bear the costs of subsidizing overseas producers? They get the right to promote their chocolate products not only as "fair-trade" but, often, as "organic" products as well—both of which categories typically command premium retail prices. In fact, organic fair-trade chocolate products are priced in the same range as luxury chocolates, but consumers appear to be willing to pay the relatively high asking prices—not only for organic products but for all kinds of chocolate products bearing the "Fair Trade Certified™" label. TransFair USA chief executive Paul Rice explains that when consumers know they're supporting programs to empower farmers in developing countries, sellers and resellers can charge "dramatically higher prices, often two to three times higher." Consumers, he says, "put their money where their mouth is and pay a little more."

A 3.5-ounce candy bar labeled "organic fair trade" may sell for $3.49, compared to about $1.50 for one that's not. Why so much? Because the fair-trade candy bar, says TransFair USA spokesperson Nicole Chettero, still occupies a niche market. She predicts, however, that, "as the demand and volume of Fair Trade-certified products increase, the market will work itself out. . . . [R]etailers will naturally start to drop prices to remain competitive." Ultimately, she concludes, "there is no reason why fair-trade [products] should cost astronomically more than traditional products."

Some critics of fair-trade practices and prices agree in principle but contend that consumers don't need to be paying such excessive prices even under current market conditions. They point out that, according to TransFair's own data, cocoa farmers get only 3 cents of the $3.49 that a socially conscious consumer pays for a Fair Trade–certified candy bar. "Farmers often receive very little," reports consumer researcher Lawrence Solomon. "Often fair trade is sold at a premium," he charges, "but the entire premium goes to the middlemen."

Critics like Solomon suggest that sellers of fair-trade products are taking advantage of consumers who are socially but not particularly price conscious. They point out that if sellers priced that $3.49 candy bar at $2.49, farmers would still be entitled to 3 cents. The price, they allege, is inflated to $3.49 simply because there's a small segment of the market willing to pay it (while farmers still get only 3 cents). Fair-trade programs, advises English economist Tim Harford, "make a promise that the producers will get a good deal. They do not promise that the consumer will get a good deal. That's up to you as a savvy shopper."[1]

Businesses everywhere need to earn profits to remain in existence. But there are disparate views on how a firm can legitimately pursue and then use those profits. Some companies aggressively seek to maximize their profits, grow at any cost, and focus on nothing but what is best for the company. Others take a much different approach to business and actively work for the betterment of society, even when it means less profit for the owners. Most businesses, however, adopt a position somewhere between these extremes. Decisions about which of these approaches to take are affected in turn by managerial ethics and social responsibility.

This chapter explores the basic issues of ethics and social responsibility in detail. We first look at individual ethics and their organizational context and then note several emerging ethical issues in organizations today. Next, we expand our discussion to the more general subject of social responsibility. After we explore the relationships between businesses and the government regarding socially responsible behavior, we examine the activities organizations sometimes undertake to be more socially responsible.

Individual Ethics in Organizations

We define ethics as an individual's personal beliefs about whether a behavior, action, or decision is right or wrong.[2] Note that we define ethics in the context of the individual—people have ethics; organizations do not. Likewise, what constitutes ethical behavior varies from one person to another. For example, one person who finds a twenty-dollar bill on the floor of an empty room believes that it is okay to keep it, whereas another feels compelled to turn it in to the lost-and-found department. Further, although ethical behavior is in the eye of the beholder, it usually refers to behavior that conforms to generally accepted social norms. Unethical behavior, then, is behavior that does not conform to generally accepted social norms.

A society generally adopts formal laws that reflect the prevailing ethical standards—the social norms—of its citizens. For example, because most people consider theft to be unethical, laws have been passed to make such behaviors illegal and to prescribe ways of punishing those who do steal. But although laws attempt to be clear and unambiguous, their application and interpretation still lead to ethical ambiguities. For example, virtually everyone would agree that forcing employees to work excessive hours, especially for no extra compensation, is unethical. Accordingly, laws have been established to define work and pay standards. But applying the law to organizational settings can still result in ambiguous situations, which can be interpreted in different ways.

An individual's ethics are determined by a combination of factors. People start to form ethical standards as children, in response to their perceptions of their parents' and other adults' behaviors and in response to the behaviors they are allowed to choose. As children grow and enter school, they are also influenced by peers with whom they interact every day. Dozens of important individual events shape people's lives and contribute to their ethical beliefs and behavior as they grow into adulthood. Values and morals also contribute to ethical standards, as do religious beliefs. People who place financial gain and personal advancement at the top of their list of priorities, for example, will adopt personal codes of ethics that promote the pursuit of wealth. Thus they may be ruthless in efforts to gain these rewards, regardless of the costs to others. In contrast, people who clearly establish their family and friends as their top priorities will adopt different ethical standards.

Managerial Ethics

Managerial ethics are the standards of behavior that guide individual managers in their work.[3] Although ethics can affect managerial work in any number of ways, three areas of special concern for managers are shown in Figure 4.1.

How an Organization Treats Its Employees One important area of managerial ethics is the treatment of employees by the organization. This area includes policies such as hiring and firing, wages and working conditions, and employee privacy and respect. For example, both ethical and legal guidelines suggest that hiring and firing decisions should be based solely on an individual's ability to perform the job. A manager who discriminates against African Americans in hiring is exhibiting both unethical and illegal behavior. But consider the case of a manager who does not discriminate in general, but who hires a family friend when other applicants might be just as qualified. Although these hiring decisions may not be illegal, they may be objectionable on ethical grounds.

Wages and working conditions, although tightly regulated, are also areas for potential controversy. For example, a manager paying an employee less than he deserves, simply because the manager knows the employee cannot afford to quit or risk losing his job by complaining, might be considered unethical. The same goes for his benefits, especially if an organization takes action that affects the compensation packages—and welfare—of an entire work force. It happens, as you can see from the *Ethically Speaking* box on page 82, entitled " 'What Are They Going to Do—Cut My Pension in Half?' "

ethics
An individual's personal beliefs about whether a behavior, action, or decision is right or wrong

ethical behavior
Behavior that conforms to generally accepted social norms

unethical behavior
Behavior that does not conform to generally accepted social norms

managerial ethics
Standards of behavior that guide individual managers in their work

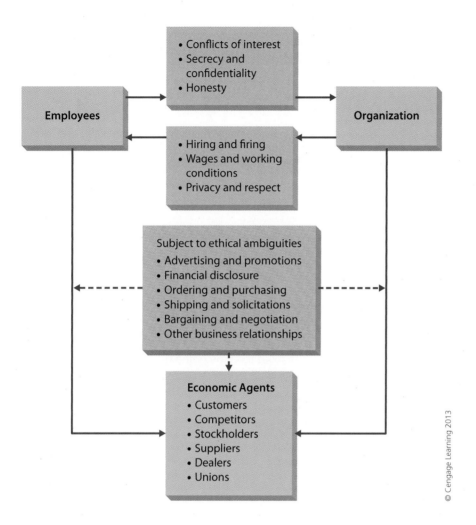

FIGURE 4.1
MANAGERIAL ETHICS

The three basic areas of concern for managerial ethics are the relationships of the firm to the employee, the employee to the firm, and the firm to other economic agents. Managers need to approach each set of relationships from an ethical and moral perspective.

Finally, most observers would also agree that an organization is obligated to protect the privacy of its employees. A manager's divulging to employees that one of their coworkers has AIDS or is having an affair is generally seen as an unethical breach of privacy. Likewise, the manner in which an organization addresses issues associated with sexual harassment involves employee privacy and related rights.

How Employees Treat the Organization Numerous ethical issues stem from how employees treat the organization, especially in regard to conflicts of interest, secrecy and confidentiality, and honesty. A conflict of interest occurs when a decision potentially benefits the individual to the possible detriment of the organization. To guard against such practices, most companies have policies that forbid their buyers to accept gifts from suppliers. Divulging company secrets is also clearly unethical. Employees who work for businesses in highly competitive industries—electronics, software, and fashion apparel, for example—might be tempted to sell information about company plans to competitors. A third area of concern is honesty in general. Relatively common problems in this area include such activities as using a business telephone to make personal long-distance calls, stealing supplies, and padding expense accounts.

In recent years, new issues regarding such behaviors as personal Internet use at work have also become more pervasive. Another disturbing trend is that more workers are calling in sick simply to get extra time off. One survey, for instance, found that the number of workers who reported taking more time off for personal needs was increasing substantially. A more recent

"[The alleged theft of corporate documents is] the clearest imaginable case of corporate espionage, theft of trade secrets, unfair competition, and computer fraud."

—STARWOOD LEGAL FILINGS AGAINST HILTON[4]

ETHICALLY SPEAKING

"What Are They Going to Do—Cut My Pension in Half?"

Christopher Parypa/Shutterstock.com

When Ellen Saracini's husband Victor, a pilot for United Airlines, was killed in a crash in 2001, she had his life insurance to protect her house, and she could count on her widow's pension to pay for the two biggest expenses looming in her life—college tuition for her daughters and assisted living for her elderly parents. A little over a year after Victor Saracini's death, however, United filed for bankruptcy. In 2005, a federal judge allowed United to default on its pension obligations and turn them over to the Pension Benefit Guaranty Corporation (PBGC), a federal agency that pays pension-fund participants when their employers can't. Ellen Saracini's financial prospects were about to change.

United's pension plan, it seems, was underfunded by $7.8 billion, and its obligations—the money that it owed to workers and retirees—came to $9.8 billion. Because of caps on the amount that it can pay out, PBGC picked up only $6.6 billion of that obligation. The remaining $3.2 billion—roughly $267,000 for every current or retired United pilot, flight attendant, and mechanic—was simply wiped out. A pilot, for example, who had earned a yearly pension of $125,000 was now entitled to no more than the $45,000 maximum amount payable by PBGC at the time. Ellen Saracini was among 122,000 United workers and dependents affected by the new math: She stood to lose 50 to 70 percent of her projected pension. Why so much? Like Social Security, PBGC pays maximum amounts to those who retire at age 65 (or 66) and lesser amounts to those who, for whatever reason, leave pension plans earlier. As it

happens, Victor Saracini was only 51 when his plane, United Flight 175, was crashed into the World Trade Center by terrorists on September 11, 2001.

Ellen Saracini was also one of about 2,000 United employees and pensioners who e-mailed their stories of sexagenarian job hunting, unaffordable medical costs, uprooted families, and lost retirement funds to Rep. George Miller of California, who was investigating such agreements as the United default and their effects on the finances of PBGC. "My own situation is not a crisis," she told Miller. "But a lot of other people have real hardship. . . . If I can help draw attention to them, I'll do it in a heartbeat." Pilot Klaus Meyer, for example, who was 47 at the time of the default, is one of those people. "I call it legalized crime," said Meyer. "I lost all my United stock value in the bankruptcy, and here's another part of the retirement I was promised that's gone. And now," he added, "my Social Security is at risk. Where does it all end? You feel brutalized by the system." According to Meyer, he'd agreed to cooperate with Miller's office despite warnings from fellow workers that United might retaliate against current employees. "What are they going to do," he replied, "cut my pension in half?"

Meanwhile, United CEO Glenn Tilton was in the process of collecting $4.5 million in benefits, ostensibly to replace those he'd lost when he left his former employer, Texaco. Asked why he hadn't felt moved by the plight of his employees to pare back his own benefits package, Tilton told a Senate committee looking into the United bankruptcy, "It's part of my contract." The company, he explained, had not only promised it but had guaranteed it.

"Why is the promise made to him understandable," wondered a retired pilot whose pension had been cut by 70 percent, "and the one made to me can go by the wayside?"

References: Dale Russakoff, "Human Toll of a Pension Default," *Washington Post*, June 13, 2005, www.washingtonpost.com on February 28, 2011; "While Worker Pensions Fail, CEOs Get Rich," *CBS News.com*, November 19, 2009, www.cbsnews.com on February 28, 2011; Pension Benefit Guaranty Corporation, *2009 Annual Management Report*, November 13, 2009, www.pbgc.gov on February 28, 2011; Barbara Hollingsworth, "Pilots: United Airlines Bankruptcy Never Should Have Happened," *Washington Examiner*, March 9, 2010, http://washingtonexaminer.com on February 28, 2011; John Crawley, "U.S. Oversight of UAL Pension Audits Questioned," *Reuters*, July 23, 2010, www.reuters.com on February 28, 2011.

CareerBuilder survey found that 29 percent of workers surveyed admitted to having called in sick when they were actually well.[5] And yet another survey found that two-thirds of U.S. workers who call in sick do so for reasons other than illness. Although most employees are basically honest, organizations must nevertheless be vigilant to avoid problems resulting from such behaviors.

How Employees and the Organization Treat Other Economic Agents Managerial ethics also come into play in the relationship between the firm and its employees with other economic agents. As shown above in Figure 4.1, the primary agents of interest include customers, competitors, stockholders, suppliers, dealers, and unions. The interactions between the organization and these agents that may be subject to ethical ambiguity include advertising and promotions, financial disclosures, ordering and purchasing, shipping and solicitations, bargaining and negotiation, and other business relationships.

For example, state pharmacy boards are charged with overseeing prescription drug safety in the United States. All told, there are almost 300 pharmacists who serve on such boards. It was recently reported that 72 of these pharmacists were employees of major drugstore chains and supermarket pharmacies. These arrangements, while legal, could create the potential for conflicts of interest, because they might give the pharmacist's employers influence over the regulatory system designed to monitor their own business practices.[6]

Another area of concern in recent years involves financial reporting by some e-commerce firms. Because of the complexities inherent in valuing the assets and revenues of these firms, some of them have been very aggressive in presenting their financial positions in highly positive lights. In at least a few cases, some firms have substantially overstated their earnings projections to entice more investment. After Time-Warner merged with AOL, it discovered that its new online partner had overstated its value through various inappropriate accounting methods. Some of today's accounting scandals in traditional firms have stemmed from similarly questionable practices.[7]

Hilton Hotels recently hired two senior executives away from rival Starwood Hotels. It was later determined that the executives took eight boxes of electronic and paper documents with them; much of the material in the boxes related to plans and details for starting a new luxury-hotel brand. When Hilton announced plans to start such a chain itself, to be called Denizen Hotels, officials at Starwood became suspicious and investigated. When they learned about the theft of confidential materials, which Hilton subsequently returned, Starwood filed a lawsuit against Hilton.[8]

Additional complexities faced by many firms today include the variations in ethical business practices in different countries. In some countries, bribes and side payments are a normal and customary part of doing business. However, U.S. laws forbid these practices, even if a firm's rivals from other countries are paying them. For example, a U.S. power-generating company once lost a $320 million contract in the Middle East because government officials demanded a $3 million bribe. A Japanese firm paid the bribe and won the contract. Another major American company once had a big project in India cancelled because newly elected officials demanded bribes. Although such payments are illegal under U.S. law, other situations are more ambiguous. In China, for example, local journalists expect their cab fare to be paid if they are covering a business-sponsored news conference. In Indonesia, the normal time for a foreigner to get a driver's license is over a year, but it can be "expedited" for an extra $100. In Romania, building inspectors routinely expect a "tip" for a favorable review.[9] And the government of Bahrain recently charged Alcoa with involvement in a 15-year conspiracy involving overcharging, fraud, and bribery.[10]

"[Enron] took on the monopolies. I believe we were on the side of consumers. I was proud walking into the lobby. . . . By making things happen, we were making the world better."

—JEFFREY SKILLING, FORMER ENRON CEO[11]

Ethics in an Organizational Context

Of course, although ethics are an individual phenomenon, ethical or unethical actions by particular managers do not occur in a vacuum. Indeed, they most often occur in an organizational context that is conducive to them. Actions of peer managers and top managers, as well as the organization's culture, all contribute to the ethical context of the organization.[12]

The starting point in understanding the ethical context of management is, of course, the individual's own ethical standards. Some people, for example, would risk personal embarrassment or lose their jobs before they would do something unethical. Other people are much more easily swayed by the unethical behavior they see around them and by other situational factors, and they may even be willing to commit major crimes to further their own careers or for financial gains. Organizational practices may strongly influence the ethical standards of employees. Some organizations openly permit unethical business practices as long as they are in the firm's best interests.

If managers become aware of unethical practices and allow them to continue, they contribute to an organization culture that says such activity is permitted. For example, Hypercom Corporation, a Phoenix company that makes card-swiping machines for retailers, came under fire because of the actions and alleged wrongdoing of a senior marketing executive named Jairo Gonzalez. Gonzalez was accused of rape by his former secretary (she was paid a $100,000 settlement by the firm), and three other women accused him of sexual harassment. He also set up his own outside business—run by his father—to charge Hypercom for handling overseas shipping. Gonzalez got a job for his girlfriend at a video production firm used by Hypercom in Miami; when she moved to Phoenix, the firm switched its account to the video production firm she joined there. But the firm's CEO, George Wallner, defended his decision to retain Gonzalez because of the huge revenues Gonzalez generated. In Wallner's words, "He [is] bringing in $70 million a year. Do you fire your number one rock star because he's difficult?" Regarding the payment to Gonzalez's former secretary, Wallner asserted, "On a moral level this is confusing. But if you think of only the business decision, it was dead right." Perhaps it is not surprising, then, that another Hypercom manager married a temp and then got her a job at the firm, or that Wallner and his brother borrowed $4.5 million from the firm, some of it interest free.[13]

The organization's environment also contributes to the context for ethical behavior. In a highly competitive or regulated industry, for example, a manager may feel more pressure to achieve high performance. When managers feel pressure to meet goals or lower costs, they may explore a variety of alternatives to help achieve these ends. And, in some cases, the alternative they choose may be unethical or even illegal.

Managing Ethical Behavior

Spurred partially by increased awareness of ethics scandals in business and partially by a sense of enhanced corporate consciousness about the importance of ethical and unethical behaviors, many organizations have reemphasized ethical behavior on the part of employees. This emphasis takes many forms, but any effort to enhance ethical behavior must begin with top management. It is top managers, for example, who establish the organization's culture and define what will and will not be acceptable behavior. Some companies also offer employees training in how to cope with ethical dilemmas. At Boeing, for example, line managers lead training sessions for other employees, and the company also has an ethics committee that reports directly to the board of directors. The training sessions involve discussions of different ethical dilemmas that employees might face and how managers might handle those dilemmas. Citibank and Xerox also have ethics training programs for their managers.[14]

Creating Ethics Codes Organizations are also going to greater lengths to formalize their ethical standards. Some, such as General Mills and Johnson & Johnson, have guidelines that detail how employees are to treat suppliers, customers, competitors, and other constituents. Others, such as Whirlpool, Texas Instruments, and Hewlett-Packard, have a formal code of ethics—written statements of the values and ethical standards that guide the firms' actions. Of course, firms must adhere to such codes if they are to be of value. In one now-infamous case, Enron's board of directors voted to set aside the firm's code of ethics to implement a business plan that violated the code.[15]

code of ethics
A formal, written statement of the values and ethical standards that guide a firm's actions

And, of course, no code, guideline, or training program can truly make up for the quality of an individual's personal judgment about what is right behavior and what is wrong behavior in a particular situation. Such devices may prescribe what people should do, but they often fail to help people understand and live with the consequences of their choices. Making ethical choices may lead to very unpleasant outcomes—firing, rejection by colleagues, and forfeiture of monetary gain, to name a few. Thus managers must be prepared to confront their own conscience and weigh the options available when making difficult ethical decisions.[16]

Applying Moral Judgment Unfortunately, what distinguishes ethical from unethical behavior is often subjective and subject to differences of opinion. So how does one go about deciding whether a particular action or decision is ethical? Traditionally, experts have suggested a three-step model for applying ethical judgments to situations that may arise during the course of business activities. These steps are: (1) Gather the relevant factual information, (2) determine the most appropriate moral values, and (3) make an ethical judgment based on the rightness or wrongness of the proposed activity or policy.

But the analysis is seldom as simple as these steps might imply. For instance, what if the facts are not clear-cut? What if there are no agreed-upon moral values? Nevertheless, a judgment and a decision must be made. Experts point out that, otherwise, trust is impossible, and trust, they add, is indispensable to any business transaction. Thus, to more completely assess the ethics of a particular behavior, a more complex perspective is necessary. To illustrate this perspective, consider the following common dilemma faced by managers who are given expense accounts.[17]

Companies routinely provide their managers with accounts to cover their work-related expenses when they are traveling on company business or entertaining clients for business purposes. Common examples of such expenses include hotel bills, meals, rental cars or taxis, and so forth. But employees, of course, are expected to claim only expenses that are accurate and work related. For example, if a manager takes a client out to dinner while in another city on business and spends $200 for dinner, submitting a receipt for that $200 dinner is clearly accurate and appropriate. Suppose, however, that the manager has a $200 dinner the next night in that same city with a good friend for purely social purposes. Submitting that receipt for full reimbursement would be unethical. A few managers, however, might rationalize that it would be okay to submit a receipt for dinner with a friend. They might argue, for example, that they are underpaid, so this is just a way for them to increase their income.

Other principles that come into play in a case like this include various ethical norms. Four such norms involve utility, rights, justice, and caring. By utility, we mean whether a particular act optimizes what is best for the organization's constituencies. By rights, we mean whether the act respects the rights of the individuals involved. By justice, we mean whether the act is consistent with what most people would see as fair. And by caring, we mean whether the act is consistent with people's responsibilities to one another. Figure 4.2 illustrates a model that incorporates these ethical norms.

Now, reconsider the case of the inflated expense account. Although the utility norm would acknowledge that the manager benefits from padding an expense account, others, such as coworkers and owners, would not. Similarly, most experts would agree that such an action does not respect the rights of others. Moreover, it is clearly unfair and compromises responsibilities to others. Thus this particular act would appear to be clearly unethical. However, the figure also provides mechanisms for considering unique circumstances that might fit only in certain limited situations. For example, suppose the manager loses the receipt for the legitimate dinner but has the receipt for the same amount for the social dinner. Some people would now argue that it is okay to submit the social dinner receipt because the manager is only doing so to get what he or she is entitled to. Others, however, would still argue that submitting the social receipt is wrong under any circumstances. The point, simply, is that changes in the situation can make things more or less clear-cut.

FIGURE 4.2 A GUIDE FOR ETHICAL DECISION MAKING

Managers should attempt to apply ethical judgment to the decisions they make. For example, this useful framework for guiding ethical decision making suggests that managers apply a set of four criteria based on utility, rights, justice, and caring when assessing decision options. The resulting analysis allows a manager to make a clear assessment of whether a decision or policy is ethical.

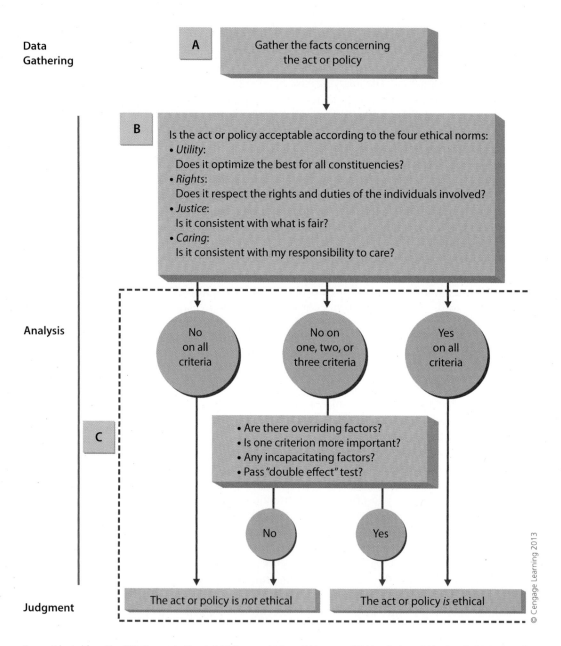

Data Gathering

Analysis

Judgment

Source: Adapted from Gerald F. Cavanagh, Dennis J. Moberg, and Manuel Velasquez, "Making Business Ethics Practical," *Business Ethics Quarterly*, 1995, Vol. 5, No. 3, pp. 399–418; Manuel Velasquez, Gerald F. Cavanagh, and Dennis Moberg, "Organizational Statesmanship and Dirty Politics," *Organizational Dynamics*, Autumn 1983, p. 84. Copyright 1983, with permission from Elsevier Science. Reprinted from Gerald F. Cavanagh, *American Business Values*, 4th ed. (Upper Saddle River, NJ: Prentice-Hall, 1998). Reprinted by permission of Prentice-Hall, Inc.

Maintaining Organizational Justice Another important consideration in managing ethical behavior in organizations is ensuring that people perceive decisions as being made in a fair and just manner. Organizational justice refers to the perceptions of people in an organization regarding fairness.[18] There are four basic forms of organizational justice.

Distributive justice refers to people's perceptions of the fairness with which rewards and other valued outcomes are distributed within the organization. Distributive justice takes a more holistic view of reward distribution than simply a comparison between one person and another. For instance, the compensation paid to top managers (especially the CEO), to peers and colleagues at the same level in an organization, and even to entry-level hourly workers can all be assessed in terms of their relative fairness vis-à-vis anyone else in the organization. Perceptions of distributive justice affect individual satisfaction with various work-related outcomes such as pay, work assignments, recognition, and opportunities for advancement. Specifically, the more people see rewards being distributed in a just and ethical manner, the more satisfied they will be with those rewards; the more unjustly they see rewards being distributed, the less satisfied they will be. Moreover, individuals who feel that rewards are not distributed justly may be inclined to attribute such injustice to a breach of ethical conduct.

Another important form of organizational justice is *procedural justice*—individual perceptions of the fairness used to determine various outcomes. For instance, suppose an employee's performance is evaluated by someone very familiar with the job being performed. Moreover, the evaluator clearly explains the basis for the evaluation and then discusses how that evaluation will translate in other outcomes such as promotions and pay increases. The individual will probably see this set of procedures as being ethical, fair, and just. But if the evaluation is conducted by someone unfamiliar with the job and who provides no explanation as to how the evaluation is being done or what it will mean, the individual is likely to see the process as unethical, less fair, and unjust.

When workers perceive a high level of procedural justice, they are somewhat more likely to be motivated to participate in activities, to follow rules, to accept relevant outcomes as being fair, and to view the organization in an ethical light. But if workers perceive more procedural injustice, they will tend to withdraw from opportunities to participate, to pay less attention to rules and policies, to see relevant outcomes as being unfair, and to assess the organization in a less ethical light. In addition, perceptions of procedural injustice may be accompanied by interpretations based on the ethical conduct of others.

Interpersonal justice relates to the degree of fairness people see in how they are treated by others in their organization. For instance, suppose an employee is treated by his boss with dignity and respect. The boss also provides information on a timely basis and is always open and honest in her dealings with the subordinate. The subordinate will express high levels of interpersonal justice and see the boss as an ethical leader. But if the boss treats her subordinate with disdain and a clear lack of respect, and withholds important information and is often ambiguous or dishonest in her dealings with the subordinate, he will experience more interpersonal injustice and see the boss as being less ethical. Perceptions of interpersonal justice will most affect how individuals feel about those with whom they interact and communicate. If they experience interpersonal justice, they are likely to reciprocate by treating others with respect and openness and in an ethical manner. But if they experience interpersonal injustice, they may be less respectful in turn, and may be less inclined to follow the directives of their leader.

Finally, *informational justice* refers to the perceived fairness of information used to arrive at decisions. If someone feels that another manager made a decision based on relatively complete and accurate information, and that the information was appropriately processed and considered, the person will likely experience informational justice even if they don't completely agree with the decision. That is, they will see the decision as having been made in an ethical manner. But if the person feels that the decision was based on incomplete and inaccurate information and/or that important information was ignored, the individual will experience less informational justice and may see the decision as having been made in a less ethical manner.

organizational justice
The perceptions of people in an organization regarding fairness

What are the three basic areas of managerial ethics?

Identify an ethical situation you have experienced or observed and analyze it in terms of the framework presented in Figure 4.2.

Emerging Ethical Issues in Organizations

Ethical scandals have become almost commonplace in today's world. Ranging from business to sports to politics to the entertainment industry, these scandals have rocked stakeholder confidence and called into question the moral integrity of our society. But, at the same time, it is important to remember that most women and men today conduct themselves and their affairs with nothing but the highest ethical standards. Hence, as we summarize several emerging ethical issues in organizations, it is important to remember that one cannot judge everyone by the transgressions of a few.

Ethical Leadership

For every unethical senior manager, there are many highly ethical ones. But over the past decade the actions of such high-profile deposed executives as Bernard Madoff, Dennis Kozlowski (Tyco), Kenneth Lay (Enron), and Bernard Ebbers (WorldCom) have substantially increased the scrutiny directed at all executives. As a direct result, executives everywhere are being expected to exhibit nothing but the strongest ethical conduct. This leadership, in turn, is expected to help set the tone for the rest of the organization and to help establish both norms and a culture that reinforce the importance of ethical behavior.

The basic premise behind ethical leadership is that because leaders serve as role models for others, their every action is subject to scrutiny. If a senior executive exercises questionable judgment, this sends a signal to others that such actions are acceptable. This signal may, in turn, be remembered by others when they face similar situations. As a result, CEOs like Aramark's Joseph Neubauer and Costco's James Sinegal are now being held up as the standard against which others are being measured. The basic premise is that a CEO must set the company's moral tone by being honest and straightforward and by taking responsibility for any identified shortcomings. And, to support this view, Congress passed the **Sarbanes-Oxley Act**, requiring CEOs and CFOs to personally vouch for the truthfulness and fairness of their firms' financial disclosures. The law also imposes tough new measures to deter and punish corporate and accounting fraud and corruption.

Ethical Issues in Corporate Governance

A related area of emerging concern relates to ethical issues in corporate governance. As discussed in Chapter 3, the board of directors of a public corporation is expected to ensure that the business is being properly managed and that the decisions made by its senior management are in the best interests of shareholders and other stakeholders. But in far too many cases, recent ethical scandals such as those alluded to above have actually started with a breakdown in the corporate governance structure. For instance, WorldCom's board approved a personal loan to the firm's CEO, Bernard Ebbers, for $366 million, when there was little evidence that he could repay it. Likewise, Tyco's board approved a $20 million bonus for one of its own members for helping with the acquisition of another firm.

Sarbanes-Oxley Act
A law passed in 2002 that requires CEOs and CFOs to personally vouch for the truthfulness and fairness of their firms' financial disclosure

But boards of directors are also increasingly being criticized even when they are not directly implicated in wrongdoing. The Swiss company Panalpina World Transport Ltd. and its U.S. subsidiary Panalpina Inc. admitted to paying $27 million in bribes to various foreign officials on behalf of their oil and gas customers to avoid local rules and regulations regarding the import of goods to foreign countries. The firm agreed to pay $156 million in criminal fines and forfeited profits of $80 million. Part of the problem, critics charge, was that some members of Panalpina's board were not sufficiently knowledgeable about the industry and other board members were close friends with senior management.[19] Although board members need to have some familiarity with both the firm and its industry to function effectively, they also need to have sufficient independence to carry out their oversight function. And increasingly, corporate boards are creating strict rules dictating governance standards that provide a clear separation of authority between the board and the CEO.[20]

> "[New rules governing CEO conduct] . . . show dramatic change and it's all motivated by the desire for good corporate governance."
>
> —STEVE ODLAND, CEO OF OFFICE DEPOT[21]

Ethical Issues in Information Technology

A final set of issues that has emerged in recent times involves information technology. Among the specific questions in this area are individual rights to privacy and the potential abuse of information technology by individuals. Indeed, online privacy has become a hot topic as companies sort out the ethical and management issues. DoubleClick, an online advertising network, is one of the firms at the eye of the privacy storm. The company has collected data on the habits of millions of web surfers, recording which sites they visit and which ads they click on. DoubleClick insists the profiles are anonymous and are used to better match surfers with appropriate ads. However, after the company announced a plan to add names and addresses to its database, it was forced to back down because of public concerns over invasion of online privacy.

DoubleClick is not the only firm gathering personal data about people's Internet activities. People who register at Yahoo! are asked to list date of birth, among other details. Amazon.com, eBay, and other sites also ask for personal information. As Internet usage increases, however, surveys show that people are troubled by the amount of information being collected and who gets to see it.

One way management can address these concerns is to post a privacy policy on their website. The policy should explain exactly what data the company collects and who gets to see the data. It should also allow people a choice about having their information shared with others and indicate how people can opt out of data collection. Disney, IBM, and other companies support this position by refusing to advertise on websites that have no posted privacy policies.

In addition, companies can offer web surfers the opportunity to review and correct information that has been collected, especially medical and financial data. In the offline world, consumers are legally allowed to inspect credit and medical records. In the online world, this kind of access can be costly and cumbersome because data are often spread across several computer systems. Despite the technical difficulties, government agencies are already working on Internet privacy guidelines, which means that companies will need internal guidelines, training, and leadership to ensure compliance.[22]

DoubleClick is an online advertising network. The firm collects data on millions of Internet users, including the sites they visit and the advertising links they click. This information is then sold to other sites in order to attract more visitors.

REUTERS/Rick Wilking/Thomson Reuters

> "We should be concerned about things like accidental social oversharing, purposeful but unwanted social sharing, government overreaching and security breaches."
>
> —JONATHAN MAYER, STANFORD RESEARCH FELLOW[23]

What are three emerging ethical issues in business today?

In what ways are information privacy and information technology relevant to you?

Social Responsibility and Organizations

As we have seen, ethics relate to individuals and their decisions and behaviors. Organizations themselves do not have ethics, but do relate to their environment in ways that often involve ethical dilemmas and decisions. These situations are generally referred to within the context of the organization's social responsibility. Specifically, social responsibility is the set of obligations an organization has to protect and enhance the societal context in which it functions.

Areas of Social Responsibility

Organizations may exercise social responsibility toward their stakeholders, toward the natural environment, and toward general social welfare. Some organizations acknowledge their responsibilities in all three areas and strive diligently to meet each of them, whereas others emphasize only one or two areas of social responsibility. And a few acknowledge no social responsibility at all. Moreover, views of social responsibility vary among different countries.[24]

Organizational Stakeholders In Chapter 3 we described the task environment as comprising those elements in an organization's external environment that directly affect the organization in one or more ways. Another way to describe these same elements is from the perspective of organizational stakeholders, or those people and organizations who are directly affected by the practices of an organization and have a stake in its performance.[25] Major stakeholders are depicted in Figure 4.3.

Most companies that strive to be responsible to their stakeholders concentrate first and foremost on three main groups: customers, employees, and investors. They then select other stakeholders that are particularly relevant or important to the organization and attempt to address their needs and expectations as well.

Organizations that are responsible to their customers strive to treat them fairly and honestly. They also seek to charge fair prices, to honor warranties, to meet delivery commitments, and to stand behind the quality of the products they sell. Companies that have established excellent reputations in this area include L.L. Bean, Lands' End, Dell Computer, and Johnson & Johnson.

Organizations that are socially responsible in their dealings with employees treat their workers fairly, make them a part of the team, and respect their dignity and basic human needs. Organizations such as 3M Company, Hoescht AG, SAS Institute, and Southwest Airlines have all established strong reputations in this area. In addition, they go to great lengths to find, hire, train, and promote qualified minorities.

To maintain a socially responsible stance toward investors, managers should follow proper accounting procedures, provide appropriate information to shareholders about the financial performance of the firm, and manage the organization to protect shareholder rights and investments. Moreover, they should be accurate and candid in their assessment of future growth and profitability, and should avoid even the appearance of improprieties involving such sensitive areas as insider trading, stock price manipulation, and the withholding of financial data.[26]

The Natural Environment A second critical area of social responsibility relates to the natural environment.[27] Not long ago, many organizations indiscriminately dumped sewage,

social responsibility
The set of obligations an organization has to protect and enhance the societal context in which it functions

organizational stakeholder
Person or organization who is directly affected by the practices of an organization and has a stake in its performance

FIGURE 4.3
ORGANIZATIONAL STAKEHOLDERS

All organizations have a variety of stakeholders who are directly affected by the organization and who have a stake in its performance. These are people and organizations to whom an organization should be responsible.

© Cengage Learning 2013

waste products from production, and trash into streams and rivers, into the air, and on vacant land. When Shell Oil first explored the Amazon River Basin for potential drilling sites in the late 1980s, its crews ripped down trees and left a trail of garbage in their wake. Now, however, many laws regulate the disposal of waste materials. In many instances, companies themselves have become more socially responsible in their release of pollutants and general treatment of the environment. For example, when Shell launched its most recent exploratory expedition into another area of the Amazon Basin, the group included a biologist to oversee environmental protection and an anthropologist to help the team interact more effectively with native tribes.[28]

Still, much remains to be done. Companies need to develop economically feasible ways to avoid contributing to acid rain, global warming, and depletion of the ozone layer, and to develop alternative methods of handling sewage, hazardous wastes, and ordinary garbage.[29] Procter & Gamble, for example, is an industry leader in using recycled materials for containers. Hyatt Corporation established a new company to help recycle waste products from its hotels. Monsanto launched an entire new product line aimed at improving the environment with genetically engineered crops.[30] Ford and other automakers are working to create low-pollution and electrically powered vehicles.[31] The Internet is also seen as having the potential to play an important role in resource conservation, as many e-commerce businesses and transactions are reducing both energy costs and pollution.[32]

Companies also need to develop safety policies that cut down on accidents that may have potentially disastrous environmental results. When one of Ashland Oil's storage tanks ruptured, spilling more than 500,000 gallons of diesel fuel into Pennsylvania's Monongahela River, the company moved quickly to clean up the spill but was still indicted for violating U.S. environmental laws.[33] After the oil tanker *Exxon Valdez* spilled millions of gallons of oil off the coast of Alaska, the tanker's owner, ExxonMobil, adopted new and more stringent procedures to keep another disaster from happening. Similarly, after the disastrous oil spill in the Gulf of Mexico in 2010, BP also adopted new procedures to help avoid other problems in the future.

General Social Welfare Some people believe that, in addition to treating constituents and the environment responsibly, business organizations also should promote the general welfare of society. Examples include contributing financially to charities, philanthropic organizations, and not-for-profit foundations and associations; providing other support (such as buying advertising space in programs) to museums, symphonies, and public radio and television; and taking a role in improving public health and education. Some people also believe that organizations should act even more broadly to correct the political inequities that exist in the world. For example, these observers would argue that businesses should not conduct operations in countries with a record of human rights violations. Thus they stand in opposition to companies doing business in China and Vietnam. The *Technically Speaking* box entitled "CSI: Criminal Science for the Incarcerated" on page 93 introduces an organization whose commitment to justice promotes general social welfare by working to free unjustly jailed individuals.

Arguments For and Against Social Responsibility

On the surface, there seems to be little disagreement about the need for organizations to be socially responsible. In truth, though, those who oppose broad interpretations of social responsibility use several convincing arguments.[34] Some of the more salient arguments on both sides of this contemporary debate are summarized in Figure 4.4 and further explained in the following sections.

Arguments For Social Responsibility People who argue in favor of social responsibility claim that because organizations create many of the problems that need to be addressed, such as air and water pollution and resource depletion, they should play a major role in solving them. They also argue that because corporations are legally defined entities with most of the same privileges as private citizens, businesses should not try to avoid their obligations as citizens. Advocates of social responsibility point out that whereas

FIGURE 4.4 ARGUMENTS FOR AND AGAINST SOCIAL RESPONSIBILITY

While many people want everyone to see social responsibility as a desirable aim, there are several strong arguments that can be used both for and against social responsibility. Hence, organizations and their managers should carefully assess their own values, beliefs, and priorities when deciding which stance and approach to take regarding social responsibility.

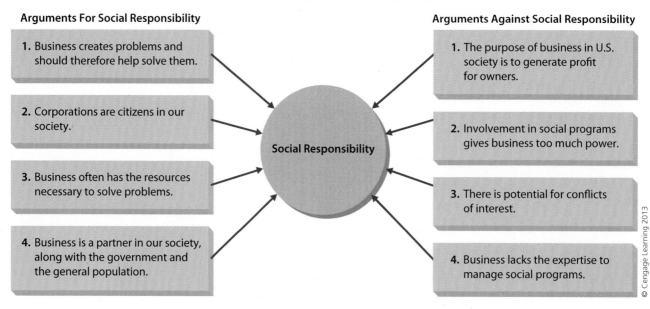

Arguments For Social Responsibility

1. Business creates problems and should therefore help solve them.

2. Corporations are citizens in our society.

3. Business often has the resources necessary to solve problems.

4. Business is a partner in our society, along with the government and the general population.

Social Responsibility

Arguments Against Social Responsibility

1. The purpose of business in U.S. society is to generate profit for owners.

2. Involvement in social programs gives business too much power.

3. There is potential for conflicts of interest.

4. Business lacks the expertise to manage social programs.

TECHNICALLY SPEAKING

CSI: Criminal Science for the Incarcerated

Bita Honarvar/MCT/Newscom

In 1988, Byron Halsey was convicted in New Jersey of sexually assaulting and brutally murdering two children, ages 7 and 8. Narrowly escaping the death penalty, he spent the next 19 years in prison, until May 2007, when a judge vacated his conviction. Halsey's lawyers were associated with the Cardozo Law School of New York's Yeshiva University, and he was a beneficiary of the Innocence Project, which describes itself as "a national litigation and public policy organization dedicated to exonerating wrongfully convicted people through DNA testing and reforming the criminal justice system to prevent future injustice." In Halsey's case, DNA evidence that wasn't available at the time of his trial pointed conclusively to another man.

Like Halsey, many of the Innocence Project's clients have been convicted of such crimes as assault, murder, or rape. Convictions are often aided by eyewitness testimony, physical evidence, or both, but as the Project frequently demonstrates, eyewitnesses are sometimes mistaken and evidence-processing laboratories (the sterling records of the criminologists on *CSI* notwithstanding) occasionally make errors. The only evidence against the learning-disabled Halsey was a highly questionable confession made after a 30-hour marathon of sleep-deprived interrogation. Halsey, noted Project Co-Director Barry Scheck when his client was exonerated, "is lucky he is alive to see the DNA results in this case. The state fought hard to execute him for a crime that, two decades later, science proves he did not commit."

Now located in 43 states and the District of Columbia, most Innocence Project offices are associated with law schools, and Project lawyers are law students or attorneys who work *pro bono*—*free* of charge. Staffers are predominantly middle class or affluent and white. Many are female. Clients are accepted without regard to race, sex, or economic status, but the typical client, like Byron Halsey, is an African American or Hispanic male who was young at the time of the alleged crime. Almost all are poor and were aided at trial by public defenders.

The close association between these two diverse groups is fostered by their empathy and a mutual interest in justice. The convicts, of course, want to regain their freedom and restore their lives. The volunteers gain practical experience while giving back. "I can't think of a job that I would rather be doing," says Vanessa Potkin, who helped head up Halsey's legal team. "When people come to us, they've exhausted every appeal. The Innocence Project for most is the last resort. . . . Every day it's an honor to be a part of it."

Not surprisingly, a lot of people disapprove of projects for aiding criminals, and many of them argue that victims deserve more attention and sympathy than convicts do. Innocence Project advocates point out, however, that their exonerated clients are victims, too. Potkin observes that Halsey, who was raising the children that he was accused of killing, lost not only his freedom but his family. "He was victimized by the wrongful conviction, he lost two decades of his life, and he never had the opportunity to grieve for his family. And," she adds, "the state tried to kill him."

Project co-founder Peter Neufeld admits that "about half the time, we go to the lab, and it turns out the DNA testing confirms guilt. But that means," he hastens to points out, that "in 50 percent of the cases we take on, it turns out they're innocent." Founded in 1992, the Innocence Project secured 100 exonerations in its first ten years. By February 2011, the number stood at 266. Seventeen were on death row, and they'd spent an average of 13 years in prison.

References: Innocence Project, "About the Innocence Project," "Mission Statement," 2011, www.innocenceproject.org on February 5, 2011; Elizabeth Salemme, "Innocence Project Marks 15th Year," *Time*, June 5, 2007, www.time.com on February 5, 2011; Innocence Project, "After 19 Years in Prison for One of the Most Heinous Crimes in NJ History, Byron Halsey Is Proven Innocent Through DNA," May 15, 2007, www.innocenceproject.org on January 7, 2009; Tina Kelley, "New Jersey Drops Charges for Man Imprisoned 19 Years," *New York Times*, July 10, 2007, www.nytimes.com on February 5, 2011.

governmental organizations have stretched their budgets to the limit, many large businesses often have surplus revenues that could be used to help solve social problems. For example, IBM routinely donates surplus computers to schools, and many restaurants give leftover food to homeless shelters.

Although each of the arguments just summarized is a distinct justification for socially responsible behaviors on the part of organizations, another more general reason for social responsibility is profit itself. For example, organizations that make clear and visible contributions to society can achieve an enhanced reputation and garner greater market share for their products. Although claims of socially responsible activities can haunt a company if they are exaggerated or untrue, they can also work to the benefit of both the organization and society if the advertised benefits are true and accurate.

Arguments Against Social Responsibility Some people, however, including the famous economist Milton Friedman, argue that widening the interpretation of social responsibility will undermine the U.S. economy by detracting from the basic mission of business: to earn profits for owners. For example, money that Chevron or General Electric contributes to social causes or charities is money that could otherwise be distributed to owners as a dividend. Shareholders of Ben & Jerry's Homemade Holdings once expressed outrage when the firm refused to accept a lucrative exporting deal to Japan simply because the Japanese distributor did not have a strong social agenda.[35]

Another objection to deepening the social responsibility of businesses points out that corporations already wield enormous power and that their activity in social programs gives them even more power. Still another argument against social responsibility focuses on the potential for conflicts of interest. Suppose, for example, that one manager is in charge of deciding which local social program or charity will receive a large grant from her business. The local civic opera company (a not-for-profit organization that relies on contributions for its existence) might offer her front-row tickets for the upcoming season in exchange for her support. If opera is her favorite form of music, she might be tempted to direct the money toward the local company, when it might actually be needed more in other areas.[36]

ExxonMobil makes substantial contributions each year to support breeding programs for the Bengal tiger, the firm's corporate symbol. But critics of social responsibility point out that the money might be more effectively directed to the elimination of poaching, stopping the illegal trade of tiger fur, or stopping the destruction of the tigers' natural habitat.

Mario FOURMY/REA/Redux Mario FOURMY/REA/Redux

Finally, critics argue that organizations lack the expertise to understand how to assess and make decisions about worthy social programs. How can a company truly know, they ask, which cause or program is most deserving of its support or how money might best be spent? For example, ExxonMobil makes substantial contributions to help save the Bengal tiger, an endangered species that happens also to serve as the firm's corporate symbol. ExxonMobil gives most of the money to support breeding programs in zoos and to help educate people about the tiger. But conservationists criticize the firm and its activities, arguing that the money might be better spent instead on eliminating poaching, the illegal trade of tiger fur, and the destruction of the tiger's natural habitat.

Organizational Approaches to Social Responsibility As we have seen, some people advocate a larger social role for organizations, and others argue that their role is already too large. Not surprisingly, organizations themselves adopt a wide range of positions on social responsibility. As Figure 4.5 illustrates, the four stances that an organization can take concerning its obligations to society fall along a continuum ranging from the lowest to the highest degree of socially responsible practices.

FIGURE 4.5 APPROACHES TO SOCIAL RESPONSIBILITY

Organizations can adopt a variety of approaches to social responsibility. For example, a firm that never considers the consequences of its decisions and tries to hide its transgressions is taking an obstructionist stance. At the other extreme, a firm that actively seeks to identify areas where it can help society is pursuing a proactive stance toward social responsibility.

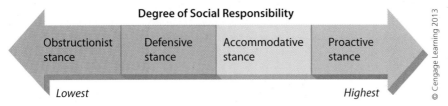

© Cengage Learning 2013

Obstructionist Stance The few organizations that take what might be called an **obstructionist stance** to social responsibility usually do as little as possible to solve social or environmental problems. When they cross the ethical or legal line that separates acceptable from unacceptable practices, their typical response is to deny or avoid accepting responsibility for their actions. A Georgia peanut processing plant owned by Peanut Corporation of America recently shipped products that were contaminated with salmonella. Preliminary tests of the products were positive for salmonella. But when a retest came back negative, rather than investigate further the firm simply ignored the first results and shipped anyway.[37] Similarly, UBS, Switzerland's largest bank, recently admitted that it had helped about 19,000 wealthy U.S. citizens evade income taxes by refusing to disclose their identities or report income earned on accounts maintained by the bank.[38] GlaxoSmithKline, a major British pharmaceutical company, came under fire in 2010 when its former vice president and associate general counsel, Lauren Stevens, denied initial claims that the company had been unlawfully marketing an antidepressant drug for use as a weight-loss aid.[39] Similarly, several automobile rental firms, including Enterprise, Hertz, and Avis have been slow to respond to recall notices from manufacturers and continue to rent vehicles that may have known safety defects.[40]

> "We are shocked at what's been going on in [Peanut Corporation of America]."
>
> —REPRESENTATIVE HENRY WAXMAN, DURING CONGRESSIONAL PROBE OF SALMONELLA OUTBREAK[41]

Defensive Stance One step removed from the obstructionist stance is the **defensive stance**, whereby the organization does everything that is required of it legally, but nothing more. This approach is most consistent with the arguments used against social responsibility. Managers in organizations that take a defensive stance insist that their job is to generate profits. For example, such a firm would install pollution control equipment dictated by law, but would not install higher-quality but slightly more expensive equipment even though it might limit pollution further.

Tobacco companies like Philip Morris take this position in their marketing efforts. In the United States, they are legally required to include warnings to smokers on their products and to limit their advertising to prescribed media. Domestically they follow these rules to the letter of the law but use stronger marketing methods in countries that have no such rules. In many African countries, for example, cigarettes are heavily promoted, contain higher levels of tar and nicotine than those sold in the United States, and carry few or no health warning labels. Philip Morris is also aggressively trying to gain market share in Russia, where over 70 percent of all men smoke, and in China, where over 63 percent of all men smoke.[42] Firms that take this position are, however, unlikely to cover up wrongdoing, and will generally admit their mistakes and take appropriate corrective actions.

> "[We're] being very socially responsible in a rather controversial industry."
>
> —LOUIS CAMILLERI, CEO OF PHILIP MORRIS INTERNATIONAL[43]

obstructionist stance
An approach to social responsibility in which firms do as little as possible to solve social or environmental problems

defensive stance
A social responsibility stance in which an organization does everything that is required of it legally, but nothing more

"If we find evidence of systematic [worker abuse], we're not going to do business with you."

—JIM WALTER, MATTEL SENIOR VICE PRESIDENT[44]

Accommodative Stance A firm that adopts an **accommodative stance** meets its legal and ethical obligations but will also go beyond these obligations in selected cases. Such firms voluntarily agree to participate in social programs, but solicitors have to convince the organization that the programs are worthy of its support. Both ExxonMobil and IBM, for example, will match contributions made by their employees to selected charitable causes. And many organizations will respond to requests for donations to Little League, Girl Scouts, youth soccer programs, and so forth. The point, though, is that someone has to knock on the door and ask—the organizations do not proactively seek such avenues for contributing.

Proactive Stance The highest degree of social responsibility that a firm can exhibit is the **proactive stance**. Firms that adopt this approach take to heart the arguments in favor of social responsibility. They view themselves as citizens in a society and proactively seek opportunities to contribute. An excellent example of a proactive stance is the Ronald McDonald House program undertaken by McDonald's. These houses, located close to major medical centers, can be used by families for minimal cost while their sick children are receiving medical treatment nearby. Target stopped selling guns in its stores, and Toys "R" Us stopped selling realistic toy guns, both due to concerns about escalating violence. Increasingly, some firms, such as Mattel, Nike, and Home Depot, are severing relationships with foreign suppliers found not to be treating their employees fairly.[45]

When the founder of L'Occitane en Provence, a French bath-and-body firm, noticed a blind woman having difficulty while shopping for perfume in one of his stores, he launched an initiative to have Braille labels applied to most L'Occitane products.[46] Peet's Coffee, a Seattle-based coffee business, is working with TechnoServe, a nonprofit organization funded by the Bill & Melinda Gates Foundation, to help develop coffee farming in war-ravaged Rwanda.[47] And drug-maker Pfizer donated prescription medicines to people who lost their jobs during the 2008–2010 recession and did not have prescription insurance.[48] Subway, the world's largest fast-food company (based on number of outlets) recently announced a voluntary measure to reduce the sodium content of most of its sandwiches.[49] These and related activities and programs exceed the accommodative stance—they indicate a sincere and potent commitment to improving the general social welfare in this country and thus represent a proactive stance to social responsibility.

Remember, too, that these categories are not discrete but merely define stages along a continuum of approaches. Organizations do not always fit neatly into one category. The Ronald McDonald House program has been widely applauded, for example, but McDonald's also has come under fire for allegedly misleading consumers about the nutritional value of its food products. Nestlé, along with others, created the World Cocoa Foundation, focused on increasing farmer income, educating cocoa farmers on sustainable farming techniques, and encouraging social and environmental programs. At the same time, though, Nestlé is being criticized for its heavy use of palm oil in its products. This is contributing to deforestation in Indonesia for the creation of palm oil plantations, which is harming various species.[50] And even though the unethical conduct of a small number of people at an organization might tarnish the firm's reputation, other employees at the same organization may be highly ethical people who would never consider an unethical action.

accommodative stance
A social responsibility stance in which an organization meets its legal and ethical obligations but will also go beyond these obligations in selected cases

proactive stance
A social responsibility stance in which an organization views itself as a citizen in a society and proactively seeks opportunities to contribute

---

What are the basic areas of social responsibility?

Which do you find most compelling: the arguments for or the arguments against social responsibility? Why?

CONCEPT CHECK

The Government and Social Responsibility

An especially important element of social responsibility is the relationship between business and government. For example, in planned economies the government heavily regulates business activities, ostensibly to ensure that business supports some overarching set of social ideals. And even in market economies there is still considerable government control of business, much of it again directed at making sure that social interests are not damaged by business interests. On the other side of the coin, business also attempts to influence the government. Such efforts are usually undertaken in an effort to offset or reverse government restrictions. As Figure 4.6 shows, organizations and the government use several methods in their attempts to influence each other.

How Government Influences Organizations

The government attempts to shape social responsibility practices through both direct and indirect channels. Direct influence most frequently is manifested through regulation, whereas indirect influence can take a number of forms, most notably taxation policies.[51]

Direct Regulation The government most often directly influences organizations through regulation, or the establishment of laws and rules that dictate what organizations can and cannot do. As noted earlier in this chapter, such regulation usually evolves from societal beliefs about what businesses should or should not be allowed to do. To implement legislation, the government generally creates special agencies to monitor and control certain aspects of business activity. For example, the Environmental Protection Agency handles environmental issues; the Federal Trade Commission and the Food and Drug Administration focus on consumer-related concerns; the Equal Employee Opportunity Commission, the National Labor Relations Board, and the Department of Labor help protect employees; and the Securities and Exchange Commission handles investor-related issues. These agencies have the power to levy fines or bring charges against organizations that violate regulations.

regulation
Government's attempts to influence business by establishing laws and rules that dictate what businesses can and cannot do

---

FIGURE 4.6 HOW BUSINESS AND THE GOVERNMENT INFLUENCE EACH OTHER

Business and the government influence each other in a variety of ways. Government influence can be direct or indirect. Business influence relies on personal contacts, lobbying, political action committees (PACs), and favors. Federal Express, for example, has a very active PAC.

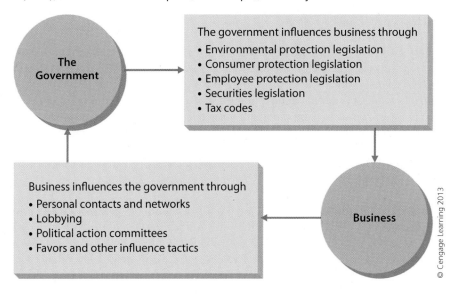

Another approach that governments can use to regulate business practices is through legislation. For instance, among other things the U.S. Foreign Corrupt Practices Act provides for financial sanctions against businesses or business officials who engage in bribery. Siemens AG, a large German engineering firm, has been under investigation for practices that include routine bribery of foreign officials to win infrastructure construction projects. All told, the firm is alleged to have spent over $1 billion in bribing officials in at least ten different countries. Siemens recently agreed to pay the U.S. government a fine of $800 million; German officials, meanwhile, are continuing to investigate both criminal and civil misconduct at the firm. (The U.S. government had the authority to fine Siemens because the German firm has a class of stock listed on the New York Stock Exchange and was thus subject to the Foreign Corrupt Practices Act.)[52] Similarly, another German firm, Daimler AG, has been charged with bribery in 22 countries, helping the company earn over $50 million in profit. The company was alleged to have given millions of dollars in bribes to foreign officials in order to win contracts supplying their governments with vehicles. Charges include conspiracy and falsifying records. Daimler agreed to pay $185 million in its settlement.[53]

Indirect Regulation   Other forms of regulation are indirect. For example, the government can indirectly influence the social responsibility of organizations through its tax codes. In effect, the government can influence how organizations spend their social responsibility dollars by providing greater or lesser tax incentives. For instance, suppose that the government wanted organizations to spend more on training the hard-core unemployed. Congress could then pass laws that provided tax incentives to companies that opened new training facilities. As a result, more businesses would probably do so. Of course, some critics argue that regulation is already excessive. They maintain that a free market system would eventually accomplish the same goals as regulation, with lower costs to both organizations and the government.

How Organizations Influence Government

As we mentioned in Chapter 3, organizations can influence their environment in many different ways. In particular, businesses have four main methods of addressing governmental pressures for more social responsibility. During the early days of President Barrack Obama's administration, however, he implemented several measures designed to restrict or regulate business influence on the government, especially through lobbying.[54]

Personal Contacts   Because many corporate executives and political leaders travel in the same social circles, personal contacts and networks offer one method of influence. A business executive, for example, may be able to contact a politician directly and present his or her case regarding a piece of legislation being considered.

Lobbying   Lobbying, or the use of persons or groups to formally represent an organization or group of organizations before political bodies, is also an effective way to influence the government. The National Rifle Association (NRA), for example, has a staff of lobbyists in Washington, with a substantial annual budget. These lobbyists work to represent the NRA's position on gun control and to potentially influence members of Congress when they vote on legislation that affects the firearms industry and the rights of gun owners. As noted above, President Obama has taken numerous steps to control or limit lobbying. For instance, any discussion between a lobbyist and a member of Congress that goes beyond general conversation has to be written in the form of a letter and posted online.

Political Action Committees   Companies themselves cannot legally make direct donations to political campaigns, so they influence the government through political action committees. Political action committees (PACs) are special organizations created to solicit money and then distribute it to political candidates. Employees of a firm may be encouraged to make donations to a particular PAC because managers know that it will support candidates with

lobbying
The use of persons or groups to formally represent a organization or group of organizations before political bodies to influence the government

political action committee (PAC)
An organization created to solicit and distribute money to political candidates

political views similar to their own. PACs, in turn, make the contributions themselves, usually to a broad slate of state and national candidates. For example, Federal Express's PAC is called FedExpac. FedExpac makes regular contributions to the campaign funds of political candidates who are most likely to work in the firm's best interests. As with lobbying, President Obama has implemented measures to limit the influence of PACs.

Favors Finally, organizations sometimes rely on favors and other influence tactics to gain support. Although these favors may be legal, they are still subject to criticism. A few years back, for example, two influential members of a House committee attending a fund-raising function in Miami were needed in Washington to finish work on a piece of legislation that Federal Express wanted passed. The law being drafted would allow the company and its competitors to give their employees standby seats on airlines as a tax-free benefit. As a favor, Federal Express provided one of its corporate jets to fly the committee members back to Washington. Federal Express was eventually reimbursed for its expenses, so its assistance was not illegal, but some people argue that such actions are dangerous because of how they might be perceived.

Identify the specific ways in which the government and organizations influence each other.

Do you think current levels of government regulation of business are excessive? Why or why not?

Managing Social Responsibility

The demands for social responsibility placed on contemporary organizations by an increasingly sophisticated and educated public are probably stronger than ever. As we have seen, there are pitfalls for managers who fail to adhere to high ethical standards and for companies that try to circumvent their legal obligations. Organizations therefore need to fashion an approach to social responsibility in the same way that they develop any other business strategy. In other words, they should view social responsibility as a major challenge that requires careful planning, decision making, consideration, and evaluation. They may accomplish this through both formal and informal dimensions of managing social responsibility.

Formal Organizational Dimensions

Some dimensions of managing social responsibility involve a formal and planned activity on the part of the organization. Indeed, some businesses are approaching social responsibility from a strategic perspective.[55] Formal organizational dimensions that can help manage social responsibility are legal compliance, ethical compliance, and philanthropic giving.

Legal Compliance Legal compliance is the extent to which the organization conforms to local, state, federal, and international laws. The task of managing legal compliance is generally assigned to the appropriate functional managers. For example, the organization's top human resource executive is responsible for ensuring compliance with regulations concerning hiring, pay, and workplace safety and health. Likewise, the top financial executive generally oversees compliance with securities and banking regulations. The organization's legal department is also likely to contribute to this effort by providing general oversight and answering queries from managers about the appropriate interpretation of laws and regulations. Unfortunately, though, legal compliance may not be enough—in some cases, for instance, perfectly legal accounting practices have still resulted in deception and other problems.[56]

legal compliance
The extent to which an organization complies with local, state, federal, and international laws

Ethical Compliance Ethical compliance is the extent to which the members of the organization follow basic ethical (and legal) standards of behavior. We noted earlier that organizations have increased their efforts in this area—providing training in ethics and developing guidelines and codes of conduct, for example. These activities serve as vehicles for enhancing ethical compliance. Many organizations also establish formal ethics committees, which may be asked to review proposals for new projects, help evaluate new hiring strategies, or assess a new environmental protection plan. They might also serve as a peer review panel to evaluate alleged ethical misconduct by an employee.[57]

Philanthropic giving is the awarding of funds to charities and other worthy causes. Following the earthquake and tsunami that struck Japan in 2011, millions of individuals and organizations made contributions to relief efforts.

Philanthropic Giving Finally, philanthropic giving is the awarding of funds or gifts to charities or other worthy causes. Target Corporation routinely gives 5 percent of its taxable income to charity and social programs. Omaha Steaks gives more than $100,000 per year to support the arts.[58] Giving across national boundaries is also becoming more common. For example, Alcoa gave $112,000 to a small town in Brazil to build a sewage treatment plant. And Japanese firms like Sony and Mitsubishi make contributions to a number of social programs in the United States. However, in the current climate of cutbacks, many corporations have also had to limit their charitable gifts over the past several years as they continue to trim their own budgets.[59] And many firms that continue to make contributions are increasingly targeting them to programs or areas where the firm will get something in return. For example, firms today are more likely to give money to job training programs than to the arts. The logic is that they get more direct payoff from the former type of contribution—in this instance, a better-trained workforce from which to hire new employees.[60] And indeed, corporate donations to arts programs declined 5 percent between 2003 and 2009.[61]

"When the economy is struggling, the arts help people move forward. We take a long-term view of our business and a long-term view of our community."

—TODD SIMON, SENIOR VICE PRESIDENT OF FAMILY-OWNED OMAHA STEAKS[62]

Informal Organizational Dimensions

In addition to these formal dimensions for managing social responsibility, there are also informal ones. Leadership, organization culture, and how the organization responds to whistleblowers all help shape and define people's perceptions of the organization's stance on social responsibility.

ethical compliance
The extent to which an organization and its members follow basic ethical standards of behavior

philanthropic giving
Awarding funds or gifts to charities or other worthy causes

Organization Leadership and Culture Leadership practices and organization culture can go a long way toward defining the social responsibility stance an organization and its members will adopt.[63] As described earlier, ethical leadership often sets the tone for the entire organization. For example, Johnson & Johnson executives for years provided a consistent message to employees that customers, employees, communities where the company did business, and shareholders were all important—and primarily in that order. Thus, when packages of poisoned Tylenol showed up on store shelves in the 1980s, Johnson & Johnson employees did not need to wait for orders from headquarters to know what to do: They immediately pulled all the packages from shelves before any other customers could buy them.[64] By contrast, the message sent to Hypercom employees by the actions of their top managers communicated much less regard for social responsibility.

Whistle-Blowing Whistle-blowing is the disclosure by an employee of illegal or unethical conduct on the part of others within the organization.[65] How an organization responds to this practice often indicates its stance on social responsibility. Whistle-blowers may have to proceed through a number of channels to be heard, and they may even get fired for their efforts.[66] Many organizations, however, welcome their contributions. A person who observes questionable behavior typically first reports the incident to his or her boss. If nothing is done, the whistle-blower may then inform higher-level managers or an ethics committee, if one exists. Eventually, the person may have to go to a regulatory agency or even the media to be heard. For example, Charles W. Robinson, Jr., worked as a director of a SmithKline lab in San Antonio. One day he noticed a suspicious billing pattern that the firm was using to collect lab fees from Medicare: The bills were considerably higher than the firm's normal charges for the same tests. He pointed out the problem to higher-level managers, but his concerns were ignored. He subsequently took his findings to the U.S. government, which sued SmithKline and eventually reached a settlement of $325 million.[67]

More recently, David Magee, a former employee of Mississippi's Stennis Space Center, reported to superiors and federal agents that government employees conspired with Lockheed Martin and Science Applications International Corp. to ensure they would win the contract to work on the Naval Oceanographic Office Major Shared Resource Center, violating the False Claims Act. Allegedly, the defendants shared secret information about the bidding process, ensuring a successful bid. For filing the suit, Magee will receive $560,000 of the $2 million settlement against Lockheed.[68] Harry Markopolos, a portfolio manager at Rampart Investments, spent nine years trying to convince the Securities and Exchange Commission that a money-management firm run by Bernard Madoff was falsifying the results it was reporting to investors. Only when the U.S. economy went into recession in 2008 did the truth about Madoff come out.[69] In response, the SEC announced plans to overhaul its whistle-blowing system.[70]

Evaluating Social Responsibility

Any organization that is serious about social responsibility must ensure that its efforts are producing the desired benefits. Essentially this requires applying the concept of control to social responsibility. Many organizations now require current and new employees to read their guidelines or code of ethics and then sign a statement agreeing to abide by it. An organization should also evaluate how it responds to instances of questionable legal or ethical conduct. Does it follow up immediately? Does it punish those involved? Or does it use delay and cover-up tactics? Answers to these questions can help an organization form a picture of its approach to social responsibility.

More formally, an organization may sometimes actually evaluate the effectiveness of its social responsibility efforts. For example, when BP Amoco established a job-training program in Chicago, it allocated additional funds to evaluate how well the program was meeting its goals. Additionally, some organizations occasionally conduct corporate social audits. A corporate social audit is a formal and thorough analysis of the effectiveness of a firm's social performance. The audit is usually conducted by a task force of high-level managers from within the firm. It requires that the organization clearly define all of its social goals, analyze the resources it devotes to each goal, determine how well it is achieving the various goals, and make recommendations about which areas need additional attention. Recent estimates suggest that around 80 percent of the world's 250 largest firms now issue annual reports summarizing their efforts in the areas of environmental and social responsibility.

whistle-blowing
The disclosure by an employee of illegal or unethical conduct on the part of others within the organization

corporate social audit
A formal and thorough analysis of the effectiveness of a firm's social performance

What formal and informal organizational dimensions can be used to manage social responsibility?

What are the advantages and disadvantages of requiring organizations to perform annual social audits?

CONCEPT CHECK

Summary of Learning Objectives and Key Points

1. Discuss managerial ethics, three areas of special ethical concern for managers, and how organizations manage ethical behavior.

   - Ethics are an individual's personal beliefs about what constitutes right and wrong behavior.
   - Important areas of ethical concern for managers are how the organization treats its employees, how employees treat the organization, and how the organization and its employees treat other economic agents.
   - The ethical context of organizations consists of each manager's individual ethics and messages sent by organizational practices.
   - Organizations use leadership, culture, training, codes, guidelines, and justice to help them manage ethical behavior.

2. Identify and summarize key emerging ethical issues in organizations today.

   - One emerging ethical issue is ethical leadership and its key role in shaping ethical norms and the culture of the organization.
   - Another involves corporate governance and focuses on the need for the board of directors to maintain appropriate oversight of senior management.
   - Third, ethical issues in information technology relate to issues such as individual privacy and the potential abuse of an organization's information technology resources by individuals.

3. Discuss the concept of social responsibility, specify to whom or what an organization might be considered responsible, and describe four types of organizational approaches to social responsibility.

   - Social responsibility is the set of obligations an organization has to protect and enhance the society in which it functions.

   - Organizations may be considered responsible to their stakeholders, to the natural environment, and to the general social welfare.
   - There are strong arguments both for and against social responsibility.
   - The approach an organization adopts toward social responsibility falls along a continuum of lesser to greater commitment: the obstructionist stance, the defensive stance, the accommodative stance, and the proactive stance.

4. Explain the relationship between the government and organizations regarding social responsibility.

   - Government influences organizations through regulation, which is the establishment of laws and rules that dictate what businesses can and cannot do in prescribed areas.
   - Organizations rely on personal contacts, lobbying, political action committees, and favors to influence the government.

5. Describe some of the activities organizations may engage in to manage social responsibility.

   - Organizations use three types of activities to formally manage social responsibility: legal compliance, ethical compliance, and philanthropic giving.
   - Leadership, culture, and allowing for whistleblowing are informal means of managing social responsibility.
   - Organizations should evaluate the effectiveness of their socially responsible practices as they would any other strategy.

Discussion Questions

Questions for Review

1. Define ethical and unethical behavior. Give three specific examples of ethical behavior and three specific examples of unethical behavior.
2. Summarize the basic stances that an organization can take regarding social responsibility.

3. Who are the important stakeholders of your college or university? What does each stakeholder group get from the school? What does each give to the school?
4. Describe the formal and informal dimensions of social responsibility.

Questions for Analysis

5. What is the relationship between the law and ethical behavior? Can illegal behavior possibly be ethical?
6. Where do organizational ethics come from? Describe the contributions made by the organization's founder, managers, and workers, as well as laws and social norms. Which do you think is most influential? Why?

7. There are many worthy causes or programs that deserve support from socially responsible companies. In your opinion, which types of causes or programs are the most deserving? Explain your reasoning.

Questions for Application

8. Since 2000 a number of corporate scandals have been brought to light. Many organizations have responded by, for example, appointing a chief ethics officer, beginning an ethics training program for workers, writing a formal code of ethics, or setting up a hotline for whistle-blowers. In your opinion, are these measures likely to increase organizational ethics in the long run? If so, why? If not, what would be effective in improving organizational ethics?
9. Review the arguments for and against social responsibility. On a scale of 1 to 10, rate the validity and importance

of each point. Use these ratings to develop a position regarding how socially responsible an organization should be. Now compare your ratings and position with those of two of your classmates. Discuss your respective positions, focusing primarily on disagreements.

10. Give three specific examples of a way in which the government has influenced an organization. Then give three specific examples of a way in which an organization has influenced the government. Do you think the government's actions were ethical? Were the company's actions ethical? Why or why not?

CengageNow™ Highlights

Now use your CengageNow™ homework to help you:
- Apply management theories in your life
- Assess your management skills
- Master management terms and concepts
- Apply your knowledge to real-world situations
- Analyze and solve challenging management problems

In order to take advantage of these elements, your instructor will need to have set up a course for your class within CengageNow™. Ask your instructor to contact his/her Cengage sales representative and Digital Solutions Manager to explore testing CengageNow™ in your course this term.

5

CHAPTER

The Global Environment

LEARNING OBJECTIVES

After studying this chapter, you should be able to:

1. Describe the nature of international business, including its meaning, recent trends, management of globalization, and competition in a global market.

2. Discuss the structure of the global economy and describe the GATT and the WTO.

3. Identify and discuss the environmental challenges inherent in international management.

4. Describe the basic issues involved in competing in a global economy, including organization size and the management challenges in a global economy.

MANAGEMENT IN ACTION   The Embargo Grinds On

ounded in 1994 and headquartered in Toronto, Canada, Merchants of Green Coffee sells coffee beans and coffee-making equipment. Its mission "is to deliver the best-tasting coffee experience to discerning consumers through a supply chain with integrity and a unique commitment to quality." The company buys only the finest beans from small growers in Africa and Latin America, and products like Cuba Turquino are typically made from beans grown under shade-tree canopies at elevations above 3,000 feet. As the name indicates, Cuba Turquino is made from Cuban coffee beans, and for that reason, American coffee connoisseurs can't buy it. Americans can buy coffee that's labeled "Cuban," but such brands as Nescafé Café con Leche and Pilon Café Cubano aren't actually made from Cuban coffee beans: Because of a U.S. embargo against Cuban products, the so-called "Cuban coffee" available in this country comes from beans grown in such countries as Nicaragua, Mexico, or Guatemala—basically, anywhere but Cuba, an island nation located just 90 miles off the coast of Florida.

Now, coffee beans from these and other Latin American nations are also of high quality, and they're often certified organic. They're just not *Cuban* coffee beans, and to some people in the coffee business, it's the principle

> "When the embargo is over, I want to be there."
>
> —PAUL KATZEFF, CEO OF THANKSGIVING COFFEE CO.

that matters. Paul Katzeff, founder of Thanksgiving Coffee Co., a California producer of specialty coffees, regards the U.S. embargo as impractical (on the grounds that it hasn't achieved its goals) and immoral (on the grounds that it punishes the Cuban people rather than their government). That's why his company has been marketing a line of beans called "End the Embargo Coffee" for over a decade. The coffee actually comes from Nicaragua, but the packaging, emblazoned with the image of Cuban revolutionary Che Guevara, gets the point across. Katzeff hastens to point out that he's not going "to risk everything I've worked for [for] over 30 years" by violating U.S. law, but in addition to selling distinctive, high-quality coffee, he's determined "to bring awareness to U.S. consumers on Cuba issues." Explains Johanna Schulz, director of Thanksgiving's social and environmental policy: "Since we can't import Cuban coffee directly, we're using [End the Embargo] as an awareness tool to educate customers about the embargo on Cuba." For the past eight years, Thanksgiving has

For years the U.S. government has imposed a ban on the importation of coffee beans from Cuba.

PeterKrenzar/Shutterstock.com

also donated 15 cents from every package sold to the U.S.-Cuba Sister Cities Association, a nonprofit that works to establish relationships between similar-sized cities in the two countries.

The U.S. embargo, which was first imposed in 1962 in response to the revolutionary communist government's appropriation of American land holdings in the country, prevents "U.S. persons" and entities "owned or controlled" by "U.S. persons" from engaging in any transactions in which Cuba has an "interest of any nature whatsoever, direct or indirect." Cuba, therefore, has no access to the American market, does without U.S. imports, and amasses substantial debts to other trading partners. But, says a Canadian businessman with investments in Cuba, "anyone who thinks there will be a 'for sale' sign [put] up by a bankrupt Cuban government is wrong." Why? Basically because the embargo doesn't have much effect on non-U.S. persons and entities.

Cubans now buy ice cream and soft drinks from Swiss-based Nestlé, soap and shampoo from Anglo-Dutch Unilever, and cigarettes from Brazil's Souza Cruz. The fact that the United States is the world's largest market for rum did not deter French-owned Pernod-Ricard from building a new distillery in Cuba, and Britain's Imperial Tobacco expects to double sales when Americans can once again purchase premium hand-rolled Cuban cigars. Most of the directors of Canada's Sherritt International are barred from the United States by provisions of the embargo, but they apparently regard the ban as a small price to pay for future returns on a $1.5 billion investment in Cuba's nickel and oil and gas industries. Cuba has also lifted restrictions on many products once unavailable to Cuban consumers, such as computers, DVDs, and mobile phones, and sales of all these products will be a boon to Telecom Italia, which holds a 27 percent stake in the country's state-owned telecom operations.

Thanksgiving Coffee's Paul Katzeff is thinking the same thing that a lot of American businesspeople are undoubtedly thinking: "When the embargo is over," he says, "I want to be there." As he sees it, Cuban coffee has a promising post-embargo future: Its potential, he points out, "is phenomenal. The climate hasn't changed. The soil hasn't changed." And while Katzeff's geopolitics may rankle some people, his business sense seems sound. At present, of course, he can't actually do business with Cuban coffee growers, but he has figured out a way to lay the groundwork. He has already established working relationships with coffee cooperatives—groups of individual growers who pool their crops to enter the export market and secure higher prices—in Latin America and Africa. "Right now," he says, "my objective is to show those cooperatives that I'm willing to risk something on their behalf," but a longer-term goal is to invest the same capital and acquired know-how in relationships with Cuban growers.

The director of Thanksgiving's Cuba project, Nick Hoskins, has already developed contacts in Cuba's coffee-growing regions, and Katzeff hopes to establish a *twinning agreement*—an exchange of people-to-people programs—with cooperatives in the coffee-growing province of Santiago de Cuba. "We're trying to create models that other companies can use and benefit from," explains Katzeff, who is meanwhile willing to settle for a public relations program of transactions—monetary and otherwise—with American coffee drinkers.[1]

Although every business is unique—and certainly Thanksgiving Coffee Co. goes about things differently than most companies—the challenges and opportunities posed by an increasingly global business environment are much the same for any firm with international aspirations. In particular, businesses must make critical decisions about allocating their resources in different markets and about the best means of gaining a competitive advantage in those markets. To be successful today, managers like Paul Katzeff need a clear understanding of the global context in which they intend to carry out their plans.

This chapter explores the global context of management. We start by describing the nature of international business. We then discuss the structure of the global market in terms of different economies and economic systems. The basic environmental challenges of management are introduced and discussed next. We then focus on issues of competition in a global economy. Finally, we conclude by characterizing the managerial functions of planning and decision making, organizing, leading, and controlling as management challenges in a global economy.

It is also important to remember, though, that it is no longer feasible to segregate a discussion of "international" management from a discussion of "domestic" management as if they were unrelated activities. Hence, although we highlight the central issues of international management in this chapter, we also integrate international issues, examples, opportunities, and challenges throughout the rest of this book. This treatment provides the most realistic possible survey and discussion of the international environment of management.

The Nature of International Business

As you prepared breakfast this morning, you may have plugged in a coffee pot manufactured in China and perhaps ironed a shirt or blouse made in Taiwan with an iron made in Mexico. The coffee you drank was probably made from beans grown in South America or Africa (but not Cuba). To get to school, you may have driven a Japanese car. Even if you drove a Ford or a Chevrolet, some of its parts were engineered or manufactured abroad. Perhaps you did not drive a car to school but rode a bus (manufactured by Daimler AG, a German company) or a motorcycle (manufactured by Honda, Kawasaki, Suzuki, or Yamaha—all Japanese firms).

Our daily lives are strongly influenced by businesses from around the world. But no country is unique in this respect. For instance, people drive Fords in Germany, use Dell computers in China, eat McDonald's hamburgers in France, and snack on Mars candy bars in England. They drink Pepsi and wear Levi Strauss jeans in China and South Africa. The Japanese line up to see Disney movies and pay with American Express credit cards. People around the world fly on United Airlines in planes made by Boeing. Their buildings are constructed with Caterpillar machinery, their factories are powered by General Electric engines, and they buy Chevron oil.

In truth, we have become part of a global village and have a global economy where no organization is insulated from the effects of foreign markets and competition.[2] Indeed, more and more firms are reshaping themselves for international competition and discovering new ways to exploit markets in every corner of the world. Failure to take a global perspective is one of the biggest mistakes managers can make.[3] Thus we start laying the foundation for our discussion by introducing and describing the basics of international business.

The Meaning of International Business

There are many different forms and levels of international business. Although the lines that distinguish one from another may be arbitrary, we can identify four general levels of international activity that differentiate organizations.[4] These are illustrated in Figure 5.1. A domestic business acquires essentially all of its resources and sells all of its products or services within a single country. Most small businesses are essentially domestic in nature; this category includes local retailers and restaurants, agricultural enterprises, and small service

FIGURE 5.1 LEVELS OF INTERNATIONAL BUSINESS ACTIVITY

There are four levels of international business activity. These range from domestic business (the lowest level of international activity) to global business (the highest level).

domestic business
A business that acquires all of its resources and sells all of its products or services within a single country

firms such as dry cleaners and hair salons. However, there are very few large domestic businesses left in the world today.

Indeed, most large firms today are either international or multinational companies. An **international business** is one that is based primarily in a single country but acquires some meaningful share of its resources or revenues (or both) from other countries. Sears fits this description. Most of its stores are in the United States, for example, and the retailer earns around 90 percent of its revenues from its U.S. operations, with the remaining 10 percent coming from Sears stores in Canada. At the same time, however, many of the products it sells, such as tools and clothing, are made abroad.[5]

A **multinational business** has a worldwide marketplace from which it buys raw materials, borrows money, where it manufactures its products, and to which it subsequently sells its products. Coca-Cola, long considered the quintessential American business, derives more than 75 percent of its revenues and 80 percent of its profits from outside of the United States. Coke promotes global advertising campaigns but also dozens of local campaigns as well. The firm markets hundreds of beverages in other countries that have never been sold in the United States. It also sponsors over 50 different national Olympic teams.[6] Multinational businesses like Coca-Cola are often called *multinational corporations*, or MNCs.[7]

Philip Morris International, or PMI, is truly a global business. The firm was started in the United States but is currently headquartered in Geneva, Switzerland. PMI has an internationally diverse top management team and thinks purely in terms of global markets and operations.

FABRICE COFFRINI/AFP/Getty Images/Newscom

The final form of international business is the global business. A **global business** is one that transcends national boundaries and is not committed to a single home country. Although no business has truly achieved this level of internationalization, a few are edging closer and closer. For example, Hoechst AG, a large German chemical company, portrays itself as a "non-national company." Similarly, Unocal Corporation is legally headquartered in California, but in its company literature, Unocal says it "no longer considers itself as a U.S. company" but is, instead, a "global energy company."[8] Firms that take this approach often have senior leadership that is well grounded in global thinking. For instance, Philip Morris International (PMI) is headed up by an executive who was born in Egypt, raised in England, educated in Switzerland, and spent most of his career in New York. PMI is incorporated in New York, is run out of an operations center in Geneva, Switzerland, and represents itself purely as a global corporation.[9]

Trends in International Business

To understand why and how these different levels of international business have emerged, we must look briefly to the past. Most of the industrialized countries in Europe were devastated during World War II. Many Asian countries, especially Japan, fared no better. There were few passable roads, few standing bridges, and even fewer factories dedicated to the manufacture of peacetime products. And those regions less affected by wartime destruction—Canada, Latin America, and Africa—had not yet developed the economic muscle to threaten the economic preeminence of the United States.

Businesses in war-torn countries like Germany and Japan had no choice but to rebuild from scratch. Because of this position, they essentially had to rethink every facet of their operations, including technology, production, finance, and marketing. Although it took many years for these countries to recover, they eventually did so, and their economic systems

international business
A business that is based primarily in a single country but acquires some meaningful share of its resources or revenues (or both) from other countries

multinational business
A business that has a worldwide marketplace from which it buys raw materials, borrows money, where it manufactures its products, and to which it subsequently sells its products

global business
A business that transcends national boundaries and is not committed to a single home country

"We regard ourselves as having a home base in each of the 23 countries where we operate."

—MARC BECKER, EXECUTIVE AT UNICREDITO ITALIANO, A LARGE LENDER INCORPORATED IN ITALY BUT TRYING TO PRESENT A GLOBAL IMAGE[10]

were subsequently poised for growth. During the same era, many U.S. companies grew somewhat complacent. Their customer base was growing rapidly. Increased population spurred by the baby boom and increased affluence resulting from the postwar economic boom greatly raised the average person's standard of living and expectations. The U.S. public continually wanted new and better products and services. Many U.S. companies profited greatly from this pattern, but most were also perhaps guilty of taking the status quo for granted.

But U.S. firms are no longer isolated from global competition or the global market. A few simple numbers help tell the full story of international trade and industry. First of all, the volume of international trade increased more than 3,000 percent between 1960 and 2000. Further, although 139 of the world's largest corporations are headquartered in the United States, there are also 71 in Japan, 39 in France, 37 in Germany, and 46 in China.[11] Within certain industries, the preeminence of non-U.S. firms is even more striking. For example, only two of the world's ten largest banks and none of the largest electronics companies are based in the United States. Only three of the ten largest chemical companies are U.S. firms. On the other hand, U.S. firms comprise seven of the ten largest aerospace companies, three of the six largest airlines, three of the nine largest computer companies, and five of the ten largest.

U.S. firms are also finding that international operations are an increasingly important element of their sales and profits. For example, in 2010 Yum! Brands (owners of Pizza Hut, Taco Bell, and KFC) realized 65 percent of its profits abroad.[12] Similarly, General Electric generated more than half of its 2010 profits from foreign markets.[13] From any perspective, then, it is clear that we live in a truly global economy. Virtually all businesses today must be concerned with the competitive situations they face in lands far from home and with how companies from distant lands are competing in their homelands.

Managing the Process of Globalization

Managers should also recognize that their global context dictates two related but distinct sets of challenges. One set of challenges must be confronted when an organization chooses to change its level of international involvement. For example, a firm that wants to move from being an international to a multinational business has to manage that transition.[14] The other set of challenges occurs when the organization has achieved its desired level of international involvement and must then function effectively within that environment. This section highlights the first set of challenges, and the next section introduces the second set of challenges. When an organization makes the decision to increase its level of international activity, there are several alternative strategies that can be adopted.

Importing and Exporting Importing or exporting (or both) is usually the first type of international business in which a firm gets involved. Exporting, or making the product in the firm's domestic marketplace and selling it in another country, can involve both merchandise and services. Importing is bringing a good, service, or capital into a firm's home country from abroad. For example, automobiles (Mazda, Ford, Volkswagen, Mercedes-Benz, Ferrari) and stereo equipment (Sony, Bang & Olufsen, Sanyo) are routinely exported by their manufacturers to other countries. Likewise, many wine distributors buy products from vineyards in France, Italy, or California and import them into their own country for resale. U.S. sports brands like Nike have become one of the latest hot exports.

An import/export operation has several advantages. For example, it is the easiest way of entering a market with a small outlay of capital. Because the products are usually sold "as is," there is no need to adapt the product to the local conditions, and little risk is involved. Nevertheless, there are also disadvantages. For example, imports and exports are subject to taxes, tariffs, and higher transportation expenses. Furthermore, because the products are not adapted to local conditions, they may miss the needs of a large segment of the

exporting
Making a product in the firm's domestic marketplace and selling it in another country

importing
Bringing a good, service, or capital into the home country from abroad

market. Finally, some products may be restricted and thus can be neither imported nor exported.

Licensing A company may prefer to arrange for a foreign company to manufacture or market its products under a licensing agreement. Factors that may lead to this decision include excessive transportation costs, government regulations, and home production costs. Licensing is an arrangement whereby a firm allows another company to use its brand name, trademark, technology, patent, copyright, or other assets. In return, the licensee pays a royalty, usually based on sales. For example, Kirin Brewery, Japan's largest producer of beer, wanted to expand its international operations but feared that the time involved in shipping it from Japan would cause the beer to lose its freshness. Thus it has entered into a number of licensing arrangements with breweries in other markets. These brewers make beer according to strict guidelines provided by the Japanese firm and then package and market it as Kirin Beer. They then pay a royalty back to Kirin for each case sold. Molson produces Kirin in Canada under such an agreement, while the Charles Wells Brewery does the same in England.

Licensing can allow a company to extend the life of its technology. For instance, older versions of computer hardware and software that have limited markets in industrialized countries may still be widely used in less developed parts of the world. This Egyptian library, for example, uses computers that have little market value in the United States.

Two advantages of licensing are increased profitability and extended profitability. This strategy is frequently used for entry into less-developed countries where older technology is still acceptable and, in fact, may be state of the art. For instance, in countries with little or no wireless Internet access, dial-up modems are still the norm. A primary disadvantage of licensing is inflexibility. A firm can tie up control of its product or expertise for a long period of time. And, if the licensee does not develop the market effectively, the licensing firm can lose profits. A second disadvantage is that licensees can take the knowledge and skill to which they have been given access for a foreign market and exploit them in the licensing firm's home market. When this happens, what used to be a business partner becomes a business competitor.

Strategic Alliances In a strategic alliance, two or more firms jointly cooperate for mutual gain.[15] FedEx subsidiary FedEx Trade Networks recently joined with Fritz Companies Israel to make the company its only regional service provider in the area. The alliance is expected to increase FedEx Trade Networks' global presence by offering customers greater international ocean and air freight services and will provide Fritz Companies Israel clients with the strength of the FedEx brand. The move is also intended to show customers that both companies are hearing and acting on their desires for more reliable global reach and supply chain solutions.[16] Starbucks recently announced a partnership with India-based Tata Coffee to purchase its coffee beans. They plan on also working with the company to open stores in hotels and other retail stores.[17]

A joint venture is a special type of strategic alliance in which the partners actually share ownership of a new enterprise. General Mills and Nestlé formed a separate new company called Cereal Partners Worldwide (CPW) to produce and market cereals. General Mills supplied the technology and proven formulas, while Nestlé provided its international distribution network. The two partners share equally in ownership and profits from CPW. Strategic alliances have enjoyed a tremendous upsurge in the past few years. In most cases, each party provides a portion of the equity or the equivalent in physical plant, raw materials, cash, or other assets. The proportion of the investment then determines the percentage of ownership in the venture.[18]

Strategic alliances have both advantages and disadvantages.[19] For example, they can allow quick entry into a market by taking advantage of the existing strengths of participants.

licensing
An arrangement whereby one company allows another company to use its brand name, trademark, technology, patent, copyright, or other assets in exchange for a royalty based on sales

strategic alliance
A cooperative arrangement between two or more firms for mutual gain

joint venture
A special type of strategic alliance in which the partners share in the ownership of an operation on an equity basis

Japanese automobile manufacturers employed this strategy to their advantage to enter the U.S. market by using the already-established distribution systems of U.S. automobile manufacturers. Strategic alliances are also an effective way to gain access to technology or raw materials. And they allow the firms to share the risk and cost of the new venture. One major disadvantage lies with the shared ownership of joint ventures. Although it reduces the risk for each participant, it also limits the control and return that each firm can enjoy.[20] Another is political interference or intrusion in countries where the government plays an active role in international joint ventures. For example, BP recently lost control of a long-standing and highly lucrative joint venture in Russia when its senior management misread the wishes and intentions of some key government officials regarding how a new venture was to be structured.[21] Blending disparate corporate cultures can also be a challenge.[22]

Direct Investment Another level of commitment to internationalization is direct investment. Direct investment occurs when a firm headquartered in one country builds or purchases operating facilities or subsidiaries in a foreign country. Disney's theme park in Hong Kong is a direct investment. Similarly, Coca-Cola spent $150 million to build a new bottling and distribution network in India. And Harley-Davidson recently announced that it will be building an assembly plant in India to better serve that country's market.[23]

A major reason many firms make direct investments is to capitalize on lower labor costs. In other words, the goal is often to transfer production to locations where labor is cheap. Japanese businesses have moved much of their production to Thailand because labor costs are much lower there than in Japan. Many U.S. firms have been using maquiladoras for the same purpose. Maquiladoras are light assembly plants built in northern Mexico close to the U.S. border. The plants are given special tax breaks by the Mexican government, and the area is populated with workers willing to work for very low wages. More than 3,000 plants in the region employ about 1.2 million workers. The plants are owned by major corporations, primarily from the United States, Japan, South Korea, and major European industrial countries. This concentrated form of direct investment benefits the country of Mexico, the companies themselves, and workers who might otherwise be without jobs. Some critics argue, however, that the low wages paid by the maquiladoras amount to little more than slave labor.[24] In recent years, some of the production in this area has been moving to China, where there is also a large pool of talented workers, most of whom will work for even lower wages.

Like the other approaches for increasing a firm's level of internationalization, direct investment carries with it a number of benefits and liabilities. Managerial control is more complete, and profits do not have to be shared as they do in joint ventures. Purchasing an existing organization provides additional benefits in that the human resources and organizational infrastructure (administrative facilities, plants, warehouses, and so forth) are already in place. Acquisition is also a way to purchase the brand-name identification of a product. This could be particularly important if the cost of introducing a new brand is high. When Nestlé bought the U.S. firm Carnation Company, it retained the firm's brand names for all of its products sold in the United States. Likewise, when Ford bought Volvo it retained that brand name; and when Ford sold Volvo to a Chinese company the name was again retained by its new owners. Notwithstanding these advantages, a company that does this is now operating a part of itself entirely within the borders of a foreign country. The additional complexity in the decision making, the economic and political risks, and so forth may outweigh the advantages that can be obtained by international expansion.

Of course, we should also note that these approaches to internationalization are not mutually exclusive. Indeed, most large firms use all of them simultaneously. MNCs have a global orientation and worldwide approach to foreign markets and production. They search for opportunities all over the world and select the best strategy to serve each market. In some settings, they may use direct investment, in others licensing, in others strategic alliances; in still others they might limit their involvement to exporting and importing. The advantages and disadvantages of each approach are summarized in Table 5.1.

direct investment
When a firm headquartered in one country builds or purchases operating facilities or subsidiaries in a foreign country

maquiladoras
Light assembly plants built in northern Mexico close to the U.S. border that are given special tax breaks by the Mexican government

TABLE 5.1 ADVANTAGES AND DISADVANTAGES OF DIFFERENT APPROACHES TO INTERNATIONALIZATION

When organizations decide to increase their level of internationalization, they can adopt several strategies. Each strategy is a matter of degree, as opposed to being a discrete and mutually exclusive category. And each has unique advantages and disadvantages that must be considered.

Approach to Internationalization	Advantages	Disadvantages
Importing or Exporting	• Small cash outlay • Little risk • No adaptation necessary	• Tariffs and taxes • High transportation costs • Government restrictions
Licensing	• Increased profitability • Extended profitability	• Inflexibility • Competition
Strategic Alliances/Joint Ventures	• Quick market entry • Access to materials and technology	• Shared ownership (limits control and profits)
Direct Investment	• Enhanced control • Existing infrastructure	• Complexity • Greater economic and political risk • Greater uncertainty

© Cengage Learning 2013

Competing in a Global Market

Even when a firm is not actively seeking to increase its desired level of internationalization, its managers are still responsible for seeing that it functions effectively within whatever level of international involvement the organization has achieved. Moreover, local firms must be prepared to compete with multinationals with aggressive globalization goals.[25] In one sense, the job of a manager in an international business may not be that much different from the job of a manager in a domestic business. Each may be responsible for acquiring resources and materials, making products, providing services, developing human resources, advertising, or monitoring cash flow.

In another sense, however, the complexity associated with each of these activities may be much greater for managers in international firms. Rather than buying raw materials from sources in California, Texas, and Missouri, an international purchasing manager may buy materials from sources in Peru, India, and Spain. Rather than training managers for new plants in Michigan, Florida, and Oregon, the international human resources executive may be training new plant managers for facilities in China, Mexico, and Scotland. And instead of developing a single marketing campaign for the United States, an advertising director may be working on promotional efforts in France, Brazil, and Japan. The *Technically Speaking* box on page 114 entitled " 'Walmart's Worst Nightmare'?" serves up some food for thought on the role played by technology in the entry of Britain's Tesco into the U.S. grocery market.

Finally, the key question that must be addressed by any manager trying to be effective in an international market is whether to focus on globalization or on regionalism. A global thrust requires that activities be managed from an overall global perspective as part of an integrated system. Regionalism, on the other hand, involves managing within each region with less regard for the overall organization. In reality, most larger MNCs manage some activities globally (for example, finance and manufacturing are commonly addressed globally) and others locally (human resource management and advertising are frequently handled this way).

TECHNICALLY SPEAKING

"Walmart's Worst Nightmare"?

It's no secret that Walmart is the largest retailer on the planet. The business-information service Hoover's calls it "an irresistible (or at least unavoidable) retail force that has yet to meet any immovable objects." Not quite everyone, however, agrees with Hoover's assessment. For one, food-retail analyst Kevin Coupe points out that "there isn't a place in the world where Tesco has gone one-on-one with Walmart and Tesco hasn't won."

In its home base of Britain, for example, Tesco, the world's third largest retailer, commands a 35 percent market share—nearly double that of Walmart-owned Asda. In 2007, moreover, Tesco launched a bold counteroffensive against Walmart on the retail superpower's home turf, rolling out a chain of food stores called Fresh & Easy as the first stage in a strategy originally calling for as many as 5,000 stores by 2020. These plans quickly hit a snag due to the recession that began in 2008, and by the end of 2009, there were only 125 Fresh & Easy outlets in the United States. Tesco officials were forced to push back their due date for profitability, but by the end of 2010, they had reaccelerated their store-opening schedule, announcing a goal of 400 outlets by 2013.

Fast & Easy outlets are about the size of a Trader Joe's, offer the kind of products that you'd find at Whole Foods, and feature prices calculated to make you think Costco. The format is one of five that Tesco operates among 4,800 stores in 14 countries, and its ability to manage stores in multiple formats as well as multiple markets is one of the company's greatest strengths. The key to this core competence is technology—or more precisely, data management, which is critical in any effort to optimize inventory selection, size, and distribution. In the United Kingdom, for instance, a wireless network connecting all Tesco stores facilitates real-time management of distribution and transportation. Workers use handheld PDAs for data entry and reporting, and radio frequency identification (RFID) tags allow them to route crates and pallets to stores carrying anywhere from 3,500 to 60,000 different products in countries located anywhere from Sussex to Seoul.

In addition, Tesco is good not only at applying data management to supply-chain management: It has also developed considerable skill in applying data management to the analysis of consumer preferences in different markets. Tesco relies on a data-mining firm called Dunnhumby (of which it has majority control) to manage everything from targeting sales promotions to designing store formats and, perhaps most importantly, developing private-label products.

Along with its ability to manage multiple store formats, many analysts regard Tesco's ability to provide a better and broader range of private brands—products manufactured for

John Crowe Alamy

retailers who sell them under their own names—as one of the most important factors in the company's marketing success. U.S. retailers, on the other hand, have never quite been able to convince consumers that private-label products are as good as their brand-name counterparts. Walmart, for example, struggles to get 35 percent of its sales from private-label goods. In many countries, however, Tesco gets as much as 60 percent of its revenue from private-label sales, and 70 percent of Fast & Easy sales come from private-label products.

According to New York retail consultant Burt P. Flickinger, "Tesco is arguably the finest food retailer in the world," and he suggests that, armed with a unique set of competencies with which to invade the U.S. market, the British grocer may well be "Walmart's worst nightmare." On a less dramatic note, he predicts that, at the very least, Tesco will "take a little piece out of everybody from Walmart to Whole Foods."

References: Alexandra Biesada, "Wal-Mart, Inc.," Hoover's, 2011, www.hoovers.com on February 8, 2011; Bruce Horowitz, "British Grocery Chain Hits America with Fresh Ideas," *USA Today*, April 11, 2008, www.usatoday.com on February 8, 2011; Julia Finch, "Tesco Feels US Downturn as Fresh & Easy Turns Stale," *The Guardian*, April 20, 2009, www.guardian.co on February 8, 2011; Kathy Gordon, "Not So Fresh & Easy for Tesco in the U.S.," *Wall Street Journal*, January 12, 2010, http://blogs.wsj.com on February 8, 2011; James Hall, "Tesco Unveils US Food Chain Expansion," *The Telegraph*, October 6, 2010, www.telegraph.co on February 8, 2011; Kerry Capell, "Tesco: 'Wal-Mart's Worst Nightmare,' " *BusinessWeek*, December 29, 2008, www.businessweek.com on February 8, 2011.

Identify and describe the four levels of international involvement.

Identify a product you recently purchased that was made in another country. What factors do you think caused it to be made there rather than at a domestic location?

The Structure of the Global Economy

One thing that can be helpful to managers seeking to operate in a global environment is to better understand the structure of the global economy. Although each country and indeed many regions within any given country are unique, we can still note some basic similarities and differences. We describe three different elements of the global economy: mature market economies and systems, high-potential/high-growth economies, and other economies.[26]

Mature Market Economies and Systems

A market economy is based on the private ownership of business and allows market factors such as supply and demand to determine business strategy. Mature market economies include the United States, Japan, the United Kingdom, France, Germany, and Sweden. These countries have several things in common. For example, they tend to employ market forces in the allocation of resources. They also tend to be characterized by private ownership of property, although there is some variance along this dimension. France, for example, has a relatively high level of government ownership among the market economies.

U.S. managers have relatively few problems operating in market economies. Many of the basic business "rules of the game" that apply in the United States also apply, for example, in Germany or England. And consumers there often tend to buy the same kinds of products. For these reasons, it is not unusual for U.S. firms seeking to expand geographically to begin operations in other market economies. Although the task of managing an international business in an industrial market economy is somewhat less complicated than operating in some other type of economy, it still poses some challenges. Perhaps foremost among them is that the markets in these economies are typically quite mature. Many industries, for example, are already dominated by large and successful companies. Thus competing in these economies poses a major challenge.

The map in Figure 5.2 highlights three relatively mature market systems. Market systems are clusters of countries that engage in high levels of trade with one another. One mature market system is North America. The United States, Canada, and Mexico are major trading partners with one another; more than 80 percent of Mexico's exports go to the United States, and more than 48 percent of what Mexico imports comes from the United States.[27] During the last several years, these countries have negotiated a variety of agreements to make trade even easier. The most important of these, the North American Free Trade Agreement (NAFTA), eliminates many of the trade barriers—quotas and tariffs, for example—that existed previously.

Another mature market system is Europe. For most of the twentieth century Europe was really two distinct economic areas. The eastern region consisted of communist countries such as Poland, Czechoslovakia, and Romania. These countries relied on government ownership of business and greatly restricted trade. In contrast, Western European countries with traditional market economies have been working together to promote international trade for decades. In particular, the European Union (or *EU*, as it is often called), currently comprised of 27 members, has long been a formidable market system. The EU's origins can be traced to 1957 when Belgium, France, Luxembourg, Germany,

market economy
An economy based on the private ownership of business that allows market factors such as supply and demand to determine business strategy

market systems
Clusters of countries that engage in high levels of trade with one another

North American Free Trade Agreement (NAFTA)
An agreement made by the United States, Canada, and Mexico to promote trade with one another

European Union (EU)
The first and most important international market system

FIGURE 5.2 THE GLOBAL ECONOMY

The global economy is dominated by three relatively mature market systems. As illustrated here, these market systems consist of North America, Europe (especially those nations in the European Union), and Pacific Asia (parts of which are high-potential/high-growth economies). Other areas of Asia, as well as Africa and South America, have the potential for future growth but currently play only a relatively small role in the global economy.

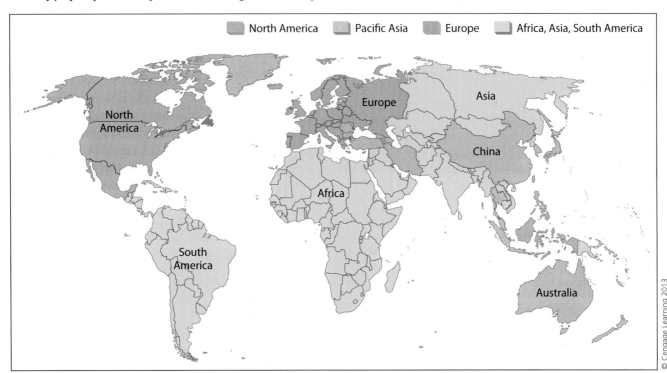

Italy, and the Netherlands signed the Treaty of Rome to promote economic integration. Between 1973 and 1986, these countries were joined by Denmark, Ireland, the United Kingdom, Greece, Spain, and Portugal, and the group became known first as the European Community and then the European Union. Austria, Finland, and Sweden joined the EU in 1995. Ten other countries, including Poland, Estonia, and Hungary, joined in 2004; Romania and Bulgaria became members in 2007. For years these countries have followed a basic plan that led to the systematic elimination of most trade barriers. The new market system achieved significantly more potential when on January 1, 2002, 11 of the EU members eliminated their home currencies (such as French francs and Italian lira) and adopted a new common currency called the *euro*.

The European situation has grown more complex, however. With the collapse of communism, the market economies adopted by the Eastern countries are not as developed as those in Western Europe, for instance. These countries also want greater participation in trade with the Western European countries and more voice in the EU. Indeed, in some ways the emergence of the East has slowed and complicated business activities in the West. Most members agree that the governance structure created for a six-member alliance needs revision since the EU has become so big, but there is little agreement on how to approach such a revision. Sharp divisions among EU members regarding the U.S.-led war in Iraq have also strained relations among such key nations as Spain and the United Kingdom (which supported the war) and France and Germany (which opposed the war). And economic turmoil in some EU countries—such as Greece—has created even more difficulties. In the long term, however, the EU is almost certain to remain an important force in the global economy.

Yet another mature market system is Pacific Asia. As shown in Figure 5.2, this market system includes Japan, China, Thailand, Malaysia, Singapore, Indonesia, South Korea, Taiwan, the Philippines, and Australia. Indeed, Japan, Taiwan, Singapore, Thailand, and South Korea were major economic powerhouses until a regional currency crisis slowed their growth in the late 1990s. Although that crisis has passed, the global effects of the 2008–2010 recession continue to affect all parts of the global economy, including Pacific Asia. The earthquake and tsunami that struck Japan in 2011 have also had disastrous effects on that country in particular.

High-Potential/High-Growth Economies

In contrast to the highly developed and mature market economies just described, other countries have what can be termed *high-potential/high-growth economies*. These economies have been relatively underdeveloped and immature and, until recently, were characterized by weak industry, weak currency, and relatively poor consumers.[28] The governments in these countries, however, have been actively working to strengthen their economies by opening their doors to foreign investment and by promoting international trade. Some of these countries have only recently adopted market economies, while others still use a command economy.

Even though it is technically part of Pacific Asia, the People's Republic of China is largely underdeveloped. But its market potential is enormous. For example, it is already the world's third largest automobile market and has recently become the world's second largest economy. The transfer of control of Hong Kong from Great Britain to China focused even more attention on the market potential in the world's most populous country.[29] This fact is the primary reason that Disney chose to build its newest theme park in China. India is also emerging as a major force in the global economy. Marvel Comics recently launched an Indian version of its popular Spider-Man comic book in India.[30] And Walmart launched a joint venture in India under the brand name Best Price Modern Wholesale.[31] Vietnam has become a potentially important market, and Brazil is becoming more important as well.[32] Likewise, Russia and the other states and republics that previously made up the Commonwealth of Independent States are being closely watched by many companies for emerging market opportunities.[33] South Africa also holds considerable promise.

The primary challenges presented by the developing economies to those interested in conducting international business there are potential consumers' lack of wealth and an underdeveloped infrastructure. Developing economies have enormous economic potential, but much of it remains untapped. Thus international firms entering these markets often have to invest heavily in distribution systems, in training consumers how to use their products, and even in providing living facilities for their workers. They also run the risk of major policy changes that can greatly distort the value of their investments.[34]

Other Economies

There are some economic systems around the world that defy classification as either mature markets or high-potential/high-growth economies. One major area that falls outside of these categories is the oil-exporting region generally called the Middle East. The oil-exporting countries present mixed models of resource allocation, property ownership, and infrastructure development. These countries all have access to major amounts of crude oil, however, and thus are important players in the global economy.

These countries include Iran, Iraq, Kuwait, Saudi Arabia, Libya, Syria, and the United Arab Emirates. High oil prices in the last four decades have created enormous wealth in these countries. Many of them invested heavily in their infrastructures. Whole new cities were built, airports were constructed, and the population was educated. The per capita incomes of the United Arab Emirates and Qatar, for example, are among the highest in the

Pacific Asia
A market system located in Southeast Asia

> "The dominant logic holds that innovation comes from the U.S., goes to Europe and Japan, and then gravitates to poor countries. But now we're starting to see a reversal of that flow."
>
> —C. K. PRAHALAD, LEADING STRATEGY EXPERT[35]

world. Although there is great wealth in the oil-producing nations, they provide great challenges to managers. Political instability (as evidenced by the Persian Gulf War in 1991, the U.S.-led war in Iraq starting in 2003, and the political turmoil that swept the region in 2011) and tremendous cultural differences, for example, combine to make doing business in many parts of the Middle East both very risky and very difficult.

Other countries pose risks of a different sort to business. Politically and ethnically motivated violence, for example, still characterizes some countries. Foremost among these are Peru, El Salvador, Turkey, Colombia, and Northern Ireland. Cuba presents special challenges because it is so insulated from the outside world. With the demise of other communist regimes, some experts believe that Cuba will eventually join the ranks of the market economies. If so, its strategic location will quickly make it an important business center.

The Role of the GATT and the WTO

The global economy is also increasingly being influenced by the General Agreement on Tariffs and Trade (GATT) and the World Trade Organization (WTO).

General Agreement on Tariffs and Trade (GATT) The General Agreement on Tariffs and Trade, or GATT, was first negotiated following World War II in an effort to avoid trade wars that would benefit rich nations and harm poorer ones. Essentially, the GATT is a trade agreement intended to promote international trade by reducing trade barriers and making it easier for all nations to compete in international markets. The GATT was a major stimulus to international trade after it was first ratified in 1948 by 23 countries.

One key component of the GATT was the identification of the so-called *most favored nation* (MFN) principle. This provision stipulates that if a country extends preferential treatment to any other nation that has signed the agreement, the same preferential treatment must be extended to all signatories of the agreement. Members can extend such treatment to nonsignatories as well, but are not required to do so.

GATT
A trade agreement intended to promote international trade by reducing trade barriers and making it easier for all nations to compete in international markets

World Trade Organization (WTO)
An organization, which currently includes 140 member nations and 32 observer countries, that requires members to open their markets to international trade and follow WTO rules

World Trade Organization (WTO) The World Trade Organization, or WTO, came into existence on January 1, 1995. The WTO replaced the GATT and absorbed its mission. The WTO is headquartered in Geneva, Switzerland, and currently includes 149 member nations and 32 observer countries. Members are required to open their markets to international trade and follow WTO rules. The WTO has three basic goals:

1. To promote trade flows by encouraging nations to adopt nondiscriminatory and predictable trade policies
2. To reduce remaining trade barriers through multilateral negotiations
3. To establish impartial procedures for resolving trade disputes among its members

The World Trade Organization is certain to continue to play a major role in the evolution of the global economy. At the same time, it has also become a lightning rod for protesters and other activists who argue that the WTO focuses too narrowly on globalization issues to the detriment of human rights and the environment.

What are the three major mature market systems? What are the GATT and WTO?

What impact has the U.S.-led war in Iraq had on international business?

CONCEPT CHECK

Environmental Challenges of International Management

We noted earlier that managing in a global context both poses and creates additional challenges for the manager. As illustrated in Figure 5.3, three environmental challenges in particular warrant additional exploration at this point—the economic environment, the political/legal environment, and the cultural environment of international management.[36]

The Economic Environment

Every country is unique and creates a unique set of challenges for managers trying to do business there. However, there are three aspects of the economic environment in particular that can help managers anticipate the kinds of economic challenges they are likely to face in working abroad.

Economic System The first of these is the economic system used in the country. As we described earlier, most countries today are moving toward a market economy. In a mature market economy, the key element for managers is freedom of choice. Consumers are free to make decisions about which products they prefer to purchase, and firms are free to decide what products and services to provide. As long as both the consumer and the firm are free to decide to be in the market, then supply and demand determine which firms and which products will be available.

A related characteristic of market economies that is relevant to managers concerns the nature of property ownership. There are two pure types—complete private ownership and complete public ownership. In systems with private ownership, individuals and organizations—not the government—own and operate the companies that conduct business. In systems with public ownership, the government directly owns the companies that manufacture and sell products. Few countries have pure systems of private ownership or pure systems of public ownership. Most countries tend toward one extreme or the other, but usually a mix of public and private ownership exists.

Natural Resources Another important aspect of the economic environment in different countries is the availability of natural resources. A very broad range of resources is available in different countries. Some countries, like Japan, have relatively few natural resources of their own. Japan is thus forced to import all of the oil, iron ore, and other natural resources it needs

---

FIGURE 5.3 ENVIRONMENTAL CHALLENGES OF INTERNATIONAL MANAGEMENT

Managers functioning in a global context must be aware of several environmental challenges. Three of the most important include economic, political/legal, and cultural challenges.

© Cengage Learning 2013

to manufacture products for its domestic and overseas markets. The United States, in contrast, has enormous natural resources and is a major producer of oil, natural gas, coal, iron ore, copper, uranium, and other metals and materials that are vital to the development of a modern economy.

One natural resource that is particularly important in the modern global economy is oil. As we noted earlier, a small set of countries in the Middle East, including Saudi Arabia, Iraq, Iran, and Kuwait, controls a very large percentage of the world's total known reserves of crude oil. Access to this single natural resource has given these oil-producing countries enormous clout in the international economy. One of the more controversial global issues today involving natural resources is the South American rain forest. Developers and farmers in Brazil, Peru, and other countries are clearing vast areas of rain forest, arguing that it is their land and that they can do what they want with it. Many environmentalists, however, fear the deforestation is wiping out entire species of animals and may so alter the environment as to affect weather patterns around the world.[37]

Infrastructure Yet another important aspect of the economic environment of relevance to international management is infrastructure. A country's **infrastructure** consists of its schools, hospitals, power plants, railroads, highways, shipping ports, communication systems, airfields, commercial distribution systems, and so forth. The United States has a highly developed infrastructure. For example, its educational system is modern, roads and bridges are well developed, and most people have access to medical care. Overall, the United States has a relatively complete infrastructure sufficient to support most forms of economic development and activity.

Some countries, on the other hand, lack a well-developed infrastructure. Some countries do not have enough electrical generating capacity to meet demand. Such countries—Kenya, for example—often schedule periods of time during which power is turned off or reduced. These planned power failures reduce power demands but can be an enormous inconvenience to business. In the extreme, when a country's infrastructure is greatly underdeveloped, firms interested in beginning businesses may have to build an entire township, including housing, schools, hospitals, and perhaps even recreational facilities, to attract a sufficient overseas workforce.

As this section indicates, a country's economic *environment* involves much more than its economic system. Its economic environment is linked not only to the state of its infrastructure and to its supply of natural resources, but also to the conditions of its natural environment. The *Greening* box entitled "Changing the Climate of Global Aid" on page 121 shows how a major supplier of humanitarian assistance addresses issues in all of these areas when it delivers aid to nations around the world.

The Political/Legal Environment

A second environmental challenge facing the international manager is the political-legal environment in which he or she will do business. Four especially important aspects of the political-legal environment of international management are government stability, incentives for multinational trade, controls on international trade, and the influence of economic communities on international trade.

infrastructure
The schools, hospitals, power plants, railroads, highways, ports, communication systems, airfields, and commercial distribution systems of a country

Government Stability Stability can be viewed in two ways—as the ability of a given government to stay in power against opposing factions in the country and as the permanence of government policies toward business. A country that is stable in both respects is preferable because managers have a higher probability of successfully predicting how government will affect their businesses. Civil war in countries such as Angola has made it virtually impossible for international managers to predict what government policies are likely to

"Europe in many ways is the global regulatory superpower."

—JEFFREY IMMELT, CEO OF GENERAL ELECTRIC[38]

GREENING THE BUSINESS ENVIRONMENT

Changing the Climate of Global Aid

JB Russel/Sygma/Corbis

As you'll recall, we introduced Mercy Corps in the *World of Difference* box in Chapter 1, where we discussed the organization's efforts to bring financial assistance to such impoverished countries as Indonesia. Mercy Corps, however, has a much broader mission: Since its founding in 1979, the Oregon-based nonprofit has provided $1.95 billion in humanitarian aid and development assistance to people in 107 countries and annually reaches nearly 17 million people in 36 nations. In the aftermath of the devastating earthquake and tsunami that struck Japan in March 2011, Mercy Corps delivered emergency supplies and set up a program called Comfort for Kids to help children deal with the emotional effects of a large-scale disaster.

Mercy Corps' approach to on-the-ground assistance also involves more than immediate response and emergency relief services. According to its mission statement,

> Mercy Corps has learned that communities recovering from war or social upheaval must be the agents of their own transformation for change to endure. It's only when communities set their own agendas, raise their own resources, and implement programs themselves that the first successes result in the renewed hope, confidence and skills to continue their development independently.

Mercy Corps thus works to foster "sustainable community development that integrates agriculture, health, housing and infrastructure, economic development, education and environment and local management," as well as launching "initiatives that promote citizen participation, accountability, conflict management, and the rule of law." In India, for example, Mercy

Corps has taught small-scale tea farmers sustainable ways to grow organic teas and get fair prices for them. In Indonesia, assistance includes equipment for harvesting rainwater and projects for removing solid waste from residential neighborhoods.

In addition to the devastating effects of war, social upheaval, and natural disaster, Mercy Corps is also concerned with the effects of climate change on developing communities. Thus it works to provide "viable economic options as communities adapt to new environmental realities," especially in helping poor communities to cope with "the rising incidence of climate-related disasters such as flooding and drought." According to Mercy Corps, its climate-related programs fall into three main areas:

- *Alternative energy:* promoting energy sources that support sustainable economic activities
- *Sustainable resource management:* supporting a community's ability to provide its own environmental and ecological services
- *Advocacy, outreach, and models that work:* inspiring governments and communities to rely on proven environment- and climate-friendly programs

In 2010, for example, when drought in the African nation of Niger threatened nearly 8 million people with malnutrition and starvation, Mercy Corps not only mobilized efforts to provide food commodities but also helped local farmers deal with chronic debt arising from inefficient methods and previous crop failures. A year later, Mercy Corps responded when Timor-Leste, an island nation northwest of Australia, faced just the opposite in climate-related crises: Because seasonal rains continued throughout the dry season, when farmers plant and harvest the country's food supply, drainage systems failed and crops could not be delivered over impassable roads. In addition to providing immediate relief, Mercy Corps trained local blacksmiths to make portable silos for storing rice and corn, the country's main staples.

References: Mercy Corps, "Mercy Corps Timeline," "Climate Change," "A Growing Opportunity for Action," 2011, www.mercycorps.org on April 5, 2011; Roger Burks, "Change Brewing in the Tea Lands," Mercy Corps, April 9, 2008, www.mercycorps.org on April 5, 2011; Mercy Corps Indonesia, "Our Work," 2009, http://indonesia.mercycorps.org on January 27, 2010; Roger Burks, "Responding to Niger's Latest Hunger Crisis," Mercy Corps, July 23, 2010, www.mercycorps.org on April 5, 2011; USAID, "USAID Helps Drought-Affected Niger with First Award under the Emergency Food Security Program," June 17, 2010, press release, www.usaid.gov on April 5, 2011; Wahyu Nugroho, "Farmers in Timor-Leste Store Up for a Better Future," Mercy Corps, March 22, 2011, www.mercycorps.org on April 5, 2011.

Swiss giant Nestlé is one of the world's largest firms. Among myriad other products, Nestlé processes and sells milk and milk products in over 100 countries around the world. But a few years ago, the company's operations in Peru were taken over by the Peruvian government.

be and whether the government will be able to guarantee the safety of international workers. Consequently, international firms have been very reluctant to invest in Angola.

In many countries—the United States, Great Britain, and Japan, for example—changes in government occur with very little disruption. In other countries—India, Argentina, and Greece, for example—changes are likely to be somewhat chaotic. Even if a country's government remains stable, the risk remains that the policies adopted by that government might change. In some countries, foreign businesses may be **nationalized** (taken over by the government) with little or no warning. For example, the government of Peru nationalized Perulac, a domestic milk producer owned by Nestlé, because of a local milk shortage.

Incentives for International Trade Another facet of the political environment is incentives to attract foreign business. For example, the state of Alabama offered Mercedes-Benz huge tax breaks and other incentives to entice the German firm to select a location for a new factory in that state. In like fashion, the French government sold land to the Walt Disney Company far below its market value and agreed to build a connecting freeway in exchange for the company's agreeing to build a European theme park outside of Paris.

Such incentives can take a variety of forms. Some of the most common include reduced interest rates on loans, construction subsidies, and tax incentives. Less-developed countries tend to offer different packages of incentives. In addition to lucrative tax breaks, for example, they can also attract investors with duty-fee entry of raw materials and equipment, market protection through limitations on other importers, and the right to take profits out of the country. They may also have to correct deficiencies in their infrastructures, as noted above, to satisfy the requirements of foreign firms.

Controls on International Trade A third element of the political environment that managers need to consider is the extent to which there are controls on international trade. In some instances, a country's government might decide that foreign competition is hurting domestic trade. To protect domestic business, such governments may enact barriers to international trade. These barriers include tariffs, quotas, export restraint agreements, and "buy national" laws. During the global economic recession that started in 2008, many countries began to raise tariffs on imports from other countries and/or subsidize their own exports in order to protect domestic businesses despite the opinions of experts who argue that such practices, over the long run, tend to make things worse instead of better.[40]

"[Russian Prime Minister Vladimir] Putin visits a combine harvester factory and decides on the spot he will raise tariffs."

—UNNAMED EU TRADE OFFICIAL[39]

A **tariff** is a tax collected on goods shipped across national boundaries. Tariffs can be collected by the exporting country, countries through which goods pass, and the importing country. Import tariffs, which are the most common, can be levied to protect domestic companies by increasing the cost of foreign goods. Japan charges U.S. tobacco producers a tariff on cigarettes imported into Japan as a way to keep their prices higher than the prices charged by domestic firms. Tariffs can also be levied, usually by less-developed countries, to raise money for the government.

In the United States, the Byrd Amendment (named after West Virginia Senator Robert Byrd) stipulates that, if a domestic firm successfully demonstrates that a foreign company is dumping (selling for less than fair-market value) its products in the U.S. market, those

nationalized
Taken over by the government

tariff
A tax collected on goods shipped across national boundaries

products will be hit with a tariff and the proceeds given to the domestic company filing the complaint. U.S. ball-bearing maker Torrington received $63 million under provisions of this statute.[41]

Quotas are the most common form of trade restriction. A *quota* is a limit on the number or value of goods that can be traded. The quota amount is typically designed to ensure that domestic competitors will be able to maintain a certain market share. Honda is allowed to import 425,000 autos each year into the United States. This quota is one reason why Honda opened manufacturing facilities in the United States. The quota applies to cars imported into the United States, but the company can produce as many cars within U.S. borders as it wants because those cars are not considered imports. Export restraint agreements are designed to convince other governments to voluntarily limit the volume or value of goods exported to or imported from a particular country. They are, in effect, export quotas. Japanese steel producers voluntarily limit the amount of steel they send to the United States each year.

"Buy national" legislation gives preference to domestic producers through content or price restrictions. Several countries have this type of legislation. Brazil requires that Brazilian companies purchase only Brazilian-made computers. The United States requires that the Department of Defense purchases only military uniforms manufactured in the United States, even though the price of foreign uniforms would be half as much. Mexico requires that 50 percent of the car parts sold in Mexico be manufactured inside its own borders.

Economic Communities Just as government policies can either increase or decrease the political risk facing international managers, trade relations between countries can either help or hinder international business. Relations dictated by quotas, tariffs, and so forth can hurt international trade. There is currently a strong movement around the world to reduce many of these barriers. This movement takes its most obvious form in international economic communities.

An international economic community is a set of countries that agree to markedly reduce or eliminate trade barriers among member nations. The first and in many ways still the most important of these economic communities is the European Union (EU), discussed earlier. The passage of NAFTA, as also noted earlier, represents perhaps the first step toward the formation of a North American economic community. Other important economic communities include the Latin American Integration Association (Bolivia, Brazil, Colombia, Chile, Argentina, and other South American countries) and the Caribbean Common Market (the Bahamas, Belize, Jamaica, Antigua, Barbados, and 12 other countries).

The Cultural Environment

Another environmental challenge for the international manager is the cultural environment and how it affects business. Disney's Hong Kong theme park struggled after it first opened, in large part because Disney made the mistake of minimizing all elements of Chinese culture in the park—essentially, making it a generic miniature reproduction of the original Disneyland in California. Disney also confused potential visitors with ads showing a father, mother, and two children walking hand-in-hand toward the theme park—overlooking China's laws that restrict many families to a single child. Only after a refurbishment to make the park more Chinese and a revised ad campaign did attendance begin to improve.[42] A country's culture includes all the values, symbols, beliefs, and language that guide behavior.

Values, Symbols, Beliefs, and Language Cultural values and beliefs are often unspoken; they may even be taken for granted by those who live in a particular country. Cultural

quota
A limit on the number or value of goods that can be traded

export restraint agreements
Accords reached by governments in which countries voluntarily limit the volume or value of goods they export to or import from one another

economic community
A set of countries that agree to markedly reduce or eliminate trade barriers among member nations (a formalized market system)

factors do not necessarily cause problems for managers when the cultures of two countries are similar. Difficulties can arise, however, when there is little overlap between the home culture of a manager and the culture of the country in which business is to be conducted. For example, most U.S. managers find the culture and traditions of England relatively familiar. The people of both countries speak the same language and share strong historical roots, and there is a history of strong commerce between the two countries. When U.S. managers begin operations in Japan or the People's Republic of China, however, most of those commonalities disappear.

In Japanese, the word *hai* (pronounced "hi") means "yes." In conversation, however, this word is used much like people in the United States use "uh-huh"; it moves a conversation along or shows the person with whom you are talking that you are paying attention. So when does *hai* mean "yes" and when does it mean "uh-huh"? This turns out to be a relatively difficult question to answer. If a U.S. manager asks a Japanese manager if he agrees to some trade arrangement, the Japanese manager is likely to say, "Hai"—but this may mean "Yes, I agree," "Yes, I understand," or "Yes, I am listening." Many U.S. managers become frustrated in negotiations with the Japanese because they believe that the Japanese continue to raise issues that have already been settled (because the Japanese managers said "Yes"). What many of these managers fail to recognize is that "yes" does not always mean "yes" in Japan.

Cultural differences between countries can have a direct impact on business practice. For example, the religion of Islam teaches that people should not make a living by exploiting the misfortune of others; as a result, charging interest payments, for example, is seen as immoral. This means that in Saudi Arabia there are few businesses that provide auto-wrecking services to tow stalled cars to the garage (because that would be capitalizing on misfortune), and in the Sudan banks cannot pay or charge interest. Given these cultural and religious constraints, those two businesses—automobile towing and banking—do not seem to hold great promise for international managers in those particular countries!

Some cultural differences between countries can be even more subtle and yet have a major impact on business activities. For example, in the United States, most managers clearly agree about the value of time. Most U.S. managers schedule their activities very tightly and then try to adhere to their schedules. Other cultures do not put such a premium on time. In the Middle East, managers do not like to set appointments, and they rarely keep appointments set too far into the future. U.S. managers interacting with managers from the Middle East might misinterpret the late arrival of a potential business partner as a negotiation ploy or an insult, when it is rather a simple reflection of different views of time and its value.[43]

Language itself can be an important factor. Beyond the obvious and clear barriers posed by people who speak different languages, subtle differences in meaning can also play a major role. For example, Imperial Oil of Canada markets gasoline under the brand name Esso. When the firm tried to sell its gasoline in Japan, it learned that *esso* means "stalled car" in Japanese. Likewise, when Chevrolet first introduced a U.S. model called the Nova in Latin America, General Motors executives could not understand why the car sold poorly. They eventually learned, though, that, in Spanish, *no va* means "it doesn't go." The color green is used extensively in Muslim countries, but it signifies death in some other countries. The color associated with femininity in the United States is pink, but in many other countries, yellow is the most feminine color.

Individual Behaviors Across Cultures   There also appear to be clear differences in individual behaviors and attitudes across different cultures. For example, Geert Hofstede, a Dutch researcher, studied 116,000 people working in dozens of different countries and found several interesting differences.[44] Hofstede's initial work identified four important dimensions along which people seem to differ across cultures. More recently, he has added a fifth dimension. These dimensions are illustrated in Figure 5.4.

FIGURE 5.4 INDIVIDUAL DIFFERENCES ACROSS CULTURES

Hofstede identified five fundamental differences that can be used to characterize people in different cultures. These dimensions are social orientation, power orientation, uncertainty orientation, goal orientation, and time orientation. Different levels of each dimension affect the perceptions, attitudes, values, motivations, and behaviors of people in different cultures.

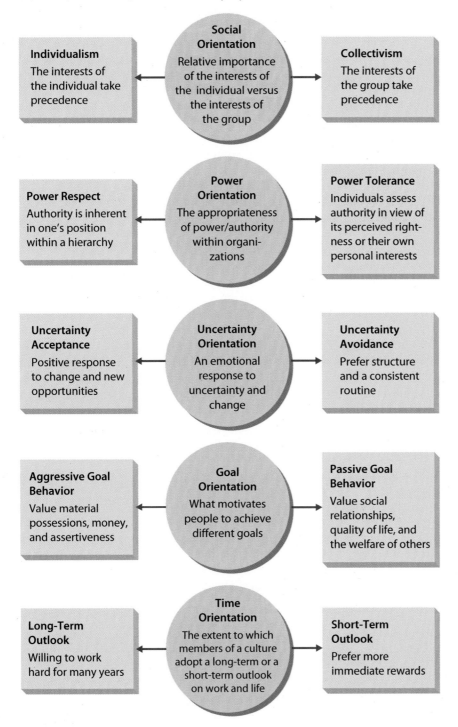

Source: Griffin, Ricky W., Pustay, Michael, *International Business*, 6th ed., © 2010, p. 104.
Adapted by permission of Pearson Education, Inc., Upper Saddle River, NJ.

The first dimension identified by Hofstede is social orientation.[45] Social orientation is a person's beliefs about the relative importance of the individual versus groups to which that person belongs. The two extremes of social orientation are individualism and collectivism. *Individualism* is the cultural belief that the person comes first. Hofstede's research suggested that people in the United States, the United Kingdom, Australia, Canada, New Zealand, and the Netherlands tend to be relatively individualistic. *Collectivism*, the opposite of individualism, is the belief that the group comes first. Hofstede found that people from Mexico, Greece, Hong Kong, Taiwan, Peru, Singapore, Colombia, and Pakistan tend to be relatively collectivistic in their values. In countries with higher levels of individualism, many workers may prefer reward systems that link pay with the performance of individual employees. In a more collectivistic culture, such a reward system may in fact be counterproductive.

A second important dimension is power orientation, the beliefs that people in a culture hold about the appropriateness of power and authority differences in hierarchies such as business organizations. Some cultures are characterized by *power respect*. This means that people tend to accept the power and authority of their superiors simply on the basis of their position in the hierarchy and to respect their right to hold that power. Hofstede found that people in France, Spain, Mexico, Japan, Brazil, Indonesia, and Singapore are relatively power accepting. In contrast, people in cultures with a *power tolerance* orientation attach much less significance to a person's position in the hierarchy. These individuals are more willing to question a decision or mandate from someone at a higher level or perhaps even refuse to accept it. Hofstede's work suggested that people in the United States, Israel, Austria, Denmark, Ireland, Norway, Germany, and New Zealand tend to be more power tolerant.

The third basic dimension of individual differences studied by Hofstede was uncertainty orientation. Uncertainty orientation is the feeling individuals have regarding uncertain and ambiguous situations. People in cultures with *uncertainty acceptance* are stimulated by change and thrive on new opportunities. Hofstede suggested that many people in the United States, Denmark, Sweden, Canada, Singapore, Hong Kong, and Australia are among those in this category. In contrast, people with *uncertainty avoidance* tendencies dislike and will avoid ambiguity whenever possible. Hofstede found that many people in Israel, Austria, Japan, Italy, Colombia, France, Peru, and Germany tend to avoid uncertainty whenever possible.

The fourth dimension of cultural values measured by Hofstede is goal orientation. In this context, goal orientation is the manner in which people are motivated to work toward different kinds of goals. One extreme on the goal orientation continuum is *aggressive goal behavior*. People who exhibit aggressive goal behaviors tend to place a high premium on material possessions, money, and assertiveness. On the other hand, people who adopt *passive goal behavior* place a higher value on social relationships, quality of life, and concern for others. According to Hofstede's research, many people in Japan tend to exhibit relatively aggressive goal behaviors, whereas many people in Germany, Mexico, Italy, and the United States reflect moderately aggressive goal behaviors. People from the Netherlands and the Scandinavian countries of Norway, Sweden, Denmark, and Finland all tend to exhibit relatively passive goal behaviors.

A fifth dimension, called time orientation, was recently added to the framework.[46] Time orientation is the extent to which members of a culture adopt a long-term versus a short-term outlook on work, life, and other elements of society. Some cultures, such as Japan, Hong Kong, Taiwan, and South Korea, have a longer-term orientation. One implication of this orientation is that people from these cultures are willing to accept that they may have to work hard for many years before achieving their goals. Other cultures, like Pakistan and West Africa, are more likely to have a short-term orientation. As a result, people from these cultures may prefer jobs that provide more immediate rewards. Hofstede's work suggests that the United States and Germany tend to have an intermediate time orientation.

social orientation
A person's beliefs about the relative importance of the individual versus groups to which that person belongs

power orientation
The beliefs that people in a culture hold about the appropriateness of power and authority differences in hierarchies such as business organizations

uncertainty orientation
The feeling individuals have regarding uncertain and ambiguous situations

goal orientation
The manner in which people are motivated to work toward different kinds of goals

time orientation
The extent to which members of a culture adopt a long-term versus a short-term outlook on work, life, and other elements of society

What are the four elements of the political-legal environment that are most relevant to international managers?

How might cultural factors influence a computer manufacturer differently than they might influence a fashion-oriented apparel company?

Competing in a Global Economy

Competing in a global economy is both a major challenge and an opportunity for businesses today. The nature of these challenges depends on a variety of factors, including the size of the organization. In addition, international management has implications for the basic functions of planning and decision making, organizing, leading, and controlling.

Globalization and Organization Size

Although organizations of any size may compete in international markets, there are some basic differences in the challenges and opportunities faced by MNCs, medium-size organizations, and small organizations.

Multinational Corporations The large MNCs have long since made the choice to compete in a global marketplace. In general, these firms take a global perspective. They transfer capital, technology, human resources, inventory, and information from one market to another. They actively seek new expansion opportunities wherever feasible. MNCs tend to allow local managers a great deal of discretion in addressing local and regional issues. At the same time, each operation is ultimately accountable to a central authority. Managers at this central authority (headquarters, a central office) are responsible for setting the overall strategic direction for the firm, making major policy decisions, and so forth. MNCs need senior managers who understand the global economy and who are comfortable dealing with executives and government officials from a variety of cultures. Table 5.2 lists the world's largest multinational enterprises.

Medium-Size Organizations Many medium-size businesses remain primarily domestic organizations, but they still may buy and sell products made abroad and compete with businesses from other countries in their own domestic markets. Increasingly, however, medium-size organizations are expanding into foreign markets as well. For example, Gold's Gym, a U.S. fitness chain, has successfully opened facilities in a few foreign locations, including Moscow.[47] In contrast to MNCs, medium-size organizations doing business abroad are much more selective about the markets they enter. They also depend more on a few international specialists to help them manage their foreign operations.

Small Organizations More and more small organizations are also finding that they can benefit from the global economy. Some, for example, serve as local suppliers for MNCs. A dairy farmer who sells milk to Carnation Company, for example, is actually transacting business with Nestlé. Local parts suppliers also have been successfully selling products to the Toyota and Honda plants in the United States. Beyond serving as local suppliers, some small businesses buy and sell products and services abroad. For example, the Collin Street Bakery, based in Corsicana, Texas, ships fruitcakes around the world. In 2010 the firm shipped over 150,000 pounds of fruitcake to Japan. Most small businesses rely on simple importing or exporting operations (or both) for their international sales. Thus only a few specialized management positions are needed. Collin Street Bakery, for example, has one local manager who handles international activities. Mail-order activities within each country are subcontracted to local firms in each market.

TABLE 5.2 THE WORLD'S LARGEST MNCs: INDUSTRIAL CORPORATIONS

Rank 2010	2009	Company	Country	Revenues $ (millions)	% Change from 2009
1	1	Walmart Stores	U.S.	421,848.0	3.3
2	2	Royal Dutch Shell	Netherlands	378,152.0	32.6
3	3	Exxon Mobil	U.S.	354,674.0	24.8
4	4	BP	Britain	308,928.0	25.5
5	7	Sinopec Group	China	273,421.9	45.8
6	10	China National Petroleum	China	240,192.4	45.1
7	8	State Grid	China	226,294.0	22.7
8	5	Toyota Motor	Japan	221,760.2	8.6
9	6	Japan Post Holdings	Japan	203,958.1	0.9
10	11	Chevron	U.S.	196,337.0	20.1
11	14	Total	France	186,055.0	19.4
12	17	ConocoPhillips	U.S.	184,968.0	32.8
13	16	Volkswagen	Germany	168,041.0	14.9
14	9	AXA	France	162,235.9	[7.4]
15	270	Fannie Mae	U.S.	153,825.0	429.2
16	13	General Electric	U.S.	151,628.0	[3.3]
17	12	ING Group	Netherlands	147,052.2	[9.9]
18	•	Glencore International	Switzerland	144,978.0	36.3
19	28	Berkshire Hathaway	U.S.	136,185.0	21.1
20	38	General Motors	U.S.	135,592.0	29.8
21	15	Bank of America Corp.	U.S.	134,194.0	[10.8]
22	32	Samsung Electronics	South Korea	133,780.5	22.8
23	24	Eni	Italy	131,758.0	12.4
24	30	Daimler	Germany	129,480.6	18.0
25	23	Ford Motor	U.S.	128,954.0	9.0

© Cengage Learning 2013

Management Challenges in a Global Economy

The management functions that constitute the framework for this book—planning and decision making, organizing, leading, and controlling—are just as relevant to international managers as to domestic managers. International managers need to have a clear view of where they want their firm to be in the future; they have to organize to implement their plans; they have to motivate those who work for them; and they have to develop appropriate control mechanisms.[48]

Planning and Decision Making in a Global Economy To effectively plan and make decisions in a global economy, managers must have a broad-based understanding of both environmental issues and competitive issues. They need to understand local market conditions and technological factors that will affect their operations. At the corporate level, executives need a great deal of information to function effectively. Which markets are growing? Which markets are shrinking? What are our domestic and foreign competitors doing in each market? They must also make a variety of strategic decisions about their organizations. For example, if a firm wishes to enter the market in France, should it buy a local firm there, start a new operation, or seek a strategic alliance? Critical issues include understanding environmental circumstances, the role of goals and planning in a global organization, and how decision making affects the global organization. We note special implications for global managers as we discuss planning and decision making in Chapters 7 through 10.

Controlling in a Global Economy Managers in international organizations must also be concerned with control. Distances, time zone differences, and cultural factors also play a role in control. For example, in some cultures close supervision is seen as being appropriate, whereas in other cultures it is not. Likewise, executives in the United States and Japan may find it difficult to communicate vital information to one another because of the time zone differences. Basic control issues for the international manager revolve around operations management, productivity, quality, technology, and information systems. These issues are integrated throughout our discussion of control in Chapters 11 through 13.

Organizing in a Global Economy Managers in international businesses must also attend to a variety of organizing issues. For example, General Electric has operations scattered around the globe. The firm has made the decision to give local managers a great deal of responsibility for how they run their business. In contrast, many Japanese firms give managers of their foreign operations relatively little responsibility. As a result, those managers must frequently travel back to Japan to present problems or get decisions approved. Managers in an international business must address the basic issues of organization structure and design, managing change, and dealing with human resources. Strategically, too, organizing decisions can be used to help promote everything from organizational flexibility to the development of expatriate managers.[49] We address the special issues of organizing the international organization in Chapters 14 through 17.

Leading in a Global Economy We noted earlier some of the cultural factors that affect international organizations. Individual managers must be prepared to deal with these and other factors as they interact with people from different cultural backgrounds. Supervising a group of five managers, each of whom is from a different state in the United States, is likely to be much simpler than supervising a group of five managers, each of whom is from a different culture. Managers must understand how cultural factors affect individuals, how motivational processes vary across cultures, how the role of leadership changes in different cultures, how communication varies across cultures, and how interpersonal and group processes depend on cultural background. In Chapters 18 through 22, we note special implications for international managers that relate to leading and interacting with others.

How do the four basic management functions relate to international business?

What kinds of small business might have the greatest success in international markets? What kinds might have the least success?

CONCEPT CHECK

Summary of Learning Objectives and Key Points

1. Describe the nature of international business, including its meaning, recent trends, management of globalization, and competition in a global market.

   - Learning to operate in a global economy is an important challenge facing many managers today.
   - Businesses can be primarily domestic, international, multinational, or global in scope.
   - Managers need to understand both the process of internationalization and how to manage within a given level of international activity.

2. Discuss the structure of the global economy and describe the GATT and the WTO.

   - Mature market economies and systems dominate the global economy today.

   - North America, the European Union, and Pacific Asia are especially important.
   - High-potential/high-growth economies in Eastern Europe, Latin America, the People's Republic of China, India, and Vietnam are increasingly important to managers.
   - The oil-exporting economies in the Middle East are also important.
   - The GATT and the WTO play critical roles in the evolution of the global economy.

3. Identify and discuss the environmental challenges inherent in international management.

   - Many of the challenges of management in a global context are unique issues associated with the international environmental context.

- These challenges reflect the economic, political-legal, and cultural environments of international management.

4. Describe the basic issues involved in competing in a global economy, including organization size and the management challenges in a global economy.

- Basic issues of competing in a global economy vary according to whether the organization is an MNC, a medium-size organization, or a small organization.
- In addition, the basic managerial functions of planning and decision making, organizing, leading, and controlling must all be addressed in international organizations.

Discussion Questions

Questions for Review

1. Describe the four basic levels of international business activity. Do you think any organization will achieve the fourth level? Why or why not?
2. For each of the four globalization strategies, describe the risks associated with that strategy and the potential returns from that strategy.

Questions for Analysis

5. What are the advantages and disadvantages for a U.S.-based multinational firm entering a mature market economy? What are the advantages and disadvantages for such a firm entering a high-potential/high-growth economy?
6. Choose an industry. Describe the impact that international business has had on firms in that industry. Are there any industries that might not be affected by the

3. Describe the various types of political controls on international trade. Be sure to highlight the differences between the types.
4. Explain the relationship between organizational size and globalization. Are large firms the only ones that are global?

trend toward international business? If so, what are they? If not, why are there none?
7. You are the CEO of an up-and-coming toy company and have plans to go international soon. What steps would you take to carry out that strategy? What areas would you stress in your decision-making process? How would you organize your company?

Questions for Application

8. Use the Internet to locate information about a company that is using a global strategic alliance or global joint venture. (*Hint*: Almost any large multinational firm will be involved in these ventures, and you can find information at corporate home pages.) What do you think are the major goals for the venture? Do you expect that the firm will accomplish its goals? If so, why? If not, what stands in its way?

9. Assume that you are the CEO of Walmart. What are the basic environmental challenges you face as your company continues its globalization efforts? Give some specific examples that relate to Walmart.
10. Review the following chart of Hofstede's cultural dimensions. Based on the chart, tell which country you would most like to work in and why. Tell which country you would like least to work in and why.

	Power Distance Range: 11–104	Individualism Range: 6–91	Uncertainty Avoidance Range: 8–112	Aggressiveness Range: 5–95
Germany	35	67	65	66
India	77	48	40	56
Israel	13	54	81	47
United Kingdom	35	89	35	66
United States	40	91	46	62

Adapted from: Geert Hofstede, *Cultures and Organizations: Software of the Mind: Intercultural Cooperation and Its Importance for Survival* (London: HarperCollins, 1994), pp. 26, 55, 84, 113.

CengageNow™ Highlights

Now use your CengageNow™ homework to help you:

- Apply management theories in your life
- Assess your management skills
- Master management terms and concepts
- Apply your knowledge to real-world situations
- Analyze and solve challenging management problems

In order to take advantage of these elements, your instructor will need to have set up a course for your class within CengageNow™. Ask your instructor to contact his/her Cengage sales representative and Digital Solutions Manager to explore testing CengageNow™ in your course this term.

The Multicultural Environment

LEARNING OBJECTIVES

After studying this chapter, you should be able to:

1. Describe the nature of diversity and multiculturalism.

2. Identify and describe the major trends and dimensions of diversity and multiculturalism in organizations.

3. Discuss the primary effects of diversity and multiculturalism in organizations.

4. Describe individual strategies for and organizational approaches to managing diversity and multiculturalism in organizations.

5. Discuss the characteristics of the fully multicultural organization.

MANAGEMENT IN ACTION   Are Minorities Subprime Citizens?

From 1995 to 2006, the United States experienced a housing boom, with cheap mortgage rates spurring record numbers of sales until home ownership had been attained by 69 percent of all U.S. households. Black and Hispanic buyers accounted for 49 percent of the increase in home ownership over the decade, but a disproportionately large number of these mortgagees received subprime or other "higher-rate" or "higher-cost" loans—general terms for mortgages carrying interest rates 3 points higher than select rates on U.S. Treasury bills. In Chicago, for example, one study found that African American homebuyers received 64.2 percent more higher-rate loans than whites. Another study revealed that although blacks accounted for just 10 percent of the loan pool, they received 19 percent of subprime loans. Similarly, Hispanics, who made up 14 percent of borrowers, received 20 percent of the subprime loans; whites, while accounting for 71 percent of all borrowers, received only 56 percent.

Economists, housing analysts, and real estate agents aren't necessarily surprised by such numbers, as subprime loans have been prevalent in minority communities for

> ## "This country has a very long history of predatory lending in communities of color."
>
> —BRIAN MILLER, EXECUTIVE DIRECTOR, UNITED FOR A FAIR ECONOMY

a long time. "This country," says Brian Miller, director of Boston-based United for a Fair Economy, "has a very long history of predatory lending in communities of color." African American households, for example, have accumulated about one-tenth of the wealth possessed by white households, and black home-loan applicants are likely to be among the first generation to go to college or hold professional jobs. Thus they usually lack the assets available to white borrowers (savings, investments, real estate) and often can't bring comparable down payments to the table. In fact, some subprime lenders write so-called "100-percent" mortgages—loans that finance the entire purchase price of the home. Higher interest rates, of course, are designed to compensate lenders for the risks entailed by loans made to customers with few assets, low credit ratings, or heavy debt.

Countrywide is one of several large mortgage lenders accused of predatory lending practices.

Jodi Hilton/The New York Times

FIGURE 6.3 PERCENTAGE OF JAPAN'S POPULATION OVER 65

Aging populations represent new challenges for industrialized countries. As the proportion of working people drops, there are increased pressures on retirement funds, for example. An aging population also means higher healthcare costs. As this graph illustrates, the average age in Japan, Germany, China, and the United States continues to grow. Japan, with the world's longest average life span, has especially significant challenges ahead.

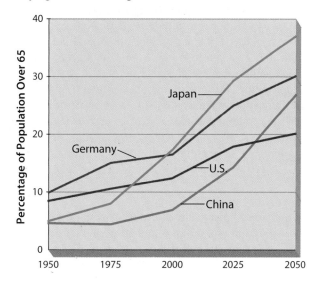

Source: "International Data Base (IDB)," U.S. Census Bureau, December 2010.

Moreover, as shown in Figure 6.3, this trend is truly an international phenomenon, with Japan leading the way. Several factors are contributing to this pattern. For one, the baby boom generation (a term used to describe the unusually large number of people who were born in the 20-year period after World War II) continues to age. Declining birthrates among the post–baby boom generations simultaneously account for smaller percentages of new entrants into the labor force. Another factor that contributes to the aging workforce is improved health and medical care. As a result of these improvements, people are able to remain productive and active for longer periods of time. Finally, and unfortunately, many people approaching traditional retirement ages do not have sufficient savings to pay for retirement and so must work longer. These factors combine to result in more and more people working beyond the age at which they might have retired just a few years ago.

How does this trend affect organizations? Older workers tend to have more experience, to be more stable, and to make greater contributions to productivity than younger workers. On the other hand, despite the improvements in health and medical care, older workers are nevertheless likely to require higher levels of insurance coverage and medical benefits. And the declining labor pool of younger workers will continue to pose problems for organizations as they find fewer potential new entrants into the labor force.[4]

"[Many younger workers] believe workers in the older generations have been too slow to adopt social media and other tools, and place too much value on tenure rather than knowledge and performance."

—ADRIENNE FOX, HR CONSULTANT[5]

Gender As more and more women have entered the workforce, organizations have subsequently experienced changes in the relative proportions of male and female employees. In the United States, for example, the workforce in 1964 was 66 percent male and 34 percent female. By 2010 the proportions were around 50.1 percent male and 49.9 percent female.

During the next ten years, the percentage of women in the U.S. workforce is expected to surpass the percentage of men.[6]

These trends aside, a major gender-related problem that many organizations face today is the so-called glass ceiling. The **glass ceiling** describes a barrier that keeps women from advancing to top management positions in many organizations.[7] This ceiling is a real barrier that is difficult to break, but it is also so subtle as to be hard to see. Indeed, whereas women comprise about 40 percent of all managers, there are very few female CEOs among the 1,000 largest businesses in the United States. Further, their distribution across functional areas is uneven, with relatively more of them holding marketing and human resource positions and relatively fewer of them holding finance and operations positions.[8] Similarly, the average pay of women in organizations is lower than that of men. Although the pay gap is gradually shrinking, inequalities are present nonetheless.

Why does the glass ceiling still seem to exist? One reason may be that real obstacles to advancement for women, such as subtle discrimination, may still exist in some organizations.[9] Another is that many talented women choose to leave their job in a large organization and start their own business. Still another factor is that some women choose to suspend or slow their career progression to have children. But there are also many talented women continuing to work their way up the corporate ladder and getting closer and closer to a corporate "top spot."[10]

glass ceiling
A perceived barrier in some organizations that keeps women from advancing to top management positions

ethnicity
The ethnic composition of a group or organization

Ethnicity A third major dimension of cultural diversity in organizations is ethnicity. **Ethnicity** refers to the ethnic composition of a group or organization. Within the United States, most organizations reflect varying degrees of ethnicity, comprising whites, African Americans, Latinos, and Asians. Figure 6.4 shows the ethnic composition of the U.S. population in 2000 and as projected for the year 2050 in terms of these ethnic groups.[11]

The biggest projected changes involve whites and Latinos. In particular, the percentage of whites in the United States is expected to drop from 72 percent to 53 percent. At the same

FIGURE 6.4 ETHNICITY DISTRIBUTION TRENDS IN THE UNITED STATES

Ethnic diversity in the United States is also increasing. For example, although 72 percent of the U.S. population was white in 1999, this will drop to 53% by 2050. Latinos will reflect the largest percentage increase, moving from 11.5 percent in 2000 to 24.5 percent of the U.S. population by 2050.

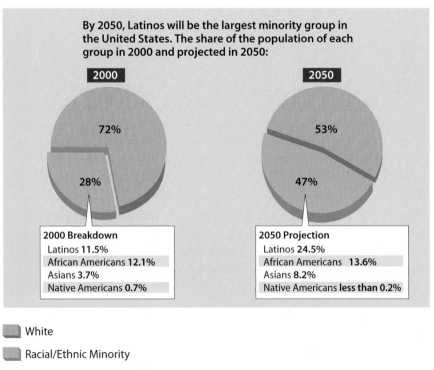

By 2050, Latinos will be the largest minority group in the United States. The share of the population of each group in 2000 and projected in 2050:

2000
72%
28%

2050
53%
47%

2000 Breakdown
Latinos **11.5%**
African Americans **12.1%**
Asians **3.7%**
Native Americans **0.7%**

2050 Projection
Latinos **24.5%**
African Americans **13.6%**
Asians **8.2%**
Native Americans **less than 0.2%**

White

Racial/Ethnic Minority

Source: U.S. Census Bureau.

TECHNICALLY SPEAKING

"We're All Potential Users"

Lonnie Duka

Rick, a construction engineer who broke his back in an auto accident, is a paraplegic suffering from vocal-cord damage. Rick, however, holds a productive job, managing complaints for building-construction projects. At both home and office, he uses a mouse activated by one finger and an on-screen keyboard because his voice is too soft for most voice-recognition software. David, whose job requires speech-recognition software and a trackball mouse to compensate for impaired manual dexterity and verbal communication, coordinates healthcare strategies and operations at the Department of Defense (DoD).

Both Rick and David depend on employer-provided *assistive technology*, and according to David, it's "a real equalizer for people with disabilities. . . . It not only raises your productivity but also your expectations for yourself. That's a good feeling for the individual and good for the employer, too." In addition to the sort of hardware, software, and peripherals that help people like Rick and David perform jobs requiring computer access, assistive technology includes such

lower-tech equipment as walkers and wheelchairs—much of which makes accommodating disabled workers less expensive than you might think. Low-tech, low-cost accommodation for a visually impaired person might entail nothing more than adjusting the lighting, supplying magnification devices, and fitting the work schedule to mass transit. More severely impaired individuals may need higher-tech assistance, but the technology is usually reasonably priced. (You can purchase Dragon NaturallySpeaking, the speech-recognition software that David uses, for $199.)

Both Rick and David suffer from permanent disabilities, but experts estimate that as many as 20 percent of us will experience some form of physical disability at some point in our careers or lives. In addition, it's worth remembering that currently employed baby boomers are getting older. "The population is aging," says Diana Burke, VP for information security at RBC Financial Group, "and people are losing hearing, vision, and mobility as the years progress. This affects employees and customers. We have to keep up with their declining abilities, or we'll find ourselves in the position of not being able to serve our customers or leverage employees' talents." Adds Dinah Cohen, director of DoD's Computer/Electronic Accommodations Program (CAP), "It's not just people born with disabilities who need assistive technology. More and more, [CAP is] serving people who acquire disabilities later in life. . . . We're all potential users."

References: "Assistive Technology Reconnects Employees to the Workplace While Recovering from Temporary Disabilities," *Accessibility in Action Case Studies* (Microsoft Corp., 2011), www.microsoft.com on February 22, 2011; National Council on Disability, *Empowerment for Americans with Disabilities: Breaking Barriers to Careers and Full Employment,* October 2007, www.ncd.gov on February 22, 2011; "What Is Assistive Technology?" *AccessIT* (University of Washington, 2009), www.washington.edu on February 22, 2011; American Federation for the Blind, "Types of Accommodations," "Cost of Accommodations," *AFB CareerConnect,* 2009, www.afb.org on February 22, 2011.

time, the percentage of Latinos is expected to climb from 11.5 percent to 24.5 percent.[12] The percentage of African Americans, Asians, and others is also expected to climb, but at lower rates. As with women, members of the African American, Latino, and Asian groups are generally underrepresented in the executive ranks of most organizations today. And their pay is similarly lower than might be expected. But, as is also the case for women, the differences are gradually disappearing as organizations fully embrace equal employment opportunity and recognize the higher overall level of talent available to them.[13]

Other Dimensions of Diversity In addition to age, gender, and ethnicity, organizations are confronting other dimensions of diversity. Different religious beliefs, for example, constitute an important dimension of diversity.[14] Single parents, dual-career couples, gays and lesbians, people with special dietary preferences (such as vegetarians), and people with different political ideologies and viewpoints also represent major dimensions of diversity in today's organizations.[15] And of course handicapped and physically challenged employees are increasingly important in many organizations, especially since the 1990 passage of the Americans with Disabilities Act. The *Technically Speaking* box on page 141 entitled " 'We're All Potential Users' " discusses some of the latest developments in technology designed to help disabled individuals accomplish workplace tasks.

Multicultural Differences In addition to these various diversity-related dimensions, organizations are increasingly being characterized by multicultural differences as well. Some organizations, especially international businesses, are actively seeking to enhance the multiculturalism of their workforce. But even organizations that are more passive in this regard may still become more multicultural because of changes in the external labor market. Immigration into the United States is at its highest rate since 1910, for example. Between 2000 and 2007, 10.3 million immigrants arrived in the United States. This is the highest seven-year period of immigration in the country's history. (An estimated 5.6 million of these immigrants are illegal aliens.)[16]

Identify several dimensions of diversity that are most relevant to organizations.

How might these dimensions be related to one another?

Effects of Diversity and Multiculturalism in Organizations

There is no question that organizations are becoming ever more diverse and multicultural. But how does this affect organizations? As we see, diversity and management provide both opportunities and challenges for organizations. They also play a number of important roles in organizations today.

Diversity, Multiculturalism, and Competitive Advantage

Many organizations are finding that diversity and multiculturalism can be a source of competitive advantage in the marketplace. In general, six arguments have been proposed for how they contribute to competitiveness.[17] These are illustrated in Figure 6.5.

The *cost argument* suggests that organizations that learn to manage diversity and multiculturalism generally have higher levels of productivity and lower levels of turnover and absenteeism. Those organizations that do a poor job of managing diversity and multiculturalism, on the other hand, suffer from problems of lower productivity and higher levels of turnover and absenteeism. Because each of these factors has a direct impact on costs, the former types of organizations remain more competitive than will the latter. Ortho McNeil Pharmaceutical estimates that it saved $500,000 within a five-year period by lowering turnover among women and ethnic minorities.[18]

The *resource acquisition argument* suggests that organizations that manage diversity and multiculturalism effectively become known among women and minorities as good places to work. These organizations are thus better able to attract qualified employees from among

FIGURE 6.5 HOW DIVERSITY AND MULTICULTURALISM PROMOTE COMPETITIVE ADVANTAGE

Many organizations today are finding that diversity and multiculturalism can be sources of competitive advantage. Various arguments have been developed to support this viewpoint. For example, an African American sales representative for Revlon helped that firm improve its packaging and promotion for its line of darker skin-tone cosmetics.

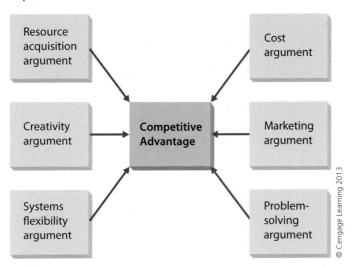

© Cengage Learning 2013

these groups. Given the increased importance of these groups in the overall labor force, organizations that can attract talented employees from all segments of society are likely to be more competitive.[19] Every year *Fortune* magazine compiles a list of the "100 Best Companies to Work for in the United States." As part of this report, the magazine also indicates which organizations have the most diverse workforces as determined by the percentage of the workforce that is ethnic minority (but in so doing excludes other key elements such as age, religion, and so forth). Among the major firms on the most recent list, and the percentage of minorities in their workforces, are the following:[20]

- Four Seasons Hotels (67%)
- The Methodist Hospital System (66%)
- Marriott International (61%)
- Men's Wearhouse (53%)
- Cisco (45%)
- Whole Foods Market (44%)
- CarMax (42%)
- Nordstrom (41%)
- Intel (40%)

- Aflac (39%)
- American Express (36%)
- Goldman Sachs (36%)
- Microsoft (33%)
- Deloitte (33%)
- Zappos.com (32%)
- Starbucks (31%)
- Ernst & Young (29%)
- KPMG (27%)

The *marketing argument* suggests that organizations with a diverse and multicultural workforce are better able to understand different market segments than are less diverse organizations. For example, a cosmetics firm such as Avon, which wants to sell its products to women and African Americans, can better understand how to create such products and effectively market them if women and African American managers are available to provide inputs into product development, design, packaging, advertising, and so forth.[21] Similarly, both Sears and Target have profited by focusing part of their marketing efforts on building consumer awareness among Latinos.[22]

The *creativity argument* suggests that organizations with diverse and multicultural workforces are generally more creative and innovative than other organizations. If an organization is dominated by one population segment, it follows that its members will generally adhere to norms and ways of thinking that reflect that segment. Moreover, they have little insight or stimulus for new ideas that might be derived from different perspectives. The diverse and multicultural organization, in contrast, is characterized by multiple perspectives and ways of thinking and is therefore more likely to generate new ideas and ways of doing things.[23]

Related to the creativity argument is the *problem-solving argument*. Diversity and multiculturalism are accompanied by an increased pool of information. In virtually any organization there is some information that everyone has and other information that is unique to each individual. In an organization with little diversity, the larger pool of information is common, and the smaller pool is unique. But in a more diverse organization, the pool of unique information is larger. Thus, because more information can be brought to bear on a problem, there is a higher probability that better solutions can be identified.[24]

Finally, the *systems flexibility argument* suggests that organizations must become more flexible as a way of managing a diverse and multicultural workforce. As a direct consequence, the overall organizational system also becomes more flexible. As we discuss in Chapters 3 and 16, organizational flexibility enables the organization to better respond to changes in its environment. Thus, by effectively managing diversity and multiculturalism within its workforce, an organization becomes better equipped to address its environment.[25]

"It strikes me as foreign to not have foreigners on a major U.S. corporation's board."

—PAUL ANDERSON, CHAIRMAN OF DUKE ENERGY[26]

Diversity, Multiculturalism, and Conflict

Unfortunately, diversity and multiculturalism in an organization can also create conflict. This conflict can arise for a variety of reasons.[27] One potential avenue for conflict occurs when an individual thinks that someone has been hired, promoted, or fired because of her or his diversity status. For example, suppose that a male executive loses a promotion to a female executive. If he believes that she was promoted because the organization simply wanted to have more female managers, rather than because she was the better candidate for the job, he will likely feel resentful toward both her and the organization.

Another source of conflict stemming from diversity or multiculturalism occurs through misunderstood, misinterpreted, or inappropriate interactions among people of different groups.[28] For example, suppose that a male executive tells a sexually explicit joke to a new female executive. He may be intentionally trying to embarrass her, he may be clumsily trying to show her that he treats everyone the same, or he may think he is making her feel part of the team. Regardless of his intent, however, if she finds the joke offensive, she will justifiably feel anger and hostility. These feelings may be directed at only the offending individual or more generally toward the entire organization if she believes that its culture facilitates such behavior. And, of course, sexual harassment is both unethical and illegal.

Conflict can also arise as a result of other elements of multiculturalism. For example, when a U.S. manager publicly praises a Japanese employee for his outstanding work, the action stems from the dominant cultural belief in the United States that such recognition is important and rewarding. But because the Japanese culture places a much higher premium on group loyalty and identity than on individual accomplishment, the employee likely will feel ashamed and embarrassed. Thus a well-intentioned action may backfire and result in unhappiness. In 2011, U.S.-based Groupon joined with Tencent, China's leading Internet service provider, to expand its discount offerings into Chinese markets. Groupon's international expansion was being run by a management team from Germany. However, the joint venture was reported to have a rocky start early on due to vast differences in the cultures' decision-making styles. Groupon sought to hire people and launch the Western-style site quickly, while Tencent wanted to make decisions more slowly and develop a Chinese-style website.[29]

GREENING THE BUSINESS ENVIRONMENT

Wayward Winds on the Legislative Horizon

When it comes to fighting greenhouse-gas emissions, most environmentalists will tell you that the line in the sand has to be drawn at CO_2—the carbon dioxide emitted by coal-fueled power plants. CO_2 is responsible for 40 percent of the country's greenhouse-gas emissions, and scientists agree that it's the number-one cause of global climate change. So, in November 2008, when the Environmental Protection Agency (EPA) was given the authority to regulate CO_2 emissions from new coal-powered plants, the environmental movement celebrated a significant victory.

Flash forward to 2010, when U.S. Senators John Kerry and Joseph Lieberman are trying to incorporate climate-control provisions into an upcoming energy bill. The lawmakers had already negotiated several concessions from opposing parties—namely, environmental groups on the one hand and big power companies on the other. When it came to climate control, however, the utility companies were willing to accept new EPA rules on greenhouse-gas emissions only in exchange for relaxed rules on emissions of other pollutants, such as particulate matter from lead and mercury. Environmentalists were adamant in rejecting any compromise. "Such provisions," said 31 groups in a joint letter to the senators, "are simply unacceptable."

Kerry promised that "there is not going to be a rollback of current requirements" on the control of particulate matter, but not everyone was convinced that a compromise could be avoided. Phaedra Ellis-Lamkins, CEO of Green for All, and Ben Jealous, president of the NAACP, warned that if the finalized

energy bill "limits the ability of the EPA . . . to enforce regulation of mercury . . . the American people will suffer immediate and long-term health consequences, from asthma to early death." Particulate emissions may not present the same planet-wide threat as greenhouse-gas emissions, but mercury pollution is responsible for 17,000 premature deaths and 10,000 cases of childhood asthma in the United States every year.

Green for All founder Van Jones echoed concerns about "a climate bill that saves carbon but takes away the EPA's authority to protect communities against toxic hazards." Jones, who, like Ellis-Lamkins and Jealous, is black, was more specific about the communities that need protection from legislative compromise: The power industry's "literal 'poison pill' proposal," charged Green, ". . . would inflict the most harm on the people who are already suffering. After all: who lives near power plants? Disproportionately low-income people and people of color." Those people, Green pointed out, were already 70 percent more likely to live in neighborhoods exposed to industrial pollution.

As it happens, Congress didn't manage to pass any energy bill in 2010, with or without unacceptable compromises. In March 2011, the EPA proceeded to propose the first nationwide set of standards for emissions of mercury and other pollutants. EPA Administrator Lisa P. Jackson called the initiative "an important step forward in EPA's efforts to safeguard the health of millions of Americans." Meanwhile, the utilities industry was moving forward with its own legislative agenda: Earlier in the same month, opponents of the EPA in Congress introduced the Upton-Inhofe bill, which would permanently prevent the agency from implementing guidelines designed to curb power-plant emissions.

References: Bryan Walsh, "Environmentalists Win Big EPA Ruling," *Time*, November 13, 2008, www.time.com on April 11, 2011; Darren Goode and Ben German, "Talks Inch Ahead as Political Sands Run on Climate Change Bill," *E² Wire*, July 15, 2010, http://thehill.com on April 11, 2011; Phaedra Ellis-Lamkins and Ben Jealous, "We Won't Accept More Poison for Less Carbon," *Huffington Post*, July 16, 2010, www.huffingtonpost.com on April 11, 2011; Van Jones, "Accept More Poison to Get Less Carbon? Kill This Crazy Idea NOW," *Grist*, July 20, 2010, www.grist.org on April 11, 2011; "EPA Proposes New Mercury Standards for Power Plants," *CNN.com*, March 23, 2011, www.cnn.com on April 11, 2011.

Conflict may also arise as a result of fear, distrust, or individual prejudice. Members of the dominant group in an organization may worry that newcomers from other groups pose a personal threat to their own positions in the organization. For example, when U.S. firms have been taken over by Japanese firms, U.S. managers have sometimes been resentful about or hostile toward Japanese managers assigned to work with them. People may also be unwilling to accept people who are different from themselves. And personal bias and prejudices are still very real among some people today and can lead to potentially harmful conflict.

Several high-profile problems involving diversity and multiculturalism have focused attention on the potential for conflict and how important it is that managers respond appropriately when problems occur. Shoney's, Inc., a southern restaurant chain, was charged with racism throughout its managerial ranks. At Texaco, senior executives used racial slurs on a tape subsequently released to the public. A class-action lawsuit against the financial brokerage giant Smith Barney alleged widespread hostility and discrimination toward women throughout the firm. Walmart has been scrutinized for similar practices.[30] In each of these cases, fortunately, the organization involved has undertaken major programs designed to eliminate such problems in the future. Denny's, for example, has taken such aggressive action that it has now become recognized as one of the best companies in the United States for minorities.[31]

Finally, conflict can occur because different ethnic or economic groups can account for different constituencies among an organization's stakeholders. In the *Greening the Business Environment* box on page 145, entitled "Wayward Winds on the Legislative Horizon," the organization is the U.S. government, and its constituencies include both powerful business interests and low-income communities.

How does diversity promote competitive advantage?

Which causes of diversity-related conflict are most likely to disappear in the future?

 CONCEPT CHECK

Managing Diversity and Multiculturalism in Organizations

Because of the tremendous potential that diversity and multiculturalism hold for competitive advantage, as well as the possible consequences of associated conflict, much attention has been focused in recent years on how individuals and organizations can better manage diversity and multiculturalism. In the sections that follow, we first discuss individual strategies for dealing with diversity and multiculturalism, and then summarize organizational approaches to managing diversity and multiculturalism.

Individual Strategies

One important element of managing diversity and multiculturalism in an organization consists of things that individuals themselves can do. The four basic attitudes that individuals can strive for are understanding, empathy, tolerance, and willingness to communicate.

Understanding The first of these is understanding the nature and meaning of diversity and multiculturalism. Some managers, for example, have taken the basic concepts of equal employment opportunity to an unnecessary extreme. They know that, by law, they cannot discriminate against people on the basis of sex, race, and so forth. Thus, in following this mandate, they come to believe that they must treat everyone the same.

But this belief can cause problems when translated into workplace behaviors among people after they have been hired, because people are not the same. Although people need to be treated fairly and equitably, managers must understand that differences among people do, in fact, exist. Thus any effort to treat everyone the same, without regard for their fundamental human differences, will only lead to problems. Managers must understand that cultural factors cause people to behave in different ways and that these differences should be accepted.

Empathy Related to understanding is empathy. People in an organization should try to understand the perspectives of others. For example, suppose a woman joins a group that has traditionally consisted of white men. Each man may be a little self-conscious about how to act toward the new member and may be interested in making her feel comfortable and welcome. But they may be able to do this even more effectively by empathizing with how she may feel. For example, she may feel disappointed or elated about her new assignment, she may be confident or nervous about her position in the group, or she may be experienced or inexperienced in working with male colleagues. By learning more about her feelings, the group members can further facilitate their ability to work together effectively.

There are several things individuals can do to promote diversity. For instance, understanding, empathy, tolerance, and a willingness to communicate are all useful. In this meeting, for example, most of the participants are white males. But if they practice the techniques noted, they can make the others in the group feel more welcome and improve the overall functioning of the team.

Tolerance A third related individual strategy for dealing with diversity and multiculturalism is tolerance. Even though people learn to understand others, and even though they may try to empathize with others, the fact remains that they still may not accept or enjoy some aspect of their behavior. For example, one organization reported that it had experienced considerable conflict among its U.S. and Israeli employees. The Israeli employees always seemed to want to argue about every issue that arose. The U.S. managers preferred to conduct business more harmoniously and became uncomfortable with the conflict. Finally, after considerable discussion, the employees realized that many of the Israeli employees actually enjoyed debating or arguing and simply saw it as part of getting the work done. The firm's U.S. employees still did not enjoy the arguing, but they were more willing to tolerate it as a fundamental cultural difference between themselves and their colleagues from Israel after they realized that it was not hostile in nature.[32]

Willingness to Communicate A final individual approach to dealing with diversity and multiculturalism is communication. Problems often get magnified over these issues because people are afraid or otherwise unwilling to openly discuss issues that relate to diversity or multiculturalism. For example, suppose that a young employee has a habit of making jokes about the age of an older colleague. Perhaps the young colleague means no harm and is just engaging in what she sees as good-natured kidding. But the older employee may find the jokes offensive. If the two do not communicate, the jokes will continue, and the resentment will grow. Eventually, what started as a minor problem may erupt into a much bigger one.

For communication to work, it must work two ways. If a person wonders whether a certain behavior on her or his part is offensive to someone else, the curious individual should just ask. Similarly, if someone is offended by the behavior of another person, he or she should explain to the offending individual how the behavior is perceived and request that it stop. As long as such exchanges are friendly, low key, and nonthreatening, they will generally have a positive outcome. Of course, if the same message is presented in an overly combative manner or if a person continues to engage in offensive behavior after having been asked to stop, problems will only escalate. At this point, third parties within the organization may have to intervene. Most organizations today, in fact, have one or more systems in place to address questions and problems that arise as a result of diversity. We now turn our attention to various ways that organizations can better manage diversity.

Organizational Approaches

Whereas individuals are important in managing diversity and multiculturalism, the organization itself must play a fundamental role.[33] Through the organization's various policies and practices, people in the organization come to understand what behaviors are and are not appropriate. Diversity and multicultural training is an even more direct method for managing diversity. And the organization's culture is the ultimate context in which diversity and multiculturalism must be addressed.

Organizational Policies The starting point in managing diversity and multiculturalism is the policies an organization adopts that directly or indirectly affect how people are treated. The extent to which an organization embraces the premise of equal employment opportunity, for instance, will help determine the potential diversity within it. But the organization that follows the law to the letter and practices only passive discrimination differs from the organization that actively seeks a diverse and varied workforce.

Another aspect of organizational policies that affects diversity and multiculturalism is how the organization addresses and responds to problems that arise from differences among people. For example, consider the example of a manager charged with sexual harassment. If the organization's policies put an excessive burden of proof on the individual being harassed and invoke only minor sanctions against the guilty party, it is sending a clear signal about the importance of such matters. A scandal at the International Monetary Fund (IMF) in 2011 uncovered an organizational culture that many people believed actually reinforced sexual harassment by some senior managers. But the organization that has a balanced set of policies for addressing questions like sexual harassment sends its employees a message that diversity and individual rights and privileges are important.

Indeed, perhaps the major policy through which an organization can reflect its stance on diversity and multiculturalism is its mission statement. If the organization's mission statement articulates a clear and direct commitment to differences among people, it follows that everyone who comes in contact with that mission statement will grow to understand and accept the importance of diversity and multiculturalism, at least to that particular organization. At Marriott International, CEO Bill Marriott's annual letter to employees is translated and distributed in 28 languages to reach its diverse workforce. Like its mission statement, this serves to reinforce the firm's proactive and pluralistic stance on diversity and multiculturalism.

Organizational Practices Organizations can also help manage diversity and multiculturalism through a variety of ongoing practices and procedures. Avon's creation of networks for various groups represents one example of an organizational practice that fosters diversity. Verizon Wireless provides mentoring and leadership development programs for various minority and cultural groups, including the Black Managers Workshop, the Asian Professional Development Workshop, the Hispanic Professional Development Workshop, and the Women's Leadership Workshop. In general, the idea is that, because diversity and multiculturalism are characterized by differences among people, organizations can more effectively manage that diversity by following practices and procedures that are based on flexibility rather than on rigidity.

Benefits packages, for example, can be structured to better accommodate individual situations. An employee who is part

Organization practices can go a long way toward enhancing diversity. For instance, giving working parents the flexibility they need to pick their children up from school or to attend school functions for their children can be very useful practices.

Lonnie Duka/PhotoLibrary

of a dual-career, childless couple may require relatively less health insurance (perhaps because his spouse's employer provides more complete coverage) and may request vacation time that coincides with those of his spouse. An employee who is a single parent may need a wide variety of health insurance coverage and prefer to schedule his vacation time to coincide with school holidays.

Flexible working hours are also a useful organizational practice for accommodating diversity. Differences in family arrangements, religious holidays, cultural events, and so forth may dictate that employees have some degree of flexibility in when they work. For example, a single parent may need to leave the office every day at 4:30 P.M. to pick up children from their day care center. An organization that truly values diversity will make reasonable attempts to accommodate such a need.

Organizations can also facilitate diversity and multiculturalism by making sure that their important committees and executive teams are diverse. Even if diversity exists within the broader organizational context, an organization that does not reflect diversity in groups such as committees and teams implies that diversity is not a fully ingrained element of its culture. In contrast, if all major groups and related work assignments reflect diversity, the message is a quite different one.

Diversity and Multicultural Training Many organizations are finding that diversity and multicultural training is an effective means for managing diversity and minimizing its associated conflict. More specifically, diversity and multicultural training is designed to better enable members of an organization to function in a diverse and multicultural workplace.[34] This training can take a variety of forms. For example, many organizations find it useful to help people learn more about their similarities to and differences from others. Men and women can be taught to work together more effectively and can gain insights into how their own behaviors affect and are interpreted by others. In one organization, a diversity training program helped male managers gain insights into how various remarks they made to one another could be interpreted by others as being sexist. In the same organization, female managers learned how to point out their discomfort with those remarks without appearing overly hostile.[35]

Similarly, white and African American managers may need training to better understand each other. Managers at Mobil Corporation (now a part of ExxonMobil) once noticed that four black colleagues never seemed to eat lunch together. After a diversity training program, they came to realize that the black managers felt that, if they ate together, their white colleagues would be overly curious about what they might be talking about. Thus they avoided close association with one another because they feared calling attention to themselves.[36]

Some organizations even go so far as to provide language training for their employees as a vehicle for managing diversity and multiculturalism. Motorola, for example, provides English-language training for its foreign employees on assignment in the United States. At Pace Foods in San Antonio, with a total payroll of over 450 employees, staff meetings and employee handbooks are translated into Spanish for the benefit of the company's 200 or so Latino employees.

Organization Culture The ultimate test of an organization's commitment to managing diversity and multiculturalism, as discussed earlier in this chapter, is its culture.[37] Regardless of what managers say or put in writing, unless there is a basic and fundamental belief that diversity and multiculturalism are valued, it cannot ever become a truly integral part of an organization. An organization that really wants to promote diversity and multiculturalism must shape its culture so that it clearly underscores top management's commitment to and support of diversity and multiculturalism in all of its forms throughout every part of the organization. With top management's support, however, and reinforced with a clear and consistent set of organizational policies and practices, diversity and multiculturalism can become a fundamental part of an organization.[38]

diversity and multicultural training Training that is designed to better enable members of an organization to function in a diverse and multicultural workforce

Name the individual strategies for managing diversity and multiculturalism in organizations.

In your opinion, which organizational approaches to managing diversity and multiculturalism are most and least likely to be effective? Why?

CONCEPT CHECK

Toward the Multicultural Organization

Many organizations today are grappling with cultural diversity. We noted in Chapter 5 that, although many organizations are becoming increasingly global, no truly global organization exists. In similar fashion, although organizations are becoming ever more diverse, few are truly multicultural. The multicultural organization is one that has achieved high levels of diversity, is able to fully capitalize on the advantages of diversity, and has few diversity-related problems. Some experts believe that such an organization would have six basic characteristics.[39] These characteristics are illustrated in Figure 6.6.

First, the multicultural organization is characterized by *pluralism*. This means that every group represented in the organization works to better understand every other group. Thus African American employees try to understand white employees, and white employees try just as hard to understand their African American colleagues. In addition, every group represented within an organization has the potential to influence the organization's culture and fundamental norms.

Second, the multicultural organization achieves *full structural integration*. Full structural integration suggests that the diversity within an organization is a complete and accurate reflection of the organization's external labor market. If around half of the labor market is female, then about half of the organization's employees are female. Moreover, this same proportion is reflected at all levels of the organization. There are no glass ceilings or other subtle forms of discrimination.

Third, the multicultural organization achieves *full integration of the informal network*. This characteristic suggests that there are no barriers to entry or participation in any organizational activity. For example, people enter and exit lunch groups, social networks, communication grapevines, and other informal aspects of organizational activity without regard to age, gender, ethnicity, or other dimension of diversity.

multicultural organization
An organization that has achieved high levels of diversity, is able to fully capitalize on the advantages of diversity, and has few diversity-related problems

FIGURE 6.6 THE MULTICULTURAL ORGANIZATION

Few, if any, organizations have become truly multicultural. At the same time, more and more organizations are moving in this direction. When an organization becomes multicultural, it reflects the six basic characteristics shown here.

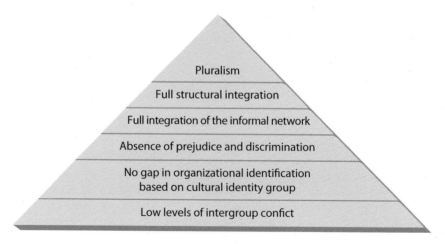

Pluralism
Full structural integration
Full integration of the informal network
Absence of prejudice and discrimination
No gap in organizational identification based on cultural identity group
Low levels of intergroup conflct

Source: Based on Taylor H. Cox, "The Multicultural Organization," *Academy of Management Executive*, May 1991, pp. 34–47. Reprinted with permission.

Fourth, the multicultural organization is characterized by an *absence of prejudice and discrimination*. No traces of bias exist, and prejudice is eliminated. Discrimination is not practiced in any shape, form, or fashion. And discrimination is nonexistent, not because it is illegal, but because of the lack of prejudice and bias. People are valued, accepted, and rewarded purely on the basis of their skills and what they contribute to the organization.

Fifth, in the multicultural organization there is *no gap in organizational identification based on cultural identity group*. In many organizations today, people tend to make assumptions about organizational roles based on group identity. For example, many people walking into an office and seeing a man and woman conversing tend to assume that the woman is the secretary and the man is the manager. No such tendencies exist in the multicultural organization. People recognize that men and women are equally likely to be managers or secretaries.

Finally, there are *low levels of intergroup conflict* in the multicultural organization. We noted earlier that conflict is a likely outcome of increased diversity. The multicultural organization has evolved beyond this point to a state of virtually no conflict among people who differ. People within the organization fully understand, empathize with, have tolerance for, and openly communicate with everyone else. Values, premises, motives, attitudes, and perceptions are so well understood by everyone that any conflict that does arise is over meaningful and work-related issues as opposed to differences in age, gender, ethnicity, or other dimensions of diversity.

What dimensions will characterize the multicultural organization?

Do you think a truly multicultural business organization will ever exist? Why or why not?

CONCEPT CHECK

Summary of Learning Objectives and Key Points

1. Describe the nature of diversity and multiculturalism.

   - Diversity exists in a community of people when its members differ from one another along one or more important dimensions.
   - Multiculturalism is reflected when the people comprising an organization represent different cultures and have different values, beliefs, behaviors, customs, and attitudes.

2. Identify and describe the major trends and dimensions of diversity and multiculturalism in organizations.

   - Diversity and multiculturalism are increasing in organizations today because of changing demographics, the desire of organizations to improve their workforces, legal pressures, and increased globalization.
   - There are several important dimensions of diversity, including age, gender, and ethnicity. The overall age of the workforce is increasing.

3. Discuss the primary effects of diversity and multiculturalism in organizations.

   - Diversity and multiculturalism can be a source of competitive advantage (cost, resource acquisition,

   marketing, creativity, problem-solving, and systems flexibility arguments).
   - Diversity and multiculturalism can also be sources of conflict in an organization.

4. Describe individual strategies for and organizational approaches to managing diversity and multiculturalism in organizations.

   - Individual strategies include understanding, empathy, tolerance, and willingness to communicate.
   - Major organizational approaches are through policies, practices, diversity training, and culture.

5. Discuss the characteristics of the fully multicultural organization.

   - The major dimensions that characterize organizations as they eventually achieve this state are pluralism, full structural integration, full integration of the informal network, an absence of prejudice and discrimination, no gap in organizational identification based on cultural identity group, and low levels of intergroup conflict attributable to diversity.

Discussion Questions

Questions for Review

1. What are the primary dimensions of diversity?
2. Summarize the six arguments used to describe how the effective management of diversity can lead to a competitive advantage.
3. Discuss the four basic individual approaches and the four basic organizational approaches to diversity and multiculturalism.
4. What are the characteristics of a multicultural organization?

Questions for Analysis

5. In your opinion, are the "other" dimensions of diversity likely to have a greater or a lesser impact than the basic dimensions? Explain your answer.
6. The text outlines many different advantages of diversity and multiculturalism in organizations. Can you think of any disadvantages?
7. Think of a time when issues of diversity or multiculturalism created an advantage or led to positive outcomes at school or work. What actions did the participants take to lead to that positive outcome?

Questions for Application

8. Visit the registrar's office or admissions office at your college or university, or find information about admissions from your school's website. What actions, if any, is your school taking to increase diversity? If it is not taking any action, why do you think that is the case? If it is taking action, do you think the actions are likely to be effective, and why?
9. Consider the case of an employee who is part of a minority group on one dimension of diversity. What are some of the potential problems that this employee might encounter? What are some ways that this employee's supervisor can help alleviate these problems?
10. Assume that you work for a large multinational organization. You have just learned that you are being transferred overseas, to an office in which you will be the first person of your ethnicity to work there. What steps might you take before you go to minimize problems that your presence might cause?

CengageNow™ Highlights

Now use your CengageNow™ homework to help you:

- Apply management theories in your life
- Assess your management skills
- Master management terms and concepts
- Apply your knowledge to real-world situations
- Analyze and solve challenging management problems

In order to take advantage of these elements, your instructor will need to have set up a course for your class within CengageNow™. Ask your instructor to contact his/her Cengage sales representative and Digital Solutions Manager to explore testing CengageNow™ in your course this term.

Basic Elements of Planning and Decision Making

LEARNING OBJECTIVES

After studying this chapter, you should be able to:

1. Summarize the functions of decision making and the planning process.

2. Discuss the purpose of organizational goals, identify different kinds of goals, discuss who sets goals, and describe how to manage multiple goals.

3. Identify different kinds of organizational plans, note the time frames for planning, discuss who plans, and describe contingency planning.

4. Discuss how tactical plans are developed and executed.

5. Describe the basic types of operational plans used by organizations.

6. Identify the major barriers to goal setting and planning, how organizations overcome those barriers, and how to use goals to implement plans.

MANAGEMENT IN ACTION Did AIG Ensure Risky Decisions?

Obviously, insurance companies incur immense risks because of the number of policies they issue, but you may not know that most of them also share their biggest risks with other insurers. Here's how it works.* Let's say that Insurance Co. 1 (IC#1) learns of a hurricane that will obligate it to pay out a large sum of money to people whose property is damaged. It doesn't know exactly how much it will have to pay out—its liability—but it estimates a total of $100 million. IC#1 thus makes a deal with Insurance Co. 2 (IC#2). It gives IC#2 a check for $75 million, and in return, IC#2 agrees that IC#1's liability is limited to $100 million; if damages are ultimately greater than $100 million, IC#2 will pay the difference. What's the advantage to IC#2? It can invest and earn money on the $75 million while waiting for claims that may or may not be filed. In other words, *buying liability* can be a lot like *selling insurance*.

Now, IC#2 might be tempted to claim some of the $75 million as income, but that's not a good idea. Why? Because IC#2 holds the money at too great a risk: What if it has to pay it to policyholders who file claims? Let's say, however, that IC#2 is having a bad year and decides to prop up its share price by including a good chunk of the $75 million in its annual earnings report. In that case,

"[Joseph Cassano is] almost single-handedly responsible for bringing AIG down and [in the process] the economy of this country. [He] basically took people's hard-earned money, gambled it, and lost everything."

—CONGRESSWOMAN JACKIE SPEIER OF CALIFORNIA

IC#2 has committed fraud (it's misled investors about its performance), and the question now facing its decision makers is twofold: What will be the compound repercussions of a bad business decision (making the deal with IC#1) *and* a bad legal decision (defrauding investors)?

How likely is it that insurance company decision makers in the real world would place themselves in such a dilemma? Consider the case of American International Group (AIG), which had become the world's number-one international insurance company by being Insurance Co. 2 to just about the whole world. In the mid-1980s, AIG branched out from the insurance business and started dealing in the financial market. This end of the business was handled by a branch located

Joseph Cassano, former CEO of AIG, has been accused of making overly risky decisions that resulted in the firm's financial disaster.

Mary F. Calvert/The New York Times/ReduxPictures

*This example is based on a scenario created by Charles Ortel of Newport Value Partners, a firm that provides research to professional investors.

in London and called AIG Financial Products (AIGFP). AIGFP was basically in the business of taking on financial risk from banks and other insurers that didn't want it, and it made a great deal of money by investing the premiums that companies paid it to take on their risk. In addition, in about 2001, AIGFP increasingly started acting like Insurance Co. 1 in our example: In particular, under new head Joseph Cassano, it began selling billions in risky loans to banks. The banks stood to make money by using the loans—that is, the money owed on them—to back securities which, in turn, they sold to various investors, while AIG pocketed fees for handling the sales. What if borrowers of the original loans—say, U.S. homebuyers—defaulted? AIG would have to reimburse the banks to which it had sold those loans. It was risky business, but in August 2007, Cassano assured investors that "it's hard for us . . . to even see a scenario, within any kind of realm or reason, that would see us losing $1 in any of those transactions."

In late 2007, when the bottom fell out of the U.S. housing market—which in fact furnished the bulk of the risky loans that AIG had been selling—the company lost $5 billion in the final three months of the year. And then it had a *really* bad year. It's a long story, but we'll simply report here that AIG lost $61.7 billion in the third quarter of 2008 alone (that's $28 million an hour, every hour on the hour, for three months). As it turns out, AIG didn't have nearly enough money to pay off the loans on which it had gambled, and in retrospect, Cassano's transactions through early 2006 look more and more like a giant Ponzi scheme: He was attracting new investments with guarantees backed by profits that earlier investments had in fact failed to deliver.

Evidence also suggests that Cassano *knew* that AIG was in serious trouble as early as 2001 or 2002. So what, then, were his motives? Why did he compound a bad business decision by continuing to make transactions that were all but certain to lose large sums of money? And why did he expose himself to potential criminal liability by understating

both the risk and the losses to investors? Such questions still mystify more than one Wall Street expert. Cassano was asked to step down in March 2008, as losses continued to pile up. Before the year was out, the U.S. government, fearing the repercussions of an AIG bankruptcy, had agreed to a bailout which, between September 2008 and June 2010, eventually poured $182 billion into the company—more than the value of the gold reserves at Fort Knox.

Congresswoman Jackie Speier of California didn't particularly care what Cassano's motives were, but she was convinced that he was

almost single-handedly responsible for bringing AIG down and [in the process] the economy of this country. [He and his cohorts] basically took people's hard-earned money, gambled it, and lost everything. [H]e must be held accountable for the dereliction of his duty and for the havoc he's wrought on America. I don't think the American people will be content . . . until we hear the click of the handcuffs on his wrists.

Unfortunately, it's hard to build a criminal case against someone for risking a trillion-dollar company (or even the whole financial system), so the U.S. government opted to investigate Cassano and his AIGFP team for misleading investors. In September 2007, for example—just two months after Cassano's assurance that AIG wasn't likely to lose as much as $1 on any of his transactions—the company confirmed probable losses of $352 million. By the end of the year, AIG had upped the total to a more realistic $11.1 billion in expected losses. As a former federal prosecutor put it, "A jump like that in three months raises real questions," but AIG issued a statement saying that "neither AIG nor AIGFP is aware of any fraud or malfeasance in connection" with Cassano's transactions; AIG's collapse, asserted company officials, resulted from "what, with hindsight, turned out to be bad business decisions." Two years later, federal prosecutors have yet to bring charges against Cassano or anyone else at AIG.[1]

Hindsight isn't always 20-20. Even the U.S. government, it seems, can't determine exactly what goals Joseph Cassano had in mind when he made the decisions that he made as head of AIGFP. There are also several questions about the connection between those decisions and the overall strategy of his employer. As we noted in Chapter 1, planning and decision making comprise the first managerial functions that organizations must address. This chapter is the first of four that explore the planning process in detail. We begin by briefly relating decision making and planning, and then explaining the planning process that most organizations follow. We then discuss the nature of organizational goals and introduce the basic concepts of planning. Next we discuss tactical and operational planning more fully. Finally, we conclude with a discussion of how to manage the goal-setting and planning processes.

Decision Making and the Planning Process

Decision making is the cornerstone of planning. Several years ago, Procter & Gamble (P&G) set a goal of doubling its revenues over a ten-year period. The firm's top managers could have adopted an array of alternative options, including increasing revenues by only 25 percent or increasing revenues threefold. The time frame for the projected revenue growth could also have been somewhat shorter or longer than the ten-year period that was actually specified. Alternatively, the goal could have included diversifying into new markets, cutting costs, or buying competing businesses. Thus P&G's exact mix of goals and plans for growth rate and time frame reflected choices from among a variety of alternatives. More recently, IBM announced its plan to achieve earnings per share of $20 (up from $11.52 in 2010) by 2015. The company also plans to reach $100 billion in cash flow and return 70 percent to shareholders by that same year.[2] This goal, while different from P&G's in several ways, nevertheless reflects the same mix of decisions regarding area, level, and time frame.

Clearly, then, decision making is the catalyst that drives the planning process. An organization's goals follow from decisions made by various managers. Likewise, deciding on the best plan for achieving particular goals also reflects a decision to adopt one course of action as opposed to others. We discuss decision making *per se* in Chapter 9. Our focus here is on the planning process itself. As we discuss goal setting and planning, however, keep in mind that decision making underlies every aspect of setting goals and formulating plans.[3]

The planning process itself can best be thought of as a generic activity. All organizations engage in planning activities, but no two organizations plan in exactly the same fashion. Figure 7.1 is a general representation of the planning process that many organizations attempt to follow. But, although most firms follow this general framework, each also has its own nuances and variations.[4]

As Figure 7.1 shows, all planning occurs within an environmental context. If managers do not understand this context, they will be unable to develop effective plans. Thus understanding

FIGURE 7.1 THE PLANNING PROCESS

The planning process takes place within an environmental context. Managers must develop a complete and thorough understanding of this context to determine the organization's mission and to develop its strategic, tactical, and operational goals and plans.

© Cengage Learning 2013

the environment is essentially the first step in planning. The four previous chapters cover many of the basic environmental issues that affect organizations and how they plan. With this understanding as a foundation, managers must then establish the organization's mission. The mission outlines the organization's purpose, premises, values, and directions. Flowing from the mission are parallel streams of goals and plans. Directly following the mission are strategic goals. These goals and the mission help determine strategic plans. Strategic goals and plans are primary inputs for developing tactical goals. Tactical goals and the original strategic plans help shape tactical plans. Tactical plans, in turn, combine with the tactical goals to shape operational goals. These goals and the appropriate tactical plans determine operational plans. Finally, goals and plans at each level can also be used as input for future activities at all levels. This chapter discusses goals and tactical and operational plans. Chapter 8 covers strategic plans.

What is the relationship between decision making and planning?

Which do you think is easier for a top manager—making a decision or developing a plan?

CONCEPT CHECK

Organizational Goals

Goals are critical to organizational effectiveness, and they serve a number of purposes. Organizations can also have several different kinds of goals, all of which must be appropriately managed. And a number of different kinds of managers must be involved in setting goals.

Purposes of Goals

Goals serve four important purposes.[5] First, they provide guidance and a unified direction for people in the organization. Goals can help everyone understand where the organization is going and why getting there is important.[6] Top managers at General Electric have set a goal that every business owned by the firm will be either number one or number two in its industry. This goal helps set the tone for decisions made by GE managers as it competes with other firms like Whirlpool and Electrolux.[7] Likewise, P&G's goal of doubling revenues, noted above, helps everyone in the firm recognize the strong emphasis on growth and expansion that is driving the firm, while IBM's goal reflects a clear focus on financial performance.

Second, goal-setting practices strongly affect other aspects of planning. Effective goal setting promotes good planning, and good planning facilitates future goal setting. For example, the ambitious revenue goal set for P&G demonstrates how setting goals and developing plans to reach them should be seen as complementary activities. The strong growth goal should encourage managers to plan for expansion by looking for new market opportunities, for example. Similarly, they must also always be alert for competitive threats and new ideas that will help facilitate future expansion. IBM, meanwhile, is focusing on balancing revenue growth with cost reductions.

Third, goals can serve as a source of motivation for employees of the organization. Goals that are specific and moderately difficult can motivate people to work harder, especially if attaining the goal is likely to result in rewards.[8] The Italian furniture manufacturer Industrie Natuzzi SpA uses goals to motivate its workers. Each craftsperson has a goal for how long it should take to perform her or his job, such as sewing leather sheets together to make a sofa cushion or building wooden frames for chair arms. At the completion of assigned tasks, workers enter their ID numbers and job numbers into the firm's computer system. If they get a job done faster than their goal, a bonus is automatically added to their paycheck.[9]

Finally, goals provide an effective mechanism for evaluation and control. This means that performance can be assessed in the future in terms of how successfully today's goals are accomplished. For example, suppose that officials of the United Way of America set a goal of collecting $250,000 from a particular small community. If, midway through the campaign, they have raised only $50,000, they know that they need to change or intensify their efforts. If they raise only $100,000 by the end of their drive, they will need to carefully study why they did not reach their goal and what they need to do differently next year. On the other hand, if they succeed in raising $265,000, evaluations of their efforts will take on an entirely different character. In 2009 the Food and Drug Administration (FDA) revealed that it was not meeting the goals it had set for itself for auditing food safety inspection programs. To address the issue, the FDA also announced plans to overhaul its inspection program and to tie individual performance ratings to food safety audits.[11]

Kinds of Goals

Organizations establish many different kinds of goals. In general, these goals vary by level, area, and time frame.[12] Figure 7.2 provides examples of each type of goal for a fast-food chain.

Level Goals are set for and by different levels within an organization. As we noted earlier, the four basic levels of goals are the mission and strategic, tactical, and operational goals. An organization's **mission** is a statement of its "fundamental, unique purpose that sets a business apart from other firms of its type and identifies the scope of the business's operations in product and market terms."[13] For instance, Starbucks' mission statement is to be "the premier purveyor of the finest coffee in the world while maintaining our uncompromising principles while we grow." The principles referred to in the mission statement include:

- Provide a great work environment and treat each other with respect and dignity.
- Embrace diversity as an essential component in the way we do business.
- Apply the highest standards of excellence to the purchasing, roasting, and fresh delivery of our coffee.
- Develop enthusiastically satisfied customers all of the time.
- Contribute positively to our communities and our environment.
- Recognize that profitability is essential to our future success.[14]

Hence, the mission statement and basic principles help managers at Starbucks make decisions and direct resources in clear and specific ways.

Strategic goals are goals set by and for top management of the organization. They focus on broad, general issues. For example, Starbucks has a strategic goal of increasing the profitability of each of its coffee stores by 25 percent over the next five years. **Tactical goals** are set by and for middle managers. Their focus is on how to operationalize actions necessary to achieve the strategic goals. To achieve Starbucks' goal of increasing its per-store profitability, managers are working on tactical goals related to company-owned versus licensed stores and the global distribution of stores in different countries.

Operational goals are set by and for lower-level managers. Their concern is with shorter-term issues associated with the tactical goals. An operational goal for Starbucks might be to boost the profitability of a certain number of stores in each of the next five years. (Some managers use the words *objective* and *goal* interchangeably. When they are differentiated, however, the term *objective* is usually used instead of *operational goal*.)

Area Organizations also set goals for different areas. The restaurant chain shown in Figure 7.2 has goals for operations, marketing, and finance. Hewlett-Packard (HP)

mission
A statement of an organization's fundamental purpose

strategic goal
A goal set by and for top management of the organization

tactical goal
A goal set by and for middle managers of the organization

operational goal
A goal set by and for lower-level managers of the organization

FIGURE 7.2 KINDS OF ORGANIZATIONAL GOALS FOR A REGIONAL FAST-FOOD CHAIN

Organizations develop many different types of goals. A regional fast-food chain, for example, might develop goals at several different levels and for several different areas.

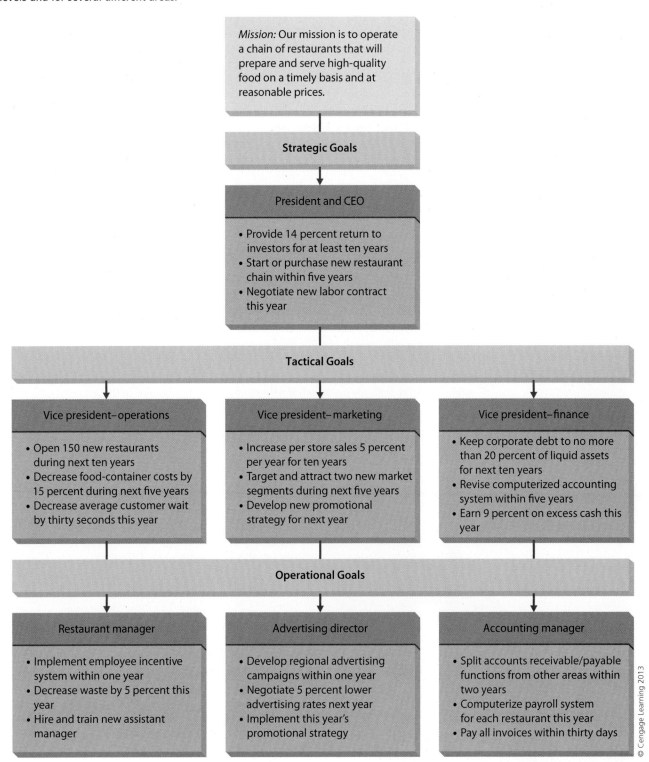

routinely sets production goals for quality, productivity, and so forth. By keeping activities focused on these important areas, HP has managed to remain competitive against organizations from around the world. Human resource goals might be set for employee turnover and absenteeism. 3M and Rubbermaid set goals for product innovation. Similarly, Bath & Body Works has a goal that 30 percent of the products sold in its retail outlets each year will be new. In addition to its profit growth goals, Starbucks also has financial goals related to return on investment and return on assets.

Time Frame Organizations also set goals across different time frames. In Figure 7.2, three goals are listed at the strategic, tactical, and operational levels. The first is a long-term goal, the second an intermediate-term goal, and the third a short-term goal. Some goals have an explicit time frame (open 150 new restaurants during the next ten years), and others have an open-ended time horizon (maintain 10 percent annual growth). Finally, we should also note that the meaning of different time frames varies by level. For example, at the strategic level, "long term" often means ten years or longer, "intermediate term" around five years or so, and "short term" around one year. But two or three years may be long term at the operational level, while short term may mean a matter of weeks or even days.

Responsibilities for Setting Goals

Who sets goals? The answer is actually quite simple: All managers should be involved in the goal-setting process. Each manager, however, generally has responsibilities for setting goals that correspond to his or her level in the organization. The mission and strategic goals are generally determined by the board of directors and top managers. Top and middle managers then work together to establish tactical goals. Finally, middle and lower-level managers are jointly responsible for operational goals. Many managers also set individual goals for themselves. These goals may involve career paths, informal work-related goals outside the normal array of official goals, or just about anything of interest or concern to the manager.

optimizing
Balancing and reconciling possible conflicts among goals

Nike has found an effective way to optimize its goals of producing high-quality and fashionable athletic shoes. In particular, the firm has enlisted the assistance of fashion designers to help create new products and has started to sell its shows at new outlets such as Urban Outfitters.

Samuel Granado/MCT/Newscom

Managing Multiple Goals

Organizations set many different kinds of goals and sometimes experience conflicts or contradictions among goals. Nike had problems with inconsistent goals a few years ago. The firm was producing high-quality shoes (a manufacturing goal), but they were not particularly stylish (a marketing goal). As a result, the company lost substantial market share when Reebok and Adidas started making shoes that were both high quality and fashionable. When Nike management recognized and corrected the inconsistencies, Nike regained its industry standing.

To address such problems, managers must understand the concept of optimizing. **Optimizing** involves balancing and reconciling possible conflicts among goals. Because goals may conflict with one another, the manager must look for inconsistencies and decide whether to pursue one goal to the exclusion of another or to find a midrange target between the extremes. For example, Home Depot first achieved success in the retailing industry by offering do-it-yourselfers high-quality home improvement products at low prices and with good service. The firm then added an additional goal of doubling its revenues from professional contractors. To help achieve this, many Home Depot stores have separate checkout areas and special products for contractors. The challenge, however, has been to keep loyal individual customers while also satisfying professional contractors.[15] Home Depot's biggest competitor, Lowe's, is also optimizing, but among different alternatives—trying to retain its core customer group (primarily male) while also appealing more to women.[16] Starbucks faces optimization challenges as it attempts to maintain its cachet as an upscale purveyor of fine coffees while also opening roadside drive-through stores. And the airlines almost always seem to face a classic optimizing question—carrying more passengers for lower prices or fewer passengers for higher prices.[17]

"Growth is a new skill to learn for us. We've been good at restructuring businesses over the last decade. Growth takes practice.

—LEWIS BOOTH, FORD MOTOR'S CHIEF FINANCIAL OFFICER[18]

What are the four fundamental purposes of goals in an organization?

Identify a recent situation in which you had to optimize among conflicting goals.

Organizational Planning

Given the clear link between organizational goals and plans, we now turn our attention to various concepts and issues associated with planning itself. In particular, this section identifies kinds of plans, time frames for planning, who is responsible for planning, and contingency planning.

Kinds of Organizational Plans

Organizations establish many different kinds of plans. At a general level, these include strategic, tactical, and operational plans.

Strategic Plans Strategic plans are the plans developed to achieve strategic goals. More precisely, a strategic plan is a general plan outlining decisions of resource allocation, priorities, and action steps necessary to reach strategic goals. These plans are set by the board of directors and top management, generally have an extended time horizon, and address questions of scope, resource deployment, competitive advantage, and synergy. We discuss strategic planning further in Chapter 8.

Tactical Plans A tactical plan, aimed at achieving tactical goals, is developed to implement specific parts of a strategic plan. Tactical plans typically involve upper and middle management and, compared with strategic plans, have a somewhat shorter time horizon and a more specific and concrete focus. Thus tactical plans are concerned more with actually getting things done than with deciding what to do. Tactical planning is covered in detail in a later section.

Operational Plans An operational plan focuses on carrying out tactical plans to achieve operational goals. Developed by middle and lower-level managers, operational plans have a short-term focus and are relatively narrow in scope. Each one deals with a fairly small set of activities. We also cover operational planning in more detail later.

Time Frames for Planning

As we noted previously, strategic plans tend to have a long-term focus, tactical plans an intermediate-term focus, and operational plans a short-term focus. The sections that follow address these time frames in more detail. Of course, we should also remember that time frames vary widely from industry to industry.

strategic plan
A general plan outlining decisions of resource allocation, priorities, and action steps necessary to reach strategic goals

tactical plan
A plan aimed at achieving tactical goals, developed to implement parts of a strategic plan

operational plan
Focuses on carrying out tactical plans to achieve operational goals

"Picking up and disposing of people's waste is not going to be the way this company survives long term. Our opportunities all arise from the sustainability movement."

—DAVID STEINER,
CEO OF WASTE MANAGEMENT[20]

Long-Range Plans A long-range plan covers many years, perhaps even decades. The founder of Matsushita Electric (maker of Panasonic and JVC electronic products), Konosuke Matsushita, once wrote a 250-year plan for his company![19] Today, however, most managers recognize that environmental change makes it unfeasible to plan too far ahead, but large firms like Ford Motor Company and ExxonMobil still routinely develop plans for five- to ten-year intervals. Ford executives, for example, have a pretty good idea today about new car models that they plan to introduce during the next decade. The time span for long-range planning varies from one organization to another. For our purposes, we regard any plan that extends beyond five years as long range. Managers of organizations in complex, volatile environments face a special dilemma. These organizations probably need a longer time horizon than do organizations in less dynamic environments, yet the complexity of their environment makes long-range planning difficult. Managers at these companies therefore develop long-range plans but also must constantly monitor their environment for possible changes.

Intermediate Plans An intermediate plan is somewhat less tentative and subject to change than is a long-range plan. Intermediate plans usually cover periods from one to five years and are especially important for middle and first-line managers. Thus they generally parallel tactical plans. For many organizations, intermediate planning has become the central focus of planning activities. Nissan, for example, fell behind its domestic rivals Toyota and Honda in profitability and productivity. To turn things around, the firm developed several plans ranging in duration from two to four years, each intended to improve some part of the company's operations. One plan (three years in duration) involved updating the manufacturing technology used in each Nissan assembly factory. Another (four years in duration) called for shifting more production to foreign plants to lower labor costs. And the successful implementation of these plans helped turn things around for Nissan.

Short-Range Plans Managers also develop short-range plans, which have a time frame of one year or less. Short-range plans greatly affect the manager's day-to-day activities. There are two basic kinds of short-range plans. An action plan operationalizes any other kind of plan. When a specific Nissan plant was ready to have its technology overhauled, its managers focused their attention on replacing the existing equipment with new equipment as quickly and as efficiently as possible, to minimize lost production time. In most cases, this was done in a matter of a few months, with actual production halted for only a few weeks. An action plan thus coordinates the actual changes at a given factory. A reaction plan, in turn, is a plan designed to allow the company to react to an unforeseen circumstance. At one Nissan factory, the new equipment arrived earlier than expected, and plant managers had to shut down production more quickly than expected. These managers thus had to react to events beyond their control in ways that still allowed their goals to be achieved. In fact, reacting to any form of environmental turbulence, as described in Chapter 3, is a form of reaction planning. The *Change* box entitled "How to Price a Body Wrap in a Recession" on page 163 shows how events in the economic environment may present a small business owner with a new wrinkle in her pricing strategy.

Responsibilities for Planning

Earlier we noted briefly who is responsible for setting goals. We can now expand that initial perspective and examine more fully how different parts of the organization participate in the overall planning process. All managers engage in planning to some degree. Marketing sales managers develop plans for target markets, market penetration, and sales increases. Operations managers plan cost-cutting programs and better inventory control methods. As a

long-range plan
A plan that covers many years, perhaps even decades; common long-range plans are for five years or more

intermediate plan
A plan that generally covers from one to five years

short-range plan
A plan that generally covers a span of one year or less

action plan
A plan used to operationalize any other kind of plan

reaction plan
A plan developed to react to an unforeseen circumstance

THE MORE THINGS CHANGE

How to Price a Body Wrap in a Recession

Let's say that you run a day spa and that one of your best-selling products is a special package which you offer for $100. We are, however, in a recession and business is sluggish. So you begin to think: Perhaps you'd make more profit if you lowered your prices. Maybe you'd attract more customers if you cut the price of your special package by a modest 10 percent, from $100 to $90. After all, it only costs you $50 to provide it and you'd still make $40 on every sale.

As a business planning idea, it seems to make sense, but in fact it probably doesn't. Think of it this way: How many more packages would you have to sell at $90 in order to make as much profit as you make when you sell them at $100?

Let's do the math. If you sold 100 packages at $100, you'd make a profit of $50 per package ($100 minus your cost of $50), for a total profit of $5,000 ($50 × 100). If, however, you sold 100 packages at $90, you'd make a profit of $40 per package, for a total profit of $4,000. In order to recover the $1,000 difference, you'd have to sell another 25 packages at a per-package profit of $40 each. Thus in order to recover the profit that you're sacrificing with your 10 percent price cut, you'd have to sell 125 packages, which is a 25 percent increase over 100 packages.

Cutting prices during a recession is a tempting idea, but most experts recommend that you think it through. In fact, most big companies try to hold the line. According to the consulting firm McKinsey & Company, the average S&P 1500 company would have to increase sales by 19 percent in order to justify a price cut of just 5 percent. That 19 percent bump in sales isn't very likely—nor is an increase of 25 percent at your day spa. In many cases, firms also prefer to maintain prices in order to protect the value of their products. Some products, for instance, have added value because consumers know them and have had positive experiences with them. A lower price—even if it's temporary—may suggest that such a product is, after all, of the same value as its lower-priced competitors, and it may take the firm a long time to reestablish the perception of the product's higher value.

It's also important to remember that consumer sensitivity to price varies from one product category to another. For example, consumer preferences for brand-name personal-care products—e.g., toothpaste—are quite deeply ingrained, and brand-loyal

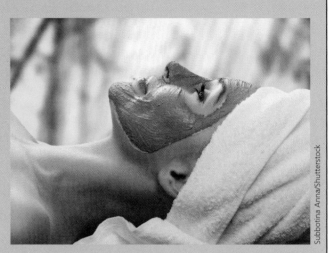

Subbotina Anna/Shutterstock

users will pay a few cents more for their preferred toothpaste because they aren't willing to substitute some other brand. In short, they're not *price sensitive* when it comes to their favorite toothpaste. Potential users of air travel, on the other hand, are highly price sensitive. Most air travel is discretionary, and while people will brush their teeth just as often in a recession, they certainly won't take as many airplane trips.

What about your special day-spa package? Are your potential customers likely to be price sensitive? Probably not. Your product, of course, is discretionary—no one *needs* a trip to a day spa. But unlike air travel, it's also more or less unique. There are other ways of indulging oneself in a respite of personal-care luxury—getting a massage, for example—but the competing products aren't necessarily substitutes for one another: A customer who wants a body wrap and a European facial isn't likely to consider a deep-tissue massage an acceptable substitute, even if the combination body wrap and facial is a little more expensive. That customer will probably pay $100 for the product as readily as $90 because, all things considered, she isn't particularly price sensitive about it.

References: Steven Nelson, "Bad Business Planning Mistakes in a Recession," *EzineArticles*.com, February 7, 2009, http://ezinearticles.com on February 23, 2011; Geoff Colvin, "How to Manage Your Business in a Recession," *CNNMoney.com*, January 8, 2009, http://money.cnn.com on February 23, 2011; Geoff Colvin, "Yes, You Can Raise Prices," *CNNMoney.com*, http://money.cnn.com on February 23, 2011; Vinnee Tong, "Higher Prices Boost Colgate-Palmolive 4Q Profit," *Toronto Telegraph*, January 29, 2009, http://story.torontotelegraph.com on February 23, 2011.

general rule, however, the larger an organization becomes, the more the primary planning activities become associated with groups of managers rather than with individual managers.

Planning Staff Some large organizations maintain a professional planning staff. General Motors, Caterpillar, Raytheon, Ford, and Boeing all have planning staffs. And although the planning staff was pioneered in the United States, foreign firms like Nippon Telegraph and Telephone have also started using them. Organizations might use a planning staff for a variety of reasons. In particular, a planning staff can reduce the workload of individual managers, help coordinate the planning activities of individual managers, bring to a particular problem many different tools and techniques, take a broader view than individual managers, and go beyond pet projects and particular departments. In recent years, though, some businesses have realized that they can plan more effectively by diffusing planning responsibility throughout their organization and/or by using planning task forces. For instance, Disney and Shell Oil have eliminated or downsized their centralized planning units.[21]

Planning Task Force Organizations sometimes use a planning task force to help develop plans. Such a task force often comprises line managers with a special interest in the relevant area of planning. The task force may also have members from the planning staff if the organization has one. A planning task force is most often created when the organization wants to address a special circumstance. For example, when Electronic Data Systems (EDS) decided to expand its information management services to Europe, managers knew that the firm's normal planning approach would not suffice, and top management created a special planning task force. The task force included representatives from each of the major units within the company, the corporate planning staff, and the management team that would run the European operation. Once the plan for entering the European market was formulated and implemented, the task force was eliminated.

The chief executive officer plays a critical role in the organization's planning process. When Anne Mulcahy was appointed CEO of Xerox the firm was in dire financial straits and seemed destined for a long period of decline. But Mulcahy changed the firm's approach to planning and returned Xerox to profitability and stability.

REUTERS/STR New

Board of Directors Among its other responsibilities, the board of directors establishes the corporate mission and strategy. In some companies the board takes an active role in the planning process.[22] At CBS, for example, the board of directors has traditionally played a major role in planning. In other companies the board selects a competent chief executive and delegates planning to that individual.

Chief Executive Officer The chief executive officer (CEO) is usually the president or the chair of the board of directors. The CEO is probably the single most important individual in any organization's planning process. The CEO plays a major role in the complete planning process and is responsible for implementing the strategy. The board and CEO, then, assume direct roles in planning. The other organizational players involved in the planning process have more of an advisory or a consulting role.

Executive Committee The executive committee is usually composed of the top executives in the organization working together as a group. Committee members usually meet regularly to provide input to the CEO on the proposals that affect their own units and to review the various strategic plans that develop from this input. Members of the executive committee are frequently assigned to various staff committees, subcommittees, and task forces to concentrate on specific projects or problems that might confront the entire organization at some time in the future.

Line Management The final component of most organizations' planning activities is line management. Line managers are those persons with formal authority and responsibility for the management of the organization. They play an important role in an organization's planning process for two reasons. First, they are a valuable source of inside information for other managers as plans are formulated and implemented. Second, the line managers at the middle and lower levels of the organization usually must execute the plans developed by top management. Line management identifies, analyzes, and recommends program alternatives, develops budgets and submits them for approval, and finally sets the plans in motion.

Contingency Planning and Crisis Management

Another important type of planning is contingency planning—the determination of alternative courses of action to be taken if an intended plan of action is unexpectedly disrupted or rendered inappropriate.[23] Crisis management, a related concept, is the set of procedures the organization uses in the event of a disaster or other unexpected calamity. Some elements of crisis management may be orderly and systematic, whereas others may be more ad hoc and develop as events unfold.

An excellent example of widespread contingency planning occurred during the late 1990s in anticipation of what was popularly known as the "Y2K bug." Concerns about the impact of technical glitches in computers stemming from their internal clocks' changing from 1999 to 2000 resulted in contingency planning for most organizations. Many banks and hospitals, for example, had extra staff available; some organizations created backup computer systems; and some even stockpiled inventory in case they could not purchase new products or materials.[24]

The devastating hurricanes that hit the Gulf Coast in 2005—Katrina and Rita—dramatically underscored the importance of effective crisis management. For example, inadequate and ineffective responses by the Federal Emergency Management Agency (FEMA) illustrated to many people that organization's weaknesses in coping with crisis situations. On the other hand, some organizations responded much more effectively. Walmart began ramping up its emergency preparedness on the same day that Katrina was upgraded from a tropical depression to a tropical storm. In the days before the storm struck, Walmart stores in the region were supplied with powerful generators and large supplies of dry ice so they could reopen as quickly as possible after the storm had passed. In neighboring states, the firm also had scores of trucks standing by crammed with both emergency-related inventory for its stores and emergency supplies it was prepared to donate—bottled water, medical supplies, and so forth. And Walmart often beat FEMA by several days in getting those supplies delivered.[25]

Seeing the consequences of poor crisis management after the terrorist attacks of September 11, 2001, and the 2005 hurricanes, many firms today are actively working to create new and better crisis management plans and procedures. For example, both Reliant Energy and Duke Energy rely on computer trading centers where trading managers actively buy and sell energy-related commodities. If a terrorist attack or natural disaster such as a hurricane were to strike their trading centers, they would essentially be out of business. Prior to September 11, each firm had relatively vague and superficial crisis plans. But now they and most other companies have much more detailed and comprehensive plans in the event of another crisis. Both Reliant and Duke, for example, have created secondary trading centers at other locations. In the event of a shutdown at their main trading centers, these firms can quickly transfer virtually all their core trading activities to their secondary centers within 30 minutes or less.[26]

contingency planning
The determination of alternative courses of action to be taken if an intended plan is unexpectedly disrupted or rendered inappropriate

crisis management
The set of procedures the organization uses in the event of a disaster or other unexpected calamity

FIGURE 7.3 CONTINGENCY PLANNING

Most organizations develop contingency plans. These plans specify alternative courses of action to be taken if an intended plan is unexpectedly disrupted or rendered inappropriate.

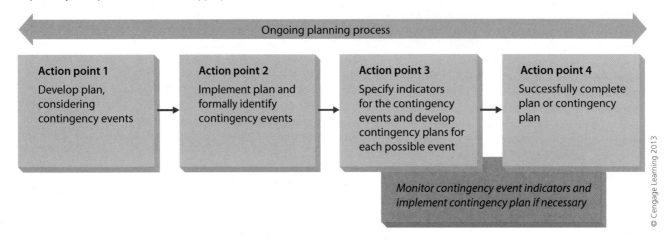

© Cengage Learning 2013

Unfortunately, however, because it is impossible to forecast the future precisely, no organization can ever be perfectly prepared for all crises. For example, due to 2011's disastrous earthquake and tsunami in Japan, many U.S. companies faced shortages of goods and materials imported from that country. General Motors was the first automaker forced to temporarily shut down one of its truck plants because it could not get enough Japanese-made parts. Two months after the disaster, Toyota's facilities in the United States were operating at less than 30 percent of capacity and did not return to full production until several months later.[27]

> "[G.M. has contingency plans for supply disruptions] but nothing on this kind of scale or scope."
>
> —STEPHEN GIRSKY, GENERAL MOTORS VICE CHAIRMAN[28]

The mechanics of contingency planning are shown in Figure 7.3. In relation to an organization's other plans, contingency planning comes into play at four action points. At action point 1, management develops the basic plans of the organization. These may include strategic, tactical, and operational plans. As part of this development process, managers usually consider various contingency events. Some management groups even assign someone the role of devil's advocate to ask, "But what if . . ." about each course of action. A variety of contingencies are usually considered.

At action point 2, the plan that management chooses is put into effect. The most important contingency events are also defined. Only the events that are likely to occur and whose effects will have a substantial impact on the organization are considered in the contingency-planning process. Next, at action point 3, the company specifies certain indicators or signs that suggest that a contingency event is about to take place. A bank might decide that a 2 percent drop in interest rates should be considered a contingency event. An indicator might be two consecutive months with a drop of 0.5 percent in each. As indicators of contingency events are being defined, the contingency plans themselves should also be developed. Examples of contingency plans for various situations are delaying plant construction, developing a new manufacturing process, and cutting prices.

After this stage, the managers of the organization monitor the indicators identified at action point 3. If the situation dictates, a contingency plan is implemented. Otherwise, the primary plan of action continues in force. Finally, action point 4 marks the successful completion of either the original or a contingency plan.

Contingency planning is becoming increasingly important for most organizations, especially for those operating in particularly complex or dynamic environments. Few managers have such an accurate view of the future that they can anticipate and plan for everything.

Contingency planning is a useful technique for helping managers cope with uncertainty and change. Crisis management, by its very nature, however, is more difficult to anticipate. But organizations that have a strong culture, strong leadership, and a capacity to deal with the unexpected stand a better chance of successfully weathering a crisis than do other organizations.[29]

Distinguish between contingency planning and crisis management.

How might time frames for planning vary across firms in different industries?

Tactical Planning

As we noted earlier, tactical plans are developed to implement specific parts of a strategic plan. You have probably heard the saying about winning the battle but losing the war. Tactical plans are to battles what strategy is to a war: an organized sequence of steps designed to execute strategic plans. Strategy focuses on resources, environment, and mission, whereas tactics focus primarily on people and action.[30] Figure 7.4 identifies the major elements in developing and executing tactical plans.

Developing Tactical Plans

Although effective tactical planning depends on many factors, which vary from one situation to another, we can identify some basic guidelines. First, the manager needs to recognize that tactical planning must address a number of tactical goals derived from a broader strategic goal.[31] An occasional situation may call for a stand-alone tactical plan, but most of the time tactical plans flow from and must be consistent with a strategic plan.

For example, top managers at Coca-Cola once developed a strategic plan for cementing the firm's dominance of the soft-drink industry. As part of developing the plan, they identified a critical environmental threat—considerable unrest and uncertainty among the independent bottlers that packaged and distributed Coca-Cola's products. To simultaneously counter this threat and strengthen the company's position, Coca-Cola bought several large independent bottlers and combined them into one new organization called "Coca-Cola

FIGURE 7.4 DEVELOPING AND EXECUTING TACTICAL PLANS

Tactical plans are used to accomplish specific parts of a strategic plan. Each strategic plan is generally implemented through several tactical plans. Effective tactical planning involves both development and execution.

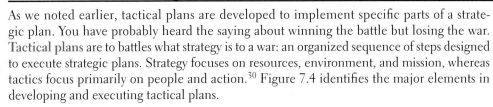

Developing tactical plans
- Recognize and understand overarching strategic plans and tactical goals
- Specify relevant resource and time issues
- Recognize and identify human resource commitments

Executing tactical plans
- Evaluate each course of action in light of its goal
- Obtain and distribute information and resources
- Monitor horizontal and vertical communication and integration of activities
- Monitor ongoing activities for goal achievement

© Cengage Learning 2013

tactical plan
A plan aimed at achieving tactical goals, developed to implement specific parts of a strategic plan

Enterprises." Selling half of the new company's stock reaped millions in profits while effectively keeping control of the enterprise in Coca-Cola's hands. Thus the creation of the new business was a tactical plan developed to contribute to the achievement of an overarching strategic goal.[32]

Second, although strategies are often stated in general terms, tactics must specify resources and time frames. A strategy can call for being number one in a particular market or industry, but a tactical plan must specify precisely what activities will be undertaken to achieve that goal. Consider the Coca-Cola example again. Another element of its strategic plan involves increased worldwide market share. To facilitate additional sales in Europe, managers developed tactical plans for building a new plant in the south of France to make soft-drink concentrate and for building another canning plant in Dunkirk. The firm has also invested heavily in India.[33] Building these plants represents a concrete action involving measurable resources (funds to build the plants) and a clear time horizon (a target date for completion).

Finally, tactical planning requires the use of human resources. Managers involved in tactical planning spend a great deal of time working with other people. They must be in a position to receive information from others within and outside the organization, process that information in the most effective way, and then pass it on to others who might make use of it. Coca-Cola executives have been intensively involved in planning the new plants, setting up the new bottling venture noted earlier, and exploring a joint venture with Cadbury Schweppes in the United Kingdom. Each activity has required considerable time and effort from dozens of managers. One manager, for example, crossed the Atlantic 12 times while negotiating the Cadbury deal.

Executing Tactical Plans

Regardless of how well a tactical plan is formulated, its ultimate success depends on the way it is carried out. Successful implementation, in turn, depends on the astute use of resources, effective decision making, and insightful steps to ensure that the right things are done at the right times and in the right ways. A manager can see an absolutely brilliant idea fail because of improper execution.

Proper execution depends on a number of important factors. First, the manager needs to evaluate every possible course of action in light of the goal it is intended to reach. Next, he or she needs to make sure that each decision maker has the information and resources necessary to get the job done. Vertical and horizontal communication and integration of activities must be present to minimize conflict and inconsistent activities. And, finally, the manager must monitor ongoing activities derived from the plan to make sure they are achieving the desired results. This monitoring typically takes place within the context of the organization's ongoing control systems.

For example, managers at Walt Disney Company recently developed a new strategic plan aimed at spurring growth in and profits from foreign markets. One tactical plan developed to stimulate growth involves expanding the cable Disney Channel into more and more foreign markets; another involved expanding the relatively small Disney theme park near Hong Kong that opened in 2006 into a much larger park. Although expanding cable television and expanding a theme park are big undertakings in their own right, they are still tactical plans within the overall strategic plan focusing on international growth.[34]

How are tactical plans developed?

Which do you think is easier—developing tactical plans or implementing them? Why?

CONCEPT CHECK

Operational Planning

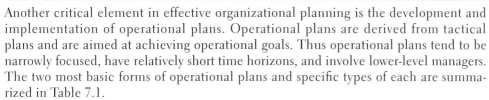

Another critical element in effective organizational planning is the development and implementation of operational plans. Operational plans are derived from tactical plans and are aimed at achieving operational goals. Thus operational plans tend to be narrowly focused, have relatively short time horizons, and involve lower-level managers. The two most basic forms of operational plans and specific types of each are summarized in Table 7.1.

Single-Use Plans

A single-use plan is developed to carry out a course of action that is not likely to be repeated in the future. As Disney plans the expansion of its theme park in Hong Kong, it will develop numerous single-use plans for individual rides, attractions, and hotels. The two most common forms of single-use plans are programs and projects.

Programs A program is a single-use plan for a large set of activities. It might consist of identifying procedures for introducing a new product line, opening a new facility, or changing the organization's mission. As part of its own strategic plans for growth several years ago, Black & Decker bought General Electric's small-appliance business. The deal involved the largest brand-name switch in history: 150 products were converted from the GE to the Black & Decker label. Each product was carefully studied, redesigned, and reintroduced with an extended warranty. A total of 140 steps were followed for each product. It took three years to convert all 150 products over to Black & Decker. The total conversion of the product line was a program.

Projects A project is similar to a program but is generally of less scope and complexity. A project may be a part of a broader program, or it may be a self-contained single-use plan. For Black & Decker, the conversion of each of the 150 products was a separate project in its own right. Each product had its own manager, its own schedule, and so forth. Projects are also used to introduce a new product within an existing product line or to add a new benefit option to an existing salary package.

single-use plan
Developed to carry out a course of action that is not likely to be repeated in the future

program
A single-use plan for a large set of activities

project
A single-use plan of less scope and complexity than a program

Plan	Description
Single-use plan	Developed to carry out a course of action not likely to be repeated in the future
Program	Single-use plan for a large set of activities
Project	Single-use plan of less scope and complexity than a program
Standing plan	Developed for activities that recur regularly over a period of time
Policy	Standing plan specifying the organization's general response to a designated problem or situation
Standard operating procedure	Standing plan outlining steps to be followed in particular circumstances
Rules and regulations	Standing plans describing exactly how specific activities are to be carried out

TABLE 7.1 TYPES OF OPERATIONAL PLANS

Organizations develop various operational plans to help achieve operational goals. In general, there are two types of single-use plans and three types of standing plans.

© Cengage Learning 2013

Standing Plans

Whereas single-use plans are developed for nonrecurring situations, a **standing plan** is used for activities that recur regularly over a period of time. Standing plans can greatly enhance efficiency by making decision making routine. Policies, standard operating procedures, and rules and regulations are three kinds of standing plans.

Policies As a general guide for action, a policy is the most general form of standing plan. A **policy** specifies the organization's general response to a designated problem or situation. For example, McDonald's has a policy that it will not grant a franchise to an individual who already owns another fast-food restaurant. Similarly, Starbucks has a policy that it will not franchise at all, instead retaining ownership of all Starbucks coffee shops. Likewise, a university admissions office might establish a policy that admission will be granted only to applicants with a minimum SAT score of 1,200 and a ranking in the top quarter of their high school class. Admissions officers may routinely deny admission to applicants who fail to reach these minimums. A policy is also likely to describe how exceptions are to be handled. The university's policy statement, for example, might create an admissions appeals committee to evaluate applicants who do not meet minimum requirements but may warrant special consideration.

Standard Operating Procedures Another type of standing plan is the **standard operating procedure**, or SOP. An SOP is more specific than a policy, in that it outlines the steps to be followed in particular circumstances. The admissions clerk at the university, for example, might be told that, when an application is received, he or she should (1) set up an electronic file for the applicant; (2) merge test-score records, transcripts, and letters of reference to the electronic file as they are received; and (3) forward the electronic file to the appropriate admissions director when it is complete. Gallo Vineyards in California has a 300-page manual of SOPs. This planning manual is credited with making Gallo one of the most efficient wine operations in the United States. McDonald's has SOPs explaining exactly how Big Macs are to be cooked, how long they can stay in the warming rack, and so forth.

Food handling is subject to myriad federal and state regulations. In order to more effectively comply with these regulations, businesses such as Fresh Direct in Queens, New York, rely on standard operating procedures and their own internal rules and regulations. Note that this food handler is wearing gloves and hair protection as she adds icing to a fresh batch of cupcakes.

standing plan
Developed for activities that recur regularly over a period of time

policy
A standing plan that specifies the organization's general response to a designated problem or situation

standard operating procedure (SOP)
A standard plan that outlines the steps to be followed in particular circumstances

rules and regulations
Describe exactly how specific activities are to be carried out

Rules and Regulations The narrowest of the standing plans, **rules and regulations**, describe exactly how specific activities are to be carried out. Rather than guiding decision making, rules and regulations actually take the place of decision making in various situations. Each McDonald's restaurant has a rule prohibiting customers from using its telephones, for example. The university admissions office might have a rule stipulating that if an applicant's file is not complete two months before the beginning of a semester, the student cannot be admitted until the next semester. Of course, in most organizations a manager at a higher level can suspend or bend the rules. If the high school transcript of the child of a prominent university alumnus and donor arrives a few days late, the director of admissions might waive the two-month rule. Indeed, rules and regulations can become problematic if they are excessive or enforced too rigidly.

Rules and regulations and SOPs are similar in many ways. They are both relatively narrow in scope, and each can serve as a substitute for decision making. An SOP typically describes a sequence of activities, however, whereas rules and regulations focus on one activity. Recall our examples: The admissions SOP consisted of three activities, whereas the two-month rule related to only one activity. In an industrial setting, the SOP for orienting a new employee could involve enrolling the person in various benefit options, introducing him or her to co-workers and supervisors, and providing a tour of the facilities. A pertinent rule for the new employee might involve when to come to work each day.

Distinguish between single-use and standing plans.

Identify a rule or regulation that relates to you but that you think is excessive or too restrictive.

CONCEPT CHECK

Managing Goal-Setting and Planning Processes

Obviously, all of the elements of goal setting and planning discussed to this point involve managing these processes in some way or another. In addition, however, because major barriers sometimes impede effective goal setting and planning, knowing how to overcome some of the barriers is important.

Barriers to Goal Setting and Planning

Several circumstances can serve as barriers to effective goal setting and planning; the more common ones are listed in Table 7.2.

Inappropriate Goals Inappropriate goals come in many forms. Paying a large dividend to stockholders may be inappropriate if it comes at the expense of research and development. Goals may also be inappropriate if they are unattainable. If Kmart were to set a goal of having more revenues than Walmart next year, people at the company would probably be embarrassed because achieving such a goal would be impossible. Goals may also be inappropriate if they place too much emphasis on either quantitative or qualitative measures of success. Some goals, especially those relating to financial areas, are quantifiable, objective, and verifiable. Other goals, such as employee satisfaction and development, are difficult, if not impossible, to quantify. Organizations are asking for trouble if they put too much emphasis on one type of goal to the exclusion of the other. A few years ago Starbucks set an ambitious goal of having

Major barriers	Inappropriate goals
	Improper reward system
	Dynamic and complex environment
	Reluctance to establish goals
	Resistance to change
	Constraints
Overcoming the barriers	Understanding the purposes of goals and planning
	Communication and participation
	Consistency, revision, and updating
	Effective reward system

TABLE 7.2 BARRIERS TO GOAL SETTING AND PLANNING

As part of managing the goal-setting and planning processes, managers must understand the barriers that can disrupt them. Managers must also know how to overcome the barriers.

© Cengage Learning 2013

40,000 locations globally. But in its zeal to meet this target, the company made numerous poor decisions for new sites, cluttered its stores with too much merchandise, and lost its focus on coffee. As a result, when the global recession hit in 2009 Starbucks was forced to postpone new openings, close several hundred underperforming stores, and eliminate several thousand jobs.[35] This also stimulated its current focus on improving profitability for individual stores as opposed to simply adding new stores.

Improper Reward System   In some settings, an improper reward system acts as a barrier to goal setting and planning. For example, people may inadvertently be rewarded for poor goal-setting behavior or go unrewarded or even be punished for proper goal-setting behavior. Suppose that a manager sets a goal of decreasing turnover next year. If turnover is decreased by even a fraction, the manager can claim success and perhaps be rewarded for the accomplishment. In contrast, a manager who attempts to decrease turnover by 5 percent but actually achieves a decrease of only 4 percent may receive a smaller reward because of her or his failure to reach the established goal. And if an organization places too much emphasis on short-term performance and results, managers may ignore longer-term issues as they set goals and formulate plans to achieve higher profits in the short term.

Dynamic and Complex Environment   The nature of an organization's environment is also a barrier to effective goal setting and planning. Rapid change, technological innovation, and intense competition can all increase the difficulty of an organization's accurately assessing future opportunities and threats. For example, when an electronics firm like IBM develops a long-range plan, it tries to take into account how much technological innovation is likely to occur during that interval. But forecasting such events is extremely difficult. During the early boom years of personal computers, data were stored primarily on floppy disks. Because these disks had a limited storage capacity, hard disks were developed. Whereas the typical floppy disk can hold hundreds of pages of information, a hard disk can store thousands of pages. Today, computers increasingly store information on shared servers or other devices capable of holding millions of pages. The manager attempting to set goals and plan in this rapidly changing environment faces a truly formidable task.

Reluctance to Establish Goals   Another barrier to effective planning is some managers' reluctance to establish goals for themselves and their units of responsibility. The reason for this reluctance may be lack of confidence or fear of failure. If a manager sets a goal that is specific, concise, and time related, then whether he or she attains it is obvious. Managers who consciously or unconsciously try to avoid this degree of accountability are likely to hinder the organization's planning efforts. Pfizer, a large pharmaceutical company, ran into problems because its managers did not set goals for research and development. Consequently, the organization fell further and further behind because managers had no way of knowing how effective their R&D efforts actually were.

"My advice . . . is to be ready to revise any system, scrap any methods, abandon any theory if the success of the job demands it."

—HENRY FORD[36]

Resistance to Change   Another barrier to goal setting and planning is resistance to change. Planning essentially involves changing something about the organization. As we will see in Chapter 16, people tend to resist change. Avon Products almost drove itself into bankruptcy several years ago because it insisted on continuing a policy of large dividend payments to its stockholders. When profits started to fall, managers resisted cutting the dividends and started borrowing to pay them. The company's debt grew from $3 million to $1.1 billion in eight years. Eventually, managers were forced to confront the problem and cut dividends.

Constraints   Constraints that limit what an organization can do are another major obstacle. Common constraints include a lack of resources, government restrictions, and strong competition. For example, Owens-Corning Fiberglass took on an enormous debt burden as part of its fight to avoid a takeover by Wickes Ltd. The company then had such a large debt that it was forced to cut back on capital expenditures and research and development. And those cutbacks greatly constrained what the firm could plan for the future. Time constraints are also a factor. It is easy to say, "I'm too busy to plan today; I'll do it tomorrow." Effective planning takes time, energy, and an unwavering belief in its importance.

Overcoming the Barriers

Fortunately, there are several guidelines for making goal setting and planning effective. Some of the guidelines are listed in Table 7.2.

Understand the Purposes of Goals and Planning One of the best ways to facilitate goal-setting and planning processes is to recognize their basic purposes. Managers should also recognize that there are limits to the effectiveness of setting goals and making plans. Planning is not a panacea that will solve all of an organization's problems, nor is it an ironclad set of procedures to be followed at any cost. And effective goals and planning do not necessarily ensure success; adjustments and exceptions are to be expected as time passes. For example, Coca-Cola followed a logical and rational approach to setting goals and planning a few years ago when it introduced a new formula to combat Pepsi's increasing market share. But all the plans proved to be wrong as consumers rejected the new version of Coca-Cola. Managers quickly reversed the decision and reintroduced the old formula as Coca-Cola Classic. Thus, even though careful planning resulted in a big mistake, the company was able to recover from its blunder.

Communication and Participation Although goals and plans may be initiated at high levels in the organization, they must also be communicated to others in the organization. Everyone involved in the planning process should know what the overriding organizational strategy is, what the various functional strategies are, and how they are all to be integrated and coordinated. People responsible for achieving goals and implementing plans must have a voice in developing them from the outset. These individuals almost always have valuable information to contribute, and because they will be implementing the plans, their involvement is critical: People are usually more committed to plans that they have helped shape. Even when an organization is somewhat centralized or uses a planning staff, managers from a variety of levels in the organization should be involved in the planning process.

Meanwhile, in discussing the uses of an information-gathering tool called the *digital dashboard*, our *Technically Speaking* box on page 174, entitled "A New Tool for Driving Decisions," touches upon some interesting arguments both for and against the intensive involvement of top managers in the planning process.

Consistency, Revision, and Updating Goals should be consistent both horizontally and vertically. Horizontal consistency means that goals should be consistent across the organization, from one department to the next. Vertical consistency means that goals should be consistent up and down the organization—strategic, tactical, and operational goals must agree with one another. Because goal setting and planning are dynamic processes, they must also be revised and updated regularly. Many organizations are seeing the need to revise and update on an increasingly frequent basis. Citigroup, for example, once used a three-year planning horizon for developing and providing new financial services. That cycle was subsequently cut to two years, and the bank now often uses a one-year horizon.

Effective Reward Systems In general, people should be rewarded both for establishing effective goals and plans and for successfully achieving them. Because failure sometimes results from factors outside the manager's control, however, people should also be assured that failure to reach a goal will not necessarily bring punitive consequences. Frederick Smith, founder and CEO of Federal Express, has a stated goal of encouraging risk. Thus, when

TECHNICALLY SPEAKING

A New Tool for Driving Decisions

Traditionally, the desk accessories of big-time CEOS did not include computers. Indeed, a desk with nothing but a phone was something of a status symbol, indicating that a company's number-one strategist spent his or her days thinking and communicating deep thoughts, not data grubbing. Oracle Corp. CEO Lawrence Ellison remembers a time when he'd get financial reports by calling up a few people and "work[ing] on feelings." After all, it would take days for people to work out elaborate spreadsheets and get written reports on his desk, and by that time, they were usually old news.

The Internet and web technology, of course, have changed all that. Nowadays, Ellison gets up-to-the-minute information on his *digital dashboard*—an easy-to-read interface app that can get information from a computer's local operating system, from an application that the computer is running, or from remote websites that it has accessed. Data from a variety of sources are merged into single views, and dashboard technology makes it possible to start from surface-level processes and then "drill down" to data stored at lower levels, including levels that senior executives don't ordinarily access.

The dashboard in the office of Verizon CIO Shaygan Kheradpir is actually a 52-inch plasma video screen. Dubbed the "Wall of Shaygan" by coworkers, it represents every single node in the company's network and uses traffic-light color coding to tell Keradpir how various aspects of the business are faring at the moment. If a sector is green, things are going fine; if it's yellow, Keradpir may slow down to take a look; if it's red, he knows that something has stopped performing the way it should.

Keradpir's outsized dashboard displays such key pieces of information as the *number of customers who sign up for a Verizon service on the Internet* and the *number of customers who do their bill paying via the web*. These are among his key *metrics*—the performance measurements that Keradpir wants to track. Different managers, of course, need to keep up with different metrics, but the common denominator is the ability of the dashboard technology to put different perspectives on performance into such commonly quantified graphics as bar and pie charts, sparklines, gauges, and heat maps. In a sense, all of this so-called "data visualization" amounts to a collection of information charts that track changes in selected ratios in real time. "You can't manage something you can't measure," argues Ken Rau, a San Francisco–area consultant.

Tetra Images/Getty Images

Like Verizon, many companies develop their own digital dashboards to incorporate data that they're already gathering in various information systems. At large companies, business units are typically selected as primary drivers of pertinent data, but dashboards can also be specialized according to corporate function—human resources, operations management, information technology, customer-relationship management, and so forth. The technology is also available from many software providers, with common features including such tools as key performance indicators and balanced scorecards.

In addition, digital dashboards aren't just for executives any more. More and more companies are using them to make real-time information available to managers who can make real-time use of it. Verizon, for example, uses its dashboard to provide managers with updated data on customer complaints and power outages. Finally, a more recent trend is the extension of dashboard technology to cell phones, PDAs, and other wireless devices. Verizon has launched a portal called (what else?) Dashboard to deliver multimedia information and entertainment services to users of Mobile Web, GetItNow, and other wireless services.

References: Spencer E. Ante, "Giving the Boss the Big Picture," *BusinessWeek*, February 13, 2006, www.businessweek.com on February 23, 2011; Danny Bradbury, "Go Straight to the Info You Need," *ComputerWeekly.com*, April 20, 2006, www.computerweekly.com on February 23, 2011; Kirsty Lee, "Prepackaged Dashboards or Adhoc Analysis: What's the Best?" *Dashboard Insight*, December 24, 2010, www.dashboardinsight.com on February 23, 2011; Alexander Chiang, "Data Visualization on Smart Phones," *Dashboard Insight*, February 18, 2011, www.dashboardinsight.com on February 23, 2011; Ovidiu Rautu, "Verizon Wireless Launches Dashboard," *Softpedia*, September 25, 2008, http://news.softpedia.com on February 23, 2011.

Federal Express lost $233 million on an unsuccessful service called ZapMail, no one was punished. Smith believed that the original idea was a good one but was unsuccessful for reasons beyond the company's control.

Using Goals to Implement Plans

Goals are often used to implement plans. Formal goal-setting programs represent one widely used method for managing the goal-setting and planning processes concurrently to ensure that both are done effectively. Some firms call this approach **management by objectives**, or **MBO**. We should also note, however, that although many firms use this basic approach, they frequently tailor it to their own special circumstances and use a special term or name for it.[37] For example, Tenneco Inc. uses an MBO-type system but calls it the "Performance Agreement System," or PAS.

The Nature and Purpose of Formal Goal Setting The purpose of formal goal setting is generally to give subordinates a voice in the goal-setting and planning processes and to clarify for them exactly what they are expected to accomplish in a given time span. Thus formal goal setting is often concerned with goal setting and planning for individual managers and their units or work groups.

The Formal Goal-Setting Process The basic mechanics of the formal goal-setting process are shown in Figure 7.5. This process is described here from an ideal perspective. In any given organization, the steps of the process are likely to vary in importance and may even take a different sequence. As a starting point, however, most managers believe that, if a formal goal-setting program is to be successful, it must start at the top of the organization. Top managers must communicate why they have adopted the program, what they think it will do, and that they have accepted and are committed to formal goal setting. Employees must also be educated about what goal setting is and what their roles in it will be. Having committed to formal goal setting, managers must implement it in a way that is consistent with overall organizational goals and plans. The idea is that goals set at the top will systematically cascade down throughout the organization.

Although establishing the organization's basic goals and plans is extremely important, collaborative goal setting and planning are the essence of formal goal setting. The collaboration

management by objectives (MBO)
A formal goal-setting process involving collaboration between managers and subordinates; the extent to which goals are accomplished is a major factor in evaluating and rewarding subordinates' performance

FIGURE 7.5 THE FORMAL GOAL-SETTING PROCESS

Formal goal setting is an effective technique for integrating goal setting and planning. This figure portrays the general steps that most organizations use when they adopt formal goal setting. Of course, most organizations adapt this general process to fit their own unique needs and circumstances.

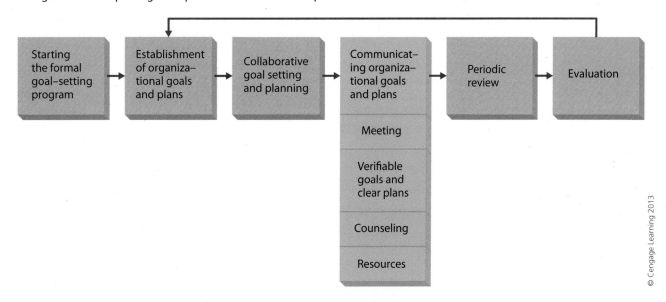

© Cengage Learning 2013

involves a series of distinct steps. First, managers tell their subordinates what organizational and unit goals and plans top management has established. Then managers meet with their subordinates on a one-to-one basis to arrive at a set of goals and plans for each subordinate that both the subordinate and the manager have helped develop and to which both are committed. Next, the goals are refined to be as verifiable (quantitative) as possible and to specify a time frame for their accomplishment. They should also be written. Further, the plans developed to achieve the goals need to be as clearly stated as possible and directly relate to each goal. Managers must play the role of counselors in the goal-setting and planning meeting. For example, they must ensure that the subordinates' goals and plans are attainable and workable and that they will facilitate both the unit's and the organization's goals and plans. Finally, the meeting should spell out the resources that the subordinate will need to implement his or her plans and work effectively toward goal attainment.

Conducting periodic reviews as subordinates are working toward their goals is advisable. If the goals and plans are for a one-year period, meeting quarterly to discuss progress may be a good idea. At the end of the period, the manager meets with each subordinate again to review the degree of goal attainment. They discuss which goals were met and which were not met in the context of the original plans. The reasons for both success and failure are explored, and the employee is rewarded on the basis of goal attainment. In an ongoing goal-setting program, the evaluation meeting may also serve as the collaborative goal-setting and planning meeting for the next time period.

The Effectiveness of Formal Goal Setting A large number of organizations, including Alcoa, Tenneco, DuPont, General Motors, Boeing, Caterpillar, and Black & Decker, all use some form of goal setting. As might be expected, goal setting has both strengths and weaknesses. A primary benefit of goal setting is improved employee motivation. By clarifying exactly what is expected, by allowing the employee a voice in determining expectations, and by basing rewards on the achievement of those expectations, organizations create a powerful motivational system for their employees.

Communication is also enhanced through the process of discussion and collaboration. And performance appraisals may be done more objectively, with less reliance on arbitrary or subjective assessment. Goal setting focuses attention on appropriate goals and plans, helps identify superior managerial talent for future promotion, and provides a systematic management philosophy that can have a positive effect on the overall organization. Goal setting also facilitates control. The periodic development and subsequent evaluation of individual goals and plans helps keep the organization on course toward its own long-run goals and plans.

On the other hand, goal setting occasionally fails because of poor implementation. Perhaps the major problem that can derail a goal-setting program is lack of top-management support. Some organizations decide to use goal setting, but then its implementation is delegated to lower management. This limits the program's effectiveness because the goals and plans cascading throughout the organization may not actually be the goals and plans of top management and because others in the organization are not motivated to accept and become committed to them. Another problem with goal setting is that some firms overemphasize quantitative goals and plans and burden their systems with too much paperwork and record keeping. Some managers will not or cannot sit down to work out goals and plans with their subordinates. Rather, they "suggest" or even "assign" goals and plans to people. The result is resentment and a lack of commitment to the goal-setting program.[38]

What are the primary barriers to goal setting and planning?

Describe how a goal-setting system such as MBO might be used in a college classroom setting.

CONCEPT CHECK

Summary of Learning Objectives and Key Points

1. Summarize the functions of decision making and the planning process.

   - The planning process is the first basic managerial function that organizations must address.
   - With an understanding of the environmental context, managers develop a number of different types of goals and plans.
   - Decision making is the underlying framework of all planning because every step of the planning process involves a decision.

2. Discuss the purpose of organizational goals, identify different kinds of goals, discuss who sets goals, and describe how to manage multiple goals.

   - Goals serve four basic purposes:
     - provide guidance and direction
     - facilitate planning
     - inspire motivation and commitment
     - promote evaluation and control
   - Goals can be differentiated by level, area, and time frame.
   - All managers within an organization need to be involved in the goal-setting process.
   - Managers need to pay special attention to the importance of managing multiple goals through optimizing and other approaches.

3. Identify different kinds of organizational plans, note the time frames for planning, discuss who plans, and describe contingency planning.

   - The major types of plans are strategic, tactical, and operational.
   - Plans are developed across a variety of time horizons, including long-range, intermediate, and short-range time frames.
   - Essential people in an organization responsible for effective planning are the planning staff, planning task forces, the board of directors, the CEO, the executive committee, and line management.
   - Contingency planning helps managers anticipate and plan for unexpected changes.

4. Discuss how tactical plans are developed and executed.

   - Tactical plans are at the middle of the organization, have an intermediate time horizon, and are of moderate scope.

   - Tactical plans are developed to implement specific parts of a strategic plan.
   - Tactical plans must flow from strategy, specify resource and time issues, and commit human resources.
   - Tactical plans must be effectively executed.

5. Describe the basic types of operational plans used by organizations.

   - Operational plans are at the lower levels of the organization, have a shorter time horizon, and are narrower in scope.
   - Operational plans are derived from a tactical plan and are aimed at achieving one or more operational goals.
   - Two major types of operational plans are single-use and standing plans.
     - Single-use plans are designed to carry out a course of action that is not likely to be repeated in the future. Programs and projects are examples of single-use plans.
     - Standing plans are designed to carry out a course of action that is likely to be repeated several times. Policies, standard operating procedures, and rules and regulations are all standing plans.

6. Identify the major barriers to goal setting and planning, how organizations overcome those barriers, and how to use goals to implement plans.

   - Several barriers exist to effective goal setting and planning:
     - improper reward system
     - dynamic and complex environment
     - reluctance to establish goals
     - resistance to change
     - various constraints
   - Methods for overcoming these barriers include:
     - understanding the purposes of goals and plans
     - communication and participation
     - consistency, revision, and updating
     - an effective reward system
   - One particularly useful technique for managing goal setting and planning is formal goal setting, a process of collaborative goal setting and planning.

Discussion Questions

Questions for Review

1. Describe the nature of organizational goals. Be certain to include both the purposes and the kinds of goals.
2. Describe the scope, responsible personnel, and time frames for each kind of organizational plan. How are plans of different kinds related?
3. Explain the various types of operational plans. Give a real or hypothetical business example for each type. Do not use examples from the text.
4. List the steps in the formal goal-setting process. What are some of the advantages for companies that use this approach? What are some of the problems that may arise from use of this approach?

Questions for Analysis

5. Managers are frequently criticized for focusing too much attention on the achievement of short-term goals. In your opinion, how much attention should be given to long-term versus short-term goals? In the event of a conflict, which should be given priority? Explain your answers.
6. What types of plans and decisions most likely require board of director involvement, and why? What types of decisions and plans are not appropriate for board involvement, and why?
7. Standing plans help make an organization more effective. However, they may inhibit experimentation and organizational learning. Under what conditions, if any, should organizations ignore their own standing plans? In the area of planning, how can an organization balance the need for effectiveness against the need for creativity?

Questions for Application

8. Interview the head of the department in which you are majoring. What kinds of goals exist for the department and for the members of the department? Share your findings with the rest of the class.
9. Tell about a time when an organization was not able to fully achieve all of its goals simultaneously. Why did this occur? Is complete realization of all goals impossible for an organization? Why or why not?
10. From your library or the Internet, find information about a company's mission statement and goals. List its mission and some of its strategic, tactical, and operational goals. Explain the relationship you see among the goals at different levels.

 CengageNow™ Highlights

Now use your CengageNow™ homework to help you:
- Apply management theories in your life
- Assess your management skills
- Master management terms and concepts
- Apply your knowledge to real-world situations
- Analyze and solve challenging management problems

In order to take advantage of these elements, your instructor will need to have set up a course for your class within CengageNow™. Ask your instructor to contact his/her Cengage sales representative and Digital Solutions Manager to explore testing CengageNow™ in your course this term.

CHAPTER

Managing Strategy and Strategic Planning

LEARNING OBJECTIVES

After studying this chapter, you should be able to:

1. Discuss the components of strategy, types of strategic alternatives, and the distinction between strategy formulation and strategy implementation.

2. Describe how to use SWOT (**S**trengths, **W**eaknesses, **O**pportunities, and **T**hreats) analysis in formulating strategy.

3. Identify and describe various alternative approaches to business-level strategy formulation.

4. Describe how business-level strategies are implemented.

5. Identify and describe various alternative approaches to corporate-level strategy formulation.

6. Describe how corporate-level strategies are implemented.

7. Discuss international and global strategies.

MANAGEMENT IN ACTION   The Hype about Hybrids

In the mid-1990s, Japanese carmakers developed a number of small, innovative, affordable cars, including "hybrids" that run on tandem gas-fueled and electric engines. Toyota's Prius, the world's first mass-produced hybrid vehicle, was introduced in Japan in 1997 and in the United States in 2000. It wasn't much fun to drive, but consumers apparently didn't care: It got better mileage, boasted lower emissions, and retained 57 percent of its value after three years. The second-generation Prius hit the U.S. market in 2003. It was faster and more fashionable and even more fuel efficient and produced even lower emissions. U.S. sales topped 25,000 and then doubled in 2004 and again in 2005. In 2006, *Consumer Reports* ranked the Prius with the Chevy Corvette as the country's "Most Satisfying" cars to own, with even more Prius owners than 'Vette owners saying that they'd buy another one (95 to 93 percent).

In 2007, Prius sales went up a staggering 67 percent (to more than 180,000) and, although bound to drop to a more sustainable level, actually continued to go up in early 2008 before falling by the end of the year (to a total just short of 160,000). Interestingly,

"Like it or not, Americans will continue to want variety, including pickups and SUVs."

—IRV MILLER, TOYOTA VP FOR CORPORATE COMMUNICATIONS

however, after selling more than 90,000 vehicles in the first half of the year, Prius dealers sold fewer than 70,000 in the second half. Why the rollercoaster sales figures? The answer is gasoline prices, which had topped $4 per gallon by July but had tumbled to an average of $1.62 by December.*

"At $1.50 a gallon, the American public is not willing to pay for fuel-saving technology," observes one U.S. auto executive, who underscores an interesting point about the economics of hybrid cars: While you pay less for fuel to drive a hybrid car, the sticker price reflects the premium that automakers charge for the vehicle's fuel-efficient technology. A recent comparison of four hybrid vehicles and their non-hybrid counterparts revealed an average difference in price—the hybrid premium—of $4,662 and an average improvement in fuel economy of 10 mpg. Technically, then, you'd be paying a surcharge

Toyota recently previewed the A-BAT, an environmentally friendly pickup truck.

*Prius sales continued to drop off in 2009 and 2010 as gas prices settled below the 2008 annual average of $3.26 per gallon (at $2.34 in 2009 and $2.73 in 2010). In addition, Toyota sales fell overall because of a series of recalls which, between mid-2009 and the end of 2010, involved well over 10 million vehicles.

of $446 per additional mpg for your hybrid vehicle. Obviously, the variables are quite complex, but one reasonable set of calculations estimates that you'd need to drive your hybrid vehicle 15,000 miles a year for 10 years before you started to see any savings.

On the other hand, you'd certainly be doing a service to the environment. After all, when you burn a gallon of gas, you're emitting 20 pounds of carbon dioxide into the atmosphere, and it shouldn't be surprising that environmental organizations have welcomed the appearance of hybrids and alternative-fuel vehicles that consume less fuel and emit fewer pollutants. The most efficient hybrid vehicles increase fuel economy by 40 to 80 percent, and according to Don MacKenzie, Clean Vehicles Engineer for the Union of Concerned Scientists (UCS), such cars as the Toyota Prius and Toyota Camry hybrid "have the potential to help reduce America's dependence on oil, lessen the impact of . . . high gas prices, and address the automobile's impact on climate change." The UCS, a science-based nonprofit environmental group, also cited Toyota as "the only major automaker to consistently improve global-warming performance since 2001, thanks to hybrids and better conventional technology."

In the fall of 2007, however, the UCS accused Toyota of "trying to scuttle strong fuel-economy standards" proposed by Congress. What soured the relationship between the environmental group and the environmentally conscious automaker? At issue were Corporate Average Fuel Economy (CAFE) standards contained in the National Energy and Environmental Security Act of 2007. In its original version, the legislation required U.S. vehicles—including passenger cars, SUVs, pickups, and vans—to attain an average mpg of 35 by the year 2020. A compromise revision of the 2007 standards—"a weak, loophole-ridden alternative," according to the UCS—sought to reduce this requirement, calling for an average mpg of 32 to 35 by 2022. The UCS opposed the revised standards on the grounds that the stricter original standards would cut 140 percent more oil consumption and 240 percent more global-warming pollution. Toyota, however, joined with the Big 3 U.S. automakers—GM, Ford, and Chrysler—in lobbying for the passage of the weaker legislation.

Toyota explained its position in a company blog posted by VP for corporate communications Irv Miller:

> Like other major automakers, Toyota is in the business of offering a full lineup of cars and trucks to meet the needs of American motorists. Its success is the result of listening to customers and offering products they want. . . . Like it or not, Americans will continue to want variety, including pickups and SUVs. Nobody forces cars and trucks on consumers. They vote with their wallets.

"Our passenger-car lineup," added Miller, "has the highest CAFE rating in the industry." The company's critics suggest that its rationale for opposing tougher CAFE standards can be explained by the distinctions that Miller makes among types of vehicles. Toyota sells a lot of passenger cars and a lot of passenger cars with hybrid technology, but history shows that when gas prices get lower, Americans get bigger cars—and not only cars, but SUVs and trucks as well. Since Ford introduced the Escape hybrid in 2004, for example, more hybrid vehicles have been introduced as SUVs than in any other segment. Toyota came out with the hybrid Highlander the next year, but its average mpg is a mere 26—a far cry from the 46 mpg offered by the Prius. In 2008, Toyota unveiled its A-BAT hybrid pickup, which, as one might expect, is even less fuel efficient, at 20 mpg.†

In short, Toyota wants to grow in the American market for larger vehicles—notably, SUVs and pickups—but it's betting that hybrid technology and fuel economy won't be the critical factors in any success to be had in those markets. As long as hybrids constitute a mere one-quarter of 1 percent of all vehicles on U.S. roads, even a successful effort to bring ratings like those of the Highlander and the A-BAT up to tough fuel-efficiency standards isn't likely to pay off in the kind of growth called for in the company's long-term strategy.[1]

Devising successful strategies is a complex task affected by a lot of factors. As our opening story shows, some of those factors—and often the most important—are external to the firm, such as changes in the economic environment in which it operates and in the customer market that it serves. This chapter discusses how organizations manage strategy and strategic planning. We begin by examining the nature of strategic management, including

†The legal wrangling ended in May 2009, when the Obama administration and the auto industry reached an agreement that actually accelerates the original CAFE goals set in 2007. Vehicles sold in the United States, for example, must get an average of 35.5 mpg not by 2020 but by 2016.

its components and alternatives. We then describe the kinds of analysis needed for firms to formulate their strategies. Next we examine how organizations first formulate and then implement business-level strategies, followed by a parallel discussion at the corporate strategy level. We conclude with a discussion of international and global strategies.

The Nature of Strategic Management

A strategy is a comprehensive plan for accomplishing an organization's goals. Strategic management, in turn, is a way of approaching business opportunities and challenges—it is a comprehensive and ongoing management process aimed at formulating and implementing effective strategies. Finally, effective strategies are those that promote a superior alignment between the organization and its environment and the achievement of strategic goals.[2]

The Components of Strategy

In general, a well-conceived strategy addresses three areas: distinctive competence, scope, and resource deployment. A distinctive competence is something the organization does exceptionally well. (We discuss distinctive competencies more fully later.) A distinctive competence of Abercrombie & Fitch is its ability to manage its supply chain more effectively than most firms. It has traditionally tracked consumer preferences daily with point-of-sale computers, electronically transmitting orders to suppliers in Hong Kong, chartering 747s to fly products to the United States, and having products in stores 48 hours later. Because other retailers generally have needed weeks or sometimes months to accomplish the same things, Abercrombie & Fitch has used this distinctive competence to remain competitive.[3] But A&F also continues to innovate. In 2010, Abercrombie & Fitch implemented what it calls Management Dynamics' Supply Chain Visibility to streamline its supply chain process and provide real-time visibility. The system will provide one detailed view of shipments to track, display any in-transit delays, and respond to potential crises across A&F's 30 trading partners and international business units. A&F expects the new system to further decrease cycle time and increase availability through improvements in stores' inventory allocations.[4]

The scope of a strategy specifies the range of markets in which an organization will compete. Hershey Foods has essentially restricted its scope to the confectionery business, with a few related activities in other food-processing areas. In contrast, its biggest competitor, Mars, has adopted a broader scope by competing in the pet food business and the electronics industry, among others. Some organizations, called conglomerates, compete in dozens or even hundreds of markets.

A strategy should also include an outline of the organization's projected resource deployment—how it will distribute its resources across the areas in which it competes. General Electric, for example, uses profits from its U.S. operations to invest in new businesses in Europe and Asia. Alternatively, the firm might have chosen to invest in different industries in its domestic market or to invest more heavily in Latin America. The choices it makes as to where and how much to invest reflect issues of resource deployment.

Types of Strategic Alternatives

Most businesses today also develop strategies at two distinct levels. These levels provide a rich combination of strategic alternatives for organizations. The two general levels are business-level strategies and corporate-level strategies. Business-level strategy is the set of strategic alternatives from which an organization chooses as it conducts business in a particular industry or market. Such alternatives help the organization focus its competitive efforts for each industry or market in a targeted and focused manner.

Corporate-level strategy is the set of strategic alternatives from which an organization chooses as it manages its operations simultaneously across several industries and several markets. As we discuss later, most large companies today compete in a variety of industries and

strategy
A comprehensive plan for accomplishing an organization's goals

strategic management
A comprehensive and ongoing management process aimed at formulating and implementing effective strategies; a way of approaching business opportunities and challenges

effective strategy
A strategy that promotes a superior alignment between the organization and its environment and the achievement of strategic goals

distinctive competence
An organizational strength possessed by only a small number of competing firms

scope
When applied to strategy, it specifies the range of markets in which an organization will compete

resource deployment
How an organization distributes its resources across the areas in which it competes

business-level strategy
The set of strategic alternatives from which an organization chooses as it conducts business in a particular industry or market

corporate-level strategy
The set of strategic alternatives from which an organization chooses as it manages its operations simultaneously across several industries and several markets

markets. Thus, although they develop business-level strategies for each industry or market, they also develop an overall strategy that helps define the mix of industries and markets that are of interest to the firm.

Strategy Formulation and Implementation

Drawing a distinction between strategy formulation and strategy implementation is also instructive. Strategy formulation is the set of processes involved in creating or determining the strategies of the organization, whereas strategy implementation is the methods by which strategies are operationalized or executed within the organization. The primary distinction is along the lines of content versus process: The formulation stage determines what the strategy is, and the implementation stage focuses on how the strategy is achieved.

Sometimes the processes of formulating and implementing strategies are rational, systematic, and planned. This is often referred to as a deliberate strategy—a plan chosen and implemented to support specific goals.[5] Texas Instruments (TI) excels at formulating and implementing deliberate strategies. TI uses a planning process that assigns most senior managers two distinct responsibilities: an operational, short-term responsibility and a strategic, long-term responsibility. Thus, one manager may be responsible for both increasing the efficiency of semiconductor operations over the next year (operational, short term) and investigating new materials for semiconductor manufacturing in the twenty-first century (strategic, long term). TI's objective is to help managers make short-term operational decisions while keeping in mind longer-term goals and objectives.

The *Greening the Business Environment* box on page 184, entitled "You, Too, Can Afford a Place in the Sun," discusses a California company that came up with an innovative deliberative strategy to become a frontrunner in the emergent market for clean energy.

Other times, however, organizations use an emergent strategy—a pattern of action that develops over time in an organization in the absence of mission and goals or despite mission and goals.[6] Implementing emergent strategies involves allocating resources even though an organization has not explicitly chosen its strategies. 3M has at times benefited from emergent strategies. The invention of invisible tape, for instance, provides a good example. Entrepreneurial engineers working independently took the invention to their boss, who concluded that it did not have major market potential because it was not part of an approved research and development plan. Only when the product was evaluated at the highest levels in the organization was it accepted and made part of 3M's product mix. Of course, 3M's Scotch tape became a major success despite the fact that it arose outside of the firm's established practices. 3M now counts on emergent strategies to help expand its numerous businesses.

strategy formulation
The set of processes involved in creating or determining the strategies of the organization; it focuses on the content of strategies

strategy implementation
The methods by which strategies are operationalized or executed within the organization; it focuses on the processes through which strategies are achieved

deliberate strategy
A plan of action that an organization chooses and implements to support specific goals

emergent strategy
A pattern of action that develops over time in an organization in the absence of mission and goals or despite mission and goals

SWOT
An acronym that stands for strengths, weaknesses, opportunities, and threats

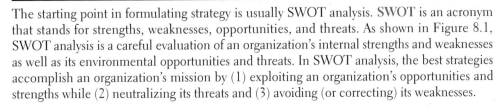

What are the basic components of strategy?

Distinguish between business- and corporate-level strategies. Is one or the other more likely to be deliberate or emergent?

CONCEPT CHECK

Using SWOT Analysis to Formulate Strategy

The starting point in formulating strategy is usually SWOT analysis. SWOT is an acronym that stands for strengths, weaknesses, opportunities, and threats. As shown in Figure 8.1, SWOT analysis is a careful evaluation of an organization's internal strengths and weaknesses as well as its environmental opportunities and threats. In SWOT analysis, the best strategies accomplish an organization's mission by (1) exploiting an organization's opportunities and strengths while (2) neutralizing its threats and (3) avoiding (or correcting) its weaknesses.

GREENING THE BUSINESS ENVIRONMENT

You, Too, Can Afford a Place in the Sun

Josef Becker/iStockphoto.com

Darin Budwig, a registered nurse in Glendale, California, wanted to do the green thing by going solar. Price, however, was a problem: "I wanted to do the right thing for the environment," says Budwig, "but I really had to ask whether it was worth taking on $30,000 in debt." According to Lyndon Rive, CEO of Solar-City, a provider of solar-energy systems located in Foster City, California, the average cost is actually closer to $20,000, but he understands Budwig's reservations. "Even those who really want to make an environmental change," admits Rive, "can't part with $20,000. . . . The solution is just too costly for them."

That's why Rive revamped his business model in order to make solar panels affordable for a much broader range of environmentally conscious consumers. He realized that he could put solar panels on people's roofs in much the same way that automakers put more expensive vehicles in their garages: by leasing them rather than selling them outright. So instead of borrowing $20,000, Darin Budwig only had to put $1,000 down and agree to lease a SolarCity system for 15 years. At a cost of $73 a month, Budwig figured to save about $95 a month and recoup his $1,000 in less than a year. Too good to be true? "We hear that a lot," says Rive. "But we do save you money, and it doesn't cost you a cent to go solar." With leasing, he adds, "we can essentially make it so that everybody can now afford clean power."

At the same time, however, Rive understands that price isn't the only consideration for potential customers like Darin Budwig. "Widespread adoption," he admits, "will come if you can take away the complexity and hassle of installing solar."

SolarCity thus made things easier for Budwig by lining up building permits, financing, and tax breaks. The company also streamlined costs by using innovative computer automation to custom-design Budwig's installation, which was based on satellite images of his rooftop. SolarCity even compiled utility-rate data to estimate Budwig's return on his solar investment.

In 2010, the company added another automated service to its innovative product line. With the acquisition of Building Solutions, a firm specializing in software-controlled home energy audits, SolarCity entered the market for home-efficiency upgrades. Company auditors now come into a house armed with duct blowers, infrared cameras, and combustion analyzers to check for leaks and test heaters. The data are then analyzed to determine what can be done at what cost and to calculate the homeowner's best return on his or her upgrade investment. COO Peter Rive (Lyndon's older brother) is especially optimistic about the company's ability to combine panel-installation services with such services as energy audits and building-envelope sealing (sealing leaks in walls, doors, and windows). "As of right now," he points out, "there aren't residential energy-efficiency providers with any serious scale. We're going to be able to bring serious economies of scale" to bear on the costs to both the provider and the customer.

Like Darin Budwig, Google engineer Michael Flaster leased a SolarCity system for his home in Menlo Park, California. He saves $100 a month on his energy bill and expects to save more than $16,000 over the 15 years of his lease. His employers at Google, a longtime supporter of clean-energy innovations, were impressed and, in June 2011, announced a $280 million fund to help SolarCity finance solar installations across the country.

References: Pete Engardio and Adam Aston, "The Next Energy Innovators," *Business-Week*, July 16, 2009, www.businessweek.com on June 14, 2011; "Solar Power for Less Than Your Cable Bill," *Environmental Forum*, April 24, 2008, http://blogs.reuters.com on June 14, 2011; Julie Schmidt, "SolarCity Aims to Make Solar Power More Affordable," *USA Today*, November 10, 2009, www.usatoday.com on June 14, 2011; Eric Wesoff, "SolarCity Adds Energy Efficiency to Solar Finance, Design and Monitoring," *Greentech Media*, October 14, 2010, www.greentechmedia.com on June 14, 2011; David A. Hill, "Solar City Takes Aim at Home Energy Audit Market," *Colorado Energy News*, May 14, 2010, http://coloradoenergynews.com on June 14, 2011; Rick Needham, "Helping Homeowners Harness the Sun," *The Official Google Blog*, June 14, 2011, http://googleblog.blogspot.com on June 14, 2011.

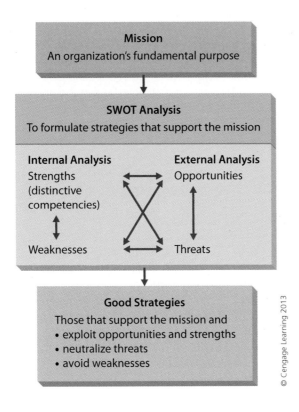

FIGURE 8.1 SWOT ANALYSIS

SWOT analysis is one of the most important steps in formulating strategy. Using the organization's mission as a context, managers assess internal strengths (distinctive competencies) and weaknesses as well as external opportunities and threats. The goal is then to develop good strategies that exploit opportunities and strengths, neutralize threats, and avoid weaknesses.

Evaluating an Organization's Strengths

Organizational strengths are skills and capabilities that enable an organization to conceive of and implement its strategies. Strengths may include such things as a deep pool of managerial talent, surplus capital, a unique reputation and/or brand name, and well-established distribution channels.[7] Sears, for example, has a nationwide network of trained service employees who repair Sears appliances. Jane Thompson, a Sears executive, conceived of a plan to consolidate repair and home improvement services nationwide under the well-known Sears brand name and to promote them as a general repair operation for all appliances, not just those purchased from Sears. Thus the firm capitalized on existing capabilities and the strength of its name to launch a new operation. Different strategies call on different skills and capabilities. For example, Matsushita Electric has demonstrated strengths in manufacturing and selling consumer electronics under the brand name Panasonic. Matsushita's strength in electronics does not ensure success, however, if the firm expands into insurance, swimming pool manufacturing, or retail. Different strategies like these require different organizational strengths. SWOT analysis divides organizational strengths into two categories: common strengths and distinctive competencies.

Common Organizational Strengths A *common strength* is an organizational capability possessed by a large number of competing firms. For example, all the major Hollywood film studios possess common strengths in lighting, sound recording, set and costume design, and makeup. *Competitive parity* exists when large numbers of competing firms are able to implement the same strategy. In this situation, organizations generally attain only average levels of performance. Thus a film company that exploits only its common strengths in choosing and implementing strategies is not likely to go beyond average performance.

Distinctive Competencies A *distinctive competence* is a strength possessed by only a small number of competing firms. Distinctive competencies are rare among a set of competitors. George Lucas's Industrial Light & Magic (ILM), for example, brought the cinematic art of

organizational strength
A skill or capability that enables an organization to conceive of and implement its strategies

common strength
A skill or capability held by numerous competing firms

special effects to new heights. Some of ILM's special effects can be produced by no other organization; these rare special effects are thus ILM's distinctive competencies. Organizations that exploit their distinctive competencies often obtain a *competitive advantage* and attain above-normal economic performance.[8] Indeed, a main purpose of SWOT analysis is to discover an organization's distinctive competencies so that the organization can choose and implement strategies that exploit its unique organizational strengths.

Imitation of Distinctive Competencies An organization that possesses distinctive competencies and exploits them in the strategies it chooses can expect to obtain a competitive advantage and above-normal economic performance. However, its success will lead other organizations to duplicate these advantages. Strategic imitation is the practice of duplicating another firm's distinctive competence and thereby implementing a valuable strategy. Although some distinctive competencies can be imitated, others cannot be. When a distinctive competence cannot be imitated, strategies that exploit these competencies generate sustained competitive advantage. A sustained competitive advantage is a competitive advantage that exists after all attempts at strategic imitation have ceased.[9]

A distinctive competence might not be imitated for three reasons. First, the acquisition or development of the distinctive competence may depend on unique historical circumstances that other organizations cannot replicate. Caterpillar, for example, obtained a sustained competitive advantage when the U.S. Army granted it a long-term contract during World War II. The army felt obligated to offer this contract because of the acute international construction requirements necessary to meet the army's needs. Caterpillar's current competitors, including Komatsu and John Deere & Company, cannot re-create these circumstances.

Second, a distinctive competence might be difficult to imitate because its nature and character might not be known or understood by competing firms. Procter & Gamble, for example, considers that its sustained competitive advantage is based on its manufacturing practices. Large sections of Procter & Gamble's plants are screened off to keep this information secure. Industrial Light & Magic also refuses to disclose how it creates some of its special effects.

Finally, a distinctive competence can be difficult to imitate if it is based on complex social phenomena, like organizational teamwork or culture. Competing organizations may know, for example, that a firm's success is directly traceable to the teamwork among its managers but, because teamwork is a difficult thing to create, may not be able to imitate this distinctive competence. Southwest Airlines is successful in part because of the unique culture that has existed within the company for decades.

Evaluating an Organization's Weaknesses

Organizational weaknesses are skills and capabilities that do not enable an organization to choose and implement strategies that support its mission. An organization has essentially two ways of addressing weaknesses. First, it may need to make investments to obtain the strengths required to implement strategies that support its mission. Second, it may need to modify its mission so that it can be accomplished with the skills and capabilities that the organization already possesses.

In practice, organizations have a difficult time focusing on weaknesses, in part because organization members are often reluctant to admit that they do not possess all the skills and capabilities needed. Evaluating weaknesses also calls into question the judgment of managers who chose the organization's mission in the first place and who failed to invest in the skills and capabilities needed to accomplish it.

Organizations that fail either to recognize or to overcome their weaknesses are likely to suffer from competitive disadvantages. An organization has a competitive disadvantage when it is not implementing valuable strategies that are being implemented by competing organizations. Organizations with a competitive disadvantage can expect to attain below-average levels of performance.

strategic imitation
The practice of duplicating another organization's distinctive competence and thereby implementing a valuable strategy

sustained competitive advantage
A competitive advantage that exists after all attempts at strategic imitation have ceased

organizational weaknesses
A skill or capability that does not enable an organization to choose and implement strategies that support its mission

competitive disadvantage
A situation in which an organization is not implementing valuable strategies that are being implemented by competing organizations

Evaluating an Organization's Opportunities and Threats

Whereas evaluating strengths and weaknesses focuses attention on the internal workings of an organization, evaluating opportunities and threats requires analyzing an organization's environment. Organizational opportunities are areas that may generate higher performance. Organizational threats are areas that increase the difficulty of an organization's performing at a high level.

Porter's "five forces" model of the competitive environment, as discussed in Chapter 3, can be used to characterize the extent of opportunity and threat in an organization's environment. Recall that Porter's five forces are level of competitive rivalry, power of suppliers, power of buyers, threat of substitutes, and threat of new entrants. In general, when the level of competitive rivalry, the power of suppliers and buyers, and the threat of substitutes and new entrants are all high, an industry has relatively few opportunities and numerous threats. Firms in these types of industries typically have the potential to achieve only normal economic performance. On the other hand, when the level of rivalry, the power of suppliers and buyers, and the threat of substitutes and new entrants are all low, then an industry has numerous opportunities and relatively few threats. These industries hold the potential for above-normal performance for organizations in them.[10]

What do the letters *S*, *W*, *O*, and *T* represent when conducting a SWOT analysis?

Under what circumstances might a firm find it advantageous to share with others the details of one of its distinctive competencies?

CONCEPT CHECK

Formulating Business-Level Strategies

A number of frameworks have been developed for identifying the major strategic alternatives that organizations should consider when choosing their business-level strategies. Three important classification schemes are Porter's generic strategies, the Miles and Snow typology, and strategies based on the product life cycle.

Porter's Generic Strategies

According to Michael Porter, organizations may pursue a differentiation, overall cost leadership, or focus strategy at the business level.[11] Table 8.1 summarizes each of these strategies. An organization that pursues a differentiation strategy seeks to distinguish itself from competitors through the quality (broadly defined) of its products or services. Firms that successfully implement a differentiation strategy are able to charge more than competitors because customers are willing to pay more to obtain the extra value they perceive.[12] Rolex pursues a differentiation strategy. Rolex watches are handmade of precious metals like gold or platinum and stainless steel, and they are subjected to strenuous tests of quality and reliability. The firm's reputation enables it to charge thousands of dollars for its watches. Coca-Cola and Pepsi compete in the market for bottled water on the basis of differentiation. Coke touts its Dasani brand on the basis of its fresh taste, whereas Pepsi promotes its Aquafina brand on the basis of its purity.[13] Other firms that use differentiation strategies are Lexus, Godiva, Nikon, Mont Blanc, and Ralph Lauren. During the economic meltdown in 2009, most youth-oriented retailers like American Eagle Outfitters, Quicksilver, and Aeropostale slashed prices in order to generate sales. But Abercrombie & Fitch decided to hold firm to standard pricing in an attempt to maintain a differentiated image for its products.[14] Similarly, other firms tried to provide strong differentiation on the basis of outstanding customer service.[15]

organizational opportunity An area in the environment that, if exploited, may generate higher performance

organizational threat An area in the environment that increases the difficulty of an organization's achieving high performance

differentiation strategy A strategy in which an organization seeks to distinguish itself from competitors through the quality of its products or services

TABLE 8.1 PORTER'S GENERIC STRATEGIES

Michael Porter has proposed three generic strategies. Each of these strategies—differentiation, overall cost leadership, and focus—is presumed to be widely applicable to many different competitive situations.

Strategy Type	Definition	Examples
Differentiation	Distinguish products or services	Rolex (watches) Godiva (chocolate) Mercedes-Benz (automobiles) Nikon (cameras) Cross (writing instruments)
Overall cost leadership	Reduce manufacturing and other costs	Timex (watches) Hershey (chocolate) Kia (automobiles) Kodak (cameras) BIC (writing instruments)
Focus	Concentrate on specific regional market, product market, or group of buyers	Tag Heuer (watches) Vosges (chocolate) Fiat, Alfa Romeo (automobiles) Hasselblad (cameras) Waterman (writing instruments)

overall cost leadership strategy
A strategy in which an organization attempts to gain a competitive advantage by reducing its costs below the costs of competing firms

focus strategy
A strategy in which an organization concentrates on a specific regional market, product line, or group of buyers

An organization implementing an overall cost leadership strategy attempts to gain a competitive advantage by reducing its costs below the costs of competing firms. By keeping costs low, the organization is able to sell its products at low prices and still make a profit. Timex uses an overall cost leadership strategy. For decades, this firm has specialized in manufacturing relatively simple, low-cost watches for the mass market. The price of Timex watches, starting around $39.95, is low because of the company's efficient high-volume manufacturing capacity. Poland Springs and Crystal Geyser bottled waters are also promoted on the basis of their low cost. Other firms that implement overall cost leadership strategies are Hyundai, BIC, Old Navy, and Hershey. When the economic recession hit in 2009, Hershey experienced a jump in sales—during hard times consumers started cutting back on high-end chocolate products from Godiva but weren't willing to forgo chocolate altogether.[16] Likewise, other low-cost producers also benefited as consumers avoided higher-priced name-brand products (that is, those with a differentiation strategy) in favor of lower-priced goods. For instance, both Proctor & Gamble and Colgate saw sales of products such as Tide, Pampers, and Colgate toothpaste decline, while sales of lower-priced private-label products jumped.[17]

A firm pursuing a focus strategy concentrates on a specific regional market, product line, or group of buyers. This strategy may have either a differentiation focus, whereby the firm differentiates its products in the focus market, or an overall cost leadership focus, whereby the firm manufactures and sells its products at low cost in the focus market. In the watch industry, Tag Heuer follows a focus differentiation strategy by selling only rugged waterproof watches to active consumers. Fiat follows a focus cost leadership strategy by selling its automobiles only in Italy and in selected regions of Europe; Alfa Romeo uses focus differentiation to sell its high-performance cars in these same markets. Hasselblad makes expensive cameras targeted at professional photographers. Fisher-Price uses focus differentiation to sell electronic calculators with large, brightly colored buttons to the parents of preschoolers; stockbroker Edward Jones focuses on small-town settings. General Mills focuses one part of its new-product development on consumers who eat meals while driving—their watchword is "Can we make it 'one-handed'?" so that drivers can safely eat or drink it. Two investors realized that most Las Vegas casinos were targeting either high-end big spenders or the young hip market. So, they bought the venerable old Tropicana casino, renovated it, and began marketing it to so-called "Middle America"—middle aged or older gamblers who aren't into big-dollar wagering. Their occupancy rates have soared, as have their profits.[18]

The Miles and Snow Typology

A second classification of strategic options was developed by Raymond Miles and Charles Snow.[19] These authors suggested that business-level strategies generally fall into one of four categories: prospector, defender, analyzer, and reactor. Table 8.2 summarizes each of these strategies. Of course, different businesses within the same company might pursue different strategies.

A firm that follows a prospector strategy is a highly innovative firm that is constantly seeking out new markets and new opportunities and is oriented toward growth and risk taking. Over the years, 3M has prided itself on being one of the most innovative major corporations in the world. Employees at 3M are constantly encouraged to develop new products and ideas in a creative and entrepreneurial way. This focus on innovation has led 3M to develop a wide range of new products and markets, including invisible tape and anti-stain fabric treatments. Amazon.com also follows a prospector strategy as it constantly seeks new market opportunities for selling different kinds of products through its websites.[20]

Rather than seeking new growth opportunities and innovation, a company that follows a defender strategy concentrates on protecting its current markets, maintaining stable growth, and serving current customers, generally by lowering its costs and improving the performance of its existing products. With the maturity of the market for writing instruments, BIC has used this approach—it has adopted a less aggressive, less entrepreneurial style of management and has chosen to defend its substantial market share in the industry. It has done this by emphasizing efficient manufacturing and customer satisfaction. Although eBay is expanding into foreign markets, the online auctioneer is still pursuing what amounts to a defender strategy, in that it is keeping its focus primarily on the auction business. Thus, while it is prospecting for new markets, it is defending its core business focus.

A business that uses an analyzer strategy, in which it attempts to maintain its current businesses and to be somewhat innovative in new businesses, combines elements of prospectors and defenders. Most large companies use this approach because they want to both protect their base of operations and create new market opportunities. IBM uses analyzer strategies. DuPont is currently using an analyzer strategy; the firm is relying heavily on its existing chemical and fiber operations to fuel its earnings for the foreseeable future. At the same time, though, DuPont is moving systematically into new business areas such as biotech agriculture and pharmaceuticals. Yahoo! is also using this strategy by keeping its primary focus on its role as an Internet portal while simultaneously seeking to extend that portal into more and more applications.

prospector strategy
A strategy in which the firm encourages creativity and flexibility and is often decentralized

defender strategy
A strategy in which the firm focuses on lowering costs and improving the performance of current products

analyzer strategy
A strategy in which the firm attempts to maintain its current businesses and to be somewhat innovative in new businesses

Strategy Type	Definition	Examples
Prospector	Is innovative and growth oriented, searches for new markets and new growth opportunities, encourages risk taking	Amazon.com 3M Rubbermaid
Defender	Protects current markets, maintains stable growth, serves current customers	BIC eBay Mrs. Fields
Analyzer	Maintains current markets and current customer satisfaction with moderate emphasis on innovation	DuPont IBM Yahoo!
Reactor	No clear strategy, reacts to changes in the environment, drifts with events	International Harvester Joseph Schlitz Brewing Co. Kmart Montgomery Ward

TABLE 8.2 THE MILES AND SNOW TYPOLOGY

The Miles and Snow typology identifies four strategic types of organizations. Three of these—the prospector, the defender, and the analyzer—can all be effective in certain circumstances. The fourth type—the reactor—represents an ineffective approach to strategy.

Finally, a business that follows a **reactor strategy** has no consistent strategic approach; it drifts with environmental events, reacting to but failing to anticipate or influence those events. Not surprisingly, these firms usually do not perform as well as organizations that implement other strategies. Although most organizations would deny using reactor strategies, a firm called International Harvester Company (IH) was clearly a reactor. At a time when IH's market for trucks, construction equipment, and agricultural equipment was booming, the company failed to keep pace with its competitors. By the time a recession cut demand for its products, it was too late for IH to respond, and the company lost millions of dollars. The firm was forced to sell off virtually all of its businesses, except its truck-manufacturing business. IH, now renamed Navistar, moved from being a dominant firm in trucking, agriculture, and construction to a medium-size truck manufacturer because it failed to anticipate changes in its environment. Kmart, Eddie Bauer, and Chrysler have all shown signs of being reactors in recent years.

Strategies Based on the Product Life Cycle

The **product life cycle** is a model that shows how sales volume changes over the life of products. Understanding the four stages in the product life cycle helps managers recognize that strategies need to evolve over time. As Figure 8.2 shows, the cycle begins when a new product or technology is first introduced. In this *introduction stage*, demand may be very high, sometimes outpacing the firm's ability to supply the product. At this stage, managers need to focus their efforts on "getting product out the door" without sacrificing quality. Managing growth by hiring new employees and managing inventories and cash flow are also concerns during this stage.

During the *growth stage*, more firms begin producing the product, and sales continue to grow. Important management issues include ensuring quality and delivery and beginning to differentiate an organization's product from competitors' products. Entry into the industry during the growth stage may threaten an organization's competitive advantage; thus, strategies to slow the entry of competitors are important.

After a period of growth, products enter a third phase. During this *maturity stage*, overall demand growth for a product begins to slow down, and the number of new firms producing the product begins to decline. The number of established firms producing the product may

reactor strategy
A strategy in which a firm has no consistent approach to strategy

product life cycle
A model that portrays how sales volume for products changes over the life of products

FIGURE 8.2 THE PRODUCT LIFE CYCLE

Managers can use the framework of the product life cycle—introduction, growth, maturity, and decline—to plot strategy. For example, management may decide on a differentiation strategy for a product in the introduction stage and a prospector approach for a product in the growth stage. By understanding this cycle and where a particular product falls within it, managers can develop more effective strategies for extending product life.

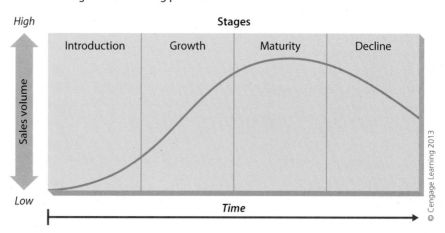

© Cengage Learning 2013

also begin to decline. This period of maturity is essential if an organization is going to survive in the long run. Product differentiation concerns are still important during this stage, but keeping costs low and beginning the search for new products or services are also important strategic considerations.

In the *decline stage*, demand for the product or technology decreases, the number of organizations producing the product drops, and total sales drop. Demand often declines because all those who were interested in purchasing a particular product have already done so. Organizations that fail to anticipate the decline stage in earlier stages of the life cycle may go out of business. Those that differentiate their product, keep their costs low, or develop new products or services may do well during this stage.

Describe Porter's generic strategies and identify an example of each.

Identify examples beyond those noted above for each of the strategies in the Miles and Snow typology.

Implementing Business-Level Strategies

As we noted earlier, after business strategies are formulated, they must then be implemented. To do this effectively, managers must integrate the activities of several different functions. *Marketing* and *sales*, for example, are used to promote products or services and the overall public image of the organization (often through various types of advertising), price products or services, directly contact customers, and make sales. *Accounting* and *finance* control the flow of money both within the organization and from outside sources to the organization, and *manufacturing* creates the organization's products or services.[21] Organizational *culture*, as discussed in Chapter 3, also helps firms implement their strategies.[22]

Implementing Porter's Generic Strategies

Differentiation and cost leadership can each be implemented through these basic organizational functions. (Focus is implemented through the same approaches, depending on which one it is based on.)

Differentiation Strategy In general, to support differentiation, marketing and sales must emphasize the high-quality, high-value image of the organization's products or services. Neiman Marcus, a department store for financially secure consumers, has excelled at using marketing to support its differentiation strategy. People do not go to Neiman Marcus just to buy clothes or to shop for home electronics. Instead, a trip to Neiman Marcus is advertised as a "total shopping experience." Customers who want to shop for $3,000 pet houses, $50,000 mink coats, and $7,000 exercise machines recognize that the store caters to their needs. Other organizations that have used their marketing function to implement a differentiation strategy include Chanel, Calvin Klein, and Bloomingdale's.

The function of accounting and finance in a business that is implementing a differentiation strategy is to control the flow of funds without discouraging the creativity needed to constantly develop new products and services to meet customer needs. If keeping track of and controlling the flow of money become more important than determining how money and resources are best spent to meet customer needs, then no organization, whether high-tech firm or fashion designer, will be able to implement a differentiation strategy effectively. In manufacturing, a firm implementing a differentiation strategy

Mark Peterson/CORBIS

Neiman Marcus uses a differentiation strategy. The retailer offers upscale products combined with superior customer service, and is able to charge premium prices as a result. This shopper, for instance, is being assisted with a new jacket by a designer at the Neiman-Marcus store in Atlanta.

must emphasize quality and meeting specific customer needs, rather than simply reducing costs. Manufacturing may sometimes have to keep inventory on hand so that customers will have access to products when they want them. Manufacturing also may have to engage in costly customization to meet customer needs.

The culture of a firm implementing a differentiation strategy, like the firm's other functions, must also emphasize creativity, innovation, and response to customer needs. Lands' End's culture puts the needs of customers ahead of all other considerations. This firm, which sells men's and women's leisure clothing through a catalog service, offers a complete guarantee on merchandise. Dissatisfied customers may return clothes for a full refund or exchange, with no questions asked. Lands' End takes orders 24 hours a day and will ship most orders within 24 hours. Items with lost buttons and broken zippers are replaced immediately. The priority given to customer needs is typical of an organization that is successfully implementing a differentiation strategy.

Overall Cost Leadership Strategy To support cost leadership, marketing and sales are likely to focus on simple product attributes and how these product attributes meet customer needs in a low-cost and effective manner. These organizations are very likely to engage in advertising. Throughout this effort, however, emphasis is on the value that an organization's products provide for the price, rather than on the special features of the product or service. Advertising for BIC pens ("Writes first time, every time"), Timex watches ("Takes a licking and keeps on ticking"), and Walmart stores ("Always the low price brands you trust—always") helps these firms implement cost leadership strategies.

Proper emphasis in accounting and finance is also pivotal. Because the success of the organization depends on having costs lower than the competitors, management must take care to reduce costs wherever possible. Tight financial and accounting controls at Walmart, Costco, and Wells Fargo have helped these organizations implement cost leadership strategies. Manufacturing typically helps, with large runs of highly standardized products. Products are designed both to meet customer needs and to be easily manufactured.

Manufacturing emphasizes increased volume of production to reduce the per-unit costs of manufacturing. Organizations such as Toshiba (a Japanese semiconductor firm) and Texas Instruments have used this type of manufacturing to implement cost leadership strategies.

The culture of organizations implementing cost leadership strategies tends to focus on improving the efficiency of manufacturing, sales, and other business functions. Managers in these organizations are almost fanatical about keeping their costs low. Walmart appeals to its customers to leave shopping carts in designated areas in its parking lots with signs that read, "Please—help us keep *your* costs low." Fujitsu Electronics, in its Tokyo manufacturing facilities, operates in plain, unpainted, cinderblock and cement facilities to keep its costs as low as possible. Family Dollar, a thriving low-cost retailer, concentrates on second- and third-tier brands, which cost less but have higher profit margins than do first-tier brands (Gain detergent rather than Tide, for example) and locates its stores in low-rent strip centers in unglamorous locations.[24]

" . . . in the absence of sufficient product differentiation or innovation, it's harder to create consumer value and shareholder value."

—A. G. LAFLEY,
FORMER CEO OF PROCTER & GAMBLE[23]

Implementing Miles and Snow's Strategies

Similarly, a variety of issues must be considered when implementing any of Miles and Snow's strategic options. (Of course, no organization would purposefully choose to implement a reactor strategy.)

Prospector Strategy An organization implementing a prospector strategy is innovative, seeks new market opportunities, and takes numerous risks. To implement this strategy, organizations need to encourage creativity and flexibility.[25] Creativity helps an organization perceive, or even create, new opportunities in its environment; flexibility enables it to change quickly to take advantage of these new opportunities. Organizations often increase creativity and flexibility by adopting a decentralized organization structure. (An organization is decentralized when major decision-making responsibility is delegated to middle- and lower-level managers.) Johnson & Johnson links decentralization with a prospector strategy. Each of the firm's different businesses is organized into a separate unit, and the managers of these units hold full decision-making responsibility and authority. Often these businesses develop new products for new markets. As the new products develop and sales grow, Johnson & Johnson reorganizes so that each new product is managed in a separate unit.

Defender Strategy An organization implementing a defender strategy attempts to protect its market from new competitors. It tends to downplay creativity and innovation in bringing out new products or services and to focus its efforts instead on lowering costs or improving the performance of current products. Often a firm implementing a prospector strategy will switch to a defender strategy. This happens when the firm successfully creates a new market or business and then attempts to protect its market from competition. A good example is Mrs. Fields. One of the first firms to introduce high-quality, high-priced cookies, Mrs. Fields sold its product in special cookie stores and grew very rapidly. This success, however, encouraged numerous other companies to enter the market. Increased competition, plus reduced demand for high-priced cookies, threatened Mrs. Fields's market position and eventually forced the firm to scale back its operations and defend its current market share rather than seeking additional growth.

Analyzer Strategy An organization implementing an analyzer strategy attempts to maintain its current business and to be somewhat innovative in new businesses. Because the analyzer strategy falls somewhere between the prospector strategy (with focus on innovation) and the defender strategy (with focus on maintaining and improving current businesses), the attributes of organizations implementing the analyzer strategy tend to be similar to both of these other types of organizations. They have tight accounting and financial controls as well as high flexibility, efficient production as well as customized products, and creativity along with low costs. Organizations maintain these multiple and contradictory processes with difficulty.

Starbucks is implementing an analyzer strategy. Although the firm is growing rapidly, its fundamental business is still coffee. At the same time, however, the firm is cautiously branching out into music and ice cream and other food products, and is experimenting with restaurants with more comprehensive menu selections. This approach is allowing Starbucks to remain focused on its core coffee business but to explore new business opportunities at the same time. Similarly, Procter & Gamble has also revised some of its business strategies in an attempt to both protect its core businesses and also expand into new ones.[26]

Identify common implementation issues for Porter's generic strategies and Miles and Snow's strategies.

CONCEPT CHECK

What role might organization culture play in implementing business-level strategies?

Formulating Corporate-Level Strategies

Most large organizations are engaged in several businesses, industries, and markets. Each business or set of businesses within such an organization is frequently referred to as a *strategic business unit*, or *SBU*. An organization such as General Electric operates hundreds of different businesses, making and selling products as diverse as jet engines, nuclear power plants, and light bulbs. GE organizes these businesses into approximately 20 SBUs. Even organizations that sell only one product may operate in several distinct markets.

Decisions about which businesses, industries, and markets an organization will enter, and how to manage these different businesses, are based on an organization's corporate strategy. The most important strategic issue at the corporate level concerns the extent and nature of organizational diversification. Diversification describes the number of different businesses that an organization is engaged in and the extent to which these businesses are related to one another. There are three types of diversification strategies: single-product strategy, related diversification, and unrelated diversification.[27]

Single-Product Strategy

An organization that pursues a single-product strategy manufactures just one product or service; this product is also often sold in a single market. The WD-40 Company, for example, basically manufactures one product, WD-40 spray lubricant, and for years sold it just in North America. WD-40 has started selling its lubricant in Europe and Asia, but it continues to center all manufacturing, sales, and marketing efforts on one product.

The single-product strategy has one major strength and one major weakness. By concentrating its efforts so completely on one product and market, a firm is likely to be very successful in manufacturing and marketing the product. Because it has staked its survival on a single product, the organization works very hard to make sure that the product is a success. Of course, if the product is not accepted by the market or is replaced by a new one, the firm will suffer. This happened to slide-rule manufacturers when electronic calculators became widely available and to companies that manufactured only black-and-white televisions when low-priced color televisions were first mass-marketed. Similarly, Wrigley long practiced what amounted to a single-product strategy with its line of chewing gums. But, because younger consumers are buying less gum than earlier generations, Wrigley experienced declining revenues and lower profits. As a result, the Wrigley family eventually sold their business to Mars.[28]

Related Diversification

diversification
The number of different businesses that an organization is engaged in and the extent to which these businesses are related to one another

single-product strategy
A strategy in which an organization manufactures just one product or service and sells it in a single geographic market

related diversification
A strategy in which an organization operates in several businesses that are somehow linked with one another

Given the disadvantage of the single-product strategy, most large businesses today operate in several different businesses, industries, or markets.[29] If the businesses are somehow linked, that organization is implementing a strategy of related diversification. Virtually all larger businesses in the United States practice related diversification.

Bases of Relatedness Organizations link their different businesses, industries, or markets in different ways. Table 8.3 gives some typical bases of relatedness. In companies such as Philips, a European consumer electronics company, a similar type of electronics technology underlies all the businesses. A common technology in aircraft design links Boeing's commercial and military aircraft divisions, and a common computer design technology links Dell's various computer products and peripherals.

Organizations such as Philip Morris, Kraft Foods, and Procter & Gamble operate multiple businesses related by a common distribution network (grocery stores) and common marketing skills (advertising). Disney and Universal rely on strong brand names and reputations to link their diverse businesses, which include movie studios and theme parks. Pharmaceutical firms such as Merck sell numerous products to a single set of customers: hospitals,

TABLE 8.3 BASES OF RELATEDNESS IN IMPLEMENTING RELATED DIVERSIFICATION

Firms that implement related diversification can do so using any number of bases of relatedness. Four frequently used bases of related uses for diversification are similar technology, common distribution and marketing skills, common brand name and reputation, and common customers.

Basis of Relatedness	Examples
Similar technology	Philips, Boeing, Westinghouse
Common distribution and marketing skills	Kraft Foods, Philip Morris, Procter & Gamble
Common brand name and reputation	Disney, Universal
Common customers	Merck, IBM, AMF-Head

© Cengage Learning 2013

doctors, patients, and drugstores. Similarly, AMF-Head sells snow skis, tennis rackets, and sportswear to active, athletic customers.

Advantages of Related Diversification Pursuing a strategy of related diversification has three primary advantages. First, it reduces an organization's dependence on any one of its business activities and thus reduces economic risk. Even if one or two of a firm's businesses lose money, the organization as a whole may still survive because the healthy businesses will generate enough cash to support the others.[30] At Disney, a decline in theme park attendance may be offset by an increase in box office and DVD sales for Disney movies.

Second, by managing several businesses at the same time, an organization can reduce the overhead costs associated with managing any one business. In other words, if the normal administrative costs required to operate any business, such as legal services and accounting, can be spread over a large number of businesses, then the overhead costs *per business* will be lower than they would be if each business had to absorb all costs itself. Thus the overhead costs of businesses in a firm that pursues related diversification are usually lower than those of similar businesses that are not part of a larger corporation.[31]

Third, related diversification allows an organization to exploit its strengths and capabilities in more than one business. When organizations do this successfully, they capitalize on synergies, which are complementary effects that exist among their businesses. *Synergy* exists among a set of businesses when the businesses' economic value together is greater than their economic value separately. McDonald's is using synergy as it diversifies into other restaurant and food businesses. For example, its McCafe premium coffee stands in some McDonald's restaurants allows the firm to create new revenue opportunities while using the firm's existing strengths in food-product purchasing and distribution. Similarly, Starbucks is experimenting with an evening menu featuring wine and cheese in a select number of stores.

Unrelated Diversification

Firms that implement a strategy of unrelated diversification operate multiple businesses that are not logically associated with one another. At one time, for example, Quaker Oats owned clothing chains, toy companies, and a restaurant business. Unrelated diversification was a very popular strategy in the 1970s. During that time, several conglomerates like ITT and Transamerica grew by acquiring literally hundreds of other organizations and then running these numerous businesses as independent entities. Even if there are important potential synergies among their different businesses, organizations implementing a strategy of unrelated diversification do not attempt to exploit them.

unrelated diversification
A strategy in which an organization operates multiple businesses that are not logically associated with one another

In theory, unrelated diversification has two advantages. First, a business that uses this strategy should have stable performance over time. During any given period, if some businesses owned by the organization are in a cycle of decline, others may be in a cycle of growth. Unrelated diversification is also thought to have resource allocation advantages. Every year, when a corporation allocates capital, people, and other resources among its various businesses, it must evaluate information about the future of those businesses so that it can place its resources where they have the highest potential for return. Given that it owns the businesses in question and thus has full access to information about the future of those businesses, a firm implementing unrelated diversification should be able to allocate capital to maximize corporate performance.

Despite these presumed advantages, research suggests that unrelated diversification usually does not lead to high performance. First, corporate-level managers in such a company usually do not know enough about the unrelated businesses to provide helpful strategic guidance or to allocate capital appropriately. To make strategic decisions, managers must have complete and subtle understanding of a business and its environment. Because corporate managers often have difficulty fully evaluating the economic importance of investments for all the businesses under their wing, they tend to concentrate only on a business's current performance. This narrow attention at the expense of broader planning eventually hobbles the entire organization. Many of International Harvester's problems noted earlier grew from an emphasis on current performance at the expense of investments for the future success of the firm.

Second, because organizations that implement unrelated diversification fail to exploit important synergies, they are at a competitive disadvantage compared to organizations that use related diversification. Universal Studios has been at a competitive disadvantage relative to Disney because its theme parks, movie studios, and licensing divisions are less integrated and therefore achieve less synergy.

> "[Sara Lee] took a brand with pedigree and stretched it until it had no meaning at all."
>
> —PAM MURTAUGH, BRANDING CONSULTANT[32]

For these reasons, almost all organizations have abandoned unrelated diversification as a corporate-level strategy. Transamerica sold off numerous businesses and now concentrates on a core set of related businesses and markets. Large corporations that have not concentrated on a core set of businesses have eventually been acquired by other companies and then broken up. Research suggests that these organizations are actually worth more when broken up into smaller pieces than when joined.[33]

Distinguish between related and unrelated diversification.

The discussion above cites research that suggests that unrelated diversification is not likely to be a successful corporate strategy. If this is so, explain why General Electric remains so successful.

CONCEPT CHECK

Implementing Corporate-Level Strategies

In implementing a diversification strategy, organizations face two important questions. First, how will the organization move from a single-product strategy to some form of diversification? Second, once the organization diversifies, how will it manage diversification effectively?

Becoming a Diversified Firm

Most organizations do not start out completely diversified. Rather, they begin operations in a single business, pursuing a particular business-level strategy. Success in this strategy then creates resources and strengths that the organization can use in related businesses.[34]

Development of New Products Some firms diversify by developing their own new products and services within the boundaries of their traditional business operations. Honda followed this path to diversification. Relying on its traditional strength in the motorcycle market, over the years Honda learned how to make fuel-efficient, highly reliable small engines. Honda began to apply its strengths in a new business: manufacturing small, fuel-efficient cars for the Japanese domestic market. These vehicles were first sold in the United States in the late 1960s. Honda's success in the U.S. market led the company to increase the size and improve the performance of its cars. Over the years, Honda has introduced automobiles of increasing quality, culminating in the Acura line of luxury cars. While diversifying into the market for automobiles, Honda also applied its engine-building strengths to produce a line of all-terrain vehicles, portable electric generators, and lawn mowers. In each case, Honda was able to parlay its strengths and resources into successful new businesses.

Replacement of Suppliers and Customers
Firms can also become diversified by replacing their former suppliers and customers. A company that stops buying supplies (either manufactured goods or raw materials) from other companies and begins to provide its own supplies has diversified through backward vertical integration. Campbell Soup once bought soup cans from several different manufacturers but later began manufacturing its own cans. In fact, Campbell is currently one of the largest can-manufacturing companies in the world, although almost all the cans it makes are used in its own soup operations.

Campbell's Soup used to buy cans from other companies. But now the soup giant manufactures its own cans. This practice is a form of backward vertical integration.

An organization that stops selling to one customer and sells instead to that customer's customers has diversified through forward vertical integration. G.H. Bass used forward vertical integration to diversify its operations. Bass once sold its shoes and other products only to retail outlets. More recently, however, Bass opened numerous factory outlet stores, which now sell products directly to consumers. Nevertheless, Bass has not abandoned its former customers, retail outlets. Many firms are also employing forward vertical integration today, as they use the Internet to market their products and services directly to consumers.

Mergers and Acquisitions Another common way for businesses to diversify is through mergers and acquisitions—that is, through purchasing another organization. Such a purchase is called a merger when the two organizations being combined are approximately the same size. In 2011 United and Continental airlines merged to create a new airline. The firm will keep United's name but Continental's logo and livery. An acquisition, in contrast, occurs when one of the organizations involved is larger than the other. In most cases, the acquired firm's "identity" disappears altogether. When Delta bought Northwest airlines, Northwest was simply folded into Delta. Organizations engage in mergers and acquisitions to diversify through vertical integration by acquiring former suppliers or former customers. Mergers and acquisitions are also becoming more common in other countries, such as Germany and China.[35]

Most organizations use mergers and acquisitions to acquire complementary products or complementary services, which are products or services linked by a common technology and common customers. The objective of most mergers and acquisitions is the creation or exploitation of synergies.[36] Synergy can reduce the combined organizations' costs

backward vertical integration
An organization's beginning the business activities formerly conducted by its suppliers

forward vertical integration
An organization's beginning the business activities formerly conducted by its customers

merger
The purchase of one firm by another firm of approximately the same size

acquisition
The purchase of a firm by a firm that is considerably larger

"Our focus is on long-term, sustainable growth. Acquisitions and divestitures have always been a part of that strategy and will continue to be in the future."

—A. G. LAFLEY,
FORMER PROCTOR & GAMBLE CEO[37]

of doing business; it can increase revenues; and it may open the way to entirely new businesses for the organization to enter. For example, Procter & Gamble made a decision to launch a nationwide chain of car washes under the widely recognized brand name of Mr. Clean, one of its leading brands of cleaning products. To jump-start the Mr. Clean Car Wash venture, the firm acquired the assets of Atlanta-based Carnett's Car Wash and its 14 locations.[38]

Managing Diversification

However an organization implements diversification—whether through internal development, vertical integration, or mergers and acquisitions—it must monitor and manage its strategy. The two major tools for managing diversification are (1) organization structure and (2) portfolio management techniques. How organization structure can be used to manage a diversification strategy is discussed in detail in Chapter 15.[39] **Portfolio management techniques** are methods that diversified organizations use to determine which businesses to engage in and how to manage these businesses to maximize corporate performance. Two important portfolio management techniques are the BCG matrix and the GE Business Screen.

BCG Matrix The **BCG** (for Boston Consulting Group) **matrix** provides a framework for evaluating the relative performance of businesses in which a diversified organization operates. It also prescribes the preferred distribution of cash and other resources among these businesses.[40] The BCG matrix uses two factors to evaluate an organization's set of businesses: the growth rate of a particular market and the organization's share of that market. The matrix suggests that fast-growing markets in which an organization has the highest market share are more attractive business opportunities than slow-growing markets in which an organization has a small market share. Dividing market growth and market share into two categories (low and high) creates the simple matrix shown in Figure 8.3.

FIGURE 8.3 THE BCG MATRIX

The BCG matrix helps managers develop a better understanding of how different strategic business units contribute to the overall organization. By assessing each SBU on the basis of its market growth rate and relative market share, managers can make decisions about whether to commit further financial resources to the SBU or to sell or liquidate it.

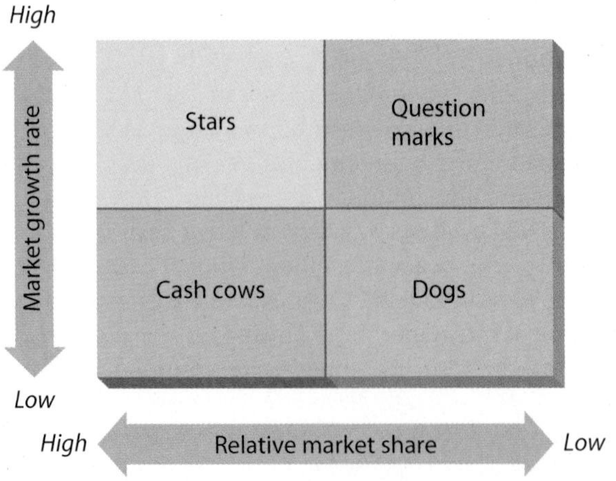

portfolio management technique
A method of determining which businesses to engage in and how to manage these businesses to maximize corporate performance

BCG matrix
A method of evaluating businesses relative to the growth rate of their market and the organization's share of the market

Source: Adapted from the BCG Portfolio Matrix from the "Product Portfolio Matrix," © 1970, The Boston Consulting Group.

The matrix classifies the types of businesses in which a diversified organization can engage as dogs, cash cows, question marks, and stars. *Dogs* are businesses that have a very small share of a market that is not expected to grow. Because these businesses do not hold much economic promise, the BCG matrix suggests that organizations either should not invest in them or should consider selling them as soon as possible. *Cash cows* are businesses that have a large share of a market that is not expected to grow substantially. These businesses characteristically generate high profits that the organization should use to support question marks and stars. (Cash cows are "milked" for cash to support businesses in markets that have greater growth potential.) *Question marks* are businesses that have only a small share of a quickly growing market. The future performance of these businesses is uncertain. A question mark that is able to capture increasing amounts of this growing market may be very profitable. On the other hand, a question mark unable to keep up with market growth is likely to have low profits. The BCG matrix suggests that organizations should invest carefully in question marks. If their performance does not live up to expectations, question marks should be reclassified as dogs and divested. *Stars* are businesses that have the largest share of a rapidly growing market. Cash generated by cash cows should be invested in stars to ensure their preeminent position. For example, BMW bought Rover a few years ago, thinking that its products would help the German automaker reach new consumers. But the company was not able to capitalize on this opportunity, so it ended up selling Rover's car business to a British firm and Land Rover to Ford. Ford couldn't get leverage out of Rover either and ended up selling it (along with Jaguar) to India's up-and-coming Tata Motors.

More recently, Yum Brands has also made significant decisions based on the BCG matrix approach. For several years Yum owned and operated five restaurant chains—KFC, Pizza Hut, Taco Bell, A&W, and Long John Silver's. As the U.S. fast food market has approached saturation Yum managers started to expand aggressively into foreign markets. The firm's three flagship brands, KFC, Pizza Hut, and Taco Bell, had been successfully launched in numerous foreign markets. Overseas profits now account for around 65 percent of Yum's total profits. But A&W and Long John Silver's have few foreign outlets and little potential for overseas growth. So, in 2011 Yum announced it would sell those two businesses in order to more effectively concentrate on the other three.[41]

GE Business Screen Because the BCG matrix is relatively narrow and overly simplistic, General Electric (GE) developed the **GE Business Screen**, a more sophisticated approach to managing diversified business units. The Business Screen is a portfolio management technique that can also be represented in the form of a matrix. Rather than focusing solely on market growth and market share, however, the GE Business Screen considers industry attractiveness and competitive position. These two factors are divided into three categories each, to make the nine-cell matrix shown in Figure 8.4.[42] These cells, in turn, classify business units as winners, losers, question marks, average businesses, or profit producers.

As Figure 8.4 shows, both market growth and market share appear in a broad list of factors that determine the overall attractiveness of an industry and the overall quality of a firm's competitive position. Other determinants of an industry's attractiveness (in addition to market growth) include market size, capital requirements, and competitive intensity. In general, the greater the market growth, the larger the market, the smaller the capital requirements, and the less the competitive intensity, the more attractive an industry will be. Other determinants of an organization's competitive position in an industry (besides market share) include technological know-how, product quality, service network, price competitiveness, and operating costs. In general, businesses with large market share, technological know-how, high product quality, a quality service network, competitive prices, and low operating costs are in a favorable competitive position.

Think of the GE Business Screen as a way of applying SWOT analysis to the implementation and management of a diversification strategy. The determinants of industry attractiveness are similar to the environmental opportunities and threats in SWOT analysis, and the determinants of competitive position are similar to organizational strengths and weaknesses.

GE Business Screen
A method of evaluating businesses along two dimensions: (1) industry attractiveness and (2) competitive position; in general, the more attractive the industry and the more competitive the position, the more an organization should invest in a business

FIGURE 8.4 THE GE BUSINESS SCREEN

The GE Business Screen is a more sophisticated approach to portfolio management than the BCG matrix. As shown here, several factors combine to determine a business's competitive position and the attractiveness of its industry. These two dimensions, in turn, can be used to classify businesses as winners, question marks, average businesses, losers, or profit producers. Such a classification enables managers to allocate the organization's resources more effectively across various business opportunities.

	Good	Medium	Poor
High	Winner	Winner	Question mark
Medium	Winner	Average business	Loser
Low	Profit producer	Loser	Loser

(Vertical axis: Industry attractiveness — High, Medium, Low)

(Horizontal axis: Competitive position — Good, Medium, Poor)

Competitive position
1. Market share
2. Technological know-how
3. Product quality
4. Service network
5. Price competitiveness
6. Operating costs

Industry attractiveness
1. Market growth
2. Market size
3. Capital requirements
4. Competitive intensity

Source: From *Strategy Formulation: Analytical Concepts*, 1st edition, by Charles W. Hofer and Dan Schendel. Copyright © 1978. Reprinted with permission of South-Western, a division of Thomson Learning: www.thomsonrights.com. Fax 800-730-2215.

By conducting this type of SWOT analysis across several businesses, a diversified organization can decide how to invest its resources to maximize corporate performance. In general, organizations should invest in winners and in question marks (where industry attractiveness and competitive position are both favorable); should maintain the market position of average businesses and profit producers (where industry attractiveness and competitive position are average); and should sell losers. For example, Unilever recently assessed its business portfolio using a similar framework and, as a result, decided to sell off several specialty chemical units that were not contributing to the firm's profitability as much as other businesses. The firm then used the revenues from these divestitures and bought more related businesses such as Ben & Jerry's Homemade and Slim-Fast.[43] During the economic recession that started in 2008, many diversified businesses took an especially aggressive approach to selling or closing underperforming businesses. For instance, Japan's Pioneer electronics business sold its television business, Home Depot shut down its Expo home-design stores, and Textron closed a business unit that financed real estate deals.[44]

Compare and contrast the BCG matrix and the GE Business Screen.

When, if ever, would it make sense for a corporation to retain ownership of a money-losing business with limited opportunities for a turnaround?

CONCEPT CHECK

International and Global Strategies

Strategic management is in many ways a continuing challenge for managers. But an increasingly important and special set of challenges confronting today's managers relates to international and global strategies.

Developing International and Global Strategies

Developing an international strategy is far more complex than developing a domestic one.[45] Managers developing a strategy for a domestic firm must deal with one national government, one currency, one accounting system, one political system, one legal system, and usually a single language and a comparatively homogeneous culture. Conversely, managers responsible for developing a strategy for an international firm must understand and deal with multiple governments, multiple currencies, multiple accounting systems, multiple political systems, multiple legal systems, and a variety of languages and cultures.

Moreover, managers in an international business must also coordinate the implementation of their firm's strategy among business units located in different parts of the world, with different time zones, different cultural contexts, and different economic conditions, as well as monitor and control their performance. Managers usually consider these complexities acceptable trade-offs for the additional opportunities that come with global expansion. Indeed, international businesses have the ability to exploit three sources of competitive advantage unavailable to domestic firms.

Global Efficiencies International firms can improve their efficiency through several means not accessible to a domestic firm. They can capture *location efficiencies* by locating their facilities anywhere in the world that yields them the lowest production or distribution costs or that best improves the quality of service they offer their customers. Production of athletic shoes, for example, is very labor intensive, and Nike, like many of its competitors, centers its manufacturing in countries where labor costs are especially low.[46] Similarly, by building factories to serve more than one country, international firms may also lower their production costs by capturing *economies of scale*. By broadening their product lines in each of the countries they enter, international firms may enjoy *economies of scope*, lowering their production and marketing costs and enhancing their bottom line.

Finally, firms can take action to centralize operations in order to increase control over far-flung activities. The *Ethically Speaking* box on page 202, entitled "The Little-White-Lie Strategy," shows that although such strategies are designed to benefit the broadest range of a firm's stakeholders, they often require managers to walk a thin ethical line when the interests of different stakeholders aren't quite the same.

Multimarket Flexibility As we discussed in earlier chapters, there are wide variations in the political, economic, legal, and cultural environments of countries. Moreover, these environments are constantly changing: New laws are passed, new governments are elected, economic policies are changed, new competitors may enter (or leave) the national market, and so on. International businesses thus face the challenge of responding to these multiple diverse and changing environments. Often firms find it beneficial to empower local managers to respond quickly to such changes. However, unlike domestic firms, which operate in and respond to changes in the context of a single domestic environment, international businesses may also respond to a change in one country by implementing a change in another country. Chicken processor Tyson Foods, for example, has benefited from the increased demand by health-conscious U.S. consumers for chicken breasts. In producing more chicken breasts, Tyson also produced more chicken legs and thighs, which are considered less desirable by U.S. consumers. Tyson capitalized on its surplus by targeting the Russian market, where dark meat is preferred over light, and the Chinese market, where chicken feet are considered a tasty delicacy. Tyson exports over $250 million worth of chicken thighs and legs to Russia and China.[47]

ETHICALLY SPEAKING

The Little-White-Lie Strategy

It may surprise you to learn that The Coca-Cola Company does not make Coca-Cola. Coke and the other beverage brands owned by The Coca-Cola Company are actually manufactured by what the company calls "bottling partners"—more than 300 franchises worldwide that both make and distribute final Coke products to grocery stores, restaurants, and other places where consumers can purchase them. Up until 2010, the largest of these franchises had been Coca-Cola Enterprises (CCE), which held the franchise for most of North America and much of Europe.

According to Coke CEO Muhtar Kent, "the franchise model is the best way to win in the marketplace," and in November 2009 he extolled the Coke franchise system for fostering a "magnificent fusion of scalable, global brands." Three months later, however, Coke announced plans to purchase CCE's North American operations in a "substantially cashless" deal that would make CCE a European-oriented bottler and give Coke 90 percent control of its own bottling operations in North America. The deal was finalized in February 2010.

a11/ZUMA Press/Newscom

Coke admitted that negotiations with CCE had been in the works for about 18 months and that a confidentiality agreement between the two firms had been in effect since November 2008, long before Kent and other Coke executives had gone on record to support the company's franchise-bottling system. Had they been saying one thing in public while doing another behind boardroom doors? "There's no question," says Wall Street analyst Phil Gorham, that the CCE deal "flies in the face of what they've done in the past. This acquisition is absolutely an about-face." Does Gorham believe that Kent and other Coke leaders damaged the company's credibility? "I think so," he says. "I think investors will think twice from now on when they're told something from Coke."

Many corporate-governance experts, however, observe that Kent was not legally obligated to explain the fine distinction between his simultaneous support of Coke's franchise system and his intention to take over its largest franchise. Legally speaking, executives cannot deny outright that they're engaged in negotiations, but they're also barred from mentioning

negotiations in public: Such statements would amount to leaking inside information and might affect stock prices—in which case, investors who lost money when the market reacted to an executive's statement could sue the company.

"Part of this is the artful use of words," suggests Paul Lapides, director of the Corporate Governance Center at Kennesaw State University, who does not feel that Coke CEO Kent was misleading his investors. "Shareholders would really like to know everything that management is thinking about," says Lapides, "but that's just bad business." In this case, for example, hints of an imminent deal could have driven up the price that Coke ultimately paid for CCE. According to John Sicher, a former corporate lawyer who's now editor of *Beverage Digest*, Kent had skillfully walked a thin legal and ethical line. "He couldn't say too little or too much. His 'committed to the franchise system' message was accurate and an appropriate communication."

On the point that Kent saved money for Coke investors, even Gorham tends to agree: "If it involves telling a little white lie for a few months while negotiations are going on," he admits, "that's probably the best way to go about it."

References: Michael J. de la Merced, "Coke Confirms Purchase of a Bottling Unit," *New York Times*, February 26, 2010, www.nytimes.com on March 2, 2011; Jeremiah McWilliams, "Coca-Cola's Mixed Message Draws Critics," *Atlanta Journal-Constitution*, March 13, 2010, www.ajc.com on March 2, 2011; The Coca-Cola Co., "The Coca-Cola Company and Coca-Cola Enterprises Strategically Advance and Strengthen Their Partnership," press release, February 25, 2010, www.thecoca-colacompany.com on March 3, 2011; "Coca-Cola Acquires CCE North America Business, Closes Sale of Norway and Swedish Bottling Operations to CCE," *DBR*, October 2, 2010, http://softdrinks.drinks-business-review.com on March 2, 2011.

Worldwide Learning The diverse operating environments of multinational corporations (MNCs) may also contribute to organizational learning.[48] Differences in these operating environments may cause the firm to operate differently in one country than in another. An astute firm may learn from these differences and transfer this learning to its operations in other countries.[49] For example, McDonald's U.S. managers once believed that its restaurants should be freestanding entities located in suburbs and small towns. A Japanese franchisee convinced McDonald's to allow it to open a restaurant in an inner-city office building. That restaurant's success caused McDonald's executives to rethink their store location criteria. Nontraditional locations—office buildings, Walmart superstores, even airplanes—are now an important source of new growth for the firm.

Unfortunately, it is difficult to exploit these three factors simultaneously. Global efficiencies can be more easily obtained when a single unit of a firm is given worldwide re-

For years engineers at BMW refused to design and install cup holders in the firm's cars. They felt that cup holders were not important and could potentially be dangerous. Only after being presented with overwhelming data supporting the importance of cup holders in purchase decisions did they reluctantly change their minds and start designing cup holders like this one.

sponsibility for the task at hand. BMW's engineering staff at headquarters in Munich, for example, is responsible for the research and design of the company's new automobiles. By focusing its research and development (R&D) efforts at one location, BMW engineers designing new transmissions are better able to coordinate their activities with their counterparts designing new engines. However, centralizing control of its R&D operations also hinders BMW's ability to customize its product to meet the differing needs of customers in different countries. Consider the simple question of whether to include cup holders in its cars. In designing cars to be driven safely at the prevailing high speeds of Germany's autobahn, the company's engineers decided that cup holders were both irrelevant and dangerous. Driving speeds in the United States, however, are much lower, and cup holders are an important comfort feature in autos sold to U.S. consumers. Lengthy battles were fought between BMW's German engineers and its U.S. marketing managers over this seemingly trivial issue. Only after years of debate did cup holders finally become a standard feature in the firm's automobiles sold in North America.

As this example illustrates, if too much power is centralized in one unit of a firm, the unit may ignore the needs of consumers in other markets. Conversely, multimarket flexibility is enhanced when a firm delegates responsibility to the managers of local subsidiaries. Vesting power in local managers allows each subsidiary to tailor its products, personnel policies, marketing techniques, and other business practices to meet the specific needs and wants of potential customers in each market the firm serves. However, this increased flexibility will reduce the firm's ability to obtain global efficiencies in such areas as production, marketing, and R&D.

Furthermore, the unbridled pursuit of global efficiencies or multimarket flexibility may stifle the firm's attempts to promote worldwide learning. Centralizing power in a single unit of the firm to capture global efficiencies may cause the unit to ignore lessons and information acquired by other units of the firm. Moreover, the other units may have little incentive or ability to acquire such information if they know that the "experts" at headquarters will ignore them. Decentralizing power in the hands of local subsidiary managers may create similar problems. A decentralized structure may make it difficult to transfer learning from one subsidiary to another. Local subsidiaries may be disposed

"From the very beginning, we decided we didn't want to export the same vision of beauty around the world. . . . We wanted to offer consumers the choice between very different options."

—JEAN-PAUL AGON,
CEO OF L'OREAL[50]

to automatically reject outside information as not being germane to the local situation. Firms wishing to promote worldwide learning must use an organizational structure that promotes knowledge transfer among its subsidiaries and corporate headquarters. The firms must also create incentive structures that motivate managers at headquarters and in subsidiaries to acquire, disseminate, and act on worldwide learning opportunities.

Consider the success of Nokia, headquartered in Helsinki, Finland, which is among the world's leaders in the cellular telephone and telecommunications industries. Nokia, like other telecommunications equipment manufacturers, was struggling to keep pace with rapid shifts in its worldwide markets. Managers in different regions had little idea what their counterparts in other markets were doing, and Nokia factories were grappling with excess inventories of some products and inventory shortages of others. In some instances, Nokia factories in one country would shut down for lack of a critical part that a Nokia factory in another country had in surplus. In response, the firm's CEO, Jorma Ollila, established what he called "commando teams" to attack these problems. The teams were charged with improving efficiency throughout the firm. Using a new worldwide information system, Nokia managers now monitor global, regional, and local sales and inventory on a real-time basis. This allows them to make internal transfers of parts and finished goods efficiently. More importantly, this approach has allowed Nokia to spot market trends and new product developments that arise in one region of the world and to transfer this knowledge to improve its competitiveness in other areas and product lines.[51]

Strategic Alternatives for International Business

International businesses typically adopt one of four strategic alternatives in their attempt to balance the three goals of global efficiencies, multimarket flexibility, and worldwide learning. The first of these strategic alternatives is the home replication strategy. In this approach, a firm uses the core competency or firm-specific advantage it developed at home as its main competitive weapon in the foreign markets that it enters. In other words, the firm takes what it does exceptionally well in its home market and attempts to duplicate it in foreign markets. Mercedes-Benz's home replication strategy, for example, relies on its well-known brand name and its reputation for building well-engineered, luxurious cars capable of traveling safely at very high speeds. It is this market segment that Mercedes-Benz has chosen to exploit internationally, despite the fact that only a very few countries have both the high income levels and the high speed limits appropriate for its products. But consumers in Asia, the rest of Europe, and the Americas are nevertheless attracted by the car's mystique.

The multidomestic strategy is a second alternative available to international firms. A multidomestic corporation manages itself as a collection of relatively independent operating subsidiaries, each of which focuses on a specific domestic market. In addition, each of these subsidiaries is free to customize its products, its marketing campaigns, and its operating techniques to best meet the needs of its local customers. The multidomestic approach is particularly effective when there are clear differences among national markets; when economies of scale for production, distribution, and marketing are low; and when the cost of coordination between the parent corporation and its various foreign subsidiaries is high. Because each subsidiary must be responsive to the local market, the parent company usually delegates considerable power and authority to managers of its subsidiaries in various host countries. International businesses operating before World War II often adopted this approach because of the difficulties in controlling distant foreign subsidiaries, given the communication and transportation technologies of that time.

home replication strategy
International strategy in which a company uses the core competency or firm-specific advantage it developed at home as its main competitive weapon in the foreign markets that it enters

multidomestic strategy
International strategy in which a company manages itself as a collection of relatively independent operating subsidiaries, each of which focuses on a specific domestic market

The global strategy is the third alternative philosophy available for international firms. A global corporation views the world as a single marketplace and has as its primary goal the creation of standardized goods and services that will address the needs of customers worldwide. The global strategy is almost the exact opposite of the multidomestic strategy. Whereas the multidomestic firm believes that its customers in every country are fundamentally different and must be approached from that perspective, a global corporation assumes that customers are fundamentally the same regardless of nationality. Thus the global corporation views the world market as a single entity as the corporation develops, produces, and sells its products. It tries to capture economies of scale in production and marketing by concentrating its production activities in a handful of highly efficient factories and then creating global advertising and marketing campaigns to sell the goods produced in those factories. Because the global corporation must coordinate its worldwide production and marketing strategies, it usually concentrates power and decision-making responsibility at a central headquarters.

The home replication strategy and the global strategy share an important similarity: Under either approach, a firm conducts business the same way anywhere in the world. There is also an important difference between the two approaches. A firm using the home replication strategy takes its domestic way of doing business and uses that approach in foreign markets as well. In essence, a firm using this strategy believes that if its business practices work in its domestic market, then they should also work in foreign markets. Conversely, the starting point for a firm adopting a global strategy has no such home-country bias. In fact, the concept of a home market is irrelevant because the global firm thinks of its market as a global one, not one divided into domestic and foreign segments. The global firm tries to figure out the best way to serve all of its customers in the global market and then does so.

A fourth approach available to international firms is the transnational strategy. The transnational corporation attempts to combine the benefits of global scale efficiencies, such as those pursued by a global corporation, with the benefits and advantages of local responsiveness, which is the goal of a multidomestic corporation. To do so, the transnational corporation does not automatically centralize or decentralize authority. Rather, it carefully assigns responsibility for various organizational tasks to the unit of the organization best able to achieve the dual goals of efficiency and flexibility.

A transnational corporation may choose to centralize certain management functions and decision making, such as R&D and financial operations, at corporate headquarters. Other management functions, such as human resource management and marketing, may be decentralized, allowing managers of local subsidiaries to customize their business activities to better respond to the local culture and business environment. Microsoft, for example, locates most of its product development efforts in the United States, whereas responsibility for marketing is delegated to its foreign subsidiaries. Often, transnational corporations locate responsibility for one product line in one country and responsibility for a second product line in another country. To achieve an interdependent network of operations, transnational corporations focus considerable attention on integration and coordination among their various subsidiaries.

global strategy
International strategy in which a company views the world as a single marketplace and has as its primary goal the creation of standardized goods and services that will address the needs of customers worldwide

transnational strategy
International strategy in which a company attempts to combine the benefits of global scale efficiencies with the benefits and advantages of local responsiveness

---

What are the basic strategic options available to multinational businesses?

In what ways is international strategic planning most similar to and most different from domestic strategic planning?

CONCEPT CHECK

Summary of Learning Objectives and Key Points

1. Discuss the components of strategy, types of strategic alternatives, and the distinction between strategy formulation and strategy implementation.

   - A strategy is a comprehensive plan for accomplishing the organization's goals.
   - Effective strategies address three organizational issues: distinctive competence, scope, and resource deployment.
   - Most large companies have both business-level and corporate-level strategies.
   - Strategy formulation is the set of processes involved in creating or determining the strategies of an organization.
   - Strategy implementation is the process of executing strategies.

2. Describe how to use SWOT (**S**trengths, **W**eaknesses, **O**pportunities, and **T**hreats) analysis in formulating strategy.

   - SWOT analysis considers an organization's strengths, weaknesses, opportunities, and threats.
   - Using SWOT analysis, an organization chooses strategies that support its mission and
     - exploit its opportunities and strengths
     - neutralize its threats
     - avoid its weaknesses
   - Common strengths cannot be ignored, but distinctive competencies hold the greatest promise for superior performance.

3. Identify and describe various alternative approaches to business-level strategy formulation.

   - A business-level strategy is the plan an organization uses to conduct business in a particular industry or market.
   - Porter suggests that businesses may formulate:
     - a differentiation strategy
     - an overall cost leadership strategy
     - a focus strategy
   - According to Miles and Snow, organizations may choose one of four business-level strategies:
     - prospector
     - defender
     - analyzer
     - reactor
   - Business-level strategies may also take into account the stages in the product life cycle.

4. Describe how business-level strategies are implemented.

   - Strategy implementation at the business level takes place in the areas of marketing, sales, accounting and finance, and manufacturing.
   - Culture also influences strategy implementation.
   - Implementation of Porter's generic strategies requires different emphases in each of these organizational areas.
   - Implementation of Miles and Snow's strategies affects organization structure and practices.

5. Identify and describe various alternative approaches to corporate-level strategy formulation.

   - A corporate-level strategy is the plan an organization uses to manage its operations across several businesses.
   - A firm that does not diversify is implementing a single-product strategy.
   - An organization pursues a strategy of related diversification when it operates a set of businesses that are somehow linked.
   - An organization pursues a strategy of unrelated diversification when it operates a set of businesses that are not logically associated with one another.

6. Describe how corporate-level strategies are implemented.

   - Strategy implementation at the corporate level addresses two issues:
     - how the organization will go about its diversification
     - the way an organization is managed once it has diversified
   - Businesses accomplish this in three ways:
     - developing new products internally
     - replacing suppliers (backward vertical integration) or customers (forward vertical integration)
     - engaging in mergers and acquisitions
   - Organizations manage diversification through the organization structure that they adopt and through portfolio management techniques.
   - The BCG matrix classifies an organization's diversified businesses as dogs, cash cows, question marks, or stars according to market share and market growth rate.
   - The GE Business Screen classifies businesses as winners, losers, question marks, average businesses, or profit producers according to industry attractiveness and competitive position.

7. Discuss international and global strategies.

- Although there are many similarities in developing domestic and international strategies, international firms have three additional sources of competitive advantage unavailable to domestic firms. These are
  - global efficiencies
  - multimarket flexibility
  - worldwide learning

- Firms participating in international business usually adopt one of four strategic alternatives:
  - the home replication strategy
  - the multidomestic strategy
  - the global strategy
  - the transnational strategy
- Each of these strategies has advantages and disadvantages in terms of its ability to help firms be responsive to local circumstances and to achieve the benefits of global efficiencies.

Discussion Questions

Questions for Review

1. Define the four parts of a SWOT analysis.
2. Describe the relationship between a distinctive competency, a competitive advantage, and a sustained competitive advantage.
3. List and describe Porter's generic strategies and the Miles and Snow typology of strategies.
4. What are the characteristics of businesses in each of the four cells of the BCG matrix?

Questions for Analysis

5. Describe the process that an organization follows when using a deliberate strategy. How does this process differ when an organization implements an emergent strategy?
6. Which strategy should a firm develop first—its business-level or its corporate-level strategy? Describe the relationship between a firm's business- and corporate-level strategies.
7. Volkswagen sold its original Beetle automobile in the United States until the 1970s. The original Beetle

was made of inexpensive materials, was built using an efficient mass-production technology, and offered few options. Then, in the 1990s Volkswagen introduced its new Beetle, which has a distinctive style, provides more optional features, and is priced for upscale buyers. What was Volkswagen's strategy with the original Beetle—product differentiation, low cost, or focus? Which strategy did Volkswagen implement with its new Beetle? Explain your answers.

Questions for Application

8. Assume that you are the owner and manager of a small business. Write a strategy for your business. Be sure to include each of the three primary strategic components.
9. Interview a manager and categorize the business- and corporate-level strategies of his or her organization according to Porter's generic strategies, the Miles and Snow typology, and extent of diversification.
10. Give an example of a corporation following a single-product strategy, a related diversification strategy, and an unrelated diversification strategy. What level of performance would you expect from each firm, based on its strategy? Examine the firm's profitability to see whether your expectations were accurate.

CengageNow™ Highlights

Now use your CengageNow™ homework to help you:
- Apply management theories in your life
- Assess your management skills
- Master management terms and concepts
- Apply your knowledge to real-world situations
- Analyze and solve challenging management problems

In order to take advantage of these elements, your instructor will need to have set up a course for your class within CengageNow™. Ask your instructor to contact his/her Cengage sales representative and Digital Solutions Manager to explore testing CengageNow™ in your course this term.

Managing Decision Making and Problem Solving

LEARNING OBJECTIVES

After studying this chapter, you should be able to:

1. Define decision making and discuss types of decisions and decision-making conditions.

2. Discuss rational perspectives on decision making, including the steps in rational decision making.

3. Describe the behavioral aspects of decision making.

4. Discuss group and team decision making, including the advantages and disadvantages of group and team decision making and how it can be more effectively managed.

MANAGEMENT IN ACTION Citi ODs on CDOs

When the closing bell tolled at the New York Stock Exchange on Friday, November 21, 2008, shares of Citigroup closed at $3.77, making the country's largest financial institution worth about $20.5 billion. Two years earlier, Citigroup's stock price had put its value at $244 billion.

It was, to say the least, a significant loss in shareholder value.

Obviously, the reasons behind such a monumental collapse are extremely complex, but in order to see what happened, let's focus on just a few factors—in particular, some miscalculated strategy initiatives and some mismanaged tactical policies.

When Charles O. Prince III took over as Citigroup CEO in October 2003, he targeted the bank's trading operations as a source of increased earnings. Now, one of the specialties of traders in the financial industry was creating *collateralized debt obligations*, or *CDOs*: securities that pool various forms or classes of debt—or fixed-income assets—into bundles for resale to investors. As you might recall from our *Management in Action* features in Chapters 6 and 7, one class of these fixed-income assets is home mortgages: A financial institution like Citi might buy mortgages from original lenders (mostly small banks and non-bank lenders), pool the projected revenue (payments to be made in the future by the original homebuyers), and sell securities backed by the pooled revenue.

> "[Risk management] has to be independent, and it wasn't independent at Citigroup."
>
> —FORMER CITIGROUP EXECUTIVE

In return for the promise to redeem the securities at interest, the bank that issues them takes fees of up to 2.5 percent of the amount of the securities sold.

In the heady days of the housing boom that lasted from about 1995 to mid-2006, there was a lot of money to be made in CDOs, and between 2003 and 2005 Citi tripled the volume of CDOs that it issued. In 2005, its trading operations generated $500 million in fees, and in that year Prince made a concerted effort to produce even more revenue from the group responsible for trading CDOs and similar instruments. He bulked up the unit, recruited key personnel from competitors, and doubled and tripled bonuses for traders. Randall H. Barker, who oversaw the buildup in the department, received $20 million a year in compensation, and Thomas G. Maheras, who headed it, took home $30 million.

CDOs may be profitable, but they can also be tricky. Mortgages became a popular component of CDOs because of the housing boom, but CDOs typically contain several different classes of fixed-income assets—from mortgages and credit-card loans to junk bonds to aircraft leases and movie revenues. Because the risk entailed by

Flawed decision making at Citi has caused the banking giant's market value to plummet.

Financial Center

Dan Moore/iStockphoto

each class of assets may depend on very different factors, overall risk can be quite difficult to determine.

Charles Prince was aware of the risks entailed by investment in fixed-asset securities, but as one former Citigroup executive puts it, "he didn't know a CDO from a grocery list." Like any responsible manager, he thus sought advice, turning to Robert E. Rubin, a onetime Wall Street executive and Secretary of the Treasury in the Clinton administration who had chaired Citi's executive committee since 1999. As Treasury secretary, Rubin had helped relax federal oversight of such exotic financial instruments as CDOs, and according to the same former executive, Rubin "had always been an advocate of being more aggressive in the [trading] arena. He would say, 'You have to take more risk if you want to earn more.' " At the time, the housing market was going strong, and as traders invented newer and more profitable types of fixed-asset securities, the CDO market was still expanding. So Prince and Rubin endorsed a strategy that called for taking greater risks in the interest of expanding business and generating higher profits.

Unfortunately, housing prices started to drop in 2006. Refinancing became more difficult, initial terms on adjustable-rate mortgages (ARMs) were expiring, higher interest rates were taking effect, and before long, 16 percent of all subprime ARMs were delinquent or in foreclosure proceedings. In September 2007, Prince learned that Citi was sitting on $43 billion in mortgage-related assets. As he had for months, Thomas Maheras, head of the trading unit, assured Prince that the bank was not facing big losses. To be on the safe side, however, Prince dispatched a risk-management team to take a closer look at Citi's mortgage-related holdings. What they discovered was that it was too late to be on the safe side. Four months later, Citi announced a fourth-quarter loss of nearly $10 billion.

By the end of 2008, losses would total $65 billion—more than half of which stemmed from the mortgage-related securities for which Maheras had vouched back in September 2007. To say the least, Citi—indeed, the banking industry as a whole—had misjudged the risk that it had been taking in the CDO market. Why

were CDOs so much riskier than most investment managers thought? Because so many of the mortgages that backed them were much riskier than they cared to believe. As JPMorgan CEO Jamie Dimon put it, "underwriting standards were deteriorating across the industry."

At Citi, the problem was made worse by a breakdown in internal risk-management practices. Normally, risk managers carefully monitor the activities of managers in lending and trading units in order to guard against excessive risk taking. Clearly, Thomas Maheras's trading unit had taken huge risks in saddling the bank with $43 billion in mortgage-related assets, but as we've seen, when CEO Prince wanted to know if those risks were excessive, he asked Maheras. Maheras, whose unit was generating immense profits (and hefty bonuses) from CDO trading, said no.

Apparently, Prince was no better served by David C. Bushnell, his senior risk officer and the manager responsible for putting the brakes on potentially dangerous trading activities. Maheras and Bushnell were longtime friends, having climbed the Citi corporate ladder together, and some insiders at the bank report that the boundaries between their two units weren't as rigorous as they should have been. Risk management, says one former employee, "has to be independent, and it wasn't independent at Citigroup, at least when it came to [trading]." In fact, at one point, risk managers responsible for overseeing trading activities reported to Maheras as well as Bushnell, thus giving the trading unit leverage over the very same managers who were supposed to be keeping an eye on the activities of traders.

Maheras and Bushnell were eventually fired, Prince resigned, and Citigroup received $45 billion in cash infusions from the federal government. The bank has a new CEO, Vikram S. Pandit, who has announced plans to streamline the organization, and a new chief risk officer, Brian Leach, who has promised to see that Citi "takes the lessons learned from recent events and makes critical enhancements to its risk-management framework. A change in culture," Leach adds, "is [also] required at Citi."[1]

Making effective decisions, as well as recognizing when bad decisions have been made and quickly responding to mistakes, is a key ingredient in organizational effectiveness. Indeed, some experts believe that decision making is the most basic and fundamental of all managerial activities.[2] Thus we discuss it here in the context of the first management function, planning. Keep in mind, however, that although decision making is perhaps most closely linked to the planning function, it is also part of organizing, leading, and controlling.

We begin our discussion by exploring the nature of decision making. We then describe rational perspectives on decision making. Behavioral aspects of decision making are then introduced and described. We conclude with a discussion of group and team decision making.

The Nature of Decision Making

Managers at Disney recently made the decision to buy Marvel Comics for $4.3 billion. At about the same time, the general manager of the Ford dealership in Bryan, Texas, made a decision to sponsor a local youth soccer team for $200. Each of these examples reflects a decision, but the decisions differ in many ways. Thus, as a starting point in understanding decision making, we must first explore the meaning of decision making as well as types of decisions and conditions under which decisions are made.[3]

Decision Making Defined

Decision making can refer to either a specific act or a general process. **Decision making** *per se* is the act of choosing one alternative from among a set of alternatives. The decision-making process, however, is much more than this. One step of the process, for example, is that the person making the decision must both recognize that a decision is necessary and identify the set of feasible alternatives before selecting one. Hence, the **decision-making process** includes recognizing and defining the nature of a decision situation, identifying alternatives, choosing the "best" alternative, and putting it into practice.[4]

The word *best*, of course, implies effectiveness. Effective decision making requires that the decision maker understand the situation driving the decision. Most people would consider an effective decision to be one that optimizes some set of factors, such as profits, sales, employee welfare, and market share. In some situations, though, an effective decision may be one that minimizes losses, expenses, or employee turnover. It may even mean selecting the best method for going out of business, laying off employees, or terminating a strategic alliance.

"The dumbest thing to do is sit on too much cash. It's not a good return on shareholders' capital."

—BRYANT RILEY, MARKET ANALYST[5]

We should also note that managers make decisions about both problems and opportunities. For example, making decisions about how to cut costs by 10 percent reflects a problem—an undesirable situation that requires a solution. But decisions are also necessary in situations of opportunity. Learning that the firm is earning higher-than-projected profits, for example, requires a subsequent decision. Should the extra funds be used to increase shareholder dividends, reinvest in current operations, or expand into new markets?

Of course, it may take a long time before a manager can know if the right decision was made. For example, in 2009 government leaders made the decision to invest billions of dollars in failing financial institutions and other businesses. It will be years—or perhaps decades—before economists and other experts will know if those were sound decisions or if the United States would have been better off allowing those businesses to fail.

decision making
The act of choosing one alternative from among a set of alternatives

decision-making process
Recognizing and defining the nature of a decision situation, identifying alternatives, choosing the "best" alternative, and putting it into practice

programmed decision
A decision that is fairly structured or recurs with some frequency (or both)

nonprogrammed decision
A decision that is relatively unstructured and occurs much less often than a programmed decision

Types of Decisions

Managers must make many different types of decisions. In general, however, most decisions fall into one of two categories: programmed and nonprogrammed.[6] A **programmed decision** is one that is relatively structured or recurs with some frequency (or both). Starbucks uses programmed decisions to purchase new supplies of coffee beans, cups, and napkins, and Starbucks employees are trained in exact procedures for brewing coffee. Likewise, the Bryan Ford dealer made a decision that he will sponsor a youth soccer team each year. Thus, when the soccer club president calls, the dealer already knows what he will do. Many decisions regarding basic operating systems and procedures and standard organizational transactions are of this variety and can therefore be programmed.[7]

Nonprogrammed decisions, on the other hand, are relatively unstructured and occur much less often. Disney's decision to buy Pixar was a nonprogrammed decision. Managers faced with such decisions must treat each one as unique, investing enormous amounts of time, energy, and resources into exploring the situation from all perspectives. Intuition and experience are major factors in nonprogrammed decisions. Most of the decisions made by top managers involving strategy (including mergers, acquisitions, and takeovers) and organization design are nonprogrammed. So are decisions about new facilities, new products, labor contracts, and legal issues.

Decision-Making Conditions

Just as there are different kinds of decisions, there are also different conditions in which decisions must be made. Managers sometimes have an almost perfect understanding of conditions surrounding a decision, but at other times they have few clues about those conditions. In general, as shown in Figure 9.1, the circumstances that exist for the decision maker are conditions of certainty, risk, or uncertainty.[8]

Decision Making under Certainty When the decision maker knows with reasonable certainty what the alternatives are and what conditions are associated with each alternative, a state of certainty exists. Suppose, for example, that managers at Singapore Airlines make a decision to buy five new jumbo jets. Their next decision is from whom to buy them. Because there are only two companies in the world that make jumbo jets, Boeing and Airbus, Singapore Airlines knows its options exactly. Each has proven products and will guarantee prices and delivery dates. The airline thus knows the alternative conditions associated with each. There is little ambiguity and relatively little chance of making a bad decision.

Few organizational decisions, however, are made under conditions of true certainty. The complexity and turbulence of the contemporary business world make such situations rare. Even the airplane purchase decision we just considered has less certainty than it appears. The aircraft companies may not be able to really guarantee delivery dates, so they may write cost-increase or inflation clauses into contracts. Thus the airline may be only partially certain of the conditions surrounding each alternative.

Decision Making under Risk A more common decision-making condition is a state of risk. Under a state of risk, the availability of each alternative and its potential payoffs and costs are all associated with probability estimates.[9] Suppose, for example, that a labor contract negotiator for a company receives a "final" offer from the union right before a strike deadline. The negotiator has two alternatives: to accept or to reject the offer. The risk centers on whether the union representatives are bluffing. If the company negotiator accepts the offer, she avoids a strike but commits to a relatively costly labor contract. If she rejects the contract, she may get a more favorable contract if the union is bluffing, but she may provoke a strike if it is not.

On the basis of past experience, relevant information, the advice of others, and her own judgment, she may conclude that there is about a 75 percent chance that union representatives are bluffing and about a 25 percent chance that they will back up their threats. Thus she can base a calculated decision on the two alternatives (accept or reject the contract demands) and the probable consequences of each. When making decisions under a state of risk, managers

state of certainty
A condition in which the decision maker knows with reasonable certainty what the alternatives are and what conditions are associated with each alternative

state of risk
A condition in which the availability of each alternative and its potential payoffs and costs are all associated with probability estimates

FIGURE 9.1 DECISION-MAKING CONDITIONS

Most major decisions in organizations today are made under a state of uncertainty. Managers making decisions in these circumstances must be sure to learn as much as possible about the situation and approach the decision from a logical and rational perspective.

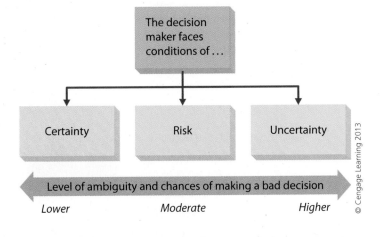

Jim West/Alamy

When negotiators for Ford Motor Company and the United Auto Workers meet to discuss new labor contracts, they make decisions under conditions of risk. Each side tries to understand what its counterparts want and how much they are willing to compromise. If they manage risk properly, then each side can get an acceptable outcome. But if they manage risk incorrectly, the result might be a costly strike.

must reasonably estimate the probabilities associated with each alternative. For example, if the union negotiators are committed to a strike if their demands are not met, and the company negotiator rejects their demands because she guesses they will not strike, her miscalculation will prove costly.

As indicated in Figure 9.1, decision making under conditions of risk is accompanied by moderate ambiguity and chances of a bad decision. For instance, like many other automobile companies, Ford laid off thousands of workers early in the recent recession. But during the depths of the recession Ford executives noted that as fuel prices were dropping, demand for its new F-150 pickup was increasing. So the firm rehired 1,000 of its former workers to help build more pickups. The risk was that if gas prices had surged unexpectedly and/or demand for the F-150 had cooled, Ford would have been in the embarrassing position of having recalled workers and then once again terminating them. But the upside was that if Ford's assessments were correct, the firm would generate new revenues and more profits.[10]

The *Technically Speaking* box on page 215, entitled "Big Pharma Puts R&D to the Test," shows how one manager at a major pharmaceutical company turned the willingness to make riskier decisions into a key factor in the firm's ability to develop new products more efficiently and (for the most part) more effectively.

Decision Making under Uncertainty Most of the major decision making in contemporary organizations is done under a **state of uncertainty**. The decision maker does not know all the alternatives, the risks associated with each, or the likely consequences of each alternative. This uncertainty stems from the complexity and dynamism of contemporary organizations and their environments. The emergence of the Internet as a significant force in today's competitive environment has served to increase both revenue potential and uncertainty for most managers.

To make effective decisions in these circumstances, managers must acquire as much relevant information as possible and approach the situation from a logical and rational perspective. Intuition, judgment, and experience always play major roles in the decision-making process under conditions of uncertainty. Even so, uncertainty is the most ambiguous condition for managers and the one most prone to error.[11] Lorraine Brennan O'Neil is the founder and CEO of 10 Minute Manicure, a quick service salon located in airports. The company found quick success and experienced rapid growth from its start in 2006, but the economic downturn required O'Neil to rethink her plans in an attempt to stay afloat through a rocky and unknown future. Knowing that the company no longer had the time to wait and monitor new stores' success, she opted to focus solely on existing stores with profits, shutting down those with losses. Aside from this, she restructured her business plan, seeking nontraditional locations, reducing corporate overhead, cutting products, and developing an online product line as a second source of income.[12]

state of uncertainty
A condition in which the decision maker does not know all the alternatives, the risks associated with each, or the consequences each alternative is likely to have

What are the two basic types of decisions? Provide an example of each.

Identify examples of decisions you have recently made under each of the three general conditions.

CONCEPT CHECK

TECHNICALLY SPEAKING

Big Pharma Puts R&D to the Test

SCPhotos/Alamy

More than companies in most industries, pharmaceutical firms have to deal with a basic paradox in the product-development process. On the one hand, they have to ensure that products work—which in the pharmaceuticals business means that they've been thoroughly tested and proven both effective and safe. On the other hand, firms also have to take certain risks. If they don't, the new-product pipeline dries up—an especially important consideration in an industry in which profitability depends on patents that eventually expire.

When Robert Ruffolo took over as executive VP for R&D operations at Wyeth, a major U.S. supplier of pharmaceuticals and over-the-counter healthcare products, he was instructed by CEO Robert Essner to "rattle the cage." Ruffolo was determined to spark innovation, but in order to set controls on the new-product process, he first announced a review of every product then under development. He was surprised to find, however, that this plan did not meet with the wholehearted approval of his staff of 70 research scientists, some of whom expressed concern that the review process would actually stifle personal productivity.

Why the unexpected concern with personal productivity? Ruffolo discovered why when he sat down to assess probable outcomes on a project-by-project basis. During the course of his review, he ran across a curious phenomenon: Projects that appeared to be failing—and which were least likely to pay

off—often received an inordinate share of available resources. Ruffolo quickly came to the conclusion that Wyeth scientists were willing to reroute resources from more promising projects to those which, for a variety of reasons, they wanted to safeguard despite low probabilities of success. Hence the concern for personal productivity: "Everybody was convinced," admits researcher Steven Projan, "that it was a tool to kill off their favorite project."

Nevertheless, Ruffolo instituted a policy of annual reviews aimed at evaluating projects according to such factors as development costs, likelihood of success, and expected sales. He also set firm targets for how many products should move forward at each stage of the new-product development process, which in the pharmaceuticals industry is usually measured in testing stages. The policy began to get results almost immediately. When Ruffolo first got to Wyeth, for example, the so-called "discovery" team—which creates compounds to be passed along to other groups for further development—was turning out a mere four drugs per year. Ruffolo set a new target of 12, which had to be met with no increase in personnel or resources. Over the next five years, the group met the new target, which was then bumped to 15.

Not everybody, however, agrees that such targets are a good idea in the pharmaceuticals industry. Quotas, argues one former Wyeth researcher, can seduce researchers into "overlooking problems" in order to make their numbers. Within a few years, Wyeth had in fact begun experiencing problems with increased failure rates during human testing and clinical trials, and the problem reached a head when the U.S. Food and Drug Administration withheld approval of three major drugs that Wyeth deemed crucial to its plans for future growth. To be fair, however, such setbacks shouldn't be laid at the feet of Robert Ruffolo: The decision to advance products from development to testing is made at Wyeth by a council consisting of scientists, regulatory experts, and marketing executives, not by researchers laboring under quota requirements.*

References: Amy Barrett, "Cracking the Whip at Wyeth," *BusinessWeek*, February 6, 2006, www.businessweek.com on March 4, 2011; Matthew Herper, "Wyeth's Worries," *Forbes*, August 13, 2007, www.forbes.com on March 4, 2011; "Wyeth Joins R&D Restructuring Parade," *Wall Street Journal*, October 28, 2008, http://blogs.wsj.com on March 4, 2011; Aaron Smith, "Pfizer Eyes Wyeth's Drug Pipeline," *CNNMoney.com*, January 23, 2009, http://money.cnn.com on March 4, 2011; Rick Mullin, "R&D Heads Shift at Big Pharma," *C&EN*, May 31, 2010, http://pubs.acs.org on March 4, 2011.

*Ruffolo retired from Wyeth in 2008 and now serves on the board of Trevena Inc., a biotechnology firm. In 2009, Wyeth was purchased for $68 billion by Pfizer, the world's largest research-based pharmaceuticals firm. Many analysts believe that Pfizer was motivated by dissatisfaction with its own R&D activities and a need to bolster its own new-product pipeline.

Rational Perspectives on Decision Making

Most managers like to think of themselves as rational decision makers. And, indeed, many experts argue that managers should try to be as rational as possible in making decisions.[13] This section highlights the fundamental and rational perspectives on decision making.

The Classical Model of Decision Making

The classical decision model is a prescriptive approach that tells managers how they should make decisions. It rests on the assumptions that managers are logical and rational and that they make decisions that are in the best interests of the organization. Figure 9.2 shows how the classical model views the decision-making process.

1. Decision makers have complete information about the decision situation and possible alternatives.
2. They can effectively eliminate uncertainty to achieve a decision condition of certainty.
3. They evaluate all aspects of the decision situation logically and rationally.

As we will see later, these conditions rarely, if ever, actually exist.

Steps in Rational Decision Making

A manager who really wants to approach a decision rationally and logically should try to follow the steps in rational decision making, listed in Table 9.1. These steps in rational decision making help keep the decision maker focused on facts and logic and help guard against inappropriate assumptions and pitfalls.

Recognizing and Defining the Decision Situation The first step in rational decision making is recognizing that a decision is necessary—that is, there must be some stimulus or spark to initiate the process. For many decisions and problem situations, the stimulus may occur without any prior warning. When equipment malfunctions, the manager must decide whether to repair or replace it. Or, when a major crisis erupts, as described in Chapter 3, the manager must quickly decide how to deal with it. As we already noted, the stimulus for a decision may be either positive or negative. A manager who must decide how to invest surplus funds, for example, faces a positive decision situation. A negative financial stimulus could involve having to trim budgets because of cost overruns.

Inherent in problem recognition is the need to define precisely what the problem is. The manager must develop a complete understanding of the problem, its causes, and its relationship to other factors. This understanding comes from careful analysis and thoughtful consideration of the situation. Consider the situation currently being faced in the international air travel industry. Because of the growth of international travel related to business, education, and tourism, global carriers like Singapore Airlines, KLM, JAL, British Airways, American Airlines, and others need to increase their capacity for international travel. Because most major

classical decision model
A prescriptive approach to decision making that tells managers how they should make decisions; assumes that managers are logical and rational and that their decisions will be in the best interests of the organization

steps in rational decision making
Recognize and define the decision situation; identify appropriate alternatives; evaluate each alternative in terms of its feasibility, satisfactoriness, and consequences; select the best alternative; implement the chosen alternative; follow up and evaluate the results of the chosen alternative

FIGURE 9.2 THE CLASSICAL MODEL OF DECISION MAKING

The classical model of decision making assumes that managers are rational and logical. It attempts to prescribe how managers should approach decision situations.

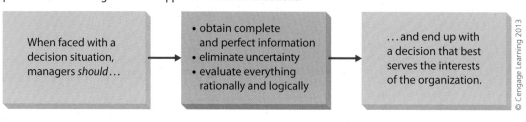

© Cengage Learning 2013

Step	Detail	Example
1. Recognizing and defining the decision situation	Some stimulus indicates that a decision must be made. The stimulus may be positive or negative.	A plant manager sees that employee turnover has increased by 5 percent.
2. Identifying alternatives	Both obvious and creative alternatives are desired. In general, the more important the decision, the more alternatives should be generated.	The plant manager can increase wages, increase benefits, or change hiring standards.
3. Evaluating alternatives	Each alternative is evaluated to determine its feasibility, its satisfactoriness, and its consequences.	Increasing benefits may not be feasible. Increasing wages and changing hiring standards may satisfy all conditions.
4. Selecting the best alternative	Consider all situational factors and choose the alternative that best fits the manager's situation.	Changing hiring standards will take an extended period of time to cut turnover, so increase wages.
5. Implementing the chosen alternative	The chosen alternative is implemented into the organizational system.	The plant manager may need permission from corporate headquarters. The human resource department establishes a new wage structure.
6. Following up and evaluating the results	At some time in the future, the manager should ascertain the extent to which the alternative chosen in step 4 and implemented in step 5 has worked.	The plant manager notes that, six months later, turnover dropped to its previous level.

TABLE 9.1 STEPS IN THE RATIONAL DECISION-MAKING PROCESS

Although the presumptions of the classical decision model rarely exist, managers can still approach decision making with rationality. By following the steps of rational decision making, managers ensure that they are learning as much as possible about the decision situation and its alternatives.

© Cengage Learning 2013

international airports are already operating at or near capacity, adding a significant number of new flights to existing schedules is not feasible. As a result, the most logical alternative is to increase capacity on existing flights. Thus Boeing and Airbus, the world's only manufacturers of large commercial aircraft, recognized an important opportunity and defined their decision situation as how to best respond to the need for increased global travel capacity.[14]

Identifying Alternatives Once the decision situation has been recognized and defined, the second step is to identify alternative courses of effective action. Developing both obvious, standard alternatives and creative, innovative alternatives is generally useful.[15] In general, the more important the decision, the more attention is directed to developing alternatives.[16] If the decision involves a multimillion-dollar relocation, a great deal of time and expertise will be devoted to identifying the best locations. JetBlue announced in 2009 that it would be seeking a new location for its corporate offices. After a year of searching and analyzing incentives to relocate to Orlando, the airline decided it would keep its headquarters in Queens, New York.[17] If the problem is to choose a color for the company softball team uniforms, less time and expertise will be brought to bear.

Although managers should seek creative solutions, they must also recognize that various constraints often limit their alternatives. Common constraints include legal restrictions, moral and ethical norms, authority constraints, and constraints imposed by the power and authority of the manager, available technology, economic considerations, and unofficial social norms. Boeing and Airbus identified three different alternatives to address the decision situation of increasing international airline travel capacity: They could independently develop new large planes, they could collaborate in a joint venture to create a single new large plane, or they could modify their largest existing planes to increase their capacity.

FIGURE 9.3 EVALUATING ALTERNATIVES IN THE DECISION-MAKING PROCESS

Managers must thoroughly evaluate all the alternatives, which increases the chances that the alternative finally chosen will be successful. Failure to evaluate an alternative's feasibility, satisfactoriness, and consequences can lead to a wrong decision.

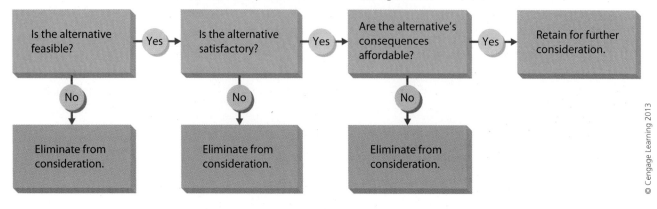

© Cengage Learning 2013

Evaluating Alternatives The third step in the decision-making process is evaluating each of the alternatives. Figure 9.3 presents a decision tree that can be used to judge different alternatives. The figure suggests that each alternative be evaluated in terms of its *feasibility*, its *satisfactoriness*, and its *consequences*. The first question to ask is whether an alternative is feasible. Is it within the realm of probability and practicality? For a small, struggling firm, an alternative requiring a huge financial outlay is probably out of the question. Other alternatives may not be feasible because of legal barriers. And limited human, material, and information resources may make other alternatives impractical.

When an alternative has passed the test of feasibility, it must next be examined to see how well it satisfies the conditions of the decision situation. For example, a manager searching for ways to double production capacity might initially consider purchasing an existing plant from another company. If more detailed analysis reveals that the new plant would increase production capacity by only 35 percent, this alternative may not be satisfactory. Finally, when an alternative has proven both feasible and satisfactory, its probable consequences must still be assessed. To what extent will a particular alternative influence other parts of the organization? What financial and nonfinancial costs will be associated with such influences? For example, a plan to boost sales by cutting prices may disrupt cash flows, require a new advertising program, and alter the behavior of sales representatives because it requires a different commission structure. The manager, then, must put "price tags" on the consequences of each alternative. Even an alternative that is both feasible and satisfactory must be eliminated if its consequences are too expensive for the total system. Airbus felt it would be at a disadvantage if it tried to simply enlarge its existing planes, because the Boeing 747 was already the largest aircraft being made and could readily be expanded to remain the largest. Boeing, meanwhile, was seriously concerned about the risk inherent in building a new and even larger plane, even if it shared the risk with Airbus as a joint venture.

> "We don't think [building the A380] is a very smart thing to do."
>
> —RANDY BAESLER, BOEING EXECUTIVE[18]

Selecting an Alternative Even though many alternatives fail to pass the triple tests of feasibility, satisfactoriness, and affordable consequences, two or more alternatives may remain. Choosing the best of these is the real crux of decision making. One approach is to choose the alternative with the optimal combination of feasibility, satisfactoriness, and affordable consequences. Even though most situations do not lend themselves to objective, mathematical analysis, the manager can often develop subjective estimates and weights for choosing an alternative.

Optimization is also a frequent goal. Because a decision is likely to affect several individuals or units, any feasible alternative will probably not maximize all of the relevant goals. Suppose that the manager of the Kansas City Royals needs to select a new outfielder for the upcoming baseball season. Bill hits .350 but has difficulty catching fly balls; Joe hits only .175 but is outstanding in the field; and Sam hits .290 and is a solid but not outstanding fielder. The manager probably would select Sam because of the optimal balance of hitting and fielding. Decision makers should also remember that finding multiple acceptable alternatives may be possible; selecting just one alternative and rejecting all the others might not be necessary. For example, the Royals' manager might decide that Sam will start each game, Bill will be retained as a pinch hitter, and Joe will be retained as a defensive substitute. In many hiring decisions, the candidates remaining after evaluation are ranked. If the top candidate rejects the offer, it may be automatically extended to the number-two candidate and, if necessary, to the remaining candidates in order. For the reasons noted earlier, Airbus proposed a joint venture with Boeing. Boeing, meanwhile, decided that its best course of action was to modify its existing 747 to increase its capacity. As a result, Airbus then decided to proceed on its own to develop and manufacture a new jumbo jet. Boeing, however, also decided that in addition to modifying its 747 it would also develop a new plane to offer as an alternative, albeit one not as large as the 747 or the proposed Airbus plane.

Implementing the Chosen Alternative After an alternative has been selected, the manager must put it into effect. In some decision situations, implementation is fairly easy; in others, it is more difficult. In the case of an acquisition, for example, managers must decide how to integrate all the activities of the new business, including purchasing, human resource practices, and distribution, into an ongoing organizational framework. For example, when Hewlett-Packard made the decision to buy Compaq Computer, managers estimated that it would take at least a year to integrate the two firms into a single one. Operational plans, which we discussed in Chapter 7, are useful in implementing alternatives.

Managers must also consider people's resistance to change when implementing decisions. The reasons for such resistance include insecurity, inconvenience, and fear of the unknown. When JCPenney decided to move its headquarters from New York to Texas, many employees resigned rather than relocate. Managers should anticipate potential resistance at various stages of the implementation process. (Resistance to change is covered in Chapter 16.) Managers should also recognize that even when all alternatives have been evaluated as precisely as possible and the consequences of each alternative weighed, unanticipated consequences are still likely. Any number of factors—unexpected cost increases, a less-than-perfect fit with existing organizational subsystems, or unpredicted effects on cash flow or operating expenses, for example—could develop after implementation has begun. Boeing set its engineers to work expanding the capacity of its 747 from 416 passengers to as many as 520 passengers by adding 30 feet to the plane's body. The company has also been developing its new plane intended for international travel, the Boeing 787 Dreamliner. Airbus engineers, meanwhile, spent years developing and constructing its new jumbo jet, the A380, equipped with escalators and elevators, and capable of carrying 655 passengers. Airbus's development costs alone are estimated to be more than $12 billion.

Boeing's 787 Dreamliner first went into passenger service in late 2011. Years earlier Boeing and Airbus, the two largest commercial aircraft companies in the world, had looked at the same market and arrived at very different decisions as to how best to serve that market. The Boeing 787 and Airbus 380 each represent major decisions for the firms.

mirounga/Shutterstock.com

Following Up and Evaluating the Results The final step in the decision-making process requires that managers evaluate the

THE MORE THINGS CHANGE

Hard Facts and Half-Truths

altrendo images/Getty images

Stanford University professors Jeffrey Pfeffer and Bob Sutton, authors of *Hard Facts, Dangerous Half-Truths, and Total Non-sense*, have put out a call for a renewed reliance on rationality in managerial decision making—an approach that they call *evidence-based management* (*EBM*). "Management decisions," they argue, "[should] be based on the best evidence, managers [should] systematically learn from experience, and organizational practices [should] reflect sound principles of thought and analysis." They define evidence-based management as "a commitment to finding and using the best theory and data available at the time to make decisions," but their "Five Principles of Evidence-Based Management" make it clear that EBM means more than just sifting through data and crunching numbers. Here's what they recommend:

1. Face the hard facts and build a culture in which people are encouraged to tell the truth, even if it's unpleasant.
2. Be committed to "fact-based" decision making—which means being committed to getting the best evidence and using it to guide actions.
3. Treat your organization as an unfinished prototype—encourage experimentation and learning by doing.
4. Look for the risks and drawbacks in what people recommend (even the best medicine has side effects).

5. Avoid basing decisions on untested but strongly held beliefs, what you have done in the past, or on uncritical "bench-marking" of what winners do.

Pfeffer and Sutton are particularly persuasive when they use EBM to question the outcomes of decisions based on "untested but strongly held beliefs" or on "uncritical 'bench-marking.'" Take, for instance, the popular policy of paying high performers significantly more than low performers. Pfeffer and Sutton's research shows that pay-for-performance policies get good results when employees work solo or independently. But it's another matter altogether when it comes to collaborative teams—the kind of teams that make so many organizational decisions today. Under these circumstances, the greater the gap between highest- and lowest-paid executives, the weaker the firm's financial performance. Why? According to Pfeffer and Sutton, wide disparities in pay often weaken both trust among team members and the social connectivity that contributes to strong team-based decision making.

Or consider another increasingly prevalent policy for evaluating and rewarding talent. Pioneered at General Electric by the legendary Jack Welch, the practice of "forced ranking" divides employees into three groups based on performance—the top 20 percent, middle 70 percent, and bottom 10 percent—and terminates those at the bottom. Pfeffer and Sutton found that, according to many HR managers, forced ranking impaired morale and collaboration and ultimately reduced productivity. They also concluded that automatically firing the bottom 10 percent resulted too often in the unnecessary disruption of otherwise effective teamwork. That's how they found out that 73 percent of the errors committed by commercial airline pilots occur on the first day that reconfigured crews work together.

References: Jeffrey Pfeffer and Robert I. Sutton, *Hard Facts, Dangerous Half-Truths, and Total Nonsense: Profiting from Evidence-Based Management* (Cambridge, MA: Harvard Business School Press, 2006); Pfeffer and Sutton, "Evidence-Based Management," 2010, www.evidence-basedmanagement.com on March 4, 2011; Donald W. McCormick, "Ethics and the 15 Minute Evidence-Based Manager," *Organization Management Journal*, Vol. 7 (2010), www.palgrave-journals.com on March 4, 2011; Kate Grey, "Evidence-Based Management: My No.-1 Top Hit," *Grey Matter*, March 29, 2010, wwwkateegrey.com on March 4, 2011.

effectiveness of their decision—that is, they should make sure that the chosen alternative has served its original purpose. If an implemented alternative appears not to be working, the manager can respond in several ways. Another previously identified alternative (the original second or third choice, for instance) could be adopted. Or the manager might recognize that the situation was not correctly defined to begin with and start the process all over again. Finally, the manager might decide that the original alternative is in fact appropriate but has not yet had time to work or should be implemented in a different way.[19]

Failure to evaluate decision effectiveness may have serious consequences. The Pentagon once spent $1.8 billion and eight years developing the Sergeant York anti-aircraft gun. From the beginning, tests revealed major problems with the weapon system, but not until it was in its final stages, when it was demonstrated to be completely ineffective, was the project scrapped.

At this point, both Boeing and Airbus are still learning about the consequences of their decisions. Airbus's A380 has been placed in commercial service. However, the plane has suffered numerous mechanical problems. Moreover, because the weakened economy has dealt a blow to large international airlines, some of them—such as Qantas Airways and Emirates Airlines—deferred or cancelled orders for the plane. Airbus estimated that it needs to sell 420 A380s before it starts making a profit. Current projections suggest that sales of the plane may not hit that target until at least 2020.[20] Meanwhile, it appeared for a while that Boeing's commitment to the new 787 might prove to be the best decision of all. A key element of the new plane is that it is much more fuel-efficient than other international airplanes. Given the dramatic surge in fuel costs in recent years, a fuel-efficient option like the 787 is likely to be an enormous success. However, the 787 suffered from numerous manufacturing problems and delays and was not placed into service until late 2011. So its real impact will not be known for a few more years.[21]

Setting your mind to making rational decisions may seem like a no-brainer, but some researchers worry that managers tend all too often to slip into bad decision-making habits. The *Change* box on page 220, entitled "Hard Facts and Half-Truths," explains why one team of researchers recommends a logical approach to the art and science of deciding what to do and what not to do in business.

What are the steps in rational decision making?

Recall a decision you recently made and believed to be rational. Trace the process through each of the steps noted above and reassess its real rationality.

CONCEPT CHECK

Behavioral Aspects of Decision Making

If all decision situations were approached as logically as described in the previous section, more decisions might prove to be successful. Yet decisions are often made with little consideration for logic and rationality. Some experts have estimated that U.S. companies use rational decision-making techniques less than 20 percent of the time.[22] And even when organizations try to be logical, they sometimes fail. For example, when Starbucks opened its first coffee shops in New York, it relied on scientific marketing research, taste tests, and rational deliberation in making a decision to emphasize drip over espresso coffee. However, that decision still proved wrong, as New Yorkers strongly preferred the same espresso-style coffees that were Starbucks mainstays in the West. Hence, the firm had to hastily reconfigure its stores to better meet customer preferences.

On the other hand, sometimes when a decision is made with little regard for logic, it can still turn out to be correct.[23] An important ingredient in how these forces work is the behavioral aspect of decision making. The administrative model better reflects these subjective considerations. Other behavioral aspects include political forces, intuition and escalation of commitment, risk propensity, and ethics.

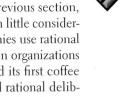

"... I'm a bit of a maverick. I listen, but I've got the final say. Then it's up to me to make it work so I don't lose my credibility."

—RICHARD BRANSON, FOUNDER, OWNER, AND CEO OF VIRGIN GROUP[24]

The Administrative Model

Herbert A. Simon was one of the first experts to recognize that decisions are not always made with rationality and logic.[25] Simon was subsequently awarded the Nobel Prize in economics. Rather than prescribing how decisions should be made, his view of decision making, now called the **administrative model**, describes how decisions often actually are made. As illustrated in Figure 9.4, the model holds that managers (1) use incomplete and imperfect information, (2) are constrained by bounded rationality, and (3) tend to "satisfice" when making decisions.

Bounded rationality suggests that decision makers are limited by their values and unconscious reflexes, skills, and habits. They are also limited by less-than-complete information and knowledge. Bounded rationality partially explains how U.S. auto executives allowed Japanese automakers to get such a strong foothold in the U.S. domestic market. For years, executives at GM, Ford, and Chrysler compared their companies' performance only to one another's and ignored foreign imports. The foreign "threat" was not acknowledged until the domestic auto market had been changed forever. If managers had gathered complete information from the beginning, they might have been better able to thwart foreign competitors. Essentially, then, the concept of bounded rationality suggests that although people try to be rational decision makers, their rationality has limits.

Another important part of the administrative model is **satisficing**. This concept suggests that rather than conducting an exhaustive search for the best possible alternative, decision makers tend to search only until they identify an alternative that meets some minimum standard of sufficiency. A manager looking for a site for a new plant, for example, may select the first site she finds that meets basic requirements for transportation, utilities, and price, even though further search might yield a better location. People satisfice for a variety of reasons. Managers may simply be unwilling to ignore their own motives (such as reluctance to spend time making a decision) and therefore may not be able to continue searching after a minimally acceptable alternative is identified. The decision maker may be unable to weigh and evaluate large numbers of alternatives and criteria. Also, subjective and personal considerations often intervene in decision situations.

Because of the inherent imperfection of information, bounded rationality, and satisficing, the decisions made by a manager may or may not actually be in the best interests of the organization. A manager may choose a particular location for the new plant because it offers the lowest price and best availability of utilities and transportation. Or she may choose the site because it is located in a community where she wants to live.

In summary, then, the classical and administrative models paint quite different pictures of decision making. Which is more correct? Actually, each can be used to better understand how managers make decisions. The classical model is prescriptive: It explains how managers can at least attempt to be more rational and logical in their approaches to decisions. The administrative model can be used by managers to develop a better understanding of their inherent biases and limitations.[26] In the following sections, we describe more fully other behavioral forces that can influence decisions.

administrative model
A decision-making model that argues that decision makers (1) use incomplete and imperfect information, (2) are constrained by bounded rationality, and (3) tend to "satisfice" when making decisions

bounded rationality
A concept suggesting that decision makers are limited by their values and unconscious reflexes, skills, and habits

satisficing
The tendency to search for alternatives only until one is found that meets some minimum standard of sufficiency

FIGURE 9.4 THE ADMINISTRATIVE MODEL OF DECISION MAKING

The administrative model is based on behavioral processes that affect how managers make decisions. Rather than prescribing how decisions should be made, it focuses more on describing how they are made.

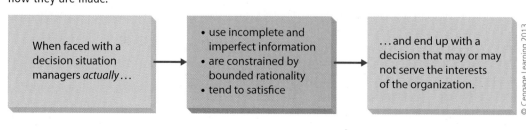

When faced with a decision situation managers *actually*...
- use incomplete and imperfect information
- are constrained by bounded rationality
- tend to satisfice

...and end up with a decision that may or may not serve the interests of the organization.

© Cengage Learning 2013

Political Forces in Decision Making

Political forces are another major element that contributes to the behavioral nature of decision making. Organizational politics is covered in Chapter 20, but one major element of politics, coalitions, is especially relevant to decision making. A **coalition** is an informal alliance of individuals or groups formed to achieve a common goal. This common goal is often a preferred decision alternative. For example, coalitions of stockholders frequently band together to force a board of directors to make a certain decision.

When General Motors decided (several years ago) to launch Saturn as a new automobile company, the idea had the full backing and support of GM CEO Roger Smith. Saturn was to have its own factories, design teams, and dealer networks and was to compete directly with high-quality foreign imports like Toyota and Honda. Just as the first Saturn cars were being introduced, however, Smith retired. As it turned out, there was a coalition of senior GM executives who had opposed the Saturn concept but had been unable to do anything about it since Smith was such a powerful product champion. When Smith left GM, though, the coalition managed to divert resources intended for Saturn to other GM brands. As a result, new Saturn products were delayed, the brand received weak marketing support, and it never lived up to expectations. GM eventually shut Saturn down as it restructured its business during the global recession.[27]

The impact of coalitions can be either positive or negative. They can help astute managers get the organization on a path toward effectiveness and profitability, or they can strangle well-conceived strategies and decisions. Managers must recognize when to use coalitions, how to assess whether coalitions are acting in the best interests of the organization, and how to constrain their dysfunctional effects.[28]

Intuition and Escalation of Commitment

Two other important decision processes that go beyond logic and rationality are intuition and escalation of commitment to a chosen course of action.

Intuition Intuition is an innate belief about something, without conscious consideration. Managers sometimes decide to do something because it "feels right" or they have a "hunch." This feeling usually is not arbitrary, however. Rather, it is based on years of experience and practice in making decisions in similar situations.[29] An inner sense may help managers make an occasional decision without going through a full-blown rational sequence of steps. For example, Kip Tindell, CEO of The Container Store, emphasizes the use of intuition throughout his company and urges employees to believe that it is critical in the workplace. He is quoted as saying, "Intuition is only the sum total of your life experiences. So why would you want to leave it at home when you come to work in the morning?"[30] Of course, all managers, but most especially inexperienced ones, should be careful not to rely too heavily on intuition. If rationality and logic are continually flouted in favor of "what feels right," the odds are that disaster will strike one day.

> "Nothing is more difficult, and therefore more precious, than to be able to decide."
>
> —NAPOLEON BONAPARTE[31]

Escalation of Commitment Another important behavioral process that influences decision making is escalation of commitment to a chosen course of action. In particular, decision makers sometimes make decisions and then become so committed to the courses of action suggested by those decisions that they stay with them even when the decisions appear to have been wrong.[32] For example, when people buy stock in a company, they sometimes refuse to sell it even after repeated drops in price. They choose a course of action—buying the stock in anticipation of making a profit—and then stay with it even in the face of increasing losses. Moreover, after the value drops, they rationalize that they can't sell now because they will lose money.

coalition
An informal alliance of individuals or groups formed to achieve a common goal

intuition
An innate belief about something, without conscious consideration

escalation of commitment
A decision maker's staying with a decision even when it appears to be wrong

For years Pan American World Airways ruled the skies and used its profits to diversify into real estate and other businesses. But with the advent of deregulation, Pan Am began to struggle and lose market share to other carriers. When Pan Am managers finally realized how ineffective their airline operations had become, experts today point out, the "rational" decision would have been to sell off the remaining airline operations and concentrate on the firm's more profitable businesses. But because they still saw the company as being first and foremost an airline, they instead began to slowly sell off the firm's profitable holdings to keep the airline flying. Eventually, the company was left with nothing but an ineffective and inefficient airline, and then had to sell off its more profitable routes before eventually being taken over by Delta. Had Pan Am managers made the more rational decision years earlier, chances are the firm could still be a profitable enterprise today, albeit one with no involvement in the airline industry.[33]

In contrast, a group of investors licensed the use of Hard Rock logos and trademarks for a theme park—Hard Rock Park—to be built in South Carolina. After six years of planning and construction and an investment of over $400 million, the park opened in Myrtle Beach to dismal reviews and poor attendance. Rather than increasing their investment and trying to increase attendance, owners decided after only nine months to shut the park down and sell off its assets.[34]

Thus decision makers must walk a fine line. On the one hand, they must guard against sticking too long with an incorrect decision. To do so can bring about financial decline. On the other hand, managers should not bail out of a seemingly incorrect decision too soon, as Adidas once did. Adidas had dominated the market for professional athletic shoes. It subsequently entered the market for amateur sports shoes and did well there also. But managers interpreted a sales slowdown as a sign that the boom in athletic shoes was over. They thought that they had made the wrong decision and ordered drastic cutbacks. The market took off again with Nike at the head of the pack, and Adidas never recovered. Fortunately, a new management team has changed the way Adidas makes decisions, and the firm is again on its way to becoming a force in the athletic shoe and apparel markets.

A group of investors licensed the use of Hard Rock logos and trademarks for a new theme park in South Carolina. However, shortly after the park opened to low attendance and bad publicity, the investors decided to pull the plug on their $400 million investment. The action helped them avoid escalation of commitment to what was clearly a bad decision from the beginning.

RANDALL HILL/MCT /Landov

Risk Propensity and Decision Making

The behavioral element of **risk propensity** is the extent to which a decision maker is willing to gamble when making a decision. Some managers are cautious about every decision they make. They try to adhere to the rational model and are extremely conservative in what they do. Such managers are more likely to avoid mistakes, and they infrequently make decisions that lead to big losses.[35] Other managers are extremely aggressive in making decisions and are willing to take risks.[35] They rely heavily on intuition, reach decisions quickly, and often risk big investments on their decisions. As in gambling, these managers are more likely than their conservative counterparts to achieve big successes with their decisions; they are also more likely to incur greater losses.[36] The organization's culture is a prime ingredient in fostering different levels of risk propensity.

Ethics and Decision Making

As we introduced in Chapter 4, individual ethics are personal beliefs about right and wrong behavior. Ethics are clearly related to decision making in a number of ways. For example, suppose that, after careful analysis, a manager realizes that his company could save money

risk propensity
The extent to which a decision maker is willing to gamble when making a decision

by closing his department and subcontracting with a supplier for the same services. But to recommend this course of action would result in the loss of several jobs, including his own. His own ethical standards will clearly shape how he proceeds.[37] Indeed, each component of managerial ethics (relationships of the firm to its employees, of employees to the firm, and of the firm to other economic agents) involves a wide variety of decisions, all of which are likely to have an ethical component. A manager must remember, then, that, just as behavioral processes such as politics and risk propensity affect the decisions he makes, so, too, do his ethical beliefs.[38]

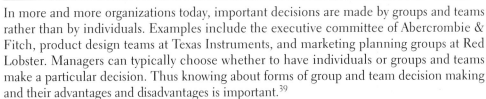

Summarize the essential components of the administrative model of decision making.

Recall a recent decision that you observed or were involved in that had strong behavioral overtones. Describe how various behavioral elements affected the process or outcome.

CONCEPT CHECK

Group and Team Decision Making in Organizations

In more and more organizations today, important decisions are made by groups and teams rather than by individuals. Examples include the executive committee of Abercrombie & Fitch, product design teams at Texas Instruments, and marketing planning groups at Red Lobster. Managers can typically choose whether to have individuals or groups and teams make a particular decision. Thus knowing about forms of group and team decision making and their advantages and disadvantages is important.[39]

Forms of Group and Team Decision Making

The most common methods of group and team decision making are interacting groups, Delphi groups, and nominal groups. Increasingly, these methods of group decision making are being conducted online.[40]

Interacting Groups and Teams Interacting groups and teams are the most common form of decision-making group. The format is simple—either an existing or a newly designated group or team is asked to make a decision. Existing groups or teams might be functional departments, regular work teams, or standing committees. Newly designated groups or teams can be ad hoc committees, task forces, or newly constituted work teams. The group or team members talk among themselves, argue, agree, argue some more, form internal coalitions, and so forth. Finally, after some period of deliberation, the group or team makes its decision. An advantage of this method is that the interaction among people often sparks new ideas and promotes understanding. A major disadvantage, though, is that political processes can play too big a role.

Delphi Groups A Delphi group is sometimes used to develop a consensus of expert opinion. Developed by the Rand Corporation, the Delphi procedure solicits input from a panel of experts who contribute individually. Their opinions are combined and, in effect, averaged. Assume, for example, that the problem is to establish an expected date for a major technological breakthrough in converting coal into usable energy. The first step in using the Delphi procedure is to obtain the cooperation of a panel of experts. For this situation, experts might include various research scientists, university researchers, and executives in a relevant energy industry. At first, the experts are asked to anonymously predict a time frame for the expected

interacting group or team
A decision-making group or team in which members openly discuss, argue about, and agree on the best alternative

Delphi group
A form of group decision making in which a group is used to achieve a consensus of expert opinion

breakthrough. The persons coordinating the Delphi group collect the responses, average them, and ask the experts for another prediction. In this round, the experts who provided unusual or extreme predictions may be asked to justify them. These explanations may then be relayed to the other experts. When the predictions stabilize, the average prediction is taken to represent the decision of the group of experts. The time, expense, and logistics of the Delphi technique rule out its use for routine, everyday decisions, but it has been successfully used for forecasting technological breakthroughs at Boeing, market potential for new products at General Motors, research and development patterns at Eli Lilly, and future economic conditions by the U.S. government.[41] Moreover, the Delphi method originally relied on paper-and-pencil responses obtained and shared through the mail; modern communication technologies such as e-mail and the Internet have enabled Delphi users to get answers much more quickly than in the past.

Nominal Groups Another useful group and team decision-making technique that is occasionally used is the nominal group. Unlike the Delphi method, in which group members do not see one another, nominal group members are brought together in a face-to-face setting. The members represent a group in name only, however; they do not talk to one another freely like the members of interacting groups. Nominal groups are used most often to generate creative and innovative alternatives or ideas. To begin, the manager assembles a group of knowledgeable experts and outlines the problem to them. The group members are then asked to individually write down as many alternatives as they can think of. The members then take turns stating their ideas, which are recorded on a flip chart or board at the front of the room. Discussion is limited to simple clarification. After all alternatives have been listed, more open discussion takes place. Group members then vote, usually by rank-ordering the various alternatives. The highest-ranking alternative represents the decision of the group. Of course, the manager in charge may retain the authority to accept or reject the group decision.[42]

Advantages of Group and Team Decision Making

The advantages and disadvantages of group and team decision making relative to individual decision making are summarized in Table 9.2. One advantage is simply that more information is available in a group or team setting—as suggested by the old axiom, "Two heads are better than one." A group or team represents a variety of education, experience, and perspective. Partly as a result of this increased information, groups and teams typically can identify

nominal group
A structured technique used to generate creative and innovative alternatives or ideas

TABLE 9.2 ADVANTAGES AND DISADVANTAGES OF GROUP AND TEAM DECISION MAKING

To increase the chances that a group or team decision will be successful, managers must learn how to manage the process of group and team decision making. Federal Express and IBM are increasingly using groups and teams in the decision-making process.

Advantages	Disadvantages
1. More information and knowledge are available.	1. The process takes longer than individual decision making, so it is costlier.
2. More alternatives are likely to be generated.	2. Compromise decisions resulting from indecisiveness may emerge.
3. More acceptance of the final decision is likely.	
4. Enhanced communication of the decision may result.	3. One person may dominate the group.
5. Better decisions generally emerge.	4. Groupthink may occur.

© Cengage Learning 2013

and evaluate more alternatives than can one person.[43] The people involved in a group or team decision understand the logic and rationale behind it, are more likely to accept it, and are equipped to communicate the decision to their work group or department.[44]

Disadvantages of Group and Team Decision Making

Perhaps the biggest drawback of group and team decision making is the additional time and hence the greater expense entailed. The increased time stems from interaction and discussion among group or team members. If a given manager's time is worth $50 an hour, and if the manager spends two hours making a decision, the decision "costs" the organization $100. For the same decision, a group of five managers might require three hours of time. At the same $50-an-hour rate, the decision "costs" the organization $750. Assuming the group or team decision is better, the additional expense may be justified, but the fact remains that group and team decision making is more costly.

Group or team decisions may also represent undesirable compromises.[45] For example, hiring a compromise top manager may be a bad decision in the long run because he or she may not be able to respond adequately to various subunits in the organization nor have everyone's complete support. Sometimes one individual dominates the group process to the point where others cannot make a full contribution. This dominance may stem from a desire for power or from a naturally dominant personality. The problem is that what appears to emerge as a group decision may actually be the decision of one person.

Finally, a group or team may succumb to a phenomenon known as "groupthink." Groupthink occurs when the desire for consensus and cohesiveness overwhelms the goal of reaching the best possible decision.[46] Under the influence of groupthink, the group may arrive at decisions that are made not in the best interests of either the group or the organization, but rather to avoid conflict among group members. One of the most clearly documented examples of groupthink involved the space shuttle *Challenger* disaster. As NASA was preparing to launch the shuttle, numerous problems and questions arose. At each step of the way, however, decision makers argued that there was no reason to delay and that everything would be fine. Shortly after its launch, the shuttle exploded, killing all seven crew members.

Managing Group and Team Decision-Making Processes

Managers can do several things to help promote the effectiveness of group and team decision making. One is simply being aware of the pros and cons of having a group or team make a decision to start with. Time and cost can be managed by setting a deadline by which the decision must be made final. Dominance can be at least partially avoided if a special group is formed just to make the decision. An astute manager, for example, should know who in the organization may try to dominate and can either avoid putting that person in the group or put several strong-willed people together.

To avoid groupthink, each member of the group or team should critically evaluate all alternatives. So that members present divergent viewpoints, the leader should not make his or her own position known too early. At least one member of the group or team might be assigned the role of devil's advocate. And after reaching a preliminary decision, the group or team should hold a follow-up meeting wherein divergent viewpoints can be raised again if any group members wish to do so.[47] Gould Paper Corporation used these methods by assigning managers to two different teams. The teams then spent an entire day in a structured debate, presenting the pros and cons of each side of an issue to ensure the best possible decision.

groupthink
A situation that occurs when a group or team's desire for consensus and cohesiveness overwhelms its desire to reach the best possible decision

Summarize the advantages and disadvantages of group decision making.

Are some of the different types of decisions and decision-making conditions more amenable to group decision making than others? Explain how and why.

CONCEPT CHECK

Summary of Learning Objectives and Key Points

1. Define decision making and discuss types of decisions and decision-making conditions.

    - Decision making is the act of choosing one alternative from among a set of alternatives.
    - The decision-making process includes recognizing and defining the nature of a decision situation, identifying alternatives, choosing the "best" alternative, and putting it into practice.
    - Two common types of decisions are programmed and nonprogrammed.
    - Decisions may be made under states of certainty, risk, or uncertainty.

2. Discuss rational perspectives on decision making, including the steps in rational decision making.

    - Rational perspectives on decision making rest on the classical model.
    - This model assumes that managers have complete information and that they will behave rationally. The primary steps in rational decision making are
        - recognizing and defining the situation
        - identifying alternatives
        - evaluating alternatives
        - selecting the best alternative
        - implementing the chosen alternative
        - following up and evaluating the effectiveness of the alternative after it is implemented

3. Describe the behavioral aspects of decision making.

    - Behavioral aspects of decision making rely on the administrative model.
    - This model recognizes that managers use incomplete information and that they do not always behave rationally.
    - The administrative model also recognizes the concepts of bounded rationality and satisficing.
    - Political activities by coalitions, managerial intuition, and the tendency to become increasingly committed to a chosen course of action are all important.
    - Risk propensity is also an important behavioral perspective on decision making.
    - Ethics also affect how managers make decisions.

4. Discuss group and team decision making, including the advantages and disadvantages of group and team decision making and how it can be more effectively managed.

    - To help enhance decision-making effectiveness, managers often use interacting, Delphi, or nominal groups or teams.
    - Group and team decision making in general has several advantages as well as disadvantages relative to individual decision making.
    - Managers can adopt a number of strategies to help groups and teams make better decisions.

Discussion Questions

Questions for Review

1. Describe the differences between programmed and non-programmed decisions. What are the implications of these differences for decision makers?
2. Describe the behavioral nature of decision making. Be certain to provide some detail about political forces, risk propensity, ethics, and commitment in your description.

3. What is meant by the term *escalation of commitment*? In your opinion, under what conditions is escalation of commitment likely to occur?
4. Explain the differences between three common methods of group decision making—interacting groups, Delphi groups, and nominal groups.

Questions for Analysis

5. Was your decision about what college or university to attend a rational decision? Did you go through each step in rational decision making? If not, why not?
6. Most business decisions are made under conditions of either risk or uncertainty. In your opinion, is it easier to make a decision under a condition of risk or a condition of uncertainty? Why?
7. Consider the following list of business decisions. Which decisions would be handled most effectively by group or team

decision making? Which would be handled most effectively by individual decision making? Explain your answers.

- A decision about switching pencil suppliers
- A decision about hiring a new CEO
- A decision about firing an employee for stealing
- A decision about calling 911 to report a fire in the warehouse
- A decision about introducing a brand new product

Questions for Application

8. Interview a local business manager about a major decision that he or she made recently. Try to determine whether the manager used a rational decision-making process or whether behavioral elements were also present. If the process was wholly rational, why do you think there was no behavioral component? If the process contained behavioral components, why were these components present?

9. Describe a recent decision you made that relied on intuition. In your opinion, what experiences formed the source of your intuition? Did the decision lead to attainment of the desired outcomes? Did your intuition play a positive or negative role in goal attainment? Explain.

10. Interview a department head at your college or university to determine whether group or team decision making is used. If it is, how does the head attempt to overcome the disadvantages of group decision making? Are the attempts successful? Why or why not?

 ## CengageNow™ Highlights

Now use your CengageNow™ homework to help you:

- Apply management theories in your life
- Assess your management skills
- Master management terms and concepts
- Apply your knowledge to real-world situations
- Analyze and solve challenging management problems

In order to take advantage of these elements, your instructor will need to have set up a course for your class within CengageNow™. Ask your instructor to contact his/her Cengage sales representative and Digital Solutions Manager to explore testing CengageNow™ in your course this term.

10
CHAPTER

Managing New Venture Formation and Entrepreneurship

LEARNING OBJECTIVES

After studying this chapter, you should be able to:

1. Discuss the nature of entrepreneurship.

2. Describe the role of entrepreneurship in society.

3. Understand the major issues involved in choosing strategies for small firms and the role of international management in entrepreneurship.

4. Discuss the structural challenges unique to entrepreneurial firms.

5. Understand the determinants of the performance of small firms.

MANAGEMENT IN ACTION The Creative Imprint at Bigfoot

Have you seen *Midnight Movie*? You wouldn't have caught it in a theater because it went straight to DVD, but that doesn't prevent hardcore horror-film fans from tracking it down—after all, it was selected as the Best Feature Film at the 10th Annual Chicago Horror Film Festival. It also found an audience outside the United States, with producer Bigfoot selling distribution rights in such countries as Germany, Greece, Thailand, and Japan. How about *3 Needles*, a Canadian-made movie about the worldwide AIDS crisis? It was no blockbuster, but it was endorsed by the United Nations and did well enough at international film festivals to find distributors in such countries as Australia, New Zealand, and Brazil. Bigfoot CEO Kacy Andrews was pleased with the film's reception: "The positive response from critics and audiences," she said, ". . . once again affirms our conviction to promote independent filmmakers."

Bigfoot Entertainment is responsible for a host of independently produced films, many of which follow similar distribution paths to venues and audiences around the world. The company, says Andrews, "is dedicated to the community of filmmakers who possess the vision and passion to create critically acclaimed independent films." It was founded in 2004 by a German serial entrepreneur named Michael Gleissner, who is in some ways a model for the sort of creative people that Bigfoot likes to back. He was certainly the model for the hero of *Hui Lu*, a 2007 Bigfoot film that Gleissner wrote and directed about a highly successful young entrepreneur who sells his company but finds himself pushed to the edge despite his millions. "What was I going to do," Gleissner replied when asked about his unusual career move, "buy more boats, buy more houses? I discovered there's a creative side in me."

Gleissner was an e-commerce pioneer in Germany, where he founded Telebook, Germany's number-one online bookstore, and WWW-Service GmbH, the country's first, and one of its most

> "What was I going to do—buy more boats, buy more houses? I discovered there's a creative side in me."
>
> —MICHAEL GLEISSNER, FOUNDER OF BIGFOOT ENTERTAINMENT

successful, web-hosting companies. In 1998, he sold Telebook to Amazon.com, where he served two years as a VP before cashing in and, in 2001, moving to Asia as a base for a new round of entrepreneurial activities. When he bought Bigfoot, it was an e-mail management firm, but

Bigfoot Entertainment has been successful by finding unique distribution channels for niche independent movies.

Gleissner quickly re-created it as an international entertainment company whose main business, according to its mission statement, is producing and financing "innovative entertainment content, including independent feature films, television series, and reality shows." As head of Bigfoot, Gleissner served as executive producer on *Midnight Movie* and *3 Needles*, as well as on *Irreversi*, his second effort at writing and directing, and on *Shanghai Kiss*, in which he also tried his hand at acting.

Bigfoot maintains offices in Los Angeles and a small production facility in Venice, California, but the centerpiece of its operations is Bigfoot Studios, which opened in 2004 on the island of Mactan, in Cebu, home to the second-largest city in the Philippines. The state-of-the-art facility features six large soundstages, fully equipped editing suites and sound-mixing studios, and the latest in high-tech cameras and other equipment. In 2007, under the auspices of Bigfoot Properties, Gleissner expanded Bigfoot Studios as the first phase of Bigfoot Center, a complex that will eventually house not only film- and TV-production facilities but Bigfoot Executive Hotel, an array of restaurants, boutiques, and sidewalk shops, and an 11-story office building (home to Bigfoot Outsourcing, which specializes in business-process services). The Bigfoot Center in the Philippines, by the way, should not be confused with the 26-story Bigfoot Centre in Hong Kong, where Bigfoot Properties is headquartered.

Gleissner's goal is to turn Cebu into a destination of choice for filmmakers who want to cut costs by shooting and finishing movies outside the United States, and when Bigfoot Entertainment finds a film suitable for financing and development, the deal usually requires the director to do some production work at the Cebu facility. By the time the studio opened in 2004, the Philippines were already an attractive location for animators looking for cheap post-production help, but the pool of talent available for work on live-action films was quite limited. Gleissner's solution? He founded the International Academy of Film and Television (IAFT), not only to staff Bigfoot Studios but to train what executive director Keith Sensing calls "the next generation of global filmmakers." IAFT, says Sensing, looks for creative people who "have a desire for adventure" and "an education that will set them apart from people who have a strictly Hollywood background."

IAFT enrollment is currently 60 percent international and 40 percent Filipino, but "all of our students," says Sensing, "have the opportunity to participate in real projects going on at Bigfoot Studios. . . . Many IAFT graduates," he adds, "have gone on to write, produce, and direct their own films" and often follow in Bigfoot's steps by finding distribution for their independent features on the international festival circuit. Three recent graduates landed jobs on Gleissner's most recent project, a Philippines-set thriller revolving around a female diver. Gleissner not only co-wrote and directed *Deep Gold* but drew on his experience as an underwater photographer to shoot key scenes in Bigfoot's specially designed 170,000-gallon Underwater Studio.

In 2010, Bigfoot moved to expand into the areas of acquisition, distribution, and foreign sales with the purchase of Ascendant Pictures. Much like Bigfoot itself, Ascendant carved out its niche in the industry by integrating the budgeting sensibility of "indie" producers with the marketing skills of larger studios. "Our schools are profitable," explains Andrews, "but overall we're not profitable yet. We're hoping the distribution side will get us there in one or two years."

The new unit, called Bigfoot Ascendant Distribution, will buy four to six English-language movies annually— "genre films," says Andrews, "horror and action that will sell well internationally and play well theatrically, too." In order to bolster its ability to get its films into theaters (most of the company's features have gone straight to DVD or sold to cable TV), Bigfoot has also become the largest shareholder in Carmike Cinemas, the fourth-largest theater chain in the United States. In 2010, it also purchased the historic Majestic Crest theater in Los Angeles. The acquisition, says Andrews, goes hand in hand with Bigfoot's purchase of Ascendant: "We wanted a great theater to showcase our films—not only ones we produce but ones we plan to acquire. Everyone knows the Crest," she adds. "It gives us a lot of prestige."[1]

Just like Michael Gleissner, thousands of people all over the world start new businesses each year. Some of them succeed but many, unfortunately, fail. Some of those who fail in a new business try again, and sometimes it takes two or more failures before a successful business gets under way. Henry Ford, for example, went bankrupt twice before succeeding with Ford Motor Company. On the other hand, of course, there are the Michael Gleissners who succeed at first, try again, and succeed a second time.

This process of starting a new business or business venture, sometimes failing and sometimes succeeding, is part of what is called "entrepreneurship," the subject of this chapter. We begin by exploring the nature of entrepreneurship. We then examine the role of entrepreneurship in the business world and discuss strategies for entrepreneurial organizations. We then describe the structure and performance of entrepreneurial organizations.

The Nature of Entrepreneurship

Entrepreneurship is the process of planning, organizing, operating, and assuming the risk of a business venture. An entrepreneur, in turn, is someone who engages in entrepreneurship. Michael Gleissner, who's featured in our opening story, fits this description. He put his own resources on the line and took a personal stake in the success or failure of Bigfoot. Business owners who hire professional managers to run their businesses and then turn their attention to other interests are not true entrepreneurs. Although they are assuming the risk of the venture, they are not actively involved in organizing or operating it. Likewise, professional managers whose job is running someone else's business are not entrepreneurs, for they assume less than total personal risk for the success or failure of the business.

Entrepreneurs start new businesses. We define a small business as one that is privately owned by one individual or a small group of individuals and has sales and assets that are not large enough to influence its environment. A small, two-person software development company with annual sales of $100,000 would clearly be a small business, whereas Microsoft Corporation is just as clearly a large business. But the boundaries are not always this clear-cut. For example, a regional retailing chain with 20 stores and annual revenues of $30 million may sound large but is really very small when compared to such giants as Walmart and Sears.

What is a small business?

How easy or difficult is it to distinguish between a small and a large business?

CONCEPT CHECK

The Role of Entrepreneurship in Society

The history of entrepreneurship and of the development of new businesses is in many ways the history of great wealth and of great failure. Some entrepreneurs have been very successful and have accumulated vast fortunes from their entrepreneurial efforts. For example, when Microsoft Corporation first sold its stock to the public in 1986, Bill Gates, then just 30 years old, received $350 million for his share of Microsoft.[2] Today his holdings—valued at over $53 billion—make him the richest person in the United States and one of the richest in the world.[3] Many more entrepreneurs, however, have lost a great deal of money. Research suggests that the majority of new businesses fail within the first few years after founding.[4] Many that last longer do so only because the entrepreneurs themselves work long hours for very little income.

As Figure 10.1 shows, most U.S. businesses employ fewer than 100 people, and most U.S. workers are employed by small firms. For example, Figure 10.1(a) shows that approximately 86 percent of all U.S. businesses employ fewer than 20 people; another 11.7 percent employ between 20 and 99 people. In contrast, only about 2.1 percent employ between 100 and 499 workers and another .2 percent employee 500 or more. Figure 10.1(b) shows that 24.5 percent of all U.S. workers are employed by firms with fewer than 20 people; another 29.6 percent work in firms that employ between 20 and 99 people. The vast majority of these companies are owner-operated.[5] Figure 10.1(b) also shows that 25.5 percent of U.S. workers are employed by firms with 100 to 499 employees and another 20.3 percent work for businesses that employ 500 or more total employees.

entrepreneurship
The process of planning, organizing, operating, and assuming the risk of a business venture

entrepreneur
Someone who engages in entrepreneurship

small business
A business that is privately owned by one individual or a small group of individuals and has sales and assets that are not large enough to influence its environment

FIGURE 10.1 THE IMPORTANCE OF SMALL BUSINESS IN THE UNITED STATES

(a) Approximately 86 percent of all U.S. businesses employ fewer than 20 people; another 11.7 percent employ between 20 and 99 people. In contrast, only about 2.1 percent employ between 100 and 400 workers, and another .2 percent employ 500 or more. (b) 24.5 percent of all U.S. workers are employed by firms with fewer than 20 people; another 29.6 percent work in firms that employ between 20 and 99 people. 25.5 percent of U.S. workers are employed by firms with 100–499 employees, and another 20.3 percent work for businesses that employ 500 or more total employees.

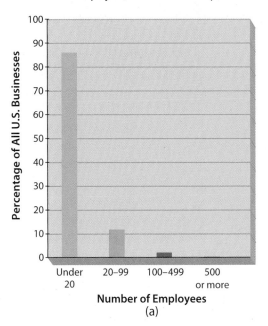

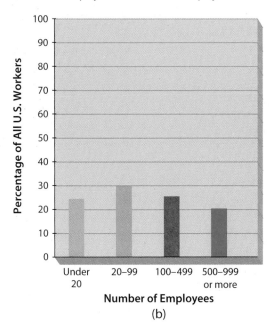

Source: U.S. Census Bureau, *Statistical Abstract of the United States*, 2010 (Washington, DC: Government Printing Office, 2011).

On the basis of numbers alone, then, small business is a strong presence in the economy, which is also true in virtually all of the world's mature economies. In Germany, for example, companies with fewer than 500 employees produce two-thirds of the nation's gross national product, train nine of ten apprentices, and employ four of every five workers. Small businesses also play major roles in the economies of Italy, France, and Brazil. In addition, experts agree that small businesses will be quite important in the emerging economies of countries such as Russia and Vietnam. The contribution of small business can be measured in terms of its effects on key aspects of an economic system. In the United States, these aspects include job creation, innovation, and importance to big business.

Job Creation

In the early 1980s, a widely cited study suggested that small businesses are responsible for creating eight of every ten new jobs in the United States. This contention touched off considerable interest in the fostering of small business as a matter of public policy. As we will see, though, relative job growth among businesses of different sizes is not easy to determine. But it is clear that small business—especially in certain industries—is an important source of new (and often well-paid) jobs in the United States. According to the Small Business Administration (SBA), for example, seven of the ten industries that added the most new jobs in 2007 were in sectors dominated by small businesses. Moreover, small businesses currently account for over one-third of all jobs in high-technology sectors of the economy.[6]

Note that new jobs are also being created by small firms specializing in international business. For example, Bob Knosp operates a small business in Bellevue, Washington, that

FIGURE 10.2

REPRESENTATIVE JOBS CREATED AND LOST IN 2009

All businesses create and eliminate jobs. Because of their size, the magnitude of job creation and elimination is especially pronounced in bigger businesses. This figure provides several representative examples of job creation and elimination at several big U.S. businesses during 2009. For example, while Caterpillar cut 20,000 jobs and Pfizer cut 19,500 jobs, Whole Foods created 8,570 jobs and Microsoft added another 7,130 during this same period.

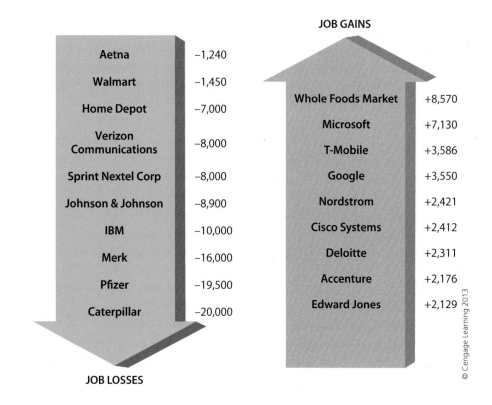

JOB LOSSES	
Aetna	−1,240
Walmart	−1,450
Home Depot	−7,000
Verizon Communications	−8,000
Sprint Nextel Corp	−8,000
Johnson & Johnson	−8,900
IBM	−10,000
Merk	−16,000
Pfizer	−19,500
Caterpillar	−20,000

JOB GAINS	
Whole Foods Market	+8,570
Microsoft	+7,130
T-Mobile	+3,586
Google	+3,550
Nordstrom	+2,421
Cisco Systems	+2,412
Deloitte	+2,311
Accenture	+2,176
Edward Jones	+2,129

makes computerized sign-making systems. Knosp gets over half his sales from abroad and has dedicated almost 75 percent of his workforce to handling international sales. Indeed, according to the SBA, small businesses account for 92 percent of all U.S. exporters.[7]

It is important to note, though, that tracking job gains and losses is very complicated and somewhat imprecise. For instance, suppose a business eliminates one full-time job but later replaces it with two part-time jobs. Some statistics would count this as a loss of one job followed by a gain of two jobs. Similarly, the jobs within a company can fluctuate when it acquires or sells a business unit. For instance, a few years ago Halliburton "cut" 53,000 jobs. But in reality, these "losses" actually came when the firm sold its largest subsidiary, KBR. Only a handful of jobs were actually eliminated; instead, over 50,000 jobs were simply moved to a new firm. And while Walmart cut 1,450 jobs in 2009, it had added almost 200,000 over the preceding three years.

At least one message is clear: Entrepreneurial business success, more than business size, accounts for most new job creation. Whereas successful retailers like Walmart and Best Buy have been growing and adding thousands of new jobs, struggling chains like Kmart have been eliminating thousands. Hence, most firms, especially those in complex and dynamic environments, go through periods of growth when they add new jobs but also have periods when they cut jobs.

The reality, then, is that jobs are created by entrepreneurial companies of all sizes, all of which hire workers and all of which lay them off. Although small firms often hire at a faster rate than large ones, they are also likely to eliminate jobs at a far higher rate. Small firms are also usually the first to hire in times of economic recovery, whereas large firms are generally the last. Conversely, however, big companies are also the last to lay off workers during economic downswings.

Innovation

History has shown that major innovations are as likely to come from small businesses (or individuals) as from big businesses. For example, small firms and individuals invented the personal computer and the stainless-steel razor blade, the transistor radio and the photocopying machine, the jet engine and the self-developing photograph. They also gave us the helicopter and power steering, automatic transmissions and air conditioning, cellophane and the

A WORLD OF DIFFERENCE

The Invisibib Woman

Head Injury Association
A BRIDGE TO HOPE AND HEALING

Home | Contact Us

What is TBI | Who We Are | Services & Programs | Donor Support | Employment | News & Events

INTRODUCING

invisibib
the invisible adult bib

The **INVISIBIB** is a transparent, light weight, easy-to-use adult bib that allows the wearer's attire to be seen, while protecting his or her clothing. Its generous size insures full coverage and protection.

It features:
- Simple 'one-button' Velcro closure with universal collar fit
- Clear vinyl for extra pliability, flexibility and comfort
- Convenient pouch pockets to hold items and catch food spills
- Easy clean-up and machine-washable
- Folds up easily for travel • Exclusively at People Products

INVENTED BY

Alison Schuback, Inc. Magazine 2008 Entrepreneur of the Year

At 23, Alison was busy working on her master's degree in family therapy, had an active social life and envisioned a life spent helping others. Then, on October 17, 1997, an SUV ran a red light and plowed into the side of her car. She became a Traumatic Brain Injury (TBI) survivor. Only for Alison, victim-hood was not a viable option. She still had her dream for a successful career.

After rehab, Alison saw she had a problem and decided to solve it. When she ate out, she needed to protect her clothing but she didn't want to be embarrassed and still wanted to look fashionable. So, she solved the problem and invented the INVISIBIB.

Through a twist of fate Alison's path crossed with the Head Injury Association and out of that has grown a unique relationship. **Head Injury Association** formed a company, **People Products**, the place for **Special Products for Special People**, staffed by TBI survivors, selling the **INVISIBIB** Alison had invented.

Alison's career dream is coming true and will grow along with People Products.

AVAILABLE AT

PeopleProducts
Special Products for Special People

People Products, the place for **Special Products for Special People**, is a company founded by the Head Injury Association staffed by Traumatic Brain Injury (TBI) survivors. Its goal is to provide special products for special people to help make their lives easier, while giving those challenged with TBI a meaningful career.

Invisibib, courtesy of Head Injury Association

Alison Schuback developed the idea for her signature product because she needed it. She suffered traumatic brain damage in an automobile accident in 1997, and she now gets around in an electric wheelchair; her voice is weak, and a battery pack implanted below her shoulder helps to control tremors in her brain. Although she has enough motor control to raise a utensil to her mouth, her hand shakes and her food spills. She tried tying an apron around her neck, but people kept looking at her in restaurants. "I wanted something to cover me that wasn't noticeable," she recalls. "People already had so many other reasons to look at me. Why give them another?"

That's how Schuback came up with an enterprising solution to her problem: She decided to develop an inconspicuous adult bib for her own personal use, and then she'd manufacture it and sell it and pay off a few medical bills in the process. The result was the Invisibib, a transparent vinyl bib with a pouch in front. Using $80,000 of her settlement money as startup capital, Schuback partnered with a disability consultant named Karen Weatherford to launch a company called Independent Empowerment to sell the adult bib and a few other products specially customized for the

disabled. For the next two years, the partners hit the trade-show circuit and made sales calls at seniors' homes and physical-rehab facilities. They made about $20,000 in sales before the money ran out.

That's when Schuback decided to audition for the PBS program *Everyday Edisons*. Conceived in 2005, the program features inventors and their inventions and, more importantly, shows them (and viewers) the path from invention to entrepreneurship: The purpose of the program, explains co-creator Michael Cable, is "to show that ordinary people do have extraordinary ideas. They just don't know what to do with them."

Because of Schuback's appearance on *Everyday Edisons*, the Invisibib came to the attention of Len Feinstein, co-founder and co-chairman of Bed Bath & Beyond, the country's number-one domestic-products retailer. Feinstein, the father of a son who, like Schuback, had suffered severe brain trauma in a car accident, was also the founder of the Head Injury Association (HIA), a nonprofit institution that maintains facilities for disabled people like his son, and he proposed that HIA sponsor a for-profit company to sell the Invisibib. Schuback, who would be mentored by members of Bed Bath & Beyond's executive team, would be involved in all aspects of the operation, including marketing and new-product decisions. As part of its agreement with the would-be entrepreneurs who appear on the show, *Everyday Edison* took charge of industrial design and manufacture, contracting to supply finished products at cost. The program also underwrote Schuback's compensation. After all, says Cable, she "did her homework, she networked, she spent her own money." In other words, she took the risk and did the work.

Launched in 2009, the enterprise is called People Products. It sells over the web and through Bed Bath & Beyond and other retailers, primarily to nursing homes and chains of assisted-living facilities. The company is also exploring other Invisibib applications, including use by children in art classes, coffee-drinking commuters, and brides sitting through makeup refreshes.

References: Leigh Buchanan, "Entrepreneur of the Year: What Alison Schuback Wants," *Inc.*, December 2008, www.inc.com on March 7, 2011; Alison Schuback, "The Invisibib: Bringing Dignity into View," The Hotmommas Project Case Study Competition, 2007–2008, www.hotmommasproject.org on March 7, 2011; "Alison Schuback," interview, *The Brand Show* (Two West Inc., September 2010), www.twowest.com on March 7, 2011; People Products, "About People Products," 2010, www.peopleproducts.com on March 7, 2011.

disposable ballpoint pen. Today, says the SBA, small businesses consistently supply over half of all "innovations" introduced into the U.S. marketplace each year.[8]

Not surprisingly, history is repeating itself with increasing rapidity in the age of computers and high-tech communication. For example, much of today's most innovative software is being written at relatively new start-up companies. Yahoo! and Netscape brought the Internet into the average U.S. living room, and online companies such as Amazon.com, eBay, and Google are using it to redefine our shopping habits. MySpace, Facebook, and Twitter have changed how we interact with one another.[9] Each of these firms started out as a small business.

> "[Twitter's founders] created a new way for people to communicate publicly and instantaneously."
>
> —FRED WILSON, VENTURE CAPITALIST[10]

Of course, not all successful new start-ups are leading-edge dot-com enterprises. Take Sacha White, for example. He moved to Oregon a few years ago and got a job as a bicycle messenger. He began to tinker with his bike, and eventually built himself a custom one from scratch. Other riders took note, and started wanting him to build bikes for them as well. White eventually started his own business called Vanilla Bicycles. He handcrafts each one and has a waiting list of four years. All told, he makes between 40 and 50 bikes per year; about 40 percent of these bikes are sold domestically, the rest to international customers. The average price of each of his custom bikes is around $7,000.[11] Entrepreneurs have also achieved success in such diverse fields as specialized dog training, hand-crafted musical instruments, and delicate fly fishing reels. The *World of Difference* box on page 237, entitled "The Invisibib Woman," tells the story of one young entrepreneur who turned adversity into an occasion for innovative thinking.

Importance to Big Business

Most of the products made by big manufacturers are sold to consumers by small businesses. For example, the majority of dealerships selling Fords, Chevrolets, Toyotas, and Kias are independently owned and operated. Moreover, small businesses provide big businesses with many of the services, supplies, and raw materials they need. Likewise, Microsoft relies heavily on small businesses in the course of its routine business operations. For example, the software giant outsources much of its routine code-writing function to hundreds of sole proprietorships and other small firms. It also outsources much of its packaging, delivery, and distribution to smaller companies. Dell Computer uses this same strategy, buying most of the parts and components used in its computers from small suppliers around the world.

Compare job creation success between small and large business in the United States.

Why do so many innovations seem to come from entrepreneurs and small business?

CONCEPT CHECK

Strategy for Entrepreneurial Organizations

One of the most basic challenges facing an entrepreneurial organization is choosing a strategy. The three strategic challenges facing small firms are choosing an industry in which to compete, emphasizing distinctive competencies, and writing a business plan.[12]

Choosing an Industry

Not surprisingly, small businesses are more common in some industries than in others. The major industry groups that include successful new ventures and small businesses are services, retailing, construction, financial and insurance, wholesaling, transportation, and manufacturing. Obviously, each group differs in its requirements for employees, money, materials, and machines.

In general, the more resources an industry requires, the harder it is to start a business and the less likely that the industry is dominated by small firms. Remember, too, that *small* is a relative term: The criteria (number of employees and total annual sales) differ from industry to industry and are often meaningful only when compared with businesses that are truly large. Figure 10.3 shows the distribution of all U.S. businesses employing fewer than 20 people across industry groups.

> "Entrepreneurship is certainly not the exclusive province of business. It can mushroom anywhere."
>
> —BARRON HARVEY, DEAN OF HOWARD UNIVERSITY'S BUSINESS SCHOOL[13]

Services Primarily because they require few resources, service businesses are the fastest-growing segment of small-business enterprise. In addition, no other industry group offers a higher return on time invested. Finally, services appeal to the talent for innovation typified by many small enterprises. As Figure 10.3 shows, 35.26 percent of all businesses with fewer than 20 employees are services.

Small-business services range from shoeshine parlors to car rental agencies, from marriage counseling to computer software, from accounting and management consulting to professional dog walking. In Dallas, for example, Jani-King has prospered by selling commercial cleaning services to local companies. In Virginia Beach, Virginia, Jackson Hewitt Tax Services has found a profitable niche in providing computerized tax preparation and electronic tax-filing services. Great Clips, Inc. is a fast-growing family-run chain of hair salons headquartered in Minneapolis.

David Flanary, Richard Sorenson, and Michael Holloway recently established an Internet-based long-distance telephone service in Austin, Texas, called PointOne Telecommunications. The basic idea was hatched during a tennis match. Recalls Sorenson, "We started getting excited, volleying at the net, and then finally we put the rackets down and went to the side to talk." The firm is off to a great start. Currently it acts as a wholesale voice carrier, but as soon as its network is completed, PointOne will start signing up its own commercial customers. Investors agree that the company will soon be a major force in telecommunications.[14]

FIGURE 10.3 SMALL BUSINESSES (BUSINESSES WITH FEWER THAN 20 EMPLOYEES) BY INDUSTRY

Small businesses are especially strong in certain industries, such as retailing and services. On the other hand, there are relatively fewer small businesses in industries such as transportation and manufacturing. The differences are affected primarily by factors such as the investment costs necessary to enter markets in these industries. For example, starting a new airline would require the purchase of large passenger aircraft and airport gates, and hiring an expensive set of employees.

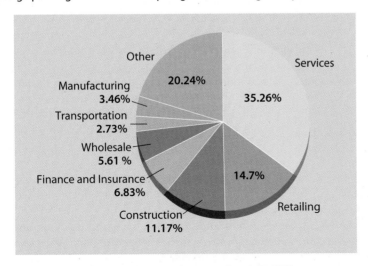

Source: U.S. Census Bureau, *Statistical Abstract of the United States*, 2010, May 25, 2011.

Retailing A retail business sells directly to consumers products manufactured by other firms. There are hundreds of different kinds of retailers, ranging from wig shops and frozen yogurt stands to automobile dealerships and department stores. Usually, however, people who start small businesses favor specialty shops—for example, big-men's clothing or gourmet coffees—which let them focus limited resources on narrow market segments. Retailing accounts for 14.7 percent of all businesses with fewer than 20 employees.

John Mackey, for example, launched Whole Foods out of his own frustration at being unable to find a full range of natural foods at other stores. He soon found, however, that he had tapped a lucrative market and started an ambitious expansion program. Today, with 299 outlets scattered across the United States, Canada, and the United Kingdom, Whole Foods is the world's leader in natural and organic foods supermarkets.[15] Likewise, when Olga Tereshko found it difficult to locate just the right cloth diapers and breast-feeding supplies for her newborn son, she decided to start selling them herself. Instead of taking the conventional retailing route, however, Tereshko set up shop on the Internet. Her business, called Little Koala, has established a customer base of over 10,000 loyal customers.

mathieu boivin/istockphoto.com

Finding just the right diapers can be a surprisingly daunting task for new parents. When Olga Tereshko couldn't locate the diapers she wanted for her baby, she concluded that others would be in the same predicament. So, she launched an Internet business, Little Koala, that quickly established a loyal customer base of over 10,000 customers.

Construction About 11.17 percent of businesses with fewer than 20 employees are involved in construction. Because many construction jobs are relatively small local projects, local construction firms are often ideally suited as contractors. Many such firms are begun by skilled craftspeople who start out working for someone else and subsequently decide to work for themselves. Common examples of small construction firms include home builders, wood finishers, roofers, painters, and plumbing, electrical, and roofing contractors.

For example, Marek Brothers Construction in College Station, Texas, was started by two brothers, Pat and Joe Marek. They originally worked for other contractors but started their own partnership in 1980. Their only employee is a receptionist. They manage various construction projects, including new-home construction and remodeling, subcontracting out the actual work to other businesses or to individual craftspeople. Marek Brothers has annual gross income of about $5 million.

Finance and Insurance Financial and insurance businesses also comprise about 6.8 percent of all firms with fewer than 20 employees. In most cases, these businesses are either affiliates of or sell products provided by larger national firms. Although the deregulation of the banking industry has reduced the number of small local banks, other businesses in this sector are still doing quite well.

Typically, for example, local State Farm Mutual offices are small businesses. State Farm itself is a major insurance company, but its local offices are run by 16,500 independent agents. In turn, agents hire their own staff, run their own offices as independent businesses, and so forth. They sell various State Farm insurance products and earn commissions from the premiums paid by their clients. Some local savings and loan operations, mortgage companies, and pawn shops also fall into this category.

Wholesaling Small-business owners often do very well in wholesaling, too; about 5.6 percent of businesses with fewer than 20 employees are wholesalers. A wholesale business buys products from manufacturers or other producers and then sells them to retailers. Wholesalers usually buy goods in bulk and store them in quantity at locations that are convenient for retailers. For a given volume of business, therefore, they need fewer employees than manufacturers, retailers, or service providers.

They also serve fewer customers than other providers—usually those who repeatedly order large volumes of goods. Wholesalers in the grocery industry, for instance, buy packaged food in bulk from companies like Del Monte and Campbell and then sell it to both large grocery chains and smaller independent grocers. Luis Espinoza has found a promising niche for Inca Quality Foods, a midwestern wholesaler that imports and distributes Latino foods for consumers from Mexico, the Caribbean, and Central America. Partnered with the large grocery-store chain Kroger, Espinoza's firm continues to grow steadily.[16]

Transportation Some small firms—about 3 percent of all companies with fewer than 20 employees—do well in transportation and transportation-related businesses. Such firms include local taxi and limousine companies, charter airplane services, and tour operators. In addition, in many smaller markets, bus companies and regional airlines subcontract local equipment maintenance to small businesses.

Consider, for example, some of the transportation-related small businesses at a ski resort like Steamboat Springs, Colorado. Most visitors fly to the town of Hayden, about 15 miles from Steamboat Springs. Although some visitors rent vehicles, many others use the services of Alpine Taxi, a small local operation, to transport them to their destinations in Steamboat Springs. While on vacation, they also rely on the local bus service, which is subcontracted by the town to another small business, to get to and from the ski slopes each day. Other small businesses offer van tours of the region, hot-air balloon rides, and helicopter lifts to remote areas for extreme skiers. Still others provide maintenance support at Hayden for the American and United aircraft that serve the area during ski season.

Manufacturing More than any other industry, manufacturing lends itself to big business—and for good reason. Because of the investment normally required in equipment, energy, and raw materials, a good deal of money is usually needed to start a manufacturing business. Automobile manufacturing, for example, calls for billions of dollars of investment and thousands of workers before the first automobile rolls off the assembly line. Obviously, such requirements shut out most individuals. Although Henry Ford began with $28,000, it has been a long time since anyone started a new U.S. car company from scratch.

Research has shown that manufacturing costs often fall as the number of units produced by an organization increases. This relationship between cost and production is called an *economy of scale*.[17] Small organizations usually cannot compete effectively on the basis of economies of scale. As depicted in Figure 10.4(a), organizations with higher levels of production have a major cost advantage over those with lower levels of production. Given the cost positions of small and large firms when there are strong economies of scale in manufacturing, it is not surprising that small manufacturing organizations generally do not do as well as large ones.

Interestingly, when technology in an industry changes, it often shifts the economies-of-scale curve, thereby creating opportunities for smaller organizations. For example, steel manufacturing was historically dominated by a few large companies, which owned several huge facilities. With the development of mini-mill technology, however, extracting economies of scale at a much smaller level of production became possible. This type of shift is depicted in Figure 10.4(b). Point A in this panel is the low-cost point with the original economies of scale. Point B is the low-cost point with the economies of scale brought on by the new technology. Notice that the number of units needed for low costs is considerably lower for the new technology. This has allowed the entry of numerous smaller firms into the steel industry. Such entry would not have been possible with the older technology.

This is not to say that there are no small-business owners who do well in manufacturing—about 3.46 percent of businesses with fewer than 20 employees are involved in some aspect of manufacturing. Indeed, it is not uncommon for small manufacturers to

FIGURE 10.4 ECONOMIES OF SCALE IN SMALL-BUSINESS ORGANIZATIONS

Small businesses sometimes find it difficult to compete in manufacturing-related industries because of the economies of scale associated with plant, equipment, and technology. As shown in (a), firms that produce a large number of units (that is, larger businesses) can do so at a lower per-unit cost. At the same time, however, new forms of technology occasionally cause the economies-of-scale curve to shift, as illustrated in (b). In this case, smaller firms may be able to compete more effectively with larger ones because of the drop in per-unit manufacturing cost.

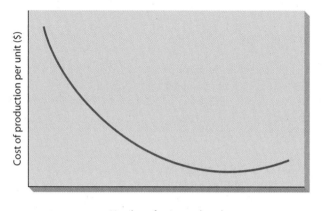

(a) Standard economies-of-scale curve

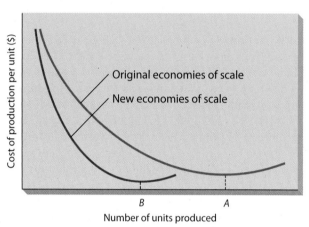

(b) Change in technology that shifts economies of scale and may make small-business manufacturing possible

© Cengage Learning 2013

outperform big business in such innovation-driven industries as chemistry, electronics, toys, and computer software. Some small manufacturers prosper by serving as suppliers to large manufacturers.

Other small manufacturers prosper by locating profitable niches. For example, brothers Dave and Dan Hanlon and Dave's wife Jennie started a new motorcycle-manufacturing business called Excelsior-Henderson. (Excelsior and Henderson are actually names of classic motorcycles from the early years of the twentieth century; the Hanlons acquired the rights to these brand names because of the images they evoke among motorcycle enthusiasts.) The Hanlons built 4,000 bikes their first year and now have annual production of 20,000 per year. So far, Excelsior-Henderson motorcycles have been well received (the top-end Excelsior-Henderson Super X sells for about $18,000), and many Harley-Davidson dealers have started to sell them as a means of diversifying their product line.[18]

Emphasizing Distinctive Competencies

As we defined in Chapter 8, an organization's distinctive competencies are the aspects of business that the firm performs better than its competitors. The distinctive competencies of small business usually fall into three areas: the ability to identify new niches in established markets, the ability to identify new markets, and the ability to move quickly to take advantage of new opportunities.

Identifying Niches in Established Markets   An established market is one in which several large firms compete according to relatively well-defined criteria. For example, throughout the 1970s, several well-known computer-manufacturing companies, including IBM, Digital Equipment, and Hewlett-Packard, competed according to three product criteria: computing power, service, and price. Over the years, the computing power and quality of service delivered by these firms continued to improve, while prices (especially relative to computing power) continued to drop.

established market
A market in which several large firms compete according to relatively well-defined criteria

Enter Apple Computer and the personal computer. For Apple, user-friendliness, not computing power, service, or price, was to be the basis of competition. Apple targeted every manager, every student, and every home as the owner of a personal computer. Apple's major entrepreneurial act was not to invent a new technology (indeed, the first Apple computers used all standard parts taken from other computers), but to recognize a new kind of computer and a new way to compete in the computer industry.

Apple's approach to competition was to identify a new niche in an established market. A niche is simply a segment of a market that is not currently being exploited. In general, small entrepreneurial businesses are better at discovering these niches than are larger organizations. Large organizations usually have so many resources committed to older, established business practices that they may be unaware of new opportunities. Entrepreneurs can see these opportunities and move quickly to take advantage of them.[19]

Dave Gilboa and Neil Blumenthal recently founded Warby Parker, a business that sells prescription eyewear through the mail. The entrepreneurs realized that most consumers disliked the experience of going to an optical shop to try on glasses and then were irritated at the price of those glasses. So, Warby Parker offers lower-priced glasses with hip designs and a money-back guarantee. Astute marketing then allowed them to get a quick start with their niche business, selling over 50,000 pairs of glasses and generating profits after only a single year of operation.[20]

Identifying New Markets Successful entrepreneurs also excel at discovering whole new markets. Discovery can happen in at least two ways. First, an entrepreneur can transfer a product or service that is well established in one geographic market to a second market. This is what Marcel Bich did with ballpoint pens, which occupied a well-established market in Europe before Bich introduced them to this country. Bich's company, Société Bic, eventually came to dominate the U.S. market.

Second, entrepreneurs can sometimes create entire industries. Entrepreneurial inventions of the dry paper copying process and the semiconductor have created vast new industries. Not only have the first companies into these markets been very successful (Xerox and National Semiconductor, respectively), but their entrepreneurial activity has spawned the development of hundreds of other companies and hundreds of thousands of jobs. Again, because entrepreneurs are not encumbered with a history of doing business in a particular way, they are usually better at discovering new markets than are larger, more mature organizations.

First-Mover Advantages A first-mover advantage is any advantage that comes to a firm because it exploits an opportunity before any other firm does. Sometimes large firms discover niches within existing markets or new markets at just about the same time small entrepreneurial firms do, but are not able to move as quickly as small companies to take advantage of these opportunities.

There are numerous reasons for this difference. For example, many large organizations make decisions slowly because each of their many layers of hierarchy has to approve an action before it can be implemented. Also, large organizations may sometimes put a great deal of their assets at risk when they take advantage of new opportunities. Every time Boeing decides to build a new model of a commercial jet, it is making a decision that could literally bankrupt the company if it does not turn out well. The size of the risk may make large organizations cautious. The dollar value of the assets at risk in a small organization, in contrast, is quite small. Managers may be willing to "bet the company" when the value of the company is only $100,000. They might be unwilling to "bet the company" when the value of the company is $1 billion.

Writing a Business Plan

Once an entrepreneur has chosen an industry to compete in and determined which distinctive competencies to emphasize, these choices are usually included in a document called a business plan. In a business plan the entrepreneur summarizes the business strategy and how that strategy is to be implemented. The very act of preparing a business plan forces prospective

niche
A segment of a market not currently being exploited

first-mover advantage
Any advantage that comes to a firm because it exploits an opportunity before any other firm does

business plan
A document that summarizes the business strategy and structure

entrepreneurs to crystallize their thinking about what they must do to launch their business successfully and obliges them to develop their business on paper before investing time and money in it. The idea of a business plan is not new. What is new is the growing use of specialized business plans by entrepreneurs, mostly because creditors and investors demand them for use in deciding whether to help finance a small business.[21]

The plan should describe the match between the entrepreneur's abilities and the requirements for producing and marketing a particular product or service. It should define strategies for production and marketing, legal aspects and organization, and accounting and finance. In particular, it should answer three questions: (1) What are the entrepreneur's goals and objectives? (2) What strategies will the entrepreneur use to obtain these goals and objectives? (3) How will the entrepreneur implement these strategies?

Business plans should also account for the sequential nature of much strategic decision making in small businesses. For example, entrepreneurs cannot forecast sales revenues without first researching markets. The sales forecast itself is one of the most important elements in the business plan. Without such forecasts, it is all but impossible to estimate intelligently the size of a plant, store, or office, or to determine how much inventory to carry or how many employees to hire.

Another important component of the overall business plan is financial planning, which translates all other activities into dollars. Generally, the financial plan is made up of a cash budget, an income statement, balance sheets, and a breakeven chart. The most important of these statements is the cash budget because it tells entrepreneurs how much money they need before they open for business and how much money they need to keep the business operating.

Kurita KAKU/Gamma-Rapho via Getty Images

Some entrepreneurial organizations find major new market opportunities abroad. While Apple is no longer a small business, of course, it remains on the forefront of entrepreneurial initiatives. For example, when the first Apple store opened in Tokyo, lines of people waiting to get into the store stretched for three blocks.

Entrepreneurship and International Management

Finally, although many people associate international management with big business, many smaller companies are also finding expansion and growth opportunities in foreign countries. For example, Fuci Metals, a small but growing enterprise, buys metal from remote locations in areas such as Siberia and Africa, and then sells it to big automakers like Ford and Toyota. Similarly, California-based Gold's Gym is expanding into foreign countries and has been especially successful in Russia. And Markel Corporation, a small Philadelphia-based firm that manufactures tubing and insulated wiring, derives 40 percent of its annual revenues (currently around $32 million) from international sales. Although such ventures are accompanied by considerable risks, they also give entrepreneurs new opportunities and can be a real catalyst for success.

Which industries seem most and least hospitable for entrepreneurship and small business?

Identifying a distinctive competence seems like a straightforward concept, yet many entrepreneurs fail to grasp its significance. Why do you think this is the case?

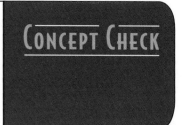

CONCEPT CHECK

Structure of Entrepreneurial Organizations

With a strategy in place and a business plan in hand, the entrepreneur can then proceed to devise a structure that turns the vision of the business plan into a reality. Many of the same concerns in structuring any business, which are described in Chapters 14 through 18 of this book, are also relevant to small businesses. For example, entrepreneurs need to consider organization design and develop job descriptions, organization charts, and management control systems.

The Internet, of course, has rewritten virtually all of the rules for starting and operating a small business. Getting into business is easier and faster than ever before, there are many more potential opportunities than at any other time in history, and the ability to gather and assimilate information is at an all-time high. Even so, would-be entrepreneurs must still make the right decisions when they start. They must decide, for example, precisely how to get into business. Should they buy an existing business or build from the ground up? In addition, would-be entrepreneurs must find appropriate sources of financing and decide when and how to seek the advice of experts.

Starting the New Business

The first step in starting a new business is the individual's commitment to becoming a business owner. Next comes choosing the goods or services to be offered—a process that means investigating one's chosen industry and market. Making this choice also requires would-be entrepreneurs to assess not only industry trends but also their own skills. Like the managers of existing businesses, new business owners must also be sure that they understand the true nature of the enterprise in which they are engaged.

Buying an Existing Business After choosing a product and making sure that the choice fits their own skills and interests, entrepreneurs must decide whether to buy an existing business or to start from scratch. Consultants often recommend the first approach. Quite simply, the odds are better: If successful, an existing business has already proved its ability to draw customers at a profit. It has also established working relationships with lenders, suppliers, and the community. Moreover, the track record of an existing business gives potential buyers a much clearer picture of what to expect than any estimate of a new business's prospects. Around 30 percent of the new businesses started in the past decade were bought from someone else. The McDonald's empire, for example, was started when Ray Kroc bought an existing hamburger business and then turned it into a global phenomenon. Likewise, Starbucks was a struggling mail-order business when Howard Schultz bought it and turned his attention to retail expansion.

Starting from Scratch Some people, however, prefer the satisfaction that comes from planting an idea, nurturing it, and making it grow into a strong and sturdy business. There are also practical reasons to start a business from scratch. A new business does not suffer the ill effects of a prior owner's errors. The start-up owner is also free to choose lenders, equipment, inventories, locations, suppliers, and workers, unbound by a predecessor's commitments and policies. Of the new businesses begun in the past decade, 64 percent were started from scratch.

Not surprisingly, though, the risks of starting a business from scratch are greater than those of buying an existing firm. Founders of new businesses can only make predictions and projections about their prospects. Success or failure thus depends heavily on identifying a genuine business opportunity—a product for which many customers will pay well but which is currently unavailable to them. To find openings, entrepreneurs must study markets and answer the following questions: (1) Who are my customers?

> "If I end up sacrificing what made Vanilla [Bicycles] special just to make more bikes, that wouldn't be worth it to me."
>
> —SACHA WHITE, FOUNDER OF VANILLA BICYCLES[22]

(2) Where are they? (3) At what price will they buy my product? (4) In what quantities will they buy? (5) Who are my competitors? (6) How will my product differ from those of my competitors?

Finding answers to these questions is a difficult task even for large, well-established firms. But where can the new business owner get the necessary information? Other sources of assistance are discussed later in this chapter, but we briefly describe three of the most accessible here. For example, the best way to gain knowledge about a market is to work in it before going into business in it. If you once worked in a bookstore and now plan to open one of your own, you probably already have some idea about the kinds of books people request and buy. Second, a quick scan of the local Yellow Pages or an Internet search will reveal many potential competitors, as will advertisements in trade journals. Personal visits to these establishments and websites can give you insights into their strengths and weaknesses. And, third, studying magazines, books, and websites aimed specifically at small businesses can also be of help, as can hiring professionals to survey the market for you.

Financing the New Business

Although the choice of how to start is obviously important, it is meaningless unless a new business owner can obtain the money to set up shop. Among the more common sources for funding are family and friends, personal savings, banks and similar lending institutions, investors, and government agencies. Lending institutions are more likely to help finance the purchase of an existing business than a new business because the risks are better understood. Individuals starting up new businesses, on the other hand, are more likely to have to rely on their personal resources.

Personal Resources According to a study by the National Federation of Independent Business, an owner's personal resources, not loans, are the most important source of money. Including money borrowed from friends and relatives, personal resources account for over two-thirds of all money invested in new small businesses and one-half of that invested in the purchase of existing businesses. John Mackey started Whole Foods with a $10,000 loan from his father. Fred Smith used $4 million he had inherited from his father to launch FedEx. And Rebecca Boenigk started Neutral Posture, an ergonomic chair company, with personal savings and loans from several family members.

Strategic Alliances Strategic alliances are also becoming a popular method for financing business growth. When Steven and Andrew Grundy decided to launch an Internet CD-exchange business called Spun.com, they had very little capital and thus made extensive use of alliances with other firms. They partnered, for example, with wholesaler Alliance Entertainment Corporation as a CD supplier. Orders to Spun.com actually go to Alliance, which ships products to customers and bills Spun.com directly. This setup has allowed Spun.com to promote a vast inventory of labels without actually having to buy inventory. All told, the firm created an alliance network that has provided the equivalent of $40 million in capital.[23]

Lenders Although banks, independent investors, and government loans all provide much smaller portions of start-up funds than the personal resources of owners, they are important in many cases. Getting money from these sources, however, requires some extra effort. Banks and private investors usually want to see formal business plans—detailed outlines of proposed businesses and markets, owners' backgrounds, and other sources of funding. Government loans have strict eligibility guidelines.

venture capital company
A group of small investors seeking to make profits on companies with rapid growth potential

Venture Capital Companies Venture capital companies are groups of small investors seeking to make profits on companies with rapid growth potential. Most of these firms do not lend money: They invest it, supplying capital in return for stock. The venture capital company may also demand a representative on the board of directors. In some cases, managers may even need approval from the venture capital company before making major decisions. Of all venture capital currently committed in the United States, around 25 percent comes from true venture capital firms.[24] In 2009, venture capital firms invested $18 billion in new start-ups in the United States.

As noted earlier, Fred Smith used his inheritance to launch FedEx. Once he got his business plan developed and started service, though, he needed an infusion of substantial additional capital. All told, he raised about $80 million in venture capital to buy his first small fleet of planes. Venture capital was also important in the launch of both Facebook and Twitter.

Small-Business Investment Companies   Taking a more balanced approach in their choices than venture capital companies, small-business investment companies (SBICs) seek profits by investing in companies with potential for rapid growth. Created by the Small Business Investment Act of 1958, SBICs are federally licensed to borrow money from the SBA and to invest it in or lend it to small businesses. They are themselves investments for their shareholders. Past beneficiaries of SBIC capital include Apple Computer, Intel, and Federal Express. In addition, the government has recently begun to sponsor minority enterprise small-business investment companies (MESBICs). As the name suggests, MESBICs specialize in financing businesses that are owned and operated by minorities.

SBA Financial Programs   Since its founding in 1953, the SBA has offered more than 20 financing programs to small businesses that meet standards of size and independence. Eligible firms must also be unable to get private financing at reasonable terms. Because of these and other restrictions, SBA loans have never been a major source of small-business financing. In addition, budget cutbacks at the SBA have reduced the number of firms benefiting from loans. Nevertheless, several SBA programs currently offer funds to qualified applicants.

For example, under the SBA's guaranteed loans program, small businesses can borrow from commercial lenders. The SBA guarantees to repay 75 to 85 percent of the loan amount, not to exceed $1.5 million. Under a related program, companies engaged in international trade can borrow up to $1.75 million. Such loans may be made for as long as 15 years for machinery and equipment and up to 25 years for real estate. Most SBA lending activity flows through this program.

Sometimes, however, both desired bank and SBA-guaranteed loans are unavailable (perhaps because the business cannot meet stringent requirements). In such cases, the SBA may help finance the entrepreneur through its immediate participation loan program. Under this arrangement, the SBA and the bank each puts up a share of the money, with the SBA's share not to exceed $150,000. Under the local development companies (LDCs) program, the SBA works with a corporation (either for-profit or nonprofit) founded by local citizens who want to boost the local economy. The SBA can lend up to $500,000 for each small business to be helped by an LDC.

Spurred in large part by the boom in Internet businesses, both venture capital and loans are in general becoming easier to get. Most small businesses, for example, report that it became increasingly easier to obtain loans between 1995 and 2005. And firms like Facebook and Twitter are being offered so much venture capital that they are turning down part of it to keep from unnecessarily diluting their ownership. Unfortunately, the credit crunch that began in 2008 has made it harder for most entrepreneurs to obtain funds, but experts believe this is only a short-term problem.[25]

Sources of Management Advice

Financing is not the only area in which small businesses need help. Until World War II, for example, the business world involved few regulations, few taxes, few records, few big competitors, and no computers. Since then, simplicity has given way to complexity.

Today, few entrepreneurs are equipped with all the business skills they need to survive. Small-business owners can no longer be their own troubleshooters, lawyers, bookkeepers, financiers, and tax experts. For these jobs, they rely on professional help. To survive and grow, however, small businesses also need advice regarding management. This advice is usually available from four sources: advisory boards, management consultants, the SBA, and a process called "networking."

Advisory Boards All companies, even those that do not legally need boards of directors, can benefit from the problem-solving abilities of advisory boards. Thus some small businesses create boards to provide advice and assistance. For example, an advisory board might help an entrepreneur determine the best way to finance a plant expansion or to start exporting products to foreign markets.

Management Consultants Opinions vary widely about the value of management consultants—experts who charge fees to help managers solve problems. They often specialize in one area, such as international business, small business, or manufacturing. Thus they can bring an objective and trained outlook to problems and provide logical recommendations. They can be quite expensive, however, as some consultants charge $1,000 or more for a day of assistance.

Like other professionals, consultants should be chosen with care. They can be found through major corporations that have used their services and that can provide references and reports on their work. Not surprisingly, they are most effective when the client helps (for instance, by providing schedules and written proposals for work to be done).

The Small Business Administration Even more important than its financing role is the SBA's role in helping small-business owners improve their management skills. It is easy for entrepreneurs to spend money; SBA programs are designed to show them how to spend it wisely. The SBA offers small businesses four major management-counseling programs at virtually no cost.

A small-business owner who needs help in starting a new business can get it free through the Service Corps of Retired Executives (SCORE). All SCORE members are retired executives, and all are volunteers. Under this program, the SBA tries to match the expert to the need. For example, if a small-business owner needs help putting together a marketing plan, the SBA will send a SCORE counselor with marketing expertise.

Like SCORE, the Active Corps of Executives (ACE) program is designed to help small businesses that cannot afford consultants. The SBA recruits ACE volunteers from virtually every industry. All ACE volunteers are currently involved in successful activities, mostly as small-business owners themselves. Together, SCORE and ACE have more than 13,000 counselors working out of 350 chapters throughout the United States. They provide assistance to some 350,000 entrepreneurs and 20,000 ongoing small businesses each year.

The talents and skills of students and instructors at colleges and universities are fundamental to the Small Business Institute (SBI). Under the guidance of seasoned professors of business administration, students seeking advanced degrees work closely with small-business owners to help solve specific problems, such as sagging sales or rising costs. Students earn credit toward their degree, with their grades depending on how well they handle a client's problems. Several hundred colleges and universities counsel thousands of small-business owners through this program every year.

Finally, another SBA management counseling project is its Small Business Development Center (SBDC) program. SBDCs are designed to consolidate information from various disciplines and institutions, including technical and professional schools. Then they make this knowledge available to new and existing small businesses. Currently, universities in 36 states take part in the program.

Networking More and more, small-business owners are discovering the value of networking—meeting regularly with one another to discuss common problems and opportunities and, perhaps most important, to pool resources. Businesspeople have long joined organizations such as the local chamber of commerce and the National Federation of Independent Businesses (NFIB) to make such contacts.

Today, organizations are springing up all over the United States to facilitate small-business networking. One such organization, the Council of Smaller Enterprises of Cleveland, boasts a total membership of more than 10,000 small-business owners, the largest number in the country. This organization offers its members not only networking possibilities but also educational programs and services tailored to their needs. In a typical year, its 85 educational programs draw more than 8,500 small-business owners.

In particular, women and minorities have found networking to be an effective problem-solving tool. The National Association of Women Business Owners (NAWBO), for example, provides a variety of networking forums. The NAWBO also has chapters in most major cities, where its members can meet regularly. Increasingly, women are relying more on other women to help locate venture capital, establish relationships with customers, and provide such essential services as accounting and legal advice. According to Patty Abramson of the Women's Growth Capital Fund, all of these tasks have traditionally been harder for women because, until now, they have never had friends in the right places. "I wouldn't say this is about discrimination," adds Abramson. "It's about not having the relationships, and business is about relationships."

Networking is an important activity for small business owners. Networking allows entrepreneurs to make important contacts with customers, suppliers, lenders, and other important people. For instance, the National Association of Women Business Owners recently sponsored a conference to assist women and minority business owners better understand future business opportunities.

Franchising

The next time you drive or walk around town, be on the alert for a McDonald's, Taco Bell, Subway, Denny's, or KFC restaurant; a 7-Eleven or Circle K convenience store; a RE/MAX or Coldwell Banker real estate office; a Super 8 or Ramada Inn motel; a Blockbuster Video store; a Sylvan Learning Center educational center; an Express Oil Change or Precision Auto Wash service center; or a Supercuts hair salon. What do these businesses have in common? In most cases, they are franchised operations, operating under licenses issued by parent companies to local entrepreneurs who own and manage them.

As many would-be businesspeople have discovered, **franchising agreements** are an accessible doorway to entrepreneurship. A franchise is an arrangement that permits the *franchisee* (buyer) to sell the product of the *franchiser* (seller, or parent company). Franchisees can thus benefit from the selling corporation's experience and expertise. They can also consult the franchiser for managerial and financial help.[26]

For example, the franchiser may supply financing. It may pick the store location, negotiate the lease, design the store, and purchase necessary equipment. It may train the first set of employees and managers and provide standardized policies and procedures. Once the business is open, the franchiser may offer franchisees savings by allowing them to purchase from a central location. Marketing strategy (especially advertising) may also be handled by the franchiser. Finally, franchisees may benefit from continued management counseling. In short, franchisees receive—that is, invest in—not only their own ready-made business but also expert help in running it.

franchising agreement
A contract between an entrepreneur (the franchisee) and a parent company (the franchiser); the entrepreneur pays the parent company for the use of its trademarks, products, formulas, and business plans

Franchises offer many advantages to both sellers and buyers. For example, franchisers benefit from the ability to grow rapidly by using the investment money provided by franchisees. This strategy has enabled giant franchisers such as McDonald's and Subway to mushroom into billion-dollar concerns in a brief time.

For the franchisee, the arrangement combines the incentive of owning a business with the advantage of access to big-business management skills. Unlike the person who starts from scratch, the franchisee does not have to build a business step by step. Instead, the business is established virtually overnight. Moreover, because each franchise outlet is probably a carbon copy of every other outlet, the chances of failure are reduced. McDonald's, for example, is a model of consistency—Big Macs taste the same everywhere.

Of course, owning a franchise also involves certain disadvantages. Perhaps the most significant is the start-up cost. Franchise prices vary widely. Fantastic Sams hair salon franchise fees are $30,000. Extremely profitable or hard-to-get franchises are much more expensive, though. A McDonald's franchise costs $500,000 and additional reopening costs of up to $1,840,000; a professional sports team can cost several hundred million dollars. Franchisees may also have continued obligations to contribute percentages of sales to the parent corporation.

Buying a franchise also entails less tangible costs. For one thing, the small-business owner sacrifices some independence. A McDonald's franchisee cannot change the way its hamburgers or milkshakes are made. Nor can franchisees create an individual identity in their community; for all practical purposes, the McDonald's owner is anonymous. In addition, many franchise agreements are difficult to terminate.

Finally, although franchises minimize risks, they do not guarantee success. Many franchisees have seen their investments—and their dreams—disappear because of poor location, rising costs, or lack of continued franchiser commitment. Moreover, figures on failure rates are artificially low because they do not include failing franchisees bought out by their franchising parent companies. An additional risk is that the chain itself could collapse. In any given year, dozens—sometimes hundreds—of franchisers close shop or stop selling franchises.

What are the pros and cons of starting a new business from scratch versus buying an existing business?

Many people assume that Starbucks coffee shops are franchises, but in reality they are not. Why do you think Starbucks insists on owning all of its own retail outlets?

The Performance of Entrepreneurial Organizations

The formulation and implementation of an effective strategy plays a major role in determining the overall performance of an entrepreneurial organization. This section examines how entrepreneurial firms evolve over time and the attributes of these firms that enhance their chances of success. For every Henry Ford, Walt Disney, Mary Kay Ash, or Bill Gates—people who transformed small businesses into major corporations—there are many small-business owners and entrepreneurs who fail.

Exact numbers of start-ups and failures are surprisingly difficult to determine, however. For instance, a business may shut down because it is out of money (a failure) or simply because the owner decides to do something else; or the business may be sold to another business and cease to exist as an independent entity. Likewise, an ongoing sole proprietorship that becomes a partnership or corporation is not really a new business but may be counted as such in some statistics; similarly, a large corporation might launch a new enterprise as a new wholly owned but separately incorporated enterprise.

In general, though, experts believe that new business start-ups generally run between around 150,000 and 200,000 per year and that business failures generally run between 50,000 and 100,000 per year. In this section, we look first at a few key trends in small-business start-ups. Then we examine some of the main reasons for success and failure in small-business undertakings.

Trends in Small-Business Start-Ups

Thousands of new businesses are started in the United States every year. Several factors account for this trend, and in this section we focus on four of them.

Emergence of E-Commerce Clearly, one of the most significant recent trends in small-business start-ups is the rapid emergence of electronic commerce. Because the Internet has provided fundamentally new ways of doing business, savvy entrepreneurs have been able to create and expand new businesses faster and more easily than ever before. Such leading-edge firms as Google, Amazon, eBay, and Facebook, for example, owe their very existence to the Internet. At the same time, however, many would-be Internet entrepreneurs have gone under in the last few years, as the so-called dot-com boom quickly faded. Still, in 2010, online retail sales exceeded $142 billion, an increase of 3.3 percent from the previous year.

Indeed, it seems as if new ideas emerge virtually every day. Andrew Beebe, for example, is scoring big with Bigstep, a web business that essentially creates, hosts, and maintains websites for other small businesses. So far, Bigstep has signed up over 100,000 small-business clients. Beebe actually provides his basic services for free but earns money by charging for such so-called premium services as customer billing. Karl Jacob's Keen.com is a web business that matches people looking for advice with experts who have the answers. Keen got the idea when he and his father were struggling to fix a boat motor and did not know where to turn for help. Keen.com attracted 100,000 subscribers in just three months.[27]

Crossovers from Big Business It is interesting to note that increasing numbers of businesses are being started by people who have opted to leave big corporations and put their experience and know-how to work for themselves. In some cases, these individuals see great new ideas they want to develop. Often, they get burned out working for a big corporation. Sometimes they have lost their job, only to discover that working for themselves was a better idea anyway.

Cisco Systems CEO John Chambers is acknowledged as one of the best entrepreneurs around. But he spent several years working first at IBM and then at Wang Laboratories before he set out on his own. Under his leadership, Cisco has become one of the most important technology companies in the world. In a more unusual case, Gilman Louie recently left an executive position at Hasbro toy company's online group to head up a CIA-backed venture capital firm called In-Q-It. The firm's mission is to help nurture high-tech companies making products of interest to the nation's intelligence community.[28]

Opportunities for Minorities and Women In addition to big-business expatriates, minorities and women are starting more small businesses. For example, the number of African American–owned businesses totals about 1.9 million, an increase of 60.5 percent since 2002. These businesses account for around 7.1 percent of all U.S. businesses, generate $137.5 billion in revenue, and employ 921,032 people. African American purchasing power is expected to hit $1.2 trillion by 2013, an increase of 35 percent since 2008.[29]

Latino-owned businesses have grown at a rate of 43.6 percent and now number about 2.3 million. Other ethnic groups are also making their presence felt among U.S. business owners. Business ownership among Asians and Pacific Islanders has increased 34.3 percent, to over 1.6 million. Although the number of businesses owned by American Indians and Alaska Natives is still somewhat small, at slightly over 235,000, the total nevertheless represents a five-year increase of 17.9 percent.

The number of women entrepreneurs is also growing rapidly. There are now 7.8 million businesses owned by women—about 28.7 percent of all businesses in the United States and an increase of 20.1 percent since 2002. Combined, they generate nearly $1.2 trillion in revenue a year and employ 7.6 million people. Celeste Johnson, for example, left a management position at Pitney Bowes to launch Obex, Inc., which makes gardening and landscaping products from mixed recycled plastics. Katrina Garnett gave up a lucrative job at Oracle to start her own software company, Crossworlds Software. Laila Rubenstein closed her management-consulting practice to create Greeting Cards.com, Inc., an Internet-based business selling customizable electronic greetings. "Women-owned business," says Teresa Cavanaugh, director of the Women Entrepreneurs' Connection at BankBoston, "is the largest emerging segment of the small-business market. Women-owned businesses are an economic force that no bank can afford to overlook."

> "Attitudes about women in the workplace, period, have changed, let alone women running their own businesses."
>
> —ERIN FULLER, EXECUTIVE DIRECTOR OF THE NATIONAL ASSOCIATION OF WOMEN BUSINESS OWNERS[30]

Better Survival Rates Finally, more people are encouraged to test their skills as entrepreneurs because the failure rate among small businesses has been declining in recent years. As of 2008, seven out of ten new businesses survived at least two years, whereas about 49 percent survived five years; 34 percent of businesses survive at least ten years, and 26 percent last 15 years or longer. For reasons discussed in the next section, small businesses suffer a higher mortality rate than larger concerns. Among those that manage to stay in business for six to ten years, however, the survival rate levels off.

Reasons for Failure

Why do some businesses succeed and others fail? Although no set pattern has been established, four general factors contribute to new business failure. One factor is managerial incompetence or inexperience. Some would-be entrepreneurs assume that they can succeed through common sense, overestimate their own managerial acumen, or think that hard work alone will lead to success. But if managers do not know how to make basic business decisions or understand the basic concepts and principles of management, they are unlikely to be successful in the long run. In the *Technically Speaking* box entitled "What Went Wrong with Wesabe?" on page 253, one of the founders of a seemingly successful web startup attributes its demise to an early decision that seemed right at the time but which turned out to have unforeseen consequences.

Neglect can also contribute to failure. Some entrepreneurs try either to launch their ventures in their spare time or to devote only a limited amount of time to a new business. But starting a new business requires an overwhelming time commitment. Entrepreneurs who are not willing to put in the time and effort that a business requires are unlikely to survive.

Third, weak control systems can lead to serious problems. Effective control systems are needed to keep a business on track and to help alert entrepreneurs to potential trouble. If control systems do not signal impending problems, managers may be in serious trouble before more visible difficulties alert them.

Finally, insufficient capital can contribute to new business failure. Some entrepreneurs are overly optimistic about how soon they will start earning profits. In most cases, however, it takes months or years before a business is likely to start turning a profit. Amazon.com, for example, has only recently started to generate profits. Most experts say that a new business should have enough capital to operate for at least six months without earning a profit; some recommend enough to last a year.[31]

TECHNICALLY SPEAKING

What Went Wrong with Wesabe?

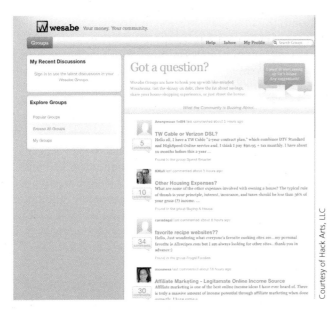

Courtesy of Hack Arts, LLC

As far as U.S. small business was concerned, the first quarter of 2010 could have been worse: There was a net loss of only 96,000 companies with fewer than 100 employees. As a matter of fact, the first quarter of 2009 *was* worse—a *lot* worse: By the end of the quarter, there were 400,000 fewer small businesses than there were at the beginning.

One of the companies that shut down in 2010 was Wesabe, which had launched in 2006 as an online site to help people manage their money and make better financial decisions. It was one of the first companies to enter the financial sector of what's often referred to as *Web 2.0*—the world of web applications that allow users to interact and collaborate on content that they create themselves. The idea was to let customers access data from several financial institutions and then compare their own money-management practices to those of online peers.

Wesabe actually got off to a reasonably good start. Within the first year, founders Marc Hedlund and Jason Knight secured venture capital totaling $4.7 million and attracted 150,000 members. The first signs of trouble appeared in the second year, just after

a competitor called Mint.com came online. Nine months after its launch, Mint.com boasted $17 million in venture capital and 300,000 users. In 2009, Intuit, a creator of financial and tax-preparation software, purchased Mint.com for $170 million. Wesabe held on until mid-2010, when Hedlund and Knight announced that the company could no longer handle users' highly sensitive data "with shoestring operations and security staff."

So what went wrong? Naturally, there's no single reason for Wesabe's failure, but both Hedlund, who blogged a postmortem shortly after the shutdown, and independent observers point to one crucial business decision as a key factor. In the early stages of the startup process, Hedlund and Knight rejected a partnership with a firm called Yodlee, which had already developed a system for accessing transaction data from banks. But because the Yodlee process worked with users' passwords, Wesabe considered it too big a security risk and proceeded to work on its own process, which, though more secure, was also more cumbersome.

"Everyone—I mean 90-percent-plus of everybody," says Hedlund, "told me that they would never in a million years use a startup website that asked them for their bank passwords." When Mint came online in 2007, it was using Yodlee technology, password-access included, and Hedlund acknowledges that he'd made a mistake by relying on his own informal market research: "We should have known," he admits, "that somebody would go with Yodlee, and we should have aimed at [Yodlee] as what we needed to achieve." By 2008, Wesabe, too, was accepting users' passwords in order to simplify the process of pulling bank data into its system.

"We just didn't build it nearly fast enough," says Hedlund of Wesabe's own data-access system. "That one mistake—not using or replacing Yodlee before Mint had a chance to launch on Yodlee—was probably enough to kill Wesabe alone."

References: Eilene Zimmerman, "How Six Companies Failed to Survive 2010," *New York Times*, January 5, 2011, www.nytimes.com on April 19, 2011; Anthony Ha, "Personal Finance Startup Wesabe to Shut Down," *VentureBeat*, June 30, 2010, http://venturebeat.com on April 19, 2011; Marc Hedlund, "Why Wesabe Lost to Mint," *Marc Hedlund's Blog*, October 1, 2010, http://blog.precipice.org on April 19, 2011; "Some Lessons Learned from the Rise and Fall of Wesabe," *Credit Union Journal*, December 16, 2010, www.cunatechnologycouncil.org on April 19, 2011.

Reasons for Success

Similarly, four basic factors are typically cited to explain new business success. One factor is hard work, drive, and dedication. New business owners must be committed to succeeding and be willing to put in the time and effort to make it happen. Having positive feelings and a good outlook on life may also play an important role.[32] Gladys Edmunds, a single teenage mother in Pittsburgh, washed laundry, made chicken dinners to sell to cab drivers, and sold fire extinguishers and Bibles door to door to earn money to launch her own business. Today, Edmunds Travel Consultants employs eight people and earns about $6 million in annual revenues.[33]

Careful analysis of market conditions can help new business owners assess the probable reception of their products in the marketplace. This will provide insights about market demand for proposed products and services. Whereas attempts to expand local restaurants specializing in baked potatoes, muffins, and gelato have been largely unsuccessful, hamburger and pizza chains continue to have an easier time expanding into new markets.

Managerial competence also contributes to success. Successful new business owners may acquire competence through training or experience or by using the expertise of others. Few successful entrepreneurs succeed alone or straight out of college. Most spend time working in successful companies or partner with others in order to bring more expertise to a new business.

Finally, luck also plays a role in the success of some firms. For example, after Alan McKim started Clean Harbors, an environmental cleanup firm based in New England, he struggled to keep his business afloat. Then the U.S. government committed $1.6 billion to toxic waste cleanup—McKim's specialty. He was able to get several large government contracts and put his business on solid financial footing. Had the government fund not been created at just the right time, McKim may well have failed. Similarly, when several major retailers closed their doors in 2009, other firms that specialize in liquidating inventories of bankrupt companies flourished and most saw a big jump in revenues and profits.[34]

What are the fundamental reasons for new business failure and success?

What current trends in business start-ups can you identify?

CONCEPT CHECK

Summary of Learning Objectives and Key Points

1. Discuss the nature of entrepreneurship.

   - Entrepreneurship is the process of planning, organizing, operating, and assuming the risk of a business venture.
   - An entrepreneur is someone who engages in entrepreneurship. In general, entrepreneurs start small businesses.

2. Describe the role of entrepreneurship in society.

   - Small businesses are an important source of innovation.
   - Small businesses create numerous jobs.
   - Small businesses contribute to the success of large businesses.

3. Understand the major issues involved in choosing strategies for small firms and the role of international management in entrepreneurship.

   - In choosing strategies, entrepreneurs have to consider the characteristics of the industry in which they are going to conduct business.

   - Small businesses generally have several distinctive competencies that they should exploit in choosing their strategy. Small businesses are usually skilled at identifying niches in established markets, identifying new markets, and acting quickly to obtain first-mover advantages.
   - Small businesses are usually not skilled at exploiting economies of scale.
   - Once an entrepreneur has chosen a strategy, the strategy is normally written down in a business plan. Writing a business plan forces an entrepreneur to plan thoroughly and to anticipate problems that might occur.

4. Discuss the structural challenges unique to entrepreneurial firms.

   - With a strategy and business plan in place, entrepreneurs must choose a structure to implement them. All of the structural issues summarized in Chapters 14 through 18 of this book are relevant to the entrepreneur.
   - In addition, the entrepreneur has some unique structural choices to make. For example, the entrepreneur can buy an existing business or start a new one.

- In determining financial structure, an entrepreneur has to decide how much personal capital to invest in an organization, how much bank and government support to obtain, and whether to encourage venture capital firms to invest.
- Entrepreneurs can also rely on various sources of advice.

5. Understand the determinants of the performance of small firms.
   - Several interesting trends characterize new business start-ups today.
   - There are several reasons why some new businesses fail and others succeed.

Discussion Questions

Questions for Review

1. Describe the similarities and differences between entrepreneurial firms and large firms in terms of their job creation and innovation.
2. What characteristics make an industry attractive to entrepreneurs? Based on these characteristics, which industries are most attractive to entrepreneurs?

3. Describe recent trends in new business start-ups.
4. What are the different sources of advice for entrepreneurs? What type of information would an entrepreneur be likely to get from each source? What are the drawbacks or limitations of each source?

Questions for Analysis

5. Entrepreneurs and small businesses play a variety of important roles in society. If these roles are so important, do you think that the government should do more to encourage the development of small business? Why or why not?
6. Consider the four major reasons for new business failure. What actions can entrepreneurs take to minimize or avoid each cause of failure?

7. The U.S. automotive industry is well established, with several large and many small competitors. Describe the unexploited niches in the U.S. auto industry and tell how entrepreneurs could offer products that fill those niches.

Questions for Application

8. Assume that you are opening a small business in your town. What are your financing options? Which option or options are you likely to choose, and why?
9. List five entrepreneur-owned businesses in your community. In which industry does each business compete? Based on the industry, how do you rate each business's long-term chances for success? Explain your answers.

10. Using the information about managing a small business presented in this chapter, analyze whether you would like to work in a small business—either as an employee or as a founder. Given your personality, background, and experience, does working in or starting a new business appeal to you? What are the reasons for your opinion?

CengageNow™ Highlights

Now use your CengageNow™ homework to help you:
- Apply management theories in your life
- Assess your management skills
- Master management terms and concepts
- Apply your knowledge to real-world situations
- Analyze and solve challenging management problems

In order to take advantage of these elements, your instructor will need to have set up a course for your class within CengageNow™. Ask your instructor to contact his/her Cengage sales representative and Digital Solutions Manager to explore testing CengageNow™ in your course this term.

Basic Elements of Control

LEARNING OBJECTIVES

After studying this chapter, you should be able to:

1. Explain the purpose of control, identify different types of control, and describe the steps in the control process.

2. Identify and explain the three forms of operations control.

3. Describe budgets and other tools for financial control.

4. Identify and distinguish between two opposing forms of structural control.

5. Discuss the relationship between strategy and control, including international strategic control.

6. Identify characteristics of effective control, why people resist control, and how managers can overcome this resistance.

Facets of Jamie Dimon's
MANAGEMENT IN ACTION Strategy at JPMorgan

In October 2006, the head of the mortgage-servicing department, which collects payments on home loans, informed JPMorgan CEO Jamie Dimon that late payments were increasing at an alarming rate. When Dimon reviewed the report, he confirmed not only that late payments were a problem at Morgan, but that things were even worse for other lenders. "We concluded," recalls Dimon, "that underwriting standards were deteriorating across the industry." Shortly thereafter, Dimon was informed that the cost of insuring securities backed by subprime mortgages was going up even though ratings agencies persisted in rating them AAA. At the time, creating securities backed by subprime mortgages was the hottest and most profitable business on Wall Street, but by the end of the year, Dimon had decided to get out of it. "We saw no profit, and lots of risk," reports Bill Winters, co-head of Morgan's investment arm. "It was Jamie," he adds, "who saw all the pieces."

Dimon's caution—and willingness to listen to what his risk-management people were telling him—paid off in a big way. Between July 2007 and July 2008, when the full force of the crisis hit the country's investment banks, Morgan recorded losses of $5 billion on mortgage-backed securities. That's a lot of money, but relatively little compared to the losses sustained by banks that didn't see the writing on the wall—$33 billion at Citibank, for example, and $26 billion at

"It's offensive to be called a cost cutter."

—JAMIE DIMON, CEO, JPMORGAN CHASE

Merrill Lynch. Citi is still in business, thanks to $45 billion in cash infusions from the federal government, but Merrill Lynch isn't—it was forced to sell itself to Bank of America. Morgan, though hit hard, weathered the storm and is still standing on its own Wall Street foundations. "You know," said President-elect Barack Obama as he surveyed the damage sustained by the U.S. banking industry in 2008, ". . . there are a lot of banks that are actually pretty well managed, JPMorgan being a good example. Jamie Dimon . . . is doing a pretty good job managing an enormous portfolio."

Ironically, Dimon got his start in banking at Citibank, where he worked closely with legendary CEO Sandy

Jamie Dixon, CEO of JPMorgan Chase, has used control effectively to help his firm avoid some of the mistakes made by other large financial institutions in recent years.

Scott J. Ferrell/Congressional Quarterly/Alamy

Weill for 12 years, helping to transform what's now known as Citigroup into the largest financial institution in the United States. Dimon left Citi in 1998 and, two years later, became CEO of Bank One, then the country's fifth-largest bank. He sold a revitalized Bank One to JPMorgan Chase in 2004, and in 2006, he became CEO and chairman of JPMorgan Chase & Co., a financial-services institution which includes JPMorgan Chase Bank, a commercial-retail bank, and JPMorgan Trust Company, an investment bank. With assets of $176.8 billion, JPMorgan Chase boasts the largest market-capitalization and deposit bases in the U.S. financial industry.

Dimon came to JPMorgan Chase with a few ideas about how to manage an enormous portfolio. Shortly after he took over, he increased oversight and control of Bank One's operations and expenses, using cost-saving measures to free up $3 billion annually by 2007. He then used the cash to finance the expansion of Morgan Chase operations, including the installation of more ATM machines and the creation of new products. As improved fundamentals and expanded operations yielded greater revenues, the bank's stock price went up (at least until the subprime crisis hit), freeing up further funds for new growth. Once the basics are right, says Dimon, "you earn the right to do a deal," and he set about building a Citi-like financial empire, relying mostly on mergers to jump-start growth in underserved regional and international markets.

Experience had shown Dimon that a large organization "can get arrogant and . . . lose focus, like the Roman Empire." In 2006, for example, JPMorgan Chase was enjoying high sales but spending a lot more than Dimon was used to spending at Bank One. Moreover, Dimon had inherited a company that had engineered multiple mergers without making much effort to integrate operations. The twofold result was ho-hum profits and a loose collection of incompatible structures and systems. Financial results from different divisions, for instance, were simply being combined, and the upshot, according to CFO Michael Cavanagh, was that even though "strong businesses were subsidizing weak ones . . . the numbers didn't jump out at you. With the results mashed together, it was easy for managers to hide."

Dimon thus set out to exercise more effective operational oversight, and his control practices currently extend to virtually every aspect of JPMorgan Chase operations:

- Every month, managers must submit 50-page reports showing financial ratios and results, product sales, and even detailed expenses for every worker.

Then Dimon and his top executives spend hours combing through the data, with the CEO asking tough questions and demanding frank answers.

- One of Dimon's top priorities is slashing bloated budgets. "Waste hurt[s] our customers," he reminds his management team. "Cars, phones, clubs, perks—what's that got to do with customers?" He's also eliminated such amenities as fresh flowers, lavish expense accounts, and oversized offices and closed the in-house gym. One time, he asked a line of limousine drivers outside company headquarters for the names of the executives they were waiting for. Then he called up each one, asking, "Too good for the subway?" or "Why don't you try walking?" Dimon denies the story, but limo service at JPMorgan Chase is way down.

- Dimon also takes a close look at compensation. Regional bank managers at JPMorgan Chase once earned $2 million a year, compared with Bank One's modest salary of $400,000. "I'd tell people they were way overpaid," says Dimon, and as he suspected, "they already knew it." He cut pay for most staff by 20 to 50 percent, but most people elected to stay with the company. Today, a strict pay-for-performance formula keeps compensation in line.

- "In a big company," Dimon advises, "it's easy for people to b.s. you. A lot of them have been practicing for decades." So he gathers outcome data from every manager, various forms of information from low-level staffers, and even candid performance critiques from suppliers. "If you just want to run your business on your own and report results," warns Steve Black, co-head of investment banking, "you won't like working for Jamie."

- Finally, Dimon is convinced that IT is critical to the bank's long-term strategy and once cancelled a long-running information-services contract with IBM. "When you're outsourcing," he explained, ". . . people don't care" about your performance. At JPMorgan Chase, "we want patriots, not mercenaries." Between 2007 and 2008, he invested $2 billion in technology developed in-house and considers it money well spent.

Dimon, however, doesn't like being thought of as a control freak. "It's offensive . . . to be called a cost cutter," he complains, and besides, his long-run goal isn't merely control—it's growth. "It's [a] thousand-mile march," observes one JPMorgan analyst, "and not everyone will survive."[1]

Jamie Dimon is almost single-handedly remaking JPMorgan Chase. Among other things, he is bringing compensation in line with industry standards, cutting costs, streamlining operations, and slashing budgets. He is also setting clear targets for profitability and growth, and managers throughout the company are then being held accountable for meeting these targets. At the heart of all these efforts is a comprehensive control system that helps him monitor all aspects of performance. In a nutshell, effective control helps managers like Jamie Dimon decide where they want their business to go, point it in that direction, and monitor results to keep it on track. Ineffective control, on the other hand, can result in a lack of focus, weak direction, and poor overall performance.

As we discussed in Chapter 1, control is one of the four basic managerial functions that provide the organizing framework for this book. This is the first of three chapters devoted to this important area. In the first section of the chapter we explain the purpose of control. We then look at types of control and the steps in the control process. The rest of the chapter examines the four levels of control that most organizations must employ to remain effective: operations, financial, structural, and strategic control. We conclude by discussing the characteristics of effective control, noting why some people resist control and describing what organizations can do to overcome this resistance. The remaining two chapters in this part focus on managing operations and managing information.

The Nature of Control

Control is the regulation of organizational activities so that some targeted element of performance remains within acceptable limits. Without this regulation, organizations have no indication of how well they are performing in relation to their goals. Control, like a ship's rudder, keeps the organization moving in the proper direction. At any point in time, it compares where the organization is in terms of performance (financial, productive, or otherwise) to where it is supposed to be. Like a rudder, control provides an organization with a mechanism for adjusting its course if performance falls outside of acceptable boundaries. For example, FedEx has a performance goal of delivering 99.9 percent of its packages on time. If on-time deliveries fall to 99.6 percent, control systems will signal the problem to managers, so that they can make necessary adjustments in operations to regain the target level of performance.[2] An organization without effective control procedures is not likely to reach its goals—or, if it does reach them, to know that it has!

The Purpose of Control

As Figure 11.1 illustrates, control provides an organization with ways to adapt to environmental change, to limit the accumulation of error, to cope with organizational complexity, and to minimize costs. These four functions of control are worth a closer look.

Adapting to Environmental Change In today's complex and turbulent business environment, all organizations must contend with change.[3] If managers could establish goals and achieve them instantaneously, control would not be needed. But between the time a goal is established and the time it is reached, many things can happen in the organization and its environment to disrupt movement toward the goal—or even to change the goal itself. A properly designed control system can help managers anticipate, monitor, and respond to changing circumstances.[4] In contrast, an improperly designed system can result in organizational performance that falls far below acceptable levels.

For example, Michigan-based Metalloy, a 56-year-old, family-run metal-casting company, signed a contract to make engine-seal castings for NOK, a big Japanese auto parts maker. Metalloy was satisfied when its first 5,000-unit production run yielded 4,985

control
The regulation of organizational activities in such a way as to facilitate goal attainment

FIGURE 11.1 THE PURPOSE OF CONTROL

Control is one of the four basic management functions in organizations. The control function, in turn, has four basic purposes. Properly designed control systems can fulfill each of these purposes.

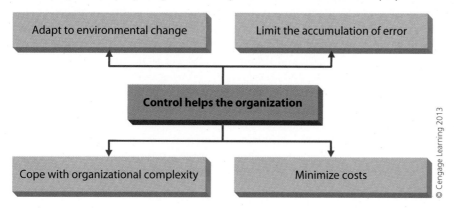

© Cengage Learning 2013

acceptable castings and only 15 defective ones. NOK, however, was quite unhappy with this performance and insisted that Metalloy raise its standards. In short, global quality standards in most industries are such that customers demand near-perfection from their suppliers. A properly designed control system can help managers like those at Metalloy stay better attuned to rising standards.

Limiting the Accumulation of Error Small mistakes and errors do not often seriously damage the financial health of an organization. Over time, however, small errors may accumulate and become very serious. For example, Whistler Corporation, a large radar detector manufacturer, was once faced with such rapidly escalating demand that quality essentially became irrelevant. The defect rate rose from 4 percent to 9 percent to 15 percent and eventually reached 25 percent. One day, a manager realized that 100 of the plant's 250 employees were spending all their time fixing defective units and that $2 million worth of inventory was awaiting repair. Had the company adequately controlled quality as it responded to increased demand, the problem would never have reached such proportions. Similarly, a routine quality control inspection of a prototype of Boeing's 787 much-delayed Dreamliner revealed that a fastener had not been installed correctly. Closer scrutiny then revealed that literally thousands of fasteners had been installed wrong in each prototype under construction. As a result, the entire project was delayed several months. If the inspection process had been more rigorous to begin with, the error would likely have been found and corrected much earlier, rather than accumulating into a major problem for Boeing.[5]

Coping with Organizational Complexity When a firm purchases only one raw material, produces one product, has a simple organization design, and enjoys constant demand for its product, its managers can maintain control with a very basic and simple system. But a business that produces many products from myriad raw materials and has a large market area, a complicated organization design, and many competitors needs a sophisticated system to maintain adequate control. When large firms merge, the short-term results are often disappointing. The typical reason for this is that the new enterprise is so large and complex that the existing control systems are simply inadequate. Hewlett-Packard and Compaq Computer faced just this problem when HP acquired Compaq and had to address myriad issues to transform the two firms into one. Similarly, when United and Continental Airlines merged, the entire process took over two years, in large part because of the complexity of each firm.

Minimizing Costs When it is practiced effectively, control can also help reduce costs and boost output. For example, Georgia-Pacific Corporation, a large wood-products company, learned of a new technology that could be used to make thinner blades for its saws. The firm's control system was used to calculate the amount of wood that could be saved from each cut made by the thinner blades relative to the costs used to replace the existing blades. The results have been impressive—the wood that is saved by the new blades each year fills 800 rail cars. As Georgia-Pacific discovered, effective control systems can eliminate waste, lower labor costs, and improve output per unit of input. Starbucks recently instructed its coffee shops to stop automatically brewing decaffeinated coffee after lunch. Sales of decaf plummet after lunch, and Starbucks realized that baristas were simply pouring most of it down the drain. Now, between noon and early evening they brew decaf only by the cup and only when a customer orders it.[6] A Cadbury chewing gum factory located in Taiwan significantly lowered its operating expenses through the simple replacement of its dehumidifier. Moisture and temperature control is critical to the gum manufacturing process, so Cadbury adopted the new dehumidifying system to reduce these costs. With the system, Cadbury reduced its energy usage by 60% (300,000 kW per year) and its operating expenses by 50 percent.[7] Similarly, many businesses are cutting back on everything from health insurance coverage to overnight shipping to business lunches for clients in their quest to lower costs.[8]

Types of Control

The examples of control given thus far have illustrated the regulation of several organizational activities, from producing quality products to coordinating complex organizations. Organizations practice control in a number of different areas and at different levels, and the responsibility for managing control is widespread.

Areas of Control Control can focus on any area of an organization. Most organizations define areas of control in terms of the four basic types of resources they use: physical, human, information, and financial.[9] Control of physical resources includes inventory management (stocking neither too few nor too many units in inventory), quality control (maintaining appropriate levels of output quality), and equipment control (supplying the necessary facilities and machinery). Control of human resources includes selection and placement, training and development, performance appraisal, and compensation. Relatedly, organizations also attempt to control the behavior of their employees—directing them toward higher performance, for example, and away from unethical behaviors.[10] Control of information resources includes sales and marketing forecasting, environmental analysis, public relations, production scheduling, and economic forecasting.[11] Financial control involves managing the organization's debt so that it does not become excessive, ensuring that the firm always has enough cash on hand to meet its obligations but does not have excess cash in a checking account, and that receivables are collected and bills are paid on a timely basis.

In many ways, the control of financial resources is the most important area, because financial resources are related to the control of all the other resources in an organization. Too much inventory leads to storage costs; poor selection of personnel leads to termination and rehiring expenses; inaccurate sales forecasts lead to disruptions in cash flows and other financial effects. Financial issues tend to pervade most control-related activities.

The crisis in the U.S. airline industry precipitated by the terrorist attacks on September 11, an economic downturn that reduced business travel, and rising fuel costs can be fundamentally traced back to financial issues. Essentially, airline revenues dropped while their costs increased. Because of high labor costs and other expenses, the airlines have faced major problems in making appropriate adjustments.[12] United Airlines, for instance, spends over half of its revenues on labor; in contrast, JetBlue spends less than 25 percent of its revenues on labor.[13]

FIGURE 11.2 LEVELS OF CONTROL

Managers use control at several different levels. The most basic levels of control in organizations are strategic, structural, operations, and financial control. Each level must be managed properly if control is to be most effective.

© Cengage Learning 2013

Levels of Control Just as control can be broken down by area, Figure 11.2 shows that it can also be broken down by level within the organizational system. Operations control focuses on the processes the organization uses to transform resources into products or services.[14] Quality control is one type of operations control. Financial control is concerned with the organization's financial resources. Monitoring receivables to make sure customers are paying their bills on time is an example of financial control. Structural control is concerned with how the elements of the organization's structure are serving their intended purpose. Monitoring the administrative ratio to make sure staff expenses do not become excessive is an example of structural control. Finally, strategic control focuses on how effectively the organization's corporate, business, and functional strategies are succeeding in helping the organization meet its goals. For example, if a corporation has been unsuccessful in implementing its strategy of related diversification, its managers need to identify the reasons and either change the strategy or renew their efforts to implement it. We discuss these four levels of control more fully later in this chapter.

Responsibilities of Control Traditionally, managers have been responsible for overseeing the wide array of control systems and concerns in organizations. They decide which types of control the organization will use, and they implement control systems and take actions based on the information provided by control systems. Thus ultimate responsibility for control rests with all managers throughout an organization.

Most larger organizations also have one or more specialized managerial positions called *controllers*. A controller is responsible for helping line managers with their control activities, for coordinating the organization's overall control system, and for gathering and assimilating relevant information. Many businesses that use an H-form or M-form organization design have several controllers: one for the corporation and one for each division. The job of controller is especially important in organizations where control systems are complex.[15]

In addition, many organizations are also beginning to use operating employees to help maintain effective control. Indeed, employee participation is often used as a vehicle for allowing operating employees an opportunity to help facilitate organizational effectiveness. For example, Whistler Corporation increased employee participation in an effort to turn its quality problems around. As a starting point, the quality control unit, formerly responsible for checking product quality at the end of the assembly process, was eliminated. Next, all

operations control
Focuses on the processes the organization uses to transform resources into products or services

financial control
Concerned with the organization's financial resources

structural control
Concerned with how the elements of the organization's structure are serving their intended purpose

strategic control
Focuses on how effectively the organization's strategies are succeeding in helping the organization meet its goals

controller
A position in organizations that helps line managers with their control activities

operating employees were encouraged to check their own work and told that they would be responsible for correcting their own errors. As a result, Whistler has eliminated its quality problems and is now highly profitable once again.

Steps in the Control Process

Regardless of the type or levels of control systems an organization needs, there are four fundamental steps in any control process.[16] These are illustrated in Figure 11.3.

Establishing Standards The first step in the control process is establishing standards. A *control standard* is a target against which subsequent performance will be compared.[17] Employees at a Taco Bell fast-food restaurant, for example, work toward the following service standards:

1. A minimum of 95 percent of all customers will be greeted within three minutes of their arrival.
2. Preheated tortilla chips will not sit in the warmer more than 30 minutes before they are served to customers or discarded.
3. Empty tables will be cleaned within five minutes after being vacated.

Standards established for control purposes should be expressed in measurable terms. Note that standard 1 above has a time limit of three minutes and an objective target of 95 percent of all customers. In standard 3, the objective target of "all" empty tables is implied.

Control standards should also be consistent with the organization's goals. Taco Bell has organizational goals involving customer service, food quality, and restaurant cleanliness. A control standard for a retailer like Home Depot should be consistent with its goal of increasing its annual sales volume by 25 percent within five years. A hospital trying to shorten the average hospital stay for a patient will have control standards that reflect current averages. A university reaffirming its commitment to academics might adopt a standard of graduating 80 percent of its student athletes within five years of their enrollment. Control standards can be as narrow or as broad as the level of activity to which they apply and must follow logically from organizational goals and objectives. When Airbus introduced the A380, the world's largest passenger airplane, managers indicated that the firm needed to ship 270 planes in order to break even, and set a goal of delivering 18 per year. Managers also forecast that demand for very large aircraft like the A380 and Boeing's revamped 747 would exceed 1,200 planes during the next 20 years.[18]

A final aspect of establishing standards is to identify performance indicators. Performance indicators are measures of performance that provide information that is directly relevant to

control standard
A target against which subsequent performance will be compared

FIGURE 11.3 STEPS IN THE CONTROL PROCESS

Having an effective control system can help ensure that an organization achieves its goals. Implementing a control system, however, is a systematic process that generally proceeds through four interrelated steps.

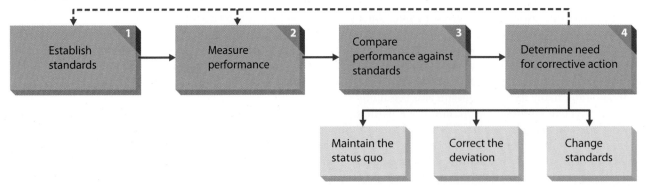

© Cengage Learning 2013

what is being controlled. For example, suppose an organization is following a tight schedule in building a new plant. Relevant performance indicators could be buying a site, selecting a building contractor, and ordering equipment. Monthly sales increases are not, however, directly relevant. On the other hand, if control is being focused on revenue, monthly sales increases are relevant, whereas buying land for a new plant is less relevant.

Measuring Performance The second step in the control process is measuring performance. Performance measurement is a constant, ongoing activity for most organizations. For control to be effective, performance measures must be valid. Daily, weekly, and monthly sales figures measure sales performance, and production performance may be expressed in terms of unit cost, product quality, or volume produced. Employees' performance is often measured in terms of quality or quantity of output, but for many jobs, measuring performance is not so straightforward.

A research and development scientist at Merck, for example, may spend years working on a single project before achieving a breakthrough. A manager who takes over a business on the brink of failure may need months or even years to turn things around. Valid performance measurement, however difficult to obtain, is nevertheless vital in maintaining effective control, and performance indicators usually can be developed. The scientist's progress, for example, may be partially assessed by peer review, and the manager's success may be evaluated by her ability to convince creditors that she will eventually be able to restore profitability.

As Airbus completed the design and manufacture of its A380 jumbo jet, managers recognized that delays and cost overruns had changed its breakeven point. New calculations indicated that the company would need to sell 420 planes before it would become profitable. Its annual sales, of course, remained relatively easy to measure.

Comparing Performance Against Standards The third step in the control process is comparing measured performance against established standards. Performance may be higher than, lower than, or identical to the standard. In some cases comparison is easy. The goal of each product manager at General Electric is to make the product either number one or number two (on the basis of total sales) in its market. Because this standard is clear and total sales are easy to calculate, it is relatively simple to determine whether this standard has been met. Sometimes, however, comparisons are less clear-cut. If performance is lower than expected, the question is how much deviation from standards to allow before taking remedial action. For example, is increasing sales by 7.9 percent when the standard was 8 percent close enough?

The timetable for comparing performance to standards depends on a variety of factors, including the importance and complexity of what is being controlled. For longer-run and higher-level standards, annual comparisons may be appropriate. In other circumstances, more frequent comparisons are necessary. For example, a business with a severe cash shortage may need to monitor its on-hand cash reserves daily. In its first year of production, Airbus did indeed deliver 18 A380s, just as it had forecast.

Considering Corrective Action The final step in the control process is determining the need for corrective action. Decisions regarding corrective action draw heavily on a manager's analytic and diagnostic skills. For example,

Taking corrective action, a vital step in the control process, is important to retailers like Ann Taylor. For example, as the selling season for seasonal apparel is ending, retailers usually mark down their prices—it's generally preferable to get lower revenue than to have unsold merchandise that has to be stored. At the extreme, retailers also sometimes find it necessary to close underperforming stores altogether.

Fred Prouser/REUTERS

as healthcare costs have risen, many firms have sought ways to keep their own expenses in check. Some have reduced benefits; others have opted to pass on higher costs to their employees.[19]

After comparing performance against control standards, one of three actions is appropriate: maintain the status quo (do nothing), correct the deviation, or change the standards.

> "Closing underperforming stores is a natural part of business of any smart retailer."
>
> —MARIA SCEPPAGUERICO, SPOKESPERSON FOR ANN TAYLOR[20]

Maintaining the status quo is preferable when performance essentially matches the standards, but it is more likely that some action will be needed to correct a deviation from the standards.

Sometimes, performance that is higher than expected may also cause problems for organizations. For example, when highly anticipated new video games or game systems are first introduced, the demand may be so strong that customers are placed on waiting lists. And even some people who are among the first to purchase such products immediately turn around and list them for sale on eBay for an inflated price. The manufacturer may be unable to increase production in the short term, though, and also knows that demand will eventually drop. At the same time, however, the firm would not want to alienate potential customers. Consequently, it may decide to simply reduce its advertising. This may curtail demand a bit and limit customer frustration.

Changing an established standard usually is necessary if it was set too high or too low at the outset. This is apparent if large numbers of employees routinely beat the standard by a wide margin or if no employees ever meet the standard. Also, standards that seemed perfectly appropriate when they were established may need to be adjusted because circumstances have since changed.

As the 2008–2009 global recession began to take its toll, two major Airbus customers, Qantas and Emirates, indicated that they wanted to defer delivery of some previously ordered A380s. As a result, Airbus found it necessary to reduce its production in 2009 from 18 to only 14. It also indicated that the plane's breakeven point had increased, but would not reveal the new target. In 2011, the devastating tsunami in Japan forced Toyota to adjust its production levels as several of its parts and vehicles were manufactured in the country. As a result, Toyota cut production by 75 percent in its North American plants.[21]

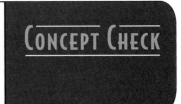

What are the basic purposes and types of control used in organizations?

Identify a goal you have set for yourself (such as raising your grade point average or buying a car) and then outline a control framework patterned after Figure 11.3 for achieving that goal.

CONCEPT CHECK

Operations Control

One of the four levels of control practiced by most organizations, **operations control**, is concerned with the processes the organization uses to transform resources into products or services. As Figure 11.4 shows, the three forms of operations control—preliminary, screening, and postaction—occur at different points in relation to the transformation processes used by the organization.

Preliminary Control

Preliminary control concentrates on the resources—financial, material, human, and information—the organization brings in from the environment. Preliminary control attempts to monitor the quality or quantity of these resources before they enter the organization. Firms like PepsiCo and General Mills hire only college graduates for their management training programs, and even then only after applicants satisfy several interviewers and

operations control
Focuses on the processes the organization uses to transform resources into products or services

preliminary control
Attempts to monitor the quality or quantity of financial, physical, human, and information resources before they actually become part of the system

FIGURE 11.4 FORMS OF OPERATIONS CONTROL

Most organizations develop multiple control systems that incorporate all three basic forms of control. For example, the publishing company that produced this book screens inputs by hiring only qualified employees, typesetters, and printers (preliminary control). In addition, quality is checked during the transformation process, such as after the manuscript is typeset (screening control), and the outputs—printed and bound books—are checked before they are shipped from the bindery (postaction control).

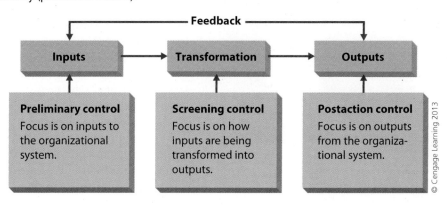

selection criteria. In this way, they control the quality of the human resources entering the organization. When Sears orders merchandise to be manufactured under its own brand name, it specifies rigid standards of quality, thereby controlling physical inputs. Organizations also control financial and information resources. For example, privately held companies like Toys "R" Us and Mars limit the extent to which outsiders can buy their stock, and television networks verify the accuracy of news stories before they are broadcast.

Screening Control

Screening control focuses on meeting standards for product or service quality or quantity during the actual transformation process itself. Screening control relies heavily on feedback processes. For example, in a Dell Computer assembly factory, computer system components are checked periodically as each unit is being assembled. This is done to ensure that all the components that have been assembled up to that point are working properly. The periodic quality checks provide feedback to workers so that they know what, if any, corrective actions to take. Because they are useful in identifying the cause of problems, screening controls tend to be used more often than other forms of control.

More and more companies are adopting screening controls because they are an effective way to promote employee participation and catch problems early in the overall transformation process. For example, Corning adopted screening controls for use in manufacturing television glass. In the past, finished television screens were inspected only after they were finished. Unfortunately, over 4 percent of them were later returned by customers because of defects. Now the glass screens are inspected at each step in the production process, rather than at the end, and the return rate from customers has dropped to .03 percent.

screening control
Relies heavily on feedback processes during the transformation process

Postaction Control

Postaction control focuses on the outputs of the organization after the transformation process is complete. Corning's old system was postaction control—final inspection after the product was completed. Although Corning abandoned its postaction control system, this still may be an effective method of control, primarily if a product can be manufactured in

postaction control
Monitors the outputs or results of the organization after the transformation process is complete

Honda uses post-action control by inspecting each of its vehicles as they roll off the assembly line. This gives the automaker a chance to identify and correct any minor problems or pull the vehicles aside for more significant repairs before it is shipped to Honda dealers. This practice helps Honda maintain a stellar reputation for product quality.

only one or two steps or if the service is fairly simple and routine. Although post-action control alone may not be as effective as preliminary or screening control, it can provide management with information for future planning. For example, if a quality check of finished goods indicates an unacceptably high defect rate, the production manager knows that he or she must identify the causes and take steps to eliminate them. Postaction control also provides a basis for rewarding employees. Recognizing that an employee has exceeded personal sales goals by a wide margin, for example, may alert the manager that a bonus or promotion is in order.

Most organizations use more than one form of operations control. For example, Honda's preliminary control includes hiring only qualified employees and specifying strict quality standards when ordering parts from other manufacturers. Honda uses numerous screening controls in checking the quality of components during the assembly of cars. A final inspection and test drive as each car rolls off the assembly line is part of the company's postaction control.[22] Indeed, most successful organizations employ a wide variety of techniques to facilitate operations control.

 CONCEPT CHECK

Distinguish between preliminary, screening, and postaction control.

Describe how a college or university is likely to use each type of operations control to monitor student progress.

◆ Financial Control

financial control
Concerned with the organization's financial resources

Financial control is the control of financial resources as they flow into the organization (revenues, shareholder investments), are held by the organization (working capital, retained earnings), and flow out of the organization (pay, expenses). Businesses must manage their finances so that revenues are sufficient to cover costs and still return a profit to the firm's owners. Not-for-profit organizations such as universities have the same concerns: Their revenues (from tax dollars or tuition) must cover operating expenses and overhead. U.S. automakers Ford and General Motors have come to realize that they have to reduce the costs of paying employees they do not need but whom they are obligated to keep due to longstanding labor agreements. A few years ago Ford offered to cover the full costs of a college education for certain of its employees if they would resign; GM, for its part, offered lump-sum payments of varying amounts to some of its workers in return for their resignations.[23] A complete discussion of financial management is beyond the scope of this book, but we will examine the control provided by budgets and other financial control tools.

Budgetary Control

A budget is a plan expressed in numerical terms.[24] Organizations establish budgets for work groups, departments, divisions, and the whole organization. The usual time period for a budget is one year, although breakdowns of budgets by the quarter or month are also common. Budgets are generally expressed in financial terms, but they may occasionally be expressed in units of output, time, or other quantifiable factors. When Disney launches the production of a new animated cartoon feature, it creates a budget for how much the movie should cost. Several years ago, when movies like *The Lion King* were raking in hundreds of millions of dollars, Disney executives were fairly flexible about budget overruns. But, on the heels of several animated flops, such as *Atlantis: The Lost Empire* and *Treasure Planet*, the company had to take a much harder line on budget overruns.[25]

Because of their quantitative nature, budgets provide yardsticks for measuring performance and facilitate comparisons across departments, between levels in the organization, and from one time period to another. Budgets serve four primary purposes. They help managers coordinate resources and projects (because they use a common denominator, usually dollars). They help define the established standards for control. They provide guidelines about the organization's resources and expectations. Finally, budgets enable the organization to evaluate the performance of managers and organizational units.

Types of Budgets Most organizations develop and make use of three different kinds of budgets—financial, operating, and nonmonetary. Table 11.1 summarizes the characteristics of each of these.

A *financial budget* indicates where the organization expects to get its cash for the coming time period and how it plans to use it. Because financial resources are critically important, the organization needs to know where those resources will be coming from and how they are to be used. The financial budget provides answers to both these questions. Usual sources of cash include sales revenue, short- and long-term loans, the sale of assets, and the issuance of new stock.

budget
A plan expressed in numerical terms

Types of Budget	What Budget Shows
Financial Budget	*Sources and Uses of Cash*
Cash flow or cash budget	All sources of cash income and cash expenditures in monthly, weekly, or daily periods
Capital expenditures budget	Costs of major assets such as a new plant, machinery, or land
Balance sheet budget	Forecast of the organization's assets and liabilities in the event all other budgets are met
Operating Budget	*Planned Operations in Financial Terms*
Sales or revenue budget	Income the organization expects to receive from normal operations
Expense budget	Anticipated expenses for the organization during the coming time period
Profit budget	Anticipated differences between sales or revenues and expenses
Nonmonetary Budget	*Planned Operations in Nonfinancial Terms*
Labor budget	Hours of direct labor available for use
Space budget	Square feet or meters of space available for various functions
Production budget	Number of units to be produced during the coming time period

© Cengage Learning 2013

TABLE 11.1
DEVELOPING BUDGETS IN ORGANIZATIONS

Organizations use various types of budgets to help manage their control functions. The three major categories of budgets are financial, operating, and nonmonetary. There are several different types of budgets in each category. To be most effective, each budget must be carefully matched with the specific function being controlled.

For years Exxon was very conservative in its capital budgeting. As a result, the firm amassed a huge financial reserve but was being overtaken in sales by Royal Dutch/Shell. But executives at Exxon were then able to use their reserves to help finance the firm's merger with Mobil, creating ExxonMobil, and to regain the number-one sales position. Since that time, the firm has become more aggressive in capital budgeting to stay ahead of its European rival.

An *operating budget* is concerned with planned operations within the organization. It outlines what quantities of products or services the organization intends to create and what resources will be used to create them. IBM creates an operating budget that specifies how many of each model of its personal computer will be produced each quarter.

A *nonmonetary budget* is simply a budget expressed in nonfinancial terms, such as units of output, hours of direct labor, machine hours, or square-foot allocations. Nonmonetary budgets are most commonly used by managers at the lower levels of an organization. For example, a plant manager can schedule work more effectively knowing that he or she has 8,000 labor hours to allocate in a week, rather than trying to determine how to best spend $86,451 in wages in a week.

Developing Budgets Traditionally, budgets were developed by top management and the controller and then imposed on lower-level managers. Although some organizations still follow this pattern, many contemporary organizations now allow all managers to participate in the budget process. As a starting point, top management generally issues a call for budget requests, accompanied by an indication of overall patterns the budgets may take. For example, if sales are expected to drop in the next year, managers may be told up front to prepare for cuts in operating budgets.

As Figure 11.5 shows, the heads of each operating unit typically submit budget requests to the head of their division. An operating unit head might be a department manager in a

FIGURE 11.5 DEVELOPING BUDGETS IN ORGANIZATIONS

Most organizations use the same basic process to develop budgets. Operating units are requested to submit their budget requests to divisions. These divisions, in turn, compile unit budgets and submit their own budgets to the organization. An organizational budget is then compiled for approval by the budget committee, controller, and CEO.

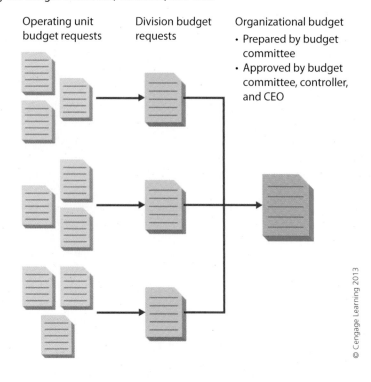

Operating unit budget requests

Division budget requests

Organizational budget
- Prepared by budget committee
- Approved by budget committee, controller, and CEO

© Cengage Learning 2013

manufacturing or wholesaling firm or a program director in a social service agency. The division heads might include plant managers, regional sales managers, or college deans. The division head integrates and consolidates the budget requests from operating unit heads into one overall division budget request. A great deal of interaction among managers usually takes place at this stage, as the division head coordinates the budgetary needs of the various departments.

Division budget requests are then forwarded to a budget committee. The budget committee is usually composed of top managers. The committee reviews budget requests from several divisions, and once again, duplications and inconsistencies are corrected. Finally, the budget committee, the controller, and the CEO review and agree on the overall budget for the organization, as well as specific budgets for each operating unit. These decisions are then communicated back to each manager.

Strengths and Weaknesses of Budgeting Budgets offer a number of advantages, but they also have weaknesses. On the plus side, budgets facilitate effective control. Placing dollar values on operations enables managers to monitor operations better and pinpoint problem areas. Budgets also facilitate coordination and communication between departments because they express diverse activities in a common denominator (dollars). Budgets help maintain records of organizational performance and are a logical complement to planning. In other words, as managers develop plans, they should simultaneously consider control measures to accompany them. Organizations can use budgets to link plans and control by first developing budgets as part of the plan and then using those budgets as part of control.

On the other hand, some managers apply budgets too rigidly. Budgets are intended to serve as frameworks, but managers sometimes fail to recognize that changing circumstances may warrant budget adjustments. The process of developing budgets can also be very time consuming. Finally, budgets may limit innovation and change. When all available funds are allocated to specific operating budgets, it may be impossible to procure additional funds to take advantage of an unexpected opportunity. Indeed, for these very reasons, some organizations are working to scale back their budgeting systems. Although most organizations are likely to continue to use budgets, the goal is to make them less confining and rigid.

Finally, the *Change* box entitled "The Grift That Keeps on Giving" on page 272 shows what can happen to the best-laid plans and best-prepared budgets when an organization's financial control spirals out of its control.

Other Tools for Financial Control

Although budgets are the most common means of financial control, other useful tools are financial statements, ratio analysis, and financial audits.

Financial Statements A financial statement is a profile of some aspect of an organization's financial circumstances. There are commonly accepted and required ways that financial statements must be prepared and presented.[26] The two most basic financial statements prepared and used by virtually all organizations are a balance sheet and an income statement.

The balance sheet lists the assets and liabilities of the organization at a specific point in time, usually the last day of an organization's fiscal year. For example, the balance sheet may summarize the financial condition of an organization on December 31, 2012. Most balance sheets are divided into current assets (assets that are relatively liquid, or easily convertible into cash), fixed assets (assets that are longer term in nature and less liquid), current liabilities (debts and other obligations that must be paid in the near future), long-term liabilities (payable over an extended period of time), and stockholders' equity (the owners' claim against the assets).

Whereas the balance sheet reflects a snapshot profile of an organization's financial position at a single point in time, the income statement summarizes financial performance over a period of time, usually one year. For example, the income statement might be for

financial statement
A profile of some aspect of an organization's financial circumstances

balance sheet
List of assets and liabilities of an organization at a specific point in time

income statement
A summary of financial performance over a period of time

THE MORE THINGS CHANGE

The Grift That Keeps on Giving

Elena Elisseeva, 2010/Used under license from Shutterstock.Com

Established in 1955 by insurance magnate Cornelius Vander Starr, the Starr Foundation is the 16th-largest charitable foundation in the United States. Focusing on education, health care, and social services, the Starr Foundation helps to fund medical research, teacher training, literacy, and scholarship programs and has, in its 53 years of operation, given nearly $2 billion in grants.

Starr's wealth came from American International Group, which he founded in 1919 and which, by 1962, was the world's number-one international insurance and financial-services company. Starr's legacy included a bequest of 39 million shares of AIG stock in 1968, and from the outset, the charitable organization has been financed and managed by AIG insiders and executives. The relationship between the two organizations hasn't always been fiscally amicable, but it's kept the nonprofit foundation financially stable for more than half a century. As of December 2006, the Starr Foundation had assets of $3.3 billion, the bulk of it deriving from Starr's endowment.

At the same time, AIG itself boasted assets of slightly more than $1 trillion. Shortly thereafter, however, the company's financial superstructure was washed away in the tidal wave of greed and monetary misjudgment known as the "subprime

crisis." From a total of $14 billion in 2006, AIG's income plummeted to $6.2 billion in 2007. Its stock price, which had been at $73 a share in May 2007, dropped to under $5 in October 2008. (Underwritten by $85 billion in loans from U.S. taxpayers, the price had climbed to just over $30 by April 2011.)

Needless to say, these weren't good times for the Starr Foundation either. It was, however, luckier than most AIG stockholders. Between January 2006 and May 2008, the Foundation had sold about 30 million shares of AIG, taking advantage of prices that still hovered between $40 and $73 a share. In mid-2008, however, it was still holding 15.5 million shares of AIG among its assets, and between the end of 2006 and October of 2008, the Starr Foundation lost at least $1 billion in assets—about one-third of its 2006 value. As of 2011, the Foundation's assets totaled about $1.25 billion, representing a loss of more than $2 billion since 2006. "You will see smaller grants from us," reported President Florence A. Davis. "At least for the time being, some of our initiatives will be put on hold."

In the meantime, Davis and Starr chairman Maurice R. Greenberg, one-time CEO of AIG, took stock of their fiduciary responsibility to the Foundation and decided to sue the corporate hand that funded them. AIG management, charged a suit filed in May 2008, had "fraudulently reassured" shareholders in February that it foresaw no more than $900 million in future losses from the subprime fiasco. The fictitious projection, argued Starr, "caused the Foundation to retain stock in AIG which it would otherwise have sold." In reality, the complaint reminded the court, AIG's losses came in at "billions more than AIG has previously acknowledged" (about $10 billion, to be more or less precise), and the Foundation sought $300 million in damages.*

References: Geraldine Fabrikant, "Economy Expected to Take a Toll on Charitable Giving," *New York Times*, September 29, 2008, www.nytimes.com on May 1, 2011; Philip Boroff and Ryan J. Donmoyer, "Starr Foundation Plans Smaller Grants after AIG Stock Plunges," *Bloomberg.com*, October 3, 2008, www.bloomberg.com on May 1, 2011; Lila Zuill, "Greenberg's Starr Foundation Sues AIG, Alleging Fraud," *Insurance Journal*, May 9, 2008, www.insurancejournal.com on May 1, 2011; Patricia Hurtado, "Starr Foundation Sues AIG Chief Sullivan for Fraud over Loss," *Bloomberg.com*, October 1, 2008, www.bloomberg.com on May 1, 2011; Eric Lichtblau, "Chamber of Commerce Accused of Tax Fraud," *New York Times*, September 10, 2010, www.nytimes.com on May 1, 2011.

* An interesting—and ironic—sidebar: The Starr Foundation was cited in a 2010 complaint filed with the Internal Revenue Service by a group called U.S. Chamber Watch, which charged that the U.S. Chamber of Commerce violated tax codes by laundering $12 million in loans from the Starr Foundation. The complaint alleges that the Chamber, in violation of restrictions on nonprofit organizations, had failed to repay the money, which it used to fund political causes favored by current and former executives at AIG, including Maurice Greenberg.

the period January 1, 2012, through December 31, 2012. The income statement summarizes the firm's revenues less its expenses to report net income (profit or loss) for the period. Information from the balance sheet and income statement is used in computing important financial ratios.

Ratio Analysis   Financial ratios compare different elements of a balance sheet or income statement to one another. Ratio analysis is the calculation of one or more financial ratios to assess some aspect of the financial health of an organization. Organizations use a variety of different financial ratios as part of financial control. For example, *liquidity ratios* indicate how liquid (easily converted into cash) an organization's assets are. *Debt ratios* reflect ability to meet long-term financial obligations. *Return ratios* show managers and investors how much return the organization is generating relative to its assets. *Coverage ratios* help estimate the organization's ability to cover interest expenses on borrowed capital. *Operating ratios* indicate the effectiveness of specific functional areas rather than of the total organization. Walt Disney is an example of a company that relies heavily on financial ratios to keep its financial operations on track.[27]

Financial Audits   Audits are independent appraisals of an organization's accounting, financial, and operational systems. The two major types of financial audits are the external audit and the internal audit.

External audits are financial appraisals conducted by experts who are not employees of the organization.[28] External audits are typically concerned with determining that the organization's accounting procedures and financial statements are compiled in an objective and verifiable fashion. The organization contracts with a certified public accountant (CPA) for this service. The CPA's main objective is to verify for stockholders, the IRS, and other interested parties that the methods by which the organization's financial managers and accountants prepare documents and reports are legal and proper. External audits are so important that publicly held corporations are required by law to have external audits regularly, as assurance to investors that the financial reports are reliable.

Unfortunately, flaws in the auditing process played a major role in the downfall of Enron and several other major firms. The problem can be traced back partially to the auditing groups' problems with conflicts of interest and eventual loss of objectivity. For instance, Enron was such an important client for its auditing firm, Arthur Andersen, that the auditors started letting the firm take liberties with its accounting systems for fear that if they were too strict, Enron might take its business to another auditing firm. In the aftermath of the resulting scandal, Arthur Andersen was forced to close its doors, Enron is a shell of its former self, indictments continue to be handed down, and the entire future of the accounting profession has been called into question.[29]

Some organizations are also starting to employ external auditors to review other aspects of their financial operations. For example, some auditing firms now specialize in checking corporate legal bills. An auditor for the Fireman's Fund Insurance Company uncovered several thousands of dollars in legal fee errors. Other auditors are beginning to specialize in real estate, employee benefits, and pension plan investments.

Whereas external audits are conducted by external accountants, an *internal audit* is handled by employees of the organization. Its objective is the same as that of an external audit—to verify the accuracy of financial and accounting procedures used by the organization. Internal audits also examine the efficiency and appropriateness of financial and accounting procedures. Because the staff members who conduct them are a permanent part of the organization, internal audits tend to be more expensive than external audits. But employees, who are more familiar with the organization's practices, may also point out significant aspects of the accounting system besides its technical correctness. Large organizations like Halliburton and Ford have an internal auditing staff that spends all its time conducting audits of different divisions and functional areas of the organization. Smaller organizations may assign accountants to an internal audit group on a temporary or rotating basis.

ratio analysis
The calculation of one or more financial ratios to assess some aspect of the organization's financial health

audit
An independent appraisal of an organization's accounting, financial, and operational systems

Satyam Computer Services in India falsely reported profits of over $1 billion when in reality it had only $66 million. The Indian affiliate of PricewaterhouseCoopers, PW India, was in charge of routinely auditing the firm, but failed to follow basic auditing procedures. Rather than confirming the supposed $1 billion cash balances with the banks, PW India relied solely on the information provided by the firm's management. In some cases, auditors failed to follow up on confirmations sent independently by the banks that showed significant differences from the balances reported by management. PW India was eventually fined $7.5 million—the largest penalty ever imposed by India on a foreign accounting firm.[30]

What are the basic kinds of budgets used in most organizations?

Given that financial control relies so heavily on numbers, how can problems like those at Enron occur?

CONCEPT CHECK

Structural Control

Organizations can create designs for themselves that result in very different approaches to control. Two major forms of structural control, bureaucratic control and decentralized control, represent opposite ends of a continuum, as shown in Figure 11.6.[31] The six dimensions shown in the figure represent perspectives adopted by the two extreme types of structural control. In other words, they have different goals, degrees of formality, performance expectations, organization designs, reward systems, and levels of participation. Although a few organizations fall precisely at one extreme or the other, most tend toward one end but may have specific characteristics of either.

FIGURE 11.6 ORGANIZATIONAL CONTROL

Organizational control generally falls somewhere between the two extremes of bureaucratic and decentralized control. NBC television uses bureaucratic control, whereas Levi Strauss uses decentralized control.

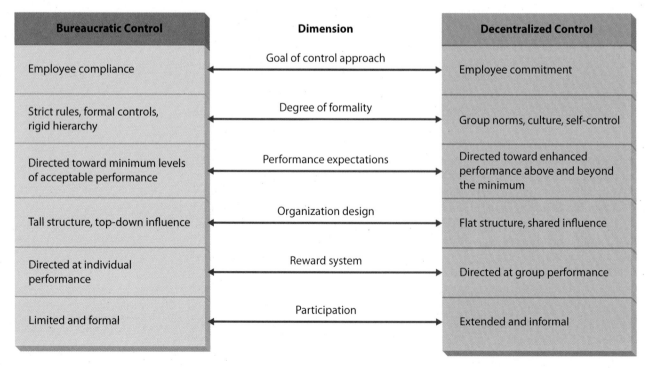

Bureaucratic Control	Dimension	Decentralized Control
Employee compliance	Goal of control approach	Employee commitment
Strict rules, formal controls, rigid hierarchy	Degree of formality	Group norms, culture, self-control
Directed toward minimum levels of acceptable performance	Performance expectations	Directed toward enhanced performance above and beyond the minimum
Tall structure, top-down influence	Organization design	Flat structure, shared influence
Directed at individual performance	Reward system	Directed at group performance
Limited and formal	Participation	Extended and informal

© Cengage Learning 2013

Bureaucratic Control

Bureaucratic control is an approach to organization design characterized by formal and mechanistic structural arrangements. As the term suggests, it follows the bureaucratic model. The goal of bureaucratic control is employee compliance. Organizations that use it rely on strict rules and a rigid hierarchy, insist that employees meet minimally acceptable levels of performance, and often have a tall structure. They focus their rewards on individual performance and allow only limited and formal employee participation.

NBC television applies structural controls that reflect many elements of bureaucracy. The organization relies on numerous rules to regulate employee travel, expense accounts, and other expenses. A new performance appraisal system precisely specifies minimally acceptable levels of performance for everyone. The organization's structure is considerably taller than those of the other major networks, and rewards are based on individual contributions. Perhaps most significantly, many NBC employees have argued that they have too small a voice in how the organization is managed.

In another example, a large oil company recently made the decision to allow employees to wear casual attire to work. But a committee then spent weeks developing a 20-page set of guidelines on what was and was not acceptable. For example, denim pants are not allowed. Similarly, athletic shoes may be worn as long as they are not white. And all shirts must have a collar. Nordstrom, the department store chain, is also moving toward bureaucratic control as it works to centralize all of its purchasing in an effort to lower costs.[32] Similarly, Home Depot is moving more toward bureaucratic control to cut its costs and more effectively compete with its hard-charging rival, Lowe's.[33]

Decentralized Control

Decentralized control, in contrast, is an approach to organizational control characterized by informal and organic structural arrangements. As Figure 11.6 shows, its goal is employee commitment to the organization. Accordingly, it relies heavily on group norms and a strong corporate culture, and gives employees the responsibility for controlling themselves. Employees are encouraged to perform beyond minimally acceptable levels. Organizations using this approach are usually relatively flat. They direct rewards at group performance and favor widespread employee participation.

Levi Strauss practices decentralized control. The firm's managers use groups as the basis for work and have created a culture wherein group norms help facilitate high performance. Rewards are subsequently provided to the higher-performing groups and teams. The company's culture also reinforces contributions to the overall team effort, and employees have a strong sense of loyalty to the organization. Levi's has a flat structure, and power is widely shared. Employee participation is encouraged in all areas of operation.[34] Another company that uses this approach is Southwest Airlines. When Southwest made the decision to "go casual," the firm resisted the temptation to develop dress guidelines. Instead, managers decided to allow employees to exercise discretion over their attire and to deal with clearly inappropriate situations on a case-by-case basis.

bureaucratic control
A form of organizational control characterized by formal and mechanistic structural arrangements

decentralized control
An approach to organizational control based on informal and organic structural arrangements

Identify the fundamental differences between bureaucratic and decentralized control.

What are the most obvious advantages and disadvantages of bureaucratic versus decentralized control?

CONCEPT CHECK

Strategic Control

Given the obvious importance of an organization's strategy, it is also important that the organization assess how effective that strategy is in helping the organization meet its goals.[35] To do this requires that the organization integrate its strategy and control systems. This is especially true for the global organization.

Integrating Strategy and Control

Strategic control generally focuses on five aspects of organizations—structure, leadership, technology, human resources, and information and operational control systems. For example, an organization should periodically examine its structure to determine whether it is facilitating the attainment of the strategic goals being sought. Suppose a firm using a functional (U-form) design has an established goal of achieving a 20 percent sales growth rate per year, but performance indicators show that it is currently growing at a rate of only 10 percent per year. Detailed analysis might reveal that the current structure is inhibiting growth in some way (for example, by slowing decision making and inhibiting innovation) and that a divisional (M-form) design is more likely to bring about the desired growth (by speeding decision making and promoting innovation).

In this way, strategic control focuses on the extent to which implemented strategy achieves the organization's strategic goals. If, as outlined above, one or more avenues of implementation are inhibiting the attainment of goals, that avenue should be changed. Consequently, the firm might find it necessary to alter its structure, replace key leaders, adopt new technology, modify its human resources, or change its information and operational control systems.

For several years, Pfizer, the world's largest pharmaceutical company, has invested billions of dollars in research and development. In 2009, though, the firm acknowledged that it was not getting an adequate return on its investment. Consequently, Pfizer announced that it was laying off 800 senior researchers. The firm also signaled a strategic reorientation by suggesting it would look for other drug companies to buy in order to acquire new patents and drug formulas.[36] In contrast, 3M is a company that is known for its innovation and product development, with staples like Scotch tape and Post-it notes. As the company began emerging from the recession, it announced that it would increase its R&D spending to $100 million, hire 60 to 80 Ph.D. scientists, and increase capital expenditures to nearly $1.05 billion to come out ahead of weaker competitors. However, the company also worked to reduce its stock-keeping units by half to focus only on those products that make up 95 percent of company sales.

Kohl's department stores essentially redefined how to compete effectively in the midtier retailing market and was on trajectory to leave competitors like Sears and Dillard's in its dust. But then the firm inexplicably stopped doing many of the very things that had led to its success—such as keeping abreast of current styles, maintaining low inventories, and keeping its stores neat and clean—and began to stumble. Now, managers are struggling to rejuvenate Kohl's strategic focus and get it back on track.[37] The *Technically Speaking* box on page 277, entitled "Engineering Time at FedEx," shows how a pioneer in an entirely different industry has been more successful in managing a strategic control system that takes advantage of advances in technology.

"Kohl's single-handedly turned the department store industry on its ear, a condition that lasted until rivals woke up and said, 'Hey, I can do that, too.'"

—KURT BARNARD, PRESIDENT, RETAIL FORECASTING[38]

strategic control
Control aimed at ensuring that the organization is maintaining an effective alignment with its environment and moving toward achieving its strategic goals

International Strategic Control

Because of both their relatively large size and the increased complexity associated with international business, global organizations must take an especially pronounced strategic view of their control systems. One very basic question that has to be addressed is whether to manage control from a centralized or a decentralized perspective.[39] Under a centralized system, each

TECHNICALLY SPEAKING

Engineering Time at FedEx

AP Photo/Paul Sakuma

Among the reasons for FedEx's long-term success are its commitments to customer service and prompt, accurate delivery. The company's information systems are critical to its ability to keep these commitments because they support the firm's complex operations (including 90,000 vehicles, 677 airplanes, and 200,000 employees in 220 countries) and allow it to deliver 6 million packages daily.

"We engineer time," explains executive VP and chief information officer Rob Carter. "We . . . allow you to engineer time to make things happen along time schedules that weren't possible [before]." Texas-based Motion Computing, for example, outsources assembly to a factory in China, and FedEx is able to transport a finished PC from the assembly plant directly to the consumer in about five days. Why is such speed so important to Motion? "We have no inventory tied up in the process anywhere," says CEO Scott Eckert. "Frankly, our business is enabled by FedEx."

FedEx founder and CEO Fred Smith once remarked that information about a package is as important as the package itself, and his company has for a long time been putting this insight into practice by means of an extensive online tracking system. Recently, the entire system has been reconfigured so that customers can stay ahead of deliveries rather than merely keeping up with them. "[We] took the whole tracking mechanism and turned it around," reports Carter, "so that as opposed to having to track a package, you say, 'I want to know what's coming to me today.' You can go out there now and see every inbound package, regardless of whether you knew someone was sending it."

It's important to FedEx that it was the first company in the package-delivery industry to recognize the strategic value of information systems. Rival UPS, asserts Carter, still lags behind even though "it's easier to copy than it is to innovate." While granting that UPS offers many of the same information services as FedEx, Carter hastens to underscore what he considers some significant differences between the two competitors. "We've been in a battle on customer-based technology," but FedEx, he explains, "tends to focus slightly less on operational technology. We focus a little more on revenue-generating, customer-satisfaction–generating, strategic-advantage technology.

"The key focus of my job," Carter adds, "is driving technology that increases the top line." As CIO, he puts the emphasis on effectiveness, quality, and satisfaction rather than on bottom-line efficiency and cost control. With a veteran team committed to innovation and an annual budget of $1 billion, Carter expects FedEx's IT operations to be a source of both strategic control and advantage for some time to come.

References: Geoffrey Colvin, "The FedEx Edge," *Fortune*, April 3, 2006, http://money.cnn.com on July 9, 2011; Dean Foust, "FedEx: Taking Off Like 'A Rocket Ship,'" *BusinessWeek*, April 3, 2006, www.businessweek.com on June 2, 2009; "FedEx Recognized as One of Fortune Magazine's 2009 '100 Best Companies to Work For,'" *Business Wire*, January 22, 2009, www.businesswire.com on June 2, 2009; "100 Best Companies to Work For," *Fortune*, February 2, 2009, http://money.cnn.com on July 9, 2011.

organizational unit around the world is responsible for frequently reporting the results of its performance to headquarters. Managers from the home office often visit foreign branches to observe firsthand how the units are functioning.

BP, Unilever, Procter & Gamble, and Sony all use this approach. They believe centralized control is effective because it allows the home office to stay better informed of the performance of foreign units and to maintain more control over how decisions are made. For example, BP discovered that its Australian subsidiary was not billing its customers for charges as quickly as were its competitors. By shortening the billing cycle, BP now receives customer payments five days faster than before. Managers believe that they discovered this oversight only because of a centralized financial control system.

Organizations that use a decentralized control system require foreign branches to report less frequently and in less detail. For example, each unit may submit summary performance statements on a quarterly basis and provide full statements only once a year. Similarly, visits from the home office are less frequent and less concerned with monitoring and assessing performance. IBM, Ford, and Shell all use this approach. Because Ford practices decentralized control of its design function, European designers have developed several innovative automobile design features. Managers believe that if they had been more centralized, designers would not have had the freedom to develop their new ideas.

How are strategy and control most commonly integrated?

In what ways are domestic and international control issues similar, and in what ways do they differ?

Managing Control in Organizations

Effective control, whether at the operations, financial, structural, or strategic level, successfully regulates and monitors organizational activities. To use the control process, managers must recognize the characteristics of effective control and understand how to identify and overcome occasional resistance to control.[40]

Characteristics of Effective Control

Control systems tend to be most effective when they are integrated with planning and when they are flexible, accurate, timely, and objective.

Integration with Planning Control should be linked with planning. The more explicit and precise this linkage, the more effective the control system is. The best way to integrate planning and control is to account for control as plans develop. In other words, as goals are set during the planning process, attention should be paid to developing standards that will reflect how well the plan is realized. Managers at Champion Spark Plug Company decided to broaden their product line to include a full range of automotive accessories—a total of 21 new products. As part of this plan, managers decided in advance what level of sales they wanted to realize from each product for each of the next five years. They established these sales goals as standards against which actual sales would be compared. Thus, by accounting for their control system as they developed their plan, managers at Champion did an excellent job of integrating planning and control.

Flexibility The control system itself must be flexible enough to accommodate change. Consider, for example, an organization whose diverse product line requires 75 different raw materials. The company's inventory control system must be able to manage and monitor current levels of inventory for all 75 materials. When a change in product line changes the number of raw materials needed, or when the required quantities of the existing materials change, the control system should be flexible enough to handle the revised requirements. The alternative—designing and implementing a new control system—is an avoidable expense. Champion's control system included a mechanism that automatically shipped products to major customers to keep their inventories at predetermined levels. The firm had to adjust this system when one of its biggest customers decided not to stock the full line of Champion products. Because its control system was flexible, though, modifying it for the customer was relatively simple.

Accuracy Managers make a surprisingly large number of decisions based on inaccurate information. Field representatives may hedge their sales estimates to make themselves look better. Production managers may hide costs to meet their targets. Human resource managers may overestimate their minority recruiting prospects to meet affirmative action goals. In each case, the information that other managers receive is inaccurate, and the results of inaccurate information may be quite dramatic. If sales projections are inflated, a manager might cut advertising (thinking it is no longer needed) or increase advertising (to further build momentum). Similarly, a production manager unaware of hidden costs may quote a sales price much lower than desirable. Or a human resources manager may speak out publicly on the effectiveness of the company's minority recruiting, only to find out later that these prospects have been overestimated. In each case, the result of inaccurate information is inappropriate managerial action.

Timeliness Timeliness does not necessarily mean quickness. Rather, it describes a control system that provides information as often as is necessary. Because Champion has a wealth of historical data on its sparkplug sales, it does not need information on sparkplugs as frequently as it needs sales feedback for its newer products. Retail organizations usually need sales results daily so that they can manage cash flow and adjust advertising and promotion. In contrast, they may require information about physical inventory only quarterly or annually. In general, the more uncertain and unstable the circumstances, the more frequently measurement is needed.

Objectivity The control system should provide information that is as objective as possible. To appreciate this, imagine the task of a manager responsible for control of his organization's human resources. He asks two plant managers to submit reports. One manager notes that morale at his plant is "okay," that grievances are "about where they should be," and that turnover is "under control." The other reports that absenteeism at her plant is running at 4 percent, that 16 grievances have been filed this year (compared with 24 last year), and that turnover is 12 percent. The second report will almost always be more useful than the first. Of course, managers also need to look beyond the numbers when assessing performance. For example, a plant manager may be boosting productivity and profit margins by putting too much pressure on workers and using poor-quality materials. As a result, impressive short-run gains may be overshadowed by longer-run increases in employee turnover and customer complaints.

Resistance to Control

Managers sometimes make the mistake of assuming that the value of an effective control system is self-evident to employees. This is not always so, however. Many employees resist control, especially if they feel overcontrolled, if they think control is inappropriately focused or rewards inefficiency, or if they are uncomfortable with accountability.

Overcontrol Occasionally, organizations try to control too many things. This becomes especially problematic when the control directly affects employee behavior. An organization that instructs its employees when to come to work, where to park, when to have morning coffee, and when to leave for the day exerts considerable control over people's daily activities. Yet many organizations attempt to control not only these but other aspects of work behavior as well. Of particular relevance in recent years is some companies' efforts to control their employees' access to private e-mail and the Internet during work hours. Some companies

Site
entrance

No hat
No boots
No vest
No job

picturesbyrob/Alamy

Many businesses have formal dress codes. In some cases, such as the one shown here, certain clothing articles are necessary for reasons related to safety, health, or cleanliness. But when organizations go further and attempt to impose standards of general "acceptability" they must careful so as to avoid being too rigid or intrusive. That is, they should avoid overcontrol.

have no policies governing these activities, some attempt to limit it, and some attempt to forbid it altogether.[41]

Troubles arise when employees perceive these attempts to limit their behavior as being unreasonable. A company that tells its employees how to dress, how to arrange their desks, and how to wear their hair may meet with more resistance. Employees at Chrysler who drove non-Chrysler vehicles used to complain because they were forced to park in a distant parking lot. People felt that these efforts to control their personal behavior (what kind of car to drive) were excessive. Managers eventually removed these controls and now allow open parking. Some employees at Abercrombie & Fitch argue that the firm is guilty of overcontrol because of its strict dress and grooming requirements—for example, no necklaces or facial hair for men and only natural nail polish and earrings no larger than a dime for women. Likewise, Enterprise Rent-A-Car has a set of 30 dress-code rules for women and 26 rules for men. The firm was recently sued by one former employee who was fired because of the color of her hair.[42] UBS, the large Swiss bank, had (until recently) a 44-page dress code that prescribed, among other things, that employees should avoid eating garlic and onions (so as to not offend customers), keep their toenails trimmed (so as to not tear their stockings or socks), and wear only skin-colored underwear (so it could remain unseen). Men were instructed in how to knot a tie, and everyone was encouraged to keep their glasses clean. (When the dress code was made public in early 2011, UBS indicated that it would be making some revisions!)[43]

> "Glasses should always be kept clean. On the one hand this gives you optimal vision, and on the other hand dirty glasses create an appearance of negligence."
>
> —UBS DRESS CODE[44]

Inappropriate Focus The control system may be too narrow, or it may focus too much on quantifiable variables and leave no room for analysis or interpretation. A sales standard that encourages high-pressure tactics to maximize short-run sales may do so at the expense of goodwill from long-term customers. Such a standard is too narrow. A university reward system that encourages faculty members to publish large numbers of articles but fails to consider the quality of the work is also inappropriately focused. Employees resist the intent of the control system by focusing their efforts only on the performance indicators being used.

Rewards for Inefficiency Imagine two operating departments that are approaching the end of their fiscal years. Department 1 expects to have $25,000 of its budget left over; department 2 is already $10,000 in the red. As a result, department 1 is likely to have its budget cut for the next year ("They had money left, so they obviously got too much to begin with"), and department 2 is likely to get a budget increase ("They obviously haven't been getting enough money"). Thus department 1 is punished for being efficient, and department 2 is rewarded for being inefficient. (No wonder departments commonly hasten to deplete their budgets as the end of the year approaches!) As with inappropriate focus, people resist the intent of this control and behave in ways that run counter to the organization's intent.

Too Much Accountability Effective controls allow managers to determine whether employees successfully discharge their responsibilities. If standards are properly set and performance accurately measured, managers know when problems arise and which departments and individuals are responsible. People who do not want to be answerable for their mistakes or who do not want to work as hard as their boss might like therefore resist control. For example, American Express has a system that provides daily information on how many calls each of its customer service representatives handles. If one representative has typically worked at a slower pace and handled fewer calls than other representatives, that individual's deficient performance can now more easily be pinpointed.

Overcoming Resistance to Control

Perhaps the best way to overcome resistance to control is to create effective control to begin with. If control systems are properly integrated with organizational planning and if the controls are flexible, accurate, timely, and objective, the organization will be less likely to overcontrol, to focus on inappropriate standards, or to reward inefficiency. Two other ways to overcome resistance are encouraging employee participation and developing verification procedures.

Encourage Employee Participation In Chapter 16, we'll learn how participation can help overcome resistance to change. By the same token, when employees are involved with planning and implementing the control system, they are less likely to resist it. For instance, employee participation in planning, decision making, and quality control at the Chevrolet Gear and Axle plant in Detroit resulted in increased employee concern for quality and a greater commitment to meeting standards.

Develop Verification Procedures Multiple standards and information systems provide checks and balances in control and allow the organization to verify the accuracy of performance indicators. Suppose a production manager argues that she failed to meet a certain cost standard because of increased prices of raw materials. A properly designed inventory control system will either support or contradict her explanation. Suppose that an employee who was fired for excessive absences argues that he was not absent "for a long time." An effective human resource control system should have records that support the termination. Resistance to control declines because these verification procedures protect both employees and management. If the production manager's claim about the rising cost of raw materials is supported by the inventory control records, she will not be held solely accountable for failing to meet the cost standard, and some action probably will be taken to lower the cost of raw materials.

What are the essential characteristics of effective control?

Recall an incident in which you resisted control. What was done, or what might have been done better, to help overcome your resistance?

CONCEPT CHECK

Summary of Learning Objectives and Key Points

1. Explain the purpose of control, identify different types of control, and describe the steps in the control process.

   - Control is the regulation of organizational activities so that some targeted element of performance remains within acceptable limits.
   - Control provides ways to adapt to environmental change, to limit the accumulation of errors, to cope with organizational complexity, and to minimize costs.
   - Control can focus on financial, physical, information, and human resources and includes operations, financial, structural, and strategic levels.
   - Control is the function of managers, the controller, and, increasingly, of operating employees.
   - Steps in the control process are
     - to establish standards of expected performance
     - to measure actual performance
     - to compare performance to the standards
     - to evaluate the comparison and take appropriate action

2. Identify and explain the three forms of operations control.

   - Operations control focuses on the processes the organization uses to transform resources into products or services.
   - Preliminary control is concerned with the resources that serve as inputs to the system.
   - Screening control is concerned with the transformation processes used by the organization.
   - Postaction control is concerned with the outputs of the organization.
   - Most organizations need multiple control systems because no one system can provide adequate control.

3. Describe budgets and other tools for financial control.

   - Financial control focuses on controlling the organization's financial resources.
   - The foundation of financial control is budgets, which are plans expressed in numerical terms.
   - Most organizations rely on financial, operating, and nonmonetary budgets.
   - Financial statements, various kinds of ratios, and external and internal audits are also important tools organizations use as part of financial control.

4. Identify and distinguish between two opposing forms of structural control.

   - Structural control addresses how well an organization's structural elements serve their intended purpose.
   - Two basic forms of structural control are bureaucratic and decentralized control.
     - Bureaucratic control is relatively formal and mechanistic.
     - Decentralized control is informal and organic.
   - Most organizations use a form of organizational control somewhere between total bureaucratic and total decentralized control.

5. Discuss the relationship between strategy and control, including international strategic control.

   - Strategic control focuses on how effectively the organization's strategies are succeeding in helping the organization meet its goals.
   - The integration of strategy and control is generally achieved through organization structure, leadership, technology, human resources, and information and operational control systems.
   - International strategic control is also important for multinational organizations.
   - The foundation of international strategic control is whether to practice centralized or decentralized control.

6. Identify characteristics of effective control, why people resist control, and how managers can overcome this resistance.

   - One way to increase the effectiveness of control is to fully integrate planning and control.
   - The control system should also be as flexible, accurate, timely, and objective as possible.
   - Employees may resist organizational controls because of overcontrol, inappropriate focus, rewards for inefficiency, and a desire to avoid accountability.
   - Managers can overcome this resistance by improving the effectiveness of controls and by allowing employee participation and developing verification procedures.

Discussion Questions

Questions for Review

1. What is the purpose of organizational control? Why is it important?
2. What are the different levels of control? What are the relationships between the different levels?
3. Describe how a budget is created in most organizations. How does a budget help a manager with financial control?
4. Describe the differences between bureaucratic and decentralized control. What are the advantages and disadvantages of each?

Questions for Analysis

5. How can a manager determine whether his or her firm needs improvement in control? If improvement is needed, how can the manager tell what type of control needs improvement (operations, financial, structural, or strategic)? Describe some steps a manager can take to improve each of these types of control.
6. One company uses strict performance standards. Another has standards that are more flexible. What are the advantages and disadvantages of each system?
7. Are the differences in bureaucratic control and decentralized control related to differences in organization structure? If so, how? If not, why not? (The terms do sound similar to those used to discuss the organizing process.)

Questions for Application

8. Many organizations today are involving lower-level employees in control. Give at least two examples of specific actions that a lower-level worker could take to help his or her organization better adapt to environmental change. Then do the same for limiting the accumulation of error, coping with organizational complexity, and minimizing costs.
9. Describe ways that the top management team, midlevel managers, and operating employees can participate in each step of the control process. Do all participate equally in each step, or are some steps better suited for personnel at one level? Explain your answer.
10. Interview a worker to determine which areas and levels of control exist for him or her on the job. Does the worker resist efforts at control? Why or why not?

 ## CengageNow™ Highlights

Now use your CengageNow™ homework to help you:
- Apply management theories in your life
- Assess your management skills
- Master management terms and concepts
- Apply your knowledge to real-world situations
- Analyze and solve challenging management problems

In order to take advantage of these elements, your instructor will need to have set up a course for your class within CengageNow™. Ask your instructor to contact his/her Cengage sales representative and Digital Solutions Manager to explore testing CengageNow™ in your course this term.

12
CHAPTER

Managing Operations, Quality, and Productivity

LEARNING OBJECTIVES

After studying this chapter, you should be able to:

1. Describe and explain the nature of operations management.

2. Identify and discuss the components involved in designing effective operations systems.

3. Discuss organizational technologies and their role in operations management.

4. Identify and discuss the components involved in implementing operations systems through supply chain management.

5. Explain the meaning and importance of managing quality and total quality management.

6. Explain the meaning and importance of managing productivity, productivity trends, and ways to improve productivity.

MANAGEMENT IN ACTION   Orchestrating Outcomes

Reviewing a recent concert by the Orpheus Chamber Orchestra, *New York Times* music critic Vivien Schweitzer wrote that the orchestra played Robert Schumann's Symphony No. 2 "with remarkable coordination"; the "balance among strings, winds, and brass," she added, "was impressively well proportioned."

Was Schweitzer, as we sometimes say, damning with faint praise? Isn't a *symphony*, which means "harmony of sounds," *supposed* to be played with remarkable coordination? Aren't the various sections of the orchestra *supposed* to be well balanced? Had the conductor, whose job is to ensure a consummate performance of the music, achieved little more than coordination and balance? Actually, New York–based Orpheus doesn't play with a conductor, and Schweitzer was remarking on the fact the orchestra had "bravely—and successfully—attempted" such a complex work without the artistic and managerial leadership of someone who directs rehearsals and stands at a podium waving an authoritative baton.

"For us at Orpheus," explains executive director Graham Parker, "it's the *way* we make the music that's the difference." Orpheus holds to the principle that its

> "[T]hey feel empowered. They don't have anyone telling them what to do. They walk into the rehearsal hall and it's their opportunity to influence [and] shape music."
>
> —EXECUTIVE DIRECTOR GRAHAM PARKER ON THE MUSICIANS OF THE ORPHEUS CHAMBER ORCHESTRA

product—the music performed for audiences—is of the highest quality when its workers—the musicians—are highly satisfied with their jobs. All professional orchestra musicians, of course, are highly trained and skilled, but make no mistake about it: A lot of them are not very happy workers. J. Richard Hackman, an organizational psychologist at Harvard, surveyed workers in 13 different occupational categories, including orchestra players, to determine relative levels of job motivation and satisfaction. On the one hand, musicians ranked at the top in motivation, "fueled by their own pride and professionalism," according to Hackman. But when it came to general satisfaction with their jobs, orchestra players ranked

The Orpheus Chamber Orchestra is unique in that it performs without a conductor.

seventh (just below federal prison guards and slightly above beer sales and delivery teams). On the question of satisfaction with growth opportunities, they ranked ninth (again, below prison guards, though a little higher than OR nurses and hockey players).

It's this disconnect between motivation and satisfaction—and between motivation and product quality—that Orpheus was conceived to rectify, and the first principle in what's now known as the "Orpheus Process" is: "Put power in the hands of the people doing the work." According to Harvey Seifter, a consultant specializing in relationships between business and the arts, the Orpheus Process consists of five elements designed to put this principle into practice:

1. *Choosing Leaders.* For each piece of music that the orchestra decides to perform, members select a leadership team composed of five to seven musicians. This "core team" then leads rehearsals and serves as a conduit for members' input. It's also responsible for seeing that the final performance reflects "a unified vision."

2. *Developing Strategies.* Prior to rehearsals, the core team decides how a piece of music will be played. Its ultimate goal is to ensure "an overall interpretive approach to the music," and it works to meet this goal by trying out various approaches to the music during rehearsals with the full orchestra.

3. *Developing the Product.* Once an interpretive approach has been chosen, rehearsals are geared toward refining it. At this point, players make suggestions and critique the playing of their colleagues. It is, of course, a highly collaborative stage in the process, and its success depends upon mutual respect. "We're all specialists—that's the beginning of the discussion," says violinist Martha Caplin. "When I talk to . . . another musician in the group, it's on an equal level. It's absolutely crucial that we have that attitude." When disagreements arise, everyone works toward a consensus, and if a consensus can't be reached, the issue is settled by a vote. Violinist Eriko Sato also emphasizes that the process of collaborative input works best when members focus their contributions on outcomes of the highest possible quality: "Fundamentally," she says, "I don't think everybody's opinion should be addressed at all times. There are certain places and times for certain things to be said. The appropriate moment. Everybody knows what's wrong, everybody can feel what's wrong. But do you have a *solution*? Do you know how to solve a *problem*?"

4. *Perfecting the Product.* Just before each concert, a couple of members take seats in the hall to listen to the performance from the audience's perspective. Then they report to the full ensemble and may suggest some final adjustments.

5. *Delivering the Product.* The final performance is the ultimate result of the Orpheus Process, but it isn't the last step. When the concert is over, members get together to share their impressions of the performance and make suggestions for even further refinements.

"If you ask any musician in the orchestra why they love playing with Orpheus," says Parker, "it's because they feel empowered. They don't have anyone telling them what to do. They walk into the rehearsal hall and it's their opportunity to influence [and] shape music, to make music with all their experience, all their training coming together." Ask double-bass player Don Palma, for instance. Palma took a sabbatical after one year with Orpheus to play with the Los Angeles Philharmonic. "I just hated it," he says. "I didn't like to be told what to do all the time, being treated like I wasn't really worth anything other than to be a good soldier and just sit there and do as I was told. I felt powerless to affect things. . . . I felt frustrated, and there was nothing I could . . . do to help make things better." By contrast, says Palma, "Orpheus keeps me involved. I have some measure of participation in the direction the music is going to take. I think that's why a lot of us have stayed involved so long."

In most orchestras, the conductor makes more or less autocratic decisions about what will be played and how. The input of musicians is neither sought nor welcomed, and unsolicited advice may be sharply rebuffed—and may, in fact, serve as grounds for dismissal. At Orpheus, says Parker, "we have a completely different structure to the way we approach rehearsal": A core team of players selected by the orchestra from each instrument section plans and leads rehearsals for a given piece of music.

To assist in meeting the inevitable challenges posed by its democratic structure, Orpheus recruited Harvard's Hackman to its board of trustees in 2007, and he immediately helped the orchestra organize itself around two leadership groups. An *artistic planning group* consists of two staff members and three "artistic directors." The executive director serves as a sort of moderator for group discussions, and the general manager keeps everyone posted on market-related events and initiatives. The three artistic directors, who are members of the orchestra, work with other members to find out what they're interested in working on and to convey their ideas to the planning group. They also serve on a *senior leadership team* with the executive director, the general manager, and the directors of finance, marketing, and operations. This team determines the best ways to do things given the organization's commitment to democratic structure, leadership, and roles—the best way to develop artistic agendas, to choose players, soloists, and composers and to make the team accountable for its own artistic decisions.

It's important to remember, however, that neither the Orpheus Process nor the Orpheus two-team structure is any guarantee of organizational effectiveness. As in any organizational endeavor, execution is the difference between success and failure, and a study of the Orpheus approach to management has revealed a variety of reasons for the effectiveness of teamwork within the ensemble. Every member, for example, clearly understands the group's purpose and mission; every member's role is clearly stated and agreed upon, and all members perform an equal amount of work in meeting the group's objectives.[1]

In this chapter, we explore operations management, quality, and productivity. Actually, all of these topics figure in our opening story about Orpheus, which has taken a highly innovative approach to each of them. To better understand why Orpheus operates as it does—and why it's successful in doing so—we'll take a closer look at the basics of each of these factors in organizational performance. We first introduce operations management and discuss its role in general management and organizational strategy. The next three sections discuss the design of operations systems, organizational technologies, and implementing operations systems. We then introduce and discuss various issues in managing for quality and total quality. Finally, we discuss productivity, which is closely related to quality.

◆ The Nature of Operations Management

Operations management is at the core of what organizations do as they add value and create products and services. But what exactly are operations? And how are they managed? **Operations management** is the set of managerial activities used by an organization to transform resource inputs into products and services. When Dell Computer buys electronic components, assembles them into PCs, and then ships them to customers, it is engaging in operations management. When a Pizza Hut employee orders food and paper products and then combines dough, cheese, and tomato paste to create a pizza, he or she is engaging in operations management.

The Importance of Operations

Operations is an important functional concern for organizations because efficient and effective management of operations goes a long way toward ensuring competitiveness and overall organizational performance, as well as quality and productivity. Inefficient or ineffective operations management, on the other hand, will almost inevitably lead to poorer performance and lower levels of both quality and productivity.

In an economic sense, operations management creates value and utility of one type or another, depending on the nature of the firm's products or services. If the product is a physical good, such as a Harley-Davidson motorcycle, operations creates value and provides form utility by combining many dissimilar inputs (sheet metal, rubber, paint, internal combustion engines, and human skills) to make something (a motorcycle) that is more valuable than the actual cost of the inputs used to create it. The inputs are converted from their incoming form into a new physical form. This conversion is typical of manufacturing operations and essentially reflects the organization's technology.

operations management
The total set of managerial activities used by an organization to transform resource inputs into products, services, or both

In contrast, the operations activities of American Airlines create value and provide time and place utility through its services. The airline transports passengers and freight according to agreed-upon departure and arrival places and times. Other service operations, such as a Coors beer distributorship or a Gap retail store, create value and provide place and possession utility by bringing together the customer and products made by others. Although the organizations in these examples produce different kinds of products or services, their operations processes share many important features.[2]

Manufacturing and Production Operations

Because manufacturing once dominated U.S. industry, the entire area of operations management used to be called "production management." **Manufacturing** is a form of business that combines and transforms resources into tangible outcomes that are then sold to others. The Goodyear Tire & Rubber Company is a manufacturer because it combines rubber and chemical compounds and uses blending equipment and molding machines to create tires. Broyhill is a manufacturer because it buys wood and metal components, pads, and fabric and then combines them into furniture.

During the 1970s, manufacturing entered a long period of decline in the United States, primarily because of foreign competition. U.S. firms had grown lax and sluggish, and new foreign competitors came onto the scene with better equipment and much higher levels of efficiency. For example, steel companies in the Far East were able to produce high-quality steel for much lower prices than were U.S. companies like Bethlehem Steel and U.S. Steel (now USX Corporation). Faced with a battle for survival, many companies underwent a long and difficult period of change, eliminating waste and transforming themselves into leaner, more efficient and responsive entities. They reduced their workforces dramatically, closed antiquated or unnecessary plants, and modernized their remaining plants. In the last decade, their efforts have started to pay dividends, as U.S. businesses have regained their competitive positions in many different industries. Although manufacturers from other parts of the world are still formidable competitors, and U.S. firms may never again be competitive in some markets, the overall picture is much better than it was just a few years ago. And prospects continue to look bright.[3]

Service Operations

During the decline of the manufacturing sector, a tremendous growth in the service sector kept the U.S. economy from declining at the same rate. A **service organization** is one that transforms resources into an intangible output and creates time or place utility for its customers. For example, Merrill Lynch makes stock transactions for its customers, Avis leases cars to its customers, and local hairdressers cut clients' hair. In 1947 the service sector was responsible for less than half of the U.S. gross national product (GNP). By 1975, however, this figure reached 65 percent, and by 2009 it was over 80 percent. The service sector has been responsible for creating approximately 40 million new jobs in the United States since 1990.[4] Managers have come to see that many of the tools, techniques, and methods that are used in a factory are also useful to a service firm. For example, managers of automobile plants and hair salons both have to decide how to design their facilities, identify the best locations for them, determine optimal capacities, make decisions about inventory storage, set procedures for purchasing raw materials, and set standards for productivity and quality.

The Role of Operations in Organizational Strategy

It should be clear by this point that operations management is very important to organizations. Beyond its direct impact on such factors as competitiveness, quality, and productivity, it also directly influences the organization's overall level of effectiveness. For example, the

manufacturing
A form of business that combines and transforms resource inputs into tangible outcomes

service organization
An organization that transforms resources into an intangible output and creates time or place utility for its customers

deceptively simple strategic decision of whether to stress high quality regardless of cost, lowest possible cost regardless of quality, or some combination of the two has numerous important implications. A highest-possible-quality strategy will dictate state-of-the-art technology and rigorous control of product design and materials specifications. A combination strategy might call for lower-grade technology and less concern about product design and materials specifications. Just as strategy affects operations management, so, too, does operations management affect strategy. Suppose that a firm decides to upgrade the quality of its products or services. The organization's ability to implement the decision is dependent in part on current production capabilities and other resources. If existing technology will not permit higher-quality work, and if the organization lacks the resources to replace its technology, increasing quality to the desired new standards will be difficult.

Distinguish between manufacturing and production operations and service operations.

Why do you think the manufacturing sector of the U.S. economy has declined while the service sector has grown?

CONCEPT CHECK

Designing Operations Systems

The problems, challenges, and opportunities faced by operations managers revolve around the acquisition and utilization of resources for conversion. Their goals include both efficiency and effectiveness. A number of issues and decisions must be addressed as operations systems are designed. The most basic ones are product-service mix, capacity, and facilities.

Determining Product-Service Mix

A natural starting point in designing operations systems is determining the **product-service mix**. This decision flows from corporate, business, and marketing strategies. Managers have to make a number of decisions about their products and services, starting with how many and what kinds to offer.[5] Procter & Gamble, for example, makes regular, tartar-control, gel, and various other formulas of Crest toothpaste and packages them in several different sizes of tubes, pumps, and other dispensers. Similarly, workers at Subway sandwich shops can combine different breads, vegetables, meats, and condiments to create hundreds of different kinds of sandwiches. Decisions also have to be made regarding the level of quality desired, the optimal cost of each product or service, and exactly how each is to be designed. GE recently reduced the number of parts in its industrial circuit breakers from 28,000 to 1,275. This whole process was achieved by carefully analyzing product design and production methods.

Capacity Decisions

product-service mix
How many and what kinds of products or services (or both) to offer

capacity
The amount of products, services, or both that can be produced by an organization

The **capacity** decision involves choosing the amount of products, services, or both that can be produced by the organization. Determining whether to build a factory capable of making 5,000 or 8,000 units per day is a capacity decision. So, too, is deciding whether to build a restaurant with 100 or 150 seats, or a bank with five or ten teller stations. The capacity decision is truly a high-risk one because of the uncertainties of future product demand and the large monetary stakes involved. An organization that builds capacity exceeding its needs may commit resources (capital investment) that will never be recovered. Alternatively, an organization can build a facility with a smaller capacity than expected demand. Doing so may result in lost market opportunities, but it may also free capital resources for use elsewhere in the organization.

A major consideration in determining capacity is demand. A company operating with fairly constant monthly demand might build a plant capable of producing an amount each month roughly equivalent to its demand. But if its market is characterized by seasonal fluctuations, building a smaller plant to meet normal demand and then adding extra shifts staffed with temporary workers or paying permanent workers extra to work more hours during peak periods might be the most effective choice. Likewise, a restaurant that needs 150 seats for Saturday night but never needs more than 100 at any other time during the week would probably be foolish to expand to 150 seats. During the rest of the week, it must still pay to light, heat, cool, and clean the excess capacity. Many customer service departments have tried to improve their capacity to deal with customers while also lowering costs by using automated voice prompts to direct callers to the right representative. As you can see in our *Change* box on page 292, entitled "How to Get2 a Human," this approach to customer relationship management isn't necessarily what a lot of customers have in mind.

Facilities Decisions

Facilities are the physical locations where products or services are created, stored, and distributed. Major decisions pertain to facilities location and facilities layout.

Location Location is the physical positioning or geographic site of facilities and must be determined by the needs and requirements of the organization. A company that relies heavily on railroads for transportation needs to be located close to rail facilities. GE decided that it did not need six plants to make circuit breakers, so it invested heavily in automating one plant and closed the other five. Different organizations in the same industry may have different facilities requirements. Benetton uses only one distribution center for the entire world, whereas Walmart has several distribution centers in the United States alone. A retail business must choose its location very carefully to be convenient for consumers.

Layout The choice of physical configuration, or the layout, of facilities is closely related to other operations decisions. The three entirely different layout alternatives shown in Figure 12.1 help demonstrate the importance of the layout decision.

A product layout is appropriate when large quantities of a single product are needed. It makes sense to custom-design a straight-line flow of work for a product when a specific task is performed at each workstation as each unit flows past. Most assembly lines use this format. For example, Dell's personal computer factories use a product layout.

Process layouts are used in operations settings that create or process a variety of products. Auto repair shops and healthcare clinics are good examples. Each car and each person is a separate "product." The needs of each incoming job are diagnosed as it enters the operations system, and the job is routed through the unique sequence of workstations needed to create the desired finished product. In a process layout, each type of conversion task is centralized in a single workstation or department. All welding is done in one designated shop location, and any car that requires welding is moved to that area. This setup is in contrast to the product layout, in which several different workstations may perform welding operations if the conversion task sequence so dictates. Similarly, in a hospital, all X-rays are done in one location, all surgeries in another, and all physical therapy in yet another. Patients are moved from location to location to get the services they need.

The fixed-position layout is used when the organization is creating a few very large and complex products. Aircraft manufacturers like Boeing and shipbuilders like Newport News use this method. An assembly line capable of moving one of Boeing's new 787 aircraft would require an enormous plant, so instead the airplane itself remains stationary, and people and machines move around it as it is assembled.

---

facilities
The physical locations where products or services are created, stored, and distributed

location
The physical positioning or geographic site of facilities

layout
The physical configuration of facilities, the arrangement of equipment within facilities, or both

product layout
A physical configuration of facilities arranged around the product; used when large quantities of a single product are needed

process layout
A physical configuration of facilities arranged around the process; used in facilities that create or process a variety of products

fixed-position layout
A physical configuration of facilities arranged around a single work area; used for the manufacture of large and complex products such as airplanes

THE MORE THINGS CHANGE

How to Get2 a Human

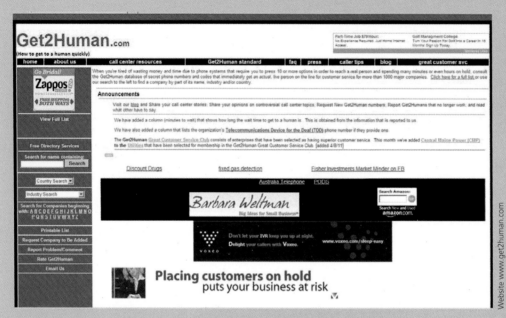

Website www.get2human.com

face of customer service in the U.S." The centerpiece of GetHuman.com is an alphabetized "cheat sheet" that tells you how you can bypass a given automated call-center system and talk to a live service representative. All you have to know is how to press the buttons on your phone. Can't get served by CompuServe? Press 1211 without waiting for the prompts. Getting zero satisfaction from NetZero? Try ###, then 32.

Granted, a company that's really bent on universal frustration could

Submitted for your consideration: the frustration associated with customer-service call centers and automated phone menus—interminable waits, unannounced hang-ups, and endless transfers. Upon even the most casual recollection, two contradictory facts should emerge: On the one hand, a company's marketing department will spend hundreds of millions of dollars to "communicate" with you; on the other hand, the same company's customer-service department acts as if it were saving hundreds of millions of dollars by refusing to communicate with you through the medium of the human voice.

It's a paradox that's by no means lost on the humanitarian website www.gethuman.com, which was founded in 2005 by technology entrepreneur Paul English. "I'm not anti-computer," avows English. "I've been a programmer for 20 years. I'm not anti-capitalist. I'm on my fifth start-up. But I am anti-arrogance. Why do the executives who run these call centers think they can decide when I deserve to speak to a human being and when I don't?"

A lot of people, of course, complain about corporate call centers, but most of us mutter under our breath, put our faith in the redial function, and prepare to be reasonably civil to the next voice we hear. We have, however, neither Paul English's tech skills nor his industry credibility. First, he started castigating customer call centers in his blog, and when that didn't work, he decided to take action. Conducting his own investigations, calling on friends who work in corporate IT departments, and collecting tips from simpatico strangers, English set up a website with the modest goal of "changing the

respond by making its phone system even more complex and difficult to use. Companies that require customers, on the other hand, could take the advice of Jim Kelly, head of customer service at ING Direct. Kelly has made his bank's online system so easy to use that customers call to complain only 1.6 times annually. And those callers get to hear the sound of a human voice every time. The thing to do, advises Kelly, is simply "eliminate most of the problems and complaints. [Then] the only reason for people to call is to do business. And those are calls you're eager to take."

Until more companies start taking Kelly's advice, there's now Get2Human, which was started in 2009 by Walt Tetschner, a veteran market researcher in the call-automation industry. Tetschner, who took over when English moved on to another startup venture, has stated the site's mission in a little more detail: "Our goal," says the Get2Human website, "is to convince enterprises that providing high-quality customer service and having satisfied customers costs much less than providing low-quality customer service and having unsatisfied customers."

References: Fuze Digital Solutions, "Gethuman.com Survey Results Reveal Significant Consumer Expectations for Online Customer Support," press release, October 21, 2008, www.content.fuze.com on May 2, 2011; Christopher Null, "How to Get a Human on the Phone," *Yahoo! Tech*, February 11, 2008, http://tech.yahoo.com on June 9, 2009; Burt Helm, "Building Good Web Buzz," *Single Articles*, April 17, 2006, www.singlearticles.com on May 2, 2011; William C. Taylor, "Your Call Should Be Important to Us, but It's Not," *New York Times*, February 26, 2006, www.nytimes.com on May 2, 2011; GetHuman, "GetHuman History," 2011, http://gethuman.com on May 2, 2011; Get2Human.com, "About Us," 2010, www.get2human.com on May 2, 2011.

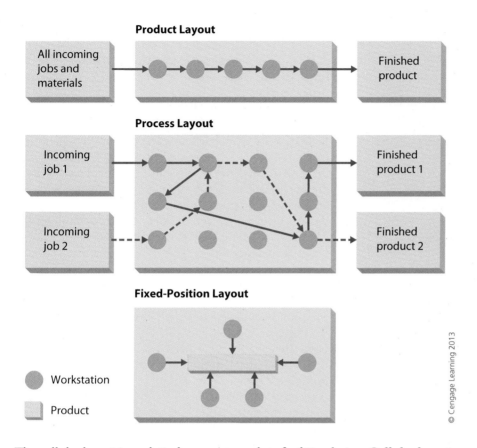

Product Layout

All incoming jobs and materials → ● → ● → ● → ● → ● → Finished product

Process Layout

Incoming job 1 → Finished product 1

Incoming job 2 → Finished product 2

Fixed-Position Layout

● Workstation

▢ Product

© Cengage Learning 2013

FIGURE 12.1
APPROACHES TO FACILITIES LAYOUT

When a manufacturer produces large quantities of a product (such as cars or computers), it may arrange its facilities in an assembly line (product layout). In a process layout, the work (such as patients in a hospital or custom pieces of furniture) moves through various workstations. Locomotives and bridges are both manufactured in a fixed-position layout.

The cellular layout is a relatively new approach to facilities design. Cellular layouts are used when families of products can follow similar flow paths. A clothing manufacturer, for example, might create a cell, or designated area, dedicated to making a family of pockets, such as pockets for shirts, coats, blouses, and slacks. Although each kind of pocket is unique, the same basic equipment and methods are used to make all of them. Hence, all pockets might be made in the same area and then delivered directly to different product layout assembly areas where the shirts, coats, blouses, and slacks are actually being assembled.

cellular layout
A physical configuration of facilities used when families of products can follow similar flow paths

What are the three basic components in designing operations systems? Identify the basic decisions that relate to each.

Think of three local restaurants or other establishments that you have visited recently. Characterize the three components of the operations systems used by each.

CONCEPT CHECK

Organizational Technologies

One central element of effective operations management is technology. In Chapter 3 we defined technology as the set of processes and systems used by organizations to convert resources into products or services.

Manufacturing Technology

Numerous forms of manufacturing technology are used in organizations. In Chapter 15, we will discuss the research of Joan Woodward. Woodward identified three forms of technology—unit or small batch, large batch or mass production, and continuous process.[6]

technology
The set of processes and systems used by organizations to convert resources into products or services

The Jacquard loom was one of the first machine-controlling devices. The loom used cards with holes punched in them to control the use of different threads as the loom helped create tapestries and rugs. While today's looms look much different than this one, the basic principles underlying how the loom operates have remain largely unchanged.

SSPL/Getty Images

Each form of technology was thought to be associated with a specific type of organization structure. Of course, newer forms of technology not considered by Woodward also warrant attention. Two of these are automation and computer-assisted manufacturing.

Automation Automation is the process of designing work so that it can be completely or almost completely performed by machines. Because automated machines operate quickly and make few errors, they increase the amount of work that can be done. Thus automation helps to improve products and services, and fosters innovation. Automation is the most recent step in the development of machines and machine-controlling devices. Machine-controlling devices have been around since the 1700s. James Watt, a Scottish engineer, invented a mechanical speed control to regulate the speed of steam engines in 1787. The Jacquard loom, developed by a French inventor, was controlled by paper cards with holes punched in them. Early accounting and computing equipment was controlled by similar punched cards.

Automation relies on feedback, information, sensors, and a control mechanism. Feedback is the flow of information from the machine back to the sensor. Sensors are the parts of the system that gather information and compare it to preset standards. The control mechanism is the device that sends instructions to the automatic machine. Early automatic machines were primitive, and the use of automation was relatively slow to develop. These elements are illustrated by the example in Figure 12.2. A thermostat has sensors that monitor air temperature and compare it to a preset value. If the air temperature falls below the preset value, the thermostat sends an electrical signal to the furnace, turning it on. The furnace heats the air. When the sensors detect that the air temperature has reached

automation
The process of designing work so that it can be completely or almost completely performed by machines

FIGURE 12.2 A SIMPLE AUTOMATIC CONTROL MECHANISM

All automation includes feedback, information, sensors, and a control mechanism. A simple thermostat is an example of automation. Another example is Benetton's distribution center in Italy. Orders are received, items pulled from stock and packaged for shipment, and invoices prepared and transmitted, with no human intervention.

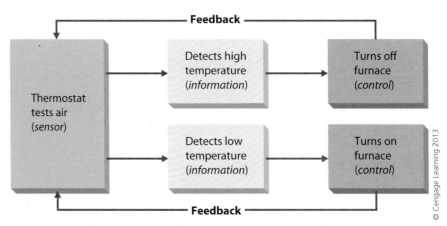

© Cengage Learning 2013

a value higher than the low preset value, the thermostat stops the furnace. The last step (shutting off the furnace) is known as *feedback*, a critical component of any automated operation.

The big move to automate factories began during World War II. The shortage of skilled workers and the development of high-speed computers combined to bring about a tremendous interest in automation. Programmable automation (the use of computers to control machines) was introduced during this era, far outstripping conventional automation (the use of mechanical or electromechanical devices to control machines). The automobile industry began to use automatic machines for a variety of jobs. In fact, the term *automation* came into use in the 1950s in the automobile industry. The chemical and oil-refining industries also began to use computers to regulate production. During the 1990s, automation became a major element in the manufacture of computers and computer components, such as electronic chips and circuits. It is this computerized, or programmable, automation that presents the greatest opportunities and challenges for management today.

The impact of automation on people in the workplace is complex. In the short term, people whose jobs are automated may find themselves without a job. In the long term, however, more jobs are created than are lost. Nevertheless, not all companies are able to help displaced workers find new jobs, so the human costs are sometimes high. In the coal industry, for instance, automation has been used primarily in mining. The output per miner has risen dramatically from the 1950s on. The demand for coal, however, has decreased, and productivity gains resulting from automation have lessened the need for miners. Consequently, many workers have lost their jobs, and the industry has not been able to absorb them. In contrast, in the electronics industry, the rising demand for products has led to increasing employment opportunities despite the use of automation.[7]

Computer-Assisted Manufacturing Current extensions of automation generally revolve around computer-assisted manufacturing. **Computer-assisted manufacturing** is technology that relies on computers to design or manufacture products. One type of computer-assisted manufacturing is *computer-aided design (CAD)*—the use of computers to design parts and complete products and to simulate performance so that prototypes need not be constructed. Boeing uses CAD technology to study hydraulic tubing in its commercial aircraft. Japan's automotive industry uses it to speed up car design. GE used CAD to change the design of circuit breakers, and Benetton uses CAD to design new styles and products. Oneida, the table flatware firm, uses CAD to design new flatware patterns; for example, it can design a new spoon in a single day. CAD is usually combined with *computer-aided manufacturing (CAM)* to ensure that the design moves smoothly to production. The production computer shares the design computer's information and is able to have machines with the proper settings ready when production is needed. A CAM system is especially useful when reorders come in because the computer can quickly produce the desired product, prepare labels and copies of orders, and send the product out to where it is wanted.

Closely aligned with this approach is *computer-integrated manufacturing (CIM)*. In CIM, CAD and CAM are linked together, and computer networks automatically adjust machine placements and settings to enhance both the complexity and the flexibility of scheduling. In settings that use these technologies, all manufacturing activities are controlled by the computer network. Because the network can access the company's other information systems, CIM is both a powerful and a complex management control tool.

Flexible manufacturing systems (FMS) usually have robotic work units or workstations, assembly lines, and robotic carts or some other form of computer-controlled transport system to move material as needed from one part of the system to another. FMS like the one at IBM's manufacturing facility in Lexington, Kentucky, rely on computers to coordinate and integrate automated production and materials-handling facilities. And after it bought Jaguar several years ago, Ford Motor Company used FMS to transform an English factory producing low-cost Ford Escorts into a Jaguar plant making Jaguar luxury cars.

computer-assisted manufacturing
A technology that relies on computers to design or manufacture products

Using traditional methods, the plant would have been closed, its workers laid off, and the facility virtually rebuilt from the ground up. But by using FMS, Ford was able to keep the plant open and running continuously while new equipment was being installed and its workers were being retrained in small groups.[8] Ford continues to be a pioneer in FMS as it adjusts plant capabilities to produce pickups, SUVs, or small hybrids depending on fluctuations in demand and supply.[9]

These systems are not without disadvantages, however. For example, because they represent fundamental change, they also generate resistance. Additionally, because of their tremendous complexity, CAD systems are not always reliable. CIM systems are so expensive that they raise the breakeven point for firms using them. This means that the firm must operate at high levels of production and sales to be able to afford the systems.

> "Lean isn't good enough anymore. The new reality requires being both lean and flexible."
>
> —DAVID COLE, AUTOMOBILE INDUSTRY EXPERT[10]

Robotics Another trend in manufacturing technology is computerized robotics. A robot is any artificial device that is able to perform functions ordinarily thought to be appropriate for human beings. Robotics refers to the science and technology of the construction, maintenance, and use of robots. The use of industrial robots has steadily increased since 1980 and is expected to continue to increase slowly as more companies recognize the benefits that accrue to users of industrial robots.[11]

Welding was one of the first applications for robots, and it continues to be the area for most applications. A close second is materials handling. Other applications include machine loading and unloading, painting and finishing, assembly, casting, and such machining applications as cutting, grinding, polishing, drilling, sanding, buffing, and deburring. Daimler, for instance, replaced about 200 welders with 50 robots on an assembly line and increased productivity about 20 percent. The use of robots in inspection work is increasing. They can check for cracks and holes, and they can be equipped with vision systems to perform visual inspections.

Robots are also beginning to move from the factory floor to all manner of other applications. The Dallas police used a robot to apprehend a suspect who had barricaded himself in an apartment building. The robot smashed a window and reached with its mechanical arm into the building. The suspect panicked and ran outside. At the Long Beach Memorial Hospital in California, brain surgeons are assisted by a robot arm that drills into the patient's skull with excellent precision. Some newer applications involve remote work. For example, the use of robot submersibles controlled from the surface can help divers in remote locations. Surveillance robots fitted with microwave sensors can do things that a human guard cannot do, such as "seeing" through nonmetallic walls and in the dark. In other applications, automated farming (called "agrimation") uses robot harvesters to pick fruit from a variety of trees.

Robots are also used by small manufacturers. One robot slices carpeting to fit the inside of custom vans in an upholstery shop. Another stretches balloons flat so that they can be spray-painted with slogans at a novelties company. At a jewelry company, a robot holds class rings while they are engraved by a laser. These robots are lighter, faster, stronger, and more intelligent than those used in heavy manufacturing and are the types that more and more organizations will be using in the future.

> "We can't [use reverse outsourcing] unless we use technology—robotics in particular—to increase our factory workers' productivity."
>
> —RODNEY BROOKS, DIRECTOR, MIT ARTIFICIAL INTELLIGENCE LABORATORY[12]

Service Technology

Service technology is also changing rapidly. And it, too, is moving more and more toward automated systems and procedures. In banking, for example, new technological breakthroughs led to automated teller machines and made it much easier to move funds between accounts or between different banks. Many people now have their paychecks deposited directly into a checking account from which many of their bills are then automatically

robot
Any artificial device that is able to perform functions ordinarily thought to be appropriate for human beings

TECHNICALLY SPEAKING

Teaming Technology and Artistry

Jeff Wheeler/Minneapolis Star Tribune

Canadian gymnast Natasha Chao joined Cirque du Soleil in 1993 and, from 1999 to 2003, performed the role of the Red Bird in *Mystère*, a production permanently staged at Treasure Island Hotel and Casino in Las Vegas. According to the show's production notes, the character of the flightless Red Bird (who is male though the performer needn't be) "leaps ever higher in his futile attempts to take to the skies. Still convinced he can fly, he struggles against his fate." As choreographed, his fate consists of a 60-foot headfirst freefall into a hidden net. "One thing all . . . Cirque artists share in common," says *Mystère* choreographer Debra Brown, "is a passion for doing art. Circus performers, who risk their lives, are the most passionate," she adds, and Chao is no exception. Working without an understudy, however, she couldn't afford to get hurt, and, passion for her art notwithstanding, she was understandably cautious in performing the stunt.

In addition to maintaining her impeccable timing and keen spatial awareness, the key for Chao was to curve her spine upright at the final moment before contact with the net. The tension in the net was continuously monitored by technicians working the theater's motion-control system, and it should come as no surprise that all of an artist's skill, preparation, and caution can do little to prevent injury if he or she doesn't get the type of support for which armies of Cirque technicians are responsible every night. Executing a stunt like the plunge of the Red Bird, says another Cirque choreographer, Jacques Heim, "is

extremely exciting, but it's . . . exciting because it's terrifying." And that's why, he explains, every Cirque performance really consists of two shows: the one that the performers are putting on in front of the audience and the one that the technicians are performing behind the scenes.

Heim did the choreography for *KÀ*, an Egyptian-themed Cirque extravaganza in residence at the MGM Grand Hotel & Casino, also in Las Vegas. Premiering in 2005 at a cost of $220 million, *KÀ* was at the time, both theatrically and technologically, the most ambitious production that Cirque du Soleil had ever mounted. "In *KÀ*," says technical director Matthew Whelan, "the machinery is so impressive that their movement becomes a [dance] number in itself. . . . The audience does see the lift movements"—the computer-controlled manipulation of the decks that comprise the mobile "stage"—"but there's also a complete other show going on in the pit where the lifts move out of sightline to allow scenic pieces to move from level to level in a specific choreography to manage limited floor space." The interaction of technicians and performers is even more critical than in most Cirque productions because, as stage architect Mark Fisher puts it, the technologically managed scenery is "actually part of the landscape in which the performers live and move to create their show."

"There's a constant risk of artists falling," admits equipment designer Jaque Paquin, and Cirque du Soleil depends on its technology and the people who run it not only to enhance the performance of its artists, but to protect them as well. Paquin, after all, is also responsible for the retractable safety net that's programmed into position beneath *KÀ*'s centerpiece scene—an aerial-acrobatics spectacle—by the theater's modular, multi-user NOMAD control system. Keith Wright, *KÀ*'s operations production manager, sees the technician's twofold responsibility as a basic reflection of Cirque du Soleil's mission: "Cirque du Soleil," he says, "is always about the artist and humanity, and the tools we use—no matter how advanced—must serve the human artists."

References: John Scott Lewinski, "Cirque du Soleil's Sophisticated *KÀ* Evolves with New Tech," *Wired*, February 16, 2010 www.wired.com on May 3, 2011; Joe Hunkins, "Cirque du Soleil: Dramatic Technologies," *Technology Report*, December 15, 2009, http:// technology-report.com on May 3, 2011; Victoria Looseleaf, "Cirque du Soleil's Magic," *Dance Magazine*, December 2007, www.dancemagazine.com on May 3, 2011; Gigi Berardi, "Circus+Dance=Cirque du Soleil," *Dance Magazine*, September 1, 2002, www .thefreelibrary.com on May 3, 2011; Stephanie Gooch, "Industrial-Scale Technology in Cirque du Soleil's *KÀ*," *Designfax*, February 1, 2005, www.thefreelibrary.com on May 3, 2011.

paid. Electronic banking—where people can access their accounts, move money between accounts, and pay bills—has become commonplace. Moreover, the capability to do these things has been extended from personal computers to cell phones and other personal electronic communication technologies.

Hotels use increasingly sophisticated technology to accept and record room reservations. People can now, for instance, check in online and stop by the front desk only long enough to pick up their room key. Universities use new technologies to electronically store and provide access to books, scientific journals, government reports, and articles. Hospitals and other healthcare organizations use new forms of service technology to manage patient records, dispatch ambulances and EMTs, and monitor patient vital signs. Restaurants use technology to record and fill customer orders, order food and supplies, and prepare food. If you've ever seen a performance by Cirque du Soleil, you probably have some idea of the role played by technology in its spectacular productions. To see how Cirque du Soleil combines technological with artistic expertise to mount such complex shows, go to the *Technically Speaking* box on page 297, entitled "Teaming Technology and Artistry." Given the increased role that service organizations—from restaurants and dry cleaners to hotels and circuses—are playing in today's economy, even more technological innovations are certain to be developed in the years to come.[13]

Identify and describe three relatively new manufacturing technologies.

Identify as many examples as you can of how service technology at your college or university has changed in recent times.

CONCEPT CHECK

Implementing Operations Systems Through Supply Chain Management

After operations systems have been properly designed and technologies developed, they must then be put into use by the organization. Their basic functional purpose is to control transformation processes to ensure that relevant goals are achieved in such areas as quality and costs. Operations management has a number of special purposes within this control framework, including purchasing and inventory management. Indeed, this area of management has become so important in recent years that a new term—*supply chain management*—has been coined. Specifically, **supply chain management** can be defined as the process of managing operations control, resource acquisition and purchasing, and inventory so as to improve overall efficiency and effectiveness.[14]

Operations Management as Control

One way of using operations management as control is to coordinate it with other functions. Monsanto Company, for example, established a consumer products division that produces and distributes fertilizers and lawn chemicals. To facilitate control, the operations function was organized as an autonomous profit center. Monsanto finds this effective because its manufacturing division is given the authority to determine not only the costs of creating the product but also the product price and the marketing program.

In terms of overall organizational control, a division like the one used by Monsanto should be held accountable only for the activities over which it has decision-making authority. It would be inappropriate, of course, to make operations accountable for profitability in an organization that stresses sales and market share over quality and productivity.

supply chain management
The process of managing operations control, resource acquisition, and inventory so as to improve overall efficiency and effectiveness

Misplaced accountability results in ineffective organizational control, to say nothing of hostility and conflict. Depending on the strategic role of operations, then, operations managers are accountable for different kinds of results. For example, in an organization using bureaucratic control, accountability will be spelled out in rules and regulations. In a decentralized system, it is likely to be understood and accepted by everyone.

Within operations, managerial control ensures that resources and activities achieve primary goals such as a high percentage of on-time deliveries, low unit-production cost, or high product reliability. Any control system should focus on the elements that are most crucial to goal attainment. For example, firms in which product quality is a major concern (as it is at Rolex) might adopt a screening control system to monitor the product as it is being created. If quantity is a higher priority (as it is at Timex), a postaction system might be used to identify defects at the end of the system without disrupting the manufacturing process itself.

For the past several years, Boeing has been grappling with problems in launching its latest major passenger airplane, the Boeing 787 Dreamliner. During its early development, the 787 was hailed as the most commercially successful new plane of all time. Airlines around the world pre-ordered over 900 of the planes at a cost of $178 million each before they ever took a test flight, based on its projected fuel efficiency, passenger comfort, low maintenance costs, flexibility, and other major design elements. But the first test flights for the plane were over two years late, largely because of supply chain issues. Boeing subcontracted out the design and assembly of major components of the 787 to firms in Japan, Italy, South Carolina, and Kansas, but did not impose adequate coordination across these various suppliers. As a result, subassemblies did not fit together properly, there were numerous quality and delivery issues, and myriad other problems. Clearly, then, poor supply chain management can be disastrous, especially for major new products.[15]

Recent events have also underscored the consequences of disruptions to supply chains. The earthquake and subsequent tsunami that devastated Japan in 2011 caused Japanese automakers in the United States to virtually cease production for several months due to the shortage of parts available from Japanese suppliers. Even U.S. automakers like General Motors and Ford suffered disruptions as well.[16]

Purchasing Management

Purchasing management, also called *procurement*, is concerned with buying the materials and resources needed to create products and services. In many ways, purchasing is at the very heart of effective supply chain management. The purchasing manager for a retailer like Sears, Roebuck is responsible for buying the merchandise the store will sell. The purchasing manager for a manufacturer buys raw materials, parts, and machines needed by the organization. Large companies like GE, IBM, and Siemens have large purchasing departments.[17] The manager responsible for purchasing must balance a number of constraints. Buying too much ties up capital and increases storage costs. Buying too little might lead to shortages and high reordering costs. The manager must also make sure that the quality of what is purchased meets the organization's needs, that the supplier is reliable, and that the best financial terms are negotiated.

Many firms have recently changed their approaches to purchasing as a means to lower costs and improve quality and productivity. In particular, rather than relying on hundreds or even thousands of suppliers, many companies are reducing their number of suppliers and negotiating special production–delivery arrangements.[18] For example, the Honda plant in Marysville, Ohio, found a local business owner looking for a new opportunity. They negotiated an agreement whereby he would start a new company to mount car stereo speakers into plastic moldings. He delivers finished goods to the plant three times a day, and Honda buys all he can manufacture. Thus he has a stable sales base, Honda has a local and reliable supplier, and both companies benefit.

purchasing management Buying materials and resources needed to produce products and services

TABLE 12.1 INVENTORY TYPES, PURPOSES, AND SOURCES OF CONTROL

Type	Purpose	Source of Control
Raw materials	Provide the materials needed to make the product	Purchasing models and systems
Work in process	Enable overall production to be divided into stages of manageable size	Shop-floor control systems
Finished goods	Provide ready supply of products on customer demand and enable long, efficient production runs	High-level production scheduling systems in conjunction with marketing
In transit (pipeline)	Distribute products to customers	Transportation and distribution control systems

© Cengage Learning 2013

Inventory Management

Inventory control, also called *materials control*, is essential for effective operations management. The four basic kinds of inventories are *raw materials, work-in-process, finished-goods*, and *in-transit* inventories. As shown in Table 12.1, the sources of control over these inventories are as different as their purposes. Work-in-process inventories, for example, are made up of partially completed products that need further processing; they are controlled by the shop-floor system. In contrast, the quantities and costs of finished-goods inventories are under the control of the overall production scheduling system, which is determined by high-level planning decisions. In-transit inventories are controlled by the transportation and distribution systems.

Like most other areas of operations management, inventory management has changed notably in recent years. One particularly important breakthrough is the **just-in-time (JIT) method**. First popularized by the Japanese, the JIT system reduces the organization's investment in storage space for raw materials and in the materials themselves. Historically, manufacturers built large storage areas and filled them with materials, parts, and supplies that would be needed days, weeks, and even months in the future. A manager using the JIT approach orders materials and parts more often and in smaller quantities, thereby reducing investment in both storage space and actual inventory. The ideal arrangement is for materials to arrive just as they are needed—or just in time.[19]

Recall our example about the small firm that assembles stereo speakers for Honda and delivers them three times a day, making it unnecessary for Honda to carry large quantities of the speakers in inventory. In an even more striking example, Johnson Controls makes automobile seats for Mercedes and ships them by small truckloads to a Mercedes plant 75 miles away. Each shipment is scheduled to arrive two hours before it is needed. Clearly, the JIT approach requires high levels of coordination and cooperation between the company and its suppliers. If shipments arrive too early, Mercedes has no place to store them. If they arrive too late, the entire assembly line may have to be shut down, resulting in enormous expense. When properly designed and used, the JIT method controls inventory very effectively.

inventory control
Managing the organization's raw materials, work in process, finished goods, and products in transit

just-in-time (JIT) method
An inventory system that has necessary materials arriving as soon as they are needed (just in time) so that the production process is not interrupted

---

What is supply chain management? What are its basic components?

Think of four situations in which the just-in-time method might be applicable. Under what circumstances would JIT not be as useful?

CONCEPT CHECK

Managing Total Quality

Quality and productivity have become major determinants of business success or failure today and are central issues in managing organizations. But, as we will see, achieving higher levels of quality is not an easy accomplishment. Simply ordering that quality be improved is about as effective as waving a magic wand.[20] The catalyst for its emergence as a mainstream management concern was foreign business, especially Japanese. And nowhere was it more visible than in the auto industry. During the energy crisis in the late 1970s, many people bought Toyotas, Hondas, and Nissans because they were more fuel-efficient than U.S. cars. Consumers soon found, however, that not only were the Japanese cars more fuel-efficient, they were also of higher quality than U.S. cars. Parts fit together better, the trim work was neater, and the cars were more reliable. Thus, after the energy crisis subsided, Japanese cars remained formidable competitors because of their reputation for quality.

The Meaning of Quality

The American Society for Quality Control defines **quality** as the totality of features and characteristics of a product or service that bear on its ability to satisfy stated or implied needs.[21] Quality has several different attributes. Table 12.2 lists eight basic dimensions that determine the quality of a particular product or service. For example, a product that has durability and is reliable is of higher quality than a product with less durability and reliability.

Quality is also relative. For example, a Lincoln is a higher-grade car than a Mercury Marquis, which, in turn, is a higher-grade car than a Ford Focus. The difference in quality stems from differences in design and other features. The Focus, however, is considered a high-quality car relative to its engineering specifications and price. Likewise, the Marquis and Lincoln may also be high-quality cars, given their standards and prices. Thus quality is both an absolute and a relative concept.

> "[Porsches] . . . cost a lot of money. When you spend that kind of money, you expect things to be right."
>
> —LYNN KINZIG, PORSCHE DEALER[22]

Quality is relevant for both products and services. Although its importance for products like cars and computers was perhaps recognized first, service firms ranging from airlines to restaurants have also come to see that quality is a vitally important determinant of their success or failure. Service quality, as we will discuss later in this chapter, has thus also become a major competitive issue in U.S. industries today.[23]

TABLE 12.2 EIGHT DIMENSIONS OF QUALITY

These eight dimensions generally capture the meaning of quality, which is a critically important contributor to organizational success today. Understanding the basic meaning of quality is a good first step toward managing it more effectively.

1. *Performance.* A product's primary operating characteristic; examples are automobile acceleration and a television's picture clarity
2. *Features.* Supplements to a product's basic functioning characteristics, such as power windows on a car
3. *Reliability.* A probability of not malfunctioning during a specified period
4. *Conformance.* The degree to which a product's design and operating characteristics meet established standards
5. *Durability.* A measure of product life
6. *Serviceability.* The speed and ease of repair
7. *Aesthetics.* How a product looks, feels, tastes, and smells
8. *Perceived quality.* As seen by a customer

Source: Reprinted by permission of *Harvard Business Review.* Exhibit from "Competing on the Eight Dimensions of Quality," by David A. Garvin, November/December 1987. Copyright © 1987 by the Harvard Business School Publishing Corporation; all rights reserved.

quality
The totality of features and characteristics of a product or service that bear on its ability to satisfy stated or implied needs

The Malcolm Baldrige Award recognizes organizations that make major improvements in quality. Vice President Joe Biden is shown here presenting the Baldrige Award to recent honorees.

AP Photo/Haraz N. Ghanbari

The Importance of Quality

To help underscore the importance of quality, the U.S. government created the **Malcolm Baldrige Award**, named after the former secretary of commerce who championed quality in U.S. industry. The award, administered by an agency of the Commerce Department, is given annually to firms that achieve major improvements in the quality of their products or services. In other words, the award is based on changes in quality, as opposed to absolute quality. In addition, numerous other quality awards have been created. For example, the Rochester Institute of Technology and *USA Today* award their Quality Cup award not to entire organizations but to individual teams of workers within organizations. Quality is also an important concern for individual managers and organizations for three very specific reasons: competition, productivity, and costs.[24]

Competition Quality has become one of the most competitive points in business today. Ford, Daimler, General Motors, and Toyota, for example, each implies that its cars and trucks are higher in quality than the cars and trucks of the others. And American, Delta, and United Airlines each claims that it provides the best and most reliable service. In the wake of the economic recession that started in 2008, many businesses have focused even more attention on service quality as a competitive advantage during lean times. While some firms, for example, cut their staff at customer call centers, others did not. What impact might this have? One study found that cutting four representatives at a call center of three dozen people sent the number of customers put on hold for four minutes from zero to 80. Firms with especially strong reputations for service quality include Amazon.com, USAA (an insurance firm), Lexus, Ritz-Carlton, Ace Hardware, and Apple.[25]

"During tough times there are plenty of other pressures customers face. We don't want a customer service issue to be what makes them blow a cork."

—JOHN VENHUIZEN, VICE PRESIDENT, ACE HARDWARE[26]

Productivity Managers have also come to recognize that quality and productivity are related. In the past, many managers thought that they could increase output (productivity) only by decreasing quality. Managers today have learned the hard way that such an assumption is almost always wrong. If a firm installs a meaningful quality enhancement program, three things are likely to result. First, the number of defects is likely to decrease, causing fewer returns from customers. Second, because the number of defects goes down, resources (materials and people) dedicated to reworking flawed output will be decreased. Third, because making employees responsible for quality reduces the need for quality inspectors, the organization is able to produce more units with fewer resources.

Costs Improved quality also lowers costs. Poor quality results in higher returns from customers, high warranty costs, and lawsuits from customers injured by faulty products. Future sales are lost because of disgruntled customers. An organization with quality problems often has to increase inspection expenses just to catch defective products. We noted in Chapter 11, for example, how at one point Whistler Corporation was using 40 percent of its workforce just to fix poorly assembled radar detectors made by the other 60 percent.[27]

Malcolm Baldrige Award
Named after a former secretary of commerce, this prestigious award is given to firms that achieve major quality improvements

Total Quality Management

Once an organization makes a decision to enhance the quality of its products and services, it must then decide how to implement this decision. The most pervasive approach to managing quality has been called **total quality management,** or **TQM** (sometimes called **quality assurance**)—a real and meaningful effort by an organization to change its whole approach to business in order to make quality a guiding factor in everything the organization does.[28] Figure 12.3 highlights the major ingredients in TQM.

Strategic Commitment The starting point for TQM is a strategic commitment by top management. Such commitment is important for several reasons. First, the organizational culture must change to recognize that quality is not just an ideal but an objective goal that must be pursued.[29] Second, a decision to pursue the goal of quality carries with it some real costs—for expenditures such as new equipment and facilities. Thus, without a commitment from top management, quality improvement will prove to be just a slogan or gimmick, with little or no real change. Just a few years ago Porsche had the lowest reliability of any automobile maker in the world. But a major commitment from top management helped turn the company around. By paying more attention to consumer preferences and using the other methods described below, Porsche shot to the top of global automobile reliability.[30]

Employee Involvement Employee involvement is another critical ingredient in TQM. Virtually all successful quality enhancement programs involve making the person responsible for doing the job responsible for making sure it is done right.[31] By definition, then, employee involvement is a critical component in improving quality. Work teams, which will be discussed in Chapter 22, are common vehicles for increasing employee involvement.

Technology New forms of technology are also useful in TQM programs. Automation and robots, for example, can often make products with higher precision and better consistency than can people. Investing in higher-grade machines capable of doing jobs more precisely and reliably often improves quality. For example, Nokia has achieved notable improvements in product quality by replacing many of its machines with new equipment. Similarly, most U.S. auto and electronics firms make regular investments in new technology to help boost quality.

Materials Another important part of TQM is improving the quality of the materials that organizations use. Suppose that a company that assembles stereos buys chips and circuits

FIGURE 12.3 TOTAL QUALITY MANAGEMENT

Quality is one of the most important issues facing organizations today. Total quality management, or TQM, is a comprehensive effort to enhance an organization's product or service quality. TQM involves the five basic dimensions shown here. Each is important and must be addressed effectively if the organization expects to truly increase quality.

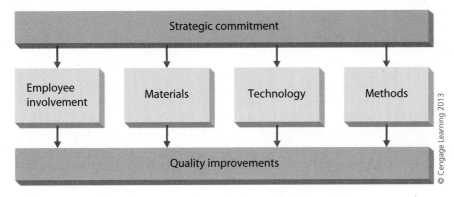

© Cengage Learning 2013

total quality management (TQM) (quality assurance)
A strategic commitment by top management to change its whole approach to business in order to make quality a guiding factor in everything it does

from another company. If the chips have a high failure rate, consumers will return defective stereos to the company whose nameplate appears on them, not to the company that made the chips. The stereo firm then loses in two ways: refunds back to customers and a damaged reputation. As a result, many firms have increased the quality requirements they impose on their suppliers as a way of improving the quality of their own products.

Methods Improved methods can improve product and service quality. Methods are operating systems used by the organization during the actual transformation process. American Express Company, for example, has found ways to cut its approval time for new credit cards from 22 to only five days. This results in improved service quality.

TQM Tools and Techniques

Beyond the strategic context of quality, managers can also rely on several specific tools and techniques for improving quality. Among the most popular today are value-added analysis, benchmarking, outsourcing, reducing cycle times, ISO 9000:2000 and ISO 14000, statistical quality control, and Six Sigma.

Value-Added Analysis Value-added analysis is the comprehensive evaluation of all work activities, materials flows, and paperwork to determine the value that they add for customers. Such an analysis often reveals wasteful or unnecessary activities that can be eliminated without jeopardizing customer service. For example, during a value-added analysis, Hewlett-Packard determined that its contracts were unnecessarily long, confusing, and hard to understand. The firm subsequently cut its standard contract form down from 20 to two pages and experienced an 18 percent increase in its computer sales.

Benchmarking Benchmarking is the process of learning how other firms do things in an exceptionally high-quality manner. Some approaches to benchmarking are simple and straightforward. For example, Xerox routinely buys copiers made by other firms and takes them apart to see how they work. This enables the firm to stay abreast of improvements and changes its competitors are using. When Ford was planning the newest version of the Taurus, it identified the 400 features customers identified as being most important to them. It then found the competing cars that did the best job on each feature. Ford's goal was to equal or surpass each of its competitors on those 400 features. Other benchmarking strategies are more indirect. For example, many firms study how L.L. Bean manages its mail-order business, how Disney recruits and trains employees, and how FedEx tracks packages for applications they can employ in their own businesses.[32]

Outsourcing Another innovation for imp-roving quality is outsourcing. Outsourcing is the process of subcontracting services and operations to other firms that can perform them more cheaply or better. If a business performs each and every one of its own administrative and business services and operations, it is almost certain to be doing at least some of them in an inefficient or low-quality manner. If those areas can be identified and outsourced, the firm will save money and realize a higher-quality service or operation.[33] For example, until recently Eastman Kodak handled all of its own computing operations. Now, however, those operations are subcontracted to IBM, which handles all of Kodak's computing. The result is higher-quality computing systems and operations at Kodak for less money than it was spending before. Firms must be careful in their

Bill Bachmann/PhotoEdit

Benchmarking is the process of learning how other firms do things in an exceptionally high-quality manner. This engineer, for example, is examining a new copy machine recently introduced by a competitor. While much of the technology within products like copiers may be protected by patents, engineers can still find useful examples that can be used to improve their own products or services.

outsourcing decisions, though, because service or delivery problems can lead to major complications. Boeing's new 787 aircraft, for example, has been running several months behind schedule because the firms to which Boeing has outsourced some of its production have been running late.[34]

Reducing Cycle Time Another popular TQM technique is reducing cycle time. Cycle time is the time needed by the organization to develop, make, and distribute products or services.[36] If a business can reduce its cycle time, quality will often improve. A good illustration of the power of cycle time reduction comes from General Electric. At one point the firm needed six plants and three weeks to produce and deliver custom-made industrial circuit breaker boxes. By analyzing and reducing cycle time, the same product can now be delivered in three days, and only a single plant is involved. Table 12.3 identifies a number of basic suggestions that have helped companies reduce the cycle time of their operations. For example, GE found it better to start from scratch with a remodeled plant. GE also wiped out the need for approvals by eliminating most managerial positions and setting up teams as a basis for organizing work. Stressing the importance of the schedule helped Motorola build a new plant and start production of a new product in only 18 months. Nokia used to need 12 to 18 months to design new cell phone models, but can do it now in six months.[37] And Ford is aggressively working on techniques that can shorten the development cycle time for new models.[38]

> "Boeing has never outsourced to this kind of level. They have big technical challenges."
>
> —RICHARD ABOULAFIA, AVIATION INDUSTRY CONSULTANT[35]

ISO 9000:2000 and ISO 14000 Still another useful technique for improving quality is ISO 9000. ISO 9000:2000 refers to a set of quality standards created by the International Organization for Standardization; the standards were revised and updated in 2000.

These standards cover such areas as product testing, employee training, record keeping, supplier relations, and repair policies and procedures. Firms that want to meet these standards apply for certification and are audited by a firm chosen by the organization's domestic affiliate (in the United States, this is the American National Standards Institute). These auditors review every aspect of the firm's business operations in relation to the standards. Many firms report that merely preparing for an ISO 9000 audit has been helpful. Many firms today, including General Electric, DuPont, Eastman Kodak, British Telecom, and Philips Electronics, are urging—or in some cases requiring—that

TABLE 12.3 GUIDELINES FOR INCREASING THE SPEED OF OPERATIONS

Many organizations today are using speed for competitive advantage. Listed in the table are six common guidelines that organizations follow when they want to shorten the time they need to get things accomplished. Although not every manager can do each of these things, most managers can do at least some of them.

1. *Start from scratch.* It is usually easier than trying to do what the organization does now faster.
2. *Minimize the number of approvals needed to do something.* The fewer people who have to approve something, the faster approval will get done.
3. *Use work teams as a basis for organization.* Teamwork and cooperation work better than individual effort and conflict.
4. *Develop and adhere to a schedule.* A properly designed schedule can greatly increase speed.
5. *Do not ignore distribution.* Making something faster is only part of the battle.
6. *Integrate speed into the organization's culture.* If everyone understands the importance of speed, things will naturally get done more quickly.

Source: From *Fortune*, February 13, 1989. Copyright © 1989 Time, Inc. All rights reserved.

cycle time
The time needed by the organization to accomplish activities such as developing, making, and distributing products or services

ISO 9000:2000
A set of quality standards created by the International Organization for Standardization and revised in 2000

their suppliers achieve ISO 9000 certification.[39] All told, more than 159 countries have adopted ISO 9000 as a national standard, and more than 610,000 certificates of compliance have been issued. ISO 14000 is an extension of the same concept to environmental performance. Specifically, ISO 14000 requires that firms document how they are using raw materials more efficiently, managing pollution, and reducing their impact on the environment.

Statistical Quality Control   Another quality control technique is statistical quality control (SQC). As the term suggests, SQC is concerned primarily with managing quality.[40] Moreover, it is a set of specific statistical techniques that can be used to monitor quality. *Acceptance sampling* involves sampling finished goods to ensure that quality standards have been met. Acceptance sampling is effective only when the correct percentage of products that should be tested (for example, 2, 5, or 25 percent) is determined. This decision is especially important when the test renders the product useless. Batteries, wine, and collapsible steering wheels, for example, are consumed or destroyed during testing. Another SQC method is *in-process sampling*. In-process sampling involves evaluating products during production so that needed changes can be made. The painting department of a furniture company might periodically check the tint of the paint it is using. The company can then adjust the color as necessary to conform to customer standards. The advantage of in-process sampling is that it allows problems to be detected before they accumulate.

ISO 14000
A set of standards for environmental performance

statistical quality control (SQC)
A set of specific statistical techniques that can be used to monitor quality; includes acceptance sampling and in-process sampling

Six Sigma   Six Sigma was developed in the 1980s for Motorola. The tool can be used by manufacturing or service organizations. The Six Sigma method tries to eliminate mistakes. Although firms rarely obtain Six Sigma quality, it does provide a challenging target. *Sigma* refers to a standard deviation, so a Six Sigma defect rate is six standard deviations above the mean rate; 1 sigma quality would produce 690,000 errors per million items. Three sigmas is challenging—66,000 errors per million. Six Sigma is obtained when a firm produces a mere 3.4 mistakes per million. Implementing Six Sigma requires making corrections until errors virtually disappear. At GE, the technique has saved the firm $8 billion in three years. GE is now teaching its customers, including Walmart and Dell, about the approach.

What are the basic components of total quality management, and what are the common tools used to manage quality?

Identify and describe three product families that illustrate the concept of absolute versus relative quality.

CONCEPT CHECK

Managing Productivity

Although the current focus on quality by U.S. companies is a relatively recent phenomenon, managers have been aware of the importance of productivity for several years. The stimulus for this attention was a recognition that the gap between productivity in the United States and that in other industrialized countries was narrowing. This section describes the meaning of productivity and underscores its importance. After summarizing recent productivity trends, we suggest ways that organizations can increase their productivity.

The Meaning of Productivity

In a general sense, productivity is an economic measure of efficiency that summarizes the value of outputs relative to the value of the inputs used to create them.[41] Productivity can be and often is assessed at different levels of analysis and in different forms.

Levels of Productivity By level of productivity we mean the units of analysis used to calculate or define productivity. For example, *aggregate productivity* is the total level of productivity achieved by a country. *Industry productivity* is the total productivity achieved by all the firms in a particular industry. *Company productivity*, just as the term suggests, is the level of productivity achieved by an individual company. *Unit* and *individual productivity* refer to the productivity achieved by a unit or department within an organization and the level of productivity attained by a single person.

Forms of Productivity There are many different forms of productivity. *Total factor productivity* is defined by the following formula:

$$\text{Productivity} = \frac{\text{Outputs}}{\text{Inputs}}$$

Total factor productivity is an overall indicator of how well an organization uses all of its resources, such as labor, capital, materials, and energy, to create all of its products and services. The biggest problem with total factor productivity is that all the ingredients must be expressed in the same terms—dollars (it is difficult to add hours of labor to number of units of a raw material in a meaningful way). Total factor productivity also gives little insight into how things can be changed to improve productivity. Consequently, most organizations find it more useful to calculate a partial productivity ratio. Such a ratio uses only one category of resource. For example, labor productivity could be calculated by this simple formula:

$$\text{Labour Productivity} = \frac{\text{Outputs}}{\text{Direct Labor}}$$

This method has two advantages. First, it is not necessary to transform the units of input into some other unit. Second, this method provides managers with specific insights into how changing different resource inputs affects productivity. Suppose that an organization can manufacture 100 units of a particular product with 20 hours of direct labor. The organization's labor productivity index is 100/20, or 5 (5 units per labor hour). Now suppose that worker efficiency is increased (through one of the ways to be discussed later in this chapter) so that the same 20 hours of labor results in the manufacture of 120 units of the product. The labor productivity index increases to 120/20, or 6 (6 units per labor hour), and the firm can see the direct results of a specific managerial action.

The Importance of Productivity

Managers consider it important that their firm maintain high levels of productivity for a variety of reasons. Firm productivity is a primary determinant of an organization's level of profitability and, ultimately, of its ability to survive. If one organization is more productive than another, it will have more products to sell at lower prices and have more profits to reinvest in other areas. Productivity also partially determines people's standard of living within a particular country. At an economic level, businesses consume resources and produce goods and services. The goods and services created within a country can be used by that country's own citizens or exported for sale in other countries. The more goods and services the businesses within a country can produce, the more goods and services the country's citizens will have. Even goods that are exported result in financial resources flowing back into the home country. Thus the citizens of a highly productive country are likely to have a notably higher standard of living than are the citizens of a country with low productivity.

productivity
An economic measure of efficiency that summarizes what is produced relative to resources used to produce it

Productivity Trends

The United States has one of the highest levels of productivity in the world. Sparked by gains made in other countries, however, U.S. business has begun to focus more attention on productivity.[42] Indeed, this was a primary factor in the decisions made by U.S. businesses to retrench, retool, and become more competitive in the world marketplace. For example, General Electric's dishwasher plant in Louisville cut its inventory requirements by 50 percent, reduced labor costs from 15 percent to only 10 percent of total manufacturing costs, and cut product development time in half. As a result of these kinds of efforts, productivity trends have now leveled out, and U.S. workers are generally maintaining their lead in most industries.[43]

One important factor that has hurt U.S. productivity indices has been the tremendous growth of the service sector in the United States. Although this sector grew, its productivity levels did not. One part of this problem relates to measurement. For example, it is fairly easy to calculate the number of tons of steel produced at a steel mill and divide it by the number of labor hours used; it is more difficult to determine the output of an attorney or a certified public accountant. Still, virtually everyone agrees that improving service-sector productivity is the next major hurdle facing U.S. business.[44]

Figure 12.4 illustrates manufacturing productivity growth from 1970 through 2010 in terms of annual average percentage of increase. As you can see, that growth slowed during the 1970s but began to rise again in the late 1980s. Some experts believe that productivity in both the United States and abroad will continue to improve at even more impressive rates. Their confidence rests on technology's potential ability to improve operations.

Improving Productivity

How does a business or industry improve its productivity? Numerous specific suggestions made by experts generally fall into two broad categories: improving operations and increasing employee involvement.

FIGURE 12.4

MANUFACTURING AND SERVICE PRODUCTIVITY GROWTH TRENDS

Both manufacturing productivity and service productivity in the United States continue to grow, although manufacturing productivity is growing at a faster pace. Total productivity, therefore, also continues to grow.

Source: U.S. Bureau of Labor Statistics.

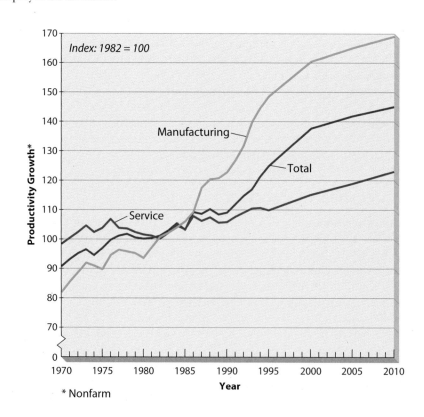

Improving Operations One way that firms can improve operations is by spending more on research and development. Research and development (R&D) spending helps identify new products, new uses for existing products, and new methods for making products. Each of these contributes to productivity. For example, Bausch & Lomb almost missed the boat on extended-wear contact lenses because the company had neglected R&D. When it became apparent that its major competitors were almost a year ahead of Bausch & Lomb in developing the new lenses, management made R&D a top-priority concern. As a result, the company made several scientific breakthroughs, shortened the time needed to introduce new products, and greatly enhanced both total sales and profits—and all with a smaller workforce than the company used to employ. Even though other countries are greatly increasing their R&D spending, the United States continues to be the world leader in this area.

Another way firms can boost productivity through operations is by reassessing and revamping their transformation facilities. We noted earlier how one of GE's modernized plants does a better job than six antiquated ones. Just building a new factory is no guarantee of success, but IBM, Ford, Caterpillar, and many other businesses have achieved dramatic productivity gains by revamping their production facilities. Facilities refinements are not limited to manufacturers. Most McDonald's restaurants now have drive-through windows, and many have moved soft-drink dispensers out to the restaurant floor so that customers can get their own drinks. Each of these moves is an attempt to increase the speed with which customers can be served, and thus to increase productivity.

Increasing Employee Involvement The other major thrust in productivity enhancement has been toward employee involvement. We noted earlier that participation can enhance quality. So, too, can it boost productivity. Examples of this involvement are an individual worker's being given a bigger voice in how she does her job, a formal agreement of cooperation between management and labor, and total involvement throughout the organization. GE eliminated most of the supervisors at its one new circuit breaker plant and put control in the hands of workers.

Another method popular in the United States is increasing the flexibility of an organization's workforce by training employees to perform a number of different jobs. Such cross-training allows the firm to function with fewer workers because workers can be transferred easily to areas where they are most needed. For example, at one Motorola plant, 397 of 400 employees have learned at least two skills under a similar program.

Rewards are essential to making employee involvement work. Firms must reward people for learning new skills and using them proficiently. At Motorola, for example, workers who master a new skill are assigned for five days to a job requiring them to use that skill. If they perform with no defects, they are moved to a higher pay grade, and then they move back and forth between jobs as they are needed. If there is a performance problem, they receive more training and practice. This approach is fairly new, but preliminary indicators suggest that it can increase productivity significantly. Many unions resist such programs because they threaten job security and reduce a person's identification with one skill or craft.

Define productivity and identify the different levels at which it can be assessed.

Will improving productivity always be worth the time and money that might be required? Why or why not?

CONCEPT CHECK

Summary of Learning Objectives and Key Points

1. Describe and explain the nature of operations management.

   - Operations management is the set of managerial activities that organizations use in creating their products and services.
   - Operations management is important to both manufacturing and service organizations.
   - It plays an important role in an organization's strategy.

2. Identify and discuss the components involved in designing effective operations systems.

   - The starting point in using operations management is designing appropriate operations systems.
   - Key decisions that must be made as part of operations systems design relate to product and service mix, capacity, and facilities.

3. Discuss organizational technologies and their role in operations management.

   - Technology also plays an important role in quality.
   - Automation is especially important today.
   - Numerous computer-aided manufacturing techniques are widely practiced.
   - Robotics is also a growing area.
   - Technology is as relevant to service organizations as to manufacturing organizations.

4. Identify and discuss the components involved in implementing operations systems through supply chain management.

   - After an operations system has been designed and put in place, it must then be implemented.

   - Major areas of interest during the use of operations systems are purchasing and inventory management.
   - Supply chain management is a comprehensive view of managing all of these activities in a more efficient manner.

5. Explain the meaning and importance of managing quality and total quality management.

   - Quality is a major consideration for all managers today.
   - Quality is important because it affects competition, productivity, and costs.
   - Total quality management is a comprehensive, organization-wide effort to enhance quality through a variety of avenues.

6. Explain the meaning and importance of managing productivity, productivity trends, and ways to improve productivity.

   - Productivity is also a major concern to managers.
   - Productivity is a measure of how efficiently an organization is using its resources to create products or services.
   - The United States is a world leader in individual productivity, but firms still work to achieve productivity gains.

Discussion Questions

Questions for Review

1. What is the relationship of operations management to overall organizational strategy? Where do productivity and quality fit into that relationship?
2. Describe three basic decisions that must be addressed in the design of operations systems. For each decision, what information do managers need to make that decision?

3. What are some approaches to facilities layout? How do they differ from one another? How are they similar?
4. What is total quality management? What are the major characteristics of TQM?

Questions for Analysis

5. Is operations management linked most closely to corporate-level, business-level, or functional strategies? Why or in what way?

6. "Automation is bad for the economy because machines will eventually replace almost all human workers, creating high unemployment and poverty." Do you agree or disagree? Explain your answer.

7. Some quality gurus claim that high-quality products or services are those that are error free. Others claim that high quality exists when customers' needs are satisfied. Still others claim that high-quality products or services must be innovative. Do you subscribe to one of these views? If not, how would you define quality? Explain how the choice of a definition of quality affects managers' behavior.

Questions for Application

8. How can a service organization use techniques from operations management? Give specific examples from your college or university (a provider of educational services).

9. Think of a firm that, in your opinion, provides a high-quality service or product. What attributes of the product or service give you the perception of high quality? Do you think that everyone would agree with your judgment? Why or why not?

10. What advice would you give to the manager of a small local service business, such as a pizza parlor or dry cleaner, about improvements in quality and productivity? Would your advice differ if the small business were a manufacturing company—for example, a T-shirt printing firm? Describe any differences you would expect to see.

CengageNow™ Highlights

Now use your CengageNow™ homework to help you:
- Apply management theories in your life
- Assess your management skills
- Master management terms and concepts
- Apply your knowledge to real-world situations
- Analyze and solve challenging management problems

In order to take advantage of these elements, your instructor will need to have set up a course for your class within CengageNow™. Ask your instructor to contact his/her Cengage sales representative and Digital Solutions Manager to explore testing CengageNow™ in your course this term.

Managing Information and Information Technology

LEARNING OBJECTIVES

After studying this chapter, you should be able to:

1. Describe the role and importance of information in the manager's job and identify the basic building blocks of information technology.

2. Discuss the basic factors that determine an organization's information technology needs and describe the basic types of information systems used by organizations.

3. Discuss how information systems can be managed.

4. Describe how information systems affect organizations.

MANAGEMENT IN ACTION   You Can't Make This Stuff Up

Let's say that there was a time when, like about 15 percent of all Americans, your connectivity needs required you to be on your cell phone for more than 1,000 minutes per month, or just over 30 minutes a day. Like just about everybody else in the same segment of the population, you were happy to report that both your business affairs and your personal life had improved significantly.

Then you ran across an article in a British Internet magazine called *Wymsey Village*. Entitled "Weekend Eating: Mobile Cooking," it showed you how to cook an egg using two cell phones. At first, you marveled at what they had in fact thought of next, but not long afterward, someone e-mailed you a copy of an article in which, complete with photographs, two Russian journalists explained how they'd replicated the process by propping a hard-boiled egg between two activated cell phones

> "You can't make this stuff up. Well, I guess you could."
>
> —BARBARA MIKKELSON, CO-FOUNDER OF SNOPES.COM

for an hour. This time, however, the article ended on an ominous note: "If the microwave radiation emitted by the mobile phones is capable of modifying the proteins in an egg, imagine what it can do to the proteins in our brains." At that point, you ditched your cell phone and had your landline reinstalled (although you routinely use the speakerphone and stay as far away as possible from the unit itself). Last but not least, you did your civic duty by e-mailing both articles to everybody you know.

Perhaps you should have Snopsed the information that you were relying on when you trashed your cell phone and

Snopes.com is a useful website people can use to check the likely truthfulness of popular stories that may sound too far-fetched to be believed.

urged everybody you know to do the same. Had you queried the fact checkers at Snopes.com—and a lot of people did—you would have found that the *Wymsey Village* article was a spoof and the article from the Russian tabloid a hoax. "The stories that arise the most," says Snopes co-founder David Mikkelson, "are those that pose a threat to readers. . . . The things that take off have to hit a nerve we're all thinking about." It's not that hard to debunk them, Mikkelson adds, if you "start off with the thought that extraordinary claims require extraordinary proof." But even so, he admits, "Most rumors never die completely." The *Wymsey Village* "article," for example, is still out there, and his only regret, says the unmasked author, "is that I didn't get a dime for every hit on that page."

Snopes.com started out in 1995 as a hobby for David Mikkelson and his wife Barbara, who share a passion for urban legends. The site, which they operate from their California home, now attracts 6.6 million visitors a month. "We quickly became the place where people mailed anything that was questionable," explains David. "If they needed verification, they'd ask us." A tech columnist for the *New York Times* has called Snopes "the Internet's authority on emailed myths," and Richard Roeper, a film critic and amateur myth-buster, declares that "Snopes is like having your own army of fact-checkers sniffing out a million wacko leads."

"Most of what we deal with," says David Mikkelson, "exists outside traditional media," but he's quick to point out that traditional media sources could perform much the same service as Snopes. "Our approach," he explains, "is going to be that something outrageous is going to be a hoax. But that's unfortunately not what a lot of people in the media do. They say, 'This is real, and we'll see if there's proof it isn't.'" Take, for instance, the famous "Hunting for Bambi" case, in which a Las Vegas TV station did a four-part story on a local outfit offering hunters the chance to shoot paintballs at naked women for a fee of $10,000. "In this case," reports Mikkelson,

we [said] is there anything that demonstrates it's real. The first thing you notice is that it's rather improbable that naked women wearing no protection whatsoever, not even helmets or goggles, will run around in front of guys with unmodified paintball guns with nothing more than a vague promise they won't shoot above the waist.

"You can't make this stuff up," adds Barbara Mikkelson, who pauses before adding, "Well, I guess you could. But if you do, I'm sure we'll get to the bottom of it."

The advent of the Internet, of course, is a key factor in the growth of the hoax and misinformation business, but the Internet, says David, "has made it easier to debunk hoaxes while at the same time making it easier to perpetrate them. . . . Really widespread Internet-based hoaxes," he adds, "are fairly uncommon. Most of them are just, 'I'm going to put up this gag and see if anyone falls for it.' Having someone go through the time and effort to do a really thought-out hoax is pretty rare, maybe happening once or twice a year." Mikkelson admits that "there's a lot on the Internet that you can't trust," but he's also well aware that "there's a lot on your bookshelf and the library shelves that you can't trust either. . . . There's never been a medium that you could inherently trust. You still have to look at who's telling you this. . . . The concept hasn't changed. . . . Nothing's really changed but the technology."

Fortunately, the Mikkelsons aren't alone in the online fact-checking business. In October 2008, an e-mail began circulating under the head "PLEASE READ!!!!!!! VERY IMPORTANT-----SNOPES EXPOSED." The anonymous e-mailer proceeded to reveal that, during the presidential election, Snopes was "owned by a flaming liberal . . . in the tank for Obama" and warned everyone receiving his urgent news that "you cannot and should not trust Snopes.com . . . for anything that remotely resembles the truth." In the spring of 2009, FactCheck.org, which describes itself as "a nonpartisan, nonprofit 'consumer advocate' for voters that aims to reduce the level of deception and confusion in U.S. politics," set out to investigate the allegations against Snopes. Researchers confirmed that Barbara Mikkelson is a nonvoting Canadian citizen and discovered that David Mikkelson, though now an independent, had last registered his party affiliation as Republican. The anti-Snopes e-mail, concluded the FactCheck report, "contains a number of false claims about the urban-legend-busting Snopes.com and its proprietors," and as for political bias, "we reviewed a sampling of their political offerings, including rumors about George W. Bush, Sarah Palin, and Barack Obama, and we found them to be utterly poker-faced."

It would appear, then, that it is indeed safe to do your fact checking at Snopes.com, where you'll continue to find thorough reviews of widely circulating information—and misinformation—of all kinds. For the record, the bad (but true) news is that Bill Gates is not giving away cash to anyone who forwards a certain e-mail message. The good (and true) news is that terrorists are not paying exorbitant prices on eBay for UPS uniforms to be used in some as-yet-unfathomed plot.[1]

As we explain later in the chapter, all "information" is not created equal: Some of it's useful and some of it not so much. At Snopes.com, the Mikkelsons are dedicated to separating useful information from the stuff that merely appears to be useful because it's presented in places where we expect to find useful information, such as the Internet. Businesses need information, but they need it to be accurate, and they need it to be accessible in a timely fashion. Thus in order to make effective use of its information, every major firm plugs all of its activities—such as designing services, ensuring product delivery and cash flow, evaluating employees, and creating advertising—into an information system. Effective information management, therefore, requires a commitment of resources to establish, maintain, and upgrade as new technologies emerge.

This chapter is about advances made by organizations doing this. We describe the role and importance of information to managers, the characteristics of useful information, and information management as control, and we identify the basic building blocks of information systems. We discuss the general and specific determinants of information technology needs. We then discuss the primary types of information technology used in organizations and describe how this technology is managed.

Information and the Manager

Information has always been an integral part of every manager's job. Its importance, however, and therefore the need to manage it, continue to grow at a rapid clip. To appreciate this trend, we need to understand the role of information in the manager's job, characteristics of useful information, and the nature of information management as control.[2]

The Role of Information in the Manager's Job

In Chapters 1 and 21 we highlight the role of communication in the manager's job. Given that information is a vital part of communication, it follows that management and information are closely related. Indeed, it is possible to conceptualize management itself as a series of steps involving the reception, processing, and dissemination of information. As illustrated in Figure 13.1, the manager is constantly bombarded with data and information (the difference between the two is noted later).

FIGURE 13.1

MANAGERS AS
INFORMATION
PROCESSORS

Managers who receive information and data must decide what to do with it. Some is stored for possible later use, and other information is combined to form new information. Subsequently, some is used immediately, some is passed on to others, and some is discarded.

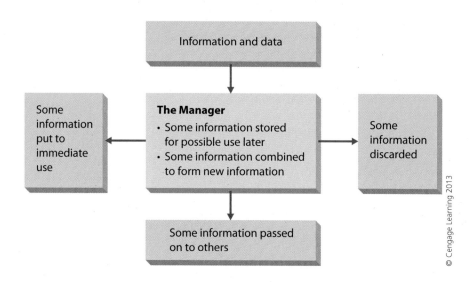

Suppose that Bob Henderson is an operations manager for a large manufacturing firm. During the course of a normal day, Bob receives many different pieces of information from formal and informal conversations and meetings, telephone calls, personal observation, e-mails, text messages, letters, reports, memos, the Internet, and trade publications. He gets a report from a subordinate that explains exactly how to solve a pressing problem, so he calls the subordinate and tells him to put the solution into effect immediately. He scans a copy of a report prepared for another manager, sees that it has no relevance to him, and discards it. He sees a *Wall Street Journal* article that he knows Sara Ferris in marketing should see, so he passes it on to her. He gets an electronic summary of yesterday's production report, but because he knows he will not need to analyze it for another week, he stores it. He observes a worker doing a job incorrectly and realizes that the incorrect method is associated with a mysterious quality problem that someone told him about last week.

A key part of information-processing activity is differentiating between data and information. Data are raw figures and facts reflecting a single aspect of reality. The independent facts that a plant has 35 machines, that each machine is capable of producing 1,000 units of output per day, that current and projected future demand for the units is 30,000 per day, and that workers sufficiently skilled to run the machines make $20 an hour are data.

Information is data presented in a way or form that has meaning.[3] Thus, combining and summarizing the four pieces of data given above provides information: The plant has excess capacity and is therefore incurring unnecessary costs. Information has meaning to a manager and provides a basis for action. The plant manager might use the information and decide to sell four machines (perhaps keeping one as a backup) and transfer five operators to other jobs.

A related term is information technology, or IT. Information technology refers to the resources used by an organization to manage information that it needs to carry out its mission. IT may consist of computers, integrated computer networks, telephones (wired and wireless), fax machines, and other pieces of hardware. In addition, IT involves software that facilitates the system's ability to manage information in a way that is useful for managers.[4]

The grocery industry uses data, information, and information technology to automate inventory and checkout facilities. The average Kroger store, for example, carries over 40,000 items. Computerized scanners at the checkout counters can provide daily sales figures for any product. These numbers alone are data and have little meaning in their pure form. But information is created from these data by other systems. Using these IT systems, managers can identify how any given product or product line is selling in any number of stores over any meaningful period of time.

Michael Dwyer/Alamy

Scanning technologies are widely used as part of the information management systems in grocery stores. Stockers use scanning devices to track inventory and checkers use them to calculate customer charges. Many stores also offer self-check lanes where customers can scan their own purchases and pay for them without interacting with a checker or other sales associate. This technology provides a wealth of information for the organization while also allowing it to function with fewer employees.

data
Raw figures and facts reflecting a single aspect of reality

information
Data presented in a way or form that has meaning

information technology (IT)
Refers to the resources used by an organization to manage information that it needs in order to carry out its mission

Characteristics of Useful Information

What factors differentiate between information that is useful and information that is not? In general, information is useful if it is accurate, timely, complete, and relevant. Indeed, part of the reason for the current lack of confidence in business is that stakeholders have long assumed that the accounting information that businesses provided was "true." But myriad scandals and controversies have shown that accounting procedures and reporting formats can vary to make things look much better than they actually are.[5]

Accurate For information to be of real value to a manager, it must be **accurate information**. Accuracy means that the information must provide a valid and reliable reflection of reality. Volkswagen's plans to fully merge with Porsche were brought to a halt after Porsche executives allegedly provided false or incomplete information to the banks involved in the merger's financing. The investigation is not set to end until 2012 at the earliest, reducing the chances of a Volkswagen takeover.[6]

Timely Information also needs to be timely. Timeliness does not necessarily mean speediness; it means only that information needs to be available in time for appropriate managerial action. What constitutes timeliness is a function of the situation facing the manager. When Marriott was gathering information for a new hotel project, managers allowed themselves a six-month period for data collection. They felt this would give them an opportunity to do a good job of getting the information they needed while not delaying things too much. In contrast, Marriott's reservation and accounting systems can provide a manager today with last night's occupancy level at any Marriott facility. In 2002, United Airlines filed for bankruptcy protection while it restructured its finances; the firm then emerged from bankruptcy and has been financially healthy ever since. But an error led a South Florida newspaper to recently post an old story about the 2002 filing on its website in a way that made it appear as a current event. The resulting panic among investors caused United's shares to drop from $12.50 a share to less than $3 a share before the error was caught and corrected.[7]

Complete Information must tell a complete story for it to be useful to a manager. If it is less than **complete information**, the manager is likely to get an inaccurate or distorted picture of reality. For example, managers at Kroger used to think that house-brand products were more profitable than national brands because they yielded higher unit profits. On the basis of this information, they gave house brands a great deal of shelf space and centered promotional activities around them. As Kroger's managers became more sophisticated in understanding their information, however, they realized that national brands were actually more profitable over time because they sold many more units than house brands during any given period of time. Hence, although a store might sell 10 cans of Kroger coffee in a day, with a profit of 50 cents per can (total profit of $5), it would also sell 15 cans of Maxwell House with a profit of 40 cents per can (total profit of $6) and 10 vacuum bags of Starbucks coffee with a profit of $1 per bag (total profit of $10). With this more complete picture, managers could do a better job of selecting the right mix of Kroger, Maxwell House, and Starbucks coffee to display and promote.

Relevant Finally, information must be relevant if it is to be useful to managers. **Relevant information**, like timely information, is defined according to the needs and circumstances of a particular manager. Operations managers need information on costs and productivity; human resource managers need information on hiring needs and turnover rates; and marketing managers need information on sales projections and advertising rates. As Walmart contemplates countries as possible expansion opportunities, it gathers information about local regulations, customs, and so forth. But the information about any given country is not as relevant before a decision is made to enter that market as it is after the firm has made a decision to enter the market.

Information Management as Control

The manager also needs to appreciate the role of information in control—indeed, to see information management as a vital part of the control process in the organization.[8] As already noted, managers receive much more data and information than they need or can use. Accordingly, deciding how to handle each piece of data and information involves a form of control.[9]

The control perspective on information management is illustrated in Figure 13.2. Information enters, is used by, and leaves the organization. For example, Marriott took great pains

accurate information
Provides a valid and reliable reflection of reality

complete information
Provides the manager with all the information he or she needs

relevant information
Information that is useful to managers in their particular circumstances for their particular needs

timely information
Available in time for appropriate managerial action

FIGURE 13.2 INFORMATION MANAGEMENT AS CONTROL

Information management can be part of the control system via preliminary, screening, and postaction control mechanisms. Because information from the environment is just as much a resource as raw materials or finances, it must be monitored and managed to promote its efficient and effective utilization.

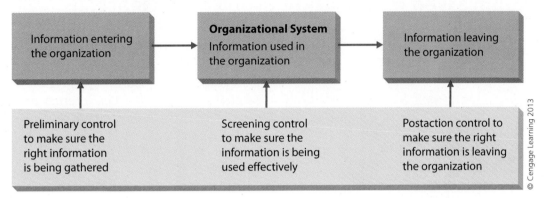

to make sure it got all the information it needed to plan for and enter the economy lodging business. Once this preliminary information was gathered, it was necessary to make sure that the information was made available in the proper form to everyone who needed it. In general, the effort to ensure that information is accurate, timely, complete, and relevant is a form of screening control. Finally, Marriott wanted to make sure that its competitors did not learn about its plans until the last possible minute. It also wanted to time and orchestrate news releases, public announcements, and advertising for maximum benefit. These efforts thus served a postaction control function.

> "Employees should go to work assuming that Big Brother is going to read over their electronic shoulder when they're sitting at the computer."
>
> —NANCY FLYNN, EXECUTIVE DIRECTOR OF EPOLICY INSTITUTE[10]

What use is information to people who are supposed to exercise control functions when it's not passed on to them? For one example, see the *Ethically Speaking* box entitled "Can Suppressed Information Break Your Heart?" on page 320.

Building Blocks of Information Technology

Information technology is generally of two types—manual or electronic. All information technology, and the systems that it defines, has five basic parts. Figure 13.3 diagrams these parts for a computer-based (electronic) information technology system. The *input medium* is the device that is used to add data and information into the system. For example, the optical scanner at Kroger enters point-of-sale information. Likewise, someone can enter data through a keyboard, with a mouse, using a barcode reader, or by transfer from other computers or the Internet.

The data that are entered into the system typically flow first to a processor. The *processor* is the part of the system that is capable of organizing, manipulating, sorting, or performing calculations or other transformations with the data. Most systems also have one or more *storage devices*—places where data can be stored for later use. Hard drives, thumb drives, CDs, DVDs, and optical disks are common forms of storage devices. As data are transformed into usable information, the resultant information must be communicated to the appropriate person by means of an *output medium*. Common ways to display output are through video displays, printers, and fax machines, as well as through transmission to other computers, web pages, or some cell phones.

Finally, the entire information technology system is operated by a *control system*—most often software of one sort or another. Simple systems in smaller organizations can use

ETHICALLY SPEAKING

Can Suppressed Information Break Your Heart?

As we saw in our *Management in Action* story in Chapter 7, AIG is the giant insurance company that suffered huge losses in the so-called "subprime" or global credit crisis and which has since received $173 billion in bailout funds from the U.S. government. Here's another chapter in the story.

In June 2006, AIG hired Joseph St. Denis, a onetime top Securities and Exchange Commission accountant, as Vice President of Accounting Policy and assigned him to oversee transactions conducted by the London office of AIG Financial Products (AIGFP). St. Denis resigned rather abruptly in October of 2007, and a year later a congressional committee investigating charges that AIG officials may have misled investors about the liability incurred from certain risky insurance contracts, wanted to know why. In a letter to the committee, St. Denis said that AIGFP head Joseph Cassano (a major character in our previous chapter) had repeatedly thwarted his efforts to do his job, mainly by blocking his access to information about the unit's finances. He'd managed to uncover some irregularities in the accounting for the risky contracts in September 2007, but later that same month, he reported, Cassano began excluding him from meetings dealing with the valuation of such contracts. Why? "Because [in Cassano's words]

'I was concerned that you would pollute the process.' My belief," St. John told the committee, "is that the 'pollution' Mr. Cassano was concerned about was the transparency I brought to the . . . process. . . . I resigned because . . . Mr. Cassano took actions that I believed were intended to prevent me from performing the job duties for which I was hired."

Apparently, the process, if not exactly "polluted," was quite faulty. In November 2007, five weeks after St. Denis' departure, AIG announced that the contracts in question had declined in value by $352 million. In February 2008, it revised the total to $11.1 billion in losses.

Shortly after he resigned, St. Denis had explained his action to AIG's chief auditor, Michael Roemer, and repeated Cassano's comment about "polluting the process." Roemer promised to report St. Denis' concerns to the company's audit committee. The congressional committee found no record of St. Denis' resignation in the notes of any board meeting, but the committee chairman, Henry Waxman of California, was convinced that the matter had in fact been brought to the board's attention. If so, he concluded, former AIG CEOs Martin Sullivan and Robert Willumstad were being less than forthright in claiming that the company's losses had been brought about by market forces entirely beyond its control. Referring to St. Denis' report, Waxman told Sullivan and Willumstad, "It looks like you both brushed it aside. He could have given you information [about activities] that later brought AIG to its knees."

"I am heartbroken over what has happened," said Sullivan, but Willumstad was apparently unconvinced: "I don't believe AIG could have done anything differently," he said.

As for St. Denis, "I never received my contractually agreed bonus," he told the committee.

References: Joseph W. St. Denis, letter to House of Representatives Committee on Oversight and Government Reform, October 4, 2008, http://oversight-archive.waxman.house.gov on July 11, 2011; Andrew G. Simpson, "Greenberg: AIG's Risky Subprime Activity 'Exploded' After He Left," *Insurance Journal*, October 10, 2008, www.insurancejournal.com on July 11, 2011; Liam Pleven and Amir Efrati, "Documents Show AIG Knew of Problems with Valuations," *Wall Street Journal*, October 11, 2008, www.freerepublic.com on July 11, 2011; Neil Roland, "AIG's Auditor Scandal," *Financial Week*, October 12, 2008, www.democraticunderground.com on July 11, 2011.

FIGURE 13.3 BUILDING BLOCKS OF A COMPUTER-BASED INFORMATION SYSTEM

Computer-based information systems generally have five basic components—an input medium, a processor, an output medium, a storage device, and a control system. Non–computer-based systems use parallel components for the same basic purposes.

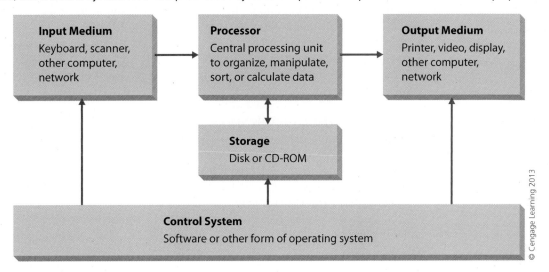

Input Medium
Keyboard, scanner, other computer, network

Processor
Central processing unit to organize, manipulate, sort, or calculate data

Output Medium
Printer, video, display, other computer, network

Storage
Disk or CD-ROM

Control System
Software or other form of operating system

© Cengage Learning 2013

off-the-shelf software. Microsoft Windows and Linux are general operating systems that control more specialized types of software. Microsoft Word and WordPerfect are popular systems for word processing. Lotus 123 and Excel are popular spreadsheet programs, and dBase and Access are frequently used for database management. Of course, elaborate systems of the type used by large businesses require a special, customized operating system. When organizations start to link computers together in a network, the operating system must be even more complex. Enterprise resource planning networks are also increasingly being used for this purpose.

As we noted earlier, information technology systems need not be computerized. Many small organizations still function quite well with a manual system using paper documents, routing slips, paper clips, file folders, file cabinets, and a single personal computer. Increasingly, however, even small businesses are abandoning their manual systems for computerized ones. As hardware prices continue to drop and software becomes more and more powerful, computerized information systems will likely be within the reach of all businesses that want to have them.

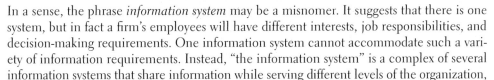

What are the characteristics of useful information?

Identify examples of both data and information that you have seen or heard in the last 24 hours.

CONCEPT CHECK

Types of Information Systems

In a sense, the phrase *information system* may be a misnomer. It suggests that there is one system, but in fact a firm's employees will have different interests, job responsibilities, and decision-making requirements. One information system cannot accommodate such a variety of information requirements. Instead, "the information system" is a complex of several information systems that share information while serving different levels of the organization, different departments, or different operations.

User Groups and System Requirements

To understand the different kinds of information systems that organizations use, it is instructive to first consider user groups and system requirements. This perspective is illustrated in Figure 13.4. In general, there are four user groups, each with different system requirements: first-line, middle, and top managers, and knowledge workers. Knowledge workers represent a special user category. Knowledge workers are specialists, usually professionally trained and certified—engineers, scientists, information technology specialists, psychologists—who rely on information technology to design new products or create new business processes.

Managers at Different Levels Because they work on different kinds of problems, first-line, middle, and top managers, as well as knowledge workers, have different information needs. First-line (or operational) managers, for example, need information to oversee the day-to-day details of their department or projects. Middle managers need summaries and analyses for setting intermediate and long-range goals for the department or projects under their supervision. Top management analyzes broader trends in the economy, the business environment, and overall company performance to conduct long-range planning for the entire organization. Finally, knowledge workers need special information for conducting technical projects.

Consider the various information needs for a flooring manufacturer. Sales managers (first-line managers) supervise salespeople, assign territories to the sales force, and handle customer service and delivery problems. They need current information on the sales and delivery of products: lists of incoming customer orders and daily delivery schedules to customers in their territory. Regional managers (middle managers) set sales quotas for each sales manager, prepare budgets, and plan staffing needs for the upcoming year. They need information on monthly sales by product and region. Top managers need both external and internal information. Internally, they use sales data summarized by product, customer type, and geographic region, along with comparisons to previous years. Equally important

knowledge workers
Specialists, usually professionally trained and certified—engineers, scientists, information technology specialists, psychologists—who rely on information technology to design new products or create new business processes

FIGURE 13.4 DETERMINANTS OF AN ORGANIZATION'S INFORMATION-PROCESSING NEEDS

Information-processing needs are determined by user groups and system requirements, as well as by such specific managerial factors as area and level in the organization.

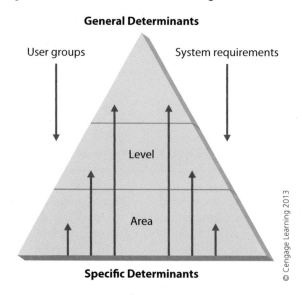

© Cengage Learning 2013

is external information on consumer behavior patterns, the competition's performance, and economic forecasts. Finally, knowledge workers developing new flooring materials need information on the chemical properties of adhesives and compression strengths for floor structures.

Functional Areas and Business Processes Each business function—marketing, human resources, accounting, operations, finance—has its own information requirements. In addition, many businesses are organized according to various business processes, and these process groups also need special information. Each of these user groups and departments, then, is represented by an information system. When organizations add to these systems the types of systems needed by the four levels of users discussed above, the total number of information systems and applications increases significantly. Top-level finance managers, for example, are concerned with long-range planning for capital expenditures for future facilities and equipment, as well as with determining sources of capital funds.

In contrast, a business process group will include users—both managers and employees—drawn from all organizational levels. The supply chain management group, for instance, may be in the process of trimming down the number of suppliers. The information system supporting this project would contain information ranging across different organizational functions and management levels. The group will need information and expert knowledge on marketing, warehousing and distribution, production, communications technology, purchasing, suppliers, and finance. It will also need different perspectives on operational, technical, and managerial issues: determining technical requirements for new suppliers, specifying task responsibilities for participating firms, and determining future financial requirements.

Major Systems by Level

In this section, we discuss different kinds of systems that provide applications at some organizational levels but not at others. For any routine, repetitive, highly structured decision, a specialized application will suffice. System requirements for knowledge workers, however, will probably vary because knowledge workers often face a variety of specialized problems. Applications of information systems for middle or top-level management decisions must also be flexible, though for different reasons. In particular, they will use a broader range of information collected from a variety of sources, both external and internal.

Transaction-Processing Systems Transaction-processing systems (TPS) are applications of information processing for basic day-to-day business transactions. Customer order-taking by online retailers, approval of claims at insurance companies, receipt and confirmation of reservations by airlines, payroll processing and bill payment at almost every company—all are routine business processes. Typically, the TPS for first-level (operational) activities is well defined, with predetermined data requirements, and follows the same steps to complete all transactions in the system.

Systems for Knowledge Workers and Office Applications Systems for knowledge workers and office applications support the activities of both knowledge workers and employees in clerical positions. They provide assistance for data processing and other office activities, including the creation of communications documents. Like other departments, the information systems department includes both knowledge workers and data workers.

Systems for Operations and Data Workers People who run the company's computer equipment are usually called *system operations workers*. They make sure that the right programs are run in the correct sequence and monitor equipment to ensure that it is operating properly. Many organizations also have employees who enter data into the system for processing.

transaction-processing system (TPS)
Application of information processing for basic day-to-day business transactions

Knowledge-Level and Office Systems Needless to say, the explosion of new support systems—word processing, document imaging, desktop publishing, computer-aided design, simulation modeling—has increased the productivity of both knowledge and office workers. Desktop publishing combines graphics and word-processing text to publish professional-quality print and web documents. Document-imaging systems can scan paper documents and images, convert them into digital form for storage on disks, retrieve them, and transmit them electronically to workstations throughout the network.

Management Information Systems Management information systems (MIS) support an organization's managers by providing daily reports, schedules, plans, and budgets. A simple MIS is shown in Figure 13.5. Each manager's information activities vary according to his or her functional area (say, accounting or marketing) and management level. Whereas midlevel managers focus mostly on internal activities and information, higher-level managers are also engaged in external activities. Middle managers, the largest MIS user group, need networked information to plan such upcoming activities as personnel training, materials movements, and cash flows. They also need to know the current status of the jobs and projects being carried out in their department: What stage is it at now? When will it be finished? Is there an opening so we can start the next job? Many of a firm's management information systems—cash flow, sales, production scheduling, shipping—are indispensable in helping managers find answers to such questions.

Decision Support Systems Middle and top-level managers receive decision-making assistance from a decision support system (DSS)—an interactive system that locates and presents information needed to support the decision-making process. Whereas some DSSs are devoted to specific problems, others serve more general purposes, allowing managers to analyze different types of problems. Thus a firm that often faces decisions on plant capacity, for example, may have a capacity DSS: The manager inputs data on anticipated levels of sales, working capital, and customer delivery requirements. Then the DSS's built-in transaction processors manipulate the data and make recommendations on the best levels of plant capacity for each future time period. In contrast, a general-purpose system, such as a marketing DSS, might respond to a variety of marketing-related problems. It may be programmed to handle "what if" questions, such as "When is the best time to introduce a new product if my main competitor introduces one in three months, our new product has an 18-month expected life, demand is seasonal with a peak in autumn, and my goal is to gain the largest possible market share?" The DSS can assist in decisions for which predetermined solutions are unknown by using sophisticated modeling tools and data analysis.

management information system (MIS)
Support managers by providing daily reports, schedules, plans, and budgets

decision support system (DSS)
An interactive system that locates and presents information needed to support the decision-making process

FIGURE 13.5 A BASIC MANAGEMENT INFORMATION SYSTEM

A basic management information system relies on an integrated database. Managers in various functional areas can access the database and get the information they need to make decisions. For example, operations managers can access the system to determine sales forecasts by marketing managers, and financial managers can check human resource files to identify possible candidates for promotion into the finance department.

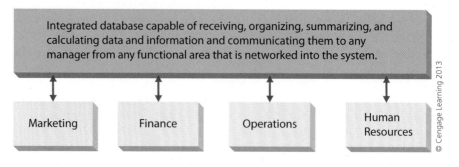

Executive Support Systems An executive support system (ESS) is a quick-reference, easy-access application of information systems specially designed for instant access by upper-level managers. ESSs are designed to assist with executive-level decisions and problems, ranging from "What lines of business should we be in five years from now?" to "Based on forecasted developments in electronic technologies, to what extent should our firm be globalized in five years? In ten years?" The ESS also uses a wide range of both internal information and external sources, such as industry reports, global economic forecasts, and reports on competitors' capabilities. Because senior-level managers do not usually possess advanced computer skills, they prefer systems that are easily accessible and adaptable. Accordingly, ESSs are not designed to address only specific, predetermined problems. Instead, they allow the user some flexibility in attacking a variety of problem situations. They are easily accessible by means of simple keyboard strokes or even voice commands.

Artificial Intelligence and Expert Systems Artificial intelligence (AI) can be defined as the construction of computer systems, both hardware and software, to imitate human behavior—in other words, systems that perform physical tasks, use thought processes, and learn. In developing AI systems, knowledge workers—business specialists, modelers, information technology experts—try to design computer-based systems capable of reasoning, so that computers, instead of people, can perform certain business activities.

One example is a credit evaluation system that decides which loan applicants are creditworthy and which are risky and then composes acceptance and rejection letters accordingly. Another example is an applicant selection system that receives interviewees' job applications, screens them, and then decides which applicants are best matched with each of several job openings. There are also AI systems that possess sensory capabilities, such as lasers that "see," "hear," and "feel." In addition, as machines become more sophisticated in processing natural language, humans can give instructions and ask questions merely by speaking to a computer.

A special form of AI program, the *expert system*, is designed to imitate the thought processes of human experts in a particular field. Expert systems incorporate the rules that an expert applies to specific types of problems, such as the judgments a physician makes in diagnosing illnesses. In effect, expert systems supply everyday users with "instant expertise." General Electric's Socrates Quick Quote, for example, imitates the decisions of a real estate expert and then places a package of recommendations about real estate transactions at the fingertips of real estate dealers on GE's private computer network. A system called MOCA (for Maintenance Operations Center Advisor), by imitating the thought processes of a maintenance manager, schedules routine maintenance for American Airlines' entire fleet. And Cisco Systems adopted Ciscopedia, a system similar to Wikipedia that allows employees to share information across the organization and encourages idea sharing.[11]

The Internet

Although not everyone would automatically think of it this way, the Internet is also an information system, one that is becoming more and more important to business every day. The Internet—the largest public data communications network—is a gigantic network of networks serving millions of computers; offering information on business, science, and government (or just about anything else, for that matter!); and providing communications flows among more than 170,000 separate networks around the world. Originally commissioned by the Pentagon as a communications tool for use during wartime, the Internet allows personal computers (including many contemporary cell phones) in virtually any location to be linked together. The Net has gained in popularity because it is an efficient tool for information retrieval that makes available an immense wealth of academic, technical, and business information.

executive support system (ESS)
A quick-reference, easy-access application of information systems specially designed for instant access by upper-level managers

artificial intelligence (AI)
The construction of computer systems, both hardware and software, to imitate human behavior, that is, to perform physical tasks, use thought processes, and learn

Internet
A gigantic network of networks serving millions of computers; offering information on business, science, government, and other topics; and providing communications flows among networks around the world

Because it can transmit information quickly and at low cost—lower than long-distance phone service, postal delivery, and overnight delivery—the Net has also become the most important e-mail system in the world. For thousands of businesses, therefore, the Net has joined—and is in many cases replacing—the telephone, fax machine, and express mail as a standard means of communication. Although individuals cannot generally connect directly to the Internet, for a small monthly usage fee they can subscribe to the Net via an **Internet service provider (ISP),** such as America Online or Earthlink. An ISP is a commercial firm that maintains a permanent connection to the Net and sells temporary connections to subscribers.[12]

The Internet's popularity continues to grow for both business and personal applications. In 2010, nearly 2 billion Internet users were active on links connecting every country in the world. Between 2000 and 2010, the number of users increased by 444.8 percent. In the United States alone, more than 239 million users are on the Internet every day. Its power to change the way business is conducted has been amply demonstrated in both large and small firms as their members use the Net to communicate both within and across organizational boundaries, to buy and sell products and services, and to glean information from myriad sources around the world.[13]

The Net has also benefited small companies, especially as a means of expanding market research and improving customer service, as well as serving as a source of information. In San Leandro, California, for example, TriNet Employer Group subscribes to Ernst & Young's online consulting program, Ernie. For $3,500 a year, TriNet controller Lyle DeWitt sends questions from his computer and gets an answer from an Ernst & Young expert within 48 hours. Aiming for small clients who cannot afford big-name consulting advice, Ernie answers questions on health insurance, benefit plans, immigration issues, and payroll taxes. Of course, as you can see from the *Change* box entitled "Your Algorithmic Alter Ego" on page 327, the constant expansion of Internet applications is not without risk, both for the marketers doing the research and for the subjects on whom they're conducting it.

The World Wide Web   Thanks to the **World Wide Web (WWW,** or simply "the web"), the Internet is easy to use and allows users around the world to communicate electronically with little effort. The World Wide Web is a system with universally accepted standards for storing, retrieving, formatting, and displaying information.[14] It provides the common language that enables us to "surf" the Net and makes the Internet available to a general audience, rather than only to technical users like computer programmers. To access a website, for example, the user must specify the *Uniform Resource Locator (URL)* that points to the resource's unique address on the Web.

> "It may sound geeky, but we need a national data-management plan."
> —FRANCINE BERMAN, DIRECTOR, SAN DIEGO SUPERCOMPUTER CENTER[15]

Internet service provider (ISP)
A commercial firm that maintains a permanent connection to the Net and sells temporary connections to subscribers

World Wide Web (WWW)
A system with universally accepted standards for storing, retrieving, formatting, and displaying information

web browser
The software that enables the user to access information on the web

Servers and Browsers   Each website opens with a *home page*—a screen display that welcomes the visitor with a greeting that may include graphics, sound, and visual enhancements introducing the user to the site. Additional pages give details on the sponsor's products and explain how to contact help in using the site. Often, they furnish URLs for related websites, to which the user can link by simply pointing and clicking. The person who is responsible for maintaining an organization's website is usually called the *webmaster*. Large websites use dedicated workstations—large computers—known as *web servers*, which are customized for managing, maintaining, and supporting websites.

With hundreds of thousands of new web pages appearing each day, cyberspace is now serving up billions of pages of publicly accessible information. Sorting through this maze would be frustrating and inefficient without access to a **web browser**—the software that enables the user to access information on the web. A browser runs on the user's PC and supports the graphics and linking capabilities needed to navigate the web. Microsoft's Internet Explorer is the world's dominant web browser today.

THE MORE THINGS CHANGE

Your Algorithmic Alter Ego

manzrussall/Shutterstock.com

It isn't the first time that the marriage of information technology and mathematics has revolutionized business—think about *business process modeling* (methods for representing business processes), *quantitative financial analysis* (techniques for standardizing financial information), and *data mining* (a tool for uncovering data patterns). It's happening again, and this time, with advances in computing capability and mathematical modeling configuring and reconfiguring vast amounts of data stored and accessed online, the subject to be mathematically "modeled" for business purposes is you.

"We turn the world of content into math," says Howard Kaushansky, founder and president of the market-analysis firm Umbria, "and we turn you into math." Marketers already analyze your buying patterns. Google, for example, sells advertising based on an analysis of customers' online browsing and buying habits, and E-LOAN, an online lender, uses a complicated algorithm to buy it. By continually adjusting the amount that it's willing to pay for 250,000 loan-related search terms, the company changes thousands of bids on key-word advertising every hour. Has anybody uncovered any useful product-related information so far? Working for PepsiCo, Umbria (which is owned by J.D. Power, a provider of global marketing information) peeked into millions of blogs and found that young men use Gatorade as a cocktail mixer in the hope of reducing hangovers. Pepsi marketers admit that it's a product use they hadn't foreseen.

As models get more sophisticated, marketers will start to analyze smaller and smaller groups and, finally, individuals. IBM, for instance, a long-time leader in process modeling, is now working to model 50,000 of its own IT consultants. The system translates education, skills, and experience into quantitative input. It investigates the use of free time by reviewing calendar software and keeps track of global location by means of mobile communication devices. By charting traffic patterns and examining the language of e-mails, it even gathers data on social habits.

Meanwhile, law-enforcement agencies collect demographic and phone-pattern data to monitor suspicious activities, and virtual libraries disseminate customized information about user reading preferences. Other modeling techniques get even more up-close and personal. Physicians and insurance companies, for example, compile data from genetic records.

Needless to say, the business of modeling people raises certain ethical issues, notably issues of privacy. In addition, a lot of critics charge that the analysts and the companies that hire them have no business wielding the kind of potential power provided by all of this personal information. Some people, however, put their faith in human ingenuity. "People are complicated," says one IBM manager who should know. "If you have a system, they figure out how to game it." At the very least, such strategies will keep the IT experts and mathematicians busy building models that adjust for human behavior.

References: Stephen Baker, "Math Will Rock Your World," *BusinessWeek*, January 23, 2006, www.businessweek on May 9, 2011; Joel Warner, "Blog-Searching Umbria Gets Power-ful," *Westword* (Denver), August 8, 2008, http://blogs.westword.com on May 9, 2011; William Holstein, "An Algorithm as a Pickax," *New York Times*, October 9, 2005, www.nytimes.com on May 9, 2011; Erik Schonfeld, "The Great Giveaway," *Business 2.0*, April 1, 2005, http://money.cnn.com on May 9, 2011.

Directories and Search Engines The web browser offers additional tools—website directories and search engines—for navigating on the web. Among the most successful cyberspace enterprises are companies like Yahoo! that maintain free directories of web content. When Yahoo! is notified about new websites, it classifies them in its directory. The user enters one or two key words (say, "Urban Outfitters" or "baseball statistics"), and the directory responds by retrieving from the directory a list of websites with titles containing those words.

In contrast to a directory, a search engine will search cyberspace's millions of web pages without preclassifying them into a directory. It searches for web pages that contain the same words as the user's search terms. Then it displays addresses for those that come closest to matching, then the next closest, and so on. A search engine such as Google or Ask.com may respond to more than 10 million inquiries per day. It is thus no surprise that both directories and search engines are packed with paid ads.[16] Yahoo! and Google are the current leaders in *portal sites*—sites used by Net surfers as primary home pages.

Intranets The success of the Internet has led some companies to extend the Net's technology internally, using it for internal websites containing information about the firm. These private networks, or **intranets**, are accessible only to employees via entry through electronic firewalls. Firewalls, discussed later, are used to limit access to an intranet. At Hewlett-Packard, the intranet allows employees to shuffle their retirement savings among various investment funds. Ford's intranet connects company workstations in Asia, South America, Europe, and the United States to thousands of Ford websites containing private information on Ford activities in production, engineering, distribution, and marketing. Sharing such information has helped reduce the lead time for getting models into production from 36 to 24 months. Ford's latest project in improving customer service through internal information sharing is called *manufacturing on demand*. Now, for example, the Mustang that required 50 days' delivery time in 1996 is available in about a week. The savings to Ford, of course, amounts to billions of dollars in inventory and fixed costs.[17]

Extranets Sometimes firms allow outsiders access to their intranets. These so-called **extranets** allow outsiders limited access to a firm's intranet. The most common application allows buyers to enter the seller's system to see which products are available for sale and delivery, thus providing product availability information quickly to outside buyers. Industrial suppliers, too, are often linked into their customers' intranets so that they can see planned production schedules and make supplies ready as needed for customers' upcoming operations.

Identify the various different levels of information systems that exist today.

Identify examples of how you use the Internet for informational purposes.

Managing Information Systems

At this point, the value and importance of information systems should be apparent. There are still important questions to be answered, however. How are such systems developed, and how are they used on a day-to-day basis? This section provides insights into these issues and related areas.

Creating Information Systems

The basic steps involved in creating an information system are outlined in Figure 13.6. The first step is to determine the information needs of the organization and to establish goals for what is to be achieved with the proposed system. It is absolutely imperative that the project have full support and an appropriate financial commitment from top management if it is to be successful. Once the decision has been made to develop and install an information system, a task force is usually constituted to oversee everything. Target users, as discussed earlier, must be well represented on such a task force.

intranet
A communications network similar to the Internet but operating within the boundaries of a single organization

extranet
A communications network that allows selected outsiders limited access to an organization's internal information system, or intranet

FIGURE 13.6 ESTABLISHING AN INFORMATION SYSTEM

Establishing an information system is a complex procedure. Managers must realize, however, that the organization's information management needs will change over time, and some steps of the process may have to be repeated in the future.

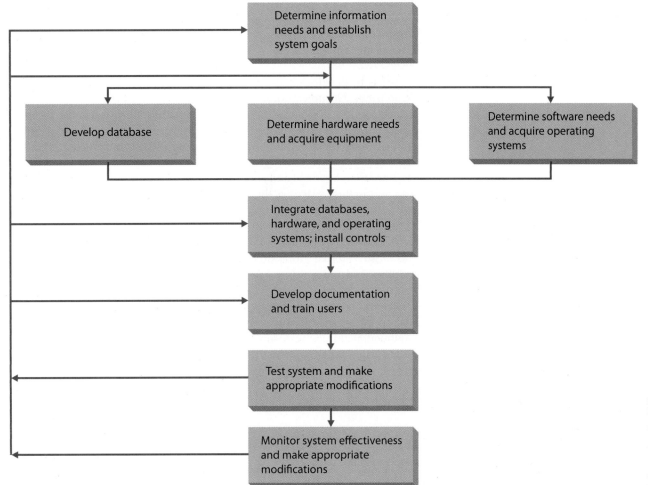

Next, three tasks can be done simultaneously. One task is to develop a database. Most organizations already possess the information they need for an information system, but it is often not in the correct form. The Pentagon has spent large sums of money to transform all of its paper records into computer records. Many other branches of the government are also working hard to computerize their data.[18]

While the database is being assembled, the organization also needs to determine its hardware needs and acquire the appropriate equipment. Some systems rely solely on one large mainframe computer; others are increasingly using personal computers. Equipment is usually obtained from large manufacturers like Hewlett-Packard, Sun, and Dell. Finally, software needs must also be determined and an appropriate operating system obtained. Again, off-the-shelf packages will sometimes work, although most companies find it necessary to do some customization to suit their needs.[19]

The actual information system is created by integrating the databases, hardware, software, and operating system. Obviously, the mechanics of doing this are beyond the scope of this discussion. However, the company usually has to rely on the expertise of outside consulting firms, along with the vendors who provided the other parts of the system, to get it all put together. During this phase, the equipment is installed, cables are strung between units (or, increasingly, wireless connections are established), the data are entered into the system, the operating system is installed and tested, and so forth. During this phase, system controls are also installed. A control is simply a characteristic of the system that limits certain forms of access or limits what a person can do with the system. For example, top managers may want to limit access to certain sensitive data to a few key people. These people may be given private codes that must be entered before the data are made available. It is important to make sure that data cannot be accidentally erased by someone who just happens to press the wrong key.

The next step is to develop documentation of how the system works and to train people in how to use it. *Documentation* refers to manuals, computerized help programs, diagrams, and instruction sheets. Essentially, it tells people how to use the system for different purposes. Beyond pure documentation, however, training sessions are also common. Such sessions allow people to practice using the system under the watchful eyes of experts.

The system must then be tested and appropriate modifications made. Regardless of how well planned an information system is, there will almost certainly be glitches. For example, the system may be unable to generate a report that needs to be made available to certain managers. Or the report may not be in the appropriate format. Or certain people may be unable to access data that they need to get other information from the system. In most cases, the consultants or the internal group that installed the system will be able to make such modifications as the need arises.

The organization must recognize that information management needs will change over time. Hence, even though the glitches get straightened out and the information system is put into normal operation, modifications may still be needed in the future. For example, as United and Continental airlines were implementing their merger in 2011 they developed an entirely new information system to better meet the needs of what was becoming the world's largest airline. Information management is a continuous process. Even if an effective information system can be created and put into use, there is still a good chance that it will occasionally need to be modified to fit changing circumstances.

Integrating Information Systems

In very large and complex organizations, information systems must also be integrated. This integration may involve linkages between different information systems within the same organization or between different organizations altogether. Within an organization, for example, it is probably necessary for the marketing system and the operations system to be able to communicate with each other.

Linking systems together is not so easy. Consider, for example, the complexities involved when Hewlett-Packard acquired Compaq Computer. Each firm had its own complex and integrated information network. But because each firm's network relied on different technologies, hardware, and operating systems, integrating the two firms has been a costly and complex undertaking. Similarly, suppose a firm installs one system in one of its divisions, using Dell equipment and Microsoft software, and then installs a different system in another division, using Hewlett-Packard equipment and Lotus software. Just as with Hewlett-Packard and Compaq, if and when the firm decides to tie its two distinct systems together, it may face considerable difficulties.

There are two ways to overcome this problem. One is to develop everything at once. Unfortunately, doing so is expensive, and sometimes managers simply cannot anticipate today exactly what their needs will be tomorrow. The other method is to adopt a standard type of system at the beginning, so that subsequent additions fit properly.[20] Even then, however, breakthroughs in information system technology may still make it necessary to change approaches in midstream.

Using Information Systems

The real test of the value of an information system is how it can be used. Ideally, an information system should be simple to use and nontechnical—that is, one should not have to be a computer expert to use the system. In theory, a manager should be able to access a modern information system by turning on a computer and clicking an icon with a mouse. The manager should also be able to enter appropriate new data or request that certain kinds of information be provided. The requested information might first be displayed on a computer screen or monitor. After the manager is satisfied, the information can then be printed out in paper form on a standard printer, or the manager can store the information back in the system for possible future use or for use by others.

One implication relates to the span of management and the number of levels of an organization. Innovations in information technology enable a manager to stay in touch with an increasingly large number of managers and subordinates. The CEO of Cypress Semiconductor uses the firm's information system to check on the progress of each of his employees every week. Using this and related approaches, spans of management are likely to widen and organizational levels to decrease. And some organizations are using their information-processing capabilities to network with other companies. Pacific Intermountain Express, a large western trucking company, gives customers access to its own computer network so they can check on the status of their shipments. And individual consumers can track shipments at UPS and FedEx if they know the specific tracking number of their package.

Travelers Insurance has made effective use of its information system by hiring a team of trained nurses to review health insurance claims. The nurses tap into the company's regular information system and analyze the medical diagnoses provided with each claim. They can use this information to determine whether a second opinion is warranted before a particular surgical procedure is approved. They enter their decision directly into the system. When the claim form is printed out, it contains a provision that spells out whether the claimant must seek a second opinion before proceeding with a particular treatment.

firewall
Software and hardware system that allows employees access to both the Internet and the company's internal computer network while barring access by outsiders

Managing Information Security

An increasingly common concern for businesses today is security. Security measures for protection against intrusion are a constant challenge. To gain entry into most systems, users have protected passwords that guard against unauthorized access, but many firms rely on additional protective software as a safeguard. To protect against intrusions by unauthorized outsiders, companies use security devices, called *electronic firewalls*, in their systems. Firewalls are software and hardware systems that allow employees access to both the Internet and the company's internal computer network while barring entry by outsiders.

Security for electronic communications is an additional concern. Electronic transmissions can be intercepted, altered, and read by intruders. To prevent unauthorized access, many firms rely on *encryption*: use of a secret numeric code to scramble the characters in the message, so that the message is not understandable during transmission. Only personnel with the deciphering codes can read them. Protection for preserving data files and databases is not foolproof and typically involves making backup copies to be stored outside the computer system, usually in a safe. Damaged system files can thus be replaced by backups.

Managing information security is one of the biggest challenges facing managers today. If unauthorized users gain access to an organization's information system, they can severely damage the organization's ability to function and acquire information that could potentially allow them to steal from the firm, its employees, or its customers. Complex layers of firewalls, encryptions, and password-protected access points, as well as physical barriers, are all used to combat this threat.

TABLE 13.1

LIMITATIONS OF INFORMATION SYSTEMS

Although information systems play a vital role in modern organizations, they are not without their limitations. In particular, information systems have six basic limitations. For example, one major limitation of installing an information system is cost. For a large company, an information system might cost several million dollars.

1. Information systems are expensive and difficult to develop, implement, maintain, and modify.
2. Information systems are not suitable for all tasks or problems.
3. Managers sometimes rely too much on information systems.
4. Information provided to managers may not be as accurate, timely, complete, or relevant as it first appears to be.
5. Managers may have unrealistic expectations of what information systems can do.
6. The information system may be subject to sabotage, computer viruses, or downtime.

© Cengage Learning 2013

Finally, the most important security factor is the people in the system. At most firms, personnel are trained in the responsibilities of computer use and warned of the penalties for violating system security. For example, each time the computer boots up, a notice displays the warning that software and data are protected and spells out penalties for unauthorized use.[21]

Understanding Information System Limitations

It is also necessary to recognize the limits of information systems. Several of these are listed in Table 13.1. First of all, as already noted, information systems are expensive and difficult to develop, implement, maintain, and modify. Thus organizations may try to cut corners too much or install a system in such a piecemeal fashion that its effectiveness suffers.

Information systems simply are not suitable for some tasks or problems. Complex problems requiring human judgment must still be addressed by humans. Information systems are often a useful tool for managers, but they can seldom actually replace managers. Managers also may come to rely too much on information systems. As a consequence, the manager may lose touch with the real-world problems he or she needs to be concerned about. Similarly, access to unlimited information can result in overload, rendering managers less effective than they would be with reduced access to information.[22]

Information may not be as accurate, timely, complete, or relevant as it appears. There is a strong tendency for people to think that because a computer performed the calculations, the answer must be correct—especially if the answer is calculated to several decimal places. But the fact of the matter is that if the initial information was flawed, all resultant computations using it are likely to be flawed as well.

Managers sometimes have unrealistic expectations about what information systems can accomplish. They may believe that the first stage of implementation will result in a full-blown Orwellian communications network that a child could use. When the manager comes to see the flaws and limitations of the system, she or he may become disappointed and as a result not use the system effectively. Finally, the information system may be subject to sabotage, computer viruses, or downtime. Disgruntled employees have been known to enter false data deliberately. And a company that relies too much on a computerized information system may find itself totally paralyzed in the event of a simple power outage or a crippling computer virus.

Describe how information systems are created.

Identify personal examples of information system limitations that you have encountered or experienced.

CONCEPT CHECK

The Impact of Information Systems on Organizations

Information systems are clearly an important part of most modern organizations. Their effects are felt in a variety of ways. Indeed, the rapid growth of information technologies has changed the very structure of business organizations.

Leaner Organizations

Information networks are leading to leaner companies with fewer employees and simpler structures. Because today's networked firm can maintain information linkages among both employees and customers, more work can be accomplished with fewer people. Bank customers, for example, can dial into a 24-hour information system and find out their current balances from a digital voice or access the information from their cell phones. In the industrial sector, assembly workers at a Dell plant used to receive instructions from supervisors or special staff. Now instructions are delivered electronically to their workstations.

Widespread reductions in middle-management positions and the shrinkage of layers in organizational structure are possible because information networks now provide direct communications between top managers and workers at lower levels. The operating managers who formerly communicated company policies, procedures, or work instructions to lower-level employees are being replaced by electronic information networks.

More Flexible Operations

Electronic networks allow businesses to offer customers greater variety and faster delivery cycles. Recovery after heart surgery, for example, is expedited by custom-tailored rehabilitation programs designed with integrated information systems. Each personalized program integrates the patient's history with information from physicians and rehabilitation specialists and then matches the patient with an electronically monitored exercise regimen. Products such as cellular phones, PCs, and audio systems can be custom-ordered, too, with your choice of features and options and next-day delivery. The underlying principle is called *mass customization*. Although companies produce in large volumes, each unit features the unique variations and options that the customer prefers.

Flexible production and fast delivery depend on an integrated network to coordinate all of the transactions, activities, and process flows necessary to make quick adjustments in the production process. The ability to organize and store massive volumes of information is crucial, as are the electronic linkages between customers, manufacturers, materials suppliers, and shippers.

Increased Collaboration

Collaboration, not only among internal units but with outside firms as well, is on the rise because networked systems make it cheaper and easier to contact everyone, whether other employees or outside organizations.[23] Aided by intranets, more companies are learning that complex problems can be solved better by means of collaboration, either in formal teams or through spontaneous interaction. In the new, networked organization, decisions that were once the domain of individuals are now shared, as both people and departments have become more interdependent. The design of new products, for example, was once an engineering responsibility. Now, in contrast, it can be a shared responsibility because so much information is accessible for evaluation from various perspectives. Marketing, finance, production, engineering, and purchasing can now share their different stores of information and determine a best overall design.

Naturally, networked systems are also helpful in business-to-business (often referred to as "B2B") relationships. Increasingly, organizational buyers and suppliers are becoming so closely networked that they sometimes seem to be working for one organization. In the financial services industry, for example, institutional investors are networked with investment bankers, thus allowing efficient buying and selling of initial stock offerings. In manufacturing, Ford's parts suppliers are linked to Ford's extranet. Because they know Ford's current production schedules and upcoming requirements, they can move materials into Ford plants more quickly and more accurately.

A step toward even greater collaboration between companies—the so-called virtual company—has become possible through networking. As we will see in Chapter 15, a virtual company can be a temporary team assembled by a single organization. But a virtual company can also be created when several firms join forces. Each contributes different skills and resources that collectively result in a competitive business that would not be feasible for any of the collaborators acting alone. A company with marketing and promotional skills, for example, may team up with firms that are experts in warehousing and distribution, engineering, and production. Networking allows collaborators to exchange ideas, plan daily activities, share customer information, and otherwise coordinate their efforts, even if their respective facilities are far apart.

One of the many advantages of modern information technology is that it allows many people to work from home. This digital artist, for example, is working from his home office as he researches images online and uses them to create new ones. This has only become possible in the last two decades.

More Flexible Work Sites

Geographic separation of the workplace from the company headquarters is more common than ever because of networked organizations. Employees no longer work only at the office or the factory, nor are all of a company's operations performed at one location. The sales manager for an advertising agency may visit the company office in New York once every two weeks, preferring instead to work over the firm's electronic network from her home office in Florida. A medical researcher for the Cleveland Clinic may work at a home office networked into the clinic's system.[24]

A company's activities may also be geographically scattered but highly coordinated, thanks to a networked system. Many e-businesses, for example, conduct no activities at one centralized location. When you order products from an Internet storefront—say, a chair, a sofa, a table, and two lamps—the chair may come from a cooperating warehouse in Philadelphia and the lamps from a manufacturer in California, while the sofa and table may be shipped directly from two manufacturers in North Carolina. All these activities are launched instantaneously by the customer's order and coordinated through the network, just as if all of them were being processed at one location.[25]

Improved Management Processes

Networked systems have changed the very nature of the management process. The activities, methods, and procedures of today's manager differ significantly from those that were common just a few years ago. Once, for example, upper-level managers did not concern themselves with all the detailed information that filtered upward in the workplace. Why? Because it was expensive to gather, slow in coming, and quickly out of date. Workplace management was delegated to middle and first-line managers.

With networked systems, however, instantaneous information is accessible in a convenient, usable format. Consequently, more and more upper managers use it routinely for planning, leading, directing, and controlling operations. Today, a top manager can find out the current status of any customer order, inspect productivity statistics for each workstation, and analyze the delivery performance of any driver and vehicle. More importantly, managers can better coordinate companywide performance. They can identify departments that are working well together and those that are creating bottlenecks. Hershey's networked system, for example, includes SAP, an enterprise resource planning model that identifies the current status of any order and traces its progress from order entry through customer delivery and receipt of payment. Progress and delays at intermediate stages—materials ordering, inventory availability, production scheduling, packaging, warehousing, distribution—can be checked continuously to determine which operations should be more closely coordinated with others to improve overall performance.

Changed Employee Behaviors

Information systems also directly affect the behaviors of people in organizations. Some of these effects are positive; others can be negative. On the plus side, information systems usually improve individual efficiency. Some people also enjoy their work more because they have fun using the new technology. Through computerized bulletin boards and e-mail, groups can form across organizational boundaries.

On the negative side, information systems can lead to isolation, as people have everything they need to do their job without interacting with others. Managers can work at home easily, with the possible side effects of being unavailable to others who need them or being removed from key parts of the social system. Computerized working arrangements also tend to be much less personal than other methods. For example, a computer-transmitted "pat on the back" will likely mean less than a real one. Researchers are just beginning to determine how individual behaviors and attitudes are affected by information systems.[26]

What are the primary impacts of information systems on organizations?

What are the primary ways in which information systems affect you personally?

CONCEPT CHECK

Summary of Learning Objectives and Key Points

1. Describe the role and importance of information in the manager's job and identify the basic building blocks of information technology.

   - Information is a vital part of every manager's job.
   - For information to be useful, it must be accurate, timely, complete, and accurate.
   - Information technology is best conceived of as part of the control process.
   - Information technology systems contain five basic components:
     ○ an input medium
     ○ a processor
     ○ an output medium
     ○ a storage device
     ○ a control system

2. Discuss the basic factors that determine an organization's information technology needs and describe the basic types of information systems used by organizations.

   - An organization's information technology needs are determined by several factors—most notably, user groups and systems requirements.

   - There are several basic levels of information systems:
     ○ transaction-processing systems
     ○ systems for various types of workers
     ○ basic management information systems
     ○ decision support systems
     ○ executive support systems
     ○ artificial intelligence systems
     ○ expert systems
   - Each provides certain types of information and is most valuable for specific types of managers.
   - Each should also be matched to the needs of user groups.

3. Discuss how information systems can be managed.

   - Managing information systems involves five basic elements:
     ○ They must be designed and created.
     ○ They must be integrated.
     ○ They must be usable.
     ○ They must be secure.
     ○ Their limitations must be recognized.

4. Describe how information systems affect organizations.

   - Information systems have an impact on organizations in a variety of ways. Major influences include:
     - leaner organizations
     - more flexible operations
     - increased collaboration
     - more flexible work sites
     - improved management processes
     - changed employee behaviors

Discussion Questions

Questions for Review

1. What are the differences between data and information? Give three examples of data and then show how those data can be turned into information.
2. Who uses information systems in organizations? What types of functions do the systems perform for each type of user?
3. Describe each of the levels of major information technology systems. Give an example of each, other than the examples in the text.
4. What are some of the positive impacts that information technology can have on organizations? What are some of the negative impacts?

Questions for Analysis

5. Very often, managers making decisions in real organizations have to work with information that does not perfectly meet all four criteria for useful information. In that case, should the manager use the imperfect information? What can the manager do to increase the usefulness of imperfect information?
6. At higher organizational levels, the information technology tools used become more sophisticated. Yet, in many organizations, higher-level managers are the least sophisticated and experienced with hands-on use of information technology. How can unsophisticated users effectively employ a sophisticated IT tool? What are some of the potential problems they should be aware of?
7. It has been said that the information revolution is like the Industrial Revolution in terms of the magnitude of its impact on organizations and society. What leads to such a view? Why might that view be an overstatement?

Questions for Application

8. Interview a business manager about the use of information in his or her organization. How is the information managed? Is a computer system used? How well is the information system integrated with other aspects of organizational control?
9. Visit a local organization, such as a university administration office, a restaurant, or a supermarket. Stand in its facility and look around you. How many different information systems can you spot? Do not look just for "computers"; also look for less obvious examples, such as the digital thermostat on the wall or the electronic cash register. What type of information system is each?
10. A knowledge worker can be defined as "someone who creates, transforms, or repackages information." Choose a knowledge worker occupation that interests you. Use the Internet to investigate the job qualifications for that occupation. What skills, knowledge, and experience are needed? How do the qualifications for knowledge workers differ from the qualifications of white-collar workers?

CengageNow™ Highlights

Now use your CengageNow™ homework to help you:

- Apply management theories in your life
- Assess your management skills
- Master management terms and concepts
- Apply your knowledge to real-world situations
- Analyze and solve challenging management problems

In order to take advantage of these elements, your instructor will need to have set up a course for your class within CengageNow™. Ask your instructor to contact his/her Cengage sales representative and Digital Solutions Manager to explore testing CengageNow™ in your course this term.

Basic Elements of Organizing

LEARNING OBJECTIVES

After studying this chapter, you should be able to:

1. Identify the basic elements of organizations.

2. Describe the basic alternative approaches to designing jobs.

3. Discuss the rationale and the most common bases for grouping jobs into departments.

4. Describe the basic elements involved in establishing reporting relationships.

5. Discuss how authority is distributed in organizations.

6. Discuss the basic coordinating activities undertaken by organizations.

7. Describe basic ways in which positions within an organization can be differentiated.

MANAGEMENT IN ACTION   Delayering as a Defense Mechanism

In October 2009, Anglo American PLC, the world's fourth-largest diversified mining company, announced that it was *delayering*—eliminating a layer of organizational structure. Analysis of its "operating model," reported the company (referring to itself as "the Group"), had resulted in "an organizational simplification and delayering across the Group, with the divisional co-ordinating level across . . . Coal and Ferrous Metals being removed." Previously, the company had been organized into two global divisions—Coal and Ferrous Metals, each with its own CEO, both of whom reported directly to the CEO of Anglo American. Below the divisional level were Anglo's various global business operations, each dealing with a different commodity (e.g., coal, platinum, iron ore) and each headed by its own CEO and functional support staff. The CEOs of these units reported directly to the CEO of his or her respective division.

As a result of "simplification and delayering," these businesses were reorganized into seven "commodity business units" (BUs), each of which is now "profit accountable"—that is, responsible for its own performance. The major criteria for this reorganization were geography and asset status. The platinum unit, for example, is headquartered in South Africa (which is also home to the parent company), the copper unit in Chile, and the metallurgical-coal unit in Australia.

> "I know what it is that we need to do."
>
> —ANGLO AMERICAN CEO CYNTHIA CARROLL

In addition, Anglo now maintains BUs only for its *core assets*—operations that are essential to producing revenue, cash flow, or profit. Going hand in hand with the company's delayering strategy is thus a strategy to divest its non-core assets: Having already shed its interests in gold and aluminum, Anglo also intends to sell its holdings in such commodities as phosphates and zinc as well as a company that manufactures steel products for the construction industry. The decision to delayer and divest, says chairman Sir John Parker, "represents an important step in creating a more streamlined business, with enhanced focus on operational effectiveness. . . . We have a truly world-class portfolio of assets, and these initiatives further improve our ability to deliver its full potential."

Streamlining and efficiency, of course, are common and logical reasons for restructuring an organization, but if we look a little more closely at the recent history of Anglo American, we'll find that these strategies also play a key role in a much more complicated game of corporate competition and, perhaps, even survival.

The year 2009 had already been a hectic one for Anglo. In February, CEO Cynthia Carroll admitted that the

Cynthia Carroll, CEO of Anglo American PLC, recently announced that the firm would eliminate one entire layer of management.

organization, like many companies, was starting to feel the impact of the global recession: "The breadth and severity of the global downturn [is] difficult to understate," she said in announcing that Anglo would cut 19,000 jobs—about a tenth of its workforce—and suspend dividend payments accrued in 2008. Carroll also reported that earnings per share had fallen from $4.40 to $4.36 and that operating profit had dropped by 0.3 percent. The slippage was hardly catastrophic, but analysts had predicted an increase of 13 percent in earnings per share and had expected operating profit to at least remain flat.

Carroll's appointment as CEO in 2007 had already been a shock to many people in what the *Times* of London calls "an irredeemably macho industry." Not only was she not a man, she was neither a mining industry veteran nor a South African (she's an American). When her appointment was announced, Anglo's stock immediately dropped $0.80 per share. The dice, observed the *Times*, were "probably loaded against her from the start," and to make her job even more difficult, she was soon forced to embark upon a $2 billion efficiency program involving a number of changes guaranteed to rile the old guard of the 91-year-old company. Her whirlwind campaign to cut costs by $450 million in the first half of 2009 earned her the nickname "Cyclone Cynthia," but many analysts and investors were unimpressed by the savings: Because the entire industry was struggling with high costs during the recession, Carroll's cost-cutting was seen as little more than the logical and obvious strategy to pursue.

Then in June 2009, the Swiss–British mining company Xstrata proposed a merger with Anglo—a move that would create a $68 billion firm to compete with industry giants like BHP Billiton, Vale, and Rio Tinto. Xstrata said in a statement that it was seeking "a merger of equals that would realize significant value for both companies' shareholders" and cited "substantial operational synergies" that could amount to savings of $1 billion a year in combined costs. From Anglo's perspective, there were drawbacks to the deal—its portfolio was worth more than Xstrata's and would be diluted by a merger of the two—but the appeal to Anglo shareholders was clear: Depending on how the new company distributed the cost savings among its investors, Anglo shareholders stood to realize an increase in the market value of their holdings of 26 to 37 percent.

Carroll and the Anglo board quickly rejected Xstrata's offer as "totally unacceptable," and in August Carroll presented both Anglo's mid-year financial results and its argument for remaining independent. Once again, however, the numbers were underwhelming: Because of the global economy, profits were off 69 percent and revenues 38 percent. Anglo investors wanted to know what management was doing to deliver the kind of returns promised by the Xstrata merger, and an analyst at Barclays Capital, Britain's biggest investment bank, announced that, "in our view, Anglo American has not yet presented a strong argument as to why a merger with Xstrata is not strategically sensible and value-creating for its shareholders." "Frankly," replied Carroll,

> I know what it is that we need to do. . . . We have a strategy, we have clear goals, we have tremendous assets . . . in the most attractive commodities in the world. The opportunities are massive. . . . We're well aware of what Xstrata does, but I'm very confident of what we can do in the future.

In October, Xstrata withdrew its offer in the face of resistance from the Anglo board. Anglo, said a company spokesman, "can now move forward and run our business without further distraction." One analyst predicted that Anglo "will likely show a renewed sense of urgency . . . and pull out all the stops to win shareholders over," and exactly one week later, Carroll announced her "simplification and delayering" plan. In making the announcement, she asked shareholders for more time to develop the firm's assets and prove its value as an independent company. "The portfolio changes we have announced," she argued, ". . . will position Anglo American well for sustained, profitable growth in the commodities we have identified as being the most attractive."[1]

All managers need the assistance of others to succeed and so must trust the members of their team to do their jobs and carry out their responsibilities. And the team members themselves need the support of their boss and a clear understanding of their role in the organization. This mutual dependence may be especially important when, as in the case of Anglo American, a new and unknown manager begins by reconfiguring the team. In any case, the working relationship between managers and their subordinates is one of the most critical elements comprising an organization.[2] As you will see in this chapter, managing the basic frameworks that organizations use to get their work done—structure—is a fundamental part of the management process.

This chapter discusses many of the critical elements of organization structure that managers can control and is the first of five devoted to organizing, the second basic managerial function identified in Chapter 1. In Part 3, we describe managerial planning—deciding what to do. Organizing, the subject of Part 5, focuses on how to do it. We first elaborate on the meaning of organization structure. Subsequent sections explore the basic elements that managers use to create an organization.

The Elements of Organizing

organizing
Deciding how best to group organizational activities and resources

organization structure
The set of elements that can be used to configure an organization

job design
The determination of an individual's work-related responsibilities

job specialization
The degree to which the overall task of the organization is broken down and divided into smaller component parts

Imagine asking a child to build a castle with a set of building blocks. She selects a few small blocks and other larger ones. She uses some square ones, some round ones, and some triangular ones. When she finishes, she has her own castle, unlike any other. Another child, presented with the same task, constructs a different castle. He selects different blocks, for example, and combines them in different ways. The children's activities—choosing certain combinations of blocks and then putting them together in unique ways—are in many ways analogous to the manager's job of organizing.[3]

Organizing is deciding how best to group organizational elements. Just as children select different kinds of building blocks, managers can choose a variety of structural possibilities. And just as the children can assemble the blocks in any number of ways, so, too, can managers put the organization together in many different ways. Understanding the nature of these building blocks and the different ways in which they can be configured can have a powerful impact on a firm's competitiveness.[4] In this chapter, our focus is on the building blocks themselves—organization structure. In Chapter 15 we focus on how the blocks can be put together—organization design.

There are six basic building blocks that managers can use in constructing an organization: designing jobs, grouping jobs, establishing reporting relationships between jobs, distributing authority among jobs, coordinating activities among jobs, and differentiating among positions. The logical starting point is the first building block—designing jobs for people within the organization.

What is the meaning of organizing as a management function?

Besides building blocks, what other analogies might seem to reflect organization structure?

CONCEPT CHECK

Designing Jobs

The first building block of organization structure is job design. **Job design** is the determination of an individual's work-related responsibilities.[5] For a machinist at Caterpillar, job design might specify what machines are to be operated, how they are to be operated, and what performance standards are expected. For a manager at Caterpillar, job design might involve defining areas of decision-making responsibility, identifying goals and expectations, and establishing appropriate indicators of success. The natural starting point for designing jobs is determining the level of desired specialization.

Job Specialization

Job specialization is the degree to which the overall task of the organization is broken down and divided into smaller component parts. Job specialization evolved from the concept of *division of labor*. Adam Smith, an eighteenth-century economist, first discussed division of labor in his case study about how a pin factory used it to improve productivity.[6] He described how one man pulled the wire from a spool, another straightened it, a third cut it, a fourth ground the point, and so on. Smith claimed that ten men working in this fashion were able to produce 48,000 pins in a day, whereas each man working alone could produce only 20 pins per day.

The first examples of the impact of specialization came from the automobile assembly line pioneered by Henry Ford and his contemporaries. Mass-production capabilities stemming from job specialization techniques have had a profound impact throughout the world. During the twentieth century, high levels of low-cost production transformed U.S. society into one of the strongest economies in the history of the world.[7]

Job specialization in its purest form is simply a normal extension of organizational growth. For example, when Walt Disney started his company, he did everything himself—wrote cartoons, drew them, added character voices, and then marketed them to theaters. As the business grew, though, he eventually hired others to perform many of these same functions. As growth continued, so, too, did specialization. For example, as animation artists work on Disney movies today, they may specialize in generating computer images of a single character or doing only background scenery. Others provide voices, and marketing specialists develop promotional campaigns. And today, the Walt Disney Company has literally thousands of different specialized jobs. Clearly, no one person could perform them all.

Benefits and Limitations of Specialization

Job specialization provides four benefits to organizations.[8] First, workers performing small, simple tasks will become very proficient at each task. Second, transfer time between tasks decreases. If employees perform several different tasks, some time is lost as they stop doing the first task and start doing the next. Third, the more narrowly defined a job is, the easier it is to develop specialized equipment to assist with that job. Fourth, when an employee who performs a highly specialized job is absent or resigns, the manager is able to train someone new at relatively low cost. Although specialization is generally thought of in terms of operating jobs, many organizations have extended the basic elements of specialization to managerial and professional levels as well.[9]

On the other hand, job specialization can have negative consequences. The foremost criticism is that workers who perform highly specialized jobs may become bored and dissatisfied. The job may be so specialized that it offers no challenge or stimulation. Boredom and monotony set in, absenteeism rises, and the quality of the work may suffer. Furthermore, the anticipated benefits of specialization do not always occur. For example, a classic study conducted at Maytag found that the time spent moving work in process from one worker to another was greater than the time needed for the same individual to change from job to job.[10] Thus, although some degree of specialization is necessary, it should not be carried to extremes, because of the possible negative consequences. Managers must be sensitive to situations in which extreme specialization should be avoided. And indeed, several alternative approaches to designing jobs have been developed in recent years.

Job specialization breaks jobs down into small, easy-to-learn components. On the one hand, specialization may improve efficiency and productivity. At the same time, though, it can also lead to monotony and boredom. This assembly line worker is helping to assemble new vehicles for Nissan at the firm's plant in Tokyo. Assembly line jobs have traditionally been highly specialized.

YOSHIKAZU TSUNO/AFP/Getty Images

"The best [Tour de France] teams have specialists to help position leaders for a win."

—PAUL HOCHMAN, BUSINESS WRITER[11]

Alternatives to Specialization

To counter the problems associated with specialization, managers have sought other approaches to job design that achieve a better balance between organizational demands for efficiency and productivity and individual needs for creativity and autonomy. Five alternative approaches are job rotation, job enlargement, job enrichment, the job characteristics approach, and work teams.[12]

Job Rotation Job rotation involves systematically moving employees from one job to another. A worker in a warehouse might unload trucks on Monday, carry incoming inventory to storage on Tuesday, verify invoices on Wednesday, pull outgoing inventory from storage on Thursday, and load trucks on Friday. Thus the jobs do not change; instead, workers move from job to job. Unfortunately, for this very reason, job rotation has not been very successful in enhancing employee motivation or satisfaction. Jobs that are amenable to rotation tend to be relatively standard and routine. Workers who are rotated to a "new" job may be more satisfied at first, but satisfaction soon wanes. Although many companies (among them American Cyanamid, Bethlehem Steel, Ford, Prudential Insurance, TRW, and Western Electric) have tried job rotation, it is most often used today as a training device to improve worker skills and flexibility. Job rotation is also being used more to increase flexibility and lower costs. That is, because workers who can perform multiple jobs can be moved around to different jobs when demand shifts, the business can often get by with fewer workers.

> "[rotating jobs]…makes the day go by. You don't get bored doing the same thing over and over."
>
> —RICK RUSH, GM ASSEMBLY LINE WORKER[13]

Job Enlargement On the assumption that doing the same basic task over and over is the primary cause of worker dissatisfaction, job enlargement was developed to increase the total number of tasks workers perform. As a result, all workers perform a wide variety of tasks, which presumably reduces the level of job dissatisfaction. Many organizations have used job enlargement, including IBM, Detroit Edison, AT&T, the U.S. Civil Service, and Maytag. At Maytag, for example, the assembly line for producing washing-machine water pumps was systematically changed so that work that had originally been performed by six workers, who passed the work sequentially from one person to another, was performed by four workers, each of whom assembled a complete pump.[14] Unfortunately, although job enlargement does have some positive consequences, these are often offset by some disadvantages: (1) Training costs usually increase, (2) unions have argued that pay should increase because the worker is doing more tasks, and (3) in many cases the work remains boring and routine even after job enlargement.

Job Enrichment A more comprehensive approach, job enrichment, assumes that increasing the range and variety of tasks is not sufficient by itself to improve employee motivation.[15] Thus job enrichment attempts to increase both the number of tasks a worker does and the control the worker has over the job. To implement job enrichment, managers remove some controls from the job, delegate more authority to employees, and structure the work in complete, natural units. These changes increase subordinates' sense of responsibility. Another part of job enrichment is to continually assign new and challenging tasks, thereby increasing employees' opportunity for growth and advancement.

AT&T was one of the earliest companies to try job enrichment. In one experiment, eight typists in a service unit prepared customer service orders. Faced with low output and high turnover, management determined that the typists felt little responsibility to clients and received little feedback. The unit was changed to create a typing team. Typists were matched with designated service representatives, the task was changed from ten specific steps to three more general steps, and job titles were upgraded. As a result, the frequency of order processing increased from 27 percent to 90 percent, the need for messenger service was eliminated, accuracy improved, and turnover became practically nil.[16] Other organizations that have tried job enrichment include Texas Instruments, IBM, and General Foods. Job enrichment is also being used in some banks today, with employees in branches being trained to work as tellers, open new accounts, and accept loan applications. By training all of its employees to perform multiple tasks, Orlando-based Anderen Bank has been able to reduce the average number of employees at each of its branches from

job rotation
An alternative to job specialization that involves systematically moving employees from one job to another

job enlargement
An alternative to job specialization that involves giving the employee more tasks to perform

job enrichment
An alternative to job specialization that involves increasing both the number of tasks the worker does and the control the worker has over the job

10 to four.[17] This approach, however, also has disadvantages. For example, work systems need to be analyzed before enrichment, but this seldom happens, and managers rarely ask for employee preferences when enriching jobs. And note that while Anderen Bank employees get to do more tasks and have greater responsibility, the firm's goal was to lower labor cost. The impact of the changes on employee morale, performance, and turnover have not been assessed.

Job Characteristics Approach The **job characteristics approach** is an alternative to job specialization that does take into account the work system and employee preferences.[18] As illustrated in Figure 14.1, the job characteristics approach suggests that jobs should be diagnosed and improved along five core dimensions:

1. *Skill variety*, the number of things a person does in a job
2. *Task identity*, the extent to which the worker does a complete or identifiable portion of the total job
3. *Task significance*, the perceived importance of the task
4. *Autonomy*, the degree of control the worker has over how the work is performed
5. *Feedback*, the extent to which the worker knows how well the job is being performed

FIGURE 14.1 THE JOB CHARACTERISTICS APPROACH

The job characteristics approach to job design provides a viable alternative to job specialization. Five core job dimensions may lead to critical psychological states that, in turn, may enhance motivation, performance, and satisfaction while also reducing absenteeism and turnover.

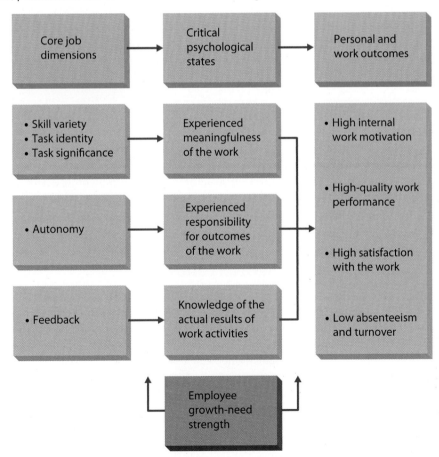

Source: J. R. Hackman and G. R. Oldham, "Motivation Through the Design of Work: Test of a Theory," *Organizational Behavior and Human Performance*, Vol. 16 (1976), pp. 250–279. Copyright © Academic Press, Inc. Reprinted by permission of Academic Press and the authors.

job characteristics approach
An alternative to job specialization that suggests that jobs should be diagnosed and improved along five core dimensions, taking into account both the work system and employee preferences

The higher a job rates on those dimensions, the more employees will experience various psychological states. Experiencing these states, in turn, presumably leads to high motivation, high-quality performance, high satisfaction, and low absenteeism and turnover. Finally, a concept called *growth-need strength* is presumed to affect how the model works for different people. People with a strong desire to grow, develop, and expand their capabilities (indicative of high growth-need strength) are expected to respond strongly to the presence or absence of the basic job characteristics; individuals with low growth-need strength are expected not to respond as strongly or consistently.

A large number of studies have been conducted to test the usefulness of the job characteristics approach. The Southwestern Division of Prudential Insurance, for example, used this approach in its claims division. Results included moderate declines in turnover and a small but measurable improvement in work quality. Other research findings have not supported this approach as strongly. Thus, although the job characteristics approach is one of the most promising alternatives to job specialization, it is probably not the final answer.

Work Teams Another alternative to job specialization is **work teams**. Under this arrangement, a group is given responsibility for designing the work system to be used in performing an interrelated set of tasks. In the typical assembly-line system, the work flows from one worker to the next, and each worker has a specified job to perform. In a work team, however, the group itself decides how jobs will be allocated. For example, the work team assigns specific tasks to members, monitors and controls its own performance, and has autonomy over work scheduling.[19] We discuss work teams more fully in Chapter 22.

What are the basic job design alternatives?

Which kind of job design best describes a job you have recently held? Do you agree or disagree with the text's assessment of that job design?

Grouping Jobs: Departmentalization

The second building block of organization structure is the grouping of jobs according to some logical arrangement. The process of grouping jobs is called **departmentalization**. After establishing the basic rationale for departmentalization, we identify some common bases along which departments are created.[20]

Rationale for Departmentalization

When organizations are small, the owner–manager can personally oversee everyone who works there. As an organization grows, however, personally supervising all the employees becomes more and more difficult for the owner–manager. Consequently, new managerial positions are created to supervise the work of others. Employees are not assigned to particular managers randomly. Rather, jobs are grouped according to some plan. The logic embodied in such a plan is the basis for all departmentalization.[21]

Common Bases for Departmentalization

Figure 14.2 presents a partial organizational chart for Apex Computers, a hypothetical firm that manufactures and sells computers and software. The chart shows that Apex uses each of the four most common bases for departmentalization: function, product, customer, and location.

work team
An alternative to job specialization that allows an entire group to design the work system it will use to perform an interrelated set of tasks

departmentalization
The process of grouping jobs according to some logical arrangement

FIGURE 14.2 BASES FOR DEPARTMENTALIZATION

Organizations group jobs into departments. Apex, a hypothetical organization, uses all four of the primary bases of departmentalization—function, product, customer, and location. Like Apex, most large organizations use more than one type of departmentalization.

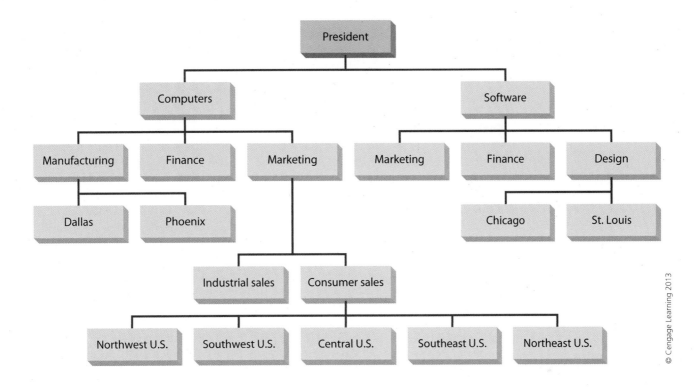

© Cengage Learning 2013

Functional Departmentalization The most common base for departmentalization, especially among smaller organizations, is by function. Functional departmentalization groups together those jobs involving the same or similar activities. (The word *function* is used here to mean organizational functions such as finance and production, rather than the basic managerial functions, such as planning or controlling.) The computer department at Apex has manufacturing, finance, and marketing departments, each an organizational function.

This approach, which is most common in smaller organizations, has three primary advantages. First, each department can be staffed by experts in that functional area. Marketing experts can be hired to run the marketing function, for example. Second, supervision is facilitated because an individual manager needs to be familiar with only a relatively narrow set of skills. And, third, coordinating activities inside each department is easier.

On the other hand, as an organization begins to grow in size, several disadvantages of this approach may emerge. For one, decision making tends to become slower and more bureaucratic. Employees may also begin to concentrate too narrowly on their own unit and lose sight of the total organizational system. Finally, accountability and performance become increasingly difficult to monitor. For example, determining whether a new product fails because of production deficiencies or a poor marketing campaign may not be possible.

Product Departmentalization Product departmentalization, a second common approach, involves grouping and arranging activities around products or product groups. Apex Computers has two product-based departments at the highest level of the firm. One is responsible for all activities associated with Apex's personal computer business, and the other handles the software business. Most larger businesses adopt this form of departmentalization for grouping activities at the business or corporate level.

functional departmentalization
Grouping jobs involving the same or similar activities

product departmentalization
Grouping activities around products or product groups

Product departmentalization has three major advantages. First, all activities associated with one product or product group can be easily integrated and coordinated. Second, the speed and effectiveness of decision making are enhanced. Third, the performance of individual products or product groups can be assessed more easily and objectively, thereby improving the accountability of departments for the results of their activities.

Product departmentalization also has two major disadvantages. For one, managers in each department may focus on their own product or product group to the exclusion of the rest of the organization. For example, a marketing manager may see her or his primary duty as helping the group rather than helping the overall organization. For another, administrative costs rise because each department must have its own functional specialists for areas such as market research and financial analysis.

Customer Departmentalization Under customer departmentalization, the organization structures its activities to respond to and interact with specific customers or customer groups. The lending activities in most banks, for example, are usually tailored to meet the needs of different kinds of customers (business, consumer, mortgage, and agricultural loans). Figure 14.2 shows that the marketing branch of Apex's computer business has two distinct departments—industrial sales and consumer sales. The industrial sales department handles marketing activities aimed at business customers, whereas the consumer sales department is responsible for wholesaling computers to retail stores catering to individual purchasers.

The basic advantage of this approach is that the organization is able to use skilled specialists to deal with unique customers or customer groups. It takes one set of skills to evaluate a balance sheet and lend a business $500,000 for operating capital, and a different set of skills to evaluate an individual's creditworthiness and lend $20,000 for a new car. However, a fairly large administrative staff is required to integrate the activities of the various departments. In banks, for example, coordination is necessary to make sure that the organization does not over-commit itself in any one area and to handle collections on delinquent accounts from a diverse set of customers.

Location Departmentalization Location departmentalization groups jobs on the basis of defined geographic sites or areas. The defined sites or areas may range in size from a hemisphere to only a few blocks of a large city. The manufacturing branch of Apex's computer business has two plants—one in Dallas and another in Phoenix. Similarly, the design division of its software design unit has two labs—one in Chicago and the other in St. Louis. Apex's consumer sales group has five sales territories corresponding to different regions of the United States. Transportation companies, police departments (precincts represent geographic areas of a city), and the Federal Reserve Bank all use location departmentalization.

The primary advantage of location departmentalization is that it enables the organization to respond easily to unique customer and environmental characteristics in the various regions. On the negative side, a larger administrative staff may be required if the organization must keep track of units in scattered locations.

Other Forms of Departmentalization Although most organizations are departmentalized by function, product, customer, or location, other forms are occasionally used. Some organizations group certain activities by time. One of the machine shops of Baker Hughes in Houston, for example, operates on three shifts. Each shift has a superintendent who reports to the plant manager, and each shift has its own functional departments. Time is thus the framework for many organizational activities. Other organizations that use time as a basis for grouping jobs include some hospitals and many airlines. In other situations, departmentalization by sequence is appropriate. Many college students, for instance, must register in sequence: seniors on Monday, juniors on Tuesday, and so on. Other areas that may be organized in sequence include credit departments (specific employees run credit checks according to customer name) and insurance claims divisions (by policy number).

customer departmentalization
Grouping activities to respond to and interact with specific customers or customer groups

location departmentalization
Grouping jobs on the basis of defined geographic sites or areas

Other Considerations Two final points about job grouping remain to be made. First, departments are often called something entirely different—*divisions, units, sections,* and *bureaus* are all common synonyms. The higher we look in an organization, the more likely we are to find departments referred to as divisions. H. J. Heinz, for example, is organized into five major divisions. Nevertheless, the underlying logic behind all the labels is the same: They represent groups of jobs that have been yoked together according to some unifying principle. Second, almost any organization is likely to employ multiple bases of departmentalization, depending on level. Although Apex Computer is a hypothetical firm that we created to explain departmentalization, it is quite similar to many real organizations in that it uses a variety of bases of departmentalization for different levels and different sets of activities.

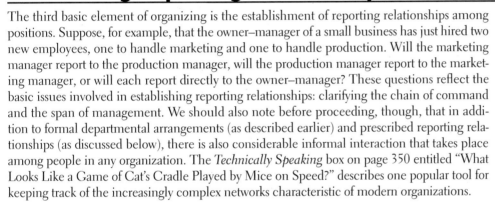

What are the common bases of departmentalization?

Identify an organization with which you have some familiarity. Based on your knowledge of the firm, describe how it is departmentalized.

Establishing Reporting Relationships

The third basic element of organizing is the establishment of reporting relationships among positions. Suppose, for example, that the owner–manager of a small business has just hired two new employees, one to handle marketing and one to handle production. Will the marketing manager report to the production manager, will the production manager report to the marketing manager, or will each report directly to the owner–manager? These questions reflect the basic issues involved in establishing reporting relationships: clarifying the chain of command and the span of management. We should also note before proceeding, though, that in addition to formal departmental arrangements (as described earlier) and prescribed reporting relationships (as discussed below), there is also considerable informal interaction that takes place among people in any organization. The *Technically Speaking* box on page 350 entitled "What Looks Like a Game of Cat's Cradle Played by Mice on Speed?" describes one popular tool for keeping track of the increasingly complex networks characteristic of modern organizations.

Chain of Command

Chain of command is an old concept, first popularized in the early years of the twentieth century. For example, early writers on the chain of command argued that clear and distinct lines of authority need to be established among all positions in an organization. The chain of command actually has two components. The first, called *unity of command*, suggests that each person within an organization must have a clear reporting relationship to one and only one boss (as we see in Chapter 15, newer models of organization design routinely—and successfully—violate this premise). The second, called the *scalar principle*, suggests that there must be a clear and unbroken line of authority that extends from the lowest to the highest position in the organization. The popular saying "The buck stops here" is derived from this idea—someone in the organization must ultimately be responsible for every decision.

chain of command
A clear and distinct line of authority among the positions in an organization

Narrow Versus Wide Spans

Another part of establishing reporting relationships is determining how many people will report to each manager. This defines the span of management (sometimes called the *span of control*). For years, managers and researchers sought to determine the optimal span of management. For example, should it be relatively narrow (with few subordinates per manager) or relatively wide

span of management
The number of people who report to a particular manager

TECHNICALLY SPEAKING

What Looks Like a Game of Cat's Cradle Played by Mice on Speed?

It's little wonder that the traditional organization chart, which displays formal lines of reporting, is becoming obsolete: In many organizations, the interconnections among people and positions tend to be much less formal than they used to be. What today's organization needs is a tool that charts its *informal* networks. That's what *social network analysis (SNA)* is designed to do.

SNA studies how people interact—who interacts, type and frequency of interactions, levels of trust, and so on. Unlike a conventional organization chart, an SNA chart resembles a spider web, with each node representing an individual and each line representing an interaction. An SNA chart, says Nion McEvoy, CEO of a small firm that underwent SNA, "looks like an advanced game of cat's cradle played by mice on speed."

Not surprisingly, SNA charts perform a lot of functions that the typical organization chart doesn't. They can, for example, pinpoint individuals whose contributions are especially valuable even if their formal positions suggest otherwise. They can identify top managers and whole units whose useful interactions are too limited because their activities are too remote from basic company operations. They can track down "bottlenecks"—people who have too many connections because too many people depend on them. They can focus on an employee who's not getting the recognition that he or she deserves because a manager is too inaccessible.

Management consultant Karen Stephenson founded NetForm International in 1997 to produce SNA software for businesses, but she prefers to work hands-on with clients. "In the work space," she says, "you've got to be able to see others and see where it is you work, why you're working there, and who it is you can interconnect and collaborate with." In 2008, for example, when San Francisco publisher Chronicle Books was preparing to move into a four-story former ironworks factory, creative director Michael Carabetta called on Stephenson for advice. He was intrigued by her concept that "organizations have their own kind of structure"—that "what you see on the flowchart of a company isn't necessarily how the work gets done."

Working closely with Chronicle's architects, Stephenson helped to fashion a workspace designed to foster interaction. Reflecting relationships rather than conventional hierarchies, Chronicle's facility takes advantage of atrium-like spaces and open stairwells to make sure that connections are vertical as well as horizontal. Employees in departments that collaborate frequently occupy airy workstations placed along open aisles. Senior offices are glass-walled and interspersed throughout the building. Carabetta is happy with the results: "There's much more democracy in terms of ideas flowing back and forth," he reports. "This has been a means to dissolve any of those real or alleged silos that can evolve in a company when it matures."

References: Rob Cross, Andrew Parker, and Stephen P. Borgatti, "A Bird's-Eye View: Using Social Network Analysis to Improve Knowledge Creation and Sharing," IBM Institute for Business Value, www.steveborgatti.com on March 15, 2011; Jena McGregor, "The Office Chart That Really Counts," *BusinessWeek*, February 27, 2006, www.businessweek.com on March 15, 2011; Ethan Watters, "The Organization Woman," *Business 2.0*, April 28, 2006, http://money.cnn.com on March 15, 2011; "A Quantum Theory of Trust," *TotalPicture Radio*, March 22, 2010, www.totalpicture.com on March 15, 2011; Karen Stephenson, keynote presentation, 2010 NTL Annual Meeting, August 27, 2010, https://custom.cvent.com on March 15, 2010; Kristin Palm, "Capturing Culture," *MetropolisMag.com*, June 2008, www.metropolismag.com on March 15, 2011.

(with many subordinates)? One early writer, A. V. Graicunas, went so far as to quantify span of management issues.[22] Graicunas noted that a manager must deal with three kinds of interactions with and among subordinates: direct (the manager's one-to-one relationship with each subordinate), cross (among the subordinates themselves), and group (between groups of subordinates).

The number of possible interactions of all types between a manager and subordinates can be determined by the following formula:

$$I = N(2^N/2 + N - 1)$$

where I is the total number of interactions with and among subordinates and N is the number of subordinates.

If a manager has only two subordinates, six potential interactions exist. If the number of subordinates increases to three, the possible interactions total 18. With five subordinates, there are 100 possible interactions. Although Graicunas offers no prescription for what N should be, his ideas demonstrate how complex the relationships become when more subordinates are added. The important point is that each additional subordinate adds more complexity than the previous one did. Going from nine to ten subordinates is very different from going from three to four.

Another early writer, Ralph C. Davis, described two kinds of spans: an operative span for lower-level managers and an executive span for middle and top managers. He argued that operative spans could approach 30 subordinates, whereas executive spans should be limited to between three and nine (depending on the nature of the managers' jobs, the growth rate of the company, and similar factors). Lyndall F. Urwick suggested that an executive span should never exceed six subordinates, and General Ian Hamilton reached the same conclusion.[23] Today we recognize that the span of management is a crucial factor in structuring organizations but that there are no universal, cut-and-dried prescriptions for an ideal or optimal span.[24] Later we summarize some important variables that influence the appropriate span of management in a particular situation. First, however, we describe how the span of management affects the overall structure of an organization.

Tall Versus Flat Organizations

Imagine an organization with 31 managers and a narrow span of management. As shown in Figure 14.3, the result is a relatively tall organization with five layers of management. With a somewhat wider span of management, however, the flat organization shown in Figure 14.3 emerges. This configuration has only three layers of management.

What difference does it make whether the organization is tall or flat? One early study at Sears found that a flat structure led to higher levels of employee morale and productivity.[25] Researchers have also argued that a tall structure is more expensive (because of the larger number of managers involved) and that it fosters more communication problems (because of the increased number of people through whom information must pass). On the other hand, a wide span of management in a flat organization may result in a manager's having more administrative responsibility (because there are fewer managers) and more supervisory responsibility (because there are more subordinates reporting to each manager). If these additional responsibilities become excessive, the flat organization may suffer.[26]

Many experts agree that businesses can function effectively with fewer layers of organization than they currently have. The Franklin Mint, for example, reduced its number of management layers from six to four. At the same time, the CEO increased his span of management from six to 12. In similar fashion, IBM has eliminated several layers of management. The British firm Cadbury PLC, maker of Cadbury Dairy chocolates, Trident gum, and other confectionary products, recently eliminated a layer of management separating the CEO and the firm's operating units. And Allergan announced in 2011 that a major reorganization will result in the elimination of an organizational layer to maintain the company's lean and efficient business model.[27] The specific reasons for the change were to improve communication between the CEO and the operating unit heads and to speed up decision making.[28] One additional reason for this trend is that improved communication technologies such as e-mail and text messaging allow managers to stay in touch with a larger number of subordinates than was possible even just a few years ago.[29]

FIGURE 14.3 TALL VERSUS FLAT ORGANIZATIONS

Wide spans of management result in flat organizations, which may lead to improved employee morale and productivity as well as increased managerial responsibility. Many organizations today, including IBM and General Electric, are moving toward flat structures to improve communication and flexibility.

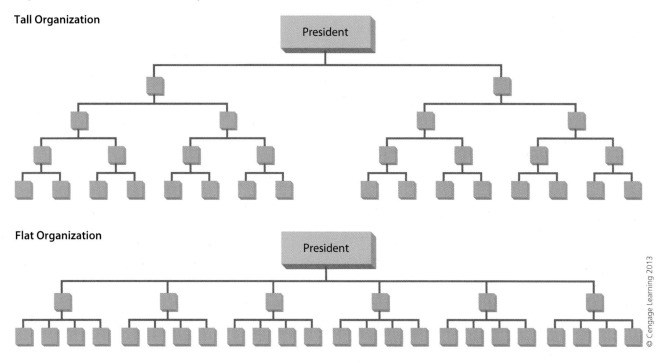

Determining the Appropriate Span

Of course, the initial question remains: How do managers determine the appropriate span for their unique situation? Although no perfect formula exists, researchers have identified a set of factors that influence the span for a particular circumstance.[30] Some of these factors are listed in Table 14.1. For example, if the manager and subordinates are competent and well trained, a wide span may be effective. Physical dispersion is also important. The more widely subordinates are scattered, the narrower the span should be. On the other hand,

TABLE 14.1 FACTORS INFLUENCING THE SPAN OF MANAGEMENT

Although researchers have found advantages to the flat organization (less expensive and with fewer communication problems than a tall organization, for example), a number of factors may favor a tall organization.

1. Competence of supervisor and subordinates (the greater the competence, the wider the potential span)
2. Physical dispersion of subordinates (the greater the dispersion, the narrower the potential span)
3. Extent of nonsupervisory work in manager's job (the more nonsupervisory work, the narrower the potential span)
4. Degree of required interaction (the less required interaction, the wider the potential span)
5. Extent of standardized procedures (the more procedures, the wider the potential span)
6. Similarity of tasks being supervised (the more similar the tasks, the wider the potential span)
7. Frequency of new problems (the higher the frequency, the narrower the potential span)
8. Preferences of supervisors and subordinates

© Cengage Learning 2013

if all the subordinates are in one location, the span can be somewhat wider. The amount of nonsupervisory work expected of the manager is also important. Some managers, especially at the lower levels of an organization, spend most or all of their time supervising subordinates. Other managers spend a lot of time doing paperwork, planning, and engaging in other managerial activities. Thus these managers may need a narrower span.

Some job situations also require a great deal of interaction between supervisor and subordinates. In general, the more interaction that is required, the narrower the span should be. Similarly, if there is a fairly comprehensive set of standard procedures, a relatively wide span is possible. If only a few standard procedures exist, however, the supervisor usually has to play a larger role in overseeing day-to-day activities and may find a narrower span more efficient. Task similarity is also important. If most of the jobs

Case manufactures a wide array of farm equipment. While this equipment was once highly standardized, today much of it is custom-built in much the same way as an automobile. This tractor, for example, has a glass-enclosed cabin, airconditioning, and a CD player.

LUDOVIC/REA/Redux

being supervised are similar, a supervisor can handle a wider span. When each employee is performing a different task, more of the supervisor's time is spent on individual supervision. Likewise, if new problems that require supervisory assistance arise frequently, a narrower span may be called for. If new problems are relatively rare, though, a wider span can be established. Finally, the preferences of both supervisor and subordinates may affect the optimal span. Some managers prefer to spend less time actively supervising their employees, and many employees prefer to be more self-directed in their jobs. A wider span may be possible in these situations.

For example, the Case Corporation factory in Racine, Wisconsin, makes farm tractors exclusively to order in five to six weeks. Farmers can select from among a wide array of options, including engines, tires, power trains, and even a CD player. A wide assortment of machines and processes is used to construct each tractor. Although workers are highly skilled operators of their particular machines, each machine is different. In this kind of setup, the complexities of each machine and the advanced skills needed by each operator mean that one supervisor can oversee only a small number of employees.[31]

In some organizational settings, other factors may influence the optimal span of management. The relative importance of each factor also varies in different settings. It is unlikely that all eight factors will suggest the same span; some may suggest a wider span, and others may indicate a need for a narrow span. Hence, managers must assess the relative weight of each factor or set of factors when deciding the optimal span of management for their unique situation.

What factors determine the appropriate span of management for a particular setting?

In your opinion, how important is it to have a clear and unambiguous chain of command? Why?

CONCEPT CHECK

Distributing Authority

Another important building block in structuring organizations is the determination of how authority is to be distributed among positions. **Authority** is power that has been legitimized by the organization.[32] Distributing authority is another normal outgrowth of increasing organizational size. For example, when an owner–manager hires a sales representative to market his products, he needs to give the new employee appropriate authority to make decisions about delivery dates, discounts, and so forth. If every decision requires the approval of the owner–manager, he is no better off than he was before he hired the sales representative. The power given to the sales representative to make certain kinds of decisions, then, represents the establishment of a pattern of authority—the sales representative can make some decisions alone and others in consultation with coworkers, and the sales representative must defer some decisions to the boss. Two specific issues that managers must address when distributing authority are delegation and decentralization.[33]

The Delegation Process

Delegation is the establishment of a pattern of authority between a superior and one or more subordinates. Specifically, **delegation** is the process by which managers assign a portion of their total workload to others.[34]

Reasons for Delegation The primary reason for delegation is to enable the manager to get more work done. Subordinates help ease the manager's burden by doing major portions of the organization's work. In some instances, a subordinate may have more expertise in addressing a particular problem than the manager does. For example, the subordinate may have had special training in developing information systems or may be more familiar with a particular product line or geographic area. Delegation also helps develop subordinates. By participating in decision making and problem solving, subordinates learn about overall operations and improve their managerial skills.

Parts of the Delegation Process In theory, as shown in Figure 14.4, the delegation process involves three steps. First, the manager assigns responsibility or gives the subordinate a job to do. The assignment of responsibility might range from telling a subordinate to prepare a report to placing the person in charge of a task force. Along with the assignment, the individual is also given the authority to do the job. The manager may give the subordinate the power to requisition needed information from confidential files or to direct a group of other workers.

FIGURE 14.4 STEPS IN THE DELEGATION PROCESS

Good communication skills can help a manager successfully delegate responsibility to subordinates. A manager must not be reluctant to delegate, nor should he or she fear that the subordinate will do the job so well that the manager's advancement is threatened.

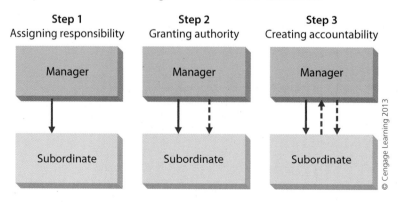

authority
Power that has been legitimized by the organization

delegation
The process by which managers assign work to subordinates

Finally, the manager establishes the subordinate's accountability—that is, the subordinate accepts an obligation to carry out the task assigned by the manager. For instance, the CEO of AutoZone will sign off for the company on financial performance only when the individual manager responsible for each unit has certified his or her own results as being accurate. The firm believes that this high level of accountability will help it avoid the kind of accounting scandal that has hit many businesses in recent times.[35]

These three steps do not occur mechanically, however. Indeed, when a manager and a subordinate have developed a good working relationship, the major parts of the process may be implied rather than stated. The manager may simply mention that a particular job must be done. A perceptive subordinate may realize that the manager is actually assigning the job to her. From past experience with the boss, she may also know, without being told, that she has the necessary authority to do the job and that she is accountable to the boss for finishing the job as "agreed."

Problems in Delegation Unfortunately, problems often arise in the delegation process. For example, a manager may be reluctant to delegate. Some managers are so disorganized that they are unable to plan work in advance and, as a result, cannot delegate appropriately. Similarly, some managers may worry that subordinates will do too well and pose a threat to their own advancement. And, finally, managers may not trust the subordinate to do the job well. Similarly, some subordinates are reluctant to accept delegation. They may be afraid that failure will result in a reprimand. They may also perceive that there are no rewards for accepting additional responsibility. Or they may simply prefer to avoid risk and therefore want their boss to take all responsibility.

There are no quick fixes for these problems. The basic issue is communication. Subordinates must understand their own responsibility, authority, and accountability, and the manager must come to recognize the value of effective delegation. With the passage of time, subordinates should develop to the point at which they can make substantial contributions to the organization. At the same time, managers should recognize that a subordinate's satisfactory performance is not a threat to their own career, but an accomplishment by both the subordinate who did the job and the manager who trained the subordinate and was astute enough to entrust the subordinate with the project. Ultimate responsibility for the outcome, however, continues to reside with the manager.

Richard Branson, the founder of Virgin Records and now the owner of over 300 companies within the Virgin Group, learned the importance of delegation early in his career. When Virgin Records first began, employees had the freedom to take charge of any responsibilities they had the ability and desire to do. However, as the employee count reached 100, Branson feared the company was becoming too slow. To maintain employee flexibility but prevent slowdown, he split the company in half and pinpointed talented employees from Virgin Records to run it. Branson has continued this strategy as his empire has grown, identifying employees with management potential and fostering employee empowerment through systematic delegation.[36]

Decentralization and Centralization

Just as authority can be delegated from one individual to another, organizations also develop patterns of authority across a wide variety of positions and departments. Decentralization is the process of systematically delegating power and authority throughout the organization to middle and lower-level managers. It is important to remember that decentralization is actually one end of a continuum anchored at the other end by centralization, the process of systematically retaining power and authority in the hands of higher-level managers. Hence, a decentralized organization is one in which decision-making power and authority are delegated as far down the chain of command as possible. Conversely, in a centralized organization, decision-making power and authority are retained at the higher levels of management. When H. Ross Perot ran EDS, he practiced centralization; his successors have used decentralization. No organization is ever completely decentralized or completely centralized; some firms position themselves toward one end of the continuum, and some lean the other way.[37]

What factors determine an organization's position on the decentralization–centralization continuum? One common determinant is the organization's external environment.

decentralization
The process of systematically delegating power and authority throughout the organization to middle and lower-level managers

centralization
The process of systematically retaining power and authority in the hands of higher-level managers

Usually, the greater the complexity and uncertainty of the environment, the greater is the tendency to decentralize. Another crucial factor is the history of the organization. Firms have a tendency to do what they have done in the past, so there is likely to be some relationship between what an organization did in its early history and what it chooses to do today in terms of centralization or decentralization. The nature of the decisions being made is also considered. The costlier and riskier the decisions, the more pressure there is to centralize. Organizations also consider the abilities of lower-level managers. If lower-level managers do not have the ability to make high-quality decisions, there is likely to be a high level of centralization. If lower-level managers are well qualified, top management can take advantage of their talents by decentralizing; in fact, if top management does not, talented lower-level managers may leave the organization.[38]

A manager has no clear-cut guidelines for determining whether to centralize or decentralize. Many successful organizations, such as General Electric and Johnson & Johnson, are quite decentralized. Equally successful firms, such as McDonald's and Walmart, have remained centralized. IBM has recently undergone a transformation from using a highly centralized approach to a much more decentralized approach to managing its operations. A great deal of decision-making authority was passed from the hands of a select group of top executives down to six product and marketing groups. The reason for the move was to speed the company's ability to make decisions, introduce new products, and respond to customers. In contrast, Royal Dutch Shell, long operated in a highly decentralized manner, has recently gone through several major changes, all intended to make the firm more centralized. New CEO Peter Voser went so far as to note that "fewer people will make strategic decisions."[39] Yahoo Inc. has also initiated a change to become more centralized.[40]

> "When you have command and control by the top 10 people, you can only do one or two things at a time. The future is about collaboration and teamwork and making decisions with a process that offers scale, speed, and flexibility."
>
> —JOHN CHAMBERS, CISCO CEO[41]

CONCEPT CHECK

What are the steps in the delegation process?

Under what circumstances would you prefer to work in a centralized organization? In a decentralized organization?

Coordinating Activities

A fifth major element of organizing is coordination. As we discuss earlier, job specialization and departmentalization involve breaking jobs down into small units and then combining those jobs into departments. Once this has been accomplished, the activities of the departments must be linked—systems must be put into place to keep the activities of each department focused on the attainment of organizational goals. This is accomplished by coordination—the process of linking the activities of the various departments of the organization.[42]

The Need for Coordination

The primary reason for coordination is that departments and work groups are interdependent—they depend on one another for information and resources to perform their respective activities. The greater the interdependence between departments, the more coordination the organization requires if departments are to be able to perform effectively. There are three major forms of interdependence: pooled, sequential, and reciprocal.[43]

Pooled interdependence represents the lowest level of interdependence. Units with pooled interdependence operate with little interaction—the output of the units is pooled

coordination
The process of linking the activities of the various departments of the organization

pooled interdependence
When units operate with little interaction; their output is simply pooled

at the organizational level. Gap clothing stores operate with pooled interdependence. Each store is considered a "department" by the parent corporation. Each has its own operating budget, staff, and so forth. The profits or losses from each store are "added together" at the organizational level. The stores are interdependent to the extent that the final success or failure of one store affects the others, but they do not generally interact on a day-to-day basis.

In sequential interdependence, the output of one unit becomes the input for another in a sequential fashion. This creates a moderate level of interdependence. At Nissan, for example, one plant assembles engines and then ships them to a final assembly site at another plant, where the cars are completed. The plants are interdependent in that the final assembly plant must have the engines from engine assembly before it can perform its primary function of producing finished automobiles. But the level of interdependence is generally one way—the engine plant is not necessarily dependent on the final assembly plant.

Reciprocal interdependence exists when activities flow both ways between units. This form is clearly the most complex. Within a Marriott hotel, for example, the reservations department, front-desk check-in, and housekeeping are all reciprocally interdependent. Reservations has to provide front-desk employees with information about how many guests to expect each day, and housekeeping needs to know which rooms require priority cleaning. If any of the three units does not do its job properly, all the others will be affected.

Structural Coordination Techniques

Because of the obvious coordination requirements that characterize most organizations, many techniques for achieving coordination have been developed. Some of the most useful devices for maintaining coordination among interdependent units are the managerial hierarchy, rules and procedures, liaison roles, task forces, and integrating departments.[44]

The Managerial Hierarchy Organizations that use the hierarchy to achieve coordination place one manager in charge of interdependent departments or units. In Walmart distribution centers, major activities include receiving and unloading bulk shipments from railroad cars and loading other shipments onto trucks for distribution to retail outlets. The two groups (receiving and shipping) are interdependent in that they share the loading docks and some equipment. To ensure coordination and minimize conflict, one manager is in charge of the whole operation.

Rules and Procedures Routine coordination activities can be handled via rules and standard procedures. In the Walmart distribution center, an outgoing truck shipment has priority over an incoming rail shipment. Thus, when trucks are to be loaded, the shipping unit is given access to all of the center's auxiliary forklifts. This priority is specifically stated in a rule. But, as useful as rules and procedures often are in routine situations, they are not particularly effective when coordination problems are complex or unusual.

Liaison Roles We introduced the liaison role of management in Chapter 1. As a device for coordination, a manager in a liaison role coordinates interdependent units by acting as a common point of contact. This individual may not have any formal authority over the groups but instead simply facilitates the flow of information between units. Two engineering groups working on component systems for a large project might interact through a liaison. The

sequential interdependence
When the output of one unit becomes the input for another in sequential fashion

reciprocal interdependence
When activities flow both ways between units

Most warehouse and distribution centers have detailed rules and procedures that specify how inventory is to be brought into and removed from the facility. This forklift operator, for example, is following a written set of procedures about how to stack boxes of inventory on storage shelves.

liaison maintains familiarity with each group as well as with the overall project. She can answer questions and otherwise serve to integrate the activities of all the groups.

Task Forces A task force may be created when the need for coordination is acute. When interdependence is complex and several units are involved, a single liaison person may not be sufficient. Instead, a task force might be assembled by drawing one representative from each group. The coordination function is thus spread across several individuals, each of whom has special information about one of the groups involved. When the project is completed, task force members return to their original positions. For example, a college overhauling its degree requirements might establish a task force made up of representatives from each department affected by the change. Each person retains her or his regular departmental affiliation and duties but also serves on the special task force. After the new requirements are agreed on, the task force is dissolved.

Integrating Departments Integrating departments are occasionally used for coordination. These are somewhat similar to task forces but are more permanent. An integrating department generally has some permanent members as well as members who are assigned temporarily from units that are particularly in need of coordination. One study found that successful firms in the plastics industry, which is characterized by complex and dynamic environments, used integrating departments to maintain internal integration and coordination.[45] An integrating department usually has more authority than a task force and may even be given some budgetary control by the organization.

In general, the greater the degree of interdependence, the more attention the organization must devote to coordination. When interdependence is pooled or simple sequential, the managerial hierarchy or rules and procedures are often sufficient. When more complex forms of sequential or simpler forms of reciprocal interdependence exist, liaisons or task forces may be more useful. When reciprocal interdependence is complex, task forces or integrating departments are needed. Of course, the manager must also rely on her or his own experience and insights when choosing coordination techniques for the organization. Moreover, informal interactions among people throughout the organization can also serve to effectively coordinate activities.

Electronic Coordination

Recent advances in electronic information technology are also providing useful mechanisms for coordination. E-mail, for example, makes it easier for people to communicate with one another. This communication, in turn, enhances coordination. Similarly, many people in organizations today use electronic scheduling, at least some of which is accessible to others. Hence, if someone needs to set up a meeting with two colleagues, he can often check their electronic schedules to determine their availability, making it easier to coordinate their activities.

Local networks, increasingly managed by hand-held electronic devices, are also making it easier to coordinate activities. Bechtel, for example, now requires its contractors, subcontractors, and suppliers to use a common web-based communication system to improve coordination among their myriad activities. The firm estimates that this improved coordination technology routinely saves it thousands of dollars on every big construction project it undertakes.

What are the three kinds of interdependence that necessitate coordination?

In the future, do you think electronic coordination will eliminate the need for structural coordination?

Differentiating Between Positions

The last building block of organization structure is differentiating between line and staff positions in the organization. A **line position** is a position in the direct chain of command that is responsible for the achievement of an organization's goals. A **staff position** is intended to provide expertise, advice, and support for line positions. In many modern organizations these differences are beginning to disappear, and in a few the difference has been eliminated altogether. However, there are still sufficient meaningful differences to warrant discussion.

Differences Between Line and Staff

The most obvious difference between line and staff is purpose—line managers work directly toward organizational goals, whereas staff managers advise and assist. But other distinctions exist as well. One important difference is authority. Line authority is generally thought of as the formal or legitimate authority created by the organizational hierarchy. Staff authority is less concrete and may take a variety of forms. One form is *advise authority*. In this instance, the line manager can choose whether to seek or to avoid input from staff; and even when advice is sought, the line manager might still choose to ignore it.

Another form of staff authority is called *compulsory advice*. In this case, the line manager must consider the advice but can choose to heed it or ignore it. For example, the pope is expected to listen to the advice of the Sacred College of Cardinals when dealing with church doctrine, but he may follow his own beliefs when making decisions. Perhaps the most important form of staff authority is called *functional authority*—formal or legitimate authority over activities related to the staff member's specialty. For example, a human resource staff manager may have functional authority when there is a question of discrimination in hiring. Conferring functional authority is probably the most effective way to use staff positions because the organization is able to take advantage of specialized expertise while also maintaining a chain of command. The *Ethically Speaking* box entitled "A Panel of Your Peers" on page 360 shows how the chief ethics officer at a major corporation exercises her staff authority.

Administrative Intensity

Organizations sometimes attempt to balance their emphasis on line versus staff positions in terms of administrative intensity. **Administrative intensity** is the degree to which managerial positions are concentrated in staff positions. An organization with high administrative intensity is one with many staff positions relative to the number of line positions; low administrative intensity reflects relatively more line positions. Although staff positions are important in many different areas, they tend to proliferate unnecessarily. All else being equal, organizations would like to devote most of their human resource investment to line managers because, by definition, they contribute to the organization's basic goals. A surplus of staff positions represents a drain on an organization's cash and an inefficient use of resources.

Many organizations have taken steps over the past few years to reduce their administrative intensity by eliminating staff positions. CBS cut hundreds of staff positions at its New York headquarters, and IBM cut its corporate staff workforce from 7,000 to 2,300. Burlington Northern generates almost $7 billion in annual sales and manages a workforce of 43,000 with a corporate staff of only 77 managers. Ford and General Motors have both downsized dramatically through job cuts and plant closings.

line position
A position in the direct chain of command that is responsible for the achievement of an organization's goals

staff position
A position intended to provide expertise, advice, and support for line positions

administrative intensity
The degree to which managerial positions are concentrated in staff positions

---

What is the basic difference between line and staff positions?

Do you think an organization can function effectively with no staff whatsoever?

CONCEPT CHECK

ETHICALLY SPEAKING

A Panel of Your Peers

Tom England/istockphoto.com

Kathleen Edmond is chief ethics officer at Best Buy, the world's largest consumer-electronics retailer. With a legal background, Edmond first came to Best Buy in 2002, when she joined a newly established ethics office whose original purpose was to assist corporate officers in dealing with laws designed to regulate their behavior. The position, however, sparked Edmond's interest in the broader concerns of ethical business culture, and she stayed on to build an ethics office that works to encourage employees at all levels to give careful thought to ethics-related issues and activities.

In January 2009, Edmond posted the following exercise (which we've edited slightly) on her website at www.kathleenedmond.com:

> In 2008, a Best Buy Supervisor (a department manager responsible for seeing that merchandising and pricing standards are met) told a direct-report employee to put an "open item" tag on an unused, undamaged product. The tag would indicate that the product might later be priced at a markdown. The Supervisor explained that he was thinking about buying the product but wasn't sure and instructed the employee to put the "open item" price tag beneath a regular price tag until he'd made up his mind. The Supervisor did not buy this particular item but did buy other products at markdowns of 55–65 percent. As it happens, the employee who had been told to place the "open item" price tag on the new product rang up these purchases. He reported that when another

manager was called to the register to authorize the markdowns, he was assured by the Supervisor that the store's Product Process Manager (a higher-level manager responsible for merchandising, inventory, and loss prevention for the whole store) knew about the transaction. When questioned later about the purchases, the Supervisor confirmed that he'd spoken about them to the Product Process Manager. The Product Process Manager said that the Supervisor had indeed expressed an interest in buying some products but had provided no specifics about products or pricing.

At the end of this summary, Edmond addressed the following questions to Best Buy employees:

- What ethical missteps do you see in this story?
- Which of the Supervisor's actions were most alarming to you and why?
- Are there procedures in place that could prevent this from happening at your store?

Following established procedure, Edmond referred the dispute, at the Supervisor's request, to a Peer Review panel, which examined statements from all employees involved as well as the company's policy on Inappropriate Conduct. After a decision had been reached by the panel, Edmond posted its Decision Summary:

1. The discount applied was not consistent with other pricing of open-box items.
2. The pricing of the Supervisor's purchases seemed to be based on the fact that the Supervisor was purchasing them rather than on the condition of the products themselves.
3. Management was not involved in these pricing decisions.
4. The instructions to the subordinate to hide a price were considered.

So, what do you think? Given the factors considered by the Peer Review panel, what action should the company have taken?*

References: Ethics and Compliance Officer Association, "Kathleen Edmond, Chief Ethics Officer, Best Buy," Board of Directors, 2011, www.theecoa.org on April 20, 2011; Best Buy Inc., "Code of Business Ethics," 2008, www.bestbuyinc.com on April 20, 2011; Kathleen Edmond, "Supervisor Takes Massive Discounts," Kathleen Edmond, Best Buy's Chief Ethics Officer, January 13, 2009, www.kathleenedmond.com on April 20, 2011.

*In order to avoid prolonging what little suspense we've managed to build, we'll report that the Supervisor was terminated. In the interest of full disclosure, we'll also confess that we've slightly reconstructed the story: The decision to terminate the Supervisor was originally made by his superiors, and his request for a hearing before the Peer Review panel was actually made as an appeal to this decision.

Summary of Learning Objectives and Key Points

1. Identify the basic elements of organizations.

   - Organizations are made up of a series of elements:
     - designing jobs
     - grouping jobs
     - establishing reporting relationships
     - distributing authority
     - coordinating activities
     - differentiating between positions.

2. Describe the basic alternative approaches to designing jobs.

   - Job design is the determination of an individual's work-related responsibilities.
   - The most common form is job specialization.
   - Other alternatives include job rotation, job enlargement, job enrichment, the job characteristics approach, and work teams.

3. Discuss the rationale and the most common bases for grouping jobs into departments.

   - The most common bases for departmentalization are:
     - function
     - product
     - customer
     - location
     - large organizations employ multiple bases of departmentalization at different levels.

4. Describe the basic elements involved in establishing reporting relationships.

   - Establishing reporting relationships starts with clarifying the chain of command.
   - The span of management partially dictates whether the organization is relatively tall or flat.

   - In recent years there has been a trend toward flatter organizations.
   - Several situational factors influence the ideal span.

5. Discuss how authority is distributed in organizations.

   - Distributing authority starts with delegation.
   - Delegation is the process by which the manager assigns a portion of his or her total workload to others.
   - Systematic delegation throughout the organization is decentralization.
   - Centralization involves keeping power and authority at the top of the organization.
   - Several factors influence the appropriate degree of decentralization.

6. Discuss the basic coordinating activities undertaken by organizations.

   - Coordination is the process of linking the activities of the various departments of the organization.
   - Pooled, sequential, or reciprocal interdependence among departments is a primary reason for coordination.
   - Managers can draw on several techniques to help achieve coordination.
   - Electronic coordination is becoming increasingly important.

7. Describe basic ways in which positions within an organization can be differentiated.

   - A line position is a position in the direct chain of command that is responsible for the achievement of an organization's goals.
   - A staff position provides expertise, advice, and support for line positions.
   - Administrative intensity is the degree to which managerial positions are concentrated in staff positions.

Discussion Questions

Questions for Review

1. Describe the five alternatives to job specialization. What is the advantage of each, as compared to specialization?
2. What is meant by unity of command? By the scalar principle? Can an organization have one without the other? Explain.
3. Describe the organizational structure that results from each of the different bases of departmentalization. What implications does each of these structures have with regard to the distribution of authority within the organization?
4. Explain the differences between line and staff positions. What are the advantages and disadvantages of high versus low administrative intensity?

Questions for Analysis

5. Some people have claimed that the increasing techno-logical sophistication required by many of today's corporations has led to a return to job specialization. In your opinion, what would be the consequences of a sharp increase in job specialization? Consider both positive and negative outcomes in your answer.

6. Try to develop a different way to departmentalize your college or university, a local fast-food restaurant, a manufacturing firm, or some other organization. What might be the advantages of your form of organization?

7. Consider the list of jobs below. In your opinion, what is the appropriate span of management for each? Describe the factors you considered in reaching your conclusion.

- A physician practices medicine in a privately owned clinic while also supervising a number of professional nurses and office staff.
- An owner–manager of an auto body shop deals with customers, directs several experienced mechanics, and also trains and oversees the work of some unskilled laborers.
- A manager in an international advertising agency directs a team of professionals who are located in offices around the world.

Questions for Application

8. Consider a job you have held. (Or, if you have not held a job, interview a worker.) Using the job characteristics approach, assess that job's core dimensions. Then describe how the core dimensions led to critical psychological states and, ultimately, to personal and work outcomes.

9. Use the Internet to locate organization charts for five different organizations. (Or use data from the Internet to draw the organization charts yourself.) Look for similarities and differences among them and try to account for what you find.

10. Contact two very different local organizations (retailing firm, manufacturing firm, church, civic club, and so on) and interview top managers to develop organization charts for each organization. How do you account for the similarities and differences between them?

CengageNow™ Highlights

Now use your CengageNow™ homework to help you:
- Apply management theories in your life
- Assess your management skills
- Master management terms and concepts
- Apply your knowledge to real-world situations
- Analyze and solve challenging management problems

In order to take advantage of these elements, your instructor will need to have set up a course for your class within CengageNow™. Ask your instructor to contact his/her Cengage sales representative and Digital Solutions Manager to explore testing CengageNow™ in your course this term.

Managing Organization Design

LEARNING OBJECTIVES

After studying this chapter, you should be
able to:

1. Describe the basic nature of organization design.

2. Identify and explain two basic universal perspectives
   on organization design.

3. Identify and explain key situational influences on
   organization design.

4. Discuss how an organization's strategy and its
   design are interrelated.

5. Describe the basic forms of organization design.

6. Describe emerging issues in organization design.

MANAGEMENT IN ACTION   Authority & Function at A&F

Along with American Eagle and Aéropostale, Abercrombie & Fitch (A&F) is one of the "Three A's" of retailing for younger consumers—the three largest specialty retailers catering to young adults ages 18 to 22 (and up). Look around your college classroom and you'll probably spy at least one A&F item—a cap, a shirt, a pair of jeans. Abercrombie & Fitch, a line of "casual luxury" apparel and other products, is actually one of five brands owned by Ohio-based A&F Corporation. The company's other brands include abercrombie ("classic cool" for pre-teens), Hollister ("SoCal" for teenagers), RUEHL 925 (a higher-priced brand for post-collegiates 22 to 30), and Gilly Hicks (Australian-themed lounge- and underwear for women).

Obviously, A&F's businesses are related, and its overall corporate strategy is best characterized as one of *related diversification* (see Chapter 8). Based on this strategy, one would assume that A&F's organizational design reflects a *divisional*, or *M-form*, structure—a form favored by companies that operate multiple related businesses. Interestingly, however, A&F relies instead on a *functional*, or *U-form*, design based on functional departments (groups responsible for specific company functions).

> "Paying $90 for torn jeans isn't that cool anymore."
>
> —ANALYST ON DECLINING SALES AT ABERCROMBIE & FITCH

Interestingly, some form of divisionalized structure is preferred by most firms that pursue strategies of related diversification. Limited Brands, for example, a close competitor (and onetime parent) of A&F, uses a divisional structure to coordinate such well-known brands as The Limited, Victoria's Secret, and Bath & Body Works. Each unit is empowered to make autonomous decisions but can also access companywide staff support in areas such as logistics, information technology, real estate, and store design. At A&F, on the other hand, every employee is assigned to one of eight basic business functions, such as planning, purchasing, distribution, or stores, each of which is headed by a president. Why this design? Basically, A&F wants every employee to develop highly specialized skills within a functional area. In addition, this design is obviously more effective in coordinating activities within a function.

The company's history also accounts in part for its choice of a functional structure. From its founding in

Abercrombie and Fitch CEO Michael Jeffries uses a divisional structure to run the retailing giant.

1892 until a bankruptcy in 1977, Abercrombie & Fitch was a high-end sporting-goods retailer. In 1978, Oshman's, a Houston-based sporting-goods chain, purchased the company brand and trademark and for 11 years operated a combination retail chain and catalog company, selling an eclectic line of products ranging from tweed jackets to exercise machines. Limited Brands purchased the brand in 1988, putting it on preppy, upscale clothing for young adults. Nine years later, Limited sold 16 percent of the company through a public stock sale, and when the remaining shares were sold to the public in 1998, A&F became an independent company. In its current incarnation, then, A&F started out as a division of a larger firm, and it makes sense that its structure would be much like that of one division in a multidivisional corporation.

It's also interesting to note that, even before the spin-off from Limited, A&F had begun to establish its own culture and its own pattern of growth. Michael Jeffries, a retail-industry veteran, became president in 1992 and undertook to transform the company into the retailer of choice for younger consumers. Jeffries quickly managed to attach the brand to an ideal lifestyle, emphasizing apparel that complemented youth, good looks, and good times. The transformation turned out to be highly profitable, with sales increasing from $85 million in 1992 to $165 million in just two years. During the same period, the number of stores in the chain grew from 36 to 67, and in 1999, with 212 stores nationwide, A&F topped $1 billion in sales. In the same year, A&F started its abercrombie division for children and preteens, and a year later, it launched Hollister, the first of its "lifestyle" chains. By the end of 2002, the multidivision company was running 485 A&F stores, 144 abercrombie shops, and 32 Hollister outlets. Sales for the year were just under $1.4 billion. RUEHL opened in 2004 and Gilly Hicks in 2008. Today, A&F Corporation operates nearly 1,100 stores.

And yet A&F is still organized as if it were one big company with one big brand. As we've already seen, the main advantage of this choice can be explained as a desire to exercise top-down control over each brand by separating and controlling all the functions on which every brand—that is, every store type—depends. Regardless of how A&F is organized and otherwise managed, one thing is clear: It's the way it is because that's the way CEO Jeffries wants it. Jeffries took over a firm that was losing $25 million a year, declared that survival depended on becoming a "young, hip, spirited company," and engineered a reversal of fortunes by turning it into something completely new—a retailer that celebrates what one observer calls "the vain, highly constructed male" (A&F has had much less influence on women's fashion).

Up until 2008, Jeffries had delivered 56 straight quarters of increased revenues (except for one quarter in 2004). "To me," says investment analyst Robert Buchanan, "it's the most amazing record . . . in U.S. retailing, period." As the company's earnings record suggests, there doesn't seem to be much wrong with the way A&F has been run, but it stands to reason that, given the thoroughness of his hands-on approach—in addition to an organizational structure that's conducive to the exercise of top-down authority—Michael Jeffries must be held responsible for the firm's debits as well as its credits.

Those debits started to mount up in 2008. Pensions, stock options, and perks had inflated Jeffries' own total compensation to $71.8 million for the year—one in which A&F's net income was down 42 percent from the previous year. In the fourth quarter alone, which Jeffries called "a catastrophe for the retail industry," net profit had plummeted by 68 percent. Over the course of the year, the company's stock had lost 74 percent of its value, and although the global economy was obviously the primary factor, analysts and investors questioned the wisdom of Jeffries' persistent refusal both to discount prices and to engage in high-profile promotional activity as a means of countering the plunge in consumer spending. One analyst, for example, disagreed strongly with "Jeffries' stubborn position not to run sales promotions in the midst of the worst retail environment in decades." Jeffries replied that "promotions are a short-term solution with dreadful long-term effects" and insisted on avoiding any strategy that would compromise the long-term value of the company's brands.

He'd taken the same stance during the post-9/11 economic slump of 2001–2002, emerging with his streak of increasingly profitable quarters intact and confirming his conviction that A&F's customers would pay premium prices for brands they regarded as worth the money. "I don't care what anyone other than our target customer thinks," said Jeffries. But this time around, his target customers apparently worried more about the value of their money than that of their apparel. In 2009, A&F netted a grand total of $254 *thousand*—a figure which makes the take of $272 *million* in 2008 look like a supernatural windfall. Between the beginning of 2008 and the end of 2009, the company's stock fell 56 percent. "Paying $90 for torn jeans," speculated one industry observer, "isn't that cool anymore." For taking home more than $70 million in compensation for a year in which his company's stock value fell by more than 70 percent, Jeffries was singled out as one of the

"Highest Paid Worst Performers" of 2008 by the Corporate Library, a firm that does research on corporate governance.

In January 2009, Jeffries reached an agreement to remain as chairman and CEO until 2014, with his compensation to remain pretty much the same: an annual base salary of $1.5 million plus bonuses up to a maximum of 240 percent of base salary. As a result, while A&F's annual revenue increased by 18 percent in 2010, Jeffries' total compensation was down by 36 percent—from $36.3 million in 2009 to $23.2 million.[1]

One of the major ingredients in managing any business is the creation of an organization design to link the various elements that comprise the organization. There is a wide array of alternatives that managers in any given organization might select for its design. As we noted above, for instance, Abercrombie & Fitch uses a functional design but could also use a divisional design if Michael Jeffries chose to do so. In Chapter 14, we identified the basic elements that go into creating an organization. In this chapter, we explore how those elements can be combined to create an overall design for the organization. We first discuss the nature of organization design. We then describe early approaches aimed at identifying universal models of organization design. Situational factors, such as technology, environment, size, and life cycle, are then introduced. Next we discuss the relationship between an organization's strategy and its structure. Basic forms of organization design are described next. We conclude by presenting four emerging issues in organization design.

The Nature of Organization Design

What is organization design? In Chapter 14, we noted that job specialization and span of management are among the common elements of organization structure. We also described how the appropriate degree of specialization can vary, as can the appropriate span of management. Not really addressed, however, were questions of how specialization and span might be related to each other. For example, should a high level of specialization be matched with a certain span? And will different combinations of each work best with different bases of departmentalization? These and related issues are associated with questions of organization design.[2]

organization design
The overall set of structural elements and the relationships among those elements used to manage the total organization

Organization design is the overall set of structural elements and the relationships among those elements used to manage the total organization. Thus organization design is a means to implement strategies and plans to achieve organizational goals.[3] As we discuss organization design, keep in mind two important points. First, organizations are not designed and then left intact. Most organizations change almost continuously as a result of factors such as situations and people. (The processes of organization change are discussed in Chapter 16.) Second, organization design for larger organizations is extremely complex, with so many nuances and variations that no description of it can ever be a full and complete explanation.

What is organization design?

How does organization design relate to organization structure?

CONCEPT CHECK

Universal Perspectives on Organization Design

In Chapter 2, we made the distinction between *contingency* and *universal* approaches to solving management problems. Recall, for example, that universal perspectives try to identify the "one best way" to manage organizations, whereas contingency perspectives suggest that appropriate managerial behavior in a given situation depends on, or is contingent on, unique elements in that situation. The foundation of contemporary thinking about organization design can be traced back to two early universal perspectives: the bureaucratic model and the behavioral model.

Bureaucratic Model

We also noted in Chapter 2 that Max Weber, an influential German sociologist, was a pioneer of classical organization theory. At the core of Weber's writings was the bureaucratic model of organizations.[4] The Weberian perspective suggests that a bureaucracy is a model of organization design based on a legitimate and formal system of authority. Many people associate bureaucracy with "red tape," rigidity, and passing the buck. For example, how many times have you heard people refer disparagingly to "the federal bureaucracy"? And many U.S. managers believe that bureaucracy in the Chinese government is a major impediment to U.S. firms' ability to do business there.

Weber viewed the bureaucratic form of organization as logical, rational, and efficient. He offered the model as a framework to which all organizations should aspire—the "one best way" of doing things. According to Weber, the ideal bureaucracy exhibits five basic characteristics:

bureaucracy
A model of organization design based on a legitimate and formal system of authority

1. The organization should adopt a distinct division of labor, and each position should be filled by an expert.

2. The organization should develop a consistent set of rules to ensure that task performance is uniform.

3. The organization should establish a hierarchy of positions or offices that creates a chain of command from the top of the organization to the bottom.

4. Managers should conduct business in an impersonal way and maintain an appropriate social distance between themselves and their subordinates.

5. Employment and advancement in the organization should be based on technical expertise, and employees should be protected from arbitrary dismissal.

Perhaps the best examples of bureaucracies today are government agencies and universities. Consider, for example, the steps you must go through and the forms you must fill out to apply for admission to college, request housing, register each semester, change majors, submit a degree plan, substitute a course, and file for graduation. Even when paper is replaced with electronic media, the steps are often the same. The reason these procedures are necessary is

While there are some advantages to using the bureaucratic model of organization design, excessive bureaucracy can lead to slow decision making and a lack of flexibility. Some managers have criticized China for being overly bureaucratic. These Chinese officials are learning about new regulations and procedures written to control foreign investment in their country. Hence, McDonald's is increasing its size as defined by its number of employees.

FREDERIC J. BROWN/AFP/Getty Images

that universities deal with large numbers of people who must be treated equally and fairly. Hence, rules, regulations, and standard operating procedures are needed. Large labor unions are also usually organized as bureaucracies.[5]

Some bureaucracies, such as the U.S. Postal Service, have been trying to portray themselves as less mechanistic and impersonal. The strategy of the Postal Service is to become more service oriented as a way to fight back against competitors like FedEx and UPS.

A primary strength of the bureaucratic model is that several of its elements (such as reliance on rules and employment based on expertise) do, in fact, often improve efficiency. Bureaucracies also help prevent favoritism (because everyone must follow the same rules) and make procedures and practices very clear to everyone. Unfortunately, however, this approach also has several disadvantages. One major disadvantage is that the bureaucratic model results in inflexibility and rigidity. Once rules are created and put in place, making exceptions or changing them is often difficult. In addition, the bureaucracy often results in neglect of human and social processes within the organization.

Behavioral Model

Another important universal model of organization design was the **behavioral model**, which paralleled the emergence of the human relations school of management thought. Rensis Likert, a management researcher, studied several large organizations to determine what made some more effective than others.[6] He found that the organizations in his sample that used the bureaucratic model of design tended to be less effective than those that used a more behaviorally oriented model consistent with the emerging human relations movement—in other words, organizations that paid more attention to developing work groups and were more concerned with interpersonal processes.

Likert developed a framework that characterized organizations in terms of eight important processes: leadership, motivation, communication, interactions, decision making, goal setting, control, and performance goals. Likert believed that all organizations could be measured and categorized along a continuum associated with each of these dimensions. He argued that the basic bureaucratic form of organization, which he called a **System 1 design**, anchored one end of each dimension. The characteristics of the System 1 organization in Likert's framework are summarized in the left column of Table 15.1.

Also summarized in the right column of this table are characteristics of Likert's other extreme form of organization design, called **System 4 design**, based on the behavioral model. For example, a System 4 organization uses a wide array of motivational processes, and its interaction processes are open and extensive. Other distinctions between System 1 and System 4 organizations are equally obvious. Between the System 1 and System 4 extremes lie the System 2 and System 3 organizations. Likert argued that System 4 should be adopted by all organizations. He suggested that managers should emphasize supportive relationships, establish high performance goals, and practice group decision making to achieve a System 4 organization. Many organizations attempted to adopt the System 4 design during its period of peak popularity. General Motors, for instance, once converted a plant in the Atlanta area from a System 2 to a System 4 organization. Over a period of three years, direct and indirect labor efficiency improved, as did tool breakage rates, scrap costs, and quality.[7]

Like the bureaucratic model, the behavioral approach has both strengths and weaknesses. Its major strength is that it emphasizes human behavior by stressing the value of an organization's employees. Likert and his associates thus paved the way for a more humanistic approach to designing organizations. Unfortunately, the behavioral approach also argues that there is one best way to design an organization—as a System 4. As we see, however, evidence is strong that there is no one best approach to organization design.[8] What works for one organization may not work for another, and what works for one organization may change as that organization's situation changes. Hence, universal models like bureaucracy and System 4 have been largely supplanted by newer models that take contingency factors into account. In the next section, we identify a number of factors that help determine the best organization design for a particular situation.

behavioral model
A model of organization design consistent with the human relations movement, stressing attention to developing work groups and concern with interpersonal processes

System 1 design
Similar to the bureaucratic model

System 4 design
Similar to behavioral model

TABLE 15.1 SYSTEM 1 AND SYSTEM 4 ORGANIZATIONS

The behavioral model identifies two extreme types of organization design called System 1 and System 4. The two designs vary in eight fundamental processes. The System 1 design is considered to be somewhat rigid and inflexible.

System 1 Organization	System 4 Organization
1. Leadership process includes no perceived confidence and trust. Subordinates do not feel free to discuss job problems with their superiors, who in turn do not solicit their ideas and opinions.	1. Leadership process includes perceived confidence and trust between superiors and subordinates in all matters. Subordinates feel free to discuss job problems with their superiors, who in turn solicit their ideas and opinions.
2. Motivational process taps only physical, security, and economic motives through the use of fear and sanctions. Unfavorable attitudes toward the organization prevail among employees.	2. Motivational process taps a full range of motives through participatory methods. Attitudes are favorable toward the organization and its goals.
3. Communication process is such that information flows downward and tends to be distorted, inaccurate, and viewed with suspicion by subordinates.	3. Communication process is such that information flows freely throughout the organization—upward, downward, and laterally. The information is accurate and undistorted.
4. Interaction process is closed and restricted. Subordinates have little effect on departmental goals, methods, and activities.	4. Interaction process is open and extensive. Both superiors and subordinates are able to affect departmental goals, methods, and activities.
5. Decision process occurs only at the top of the organization; it is relatively centralized.	5. Decision process occurs at all levels through group processes; it is relatively decentralized.
6. Goal-setting process is located at the top of the organization; discourages group participation.	6. Goal-setting process encourages group participation in setting high, realistic objectives.
7. Control process is centralized and emphasizes fixing of blame for mistakes.	7. Control process is dispersed throughout the organization and emphasizes self-control and problem solving.
8. Performance goals are low and passively sought by managers who make no commitment to developing the human resources of the organization.	8. Performance goals are high and actively sought by superiors who recognize the necessity for making a full commitment to developing, through training, the human resources of the organization.

Source: Adapted from Rensis Likert, *The Human Organization*, 1967. Copyright © 1967 The McGraw-Hill Companies, Inc. Reprinted with permission.

CONCEPT CHECK

Distinguish between the bureaucratic model and the behavioral model of organization design.

Why do you think managers have often been concerned with identifying the "one best way" of doing something?

Situational Influences on Organization Design

The **situational view of organization design** is based on the assumption that the optimal design for any given organization depends on a set of relevant situational factors. In other words, situational factors play a role in determining the best organization design for any particular circumstance.[9] As you can see in the *World of Difference* box on page 370, entitled "To Offshore or Not to Offshore," such practices as offshoring are often affected by situational factors. Four basic situational factors—technology, environment, size, and organizational life cycle—are discussed here. Another factor, strategy, is described in the next section.

situational view of organization design
Based on the assumption that the optimal design for any given organization depends on a set of relevant situational factors

A WORLD OF DIFFERENCE

To Offshore or Not to Offshore

AP Photo/Gautam Singh

From computer programmers in the Philippines and molecular biologists in Russia to customer-service agents in India, the practice of *offshoring* (or *outsourcing*) is bringing workers from around the world into the workforces of U.S. corporations in a broad range of industries. When U.S. firms "offshore," they're hiring foreign firms and foreign personnel to perform their business functions. In so doing, they're not only increasing the diversity of their workforces but altering the processes by which they conduct organizational business.

"In theory," says business journalist Pete Engardio, offshoring is making it "possible to buy, off the shelf, practically any function you need to run a company." In part, that's why the offshoring processes at some firms are almost dizzying in their complexity. At Penske Truck Leasing, for instance, drivers submit their paper logs for data entry to a facility in Mexico, which forwards them to Hyderabad, India, where they're analyzed and the results reported to Penske management back in the United States. How does a company's data-processing function come to consist of such far-flung operations? As in most other decisions, companies choose operational partners according to the value-creation capabilities that they bring to the overall process.

Ideally, of course, offshoring should benefit the contractor as well as the contracting firm. Take, for example, the case of Wisconsin-based PCMC, which designs and makes paper packaging. PCMC had a problem with its engineering function:

Although it had a large base of potential customers, it often lost them because its engineering group was too small to create new designs fast enough to keep pace with customer needs. Nor could the company afford to expand its engineering department. To solve the problem, PCMC entered into an offshoring contract with an Indian company that agreed to provide a 160-member staff to support PCMC's engineering function. The result? Not only 160 new jobs in India but more orders and more jobs in Wisconsin as well.

Obviously, offshoring arrangements don't always work out as well as the one established by PCMC and its Indian partner. Problems can arise, for example, when the process requires significant interaction between foreign contract personnel and people in the contracting firm's home country—not only its employees but its customers. For one thing, language and culture differences can make communication difficult, especially when it's conducted by e-mail or phone. When 1-800-FLOWERS tried to expand its customer-service operation by outsourcing customer calls to India, the results were disastrous. Why? When customers call, florists have to do more than merely process orders: They're often called upon to offer interior-design tips and relationship counseling and even to console the grieving. Indian workers could neither fully understand the psychology of U.S. flower buyers nor communicate the nuances necessary to serve their needs. 1-800-FLOWERS terminated the experiment after a few weeks. "The folks were difficult to understand," admitted one company executive. "We were afraid that we would lose sales, and we couldn't risk that."

The decision made sense: Typically, it costs six times as much to replace a customer as to keep one. Fortunately, the company had a plan B—"homeshoring," or hiring in-country contract workers. Homeshoring employees are more expensive than overseas contractors, but they're less expensive than full-time on-site employees. They connect with American customers, and they also alleviate the concerns that some U.S. consumers have about their private data being shipped overseas.

References: Michelle Conlin, "Call Centers in the Rec Room," *BusinessWeek*, January 23, 2006, www.businessweek.com on July 8, 2011; Pete Engardio, "The Future of Outsourcing," *BusinessWeek*, January 30, 2006, www.businessweek.com on July 8, 2011; Manjeet Kripalani with Brian Grow, "Offshoring: Spreading the Gospel," *BusinessWeek*, March 6, 2006, www.businessweek.com on July 8, 2011.

Core Technology

Technology consists of the conversion processes used to transform inputs (such as materials or information) into outputs (such as products or services). Most organizations use multiple technologies, but an organization's most important one is called its *core technology*. Although most people visualize assembly lines and machinery when they think of technology, the term can also be applied to service organizations. For example, an investment firm like Fidelity uses technology to transform investment dollars into income in much the same way that Union Carbide uses natural resources to manufacture chemical products.

The link between technology and organization design was first recognized by Joan Woodward.[10] Woodward studied 100 manufacturing firms in southern England, collecting information about such aspects as the history of each organization, its manufacturing processes, its forms and procedures, and its financial performance. Woodward expected to find a relationship between the size of an organization and its design, but no such relationship emerged. As a result, she began to seek other explanations for differences. Close scrutiny of the firms in her sample led her to recognize a potential relationship between technology and organization design. This follow-up analysis led Woodward to first classify the organizations according to their technology. Three basic forms of technology were identified by Woodward:

1. *Unit or small-batch technology*. The product is custom-made to customer specifications or produced in small quantities. Organizations using this form of technology include a tailor's shop specializing in custom suits, a print shop that produces business cards and company stationery, and a photography studio.

2. *Large-batch or mass-production technology*. The product is manufactured in assembly-line fashion by combining component parts into another part or finished product. Examples include automobile manufacturers like Subaru, appliance makers like Whirlpool Corporation, and electronics firms like Philips.

3. *Continuous-process technology*. Raw materials are transformed into a finished product by a series of machine or process transformations. The composition of the materials themselves is changed. Examples include petroleum refineries like ExxonMobil and Shell, and chemical refineries like Dow Chemical and Hoechst AG.

These forms of technology are listed in order of their assumed levels of complexity. In other words, unit or small-batch technology is presumed to be the least complex and continuous-process technology the most complex. Woodward found that different configurations of organization design were associated with each technology.

As technology became more complex in Woodward's sample, the number of levels of management increased (that is, the organization became taller). The executive span of management also increased, as did the relative size of its staff component. The supervisory span of management, however, first increased and then decreased as technology became more complex, primarily because much of the work in continuous-process technologies is automated. Fewer workers are needed, but the skills necessary to do the job increase. These findings are consistent with the discussion of the span of management in Chapter 14—the more complex the job, the narrower the span should be.

At a more general level of analysis, Woodward found that the two extremes (unit or small-batch and continuous-process) tended to be very similar to Likert's System 4 organization, whereas the middle-range organizations (large-batch or mass-production) were much more like bureaucracies or System 1. The large-batch and mass-production organizations also had a higher level of specialization.[11] Finally, she found that organizational success was related to the extent to which organizations followed the typical pattern. For example, successful continuous-process organizations tended to be more like System 4 organizations, whereas less successful firms with the same technology were less like System 4 organizations.

technology
Conversion processes used to transform inputs into outputs

TECHNICALLY SPEAKING

"Ph.D.'s for a Dollar an Hour"

AP Photo/PRNewsFoto/Netflix, Inc.

According to CEO Reed Hastings, the core technology at Netflix, the highly successful provider of by-mail movies and on-demand video, is designed to provide each customer with "the most personalized Website in the world. If the Starbucks secret is a smile when you get your latte," says Hastings, "ours is that the Website adapts to the individual's taste."

A critical component of Netflix technology (much of which has been developed in-house) is its *recommender system*—software that analyzes patterns in a subscriber's rental choices. It's important because it can help to predict other movies that the subscriber might like—and thus to maximize the number of movies that he or she rents. To get a better idea of how well-tuned recommender technology can contribute to customer satisfaction, and customer satisfaction to profitability, consider Netflix's success in renting out films from its "backlist," which includes older, independent, and foreign movies—just about everything that doesn't fall into the category of big-studio blockbuster. Netflix subscribers rent backlist movies because they show up on their recommendation lists and, more importantly, because they've come to trust Netflix's recommender system to make a high percentage of reliable recommendations. Today, about 70 percent of all Netflix rentals are backlist titles (compared to about 20 percent for traditional video stores).

In 2000, Netflix introduced a recommender system called Cinematch, which didn't work very well at first, turning out "a mix of insightful and boneheaded recommendations," as Hastings recalls. Programmers, however, improved the system over the next few years, until it was able to make some pretty surprising connections (who would have guessed that people who liked the heartwarming drama *Pay It Forward* would also like the high-tech thriller *I, Robot*?).

In 2006, however, when Netflix programmers had reached the point of diminishing returns in their efforts to enhance the system, Hastings came up with the idea of offering a $1 million prize to anyone who could improve the accuracy of Cinematch by 10 percent. It took three years (and a couple of interim "Progress Prizes"), but by September 2009, there was finally a winner: a team of researchers from Austria and the United States who'd started out as competitors but joined forces as the competition grew more complex and more intense. ("You need to think outside the box," says one member of the winning team, "and the only way to do that is find someone else's box.") As a result of its million-dollar tweaking, reports *New York Times* science writer Clive Thompson, Cinematch now functions as a sort of "video-store roboclerk" whose suggestions drive nearly 60 percent of all Netflix rentals.

And that's why improving Cinematch was worth $1 million to Netflix: "Getting to 10 percent would certainly be worth well in excess of $1 million," commented Hastings at the outset of the contest, and when it was over, he added that it had also been extremely cost effective: "You look at the cumulative hours, and you're getting Ph.D.'s for a dollar an hour."

References: Clive Thompson, "If You Liked This, You're Sure to Love That," *New York Times*, November 23, 2008, www.nytimes.com on June 30, 2010; Michael V. Copeland, "Box Office Boffo for Brainiacs: The Netflix Prize," *Fortune*, November 21, 2009, http://tech.fortune.cnn.com on July 5, 2010; C. A. Heidelberger, "Data Mining at Netflix," *CAH@DSU*, August 4, 2009, http://cahdsu.wordpress.com on July 5, 2010; Lisa Guernsey, "Making Intelligence a Bit Less Artificial," *New York Times*, May 1, 2003, www.nytimes.com on June 16, 2010; E. E. Boyd, "Netflix Prize: 'Getting PhDs for a Dollar an Hour,'" *BayNewser*, September 24, 2009, www.mediabistro.com on June 30, 2010; David Leonhardt, "What Netflix Could Teach Hollywood," *New York Times*, June 7, 2006, www.nytimes.com on June 16, 2010.

Thus technology clearly appears to play an important role in determining organization design. As future technologies become more diverse and complex, managers will have to be even more aware of different technologies' impact on the design of organizations. For example, the increased use of robotics may necessitate alterations in organization design to better accommodate different assembly methods. Likewise, increased usage of new forms of information technology will almost certainly cause organizations to redefine the nature of work and the reporting relationships among individuals.[12] The *Technically Speaking* box entitled " 'Ph.D's for a Dollar an Hour' " on page 372 shows how one extremely successful company has already gone about harnessing the latest in analytic technology in order to tailor its appeal to customer tastes.

Environment

In addition to the various relationships described in Chapter 3, environmental elements and organization design are specifically linked in a number of ways.[13] The first widely recognized analysis of environment–organization design linkages was provided by Tom Burns and G. M. Stalker.[14] Like Woodward, Burns and Stalker worked in England. Their first step was identifying two extreme forms of organizational environment: stable (one that remains relatively constant over time) and unstable (subject to uncertainty and rapid change). Next they studied the designs of organizations in each type of environment. Not surprisingly, they found that organizations in stable environments tended to have a different kind of design than did organizations in unstable environments. The two kinds of design that emerged were called mechanistic and organic organization.

A mechanistic organization, quite similar to the bureaucratic or System 1 model, was most frequently found in stable environments. Free from uncertainty, organizations structured their activities in rather predictable ways by means of rules, specialized jobs, and centralized authority. Mechanistic organizations are also quite similar to bureaucracies. Although no environment is completely stable, Abercrombie & Fitch and Wendy's use mechanistic designs. Each A&F store, for example, has prescribed methods for store design and merchandise-ordering processes. Little or no deviation is allowed from these methods. An organic organization, on the other hand, was most often found in unstable and unpredictable environments, in which constant change and uncertainty usually dictate a much higher level of fluidity and flexibility. Motorola (facing rapid technological change) and Apple (facing both technological change and constant change in consumer tastes) both use organic designs. A manager at Motorola, for example, has considerable discretion over how work is performed and how problems can be solved.

These ideas were extended in the United States by Paul R. Lawrence and Jay W. Lorsch.[16] They agreed that environmental factors influence organization design but believed that this influence varies between different units of the same organization. In fact, they predicted that each organizational unit has its own unique environment and responds by developing unique attributes. Lawrence and Lorsch suggested that organizations could be characterized along two primary dimensions.

One of these dimensions, differentiation, is the extent to which the organization is broken down into subunits. A firm with many subunits is highly differentiated; one with few subunits has a low level of differentiation. The second dimension, integration, is the degree to which the various subunits must work together in a coordinated fashion. For example, if each unit competes in a different market and has its own production facilities, they may need little integration. Lawrence and Lorsch reasoned that the degree of differentiation and integration needed by an organization depends on the stability of the environments that its subunits face.

Organizational Size

The size of an organization is yet another factor that affects its design.[17] Although several definitions of size exist, we define organizational size as the total number of full-time or full-time-equivalent employees. A team of researchers at the University of Aston in Birmingham, England, believed that Woodward had failed to find a size–structure relationship (which was her original expectation) because almost all of the organizations she studied were relatively small (three-fourths had fewer than 500 employees).[18] Thus they decided

> "Networks are becoming the locus for innovation. Firms . . . are more porous and decentralized."
>
> —WALTER POWELL, STANFORD PROFESSOR[15]

mechanistic organization
Similar to the bureaucratic or System 1 model, most frequently found in stable environments

organic organization
Very flexible and informal model of organization design, most often found in unstable and unpredictable environments

differentiation
Extent to which the organization is broken down into subunits

integration
Degree to which the various subunits must work together in a coordinated fashion

organizational size
Total number of full-time or full-time-equivalent employees

McDonald's engaged in a massive hiring blitz in spring 2011. This poster, for example, is emphasizing that there were openings at all of the McDonald's in New York City. Similar campaigns were launched in other major cities. Hence, McDonald's is increasing its size as defined by its number of employees.

to undertake a study of a wider array of organizations to determine how size and technology both individually and jointly affect an organization's design.

Their primary finding was that technology did in fact influence structural variables in small firms, probably because all of their activities tend to be centered on their core technologies. In large firms, however, the strong technology–design link broke down, most likely because technology is not as central to ongoing activities in large organizations. The Aston studies yielded a number of basic generalizations: When compared to small organizations, large organizations tend to be characterized by higher levels of job specialization, more standard operating procedures, more rules, more regulations, and a greater degree of decentralization. Walmart is a good case in point. The firm expects to continue its dramatic growth for the foreseeable future, adding several thousand new jobs in the next few years. But, as it grows, the firm acknowledges that it will have to become more decentralized for its first-line managers to stay in tune with their customers.[19] Marathon Oil, meanwhile, announced in early 2011 that it would be spinning off its downstream business, creating two independent businesses and significantly reducing the size of its business.[20] Consequently, Marathon is becoming a much smaller organization.

Organizational Life Cycle

Of course, size is not constant. As we noted in Chapter 10, for example, some small businesses are formed but soon disappear. Others remain as small, independently operated enterprises as long as their owner–manager lives. A few, like Dell Computer, JetBlue, and Starbucks, skyrocket to become organizational giants. And occasionally large organizations reduce their size through layoffs or divestitures. For example, Navistar is today far smaller than was its previous incarnation as International Harvester Company. And as noted above, Marathon Oil is making a strategic decision to reduce its size by splitting itself into two businesses.

Although no clear pattern explains changes in size, many organizations progress through a four-stage **organizational life cycle**.[21] The first stage is the *birth* of the organization. The second stage, *youth*, is characterized by growth and the expansion of organizational resources. *Midlife* is a period of gradual growth evolving eventually into stability. Finally, *maturity* is a period of stability, perhaps eventually evolving into decline. Firms like NetFlix and Starbucks, for instance, are still in their youth stage; Halliburton and Chevron are in midlife, and Ford and Boeing are in maturity. (A key challenge for managers, of course, is to avoid allowing a mature organization to begin to decline. Hence, they must be alert for opportunities to re-energize the organization with new products and new markets.)

Managers must confront a number of organization design issues as the organization progresses through these stages. In general, as an organization passes from one stage to the next, it becomes bigger, more mechanistic, and more decentralized. It also becomes more specialized, devotes more attention to planning, and takes on an increasingly large staff component. Finally, coordination demands increase, formalization increases, organizational units become geographically more dispersed, and control systems become more extensive. Thus an organization's size and design are clearly linked, and this link is dynamic because of the organizational life cycle.[22]

organizational life cycle
Progression through which organizations evolve as they grow and mature

ANDREW GOMBERT/EPA/Landov

What are the most prevalent situational factors that influence organization design?

Which situational factor is the most and which is the least likely to affect a small neighborhood retailer? Why?

CONCEPT CHECK

Strategy and Organization Design

Another important determinant of an organization's design is the strategy adopted by its top managers. In general, corporate and business strategies both affect organization design. Basic organizational functions such as finance and marketing can also affect organization design in some cases.[23]

Corporate-Level Strategy

As we noted in Chapter 8, an organization can adopt a variety of corporate-level strategies. Its choice will partially determine what type of design will be most effective. For example, a firm that pursues a single-product strategy likely relies on functional departmentalization and can use a mechanistic design. If either unrelated or related diversification is used to spur growth, managers need to decide how to arrange the various units within the organizational umbrella. For example, if the firm is using related diversification, there must be a high level of coordination among the various units to capitalize on the presumed synergistic opportunities inherent in this strategy. On the other hand, firms using unrelated diversification more likely rely on a strong hierarchical reporting system, so that corporate managers can better monitor the performance of individual units with the firm.

An organization that adopts the portfolio approach to implement its corporate-level strategies must also ensure that its design fits its strategy. For example, each strategic business unit may remain a relatively autonomous unit within the organization. But managers at the corporate level need to decide how much decision-making latitude to give the head of each unit (a question of decentralization), how many corporate-level executives are needed to oversee the operations of various units (a question of span of management), and what information, if any, is shared among the units (a question of coordination).[24]

Business-Level Strategy

Business-level strategies affect the design of individual businesses within the organization as well as the overall organization itself. An organization pursuing a defender strategy, for example, is likely to be somewhat tall and centralized, have narrow spans of management, and perhaps take a functional approach to departmentalization. Thus it may generally follow the bureaucratic approach to organization design.

In contrast, a prospecting type of organization is more likely to be flatter and decentralized. With wider spans of management, it tries to be very flexible and adaptable in its approach to doing business. A business that uses an analyzer strategy is likely to have an organization design somewhere between these two extremes (perhaps being a System 2 or 3 organization). Given that a reactor is essentially a strategic failure, its presumed strategy is probably not logically connected to its design.

Generic competitive strategies can also affect organization design. A firm using a differentiation strategy, for example, may structure departments around whatever it is using as a basis for differentiating its products (such as marketing in the case of image or manufacturing in the case of quality). A cost leadership strategy necessitates a strong commitment to efficiency and control. Thus such a firm is more centralized as it attempts to control costs.

And a firm using a focus strategy may design itself around the direction of its focus (location departmentalization if its focus is geographic region, customer departmentalization if its focus is customer groups).

Organizational Functions

The relationship between an organization's functional strategies and its design is less obvious and may be subsumed under corporate or business-level concerns. If the firm's marketing strategy calls for aggressive marketing and promotion, separate departments may be needed for advertising, direct sales, and promotion. If its financial strategy calls for low debt, it may need only a small finance department. If production strategy calls for manufacturing in diverse locations, organization design arrangements need to account for this geographic dispersion. Human resource strategy may call for greater or lesser degrees of decentralization as a way to develop skills of new managers at lower levels in the organization. And research and development strategy may dictate various designs for managing the R&D function itself. A heavy commitment to R&D, for example, may require a separate unit with a vice president in charge. A lesser commitment to R&D may be achieved with a director and a small staff.[25]

How does organization design relate to strategy?

Under what circumstances, if any, might a single-business corporation have different organization designs for its corporate operations and its business activities?

CONCEPT CHECK

◈ Basic Forms of Organization Design

Because technology, environment, size, life cycle, and strategy can all influence organization design, it should come as no surprise that organizations adopt many different kinds of designs. Most designs, however, fall into one of four basic categories. Others are hybrids based on two or more of the basic forms.

Functional (U-Form) Design

The **functional design** is an arrangement based on the functional approach to departmentalization, as detailed in Chapter 14. This design has been termed the *U form* (for unitary) by the noted economist Oliver E. Williamson.[26] Under the U-form arrangement, the members and units in the organization are grouped into functional departments such as marketing and production.

For the organization to operate efficiently in this design, there must be considerable coordination across departments. This integration and coordination are most commonly the responsibility of the CEO and members of senior management. Figure 15.1 shows the U-form design applied to the corporate level of a small manufacturing company. In a U-form organization, none of the functional areas can survive without the others. Marketing, for example, needs products from operations to sell and funds from finance to pay for advertising. The WD-40 Company, which makes a popular lubricating oil, and the McIlhenny Company, which makes TABASCO sauce, are both examples of firms that use the U-form design. Abercrombie & Fitch also uses the U-form design.

In general, this approach shares the basic advantages and disadvantages of functional departmentalization. Thus it allows the organization to staff all important positions with functional experts and facilitates coordination and integration. On the other hand, it also promotes a functional, rather than an organizational, focus and tends to promote centralization. And, as we noted in Chapter 14, functionally based designs are most commonly used

functional (U-form) design
Based on the functional approach to departmentalization

FIGURE 15.1 FUNCTIONAL OR U-FORM DESIGN FOR A SMALL MANUFACTURING COMPANY

The U-form design is based on functional departmentalization. This small manufacturing firm uses managers at the vice presidential level to coordinate activities within each functional area of the organization. Note that each functional area is dependent on the others.

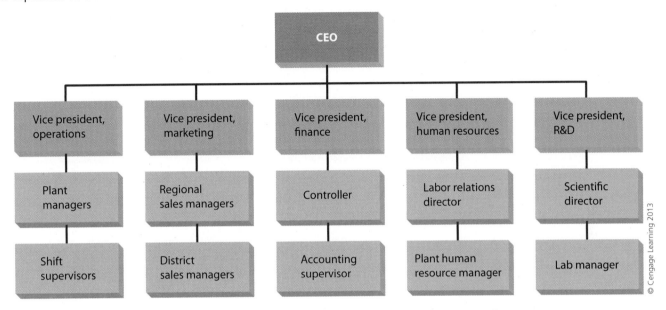

in small organizations because an individual CEO can easily oversee and coordinate the entire organization. As an organization grows, the CEO finds staying on top of all functional areas increasingly difficult.

Conglomerate (H-Form) Design

Another common form of organization design is the **conglomerate, or H-form, approach.**[27] The conglomerate design is used by an organization made up of a set of unrelated businesses. Thus the H-form design is essentially a holding company that results from unrelated diversification. (The *H* in this term thus stands for holding.)

This approach is based loosely on the product form of departmentalization (see Chapter 14). Each business or set of businesses is operated by a general manager who is responsible for its profits or losses, and each general manager functions independently of the others. Samsung Electrics Company, a South Korean firm, uses the H-form design. As illustrated in Figure 15.2, Samsung consists of four basic business groups. Other firms that use the H-form design include General Electric (aircraft engines, appliances, financial services, lighting products, plastics, and other unrelated businesses) and Tenneco (pipelines, auto parts, financial services, and other unrelated businesses).

In an H-form organization, a corporate staff usually evaluates the performance of each business, allocates corporate resources across companies, and shapes decisions about buying and selling businesses. The basic shortcoming of the H-form design is the complexity associated with holding diverse and unrelated businesses. Managers usually find comparing and integrating activities across a large number of diverse operations difficult. Research by Michael Porter suggests that many organizations following this approach achieve only average to weak financial performance.[28] Thus, although some U.S. firms are still using the H-form design, many others have abandoned it for other approaches.

conglomerate (H-form) design
Used by an organization made up of a set of unrelated businesses

FIGURE 15.2 CONGLOMERATE (H-FORM) DESIGN AT SAMSUNG

Samsung Electronics Company, a South Korean firm, uses the conglomerate form of organization design. This design, which results from a strategy of unrelated diversification, is a complex one to manage. Managers find that comparing and integrating activities among the dissimilar operations are difficult. Companies may abandon this design for another approach, such as the M-form design.

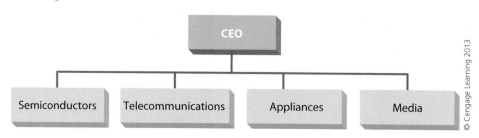

© Cengage Learning 2013

Divisional (M-Form) Design

In the divisional design, which is becoming increasingly popular, a product form of organization is also used; in contrast to the H-form, however, the divisions are related. Thus the **divisional design**, or **M form** (for multidivisional), is based on multiple businesses in related areas operating within a larger organizational framework. This design results from a strategy of related diversification.

Some activities are extremely decentralized down to the divisional level; others are centralized at the corporate level.[29] For example, as shown in Figure 15.3, Hilton Hotels uses this approach. Each of its divisions is headed by a president or executive vice president and operates with reasonable autonomy, but the divisions also coordinate their activities as appropriate. Other firms that use this approach include the Walt Disney Company (theme parks, movies, and merchandising units, all interrelated) and Hewlett-Packard (computers, printers, scanners, electronic medical equipment, and other electronic instrumentation).

The opportunities for coordination and shared resources represent one of the biggest advantages of the M-form design. Hilton's market research and purchasing departments are centralized. Thus a site selector can visit a city and look for possible locations for different Hilton brands and a buyer can purchase bed linens for multiple Hilton brands from the same supplier. The M-form design's basic objective is to optimize internal competition and cooperation. Healthy competition for resources among divisions can enhance effectiveness, but cooperation should also be promoted. Research suggests that the M-form organization

divisional (M-form) design
Based on multiple businesses in related areas operating within a larger organizational framework

FIGURE 15.3 MULTIDIVISIONAL (M-FORM) DESIGN AT HILTON HOTELS

Hilton Hotels uses the multidivisional approach to organization design. Although each unit operates with relative autonomy, all units function in the same general market. This design resulted from a strategy of related diversification. Other firms that use M-form designs include PepsiCo and the Walt Disney Company.

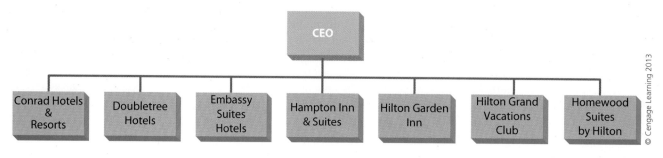

© Cengage Learning 2013

that can achieve and maintain this balance will outperform large U-form and all H-form organizations.[30]

Matrix Design

The **matrix design**, another common approach to organization design, is based on two over-lapping bases of departmentalization.[31] The foundation of a matrix is a set of functional departments. A set of product groups, or temporary departments, is then superimposed across the functional departments. Employees in a matrix are simultaneously members of a functional department (such as engineering) and of a project team.

Figure 15.4 shows a basic matrix design. At the top of the organization are functional units headed by vice presidents of engineering, production, finance, and marketing. Each of these managers has several subordinates. Along the side of the organization are a number of positions called *project manager*. Each project manager heads a project group composed of representatives or workers from the functional departments. Note from the figure that a matrix reflects a *multiple-command structure*—any given individual reports to both a functional superior and one or more project managers.

The project groups, or teams, are assigned to designated projects or programs. For example, the company might be developing a new product. Representatives are chosen from each functional area to work as a team on the new product. They also retain

matrix design
Based on two overlapping bases of departmentalization

FIGURE 15.4 A MATRIX ORGANIZATION

A matrix organization design is created by superimposing a product form of departmentalization on an existing functional organization. Project managers coordinate teams of employees drawn from different functional departments. Thus a matrix relies on a multiple-command structure.

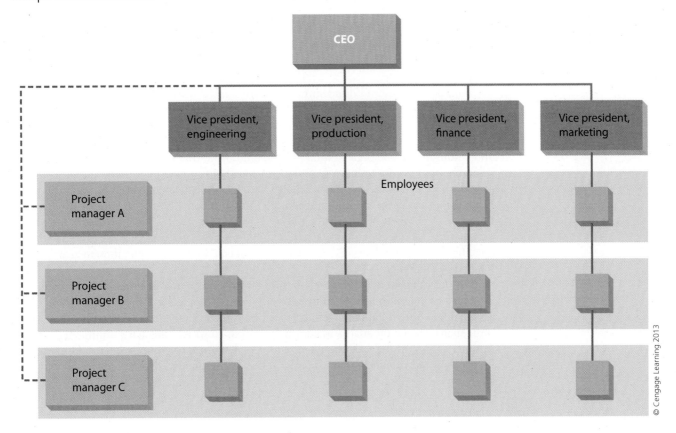

© Cengage Learning 2013

membership in the original functional group. At any given time, a person may be a member of several teams as well as a member of a functional group. Ford used this approach in creating its popular Focus automobile. It formed a group called "Team Focus" made up of designers, engineers, production specialists, marketing specialists, and other experts from different areas of the company. This group facilitated getting a very successful product to the market at least a year earlier than would have been possible using Ford's previous approaches.

Martha Stewart also uses a matrix organization for her lifestyle business. The company was first organized broadly into media and merchandising groups, each of which has specific products and product groups. Layered on top of this structure are teams of lifestyle experts organized into groups such as cooking, crafts, weddings, and so forth. Each of these groups is targeted toward specific customer needs, but they work as necessary across all of the product groups. For example, a wedding expert might contribute to an article on wedding planning for a *Martha Stewart Living* magazine, contribute a story idea for a cable television program, and supply content for a Martha Stewart website. This same individual might also help select fabrics suitable for wedding gowns for retailing.[32]

Many other organizations have also used the matrix design. Notable among them are American Cyanamid, Monsanto, NCR, Chase Manhattan Bank, Prudential, General Motors, and several state and federal government agencies. Some organizations, however, such as Citibank and the Dutch firm Philips, adopted and then dropped the matrix design. Thus it is important to recognize that a matrix design is not always appropriate.

The matrix form of organization design is most often used in one of three situations.[33] First, a matrix may work when there is strong pressure from the environment. For example, intense external competition may dictate the sort of strong marketing thrust that is best spearheaded by a functional department, but the diversity of a company's products may argue for product departments. Second, a matrix may be appropriate when large amounts of information need to be processed. For example, creating lateral relationships by means of a matrix is one effective way to increase the organization's capacity for processing information. Third, the matrix design may work when there is pressure for shared resources. For example, a company with ten product departments may have resources for only three marketing specialists. A matrix design would allow all the departments to share the company's scarce marketing resources.

Both advantages and disadvantages are associated with the matrix design. Researchers have observed six primary advantages of matrix designs. First, they enhance flexibility because teams can be created, redefined, and dissolved as needed. Second, because they assume a major role in decision making, team members are likely to be highly motivated and committed to the organization. Third, employees in a matrix organization have considerable opportunity to learn new skills. A fourth advantage of a matrix design is that it provides an efficient way for the organization to take full advantage of its human resources. Fifth, team members retain membership in their functional unit so that they can serve as a bridge between the functional unit and the team, enhancing cooperation. Sixth, the matrix design gives top management a useful vehicle for decentralization. Once the day-to-day operations have been delegated, top management can devote more attention to areas such as long-range planning.

On the other hand, the matrix design also has some major disadvantages. Employees may be uncertain about reporting relationships, especially if they are simultaneously assigned to a functional manager and to several project managers. To complicate matters, some managers see the matrix as a form of anarchy in which they have unlimited freedom. Another set of problems is associated with the dynamics of group behavior. Groups take longer than individuals to make decisions, may be dominated by one individual, and may compromise too much. They may also get bogged down in discussion and not focus on their primary objectives. Finally, in a matrix, more time may be required for coordinating task-related activities.[34]

Hybrid Designs

Some organizations use a design that represents a hybrid of two or more of the common forms of organization design.[35] For example, an organization may have five related divisions and one unrelated division, making its design a cross between an M form and an H form. Indeed, few companies use a design in its pure form; most firms have one basic organization design as a foundation for managing the business but maintain sufficient flexibility so that temporary or permanent modifications can be made for strategic purposes. Ford, for example, used the matrix approach to design the Focus and the newest Mustang, but the company is basically a U-form organization showing signs of moving to an M-form design. As we noted earlier, any combination of factors may dictate the appropriate form of design for any particular company.

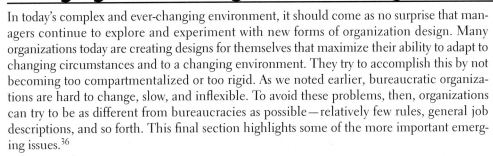

What are the basic forms of organization design?

Which basic organization designs are the most and the least clearly linked with strategy?

CONCEPT CHECK

Emerging Issues in Organization Design

In today's complex and ever-changing environment, it should come as no surprise that managers continue to explore and experiment with new forms of organization design. Many organizations today are creating designs for themselves that maximize their ability to adapt to changing circumstances and to a changing environment. They try to accomplish this by not becoming too compartmentalized or too rigid. As we noted earlier, bureaucratic organizations are hard to change, slow, and inflexible. To avoid these problems, then, organizations can try to be as different from bureaucracies as possible—relatively few rules, general job descriptions, and so forth. This final section highlights some of the more important emerging issues.[36]

The Team Organization

Some organizations today are using the team organization, an approach to organization design that relies almost exclusively on project-type teams, with little or no underlying functional hierarchy. Within such an organization, people float from project to project as necessitated by their skills and the demands of those projects. At Cypress Semiconductor, T. J. Rodgers refuses to allow the organization to grow so large that it cannot function this way. Whenever a unit or group starts getting too large, he simply splits it into smaller units. Consequently, all units within the organization are small. This allows them to change direction, explore new ideas, and try new methods without dealing with a rigid bureaucratic organizational context. Although few organizations have actually reached this level of adaptability, Apple Computer and Xerox are among those moving toward it.[37]

The Virtual Organization

Closely related to the team organization is the virtual organization. A virtual organization is one that has little or no formal structure. Such an organization typically has only a handful of permanent employees and a very small staff and administrative headquarters facility. As the needs of the organization change, its managers bring in temporary workers, lease facilities, and outsource basic support services to meet the demands of each unique situation. As the situation changes, the temporary workforce changes in parallel, with some people

team organization
An approach to organization design that relies almost exclusively on project-type teams, with little or no underlying functional hierarchy

virtual organization
One that has little or no formal structure

"When a company is as spread out as [MySQL] you have to think of virtual ways to imitate the dynamics of what goes on in a more familiar employment situation."

—THOMAS BASIL, MYSQL EXECUTIVE[39]

leaving the organization and others entering. Facilities and the services subcontracted to others change as well. Thus the organization exists only in response to its needs. And, increasingly, virtual organizations are conducting most—if not all—of their businesses online.[38]

For example, TLG Research Inc. was founded as a virtual organization focused on marketing research for automotive, aviation, marine, and industrial markets for original equipment and replacement parts. Currently, the company consists of an in-house project management staff of ten people and a virtual network of industry professionals. It also has a global business and research sources in Europe, Latin America, and Asia–Pacific to refer to for consulting and research services as needed.

The Learning Organization

Another recent approach to organization design is the so-called learning organization. Organizations that adopt this approach work to integrate continuous improvement with continuous employee learning and development. Specifically, a **learning organization** is one that works to facilitate the lifelong learning and personal development of all of its employees while continually transforming itself to respond to changing demands and needs.[40]

learning organization
One that works to facilitate the lifelong learning and personal development of all of its employees while continually transforming itself to respond to changing demands and needs

Although managers might approach the concept of a learning organization from a variety of perspectives, improved quality, continuous improvement, and performance measurement are frequent goals. The idea is that the most consistent and logical strategy for achieving continuous improvement is by constantly upgrading employee talent, skill, and knowledge. For example, if each employee in an organization learns one new thing each day and can translate that knowledge into work-related practice, continuous improvement will logically follow. Indeed, organizations that wholeheartedly embrace this approach believe that only through constant learning by employees can continuous improvement really occur.[41]

In recent years, many different organizations have implemented this approach. For example, Royal Dutch Shell owns and operates a conference center in RijsWijk, Norway, which it calls the Learning Centre for Technical courses. The center boasts state-of-the-art classrooms with instructional technology and drilling simulators, lodging facilities, a restaurant and a sandwich shop, a prayer room, and quiet spaces where people can go to reflect and meditate. The Learning Centre can accommodate 270 students per day and more than 5000 per year. Line managers at the firm rotate through the Shell Learning Centre and serve as teaching faculty. Such teaching assignments last anywhere from a few days to several months. At the same time, all Shell employees routinely attend training programs, seminars, and related activities, all the while learning the latest information that they need to contribute more effectively to the firm. Recent seminar topics have ranged from time management, to the latest oil drilling techniques, to balancing work and family demands, to international trade theory. The idea is that by continuously immersing people in shared learning experiences the firm will promote an organic design populated by people with common knowledge, goals, and expectations.

vm/istockphoto

A number of large businesses today have adopted the learning organization model. While businesses have long provided training and development opportunities for their employees, the concept of learning organization is focused on both lifetime learning and continuous organizational transformation. These managers, for example, are learning new techniques for competitive analysis and strategic thinking.

Special Issues in International Organization Design

Another emerging issue in organization design is the trend toward the internationalization of business. As we discussed in Chapter 5, most businesses today interact with suppliers, customers, or competitors (or all three) from other countries. The relevant issue for organization design is how to design the firm to most effectively deal with international forces and compete in global markets. For example, consider a moderate-size company that has just decided to "go international." Should it set up an international division, retain its current structure and establish an international operating group, or make its international operations an autonomous subunit?[42] Whatever the case, managers need to recognize that when they approach international organization design from a strategic perspective rather than simply allowing it to evolve haphazardly and without forethought, they can reap important advantages, including the development of expatriate managers and enhanced organizational flexibility.[43]

Figure 15.5 illustrates four of the most common approaches to organization design used for international purposes. The design shown in A is the simplest, relying on a separate international division. Levi Strauss & Company uses this approach. The design shown in B, used by Ford Motor Company, is an extension of location departmentalization to international settings. An extension of product departmentalization, with each product manager being responsible for all product-related activities regardless of location, is shown in C. Finally, the design shown in D, most typical of larger multinational corporations, is an extension of the multidivisional structure with branches located in various foreign markets. Nestlé and Unilever use this type of design.

FIGURE 15.5 COMMON ORGANIZATION DESIGNS FOR INTERNATIONAL ORGANIZATIONS

Companies that compete in international markets must create an organization design that fits their own unique circumstances. These four general designs are representative of what many international organizations use. Each is derived from one of the basic forms of organization design.

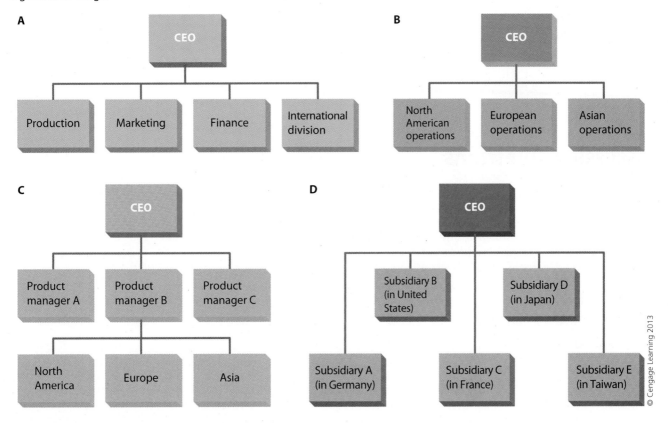

© Cengage Learning 2013

What is a team organization?

Do you think it is possible for a one-person operation, operating as a virtual organization, to grow large enough to compete with large businesses? Why or why not?

Summary of Learning Objectives and Key Points

1. Describe the basic nature of organization design.

   • Organization design is the overall set of structural elements and the relationships among those elements used to manage the total organization.

2. Identify and explain the two basic universal perspectives on organization design.

   • Two early universal models of organization design were the bureaucratic model and the behavioral model.
   • These models attempted to prescribe how all organizations should be designed.

3. Identify and explain several situational influences on organization design.

   • The situational view of organization design is based on the assumption that the optimal organization design is a function of situational factors.
   • Four important situational factors are:
     ○ technology
     ○ environment
     ○ size
     ○ organizational life cycle

4. Discuss how an organization's strategy and its design are interrelated.

   • An organization's strategy also helps shape its design.
   • In various ways, corporate- and business-level strategies both affect organization design.
   • Basic organizational functions like marketing and finance also play a role in shaping design.

5. Describe the basic forms of organization design.

   • Many organizations today adopt one of four basic organization designs:
     ○ functional (U form)
     ○ conglomerate (H form)
     ○ divisional (M form)
     ○ matrix
   • Other organizations use a hybrid design derived from two or more of these basic designs.

6. Describe emerging issues in organization design.

   • Four emerging issues in organization design are:
     ○ team organization
     ○ virtual organization
     ○ learning organization
     ○ international business organization

Discussion Questions

Questions for Review

1. Describe the three forms of core technology. Tell about the differences in organizational structure that occur in firms with each of the three types.
2. List the changes that occur as an organization grows in size. List the changes that occur as an organization ages over time. Are the two lists the same? Explain any differences you find.
3. Describe the basic forms of organization design. What are the advantages and disadvantages of each?
4. Compare and contrast the matrix organization and the team organization, describing any similarities and differences.

Questions for Analysis

5. The business world today is increasingly complex and variable, in virtually every country and industry. Thus organizations must become more organic. What are some of the outcomes that companies will experience as they become more organic and less mechanistic? Be sure to include both positive and negative outcomes.
6. Each of the organization designs is appropriate for some firms but not for others. Describe the characteristics that

a firm using the U form should have. Then do the same for the H-form, the M-form, and the matrix designs. For each item, explain the relationship between that set of characteristics and the choice of organization design.

7. What are the benefits of using the learning organization approach to design? Now consider that, in order to learn, organizations must be willing to tolerate many mistakes because it is only through the effort of understanding mistakes that learning can occur. With this statement in mind, what are some of the potential problems with the use of the learning organization approach?

Questions for Application

8. Consider an organization (such as your workplace, a club or society, a sorority or fraternity, a church, and so on) of which you are a member. Describe some structural elements of that organization that reflect the bureaucratic model. Describe some elements that reflect the behavioral model. In your opinion, is that organization more bureaucratic or more behavioral in its structure? Why?

9. Use the Internet or library to investigate a corporation's strategy. Then use the Internet or library to obtain a description of the firm's organization design. Can you identify any links between the company's strategy and structure? Share your findings with the class.

10. What form of organization does your university or college use? What form does your city or town government use? What form do other organizations with which you are familiar use? What similarities and differences do you see? Explain your answers.

CengageNow™ Highlights

Now use your CengageNow™ homework to help you:
- Apply management theories in your life
- Assess your management skills
- Master management terms and concepts
- Apply your knowledge to real-world situations
- Analyze and solve challenging management problems

In order to take advantage of these elements, your instructor will need to have set up a course for your class within CengageNow™. Ask your instructor to contact his/ her Cengage sales representative and Digital Solutions Manager to explore testing CengageNow™ in your course this term.

Managing Organization Change and Innovation

LEARNING OBJECTIVES

After studying this chapter, you should be able to:

1. Describe the nature of organization change, including forces for change and planned versus reactive change.

2. Discuss the steps in organization change and how to manage resistance to change.

3. Identify and describe major areas of organization change and discuss the assumptions, techniques, and effectiveness of organization development.

4. Describe the innovation process, forms of innovation, failure to innovate, and how organizations can promote innovation.

MANAGEMENT IN ACTION   The Science of the Deal

In 2000, OSI Pharmaceuticals, a small biotechnology company based on Long Island, New York, was looking for a partner to share in the development of a newly invented drug for the treatment of lung and pancreatic cancer. The drug was extremely promising, and with 42 companies bidding on a piece of the action, the OSI deal was the year's most competitive in the pharmaceuticals industry. The winner was San Francisco-based Genentech, a highly successful pioneer in the biotech field. In order to lock up the deal, both Genentech and its largest shareholder (and eventual parent), the Swiss pharmaceuticals company Roche Group, purchased $35 million in OSI stock and offered upfront fees totaling another $117 million.

It was certainly an attractive offer, but it wasn't actually the highest bid. OSI went with Genentech because it had more than money to offer. Joe McCracken, who negotiated the deal for Genentech, argues that OSI accepted his bid because his company paid attention to what OSI wanted (in addition to a healthy infusion of capital): "They wanted to build a company," he recalls, "and you were not going to help them build a company by giving them a whole bunch of cash. . . . What we

> "The way you maximize the value of the [biotech] business is by leveraging the resources of partners in manufacturing and development."
>
> —JOE MCCRACKEN, GLOBAL HEAD OF BUSINESS DEVELOPMENT, ROCHE GROUP

proposed . . . was a partnership where we would really work together and share the science and be partners in development." The agreement called for Genentech and OSI to share development costs and profits from U.S. sales and Roche to pay royalties on sales in all other markets.

According to McCracken (who was VP of Business Development at the time), deals like the one with OSI are mostly about the science and the organizational processes that transform scientific resources into profitable products. At Genentech, he says, "we emphasize scientific rationale and probability of approval much more than we emphasize market size. A strong underlying scientific rationale or a probability of approval will trump market size any time."

In January 2007, for instance, McCracken negotiated a deal with a biotech firm called Seattle Genetics Inc. to

Change is a fact of life in the biomedical research field as companies constantly scramble to stay abreast of the latest developments.

AVAVA/Shutterstock.Com

partner in the commercialization of a cancer drug known as SGN-40. Under the terms of the arrangement, Genentech made an upfront payment of $60 million and agreed to pay for future research, development, and manufacturing through "milestone" payments of more than $800 million based on Seattle Genetics' clinical and regulatory progress in developing the drug. It was an expensive deal, but McCracken had good reason to make it: "[F]or us to do these larger deals," he explains, ". . . we have to believe we have synergies we can exploit in maximizing the development of [the products]. In this case, we really believe we have some good insights and expertise in basic research and in development and manufacturing that we can leverage. . . . This product," he adds, "has the opportunity to address an important disease that we don't have anything else in our pipeline to address. We put a big premium on that." As of 2011, SGN-40 was performing well in clinical trials on patients with a form of blood cancer known as non-Hodgkin lymphoma.

Ironically, McCracken's first assignments in "business development" at Genentech involved selling off pieces of the company. Concerned about its direction, he left in 1993 but returned in 2000 to a much different organization. For one thing, Genentech had turned its attention to acquiring technologies rather than divesting them, and as head of business development, McCracken spent the next nine years helping to grow the company through deal making with partners like OSI and Seattle Genetics.

In the pharmaceuticals industry, in addition to the usual run of joint ventures and M&As, deals come in a variety of forms. *In-licensing* ventures, for example, are partnerships between firms with shared goals, strategies, or fields of interest; like Genentech's deals with OSI and Seattle Genetics, they're often created to share the costs of developing products from which both partners can profit. *Out-licensing* refers to ventures in which a firm seeks a partner to continue the development of a product that's previously been developed internally. Back in 1996, for example, Genentech had taken a drug called Raptiva through preclinical and mid-stage clinical trials but didn't have the financial wherewithal to take it any further. So it out-licensed the drug to a small biotech company called Xoma, which used its familiarity with similar antibodies to complete the development process ("better, faster, and cheaper," according to McCracken). Raptiva, a therapy for psoriasis, came out in 2003 and returned $500 million in revenue for Genentech over the next five years.

"Never underestimate the value of a small company that has a singular focus," advises McCracken, who points out that while Genentech was strapped for both the necessary "human resources and management attention," Raptiva was Xoma's "most important project."* In the long run, reasons McCracken, this approach to deal making means that "we have all these opportunities and [we] manage our internal growth. The way you maximize the value of the [biotech] business is by leveraging the resources of partners in manufacturing and development." Interestingly, McCracken's approach leaves little room for acquisition as a deal-making option; in fact, Genentech has only made one acquisition in its entire 33-year history. "We haven't had to do them to drive growth," he explains. "We've been able to sustain growth with our internal pipeline. We've been able to get access to the technologies and products that we needed through licensing activities."

In early 2004, as part of a major reorganization of Genentech's Development, Commercial, and Manufacturing activities, McCracken was given additional responsibilities as head of a new unit called Strategic Pipeline Development. Among the goals of the reorganization was focusing the efforts of top managers on product innovation and the firm's *product pipeline*—the flow of new-product concepts through the process that transforms them into products available to end users. McCracken's new responsibilities included heading up a team to advise the president of the Product Development unit on the expansion of the company's product pipeline.

In the next few years, McCracken's team would negotiate anywhere from 40 to 50 deals annually, but hooking up with partners soon became a secondary aspect of his job. Following the reorganization, he spent most of his time with what he called "my customers"—the people *inside* Genentech who conduct the research necessary to develop products already in the pipeline. The shift in his job description, according to McCracken, was important "because business development [at Genentech] is so integrated with our internal customers in research [and] development."

For the record, it wasn't long before McCracken was back at the job of making partnership deals, first as Roche's Head of Pharma Partnering Asia and, currently, as its Global Head of Business Development.[1]

---

*Unfortunately, Raptiva turned from asset to liability in 2009, when Genentech withdrew it from the market: Studies associated usage of the drug with the risk of a rare and usually fatal brain infection, and Genentech is now contending with a slew of lawsuits.

Managers like Joe McCracken have kept Genentech at the forefront of its industry through the astute management of innovation. In particular, the company relies on the development of innovative products to grow and prosper. On a broader level, Genentech also embraces change. As we will see, understanding when and how to implement change is a vital part of management. This chapter describes how organizations manage change. We first examine the nature of organization change and identify the basic issues of managing change. We then identify and describe major areas of change, including business process change, a major type of change undertaken by many firms recently. We then examine organization development and conclude by discussing organizational innovation as a vital form of change.

The Nature of Organization Change

Organization change is any substantive modification to some part of the organization.[2] Thus change can involve virtually any aspect of an organization: work schedules, bases for departmentalization, span of management, machinery, organization design, people themselves, and so on. It is important to keep in mind that any change in an organization may have effects extending beyond the actual area where the change is implemented. For example, when Northrop Grumman recently installed a new automated production system at one of its plants, employees were trained to operate new equipment, the compensation system was adjusted to reflect new skill levels, the span of management for supervisors was altered, and several related jobs were redesigned. Selection criteria for new employees were also changed, and a new quality-control system was installed.[3] In addition, it is quite common for multiple organization change activities to be going on simultaneously.[4]

organization change
Any substantive modification to some part of the organization

Forces for Change

Why do organizations find change necessary? The basic reason is that something relevant to the organization either has changed or is likely to change in the foreseeable future. The organization therefore may have little choice but to change as well. Indeed, a primary reason for the problems that organizations often face is failure to anticipate or respond properly to changing circumstances. The forces that compel change may be external or internal to the organization.[5]

External Forces External forces for change derive from the organization's general and task environments. For example, two energy crises, an aggressive Japanese automobile industry, floating currency exchange rates, and floating international interest rates—all manifestations of the international dimension of the general environment—have profoundly influenced U.S. automobile companies. New rules of production and competition forced them to dramatically alter the way they do business. In the political arena, new laws, court decisions, and regulations affect organizations. The technological dimension may yield new production techniques that the organization needs to explore. The economic dimension is affected by inflation, the cost of living, and money supplies. The sociocultural dimension, reflecting societal values, determines what kinds of products or services will be accepted in the market.

The need for change can be prompted by any number of things. For instance, the prices charged by competitors can force an organization to modify its own prices. But at a deeper level it may also force the organization to change its technologies, production methods, and supply chains in order to remain profitable at lower price.

David L. Moore/Alamy

Because of its proximity to the organization, the task environment is an even more powerful force for change. Competitors influence an organization through their price structures and product lines. When Hewlett-Packard lowers computer prices, Dell may have little choice but to follow suit. Because customers determine what products can be sold at what prices, organizations must be concerned with consumer tastes and preferences. Suppliers affect organizations by raising or lowering prices or changing product lines. Regulators can have dramatic effects on an organization. For example, if OSHA rules that a particular production process is dangerous to workers, it can force a firm to close a plant that uses that process until it meets stricter safety standards. Unions can force change when they have the clout to negotiate for higher wages or if they go on strike.[7]

> "Standing still is how you kill the company."
>
> —RAY DAVIS, CEO OF UMPQUA HOLDINGS[6]

Internal Forces A variety of forces inside the organization may cause change. If top management revises the organization's strategy, organization change is likely to result. A decision by an electronics company to enter the home computer market or a decision to increase a ten-year product sales goal by 3 percent would occasion many organization changes. Other internal forces for change may be reflections of external forces. As sociocultural values shift, for example, workers' attitudes toward their job may also shift—and workers may demand a change in working hours or working conditions. In such a case, even though the force is rooted in the external environment, the organization must respond directly to the internal pressure it generates.[8]

Planned Versus Reactive Change

Some change is planned well in advance; other change comes about as a reaction to unexpected events. Planned change is change that is designed and implemented in an orderly and timely fashion in anticipation of future events. Reactive change is a piecemeal response to circumstances as they develop. Because reactive change may be hurried, the potential for poorly conceived and executed change is increased. Planned change is almost always preferable to reactive change.[9]

Georgia-Pacific, a large forest products business, is an excellent example of a firm that went through a planned and well-managed change process. When A. D. Correll became CEO, he quickly became alarmed at the firm's high accident rate—nine serious injuries per 100 employees each year, and 26 deaths during the most recent five-year period. Although the forest products business is inherently dangerous, Correll believed that the accident rate was far too high and set out on a major change effort to improve things. He and other top managers developed a multistage change program intended to educate workers about safety, improve safety equipment in the plant, and eliminate a long-standing part of the firm's culture that made injuries almost a badge of courage. As a result, Georgia-Pacific soon achieved the best safety record in the industry, with relatively few injuries.[10]

On the other hand, Caterpillar was caught flat-footed by a worldwide recession in the construction industry, suffered enormous losses, and took several years to recover. Had managers at Caterpillar anticipated the need for change earlier, they might have been able to respond more quickly. Similarly, Kodak had to cut 12,000 jobs in reaction to sluggish sales and profits.[11] Again, better anticipation might have forestalled those job cuts. The importance of approaching change from a planned perspective is reinforced by the frequency of organization change. Most companies or divisions of large companies implement some form of moderate change at least every year and one or more major changes every four to five years.[12] Managers who sit back and respond only when they have to are likely to spend a lot of time hastily changing and rechanging things. A more effective approach is to anticipate forces urging change and plan ahead to deal with them.[13]

planned change
Change that is designed and implemented in an orderly and timely fashion in anticipation of future events

reactive change
A piecemeal response to circumstances as they develop

Managing Change in Organizations

Organization change is a complex phenomenon. A manager cannot simply wave a wand and implement a planned change like magic. Instead, any change must be systematic and logical to have a realistic opportunity to succeed.[14] To carry this off, the manager needs to understand the steps of effective change and how to counter employee resistance to change.[15]

Steps in the Change Process

Researchers have over the years developed a number of models or frameworks outlining steps for change.[16] The Lewin model was one of the first, although a more comprehensive approach is usually more useful in today's complex business environment.

The Lewin Model Kurt Lewin, a noted organizational theorist, suggested that every change requires three steps.[17] The first step is *unfreezing*—individuals who will be affected by the impending change must be led to recognize why the change is necessary. Next, the *change itself* is implemented. Finally, *refreezing* involves reinforcing and supporting the change so that it becomes a part of the system.[18] For example, one of the changes Caterpillar faced in response to the recession noted earlier involved a massive workforce reduction. The first step (unfreezing) was convincing the United Auto Workers to support the reduction because of its importance to long-term effectiveness. After this unfreezing was accomplished, 30,000 jobs were eliminated (implementation). Then Caterpillar worked to improve its damaged relationship with its workers (refreezing) by guaranteeing future pay hikes and promising no more cutbacks. As interesting as Lewin's model is, it unfortunately lacks operational specificity. Thus a more comprehensive perspective is often needed.

A Comprehensive Approach to Change The comprehensive approach to change takes a systems view and delineates a series of specific steps that often lead to successful change. This expanded model is illustrated in Figure 16.1. The first step is recognizing the need for change. Reactive change might be triggered by employee complaints, declines in productivity or turnover, court injunctions, sales slumps, or labor strikes. Recognition may simply be managers' awareness that change in a certain area is inevitable. For example, managers may be aware of the general frequency of organizational change undertaken by most organizations and recognize that their organization should probably follow the same pattern. The immediate stimulus might be the result of a forecast indicating new market potential, the accumulation of a cash surplus for possible investment, or an opportunity to achieve and capitalize on a major technological breakthrough. Managers might also initiate change today because indicators suggest that it will be necessary in the near future.[19]

Managers must next set goals for the change. To increase market share, to enter new markets, to restore employee morale, to settle a strike, and to identify investment opportunities all might be goals for change. Third, managers must diagnose what brought on the need for change. Turnover, for example, might be caused by low pay, poor working conditions, poor supervisors, or employee dissatisfaction. Thus, although turnover may be the immediate stimulus for change, managers must understand its causes to make the right changes.

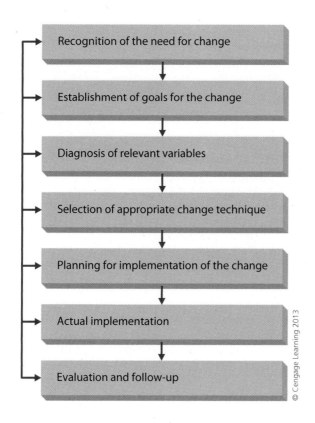

Recognition of the need for change

Establishment of goals for the change

Diagnosis of relevant variables

Selection of appropriate change technique

Planning for implementation of the change

Actual implementation

Evaluation and follow-up

© Cengage Learning 2013

FIGURE 16.1 STEPS IN THE CHANGE PROCESS

Managers must understand how and why to implement change. A manager who, when implementing change, follows a logical and orderly sequence like the one shown here is more likely to succeed than a manager whose change process is haphazard and poorly conceived.

The next step is to select a change technique that will accomplish the intended goals. If turnover is caused by low pay, a new reward system may be needed. If the cause is poor supervision, interpersonal skills training may be called for. (Various change techniques are summarized later in this chapter.) After the appropriate technique has been chosen, its implementation must be planned. Issues to consider include the costs of the change, its effects on other areas of the organization, and the degree of employee participation appropriate for the situation. If the change is implemented as planned, the results should then be evaluated. If the change was intended to reduce turnover, managers must check turnover after the change has been in effect for a while. If turnover is still too high, other changes may be necessary.[20]

Understanding Resistance to Change

Another element in the effective management of change is understanding the resistance that often accompanies change.[21] Managers need to know why people resist change and what can be done about their resistance. When Westinghouse first provided all of its managers with personal computers, most people responded favorably. One manager, however, resisted the change to the point where he began leaving work every day at noon! It was some time before he began staying in the office all day again. Such resistance is common for a variety of reasons.[22]

Uncertainty Perhaps the biggest cause of employee resistance to change is uncertainty. In the face of impending change, employees may become anxious and nervous. They may worry about their ability to meet new job demands, they may think that their job security is threatened, or they may simply dislike ambiguity. Nabisco was once the target of an extended and confusing takeover battle, and during the entire time, employees were nervous about the impending change. The *Wall Street Journal* described them this way: "Many are angry at their leaders and fearful for their jobs. They are swapping rumors and spinning scenarios for the ultimate outcome of the battle for the tobacco and food giant. Headquarters staffers in Atlanta know so little about what's happening in New York that some call their office 'the mushroom complex,' where they are kept in the dark."[23] More recently, in late 2010, 13,500 British Airways cabin crew members voted to participate in a strike over the heavily traveled holiday season. The action against the airlines was spurred by high levels of uncertainty as British Airways planned to merge with Iberia and proposed cutting 1,700 jobs and freezing employee wages in the process.[24]

Threatened Self-Interests Many impending changes threaten the self-interests of some managers within the organization. A change might diminish their power or influence within the company, so they fight it. Managers at Sears once developed a plan calling for a new type of store. The new stores would be somewhat smaller than a typical Sears store and would not be located in large shopping malls. Instead, they would be located in smaller strip centers. They would carry clothes and other "soft goods," but not hardware, appliances, furniture, or automotive products. When executives in charge of the excluded product lines heard about the plan, they raised such strong objections that the plan was cancelled.

Different Perceptions A third reason that people resist change is due to different percep-tions. A manager may make a decision and recommend a plan for change on the basis of her own assessment of a situation. Others in the organization may resist the change because they do not agree with the manager's assessment or they perceive the situation differently.[25] Executives at 7-Eleven battled this problem as they attempted to enact a major organiza-tional change. The corporation wanted to take its convenience stores a bit "upscale" and begin selling fancy fresh foods to go, the newest hardcover novels, some gourmet products, and higher-quality coffee. But many franchisees balked because they saw this move as taking the firm away from its core blue-collar customers.

Feelings of Loss Many changes involve altering work arrangements in ways that dis-rupt existing social networks. Because social relationships are important, most people resist any change that might adversely affect those relationships. Other intangibles threat-ened by change include power, status, security, familiarity with existing procedures, and self-confidence.

Overcoming Resistance to Change

Of course, a manager should not give up in the face of resistance to change. Although there are no sure-fire cures, there are several techniques that at least have the potential to over-come resistance.[26]

Participation Participation is often the most effective technique for overcoming resistance to change. Employees who participate in planning and implementing a change are better able to understand the reasons for the change. Uncertainty is reduced, and self-interests and social relationships are less threatened. Having had an opportunity to express their ideas and assume the perspectives of others, employees are more likely to accept the change gracefully. A classic study of participation monitored the introduction of a change in production methods among four groups in a Virginia pajama factory.[27] The two groups that were allowed to fully participate in planning and implementing the change improved sig-nificantly in their productivity and satisfaction relative to the two groups that did not participate. Allstate Technology created the Allstate Change Agent Network to involve employees in change by fostering their understanding and input. Those involved spend about four hours per month for one year taking part in task forces to develop ideas for change which go directly to leadership.

"People often resent change when they have no involvement in how it should be implemented. So, contrary to popular belief, people do not resist change, they resist being controlled."

—KEN BLANCHARD, MANAGEMENT CONSULTANT AND LEADERSHIP EXPERT[28]

revolves around information technology. The adoption and institutionalization of information technology innovations is almost constant in most firms today. Sun Microsystems, for example, adopted a very short-range planning cycle to be best prepared for environmental changes.[32] Another important form of technological change involves equipment. To keep pace with competitors, firms periodically find that replacing existing machinery and equipment with newer models is necessary.

A change in work processes or work activities may be necessary if new equipment is introduced or new products are manufactured. In manufacturing industries, the major reason for changing a work process is to accommodate a change in the materials used to produce a finished product. Consider a firm that manufactures battery-operated flashlights. For many years flashlights were made of metal, but now most are made of plastic. A firm might decide to move from metal to plastic flashlights because of consumer preferences, raw materials costs, or other reasons. Whatever the reason, the technology necessary to make flashlights from plastic differs importantly from that used to make flashlights from metal. Work process changes may occur in service organizations as well as in manufacturing firms. As traditional barbershops and beauty parlors are replaced by hair salons catering to both sexes, for example, the hybrid organizations have to develop new methods for handling appointments and setting prices.

A change in work sequence may or may not accompany a change in equipment or a change in work processes. Making a change in work sequence means altering the order or sequence of the workstations involved in a particular manufacturing process. For example, a manufacturer might have two parallel assembly lines producing two similar sets of machine parts. The lines might converge at one central quality-control unit, where inspectors verify tolerances. The manager, however, might decide to change to periodic rather than final inspection. Under this arrangement, one or more inspections are established farther up the line. Work sequence changes can also be made in service organizations. The processing of insurance claims, for example, could be changed. The sequence of logging and verifying claims, requesting checks, getting countersignatures, and mailing checks could be altered in several ways, such as combining the first two steps or routing the claims through one person while another handles checks. Organizational control systems may also be targets of change.[33] For example, a firm attempting to improve the quality of its products might develop and implement a set of more rigorous and comprehensive quality-control procedures.

Finally, many businesses have been working to implement technological and operations change by installing and using complex and integrated software systems. Such systems—called *enterprise resource planning*—link virtually all facets of the business, making it easier for managers to keep abreast of related developments. Enterprise resource planning, or ERP, is a large-scale information system for integrating and synchronizing the many activities in the extended enterprise. In most cases these systems are purchased from external vendors who then tailor their products to the client's unique needs and requirements. Companywide processes—such as materials management, production planning, order management, and financial reporting—can all be managed via ERP. In effect, these are the processes that cut across product lines, departments, and geographic locations.

Developing the ERP system starts by identifying the key processes that need critical attention, such as supplier relationships, materials flows, or customer order fulfillment. The system could result, for instance, in sales processes being integrated with production planning and then integrating both of these into the firm's financial accounting system. For example, a customer in Rome can place an order that is to be produced in Ireland, schedule it to be shipped via air cargo to Rome, and then have it picked up by a truck at the airport and delivered to the customer's warehouse by a specified date. All of these activities are synchronized by activities linkages in one massive database.

The ERP integrates all activities and information flows that relate to the firm's critical processes. It also keeps updated real-time information on their current status, reports recent past transactions and upcoming planned transactions, and provides electronic notices that action is required on some items if planned schedules are to be met. It coordinates internal

enterprise resource planning (ERP)
A large-scale information system for integrating and synchronizing the many activities in the extended enterprise

operations with activities by outside suppliers and notifies business partners and customers of current status and upcoming deliveries and billings. It can integrate financial flows among the firm, its suppliers, its customers, and commercial bank deposits for up-to-the-minute status reports that can be used to create real-time financial reports at a moment's notice, rather than in the traditional one-month (or longer) time span for producing a financial statement. ERP's multilanguage capabilities also allow real-time correspondence in various languages to facilitate international transactions.

Changing People, Attitudes, and Behaviors

A third area of organization change has to do with human resources. For example, an organization might decide to change the skill level of its workforce. This change might be prompted by changes in technology or by a general desire to upgrade the quality of the workforce. Thus training programs and new selection criteria might be needed. The organization might also decide to improve its workers' performance level. In this case, a new incentive system or performance-based training might be in order. Due to intense competition for talent from competitors, Microsoft has increased its employees' compensation by shifting a portion of their stock awards to their base salaries, as well as boosting funding for bonuses and stock awards to reward its top performers.[34] Volvo Construction Equipment laid off roughly 25 percent of its workforce globally, leaving the company with employees who are focused and understand the urgency necessary to facilitate change.[35]

Perceptions and expectations are also a common focus of organization change. Workers in an organization might believe that their wages and benefits are not as high as they should be. Management, however, might have evidence that shows the firm is paying a competitive wage and providing a superior benefit package. The change, then, would be centered on informing and educating the workforce about the comparative value of its compensation package. A common way to do this is to publish a statement that places an actual dollar value on each benefit provided and compares that amount to what other local organizations are providing their workers. Change might also be directed at employee attitudes and values. In many organizations today, managers are trying to eliminate adversarial relationships with workers and to adopt a more collaborative relationship. In many ways, changing attitudes and values is perhaps the hardest thing to do.[36]

Changing Business Processes

Many organizations today have also gone through massive and comprehensive change programs involving all aspects of organization design, technology, and people. Although various descriptions are used, the terms currently in vogue for these changes are *business process change* or *reengineering*. Specifically, business process change, or reengineering, is the radical redesign of all aspects of a business to achieve major gains in cost, service, or time.[37] ERP, as described above, is a common platform for changing business processes. However, business process change is a more comprehensive set of changes that goes beyond software and information systems.

Corning, for example, has undergone major reengineering over the last few years. Whereas the 150-year-old business once manufactured cookware and other durable consumer goods, it has transformed itself into a high-tech powerhouse making such products as the ultra-thin screens used in products like smart phones and laptop computers.[38] Similarly, the dramatic overhauls of Kodak away from print film to other forms of optical imaging, of Yellow into a sophisticated freight delivery firm, and of UPS into a major international delivery giant all required business process changes throughout these organizations.

business process change (reengineering)
The radical redesign of all aspects of a business to achieve major gains in cost, service, or time

The Need for Business Process Change Why are so many organizations finding it necessary to undergo business process change? We note in Chapter 2 that all systems, including organizations, are subject to entropy—a normal process leading to system decline. An organization is behaving most typically when it maintains the status quo, does not change in sync with its environment, and starts consuming its own resources to survive. In a sense, that is what happened to Kmart. In the early and mid-1970s, Kmart was in such a high-flying growth mode that it passed first JCPenney and then Sears to become the world's largest retailer. But then the firm's managers grew complacent and assumed that the discount retailer's prosperity would continue and that they need not worry about environmental shifts, the growth of Walmart, and so forth—and entropy set in. The key is to recognize the beginning of the decline and immediately move toward changing relevant business processes. For instance, Netflix required business process changes throughout the organization as it shifted its focus to delivering movies and TV over the Internet rather than through the mail. But these changes were approached in a planned and strategic fashion.[39] Major problems occur when managers either do not recognize the onset of entropy until it is well advanced or are complacent about taking steps to correct it.[40]

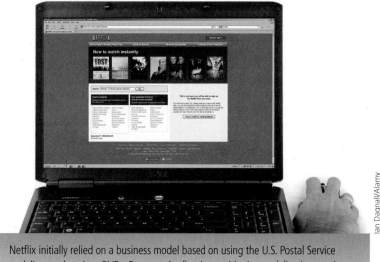

Netflix initially relied on a business model based on using the U.S. Postal Service to deliver and retrieve DVDs. But now the firm is transitioning to delivering movies online. This new business model has required major changes throughout Netflix's entire set of business processes.

Ian Dagnall/Alamy

Approaches to Business Process Change Figure 16.3 shows general steps in changing business processes, or reengineering. The first step is setting goals and developing a strategy for the changes. The organization must know in advance what new business

© Cengage Learning 2013

FIGURE 16.3 THE REENGINEERING PROCESS

Reengineering is a major redesign of all areas of an organization. To be successful, reengineering requires a systematic and comprehensive assessment of the entire organization. Goals, top management support, and a sense of urgency help the organization re-create itself and blend both top-level and bottom-up perspectives.

processes are supposed to accomplish and how those accomplishments will be achieved. Next, top managers must begin and direct the reengineering effort. If a CEO simply announces that business process change is to occur but does nothing else, the program is unlikely to be successful. But if the CEO is constantly involved in the process, underscoring its importance and taking the lead, business process change stands a much better chance of success.

Most experts also agree that successful business process change is usually accompanied by a sense of urgency. People in the organization must see the clear and present need for the changes being implemented and appreciate their importance. In addition, most successful reengineering efforts start with a new, clean slate. In other words, rather than assuming that the existing organization is a starting point and then trying to modify it, business process change usually starts by asking questions such as how customers are best served and competitors best neutralized. New approaches and systems are then created and imposed in place of existing ones.

Finally, business process change requires a careful blend of top-down and bottom-up involvement. On the one hand, strong leadership is necessary, but too much involvement by top management can make the changes seem autocratic. Similarly, employee participation is also important, but too little involvement by leaders can undermine the program's importance and create a sense that top managers do not care. Thus care must be taken to carefully balance these two countervailing forces. Our next section explores more fully one related but distinct approach called *organization development*.

Organization Development

We have noted in several places the importance of people and change. Beyond those change interests discussed above, a special area of interest that focuses almost exclusively on people is organization development (OD).

OD Assumptions Organization development is concerned with changing attitudes, perceptions, behaviors, and expectations. More precisely, **organization development (OD)** is a planned effort that is organization-wide and managed from the top, intended to increase organizational effectiveness and health through planned interventions in the organization's process, using behavioral science knowledge.[41] The theory and practice of OD are based on several very important assumptions. The first is that employees have a desire to grow and develop. Another is that employees have a strong need to be accepted by others within the organization. Still another critical assumption of OD is that the total organization and the way it is designed will influence the way individuals and groups within the organization behave. Thus some form of collaboration between managers and their employees is necessary to (1) take advantage of the skills and abilities of the employees and (2) eliminate aspects of the organization that retard employee growth, development, and group acceptance. Because of the intensely personal nature of many OD activities, many large organizations rely on one or more OD consultants (either full-time employees assigned to this function or outside experts hired specifically for OD purposes) to implement and manage their OD program.[42]

organization development (OD)
An effort that is planned, organization-wide, and managed from the top, intended to increase organizational effectiveness and health through planned interventions in the organization's process, using behavioral science knowledge

OD Techniques Several kinds of interventions or activities are generally considered part of organization development.[43] Some OD programs may use only one or a few of these; other programs use several of them at once.

- *Diagnostic activities.* Just as a physician examines patients to diagnose their current condition, an OD diagnosis analyzes the current condition of an organization. To carry out this diagnosis, managers use questionnaires, opinion or attitude surveys, interviews, archival data, and meetings to assess various characteristics of

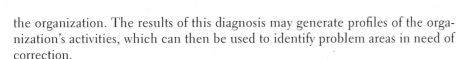

the organization. The results of this diagnosis may generate profiles of the organization's activities, which can then be used to identify problem areas in need of correction.

- *Team building*. Team-building activities are intended to enhance the effectiveness and satisfaction of individuals who work in groups or teams and to promote overall group effectiveness. Given the widespread use of teams today, these activities have taken on increased importance. An OD consultant might interview team members to determine how they feel about the group; then an off-site meeting could be held to discuss the issues that surfaced and iron out any problem areas or member concerns. Caterpillar used team building as one method for changing the working relationships between workers and supervisors from confrontational to cooperative. An interesting new approach to team building involves having executive teams participate in group cooking classes to teach them the importance of interdependence and coordination.[44]

- *Survey feedback*. In survey feedback, each employee responds to a questionnaire intended to measure perceptions and attitudes (for example, satisfaction and supervisory style). Everyone involved, including the supervisor, receives the results of the survey. The aim of this approach is usually to change the behavior of supervisors by showing them how their subordinates view them. After the feedback has been provided, workshops may be conducted to evaluate results and suggest constructive changes.

- *Education*. Educational activities focus on classroom training. Although such activities can be used for technical or skill-related purposes, an OD educational activity typically focuses on "sensitivity skills"—that is, it teaches people to be more considerate and understanding of the people they work with. Participants often go through a series of experiential or role-playing exercises to learn better how others in the organization feel.[45]

- *Intergroup activities*. The focus of intergroup activities is on improving the relationships between two or more groups. We noted in Chapter 14 that, as group interdependence increases, so do coordination difficulties. Intergroup OD activities are designed to promote cooperation or resolve conflicts that arose as a result of interdependence. Experiential or role-playing activities are often used to bring this about.

- *Third-party peacemaking*. Another approach to OD is through third-party peacemaking, which is most often used when substantial conflict exists within the organization. Third-party peacemaking can be appropriate on the individual, group, or organizational level. The third party, usually an OD consultant, uses a variety of mediation or negotiation techniques to resolve any problems or conflicts among individuals or groups.

- *Technostructural activities*. Technostructural activities are concerned with the design of the organization, the technology of the organization, and the interrelationship of design and technology with people on the job. A structural change such as an increase in decentralization, a job design change such as an increase in the use of automation, and a technological change involving a modification in work flow all qualify as technostructural OD activities if their objective is to improve group and interpersonal relationships within the organization.

- *Process consultation*. In process consultation, an OD consultant observes groups in the organization to develop an understanding of their communication patterns, decision-making and leadership processes, and methods of cooperation and conflict resolution. The consultant then provides feedback to the involved parties about the processes he or she has observed. The goal of this form of intervention is to improve the observed processes. A leader who is presented with feedback outlining deficiencies in his or her leadership style, for example, might be expected to change to overcome them.

- *Life and career planning.* Life and career planning helps employees formulate their personal goals and evaluate strategies for integrating their goals with the goals of the organization. Such activities might include specification of training needs and plotting a career map. General Electric has a reputation for doing an outstanding job in this area.
- *Coaching and counseling.* Coaching and counseling provide nonevaluative feedback to individuals. The purpose is to help people develop a better sense of how others see them and learn behaviors that will assist others in achieving their work-related goals. The focus is not on how the individual is performing today; instead, it is on how the person can perform better in the future.
- *Planning and goal setting.* More pragmatic than many other interventions are activities designed to help managers improve their planning and goal setting. Emphasis still falls on the individual, however, because the intent is to help individuals and groups integrate themselves into the overall planning process. The OD consultant might use the same approach as in process consultation, but the focus is more technically oriented on the mechanics of planning and goal setting.

The Effectiveness of OD Given the diversity of activities encompassed by OD, it is not surprising that managers report mixed results from various OD interventions. Organizations that actively practice some form of OD include American Airlines, Texas Instruments, Procter & Gamble, and BFGoodrich. Goodrich, for example, has trained 60 people in OD processes and techniques. These trained experts have subsequently become internal OD consultants to assist other managers in applying the techniques.[46] Many other managers, in contrast, report that they have tried OD but discarded it.[47]

OD will probably remain an important part of management theory and practice. Of course, there are no sure things when dealing with social systems such as organizations, and the effectiveness of many OD techniques is difficult to evaluate. Because all organizations are open systems interacting with their environments, an improvement in an organization after an OD intervention may be attributable to the intervention, but it may also be attributable to changes in economic conditions, luck, or other factors.[48]

Identify each of the major areas of organization change and provide examples to illustrate each one.

Based on your own knowledge and experiences, which, if any, of these areas of change is likely to become more prevalent in the future? Which, if any, is likely to become less prevalent? Why?

CONCEPT CHECK

 ## Organizational Innovation

innovation
The managed effort of an organization to develop new products or services or new uses for existing products or services

A final element of organization change that we address is innovation. Innovation is the managed effort of an organization to develop new products or services, or new uses for existing products or services. Innovation is clearly important because, without new products or services, any organization will fall behind its competition.[49] Our *Management in Action* story highlighted the importance of innovation in the growth of the biotech firm Genentech. The *Technically Speaking* box entitled "The F/X of Tech from the Fan's POV" on page 403 takes a close look at the role of innovation in the start-up and development of a smaller company called Sportvision.

TECHNICALLY SPEAKING

The F/X of Tech from the Fan's POV

John Storey/Contributor/TIME & LIFE Images/Getty Images

Football fans: Where were you on September 27, 1998? It was a Sunday, so you were probably watching a couple of National Football League (NFL) games, perhaps an otherwise less-than-memorable matchup between the Baltimore Ravens and Cincinnati Bengals. Fans in the stands didn't see anything out of the ordinary, but viewers of the game on Fox TV got their first look at a remarkable innovation in sports telecasting: the virtual first-and-ten line—that bright-yellow stripe that appears on your TV screen to show you where the offensive team needs to go in order to keep the football. A decade later, according to one ESPN executive, the virtual first-and-ten line has "become so much a part of the fabric [of football on TV] that if people don't see it, their reaction is that the telecast is substandard." (Football fans needn't worry: A deal reached in 2010 ensures that the 1st & Ten Line™ computer will enhance Fox NFL broadcasts through the 2013–14 season.)

The biggest innovation in sports coverage since slo-mo and instant replay (both of which appeared in the 1960s), the 1st & Ten Line is a product of Chicago-based Sportvision Inc., which has since become a pipeline of innovative technologies for revolutionizing TV sports from golf to NASCAR. Today, PITCHf/x traces the arc of pitches in Major League Baseball games, and the newly introduced Fieldf/x, which tracks the movements

of every player on the field, earned Sportvision a spot on *Fast Company* magazine's 2010 list of "The World's Most Innovative Companies." RACEf/x treats motor-sports fans to virtual dashboards and simulated flags to identify cars, and an in-car electronic device gathers and relays data on speed, RPMs, and track position. There are also applications tailored to golf, horse racing, soccer, bowling, Olympic competition, and extreme sports. Sportvision bills itself as "the nation's premier innovator of sports and entertainment products for fans, media, and marketers," and *SportsBusiness Journal* credits the company with ten of the 20 greatest all-time innovations in sports broadcasting.

Currently, about 70 percent of the company's revenues come from licensing its technology to the networks that broadcast the sporting events. Unfortunately, though 2009 revenues from such clients as Fox and ESPN reached $20 million, earnings amounted to only $3 million. Not surprisingly, the company has turned to additional sources of revenue. At the top of the list are Internet subscription packages because, as CEO Hank Adams puts it, "there's a big difference between serving a dozen clients versus serving a million customer subscribers." With Nascar Trackpass RaceView, for instance, auto-racing fans can pay $80 a year to track drivers in real time and even enjoy cockpit views from any car in the race.

Another innovative technology also involves a partnership with NASCAR: In order to further blur the increasingly fine line between real and virtual sports, Sportvision is currently developing a new generation of computer video games that will use real-time data to put racing fans in the driver's seat, barreling around the oval at Daytona and bumping fenders with the likes of Dale Earnhardt Jr.

References: Mark Hyman, "Stan Honey: Virtual Virtuoso," *BusinessWeek*, October 31, 2005, www.businessweek.com on March 28, 2011; Jeff Borden, "Second and 10 for Sportvision," *BusinessWeek*, February 29, 2008, www.businessweek.com on March 28, 2011; Sportvision Inc., "Sportvision and Fox Sports Media Group Announce New Partnership to Enhance Coverage," press release, July 13, 2010, www.sportvision.com on March 28, 2011; Chuck Salter, "#34 Sportvision," *Fast Company*, February 17, 2010, www.fastcompany.com on March 28, 2011; "Goal Oriented: How Hank Adams Applied Technology to Sports to Make Sportvision a Winner," *Smart Business*, July 2008, www.sbonline.com on March 28, 2011; Sportvision Inc., "The New View of RaceView," 2010, www.sportvision.com on March 28, 2011.

The Innovation Process

The organizational innovation process consists of developing, applying, launching, growing, and managing the maturity and decline of creative ideas.[50] This process is depicted in Figure 16.4.

Innovation Development Innovation development involves the evaluation, modification, and improvement of creative ideas. Innovation development can transform a product or service with only modest potential into a product or service with significant potential. Parker Brothers, for example, decided during innovation development not to market an indoor volleyball game but instead to sell separately the appealing little foam ball designed for the game. The firm will never know how well the volleyball game would have sold, but the Nerf ball and numerous related products generated millions of dollars in revenues for Parker Brothers.

Innovation Application Innovation application is the stage in which an organization takes a developed idea and uses it in the design, manufacturing, or delivery of new products, services, or processes. At this point the innovation emerges from the laboratory and is transformed into tangible goods or services. One example of innovation application is the use of radar-based focusing systems in Polaroid's instant cameras. The idea of using radio waves to discover the location, speed, and direction of moving objects was first applied extensively by Allied forces during World War II. As radar technology developed during the following years, the electrical components needed became smaller and more streamlined. Researchers at Polaroid applied this well-developed technology in a new way.[51]

Application Launch Application launch is the stage at which an organization introduces new products or services to the marketplace. The important question is not "Does the innovation work?" but "Will customers want to purchase the innovative product and service?" History is full of creative ideas that did not generate enough interest among customers to be successful. Some notable innovation failures include a portable seat warmer from Sony, "New" Coke, Polaroid's SX-70 instant camera (which cost $3 billion to develop, but never sold more than 100,000 units in a year), and the flip video recorder. Thus, despite development and application, new products and services can still fail at the launch phase.

Application Growth Once an innovation has been successfully launched, it then enters the stage of application growth. This is a period of high economic performance for an organization because demand for the product or service is often greater than supply. Organizations that fail to anticipate this stage may unintentionally limit their growth, as Apple did by not anticipating

FIGURE 16.4 THE INNOVATION PROCESS

Organizations actively seek to manage the innovation process. These steps illustrate the general life cycle that characterizes most innovations. Of course, as with creativity, the innovation process will suffer if it is approached too mechanically and rigidly.

© Cengage Learning 2013

demand for its iMac computer.[52] At the same time, overestimating demand for a new product can be just as detrimental to performance. Unsold products can sit in warehouses for years.

Innovation Maturity After a period of growing demand, an innovative product or service often enters a period of maturity. Innovation maturity is the stage at which most organizations in an industry have access to an innovation and are applying it in approximately the same way. The technological application of an innovation during this stage of the innovation process can be very sophisticated. Because most firms have access to the innovation, however, either as a result of their developing the innovation on their own or copying the innovation of others, it does not provide competitive advantage to any one of them. The time that elapses between innovation development and innovation maturity varies notably depending on the particular product or service. Whenever an innovation involves the use of complex skills (such as a complicated manufacturing process or highly sophisticated teamwork), moving from the growth phase to the maturity phase will take longer. In addition, if the skills needed to implement these innovations are rare and difficult to imitate, then strategic imitation may be delayed, and the organization may enjoy a period of sustained competitive advantage.

Innovation Decline Every successful innovation bears the seeds of its own decline. Because an organization does not gain a competitive advantage from an innovation at maturity, it must encourage its creative scientists, engineers, and managers to begin looking for new innovations. This continued search for competitive advantage usually leads new products and services to move from the creative process through innovation maturity, and finally to innovation decline. Innovation decline is the stage during which demand for an innovation decreases and substitute innovations are developed and applied.

Forms of Innovation

Each creative idea that an organization develops poses a different challenge for the innovation process. Innovations can be radical or incremental, technical or managerial, and product or process.

Radical Versus Incremental Innovations Radical innovations are new products, services, or technologies developed by an organization that completely replace the existing products, services, or technologies in an industry.[53] Incremental innovations are new products or processes that modify existing ones. Firms that implement radical innovations fundamentally shift the nature of competition and the interaction of firms within their environments. Firms that implement incremental innovations alter, but do not fundamentally change, competitive interaction in an industry.

Over the last several years, organizations have introduced many radical innovations. For example, compact disk technology replaced long-playing vinyl records in the recording industry, and now digital downloading is replacing CDs; DVDs have replaced videocassettes but are now being supplanted by Blu-ray DVDs and streaming video; and high-definition television is replacing regular television technology. Whereas radical innovations like these tend to be very visible and public, incremental innovations actually are more numerous. For instance, each new generation of the iPhone and the iPod represent relatively minor changes over previous versions.

Technical Versus Managerial Innovations Technical innovations are changes in the physical appearance or performance of a product or service, or of the physical processes through which a product or service is manufactured. Many of the most important innovations over the last 50 years have been technical. For example, the serial replacement of the vacuum tube with the transistor, the transistor with the integrated circuit, and the integrated circuit with the microchip has greatly enhanced the power, ease of use, and speed of operation of a wide variety of electronic products. Not all innovations developed by organizations are technical, however. Managerial innovations are changes in the management process by

radical innovation
A new product, service, or technology that completely replaces an existing one

incremental innovation
A new product, service, or technology that modifies an existing one

technical innovation
A change in the appearance or performance of products or services, or of the physical processes through which a product or service passes

managerial innovation
A change in the management process in an organization

which products and services are conceived, built, and delivered to customers.[54] Managerial innovations do not necessarily affect the physical appearance or performance of products or services directly. In effect, business process change or reengineering, as we discuss earlier, represents a managerial innovation.

Product Versus Process Innovations   Perhaps the two most important types of technical innovations are product innovations and process innovations. Product innovations are changes in the physical characteristics or performance of existing products or services or the creation of brand-new products or services. Process innovations are changes in the way products or services are manufactured, created, or distributed. Whereas managerial innovations generally affect the broader context of development, process innovations directly affect manufacturing.

The implementation of robotics, as we discussed earlier, is a process innovation. As Figure 16.5 shows, the effect of product and process innovations on economic return depends on the stage of the innovation process that a new product or service occupies. At first, during development, application, and launch, the physical attributes and capabilities of an innovation most affect organizational performance. Thus product innovations are particularly important during these beginning phases. Later, as an innovation enters the phases of growth, maturity, and decline, an organization's ability to develop process innovations, such as fine-tuning manufacturing, increasing product quality, and improving product distribution, becomes important to maintaining economic return.

So what's a good example of incremental versus radical innovation, of technical versus managerial innovation, and of both product and process innovation? You can find the answer in the *Change* box entitled "A Marriage of Technique and Technology" on page 407. (*Hint:* It has 88 keys.)

Japanese organizations have often excelled at process innovation. The market for 35mm cameras was dominated by German and other European manufacturers when, in the early 1960s, Japanese organizations such as Canon and Nikon began making cameras. Some of these early Japanese products were not very successful, but these companies continued to invest in their process technology and eventually were able to increase quality and decrease manufacturing costs.[55] The Japanese organizations came to dominate the worldwide market for 35mm cameras, and the German companies, because they were not able to maintain the same pace of process innovation, struggled to maintain market share and profitability. And as film technology gives way to digital photography, the same Japanese firms are effectively transitioning to leadership in this market as well.

product innovation
A change in the physical characteristics or performance of an existing product or service or the creation of new ones

process innovation
A change in the way a product or service is manufactured, created, or distributed

FIGURE 16.5 EFFECTS OF PRODUCT AND PROCESS INNOVATION ON ECONOMIC RETURN

As the innovation process moves from development to decline, the economic return from product innovations gradually declines. In contrast, the economic return from process innovations increases during this same process.

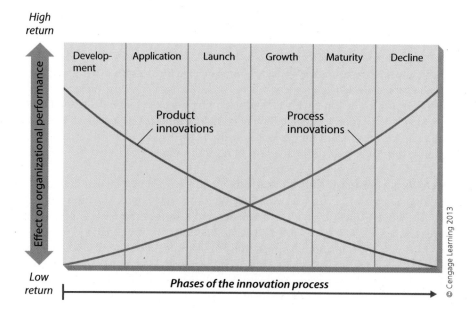

© Cengage Learning 2013

THE MORE THINGS CHANGE

A Marriage of Technique and Technology

avatra images/Alamy

In 1883, the great composer and piano virtuoso Franz Liszt wrote Heinrich Steinway, founder of Steinway & Sons, to praise the Steinway grand piano. In particular, Liszt had good things to say about the tonal effect of the piano's *scale*—the arrangement of its strings. Thirty years earlier, Henry Steinway Jr. had patented a technique for scaling called *overstringing*: Instead of running them parallel to the piano's treble strings, he fanned the bass strings above and diagonally to create a second tier of strings. As a result, he was able to improve the instrument's tone by using longer strings with superior vibratory quality.

Another feature developed by Steinway in the mid-nineteenth century made it possible to use strings that were also bigger—and thus louder. If you look under a piano, you'll see a cast-iron plate. This component was once made of wood fortified by metal braces, but Steinway had made the cast-iron plate a regular feature by the 1840s. The metal plate, of course, is much stronger and allowed the piano maker to apply much greater tension to the strings; in turn, the ability to increase string tension made it possible to tune the piano to more exacting standards of pitch.

Steinway was the first piano maker to combine the cast-iron plate with the technique of overstringing, and

very little has changed in the construction of a grand piano since these and a few other facets of traditional technology were first introduced. This isn't to say, however, that you won't find any modern technology in the present Steinway factory.

Take, for example, the soundboard, which you'll see if you open up a grand piano and look inside. A solid wooden "diaphragm" located between the strings and the metal plate, the *soundboard* is a marvel of deceptively simple design which vibrates in order to amplify the sound of the strings while withstanding the 1,000 pounds of pressure that they place on it. Because they're constructed by hand, no two soundboards are exactly the same size. Nor is any one piano *case*—the curved lateral surface that runs around the whole instrument—the same size as any other. The important thing is that the case is fitted—and fitted *precisely*—to a soundboard.

Because the soundboard is measured first and the case then fitted to it, there's only one case for each soundboard. To ensure a satisfactory fit between case and soundboard, the case (as we saw in our *Management in Action* story in Chapter 2) must be *frazed*—sawed and planed to specification. Performed by hand, this task took 14 hours, but today it's done in 1½ hours by a CNC (for *computer numerically controlled*) milling machine—a system in which a computerized storage medium issues programmed commands to a variety of specialized tools.

Granted, CNC technology is fairly new at Steinway—the million-dollar milling machine and several other pieces of CNC technology were introduced between 2000 and 2005. Most of Steinway's CNC tools are highly specialized, and the company custom-built many of them. Obviously, such technology leads to a lot of labor savings, but Steinway officials are adamant about the role of technology in maintaining rather than supplanting Steinway tradition: Some people, says Director of Quality Robert Berger, "think that Steinway is automating to save on labor costs or improve productivity. But these investments are all about quality. We're making a few specific technology investments in areas where we can improve the quality of our product."

References: Steinway & Sons, "Steinway History: Leadership Through Craftsmanship and Innovation," 2011, www.steinway.com on March 29, 2011; Steinway & Sons, "Online Factory Tour," 2009, http://archive.steinway.com on March 29, 2011; Victor Verney, "88 Keys: The Making of a Steinway Piano," *All About Jazz*, June 18, 2006, www.allaboutjazz.com on March 29, 2011; WGBH (Boston), "*Note by Note*: The Making of Steinway L1037," 2010, www.wgbh.org on March 29, 2011; M. Eric Johnson, Joseph Hall, and David Pyke, "Technology and Quality at Steinway & Sons," Tuck School of Business at Dartmouth, May 13, 2005, http://mba.tuck.dartmouth.edu on March 29, 2011.

The Failure to Innovate

To remain competitive in today's economy, organizations must be innovative. And yet many organizations that should be innovative are not successful at bringing out new products or services or do so only after innovations created by others are very mature. Organizations may fail to innovate for at least three reasons.

Lack of Resources Innovation is expensive in terms of dollars, time, and energy. If a firm does not have sufficient money to fund a program of innovation or does not currently employ the kinds of employees it needs in order to be innovative, it may lag behind in innovation. Even highly innovative organizations cannot become involved in every new product or service its employees think up. For example, numerous other commitments in the electronic instruments and computer industry forestalled Hewlett-Packard from investing in Steve Jobs and Steve Wozniak's original idea for a personal computer. With infinite resources of money, time, and technical and managerial expertise, HP might have entered this market early. Because the firm did not have this flexibility, however, it had to make some difficult choices about which innovations to invest in.[56]

Failure to Recognize Opportunities Because firms cannot pursue all innovations, they need to develop the capability to carefully evaluate innovations and to select the ones that hold the greatest potential. To obtain a competitive advantage, an organization usually must make investment decisions before the innovation process reaches the mature stage. The earlier the investment, however, the greater the risk. If organizations are not skilled at recognizing and evaluating opportunities, they may be overly cautious and fail to invest in innovations that later turn out to be successful for other firms.

Resistance to Change As we discuss earlier, many organizations tend to resist change. Innovation means giving up old products and old ways of doing things in favor of new products and new ways of doing things. These kinds of changes can be personally difficult for managers and other members of an organization. Thus resistance to change can slow the innovation process.

3M is one of the most innovative businesses in the world. The firm has made innovation an integral part of its culture, and continues to promote innovation through its reward system. For example, 3M offers grants to innovators whose projects might have difficulty obtaining normal funding.

AP Photo/Matt Rourke

Promoting Innovation in Organizations

A wide variety of ideas for promoting innovation in organizations have been developed over the years. Three specific ways for promoting innovation are through the reward system, through the organizational culture, and through a process called *intrapreneurship*.[57]

The Reward System A firm's reward system is the means by which it encourages and discourages certain behaviors by employees. Major components of the reward system include salaries, bonuses, and perquisites. Using the reward system to promote innovation is a fairly mechanical but nevertheless effective management technique. The idea is to provide financial and nonfinancial rewards to people and groups who develop innovative ideas. Once the members of an organization understand that they will be rewarded for such activities, they are more likely to work creatively. With this end in mind, Monsanto gives a

$50,000 award each year to the scientist or group of scientists who develop the biggest commercial breakthrough. 3M's Genesis Grant offers $85,000 to innovators whose projects may have trouble attaining financial backing through normal means.

It is important for organizations to reward creative behavior, but it is vital to avoid punishing creativity when it does not result in highly successful innovations. It is the nature of the creative and innovative processes that many new product ideas will simply not work out in the marketplace. Each process is fraught with too many uncertainties to generate positive results every time. An individual may have prepared herself to be creative, but an insight may not be forthcoming. Or managers may attempt to apply a developed innovation, only to recognize that it does not work. Indeed, some organizations operate according to the assumption that, if all their innovative efforts succeed, then they are probably not taking enough risks in research and development. At 3M, nearly 60 percent of the creative ideas suggested each year do not succeed in the marketplace.

Managers need to be very careful in responding to innovative failure. If innovative failure is due to incompetence, systematic errors, or managerial sloppiness, then a firm should respond appropriately, for example, by withholding raises or reducing promotion opportunities. People who act in good faith to develop an innovation that simply does not work out, however, should not be punished for failure. If they are, they will probably not be creative in the future. A punitive reward system will discourage people from taking risks and therefore reduce the organization's ability to obtain competitive advantages.

Organization Culture As we discussed in Chapter 3, an organization's culture is the set of values, beliefs, and symbols that help guide behavior. A strong, appropriately focused organizational culture can be used to support innovative activity. A well-managed culture can communicate a sense that innovation is valued and will be rewarded and that occasional failure in the pursuit of new ideas is not only acceptable but even expected. In addition to reward systems and intrapreneurial activities, firms such as Apple, Google, Nintendo, Nokia, Sony, Walt Disney, Vodafone, and Hewlett-Packard are all known to have strong, innovation-oriented cultures that value individual creativity, risk taking, and inventiveness.[58] Google, for instance, allows employees to use 20 percent of their time (one day per week) to work on their own side projects in order to foster innovation.

Intrapreneurship in Larger Organizations In recent years, many large businesses have realized that the entrepreneurial spirit that propelled their growth becomes stagnant after they transform themselves from a small but growing concern into a larger one.[59] To help revitalize this spirit, some firms today encourage what they call "intrapreneurship." Intrapreneurs are similar to entrepreneurs except that they develop a new business in the context of a large organization. There are three intrapreneurial roles in large organizations.[60] To successfully use intrapreneurship to encourage creativity and innovation, the organization must find one or more individuals to perform these roles.

The *inventor* is the person who actually conceives of and develops the new idea, product, or service by means of the creative process. Because the inventor may lack the expertise or motivation to oversee the transformation of the product or service from an idea into a marketable entity, however, a second role comes into play. A *product champion* is usually a middle manager who learns about the project and becomes committed to it. He or she helps overcome organizational resistance and convinces others to take the innovation seriously. The product champion may have only limited understanding of the technological aspects of the innovation. Nevertheless, product champions are skilled at knowing how the organization works, whose support is needed to push the project forward, and where to go to secure the resources necessary for successful development. A *sponsor* is a top-level manager who approves of and supports a project. This person may fight for the budget needed to develop an idea, overcome arguments against a project, and use organizational politics to ensure the

intrapreneurs
Similar to entrepreneurs except that they develop new businesses in the context of a large organization

project's survival. With a sponsor in place, the inventor's idea has a much better chance of being successfully developed.

Several firms have embraced intrapreneurship as a way to encourage creativity and innovation. Colgate-Palmolive has created a separate unit, Colgate Venture Company, staffed with intrapreneurs who develop new products. SC Johnson & Son established a $250,000 fund to support new product ideas. Texas Instruments refuses to approve a new innovative project unless it has an acknowledged inventor, champion, and sponsor. Lockheed Martin's Advanced Development Programs, also known as Skunk Works, focuses on innovative aerospace technologies and aircraft.[61]

Identify and describe the basic forms of innovation.

Identify several new products or variations of existing products that have been successful and several others that have been less successful.

Summary of Learning Objectives and Key Points

1. Describe the nature of organization change, including forces for change and planned versus reactive change.

   - Organization change is any substantive modification to some part of the organization.
   - Change may be prompted by forces internal or external to the organization.
   - In general, planned change is preferable to reactive change.

2. Discuss the steps in organization change and how to manage resistance to change.

   - The Lewin model provides a general perspective on the steps involved in change.
   - A comprehensive model is usually more effective.
   - People tend to resist change because of uncertainty, threatened self-interests, different perceptions, and feelings of loss.
   - Participation, education and communication, facilitation, and force-field analysis are methods for overcoming this resistance.

3. Identify and describe major areas of organization change and discuss the assumptions, techniques, and effectiveness of organization development.

   - The most common areas of change involve changing organizational structure and design, technology, and people.

   - Business process change is a more massive and comprehensive change.
   - Organization development is concerned with changing attitudes, perceptions, behaviors, and expectations. Its effective use relies on an important set of assumptions.
   - There are conflicting opinions about the effectiveness of several OD techniques.

4. Describe the innovation process, forms of innovation, failure to innovate, and how organizations can promote innovation.

   - The innovation process has six steps: development, application, launch, growth, maturity, and decline.
   - Basic categories of innovation include radical, incremental, technical, managerial, product, and process innovations.
   - Despite the importance of innovation, many organizations fail to innovate because they lack the required creative individuals or are committed to too many other creative activities, fail to recognize opportunities, or resist the change that innovation requires.
   - Organizations can use a variety of tools to overcome these problems, including the reward system, organizational culture, and intrapreneurship.

Discussion Questions

Questions for Review

1. What forces or kinds of events lead to organization change? Identify each force or event as a planned or a reactive change.
2. Compare planned and reactive change. What are the advantages of planned change, as compared to reactive change?
3. In a brief sentence or just a phrase, describe each of the organizational development (OD) techniques.
4. Consider the following list of products. Categorize each along all three dimensions of innovation, if possible (radical versus incremental, technical versus managerial, and product versus process). Explain your answers.

   - Teaching college courses by videotaping the instructor and sending the image over the Internet
   - The rise in popularity of virtual organizations (discussed in Chapter 15)
   - Checking the security of packages on airlines with the type of MRI scanning devices that are common in health care
   - A device combining features of a cell phone and a handheld computer with Internet capability
   - Robotic arms that can perform surgery that is too precise for a human surgeon's hands
   - Hybrid automobiles, which run on both batteries and gasoline
   - Using video games to teach soldiers how to plan and execute battles

Questions for Analysis

5. What are the symptoms that a manager should look for in determining whether an organization needs to change? What are the symptoms that indicate that an organization has been through too much change?
6. Assume that you are the manager of an organization that has a routine way of performing a task and now faces a major change in how it performs that task. Using Lewin's model, tell what steps you would take to implement the change. Using the comprehensive approach, tell what steps you would take. For each step, give specific examples of actions you would take at that step.
7. Think back to a time when a professor announced a change that you, the student, did not want to adopt. What were the reasons for your resistance to change? Was the professor able to overcome your resistance? If so, tell what he or she did. If not, tell what he or she could have done that might have been successful.

Questions for Application

8. Some people resist change, whereas others welcome it enthusiastically. To deal with the first group, one needs to overcome resistance to change; to deal with the second, one needs to overcome resistance to stability. What advice can you give a manager facing the latter situation?
9. Can a change made in one area of an organization—in technology, for instance—not lead to change in other areas? If you think that change in one area must lead to change in other areas, describe an example of an organization change to illustrate your point. If you think that change can occur in just one area without causing change in other areas, describe an example of an organization change that illustrates your point.
10. Research an innovation change that occurred in a real organization, by either interviewing an employee, reading the business press, or using the Internet. Describe the process by which the innovation was developed. Did the actual process follow the ideal process described in the chapter? Why or why not?

CengageNow™ Highlights

Now use your CengageNow™ homework to help you:

- Apply management theories in your life
- Assess your management skills
- Master management terms and concepts
- Apply your knowledge to real-world situations
- Analyze and solve challenging management problems

In order to take advantage of these elements, your instructor will need to have set up a course for your class within CengageNow™. Ask your instructor to contact his/ her Cengage sales representative and Digital Solutions Manager to explore testing CengageNow™ in your course this term.

Managing Human Resources in Organizations

LEARNING OBJECTIVES

After studying this chapter, you should be able to:

1. Describe the environmental context of human resource management, including its strategic importance and its relationship with legal and social factors.

2. Discuss how organizations attract human resources, including human resource planning, recruiting, and selection.

3. Describe how organizations develop human resources, including training and development, performance appraisal, and performance feedback.

4. Discuss how organizations maintain human resources, including the determination of compensation and benefits and career planning.

5. Discuss labor relations, including how employees form unions and the mechanics of collective bargaining.

6. Describe the key issues associated with managing knowledge and contingent and temporary workers.

MANAGEMENT IN ACTION No Company for Old-Fashioned Management

f you're looking for the best Parmesan cheese for your chicken parmigiana recipe, you might try Wegmans, especially if you happen to live in the vicinity of Pittsford, New York. Cheese department manager Carol Kent will be happy to recommend the best brand because her job calls for knowing cheese as well as managing some 20 subordinates. Kent is a knowledgeable employee, and knowledgeable employees, says Wegmans CEO Danny Wegman, are "something our competitors don't have and our customers couldn't get anywhere else."

Wegmans Food Markets, a family-owned East Coast chain with nearly 80 outlets in six states, prides itself on its commitment to customers, and it shows: It ranks at the top of the latest *Consumer Reports* survey of the best national and regional grocery stores. But commitment to customers is only half of Wegmans' overall strategy, which calls for reaching its customers through its employees. "How do we differentiate ourselves?" asks Wegman, who then proceeds to answer his own question: "If we can sell products that require knowledge in terms of how you use them, that's our strategy. Anything

"Anything that requires knowledge and service gives us a reason to be."

—DANNY WEGMAN, CEO OF WEGMANS FOOD MARKETS

that requires knowledge and service gives us a reason to be." That's the logic behind one of Carol Kent's recent assignments—one which she understandably regards as a perk: Wegmans sent her to Italy to conduct a personal study of Italian cheese. "We sat with the families" that make the cheeses, she recalls, "broke bread with them. It helped me understand that we're not just selling a piece of cheese. We're selling a tradition, a quality."

Kent and the employees in her department also enjoy the best benefits package in the industry, including fully paid health insurance. And that includes part-timers, who make up about two-thirds of the company's workforce of more than 37,000. In part, the strategy of extending benefits to this large segment of the labor force is intended to make sure that stores have enough good workers for crucial peak periods, but there's no denying that the costs

Wegmans Food Markets has a reputation for being among the best places to work in the United States.

Chris Mueller/Redux

of employee-friendly policies can mount up. At 15 to 17 percent of sales, for example, Wegmans' labor costs are well above the 12 percent figure for most supermarkets. But according to one company HR executive, holding down labor costs isn't necessarily a strategic priority: "We would have stopped offering free health insurance [to part-timers] a long time ago," she admits, "if we tried to justify the costs."

Besides, employee turnover at Wegmans is about 6 percent—a mere fraction of an industry average that hovers around 19 percent (and can approach 100 percent for part-timers). And this is an industry in which total turnover costs have been known to outstrip total annual profits by 40 percent. Wegmans' employees tend to be knowledgeable because about 20 percent of them have been with the company for at least ten years, and many have logged at least a quarter century. Says one 19-year-old college student who works at an upstate-New York Wegmans while pursuing a career as a high school history teacher: "I love this place. If teaching doesn't work out, I would so totally work at Wegmans." Edward McLaughlin, who directs the Food Industry Management Program at Cornell University, understands this sort of attitude: "When you're a 16-year-old kid, the last thing you want to do is wear a geeky shirt and work for a supermarket," but at Wegmans, he explains, "it's a badge of honor. You're not a geeky cashier. You're part of the social fabric."·

In 2011, Wegmans placed third in *Fortune* magazine's annual list of "100 Best Companies to Work For"—good for 14 consecutive years on the list and seven straight top-seven finishes. "It says that we're doing something

right," says a company spokesperson, "and that there's no better way to take care of our customers than to be a great place for our employees to work." In addition to its healthcare package, Wegmans has been cited for such perks as fitness center discounts, compressed work weeks, telecommuting, and domestic-partner benefits (which extend to same-sex partners).

Finally, under the company's Employee Scholarship Program, full-time workers can receive up to $2,200 a year for four years and part-timers up to $1,500. Since its inception in 1984, the program has handed out $76 million in scholarships to more than 23,500 employees. Like most Wegman policies, this one combines employee outreach with long-term corporate strategy: "This program has made a real difference in the lives of many young people," says president Colleen Wegman, who adds that it's also "one of the reasons we've been able to attract the best and the brightest to work at Wegmans."

Granted, Wegmans, which has remained in family hands since its founding in 1915, has an advantage in being as generous with its resources as its family of top executives wants to be: It doesn't have to do everything with quarterly profits in mind, and the firm likes to point out that taking care of its employees is a long-standing priority. Profit sharing and fully funded medical coverage were introduced in 1950 by Robert Wegman, son and nephew of brothers Walter and John, who opened the firm's original flagship store in Rochester, New York, in 1930. Why did Robert Wegman make such generous gestures to his employees way back then? "Because," he says simply, "I was no different from them."[1]

This chapter is about how organizations manage the people that comprise them. That's why our opening story is about a company that's reaped big dividends from a strategy that integrates customer satisfaction with employee satisfaction. The set of processes by which Wegmans and other companies manage their people is called "human resource management," or HRM. We start by describing the environmental context of HRM. We then discuss how organizations attract human resources. Next we describe how organizations seek to further develop the capacities of their human resources. We also examine how high-quality human resources are maintained by organizations. We conclude by discussing labor relations.

> **human resource management (HRM)**
> The set of organizational activities directed at attracting, developing, and maintaining an effective workforce

The Environmental Context of Human Resource Management

Human resource management (HRM) is the set of organizational activities directed at attracting, developing, and maintaining an effective workforce.[2] Human resource management takes place within a complex and ever-changing environmental context. Three particularly vital components of this context are HRM's strategic importance and the legal and social environments of HRM.

The Strategic Importance of HRM

Human resources are critical for effective organizational functioning. HRM (or "personnel," as it is sometimes called) was once relegated to second-class status in many organizations, but its importance has grown dramatically in the last two decades. Its new importance stems from increased legal complexities, the recognition that human resources are a valuable means for improving productivity, and the awareness today of the costs associated with poor human resource management.[3] For example, Microsoft recently announced that it was laying off 5,000 people in parts of its business expected to shrink. At the same time, though, the firm began developing strategies for hiring highly talented people for jobs related to Internet search, an important growth area for the company.[4] This careful and systematic approach, reducing human resources in areas where they are no longer needed and adding new human resources to key growth areas, reflects a strategic approach to human resource management.

Indeed, managers now realize that the effectiveness of their HR function has a substantial impact on the bottom-line performance of the firm. Poor human resource planning can result in spurts of hiring followed by layoffs—costly in terms of unemployment compensation payments, training expenses, and morale. Haphazard compensation systems do not attract, keep, and motivate good employees, and outmoded recruitment practices can expose the firm to expensive and embarrassing discrimination lawsuits. Consequently, the chief human resource executive of most large businesses is a vice president directly accountable to the CEO, and many firms are developing strategic HR plans and integrating those plans with other strategic planning activities.[5]

Even organizations with as few as 200 employees usually have a human resource manager and a human resource department charged with overseeing these activities. Responsibility for HR activities, however, is shared between the HR department and line managers. The HR department may recruit and initially screen candidates, but the final selection is usually made by managers in the department where the new employee will work. Similarly, although the HR department may establish performance appraisal policies and procedures, the actual evaluation and coaching of employees is done by their immediate superiors.

The growing awareness of the strategic significance of human resource management has even led to new terminology to reflect a firm's commitment to people. Human capital reflects the organization's investment in attracting, retaining, and motivating an effective workforce. Hence, just as the phrase *financial capital* is an indicator of a firm's financial resources and reserves, so, too, does *human capital* serve as a tangible indicator of the value of the people who comprise an organization.[6]

The Legal Environment of HRM

A number of laws regulate various aspects of employee–employer relations, especially in the areas of equal employment opportunity, compensation and benefits, labor relations, and occupational safety and health. Several major ones are summarized in Table 17.1.

Equal Employment Opportunity Title VII of the Civil Rights Act of 1964 forbids discrimination in all areas of the employment relationship. The intent of Title VII is to ensure that employment decisions are made on the basis of an individual's qualifications rather than on the basis of personal biases. The law has reduced direct forms of discrimination (refusing to promote African Americans into management, failing to hire men as flight attendants, refusing to hire women as construction workers) as well as indirect forms of discrimination (using employment tests that whites pass at a higher rate than African Americans).

Employment requirements such as test scores and other qualifications are legally defined as having an adverse impact on minorities and women when such individuals meet or pass the requirement at a rate less than 80 percent of the rate of majority group members.

human capital
Reflects the organization's investment in attracting, retaining, and motivating an effective workforce

Title VII of the Civil Rights Act of 1964
Forbids discrimination on the basis of sex, race, color, religion, or national origin in all areas of the employment relationship

adverse impact
When minority group members pass a selection standard at a rate less than 80 percent of the pass rate of majority group members

Equal Employment Opportunity

Title VII of the Civil Rights Act of 1964 (as amended by the Equal Employment Opportunity Act of 1972). Forbids discrimination in all areas of the employment relationship.

Age Discrimination in Employment Act. Outlaws discrimination against people older than 40 years.

Various executive orders, especially Executive Order 11246 in 1965. Requires employers with government contracts to engage in affirmative action.

Pregnancy Discrimination Act. Specifically outlaws discrimination on the basis of pregnancy.

Vietnam Era Veterans Readjustment Assistance Act. Extends affirmative action mandate to military veterans who served during the Vietnam War.

Americans with Disabilities Act. Specifically outlaws discrimination against disabled persons.

Civil Rights Act of 1991. Makes it easier for employees to sue an organization for discrimination but limits punitive damage awards if they win.

Compensation and Benefits

Fair Labor Standards Act. Establishes minimum wage and mandated overtime pay for work in excess of 40 hours per week.

Equal Pay Act of 1963. Requires that men and women be paid the same amount for doing the same job.

Employee Retirement Income Security Act of 1974 (ERISA). Regulates how organizations manage their pension funds.

Family and Medical Leave Act of 1993. Requires employers to provide up to 12 weeks of unpaid leave for family and medical emergencies.

Labor Relations

National Labor Relations Act. Spells out procedures by which employees can establish labor unions and requires organizations to bargain collectively with legally formed unions; also known as the *Wagner Act.*

Labor-Management Relations Act. Limits union power and specifies management rights during a union-organizing campaign; also known as the *Taft-Hartley Act.*

Health and Safety

Occupational Safety and Health Act of 1970 (OSHA). Mandates the provision of safe working conditions.

© Cengage Learning 2013

TABLE 17.1 THE LEGAL ENVIRONMENT OF HUMAN RESOURCE MANAGEMENT

As much as any area of management, HRM is subject to wide-ranging laws and court decisions. These laws and decisions affect the human resource function in many areas. For example, AT&T was once fined several million dollars for violating Title VII of the Civil Rights Act of 1964.

Equal Employment Opportunity Commission
Charged with enforcing Title VII of the Civil Rights Act of 1964

Age Discrimination in Employment Act
Outlaws discrimination against people older than 40 years; passed in 1967, amended in 1978 and 1986

affirmative action
Intentionally seeking and hiring qualified or qualifiable employees from racial, sexual, and ethnic groups that are underrepresented in the organization

Criteria that have an adverse impact on protected groups can be used only when there is solid evidence that they effectively identify individuals who are better able than others to do the job. The Equal Employment Opportunity Commission is charged with enforcing Title VII as well as several other employment-related laws.

The Age Discrimination in Employment Act, passed in 1967, amended in 1978, and amended again in 1986, is an attempt to prevent organizations from discriminating against older workers. In its current form, it outlaws discrimination against people older than 40 years. Both the Age Discrimination in Employment Act and Title VII require passive nondiscrimination, or equal employment opportunity. Employers are not required to seek out and hire minorities, but they must treat all who apply fairly.

Several executive orders, however, require that employers holding government contracts engage in affirmative action—intentionally seeking and hiring employees from groups that are underrepresented in the organization. These organizations must have a written affirmative action plan that spells out employment goals for underutilized groups and how those goals will be met. These employers are also required to act affirmatively in hiring Vietnam-era veterans (as a result of the Vietnam Era Veterans Readjustment Assistance Act) and qualified handicapped individuals. Finally, the Pregnancy Discrimination Act forbids discrimination against women who are pregnant.

In 1990 Congress passed the **Americans with Disabilities Act**, which forbids discrimination on the basis of disabilities and requires employers to provide reasonable accommodations for disabled employees.

More recently, the **Civil Rights Act of 1991** amended the original Civil Rights Act as well as other related laws by both making it easier to bring discrimination lawsuits (which partially explains the aforementioned backlog of cases) while simultaneously limiting the amount of punitive damages that can be awarded in those lawsuits.

Compensation and Benefits Laws also regulate compensation and benefits. The **Fair Labor Standards Act**, passed in 1938 and amended frequently since then, sets a minimum wage and requires the payment of overtime rates for work in excess of 40 hours per week. Salaried professional, executive, and administrative employees are exempt from the minimum hourly wage and overtime provisions. The **Equal Pay Act of 1963** requires that men and women be paid the same amount for doing the same job. Attempts to circumvent the law by having different job titles and pay rates for men and women who perform the same work are also illegal. Basing an employee's pay on seniority or performance is legal, however, even if it means that a man and woman are paid different amounts for doing the same job.

The provision of benefits is also regulated in some ways by state and federal laws. Certain benefits are mandatory—for example, workers' compensation insurance for employees who are injured on the job. Employers who provide a pension plan for their employees are regulated by the **Employee Retirement Income Security Act of 1974 (ERISA)**. The purpose of this act is to help ensure the financial security of pension funds by regulating how they can be invested. The **Family and Medical Leave Act of 1993** requires employers to provide up to 12 weeks of unpaid leave for family and medical emergencies.

In the last few years some large employers, most notably Walmart, have come under fire because they do not provide health care for all of their employees. In response to this, the state of Maryland passed a law, informally called the "Walmart bill," that requires employers with more than 10,000 workers to spend at least 8 percent of their payrolls on health care or else pay a comparable amount into a general fund for uninsured workers. Walmart appealed this rule and the case is still pending; meanwhile, several other states are considering the passage of similar laws.[7]

Labor Relations Union activities and management's behavior toward unions constitute another heavily regulated area. The **National Labor Relations Act** (also known as the Wagner Act), passed in 1935, sets up a procedure for employees to vote on whether to have a union. If they vote for a union, management is required to bargain collectively with the union. The **National Labor Relations Board (NLRB)** was established by the Wagner Act to enforce its provisions. Following a series of severe strikes in 1946, the **Labor-Management Relations Act** (also known as the Taft-Hartley Act) was passed in 1947 to limit union power. The law increases management's rights during an organizing campaign. The Taft-Hartley Act also contains the National Emergency Strike provision, which allows the president of the United States to prevent or end a strike that endangers national security. Taken together, these laws balance union and management power. Employees can be represented by a legally created and managed union, but the business can make nonemployee-related business decisions without interference.

National labor-relations laws have been on the books for about 80 years now, but as you can see from the *Change* box on page 419, entitled "The Law of Collective Begging," the legal environment in which organizations operate can be just as volatile as other aspects of the organizational environment.

Americans with Disabilities Act
Prohibits discrimination against people with disabilities

Civil Rights Act of 1991
Amends the original Civil Rights Act, making it easier to bring discrimination lawsuits while also limiting punitive damages

Fair Labor Standards Act
Sets a minimum wage and requires overtime pay for work in excess of 40 hours per week; passed in 1938 and amended frequently since then

Equal Pay Act of 1963
Requires that men and women be paid the same amount for doing the same job

Employee Retirement Income Security Act of 1974 (ERISA)
Regulates how organizations manage their pension funds

Family and Medical Leave Act of 1993
Requires employers to provide up to 12 weeks of unpaid leave for family and medical emergencies

National Labor Relations Act
Passed in 1935 to set up procedures for employees to vote on whether to have a union; also known as the Wagner Act

National Labor Relations Board (NLRB)
Established by the Wagner Act to enforce its provisions

Labor-Management Relations Act
Passed in 1947 to limit union power; also known as the Taft-Hartley Act

THE MORE THINGS CHANGE

The Law of Collective Begging

Mark Hirsch/Getty Images

On or about February 17, 2011, 14 members of the Wisconsin Senate disappeared—at least from the state of Wisconsin.

Actually, they were in neighboring Illinois, where they were camped out in cheap (well, inexpensive) motel rooms in an effort to avoid the long arm of the law—not a law that they had violated, but rather one that they didn't want passed. All 14 were Democrats, and they were trying to buy time to marshal public sentiment against a bill that would severely limit the rights of Wisconsin public-sector employees to bargain collectively with state and local government bodies. As long as they were absent from the state, the Senate could not—or so they thought—convene enough members to hold a vote on the bill. On March 9, however, the 19 Republican members of the Senate maneuvered the bill onto the agenda and passed it by a vote of 18-1.

The new law limits public-sector unions to bargaining only on the issue of base pay. It also pegs raises to the consumer price index, an inflation-measurement tool, unless voters approve higher increases. Other provisions further curtail union activity by making the payment of union dues voluntary and prohibiting the state from collecting dues through members' paychecks. State workers themselves must increase contributions to their pensions to 5.8 percent of their salaries and double, to 12.6 percent, contributions to their healthcare plans.

The overall effect of the new measures is a cut in take-home pay of about 8 percent.

The Wisconsin law does not apply to private-sector unions, but today's unionized workforce includes a much greater percentage of public employees than it did 35 years ago, when about 25 percent of workers in both sectors belonged to unions. Today, the union membership rate for public workers has grown and is substantially higher than the declining rate for private-sector workers—36.2 percent to 6.9 percent. Remember, however, that the total public-sector labor force is much smaller than the total private-sector labor force— a fact that only makes all the more striking the recent Bureau of Labor Statistics announcement that, for the first time ever, public-sector union employees outnumber private-sector union employees (7.6 million to 7.1 million). In short, with the collapse of union presence in the private sector, whatever strength organized labor has left depends on the endurance of public-sector unions.

Proponents of the new law see it as an efficient means of closing budget deficits faced by the state's financially strapped cities, counties, and school districts. Opponents, however, point out that budgetary problems in states all across the country are among the financial repercussions of the recession, which has decimated revenues from income and sales taxes. In Texas, for example, one public-union official observes that the state suffers from a budget deficit of $26 billion even though state law already prohibits collective bargaining for teachers and most other public workers.

Many critics of the Wisconsin measure also see it as a thinly veiled effort to curb or destroy public unions. "It's pretty much [an] evisceration of collective bargaining," says Ohio State University law professor James Brudney, and as a union official in Missouri puts it, "If you don't have collective bargaining, the best you can hope for is collective begging."

References: Monica Davey, "Wisconsin Senate Limits Bargaining by Public Workers," *New York Times*, March 9, 2011, www.nytimes.com on April 18, 2011; Ezra Klein, "Unions Aren't to Blame for Wisconsin's Budget," *Washington Post*, February 18, 2011, http://voices.washingtonpost.com on April 19, 2011; William Rogers, "Opposition to Wisconsin Union Busting Bill Gathers Momentum," *Left Labor Reporter*, February 22, 2011, http://leftlaborreporter.wordpress.com on April 19, 2011; Steven Greenhouse, "Ohio's Anti-Union Law Is Tougher Than Wisconsin's," *New York Times*, March 31, 2011, www.nytimes.com on April 15, 2011; Andrew Denney, "Wisconsin Labor Clash Ignites Debate Elsewhere," *Columbia* (MO) *Daily Tribune*, February 22, 2011, www.columbiatribune.com on April 18, 2011.

Health and Safety The Occupational Safety and Health Act of 1970 (OSHA) directly mandates the provision of safe working conditions. It requires that employers (1) provide a place of employment that is free from hazards that may cause death or serious physical harm and (2) obey the safety and health standards established by the Department of Labor. Safety standards are intended to prevent accidents, whereas occupational health standards are concerned with preventing occupational disease. For example, standards limit the concentration of cotton dust in the air because this contaminant has been associated with lung disease in textile workers. The standards are enforced by OSHA inspections, which are conducted when an employee files a complaint of unsafe conditions or when a serious accident occurs.

Spot inspections of plants in especially hazardous industries such as mining and chemicals are also made. Employers who fail to meet OSHA standards may be fined. A Miami-based company, Lead Enterprises Inc., was cited by OSHA as knowingly failing to protect employees from lead exposure despite knowing the potential hazards (brain damage, kidney disease, and reproductive system damage). The company, which produces various lead products, including fish tackles and lead diving weights, was cited for 32 safety and health violations after multiple inspections and fined more than $307,000 in penalties.[8]

Emerging Legal Issues Several other areas of legal concern have emerged during the past few years. One is sexual harassment. Although sexual harassment is forbidden under Title VII, it has received additional attention in the courts recently, as more and more victims have decided to publicly confront the problem. Why do there still seem to be more and more victims? The *World of Difference* box on page 421, entitled "Power Plays in the Workplace," explores one theory.

Another emerging human resource management issue is alcohol and drug abuse. Both alcoholism and drug dependence are major problems today. Recent court rulings have tended to define alcoholics and drug addicts as disabled, protecting them under the same laws that protect other handicapped people. AIDS is an important legal issue as well. AIDS victims, too, are most often protected under various laws protecting the disabled. Finally, employee privacy is also becoming a controversial issue in the HR arena. For instance, can employers refuse to hire an otherwise qualified applicant because of information they post on social networking sites?

Social Change and HRM

Beyond the objective legal context of HRM, various social changes are also affecting how organizations interact with their employees. First, many organizations are using more and more temporary workers today. This trend, discussed more fully later, allows them to add workers as necessary without the risk that they may have to eliminate their jobs in the future.

Second, dual-career families are much more common today than just a few years ago. Organizations are finding that they must make accommodations for employees who are dual-career partners. These accommodations may include delaying transfers, offering employment to the spouses of current employees to retain them, and providing more flexible work schedules and benefits packages. A related aspect of social change and HRM, workforce diversity, was covered more fully in Chapter 6.

Employment-at-will is also becoming an important issue. Although employment-at-will has legal implications, its emergence as an issue is socially driven. Employment-at-will is a traditional view of the workplace that says organizations can fire an employee for any reason. Increasingly, however, people are arguing that organizations should be able to fire only people who are poor performers or who violate rules and, conversely, should not be able to fire people who report safety violations to OSHA or refuse to perform unethical activities. Several court cases in recent years have upheld this emerging view and have limited many organizations' ability to terminate employees to those cases where there is clear and just cause or there is an organization-wide cutback. Further, in the wake of massive layoffs during the recession that began in 2008, several ex-workers sued their former employers, citing alleged violations of various severance laws.[9]

Occupational Safety and Health Act of 1970 (OSHA)
Directly mandates the provision of safe working conditions

employment-at-will
A traditional view of the workplace that says organizations can fire their employees for whatever reason they want; recent court judgments are limiting employment-at-will

≋ A WORLD OF DIFFERENCE ≋

Power Plays in the Workplace

Ryan McVay/Photodisc/Getty Images

Recent research shows that more than 30 percent of female workers in the United States have been harassed at work—all of them by men. Forty-three percent identified the male harasser as a supervisor, 27 percent as an employee senior to them, and 19 percent as a coworker at the same level. In 2009 (the last year for which there are complete data), nearly 13,000 charges of sexual harassment were filed with the U.S. Equal Employment Opportunity Commission (EEOC), 84 percent of them by women.

Why does sexual harassment (mostly of women) occur in the workplace?

"Power," says researcher Debbie Dougherty, who conducted a study in conjunction with a large Midwestern healthcare organization. "It was the common answer. It came up repeatedly," says Dougherty, a specialist in communications and power in organizations. She also found that men and women understand the idea of *power* differently, and that difference in understanding, she reports, may play an important part in the persistence of harassing behavior in the workplace:

• For most men, power is something that belongs to superiors—managers and supervisors—who can harass because they possess the power to do so. By definition, a male coworker cannot actually harass a female coworker who's at the same level because he doesn't possess sufficient power over her.

• Women, on the other hand, see power as something that can be introduced into a relationship as it develops; it's something more than the mere formal authority built into the superior's job description. Harassment can be initiated by anyone who's able to create the perception of power.

According to Dougherty, gender differences in the perception of power may account, at least in part, for gender differences in perceptions of behavior. "If a man," she suggests, "thinks that sexual harassment only comes from a supervisor, he may feel free to make sexual comments to a female coworker," reasoning that because he holds no power over her, she won't perceive the behavior as harassment. She, however, probably regards power as something that can be sought and gained in a relationship and may therefore "see the sexual comments as a quest for power and label it as sexual harassment."

The findings of another recent study tend to support Doughtery's conclusions. Researchers from the University of Minnesota discovered that women in supervisory positions were 137 percent more likely to be harassed than women in nonsupervisory roles. Although many of the harassers were men in superior positions, a large number were coworkers in equivalent positions. It would seem, then, that male coworkers felt free to behave in a harassing manner because they believed that their female targets would not perceive their behavior as efforts to exert power. As Dougherty predicts, however, they were wrong: The women perceived the harassing behaviors as power plays. "This study," says researcher Heather McLaughlin, "provides the strongest evidence to date supporting the theory that sexual harassment is less about sexual desire than about control and domination. . . . Male coworkers . . . and supervisors seem to be using harassment as an equalizer against women in power."

References: "Sexual Harassment in the Workplace," *Sexual Harassment Support*, 2009, www.sexualharassmentsupport.org on April 21, 2011; "Sexual Harassment Statistics in the Workplace," *Brain Contour*, March 21, 2011, www.braincontour.com on April 1, 2011; Pamela Mahabeer, "Sexual Harassment Still Pervasive in the Workplace," *AOL Jobs*, January 28, 2011, http://jobs.aol.com on April 21, 2011; "Power and Sexual Harassment—Men and Women See Things Differently," *Science Daily*, April 6, 2007, www.sciencedaily.com on April 21, 2011; "Female Supervisors More Susceptible to Workplace Sexual Harassment," *EurekAlert!*, August 8, 2009, www.eurekealert.com on April 21, 2011; Rick Moore, "Behind Harassment," UMNews, August 19, 2009, www1.umn.edu on April 21, 2011.

Identify and briefly summarize the key laws that affect human resource management.

How might the importance of human capital vary across different kinds of business?

CONCEPT CHECK

Attracting Human Resources

With an understanding of the environmental context of human resource management as a foundation, we are now ready to address its first substantive concern—attracting qualified people who are interested in employment with the organization.

"We are in the midst of a major structural shift in manufacturing. . . . The number of good-paying, middle-class jobs that have been the bulk of manufacturing is likely going to be less in the future."

—HARLEY SHAIKEN, PROFESSOR OF LABOR RELATIONS,
UNIVERSITY OF CALIFORNIA, BERKELEY[10]

Human Resource Planning

The starting point in attracting qualified human resources is planning. HR planning, in turn, involves job analysis and forecasting the demand and supply of labor.

Job Analysis Job analysis is a systematic analysis of jobs within an organization. A job analysis is made up of two parts. The job description lists the duties of a job, the job's working conditions, and the tools, materials, and equipment used to perform it. The job specification lists the skills, abilities, and other credentials needed to do the job. Job analysis information is used in many human resource activities. For instance, knowing about job content and job requirements is necessary to develop appropriate selection methods and job-relevant performance appraisal systems and to set equitable compensation rates.

Forecasting Human Resource Demand and Supply After managers fully understand the jobs to be performed within the organization, they can start planning for the organization's future human resource needs. Figure 17.1 summarizes the steps most often followed. The manager starts by assessing trends in past human resources usage, future organizational plans, and general economic trends. A good sales forecast is often the foundation, especially for smaller organizations. Historical ratios can then be used to predict demand for such employees as operating employees and sales representatives. Of course, large organizations use much more complicated models to predict their future human resource needs. About ten years ago Walmart went through an exhaustive planning process that projected that the firm would need to hire 1 million people over the next decade. Of this projected total, 800,000 would be new positions created as the firm grows, and the other 200,000 would replace current workers who leave for various reasons.[11] As time passed, of course, Walmart adjusted these figures both up and down. But as the decade drew to its close, Walmart did indeed employ about 800,000 more people than it did when the plan was completed.

Forecasting the supply of labor is really two tasks: forecasting the internal supply (the number and type of employees who will be in the firm at some future date) and forecasting the external supply (the number and type of people who will be available for hiring in the labor market at large).[12] The simplest approach merely adjusts present staffing levels for anticipated turnover and promotions. Again, though, large organizations use extremely sophisticated models to make these forecasts. Union Oil Company of California, for example, has a complex forecasting system for keeping track of the present and future distributions of professionals and managers. The Union Oil system can spot areas where there will

job analysis
A systematized procedure for collecting and recording information about jobs within an organization

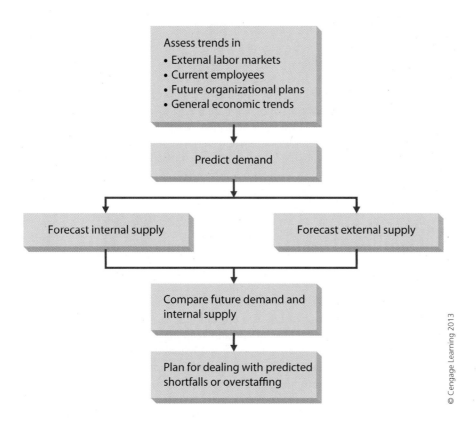

FIGURE 17.1 HUMAN RESOURCE PLANNING

Attracting human resources cannot be left to chance if an organization expects to function at peak efficiency. Human resource planning involves assessing trends, forecasting supply and demand of labor, and then developing appropriate strategies for addressing any differences.

© Cengage Learning 2013

eventually be too many qualified professionals competing for too few promotions or, conversely, too few good people available to fill important positions.[13]

At higher levels of the organization, managers plan for specific people and positions. The technique most commonly used is the **replacement chart**, which lists each important managerial position, who occupies it, how long he or she will probably stay in it before moving on, and who (by name) is now qualified or soon will be qualified to move into the position. This technique allows ample time to plan developmental experiences for persons identified as potential successors to critical managerial jobs.[14] Xerox CEO Anne Mulcahy essentially identified her eventual successor when she appointed Ursula Burns as president. And sure enough, when Mulcahy decided to retire, Burns was quickly appointed as the new CEO. This well-managed process made the transition easy and efficient.[15] Similarly, when Morgan Stanley's CEO John Mack announced he would like to step back from the CEO role, the company's board created a succession plan, announcing that Co-President James Gorman would take over as CEO when Mack retired.

To facilitate both planning and identifying persons for current transfer or promotion, some organizations also have an **employee information system**, or **skills inventory**. Such systems are usually computerized and contain information on each employee's education, skills, work experience, and career aspirations. Such a system can quickly locate all the employees in the organization who are qualified to fill a position requiring, for instance, a degree in chemical engineering, three years of experience in an oil refinery, and fluency in Spanish. Enterprise resource planning (ERP) systems, as described in Chapter 16, generally include capabilities for measuring and managing the internal supply of labor in ways that best fit the needs of the organization.

Forecasting the external supply of labor is a different problem altogether. How does a manager, for example, predict how many electrical engineers will be seeking work in Georgia three years from now? To get an idea of the future availability of labor, planners must rely on information from such outside sources as state employment commissions, government reports, and figures supplied by colleges on the number of students in major fields.

replacement chart
Lists each important managerial position in the organization, who occupies it, how long he or she will probably remain in the position, and who is or will be a qualified replacement

employee information system (skills inventory)
Contains information on each employee's education, skills, experience, and career aspirations; usually computerized

Matching Human Resource Supply and Demand After comparing future demand and internal supply, managers can make plans to manage predicted shortfalls or overstaffing. If a shortfall is predicted, new employees can be hired, present employees can be retrained and transferred into the understaffed area, individuals approaching retirement can be convinced to stay on, or labor-saving or productivity-enhancing systems can be installed.

If the organization needs to hire, the external labor supply forecast helps managers plan how to recruit, based on whether the type of person needed is readily available or scarce in the labor market. As we noted earlier, the trend in temporary workers also helps managers in staffing by affording them extra flexibility. If overstaffing is expected to be a problem, the main options are transferring the extra employees, not replacing individuals who quit, encouraging early retirement, and laying people off.

Recruiting Human Resources

Once an organization has an idea of its future human resource needs, the next phase is usually recruiting new employees.[16] Recruiting is the process of attracting qualified persons to apply for jobs that are open. Where do recruits come from? Some recruits are found internally; others come from outside the organization.

Internal recruiting means considering present employees as candidates for openings. Promotion from within can help build morale and keep high-quality employees from leaving the firm. In unionized firms, the procedures for notifying employees of internal job change opportunities are usually spelled out in the union contract. For higher-level positions, a skills inventory system may be used to identify internal candidates, or managers may be asked to recommend individuals who should be considered. Most businesses today routinely post job openings on their internal communication network, or intranet. One disadvantage of internal recruiting is its ripple effect. When an employee moves to a different job, someone else must be found to take his or her old job. In one organization, 454 job movements were necessary as a result of filling 195 initial openings!

External recruiting involves attracting persons outside the organization to apply for jobs. External recruiting methods include advertising, campus interviews, employment agencies or executive search firms, union hiring halls, referrals by present employees, and hiring "walk-ins" or "gate-hires" (people who show up without being solicited). Increasingly, firms are using the Internet to post job openings and to solicit applicants. Of course, a manager must select the most appropriate methods— using the state employment service to find maintenance workers but not a nuclear physicist, for example. Private employment agencies can be a good source of clerical and technical employees, and executive search firms specialize in locating top-management talent. Newspaper ads are often used because they reach a wide audience and thus allow minorities equal opportunity to find out about and apply for job openings.

The organization must also keep in mind that recruiting decisions often go both ways— the organization is recruiting an employee, but the prospective employee is also selecting a job.[17] For instance, when unemployment is low (meaning there are fewer people seeking work), businesses may have to work harder to

recruiting
The process of attracting individuals to apply for jobs that are open

internal recruiting
Considering current employees as applicants for higher-level jobs in the organization

external recruiting
Getting people from outside the organization to apply for jobs

Private employment agencies can be a good source of technical and clerical workers. There are also specialized private agencies that deal only with top managers, knowledge workers, and other segments of the labor market requiring special expertise.

DWImages Northern Ireland/Alamy

attract new employees. During the late 1990s, when unemployment dropped to a 25-year low, some recruiters at firms such as Sprint, PeopleSoft, and Cognex stressed how much "fun" it was to work for them, reinforcing this message with ice cream socials, karaoke contests, softball leagues, and free movie nights.[19] But when unemployment is higher (meaning there are more people looking for work), organizations may find it easier to recruit prospective employees without having to resort to expensive hiring incentives. For example, during the economic recession that began in 2008, many firms reduced jobs and/or cut back on labor hours. As a result, firms that needed to hire new workers found it much easier to do so. Avon, for instance, used this period to substantially increase the size and effectiveness of its sales force by hiring talented people who would not otherwise have had much interest in direct sales.[20]

Nevertheless, even if a firm can take its pick of the best potential employees, it still should put its best foot forward, treat all applicants with dignity, and strive for a good person–job fit. Hiring the wrong employee can cost the company about half of a low-skilled worker's annual wages or three to five times upper-level employees' annual wages. Therefore, hiring the "wrong" employee for $20,000 per year could cost the company at least $10,000. These costs stem from training, counseling, low productivity, termination, and recruiting and hiring a replacement.

One generally successful method for facilitating a good person–job fit is the so-called **realistic job preview (RJP)**. As the term suggests, the RJP involves providing the applicant with a real picture of what performing the job that the organization is trying to fill would be like.[21] For example, it would not make sense for a firm to tell an applicant that the job is exciting and challenging when in fact it is routine and straightforward, yet some managers do this to hire the best people. The likely outcome will be a dissatisfied employee who will quickly be looking for a better job. If the company is more realistic about a job, though, the person hired will be more likely to remain in the job for a longer period of time.

Selecting Human Resources

Once the recruiting process has attracted a pool of applicants, the next step is to select whom to hire. The intent of the selection process is to gather from applicants information that will predict their job success and then to hire the candidates likely to be most successful.[22] Of course, the organization can only gather information about factors that are predictive of future performance. The process of determining the predictive value of information is called **validation**.

Two basic approaches to validation are predictive validation and content validation. *Predictive validation* involves collecting the scores of employees or applicants on the device to be validated and correlating their scores with actual job performance. A significant correlation means that the selection device is a valid predictor of job performance. *Content validation* uses logic and job analysis data to establish that the selection device measures the exact skills needed for successful job performance. The most critical part of content validation is a careful job analysis showing exactly what duties are to be performed. The test is then developed to measure the applicant's ability to perform those duties.

Application Blanks The first step in selection is usually asking the candidate to fill out an application blank. Application blanks are an efficient method of gathering information about the applicant's previous work history, educational background, and other job-related demographic data. They should not contain questions about areas not related to the job, such as gender, religion, or national origin. Application blank data are generally used informally to decide whether a candidate merits further evaluation, and interviewers use application blanks to familiarize themselves with candidates before interviewing them. Unfortunately, in recent

"Everything that makes women come to Avon is amplified during slow economic times."

—LIZ SMITH, AVON PRESIDENT[18]

realistic job preview (RJP)
Provides the applicant with a real picture of what performing the job that the organization is trying to fill would be like

validation
Determining the extent to which a selection device is really predictive of future job performance

years there has been a trend toward job applicants either falsifying or inflating their credentials to stand a better chance of getting a job. Indeed, one recent survey of 2.6 million job applications found that an astounding 44 percent of them contained some false information.[23]

Tests Tests of ability, skill, aptitude, or knowledge that is relevant to the particular job are usually the best predictors of job success, although tests of general intelligence or personality are occasionally useful as well. In addition to being validated, tests should be administered and scored consistently. All candidates should be given the same directions, should be allowed the same amount of time, and should experience the same testing environment (temperature, lighting, distractions).[24]

Interviews Although a popular selection device, interviews are sometimes poor predictors of job success. For example, biases inherent in the way people perceive and judge others at a first meeting affect subsequent evaluations by the interviewer. Interview validity can be improved by training interviewers to be aware of potential biases and by increasing the structure of the interview. In a structured interview, questions are written in advance, and all interviewers follow the same question list with each candidate they interview. This procedure introduces consistency into the interview procedure and allows the organization to validate the content of the questions to be asked.[25]

For interviewing managerial or professional candidates, a somewhat less structured approach can be used. Question areas and information-gathering objectives are still planned in advance, but the specific questions vary with the candidates' backgrounds. Trammell Crow Real Estate Investors uses a novel approach in hiring managers. Each applicant is interviewed not only by two or three other managers but also by a secretary or young leasing agent. This provides information about how the prospective manager relates to nonmanagers.[26]

Assessment Centers Assessment centers are a popular method used to select managers and are particularly good for selecting current employees for promotion.[27] The assessment center is a content-valid simulation of major parts of the managerial job. A typical center lasts two to three days, with groups of 6 to 12 persons participating in a variety of managerial exercises. Centers may also include interviews, public speaking, and standardized ability tests. Candidates are assessed by several trained observers, usually managers several levels above the job for which the candidates are being considered. Assessment centers are quite valid if properly designed and are fair to members of minority groups and women.[28] For some firms, the assessment center is a permanent facility created for these activities. For other firms, the assessment activities are performed in a multipurpose location such as a conference room. AT&T pioneered the assessment center concept. For years the firm has used assessment centers to make virtually all of its selection decisions for management positions.

Other Techniques Organizations also use other selection techniques depending on the circumstances. Polygraph tests, once popular, are declining in popularity. On the other hand, more and more organizations are requiring that applicants in whom they are interested take physical exams. Organizations are also increasingly using drug tests, especially in situations in which drug-related performance problems could create serious safety hazards. For example, applicants for jobs in a nuclear power plant would likely be tested for drug use. And some organizations today even run credit checks on prospective employees.

Describe the processes of human resource planning, recruiting, and selection.

As a potential employee, what things might a firm do in its recruiting efforts to impress you?

CONCEPT CHECK

Developing Human Resources

Regardless of how effective a selection system is, however, most employees need additional training if they are to grow and develop in their jobs. Evaluating their performance and providing feedback are also necessary.

Training and Development

In HRM, **training** usually refers to teaching operational or technical employees how to do the job for which they were hired. **Development** refers to teaching managers and professionals the skills needed for both present and future jobs.[29] Most organizations provide regular training and development programs for managers and employees. For example, IBM spends more than $700 million annually on programs and has a vice president in charge of employee education. U.S. businesses spend more than $50 billion annually on training and development programs away from the workplace (in 2010 the figure was $52.8 billion).[30] And this figure does not include wages and benefits paid to employees while they are participating in such programs.

Assessing Training Needs The first step in developing a training plan is to determine what needs exist. For example, if employees do not know how to operate the machinery necessary to do their job, a training program on how to operate the machinery is clearly needed. On the other hand, when a group of office workers is performing poorly, training may not be the answer. The problem could be motivation, aging equipment, poor supervision, inefficient work design, or a deficiency of skills and knowledge. Only the last could be remedied by training. As training programs are being developed, the manager should set specific and measurable goals specifying what participants are to learn. Managers should also plan to evaluate the training program after employees complete it. The training process from start to finish is diagrammed in Figure 17.2.

Common Training Methods Many different training and development methods are available. Selection of methods depends on many considerations, but perhaps the most important is training content. When the training content is factual material (such as company rules or explanations of how to fill out forms), assigned reading, programmed learning, and lecture methods work well. When the content is interpersonal relations or group decision making, however, firms must use a method that allows interpersonal contact, such as role-playing or case discussion groups. When employees must learn a physical skill, methods allowing practice and the actual use of tools and materials are needed, as in on-the-job training or vestibule training. (Vestibule training enables participants to focus on safety, learning, and feedback rather than on productivity.)

Web-based and other electronic media–based training are becoming very popular. Such methods allow a mix of training content, are relatively easy to update and revise, let participants use a variable schedule, and lower travel costs.[31] On the other hand, they are limited in their capacity to simulate real activities and facilitate face-to-face interaction. Xerox, Massachusetts Mutual Life Insurance, and Ford have all reported tremendous success with these methods. In addition, most training programs actually rely on a mix of methods. Boeing, for example, sends managers to an intensive two-week training seminar involving tests, simulations, role-playing exercises, and flight simulation exercises.[32]

Finally, some larger businesses have started creating their own self-contained training facility, often called a *corporate university*. McDonald's was among the first to start this practice with its so-called Hamburger University in Illinois. All management trainees for the firm attend training programs there to learn exactly how long to grill a burger, how to maintain good customer service, and so on. The cult hamburger chain In-N-Out Burger also has a similar training venue it calls In-N-Out University. Other firms that use this approach include Shell Oil and General Electric.[33]

"Certainly times are tough, but we recognize that employee development needs to continue."

—DAVID METZGER, CANON USA'S DIRECTOR OF MANAGEMENT DEVELOPMENT[34]

training
Teaching operational or technical employees how to do the job for which they were hired

development
Teaching managers and professionals the skills needed for both present and future jobs

FIGURE 17.2 THE TRAINING PROCESS

Managing the training process can go a long way toward enhancing its effectiveness. If training programs are well conceived and well executed, both the organization and its employees benefit. Following a comprehensive process helps managers meet the objectives of the training program.

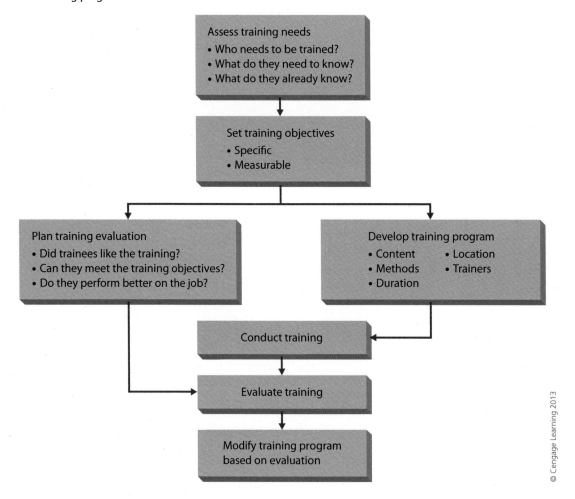

© Cengage Learning 2013

Evaluation of Training Training and development programs should always be evaluated. Typical evaluation approaches include measuring one or more relevant criteria (such as attitudes or performance) before and after the training, and determining whether the criteria changed. Evaluation measures collected at the end of training are easy to get, but actual performance measures collected when the trainee is on the job are more important. Trainees may say that they enjoyed the training and learned a lot, but the true test is whether their job performance improves after their training.

Performance Appraisal

performance appraisal
A formal assessment of how well an employee is doing his or her job

Once employees are trained and settled into their jobs, one of management's next concerns is performance appraisal.[35] Performance appraisal is a formal assessment of how well employees are doing their jobs. Employees' performance should be evaluated regularly for many reasons. One reason is that performance appraisal may be necessary for validating selection devices or assessing the impact of training programs. A second reason is administrative—to aid in making decisions about pay raises, promotions, and training. Still another reason is to provide feedback to employees to help them improve their present performance and plan their future careers.[36]

Because performance evaluations often help determine wages and promotions, they must be fair and nondiscriminatory. In the case of appraisals, content validation is used to show that the appraisal system accurately measures performance on important job elements and does not measure traits or behavior that are irrelevant to job performance.

Common Appraisal Methods Two basic categories of appraisal methods commonly used in organizations are objective methods and judgmental methods. Objective measures of performance include actual output (that is, number of units produced), scrap rate, dollar volume of sales, and number of claims processed. Objective performance measures may be contaminated by "opportunity bias" if some persons have a better chance to perform than others. For example, a sales representative selling snow blowers in Michigan has a greater opportunity than does a colleague selling the same product in Alabama. Fortunately, adjusting raw performance figures for the effect of opportunity bias and thereby arriving at figures that accurately represent each individual's performance is often possible.

Another type of objective measure, the special performance test, is a method by which each employee is assessed under standardized conditions. This kind of appraisal also eliminates opportunity bias. For example, Verizon Southwest has a series of prerecorded calls that operators in a test booth answer. The operators are graded on speed, accuracy, and courtesy in handling the calls. Performance tests measure ability but do not measure the extent to which one is motivated to use that ability on a daily basis. (A high-ability person may be a lazy performer except when being tested.) Special performance tests must therefore be supplemented by other appraisal methods to provide a complete picture of performance.

Judgmental methods, including ranking and rating techniques, are the most common way to measure performance. Ranking compares employees directly with one another and orders them from best to worst. Ranking has a number of drawbacks. Ranking is difficult for large groups, because the individuals in the middle of the distribution may be hard to distinguish from one another accurately. Comparisons of people in different work groups are also difficult. For example, an employee ranked third in a strong group may be more valuable than an employee ranked first in a weak group. Another criticism of ranking is that the manager must rank people on the basis of overall performance, even though each person likely has both strengths and weaknesses. Furthermore, rankings do not provide useful information for feedback. To be told that one is ranked third is not nearly as helpful as to be told that the quality of one's work is outstanding, its quantity is satisfactory, one's punctuality could use improvement, or one's paperwork is seriously deficient.

Rating differs from ranking in that it compares each employee with a fixed standard rather than with other employees. A rating scale provides the standard. Figure 17.3 gives examples of three graphic rating scales for a bank teller. Each consists of a performance dimension to be rated (punctuality, congeniality, and accuracy) followed by a scale on which to make the rating. In constructing graphic rating scales, performance dimensions that are relevant to job performance must be selected. In particular, they should focus on job behaviors and results rather than on personality traits or attitudes.

The **Behaviorally Anchored Rating Scale (BARS)** is a sophisticated and useful rating method. Supervisors construct rating scales with associated behavioral anchors. They first identify relevant performance dimensions and then generate anchors—specific, observable behaviors typical of each performance level. Figure 17.4 shows an example of a behaviorally anchored rating scale for the dimension "Inventory control."

The other scales in this set, developed for the job of department manager in a chain of specialty stores, include "Handling customer complaints," "Planning special promotions," "Following company procedures," "Supervising sales personnel," and "Diagnosing and solving special problems." BARS can be effective because they require that management take proper care in constructing the scales and they provide useful anchors for supervisors to use in evaluating people. They are costly, however, because outside expertise is usually needed and because scales must be developed for each job within the organization.

Behaviorally Anchored Rating Scale (BARS)
A sophisticated rating method in which supervisors construct a rating scale associated with behavioral anchors

FIGURE 17.3 GRAPHIC RATING SCALES FOR A BANK TELLER

Graphic rating scales are very common methods for evaluating employee performance. The manager who is doing the rating circles the point on each scale that best reflects her or his assessment of the employee on that scale. Graphic rating scales are widely used for many different kinds of jobs.

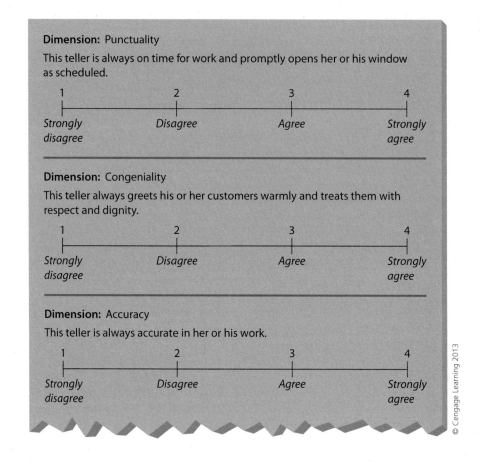

Dimension: **Punctuality**

This teller is always on time for work and promptly opens her or his window as scheduled.

1	2	3	4
Strongly disagree	Disagree	Agree	Strongly agree

Dimension: **Congeniality**

This teller always greets his or her customers warmly and treats them with respect and dignity.

1	2	3	4
Strongly disagree	Disagree	Agree	Strongly agree

Dimension: **Accuracy**

This teller is always accurate in her or his work.

1	2	3	4
Strongly disagree	Disagree	Agree	Strongly agree

© Cengage Learning 2013

Errors in Performance Appraisal   Errors or biases can occur in any kind of rating or ranking system.[37] One common problem is *recency error*—the tendency to base judgments on the subordinate's most recent performance because it is most easily recalled. Often a rating or ranking is intended to evaluate performance over an entire time period, such as six months or a year, so the recency error does introduce error into the judgment. Other errors include overuse of one part of the scale—being too lenient, being too severe, or giving everyone a rating of "average."

FIGURE 17.4 BEHAVIORALLY ANCHORED RATING SCALE

Behaviorally anchored rating scales help overcome some of the limitations of standard rating scales. Each point on the scale is accompanied by a behavioral anchor—a summary of an employee behavior that fits that spot on the scale.

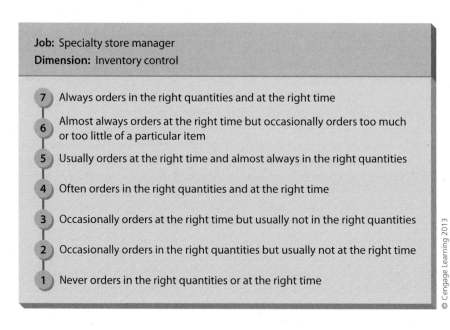

Job: Specialty store manager
Dimension: Inventory control

- 7 — Always orders in the right quantities and at the right time
- 6 — Almost always orders at the right time but occasionally orders too much or too little of a particular item
- 5 — Usually orders at the right time and almost always in the right quantities
- 4 — Often orders in the right quantities and at the right time
- 3 — Occasionally orders at the right time but usually not in the right quantities
- 2 — Occasionally orders in the right quantities but usually not at the right time
- 1 — Never orders in the right quantities or at the right time

© Cengage Learning 2013

Halo error is allowing the assessment of an employee on one dimension to "spread" to ratings of that employee on other dimensions. For instance, if an employee is outstanding on quality of output, a rater might tend to give her or him higher marks than deserved on other dimensions. Errors can also occur because of race, sex, or age discrimination, intentionally or unintentionally. The best way to offset these errors is to ensure that a valid rating system is developed at the outset and then to train managers in how to use it.

One interesting innovation in performance appraisal used in some organizations today is called 360-degree feedback, in which managers are evaluated by everyone around them—their boss, their peers, and their subordinates. Such a complete and thorough approach provides people with a far richer array of information about their performance than does a conventional appraisal given by just the boss. Of course, such a system also takes considerable time and must be handled so as not to breed fear and mistrust in the workplace.[38]

Performance Feedback

The last step in most performance appraisal systems is giving feedback to subordinates about their performance. This is usually done in a private meeting between the person being evaluated and his or her boss. The discussion should generally be focused on the facts—the assessed level of performance, how and why that assessment was made, and how it can be improved in the future. Feedback interviews are not easy to conduct. Many managers are uncomfortable with the task, especially if feedback is negative and subordinates are disappointed by what they hear. Properly training managers, however, can help them conduct more effective feedback interviews.[39]

Some firms use a very aggressive approach to terminating people who do not meet expectations. General Electric actually implemented a system whereby each year the bottom 10 percent of its workforce is terminated and replaced with new employees. Company executives claim that this approach, although stressful for all employees, helps it to continuously upgrade its workforce. Other firms have started using this same approach. However, both Ford and Goodyear recently agreed to abandon similar approaches in response to age discrimination lawsuits.[40]

360-degree feedback
A performance appraisal system in which managers are evaluated by everyone around them—their boss, their peers, and their subordinates

compensation
The financial remuneration given by the organization to its employees in exchange for their work

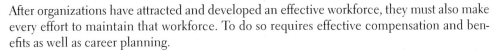

What are the most common methods for training employees and assessing their performance?

What kind of performance appraisal techniques or methods would you prefer to use as a manager? As someone being evaluated? Why?

CONCEPT CHECK

Maintaining Human Resources

After organizations have attracted and developed an effective workforce, they must also make every effort to maintain that workforce. To do so requires effective compensation and benefits as well as career planning.

Determining Compensation

Compensation is the financial remuneration given by the organization to its employees in exchange for their work. There are three basic forms of compensation. *Wages* are the hourly compensation paid to operating employees. The minimum hourly wage paid in the United States today is $7.25 (though several states have minimum wage levels that exceed this federal minimum). *Salary* refers to compensation paid for total contributions, as opposed to pay based on hours worked. For example, managers earn an annual salary, usually paid monthly. They receive the salary regardless of the number of hours they work. Some firms have started paying all their employees a salary instead of hourly wages. For example, all employees at Chaparral Steel earn a salary, starting at $35,000 a year for entry-level operating employees. Finally, *incentives* represent special compensation opportunities that are usually tied to performance. Sales commissions and bonuses are among the most common incentives.

Compensation is an important and complex part of the organization–employee relationship.[41] Basic compensation is necessary to provide employees with the means to maintain a reasonable standard of living. Beyond this, however, compensation also provides a tangible measure of the value of the individual to the organization. If employees do not earn enough to meet their basic economic goals, they will seek employment elsewhere. Likewise, if they believe that their contributions are undervalued by the organization, they may leave or exhibit poor work habits, low morale, and little commitment to the organization. Thus, designing an effective compensation system is clearly in the organization's best interests.[42]

A good compensation system can help attract qualified applicants, retain present employees, and stimulate high performance at a cost reasonable for one's industry and geographic area. To set up a successful system, management must make decisions about wage levels, the wage structure, and the individual wage determination system. Some firms used the 2009 recession as an opportunity to refine their compensation systems. While many firms reduced their workforces through layoffs, others used targeted salary cuts to avoid layoffs. For instance, at Hewlett-Packard the CEO first cut his own salary by 20 percent. The firm's very top performers kept their same pay levels. But others were given tiered salary cuts ranging from as little as 2.5 percent to as much as 20 percent. A few firms went even further. CareerBuilder.com, for instance, instituted pay cuts for all employees but also told everyone they only had to work half a day on Fridays.[43]

Wage-Level Decision The wage-level decision is a management policy decision about whether the firm wants to pay above, at, or below the going rate for labor in the industry or the geographic area. Most firms choose to pay near the average, although those that cannot afford more pay below average. Large, successful firms may like to cultivate the image of being "wage leaders" by intentionally paying more than average and thus attracting and keeping high-quality employees. Google, IBM, and Microsoft, for example, pay top dollar to get the new employees they want. McDonald's, on the other hand, often pays close to the minimum wage. The level of unemployment in the labor force also affects wage levels. Pay declines when labor is plentiful and increases when labor is scarce.

Once managers make the wage-level decision, they need information to help set actual wage rates. Managers need to know what the maximum, minimum, and average wages are for particular jobs in the appropriate labor market. This information is collected by means of a wage survey. Area wage surveys can be conducted by individual firms or by local HR or business associations. Professional and industry associations often conduct surveys and make the results available to employers.

Wage Structure Decision Wage structures are usually set up through a procedure called job evaluation—an attempt to assess the worth of each job relative to other jobs. At Ben & Jerry's Homemade, company policy once dictated that the highest-paid employee in the firm could not make more than seven times what the lowest-paid employee earned. But this policy had to be modified when the company found that it was simply unable to hire a new CEO without paying more than this amount. The simplest method for creating a wage structure is to rank jobs from those that should be paid the most (for example, the president) to those that should be paid the least (for example, a mail clerk or a janitor).

In a smaller firm with few jobs (like Ben & Jerry's, for example), this method is quick and practical, but larger firms with many job titles require more sophisticated methods. The next step is setting actual wage rates on the basis of a combination of survey data and the wage structure that results from job evaluation. Jobs of equal value are often grouped into wage grades for ease of administration.

job evaluation
An attempt to assess the worth of each job relative to other jobs

Individual Wage Decisions After wage-level and wage structure decisions are made, the individual wage decision must be addressed. This decision concerns how much to pay each employee in a particular job. Although the easiest decision is to pay a single rate for each job, more typically a range of pay rates is associated with each job. For example, the pay range for an individual job might be $10.00 to $14.40 per hour, with different employees earning different rates within the range.

A system is then needed for setting individual rates. This may be done on the basis of seniority (enter the job at $10.00, for example, and increase 50 cents per hour every six months on the job), initial qualifications (inexperienced people start at $10.00; more experienced people start at a higher rate), or merit (raises above the entering rate are given for good performance). Combinations of these bases may also be used.

The Internet is also playing a key role in compensation patterns today because both job seekers and current employees can more easily get a sense of what their true market value is. If they can document the claim that their value is higher than what their current employer now pays or is offering, they are in a position to demand a higher salary. Consider the case of one compensation executive who met recently with a subordinate to discuss her raise. He was surprised when she produced data from five different websites backing up her claim for a bigger raise than he had intended to offer.[44]

Determining Benefits

Benefits are things of value other than compensation that the organization provides to its workers. (Benefits are sometimes called *indirect compensation*.) The average company spends an amount equal to more than one-third of its cash payroll on employee benefits.

benefits
Things of value other than compensation that an organization provides to its workers

© Salary.com

Determining compensation for employees is a vital part of how businesses retain their human resources. Employees were once forced to rely on limited and imperfect information to determine the fairness of their compensation. However, the Internet has made it much easier for people to learn about how much employers are paying people with their skills and abilities. Hence, businesses must keep informed about competitive compensation practices in order to keep their most valuable employees.

Thus an average employee who is paid, say, $30,000 per year averages a bit over $10,000 more per year in benefits.

Benefits come in several forms. Pay for time not worked includes sick leave, vacation, holidays, and unemployment compensation. Insurance benefits often include life and health insurance for employees and their dependents. Workers' compensation is a legally required insurance benefit that provides medical care and disability income for employees injured on the job. Social Security is a government pension plan to which both employers and employees contribute. Many employers also provide a private pension plan to which they and their employees contribute. Employee service benefits include such extras as tuition reimbursement and recreational opportunities.

Some organizations have instituted "cafeteria benefit plans," whereby basic coverage is provided for all employees but employees are then allowed to choose which additional benefits they want (up to a cost limit based on salary). An employee with five children might choose enhanced medical and dental coverage for dependents, a single employee might prefer more vacation time, and an older employee might elect increased pension benefits. Flexible systems are expected to encourage people to stay in the organization and even help the company attract new employees.[45]

In recent years, companies have also started offering more innovative benefits as a way of accommodating different needs. On-site childcare, mortgage assistance, and paid leave programs are interesting new benefits that some firms offer.[46] A good benefits plan may encourage people to join and stay with an organization, but it seldom stimulates high performance, because benefits are tied more to membership in the organization than to performance. To manage their benefits programs effectively, companies should shop carefully, avoid redundant coverage, and provide only those benefits that employees want. Benefits programs should also be explained to employees in clear and straightforward language so that they can use the benefits appropriately and appreciate what the company is providing.

Finally, as a result of economic pressures, some firms have started to reduce employee benefits in the last few years. In 2002, for example, 17 percent of employees in the United States with employer healthcare coverage saw their benefits cut; the 2009 recession led to further reductions. Some employers have also reduced their contributions to employee retirement plans, cut the amount of annual leave they offer to employees, or both.[47] For instance, in 2009 16 major companies announced that they would reduce or eliminate employer contributions to employee retirement plans. Several others followed suit in 2010. Among these were Wells Fargo, Anheuser-Busch, Boise Cascade, Cooper Tire & Rubber, Kimberly-Clark, and Saks.[48] A Prudential survey published in 2011 found that 20 percent of executives surveyed said their companies are likely to terminate their defined benefit plans and 60 percent are implementing strategies to reduce the risk associated with these plans.[49] On average, companies have cut up to five employee-oriented benefits to reduce spending— 401(k) matching, tuition reimbursement, bonuses, and so on. For instance, while Goodyear Tire & Rubber reinstated 401(k) matching for employees, it froze its pension plan to save millions of dollars.[50]

Career Planning

A final aspect of maintaining human resources is career planning. Few people work in the same jobs their entire careers. Some people change jobs within one organization, others change organizations, and many do both. When these movements are haphazard and poorly conceived, both the individual and the organization suffer. Thus planning career progressions in advance is in everyone's best interests. Of course, planning a 30-year career for a newcomer just joining the organization is difficult. But planning can help map out what areas the individual is most interested in and help the person see what opportunities are available within the organization.[51]

Describe the fundamental components and issues involved in determining compensation in organizations.

As a prospective employee, what benefits would you assume that your employer will offer? What unusual or special benefits might you personally find appealing?

Managing Labor Relations

Labor relations is the process of dealing with employees who are represented by a union.[52] At one time, almost a third of the entire U.S. labor force belonged to a labor union. Unions enjoyed their largest membership between the years of 1940 and 1955. Membership began to decline steadily in the mid-1950s though, for several reasons: (1) increased standards of living made union membership seem less important; (2) traditionally unionized industries in the manufacturing sector began to decline; and (3) the globalization of business operations caused many unionized jobs to be lost to foreign workers. This downward trend continued until 2008, when union membership rose by the largest amount in over a quarter century, a gain of 428,000 members (12.4 percent of all U.S. workers).[53] However, union membership again declined the following two years, dropping to 11.9 percent in 2010. Much of this fluctuation was attributable to fears of job insecurity due to the recession that hit in 2008; but as the economy bottomed out and started to rebound, membership again declined. Managing labor relations is an important part of HRM. However, most large firms have separate labor relations specialists to handle these activities apart from other human resource functions.

How Employees Form Unions

For employees to form a new local union, several things must occur. First, employees must become interested in having a union. Nonemployees who are professional organizers employed by a national union (such as the Teamsters or United Auto Workers) may generate interest by making speeches and distributing literature outside the workplace. Inside, employees who want a union try to convince other workers of the benefits of a union.

The second step is to collect employees' signatures on authorization cards. These cards state that the signer wishes to vote to determine whether the union will represent him or her. To show the National Labor Relations Board (NLRB) that interest is sufficient to justify holding an election, 30 percent of the employees in the potential bargaining unit must sign these cards. Before an election can be held, however, the bargaining unit must be defined. The bargaining unit consists of all employees who will be eligible to vote in the election and to join and be represented by the union if one is formed.

The election is supervised by an NLRB representative (or, if both parties agree, the American Arbitration Association—a professional association of arbitrators) and is conducted by secret ballot. If a simple majority of those voting (not of all those eligible to vote) votes for the union, then the union becomes certified as the official representative of the bargaining unit.[54] The new union then organizes itself by officially signing up members and electing officers; it will soon be ready to negotiate the first contract. The union-organizing process is diagrammed in Figure 17.5. If workers become disgruntled with their union or if management presents strong evidence that the union is not representing workers appropriately, the NLRB can arrange a decertification election. The results of such an election determine whether the union remains certified.

Organizations usually prefer that employees not be unionized because unions limit management's freedom in many areas. Management may thus wage its own campaign to convince employees to vote against the union. "Unfair labor practices" are often committed at this

labor relations
The process of dealing with employees who are represented by a union

FIGURE 17.5 THE UNION-ORGANIZING PROCESS

If employees of an organization want to form a union, the law prescribes a specific set of procedures that both employees and the organization must follow. Assuming that these procedures are followed and the union is approved, the organization must engage in collective bargaining with the new union.

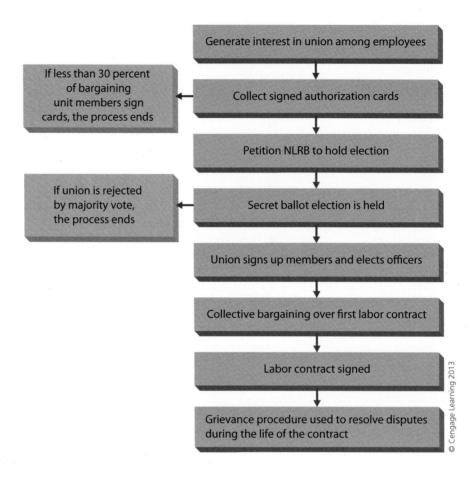

© Cengage Learning 2013

point. For instance, it is an unfair labor practice for management to promise to give employees a raise (or any other benefit) if the union is defeated. Experts agree that the best way to avoid unionization is to practice good employee relations all the time—not just when threatened by a union election. Providing absolutely fair treatment with clear standards in the areas of pay, promotion, layoffs, and discipline; having a complaint or appeal system for persons who feel unfairly treated; and avoiding any kind of favoritism will help make employees feel that a union is unnecessary. Walmart strives to avoid unionization through these practices.[55]

Collective Bargaining

The intent of **collective bargaining** is to agree on a labor contract between management and the union that is satisfactory to both parties. The contract contains agreements about such issues as wages, work hours, job security, promotion, layoffs, discipline, benefits, methods of allocating overtime, vacations, rest periods, and the grievance procedure. The process of bargaining may go on for weeks, months, or longer, with representatives of management and the union meeting to make proposals and counterproposals. The resulting agreement must be ratified by the union membership. If it is not approved, the union may strike to put pressure on management, or it may choose not to strike and simply continue negotiating until a more acceptable agreement is reached.

For example, Boeing's machinists' union went on strike in 2008 over issues of job security and the firm's plans to outsource more jobs to foreign factories.[56] In 2010, employees of a Mott's applesauce factory in New York went on a 120-day strike over Dr. Pepper Snapple Group's proposal for wage, pension, and healthcare cuts despite profits being up.[57] For its part, management can also take certain actions if a new contract is not approved. One

collective bargaining
The process of agreeing on a satisfactory labor contract between management and a union

option is called a lockout—employees are not allowed to work nor do they get paid. The NFL used this measure in 2011 when the players' union would not agree to management's contract proposal. When a final agreement was reached in July 2011, training camps were opened and the players returned to work.

Occasionally circumstances arise that cause management and labor to bargain over changes in existing contracts even before a new contract is needed. This is most likely to happen when unforeseen problems jeopardize the future of the business, and hence the jobs of union members. For example, when General Motors, Ford, and Chrysler were facing financial crisis in 2008, the United Auto Workers (UAW) agreed to contract concessions with the automakers to help give the firms the flexibility they claimed they needed to restructure their operations. Among others things, for instance, the UAW agreed to allow the companies to delay billions of dollars in payments for healthcare costs for retirees and to eliminate a controversial job banks program that allowed workers to get most of their wages even when they had been laid off.[58]

The grievance procedure is the means by which the contract is enforced. Most of what is in a contract concerns how management will treat employees. When employees feel that they have not been treated fairly under the contract, they file a grievance to correct the problem. The first step in a grievance procedure is for the aggrieved employee to discuss the alleged contract violation with her immediate superior. Often the grievance is resolved at this stage. If the employee still believes that she is being mistreated, however, the grievance can be appealed to the next level. A union official can help an aggrieved employee present her case. If the manager's decision is also unsatisfactory to the employee, additional appeals to successively higher levels are made until, finally, all in-company steps are exhausted. The final step is to submit the grievance to binding arbitration. An arbitrator is a labor law expert who is paid jointly by the union and management. The arbitrator studies the contract, hears both sides of the case, and renders a decision that both parties must obey. The grievance system for resolving disputes about contract enforcement prevents any need to strike during the term of the contract.

What are the basic steps employees follow to form a union?

In your opinion, do unions serve a useful purpose today? Why or why not?

CONCEPT CHECK

New Challenges in the Changing Workplace

As we have seen throughout this chapter, human resource managers face several ongoing challenges in their efforts to keep their organizations staffed with effective workforces. To complicate matters, new challenges arise as the economic and social environments of business change. We conclude this chapter with a look at two of the most important human resource management issues facing business today.

Managing Knowledge Workers

Employees traditionally added value to organizations because of what they did or because of their experience. In the "information age," however, many employees add value because of what they know.[59]

The Nature of Knowledge Work These employees are usually called knowledge workers, and the skill with which they are managed is a major factor in determining which firms will be successful in the future. Knowledge workers, including computer scientists, engineers, and physical scientists, provide special challenges for the HR manager. They tend to work in high-technology firms and are usually experts in some abstract knowledge

grievance procedure
The means by which a labor contract is enforced

knowledge workers
Workers whose contributions to an organization are based on what they know

Knowledge workers represent a special challenge to organizations due to their specialized expertise and high level of job mobility. This architect, for example, is reviewing construction plans with a project manager. The architect's expertise allows him to select from a wide variety of employers or to work for himself. As a result, his employer must go to extra lengths to make sure he is satisfied and has positive attitudes toward the company.

base. They often like to work independently and tend to identify more strongly with their profession than with any organization—even to the extent of defining performance in terms recognized by other members of their profession.

As the importance of information-driven jobs grows, the need for knowledge workers continues to grow as well. But these employees require extensive and highly specialized training, and not every organization is willing to make the human capital investments necessary to take advantage of these jobs. In fact, even after knowledge workers are on the job, retraining and training updates are critical to prevent their skills from becoming obsolete. It has been suggested, for example, that the "half-life" of a technical education in engineering is about three years. The failure to update such skills will not only result in the loss of competitive advantage but also increase the likelihood that the knowledge worker will go to another firm that is more committed to updating them.

Knowledge Worker Management and Labor Markets Even though overall demand for labor has slumped in recent years due to the economic downturn, the demand for knowledge workers remains strong. As a result, organizations that need these workers must introduce regular market adjustments (upward) in order to pay them enough to keep them. This is especially critical in areas in which demand is growing, as even entry-level salaries for these employees are high. Once an employee accepts a job with a firm, the employer faces yet another dilemma. Once hired, workers are more subject to the company's internal labor market, which is not likely to be growing as quickly as the external market for knowledge workers as a whole. Consequently, the longer an employee remains with a firm, the further behind the market his or her pay falls—unless, of course, it is regularly adjusted (upward).

"The world is not the same as it used to be. Companies pay for skills in an era where brains are more important than brawn, and the forces of automation, globalization, deregulation, and competition have changed what this kind of work is worth in the world."

—JOHN CHALLENGER, CEO OF OUTPLACEMENT FIRM CHALLENGER, GRAY, & CHRISTMAS[60]

Not surprisingly, strong demand for these workers has inspired some fairly extreme measures for attracting them in the first place.[61] High starting salaries and sign-on bonuses are common. BP Exploration was recently paying starting petroleum engineers with undersea platform-drilling knowledge—not experience, just knowledge—salaries in the six figures, plus sign-on bonuses of over $50,000 and immediate profit sharing. Even with these incentives, HR managers complained that, in the Gulf Coast region, they cannot retain specialists because young engineers soon leave to accept sign-on bonuses with competitors.

Contingent and Temporary Workers

A final contemporary HR issue of note involves the use of contingent or temporary workers.[62] Indeed, recent years have seen an explosion in the use of such workers by organizations. The FBI, for example, routinely employs a cadre of retired agents in various temporary jobs.[63]

Trends in Contingent and Temporary Employment In recent years, the number of contingent workers in the workforce has increased dramatically. A contingent worker is a person who works for an organization on something other than a permanent or full-time basis. Categories of contingent workers include independent contractors, on-call workers, temporary employees (usually hired through outside agencies), and contract and leased employees. Another category is part-time workers. The financial services giant Citigroup, for example, makes extensive use of part-time sales agents to pursue new clients. In 2008, a Staffing Industry Analysts survey estimated that 13 percent of the workforce was classified as contingent workers. However, this is predicted to rise to as much as 30 to 50 percent in the coming years.[64]

Managing Contingent and Temporary Workers Given the widespread use of contingent and temporary workers, HR managers must understand how to use such employees most effectively. In other words, they need to understand how to manage contingent and temporary workers.

One key is careful planning. Even though one of the presumed benefits of using contingent workers is flexibility, it is still important to integrate such workers in a coordinated fashion. Rather than having to call in workers sporadically and with no prior notice, organizations try to bring in specified numbers of workers for well-defined periods of time. The ability to do so comes from careful planning.

A second key is understanding contingent workers and acknowledging both their advantages and their disadvantages. In other words, the organization must recognize what it can and cannot achieve from the use of contingent and temporary workers. Expecting too much from such workers, for example, is a mistake that managers should avoid.

Third, managers must carefully assess the real cost of using contingent workers. We noted above, for example, that many firms adopt this course of action to save labor costs. The organization should be able to document precisely its labor-cost savings. How much would it be paying people in wages and benefits if they were on permanent staff? How does this cost compare with the amount spent on contingent workers? This difference, however, could be misleading. We also noted, for instance, that contingent workers might be less effective performers than permanent and full-time employees. Comparing employee for employee on a direct-cost basis, therefore, is not necessarily valid. Organizations must learn to adjust the direct differences in labor costs to account for differences in productivity and performance.

Finally, managers must fully understand their own strategies and decide in advance how they intend to manage temporary workers, specifically focusing on how to integrate them into the organization. On a very simplistic level, for example, an organization with a large contingent workforce must make some decisions about the treatment of contingent workers relative to the treatment of permanent, full-time workers. Should contingent workers be invited to the company holiday party? Should they have the same access to such employee benefits as counseling services and childcare? There are no right or wrong answers to such questions. Managers must understand that they need to develop a strategy for integrating contingent workers according to some sound logic and then follow that strategy consistently over time.[65]

Indeed, this last point has become part of a legal battleground in recent years as some workers hired under the rubric of contingent workers have subsequently argued that this has been a title in name only, and that their employers use this title to discriminate against them in various ways. For instance, FedEx relies on over 13,000 "contract" drivers. These individuals wear FedEx uniforms, drive FedEx trucks, and must follow FedEx rules and procedures. However, because the firm has hired them under a different employment agreement than its "regular" employees, it does not provide them with benefits. Groups of these individuals across the country sued FedEx on the grounds that, for all practical purposes, they are employees and should enjoy the same benefits as other drivers. In 2010, a U.S. district judge in Indiana ruled in favor of FedEx, upholding the drivers' status as independent contractors in 20 of 28 class-action cases. However, the court has ruled against FedEx on at least one claim.[66]

What are the fundamental issues and considerations regarding the use of contingent and temporary employees?

Have trends in employment for knowledge workers changed since the publication of this book?

Summary of Learning Objectives and Key Points

1. Describe the environmental context of human resource management, including its strategic importance and its relationship with legal and social factors.

   - Human resource management is concerned with attracting, developing, and maintaining the human resources an organization needs.
   - Its environmental context consists of its strategic importance and the legal and social environments that affect human resource management.

2. Discuss how organizations attract human resources, including human resource planning, recruiting, and selection.

   - Attracting human resources is an important part of the HRM function.
   - Human resource planning starts with job analysis and then focuses on forecasting the organization's future need for employees, forecasting the availability of employees both within and outside the organization, and planning programs to ensure that the proper number and type of employees will be available when needed.
   - Recruitment and selection are the processes by which job applicants are attracted, assessed, and hired.
   - Methods for selecting applicants include application blanks, tests, interviews, and assessment centers.
   - Any method used for selection should be properly validated.

3. Describe how organizations develop human resources, including training and development, performance appraisal, and performance feedback.

   - Organizations must also work to develop their human resources.
   - Training and development enable employees to perform their present job effectively and to prepare for future jobs.
   - Performance appraisals are important for validating selection devices, assessing the impact of training

   programs, deciding pay raises and promotions, and determining training needs.
   - Both objective and judgmental methods of appraisal can be applied, and a good system usually includes several methods.
   - The validity of appraisal information is always a concern, because it is difficult to accurately evaluate the many aspects of a person's job performance.

4. Discuss how organizations maintain human resources, including the determination of compensation and benefits and career planning.

   - Maintaining human resources is also important.
   - Compensation rates must be fair compared with rates for other jobs within the organization and with rates for the same or similar jobs in other organizations in the labor market.
   - Properly designed incentive or merit pay systems can encourage high performance, and a good benefits program can help attract and retain employees.
   - Career planning is also a major aspect of human resource management.

5. Discuss labor relations, including how employees form unions and the mechanics of collective bargaining.

   - If a majority of a company's nonmanagement employees so desire, they have the right to be represented by a union.
   - Management must engage in collective bargaining with the union in an effort to agree on a contract.
   - While a union contract is in effect, the grievance system is used to settle disputes with management.

6. Describe the key issues associated with managing knowledge and contingent and temporary workers.

   - Two important new challenges in the workplace include
     - the management of knowledge workers
     - issues associated with the use of contingent and temporary workers

Discussion Questions

Questions for Review

1. Describe the steps in the process of human resource planning. Explain the relationships between the steps.
2. Describe the common selection methods. Which method or methods are the best predictors of future job performance? Which are the worst? Why?
3. Compare training and development, noting any similarities and differences. What are some commonly used training methods?
4. Define wages and benefits. List different benefits that organizations can offer. What are the three decisions that managers must make to determine compensation and benefits? Explain each decision.

Questions for Analysis

5. The Family and Medical Leave Act of 1993 is seen as providing much-needed flexibility and security for families and workers. Others think that it places an unnecessary burden on business. Yet another opinion is that the act hurts women, who are more likely to ask for leave, and shuffles them off to a low-paid "mommy track" career path. In your opinion, what are the likely consequences of the act? You can adopt one of the viewpoints expressed above or develop another. Explain your answer.
6. How do you know a selection device is valid? What are the possible consequences of using invalid selection methods? How can an organization ensure that its selection methods are valid?
7. In a right-to-work state, workers are permitted to decide for themselves whether to join a union. In other states, workers may be required to join a union to obtain certain types of employment. If you live in a right-to-work state, do you agree that the choice to join a union should be made by each individual worker? If you do not live in a right-to-work state, do you agree that individuals should be required to join a union? Finally, if the choice were yours to make, would you join a union? Explain your answers. (*Hint*: Right-to-work states are generally in the South, Midwest, and parts of the West. If you do not know whether you live in a right-to-work state, visit the National Right to Work Legal Defense Foundation website, at **www.nrtw.org/rtws.htm**.)

Questions for Application

8. Choose three occupations that interest you. (The Labor Department's website has a full list, if you need help choosing.) Then access the Department of Labor, Bureau of Labor Statistics, online *Occupational Outlook Handbook*, at **www.bls.gov/oco**. What are the job prospects like in each of these fields? Based on what you read at the website, do you think you would enjoy any of these occupations? Why or why not?
9. Consider a job that you have held or with which you are familiar. Describe how you think an organization could best provide a realistic job preview for that position. What types of information and experiences should be conveyed to applicants? What techniques should be used to convey the information and experiences?
10. Contact a local organization to determine how that organization evaluates the performance of employees in complex jobs such as middle- or higher-level manager, scientist, lawyer, or market researcher. What problems with performance appraisal can you note?

 ## CengageNow™ Highlights

Now use your CengageNow™ homework to help you:

- Apply management theories in your life
- Assess your management skills
- Master management terms and concepts
- Apply your knowledge to real-world situations
- Analyze and solve challenging management problems

In order to take advantage of these elements, your instructor will need to have set up a course for your class within CengageNow™. Ask your instructor to contact his/her Cengage sales representative and Digital Solutions Manager to explore testing CengageNow™ in your course this term.

Basic Elements of Individual Behavior in Organizations

LEARNING OBJECTIVES

After studying this chapter, you should be able to:

1. Explain the nature of the individual–organization relationship.

2. Define personality and describe personality attributes that affect behavior in organizations.

3. Discuss individual attitudes in organizations and how they affect behavior.

4. Describe basic perceptual processes and the role of attributions in organizations.

5. Discuss the causes and consequences of stress and describe how it can be managed.

6. Describe creativity and its role in organizations.

7. Explain how workplace behaviors can directly or indirectly influence organizational effectiveness.

MANAGEMENT IN ACTION   The Psychopath in the Executive Suite

We'll assume that you know *something* about Bernie Madoff (and if you expect to have money to invest some day, you probably should). Madoff is the former Nasdaq chairman who turned his experience in courting investors into a second career as a con man extraordinaire. What started out as an asset-management business in the 1990s gradually turned, in about 2005, into a massive Ponzi scheme in which Madoff used money from new investors to pay off previous investors who wanted to cash out. By the time the scheme unraveled in 2008, Madoff had defrauded clients out of about $65 billion.

FBI profiler Gregg O. McCrary compares Madoff to Ted Bundy, who confessed to murdering 30 young women between 1974 and 1978. Isn't it going a little too far to put an elderly greed-obsessed financier in the same class as a cold-blooded serial killer? "With serial killers," explains McCrary, "they have control over the life or death of people. They're playing God. . . . Madoff [was] getting the same thing [out of his criminal activity]. He was playing financial god, ruining these people and taking their money."

"There are certainly more [psychopaths] in the business world . . . than in the general population."

—DAVID HARE, FORENSIC PSYCHOLOGIST

In fact, more and more forensic psychologists are coming to the conclusion that the behavior of people in many walks of life qualifies for a label once reserved for the acts of people like Ted Bundy. Psychologist J. Reid Meloy, for example, sees similarities between Madoff's behavior and that of many criminals he's studied: "Typically," he observes, "people with psychopathic personalities don't fear getting caught. They [also] tend to be very narcissistic with a strong sense of entitlement." Robert Hare, a forensic psychologist who consults with law-enforcement agencies, agrees that perhaps we need to lower the bar when it comes to granting someone the dubious status of "psychopath." Many criminals, explains Hare, suffer from some sort of antisocial personality disorder that causes them to act impulsively and commit violent crimes. Some of these criminals also suffer from *psychopathy*, which is

Bernie Madoff used a complex ponzi scheme to swindle his clients out of $65 billion.

ORLINSKY KATIE/SIPA/Newscom

evident in the absence of empathy for the people they hurt. Among this group, there's a smaller subset of people who suffer from psychopathy alone: These people exhibit no violence but appear to be indifferent to the well-being of others. Psychologist Michele Galietta calls those in this last group "white-collar psychopaths."

Fortunately, your odds of encountering someone like Ted Bundy on a dark night are pretty slim. On the other hand, Hare, coauthor of *Snakes in Suits: When Psychopaths Go to Work*, suspects that your odds of encountering a psychopath in the workplace are higher than you'd think: "There are certainly more people in the business world," he says, "who would score high in the psychopathic dimension than in the general population. . . . If I wasn't studying psychopaths in prison, I'd do it at the stock exchange."

Psychopaths, says Hare, are largely motivated by the desire to fulfill their own selfish needs regardless of the consequences to others. They're often superficially charming, insincere, prone to lying, manipulative, guilt free, lacking in empathy, ruthless, and unwilling to accept responsibility. Psychopaths in general often display two personality traits: (1) a "callous, selfish, remorseless use of others" and (2) a "chronically unstable and antisocial lifestyle." Psychopathic executives tend to score high on the first factor but low on the second and are often highly functional.

Why do so many of these psychopathic personalities end up in corner offices? Unfortunately, business is a very good arena in which to exercise psychopathic tendencies. Indeed, it often provides psychopaths with ample opportunity to put their particular personality traits to ostensibly good use. After all, American stockholders prefer top managers who are charismatic, visionary, and tough—characteristics that often accompany more overt psychopathic traits.

Not all successful corporate leaders, of course, are psychopaths. If your boss, for example, seems inordinately insensitive or even egotistical, he or she may simply be a *narcissist*. According to psychologists, narcissists often have good intentions but won't allow themselves to see through the eyes of the people who are affected by their efforts to get what they want. They may, for example, freely criticize others while refusing to accept criticism. But that sort of behavior is a long way from the psychopathic antics of hotel magnate Leona Helmsley, who shouted profanities at employees and summarily fired hundreds for trivial offenses.

Granted, narcissists "don't have much empathy," observes psychotherapist and consultant Michael Maccoby, author of *The Productive Narcissist: The Promise and Perils of Visionary Leadership*. "They see other people as a means toward their ends. But they do have a sense of . . . improving the world," and they manipulate people in the interest of this externalized goal. "In contrast," says Maccoby, "psychopaths are only interested in self." Entrepreneurial founder-CEOs, adds Paul Babiak, a consultant who helps organizations deal with "unique issues," are often narcissistic. He cites such successful leaders as Apple's Steve Jobs, Microsoft's Bill Gates, and Oracle's Larry Ellison. Such people, he says, "have a vested interest: Their identity is wrapped up in the company," which is typically an extension of self. The psychopath, on the other hand, "has no allegiance to the company at all, just to self." Like Bernie Madoff, the "psychopath is playing a short-term parasitic game."

Many experts agree that a moderate degree of narcissism may be helpful—even necessary—in motivating an entrepreneur to persist and excel at a difficult job in a risk-filled environment. Many people seem to accept that fact, but, unfortunately, most of us don't know how to tell the difference between a narcissist and a genuine psychopath. Indeed, we often admire highly publicized leaders who, unbeknownst to us, exhibit tendencies to cross the line. "It goes against our intuition," suggests Harvard psychologist Martha Stout, "that a small percentage of people can be so different from the rest of us—and so evil. Good people don't want to believe it," and that may be precisely why normal people are so vulnerable to psychopaths. As a rule, psychopathic tendencies eventually betray themselves in overt psychopathic behavior, but by then, to the dismay of boards and stockholders, the damage may have already been done.

Moreover, adds Babiak, lending approval to narcissistic tendencies can be dangerous because it makes us prone to overlook psychopathic tendencies: "[I]ndividuals who are really psychopaths," he argues, "are often mistaken for [mere] narcissists and chosen by organizations for leadership positions." So what *is* the best way to tell the difference? "In the case of a narcissist," says Babiak, "everything is me, me, me. With a psychopath, it's 'Is it thrilling, is it a game I can win, and does it hurt others?' My belief," he adds, "is a psychopath enjoys hurting others."[1]

The people who populate today's business world are characterized by a wide variety of personalities and behaviors. While most people in business have relatively healthy and constructive personalities and behave in ethical and productive ways, there are some who reflect different profiles. Indeed, myriad different and unique characteristics reside in each and every employee and manager. These affect how they feel about the organization, how they will alter their future attitudes about the firm, and how they perform their jobs. These characteristics reflect the basic elements of individual behavior in organizations.

This chapter describes several of these basic elements and is the first of several chapters designed to develop a more complete perspective on the leading function of management. In the next section we investigate the psychological nature of individuals in organizations. The following section introduces the concept of personality and discusses several important personality attributes that can influence behavior in organizations. We then examine individual attitudes and their role in organizations. The role of stress in the workplace is then discussed, followed by a discussion of individual creativity. Finally, we describe a number of basic individual behaviors that are important to organizations.

Understanding Individuals in Organizations

As a starting point in understanding human behavior in the workplace, we must consider the basic nature of the relationship between individuals and organizations. We must also gain an appreciation of the nature of individual differences.

The Psychological Contract

Most people have a basic understanding of a contract. Whenever we buy a car or sell a house, for example, both buyer and seller sign a contract that specifies the terms of the agreement. A psychological contract is similar in some ways to a standard legal contract but is less formal and well defined. In particular, a **psychological contract** is the overall set of expectations held by an individual with respect to what he or she will contribute to the organization and what the organization will provide in return.[2] Thus a psychological contract is not written on paper, nor are all of its terms explicitly negotiated.

The essential nature of a psychological contract is illustrated in Figure 18.1. The individual makes a variety of **contributions** to the organization—effort, skills, ability, time, loyalty, and so forth. These contributions presumably satisfy various needs and requirements of the organization. In other words, because the organization may have hired the person

FIGURE 18.1 THE PSYCHOLOGICAL CONTRACT

Psychological contracts are the basic assumptions that individuals have about their relationships with their organization. Such contracts are defined in terms of contributions by the individual relative to inducements from the organization.

Contributions from the Individual	Inducements from the Organization
• Effort	• Pay
• Ability	• Job security
• Loyalty	• Benefits
• Skills	• Career opportunities
• Time	• Status
• Competencies	• Promotion opportunities

© Cengage Learning 2013

---

psychological contract
The overall set of expectations held by an individual with respect to what he or she will contribute to the organization and what the organization will provide in return

contributions
What the individual provides to the organization

because of her skills, it is reasonable for the organization to expect that she will subsequently display those skills in the performance of her job.

In return for these contributions, the organization provides inducements to the individual. Some inducements, like pay and career opportunities, are tangible rewards. Others, like job security and status, are more intangible. Just as the contributions available from the individual must satisfy the needs of the organization, the inducements offered by the organization must serve the needs of the individual. Thus, if a person accepts employment with an organization because he thinks he will earn an attractive salary and have an opportunity to advance, he will subsequently expect that those rewards will actually be forthcoming.

If both the individual and the organization perceive that the psychological contract is fair and equitable, they will be satisfied with the relationship and will likely continue it. On the other hand, if either party sees an imbalance or inequity in the contract, they may initiate a change. For example, the individual may request a pay raise or promotion, decrease her contributed effort, or look for a better job elsewhere. The organization can also initiate change by requesting that the individual improve his skills through training, transfer the person to another job, or terminate the person's employment altogether.[3]

A basic challenge faced by the organization, then, is to manage psychological contracts. The organization must ensure that it is getting value from its employees. At the same time, it must be sure that it is providing employees with appropriate inducements. If the organization is underpaying its employees for their contributions, for example, they may perform poorly or leave for better jobs elsewhere. On the other hand, if they are being overpaid relative to their contributions, the organization is incurring unnecessary costs.[4]

> "Take a reasonably intelligent worker who has been schooled in the idea that his employer is always out to take advantage of him, [and] he may not believe his company is really in jeopardy [when managers discuss financial problems]."
>
> —JAY WAKS, EMPLOYMENT AND LABOR ATTORNEY[5]

The Person–Job Fit

One specific aspect of managing psychological contracts is managing the person–job fit. Person–job fit is the extent to which the contributions made by the individual match the inducements offered by the organization. In theory, each employee has a specific set of needs that he wants fulfilled and a set of job-related behaviors and abilities to contribute. Thus, if the organization can take perfect advantage of those behaviors and abilities and exactly fulfill his needs, it will have achieved a perfect person–job fit.

Of course, such a precise level of person-job fit is seldom achieved. There are several reasons for this. For one thing, organizational selection procedures are imperfect. Organizations can make approximations of employee skill levels when making hiring decisions and can improve them through training. But even simple performance dimensions are often hard to measure in objective and valid ways.

Another reason for imprecise person–job fits is that both people and organizations change. An individual who finds a new job stimulating and exciting may find the same job boring and monotonous after a few years of performing it. And when the organization adopts new technology, it changes the skills it needs from its employees. Still another reason for imprecision in the person–job fit is that each individual is unique. Measuring skills and performance is difficult enough. Assessing needs, attitudes, and personality is far more complex. Each of these individual differences serves to make matching individuals with jobs a difficult and complex process.[7]

> "I think it's really important to find a place where you fit in."
>
> — JULIE ROEHM, ADVERTISING EXECUTIVE[6]

inducements
What the organization provides to the individual

person–job fit
The extent to which the contributions made by the individual match the inducements offered by the organization

individual differences
Personal attributes that vary from one person to another

The Nature of Individual Differences

Individual differences are personal attributes that vary from one person to another. Individual differences may be physical, psychological, or emotional. Taken together, all of the individual differences that characterize any specific person serve to make that individual unique from everyone else. Much of the remainder of this chapter is devoted to individual differences.

Before proceeding, however, we must also note the importance of the situation in assessing the behavior of individuals.

Are specific differences that characterize a given individual good or bad? Do they contribute to or detract from performance? The answer, of course, is that it depends on the circumstances. One person may be very dissatisfied, withdrawn, and negative in one job setting, but very satisfied, outgoing, and positive in another. Working conditions, coworkers, and leadership are all important ingredients.

Thus, whenever an organization attempts to assess or account for individual differences among its employees, it must also be sure to consider the situation in which behavior occurs. Individuals who are satisfied or productive workers in one context may prove to be dissatisfied or unproductive workers in another context. Attempting to consider both individual differences and contributions in relation to inducements and contexts, then, is a major challenge for organizations as they attempt to establish effective psychological contracts with their employees and achieve optimal fits between people and jobs.[8]

What is a psychological contract, and what are its fundamental components?

Describe different jobs that would result in both a very good and a very bad person–job fit for you personally.

CONCEPT CHECK

◈ Personality and Individual Behavior

Personality traits represent some of the most fundamental sets of individual differences in organizations. **Personality** is the relatively stable set of psychological attributes that distinguish one person from another.[9] Managers should strive to understand basic personality attributes and the ways they can affect people's behavior in organizational situations, not to mention their perceptions of and attitudes toward the organization.

The "Big Five" Personality Traits

Psychologists have identified literally thousands of personality traits and dimensions that differentiate one person from another. But in recent years researchers have identified five fundamental personality traits that are especially relevant to organizations. Because these five traits are so important and because they are currently the subject of so much attention, they are now commonly referred to as the "Big Five" personality traits.[10] Figure 18.2 illustrates the Big Five traits.

Agreeableness refers to a person's ability to get along with others. Agreeableness causes some people to be gentle, cooperative, forgiving, understanding, and good-natured in their dealings with others. But it results in others' being irritable, short-tempered, uncooperative, and generally antagonistic toward other people. Although research has not yet fully investigated the effects of agreeableness, it would seem likely that highly agreeable people will be better able to develop good working relationships with coworkers, subordinates, and higher-level managers, whereas less agreeable people will not have particularly good working relationships. This same pattern might also extend to relationships with customers, suppliers, and other key organizational constituents.

Conscientiousness refers to the number of goals on which a person focuses. People who focus on relatively few goals at one time are likely to be organized, systematic, careful, thorough, responsible, and self-disciplined as they work to pursue those goals. Others, however, tend to take on a wider array of goals and, as a result, are more disorganized, careless, and

personality
The relatively permanent set of psychological and behavioral attributes that distinguish one person from another

"Big Five" personality traits
A popular personality framework based on five key traits

agreeableness
A person's ability to get along with others

conscientiousness
The number of goals on which a person focuses

FIGURE 18.2 THE "BIG FIVE" MODEL OF PERSONALITY

The "Big Five" personality model represents an increasingly accepted framework for understanding personality traits in organizational settings. In general, experts tend to agree that personality traits toward the left end of each dimension, as illustrated in this figure, are more positive in organizational settings, whereas traits closer to the right are less positive.

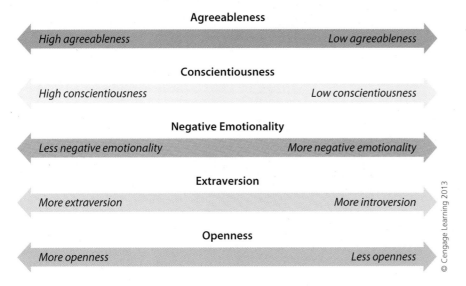

Agreeableness
High agreeableness — Low agreeableness

Conscientiousness
High conscientiousness — Low conscientiousness

Negative Emotionality
Less negative emotionality — More negative emotionality

Extraversion
More extraversion — More introversion

Openness
More openness — Less openness

© Cengage Learning 2013

irresponsible, as well as less thorough and self-disciplined. Research has found that more conscientious people tend to be higher performers than less conscientious people across a variety of different jobs. This pattern seems logical, of course, because more conscientious people will take their jobs seriously and will approach the performance of their jobs in highly responsible fashions.

The third of the Big Five personality dimensions is **negative emotionality**. People with less negative emotionality will be relatively poised, calm, resilient, and secure. But people with more negative emotionality will be more excitable, insecure, reactive, and subject to extreme mood swings. People with less negative emotionality might be expected to better handle job stress, pressure, and tension. Their stability might also lead them to be seen as more reliable than their less stable counterparts.

Extraversion refers to a person's comfort level with relationships. People who are called "extraverts" are sociable, talkative, assertive, and open to establishing new relationships. Introverts are much less sociable, talkative, and assertive, and less open to establishing new relationships. Research suggests that extraverts tend to be higher overall job performers than introverts and that they are also more likely to be attracted to jobs based on personal relationships, such as sales and marketing positions.

Finally, **openness** refers to a person's rigidity of beliefs and range of interests. People with high levels of openness are willing to listen to new ideas and to change their own ideas, beliefs, and attitudes as a result of new information. They also tend to have broad interests and to be curious, imaginative, and creative. On the other hand, people with low levels of openness tend to be less receptive to new ideas and less willing to change their minds. Further, they tend to have fewer and narrower interests and to be less curious and creative. People with more openness might be expected to be better performers, owing to their flexibility and the likelihood that they will be better accepted by others in the organization. Openness may also encompass an individual's willingness to accept change. For example, people with high levels of openness may be more receptive to change, whereas people with low levels of openness may be more likely to resist change.

negative emotionality
Extent to which a person is poised, calm, resilient, and secure

extraversion
A person's comfort level with relationships

openness
A person's rigidity of beliefs and range of interests

Extraversion is a person's comfort level with relationships. Extraverts, like these three people, are sociable and talkative. Introverts, on the other hand, are quieter and less open to establishing new relationships. Extraversion is one of the Big Five personality dimensions.

StockLite/Shutterstock.com

The Big Five framework continues to attract the attention of both researchers and managers. The potential value of this framework is that it encompasses an integrated set of traits that appear to be valid predictors of certain behaviors in certain situations. Thus managers who can develop both an understanding of the framework and the ability to assess these traits in their employees will be in a good position to understand how and why employees behave as they do.[11] On the other hand, managers must also be careful not to overestimate their ability to assess the Big Five traits in others. Even assessment using the most rigorous and valid measures, for instance, is still likely to be somewhat imprecise. Another limitation of the Big Five framework is that it is based primarily on research conducted in the United States. Thus there are unanswered questions as to how accurately it applies to workers in other cultures. And even within the United States, a variety of other factors and traits are also likely to affect behavior in organizations.[12]

The Myers–Briggs Framework

Another interesting approach to understanding personalities in organizations is the Myers–Briggs framework. This framework, based on the classic work of Carl Jung, differentiates people in terms of four general dimensions. These are defined as follows.

- *Extraversion (E) Versus Introversion (I).* Extraverts get their energy from being around other people, whereas introverts are worn out by others and need solitude to recharge their energy.
- *Sensing (S) Versus Intuition (N).* The sensing type prefers concrete things, whereas intuitives prefer abstract concepts.
- *Thinking (T) Versus Feeling (F).* Thinking individuals base their decisions more on logic and reason, whereas feeling individuals base their decisions more on feelings and emotions.
- *Judging (J) Versus Perceiving (P).* People who are the judging type enjoy completion or being finished, whereas perceiving types enjoy the process and open-ended situations.

To use this framework, people complete a questionnaire designed to measure their personality on each dimension. Higher or lower scores in each of the dimensions are used to classify people into one of 16 different personality categories.

The Myers–Briggs Type Indicator (MBTI) is one popular questionnaire that some organizations use to assess personality types. Indeed, it is among the most popular selection instruments used today, with as many as 2 million people taking it each year. Research suggests that the MBTI is a useful method for determining communication styles and interaction preferences. In terms of personality attributes, however, questions exist about both the validity and the reliability of the MBTI.

Other Personality Traits at Work

Besides the Big Five and the Myers–Briggs framework, there are several other personality traits that influence behavior in organizations. Among the most important are locus of control, self-efficacy, authoritarianism, Machiavellianism, self-esteem, and risk propensity.

Locus of control is the extent to which people believe that their behavior has a real effect on what happens to them.[13] Some people, for example, believe that if they work hard, they will succeed. They also may believe that people who fail do so because they lack ability or motivation. People who believe that individuals are in control of their lives are said to have an *internal locus of control*. Other people think that fate, chance, luck, or other people's behavior determines what happens to them. For example, an employee who fails to get a promotion may attribute that failure to a politically motivated boss or just bad luck, rather than to her or his own lack of skills or poor performance record. People who think that forces beyond their control dictate what happens to them are said to have an *external locus of control*.

Self-efficacy is a related but subtly different personality characteristic. Self-efficacy is a person's beliefs about his or her capabilities to perform a task.[14] People with high self-efficacy believe that they can perform well on a specific task, whereas people with low self-efficacy tend to doubt their ability to perform a specific task. Although self-assessments of ability contribute to self-efficacy, so, too, does the individual's personality. Some people simply have more self-confidence than do others. This belief in their ability to perform a task effectively results in their being more self-assured and more able to focus their attention on performance.

Another important personality characteristic is **authoritarianism**, the extent to which an individual believes that power and status differences are appropriate within hierarchical social systems like organizations.[15] For example, a person who is highly authoritarian may accept directives or orders from someone with more authority purely because the other person is "the boss." On the other hand, although a person who is not highly authoritarian may still carry out appropriate and reasonable directives from the boss, he or she is also more likely to question things, express disagreement with the boss, and even refuse to carry out orders if they are for some reason objectionable. A highly authoritarian manager may be autocratic and demanding, and highly authoritarian subordinates will be more likely to accept this behavior from their leader. On the other hand, a less authoritarian manager may allow subordinates a bigger role in making decisions, and less authoritarian subordinates will respond positively to this behavior.

Machiavellianism is another important personality trait. This concept is named after Niccolo Machiavelli, a sixteenth-century Italian political philosopher. In his book entitled *The Prince*, Machiavelli explained how the nobility could more easily gain and use power. *Machiavellianism* is now used to describe behavior directed at gaining power and controlling the behavior of others. Research suggests that Machiavellianism is a personality trait that varies from person to person. More Machiavellian individuals tend to be rational and nonemotional, may be willing to lie to attain their personal goals, may put little weight on loyalty and friendship, and may enjoy manipulating others' behavior. Less Machiavellian individuals are more emotional, less willing to lie to succeed, value loyalty and friendship highly, and get little personal pleasure from manipulating others. By all accounts, Dennis Kozlowski, the indicted former CEO of Tyco International currently serving prison time, had a high degree of Machiavellianism. He apparently came to believe that his position of power in the company gave him the right to do just about anything he wanted with company resources.[16]

Self-esteem is the extent to which a person believes that she is a worthwhile and deserving individual.[17] A person with high self-esteem is more likely to seek high-status jobs, be more confident in her ability to achieve higher levels of performance, and derive greater intrinsic satisfaction from her accomplishments. In contrast, a person with less self-esteem may be more content to remain in a lower-level job, be less confident of his ability, and

locus of control
The degree to which an individual believes that his or her behavior has a direct impact on the consequences of that behavior

self-efficacy
An individual's beliefs about her or his capabilities to perform a task

authoritarianism
The extent to which an individual believes that power and status differences are appropriate within hierarchical social systems like organizations

Machiavellianism
Behavior directed at gaining power and controlling the behavior of others

self-esteem
The extent to which a person believes that he or she is a worthwhile and deserving individual

focus more on extrinsic rewards. Among the major personality dimensions, self-esteem is the one that has been most widely studied in other countries. Although more research is clearly needed, the published evidence does suggest that self-esteem as a personality trait does indeed exist in a variety of countries and that its role in organizations is reasonably important across different cultures.[18]

Risk propensity is the degree to which an individual is willing to take chances and make risky decisions. A manager with a high risk propensity, for example, might be expected to experiment with new ideas and gamble on new products. She might also lead the organization in new and different directions. This manager might also be a catalyst for innovation. On the other hand, the same individual might also jeopardize the continued well-being of the organization if the risky decisions prove to be bad ones. A manager with low risk propensity might lead to a stagnant and overly conservative organization or help the organization successfully weather turbulent and unpredictable times by maintaining stability and calm. Thus the potential consequences of risk propensity to an organization are heavily dependent on that organization's environment.

Emotional Intelligence

The concept of emotional intelligence has been identified in recent years and provides some interesting insights into personality. Emotional intelligence, or EQ, refers to the extent to which people are self-aware, manage their emotions, motivate themselves, express empathy for others, and possess social skills.[19] These various dimensions can be described as follows:

- *Self-Awareness.* This is the basis for the other components. It refers to a person's capacity for being aware of how they are feeling. In general, more self-awareness allows people to more effectively guide their own lives and behaviors.
- *Managing Emotions.* This refers to a person's capacities to balance anxiety, fear, and anger so that they do not overly interfere with getting things accomplished.
- *Motivating Oneself.* This dimension refers to a person's ability to remain optimistic and to continue striving in the face of setbacks, barriers, and failure.
- *Empathy.* Empathy refers to a person's ability to understand how others are feeling, even without being explicitly told.
- *Social Skill.* This refers to a person's ability to get along with others and to establish positive relationships.

Preliminary research suggests that people with high EQ may perform better than others, especially in jobs that require a high degree of interpersonal interaction and that involve influencing or directing the work of others. Moreover, EQ appears to be something that is not biologically based but can be developed.[20]

risk propensity
The degree to which an individual is willing to take chances and make risky decisions

emotional intelligence (EQ)
The extent to which people are self-aware, manage their emotions, motivate themselves, express empathy for others, and possess social skills

attitudes
Complexes of beliefs and feelings that people have about specific ideas, situations, or other people

What is personality? Identify several basic personality dimensions.

Describe your own personality in terms of the various personality dimensions discussed in this section. For instance, do you think you have an internal or an external locus of control?

CONCEPT CHECK

Attitudes and Individual Behavior

Another important element of individual behavior in organizations is attitudes. Attitudes are complexes of beliefs and feelings that people have about specific ideas, situations, or other people.[21] Attitudes are important because they are the mechanism through which most people express their feelings. An employee's statement that he feels underpaid by the organization reflects his feelings about his pay. Similarly, when a manager says that she likes the new advertising campaign, she is expressing her feelings about the organization's marketing efforts.

Attitudes have three components. The *affective component* of an attitude reflects feelings and emotions an individual has toward a situation. The *cognitive component* of an attitude is derived from knowledge an individual has about a situation. It is important to note that cognition is subject to individual perceptions (something we discuss more fully later). Thus one person might "know" that a certain political candidate is better than another, whereas someone else might "know" just the opposite. Finally, the *intentional component* of an attitude reflects how an individual expects to behave toward or in the situation.

To illustrate these three components, consider the case of a manager who places an order for some supplies for his organization from a new office supply firm. Suppose many of the items he orders are out of stock, others are overpriced, and still others arrive damaged. When he calls someone at the supply firm for assistance, he is treated rudely and gets disconnected before his claim is resolved. When asked how he feels about the new office supply firm, he might respond, "I don't like that company [affective component]. They are the worst office supply firm I've ever dealt with [cognitive component]. I'll never do business with them again [intentional component]."

People try to maintain consistency among the three components of their attitudes as well as among all their attitudes. However, circumstances sometimes arise that lead to conflicts. The conflict individuals may experience among their own attitudes is called cognitive dissonance.[22] Say, for example, that an individual who has vowed never to work for a big, impersonal corporation intends instead to open her own business and be her own boss. Unfortunately, a series of financial setbacks leads her to have no choice but to take a job with a large company and work for someone else. Thus cognitive dissonance occurs: The affective and cognitive components of the individual's attitude conflict with intended behavior. To reduce cognitive dissonance, which is usually an uncomfortable experience for most people, the individual might tell herself that the situation is only temporary and that she can go back out on her own in the near future. Or she might revise her cognitions and decide that working for a large company is more pleasant than she had expected.

cognitive dissonance
Caused when an individual has conflicting attitudes

job satisfaction or dissatisfaction
An attitude that reflects the extent to which an individual is gratified by or fulfilled in his or her work

Work-Related Attitudes

People in organizations form attitudes about many different things. For example, employees are likely to have attitudes about their salary, promotion possibilities, their boss, employee benefits, the food in the company cafeteria, and the color of the company softball team uniforms. Of course, some of these attitudes are more important than others. Especially important attitudes are job satisfaction or dissatisfaction and organizational commitment.[23]

Job Satisfaction or Dissatisfaction Job satisfaction or dissatisfaction is an attitude that reflects the extent to which an individual is gratified by or fulfilled in his or her work. Extensive research conducted on job satisfaction has indicated that personal factors, such as an individual's needs and aspirations, determine this attitude, along with group and organizational factors, such as relationships with coworkers and supervisors, as well as working conditions, work policies, and compensation.[24]

Job satisfaction or dissatisfaction is an attitude reflecting how a person feels about her or his job. This manager, for example, seems to be quiet dissatisfied at the moment. The cause of her dissatisfaction might be the pile of work waiting for her or an email she has just received. Regardless, though, if her dissatisfaction lingers too long she may be absent from work often or start looking for another job.

Demid Borodin/Shutterstock.com

A satisfied employee also tends to be absent less often, to make positive contributions, and to stay with the organization.[25] In contrast, a dissatisfied employee may be absent more often, may experience stress that disrupts coworkers, and may be continually looking for another job. Contrary to what many managers believe, however, high levels of job satisfaction do not necessarily lead to higher levels of performance. One survey has also indicated that, contrary to popular opinion, Japanese workers are less satisfied with their jobs than their counterparts in the United States.[26]

> "People don't feel good about flying an airline where the employees don't feel good about working for them."
>
> — RICHARD CHAIFETZ, CEO OF COMPSYCH[27]

Organizational Commitment

Organizational commitment is an attitude that reflects an individual's identification with and attachment to the organization itself. A person with a high level of commitment is likely to see herself as a true member of the organization (for example, referring to the organization in personal terms like "We make high-quality products"), to overlook minor sources of dissatisfaction with the organization, and to see herself remaining a member of the organization. In contrast, a person with less organizational commitment is more likely to see himself as an outsider (for example, referring to the organization in less personal terms like "They don't pay their employees very well"), to express more dissatisfaction about things, and to not see himself as a long-term member of the organization. Research suggests that Japanese workers may be more committed to their organizations than are American workers.[28]

Research also suggests that commitment strengthens with an individual's age, years with the organization, sense of job security, and participation in decision making.[29] Employees who feel committed to an organization have highly reliable habits, plan a long tenure with the organization, and muster more effort in performance. Although there are few definitive things that organizations can do to create or promote commitment, there are a few specific guidelines available.[30] For one thing, if the organization treats its employees fairly and provides reasonable rewards and job security, those employees will more likely be satisfied and committed. Allowing employees to have a say in how things are done can also promote all three attitudes.[31]

Affect and Mood in Organizations

Researchers have recently started to focus renewed interest on the affective component of attitudes. Recall from our discussion above that the affective component of an attitude reflects our feelings and emotions. Although managers once believed that emotion and feelings varied among people from day to day, research now suggests that, although some short-term fluctuation does indeed occur, there are also underlying stable predispositions toward fairly constant and predictable moods and emotional states.[32]

Some people, for example, tend to have a higher degree of **positive affectivity**. This means that they are relatively upbeat and optimistic, have an overall sense of well-being, and usually see things in a positive light. Thus they always seem to be in a good mood. It's also recently been proposed that positive affectivity may play a role in entrepreneurial success.[33] Other people, those with more **negative affectivity**, are just the opposite. They are generally downbeat and pessimistic, and they usually see things in a negative way. They seem to be in a bad mood most of the time.

Of course, as noted above, there can be short-term variations among even the most extreme types. People with a lot of positive affectivity, for example, may still be in a bad mood if they have just received some bad news—being passed over for a promotion, getting extremely negative performance feedback, or being laid off or fired, for instance. Similarly, those with negative affectivity may still be in a good mood—at least for a short time—if they have just been promoted, received very positive performance feedback, or had other good things befall them. After the initial impact of these events wears off, however, those with positive affectivity will generally return to their normal positive mood, whereas those with negative affectivity will gravitate back to their normal bad mood.

organizational commitment
An attitude that reflects an individual's identification with and attachment to the organization itself

positive affectivity
A tendency to be relatively upbeat and optimistic, have an overall sense of well-being, see things in a positive light, and seem to be in a good mood

negative affectivity
A tendency to be generally downbeat and pessimistic, see things in a negative way, and seem to be in a bad mood

Identify and describe the three components of an attitude.

Using a job you have either held in the past or currently hold, describe the level of job satisfaction or dissatisfaction and organizational commitment you felt or feel. Describe what caused those attitudes and how they affected your behavior.

Perception and Individual Behavior

As noted earlier, an important element of an attitude is the individual's perception of the object about which the attitude is formed. Because perception plays a role in a variety of other workplace behaviors, managers need to have a general understanding of basic perceptual processes.[34] The role of attributions is also important.

Basic Perceptual Processes

Perception is the set of processes by which an individual becomes aware of and interprets information about the environment. As shown in Figure 18.3, basic perceptual processes that are particularly relevant to organizations are selective perception and stereotyping.

Selective Perception Selective perception is the process of screening out information that we are uncomfortable with or that contradicts our beliefs. For example, suppose a manager is exceptionally fond of a particular worker. The manager has a very positive attitude about the worker and thinks he is a top performer. One day the manager notices that the worker seems to be goofing off. Selective perception may cause the manager to quickly forget what he observed. Similarly, suppose a manager has formed a very negative image of a particular worker. She thinks this worker is a poor performer and never does a good job. When she happens to observe an example of high performance from the worker, she, too, may not remember it for very long. In one sense, selective perception is beneficial because it allows us to disregard minor bits of information. Of course, this is helpful only if our basic perception is accurate. If selective perception causes us to ignore important information, however, it can become quite detrimental.

FIGURE 18.3 PERCEPTUAL PROCESSES

Two of the most basic perceptual processes are selective perception and stereotyping. As shown here, selective perception occurs when we screen out information (represented by the − symbols) that causes us discomfort or that contradicts our beliefs. Stereotyping occurs when we categorize or label people on the basis of a single attribute, illustrated here by color.

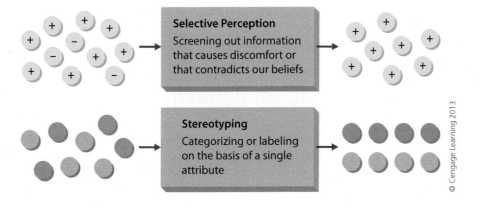

perception
The set of processes by which an individual becomes aware of and interprets information about the environment

selective perception
The process of screening out information that we are uncomfortable with or that contradicts our beliefs

Stereotyping Stereotyping is the process of categorizing or labeling people on the basis of a single attribute. Common attributes on which people often stereotype are race, gender, and age.[35] Of course, stereotypes along these lines are inaccurate and can be harmful. For example, suppose a manager forms the stereotype that women can perform only certain tasks and that men are best suited for other tasks. To the extent that this affects the manager's hiring practices, the manager is (1) costing the organization valuable talent for both sets of jobs, (2) violating federal law, and (3) behaving unethically. On the other hand, certain forms of stereotyping can be useful and efficient. Suppose, for example, that a manager believes that communication skills are important for a particular job and that speech communication majors tend to have exceptionally good communication skills. As a result, whenever he interviews candidates for jobs, he pays especially close attention to speech communication majors. To the extent that communication skills truly predict job performance and that majoring in speech communication does indeed provide those skills, this form of stereotyping can be beneficial.

Perception and Attribution

Perception is also closely linked with another process called attribution. Attribution is a mechanism through which we observe behavior and then attribute causes to it.[36] The behavior that is observed may be our own or that of others. For example, suppose someone realizes one day that she is working fewer hours than before, that she talks less about her work, and that she calls in sick more frequently. She might conclude from this that she must have become disenchanted with her job and subsequently decide to quit. Thus she observed her own behavior, attributed a cause to it, and developed what she thought was a consistent response.

More common is attributing cause to the behavior of others. For example, if the manager of the individual described above has observed the same behavior, he might form exactly the same attribution. On the other hand, he might instead decide that she has a serious illness, that he is driving her too hard, that she is experiencing too much stress, that she has a drug problem, or that she is having family problems.

The basic framework around which we form attributions is *consensus* (the extent to which other people in the same situation behave the same way), *consistency* (the extent to which the same person behaves in the same way at different times), and *distinctiveness* (the extent to which the same person behaves in the same way in other situations). For example, suppose a manager observes that an employee is late for a meeting. The manager might further realize that he is the only one who is late (low consensus), recall that he is often late for other meetings (high consistency), and subsequently realize that the same employee is sometimes late for work and returning from lunch (low distinctiveness). This pattern of attributions might cause the manager to decide that the individual's behavior is something that should be changed. As a result, the manager might meet with the subordinate and establish some punitive consequences for future tardiness.

stereotyping
The process of categorizing or labeling people on the basis of a single attribute

attribution
The process of observing behavior and attributing causes to it

stress
An individual's response to a strong stimulus, which is called a stressor

General Adaptation Syndrome (GAS)
General cycle of the stress process

Define perception and discuss two fundamental perceptual processes.

Recall a vivid example of behavior exhibited by someone and then describe that behavior from an attributional perspective.

CONCEPT CHECK

 # Stress and Individual Behavior

Another important element of behavior in organizations is stress. Stress is an individual's response to a strong stimulus.[37] This stimulus is called a *stressor*. Stress generally follows a cycle referred to as the General Adaptation Syndrome, or GAS,[38] shown in Figure 18.4. According to this view, when an individual first encounters a stressor, the GAS is initiated, and the first stage, alarm, is activated. He may feel panic, wonder how to cope, and feel helpless. For

FIGURE 18.4 THE GENERAL ADAPTATION SYNDROME

The General Adaptation Syndrome represents the normal process by which we react to stressful events. At stage 1—alarm—we feel panic and alarm, and our level of resistance to stress drops. Stage 2—resistance—represents our efforts to confront and control the stressful circumstance. If we fail, we may eventually reach stage 3—exhaustion—and just give up or quit.

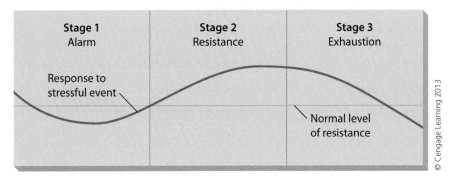

example, suppose a manager is told to prepare a detailed evaluation of a plan by his firm to buy one of its competitors. His first reaction may be, "How will I ever get this done by tomorrow?"

If the stressor is too intense, the individual may feel unable to cope and never really try to respond to its demands. In most cases, however, after a short period of alarm, the individual gathers some strength and starts to resist the negative effects of the stressor. For example, the manager with the evaluation to write may calm down, call home to say he is working late, roll up his sleeves, order out for coffee, and get to work. Thus, at stage 2 of the GAS, the person is resisting the effects of the stressor.

In many cases, the resistance phase may end the GAS. If the manager is able to complete the evaluation earlier than expected, he may drop it in his briefcase, smile to himself, and head home tired but satisfied. On the other hand, prolonged exposure to a stressor without resolution may bring on stage 3 of the GAS—exhaustion. At this stage, the individual literally gives up and can no longer resist the stressor. The manager, for example, might fall asleep at his desk at 3:00 A.M. and never finish the evaluation.

We should note that stress is not all bad. In the absence of stress, we may experience lethargy and stagnation. An optimal level of stress, on the other hand, can result in motivation and excitement. Too much stress, however, can have negative consequences. It is also important to understand that stress can be caused by "good" as well as "bad" things. Excessive pressure, unreasonable demands on our time, and bad news can all cause stress. But even receiving a bonus and then having to decide what to do with the money can be stressful. So, too, can receiving a promotion, gaining recognition, and similar good things.

One important line of thinking about stress focuses on **Type A** and **Type B** personalities.[39] Type A individuals are extremely competitive, very devoted to work, and have a strong sense of time urgency. They are likely to be aggressive, impatient, and very work oriented. They have a lot of drive and want to accomplish as much as possible as quickly as possible. Type B individuals are less competitive, less devoted to work, and have a weaker sense of time urgency. Such individuals are less likely to experience conflict with other people and more likely to have a balanced, relaxed approach to life. They are able to work at a constant pace without time urgency. Type B people are not necessarily more or less successful than are Type A people, but they are less likely to experience stress.

Causes and Consequences of Stress

Stress is obviously not a simple phenomenon. Several different things can cause stress, as listed in Figure 18.5. Note that this list includes only work-related conditions. We should keep in mind that stress can also be the result of personal circumstances.[40]

Type A
Individuals who are extremely competitive, very devoted to work, and have a strong sense of time urgency

Type B
Individuals who are less competitive, less devoted to work, and have a weaker sense of time urgency

FIGURE 18.5 CAUSES OF WORK STRESS

There are several causes of work stress in organizations. Four general sets of organizational stressors are task demands, physical demands, role demands, and interpersonal demands.

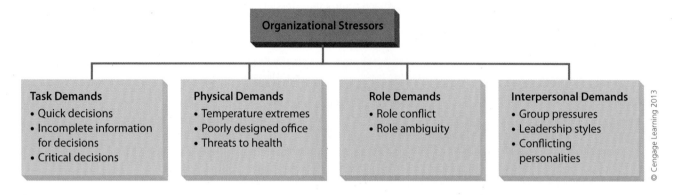

Organizational Stressors

Task Demands
- Quick decisions
- Incomplete information for decisions
- Critical decisions

Physical Demands
- Temperature extremes
- Poorly designed office
- Threats to health

Role Demands
- Role conflict
- Role ambiguity

Interpersonal Demands
- Group pressures
- Leadership styles
- Conflicting personalities

© Cengage Learning 2013

Causes of Stress Work-related stressors fall into one of four categories—task, physical, role, and interpersonal demands. *Task demands* are associated with the task itself. Some occupations are inherently more stressful than others. Having to make fast decisions, decisions with less than complete information, or decisions that have relatively serious consequences are some of the things that can make some jobs stressful. The jobs of surgeon, airline pilot, and stockbroker are relatively more stressful than the jobs of general practitioner, baggage handler, and office receptionist. Although a general practitioner makes important decisions, he is also likely to have time to make a considered diagnosis and fully explore a number of different treatments. But during surgery, the surgeon must make decisions quickly while realizing that the wrong one may endanger her patient's life.

"Increasing store hours increases the hours that the bad guys can rob you. Darkness to dawn is the highest time of exposure to armed robberies."

— BILL WISE, FORMER MANAGER OF SAFETY AND SECURITY FOR WENDY'S[41]

Physical demands are stressors associated with the job setting. Working outdoors in extremely hot or cold temperatures, or even in an improperly heated or cooled office, can lead to stress. Likewise, jobs that have rotating work shifts make it difficult for people to have stable sleep patterns. A poorly designed office—one which, for example, makes it difficult for people to have privacy or promotes too little social interaction—can result in stress, as can poor lighting and inadequate work surfaces. Even more severe are actual threats to health. Examples include jobs like coal mining, poultry processing, and toxic waste handling. Similarly, some jobs carry risks associated with higher incident rates of violence such as armed robberies and so forth. Examples include law enforcement officers, taxi drivers, and convenience store clerks.

Role demands can also cause stress. (Roles are discussed more fully in Chapter 21.) A role is a set of expected behaviors associated with a position in a group or organization. Stress can result from either role conflict or role ambiguity that people can experience in groups. For example, an employee who is feeling pressure from her boss to work longer hours or to travel more, while also being asked by her family for more time at home, will almost certainly experience stress as a result of role conflict.[42] Similarly, a new employee experiencing role ambiguity because of poor orientation and training practices by the organization will also suffer from stress. Excessive meetings are also a potential source of stress.[43] While job cuts and layoffs during the 2008–2009 recession focused attention on the stress experienced by those losing their jobs (and appropriately so), it's also the case that many of the managers imposing the layoffs experienced stress as well.[44]

Interpersonal demands are stressors associated with relationships that confront people in organizations. For example, group pressures regarding restriction of output and norm conformity can lead to stress. Leadership styles may also cause stress. An employee who feels a strong need to participate in decision making may feel stress if his boss refuses to allow such participation. And individuals with conflicting personalities may experience stress if required to work too closely together. For example, a person with an internal locus of control might be frustrated when working with someone who prefers to wait and just let things happen.[45]

Consequences of Stress   As noted earlier, the results of stress may be positive or negative. The negative consequences may be behavioral, psychological, or medical. Behaviorally, for example, stress may lead to detrimental or harmful actions, such as smoking, alcohol or drug abuse, and overeating. Other stress-induced behaviors are accident proneness, violence toward self or others, and appetite disorders. Substance abuse is also a potential consequence.[47]

> "Some of [the people I laid off] I'd worked with for a very long time. I saw such pain in their faces, but felt I couldn't show my emotions to them. . . . As soon as I could, I'd close the door, draw the blinds, and have a good sob."
>
> — ALICIA SANERA, HR EXECUTIVE[46]

As you can see from the *World of Difference* box entitled "The BOSS in Indian BPO" on page 460, the psychological consequences of stress can interfere with an individual's mental health and well-being. Problems include sleep disturbances, depression, family problems, and sexual dysfunction. Managers are especially prone to sleep disturbances when they experience stress at work.[48] Medical consequences of stress affect an individual's physiological well-being. Heart disease and stroke have been linked to stress, as have headaches, backaches, ulcers and related disorders, and skin conditions such as acne and hives.

Individual stress also has direct consequences for businesses. For an operating employee, stress may translate into poor-quality work and lower productivity. For a manager, it may mean faulty decision making and disruptions in working relationships.[49] Withdrawal behaviors can also result from stress. People who are having difficulties with stress in their job are more likely to call in sick or to leave the organization. More subtle forms of withdrawal may also occur. A manager may start missing deadlines, for example, or taking longer lunch breaks. Employees may also withdraw by developing feelings of indifference. The irritation displayed by people under great stress can make them difficult to get along with. Job satisfaction, morale, and commitment can all suffer as a result of excessive levels of stress. So, too, can motivation to perform.

Another consequence of stress is **burnout**—a feeling of exhaustion that may develop when someone experiences too much stress for an extended period of time. Burnout results in constant fatigue, frustration, and helplessness. Increased rigidity follows, as do a loss of self-confidence and psychological withdrawal. The individual dreads going to work, often puts in longer hours but gets less accomplished than before, and exhibits mental and physical exhaustion. Because of the damaging effects of burnout, some firms are taking steps to help avoid it. For example, British Airways provides all of its employees with training designed to help them recognize the symptoms of burnout and develop strategies for avoiding it.

Managing Stress

Given the potential consequences of stress, it follows that both people and organizations should be concerned about how to limit its more damaging effects. Numerous ideas and approaches have been developed to help manage stress. Some are strategies for individuals; others are strategies for organizations.[50]

One way people manage stress is through exercise. People who exercise regularly feel less tension and stress, are more self-confident, and feel more optimistic. Their better physical condition also makes them less susceptible to many common illnesses. People who do not exercise regularly, on the other hand, tend to feel more stress and are more likely to be depressed. They are also more likely to have heart attacks. And, because of their physical condition, they are more likely to contract illnesses.

Another method people use to manage stress is relaxation. Relaxation allows individuals to adapt to, and therefore better deal with, their stress. Relaxation comes in many forms, such as taking regular vacations and engaging in non-work activities on the weekends. A recent study found that people's attitudes toward a variety of workplace characteristics

burnout
A feeling of exhaustion that may develop when someone experiences too much stress for an extended period of time

A WORLD OF DIFFERENCE

The BOSS in Indian BPO

Zack Canepari/The New York Time/Redux Pictures

Twenty-one-year-old Anurag Verma has one of those jobs that tend to come up in the conversation when Americans are talking about U.S. unemployment: He works in India's burgeoning business process outsourcing (BPO) industry. He makes very good money—about $800 a month, which is 12 times the average Indian salary. He uses a BlackBerry and doesn't have to ride a crowded bus to work because he owns a car. He was getting ready to put money down on a condo until one day he collapsed at his desk and had to be taken to the hospital. In the weeks leading up to his collapse, he had been suffering from dizzy spells and migraines; he'd lost his appetite and 22 pounds.

Anurag had been on the job for eight months, and in the industry, his problem is known as BOSS—Burn Out Stress Syndrome. Symptoms include chronic fatigue, insomnia, loss of appetite, and gastrointestinal problems. Back and shoulder pain are common, as are ear and eye ailments. Experts say that BOSS affects about one-third of India's 7 million BPO workers. In the city of Bangalore (known as the "Silicon Valley of India" because it's the country's leading information technology exporter), a study of IT professionals conducted by the National Institute for Mental Health and Neurosciences (NIMHANS)

found that one in 20 workers regularly considered suicide and classified 36 percent as "probable psychiatric cases."

"You are making nice money," reports 26-year-old Vaibhav Vats, whose weight ballooned to 265 pounds after two years at an outsourced IBM call center, "but the trade-off," he warns young people just entering the industry out of college, "is also big." Those trade-offs typically include long night shifts and disrupted eating and sleeping schedules, and a common result, according to doctors, is the alteration of biorhythms—the patterns by which our bodies adapt to the patterns of day and night. One study, for example, found that BPO workers tend to develop markedly different sleeping patterns. According to researchers, they were not only sleepier but were "more depressed and suffered from anxiety disorders." Explains Dr. Anupam Mittal of Delhi's Max Hospital: "Those who put in 10 hours of work every night are unable to get adequate sleep during daytime no matter how hard they try. This causes a cumulative sleep debt leading to significant sleep deprivation, fatigue, mood swings, [and] lack of concentration."

There are also physiological repercussions. Women, for instance, suffer from menstrual and hormonal disorders when disrupted sleep patterns create imbalances in melatonin and cortisol, two hormones related to sleep and stress. "Sleep deprivation and exposure to light at night," says Dr. Swati Bhargava, a Mumbai gynecologist, "interrupts melatonin production, thereby stimulating the body to produce more estrogen, which is a known hormonal promoter of breast cancer." Bhargava's diagnosis is supported by research showing that women who work nights have a 6 percent higher risk of breast cancer.

References: Neeta Lal, "India's Outsourcing Blues," *Asia Sentinel*, May 6, 2008, www.asiasentinel.com on April 13, 2011; Pawan Budhwar, "The Good and Bad of Outsourcing to India: Emerging Problems in the Sector and the Way Forward" (Birmingham, UK: Aston University, January 26, 2010), www1.aston.ac.uk on April 13, 2011; Saritha Rai, "India Outsourcing Workers Stressed to the Limit," *ZDNet*, August 26, 2009, www.zdnet.com on April 13, 2011; "India's Outsourcing Industry Facing Mass Level Health Problems," *BPO Tiger*, January 23, 2008, www.bpotiger.com on April 13, 2011.

improved significantly following a weekend when they were able to fully disengage from their work.[51] People can also learn to relax while on the job. For example, some experts recommend that people take regular rest breaks during their normal workday.

People can also use time management to control stress. The idea behind time management is that many daily pressures can be reduced or eliminated if individuals do a better job of managing time. One approach to time management is to make a list every morning of the things to be done that day. The items on the list are then grouped into three categories: critical activities that must be performed, important activities that should be performed, and optional or trivial things that can be delegated or postponed. The individual performs the items on the list in their order of importance.

Finally, people can manage stress through support groups. A support group can be as simple as a group of family members or friends to enjoy leisure time with. Going out after work with a couple of coworkers to a basketball game or a movie, for example, can help relieve stress built up during the day. Family and friends can help people cope with stress on an ongoing basis and during times of crisis. For example, an employee who has just learned that she did not get the promotion she has been working toward for months may find it helpful to have a good friend to lean on, talk to, or yell at. People also may make use of more elaborate and formal support groups. Community centers or churches, for example, may sponsor support groups for people who have recently gone through a divorce, the death of a loved one, or some other tragedy.

Organizations are also beginning to realize that they should be involved in helping employees cope with stress. One argument for this is that because the business is at least partially responsible for stress, it should also help relieve it. Another is that stress-related insurance claims by employees can cost the organization considerable sums of money. Still another is that workers experiencing lower levels of detrimental stress will be able to function more effectively. AT&T has initiated a series of seminars and workshops to help its employees cope with the stress they face in their jobs. The firm was prompted to develop these seminars for all three of the reasons noted above.

A wellness stress program is a special part of the organization specifically created to help deal with stress. Organizations have adopted stress-management programs, health promotion programs, and other kinds of programs for this purpose. The AT&T seminar program noted earlier is similar to this idea, but true wellness programs are ongoing activities that have a number of different components. They commonly include exercise-related activities as well as classroom instruction programs dealing with smoking cessation, weight reduction, and general stress management. Corning has adopted a stress management program providing workers with resources to help them understand stress and its health effects, as well as how to adopt stress coping skills. As part of the program, the company offers various classes in tai chi, biofeedback, meditation, yoga, muscle relaxation, guided imagery, and cognitive restructuring.[52]

Some companies are developing their own programs or using existing programs of this type. Johns Manville, for example, has a gym at its corporate headquarters. Other firms negotiate discounted health club membership rates with local establishments. For the instructional part of the program, the organization can again either sponsor its own training or perhaps jointly sponsor seminars with a local YMCA, civic organization, or church. Organization-based fitness programs facilitate employee exercise, a very positive consideration, but such programs are also quite costly. Still, more and more companies are developing fitness programs for employees. Similarly, some companies are offering their employees periodic sabbaticals—extended breaks from work that presumably allow people to get revitalized and reenergized. Intel and McDonald's are among the firms offering this benefit.[53]

creativity
The ability of an individual to generate new ideas or to conceive of new perspectives on existing ideas

---

Define stress and list its primary causes and consequences.

Are you more of a Type A or a Type B person? How do you feel about this?

CONCEPT CHECK

Creativity in Organizations

Creativity is yet another important component of individual behavior in organizations. Creativity is the ability of an individual to generate new ideas or to conceive of new perspectives on existing ideas. What makes a person creative? How do people become creative? How does the creative process work? Although psychologists have not yet discovered complete answers to these questions, examining a few general patterns can help us understand the sources of individual creativity within organizations.[54]

The Creative Individual

Numerous researchers have focused their efforts on attempting to describe the common attributes of creative individuals. These attributes generally fall into three categories: background experiences, personal traits, and cognitive abilities.

Background Experiences and Creativity   Researchers have observed that many creative individuals were raised in environments in which creativity was nurtured. Mozart was raised in a family of musicians and began composing and performing music at age six. Pierre and Marie Curie, great scientists in their own right, also raised a daughter, Irene, who won the Nobel Prize in chemistry. Thomas Edison's creativity was nurtured by his mother. However, people with background experiences very different from theirs have also been creative. Frederick Douglass was born into slavery in Tuckahoe, Maryland, and had very limited opportunities for education. Nonetheless, his powerful oratory and creative thinking helped lead to the Thirteenth Amendment to the U.S. Constitution, which outlawed slavery in the United States.

Personal Traits and Creativity   Certain personal traits have also been linked to creativity in individuals. The traits shared by most creative people are openness, an attraction to complexity, high levels of energy, independence and autonomy, strong self-confidence, and a strong belief that one is, in fact, creative. Individuals who possess these traits are more likely to be creative than are those who do not have them.

Cognitive Abilities and Creativity   Cognitive abilities are an individual's power to think intelligently and to analyze situations and data effectively. Intelligence may be a precondition for individual creativity—although most creative people are highly intelligent, not all intelligent people are necessarily creative. Creativity is also linked with the ability to think divergently and convergently. *Divergent thinking* is a skill that allows people to see differences among situations, phenomena, or events. *Convergent thinking* is a skill that allows people to see similarities among situations, phenomena, or events. Creative people are generally very skilled at both divergent and convergent thinking.

Interestingly, Japanese managers have come to question their own creative abilities. The concern is that their emphasis on group harmony may have stifled individual initiative and hampered the development of individual creativity. As a result, many Japanese firms, including Omron Corporation, Fuji Photo, and Shimizu Corporation, have launched employee training programs intended to boost the creativity of their employees.[55]

The Creative Process

Although creative people often report that ideas seem to come to them "in a flash," individual creative activity actually tends to progress through a series of stages. Not all creative activity has to follow these four stages, but much of it does.

Preparation   The creative process normally begins with a period of *preparation*. To make a creative contribution to business management or business services, individuals must usually receive formal training and education in business. Formal education and training are usually the most efficient ways of becoming familiar with this vast amount of research and knowledge. This is one reason for the strong demand for undergraduate and master's level business education. Formal business education can be an effective way for an individual to get "up to speed" and begin making creative contributions quickly.

Experiences that managers have on the job after their formal training has finished can also contribute to the creative process. In an important sense, the education and training of creative people never really ends. It continues as long as they remain interested in the world and curious about the way things work. Bruce Roth earned a Ph.D. in chemistry and then spent years working in the pharmaceutical industry learning more and more about chemical compounds and how they work in human beings.

Incubation The second phase of the creative process is *incubation*—a period of less intense conscious concentration during which the knowledge and ideas acquired during preparation mature and develop. A curious aspect of incubation is that it is often helped along by pauses in concentrated rational thought. Some creative people rely on physical activity such as jogging or swimming to provide a break from thinking. Others may read or listen to music. Sometimes sleep may even supply the needed pause. Bruce Roth eventually joined Warner-Lambert, an up-and-coming drug company, to help develop medication to lower cholesterol. In his spare time, Roth read mystery novels and hiked in the mountains. He later acknowledged that this was when he did his best thinking. Similarly, twice a year Bill Gates retreats to a secluded wooded cabin to reflect on trends in technology; it is during these weeks, he says, that he develops his sharpest insights into where Microsoft should be heading.[56]

Monkey Business Images/Shutterstock

The incubation phase of creativity is a less intense period when ideas and information can mature and develop. Incubation often takes place when people do things that have little to do with their work. This young man, for example, is riding his bike on the weekend and not really thinking about his job. But at the same time, ideas about a big project at work may be developing in the back of his mind.

Insight Usually occurring after preparation and incubation, *insight* is a spontaneous breakthrough in which the creative person achieves a new understanding of some problem or situation. Insight represents a coming together of all the scattered thoughts and ideas that were maturing during incubation. It may occur suddenly or develop slowly over time. Insight can be triggered by some external event, such as a new experience or an encounter with new data, which forces the individual to think about old issues and problems in new ways, or it can be a completely internal event in which patterns of thought finally coalesce in ways that generate new understanding. One day Bruce Roth was reviewing data from some earlier studies that had found the new drug under development to be no more effective than other drugs already available. But this time he saw some statistical relationships that had not been identified previously. He knew then that he had a major breakthrough on his hands.

Verification Once an insight has occurred, *verification* determines the validity or truthfulness of the insight. For many creative ideas, verification includes scientific experiments to determine whether the insight actually leads to the results expected. Verification may also include the development of a product or service prototype. A prototype is one product or a very small number of products built just to see if the ideas behind this new product actually work. Product prototypes are rarely sold to the public but are very valuable in verifying the insights developed in the creative process. Once the new product or service is developed, verification in the marketplace is the ultimate test of the creative idea behind it. Bruce Roth and his colleagues set to work testing the new drug compound and eventually won FDA approval. The drug, named Lipitor, is already the largest-selling pharmaceutical in history.

And Pfizer, the firm that bought Warner-Lambert in a hostile takeover, earns more than $10 billion a year on the drug.

Enhancing Creativity in Organizations

Managers who wish to enhance and promote creativity in their organizations can do so in a variety of ways.[57] One important method for enhancing creativity is to make it a part of the organization's culture, often through explicit goals. Firms that truly want to stress creativity, like 3M and Rubbermaid, for example, state goals that some percentage of future revenues is to be gained from new products. This clearly communicates that creativity and innovation are valued. Best Buy recently picked four groups of salespeople in their 20s and early 30s and asked them to spend ten weeks living together in a Los Angeles apartment complex (with expenses paid by the company and still earning their normal pay). Their job? Sit around and brainstorm new business ideas that could be rolled out quickly and cheaply.[58]

Another important part of enhancing creativity is to reward creative successes, while being careful not to punish creative failures. Many ideas that seem worthwhile on paper fail to pan out in reality. If the first person to come up with an idea that fails is fired or otherwise punished, others in the organization will become more cautious in their own work. And, as a result, fewer creative ideas will emerge. Steve Jobs encourages creativity throughout Apple's culture by encouraging debate when discussing new ideas and removing passive aggressive behaviors. Dealing with conflict head-on and embracing the tension spurs new ideas and different angles, and reduces risks.[59]

Define creativity and describe its likely causes.

Think of an important idea you recently had and try to explain how you derived it, based on the creative process discussed in this section.

CONCEPT CHECK

Types of Workplace Behavior

Now that we have looked closely at how individual differences can influence behavior in organizations, let's turn our attention to what we mean by workplace behavior. **Workplace behavior** is a pattern of action by the members of an organization that directly or indirectly influences organizational effectiveness. Important workplace behaviors include performance and productivity, absenteeism and turnover, and organizational citizenship. Unfortunately, a variety of dysfunctional behaviors can also occur in organizational settings.

Performance Behaviors

workplace behavior
A pattern of action by the members of an organization that directly or indirectly influences organizational effectiveness

performance behaviors
The total set of work-related behaviors that the organization expects the individual to display

Performance behaviors are the total set of work-related behaviors that the organization expects the individual to display. Thus they derive from the psychological contract. For some jobs, performance behaviors can be narrowly defined and easily measured. For example, an assembly-line worker who sits by a moving conveyor and attaches parts to a product as it passes by has relatively few performance behaviors. He or she is expected to remain at the workstation and correctly attach the parts. Performance can often be assessed quantitatively by counting the percentage of parts correctly attached.

For many other jobs, however, performance behaviors are more diverse and much more difficult to assess. For example, consider the case of a research and development scientist at Merck. The scientist works in a lab trying to find new scientific breakthroughs that have commercial potential. The scientist must apply knowledge learned in graduate school with experience gained from previous research. Intuition and creativity are also important elements. And the desired breakthrough may take months or even years to accomplish. As we discussed in Chapter 17, organizations rely on a number of different methods for evaluating performance. The key, of course, is to match the evaluation mechanism with the job being performed.

Withdrawal Behaviors

Another important type of work-related behavior is that which results in withdrawal—absenteeism and turnover. Absenteeism occurs when an individual does not show up for work. The cause may be legitimate (illness, jury duty, death in the family, and so forth) or feigned (reported as legitimate but actually just an excuse to stay home). When an employee is absent, her or his work does not get done at all, or a substitute must be hired to do it. In either case, the quantity or quality of actual output is likely to suffer. Obviously, some absenteeism is expected. The key concern of organizations is to minimize feigned absenteeism and to reduce legitimate absences as much as possible. High absenteeism may be a symptom of other problems as well, such as job dissatisfaction and low morale.

Turnover occurs when people quit their jobs. An organization usually incurs costs in replacing individuals who have quit, but if turnover involves especially productive people, it is even more costly. Turnover seems to result from a number of factors, including aspects of the job, the organization, the individual, the labor market, and family influences. In general, a poor person–job fit is also a likely cause of turnover.[60] The current high levels of unemployment reduce employee-driven turnover, given that fewer jobs are available. But when unemployment is low (and there are many open jobs) turnover may naturally increase as people seek better opportunities, higher pay, and so forth.

Efforts to directly manage turnover are frequently fraught with difficulty, even in organizations that concentrate on rewarding good performers. Of course, some turnover is inevitable, and in some cases it may even be desirable. For example, if the organization is trying to cut costs by reducing its staff, having people voluntarily choose to leave is preferable to having to terminate their jobs. And if the people who choose to leave are low performers or express high levels of job dissatisfaction, the organization may also benefit from turnover.

Organizational Citizenship

Organizational citizenship is the behavior of individuals that makes a positive overall contribution to the organization.[61] Consider, for example, an employee who does work that is acceptable in terms of both quantity and quality. However, she refuses to work overtime, will not help newcomers learn the ropes, and is generally unwilling to make any contribution to the organization beyond the strict performance of her job. Although this person may be seen as a good performer, she is not likely to be seen as a good organizational citizen.

Another employee may exhibit a comparable level of performance. In addition, however, he will always work late when the boss asks him to, take time to help newcomers learn their way around, and is perceived as being helpful and committed to the organization's success. Although his level of performance may be seen as equal to that of the first worker, he is also likely to be seen as a better organizational citizen.

The determinant of organizational citizenship behaviors is likely to be a complex mosaic of individual, social, and organizational variables. For example, the personality, attitudes, and needs of the individual will have to be consistent with citizenship behaviors. Similarly, the social context in which the individual works, or work group, will need to facilitate and promote such behaviors (we discuss group dynamics in Chapter 21). And the organization itself, especially its culture, must be capable of promoting, recognizing, and rewarding these types of behaviors if they are to be maintained. Although the study of organizational citizenship is still in its infancy, preliminary research suggests that it may play a powerful role in organizational effectiveness.[62]

absenteeism
When an individual does not show up for work

turnover
When people quit their jobs

organizational citizenship
The behavior of individuals that makes a positive overall contribution to the organization

THE MORE THINGS CHANGE

A Disturbance in the Work Force

David Becker/ZUMA Press/Corbis

In November 2009, Jason Rodriguez, a former employee of an engineering firm in Orlando, Florida, entered the company's offices and opened fire with a handgun, killing one person and wounding five others. Rodriguez had been fired from Reynolds, Smith and Hills less than two years earlier and told police that he thought the firm was hindering his efforts to collect unemployment benefits. "They left me to rot," he told a reporter who asked him about his motive.

According to the U.S. Department of Labor, the incidence of workplace violence has actually been trending down over the past few years, in part because employers have paid more attention to the problem and taken successful preventive measures. More and more companies, for example, have set up *employee assistance programs (EAPs)* to help workers deal with various sources of stress, but EAP providers report that, in the current climate of economic uncertainty, they're being asked to deal with a different set of problems than the ones they've typically handled in the past.

In particular, financial problems have replaced emotional problems as employees' primary area of concern, and with unemployment totals approaching 27-year highs, American workers appear to be more worried about the future than about such conventional stressors as pressing deadlines and demanding bosses. Today, says Sandra Naiman, a Denver-based career coach, "off- and on-the-job stresses feed into one another" to elevate stress levels all around, and workplace stress during the current recession may reflect this unfamiliar convergence of stressors.

There are as yet no hard data to connect workplace violence with economic downturns, but many professionals and other experts in the field are convinced that the connection is real. ComPsych Corp., an EAP provider in Chicago, reports that calls are running 30 percent above normal, and according to Rick Kronberg of Perspectives Ltd., another Chicago-based EAP provider, "with the layoffs and the general financial picture, we're getting a lot of reaction . . . [from] people with a high degree of stress." Adds Tim Horner, a managing director at Kroll Inc., a security consulting firm: "There are signs out there that something's going on. It's not unusual that somebody snaps." Kenneth Springer, another security specialist whose job now includes keeping an eye on potentially dangerous ex-employees for their former employers, agrees: "Tough times," he says, "will cause people to do crazy things."

By the same token, says Laurence Miller, a forensic psychologist and author of *From Difficult to Disturbed: Understanding and Managing Dysfunctional Employees*, economic stress alone won't turn someone into a killer, nor is the average coworker likely to turn violent without warning. "People shouldn't be sitting around wondering if someone they've been working with for years who's been a regular guy [with] no real problems is going to suddenly snap and go ballistic on them," says Miller. "It's usually somebody," he warns, "that's had a long streak of problems." Unfortunately, that profile fits Jason Rodriguez, who'd been struggling for years with marital and mental-health problems, unemployment, debt, and smoldering anger. "He was a very, very angry man," reports his former mother-in-law.

References: Mark Trumbull, "Orlando Shooting Comes as Trend in Workplace Violence Drops," *Christian Science Monitor*, November 7, 2009, www.csmonitor.com on April 14, 2011; Ellen Wulhorst, "Recession Fuels Worries of Workplace Violence," *Reuters*, April 22, 2009, www.reuters.com on April 14, 2011; Scott Powers and Fernando Quintero, "Jason Rodriguez Profile: 'He Was a Very, Very Angry Man,'" *OrlandoSentinel.com*, November 6, 2009, www.orlandosentinel.com on April 14, 2011; Laurence Miller, *From Difficult to Disturbed: Understanding and Managing Dysfunctional Employees* (New York: AMACOM, 2008), http://books.google.com on April 14, 2011.

Dysfunctional Behaviors

Some work-related behaviors are dysfunctional in nature. **Dysfunctional behaviors** are those that detract from, rather than contribute to, organizational performance.[63] Two of the more common ones, absenteeism and turnover, are discussed above. But other forms of dysfunctional behavior may be even more costly for an organization. Theft and sabotage, for example, result in direct financial costs for an organization. Sexual and racial harassment also cost an organization, both indirectly (by lowering morale, producing fear, and driving off valuable employees) and directly (through financial liability if the organization responds inappropriately). So, too, can politicized behavior, intentionally misleading others in the organization, spreading malicious rumors, and similar activities. Incivility and rudeness can result in conflict and damage to morale and the organization's culture.[64]

Workplace violence is also a growing concern in many organizations. Violence by disgruntled workers or former workers results in dozens of deaths and injuries each year.[65] The factors that contribute to workplace violence—not to mention the factors involved in increases and decreases—are difficult to pin down, but the *Change* box on page 466, entitled "A Disturbance in the Work Force," discusses the possible role of the current economic downturn as a contributing factor in recent incidents of workplace violence.

dysfunctional behaviors
Those that detract from, rather than contribute to, organizational performance

---

Distinguish between performance behaviors, withdrawal behaviors, organizational citizenship, and dysfunctional behaviors.

Have you ever called in sick for work when you were well, or missed class using sickness as a false excuse? Can such actions be justified?

CONCEPT CHECK

Summary of Learning Objectives and Key Points

1. Explain the nature of the individual–organization relationship.

   - A basic framework that can be used to facilitate this understanding is the psychological contract—the set of expectations held by people with respect to what they will contribute to the organization and what they expect to get in return.
   - Organizations strive to achieve an optimal person–job fit, but this process is complicated by the existence of individual differences.

2. Define personality and describe personality attributes that affect behavior in organizations.

   - Personality is the relatively stable set of psychological and behavioral attributes that distinguish one person from another.
   - The "Big Five" personality traits are:
     - agreeableness
     - conscientiousness
     - negative emotionality
     - extraversion
     - openness

   - The Myers–Briggs framework can also be a useful mechanism for understanding personality.
   - Other important traits are:
     - locus of control
     - self-efficacy
     - authoritarianism
     - Machiavellianism
     - self-esteem
     - risk propensity
   - Emotional intelligence, a fairly new concept, may provide additional insights into personality.

3. Discuss individual attitudes in organizations and how they affect behavior.

   - Attitudes are based on emotion, knowledge, and intended behavior.
   - Whereas personality is relatively stable, some attitudes can be formed and changed easily. Others are more constant.
   - Job satisfaction or dissatisfaction and organizational commitment are important work-related attitudes.

4. Describe basic perceptual processes and the role of attributions in organizations.

   - Perception is the set of processes by which an individual becomes aware of and interprets information about the environment.
   - Basic perceptual processes include selective perception and stereotyping.
   - Perception and attribution are also closely related.

5. Discuss the causes and consequences of stress and describe how it can be managed.

   - Stress is an individual's response to a strong stimulus.
   - The General Adaptation Syndrome outlines the basic stress process.
   - Stress can be caused by task, physical, role, and interpersonal demands.
   - Consequences of stress include organizational and individual outcomes, as well as burnout.
   - Several things can be done to manage stress.

6. Describe creativity and its role in organizations.

   - Creativity is the capacity to generate new ideas.
   - Creative people tend to have certain profiles of background experiences, personal traits, and cognitive abilities.

   - The creative process itself includes preparation, incubation, insight, and verification.

7. Explain how workplace behaviors can directly or indirectly influence organizational effectiveness.

   - Workplace behavior is a pattern of action by the members of an organization that directly or indirectly influences organizational effectiveness.
   - Performance behaviors are the set of work-related behaviors that the organization expects the individual to display to fulfill the psychological contract.
   - Basic withdrawal behaviors are absenteeism and turnover.
   - Organizational citizenship refers to behavior that makes a positive overall contribution to the organization.
   - Dysfunctional behaviors can be very harmful to an organization.

Discussion Questions

Questions for Review

1. What is a psychological contract? List the things that might be included in individual contributions. List the things that might be included in organizational inducements.
2. Describe the three components of attitudes and tell how the components are related. What is cognitive dissonance? How do individuals resolve cognitive dissonance?
3. Identify and discuss the steps in the creative process. What can an organization do to increase employees' creativity?
4. Identify and describe several important workplace behaviors.

Questions for Analysis

5. Organizations are increasing their use of personality tests to screen job applicants. What are the advantages and disadvantages of this approach? What can managers do to avoid some of the potential pitfalls?
6. As a manager, how can you tell that an employee is experiencing job satisfaction? How can you tell that employees are highly committed to the organization? If a worker is not satisfied, what can a manager do to improve satisfaction? What can a manager do to improve organizational commitment?
7. Managers cannot pay equal attention to every piece of information, so selective perception is a fact of life. How does selective perception help managers? How does it create difficulties for them? How can managers increase their "good" selective perception and decrease the "bad"?

Questions for Application

8. Write the psychological contract you have in this class. In other words, what do you contribute, and what inducements are available? Ask your professor to tell the class about the psychological contract that he or she intended to establish with the students in your class. How does the professor's intended contract compare with the one you wrote? If there are differences, why do you think the differences exist? Share your ideas with the class.

9. Assume that you are going to hire three new employees for the department store you manage. One will sell shoes, one will manage the toy department, and one will work in the stockroom. Identify the basic characteristics you want in each of the people, to achieve a good person–job fit.

10. Describe a time when someone displayed each one of the Big Five personality traits at either a very high or a very low level. For example, tell about someone who appeared to be highly agreeable or highly disagreeable. Then tell about the outcomes that person experienced as a result of displaying that particular personality trait. Do the outcomes seem logical; that is, do positive personality traits usually lead to good outcomes and negative traits to bad ones? Explain your answer.

 ## CengageNow™ Highlights

Now use your CengageNow™ homework to help you:
- Apply management theories in your life
- Assess your management skills
- Master management terms and concepts
- Apply your knowledge to real-world situations
- Analyze and solve challenging management problems

In order to take advantage of these elements, your instructor will need to have set up a course for your class within CengageNow™. Ask your instructor to contact his/her Cengage sales representative and Digital Solutions Manager to explore testing CengageNow™ in your course this term.

CHAPTER

Managing Employee Motivation and Performance

LEARNING OBJECTIVES

After studying this chapter, you should be able to:

1. Characterize the nature of motivation, including its importance and historical perspectives.

2. Identify and describe the major content perspectives on motivation.

3. Identify and describe the major process perspectives on motivation.

4. Describe reinforcement perspectives on motivation.

5. Identify and describe popular motivational strategies.

6. Describe the role of organizational reward systems in motivation.

MANAGEMENT IN ACTION ## Are You Happily Productive or Productively Happy?

Sara Caputo is the founder and owner of Radiant Organizing, a training and coaching firm located in Santa Barbara, California. As a productivity consultant, her work includes both one-on-one sessions with clients and speaking engagements on how to get things done in the workplace. One day, she recalls, as she was in the middle of a presentation at a professional conference, "I just felt myself really loving what I do. . . . This got me thinking," she says. "What comes first—happiness in your work or productivity in your work? Are we *more productive* in our jobs and at work because we enjoy what we do and [because] that in itself is a motivator? Or are we *happier* in our jobs and at work because we're productive?"

At first, Caputo admits, she was willing to accept the likelihood that her question came down to "sort of a chicken/egg dilemma." Upon further reflection, however, she decided that happiness probably comes first. "At one point in your life," she reasons,

you had a calling to do what you're doing right now. Then time goes by, and what gets in the

"If you're not happy doing what you do on a daily basis, you'll just be getting things done for the sake of getting things done."

—PRODUCTIVITY CONSULTANT SARA CAPUTO

way? All the "other stuff." At the end of the day, if you're not happy doing what you do on a daily basis, you'll have a hard time sustaining your productivity because you'll just be getting things done for the sake of getting things done.

One rather suspects that Caputo's workplace experience has been somewhat happier than average, but her bottom-line perspective on the cause-and-effect relationship between happiness and productivity is pretty much in line with most thinking on the subject. Another productivity consultant, for example, advises that "if you want to get more done at work . . . you should start by liking what you do. . . . [T]he productivity gurus out there," warns Alexander Kjerulf, founder

Alexander Kjerulf leads a Danish consulting company that specializes in improving employee morale. Not everyone, though, agrees that making employees more satisfied will make them more productive.

Alexander Kjerulf

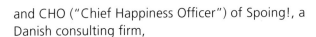

and CHO ("Chief Happiness Officer") of Spoing!, a Danish consulting firm,

> will tell you that it's all about having the right system. You need to prioritize your tasks. You must keep detailed logs of how you spend your time, [and] to-do lists are of course essential. You must learn to structure your calendar, and much, much more. . . . [But] no system, no tool or methodology in the world can beat the productivity boost you get from really, really enjoying your work.

Happiness at work, says Kjerulf, "is the #1 productivity booster," and he cites a number of reasons why: Happy people work better with others, fix problems rather than complain about them, and make better decisions; they're optimistic and "way more motivated," and they have more energy and get sick less often.

Kjerulf admits that there's still a "question of causation"—the chicken-or-the-egg issue of which came first, happiness or productivity. "The link," he concludes, "goes both ways," but "the link is strongest from happiness to productivity—which means that if you want to be more productive, the very best thing you can do is focus on being happy with what you do."

Not everyone, however, sees the happiness–productivity link from the same perspective. For Paul Larson, a veteran of operations management in a variety of industries, the "legend that happy workers are productive employees has been a part of our organizational thinking for so long that many just take for granted that it has to be true." Larson, founder and president of The Myrddin Group, a Texas-based consultancy specializing in organizational design and development, agrees that "productive workers do seem to be happier." But that, he suggests, is "where the confusion is coming from. . . . [P]roductivity leads to satisfaction and happiness," he argues, "not the other way around. People who do a good job tend to feel intrinsically good about it."

To boost productivity, Larson advises, companies should train and support managers "in their efforts to keep the troops fully engaged. It's that engagement that provides the venues for achievement and recognition."

Charles Kerns, a behavioral psychologist at Pepperdine University's Graziado School of Business and Management, agrees with Larson that engagement is the best goal for a manager who wants "to influence the happiness level of his or her employees." He's not quite so sure, however, that enhancing either personal or organizational productivity hinges on solving the chicken-or-egg dilemma. "Job satisfaction researchers," he points out, "have had a long-standing debate as to whether employees are happy first and performers second, or performers first and happy second," and he doesn't think that the matter is going to be resolved any time soon. For practical purposes, he suggests, "both happiness and job performance need to be addressed."

This is where *engagement* comes in. On the one hand, according to Kerns, managers should probably resign themselves to the fact that improving engagement is about the best they can hope for. On the other hand, improving an employee's engagement with his or her work is no small achievement. Engagement can be measured by the extent to which an individual has *more happy or positive experiences than negative ones*, and the key to increasing positive experiences, says Kerns, is engaging an employee's strengths: "An employee's level of engagement . . . and subsequent happiness," he contends, "is likely boosted when he or she has the opportunity to do what he or she does best at work: Utilizing one's strengths is a positive experience." With engagement as a starting point, Kerns thinks that the happiness–productivity equation can be formulated in more practical terms: Happiness, he explains, "comes from work experiences that yield positive emotions [and] positive thoughts," and "people who approach tasks with positivity [are] more productive."[1]

Obviously, managers can't do much about what makes people either happier or more productive. The job, however, involves encouraging productivity, and it's always worthwhile trying to figure out what makes employees more (or less) productive. Whether happiness is or isn't a key factor, the issue almost invariably comes down to motivation, which is the subject of this chapter. We first examine the nature of employee motivation and then explore the major perspectives on motivation. Newly emerging approaches are then discussed. We conclude with a description of rewards and their role in motivation.

The Nature of Motivation

Motivation is the set of forces that cause people to behave in certain ways.[2] On any given day, an employee may choose to work as hard as possible at a job, work just hard enough to avoid a reprimand, or do as little as possible. The goal for the manager is to maximize the likelihood of the first behavior and minimize the likelihood of the last. This goal becomes all the more important when we understand how important motivation is in the workplace.

The Importance of Employee Motivation in the Workplace

Individual performance is generally determined by three things: motivation (the desire to do the job), ability (the capability to do the job), and the work environment (the resources needed to do the job). If an employee lacks ability, the manager can provide training or replace the worker. If there is a resource problem, the manager can correct it. But if motivation is the problem, the task for the manager is more challenging.[3] Individual behavior is a complex phenomenon, and the manager may be hard pressed to figure out the precise nature of the problem and how to solve it. Thus motivation is important because of its significance as a determinant of performance and because of its intangible character.[4]

The motivation framework in Figure 19.1 is a good starting point for understanding how motivated behavior occurs. The motivation process begins with a need deficiency. For example, when a worker feels that she is underpaid, she experiences a need for more income. In response, the worker searches for ways to satisfy the need, such as working harder to try to earn a raise or seeking a new job. Next she chooses an option to pursue. After carrying out the chosen option—working harder and putting in more hours for a reasonable period of time, for example—she then evaluates her success. If her hard work resulted in a pay raise, she probably feels good about things and will continue to work hard. But if no raise has been provided, she is likely to try another option.

Historical Perspectives on Motivation

To appreciate what we know about employee motivation, it is helpful to review earlier approaches. The traditional, human relations, and human resource approaches have each shed partial light on motivation.[5]

The Traditional Approach The traditional approach is best represented by the work of Frederick W. Taylor.[6] As noted in Chapter 2, Taylor advocated an incentive pay system. He believed that managers knew more about the jobs being performed than did workers, and he assumed that economic gain was the primary thing that motivated everyone. Other

motivation
The set of forces that cause people to behave in certain ways

FIGURE 19.1
THE MOTIVATION FRAMEWORK

The motivation process progresses through a series of discrete steps. Content, process, and reinforcement perspectives on motivation address different parts of this process.

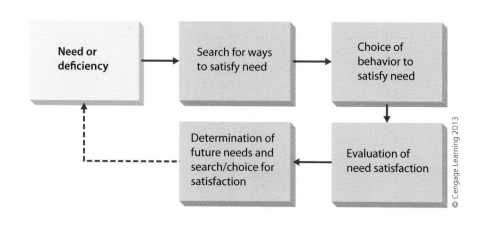

assumptions of the traditional approach were that work is inherently unpleasant for most people and that the money they earn is more important to employees than the nature of the job they are performing. Hence, people could be expected to perform any kind of job if they were paid enough. Although the role of money as a motivating factor cannot be dismissed, proponents of the traditional approach took too narrow a view of the role of monetary compensation and failed to consider other motivational factors.

The Human Relations Approach The human relations approach was also summarized in Chapter 2.[7] The human relationists emphasized the role of social processes in the workplace. Their basic assumptions were that employees want to feel useful and important, that employees have strong social needs, and that these needs are more important than money in motivating them. Advocates of the human relations approach advised managers to make workers feel important and allow them a modicum of self-direction and self-control in carrying out routine activities. The illusion of involvement and importance was expected to satisfy workers' basic social needs and result in higher motivation to perform. For example, a manager might allow a work group to participate in making a decision even though he or she had already determined what the decision would be. The symbolic gesture of seeming to allow participation was expected to enhance motivation, even though no real participation took place.

The Human Resource Approach The human resource approach to motivation carries the concepts of needs and motivation one step further. Whereas the human relationists believed that the illusion of contribution and participation would enhance motivation, the human resource view assumes that the contributions themselves are valuable to both individuals and organizations. It assumes that people want to contribute and are able to make genuine contributions. Management's task, then, is to encourage participation and to create a work environment that makes full use of the human resources available. This philosophy guides most contemporary thinking about employee motivation. At Ford, Westinghouse, Texas Instruments, and Hewlett-Packard, for example, work teams are being called on to solve a variety of problems and to make substantive contributions to the organization.

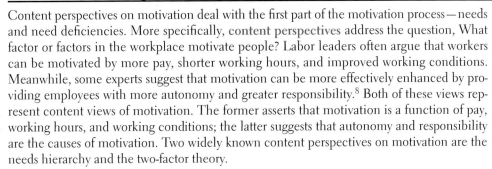

Summarize historical perspectives on employee motivation.

Use Figure 19.1 to trace through a motivational cycle you have recently experienced.

CONCEPT CHECK

Content Perspectives on Motivation

Content perspectives on motivation deal with the first part of the motivation process—needs and need deficiencies. More specifically, **content perspectives** address the question, What factor or factors in the workplace motivate people? Labor leaders often argue that workers can be motivated by more pay, shorter working hours, and improved working conditions. Meanwhile, some experts suggest that motivation can be more effectively enhanced by providing employees with more autonomy and greater responsibility.[8] Both of these views represent content views of motivation. The former asserts that motivation is a function of pay, working hours, and working conditions; the latter suggests that autonomy and responsibility are the causes of motivation. Two widely known content perspectives on motivation are the needs hierarchy and the two-factor theory.

content perspectives
Approach to motivation that tries to answer the question, What factor or factors motivate people?

The Needs Hierarchy Approach

The needs hierarchy approach has been advanced by many theorists. Needs hierarchies assume that people have different needs that can be arranged in a hierarchy of importance. The two best known are Maslow's hierarchy of needs and the ERG theory.

Maslow's Hierarchy of Needs Abraham Maslow, a human relationist, argued that people are motivated to satisfy five need levels.[9] **Maslow's hierarchy of needs** is shown in Figure 19.2. At the bottom of the hierarchy are the *physiological needs*—things like food, sex, and air, which represent basic issues of survival and biological function. In organizations, these needs are generally satisfied by adequate wages and the work environment itself, which provides restrooms, adequate lighting, comfortable temperatures, and ventilation.

Next are the *security needs* for a secure physical and emotional environment. Examples include the desire for housing and clothing and the need to be free from worry about money and job security. These needs can be satisfied in the workplace by job continuity (no layoffs), a grievance system (to protect against arbitrary supervisory actions), and an adequate insurance and retirement benefit package (for security against illness and provision of income in later life). Even today, however, depressed industries and economic decline can put people out of work and restore the primacy of security needs.

Belongingness needs relate to social processes. They include the need for love and affection and the need to be accepted by one's peers. These needs are satisfied for most people by family and community relationships outside of work and by friendships on the job. A manager can help satisfy these needs by allowing social interaction and by making employees feel like part of a team or work group.

Esteem needs actually comprise two different sets of needs: the need for a positive self-image and self-respect, and the need for recognition and respect from others. A manager can help address these needs by providing a variety of extrinsic symbols of accomplishment, such as job titles, nice offices, and similar rewards, as appropriate. At a more intrinsic level, the manager can provide challenging job assignments and opportunities for the employee to feel a sense of accomplishment.

FIGURE 19.2 MASLOW'S HIERARCHY OF NEEDS

Maslow's hierarchy suggests that human needs can be classified into five categories and that these categories can be arranged in a hierarchy of importance. A manager should understand that an employee may not be satisfied with only a salary and benefits; he or she may also need challenging job opportunities to experience self-growth and satisfaction.

Maslow's hierarchy of needs
Suggests that people must satisfy five groups of needs in order—physiological, security, belongingness, esteem, and self-actualization

Source: Adapted from Abraham H. Maslow, "A Theory of Human Motivation," *Psychology Review*, 1943, Vol. 50, pp. 370–396.

At the top of the hierarchy are the *self-actualization needs*. These involve realizing one's potential for continued growth and individual development. The self-actualization needs are perhaps the most difficult for a manager to address. In fact, it can be argued that these needs must be met entirely from within the individual. But a manager can help by promoting a culture wherein self-actualization is possible. For instance, a manager could give employees a chance to participate in making decisions about their work and the opportunity to learn new things.

Maslow suggests that the five need categories constitute a hierarchy. An individual is motivated first and foremost to satisfy physiological needs. As long as these remain unsatisfied, the individual is motivated to fulfill only them. When satisfaction of physiological needs is achieved, they cease to act as primary motivational factors, and the individual moves "up" the hierarchy and becomes concerned with security needs. This process continues until the individual reaches the self-actualization level. Maslow's concept of the needs hierarchy has a certain intuitive logic and has been accepted by many managers. But research has revealed certain shortcomings and defects in the theory. Some research has found that five levels of need are not always present and that the order of the levels is not always the same as postulated by Maslow.[11] In addition, people from different cultures are likely to have different need categories and hierarchies.

> "I wanted to do something with my life where I felt I was contributing. Somehow, selling more tacos and margaritas than the week before wasn't."
>
> —CATHEY GARDNER, FORMER RESTAURANT MANAGER, ON HER DECISION TO BECOME A NURSE[10]

The ERG Theory In response to these and similar criticisms, an alternative hierarchy of needs, called the **ERG theory of motivation**, was developed.[12] This theory collapses the needs hierarchy developed by Maslow into three levels. *Existence needs* correspond to the physiological and security needs. *Relatedness needs* focus on how people relate to their social environment. In Maslow's hierarchy, these would encompass both the need to belong and the need to earn the esteem of others. *Growth needs*, the highest level in this schema, include the needs for self-esteem and self-actualization.

Although the ERG theory assumes that motivated behavior follows a hierarchy in somewhat the same fashion as suggested by Maslow, there are two important differences. First, the ERG theory suggests that more than one level of need can cause motivation at the same time. For example, it suggests that people can be motivated by a desire for money (existence), friendship (relatedness), and the opportunity to learn new skills (growth) all at once. Second, the ERG theory has what has been called a *frustration-regression* element. Thus, if needs remain unsatisfied, the individual will become frustrated, regress to a lower level, and begin to pursue those things again. For example, a worker previously motivated by money (existence needs) may have just been awarded a pay raise sufficient to satisfy those needs. Suppose that he then attempts to establish more friendships to satisfy relatedness needs. If for some reason he finds that it is impossible to become better friends with others in the workplace, he eventually gets frustrated and regresses to being motivated to earn even more money.

The Two-Factor Theory

Another popular content perspective is the **two-factor theory of motivation**.[13] Frederick Herzberg developed his theory after interviewing 200 accountants and engineers. He asked them to recall occasions when they had been satisfied and motivated and occasions when they had been dissatisfied and unmotivated. Surprisingly, he found that different sets of factors were associated with satisfaction and with dissatisfaction—that is, a person might identify "low pay" as causing dissatisfaction but would not necessarily mention "high pay" as a cause of satisfaction. Instead, different factors—such as recognition or accomplishment—were cited as causing satisfaction and motivation.

This finding led Herzberg to conclude that the traditional view of job satisfaction was incomplete. That view assumed that satisfaction and dissatisfaction are at opposite ends of a single continuum. People might be satisfied, dissatisfied, or somewhere in between.

ERG theory of motivation
Suggests that people's needs are grouped into three possibly overlapping categories—existence, relatedness, and growth

two-factor theory of motivation
Suggests that people's satisfaction and dissatisfaction are influenced by two independent sets of factors—motivation factors and hygiene factors

FIGURE 19.3 THE TWO-FACTOR THEORY OF MOTIVATION

The two-factor theory suggests that job satisfaction has two dimensions. A manager who tries to motivate an employee using only hygiene factors, such as pay and good working conditions, will likely not succeed. To motivate employees and produce a high level of satisfaction, managers must also offer factors such as responsibility and the opportunity for advancement (motivation factors).

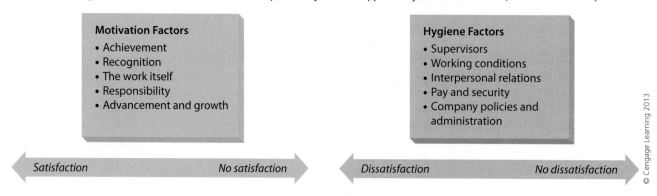

© Cengage Learning 2013

But Herzberg's interviews had identified two different dimensions altogether: one ranging from satisfaction to no satisfaction and the other ranging from dissatisfaction to no dissatisfaction. This perspective, along with several examples of factors that affect each continuum, is shown in Figure 19.3. Note that the factors influencing the satisfaction continuum—called *motivation factors*—are related specifically to the work content. The factors presumed to cause dissatisfaction—called *hygiene factors*—are related to the work environment.

Based on these findings, Herzberg argued that there are two stages in the process of motivating employees. First, managers must ensure that the hygiene factors are not deficient. Pay and security must be appropriate, working conditions must be safe, technical supervision must be acceptable, and so on. By providing hygiene factors at an appropriate level, managers do not stimulate motivation but merely ensure that employees are "not dissatisfied." Employees whom managers attempt to "satisfy" through hygiene factors alone will usually do just enough to get by. Thus managers should proceed to stage two—giving employees the opportunity to experience motivation factors such as achievement and recognition. The result is predicted to be a high level of satisfaction and motivation. Herzberg also went a step further than most other theorists and described exactly how to use the two-factor theory in the workplace. Specifically, he recommended job enrichment, as discussed in Chapter 14. He argued that jobs should be redesigned to provide higher levels of the motivation factors.

Although widely accepted by many managers, Herzberg's two-factor theory is not without its critics. One criticism is that the findings in Herzberg's initial interviews are subject to different explanations. Another charge is that his sample was not representative of the general population and that subsequent research often failed to uphold the theory.[14] At the present time, Herzberg's theory is not held in high esteem by researchers in the field. The theory has had a major impact on managers, however, and has played a key role in increasing their awareness of motivation and its importance in the workplace.

Individual Human Needs

In addition to these theories, research has focused on specific individual human needs that are important in organizations. The three most important individual needs are achievement, affiliation, and power.[15]

The need for achievement, the best known of the three, is the desire to accomplish a goal or task more effectively than in the past. People with a high need for achievement have a desire to assume personal responsibility, a tendency to set moderately difficult goals, a desire for specific and immediate feedback, and a preoccupation with their task. David C. McClelland, the psychologist who first identified this need, argues that only about 10 percent of the

need for achievement
The desire to accomplish a goal or task more effectively than in the past

U.S. population has a high need for achievement. In contrast, almost one-quarter of the workers in Japan have a high need for achievement.[16]

The **need for affiliation** is less well understood. Like Maslow's belongingness need, the need for affiliation is a desire for human companionship and acceptance. People with a strong need for affiliation are likely to prefer (and perform better in) a job that entails a lot of social interaction and offers opportunities to make friends. One recent survey found that workers with one or more good friends at work are much more likely to be committed to their work. Continental Airlines, for instance, allows flight attendants to form their own teams; those who participate tend to form teams with their friends.[16]

The need for power has also received considerable attention as an important ingredient in managerial success. The **need for power** is the desire to be influential in a group and to control one's environment. Research has shown that people with a strong need for power are likely to be superior performers, have good attendance records, and occupy supervisory positions. One study found that managers as a group tend to have a stronger power motive than the general population and that successful managers tend to have stronger power motives than less successful managers.[17] Dennis Kozlowski, disgraced former CEO of Tyco International, clearly had a strong need for power. This was reflected in the way he routinely took control over resources and used them for his own personal gain. Indeed, the things he bought with company money—gold shower curtains, for example—were probably intended to convey to the world the extent of his power.[18] The need for power might also explain why Mark Hurd, the former CEO of Hewlett-Packard, took advantage of his power and role as head of the company in 2010. Hurd was forced to resign after a sexual harassment claim by a female contractor alleging that Hurd had used corporate funds for personal gains in attempts to woo her. The former CEO had submitted personal receipts ranging from $1,000 to $20,000 over a two-year period.[19]

Mark Hurd was the highly respected CEO of Hewlett-Packard before a sexual harassment scandal forced him to step down. Part of the motivation underlying his behavior may have been a strong need for power. Indeed, most experts agree that most behaviors associated with sexual harassment are more likely to be motivated by the need for power than by physical needs.

Monica Davey/Reuters/Landov

Implications of the Content Perspectives

Managers should remember that Maslow's needs hierarchy, the ERG theory, the two-factor theory, and the needs for achievement, affiliation, and power all provide useful insights into factors that cause motivation. What they do not do is shed much light on the process of motivation. They do not explain why people might be motivated by one factor rather than by another at a given level or how people might go about trying to satisfy their different needs. These questions involve behaviors or actions, goals, and feelings of satisfaction—concepts that are addressed by various process perspectives on motivation.

need for affiliation
The desire for human companionship and acceptance

need for power
The desire to be influential in a group and to control one's environment

Summarize the needs hierarchy approaches to employee motivation.

How would you assess yourself regarding the needs for achievement, affiliation, and power?

◈ Process Perspectives on Motivation

Process perspectives are concerned with how motivation occurs. Rather than attempting to identify motivational stimuli, **process perspectives** focus on why people choose certain behavioral options to satisfy their needs and how they evaluate their satisfaction after they have attained these goals. Three useful process perspectives on motivation are the expectancy, equity, and goal-setting theories.

Expectancy Theory

Expectancy theory suggests that motivation depends on two things—how much we want something and how likely we think we are to get it.[20] Assume that you are approaching graduation and looking for a job. You see in the want ads that General Motors is seeking a new vice president with a starting salary of $500,000 per year. Even though you might want the job, you will not apply because you realize that you have little chance of getting it. The next ad you see is for someone to scrape bubble gum from underneath theater seats for a starting salary of $6 an hour. Even though you could probably get this job, you do not apply because you do not want it. Then you see an ad for a management trainee at a big company, with a starting salary of $45,000. You will probably apply for this job because you want it and because you think you have a reasonable chance of getting it.

Expectancy theory rests on four basic assumptions. First, it assumes that behavior is determined by a combination of forces in the individual and in the environment. Second, it assumes that people make decisions about their own behavior in organizations. Third, it assumes that different people have different types of needs, desires, and goals. Fourth, it assumes that people make choices from among alternative plans of behavior, based on their perceptions of the extent to which a given behavior will lead to desired outcomes.

Figure 19.4 summarizes the basic expectancy model. The model suggests that motivation leads to effort and that effort, combined with employee ability and environmental factors, results in performance. Performance, in turn, leads to various outcomes, each of which has an associated value, called its *valence*. The most important parts of the expectancy model cannot be shown in the figure, however. These are the individual's expectation that

process perspectives
Approaches to motivation that focus on why people choose certain behavioral options to fulfill their needs and how they evaluate their satisfaction after they have attained these goals

expectancy theory
Suggests that motivation depends on two things—how much we want something and how likely we think we are to get it

FIGURE 19.4 THE EXPECTANCY MODEL OF MOTIVATION

The expectancy model of motivation is a complex but relatively accurate portrayal of how motivation occurs. According to this model, a manager must understand what employees want (such as pay, promotions, or status) to begin to motivate them.

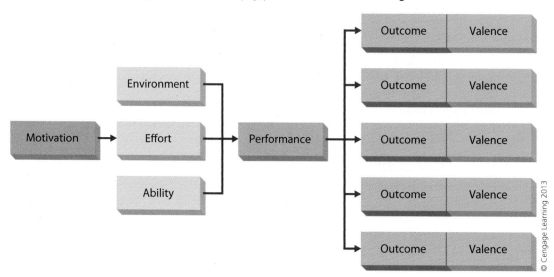

© Cengage Learning 2013

effort will lead to high performance, that performance will lead to outcomes, and that each outcome will have some kind of value.

Effort-to-Performance Expectancy   The effort-to-performance expectancy is the individual's perception of the probability that effort will lead to high performance. When the individual believes that effort will lead directly to high performance, expectancy will be quite strong (close to 1.00). When the individual believes that effort and performance are unrelated, the effort-to-performance expectancy is very weak (close to 0). The belief that effort is somewhat but not strongly related to performance carries with it a moderate expectancy (somewhere between 0 and 1.00).

Performance-to-Outcome Expectancy   The performance-to-outcome expectancy is the individual's perception that performance will lead to a specific outcome. For example, if the individual believes that high performance *will* result in a pay raise, the performance-to-outcome expectancy is high (approaching 1.00). The individual who believes that high performance *may* lead to a pay raise has a moderate expectancy (between 1.00 and 0). The individual who believes that performance has no relationship to rewards has a low performance-to-outcome expectancy (close to 0).

Outcomes and Valences   Expectancy theory recognizes that an individual's behavior results in a variety of outcomes, or consequences, in an organizational setting. A high performer, for example, may get bigger pay raises, faster promotions, and more praise from the boss. On the other hand, she may also be subject to more stress and incur resentment from coworkers. Each of these outcomes also has an associated value, or valence—an index of how much an individual values a particular outcome. If the individual wants the outcome, its valence is positive; if the individual does not want the outcome, its valence is negative; and if the individual is indifferent to the outcome, its valence is zero.

It is this part of expectancy theory that goes beyond the content perspectives on motivation. Different people have different needs, and they will try to satisfy these needs in different ways. For an employee who has a high need for achievement and a low need for affiliation, the pay raise and promotions cited above as outcomes of high performance might have positive valences, the praise and resentment zero valences, and the stress a negative valence. For a different employee, with a low need for achievement and a high need for affiliation, the pay raise, promotions, and praise might all have positive valences, whereas both resentment and stress could have negative valences.

For motivated behavior to occur, three conditions must be met. First, the effort-to-performance expectancy must be greater than 0 (the individual must believe that if effort is expended, high performance will result). The performance-to-outcome expectancy must also be greater than 0 (the individual must believe that if high performance is achieved, certain outcomes will follow). And the sum of the valences for the outcomes must be greater than 0. (One or more outcomes may have negative valences if they are more than offset by the positive valences of other outcomes. For example, the attractiveness of a pay raise, a promotion, and praise from the boss may outweigh the unattractiveness of more stress and resentment from coworkers.) Expectancy theory suggests that when these conditions are met, the individual is motivated to expend effort.

Starbucks credits its unique stock ownership program with maintaining a dedicated and motivated workforce. Based on the fundamental concepts of expectancy theory, Starbucks employees earn stock as a function of their seniority and performance. Thus their hard work helps them earn shares of ownership in the company.[21]

The Porter-Lawler Extension   An interesting extension of expectancy theory has been proposed by Porter and Lawler.[23] Recall from Chapter 2 that the human relationists assumed that employee satisfaction causes good performance. We also noted that research has not supported such a relationship. Porter and Lawler suggested that there may indeed be a relationship between

---

effort-to-performance expectancy
The individual's perception of the probability that effort will lead to high performance

performance-to-outcome expectancy
The individual's perception that performance will lead to a specific outcome

outcomes
Consequences of behaviors in an organizational setting, usually rewards

valence
An index of how much an individual desires a particular outcome; the attractiveness of the outcome to the individual

"When we're productive and we've done something good together (and we are recognized for it), we feel satisfied, not the other way around."

—J. RICHARD HACKMAN, LEADING ORGANIZATIONAL PSYCHOLOGIST[22]

FIGURE 19.5 THE PORTER–LAWLER EXTENSION OF EXPECTANCY THEORY

The Porter–Lawler extension of expectancy theory suggests that if performance results in equitable rewards, people will be more satisfied. Thus performance can lead to satisfaction. Managers must therefore be sure that any system of motivation includes rewards that are fair, or equitable, for all.

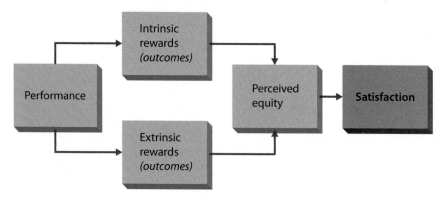

Source: Edward E. Lawler III and Lyman W. Porter, "The Effect of Performance on Job Satisfaction," *Industrial Relations*, October 1967, p. 23. Used with permission of the Wiley-Blackwell.

satisfaction and performance but that it goes in the opposite direction—that is, high performance may lead to high satisfaction. Figure 19.5 summarizes Porter and Lawler's logic. Performance results in rewards for an individual. Some of these are extrinsic (such as pay and promotions); others are intrinsic (such as self-esteem and accomplishment). The individual evaluates the equity, or fairness, of the rewards relative to the effort expended and the level of performance attained. If the rewards are perceived to be equitable, the individual is satisfied.

Equity Theory

After needs have stimulated the motivation process and the individual has chosen an action that is expected to satisfy those needs, the individual assesses the fairness, or equity, of the resultant outcome. Equity theory contends that people are motivated to seek social equity in the rewards they receive for performance.[24] Equity is an individual's belief that the treatment he or she is receiving is fair relative to the treatment received by others. According to equity theory, outcomes from a job include pay, recognition, promotions, social relationships, and intrinsic rewards. To get these rewards, the individual makes inputs to the job, such as time, experience, effort, education, and loyalty. The theory suggests that people view their outcomes and inputs as a ratio and then compare it to someone else's ratio. This other "person" may be someone in the work group or some sort of group average or composite. The process of comparison looks like this:

Both the formulation of the ratios and comparisons between them are very subjective and based on individual perceptions. As a result of comparisons, three conditions may result: The individual may feel equitably rewarded, underrewarded, or overrewarded. A feeling of equity will result when the two ratios are equal. This may occur even though the other person's outcomes are greater than the individual's own outcomes—provided that the other's inputs are also proportionately greater. Suppose that Mark has a high school education and earns $30,000. He may still feel equitably treated relative to Susan, who earns $35,000, because she has a college degree.

People who feel underrewarded try to reduce the inequity. Such an individual might decrease her inputs by exerting less effort, increase her outcomes by asking for a raise, distort the original ratios by rationalizing, try to get the other person to change her or his outcomes or inputs, leave the situation, or change the object of comparison. An individual may also feel overrewarded relative to another person. This is not likely to be terribly disturbing to most people, but research suggests that some people who experience inequity under these conditions are somewhat motivated to reduce it. Under such a circumstance, the person might increase

equity theory
Suggests that people are motivated to seek social equity in the rewards they receive for performance

his inputs by exerting more effort, reduce his outcomes by producing fewer units (if paid on a per-unit basis), distort the original ratios by rationalizing, or try to reduce the inputs or increase the outcomes of the other person.

Managers today may need to pay even greater attention to equity theory and its implications. Many firms, for example, are moving toward performance-based reward systems (discussed later in this chapter) as opposed to standard or across-the-board salary increases. Hence, they must ensure that the bases for rewarding some people more than others are clear and objective. Beyond legal issues such as discrimination, managers need to be sure that they are providing fair rewards and incentives to those who do the best work.[25] Moreover, they must be sensitive to cultural differences that affect how people may perceive and react to equity and inequity.[26]

> "People have long memories. They'll remember whether they think they were dealt with equitably."
>
> —WILLIAM CONATY, FORMER DIRECTOR OF HR FOR GENERAL ELECTRIC[27]

Goal-Setting Theory

The goal-setting theory of motivation assumes that behavior is a result of conscious goals and intentions.[28] Therefore, by setting goals for people in the organization, a manager should be able to influence their behavior. Given this premise, the challenge is to develop a thorough understanding of the processes by which people set goals and then work to reach them. In the original version of goal-setting theory, two specific goal characteristics—goal difficulty and goal specificity—were expected to shape performance.

Goal Difficulty *Goal difficulty* is the extent to which a goal is challenging and requires effort. If people work to achieve goals, it is reasonable to assume that they will work harder to achieve more difficult goals. But a goal must not be so difficult that it is unattainable. If a new manager asks her sales force to increase sales by 300 percent, the group may become disillusioned. A more realistic but still difficult goal—perhaps a 30 percent increase—would be a better incentive. A substantial body of research supports the importance of goal difficulty. In one study, for example, managers at Weyerhaeuser set difficult goals for truck drivers hauling loads of timber from cutting sites to wood yards. Over a nine-month period, the drivers increased the quantity of wood they delivered by an amount that would have required $250,000 worth of new trucks at the previous per-truck average load.[29]

Goal Specificity *Goal specificity* is the clarity and precision of the goal. A goal of "increasing productivity" is not very specific; a goal of "increasing productivity by 3 percent in the next six months" is quite specific. Some goals, such as those involving costs, output, profitability, and growth, are readily amenable to specificity. Other goals, however, such as improving employee job satisfaction, morale, company image and reputation, ethics, and socially responsible behavior, may be much harder to state in specific terms. Like difficulty, specificity has been shown to be consistently related to performance. The study of timber truck drivers mentioned above, for example, also examined goal specificity. The initial loads the truck drivers were carrying were found to be 60 percent of the maximum weight each truck could haul. The managers set a new goal for drivers of 94 percent, which the drivers were soon able to reach. Thus the goal was both specific and difficult.

Because the theory attracted so much widespread interest and research support from researchers and managers alike, an expanded model of the goal-setting process was eventually proposed. The expanded model, shown in Figure 19.6, attempts to capture more fully the complexities of goal setting in organizations.

The expanded theory argues that goal-directed effort is a function of four goal attributes: difficulty and specificity, as already discussed, and acceptance and commitment. *Goal acceptance* is the extent to which a person accepts a goal as his or her own. *Goal commitment* is the extent to which she or he is personally interested in reaching the goal. The manager who vows to take whatever steps are necessary to cut costs by 10 percent has made a commitment to achieve the goal. Factors that can foster goal acceptance and commitment include participating in the

FIGURE 19.6 THE EXPANDED GOAL-SETTING THEORY OF MOTIVATION

One of the most important emerging theories of motivation is goal-setting theory. This theory suggests that goal difficulty, specificity, acceptance, and commitment combine to determine an individual's goal-directed effort. This effort, when complemented by appropriate organizational support and individual abilities and traits, results in performance. Finally, performance is seen as leading to intrinsic and extrinsic rewards that, in turn, result in employee satisfaction.

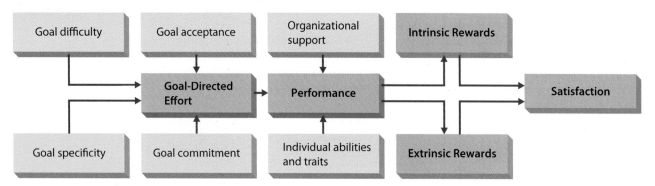

Source: Reprinted from Gary P. Latham and Edwin A. Locke, "A Motivational Technique That Works," *Organizational Dynamics*, Autumn 1979, p. 79, copyright © 1979 with permission from Elsevier Science.

goal-setting process, making goals challenging but realistic, and believing that goal achievement will lead to valued rewards.

The interaction of goal-directed effort, organizational support, and individual abilities and traits determines actual performance. Organizational support is whatever the organization does to help or hinder performance. Positive support might mean making available adequate personnel and a sufficient supply of raw materials; negative support might mean failing to fix damaged equipment. Individual abilities and traits are the skills and other personal characteristics necessary for doing a job. As a result of performance, a person receives various intrinsic and extrinsic rewards, which in turn influence satisfaction. Note that the latter stages of this model are quite similar to the Porter and Lawler expectancy model discussed earlier.[30]

Implications of the Process Perspectives

Expectancy theory can be useful for managers who are trying to improve the motivation of their subordinates. A series of steps can be followed to implement the basic ideas of the theory. First, figure out the outcomes each employee is likely to want. Second, decide what kinds and levels of performance are needed to meet organizational goals. Then make sure that the desired levels of performance are attainable. Also, make sure that desired outcomes and desired performance are linked. Next, analyze the complete situation for conflicting expectancies and ensure that the rewards are large enough. Finally, make sure the total system is equitable (fair to all). The single most important idea for managers to remember from equity theory is that if rewards are to motivate employees, they must be perceived as being equitable and fair. A second implication is that managers need to consider the nature of the "other" to whom the employee is comparing her- or himself. Goal-setting theory can be used to implement both expectancy and equity theory concepts.

Describe the basic motivational process that employees go through as reflected in expectancy theory.

Recall a situation in which you experienced inequity. Analyze the situation in terms of equity theory. Was your feeling of inequity justified?

CONCEPT CHECK

Reinforcement Perspectives on Motivation

A third element of the motivational process addresses why some behaviors are maintained over time and why other behaviors change. As we have seen, content perspectives deal with needs, whereas process perspectives explain why people choose various behaviors to satisfy needs and how they evaluate the equity of the rewards they get for those behaviors. Reinforcement perspectives explain the role of those rewards as they cause behavior to change or remain the same over time. Specifically, **reinforcement theory** argues that behavior that results in rewarding consequences is likely to be repeated, whereas behavior that results in punishing consequences is less likely to be repeated.[31]

Kinds of Reinforcement in Organizations

There are four basic kinds of reinforcement that can result from behavior—positive reinforcement, avoidance, punishment, and extinction.[32] These are summarized in Table 19.1. Two kinds of reinforcement strengthen or maintain behavior, whereas the other two weaken or decrease behavior.

Positive reinforcement, a method of strengthening behavior, is a reward or a positive outcome after a desired behavior is performed. When a manager observes an employee doing an especially good job and offers praise, the praise serves to positively reinforce the behavior of good work. Other positive reinforcers in organizations include pay raises, promotions, and awards. Employees who work at General Electric's customer service center receive clothing, sporting goods, and even trips to Disney World as rewards for outstanding performance. The other method of strengthening desired behavior is through **avoidance**. An

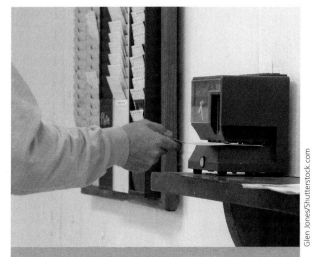

Punching a time clock to register when an employee starts and stops working each day is a practice that has been around for decades. But this method of determining employee pay—hours worked times an hourly wage rate—often has little to do with motivation. While this approach is presumably necessary in some settings, it nevertheless pays people for simply showing up rather than for what they actually accomplish in a day.

Glen Jones/Shutterstock.com

TABLE 19.1 ELEMENTS OF REINFORCEMENT THEORY

A manager who wants the best chance of reinforcing a behavior would likely offer the employee a positive reinforcement after a variable number of behaviors (variable-ratio reinforcement). For example, the manager could praise the employee after the third credit card application was received. Additional praise might be offered after the next five applications, then again after the next three, the next seven, the next four, and so on.

Arrangement of the Reinforcement Contingencies	
1. *Positive Reinforcement.* Strengthens behavior by providing a desirable consequence.	3. *Punishment.* Weakens behavior by providing an undesirable consequence.
2. *Avoidance.* Strengthens behavior by allowing escape from an undesirable consequence.	4. *Extinction.* Weakens behavior by ignoring it.

Schedules for Applying Reinforcement	
1. *Fixed-Interval.* Reinforcement is applied at fixed time intervals, regardless of behavior.	1. *Fixed-Ratio.* Reinforcement is applied after a fixed number of behaviors, regardless of time.
2. *Variable-Interval.* Reinforcement is applied at variable time intervals.	2. *Variable-Ratio.* Reinforcement is applied after a variable number of behaviors.

© Cengage Learning 2013

reinforcement theory
Approach to motivation that argues that behavior that results in rewarding consequences is likely to be repeated, whereas behavior that results in punishing consequences is less likely to be repeated

positive reinforcement
A method of strengthening behavior with rewards or positive outcomes after a desired behavior is performed

avoidance
Used to strengthen behavior by avoiding unpleasant consequences that would result if the behavior were not performed

employee may come to work on time to avoid a reprimand. In this instance, the employee is motivated to perform the behavior of punctuality to avoid an unpleasant consequence that is likely to follow tardiness.

Punishment is used by some managers to weaken undesired behaviors. When an employee is loafing, coming to work late, doing poor work, or interfering with the work of others, the manager might resort to reprimands, discipline, or fines. The logic is that the unpleasant consequence will reduce the likelihood that the employee will choose that particular behavior again. Given the counterproductive side effects of punishment (such as resentment and hostility), it is often advisable to use the other kinds of reinforcement if at all possible. Extinction can also be used to weaken behavior, especially behavior that has previously been rewarded. When an employee tells an off-color joke and the boss laughs, the laughter reinforces the behavior and the employee may continue to tell off-color jokes. By simply ignoring this behavior and not reinforcing it, the boss can cause the behavior to subside and eventually become "extinct."

Providing Reinforcement in Organizations

Not only is the kind of reinforcement important, but so is when or how often it occurs. Various strategies are possible for providing reinforcement. These are also listed in Table 19.1. The fixed-interval schedule provides reinforcement at fixed intervals of time, regardless of behavior. A good example of this schedule is the weekly or monthly paycheck. This method provides the least incentive for good work because employees know they will be paid regularly regardless of their efforts. A variable-interval schedule also uses time as the basis for reinforcement, but the time interval varies from one reinforcement to the next. This schedule is appropriate for praise or other rewards based on visits or inspections. When employees do not know when the boss is going to drop by, they tend to maintain a reasonably high level of effort all the time.

A fixed-ratio schedule gives reinforcement after a fixed number of behaviors, regardless of the time that elapses between behaviors. This results in an even higher level of effort. For example, when Sears is recruiting new credit card customers, salespersons get a small bonus for every fifth application returned from their department. Under this arrangement, motivation will be high because each application gets the person closer to the next bonus. The variable-ratio schedule, the most powerful schedule in terms of maintaining desired behaviors, varies the number of behaviors needed for each reinforcement. A supervisor who praises an employee for her second order, the seventh order after that, the ninth after that, then the fifth, and then the third is using a variable-ratio schedule. The employee is motivated to increase the frequency of the desired behavior because each performance increases the probability of receiving a reward. Of course, a variable-ratio schedule is difficult (if not impossible) to use for formal rewards such as pay because it would be too complicated to keep track of who was rewarded when.

Managers wanting to explicitly use reinforcement theory to motivate their employees generally do so with a technique called behavior modification, or OB Mod.[33] An OB Mod program starts by specifying behaviors that are to be increased (such as producing more units) or decreased (such as coming to work late). These target behaviors are then tied to specific forms or kinds of reinforcement. Although many organizations (such as Procter & Gamble and Ford) have used OB Mod, the best-known application was at Emery Air Freight. Management felt that the containers used to consolidate small shipments into fewer, larger shipments were not being packed efficiently. Through a system of self-monitored feedback and rewards, Emery increased container usage from 45 percent to 95 percent and saved over $3 million during the first three years of the program.[34]

punishment
Used to weaken undesired behaviors by using negative outcomes or unpleasant consequences when the behavior is performed

extinction
Used to weaken undesired behaviors by simply ignoring or not reinforcing them

fixed-interval schedule
Provides reinforcement at fixed intervals of time, such as regular weekly paychecks

variable-interval schedule
Provides reinforcement at varying intervals of time, such as occasional visits by the supervisor

fixed-ratio schedule
Provides reinforcement after a fixed number of behaviors regardless of the time interval involved, such as a bonus for every fifth sale

variable-ratio schedule
Provide reinforcement after varying numbers of behaviors are performed, such as the use of complements by a supervisor on an irregular basis

behavior modification (OB Mod)
Method for applying the basic elements of reinforcement theory in an organizational setting

Implications of the Reinforcement Perspectives

Reinforcement in organizations can be a powerful force for maintaining employee motivation. Of course, for reinforcement to be truly effective, managers need to use it in a manner consistent with the various types and schedules of reinforcement discussed above. In addition, managers must understand that they may be inadvertently motivating undesired or dysfunctional behaviors. For instance, if an employee routinely comes to work late but experiences no consequences, both that worker and others will see that it is all right to be late for work.

What are the basic kinds and schedules of reinforcement available to managers in organizations?

Describe a time when each of the different kinds of reinforcement affected your behavior.

CONCEPT CHECK

Popular Motivational Strategies

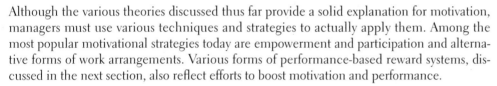

Although the various theories discussed thus far provide a solid explanation for motivation, managers must use various techniques and strategies to actually apply them. Among the most popular motivational strategies today are empowerment and participation and alternative forms of work arrangements. Various forms of performance-based reward systems, discussed in the next section, also reflect efforts to boost motivation and performance.

Empowerment and Participation

Empowerment and participation represent important methods that managers can use to enhance employee motivation. Empowerment is the process of enabling workers to set their own work goals, make decisions, and solve problems within their sphere of responsibility and authority. Participation is the process of giving employees a voice in making decisions about their own work. Thus empowerment is a somewhat broader concept that promotes participation in a wide variety of areas, including but not limited to work itself, work context, and work environment.[35]

The role of participation and empowerment in motivation can be expressed in terms of both content perspectives and expectancy theory. Employees who participate in decision making may be more committed to executing decisions properly. Furthermore, the successful process of making a decision, executing it, and then seeing the positive consequences can help satisfy one's need for achievement, provide recognition and responsibility, and enhance self-esteem. Simply being asked to participate in organizational decision making also may enhance an employee's self-esteem. In addition, participation should help clarify expectancies; that is, by participating in decision making, employees may better understand the linkage between their performance and the rewards they want most.

Areas of Participation At one level, employees can participate in addressing questions and making decisions about their own job. Instead of just telling them how to do their job, for example, managers can ask employees to make their own decisions about how to do it. Based on their own expertise and experience with their tasks, workers might be able to improve their own productivity. In many situations, they might also be well qualified to make decisions about what materials to use, what tools to use, and so forth.

It might also be helpful to let workers make decisions about administrative matters, such as work schedules. If jobs are relatively independent of one another, employees might decide when to change shifts, take breaks, go to lunch, and so forth. A work group or team might

empowerment
The process of enabling workers to set their own work goals, make decisions, and solve problems within their sphere of responsibility and authority

participation
The process of giving employees a voice in making decisions about their own work

also be able to schedule vacations and days off for all of its members. Furthermore, employees are getting increasing opportunities to participate in broader issues of product quality. Such participation has become a hallmark of successful Japanese and other international firms, and many U.S. companies have followed suit.

Techniques and Issues in Empowerment In recent years, many organizations have actively sought ways to extend participation beyond the traditional areas. Simple techniques, such as suggestion boxes and question-and-answer meetings, allow a certain degree of participation, for example. The basic motive has been to better capitalize on the assets and capabilities inherent in all employees. Thus many managers today prefer the term *empowerment* to *participation* because of its more comprehensive character.

One method used to empower workers is the use of work teams. Such teams are collections of employees empowered to plan, organize, direct, and control their own work. Their supervisor, rather than being a traditional "boss," plays more the role of a coach. The other method for empowerment is to change the team's overall method of organizing. The basic pattern is for an organization to eliminate layers from its hierarchy, thereby becoming much more decentralized. Power, responsibility, and authority are delegated as far down the organization as possible, placing control over work squarely in the hands of those who actually do it.[36]

Regardless of the specific technique or method used, however, empowerment will enhance organizational effectiveness only if certain conditions exist. First of all, the organization must be sincere in its efforts to spread power and autonomy to lower levels of the organization. Token efforts to promote participation in only a few areas are not likely to succeed. Second, the organization must be committed to maintaining participation and empowerment. Workers will be resentful if they are given more control, only to later have it reduced or taken away altogether. Third, workers must truly believe that they and their managers are working together in their joint best interests. In some factory settings, for instance, high-performing workers routinely conceal the secrets of their high output. They fear that if management learns those secrets, it will use them to ratchet up performance expectations.[37]

In addition, the organization must be systematic and patient in its efforts to empower workers. Turning over too much control too quickly can spell disaster. And finally, the organization must be prepared to increase its commitment to training. Employees given more freedom in how they work will quite likely need additional training to help them exercise that freedom most effectively.[38]

Alternative Forms of Work Arrangements

Many organizations today are also experimenting with a variety of alternative work arrangements. These alternative arrangements are generally intended to enhance employee motivation and performance by providing employees with greater flexibility in how and when they work. Among the more popular alternative work arrangements are variable work schedules, flexible work schedules, job sharing, and telecommuting.[39]

Variable Work Schedules Although there are many exceptions, of course, the traditional work schedule starts at 8:00 or 9:00 in the morning and ends at 5:00 in the evening, five days a week (and, of course, many managers work additional hours outside of these times). Unfortunately, this schedule makes it difficult to attend to routine personal business—going to the bank, seeing a doctor or dentist for a routine checkup, having a parent–teacher conference, getting an automobile serviced, and so forth. At a surface level, then, employees locked into this sort of arrangement may find it necessary to take a sick day or a vacation day to handle these activities. At a more unconscious level, some people may also feel so powerless and constrained by their job schedule as to feel increased resentment and frustration.

To help counter these problems, some businesses have adopted a **compressed work schedule**, working a full 40-hour week in fewer than the traditional five days.[40] One approach

compressed work schedule
Working a full 40-hour week in fewer than the traditional five days

involves working ten hours a day for four days, leaving an extra day off. Another alternative is for employees to work slightly less than ten hours a day, but to complete the 40 hours by lunchtime on Friday. And a few firms have tried having employees work 12 hours a day for three days, followed by four days off. Organizations that have used these forms of compressed workweeks include John Hancock, BP Amoco, and Philip Morris. One problem with this schedule is that when employees put in too much time in a single day, they tend to get tired and perform at a lower level later in the day.

A schedule that some organizations today are beginning to use is what they call a "nine-eighty" schedule. Under this arrangement, an employee works a traditional schedule one week and a compressed schedule the next, getting every other Friday off. In other words, they work 80 hours (the equivalent of two weeks of full-time work) in nine days. By alternating the regular and compressed schedules across half of its workforce, the organization can be fully staffed at all times, while still giving employees two full days off each month. Shell Oil and BP Amoco Chemicals are two of the firms that currently use this schedule.

Flexible Work Schedules Another promising alternative work arrangement is **flexible work schedules**, sometimes called *flextime*. Flextime gives employees more personal control over the times they work. The workday is broken down into two categories: flexible time and core time. All employees must be at their workstations during core time, but they can choose their own schedules during flexible time. Thus one employee may choose to start work early in the morning and leave in midafternoon, another to start in the late morning and work until late afternoon, and still another to start early in the morning, take a long lunch break, and work until late afternoon.

Organizations that have used the flexible work schedule method for arranging work include Hewlett-Packard, Microsoft, and Texas Instruments. The *World of Difference* box on page 490, entitled "The Balance of Trade-Offs," looks at the flexible-scheduling policies of a company whose program is also designed to attract and keep valuable female employees.

Job Sharing Yet another potentially useful alternative work arrangement is job sharing. In **job sharing**, two part-time employees share one full-time job. One person may perform the job from 8:00 A.M. to noon and the other from 1:00 P.M. to 5:00 P.M. Job sharing may be desirable for people who want to work only part time or when job markets are tight. For its part, the organization can accommodate the preferences of a broader range of employees and may benefit from the talents of more people.

Telecommuting An increasingly popular approach to alternative work arrangements is telecommuting—allowing employees to spend part of their time working offsite, usually at home. By using e-mail, the Internet, and other forms of information technology, many employees can maintain close contact with their organization and still get just as much (or even more) work done at home as if they were in their office. The increased power and sophistication of modern communication technology is making telecommuting easier and easier. One recent study found that nearly 40 percent of the U.S. workforce (33 million workers) are in jobs that allow for partial or complete telecommuting. Nearly half of AT&T's employees have received mobile and remote access technologies that provide them with the flexibility to work from various locations. And 40 percent of IBM's employees currently telecommute. (In the case of IBM, not only are employees more satisfied with the arrangement but the firm has saved close to $2.9 billion in office space needs.)[42]

> "I get to sit here and look out my window while I talk to customers [by telecommuting]—and watch the leaves changing, squirrels running around, and kids going off to school."
>
> —WALT SWANSON, AGILENT TECHNOLOGIES CUSTOMER SERVICE REPRESENTATIVE[41]

flexible work schedule
Work schedule in which employees have some control over the hours they choose to work; also called flextime

job sharing
When two part-time employees share one full-time job

telecommuting
Allowing employees to spend part of their time working offsite, usually at home

---

Summarize the basic concepts underlying employee empowerment and participation.

What work schedule would be most attractive to you? Least attractive?

CONCEPT CHECK

A WORLD OF DIFFERENCE

The Balance of Trade-Offs

Andresr/iStockphoto.com

The good news is that 60 percent of HR executives are satisfied with the work-life services that their companies offer employees. The bad news is that only 16 percent of their employees agree with them.

According to a study conducted in 2009 by the Corporate Executive Board (CEB), a global network of business professionals, the disconnect results from the fact that HR managers tend to value different services than employees do. They tend to assume, for example, that such expensive, high-profile services as onsite gyms and healthcare options are the kinds of things that employees want in a workplace that claims to promote good work-life balance. In reality, only about 20 percent of employees place any value on such services.

So, what *do* employees—managers and subordinates alike—really want? The answer seems to be *time*—or, more precisely, more control over it. More than 60 percent of the 50,000 workers polled in the CEB study specified *flexible schedules* as the single most important work-life benefit that an employer can offer. Flexible scheduling—or "flextime"—allows employees to adjust the time and/or place for completing their work.

One company that's happy with its experiments in flexible-work programs is KPMG, an Atlanta-based tax and audit consultancy. KPMG is in an industry in which turnover is traditionally higher for women than for men, but the numbers in the financial industry also reflect broader trends in the U.S. workforce. According to a survey reported by the *Harvard Business Review*, for instance, 24 percent of male executives take a career "off-ramp" at some point—that is, they voluntarily leave their careers for a period of time. When it comes to women, the figure is 37 percent; for women with children, it's 43 percent. Among the men, 12 percent have interrupted their careers to take care of children or elders; among the women, it's the reason cited by 44 percent.

Because of data like these, KPMG launched a campaign in 2002 to transform itself into an "employer of choice" by offering employees a range of options for balancing work and home life. Family-friendly policies fall into such categories as *flexibility* (flextime, telecommuting, job sharing) and *family resources* (backup child- and eldercare, discounts at childcare centers), and according to Barbara Wankoff, director of Workplace Solutions, 70 percent of company employees now work flexible hours. "Our employees," she says, "tend to be ambitious and career oriented. They want to develop professionally and build a career, but they also have lives as parents, sons or daughters, and spouses. So at KPMG we're promoting a culture of flexibility to help them manage the complexities of work and life."

In one recent year, KPMG managed to improve retention of female employees by 10 percent and to increase the total number of women in its workforce by 15 percent. KPMG also says that if it hadn't offered flexible scheduling to female employees with young children, it would have lost about two-thirds of them. "In order to retain the best and the brightest," says Kristen Piersol-Stockton, one of Barbara Wankoff's regional directors, "we have to be flexible in how, when, and where the work gets done."

References: Corporate Executive Board, "The Increasing Call for Work-Life Balance," *BusinessWeek*, March 27, 2009, www.businessweek.com on April 21, 2011; Georgetown University Law Center, "Flexible Work Arrangements: Selected Case Studies," *Workplace Flexibility 2010*, www.law.georgetown.edu on April 21, 2011; Network of Executive Women, "Balancing Acts: People-Friendly Policies That Build Productivity," 2007, www.newnewsletter.org on April 21, 2011; Emily Schmitt, "How a Flexible Work Schedule Can Help You Strike the Balance," *Forbes*, March 16, 2009, www.forbes.com on April 21, 2011.

Using Reward Systems to Motivate Performance

Aside from these types of motivational strategies, an organization's reward system is its most basic tool for managing employee motivation. An organizational **reward system** is the formal and informal mechanisms by which employee performance is defined, evaluated, and rewarded. Rewards that are tied specifically to performance, of course, have the greatest impact on enhancing both motivation and actual performance.

Performance-based rewards play a number of roles and address a variety of purposes in organizations. The major purposes involve the relationship of rewards to motivation and to performance. Specifically, organizations want employees to perform at relatively high levels and need to make it worth their effort to do so. When rewards are associated with higher levels of performance, employees will presumably be motivated to work harder to achieve those awards. At that point, their own self-interests coincide with the organization's interests. Performance-based rewards are also relevant regarding other employee behaviors, such as retention and citizenship.

Merit Reward Systems

Merit reward systems are one of the most fundamental forms of performance-based rewards.[43] **Merit pay** generally refers to pay awarded to employees on the basis of the relative value of their contributions to the organization. Employees who make greater contributions are given higher pay than those who make lesser contributions. **Merit pay plans**, then, are compensation plans that formally base at least some meaningful portion of compensation on merit.

The most general form of merit pay plan is to provide annual salary increases to individuals in the organization based on their relative merit. Merit, in turn, is usually determined or defined based on the individual's performance and overall contributions to the organization. For example, an organization using such a traditional merit pay plan might instruct its supervisors to give all their employees an average pay raise of, say, 4 percent. But the individual supervisor is further instructed to differentiate among high, average, and low performers. Under a simple system, for example, a manager might give the top 25 percent of her employees a 6 percent pay raise, the middle 50 percent a 4 percent or average pay raise, and the bottom 25 percent a 2 percent pay raise.

Incentive Reward Systems

Incentive reward systems are among the oldest forms of performance-based rewards. For example, some companies were using individual piece-rate incentive plans over 100 years ago.[44] Under a **piece-rate incentive plan**, the organization pays an employee a certain amount of money for every unit she or he produces. For example, an employee might be paid $1 for every dozen units of product that are successfully completed. But such simplistic systems fail to account for such facts as minimum wage levels and rely very heavily on the assumptions that performance is totally under an individual's control and that the individual employee does a single task continuously throughout his or her work time. Thus most organizations today that try to use incentive compensation systems use more sophisticated methodologies.

Incentive Pay Plans Generally speaking, *individual incentive plans* reward individual performance on a real-time basis. In other words, rather than increasing a person's base salary at the end of the year, an individual instead receives some level of salary increase or financial reward in conjunction with demonstrated outstanding performance in close proximity to when that performance occurred. Individual incentive systems are most likely to be used in cases in which performance can be objectively assessed in terms of number of units of

reward system
The formal and informal mechanisms by which employee performance is defined, evaluated, and rewarded

merit pay
Pay awarded to employees on the basis of the relative value of their contributions to the organization

merit pay plan
Compensation plan that formally bases at least some meaningful portion of compensation on merit

piece-rate incentive plan
Reward system wherein the organization pays an employee a certain amount of money for every unit she or he produces

output or similar measures, rather than on a subjective assessment of performance by a superior. WD-40 Company uses an individual incentive plan that covers almost its entire workforce. The firm's managers credit the incentive plan with motivating its employees to perform at high levels during the 2008–2010 recession in ways that enabled the firm to achieve record profits.[45]

Some variations on a piece-rate system are still fairly popular. Although many of these still resemble the early plans in most ways, a well-known piece-rate system at Lincoln Electric illustrates how an organization can adapt the traditional model to achieve better results. For years, Lincoln's employees were paid individual incentive payments based on their performance. However, the amount of money shared (the incentive pool) was based on the company's profitability. There was also a well-organized system whereby employees could make suggestions for increasing productivity. There was motivation to do this because the employees received one-third of the profits (another third went to the stockholders, and the last share was retained for improvements and seed money). Thus the pool for incentive payments was determined by profitability, and an employee's share of this pool was a function of his or her base pay and rated performance based on the piece-rate system. Lincoln Electric was most famous, however, because of the stories (which were apparently typical) of production workers' receiving a year-end bonus payment that equaled their yearly base pay.[46] In recent years, Lincoln has partially abandoned its famous system for business reasons, but it still serves as a benchmark for other companies seeking innovative piece-rate pay systems.

Perhaps the most common form of individual incentive is *sales commissions* that are paid to people engaged in sales work. For example, sales representatives for consumer products firms and retail sales agents may be compensated under this type of commission system. In general, the person might receive a percentage of the total volume of attained sales as her or his commission for a period of time. Some sales jobs are based entirely on commission, whereas others use a combination of base minimum salary with additional commission as an incentive. Notice that these plans put a considerable amount of the salespersons' earnings "at risk." In other words, although organizations often have drawing accounts to allow the salesperson to live during lean periods (the person then "owes" this money back to the organization), if he or she does not perform well, he or she will not be paid much. The portion of salary based on commission is simply not guaranteed and is paid only if sales reach some target level.

Other Forms of Incentive Occasionally organizations may also use other forms of incentives to motivate people. For example, a nonmonetary incentive, such as additional time off or a special perk, might be a useful incentive. For example, a company might establish a sales contest in which the sales group that attains the highest level of sales increase over a specified period of time will receive an extra week of paid vacation, perhaps even at an arranged place, such as a tropical resort or a ski lodge.[47]

A major advantage of incentives relative to merit systems is that incentives are typically a one-shot reward and do not accumulate by becoming part of the individual's base salary. Stated differently, an individual whose outstanding performance entitles him or her to a financial incentive gets the incentive only one time, based on that level of performance. If the individual's performance begins to erode in the future, then the individual may receive a lesser incentive or perhaps no incentive in the future. As a consequence, his or her base salary remains the same or is perhaps increased at a relatively moderate pace; he or she receives one-time incentive rewards as recognition for exemplary performance. Furthermore, because these plans, by their very nature, focus on one-time events, it is much easier for the organization to change the focus of the incentive plan. At a simple level, for example, an organization can set up an incentive plan for selling one product during one quarter, but then shift the incentive to a different product the next quarter, as the situation requires. Automobile companies like Ford and GM routinely do this by reducing sales incentives for models that are selling very well and increasing sales incentives for models that are selling below expectations or are about to be discontinued.

Team and Group Incentive Reward Systems

The merit compensation and incentive compensation systems described in the preceding sections deal primarily with performance-based reward arrangements for individuals. There also exists a different set of performance-based reward programs that are targeted for teams and groups. These programs are particularly important for managers to understand today, given the widespread trends toward team- and group-based methods of work and organization.[48]

Common Team and Group Reward Systems

There are two commonly used types of team and group reward systems. One type used in many organizations is an approach called gainsharing. Gainsharing programs are designed to share the cost savings from productivity improvements with employees. The underlying assumption of gainsharing is that employees and the employer have the same goals and thus should appropriately share in incremental economic gains.[49]

As more and more businesses start using teams to get work done, they must also consider the implications for reward systems. When people work as individuals, it is often relatively easy to assess their contributions and decide on the most appropriate rewards. But when it's the team that makes contributions to the organization, it's not always easy to know how to reward its members.

In general, organizations that use gainsharing start by measuring team- or group-level productivity. It is important that this measure be valid and reliable and that it truly reflect current levels of performance by the team or group. The team or work group itself is then given the task of attempting to lower costs and otherwise improve productivity through any measures that its members develop and its manager approves. Resulting cost savings or productivity gains that the team or group is able to achieve are then quantified and translated into dollar values. A predetermined formula is then used to allocate these dollar savings between the employer and the employees themselves. A typical formula for distributing gainsharing savings is to provide 25 percent to the employees and 75 percent to the company.

One specific type of gainsharing plan is an approach called the Scanlon plan. This approach was developed by Joseph Scanlon in 1927. The Scanlon plan has the same basic strategy as gainsharing plans, in that teams or groups of employees are encouraged to suggest strategies for reducing costs. However, the distribution of these gains is usually tilted much more heavily toward employees, with employees usually receiving between two-thirds and three-fourths of the total cost savings that the plan achieves. Furthermore, the distribution of cost savings resulting from the plan is given not just to the team or group that suggested and developed the ideas, but across the entire organization.

Other Types of Team and Group Rewards

Although gainsharing and Scanlon-type plans are among the most popular group incentive reward systems, there are other systems that are also used by some organizations. Some companies, for example, have begun to use true incentives at the team or group level. Just as with individual incentives, team or group incentives tie rewards directly to performance increases. And, like individual incentives, team or group incentives are paid as they are earned rather than being added to employees' base salary. The incentives are distributed at the team or group level, however, rather than at the individual level. In some cases, the distribution may be based on the existing salary of each employee, with incentive bonuses being given on a proportionate basis. In other settings, each member of the team or group receives the same incentive pay.

gainsharing programs
Designed to share the cost savings from productivity improvements with employees

Scanlon plan
Similar to gainsharing, but the distribution of gains is tilted much more heavily toward employees

Some companies also use nonmonetary rewards at the team or group level—most commonly in the form of prizes and awards. For example, a company might designate the particular team in a plant or subunit of the company that achieves the highest level of productivity increase, the highest level of reported customer satisfaction, or a similar index of performance. The reward itself might take the form of additional time off, as described earlier in this chapter, or a tangible award, such as a trophy or plaque. In any event, the idea is that the reward is at the team level and serves as recognition of exemplary performance by the entire team.

There are also other kinds of team- or group-level incentives that go beyond the contributions of a specific work group. These are generally organization-wide kinds of incentives. One longstanding method for this approach is *profit sharing*. In a profit-sharing approach, at the end of the year some portion of the company's profits is paid into a profit-sharing pool that is then distributed to all employees. Either this amount is distributed at that time, or it is put into an escrow account and payment is deferred until the employee retires.

The basic rationale behind profit-sharing systems is that everyone in the organization can expect to benefit when the company does well. But, on the other side of the coin, during bad economic times, when the company is perhaps achieving low or perhaps no profits, then no profit sharing is paid out. This sometimes results in negative reactions from employees, who have perhaps come to feel that profit sharing is really a part of their annual compensation.

Employee stock ownership plans (ESOPs) also represent a group-level reward system that some companies use. Under the employee stock ownership plan, employees are gradually given a major stake in ownership of a corporation. The typical form of this plan involves the company's taking out a loan, which is then used to buy a portion of its own stock in the open market. Over time, company profits are then used to pay off this loan. Employees, in turn, receive a claim on ownership of some portion of the stock held by the company, based on their seniority and perhaps on their performance. Eventually, each individual becomes an owner of the company. One recent study found that 20 percent of employees in the private sector (25 million Americans) reported owning stock in their companies, with 10 percent holding stock options.[50]

We'll end this section by pointing out that, under certain adverse circumstances, even successful approaches to employee satisfaction have limitations. For an example, see the *Change* box entitled "The NetApp Approach to Net Jobs" on page 495.

Executive Compensation

The top-level executives of most companies have separate compensation programs and plans. These are intended to reward these executives for their performance and for the performance of the organization.

Standard Forms of Executive Compensation Most senior executives receive their compensation in two forms. One form is a *base salary*. As with the base salary of any staff member or professional member of an organization, the base salary of an executive is a guaranteed amount of money that the individual will be paid. For example, in 2010 Lockheed Martin paid its CEO, Robert Stevens, $1,800,000 in base salary.[51]

Above and beyond this base salary, however, most executives also receive one or more forms of incentive pay. The traditional method of incentive pay for executives is in the form of bonuses. Bonuses, in turn, are usually determined by the performance of the organization. Thus, at the end of the year, some portion of a corporation's profits may be diverted into a bonus pool. Senior executives then receive a bonus expressed as a percentage of this bonus pool. The chief executive officer and president are obviously likely to get a larger percentage bonus than a vice president. The exact distribution of the bonus pool is usually specified ahead of time in the individual's employment contract. Some organizations intentionally leave the distribution unspecified, so that the board of directors has the flexibility to give

THE MORE THINGS CHANGE

The NetApp Approach to Net Jobs

AP Photo/Paul Sakuma

#1

In January 2009, when they placed NetApp* at the top of their list of the "100 Best Companies to Work For," the editors at *Fortune* magazine noted that the storage and data-management company "has gained market share during the slump, hasn't had layoffs, and has more than $2 billion in cash on hand to help it ride out the global financial crisis." A month later, NetApp announced that it was taking "a number of steps to better align our resources with the business outlook. This restructuring includes a reduction of about 6 percent of the global workforce, as well as the reallocation of other resources to initiatives designed to increase operating efficiency and build a foundation for additional market-share gains."

In fact, about 530 of the firm's more than 8,000 global employees were laid off, either as a result of the lingering recession or "restructuring." In any case, blogged one employee, "for 6 percent of the staff, it's no longer the best place to work."

In characterizing the firm as the number-one U.S. company to work for, the Great Place to Work Institute had attributed "the quality of the workplace at NetApp" to its "high trust culture." NetApp leaders, said Amy Lyman, the Institute's director of corporate research, "reach out to employees, sharing information, support, and time in a variety of ways." She reported that, as the recession deepened, the company took steps to ensure that all employees were "kept well informed of changes in projections with frequent communications from senior leaders." A Vice Presidents' Forum, for example, convened every two weeks to share economic information and find out what was on employees' minds. To help managers respond to questions, recognize signs of stress, and involve employees in discussions of issues facing the company, NetApp distributed a kit entitled "Communicating with Employees During Tough Times."

The goal of such programs was twofold: to let NetApp employees know that the company would provide support and to help them understand the effect of the economic downturn on the decisions being made by its leadership. At the time, however, former executive chairman Dan Warmenhoven said that "we can't predict our future. We don't know if it's going up or down." He also admitted that he wasn't optimistic about immediate prospects for growth. He wouldn't rule out modest growth per quarter, but he also warned that it would take years for NetApp to get back to the levels that it had enjoyed as recently as the fall of 2008.

"Not surprising," replied one worker whose response indicates how difficult it is for any company to juggle messages that employees often (and sometimes rightly) perceive as motivated less by the desire to reveal information than to conceal it. "Over the previous quarter," continued the anonymous employee, "Warmenhoven and [CEO Tom] Georgens slowly changed their tune from 'belt-tightening, no layoffs,' to 'we'll only do layoffs if we absolutely to have to,' to 'gee, things are looking really bad, we don't know what will happen.'"

What *did* happen turned out to be good news for both the company and its workforce. Revenue for fiscal 2010 was up 51 percent over fiscal 2009, and NetApp immediately launched efforts to fill 800 job openings worldwide.

References: "100 Best Companies to Work For," *Fortune*, February 2, 2009, http://money.cnn.com on April 21, 2011; Amy Lyman, "NetApp: Culture—Values—Leadership," Great Place to Work Institute, 2009, http://resources.greatplacetowork.com on April 21, 2011; Peter Burrows, "NetApp Rethinks the Future," *BusinessWeek*, February 11, 2009, www.businessweek.com on April 21, 2011; Sathya Mithra Ashok, "External Storage Is Back from Recession: Gartner," *Computer News Middle East*, March 9, 2011, www.computernewsme.com on April 21, 2011; John Murawski, "NetApp Trumpets Its Hiring Binge," *News Observer*, May 14, 2010, www.newsobserver.com on April 21, 2011.

*Recall that NetApp is also the subject of our *Management in Action* story in Chapter 3.

larger rewards to those individuals deemed to be most deserving. Lockheed Martin's Robert Stevens received a cash bonus of about $8.6 million in 2010.[52]

Special Forms of Executive Compensation   Beyond base salary and bonuses, many executives receive other kinds of compensation as well. A form of executive compensation that has received a lot of attention in recent years has been various kinds of stock options. A **stock option plan** is established to give senior managers the option to buy company stock in the future at a predetermined fixed price. The basic idea underlying stock option plans is that if the executives contribute to higher levels of organizational performance, then the company stock should increase in value. Then the executive will be able to purchase the stock at the predetermined price, which theoretically should be lower than its future market price. The difference then becomes profit for the individual. Lockheed Martin awarded Robert Stevens stock options with a potential value of $7 million.[53]

Stock options continue to grow in popularity as a means of compensating top managers. Options are seen as a means of aligning the interests of the manager with those of the stockholders, and given that they do not cost the organization much (other than some possible dilution of stock values), they will probably be even more popular in the future. In fact, a recent study by KPMG Peat Marwick indicates that for senior management whose salary exceeds $250,000, stock options represent the largest share of the salary mix (relative to salary and other incentives). Furthermore, when we consider all of top management (annual salary over $750,000), stock options comprise a full 60 percent of their total compensation. And the Peat Marwick report indicates that even among exempt employees at the $35,000-a-year level, stock options represent 13 percent of total compensation.

But events in recent years have raised serious questions about the use of stock options as incentives for executives. For example, several executives at Enron allegedly withheld critical financial information from the markets, cashed in their stock options (while Enron stock was trading at $80 a share), and then watched as the financial information was made public and the stock fell to less than $1 a share. Of course, these actions (if proven) are illegal, but they raise questions in the public's mind about the role of stock options and about the way organizations treat stock options from an accounting perspective. Most organizations have *not* treated stock options as liabilities, even though, when exercised, they are exactly that. There is concern that by not carrying stock options as liabilities, the managers are overstating the value of the company, which, of course, can help raise the stock price. Finally, when stock prices fall below the option price they become essentially worthless.

Aside from stock option plans, other kinds of executive compensation are also used by some companies. Among the more popular are such perquisites as memberships in private clubs, access to company recreational facilities, and similar considerations. Some organizations also make available to senior executives low- or no-interest loans. These are often given to new executives whom the company is hiring from other companies and serve as an incentive for the individual to leave his or her current job to join a new organization. Lockheed Martin's Robert Stevens received $1.6 million in other compensation during 2010 for things such as perks, tax reimbursement, and payments for life insurance.[54]

Criticisms of Executive Compensation   In recent years, executive compensation has come under fire for a variety of reasons. One major reason is that the levels of executive compensation attained by some managers seem simply too large for the average shareholder to understand. It is not uncommon, for instance, for a senior executive of a major corporation to earn total income from his or her job in a given year of well in excess of $1 million. Sometimes the income of chief executive officers can be substantially more than this. Thus, just as the typical person has difficulty comprehending the astronomical salaries paid to some movie stars and sports stars, so, too, would the average person be aghast at the astronomical salaries paid to some senior executives.

stock option plan
Established to give senior managers the option to buy company stock in the future at a predetermined fixed price

Compounding the problem created by perceptions of executive compensation is the fact that there often seems to be little or no relationship between the performance of the organization and the compensation paid to its senior executives.[55] Certainly, if an organization is performing at an especially high level and its stock price is increasing consistently, then most observers would agree that the senior executives responsible for this growth should be entitled to attractive rewards.[56] However, it is more difficult to understand a case in which executives are paid huge salaries and other forms of rewards when their company is performing at only a marginal level, yet this is fairly common today. For example, in 2010, General Electric CEO Jeffrey Immelt received stock options increasing his total compensation to $28.5 million from $9.8 million in 2009, a jump of 188 percent. However, shareholder returns have continued to fall behind that of similar companies over the past three years (24.33 percent compared to 32.21 percent in 2010).[57] Similarly, Johnson & Johnson CEO William Weldon received a substantial pay raise in 2011 despite numerous product recalls throughout the previous two years that cost the company $900 million.[58]

Finally, we should note that the gap between the earnings of the CEO and the earnings of a typical employee is enormous. First of all, the size of the gap has been increasing in the United States. In 1980 the typical CEO earned 42 times the earnings of an ordinary worker; by 1990 this ratio had increased to 85 times the earnings of an ordinary worker; in 2009 the ratio was 263 times the earnings of a typical worker. In Japan, on the other hand, the CEO-to-worker pay ratio is 16 times; in Germany the ratio is 13 times.[59]

New Approaches to Performance-Based Rewards

Some organizations have started to recognize that they can leverage the value of the incentives they offer to their employees and to groups in their organization by allowing those individuals and groups to have a say in how rewards are distributed. For example, at the extreme, a company could go so far as to grant salary increase budgets to work groups and then allow the members of those groups themselves to determine how the rewards are going to be allocated among the various members of the group. This strategy would appear to hold considerable promise if everyone understands the performance arrangements that exist in the work group and everyone is committed to being fair and equitable. Unfortunately, it can also create problems if people in a group feel that rewards are not being distributed fairly.[60]

Organizations are also getting increasingly innovative in their incentive programs. For example, some now offer stock options to all their employees, rather than just to top executives. In addition, some firms are looking into ways to purely individualize reward systems. For instance, a firm might offer one employee a paid three-month sabbatical every two years in exchange for a 20 percent reduction in salary. Another employee in the same firm might be offered a 10 percent salary increase in exchange for a 5 percent reduction in company contributions to the person's retirement account. Corning, General Electric, and Microsoft are among the firms closely studying this option.[61]

Regardless of the method used, however, it is also important that managers in an organization effectively communicate what rewards are being distributed and the basis for that distribution. In other words, if incentives are being distributed on the basis of perceived individual contributions to the organization, then members of the organization should be informed of that fact. This will presumably better enable them to understand the basis on which pay increases and other incentives and performance-based rewards have been distributed.

Summarize the essential elements of merit and incentive reward systems.

What are your personal opinions regarding executive compensation?

CONCEPT CHECK

Summary of Learning Objectives and Key Points

1. Characterize the nature of motivation, including its importance and basic historical perspectives.

   - Motivation is the set of forces that cause people to behave in certain ways.
   - Motivation is an important consideration for managers because, along with ability and environmental factors, it determines individual performance.
   - Thinking about motivation has evolved from the traditional view through the human relations approach to the human resource view.

2. Identify and describe the major content perspectives on motivation.

   - Content perspectives on motivation are concerned with what factor or factors cause motivation.
   - Popular content theories include Maslow's needs hierarchy, the ERG theory, and Herzberg's two-factor theory.
   - Other important needs are the needs for achievement, affiliation, and power.

3. Identify and describe the major process perspectives on motivation.

   - Process perspectives on motivation deal with how motivation occurs.
   - Expectancy theory suggests that people are motivated to perform if they believe that their effort will result in high performance, that this performance will lead to rewards, and that the positive aspects of the outcomes outweigh the negative aspects.
   - Equity theory is based on the premise that people are motivated to achieve and maintain social equity.
   - Attribution theory is a new process theory.

4. Describe reinforcement perspectives on motivation.

   - The reinforcement perspective focuses on how motivation is maintained.
   - Its basic assumption is that behavior that results in rewarding consequences is likely to be repeated, whereas behavior resulting in negative consequences is less likely to be repeated.
   - Reinforcement contingencies can be arranged in the form of positive reinforcement, avoidance, punishment, and extinction, and they can be provided on fixed-interval, variable-interval, fixed-ratio, or variable-ratio schedules.

5. Identify and describe popular motivational strategies.

   - Managers use a variety of motivational strategies derived from the various theories of motivation.
   - Common strategies include empowerment and participation and alternative forms of work arrangements, such as variable work schedules, flexible work schedules, and telecommuting.

6. Describe the role of organizational reward systems in motivation.

   - Reward systems also play a key role in motivating employee performance.
   - Popular methods include merit reward systems, incentive reward systems, and team and group incentive reward systems.
   - Executive compensation is also intended to serve as motivation for senior managers but has currently come under close scrutiny and criticism.

Discussion Questions

Questions for Review

1. Each historical perspective on motivation built on the earlier perspectives and differed from them in some ways. Describe the similarities and differences between the traditional approach and the human relations approach. Then describe the similarities and differences between the human relations approach and the human resource approach.

2. Compare and contrast content, process, and reinforcement perspectives on motivation.

3. Explain how goal-setting theory works. How is goal setting different from merely asking a worker to "do your best"?

4. Describe some new forms of working arrangements. How do these alternative arrangements increase motivation?

Questions for Analysis

5. Choose one theory from the content perspectives and one from the process perspectives. Describe actions that a manager might take to increase worker motivation under each of the theories. What differences do you see between the theories in terms of their implications for managers?

6. Can factors from both the content and the process perspectives be acting on a worker at the same time? Explain why or why not. Whether you answered yes or no to the previous question, explain the implications for managers.

Questions for Application

8. Think about the worst job you have held. What approach to motivation was used in that organization? Now think about the best job you have held. What approach to motivation was used there? Can you base any conclusions on this limited information? If so, what are they?

9. Interview both a manager and a worker (or administrator and faculty member) from a local organization. What views

7. How do rewards increase motivation? What would happen if an organization gave too few rewards? What would happen if it gave too many?

of or approaches to motivation seem to be in use in that organization? Do the manager's views differ from the worker's? If so, how do you explain the differing perceptions?

10. Consider a class you have taken. Using just that one class, offer examples of times when the professor used positive reinforcement, avoidance, punishment, and extinction to manage students' behavior.

CengageNow™ Highlights

Now use your CengageNow™ homework to help you:
• Apply management theories in your life
• Assess your management skills
• Master management terms and concepts
• Apply your knowledge to real-world situations
• Analyze and solve challenging management problems

In order to take advantage of these elements, your instructor will need to have set up a course for your class within CengageNow™. Ask your instructor to contact his/her Cengage sales representative and Digital Solutions Manager to explore testing CengageNow™ in your course this term.

CHAPTER

Managing Leadership and Influence Processes

LEARNING OBJECTIVES

After studying this chapter, you should be able to:

1. Describe the nature of leadership and relate leadership to management.

2. Discuss and evaluate the two generic approaches to leadership.

3. Identify and describe the major situational approaches to leadership.

4. Identify and describe three related approaches to leadership.

5. Describe three emerging approaches to leadership.

6. Discuss political behavior in organizations and how it can be managed.

When to Stand on Your Head and Other Tips from the Top

MANAGEMENT IN ACTION

It isn't easy leading a U.S. business these days. Leaving aside the global recession, the passion for "lean and mean" operations means that there are fewer workers to do more work. Globalization means keeping abreast of cross-cultural differences. Knowledge industries present unique leadership challenges requiring better communication skills and greater flexibility. Advances in technology have opened unprecedented channels of communication. Now more than ever, leaders must be able to do just about everything and more of it. As U.S. Senator and former presidential candidate John McCain puts it, "[Leadership is] a game of pinball, and you're the ball." Fortunately, a few of corporate America's veteran leaders have some tips for those who still want to follow their increasingly treacherous path.

First of all, if you think you're being overworked—if your hours are too long and your schedule is too demanding—odds are, you're right: Most people—including executives—*are* overworked. And in some industries, they're *particularly* overworked. U.S. airlines, for example, now service 100 million more passengers

> "[Leadership is] a game of pinball, and you're the ball."
>
> —U.S. SENATOR JOHN MCCAIN

annually than they did just five years ago—with 70,000 fewer workers. "I used to manage my time," quips one airline executive. "Now I manage my energy." In fact, many high-ranking managers have realized that energy is a key factor in their ability to complete tasks on tough schedules. Most top corporate leaders work 80 to 100 hours a week, and a lot of them have found that regimens that allow them to refuel and refresh make it possible for them to keep up the pace.

Carlos Ghosn, who's currently president of Renault *and* CEO of Nissan, believes in regular respites from his work-week routine. "I don't bring my work home. I play with my four children and spend time with my family on weekends," says Ghosn. "I come up with good ideas as a result of becoming stronger after being recharged." Google VP Marissa Mayer admits that "I can get by on

Bill Gates is always at the forefront of information technology. He's shown here illustrating how social networking might look in the future.

Justin Sullivan/Getty Images

four to six hours of sleep," but she also takes a week-long vacation three times a year. Global HR consultant Robert Freedman devotes two minutes every morning to doodling on napkins. Not only does it give him a chance to meditate, but he's thinking about publishing both his doodles and his meditations in a coffee-table book.

Many leaders report that playing racquetball, running marathons, practicing yoga, or just getting regular exercise helps them to recover from overwork. Hank Greenberg, who's currently CEO of the financial-services firm C. V. Starr & Co., plays tennis for most of the year and skis in the winter months. "I'm addicted to exercise," he says, because it "unwinds me." Max Levchin, founder of Slide, which makes widgets for social-networking sites, prefers "80 or 90 hard miles on a road bike . . . starting early on Saturday mornings." Eighty-eight-year-old Viacom CEO Sumner Redstone rises at 5 A.M. and hits both the exercise bike and treadmill before the markets open. (Redstone also recommends "lots of fish and plenty of antioxidants.") Finally, Strauss Zelnick, CEO and chairman of Take-Two Interactive Software, is *really* serious about exercise:

> I try to book my exercise like a meeting and try hard never to cancel it. . . . Generally I try to do an exercise class at the gym once a week; I train for an hour with a trainer once or twice a week; I cycle with a group of friends for an hour once to three times a week, and I lift weights with a friend or colleague twice or three times a week.

Effective leaders also take control of information flow—which means managing it, not reducing the flow until it's as close to a trickle as they can get it. Like most executives, for example, Mayer can't get by without multiple sources of information: "I always have my laptop with me," he reports, and "I adore my cell phone." Starbucks CEO Howard Schultz receives a morning voicemail summarizing the previous day's sales results and reads three newspapers a day. Mayer watches the news all day, and Bill Gross, a securities portfolio manager, keeps on eye on six monitors displaying real-time investment data.

On the other hand, Gross stands on his head to force himself to take a break from communicating. When he's upright again, he tries to find time to concentrate. "Eliminating the noise," he says, "is critical. . . . I only pick up the phone three or four times a day. . . . I don't want to be connected—I want to be disconnected." Ghosn,

whose schedule requires weekly intercontinental travel, uses bilingual assistants to screen and translate information—one assistant for information from Europe (where Renault is), one for information from Japan (where Nissan is), and one for information from the United States (where Ghosn often has to be when he doesn't have to be in Europe or Japan). Clothing designer Vera Wang also uses an assistant to filter information. "The barrage of calls is so enormous," she says, "that if I just answered calls I'd do nothing else. . . . If I were to go near e-mail, there'd be even more obligations, and I'd be in [a mental hospital] with a white jacket on."

Not surprisingly, Microsoft chairman Bill Gates integrates the role of his assistant into a high-tech information-organizing system:

> On my desk I have three screens, synchronized to form a single desktop. I can drag items from one screen to the next. Once you have that large display area, you'll never go back, because it has a direct impact on productivity.

> The screen on the left has my list of e-mails. On the center screen is usually the specific e-mail I'm reading and responding to. And my browser is on the right-hand screen. This setup gives me the ability to glance and see what new has come in while I'm working on something and to bring up a link that's related to an e-mail and look at it while the e-mail is still in front of me.

> At Microsoft, e-mail is the medium of choice. . . . I get about 100 e-mails a day. We apply filtering to keep it to that level. E-mail comes straight to me from anyone I've ever corresponded with, anyone from Microsoft, Intel, HP, and all the other partner companies, and anyone I know. And I always see a write-up from my assistant of any other e-mail, from companies that aren't on my permission list or individuals I don't know. . . .

> We're at the point now where the challenge isn't how to communicate effectively with e-mail—it's ensuring that you spend your time on the e-mail that matters most. I use tools like "in-box rules" and search folders to mark and group messages based on their content and importance.[1]

This chapter examines people like Bill Gates, Carlos Ghosn, and Strauss Zelnick to find out not only how they manage their physical and mental health, but how they focus on the tasks of leadership and how they see its role in management. We characterize the nature of leadership and discuss the three major approaches to studying leadership—traits, behaviors, and situations. After examining other perspectives on leadership, we conclude by describing another approach to influencing others—political behavior in organizations.

The Nature of Leadership

In Chapter 19, we described various models and perspectives on employee motivation. From the manager's standpoint, trying to motivate people is an attempt to influence their behavior. In many ways, leadership, too, is an attempt to influence the behavior of others. In this section, we first define leadership, then differentiate it from management, and conclude by relating it to power.

The Meaning of Leadership

Leadership is both a process and a property.[2] As a process—focusing on what leaders actually do—leadership is the use of noncoercive influence to shape the group or organization's goals, motivate behavior toward the achievement of those goals, and help define group or organizational culture.[3] As a property, leadership is the set of characteristics attributed to individuals who are perceived to be leaders. Thus leaders are (1) people who can influence the behaviors of others without having to rely on force or (2) people whom others accept as leaders.

Leadership and Management

From these definitions, it should be clear that leadership and management are related, but they are not the same. A person can be a manager, a leader, both, or neither.[4] Some of the basic distinctions between the two are summarized in Table 20.1. At the left side of the table are four elements that differentiate leadership from management. The two columns show how each element differs when considered from a management and from a leadership point of view. For example, when executing plans, managers focus on monitoring results, comparing them with goals, and correcting deviations. In contrast, the leader focuses on energizing people to overcome bureaucratic hurdles to reach goals.

Organizations need both management and leadership if they are to be effective. Leadership is necessary to create change, and management is necessary to achieve orderly results. Management in conjunction with leadership can produce orderly change, and leadership in conjunction with management can keep the organization properly aligned with its environment. Indeed, perhaps part of the reason why executive compensation has soared in recent years is the belief that management and leadership skills reflect a critical but rare combination that can lead to organizational success.

Leadership and Power

To fully understand leadership, it is necessary to understand power. Power is the ability to affect the behavior of others. One can have power without actually using it. For example, a football coach has the power to bench a player who is not performing up to par. The coach seldom has to use this power because players recognize that the power exists and work hard to keep their starting positions. In organizational settings, there are usually five kinds of power: legitimate, reward, coercive, referent, and expert power.[5]

leadership
As a process, the use of noncoercive influence to shape the group's or organization's goals, motivate behavior toward the achievement of those goals, and help define group or organizational culture; as a property, the set of characteristics attributed to individuals who are perceived to be leaders

leaders
People who can influence the behaviors of others without having to rely on force; those accepted by others as leaders

power
The ability to affect the behavior of others

TABLE 20.1 DISTINCTIONS BETWEEN MANAGEMENT AND LEADERSHIP

Management and leadership are related, but distinct, constructs. Managers and leaders differ in how they create an agenda, develop a rationale for achieving the agenda, execute plans, and in the types of outcomes they achieve.

Activity	Management	Leadership
Creating an agenda	*Planning and Budgeting.* Establishing detailed steps and timetables for achieving needed results; allocating the resources necessary to make those needed results happen	*Establishing Direction.* Developing a vision of the future, often the distant future, and strategies for producing the changes needed to achieve that vision
Developing a human network for achieving the agenda	*Organizing and Staffing.* Establishing some structure for accomplishing plan requirements, staffing that structure with individuals, delegating responsibility and authority for carrying out the plan, providing policies and procedures to help guide people, and creating methods or systems to monitor implementation	*Aligning People.* Communicating the direction by words and deeds to everyone whose cooperation may be needed to influence the creation of teams and coalitions that understand the visions and strategies and accept their validity
Executing plans	*Controlling and Problem Solving.* Monitoring results versus planning in some detail, identifying deviations, and then planning and organizing to solve these problems	*Motivating and Inspiring.* Energizing people to overcome major political, bureaucratic, and resource barriers by satisfying very basic, but often unfulfilled, human needs
Outcomes	Produces a degree of predictability and order and has the potential to produce consistently major results expected by various stakeholders (for example, for customers, always being on time; for stockholders, being on budget)	Produces change, often to a dramatic degree, and has the potential to produce extremely useful change (for example, new products that customers want, new approaches to labor relations that help make a firm more competitive)

Source: Reprinted with permission of The Free Press, a division of Simon & Schuster Adult Publishing Group, from *A Force for Change: How Leadership Differs from Management* by John P. Kotter. Copyright © 1990 by John P. Kotter, Inc.

Legitimate Power Legitimate power is power granted through the organizational hierarchy; it is the power defined by the organization to be accorded to people occupying a particular position. A manager can assign tasks to a subordinate, and a subordinate who refuses to do them can be reprimanded or even fired. Such outcomes stem from the manager's legitimate power as defined and vested in her or him by the organization. Legitimate power, then, is authority. All managers have legitimate power over their subordinates. The mere possession of legitimate power, however, does not by itself make someone a leader. Some subordinates follow only orders that are strictly within the letter of organizational rules and policies. If asked to do something not in their job descriptions, they refuse or do a poor job. The manager of such employees is exercising authority but not leadership.

Reward Power Reward power is the power to give or withhold rewards. Rewards that a manager may control include salary increases, bonuses, promotion recommendations, praise, recognition, and interesting job assignments. In general, the greater the number of rewards a manager controls and the more important the rewards are to subordinates, the greater is the manager's reward power. If the subordinate sees as valuable only the formal organizational rewards provided by the manager, then he or she is not a leader. If the subordinate

legitimate power
Power granted through the organizational hierarchy; the power defined by the organization to be accorded to people occupying particular positions

reward power
The power to give or withhold rewards, such as salary increases, bonuses, promotions, praise, recognition, and interesting job assignments

Barry Iverson/Alamy

Former Libyan leader Muammar Gaddafi ruled his country for years with a heavy dose of coercive power. His opponents were imprisoned, for example, and his critics constantly harassed. His heavy-handed ways played a major role in the 2011 Libyan uprising that toppled him from power.

"It is wise to persuade people to do things and make them think it was their own idea."

—NELSON MANDELA, FORMER PRESIDENT OF SOUTH AFRICA[8]

coercive power
The power to force compliance by means of psychological, emotional, or physical threat

referent power
The personal power that accrues to someone based on identification, imitation, loyalty, or charisma

expert power
The personal power that accrues to someone based on the information or expertise they possess

also wants and appreciates the manager's informal rewards, such as praise, gratitude, and recognition, however, then the manager is also exercising leadership.

Coercive Power Coercive power is the power to force compliance by means of psychological, emotional, or physical threat. In the past, physical coercion in organizations was relatively common. In most organizations today, however, coercion is limited to verbal reprimands, written reprimands, disciplinary layoffs, fines, demotion, and termination. Some managers occasionally go so far as to use verbal abuse, humiliation, and psychological coercion in an attempt to manipulate subordinates. (Of course, most people would agree that these are not appropriate managerial behaviors.) James Dutt, a legendary former CEO of Beatrice Company, once told a subordinate that if his wife and family got in the way of his working a 24-hour day seven days a week, he should get rid of them.[6] The more punitive the elements under a manager's control and the more important they are to subordinates, the more coercive power the manager possesses. On the other hand, the more a manager uses coercive power, the more likely he is to provoke resentment and hostility and the less likely he is to be seen as a leader.[7]

Referent Power Compared with legitimate, reward, and coercive power, which are relatively concrete and grounded in objective facets of organizational life, referent power is abstract. It is based on identification, imitation, loyalty, or charisma. Followers may react favorably because they identify in some way with a leader, who may be like them in personality, background, or attitudes. In other situations, followers might choose to imitate a leader with referent power by wearing the same kind of clothes, working the same hours, or espousing the same management philosophy. Referent power may also take the form of charisma, an intangible attribute of the leader that inspires loyalty and enthusiasm. Thus a manager might have referent power, but it is more likely to be associated with leadership.

Expert Power Expert power is derived from information or expertise. A manager who knows how to interact with an eccentric but important customer, a scientist who is capable of achieving an important technical breakthrough that no other company has dreamed of, and an administrative assistant who knows how to unravel bureaucratic red tape all have expert power over anyone who needs that information. The more important the information and the fewer the people who have access to it, the greater is the degree of expert power possessed by any one individual. In general, people who are both leaders and managers tend to have a lot of expert power.

Using Power How does a manager or leader use power? Several methods have been identified.[9] One method is the *legitimate request*, which is based on legitimate power. The manager requests that the subordinate comply because the subordinate recognizes that the organization has given the manager the right to make the request. Most day-to-day interactions between manager and subordinate are of this type. Another use of power is *instrumental compliance*, which is based on the reinforcement theory of motivation. In this form of exchange, a subordinate complies to get the reward the manager controls. Suppose that a manager asks a subordinate to do something outside the range of the subordinate's normal duties, such as working extra hours on the weekend, terminating a relationship with a longstanding buyer, or delivering bad news. The subordinate complies and, as a direct result, reaps praise and a bonus from the manager. The next time the subordinate is asked to perform a similar activity, that subordinate will recognize that compliance will be instrumental in her getting more rewards. Hence the basis of instrumental compliance is clarifying important performance–reward contingencies.

A manager is using *coercion* when she suggests or implies that the subordinate will be punished, fired, or reprimanded if he does not do something. *Rational persuasion* occurs when the manager can convince the subordinate that compliance is in the subordinate's best interests. For example, a manager might argue that the subordinate should accept a transfer because it would be good for the subordinate's career. In some ways, rational persuasion is like reward power, except that the manager does not really control the reward.

Still another way a manager can use power is through *personal identification*. A manager who recognizes that she has referent power over a subordinate can shape the behavior of that subordinate by engaging in desired behaviors: The manager consciously becomes a model for the subordinate and exploits personal identification. Sometimes a manager can induce a subordinate to do something consistent with a set of higher ideals or values through *inspirational appeal*. For example, a plea for loyalty represents an inspirational appeal. Referent power plays a role in determining the extent to which an inspirational appeal is successful because its effectiveness depends at least in part on the persuasive abilities of the leader.

A dubious method of using power is through *information distortion*. The manager withholds or distorts information to influence subordinates' behavior. For example, if a manager has agreed to allow everyone to participate in choosing a new group member but subsequently finds one individual whom she really prefers, she might withhold some of the credentials of other qualified applicants so that the desired member is selected. This use of power is dangerous. It may be unethical, and if subordinates find out that the manager has deliberately misled them, they will lose their confidence and trust in that manager's leadership.[10]

Summarize the key differences between leadership and management.

Identify an example you have experienced or observed to illustrate each of the five types of power discussed in this section.

CONCEPT CHECK

Generic Approaches to Leadership

Early approaches to the study of leadership adopted what might be called a "universal" or "generic" perspective. Specifically, they assumed that there was one set of answers to the leadership puzzle. One generic approach focused on leadership traits, and the other looked at leadership behavior.

Leadership Traits

The first organized approach to studying leadership analyzed the personal, psychological, and physical traits of strong leaders. The trait approach assumed that some basic trait or set of traits existed that differentiated leaders from nonleaders. If those traits could be defined, potential leaders could be identified. Researchers thought that leadership traits might include intelligence, assertiveness, above-average height, good vocabulary, attractiveness, self-confidence, and similar attributes.[11]

During the first half of the twentieth century, hundreds of studies were conducted in an attempt to identify important leadership traits. For the most part, the results of the studies were disappointing. For every set of leaders who possessed a common trait, a long list of exceptions was also found, and the list of suggested traits soon grew so long that it had little practical value. Alternative explanations usually existed even for relationships between traits and leadership that initially appeared valid. For example, it was observed that many leaders have good communication skills and are assertive. Rather than those traits being the cause of leadership, however, successful leaders may begin to display those traits after they have achieved a leadership position.

Although most researchers gave up trying to identify traits as predictors of leadership ability, many people still explicitly or implicitly adopt a trait orientation.[12] For example, politicians are all too often elected on the basis of personal appearance, speaking ability, or an aura of self-confidence. In addition, traits like honesty and integrity may very well be fundamental leadership traits that serve an important purpose. Intelligence also seems to play a meaningful role in leadership.[13]

Leadership Behaviors

Spurred on by their lack of success in identifying useful leadership traits, researchers soon began to investigate other variables, especially the behaviors or actions of leaders. The new hypothesis was that effective leaders somehow behaved differently than less effective leaders. Thus the goal was to develop a fuller understanding of leadership behaviors.

job-centered leader behavior
The behavior of leaders who pay close attention to the job and work procedures involved with that job

employee-centered leader behavior
The behavior of leaders who develop cohesive work groups and ensure employee satisfaction

initiating-structure behavior
The behavior of leaders who define the leader–subordinate role so that everyone knows what is expected, establish formal lines of communication, and determine how tasks will be performed

consideration behavior
The behavior of leaders who show concern for subordinates and attempt to establish a warm, friendly, and supportive climate

Michigan Studies Researchers at the University of Michigan, led by Rensis Likert, began studying leadership in the late 1940s.[14] Based on extensive interviews with both leaders (managers) and followers (subordinates), this research identified two basic forms of leader behavior: job centered and employee centered. Managers using job-centered leader behavior pay close attention to subordinates' work, explain work procedures, and are keenly interested in performance. Managers using employee-centered leader behavior are interested in developing a cohesive work group and ensuring that employees are satisfied with their jobs. Their primary concern is the welfare of subordinates.

The two styles of leader behavior were presumed to be at the ends of a single continuum. Although this suggests that leaders may be extremely job centered, extremely employee centered, or somewhere in between, Likert studied only the two end styles for contrast. He argued that employee-centered leader behavior generally tends to be more effective. We should also note the similarities between Likert's leadership research and his Systems 1 through 4 organization designs (discussed in Chapter 15). Job-centered leader behavior is consistent with the System 1 design (rigid and bureaucratic), whereas employee-centered leader behavior is consistent with the System 4 design (organic and flexible). When Likert advocates moving organizations from System 1 to System 4, he is also advocating a transition from job-centered to employee-centered leader behavior.

Ohio State Studies At about the same time that Likert was beginning his leadership studies at the University of Michigan, a group of researchers at Ohio State University also began studying leadership.[15] The extensive questionnaire surveys conducted during the Ohio State studies also suggested that there are two basic leader behaviors or styles: initiating-structure behavior and consideration behavior. When using initiating-structure behavior, the leader clearly defines the leader–subordinate role so that everyone knows what is expected, establishes formal lines of communication, and determines how tasks will be performed. Leaders using consideration behavior show concern for subordinates and attempt to establish a warm, friendly, and supportive climate. The behaviors identified at Ohio State are similar to those described at Michigan, but there are important differences. One major difference is that the Ohio State researchers did not interpret leader behavior as being one-dimensional; each behavior was assumed to be independent of the other. Presumably, then, a leader could exhibit varying levels of initiating structure and at the same time varying levels of consideration.

At first, the Ohio State researchers thought that leaders who exhibit high levels of both behaviors would tend to be more effective than other leaders. A study at International Harvester (now Navistar International), however, suggested a more complicated pattern.[16] The researchers found that employees of supervisors who ranked high on initiating structure were high performers but expressed low levels of satisfaction and had a higher absence rate. Conversely, employees of supervisors who ranked high on consideration had low performance ratings but high levels of satisfaction and few absences from work. Later research isolated other variables that make consistent prediction difficult and determined that situational influences also occurred. (This body of research is discussed in the section on situational approaches to leadership.[17])

Managerial Grid Yet another behavioral approach to leadership is the Managerial Grid.[18] The Managerial Grid provides a means for evaluating leadership styles and then training managers to move toward an ideal style of behavior. The Managerial Grid is shown in Figure 20.1. The horizontal axis represents concern for production (similar to job-centered and initiating-structure behaviors), and the vertical axis represents concern for people (similar to employee-centered and consideration behaviors). Note the five extremes of managerial behavior: the 1,1 manager

concern for production
The part of the Managerial Grid that deals with the job and task aspects of leader behavior

concern for people
The part of the Managerial Grid that deals with the human aspects of leader behavior

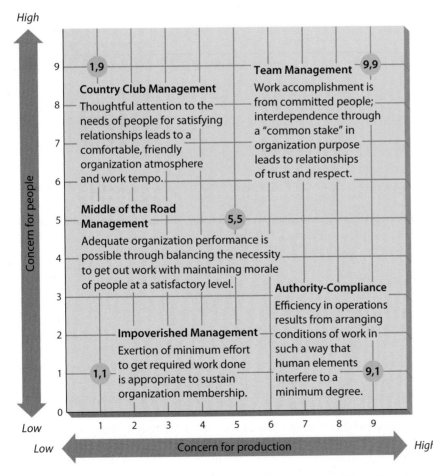

FIGURE 20.1 THE LEADERSHIP GRID

The Leadership Grid® is a method of evaluating leadership styles. The overall objective of an organization using the Grid is to train its managers using organization development techniques so that they are simultaneously more concerned for both people and production (9,9 style on the Grid).

Source: The Leadership Grid figure from *Leadership Dilemmas—Grid Solutions* by Robert R. Blake and Anne Adams McCanse. (Formerly *The Managerial Grid* by Robert R. Blake and Jane S. Mouton.) Houston: Gulf Publishing Company, p. 29. Copyright © 1997 by Grid International, Inc. Reproduced by permission of the owners.

(impoverished management), who exhibits minimal concern for both production and people; the 9,1 manager (authority-compliance), who is highly concerned about production but exhibits little concern for people; the 1,9 manager (country club management), who has exactly opposite concerns from the 9,1 manager; the 5,5 manager (middle-of-the-road management), who maintains adequate concern for both people and production; and the 9,9 manager (team management), who exhibits maximum concern for both people and production.

According to this approach, the ideal style of managerial behavior is 9,9. There is a six-phase program to assist managers in achieving this style of behavior. A.G. Edwards, Westinghouse, the FAA, Equicor, and other companies have used the Managerial Grid with reasonable success. However, there is little published scientific evidence regarding its true effectiveness.

The leader-behavior theories have played an important role in the development of contemporary thinking about leadership. In particular, they urge us not to be preoccupied with what leaders are (the trait approach) but to concentrate on what leaders do (their behaviors). Unfortunately, these theories also make universal generic prescriptions about what constitutes effective leadership. When we are dealing with complex social systems composed of complex individuals, however, few, if any, relationships are consistently predictable, and certainly no formulas for success are infallible. Yet the behavior theorists tried to identify consistent relationships between leader behaviors and employee responses in the hope of finding a dependable prescription for effective leadership. As we might expect, they often failed. Other approaches to understanding leadership were therefore needed. The catalyst for these new approaches was the realization that although interpersonal and task-oriented dimensions might be useful for describing the behavior of leaders, they were not useful for predicting or prescribing it. The next step in the evolution of leadership theory was the creation of situational models.

Describe the basic types of leader behavior identified in the generic approaches to leadership.

Setting aside the validity of the concept, what traits would you see as being most important for effective leadership?

◈ Situational Approaches to Leadership

Situational models assume that appropriate leader behavior varies from one situation to another. The goal of a situational theory, then, is to identify key situational factors and to specify how they interact to determine appropriate leader behavior. Before discussing the major situational theories, we should first discuss an important early model that laid the foundation for subsequent developments. In a 1958 study of the decision-making process, Robert Tannenbaum and Warren H. Schmidt proposed a continuum of leadership behavior. Their model is much like the original Michigan framework.[19] Besides purely job-centered behavior (or "boss-centered" behavior, as they termed it) and employee-centered ("subordinate-centered") behavior, however, they identified several intermediate behaviors that a manager might consider. These are shown on the leadership continuum in Figure 20.2.

This continuum of behavior moves from one extreme, of having the manager make the decision alone, to the other extreme, of having the employees make the decision with minimal guidance. Each point on the continuum is influenced by characteristics of the manager, the subordinates, and the situation. Managerial characteristics include the manager's value system, confidence in subordinates, personal inclinations, and feelings of security. Subordinate characteristics include the subordinates' need for independence, readiness to assume responsibility, tolerance for ambiguity, interest in the problem, understanding of goals, knowledge, experience, and expectations. Situational characteristics that affect decision making include the type of organization, group effectiveness, the problem itself, and time

FIGURE 20.2 TANNENBAUM AND SCHMIDT'S LEADERSHIP CONTINUUM

The Tannenbaum and Schmidt leadership continuum was an important precursor to modern situational approaches to leadership. The continuum identifies seven levels of leadership, which range between the extremes of boss-centered and subordinate-centered leadership.

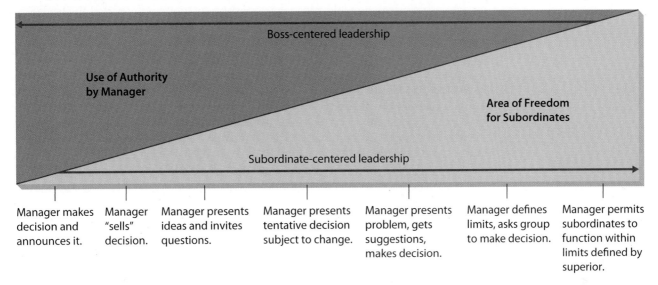

| Manager makes decision and announces it. | Manager "sells" decision. | Manager presents ideas and invites questions. | Manager presents tentative decision subject to change. | Manager presents problem, gets suggestions, makes decision. | Manager defines limits, asks group to make decision. | Manager permits subordinates to function within limits defined by superior. |

Source: Reprinted by permission of the *Harvard Business Review*. An exhibit from "How to Choose a Leadership Pattern" by Robert Tannenbaum and Warren Schmidt (May–June 1973). Copyright © 1973 by the President and Fellows of Harvard College; all rights reserved.

pressures. Although this framework pointed out the importance of situational factors, it was only speculative. It remained for others to develop more comprehensive and integrated theories. In the following sections, we describe four of the most important and widely accepted situational theories of leadership: the LPC theory, the path–goal theory, Vroom's decision tree approach, and the leader–member exchange approach.

LPC Theory

The LPC theory, developed by Fred Fiedler, was the first truly situational theory of leadership.[20] As we will discuss later, LPC stands for least-preferred coworker. Beginning with a combined trait and behavioral approach, Fiedler identified two styles of leadership: task oriented (analogous to job-centered and initiating-structure behavior) and relationship oriented (similar to employee-centered and consideration behavior). He went beyond the earlier behavioral approaches by arguing that the style of behavior is a reflection of the leader's personality and that most personalities fall into one of his two categories—task oriented or relationship oriented by nature. Fiedler measures leadership style by means of a controversial questionnaire called the **least-preferred coworker (LPC) measure.** To use the measure, a manager or leader is asked to describe the specific person with whom he or she is able to work least well—the LPC—by filling in a set of 16 scales anchored at each end by a positive or negative adjective. For example, 3 of the 16 scales are:

Helpful __ __ __ __ __ __ __ __ Frustrating
         8 7 6 5 4 3 2 1

Tense __ __ __ __ __ __ __ __ Relaxed
      1 2 3 4 5 6 7 8

Boring __ __ __ __ __ __ __ __ Interesting
       1 2 3 4 5 6 7 8

LPC theory
A theory of leadership that suggests that the appropriate style of leadership varies with situational favorableness

least-preferred coworker (LPC) measure
The measuring scale that asks leaders to describe the person with whom he or she is able to work least well

The leader's LPC score is then calculated by adding up the numbers below the line checked on each scale. Note in these three examples that the higher numbers are associated with positive qualities (helpful, relaxed, and interesting), whereas the negative qualities (frustrating, tense, and boring) have low point values. A high total score is assumed to reflect a relationship orientation and a low score a task orientation on the part of the leader. The LPC measure is controversial because researchers disagree about its validity. Some question exactly what an LPC measure reflects and whether the score is an index of behavior, personality, or some other factor.[21]

Favorableness of the Situation   The underlying assumption of situational models of leadership is that appropriate leader behavior varies from one situation to another. According to Fiedler, the key situational factor is the favorableness of the situation from the leader's point of view. This factor is determined by leader–member relations, task structure, and position power. *Leader–member relations* refer to the nature of the relationship between the leader and the work group. If the leader and the group have a high degree of mutual trust, respect, and confidence, and if they like one another, relations are assumed to be good. If there is little trust, respect, or confidence, and if they do not like one another, relations are poor. Naturally, good relations are more favorable.

Task structure is the degree to which the group's task is well defined. The task is structured when it is routine, easily understood, and unambiguous, and when the group has standard procedures and precedents to rely on. An unstructured task is nonroutine, ambiguous, and complex, with no standard procedures or precedents. You can see that high structure is more favorable for the leader, whereas low structure is less favorable. For example, if the task is unstructured, the group will not know what to do, and the leader will have to play a major role in guiding and directing its activities. If the task is structured, the leader will not have to get so involved and can devote time to nonsupervisory activities.

Position power is the power vested in the leader's position. If the leader has the power to assign work and to reward and punish employees, position power is assumed to be strong. But if the leader must get job assignments approved by someone else and does not administer rewards and punishment, position power is weak, and it is more difficult to accomplish goals. From the leader's point of view, strong position power is clearly preferable to weak position power. However, position power is not as important as task structure and leader–member relations.

Favorableness and Leader Style   Fiedler and his associates conducted numerous studies linking the favorableness of various situations to leader style and the effectiveness of the group.[22] The results of these studies—and the overall framework of the theory—are shown in Figure 20.3. To interpret the model, look first at the situational factors at the top of the figure. Good or bad leader–member relations, high or low task structure, and strong or weak leader position power can be combined to yield six unique situations. For example, good leader–member relations, high task structure, and strong leader position power (at the far left) are presumed to define the most favorable situation; bad leader–member relations, low task structure, and weak leader power (at the far right) are the least favorable. The other combinations reflect intermediate levels of favorableness.

Below each set of situations are shown the degree of favorableness and the form of leader behavior found to be most strongly associated with effective group performance for those situations. When the situation is most and least favorable, Fiedler found that a task-oriented leader is most effective. When the situation is only moderately favorable, however, a relationship-oriented leader is predicted to be most effective.

Flexibility of Leader Style   Fiedler argued that, for any given individual, leader style is essentially fixed and cannot be changed; leaders cannot change their behavior to fit a particular situation because it is linked to their particular personality traits. Thus, when a leader's style and the situation do not match, Fiedler argued that the situation should be changed to

FIGURE 20.3 THE LEAST-PREFERRED COWORKER THEORY OF LEADERSHIP

Fiedler's LPC theory of leadership suggests that appropriate leader behavior varies as a function of the favorableness of the situation. Favorableness, in turn, is defined by task structure, leader–member relations, and the leader's position power. According to the LPC theory, the most and least favorable situations call for task-oriented leadership, whereas moderately favorable situations suggest the need for relationship-oriented leadership.

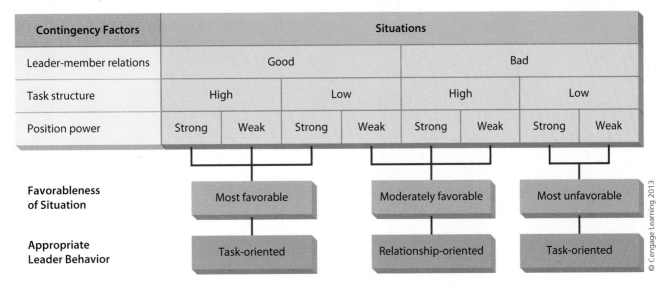

© Cengage Learning 2013

fit the leader's style. When leader–member relations are good, task structure low, and position power weak, the leader style that is most likely to be effective is relationship oriented. If the leader is task oriented, a mismatch exists. According to Fiedler, the leader can make the elements of the situation more congruent by structuring the task (by developing guidelines and procedures, for instance) and increasing power (by requesting additional authority or by other means).

Fiedler's contingency theory has been attacked on the grounds that it is not always supported by research, that his findings are subject to other interpretations, that the LPC measure lacks validity, and that his assumptions about the inflexibility of leader behavior are unrealistic.[23] However, Fiedler's theory was one of the first to adopt a situational perspective on leadership. It has helped many managers recognize the important situational factors they must contend with, and it has fostered additional thinking about the situational nature of leadership. Moreover, in recent years Fiedler has attempted to address some of the concerns about his theory by revising it and adding such additional elements as cognitive resources.

Path–Goal Theory

The path–goal theory of leadership—associated most closely with Martin Evans and Robert House—is a direct extension of the expectancy theory of motivation discussed in Chapter 19.[24] Recall that the primary components of expectancy theory included the likelihood of attaining various outcomes and the value associated with those outcomes. The path–goal theory of leadership suggests that the primary functions of a leader are to make valued or desired rewards available in the workplace and to clarify for the subordinate the kinds of behavior that will lead to goal accomplishment and valued rewards—that is, the leader should clarify the paths to goal attainment.

Leader Behavior The most fully developed version of path–goal theory identifies four kinds of leader behavior. *Directive leader behavior* lets subordinates know what is expected of them, gives guidance and direction, and schedules work. *Supportive leader behavior* is being friendly and

path–goal theory
A theory of leadership suggesting that the primary functions of a leader are to make valued or desired rewards available in the workplace and to clarify for the subordinate the kinds of behavior that will lead to those rewards

Effective leaders often rely on a variety of different behaviors to motivate their employees. This manager, for example, is showing his team the award they won for exceeding their corporate goals. He is emphasizing achievement, making them feel like a part of the success, and providing encouragement that they can continue to excel and perform at a high level.

Flying Colours Ltd/Photodisc/Jupiter images

approachable, showing concern for subordinates' welfare, and treating members as equals. *Participative leader behavior* includes consulting with subordinates, soliciting suggestions, and allowing participation in decision making. *Achievement-oriented leader* behavior means setting challenging goals, expecting subordinates to perform at high levels, encouraging subordinates, and showing confidence in subordinates' abilities.

In contrast to Fiedler's theory, path–goal theory assumes that leaders can change their style or behavior to meet the demands of a particular situation. For example, when encountering a new group of subordinates and a new project, the leader may be directive in establishing work procedures and in outlining what needs to be done. Next, the leader may adopt supportive behavior to foster group cohesiveness and a positive climate. As the group becomes familiar with the task and as new problems are encountered, the leader may exhibit participative behavior to enhance group members' motivation. Finally, achievement-oriented behavior may be used to encourage continued high performance.

Situational Factors Like other situational theories of leadership, path–goal theory suggests that appropriate leader style depends on situational factors. Path–goal theory focuses on the situational factors of the personal characteristics of subordinates and environmental characteristics of the workplace.

Important personal characteristics include the subordinates' perception of their own abilities and their locus of control. If people perceive that they are lacking in abilities, they may prefer directive leadership to help them understand path–goal relationships better. If they perceive themselves as having a lot of abilities, however, employees may resent directive leadership. Locus of control is a personality trait. People who have an internal locus of control believe that what happens to them is a function of their own efforts and behavior. Those who have an external locus of control assume that fate, luck, or "the system" determines what happens to them. A person with an internal locus of control may prefer participative leadership, whereas a person with an external locus of control may prefer directive leadership. Managers can do little or nothing to influence the personal characteristics of subordinates, but they can shape the environment to take advantage of these personal characteristics by, for example, providing rewards and structuring tasks.

Environmental characteristics include factors outside the subordinates' control. Task structure is one such factor. When structure is high, directive leadership is less effective than when structure is low. Subordinates do not usually need their boss to continually tell them how to do an extremely routine job. The formal authority system is another important environmental characteristic. Again, the higher the degree of formality, the less directive is the leader behavior that will be accepted by subordinates. The nature of the work group also affects appropriate leader behavior. When the work group provides the employee with social support and satisfaction, supportive leader behavior is less critical. When social support and satisfaction cannot be derived from the group, the worker may look to the leader for this support. Greater leadership support may also be an important factor in times of change or under unusually stressful conditions. The *Change* box entitled "Tips for Tough Times" on page 518 discusses some of the ways in which leaders adapt their support behavior in times of economic uncertainty.

The basic path–goal framework as illustrated in Figure 20.4 shows that different leader behaviors affect subordinates' motivation to perform. Personal and environmental

FIGURE 20.4 THE PATH-GOAL FRAMEWORK

The path–goal theory of leadership suggests that managers can use four types of leader behavior to clarify subordinates' paths to goal attainment. Personal characteristics of the subordinate and environmental characteristics within the organization both must be taken into account when determining which style of leadership will work best for a particular situation.

© Cengage Learning 2013

characteristics are seen as defining which behaviors lead to which outcomes. The path–goal theory of leadership is a dynamic and incomplete model. The original intent was to state the theory in general terms so that future research could explore a variety of interrelationships and modify the theory. Research that has been done suggests that the path–goal theory is a reasonably good description of the leadership process and that future investigations along these lines should enable us to discover more about the link between leadership and motivation.[25]

Vroom's Decision Tree Approach

The third major contemporary approach to leadership is **Vroom's decision tree approach**. The earliest version of this model was proposed by Victor Vroom and Philip Yetton and later revised and expanded by Vroom and Arthur Jago.[26] Most recently, Vroom has developed yet another refinement of the original model.[27] Like the path–goal theory, this approach attempts to prescribe a leadership style appropriate to a given situation. It also assumes that the same leader may display different leadership styles. But Vroom's approach concerns itself with only a single aspect of leader behavior: subordinate participation in decision making.

Basic Premises Vroom's decision tree approach assumes that the degree to which subordinates should be encouraged to participate in decision making depends on the characteristics of the situation. In other words, no one decision-making process is best for all situations. After evaluating a variety of problem attributes (characteristics of the problem or decision), the leader determines an appropriate decision style that specifies the amount of subordinate participation.

Vroom's current formulation suggests that managers use one of two different decision trees.[28] To do so, the manager first assesses the situation in terms of several factors. This assessment involves determining whether the given factor is high or low for the decision that is to be made. For instance, the first factor is decision significance. If the decision is extremely important and may have a major impact on the organization (such as choosing a location for a new plant), its significance is high. But if the decision is routine and its consequences are not terribly important (selecting a color for the firm's softball team uniforms), its significance is low. This assessment guides the manager through the paths of the decision tree to a recommended course of action. One decision tree is to be used when the manager

Vroom's decision tree approach
Predicts what kinds of situations call for different degrees of group participation

is interested primarily in making the decision as quickly as possible; the other is to be used when time is less critical and the manager is interested in helping subordinates to improve and develop their own decision-making skills.

The two decision trees are shown in Figures 20.5 and 20.6. The problem attributes (situational factors) are arranged along the top of the decision tree. To use the model, the decision maker starts at the left side of the diagram and assesses the first problem attribute (decision significance). The answer determines the path to the second node on the decision tree, where the next attribute (importance of commitment) is assessed. This process continues until a terminal node is reached. In this way, the manager identifies an effective decision-making style for the situation.

FIGURE 20.5 VROOM'S TIME-DRIVEN DECISION TREE

This matrix is recommended for situations where time is of the highest importance in making a decision. The matrix operates like a funnel. You start at the left with a specific decision problem in mind. The column headings denote situational factors that may or may not be present in that problem. You progress by selecting high or low (H or L) for each relevant situational factor. Proceed down the funnel, judging only those situational factors for which a judgment is called, until you reach the recommended process.

PROBLEM STATEMENT

Decision Significance	Importance of Commitment	Leader Expertise	Likelihood of Commitment	Group Support	Group Expertise	Team Competence	
H	H	H	H	—	—	—	Decide
H	H	H	L	H	H	H	Delegate
H	H	H	L	H	H	L	Consult (group)
H	H	H	L	H	L	—	Consult (group)
H	H	H	L	L	—	—	Consult (group)
H	H	L	H	H	H	H	Facilitate
H	H	L	H	H	H	L	Consult (individually)
H	H	L	H	H	L	—	Consult (individually)
H	H	L	H	L	—	—	Consult (individually)
H	H	L	L	H	H	H	Facilitate
H	H	L	L	H	H	L	Consult (group)
H	H	L	L	H	L	—	Consult (group)
H	H	L	L	L	—	—	Consult (group)
H	L	H	—	—	—	—	Decide
H	L	L	—	H	H	H	Facilitate
H	L	L	—	H	H	L	Consult (individually)
H	L	L	—	H	L	—	Consult (individually)
H	L	L	—	L	—	—	Consult (individually)
L	H	—	H	—	—	—	Decide
L	H	—	L	—	—	H	Delegate
L	H	—	L	—	—	L	Facilitate
L	L	—	—	—	—	—	Decide

Source: Adapted and reprinted by permission from *Leadership and Decision-Makings*, by Victor H. Vroom and Philip W. Yetton, by permission of the University of Pittsburgh Press. Copyright © 1973 by University of Pittsburgh Press.

Decision-Making Styles The various decision styles reflected at the ends of the tree branches represent different levels of subordinate participation that the manager should attempt to adopt in a given situation. The five styles are defined as follows:

- *Decide*. The manager makes the decision alone and then announces or "sells" it to the group.
- *Consult (individually)*. The manager presents the program to group members individually, obtains their suggestions, and then makes the decision.
- *Consult (group)*. The manager presents the problem to group members at a meeting, gets their suggestions, and then makes the decision.
- *Facilitate*. The manager presents the problem to the group at a meeting, defines the problem and its boundaries, and then facilitates group member discussion as they make the decision.
- *Delegate*. The manager allows the group to define for itself the exact nature and parameters of the problem and then to develop a solution.

Vroom's decision tree approach represents a very focused but quite complex perspective on leadership. To compensate for this difficulty, Vroom has developed elaborate expert system software to help managers assess a situation accurately and quickly and then to make an appropriate decision regarding employee participation.[29] Many firms, including Halliburton Company, Litton Industries, and Borland International, have provided their managers with training in how to use the various versions of this model.

FIGURE 20.6 VROOM'S DEVELOPMENT-DRIVEN DECISION TREE

This matrix is to be used when the leader is more interested in developing employees than in making the decision as quickly as possible. Just as with the time-driven tree shown in Figure 20.5, the leader assesses up to seven situational factors. These factors, in turn, funnel the leader to a recommended process for making the decision.

	Decision Significance	Importance of Commitment	Leader Expertise	Likelihood of Commitment	Group Support	Group Expertise	Team Competence	
P R O B L E M	H	H	—	H	H	H	H	Decide
							L	Facilitate
						L	—	Consult (group)
					L	—	—	
S				L	H	H	H	Delegate
T A							L	Facilitate
T						L	—	
E M					L	—	—	Consult (group)
E N		L	—	—	H	H	H	Delegate
T							L	Facilitate
						L	—	Consult (group)
					L	—	—	
	L	H	—	H	—	—	—	Decide
				L	—	—	—	Delegate
		L	—	—	—	—	—	Decide

Source: Adapted and reprinted by permission from *Leadership and Decision-Makings,* by Victor H. Vroom and Philip W. Yetton, by permission of the University of Pittsburgh Press. Copyright © 1973 by University of Pittsburgh Press.

THE MORE THINGS CHANGE

Tips for Tough Times

Bob Daemmrich/Alamy

How does one go about leading in a recession like the one we're currently going through? What adjustments do you have to make when money is scarce, markets are volatile, and morale needs boosting? Dennis Carey, vice chairman of Korn Ferry International, an executive-search firm, suggests that top managers start by acknowledging that leading in extreme circumstances means calling into question everything they do under normal circumstances. "You can't rely on a peacetime general to fight a war," he reminds fellow executives. "The wartime CEO prepares for the worst so that his or her company can take market share away from players who haven't." Hire away your competitors' best people, advises Carey, and keep them from grabbing yours. Or buy up their assets while they can be had at bargain prices.

Jack Hayhow, consultant and founder of Opus Training and ReallyEasyHR, adds that leaders need to make sure their employees know why they're making changes: "Clearly state to your people that we are in a recession . . . [and that] very little of what [they've] assumed to be true in the past will be true in the future. [Tell them]: 'You must understand that this is no longer business as usual. . . . My suggestion," says Hayhow, "would

be [something like]: 'Quit worrying about the things you can't control and focus on what you can. Find ways to contribute . . . and make it really hard for the company to let you go. . . .' If you have people who argue or debate, show them the door."

Hayhow also realizes that "when things are as bad as they are [in a recession], motivation is critical. . . . If you create an environment conducive to people motivating themselves," he contends, "you'll be able to motivate in these changing times." How do you create such an environment? "Start by matching talent with the task," says Hayhow. "Play to your employees' strengths. Figure out who does what and make sure they're spending their time where they can best utilize their talents." And don't forget to "give people some choice. . . . When people have even a little choice over what they do or how they do it, they're more committed and enthusiastic about the task." Let employees decide how to do something "or maybe even who they work with to get the job done."

Ex-Starbucks CEO Jim Donald makes a fairly simple recommendation: "Communicate, communicate, communicate. Especially at a time of crisis," he advises, "make sure your message reaches all levels, from the very lowest to the uppermost." Kip Tindell, who's been CEO of the Container Store since its founding in 1978, agrees. That's why his managers "run around like chickens relentlessly trying to communicate everything to every single employee at all times." He admits that it's an impossible task, but he's also convinced that the effort is more important than ever in times of crisis. He also contends that his company is in a better position to ride out the economic storm "because we're so dedicated to the notion that communication and leadership are the same thing." At the very least, he says, "we're fortunate to be minus the paranoia that goes with employees who feel they don't know what's going on."

References: Emily Thornton, "Managing Through a Crisis: The New Rules," *BusinessWeek*, January 8, 2009, www.businessweek.com on April 24, 2011; Anthony Portuesi, "Leading in a Recession: An Interview with Jack Hayhow," *Driven Leaders*, February 24, 2009, http://drivenleaders.com on April 24, 2011; Jim Donald, "Guest Post: Former Starbucks CEO's Tips for Tough Times," *Fortune*, April 1, 2009, http://postcards.blogs.fortune.cnn.com on April 24, 2011; Ellen Davis, "Retail Execs Offer Insights on Leadership in Tough Economic Times," *NRF Annual 2009 Convention Blog*, January 15, 2009, http://blog.nrf.com on April 24, 2011.

Evaluation and Implications Because Vroom's current approach is relatively new, it has not been fully scientifically tested. The original model and its subsequent refinement, however, attracted a great deal of attention and generally was supported by research.[30] For example, there is some support for the idea that individuals who make decisions consistent with the predictions of the model are more effective than those who make decisions inconsistent with

FIGURE 20.7 THE LEADER–MEMBER EXCHANGE (LMX) MODEL

The LMX model suggests that leaders form unique independent relationships with each of their subordinates. As illustrated here, a key factor in the nature of this relationship is whether the individual subordinate is in the leader's out-group or in-group.

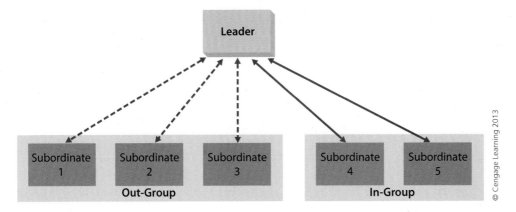

© Cengage Learning 2013

it. The model therefore appears to be a tool that managers can apply with some confidence in deciding how much subordinates should participate in the decision-making process.

The Leader–Member Exchange Approach

Because leadership is such an important area, managers and researchers continue to study it. As a result, new ideas, theories, and perspectives are continuously being developed. The leader–member exchange (LMX) model of leadership, conceived by George Graen and Fred Dansereau, stresses the importance of variable relationships between supervisors and each of their subordinates.[31] Each superior–subordinate pair is referred to as a "vertical dyad." The model differs from earlier approaches in that it focuses on the differential relationship leaders often establish with different subordinates. Figure 20.7 shows the basic concepts of the leader–member exchange theory.

The model suggests that supervisors establish a special relationship with a small number of trusted subordinates, referred to as "the in-group." The in-group usually receives special duties requiring responsibility and autonomy; they may also receive special privileges. Subordinates who are not a part of this group are called "the out-group," and they receive less of the supervisor's time and attention. Note in the figure that the leader has a dyadic, or one-to-one, relationship with each of the five subordinates.

Early in his or her interaction with a given subordinate, the supervisor initiates either an in-group or an out-group relationship. It is not clear how a leader selects members of the in-group, but the decision may be based on personal compatibility and subordinates' competence. Research has confirmed the existence of in-groups and out-groups. In addition, studies generally have found that in-group members have a higher level of performance and satisfaction than do out-group members.[32]

leader–member exchange (LMX) model
Stresses that leaders have different kinds of relationships with different subordinates

Summarize the essential elements of each of the situational approaches to leadership.

Which situational approach do you think is most useful and which the least useful for managers in organizations?

CONCEPT CHECK

Related Approaches to Leadership

Because of its importance to organizational effectiveness, leadership continues to be the focus of a great deal of research and theory building. New approaches that have attracted much attention are the concepts of substitutes for leadership and transformational leadership.[33]

Substitutes for Leadership

The concept of substitutes for leadership was developed because existing leadership models and theories do not account for situations in which leadership is not needed.[34] They simply try to specify what kind of leader behavior is appropriate. The substitutes concept, however, identifies situations in which leader behaviors are neutralized or replaced by characteristics of the subordinate, the task, and the organization. For example, when a patient is delivered to a hospital emergency room, the professionals on duty do not wait to be told what to do by a leader. Nurses, doctors, and attendants all go into action without waiting for directive or supportive leader behavior from the emergency room supervisor.

Characteristics of the subordinate that may serve to neutralize leader behavior include ability, experience, need for independence, professional orientation, and indifference toward organizational rewards. For example, employees with a high level of ability and experience may not need to be told what to do. Similarly, a subordinate's strong need for independence may render leader behavior ineffective. Task characteristics that may substitute for leadership include routineness, the availability of feedback, and intrinsic satisfaction. When the job is routine and simple, the subordinate may not need direction. When the task is challenging and intrinsically satisfying, the subordinate may not need or want social support from a leader.

Organizational characteristics that may substitute for leadership include formalization, group cohesion, inflexibility, and a rigid reward structure. Leadership may not be necessary when policies and practices are formal and inflexible, for example. Similarly, a rigid reward system may rob the leader of reward power and thereby decrease the importance of the role. Preliminary research has provided support for the concept of substitutes for leadership.[35]

Charismatic Leadership

The concept of charismatic leadership, like trait theories, assumes that charisma is an individual characteristic of the leader. Charisma is a form of interpersonal attraction that inspires support and acceptance. All else being equal, then, someone with charisma is more likely to be able to influence others than is someone without charisma. For example, a highly charismatic supervisor will be more successful in influencing subordinate behavior than a supervisor who lacks charisma. Thus influence is again a fundamental element of this perspective.

Robert House first proposed a theory of charismatic leadership, based on research findings from a variety of social science disciplines.[36] His theory suggests that charismatic leaders are likely to have a lot of self-confidence, a firm conviction in their beliefs and ideals, and a strong need to influence people. They also tend to communicate high expectations about follower performance and express confidence in followers. Donald Trump is an excellent example of a charismatic leader. Even though he has made his share of mistakes and generally is perceived as only an "average" manager, many people view him as larger than life.

There are three elements of charismatic leadership in organizations that most experts acknowledge today.[37] First, the leader needs to be able to envision the future, set high

substitutes for leadership
A concept that identifies situations in which leader behaviors are neutralized or replaced by characteristics of subordinates, the task, and the organization

charismatic leadership
Assumes that charisma is an individual characteristic of the leader

charisma
A form of interpersonal attraction that inspires support and acceptance

expectations, and model behaviors consistent with meeting those expectations. Next, the charismatic leader must be able to energize others through a demonstration of personal excitement, personal confidence, and patterns of success. And, finally, the charismatic leader enables others by supporting them, empathizing with them, and expressing confidence in them.[38]

Charismatic leadership ideas are quite popular among managers today and are the subject of numerous books and articles. Unfortunately, few studies have attempted to specifically test the meaning and impact of charismatic leadership. There are also lingering ethical issues about charismatic leadership, however, that trouble some people. For instance, President Bill Clinton was a charismatic leader. But some of his critics argued that this very charisma caused his supporters to overlook his flaws and to minimize some of his indiscretions. In contrast, President George W. Bush did not possess a high level of charisma, and this may have enabled some critics to magnify his shortcomings.

Transformational Leadership

Another new perspective on leadership has been called by a number of labels: charismatic leadership, inspirational leadership, symbolic leadership, and transformational leadership. We use the term **transformational leadership** and define it as leadership that goes beyond ordinary expectations by transmitting a sense of mission, stimulating learning experiences, and inspiring new ways of thinking.[39] Because of rapid change and turbulent environments, transformational leaders are increasingly being seen as vital to the success of business.[40]

A widely-circulated popular press article once identified seven keys to successful leadership: trusting one's subordinates, developing a vision, keeping cool, encouraging risk, being an expert, inviting dissent, and simplifying things.[41] Although this list was the result of a simplistic survey of the leadership literature, it is nevertheless consistent with the premises underlying transformational leadership. So, too, are recent examples cited as effective leadership. Take the case of 3M. The firm's new CEO is working to make the firm more efficient and profitable while simultaneously keeping its leadership role in new product innovation. He has also changed the reward system, overhauled procedures, and restructured the entire firm. And so far, at least, analysts have applauded these changes.[42]

John F. Kennedy is remembered as a charismatic leader. He was a master at inspiring support and acceptance of his beliefs. It was Kennedy, for example, who set a goal of sending an astronaut to the moon by the end of the 1960s. He is shown here in Houston promoting the economic benefits of space travel.

World History Archive/Alamy

transformational leadership
Leadership that goes beyond ordinary expectations by transmitting a sense of mission, stimulating learning experiences, and inspiring new ways of thinking

"Turnaround or growth, it's getting your people focused on the goal that is still the job of leadership."

—ANNE MULCAHY, FORMER CEO OF XEROX[43]

What are leadership substitutes? What specific substitutes might work in a classroom setting?

Identify a person you would consider to be a charismatic leader and describe why the person fits the definition.

Emerging Approaches to Leadership

Recently, three potentially very important new approaches to leadership have emerged. One is called "strategic leadership"; the others deal with cross-cultural leadership and ethical leadership.

Strategic Leadership

Strategic leadership is a new concept that explicitly relates leadership to the role of top management. We define strategic leadership as the capability to understand the complexities of both the organization and its environment and to lead change in the organization in order to achieve and maintain a superior alignment between the organization and its environment. This definition reflects an integration of the leadership concepts covered in this chapter with our discussion of strategic management in Chapter 8. Its board of directors, of course, is a key element in any firm's strategic leadership, and the *World of Difference* box on page 523, entitled "Getting on Board with Diversity," discusses a lingering issue in the composition of U.S. boards.

To be effective as a strategic leader, a manager needs to have a thorough and complete understanding of the organization—its history, its culture, its strengths, and its weaknesses. In addition, the leader needs a firm grasp of the organization's environment. This understanding must encompass current conditions and circumstances as well as significant trends and issues on the horizon. The strategic leader also needs to recognize how the firm is currently aligned with its environment—where it relates effectively and where it relates less effectively with that environment. Finally, looking at environmental trends and issues, the strategic leader works to improve both the current alignment and the future alignment.[44]

Jeffrey Immelt (CEO of General Electric), Hector Ruiz (CEO of Advanced Micro Devices), John Chambers (CEO of Cisco), Michael Dell (founder and CEO of Dell Computer), and Irene Rosenfeld (CEO of Kraft Foods) are generally seen as strong strategic leaders.[45] On the other hand, Ken Lewis (former CEO of Bank of America) and Mike Jeffries (CEO of Abercrombie & Fitch) have recently been cited as less effective strategic leaders.[46]

> [3M CEO] . . . is pulling, pushing, and driving 3M back to its R&D roots. This is a company that prides itself on developing the most iconic products. That all came out of internal innovation, and he wants to make sure that that's not lost."
>
> —ANALYST AT FBR CAPITAL MARKETS[47]

Cross-Cultural Leadership

Another new approach to leadership is based on cross-cultural issues. In this context, culture is used as a broad concept to encompass both international differences and diversity-based differences within one culture. For instance, when a Japanese firm sends an executive to head the firm's operations in the United States, that person will need to become acclimated to the cultural differences that exist between the two countries and to change his or her leadership style accordingly. As noted in Chapter 5, Japan is generally characterized by collectivism, whereas the United States is based more on individualism. The Japanese executive, then, will find it necessary to recognize the importance of individual contributions and rewards, as well as the differences in individual and group roles, that exist in Japanese and U.S. businesses.

Similarly, cross-cultural factors play a growing role in organizations as their workforces become more and more diverse. Most leadership research, for instance, has been conducted on samples or case studies involving white male leaders (until several years ago, most business leaders were white males). But as more females, African Americans, and Latinos achieve leadership positions, it may be necessary to reassess how applicable current theories and models of leadership are when applied to an increasingly diverse pool of leaders.

strategic leadership
The capability to understand the complexities of both the organization and its environment and to lead change in the organization in order to achieve and maintain a superior alignment between the organization and its environment

A WORLD OF DIFFERENCE

Getting on Board with Diversity

Chip Somodevilla/Getty Images

"It's been proven again and again," says Carl Brooks, CEO of the Executive Leadership Council, a network of senior African American executives, "that companies with board members who reflect gender and ethnic diversity also tend to have better returns on equity and sales." According to Marc H. Morial, CEO of the National Urban League, which promotes economic empowerment for African Americans, a minority presence on corporate boards is also necessary to protect the interests of minority consumers and other stakeholders: "African-American voices and perspectives," he argues, "are needed on corporate boards to ensure that business decisions affecting Black America are both responsible and sensitive to the needs of our communities."

Unfortunately, says Morial, "African Americans still represent a miniscule fraction of board-level corporate leadership in America." Citing a 2009 study by the Executive Leadership Council, Morial points out that the number of blacks on *Fortune* 500 boards actually *declined* between 2004 and 2008: Even though blacks comprise 13 percent of the U.S. population, representation on corporate boards stands at "a meager 7 percent."

The same trend was confirmed a year later, with the release, in August 2010, of the U.S. Senate Democratic Hispanic Task Force report on minority and women representation on *Fortune* 500 boards and executive teams (CEOs plus their direct reports). Here are some of the survey's findings:

- Women comprise 18 percent of all board members and just under 20 percent of executive team members (roughly 1 in 5). Those figures, of course, are far below the 50 percent proportion of women in the population.
- Minorities comprise 14.5 percent of all directors—about 1 out of every 7—and an even smaller percentage of executive-team members. That's less than half of their 35 percent proportion of the population.
- Although African Americans boast the highest minority representation on boards—8.8 percent—that's equivalent to only 69 percent of their total proportion of the population. Representation on executive teams was only 4.2 percent.
- Hispanics fared worse than any other minority. Although they represent 15 percent of the U.S. population, they comprise only 3.3 percent of board members and 3 percent of executive-team members.

The report, says, task force chair Robert Menendez (the lone Hispanic member of the U.S. Senate),

clearly confirms what we had suspected all along—that American corporations need to do better when it comes to having the board rooms on Wall Street reflect the reality on Main Street. We need to change the dynamic and make it commonplace for minorities to be part of the American corporate structure. It is not just about doing what's right, but it's a good business decision that will benefit both corporations and the communities they're tapping into and making investments in.

References: "African Americans Lost Ground on Fortune 500 Boards," *Savoy*, August 2009, http://savoynetwork.com on April 25, 2011; Marc H. Morial, "National Urban League Trains African Americans for Corporate Boards," *Philadelphia Tribune*, April 14, 2011, www.phillytrib.com on April 25, 2011; "Results of Menendez's Major Fortune 500 Diversity Survey: Representation of Women and Minorities on Corporate Boards Still Lags Far Behind National Population," *Friends Fiduciary*, August 4, 2010, www.friendsfiduciary.org on April 25, 2011.

Ethical Leadership

Most people have long assumed that top managers are ethical people. But in the wake of recent corporate scandals, faith in top managers has been shaken. Perhaps now more than ever, high standards of ethical conduct are being held up as a prerequisite for effective leadership. More specifically, top managers are being called on to maintain high ethical standards for their own conduct, to exhibit ethical behavior unfailingly, and to hold others in their organization to the same standards.

The behaviors of top leaders are being scrutinized more than ever, and those responsible for hiring new leaders for a business are looking more and more closely at the background of those being considered. And the emerging pressures for stronger corporate governance models are likely to further increase commitment to selecting only those individuals with high ethical standards and to hold them more accountable than in the past for both their actions and the consequences of those actions.[48]

> "Reputation is everything."
>
> —KEN CHENAULT,
> CEO OF AMERICAN EXPRESS[49]

CONCEPT CHECK

What are the three emerging approaches to leadership, and why are they important?

Can you identify any other emerging leadership issues that are likely to become important in the future?

Political Behavior in Organizations

Another common influence on behavior is politics and political behavior. Political behavior describes activities carried out for the specific purpose of acquiring, developing, and using power and other resources to obtain one's preferred outcomes.[50] Political behavior may be undertaken by managers dealing with their subordinates, subordinates dealing with their managers, and managers and subordinates dealing with others at the same level. In other words, it may be directed upward, downward, or laterally. Decisions ranging from where to locate a manufacturing plant to where to put the company coffee maker are subject to political action. In any situation, individuals may engage in political behavior to further their own ends, to protect themselves from others, to further goals they sincerely believe to be in the organization's best interests, or simply to acquire and exercise power. And power may be sought by individuals, by groups of individuals, or by groups of groups.[51]

Although political behavior is difficult to study because of its sensitive nature, one early survey found that many managers believed that politics influenced salary and hiring decisions in their firm. Many also believed that the incidence of political behavior was greater at the upper levels of their organization and lesser at the lower levels. More than half of the respondents felt that organizational politics was bad, unfair, unhealthy, and irrational, but most suggested that successful executives have to be good politicians and be political to get ahead.[52]

Common Political Behaviors

Research has identified four basic forms of political behavior widely practiced in organizations.[53] One form is *inducement*, which occurs when a manager offers to give something to someone else in return for that individual's support. For example, a product manager might suggest to another product manager that she will put in a good word with his boss if he supports a new marketing plan that she has developed. By most accounts, former WorldCom CEO Bernard Ebbers made frequent use of this tactic to retain his leadership position in the company. For example, he allowed board members to use the corporate jet whenever they wanted and invested heavily in their pet projects.

A second tactic is *persuasion*, which relies on both emotion and logic. An operations manager wanting to construct a new plant on a certain site might persuade others to support his goal on grounds that are objective and logical (it's less expensive; taxes are lower)

political behavior
Activities carried out for the specific purpose of acquiring, developing, and using power and other resources to obtain one's preferred outcomes

as well as subjective and personal. Ebbers also used this approach. For instance, when one board member attempted to remove him from his position, he worked behind the scenes to persuade the majority of board members to allow him to stay on.

A third political behavior involves the *creation of an obligation*. For example, one manager might support a recommendation made by another manager for a new advertising campaign. Although he might really have no opinion on the new campaign, he might think that by going along, he is incurring a debt from the other manager and will be able to "call in" that debt when he wants to get something done and needs additional support. Ebbers loaned WorldCom board members money, for example, but then forgave the loans in exchange for their continued support.

Coercion is the use of force to get one's way. For example, a manager may threaten to withhold support, rewards, or other resources as a way to influence someone else. This, too, was a common tactic used by Ebbers. He reportedly belittled any board member who dared question him, for example. In the words of one former director, "Ebbers treated you like a prince—as long as you never forgot who was king."[54]

Impression Management

Impression management is a subtle form of political behavior that deserves special mention. **Impression management** is a direct and intentional effort by someone to enhance his or her image in the eyes of others. People engage in impression management for a variety of reasons. For one thing, they may do so to further their own careers. By making themselves look good, they think they are more likely to receive rewards, to be given attractive job assignments, and to receive promotions. They may also engage in impression management to boost their self-esteem. When people have a solid image in an organization, others make them aware of it through compliments, respect, and so forth. Still another reason people use impression management is in an effort to acquire more power and hence more control.

People attempt to manage how others perceive them through a variety of mechanisms. Appearance is one of the first things people think of. Hence, a person motivated by impression management will pay close attention to choice of attire, selection of language, and use of manners and body posture. People interested in impression management are also likely to jockey for association only with successful projects. By being assigned to high-profile projects led by highly successful managers, a person can begin to link his or her own name with such projects in the minds of others.

> "Every time I turn around, there is someone sticking their head in my office reminding me what they are doing for me."
>
> —TREVOR TRAINA, SILICON VALLEY ENTREPRENEUR[56]

Sometimes people too strongly motivated by impression management become obsessed with it and may resort to dishonest or unethical means. For example, some people have been known to take credit for others' work in an effort to make themselves look better. People have also been known to exaggerate or even falsify their personal accomplishments in an effort to build an enhanced image.[55]

Managing Political Behavior

By its very nature, political behavior is tricky to approach in a rational and systematic way. But managers can handle political behavior so that it does not do excessive damage.[57] First, managers should be aware that, even if their actions are not politically motivated, others may assume that they are. Second, by providing subordinates with autonomy, responsibility, challenge, and feedback, managers reduce the likelihood of political behavior by subordinates. Third, managers should avoid using power if they want to avoid charges of political motivation. Fourth, managers should get disagreements out in the open so that subordinates will have less opportunity for political behavior through using conflict for their own purposes. Finally, managers should avoid covert activities. Behind-the-scenes activities give the

impression management
A direct and intentional effort by someone to enhance his or her image in the eyes of others

impression of political intent, even if none really exists.[58] Other guidelines include clearly communicating the bases and processes for performance evaluation, tying rewards directly to performance, and minimizing competition among managers for resources.[59]

Of course, these guidelines are much easier to list than they are to implement. The well-informed manager should not assume that political behavior does not exist or, worse yet, attempt to eliminate it by issuing orders or commands. Instead, the manager must recognize that political behavior exists in virtually all organizations and that it cannot be ignored or stamped out. It can, however, be managed in such a way that it will seldom inflict serious damage on the organization. It may even play a useful role in some situations.[60] For example, a manager may be able to use his or her political influence to stimulate a greater sense of social responsibility or to heighten awareness of the ethical implications of a decision.

What are the most common forms of political behavior in organizations?

Have you ever intentionally used impression management? When might impression management be an acceptable behavior, and when might it be an unacceptable behavior?

CONCEPT CHECK

Summary of Learning Objectives and Key Points

1. Describe the nature of leadership and relate leadership to management.

   - As a process, leadership is the use of noncoercive influence to shape the group's or organization's goals, motivate behavior toward the achievement of those goals, and help define group or organization culture.
   - As a property, leadership is the set of characteristics attributed to those who are perceived to be leaders.
   - Leadership and management are often related but are also different.
   - Managers and leaders use legitimate, reward, coercive, referent, and expert power.

2. Discuss and evaluate the two generic approaches to leadership.

   - The trait approach to leadership assumed that some basic trait or set of traits differentiated leaders from nonleaders.
   - The leadership behavior approach to leadership assumed that the behavior of effective leaders was somehow different from the behavior of nonleaders.
   - Research at the University of Michigan and Ohio State University identified two basic forms of leadership behavior—one concentrating on work and performance and the other concentrating on employee welfare and support.
   - The Managerial Grid attempts to train managers to exhibit high levels of both forms of behavior.

3. Identify and describe the major situational approaches to leadership.

   - Situational approaches to leadership recognize that appropriate forms of leadership behavior are not universally applicable and attempt to specify situations in which various behaviors are appropriate.
   - The LPC theory suggests that a leader's behaviors should be either task oriented or relationship oriented, depending on the favorableness of the situation.
   - The path–goal theory suggests that directive, supportive, participative, or achievement-oriented leader behaviors may be appropriate, depending on the personal characteristics of subordinates and the environment.
   - Vroom's decision tree approach maintains that leaders should vary the extent to which they allow subordinates to participate in making decisions as a function of problem attributes.
   - The leader–member exchange model focuses on individual relationships between leaders and followers and on in-group versus out-group considerations.

4. Identify and describe three related approaches to leadership.

   - Related leadership perspectives are
     - the concept of substitutes for leadership
     - charismatic leadership
     - the role of transformational leadership in organizations

5. Describe three emerging approaches to leadership.

   - Emerging approaches include
     - strategic leadership
     - cross-cultural leadership
     - ethical leadership

6. Discuss political behavior in organizations and how it can be managed.

- Political behavior is another influence process frequently used in organizations.
- Impression management, one especially important form of political behavior, is a direct and intentional effort by someone to enhance his or her image in the eyes of others.
- Managers can take steps to limit the effects of political behavior.

Discussion Questions

Questions for Review

1. What activities do managers perform? What activities do leaders perform? Do organizations need both managers and leaders? Why or why not?
2. What are the situational approaches to leadership? Briefly describe each and compare and contrast their findings.
3. Describe the subordinate's characteristics, leader behaviors, and environmental characteristics used in path–goal theory. How do these factors combine to influence motivation?
4. In your own words, define political behavior. Describe four political tactics and give an example of each.

Questions for Analysis

5. Even though the trait approach to leadership has no empirical support, it is still widely used. In your opinion, why is this so? In what ways is the use of the trait approach helpful to those who use it? In what ways is it harmful to those who use it?
6. The behavioral theories of leadership claim that an individual's leadership style is fixed. Do you agree or disagree? Give examples to support your position. The behavioral theories also claim that the ideal style is the same in every situation. Do you agree or disagree? Again, give examples.
7. A few universities are experimenting with alternative approaches, such as allowing students to design their own majors, develop a curriculum for that major, choose professors and design courses, or self-direct and self-evaluate their studies. These are examples of substitutes for leadership. Do you think this will lead to better outcomes for students than a traditional approach? Would you personally like to have that type of alternative approach at your school? Explain your answers.

Questions for Application

8. Consider the following list of leadership situations. For each situation, describe in detail the kinds of power the leader has. If the leader were the same but the situation changed—for example, if you thought of the president as the head of his family rather than of the military—would your answers change? Why?

   - The president of the United States is commander-in-chief of the U.S. military.
   - An airline pilot is in charge of a particular flight.
   - Fans look up to a movie star.
   - Your teacher is the head of your class.

9. Think about a decision that would affect you as a student. Use Vroom's decision tree approach to decide whether the administrator making that decision should involve students in the decision. Which parts of the model seem most important in making that decision? Why?
10. Describe a time when you or someone you know was part of an in-group or an out-group. What was the relationship between each of the groups and the leader? What was the relationship between the members of the two different groups? What was the outcome of the situation for the leader? For the members of the two groups? For the organization?

CengageNow™ Highlights

Now use your CengageNow™ homework to help you:

- Apply management theories in your life
- Assess your management skills
- Master management terms and concepts
- Apply your knowledge to real-world situations
- Analyze and solve challenging management problems

In order to take advantage of these elements, your instructor will need to have set up a course for your class within CengageNow™. Ask your instructor to contact his/her Cengage sales representative and Digital Solutions Manager to explore testing CengageNow™ in your course this term.

Managing Interpersonal Relations and Communication

LEARNING OBJECTIVES

After studying this chapter, you should be able to:

1. Describe the interpersonal nature of organizations.

2. Describe the role and importance of communication in the manager's job.

3. Identify the basic forms of communication in organizations.

4. Discuss informal communication, including its various forms and types.

5. Describe how the communication process can be managed to recognize and overcome barriers.

MANAGEMENT IN ACTION The Converse of In-Person Communication

News flash: *Interviews are stressful*. The uncomfortable dress clothes, the need to make an instant good impression, the unexpected questions. Surely phone interviews are easier, right? Wrong. A job interview is a job interview, and interviews conducted on the phone pose all the challenges of a face-to-face interview—and then some. You need to take phone interviewing seriously because nowadays many corporations use them to pre-screen applicants and, more importantly, because many HR departments rely on phone interviews exclusively.

Remember first of all that talking on the phone is a certain type of communication and that, as such, it poses certain communication challenges and requires certain communication skills. It also requires a little common sense, so here are a few tips on how to solve some of the common problems that tend to accompany phone interviews.

Problem 1: Scheduling. Interviewers usually call at mutually agreed-upon times. Sometimes, however, they want to assess a candidate's ability to think on his or her feet and are looking for unscripted responses. In that case, the call may come at an unscheduled or even inconvenient time—say, when the kids are screaming for dinner or your roommate's throwing a party.

Solution. If the interviewer calls at a time when conversation is truly out of the question, you'll have to call back. Bear in mind, however, that some interviewers are put off by the request, so if the call is merely difficult but not impossible, you're better off following through with the interview.

Problem 2: Preparation. Phone interviews require the same preparation as in-person

"I'm not looking to be sold. [I want] to get an accurate view of your experience."

—MICROSOFT JOB INTERVIEWER MATT ABERHAM

interviews, but they do have a potential benefit: "You cannot be seen," points out an advisor at CollegeGrad.com, a leading website for entry-level job seekers. "Use this [fact] to your advantage." Even while you're on the phone, for example, do what you can to relax.

Telephone interviews between recruiters and job applicants are becoming increasingly common.

ThinkStock Images/Comstock Images/Getty Images

Solution. Prepare notes (yes, it's okay to use notes) on the points that you want to cover, and be sure to arrange them near the phone so that you can actually make use of them. It's also okay to say, "Could I have just a moment to look at my notes?" Referring to your notes reminds the interviewer that you're prepared. You should also have paper and pen handy so that you can *take* notes.

Problem 3: Noise. When it comes to the process of communicating, "noise" means any sort of distraction—like trying to talk while multitasking at your computer as well as having to put up with the sounds of a nearby television. Phone conversations are especially subject to all sorts of noise, including a poor connection or the sudden demise of a cell phone battery as well as plain environmental noise.

Solution. Shut the door and try to make as little unnecessary noise of your own as possible. If you have a poor connection, ask the interviewer to speak up. If your cell phone battery isn't charged, you aren't prepared for any kind of phone communication, much less an interview for the job you want or need. (In other words, keep your phone charged.) Focus on the activity at hand and pay attention to the conversation.

Problem 4: Lack of context cues. For good or ill, an in-person conversation is affected by all sorts of nonverbal "context cues"—gesture, body language, facial expression, dress, and so forth. In fact, only a small portion of conversational meaning is determined solely by words. A phone interview, on the other hand, allows for just one nonverbal element—tone of voice.

Solution. Even though the interviewer can't see you, smile: The information that you're conveying will come across as personal and intended for the person on the other end of the line. Many experts also recommend that you feel free to use gestures, expressions, and body language, just as if you were in a face-to-face interview. Take a tip from phone-sales professionals, who often stand or walk around the room in order to sound more comfortable and more energetic.

Now that you're properly equipped to solve the most common problems that come up in phone interviews, let's run over a few do's and don'ts. First, some tips on what you should do from Job Application and Interview Advice, a website written by management and HR professionals:

- *Be positive.* Talk about the positive aspects of your present job and what you're looking forward to in a new one.

- *Know what you're talking about and be specific.* In other words, hold the interviewer's interest by taking charge of context cues. "Because [interviewers] don't have an image of your face to set you apart from others," says one job counselor, "you need to draw pictures with your words." Back up general statements with good examples; people prefer good (economical) stories to dissertations, and they get a better impression of what you've done in your work life.

- *Refer to your notes.* Don't be embarrassed about asking to look at your notes. It shows confidence and preparation to ask to refer to notes.

- *Take the initiative.* If there's something that you feel it's important to talk about but that doesn't come up, bring it up. Don't waste any opportunity to sell yourself.

- *Know when a topic's been covered (and when the conversation's over).* Don't be tempted to fill in silences by simply continuing to talk.

Finally, let's review a few things to avoid. Matt Aberham, who interviews would-be program managers and engineers for Microsoft's Online Services Business, offers the following list of five good ways to avoid failing a telephone interview (at least one that he's in charge of):

- *Keep track of the time.* Because most interviews are slated for 30–45 minutes, there's time to cover several topics thoroughly and a couple in fairly deep detail. But no matter what you're talking about, be conscious of how long you've been talking about it. Err on the side of conciseness—if the interviewer wants to know more, he or she will be sure to let you know.

- *Answer the question instead of trying to sell yourself.* Don't be afraid to discuss areas where you need (and want) further development. "I'm not looking to be sold," says Aberham. "[I want] to get an accurate view of your experience."

- *Talk about "me," not "we."* Don't get into the habit of saying "we" instead of "I" throughout the interview unless you're trying to show how you *led* a group in accomplishing its goals. Take "ownership" of what *you* did. "Showing ownership," explains Aberham, "helps me figure out if . . . your contributions are appropriate for the work we're thinking of having you do."

- *Be concrete instead of abstract.* Don't give a hypothetical answer to a specific question. "The quickest way to fail a 'Tell-me-about-a-time-when . . .' question," advises Aberham, "is to give me a

'Here's-what-I-would-do-in-that-situation . . .'
answer. . . . If [I ask you] to describe a situation you've
never handled, let me know and I'll pick a different
question."

- *Don't ask "How'd I do?"* Interviewers usually
don't mind giving you some feedback about the

match between your skills and experiences and the
employer's needs, but they're rarely ready at the end
of a phone interview to tell you what they're going to
do next about you. And Aberham particularly doesn't
like it when something like "How'd I do?" is the only
question you have for him.[1]

Businesses continue to look for effective ways to communicate with their employees, as well as job seekers, customers, and investors. The idea of telephone interviews for job seekers may seem odd to some people, but many firms are finding this method of screening prospective employees to be both efficient and effective. Of course, as noted, there are both advantages and disadvantages to telephone interviews. Communication has always been a vital part of managerial work. Indeed, managers around the world agree that communication is one of their most important tasks. It is important for them to communicate with others in order to convey their vision and goals for the organization. And it's important for others to communicate with them so that they will better understand what is going on in their environment and how they and their organization can become more effective.

This chapter is the first of two that focuses on interpersonal processes in organizations. We first establish the interpersonal nature of organizations and then discuss communication, one of the most basic forms of interaction among people. We begin by examining communication in the context of the manager's job. We then identify and discuss forms of interpersonal, group, and organizational communication. After discussing informal means of communication, we describe how organizational communication can be effectively managed. In our next chapter, we discuss other elements of interpersonal relations: group and team processes and conflict.

The Interpersonal Nature of Organizations

In Chapter 1, we noted how much of a manager's job involves scheduled and unscheduled meetings, telephone calls, e-mail, and related activities. Indeed, a great deal of what all managers do involves interacting with other people, both directly and indirectly and both inside and outside of the organization. The schedule that follows is a typical day for the president of a Houston-based company, part of a larger firm headquartered in California. He kept a log of his activities for several different days so that you could better appreciate the nature of managerial work.

6:00–6:30 A.M. Read and respond to e-mail from home; scan major news stories.

7:45–8:15 A.M. Arrive at work; review hardcopy mail sorted by assistant.

8:15–8:30 A.M. Scan the *Wall Street Journal*; read and respond to e-mail; scan cnn.com for business news and updates.

8:30–9:00 A.M. Meet with labor officials and plant manager to resolve minor labor disputes.

9:00–9:30 A.M. Review internal report; read and respond to new e-mail.

9:30–10:00 A.M. Meet with two marketing executives to review advertising campaign; instruct them to fax approvals to advertising agency.

10:00–11:30 A.M. Meet with company executive committee to discuss strategy, budgetary issues, and competition (this committee meets weekly).

11:30–12:00 noon. Send several e-mails; read and respond to new e-mail.

12:00–1:15 P.M. Lunch with the financial vice president and two executives from another subsidiary of the parent corporation. Primary topic of discussion is the Houston Rockets basketball team. Place three calls from cell phone en route to lunch and receive one call en route back to office.

1:15–1:45 P.M. Meet with human resource director and assistant about a recent OSHA inspection; establish a task force to investigate the problems identified and to suggest solutions.

1:45–2:00 P.M. Read and respond to new e-mail.

2:00–2:30 P.M. Conference call with four other company presidents.

2:30–3:00 P.M. Meet with financial vice president about a confidential issue that came up at lunch (unscheduled).

3:00–3:30 P.M. Work alone in office; read and respond to new e-mail; send several e-mails.

3:30–4:15 P.M. Meet with a group of sales representatives and the company purchasing agent.

4:15–5:30 P.M. Work alone in office.

5:30–7:00 P.M. Play racquetball at nearby athletic club with marketing vice president.

9:00–9:30 P.M. Read and respond to e-mail from home; send e-mail to assistant about an emergency meeting to be scheduled for the next day.

How did this manager spend his time? He spent most of it working, communicating, and interacting with other people. And this compressed daily schedule does not include several other brief telephone calls, brief conversations with his assistant, and brief conversations with other managers. Clearly, interpersonal relations, communication, and group processes are a pervasive part of all organizations and a vital part of all managerial activities.[2]

Interpersonal Dynamics

The nature of interpersonal relations in an organization is as varied as the individual members themselves.[3] At one extreme, interpersonal relations can be personal and positive. This occurs when the two parties know each other, have mutual respect and affection, and enjoy interacting. Two managers who have known each other for years, play golf together on weekends, and are close personal friends will likely interact at work in a positive fashion. At the other extreme, interpersonal dynamics can be personal but negative. This is most likely when the parties dislike each other, do not have mutual respect, and do not enjoy interacting. Suppose a manager has fought openly for years to block the promotion of another manager within the organization. Over the objections of the first manager, however, the other manager eventually gets promoted to the same rank. When the two of them must interact, it will most likely be in a negative manner.

Most interactions fall between these extremes, as members of the organization interact in a professional way focused primarily on goal accomplishment. The interaction deals with the job at hand, is relatively formal and structured, and is task directed. Two managers may respect each other's work and recognize the professional competence that each brings to the job. However, they may also have few common interests and little to talk about besides the job they are doing. These different types of interactions may occur between individuals, between groups, or

"You have to read people quickly to fit into the social network."

—STEPHEN MILES, EXECUTIVE COACH[4]

between individuals and groups, and they can change over time. The two managers in the second scenario, for example, might decide to bury the hatchet and adopt a detached, professional manner. The two managers in the third example could find more common ground than they anticipated and evolve to a personal and positive interaction.

Outcomes of Interpersonal Behaviors

A variety of things can happen as a result of interpersonal behaviors.[5] Recall from Chapter 19, for example, that numerous perspectives on motivation suggest that people have social needs. Interpersonal relations in organizations can be a primary source of need satisfaction for many people. For a person with a strong need for affiliation, high-quality interpersonal relations can be an important positive element in the workplace. However, when this same person is confronted with poor-quality working relationships, the effect can be just as great in the other direction.

Interpersonal relations also serve as a solid basis for social support. Suppose that an employee receives a poor performance evaluation or is denied a promotion. Others in the organization can lend support because they share a common frame of reference—an understanding of the causes and consequences of what happened. Good interpersonal relations throughout an organization can also be a source of synergy. People who support one another and who work well together can accomplish much more than people who do not support one another and who do not work well together. Another outcome, implied earlier, is conflict—people may leave an interpersonal exchange feeling angry or hostile. But a common thread is woven through all of these outcomes—communication between people in the organization.[6]

What kinds of interpersonal interactions can be identified in organizational settings?

How much of your daily life involves interacting with other people?

CONCEPT CHECK

Communication and the Manager's Job

As evidenced by the daily log presented earlier, a typical day for a manager includes doing desk work, attending scheduled meetings, placing and receiving telephone calls, reading and answering correspondence (both print and electronic), attending unscheduled meetings, and making tours.[7] Most of these activities involve communication. In fact, managers usually spend over half their time on some form of communication. Communication always involves two or more people, so other behavioral processes, such as motivation, leadership, and group and team interactions, all come into play. Top executives must handle communication effectively if they are to be true leaders.[8]

A Definition of Communication

Imagine three managers working in an office building. The first is all alone but is nevertheless yelling for a subordinate to come help. No one appears, but he continues to yell. The second is talking to a subordinate on a cell phone, but a poor signal causes the subordinate to misunderstand some important numbers being provided by the manager. As a result, the subordinate sends 1,500 crates of eggs to 150 Fifth Street, when he should have sent 150 crates of eggs to 1500 Fifteenth Street. The third manager is talking in her office with a subordinate who clearly hears and understands what is being said. Each of these managers is attempting to communicate, but with different results.

Communication is the process of transmitting information from one person to another. Did any of our three managers communicate? The last did, and the first did not. How about

communication
The process of transmitting information from one person to another

the second? In fact, she did communicate. She transmitted information, and information was received. The problem was that the message transmitted and the message received were not the same. The words spoken by the manager were distorted by static and noise. Effective communication, then, is the process of sending a message in such a way that the message received is as close in meaning as possible to the message intended. Although the second manager engaged in communication, it was not effective.

Our definition of effective communication is based on the ideas of meaning and consistency of meaning. Meaning is the idea that the individual who initiates the communication exchange wishes to convey. In effective communication, the meaning is transmitted in such a way that the receiving person understands it. For example, consider these messages:

1. The high today will be only 40 degrees.
2. It will be cold today.
3. Ceteris paribus.
4. Xn1gp bo5cz4ik ab19.

You probably understand the meaning of the first statement. The second statement may seem clear at first, but it is somewhat less clear than the first statement because cold is a relative condition and the word can mean different things to different people. Fewer still understand the third statement, because it is written in Latin. None of you understands the last statement because it is written in a secret code that your author developed as a child.

effective communication
The process of sending a message in such a way that the message received is as close in meaning as possible to the message intended

The Role of Communication in Management

We noted earlier the variety of activities that fill a manager's day. Meetings, telephone calls, and correspondence are all a necessary part of every manager's job—and all clearly involve communication. To better understand the linkages between communication and management, recall the variety of roles that managers must fill. Each of the ten basic managerial roles discussed in Chapter 1 (see Table 1.2) would be impossible to fill without communication.[9] Interpersonal roles involve interacting with supervisors, subordinates, peers, and others outside the organization. Decisional roles require managers to seek out information to use in making decisions and then communicate those decisions to others. Informational roles focus specifically on acquiring and disseminating information.

Communication also relates directly to the basic management functions of planning, organizing, leading, and controlling. Environmental scanning, integrating planning-time horizons, and decision making, for example, all necessitate communication. Delegation, coordination, and organization change and development also entail communication. Developing reward systems and interacting with subordinates as a part of the leading function would be impossible without some form of communication. And communication is essential to establishing standards, monitoring performance, and taking corrective actions as a part of control. Clearly, then, communication is a pervasive part of virtually all managerial activities.[10]

Information overload is an all too common problem today. Managers can be deluged with telephone calls, written requests, and emails that require quick responses. Occasionally people get so overwhelmed by this overload that they are unsure of what to tackle first.

Otmar Winterleitner/istockphoto.com

The Communication Process

Figure 21.1 illustrates how communication generally takes place between people. The process of communication begins when one person (the sender) wants to transmit a fact, idea, opinion, or other information to someone else (the receiver). This fact, idea, or opinion has meaning to the sender, whether it be simple and concrete or complex and abstract. For example, Linda Porter, a marketing representative at Canon, recently landed a new account and wanted to tell her boss about it. This fact and her motivation to tell her boss represented meaning.

The next step is to encode the meaning into a form appropriate to the situation. The encoding might take the form of words, facial expressions, gestures, or even artistic expressions and physical actions. For example, the Canon representative might have said, "I just landed the Acme account," "We just got some good news from Acme," "I just spoiled Xerox's day," "Acme just made the right decision," or any number of other things. She actually chose the second message. Clearly, the encoding process is influenced by the content of the message, the familiarity of sender and receiver, and other situational factors.

After the message has been encoded, it is transmitted through the appropriate channel or medium. The channel by which this encoded message is being transmitted to you is the printed page. Common channels in organizations include meetings, e-mail, memos, letters, reports, and telephone calls. Linda Porter might have written her boss a note, sent him an e-mail, called him on the telephone, or dropped by his office to convey the news. Because both she and her boss were out of the office when she got the news, she called and left a message for him on his voicemail.

After the message is received, it is decoded back into a form that has meaning for the receiver. As noted earlier, the consistency of this meaning can vary dramatically. Upon hearing about the Acme deal, the sales manager at Canon might have thought, "This'll mean a big promotion for both of us," "This is great news for the company," or "She's blowing her own horn too much again." His actual feelings were closest to the second statement. In many cases, the meaning prompts a response, and the cycle is continued when a new message is sent by the same steps back to the original sender. The manager might have called the sales

FIGURE 21.1 THE COMMUNICATION PROCESS

As the figure shows, noise can disrupt the communication process at any step. Managers must therefore understand that a conversation in the next office, a fax machine out of paper, and the receiver's worries may all thwart the manager's best attempts to communicate.

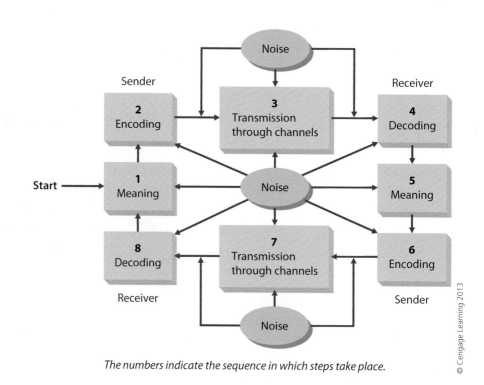

The numbers indicate the sequence in which steps take place.

© Cengage Learning 2013

representative to offer congratulations, written her a personal note of praise, offered praise in an e-mail, or sent a formal letter of acknowledgment. Linda's boss wrote her a personal note.

"Noise" may disrupt communication anywhere along the way. Noise can be the sound of someone coughing, a truck driving by, or two people talking close at hand. It can also include disruptions such as a letter lost in the mail, a dead telephone line, an interrupted cell phone call, an e-mail misrouted or infected with a virus, or one of the participants in a conversation being called away before the communication process is completed. If the note written by Linda's boss had gotten lost, she might have felt unappreciated. As it was, his actions positively reinforced not only her efforts at Acme but also her effort to keep him informed. Another form of noise might be difficulties in understanding messages due to language barriers.

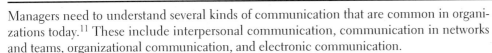

Distinguish between communication and effective communication.

Recall a recent communication exchange in which you participated and analyze it in terms of the model in Figure 21.1.

CONCEPT CHECK

Forms of Communication in Organizations

Managers need to understand several kinds of communication that are common in organizations today.[11] These include interpersonal communication, communication in networks and teams, organizational communication, and electronic communication.

Interpersonal Communication

Interpersonal communication generally takes one of two forms: oral and written. As we will see, each has clear strengths and weaknesses.

Oral Communication Oral communication takes place in conversations, group discussions, telephone calls, and other situations in which the spoken word is used to express meaning. One study (conducted before the advent of e-mail) demonstrated the importance of oral communication by finding that most managers spent between 50 and 90 percent of their time talking to people.[12] Oral communication is so prevalent for several reasons. The primary advantage of oral communication is that it promotes prompt feedback and interchange in the form of verbal questions or agreement, facial expressions, and gestures. Oral communication is also easy (all the sender needs to do is talk), and it can be done with little preparation (though careful preparation is advisable in certain situations). The sender does not need pencil and paper, a printer, or other equipment. In another survey, 55 percent of the executives sampled felt that their own written communication skills were fair or poor, so they chose oral communication to avoid embarrassment![13]

However, oral communication also has drawbacks. It may suffer from problems of inaccuracy if the speaker chooses the wrong words to convey meaning or leaves out pertinent details, if noise disrupts the process, or if the receiver forgets part of the message.[14] In a two-way discussion, there is seldom time for a thoughtful, considered response or for introducing many new facts, and there is no permanent record of what has been said. In addition, although most managers are comfortable talking to people individually or in small groups, fewer enjoy speaking to larger audiences.[15]

Written Communication "Putting it in writing" in a letter, report, memorandum, handwritten note, or e-mail can solve many of the problems inherent in oral communication. Nevertheless, and perhaps surprisingly, written communication is not as common

oral communication
Face-to-face conversation, group discussions, telephone calls, and other circumstances in which the spoken word is used to transmit meaning

written communication
Memos, letters, reports, notes, and other circumstances in which the written word is used to transmit meaning

Written communication is one of the most common forms of communication in organizations. While written communication was once dominated by letters, memorandums, and reports, today it's much more likely to be email or text messages. But the advantages and disadvantages of this form of communication remain essentially the same.

Elena Elisseeva/Shutterstock.com

as one might imagine, nor is it a mode of communication much respected by managers. One sample of managers indicated that only 13 percent of the printed mail they received was of immediate use to them.[16] Over 80 percent of the managers who responded to another survey indicated that the written communication they received was of fair or poor quality.[17]

The biggest single drawback of traditional forms of written communication is that they inhibit feedback and interchange. When one manager sends another manager a letter, it must be written or dictated, printed, mailed, received, routed, opened, and read. If there is a misunderstanding, it may take several days for it to be recognized, let alone rectified. Although the use of e-mail is, of course, much faster, both sender and receiver must still have access to a computer or other device, and the receiver must open and read the message for it to actually be received. A phone call could settle the whole matter in just a few minutes. Thus written communication often inhibits feedback and interchange and is usually more difficult and time consuming than oral communication.

Of course, written communication offers some advantages. It is often quite accurate and provides a permanent record of the exchange. The sender can take the time to collect and assimilate the information and can draft and revise it before it is transmitted. The receiver can take the time to read it carefully and can refer to it repeatedly, as needed. For these reasons, written communication is generally preferable when important details are involved. At times it is important to one or both parties to have a written record available as evidence of exactly what took place. Julie Regan, founder of Toucan-Do, an importing company based in Honolulu, relies heavily on formal business letters in establishing contacts and buying merchandise from vendors in Southeast Asia. She believes that such letters give her an opportunity to carefully think through what she wants to say, tailor her message to each individual, and avoid later misunderstandings.

Choosing the Right Form Which form of interpersonal communication should the manager use? The best medium will be determined by the situation. Oral communication or e-mail is often preferred when the message is personal, nonroutine, and brief. More formal written communication is usually best when the message is more impersonal, routine, and longer. And, given the prominent role that e-mails have played in several recent court cases, managers should always use discretion when sending messages electronically.[18] For example, private e-mails made public during legal proceedings have played major roles in litigation involving Enron, Tyco, WorldCom, and Morgan Stanley.[19]

The manager can also combine media to capitalize on the advantages of each. For example, a quick telephone call to set up a meeting is easy and gets an immediate response. Following up the call with a reminder e-mail or handwritten note helps ensure that the recipient will remember the meeting, and it provides a record of the meeting's having been called. Electronic communication, discussed more fully later, blurs the differences between oral and written communication and can help each be more effective. In some instances, electronic communication itself is also the most appropriate way to send a message. That's what one doctor found out, as you can see in the *Technically Speaking* box, entitled "The Medical Uses of Viral E-Mail," on page 539.

"I'm not a big e-mailer. I prefer face-to-face whenever possible."

—A. G. LAFLEY, FORMER PROCTER & GAMBLE CHAIRMAN[20]

TECHNICALLY SPEAKING

The Medical Uses of Viral E-Mail

Sandra O'Claire/iStockphoto.com

Dr. William H. Parker, a clinical professor of obstetrics and gynecology at the UCLA School of Medicine, says that there's a certain patient question he answers almost every day. It concerns a blood test known as CA-125, which is used to monitor the status of the disease in women diagnosed with ovarian cancer. "I probably answer maybe five or six patients a week who come in saying, 'I read this e-mail that says I'm supposed to get this test.' . . . I don't mind educating my patients," Parker explains, but the e-mail "is based on bad information." When he investigated the online message that had spurred the concerns of so many patients, Parker discovered that it had been circulating for nearly ten years.

It was written by a woman named Carolyn Benivegna, who'd had a bad experience with the diagnosis of a disease quite similar to ovarian cancer. Dispatched in July 1998, Benivegna's chain letter emphasized that her cancer could have been treated more effectively if doctors had ordered the CA-125 test earlier in the lengthy diagnostic process. She urged everyone who received her message "to give it or send it via e-mail to everybody you know." She also added: "Beware that their doctors might try to talk them out of it. Don't take no for an answer." Before long, Benivegna's warning was on a decade-long journey through cyberspace—"a full-blown viral message with seemingly unstoppable momentum," according to one medical journalist.

Hence Dr. Parker's dilemma. "To explain to [patients] why this test is not reliable, without brushing off their concerns," he says, "I have to launch into a 15-minute discussion about the science and why this e-mail presents the wrong information. And," he adds, "I still have to quell their anxiety about it." Parker can, for example, explain "the science" (and often does), but he quickly discovered that his calm recitation of the data didn't have nearly the impact of Benivegna's cautionary tale.*

"So one day," he says, "I thought to myself, 'I need to do what they did. I need to get an e-mail out there that will take on a life of its own and be passed from woman to woman.' " So Parker composed an anti-misinformation e-mail and ran it by Carla Dionne, the executive director of a nonprofit women's health organization. "It needed a lot of work," recalls Dionne. "It was extremely passive and written from the clinician's perspective. It was calm, educated, and careful. The whole business of catching attention seemed somewhat offensive to him."

Ironically, she advised Parker to consult Benivegna's original message to see how he should compose his own, and Parker came back with a revised version of his e-mail message, charging it with some emotion and putting the important information up front. It promised to be much more effective. "The content of the message," explains Jeanne Jennings, an e-mail marketing consultant in Washington, D.C., "has to be of intense interest to your target audience. Women, of course, are naturally looking out for each other. So if there's a health concern or a danger, they'll naturally pass it on to their network of friends and relatives."

Parker's revised e-mail message went out in January 2008. It took a couple of weeks before a patient mentioned it, but at least Parker knew that it was making the rounds. He keeps copies of it, along with a write-up in the *New York Times*, in his waiting room, and now, he says, "when patients ask about the test, I refer them to the e-mail and the article. Then, if they have more questions, I talk to them. It just makes my life much easier this way."

References: John McCormack, "Rumor Control: How to Battle Online Misinformation," *American Medical News*, March 17, 2008, www.ama-assn.org on April 30, 2011; "CA-125 Screening for Ovarian Cancer," *BreakTheChain.org*, June 27, 2002/September 27, 2008, www.breakthechain.org on April 30, 2011; Tara Parker-Pope, "Doctors Take On a Notorious E-Mail," *New York Times*, January 18, 2008, http://well.blogs.nytimes.com on April 30, 2011; "CA-125," *Snopes.com*, March 11, 2009, www.snopes.com on April 30, 2011.

*When she learned in 2002 that she had inadvertently passed along potentially harmful misinformation, Benivegna hastened to circulate a corrective e-mail. Unfortunately, the follow-up has never attained the popularity of the original. Benivegna died of ovarian cancer in September 2008.

Communication in Networks and Work Teams

Although communication among team members in an organization is clearly interpersonal in nature, substantial research also focuses specifically on how people in networks and work teams communicate with one another. A communication network is the pattern through which the members of a group or team communicate. Researchers studying group dynamics have discovered several typical networks in groups and teams consisting of three, four, and five members. Representative networks among members of five-member teams are shown in Figure 21.2.[21]

In the wheel pattern, all communication flows through one central person, who is probably the group's leader. In a sense, the wheel is the most centralized network because one person receives and disseminates all information. The Y pattern is slightly less centralized—two people are close to the center. The chain offers a more even flow of information among members, although two people (the ones at each end) interact with only one other person. This path is closed in the circle pattern. Finally, the all-channel network, the most decentralized, allows a free flow of information among all group members. Everyone participates equally, and the group's leader, if there is one, is not likely to have excessive power.

Research conducted on networks suggests some interesting connections between the type of network and group performance. For example, when the group's task is relatively simple and routine, centralized networks tend to perform with greatest efficiency and accuracy. The dominant leader facilitates performance by coordinating the flow of information. When a group of accounting clerks is logging incoming invoices and distributing them for payment, for example, one centralized leader can coordinate things efficiently. When the task is complex and nonroutine, such as making a major decision about organizational strategy, decentralized networks tend to be most effective because open channels of communication permit more interaction and a more efficient sharing of relevant information. Managers should recognize the effects of communication networks on group and organizational performance and should try to structure networks appropriately.

Organizational Communication

communication network
The pattern through which the members of a group communicate

Still other forms of communication in organizations are those that flow among and between organizational units or groups. Each of these involves oral or written communication, but each also extends to broad patterns of communication across the organization.[22] As shown in Figure 21.3, two of these forms of communication follow vertical and horizontal linkages in the organization.

FIGURE 21.2 TYPES OF COMMUNICATION NETWORKS

Research on communication networks has identified five basic networks for five-person groups. These networks vary in terms of information flow, position of the leader, and effectiveness for different types of tasks. Managers might strive to create centralized networks when group tasks are simple and routine. Alternatively, managers can foster decentralized groups when group tasks are complex and nonroutine.

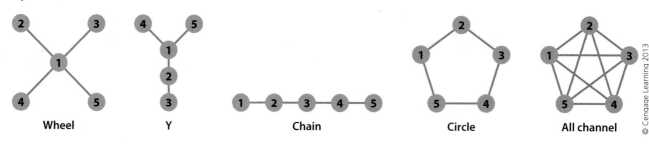

Wheel Y Chain Circle All channel

© Cengage Learning 2013

FIGURE 21.3 FORMAL COMMUNICATION IN ORGANIZATIONS

Formal communication in organizations follows official reporting relationships or prescribed channels. For example, vertical communication, shown here with the solid lines, flows between levels in the organization and involves subordinates and their managers. Horizontal communication, shown with dashed lines, flows between people at the same level and is usually used to facilitate coordination.

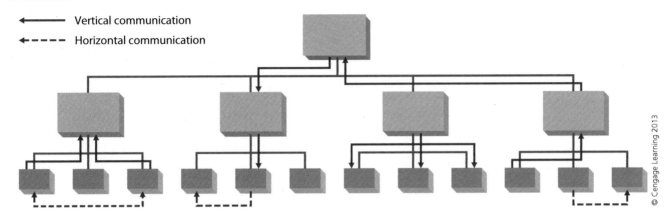

← ——— Vertical communication

← - - - - Horizontal communication

© Cengage Learning 2013

Vertical Communication Vertical communication is communication that flows up and down the organization, usually along formal reporting lines—that is, it is the communication that takes place between managers and their superiors and subordinates. Vertical communication may involve only two people, or it may flow through several different organizational levels.

Upward communication consists of messages from subordinates to superiors. This flow is usually from subordinates to their direct superior, then to that person's direct superior, and so on up the hierarchy. Occasionally, a message might bypass a particular superior. The typical content of upward communication is requests, information that the lower-level manager thinks is of importance to the higher-level manager, responses to requests from the higher-level manager, suggestions, complaints, and financial information. Research has shown that upward communication is more subject to distortion than is downward communication. Subordinates are likely to withhold or distort information that makes them look bad. The greater the degree of difference in status between superior and subordinate and the greater the degree of distrust, the more likely the subordinate is to suppress or distort information.[23] For example, subordinates might choose to withhold information about problems from their boss if they think the news will make him angry and if they think they can solve the problem themselves without his ever knowing about it.

Downward communication occurs when information flows down the hierarchy from superiors to subordinates. The typical content of these messages is directives on how something is to be done, the assignment of new responsibilities, performance feedback, and general information that the higher-level manager thinks will be of value to the lower-level manager. Vertical communication can and usually should be two-way in nature. In other words, give-and-take communication with active feedback is generally likely to be more effective than one-way communication.[24]

Horizontal Communication Whereas vertical communication involves a superior and a subordinate, horizontal communication involves colleagues and peers at the same level of the organization. For example, an operations manager might communicate to a marketing manager that inventory levels are running low and that projected delivery dates should be extended by two weeks. Horizontal communication probably occurs more among managers than among nonmanagers.

vertical communication
Communication that flows up and down the organization, usually along formal reporting lines; takes place between managers and their superiors and subordinates and may involve several different levels of the organization

horizontal communication
Communication that flows laterally within the organization; involves colleagues and peers at the same level of the organization and may involve individuals from several different organizational units

This type of communication serves a number of purposes.[25] It facilitates coordination among interdependent units. For example, a manager at Motorola was once researching the strategies of Japanese semiconductor firms in Europe. He found a great deal of information that was relevant to his assignment. He also uncovered some additional information that was potentially important to another department, so he passed it along to a colleague in that department, who used it to improve his own operations. Horizontal communication can also be used for joint problem solving, as when two plant managers at Northrop Grumman got together to work out a new method to improve productivity. Finally, horizontal communication plays a major role in work teams with members drawn from several departments.

Electronic Communication

Finally, as already noted, electronic communication has taken on much greater importance for managers in recent times. Both formal information systems and personal information technology have reshaped how managers communicate with one another. The *Change* box on page 543, entitled "The Brutally-Honest-Opinion Business," shows how some corporations are making use of a relatively new form of electronic communication—the blog.

Formal Information Systems Most larger businesses manage at least a portion of their organizational communication through information systems. Some firms go so far as to create a position for a chief information officer, or CIO. General Mills, Xerox, and Burlington Industries all have such a position. The CIO is responsible for determining the information-processing needs and requirements of the organization and then putting in place systems that facilitate smooth and efficient organizational communication.

Part of the CIO's efforts also involves the creation of one or more formal information systems linking all relevant managers, departments, and facilities in the organization. Most enterprise resource planning systems play this role very effectively. In the absence of such a system, a marketing manager, for example, may need to call a warehouse manager to find out how much of a particular product is in stock before promising shipping dates to a customer. An effective formal information system allows the marketing manager to get the information more quickly, and probably more accurately, by plugging directly into a computerized information system. Because of the increased emphasis on and importance of these kinds of information systems, we cover them in detail in Chapter 13.

Personal Electronic Technology In recent years, the nature of organizational communication has changed dramatically, mainly because of breakthroughs in personal electronic communication technology, and the future promises even more change. Electronic typewriters and photocopying machines were early breakthroughs. The photocopier, for example, made it possible for a manager to have a typed report distributed to large numbers of other people in an extremely short time. Personal computers have accelerated the process even more. E-mail networks, the Internet, corporate intranets, social networking sites, wireless communication systems, and other breakthroughs are carrying communication technology even further.

It is also becoming common to have teleconferences in which managers stay at their own location (such as offices in different cities) but are seen on television or computer monitors as they "meet." A manager in New York can keyboard a letter or memorandum at her personal computer, point and click with a mouse, and have it delivered to hundreds or even thousands of colleagues around the world in a matter of seconds. Highly detailed information can be retrieved with ease from large electronic databanks. This has given rise to a new version of an old work arrangement—cottage industry. In cottage industry, people work at home (in their "cottage") and periodically bring the products of their labors in to the company. Telecommuting is the label given to a new electronic cottage industry. In telecommuting, people work at home on their computers and transmit their work to their companies via telephone line or cable modem.

THE MORE THINGS CHANGE

The Brutally-Honest-Opinion Business

http://www.stonyfield.com/

Cell phones and fax machines? Your grandfather's technology. Video conferencing? Been there, done that. The Internet? Old news. E-mail? Business as usual. PDA? BlackBerry? Standard issue for today's manager.

Obviously, the explosion in digital-communication technology over the last 25 years has created many new media. Corporations now rely extensively on these new technologies, and they've changed the way we work. Virtual teams, global workforces, outsourcing, just-in-time inventory—these are just a few of the widely accepted business tools and methods that could never have existed without new developments in communication technology. Today, yet another new technology is at the cutting edge of business-communication strategies: *web logs*, or so-called "blogs."

A *blog* is any web-based publication consisting mainly of periodically posted articles, usually in reverse chronological order. They're similar to journals in that bloggers express thoughts or opinions over a period of time, but most blogs allow readers to add their own comments in response to original posts. Blogs allow groups of people, whether or not they're

otherwise connected, to share thoughts, and for some readers, professionally (or semiprofessionally) posted blogs actually supplement or replace traditional news media. Blogs can also function much like face-to-face grapevines to communicate information that's suppressed elsewhere.

Nowadays, organizations as disparate as General Motors, the Dallas Cowboys, and Stonyfield Farm (an organic dairy) maintain popular corporate blogs; Microsoft supports 237 blogs (at last count). What do corporations do with blogs? Naturally, they use them to communicate with customers and employees, but they've found a variety of other uses for them, too. A consumer-research firm called Umbria, for example, charges companies such as Electronic Arts, SAP, and Sprint $60,000 a year to conduct routine scans of 20 million blogs. The data is valuable to corporate marketers, in particular because bloggers are often early product adopters and blog opinions show up quickly. Marketers, however, should be prepared for the kind of input they're going to get for their money: "The blogosphere," warns Umbria CEO Howard Kaushansky, "is overflowing with brutally honest opinion."

With a survey list of merely 20 million blogs and a 10 percent share, Umbria is actually a fairly small player in the blog-research market. Larger competitors in the $20 million market include Intelliseek, with about a third of the market, and BuzzMetrics, which doesn't reveal how much business it does. There appears to be room for more competitors, however. According to the search engine Technorati, there are at least 112.8 million blogs out there (not counting another 72.8 million in China), with about 175,000 new blogs popping up every day. Bloggers put up more than 1.6 million posts per day, or more than 18 updates a second.

References: Matthew Boyle, "Do's and Don'ts of Corporate Blogging," *Fortune*, February 28, 2006, http://money.cnn.com on April 26, 2011; Justin Martin, "What Bloggers Think of Your Business," *Fortune*, December 7, 2005, http://money.cnn.com on April 26, 2011; Anne Helmond, "How Many Blogs Are There? Is Someone Still Counting?" *The Blog Herald*, February 11, 2008, www.blogherald.com on April 26, 2011; Adam Thierer, "Need Help . . . How Many Blogs Are There Out There?" *The Technology Liberation Front*, May 6, 2008, http://techliberation.com on April 26, 2011.

Cellular telephones and facsimile machines have made it even easier for managers to communicate with one another. Many now use cell phones to make calls while commuting to and from work, and carry them in their briefcases so that they can receive calls while at lunch. Facsimile machines make it easy for people to use written communication media and get rapid feedback. And other current personal computing devices, such as BlackBerrys, iPhones, and iPads are further revolutionizing how people communicate with one another.

Psychologists, however, are beginning to associate some problems with these communication advances. For one thing, managers who are seldom in their "real" offices are likely to fall behind in their fields and to be victimized by organizational politics because they are not present to keep in touch with what is going on and to protect themselves. They drop out of the organizational grapevine and miss out on much of the informal communication that takes place. Moreover, the use of electronic communication at the expense of face-to-face meetings and conversations makes it hard to build a strong culture, develop solid working relationships, and create a mutually supportive atmosphere of trust and cooperativeness.[26] Finally, electronic communication is also opening up new avenues for dysfunctional employee behavior, such as the passing of lewd or offensive materials to others. For example, the *New York Times* once fired almost 10 percent of its workers at one of its branch offices for sending inappropriate e-mails at work.[27]

What are the primary forms of communication that are used by managers in organizations today?

What kinds of electronic communication have you used in the last 24 hours?

Informal Communication in Organizations

The forms of organizational communication discussed in the previous section all represent planned and relatively formal communication mechanisms. However, in many cases some of the communication that takes place in an organization transcends these formal channels and instead follows any of several informal methods. Figure 21.4 illustrates numerous examples of informal communication. Common forms of informal communication in organizations include the grapevine, management by wandering around, and nonverbal communication.

grapevine
An informal communication network among people in an organization

The Grapevine

The grapevine is an informal communication network that can permeate an entire organization. Grapevines are found in all organizations except the very smallest, but they do not always follow

FIGURE 21.4 INFORMAL COMMUNICATION IN ORGANIZATIONS

Informal communication in organizations may or may not follow official reporting relationships or prescribed channels. It may cross different levels and different departments or work units, and may or may not have anything to do with official organizational business.

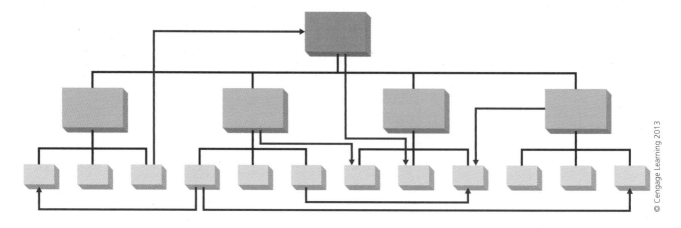

© Cengage Learning 2013

FIGURE 21.5 COMMON GRAPEVINE CHAINS FOUND IN ORGANIZATIONS

The two most common grapevine chains in organizations are the gossip chain (in which one person communicates messages to many others) and the cluster chain (in which many people pass messages to a few others).

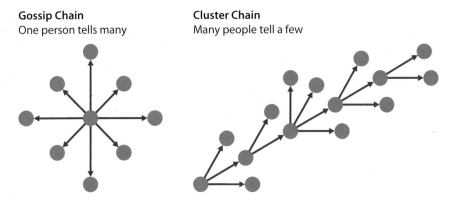

Gossip Chain
One person tells many

Cluster Chain
Many people tell a few

Source: From Keith Davis and John W. Newstrom, *Human Behavior at Work: Organizational Behavior*, Eighth Edition, 1989. Copyright © 1989 The McGraw-Hill Companies, Inc. Reprinted with permission.

the same patterns as, nor do they necessarily coincide with, formal channels of authority and communication. Research has identified several kinds of grapevines.[28] The two most common are illustrated in Figure 21.5. The gossip chain occurs when one person spreads the message to many other people. Each one, in turn, may either keep the information confidential or pass it on to others. The gossip chain is likely to carry personal information. The other common grapevine is the cluster chain, in which one person passes the information to a selected few individuals. Some of the receivers pass the information to a few other individuals; the rest keep it to themselves.

There is some disagreement about how accurate the information carried by the grapevine is, but research is increasingly finding it to be fairly accurate, especially when the information is based on fact rather than speculation. One study found that the grapevine may be between 75 percent and 95 percent accurate.[29] That same study also found that informal communication is increasing in many organizations for several basic reasons. One contributing factor is the recent increase in merger, acquisition, and takeover activity. Because such activity can greatly affect the people within an organization, it follows that they may spend more time talking about it.[30] The second contributing factor is that as more and more corporations move facilities from inner cities to suburbs, employees tend to talk less and less to others outside the organization and more and more to one another. Yet another contributing factor is simply the widespread availability of information technology that makes it easier than ever before for people to communicate quickly and easily.

More recently, another study looked at the effects of the recession and large-scale job losses on informal communication. Over half of the survey participants reported a sharp increased in gossip and rumors in their organizations. The same survey also reported an increase in the amount of eaves-dropping in most businesses.[31] Further, in another recent survey, 32 percent of people claimed to use their work e-mail inappropriately and 48 percent admitted gossiping with other employees through their e-mail.[32]

"Especially in this climate with job security, any time there's budget talk my ears perk up."

—ANONYMOUS EMPLOYEE WORKING IN A CUBICLE ENVIRONMENT[33]

Attempts to eliminate the grapevine are fruitless, but fortunately the manager does have some control over it. By maintaining open channels of communication and responding vigorously to inaccurate information, the manager can minimize the damage the grapevine can do. The grapevine can actually be an asset. By learning who the key people in the grapevine are, for example, the manager can partially control the information they receive and use the grapevine to sound out employee reactions to new ideas, such as a change in human resource policies or benefit packages. The manager can also get valuable information from the grapevine and use it to improve decision making.[34]

Management by Wandering Around

Another increasingly popular form of informal communication is called, interestingly enough, management by wandering around.[35] The basic idea is that some managers keep in touch with what is going on by wandering around and talking with people—immediate subordinates, subordinates far down the organizational hierarchy, delivery people, customers, or anyone else who is involved with the company in some way. Bill Marriott, for example, frequently visits the kitchens, loading docks, and custodial work areas whenever he tours a Marriott hotel. He claims that, by talking with employees throughout the hotel, he gets new ideas and has a better feel for the entire company. And when United Airlines CEO Jeffery Smisek travels, he makes a point of talking to flight attendants and other passengers to gain continuous insights into how the business can be run more effectively.

A related form of organizational communication that really has no specific term is the informal interchange that takes place outside the normal work setting. Employees attending the company picnic, playing on the company softball team, or taking fishing trips together will almost always spend part of their time talking about work. For example, Texas Instruments engineers at TI's Lewisville, Texas, facility often frequent a local bar in town after work. On any given evening, they talk about the Dallas Cowboys, the newest government contract received by the company, the weather, their boss, the company's stock price, local politics, and problems at work. There is no set agenda, and the key topics of discussion vary from group to group and from day to day. Still, the social gatherings serve an important role. They promote a strong culture and enhance understanding of how the organization works.

Nonverbal communication does not rely strictly on words and their literal meaning to convey information but instead relies on things like facial expressions, body language, tone, and so forth. Take this manager, for example. Her posture and expression suggest that she is worried or undecided about how to proceed.

Yuri Arcurs/Shutterstock.com

Nonverbal Communication

Nonverbal communication is a communication exchange that does not use words or uses words to carry more meaning than the strict definition of the words themselves. Nonverbal communication is a powerful but little-understood form of communication in organizations. It often relies on facial expressions, body movements, physical contact, and gestures. One study found that as much as 55 percent of the content of a message is transmitted by facial expressions and body posture and that another 38 percent derives from inflection and tone. Words themselves account for only 7 percent of the content of the message.[36]

Research has identified three kinds of nonverbal communication practiced by managers—images, settings, and body language.[37] In this context, images are the kinds of words people elect to use. "Damn the torpedoes, full speed ahead" and "Even though there are some potential hazards, we should proceed with this course of action" may convey the same meaning. Yet the person who uses the first expression may be perceived as a maverick, a courageous hero, an individualist, or a reckless and foolhardy adventurer. The person who uses the second might be described as aggressive, forceful, diligent, or narrow minded and resistant to change. At a recent meeting of Walmart executives, former CEO Lee Scott announced that "I can tell everyone what color underwear they're wearing." His meaning? There was a political issue dividing the group, and Scott wanted those in attendance to know that he was aware of which executives were on each side of the issue.[38] In short, our choice of words conveys much more than just the strict meaning of the words themselves.

The setting for communication also plays a major role in nonverbal communication. Boundaries, familiarity, the home turf, and other elements of the setting are all important. Much has been written about the symbols of power in organizations. The size and location of an office, the kinds of furniture in the office, and the accessibility of the person in the office all communicate useful information. For example, H. Ross Perot positions his desk so that it is always between him and a visitor. This keeps him in charge. When he wants a less formal dialogue, he moves around to the front of the desk and sits beside his visitor. Michael Dell of Dell Computer has his desk facing a side window so that, when he turns around to greet a visitor, there is never anything between them.

A third form of nonverbal communication is body language.[40] The distance we stand from someone as we speak has meaning. In the United States, standing very close to someone you are talking to generally signals either familiarity or aggression. The English and Germans stand farther apart than Americans when talking, whereas the Arabs, Japanese, and Mexicans stand closer together.[41] Eye contact is another effective means of nonverbal communication. For example, prolonged eye contact might suggest either hostility or romantic interest. Other kinds of body language include body and hand movement, pauses in speech, and mode of dress.

The manager should be aware of the importance of nonverbal communication and recognize its potential impact. Giving an employee good news about a reward with the wrong nonverbal cues can destroy the reinforcement value of the reward. Likewise, reprimanding an employee but providing inconsistent nonverbal cues can limit the effectiveness of the sanctions. The tone of the message, where and how the message is delivered, facial expressions, and gestures can all amplify or weaken the message or change the message altogether.

> Make no mistake. I can tell everyone what color underwear they're wearing."
>
> —FORMER WALMART CEO LEE SCOTT, MEANING THAT HE KNEW WHO IN A GROUP OF EXECUTIVES WAS ON HIS SIDE[39]

CONCEPT CHECK

What are the three fundamental kinds of informal communication that occur in an organization?

Spend 30 minutes observing other people and note the various kinds of nonverbal communication they exhibit.

Managing Organizational Communication

In view of the importance and pervasiveness of communication in organizations, it is vital for managers to understand how to manage the communication process.[42] Managers should understand how to maximize the potential benefits of communication and minimize the potential problems. We begin our discussion of communication management by considering the factors that might disrupt effective communication and how to deal with them.

Barriers to Communication

Several factors may disrupt the communication process or serve as barriers to effective communication.[43] As shown in Table 21.1, these may be divided into two classes: individual barriers and organizational barriers.

TABLE 21.1 BARRIERS TO EFFECTIVE COMMUNICATION

Numerous barriers can disrupt effective communication. Some of these barriers involve individual characteristics and processes. Others are functions of the organizational context in which communication is taking place.

Individual Barriers	Organizational Barriers
Conflicting or inconsistent signals	Semantics
Credibility about the subject	Status or power differences
Reluctance to communicate	Different perceptions
Poor listening skills	Noise
Predispositions about the subject	Overload
	Language differences

© Cengage Learning 2013

Individual Barriers Several individual barriers may disrupt effective communication. One common problem is conflicting or inconsistent signals. A manager is sending conflicting signals when she says on Monday that things should be done one way, but then prescribes an entirely different procedure on Wednesday. Inconsistent signals are being sent by a manager who says that he has an "open door" policy and wants his subordinates to drop by, but keeps his door closed and becomes irritated whenever someone stops in.

Another barrier is lack of credibility. Credibility problems arise when the sender is not considered a reliable source of information. He may not be trusted or may not be perceived as knowledgeable about the subject at hand. When a politician is caught withholding information or when a manager makes a series of bad decisions, the extent to which he or she will be listened to and believed thereafter diminishes. In extreme cases, people may talk about something they obviously know little or nothing about.

Some people are simply reluctant to initiate a communication exchange. This reluctance may occur for a variety of reasons. A manager may be reluctant to tell subordinates about an impending budget cut because he knows they will be unhappy about it. Likewise, a subordinate may be reluctant to transmit information upward for fear of reprisal or because it is felt that such an effort would be futile.

Poor listening habits can be a major barrier to effective communication. Some people are simply poor listeners. When someone is talking to them, they may be daydreaming, looking around, reading, or listening to another conversation. Because they are not concentrating on what is being said, they may not comprehend part or all of the message. They may even think that they really are paying attention, only to realize later that they cannot remember parts of the conversation.

Receivers may also bring certain predispositions to the communication process. They may already have their minds made up, firmly set in a certain way. For example, a manager may have heard that his new boss is unpleasant and hard to work with. When she calls him in for an introductory meeting, he may go into that meeting predisposed to dislike her and discount what she has to say.

"... a synergy-related headcount adjustment goal."

—WORDING USED IN A NOKIA PRESS RELEASE TO ANNOUNCE THE REDUCTION OF 9,000 JOBS[44]

Organizational Barriers Other barriers to effective communication involve the organizational context in which the communication occurs. Semantics problems arise when words have different meanings for different people. Words and phrases such as *profit*, *increased output*, and *return on investment* may have positive meanings for managers but less positive meanings for labor.

Communication problems may also arise when people of different power or status try to communicate with each other. The company president may discount a suggestion from an operating employee, thinking, "How can someone at that level help me run my business?" Or, when the president goes out to inspect a new plant, workers may be reluctant to offer suggestions because of their lower status. The marketing vice president may have more power than the human resource vice president and consequently may not pay much attention to a staffing report submitted by the human resource department.

If people perceive a situation differently, they may have difficulty communicating with one another. When two managers observe that a third manager has not spent much time in her office lately, one may believe that she has been to several important meetings, and the other may think she is "hiding out." If they need to talk about her in some official capacity, problems may arise because one has a positive impression and the other a negative impression.

Environmental factors may also disrupt effective communication. As mentioned earlier, noise may affect communication in many ways. Similarly, overload may be a problem when the receiver is being sent more information than he or she can effectively handle. Many managers report getting so many e-mail messages each day that they sometimes feel overwhelmed.[45] And when the manager gives a subordinate many jobs on which to work and at the same time the subordinate is being told by family and friends to do other things, overload may result and communication effectiveness diminishes.

Finally, as businesses become more and more global, different languages can create problems. To counter this problem, some firms are adopting an "official language." For example, when the German chemical firm Hoechst merged with the French firm Rhone-Poulenc, the new company adopted English as its official language. Indeed, English is increasingly becoming the standard business language around the world.[46]

Improving Communication Effectiveness

Considering how many factors can disrupt communication, it is fortunate that managers can resort to several techniques for improving communication effectiveness.[47] As shown in Table 21.2, these techniques include both individual and organizational skills.

Individual Skills The single most important individual skill for improving communication effectiveness is being a good listener.[48] Being a good listener requires that the individual be prepared to listen, not interrupt the speaker, concentrate on both the words and the meaning being conveyed, be patient, and ask questions as appropriate.[49] So important are good listening

TABLE 21.2 OVERCOMING BARRIERS TO COMMUNICATION

Because communication is so important, managers have developed several methods of overcoming barriers to effective communication. Some of these methods involve individual skills, whereas others are based on organizational skills.

Individual Skills	Organizational Skills
Develop good listening skills	Follow up
Encourage two-way communication	Regulate information flows
Be aware of language and meaning	Understand the richness of media
Maintain credibility	
Be sensitive to receiver's perspective	
Be sensitive to sender's perspective	

© Cengage Learning 2013

"... being a good listener for as long as you can stand it is the most important thing [for a new leader] to do."

—HENRY SCHACHT, FORMER CEO OF LUCENT TECHNOLOGIES[50]

skills that companies like Delta, IBM, and Boeing conduct programs to train their managers to be better listeners. Figure 21.6 illustrates the characteristics of poor listeners versus good listeners.

In addition to being a good listener, several other individual skills can promote effective communication. Feedback, one of the most important, is facilitated by two-way communication. Two-way communication allows the receiver to ask questions, request clarification, and express opinions that let the sender know whether he or she has been understood. In general, the more complicated the message, the more useful two-way communication is. In addition, the sender should be aware of the meanings that different receivers might attach to various words. For example, when addressing stockholders, a manager might use the word *profits* often. When addressing labor leaders, however, she may choose to use *profits* less often.

Furthermore, the sender should try to maintain credibility. This can be accomplished by not pretending to be an expert when one is not, by "doing one's homework" and checking facts, and by otherwise being as accurate and honest as possible. The sender should also try to be sensitive to the receiver's perspective. A manager who must tell a subordinate that she has not been recommended for a promotion should recognize that the subordinate will be frustrated and unhappy. The content of the message and its method of delivery should be chosen accordingly. The manager should be primed to accept a reasonable degree of hostility and bitterness without getting angry in return.[51]

Finally, the receiver should also try to be sensitive to the sender's point of view. Suppose that a manager has just received some bad news—for example, that his position is being eliminated next year. Others should understand that he may be disappointed, angry, or even depressed for a while. Thus they might make a special effort not to take too much offense if he snaps at them, and they might look for signals that he needs someone to talk to.[52]

Organizational Skills Three useful organizational skills can also enhance communication effectiveness for both the sender and the receiver—following up, regulating information flow, and understanding the richness of different media. Following up simply involves checking at a later time to be sure that a message has been received and understood. After a manager mails a report to a colleague, she might call a few days later to make sure the report has arrived. If it has, the manager might ask whether the colleague has any questions about it.

Regulating information flow means that the sender or receiver takes steps to ensure that overload does not occur. For the sender, this could mean not passing too much information

FIGURE 21.6 MORE AND LESS EFFECTIVE LISTENING SKILLS

Effective listening skills are a vital part of communication in organizations. There are several barriers that can contribute to poor listening skills by individuals in organizations. Fortunately, there are also several practices for improving listening skills.

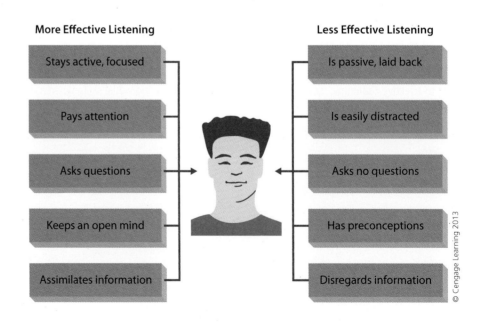

More Effective Listening

- Stays active, focused
- Pays attention
- Asks questions
- Keeps an open mind
- Assimilates information

Less Effective Listening

- Is passive, laid back
- Is easily distracted
- Asks no questions
- Has preconceptions
- Disregards information

© Cengage Learning 2013

through the system at one time. For the receiver, it might mean calling attention to the fact that he is being asked to do too many things at once. Many managers limit the influx of information by periodically weeding out the list of journals and routine reports they receive, or they train their assistant to screen phone calls and visitors. Indeed, some executives now get so much e-mail that they have it routed to an assistant. That person reviews the e-mail, discards those that are not useful (such as "spam"), responds to those that are routine, and passes on to the executive only those that require her or his personal attention.

Both parties should also understand the richness associated with different media. When a manager is going to lay off a subordinate temporarily, the message should be delivered in person. A face-to-face channel of communication gives the manager an opportunity to explain the situation and answer questions. When the purpose of the message is to grant a pay increase, written communication may be appropriate because it can be more objective and precise. The manager could then follow up the written notice with personal congratulations.

CONCEPT CHECK

What are the primary barriers to communication in organizations, and how can they most effectively be overcome?

Think of two recent situations in which you encountered a barrier to communication. How was it—or how might it have been—overcome?

Summary of Learning Objectives and Key Points

1. Describe the interpersonal nature of organizations.

   - Communication is the process of transmitting information from one person to another.
   - Effective communication is the process of sending a message in such a way that the message received is as close in meaning as possible to the message intended.

2. Describe the role and importance of communication in the manager's job.

   - Communication is a pervasive and important part of the manager's world.
   - The communication process consists of a sender's encoding meaning and transmitting it to one or more receivers, who receive the message and decode it into meaning.
   - In two-way communication, the process continues with the roles reversed.
   - Noise can disrupt any part of the overall process.

3. Identify the basic forms of communication in organizations.

   - Several forms of organizational communication exist. Interpersonal communication focuses on communication among a small number of people.
   - Two important forms of interpersonal communication, oral and written, both offer unique advantages and disadvantages.

   - The manager should weigh the pros and cons of each when choosing a medium for communication.
   - Communication networks are recurring patterns of communication among members of a group or work team.
   - Vertical communication between superiors and subordinates may flow upward or downward.
   - Horizontal communication involves peers and colleagues at the same level in the organization.
   - Organizations also use information systems to manage communication.
   - Electronic communication is having a profound effect on managerial and organizational communication.

4. Discuss informal communication, including its various forms and types.

   - There is also a great deal of informal communication in organizations.
   - The grapevine is the informal communication network among people in an organization.
   - Management by wandering around is also a popular informal method of communication.
   - Nonverbal communication includes facial expressions, body movement, physical contact, gestures, and inflection and tone.

5. Describe how the communication process can be managed to recognize and overcome barriers.

  - Managing the communication process necessitates recognizing the barriers to effective communication and understanding how to overcome them.

- Barriers can be identified at both the individual and the organizational levels.
- Both individual and organizational skills can be used to overcome these barriers.

Discussion Questions

Questions for Review

1. Describe the difference between communication and effective communication. How can a sender verify that a communication was effective? How can a receiver verify that a communication was effective?
2. Which form of interpersonal communication is best for long-term retention? Why? Which form is best for getting across subtle nuances of meaning? Why?
3. What are the similarities and differences of oral and written communication? What kinds of situations call for the use of oral methods? What situations call for written communication?
4. Describe the individual and organizational barriers to effective communication. For each barrier, describe one action that a manager could take to reduce the problems caused by that barrier.

Questions for Analysis

5. "Personal friendships have no place at work." Do you agree or disagree with this statement, and why?
6. At what points in the communication process can problems occur? Give examples of how noise can interfere with the communication process. What can managers do to reduce problems and noise?
7. How are electronic communication devices (cell phones, e-mail, and websites) likely to affect the communication process in the future? Describe both the advantages and the disadvantages of these three devices over traditional communication methods, such as face-to-face conversations, written notes, and phone calls.

Questions for Application

8. What forms of communication have you experienced today? What form of communication is involved in a face-to-face conversation with a friend? A telephone call from a customer? A traffic light or crossing signal? A picture of a cigarette in a circle with a slash across it? An area around machinery defined by a yellow line painted on the floor?
9. Keep track of your own activities over the course of a few hours of leisure time to determine what forms of communication you encounter. Which forms were most common? If you had been tracking your communications while at work, how would the list be different? Explain why the differences occur.
10. For each of the following situations, tell which form of communication you would use. Then ask the same question of someone who has been in the workforce for at least ten years. For any differences that occur, ask the worker to explain why his or her choice is better than yours. Do you agree with his or her assessment? Why or why not?

  - Describing complex changes in how healthcare benefits are calculated and administered to every employee of a large firm
  - Asking your boss a quick question about how she wants something done
  - Telling customers that a new two-for-one promotion is available at your store
  - Reprimanding an employee for excessive absences on the job
  - Reminding workers that no smoking is allowed in your facility

CengageNow™ Highlights

Now use your CengageNow™ homework to help you:
- Apply management theories in your life
- Assess your management skills
- Master management terms and concepts
- Apply your knowledge to real-world situations
- Analyze and solve challenging management problems

In order to take advantage of these elements, your instructor will need to have set up a course for your class within CengageNow™. Ask your instructor to contact his/her Cengage sales representative and Digital Solutions Manager to explore testing CengageNow™ in your course this term.

Managing Work Groups and Teams

LEARNING OBJECTIVES

After studying this chapter, you should be able to:

1. Define and identify types of groups and teams in organizations, discuss reasons why people join groups and teams, and list the stages of group and team development.

2. Identify and discuss four essential characteristics of groups and teams.

3. Discuss interpersonal and intergroup conflict in organizations.

4. Describe how organizations manage conflict.

MANAGEMENT IN ACTION

On the One Hand (Or Maybe on the Other Hand)

All of the following operating-room mishaps occurred in hospitals in the state of Rhode Island:

- A surgeon drilled into the wrong side of a patient's head in a procedure to drain blood.
- A surgeon operated on the wrong knee of a patient undergoing arthroscopic surgery.
- A surgeon operated on the wrong side of a child's mouth during surgery to correct a cleft palate.
- A surgeon anesthetized the wrong eye of a patient about to undergo eye surgery.
- A surgeon operated on the wrong finger of a patient during hand surgery.

The last instance of so-called "wrong-site surgery"—an operation conducted on a body part other than the one intended by patient and surgeon—took place at Rhode Island Hospital, the state's largest and the main teaching hospital of prestigious Brown University. According to the chief quality officer of the hospital's parent company, Lifespan, the incident served to underscore

> "Every time one of these kinds of things happens, [our] commitment is just made stronger."
>
> —ADMINISTRATOR ON A HOSPITAL'S EFFORTS TO CUT DOWN ON SURGICAL ERRORS

how difficult it is to prevent such errors. The hospital, said Mary Reich Cooper, is committed to safety, and "every time one of these kinds of things happens, that commitment is just made stronger."

There's apparently some question, however, about how many times such errors have to happen before a hospital's commitment is strong enough. Only two years earlier, the state department of health had fined Rhode Island Hospital $50,000 for the occurrence of three wrong-site surgical errors in a one-year span—all of them involving procedures in which doctors drilled into the wrong side of a patient's head. "Frustrating—in capital letters—is probably the best way to describe the mood here," said department director David R. Gifford after

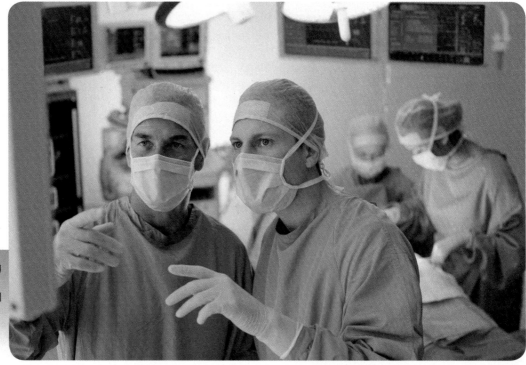

Many hospitals are working to improve communication among members of surgical teams so as to reduce the number of mistakes that could be made.

Clerkenwell/Jupiter Images

the wrong-finger incident. Asked if there might be some fundamental flaw in the hospital's procedural system, Gifford replied, "I'm wondering that myself."

All the incidents of wrong-site surgery on our list occurred in one state during a period of just over two years, and the Joint Commission on Accreditation of Healthcare Organizations, which evaluates more than 15,000 healthcare facilities and programs in the United States, estimates that wrong-site surgery occurs about 40 times a week around the country. A study in Pennsylvania conducted by the state's Patient Safety Authority added "near misses" into the mix and found that an "adverse event" (i.e., wrong-site surgery) or a "near miss" occurred every other day at Pennsylvania healthcare facilities. "To be frank," says Dr. Stan Mullens, VP of the Authority's board of directors, "wrong-site surgeries in Pennsylvania should never occur." But he hastens to add, "We're not alone. Wrong-site surgeries are no more common in Pennsylvania than they are in other states."

The Joint Commission has spent 15 years looking for ways to reduce the number of wrong-site surgical errors, but the results so far haven't been very promising; in fact, the rate of occurrence is the same as it was 15 years ago. So, what's the underlying problem? According to the Commission, it's communications breakdown, and some studies show that communications failure is a factor in two-thirds of all surgical mishaps resulting in serious patient harm or death. Surgery, of course, is performed by *teams*, and the typical surgical team has at least three core members: the surgeon, who performs the operation and leads the team; the anesthesiologist, whose responsibility is pain management and patient safety; and the operating nurse, who provides comprehensive care, assistance, and pain management at every stage of the operation. Perhaps the most logical question to start with, therefore, is: What are the barriers to communication (see Chapter 21) among the core members of a surgical team?

According to some researchers, the most serious barrier results from team members' different perceptions about the nature and quality of the group's teamwork and communications. According to a study commissioned by the Department of Veterans Affairs, the "most common pattern" of differing perceptions reflects a disparity between the perceptions of nurses and anesthesiologists on the one hand and those of surgeons on the other. In particular, surgeons tend to believe that both teamwork and communications are more effective than nurses and anesthesiologists

do. One item on the research questionnaire, for example, asked team members to respond to the statement "I am comfortable intervening in a procedure if I have concerns about what is occurring." While surgeons reported that the OR environment did indeed support intervention, nurses and anesthesiologists generally did not. Surgeons were also more likely to report that "morale on our team is high." In assessing such results as these, the authors of the study wonder, "If surgical team members have disparate perceptions about how well they are communicating or collaborating with each other, how is it possible for them to be collaborating optimally with other members of the surgical team for the care of their patients?"

When the results of a study at Johns Hopkins revealed a similar breakdown in perceptions, the lead researcher, who is also a surgeon, admitted that "the study is somewhat humbling to me. . . . We need to balance out the captain-of-the-ship doctrine," suggested Dr. Martin A. Makary. Makary believes that a standardized OR briefing program is one way to improve surgical-team communication and has helped to make brief two-minute "team meetings" a regular step in surgical procedure at Johns Hopkins and other university hospitals. During the meeting, which is conducted just after anesthesia is administered, all members of the OR team state their names and roles and the surgeon verifies the critical aspects of the procedure, including the correct site.

Where the policy has been adopted, according to Makary, researchers have observed an increase in "the awareness of OR personnel with regard to the site and procedure and their perceptions of operating room safety." Without such a policy, Makary points out, many surgeons simply walk into the OR and start operating without even asking the names of the other medical personnel in the room.

Such measures as team meetings hold some promise in the effort to reduce surgical error, as do checklists and "time outs," both of which require periodic confirmation of the critical components of a procedure. But "the unfortunate truth," cautions Dr. Mark R. Chassin, president of the Joint Commission, "is that no hospital today . . . can guarantee that [surgical errors] will never happen. We do not know how to perfect our processes. . . ." In some hospitals, he admits, the Commission has even encountered "denial or serious avoidance of the potential for real problems," and he recommends that patients everywhere ask surgeons in advance what steps will be taken to prevent errors while they're in the OR.[1]

This chapter is about the processes that lead to and follow from problems like those experienced in the operating rooms described above. More importantly, it's also about the processes leading to and following from successful operations (no pun intended), which, fortunately, happen more often in all sorts of organizational settings. In our last chapter we established the interpersonal nature of organizations. We extend that discussion here by first introducing basic concepts of group and team dynamics. Subsequent sections explain the characteristics of groups and teams in organizations. We then describe interpersonal and intergroup conflict. Finally, we conclude with a discussion of how conflict can be managed.

Groups and Teams in Organizations

Groups are a ubiquitous part of organizational life. They are the basis for much of the work that gets done, and they evolve both inside and outside the normal structural boundaries of the organization. We will define a **group** as two or more people who interact regularly to accomplish a common purpose or goal.[2] The purpose of a group or team may range from preparing a new advertising campaign, to informally sharing information, to making important decisions, to fulfilling social needs.

Types of Groups and Teams

In general, three basic kinds of groups are found in organizations—functional groups, informal or interest groups, and task groups and teams.[3] These are illustrated in Figure 22.1.

Functional Groups A *functional group* is a permanent group created by the organization to accomplish a number of organizational purposes with an unspecified time horizon. The advertising department at Target, the management department at the University of North Texas, and the nursing staff at the Mayo Clinic are functional groups. The advertising department at Target, for example, seeks to plan effective advertising campaigns, increase sales, run in-store promotions, and develop a unique identity for the company. It is assumed that the functional group will remain in existence after it attains its current objectives; those objectives will be replaced by new ones.

Informal or Interest Groups An *informal or interest group* is created by its own members for purposes that may or may not be relevant to organizational goals. It also has an unspecified time horizon. A group of employees who lunch together every day may be discussing productivity, money embezzling, or local politics and sports.[4] As long as the group members enjoy eating together, they will probably continue to do so. When lunches cease to be pleasant, they will seek other company or a different activity.

Informal groups can be a powerful force that managers cannot ignore.[5] One writer described how a group of employees at a furniture factory subverted their boss's efforts to increase production. They tacitly agreed to produce a reasonable amount of work but not to work too hard. One man kept a stockpile of completed work hidden as a backup in case he got too far behind. In another example, auto workers described how they left out gaskets and seals and put soft-drink bottles inside doors to cause customer complaints.[6] Of course, informal groups can also be a positive force, as when people work together to help out a colleague who has suffered a personal tragedy. For example, several instances of this behavior were reported in the wake of the devastating tornadoes that swept through Alabama and Missouri in 2011.

In recent years the Internet has served as a platform for the emergence of more and different kinds of informal or interest groups. As one example, Yahoo! includes a wide array of interest groups that bring together people with common interests. And increasingly, workers who lose their jobs as a result of layoffs are banding together electronically to offer moral support to one another and to facilitate networking as they all look for new jobs.[7]

group
Consists of two or more people who interact regularly to accomplish a common purpose or goal

functional group
A permanent group created by the organization to accomplish a number of organizational purposes with an unspecified time horizon

informal or interest group
Created by its members for purposes that may or may not be relevant to those of the organization

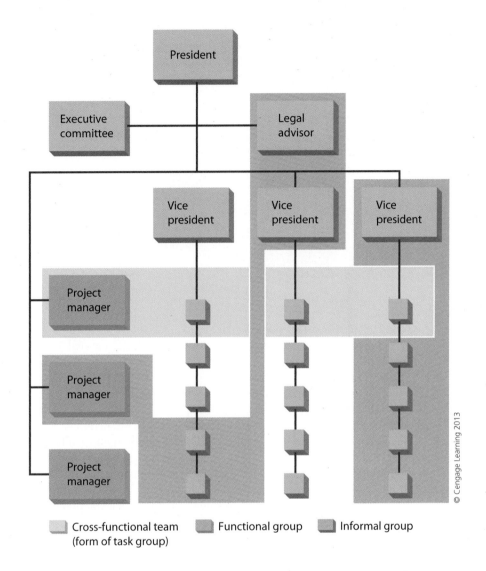

Cross-functional team (form of task group)   Functional group   Informal group

FIGURE 22.1 TYPES OF GROUPS IN ORGANIZATIONS

Every organization has many different types of groups. In this hypothetical organization, a functional group is shown within the purple area, a cross-functional team within the yellow area, and an informal group within the green area.

Task Groups A task group is a group created by the organization to accomplish a relatively narrow range of purposes within a stated or implied time horizon. Most committees and task forces are task groups. The organization specifies group membership and assigns a relatively narrow set of goals, such as developing a new product or evaluating a proposed grievance procedure. The time horizon for accomplishing these purposes is either specified (a committee may be asked to make a recommendation within 60 days) or implied (the project team will disband when the new product is developed).

Teams are a special form of task group that have become increasingly popular.[8] In the sense used here, a team is a group of workers that functions as a unit, often with little or no supervision, to carry out work-related tasks, functions, and activities. Table 22.1 lists and defines some of the various types of teams that are being used today. Earlier forms of teams included autonomous work groups and quality circles. Today, teams are also sometimes called "self-managed teams," "cross-functional teams," or "high-performance teams." Many firms today are routinely using teams to carry out most of their daily operations.[9] Further, virtual teams—teams comprised of people from remote work sites who work together online—are also becoming more and more common.[10] In fact, virtual connections are sometimes more complex than basic online hookups, and you'd be surprised at what sort of things well-connected virtual teams can do. For a good example, see our *Technically Speaking* box, entitled "What to Do When the Surgeon Asks for a Joystick," on page 561.

task group
A group created by the organization to accomplish a relatively narrow range of purposes within a stated or implied time horizon

team
A group of workers that functions as a unit, often with little or no supervision, to carry out work-related tasks, functions, and activities

virtual team
Team comprised of people from remote work sites who work together online

TABLE 22.1
TYPES OF TEAMS

Problem-solving team	Most popular type of team; comprises knowledge workers who gather to solve a specific problem and then disband
Management team	Consists mainly of managers from various functions like sales and production; coordinates work among other teams
Work team	An increasingly popular type of team; work teams are responsible for the daily work of the organization; when empowered, they are self-managed teams
Virtual team	A newer type of work team whose members interact in a virtual arena; members enter and leave the network as needed and may take turns serving as leader
Quality circle	Declining in popularity, quality circles, comprising workers and supervisors, meet intermittently to discuss workplace problems

Source: From *Fortune*, September 5, 2004. Copyright © 2004 Time Inc. All rights reserved.

Organizations create teams for a variety of reasons. For one thing, they give more responsibility for task performance to the workers who are actually performing the tasks. They also empower workers by giving them greater authority and decision-making freedom. In addition, they allow the organization to capitalize on the knowledge and motivation of their workers. Finally, they enable the organization to shed its bureaucracy and to promote flexibility and responsiveness. Ford used teams to design its new Focus. Similarly, General Motors used a team to develop its new Chevrolet Volt.

When an organization decides to use teams, it is essentially implementing a major form of organization change, as discussed in Chapter 16. Thus it is important to follow a logical and systematic approach to planning and implementing teams in an existing organization design. It is also important to recognize that resistance may be encountered. This resistance is most likely from first-line managers who will be giving up much of their authority to the team. Many organizations find that they must change the whole management philosophy of such managers away from being a supervisor to being a coach or facilitator.[11]

After teams are in place, managers should continue to monitor their contributions and how effectively they are functioning. In the best circumstances, teams will become very cohesive groups with high performance norms. To achieve this state, the manager can use any or all of the techniques described later in this chapter for enhancing cohesiveness. If implemented properly, and with the support of the workers themselves, performance norms

> "If a team can't be fed by two pizzas, it's too large."
>
> —JEFF BEZOS, FOUNDER AND CEO OF AMAZON.COM[13]

will likely be relatively high. In other words, if the change is properly implemented, the team participants will understand the value and potential of teams and the rewards they may expect to get as a result of their contributions. On the other hand, poorly designed and implemented teams will do a less effective job and may detract from organizational effectiveness.[12]

Why People Join Groups and Teams

People join groups and teams for a variety of reasons. They join functional groups simply by virtue of joining organizations. People accept employment to earn money or to practice their chosen professions. Once inside the organization, they are assigned to jobs and roles and thus become members of functional groups. People in existing functional groups are told, are asked, or volunteer to serve on committees, task forces, and teams. People join informal or interest groups for a variety of reasons, most of them quite complex.[14] Indeed, the need to be a team player has grown so strong today that many organizations will actively resist hiring someone who does not want to work with others.[15]

TECHNICALLY SPEAKING

What to Do When the Surgeon Asks for a Joystick

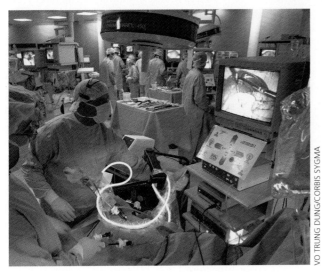

VO TRUNG DUNG/CORBIS SYGMA

In September 2001, surgeons removed the gall bladder of a 68-year-old woman in Strasbourg, France. Gall bladder removal is a pretty routine procedure, the standard of care in the use of "minimally invasive surgery." Such surgery is made possible by the laparoscope—a thin, lighted tube that allows doctors to see what they're doing with remote-controlled instruments inserted into the patient's body through small incisions. The patient in Strasbourg left the hospital after 48 hours and had an uneventful recovery. The only noteworthy aspect of the operation was the fact that the surgeon wasn't in Strasbourg. In fact, he wasn't even in a hospital: He was in the U.S. offices of France Télécom in New York, 4,300 miles away. The operation was the first complete "remote surgery" performed on a human patient—the result of a hands-on collaboration (so to speak) among Dr. Jacques Marescaux, director of the European Institute of Telesurgery; Computer Motion Inc., a maker of medical devices located in California; France Télécom, the biggest telecommunications company in France; and surgeons at Strasbourg's Hôpitaux Universitaires.

This particular operation wasn't necessarily a qualitative leap forward from conventional laparoscopic surgery. Surgeons had been performing computer-assisted procedures since the mid-1990s, though always in the same theaters with their patients. *Remote surgery*, or *telesurgery*, simply adds the technology that allows surgeons and patients to be in different places, and the breakthrough made in the 2001

New York–Strasbourg procedure was largely a matter of distance. In demonstrating "the feasibility of a transatlantic procedure," said Marescaux, his team had achieved merely "a richly symbolic milestone."

Even so, the benefits of remote surgery—say, having a world-class surgeon perform an operation on one patient in Europe in the morning and on another in South America in the afternoon—are fairly obvious. Some doctors also refer to a related benefit that Marescaux calls "telecompanionship"—the opportunity for surgeons to hone their skills and learn new ones by watching acknowledged experts at work.

In 2007, for example, Dr. Alex Gandsas, a surgeon at Sinai Hospital in Baltimore, used a telesurgery system to enable physicians in Argentina to perform a procedure for the treatment of obesity. Dr. Sergio Cantarelli had originally contacted Gandsas about the possibility of coming to the United States to learn the procedure. "He had never done this type of surgery before," recalls Gandsas, but "in practice, it wasn't possible for him to come over and train here." That's when Gandsas got the idea of mentoring Cantarelli remotely, and for nearly three months, Cantarelli and a colleague, Dr. Gabriel Egidi, studied the procedure by participating in surgeries performed in the United States.

At the end of the training period, Cantarelli and Egidi performed the operation in Argentina by means of a "remote-presence robot" that allowed Gandsas, controlling a joystick in Baltimore, to monitor the procedure and mentor the surgeons in the actual OR, 5,400 miles away. "During the surgery," explains Gandsas, "the robot allowed me to zoom in on the patient and the monitors to assess the situation" while the Argentine doctors actually operated on the patient, a 39-year-old woman. Meanwhile, Cantarelli and Egidi, who had never met their American colleague personally, reported that the long-distance collaboration benefited everyone involved. "Having a world expert from the United States looking over our shoulder," said Cantarelli, ". . . greatly enhanced our comfort level and provided the best care for the patient."

References: J[acques] Marescaux, "Code Name: Lindbergh Operation," *WebSurg*, January 2002, www.websurg.com on April 30, 2011; Vicki Brower, "The Cutting Edge in Surgery," *EMBO Reports*, Vol. 3 (2002), www.nature.com on April 30, 2011; "Remote Surgery between U.S. and Argentina," *Medical News*, October 4, 2007, www.news-medical.net on April 30, 2011; Matthew Knight, "Virtual Surgery Becoming a Reality," *CNN.com*, October 18, 2007, http://edition.cnn.com on April 30, 2011; "Robot Teaches World's First Remote Surgery," *Physorg.com*, October 3, 2007, www.physorg.com on April 30, 2011.

David Madison/Getty Images

People sometimes join a group because of the activity they can engage in as part of that group. For instance, leisure-time activities such as playing fantasy football or discussing new books generally require a group. These people are coworkers who gather regularly to play softball together.

"Give us people who are dedicated to making the team work, as opposed to a bunch of talented people with big egos, and we'll win every time."

—JOHN MCCONNELL, CEO OF WORTHINGTON INDUSTRIES[16]

Interpersonal Attraction One reason why people choose to form informal or interest groups is that they are attracted to one another. Many different factors contribute to interpersonal attraction. When people see a lot of each other, pure proximity increases the likelihood that interpersonal attraction will develop. Attraction is increased when people have similar attitudes, personalities, or economic standings.

Group Activities Individuals may also be motivated to join a group because the activities of the group appeal to them. Jogging, playing bridge, bowling, discussing poetry, playing war games, and flying model airplanes are all activities that some people enjoy. Many of them are more enjoyable to participate in as a member of a group, and most require more than one person. Many large firms like Shell Oil and Apple Computer have a football, softball, or bowling league. A person may join a bowling team, not because of any particular attraction to other group members, but simply because being a member of the group allows that person to participate in a pleasant activity. Of course, if the group's level of interpersonal attraction is very low, a person may choose to forgo the activity rather than join the group.

Group Goals The goals of a group may also motivate people to join. The Sierra Club, which is dedicated to environmental conservation, is a good example of this kind of interest group. Various fund-raising groups are another illustration. Members may or may not be personally attracted to the other fundraisers, and they probably do not enjoy the activity of knocking on doors asking for money, but they join the group because they subscribe to its goal. Workers join unions like the United Auto Workers because they support its goals.

Need Satisfaction Still another reason for joining a group is to satisfy the need for affiliation. New residents in a community may join the Newcomers Club partially as a way to meet new people and partially just to be around other people. Likewise, newly divorced people often join support groups as a way to have companionship.

Instrumental Benefits A final reason why people join groups is that membership is sometimes seen as instrumental in providing other benefits to the individual. For example, it is fairly common for college students entering their senior year to join several professional clubs or associations because listing such memberships on a résumé is thought to enhance the chances of getting a good job. Similarly, a manager might join a certain racquet club not because she is attracted to its members (although she might be) and not because of the opportunity to play tennis (although she may enjoy it). The club's goals are not relevant, and her affiliation needs may be satisfied in other ways. However, she may feel that being a member of this club will lead to important and useful business contacts. The racquet club membership is instrumental in establishing those contacts. Membership in civic groups such as the Junior League and Rotary may be solicited for similar reasons.

Stages of Group and Team Development

Imagine the differences between a collection of five people who have just been brought together to form a group or team and a group or team that has functioned like a well-oiled machine for years. Members of a new group or team are unfamiliar with how they will function together and are tentative in their interactions. In a group or team with considerable experience, members are familiar with one another's strengths and weaknesses and are more secure in their roles in the group. The former group or team is generally considered to be immature; the latter, mature. To progress from the immature phase to the mature phase, a group or team must go through certain stages of development, as shown in Figure 22.2.[17]

The first stage of development is called *forming*. The members of the group or team get acquainted and begin to test which interpersonal behaviors are acceptable and which are unacceptable to the other members. The members are very dependent on others at this point to provide cues about what is acceptable. The basic ground rules for the group or team are established, and a tentative group structure may emerge.[18] At adidas, for example, a merchandising team was created to handle its sportswear business. The team leader and his members were barely acquainted and had to spend a few weeks getting to know one another.

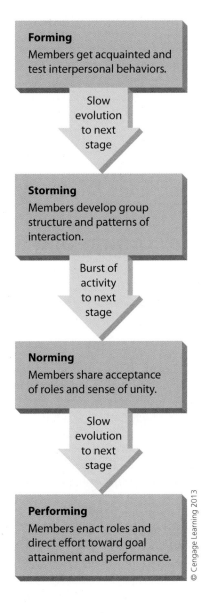

© Cengage Learning 2013

FIGURE 22.2 STAGES OF GROUP DEVELOPMENT

As groups mature, they tend to evolve through four distinct stages of development. Managers must understand that group members need time to become acquainted, accept one another, develop a group structure, and become comfortable with their roles in the group before they can begin to work directly to accomplish goals.

The second stage of development, often slow to emerge, is *storming*. During this stage, there may be a general lack of unity and uneven interaction patterns. At the same time, some members of the group or team may begin to exert themselves to become recognized as the group leader or at least to play a major role in shaping the group's agenda. In adidas's team, some members advocated a rapid expansion into the marketplace; others argued for a slower entry. The first faction won, with disastrous results. Because of the rush, product quality was poor and deliveries were late. As a result, the team leader was fired and a new manager placed in charge.

The third stage of development, called *norming*, usually begins with a burst of activity. During this stage, each person begins to recognize and accept her or his role and to understand the roles of others. Members also begin to accept one another and to develop a sense of unity. There may also be temporary regressions to the previous stage. For example, the group or team might begin to accept one particular member as the leader. If this person later violates important norms or otherwise jeopardizes his or her claim to leadership, conflict might reemerge as the group rejects this leader and searches for another. Adidas's new leader transferred several people away from the team and set up a new system and structure for managing things. The remaining employees accepted his new approach and settled into doing their jobs.

Performing, the final stage of group or team development, is also slow to develop. The team really begins to focus on the problem at hand. The members enact the roles they have accepted, interaction occurs, and the efforts of the group are directed toward goal attainment. The basic structure of the group or team is no longer an issue but has become a mechanism for accomplishing the purpose of the group. Adidas's sportswear business is now growing consistently and has successfully avoided the problems that plagued it at first.

What are the basic types of groups and teams in organizations?

Identify four groups that you belong to and describe why you joined each one.

CONCEPT CHECK

Characteristics of Groups and Teams

As groups and teams mature and pass through the four basic stages of development, they begin to take on four important characteristics—a role structure, norms, cohesiveness, and informal leadership.[19]

Role Structures

roles
The parts individuals play in groups in helping the group reach its goals

role structure
The set of defined roles and interrelationships among those roles that the group members define and accept

Each individual in a team has a part, or **role**, to play in helping the group reach its goals. Some people are leaders, some do the work, some interface with other teams, and so on. Indeed, a person may take on a *task specialist role* (concentrating on getting the group's task accomplished) or a *socioemotional role* (providing social and emotional support to others on the team). A few people, usually the leaders, perform both roles; a few others may do neither. The group's **role structure** is the set of defined roles and interrelationships among those roles that the group or team members define and accept. Each of us belongs to many groups and therefore plays multiple roles—in work groups, classes, families, and social organizations.[20]

Role structures emerge as a result of role episodes, as shown in Figure 22.3. The process begins with the expected role—what other members of the team expect the individual to do. The expected role gets translated into the sent role—the messages and cues that team members use to communicate the expected role to the individual. The perceived role is what the individual perceives the sent role to mean. Finally, the enacted role is what the individual

FIGURE 22.3 THE DEVELOPMENT OF A ROLE

Roles and role structures within a group generally evolve through a series of role episodes. The first two stages of role development are group processes, as the group members let individuals know what is expected of them. The other two parts are individual processes, as the new group members perceive and enact their roles.

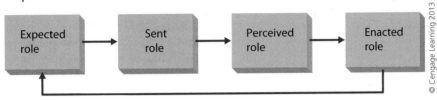

© Cengage Learning 2013

actually does in the role. The enacted role, in turn, influences future expectations of the team. Of course, role episodes seldom unfold this easily. When major disruptions occur, individuals may experience role ambiguity, conflict, or overload.[21]

Role Ambiguity Role ambiguity arises when the sent role is unclear. If your instructor tells you to write a term paper but refuses to provide more information, you will probably experience role ambiguity. You do not know what the topic is, how long the paper should be, what format to use, or when the paper is due. In work settings, role ambiguity can stem from poor job descriptions, vague instructions from a supervisor, or unclear cues from coworkers. The result is likely to be a subordinate who does not know what to do. Role ambiguity can be a significant problem for both the individual who must contend with it and the organization that expects the employee to perform.

Role Conflict Role conflict occurs when the messages and cues composing the sent role are clear but contradictory or mutually exclusive.[22] One common form is *interrole conflict*—conflict between roles. For example, if a person's boss says that one must work overtime and on weekends to get ahead, and the same person's spouse says that more time is needed at home with the family, conflict may result. In a matrix organization, interrole conflict often arises between the roles one plays in different teams as well as between team roles and one's permanent role in a functional group.

Intrarole conflict may occur when the person gets conflicting demands from different sources within the context of the same role. A manager's boss may tell her that she needs to put more pressure on subordinates to follow new work rules. At the same time, her subordinates may indicate that they expect her to get the rules changed. Thus the cues are in conflict, and the manager may be unsure about which course to follow. *Intrasender conflict* occurs when a single source sends clear but contradictory messages. This might arise if the boss says one morning that there can be no more overtime for the next month but after lunch tells someone to work late that same evening. *Person–role conflict* results from a discrepancy between the role requirements and the individual's personal values, attitudes, and needs. If a person is told to do something unethical or illegal, or if the work is distasteful (for example, firing a close friend), person–role conflict is likely. Role conflict of all varieties is of particular concern to managers. Research has shown that conflict may occur in a variety of situations and lead to a variety of adverse consequences, including stress, poor performance, and rapid turnover.

Role Overload A final consequence of a weak role structure is role overload, which occurs when expectations for the role exceed the individual's capabilities. When a manager gives an employee several major assignments at once, while increasing the person's regular workload, the employee will probably experience role overload. Role overload may also result when an individual takes on too many roles at one time. For example, a person trying to work extra hard at work, run for election to the school board, serve

role ambiguity
Arises when the sent role is unclear and the individual does not know what is expected of him or her

role conflict
Occurs when the messages and cues composing the sent role are clear but contradictory or mutually exclusive

role overload
Occurs when expectations for the role exceed the individual's capabilities to perform

on a committee in church, coach Little League baseball, maintain an active exercise program, and be a contributing member to her or his family will probably encounter role overload.

In a functional group or team, the manager can take steps to avoid role ambiguity, conflict, and overload. Having clear and reasonable expectations and sending clear and straightforward cues go a long way toward eliminating role ambiguity. Consistent expectations that take into account the employee's other roles and personal value system may minimize role conflict. Role overload can be avoided simply by recognizing the individual's capabilities and limits. In friendship and interest groups, role structures are likely to be less formal; hence, the possibility of role ambiguity, conflict, or overload may not be so great. However, if one or more of these problems does occur, they may be difficult to handle. Because roles in friendship and interest groups are less likely to be partially defined by a formal authority structure or written job descriptions, the individual cannot turn to those sources to clarify a role.

> "Some of the worst teams I've ever seen have been those where everybody was a potential CEO."
>
> —DAVID NADLER, CONSULTANT[23]

Behavioral Norms

norms
Standards of behavior that the group accepts for and expects of its members

Norms are standards of behavior that the group or team accepts for and expects of its members. Most committees, for example, develop norms governing their discussions. A person who talks too much is perceived as doing so to make a good impression or to get his or her own way. Other members may not talk much to this person, may not sit nearby, may glare at the person, and may otherwise "punish" the individual for violating the norm. Norms, then, define the boundaries between acceptable and unacceptable behavior.[24] Some groups develop norms that limit the upper bounds of behavior to "make life easier" for the group—for example, do not make more than two comments in a committee discussion or do not produce any more than you have to. In general, these norms are counterproductive. Other groups may develop norms that limit the lower bounds of behavior—for example, do not come to meetings unless you have read the reports to be discussed or produce as much as you can. These norms tend to reflect motivation, commitment, and high performance. Managers can sometimes use norms for the betterment of the organization. For example, Kodak has successfully used group norms to reduce injuries in some of its plants.[25]

Norm Generalization The norms of one group cannot always be generalized to another group. Some academic departments, for example, have a norm that suggests that faculty members dress up on teaching days. People who fail to observe this norm are "punished" by sarcastic remarks or even formal reprimands. In other departments, the norm may be casual clothes, and the person unfortunate enough to wear dress clothes may be punished just as vehemently. Even within the same work area, similar groups or teams can develop different norms. One team may strive always to produce above its assigned quota; another may maintain productivity just below its quota. The norm of one team may be to be friendly and cordial to its supervisor; that of another team may be to remain aloof and distant. Some differences are due primarily to the composition of the teams.

James Leynse/CORBIS

Group norms are standards of behavior that the group or team accepts for and expects of its members. Kodak has used norms to help reduce injuries at some of its plants. These workers, for example, are assembling Kodak single-use cameras. The injury rate at their facility has declined significantly through the use of group norms.

Norm Variation In some cases, there can also be norm variation within a group or team. A common norm is that the least senior member of a group is expected to perform unpleasant or trivial tasks for the rest of the group. These tasks might be to wait on customers who are known to be small tippers (in a restaurant), to deal with complaining customers (in a department store), or to handle the low-commission line of merchandise (in a sales department). Another example is when certain individuals, especially informal leaders, may violate some norms. If the team is going to meet at 8:00 A.M., anyone arriving late will be chastised for holding things up. Occasionally, however, the informal leader may arrive a few minutes late. As long as this does not happen too often, the group probably will not do anything about it.

Norm Conformity Four sets of factors contribute to norm conformity. First, factors associated with the group are important. For example, some groups or teams may exert more pressure for conformity than others. Second, the initial stimulus that prompts behavior can affect conformity. The more ambiguous the stimulus (for example, news that the team is going to be transferred to a new unit), the more pressure there is to conform. Third, individual traits determine the individual's propensity to conform (for example, more intelligent people are often less susceptible to pressure to conform). Finally, situational factors, such as team size and unanimity, influence conformity. As an individual learns the group's norms, he can do several different things. The most obvious is to adopt the norms. For example, the new male professor who notices that all the other men in the department dress up to teach can also start wearing a suit. A variation is to try to obey the "spirit" of the norm while retaining individuality. The professor may recognize that the norm is actually to wear a tie; thus he might succeed by wearing a tie with his sport shirt, jeans, and sneakers.

The individual may also ignore the norm. When a person does not conform, several things can happen. At first the group may increase its communication with the deviant individual to try to bring her back in line. If this does not work, communication may decline. Over time, the group may begin to exclude the individual from its activities and, in effect, ostracize the person.

Finally, we need to briefly consider another aspect of norm conformity—socialization. Socialization is generalized norm conformity that occurs as a person makes the transition from being an outsider to being an insider. A newcomer to an organization, for example, gradually begins to learn about such norms as dress, working hours, and interpersonal relations. As the newcomer adopts these norms, she is being socialized into the organizational culture. Some organizations, like Texas Instruments, work to actively manage the socialization process; others leave it to happenstance.

Cohesiveness

A third important team characteristic is cohesiveness. Cohesiveness is the extent to which members are loyal and committed to the group. In a highly cohesive team, the members work well together, support and trust one another, and are generally effective at achieving their chosen goals.[26] In contrast, a team that lacks cohesiveness is not very coordinated, its members do not necessarily support one another fully, and it may have a difficult time reaching goals. Of particular interest are the factors that increase and reduce cohesiveness and the consequences of team cohesiveness. These are listed in Table 22.2.

Factors That Increase Cohesiveness Five factors can increase the level of cohesiveness in a group or team. One of the strongest is intergroup competition. When two or more groups are in direct competition (for example, three sales groups competing for top sales honors

socialization
Generalized norm conformity that occurs as a person makes the transition from being an outsider to being an insider in the organization

cohesiveness
The extent to which members are loyal and committed to the group; the degree of mutual attractiveness within the group

TABLE 22.2

FACTORS THAT INFLUENCE GROUP COHESIVENESS

Several different factors can influence the cohesiveness of a group. For example, a manager can establish intergroup competition, assign compatible members to the group, create opportunities for success, establish acceptable goals, and foster interaction to increase cohesiveness. Other factors can be used to decrease cohesiveness.

Factors That Increase Cohesiveness	Factors That Reduce Cohesiveness
Intergroup competition	Group size
Personal attraction	Disagreement on goals
Favorable evaluation	Intragroup competition
Agreement on goals	Domination
Interaction	Unpleasant experiences

© Cengage Learning 2013

or two football teams competing for a conference championship), each group is likely to become more cohesive. Second, just as personal attraction plays a role in causing a group to form, so, too, does attraction seem to enhance cohesiveness. Third, favorable evaluation of the entire group by outsiders can increase cohesiveness. Thus a group's winning a sales contest or a conference title or receiving recognition and praise from a superior tends to increase cohesiveness.

Similarly, if all the members of the group or team agree on their goals, cohesiveness is likely to increase.[27] And the more frequently members of the group interact with one another, the more likely the group is to become cohesive. A manager who wants to foster a high level of cohesiveness in a team might do well to establish some form of intergroup competition, assign members to the group who are likely to be attracted to one another, provide opportunities for success, establish goals that all members are likely to accept, and allow ample opportunities for interaction.[28]

Factors That Reduce Cohesiveness There are also five factors that are known to reduce team cohesiveness. First of all, cohesiveness tends to decline as a group increases in size. Second, when members of a team disagree on what the goals of the group should be, cohesiveness may decrease. For example, when some members believe the group should maximize output and others think output should be restricted, cohesiveness declines. Third, intragroup competition reduces cohesiveness. When members are competing among themselves, they focus more on their own actions and behaviors than on those of the group.

Fourth, domination by one or more persons in the group or team may cause overall cohesiveness to decline. Other members may feel that they are not being given an opportunity to interact and contribute, and they may become less attracted to the group as a consequence. Finally, unpleasant experiences that result from group membership may reduce cohesiveness. A sales group that comes in last in a sales contest, an athletic team that sustains a long losing streak, and a work group reprimanded for poor-quality work may all become less cohesive as a result of their unpleasant experiences.

Consequences of Cohesiveness In general, as teams become more cohesive, their members tend to interact more frequently, conform more to norms, and become more satisfied with the team. Cohesiveness may also influence team performance. However, performance is also influenced by the team's performance norms. Figure 22.4 shows how cohesiveness and performance norms interact to help shape team performance.

When both cohesiveness and performance norms are high, high performance should result because the team wants to perform at a high level (norms) and its members are working together toward that end (cohesiveness). When norms are high and cohesiveness is low, performance will be moderate. Although the team wants to perform at a high level, its members are not necessarily working well together. When norms are low, performance will be low, regardless of whether group cohesiveness is high or low. The least desirable situation occurs when low performance norms are combined with high cohesiveness. In this case, all team members embrace the standard of restricting performance (owing to the low per-

FIGURE 22.4 THE INTERACTION BETWEEN COHESIVENESS AND PERFORMANCE NORMS

Group cohesiveness and performance norms interact to determine group performance. From the manager's perspective, high cohesiveness combined with high performance norms is the best situation, and high cohesiveness with low performance norms is the worst situation. Managers who can influence the level of cohesiveness and performance norms can greatly improve the effectiveness of a work group.

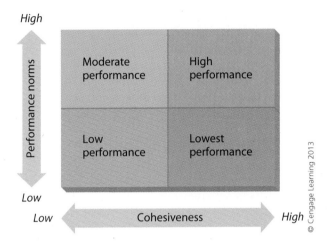

formance norm), and the group is united in its efforts to maintain that standard (owing to the high cohesiveness). If cohesiveness were low, the manager might be able to raise performance norms by establishing high goals and rewarding goal attainment or by bringing in new group members who are high performers. But a highly cohesive group is likely to resist these interventions.[29]

Formal and Informal Leadership

Most functional groups and teams have a formal leader—that is, one appointed by the organization or chosen or elected by the members of the group. Because friendship and interest groups are formed by the members themselves, however, any formal leader must be elected or designated by the members. Although some groups do designate such a leader (a softball team may elect a captain, for example), many do not. Moreover, even when a formal leader is designated, the group or team may also look to others for leadership. An **informal leader** is a person who engages in leadership activities but whose right to do so has not been formally recognized. The formal and the informal leader in any group or team may be the same person, or they may be different people. We noted earlier the distinction between the task specialist and socioemotional roles within groups. An informal leader is likely to be a person capable of carrying out both roles effectively. If the formal leader can fulfill one role but not the other, an informal leader often emerges to supplement the formal leader's functions. If the formal leader can fill neither role, one or more informal leaders may emerge to carry out both sets of functions.

Is informal leadership desirable? In many cases informal leaders are quite powerful because they draw from referent or expert power. When they are working in the best interests of the organization, they can be a tremendous asset. Notable athletes like Ben Roethlisberger and Mia Hamm are classic examples of informal leaders. However, when informal leaders work counter to the goals of the organization, they can cause significant difficulties. Such leaders may lower performance norms, instigate walkouts or wildcat strikes, or otherwise disrupt the organization.

informal leader
A person who engages in leadership activities but whose right to do so has not been formally recognized by the organization or group

Identify and describe the fundamental characteristics of groups and teams.

Assume you were assigned to manage a highly cohesive group with low performance norms. What would you do to try to change things?

Concept Check

Interpersonal and Intergroup Conflict

Of course, when people work together in an organization, things do not always go smoothly. Indeed, conflict is an inevitable element of interpersonal relationships in organizations. In this section, we look at how conflict affects overall performance. We also explore the causes of conflict between individuals, between groups, and between an organization and its environment.

The Nature of Conflict

Conflict is a disagreement among two or more individuals, groups, or organizations. This disagreement may be relatively superficial or very strong. It may be short-lived or exist for months or even years, and it may be work-related or personal. Conflict may manifest itself in a variety of ways. People may compete with one another, glare at one another, shout, or withdraw. Groups may band together to protect popular members or oust unpopular members. Organizations may seek legal remedies.

Most people assume that conflict is something to be avoided because it connotes antagonism, hostility, unpleasantness, and dissension. Indeed, managers and management theorists have traditionally viewed conflict as a problem to be avoided.[30] In recent years, however, we have come to recognize that, although conflict can be a major problem, certain kinds of conflict may also be beneficial.[31] For example, when two members of a site selection committee disagree over the best location for a new plant, each may be forced to more thoroughly study and defend his or her preferred alternative. As a result of more systematic analysis and discussion, the committee may make a better decision and be better prepared to justify it to others than if everyone had agreed from the outset and accepted an alternative that was perhaps less well analyzed.

As long as conflict is being handled in a cordial and constructive manner, it is probably serving a useful purpose in the organization. On the other hand, when working relationships are being disrupted and the conflict has reached destructive levels, it has likely become dysfunctional and needs to be addressed.[32] We discuss ways of dealing with such conflict later in this chapter.

Figure 22.5 depicts the general relationship between conflict and performance for a group or organization. If there is absolutely no conflict in the group or organization, its members may become complacent and apathetic. As a result, group or organizational performance and innovation may begin to suffer. A moderate level of conflict among group or organizational members, on the other hand, can spark motivation, creativity, innovation, and initiative, and raise performance. Too much conflict, though, can produce such undesirable results as hostility and lack of cooperation, which lower performance. The key for managers is to find and maintain the optimal amount of conflict that fosters performance. Of course, what constitutes optimal conflict varies with both the situation and the people involved.[33]

Causes of Conflict

Conflict may arise in both interpersonal and intergroup relationships. Occasionally, conflict between individuals and groups may be caused by particular organizational strategies and practices. A third arena for conflict is between an organization and its environment.

conflict
A disagreement among two or more individuals or groups

FIGURE 22.5 THE NATURE OF ORGANIZATIONAL CONFLICT

Either too much or too little conflict can be dysfunctional for an organization. In either case, performance may be low. However, an optimal level of conflict that sparks motivation, creativity, innovation, and initiative can result in higher levels of performance.

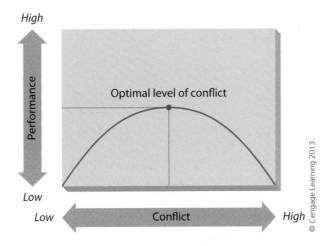

© Cengage Learning 2013

Interpersonal Conflict Conflict between two or more individuals is almost certain to occur in any organization, given the great variety in perceptions, goals, attitudes, and so forth among its members. Bill Gates, founder and CEO of Microsoft, and Kazuhiko Nishi, a former business associate from Japan, once ended a lucrative long-term business relationship because of interpersonal conflict. Nishi accused Gates of becoming too political, while Gates charged that Nishi became too unpredictable and erratic in his behavior.[34]

A frequent source of interpersonal conflict in organizations is what many people call a "personality clash"—when two people distrust each other's motives, dislike each other, or for some other reason simply cannot get along.[35] Conflict may also arise between people who have different beliefs or perceptions about some aspect of their work or their organization. For example, one manager might want the organization to require that all employees use Microsoft Office software, to promote standardization. Another manager might believe that a variety of software packages should be allowed, in order to recognize individuality. Similarly, a male manager may disagree with his female colleague over whether the organization is guilty of discriminating against women in promotion decisions. Conflict can also result from excess competitiveness among individuals. Two people vying for the same job, for example, may resort to political behavior in an effort to gain an advantage. If either competitor sees the other's behavior as inappropriate, accusations are likely to result. Even after the "winner" of the job is determined, such conflict may continue to undermine interpersonal relationships, especially if the reasons given for selecting one candidate are ambiguous or open to alternative explanations. Acer CEO and President Gianfranco Lanci resigned in 2011 due to several months of unresolved conflict with the company's board of directors. Lanci and the board had differing views on organizational growth, customer value creation, brand position enhancement, and resource allocation. Lanci pushed strongly for a move into the mobile segment to compete with Apple's iPad, while the board wanted to maintain its core PC business.[36]

Sometimes, of course, conflicts can't be resolved from within the organization, and when parties—both individuals and companies—are forced to seek resolution outside corporate headquarters, they usually find themselves in a courtroom or the offices of a governmental agency. Once in a great while, conflicts escalate to the point at which they end up in the halls of Congress. Our *Change* box on page 572, entitled "Whistle-Blowing in the Dark," provides a good example.

THE MORE THINGS CHANGE

Whistle-Blowing in the Dark

Jason Reed/Reuters

In 2008, Joseph Burke, a former manager at the advertising firm Ogilvy & Mather (O&M), filed a complaint with the Occupational Safety and Health Administration (OSHA), which is responsible for enforcing the whistle-blower protection provisions of the Sarbannes–Oxley Act (SOX). Burke charged that, in violation of SOX, he had been fired for cooperating with a federal investigation into his employer's billing practices. The story (at least so far) may seem straightforward, but it raises two fairly obvious questions:

1. Why SOX? Enacted in 2002 in the wake of corporate scandals involving such companies as Enron and Worldcom, SOX protects people who blow the whistle on firms that are registered or required to file reports with the Securities and Exchange Commission (SEC). The law states in part that covered companies "may not discharge or in any manner retaliate against an employee because he or she . . . assisted in an investigation by . . . a federal regulatory or law enforcement agency."

2. Why OSHA? Under the direction of the U.S. Department of Labor (DOL), OSHA is responsible for enforcing the whistle-blowing statutes of SOX. A complaint like Joseph Burke's goes first to an OSHA official, where it may be upheld or dismissed. It may then be appealed to a DOL administrative law judge (ALJ) and again appealed to the DOL's Administrative Review Board (ARB).

Burke's complaint didn't get very far: It was dismissed by OSHA, whose decision was upheld by an ALJ. As it happens, Burke has had a lot of company in his frustration. In the decade after SOX became law, the OSHA-DOL process ruled in favor of just 21 corporate whistle-blowers—out of nearly 1,500 complaints. And almost 1,000 others were dismissed before reaching an ALJ. Why this overwhelming preponderance in favor of corporate defendants? Under the Bush administration, DOL lawyers issued a directive declaring that there is "no legal basis for the argument that subsidiaries of covered corporations are automatically covered" by SOX; after all, said administration lawyers, the law nowhere "expressly" says "subsidiaries." Joseph Burke, as an employee of O&M, worked for a *non-public subsidiary* of publicly traded WPP Group PLC. Thus his case, according to the ALJ who presided over it, fell short because "only employees of publicly traded companies are protected" and Burke had "not established, by a preponderance of evidence, that he is an employee of a company covered under" SOX.

Not surprisingly, many people, both in government and the legal profession, were opposed to the DOL's strict interpretation of SOX. At least one ALJ, recalling the era of unchecked corporate fraud under which the law was passed, reminded his colleagues that "subsidiaries were the vehicles through which the fraud was facilitated or accomplished" in the first place. Also adamant about the broader intent of SOX was U.S. Senator Patrick Leahy, who coauthored the law's whistle-blowing provisions. Why *wouldn't* SOX cover subsidiaries? he asked. "Otherwise, a company that wants to do something shady could just do it in a subsidiary."

As Congress eventually moved to close the loophole, OSHA took steps to enforce the whistle-blowing provisions of SOX more vigorously: In March 2010, the agency issued awards totaling more than $1.6 million, plus reinstatement, to two whistle-blowers. In April 2011, the DOL's Administrative Review Board ruled that SOX does in fact protect employees of publicly traded companies.

References: Jennifer Levitz, "Shielding the Whistleblower," *Wall Street Journal*, December 1, 2009, http://online.wsj.com on April 30, 2011; David Nolte, "DOL Continues to Ignore and Rewrite SOX's Whistleblower Law," *HGExperts.com*, 2010, www.hgexperts.com on April 30, 2011; Squire, Sanders & Dempsey LLP, "Sarbannes-Oxley Whistleblower Complaints against Non-Public Subsidiaries Routinely Dismissed by OSHA," October 16, 2008, www.ssd.com on April 30, 2011; Jennifer Levitz, "Whistleblowers Are Left Dangling," *Wall Street Journal*, September 4, 2008, http://online.wsj.com on April 30, 2011; Seyfarth Shaw LLP, "OSHA Steps Up Enforcement of Sarbannes-Oxley Whistleblower Claims," March 24, 2010, www.seyfarth.com on April 30, 2011; Richard Renner, "ARB Holds That SOX Covers Subsidiaries," *Whistleblower Protection Blog*, April 1, 2011, www.whistleblowersblog.org.

Intergroup Conflict Conflict between two or more organizational groups is also quite common. For example, the members of a firm's marketing group may disagree with the production group over product quality and delivery schedules. Two sales groups may disagree over how to meet sales goals, and two groups of managers may have different ideas about how best to allocate organizational resources.

Many intergroup conflicts arise more from organizational causes than from interpersonal causes. In Chapter 14, we described three forms of group interdependence—pooled, sequential, and reciprocal. Just as increased interdependence makes coordination more difficult, it also increases the potential for conflict. For example, recall that in sequential interdependence, work is passed from one unit to another. Intergroup conflict may arise if the first group turns out too much work (the second group will fall behind), too little work (the second group will not meet its own goals), or poor-quality work.

At one JCPenney department store, conflict arose between stockroom employees and sales associates. The sales associates claimed that the stockroom employees were slow in delivering merchandise to the sales floor so that it could be priced and shelved. The stockroom employees, in turn, claimed that the sales associates were not giving them enough lead time to get the merchandise delivered and failed to understand that they had additional duties besides carrying merchandise to the sales floor.

Just like people, different departments often have different goals. Further, these goals may often be incompatible. A marketing goal of maximizing sales, achieved partially by offering many products in a wide variety of sizes, shapes, colors, and models, probably conflicts with a production goal of minimizing costs, achieved partially by long production runs of a few items. Reebok recently confronted this very situation. One group of managers wanted to introduce a new sportswear line as quickly as possible, but other managers wanted to expand more deliberately and cautiously. Because the two groups were not able to reconcile their differences effectively, conflict between the two factions led to quality problems and delivery delays that plagued the firm for months.

Competition for scarce resources can also lead to intergroup conflict. Most organizations—especially universities, hospitals, government agencies, and businesses in depressed industries—have limited resources. In one New England town, for example, the public works department and the library battled over funds from a federal construction grant. The Buick, Pontiac, and Chevrolet divisions of General Motors frequently fought over the right to manufacture various new products developed by the company. This in-fighting was identified as one of many factors that led to GM's recent problems. As part of the solution, the Pontiac brand was eventually discontinued.

Conflict Between Organization and Environment Conflict that arises between one organization and another is called *interorganizational conflict*. A moderate amount of interorganizational conflict resulting from business competition is expected, of course, but sometimes conflict becomes more extreme. For example, Starwood Hotels (owners of Sheraton, Westin, W, and other brands) sued Hilton Hotels Corporation for theft of trade secrets. In an effort to replicate Starwood's successful lifestyle hotels (most notably W), Hilton hired two Starwood executives, Ross Klein and Amar Lalvani, who were ultimately accused of stealing over 100,000 documents from Starwood to use in the development of the new Hilton brand. The suit was recently settled in favor of Starwood, with Hilton being forced to make a $75 million payment to Starwood.[37]

Conflict can also arise between an organization and other elements of its environment. For example, an organization may conflict with a consumer group over claims it makes about its products. McDonald's faced this problem a few years ago when it published nutritional information about its products that omitted details about fat content. A manufacturer might conflict with a governmental agency such as the federal Occupational Safety and Health Administration (OSHA). For example, the firm's management may believe it is in compliance with OSHA regulations, whereas officials from the agency itself believe that the firm is not in compliance. Or a firm might conflict with a supplier over the quality of raw materials.

The firm may think the supplier is providing inferior materials, while the supplier thinks the materials are adequate. Finally, individual managers obviously may have disagreements with groups of workers. For example, a manager may think her workers are doing poor-quality work and that they are unmotivated. The workers, on the other hand, may believe they are doing good jobs and that the manager is doing a poor job of leading them.

Define conflict and identify its primary causes.

Try to think of a time when you were involved in conflict that had a positive outcome.

Managing Conflict in Organizations

How do managers cope with all this potential conflict? Fortunately, as Table 22.3 shows, there are ways to stimulate conflict for constructive ends, to control conflict before it gets out of hand, and to resolve it if it does. Below we look at ways of managing conflict.[38]

Stimulating Conflict

In some situations, an organization may stimulate conflict by placing individual employees or groups in competitive situations. Managers can establish sales contests, incentive plans, bonuses, or other competitive stimuli to spark competition. As long as the ground rules are equitable and all participants perceive the contest as fair, the conflict created by the competition is likely to be constructive because each participant will work hard to win (thereby enhancing some aspect of organizational performance).

Another useful method for stimulating conflict is to bring in one or more outsiders who will shake things up and present a new perspective on organizational practices. Outsiders may be new employees, current employees assigned to an existing work group, or consultants or advisors hired on a temporary basis. Of course, this action can also provoke resentment

TABLE 22.3
METHODS FOR MANAGING CONFLICT

Conflict is a powerful force in organizations and has both negative and positive consequences. Thus managers can draw on several different techniques to stimulate, control, or resolve and eliminate conflict, depending on their unique circumstances.

Stimulating Conflict
Increase competition among individuals and teams.
Hire outsiders to shake things up.
Change established procedures.
Controlling Conflict
Expand resource base.
Enhance coordination of interdependence.
Set superordinate goals.
Match personalities and work habits of employees.
Resolving and Eliminating Conflict
Avoid conflict.
Convince conflicting parties to compromise.
Bring conflicting parties together to confront and negotiate conflict.

© Cengage Learning 2013

from insiders who feel they were qualified for the position. The Beecham Group, a British company, once hired an executive from the United States for its CEO position, expressly to change how the company did business. His arrival brought with it new ways of doing things and a new enthusiasm for competitiveness. Unfortunately, some valued employees also chose to leave Beecham because they resented some of the changes that were made.

Changing established procedures, especially procedures that have outlived their usefulness, can also stimulate conflict. Such actions cause people to reassess how they perform their job and whether they perform it correctly. For example, one university president announced that all vacant staff positions could be filled only after written justification had received his approval. Conflict arose between the president and the department heads, who felt they were having to do more paperwork than was necessary. Most requests were approved, but because department heads now had to think through their staffing needs, a few unnecessary positions were appropriately eliminated.

Controlling Conflict

One method of controlling conflict is to expand the resource base. Suppose a top manager receives two budget requests for $100,000 each. If she has only $180,000 to distribute, the stage is set for conflict because each group will believe its proposal is worth funding and will be unhappy if it is not fully funded. If both proposals are indeed worthwhile, it may be possible for the manager to come up with the extra $20,000 from some other source and thereby avoid difficulty.

As noted earlier, pooled, sequential, and reciprocal interdependence can all result in conflict. If managers use an appropriate technique for enhancing coordination, they can reduce the probability that conflict will arise. Techniques for coordination (described in Chapter 14) include making use of the managerial hierarchy, relying on rules and procedures, enlisting liaison people, forming task forces, and integrating departments. At the JCPenney store mentioned earlier, the conflict was addressed by providing salespeople with clearer forms on which to specify the merchandise they needed and in what sequence. If one coordination technique does not have the desired effect, a manager might shift to another one.[39]

Competing goals can also be a source of conflict among individuals and groups. Managers can sometimes focus employee attention on higher-level, or superordinate, goals as a way of eliminating lower-level conflict. When labor unions like the United Auto Workers make wage concessions to ensure survival of the automobile industry, they are responding to a superordinate goal. Their immediate goal may be higher wages for members, but they realize that, without the automobile industry, their members would not even have jobs.

Finally, managers should try to match the personalities and work habits of employees so as to avoid conflict between individuals. For instance, two valuable subordinates, one a chain smoker and the other a vehement antismoker, probably should not be required to work together in an enclosed space. If conflict does arise between incompatible individuals, a manager might seek an equitable transfer for one or both of them to other units.

Conflict is a normal interpersonal process in organizations. In some cases it can be functional, but in other cases it is dysfunctional. Managers need to be alert to the underlying causes and consequences of conflict so they can encourage it, control it, or resolve it as appropriate.

Mark Hatfield/istockphoto.com

Resolving and Eliminating Conflict

Despite everyone's best intentions, conflict sometimes flares up. If it is disrupting the workplace, creating too much hostility and tension, or otherwise harming the organization, attempts must be made to resolve it.[40] Some managers who are uncomfortable dealing with conflict choose to avoid the conflict and hope it will go away. Avoidance may sometimes be effective in the short run for some kinds of interpersonal disagreements, but it does little to resolve long-run or chronic conflicts. Even more unadvisable, though, is "smoothing"—minimizing the conflict and telling everyone that things will "get better." Often the conflict only worsens as people continue to brood over it.

Compromise is striking a middle-range position between two extremes. This approach can work if it is used with care, but in most compromise situations, someone wins and someone loses. Budget problems are one of the few areas amenable to compromise because of their objective nature. Assume, for example, that additional resources are not available to the manager mentioned earlier. She has $180,000 to divide, and each of two groups claims to need $100,000. If the manager believes that both projects warrant funding, she can allocate $90,000 to each. The fact that the two groups have at least been treated equally may minimize the potential conflict.

The confrontational approach to conflict resolution—also called *interpersonal problem solving*—consists of bringing the parties together to confront the conflict. The parties discuss the nature of their conflict and attempt to reach an agreement or a solution. Confrontation requires a reasonable degree of maturity on the part of the participants, and the manager must structure the situation carefully. If handled well, this approach can be an effective means of resolving conflict. In recent years, many organizations have experimented with a technique called *alternative dispute resolution*, using a team of employees to arbitrate conflict in this way.[41] Negotiation, a closely related method, is discussed in our final section.

Regardless of the approach, organizations and their managers should realize that conflict must be addressed if it is to serve constructive purposes and be prevented from bringing about destructive consequences. Conflict is inevitable in organizations, but its effects can be constrained with proper attention. For example, Union Carbide sent 200 of its managers to a three-day workshop on conflict management. The managers engaged in a variety of exercises and discussions to learn with whom they were most likely to come in conflict and how they should try to resolve it. As a result, managers at the firm later reported that hostility and resentment in the organization had been greatly diminished and that people in the firm reported more pleasant working relationships.[42]

◈ Negotiation

Negotiation is the process in which two or more parties (people or groups) reach agreement on an issue even though they have different preferences regarding that issue. In its simplest form the parties involved may be two individuals who are trying to decide who will pay for lunch. A little more complexity is involved when two people, such as an employee and a manager, sit down to decide on personal performance goals for the next year against which the employee's performance will be measured. Even more complex are the negotiations that take place between labor unions and the management of a company or between two companies as they negotiate the terms of a joint venture. The key issues in such negotiations are that at least two parties are involved, their preferences are different, and they need to reach agreement. Interest in negotiation has grown steadily in recent years.[43] Four primary approaches to negotiation have dominated this study: individual differences, situational characteristics, game theory, and cognitive approaches.

negotiation
The process in which two or more parties (people or groups) reach agreement on an issue even though they have different preferences regarding that issue

Early psychological approaches concentrated on the personality traits of the negotiators.[44] Traits investigated have included demographic characteristics and personality variables. Demographic characteristics have included age, gender, and race, among others. Personality variables have included risk taking, locus of control, tolerance for ambiguity, self-esteem, authoritarianism, and Machiavellianism. The assumption of this type of research was that the key to successful negotiation was selecting the right person to do the negotiating, one who had the appropriate demographic characteristics or personality. This assumption seemed to make sense because negotiation is such a personal and interactive process. However, the research rarely showed the positive results expected because situational variables negated the effects of the individual differences.[45]

Situational characteristics are the context within which negotiation takes place. They include such things as the types of communication between negotiators, the potential outcomes of the negotiation, the relative power of the parties (both positional and personal), the time frame available for negotiation, the number of people representing each side, and the presence of other parties. Some of this research has contributed to our understanding of the negotiation process. However, the shortcomings of the situational approach are similar to those of the individual characteristics approach. Many situational characteristics are external to the negotiators and beyond their control. Often the negotiators cannot change their relative power positions or the setting within which the negotiation occurs. So, although we have learned a lot from research on the situational issues, we still need to learn much more about the process.

Game theory was developed by economists using mathematical models to predict the outcome of negotiation situations (as illustrated in the Academy Award-winning movie *A Beautiful Mind*). It requires that every alternative and outcome be analyzed with probabilities and numerical outcomes reflecting the preferences for each outcome. In addition, the order in which different parties can make choices and every possible move are predicted, along with associated preferences for outcomes. The outcomes of this approach are exactly what negotiators want: a predictive model of how negotiation should be conducted. One major drawback is that it requires the ability to describe all possible options and outcomes for every possible move in every situation before the negotiation starts. This is often very tedious, if possible at all. Another problem is that this theory assumes that negotiators are rational at all times. Other research in negotiation has shown that negotiators often do not act rationally. Therefore, this approach, although elegant in its prescriptions, is usually unworkable in a real negotiation situation.

The fourth approach is the cognitive approach, which recognizes that negotiators often depart from perfect rationality during negotiation; it tries to predict how and when negotiators will make these departures. Howard Raiffa's decision analytic approach focuses on providing advice to negotiators actively involved in negotiation.[46] Bazerman and Neale have added to Raiffa's work by specifying eight ways in which negotiators systematically deviate from rationality.[47] The types of deviations they describe include escalation of commitment to a previously selected course of action, overreliance on readily available information, assuming that the negotiations can produce fixed-sum outcomes, and anchoring negotiation in irrelevant information. These cognitive approaches have advanced the study of negotiation a long way beyond the early individual and situational approaches. Negotiators can use them to attempt to predict in advance how the negotiation might take place.

What techniques are available to managers to stimulate, control, and resolve conflict?

What are the primary risks involved if a manager decides to stimulate conflict?

CONCEPT CHECK

Summary of Learning Objectives and Key Points

1. Define and identify types of groups and teams in organizations, discuss reasons why people join groups and teams, and list the stages of group and team development.

   - A group is two or more people who interact regularly to accomplish a common purpose or goal.
   - General kinds of groups in organizations are
     - functional groups
     - task groups and teams
     - informal or interest groups
   - A team is a group of workers that functions as a unit, often with little or no supervision, to carry out organizational functions.

2. Identify and discuss four essential characteristics of groups and teams.

   - People join functional groups and teams to pursue a career.
   - Their reasons for joining informal or interest groups include interpersonal attraction, group activities, group goals, need satisfaction, and potential instrumental benefits.
   - The stages of team development include testing and dependence, intragroup conflict and hostility, development of group cohesion, and focusing on the problem at hand.
   - Four important characteristics of teams are role structures, behavioral norms, cohesiveness, and informal leadership.

   - Role structures define task and socioemotional specialists and may be disrupted by role ambiguity, role conflict, or role overload.
   - Norms are standards of behavior for group members.
   - Cohesiveness is the extent to which members are loyal and committed to the team and to one another.
   - Informal leaders are those leaders whom the group members themselves choose to follow.

3. Discuss interpersonal and intergroup conflict in organizations.

   - Conflict is a disagreement between two or more people, groups, or organizations.
   - Too little or too much conflict may hurt performance, but an optimal level of conflict may improve performance.
   - Interpersonal and intergroup conflict in organizations may be caused by personality differences or by particular organizational strategies and practices.

4. Describe how organizations manage conflict.

   - Organizations may encounter conflict with one another and with various elements of the environment.
   - Three methods of managing conflict are
     - to stimulate it
     - to control it
     - to resolve and eliminate it

Discussion Questions

Questions for Review

1. What is a group? Describe the several different types of groups and indicate the similarities and differences among them. What is the difference between a group and a team?
2. What are the stages of group development? Do all teams develop through all the stages discussed in this chapter? Why or why not? How might the management of a mature team differ from the management of teams that are not yet mature?
3. Describe the development of a role within a group. Tell how each role leads to the next.
4. Describe the causes of conflict in organizations. What can a manager do to control conflict? To resolve and eliminate conflict?

Questions for Analysis

5. Individuals join groups for a variety of reasons. Most groups contain members who joined for different reasons. What is likely to be the result when members join a group for different reasons? What can a group leader do to reduce the negative impact of a conflict in reasons for joining the group?

6. Consider the case of a developed group, where all members have been socialized. What are the benefits to the individuals of norm conformity? What are the benefits of not conforming to the group's norms? What are the benefits to an organization of conformity? What are the benefits to an organization of nonconformity?

7. Do you think teams are a valuable new management technique that will endure, or are they just a fad that will be replaced with something else in the near future?

Questions for Application

8. Think of several groups of which you have been a member. Why did you join each? Did each group progress through the stages of development discussed in this chapter? If not, why do you think it did not?

9. Describe the behavioral norms that are in effect in your management class. To what extent are the norms generalized; in other words, how severely are students "punished" for not observing norms? To what extent is there norm variation; that is, are some students able to "get away" with violating norms to which others must conform?

10. Describe a case of interpersonal conflict that you have observed in an organization. Describe a case of intergroup conflict that you have observed. (If you have not observed any, interview a worker or manager to obtain examples.) In each case, was the conflict beneficial or harmful to the organization, and why?

CengageNow™ Highlights

Now use your CengageNow™ homework to help you:
- Apply management theories in your life
- Assess your management skills
- Master management terms and concepts
- Apply your knowledge to real-world situations
- Analyze and solve challenging management problems

In order to take advantage of these elements, your instructor will need to have set up a course for your class within CengageNow™. Ask your instructor to contact his/her Cengage sales representative and Digital Solutions Manager to explore testing CengageNow™ in your course this term.

Building Effective Skills

Chapter 1: Building Effective Time-Management Skills

Exercise Overview

Time-management skills refer to the ability to prioritize tasks, to work efficiently, and to delegate appropriately. This exercise allows you to assess your own current time-management skills and to gather some suggestions for how you can improve in this area.

Exercise Background

As we saw in Chapter 1, effective managers must be prepared to switch back and forth among the four basic activities in the management process. They must also be able to fulfill a number of different roles in their organizations, and they must exercise a variety of managerial skills in doing so. On top of everything else, their schedules are busy and full of tasks—personal and job-related activities that require them to "switch gears" frequently throughout the workday.

Stephen Covey, a management consultant and author of *The 7 Habits of Highly Effective People*, has developed a system for prioritizing tasks. First, he divides them into two categories—*urgent* and *critical*. *Urgent* tasks, such as those with approaching deadlines, must be performed right away. *Critical* tasks are tasks of high importance—say, those that will affect significant areas of one's life or work. Next, Covey plots both types of tasks on a grid with four quadrants: A task may be *urgent, critical, urgent and critical,* or *not urgent and not critical.*

Most managers, says Covey, spend too much time on tasks that are urgent when in fact they should be focused on tasks that are *critical*. He observes, for example, that managers who concentrate on urgent tasks meet their deadlines but tend to neglect such critical areas as long-term planning. (Unfortunately, the same people are also apt to neglect critical areas of their personal lives.) In short, effective managers must learn to balance the demands of urgent tasks with those of critical tasks by redistributing the amount of time devoted to each type.

Exercise Task

1. Visit the website of FranklinCovey (the firm cofounded by Stephen Covey) at **www.franklincovey.com**. Click on the tab marked *Effectiveness Zone*, and then select *Assessment Sector*. Now take the "Urgency Analysis Profile," a brief online survey that should take about 10 minutes.
2. Now look over your profile and examine the assessment of your current use of time and the suggestions for how you can improve your time management. In what ways do you agree and disagree with your personal assessment? Explain your reasons for agreeing or disagreeing.
3. Think of a task that you regularly perform and which, if you were being perfectly honest, you could label *not urgent and not critical*. How much time do you spend on this task? What might be a more appropriate amount of time? To what other tasks could you give some of the time that you spend on this *not-urgent-not-critical* task?
4. What one thing can you do today to make better use of your time? Try it to see if your time management improves.

Chapter 1: Building Effective Conceptual Skills

Exercise Overview

Your conceptual skills reflect your ability to think in the abstract. This exercise will help you extend your conceptual skills by identifying and analyzing situations that call for different kinds of management functions, roles, and skills in different kinds of organizations.

Exercise Background

Chapter 1 includes discussions of four management *functions*, ten management *roles*, and seven management *skills*. It also stresses the idea that management activities are necessary in many different kinds of organizations.

Start by identifying five different types of organizations: one large business, one small business, one educational organization, one healthcare organization, and one government organization. You might choose organizations about which you have some personal knowledge or organizations that you simply recognize by name and industry. Next, put yourself in the position of a top manager in each of your five specific organizations.

Write the names of these five organizations across the top of a sheet of paper. Then list the four functions, ten roles, and seven skills down the left side of the sheet. Now put your imagination to work: Think of a situation, a problem, or an opportunity that fits at the intersection of each row and column on the sheet. The dean of your college, for example, must perform a leadership role and apply interpersonal skills. The manager of an all-night diner must perform an organizing function and play the role of monitor.

Exercise Task

1. Do you notice any patterns of meaningful similarities in functions, roles, or skills across the five columns? Are there, for example, similarities in performing leadership roles or applying communication skills in most or all of the five types of organization? Do you notice any patterns of meaningful differences?
2. Based on your assessment of the patterns of similarities and differences that you identified in task 1, give two or three reasons why managers might find it easy to move from one type of organization to another. Give two or three reasons why managers might find it difficult to move from one type of organization to another.
3. Identify two or three places on your grid where the intersection between a type of organization and a function, role, or skill suggests something at which you might be particularly good. How about something at which, at least right now, you think you wouldn't be very good. Explain your reasoning

Chapter 2: Building Effective Decision-Making Skills

Exercise Overview

Decision-making skills include the ability to recognize and define problems or opportunities and then select the appropriate course of action. This exercise will help you develop your own decision-making skills while also underscoring the importance of subsystem interdependencies in organizations.

Exercise Background

You're the vice president of a large company that makes outdoor furniture for decks, patios, and pools. Each product line and the firm itself have grown substantially in recent years. Unfortunately, your success has attracted the attention of competitors, and several have entered the market in the last two years. Your CEO wants you to determine how to cut costs by 10 percent so that prices can be cut by the same amount. She's convinced that the move is necessary to retain market share in the face of new competition.

You've examined the situation and decided that you have three options for cutting costs:

- Begin buying slightly lower-grade materials, including hardwood, aluminum, vinyl, and nylon.
- Lay off a portion of your workforce and then try to motivate everyone who's left to work harder; this option also means selecting future hires from a lower-skill labor pool and paying lower wages.
- Replace existing equipment with newer, more efficient equipment; although this option entails substantial up-front investment, you're sure that you can more than make up the difference in lower production costs.

Exercise Task

With this background in mind, respond to the following questions:
1. Carefully examine each of your three options. In what ways might each option affect other parts of the organization?
2. Which is the most costly option *in terms of impact on other parts of the organization, not in terms of absolute dollars*? Which is the least costly?
3. What are the primary obstacles that you might face in trying to implement each of your three options?
4. Are there any other options for accomplishing your goal of reducing costs?

Chapter 2: Building Effective Interpersonal Skills

Exercise Overview

Interpersonal skills refer to your ability to communicate with, understand, and motivate both individuals and groups. This exercise asks you to examine your attitudes about how people regard work and how they behave in the workplace.

Exercise Task

Below is a series of paired statements—that is, each of the eight items consists of *two related statements*. Consider and respond to each pair as follows:

- Ask yourself: How does each statement reflect my attitude about how people regard work and behave in the workplace?
- You have 5 points to divide between each pair of statements. If the first statement, for example, totally reflects your attitude and the other does not, give the first statement 5 points and the second 0. If the first statement usually reflects your attitude, give it 4 points and the second statement 1 point. *The combined score for each pair must always equal 5 points.*

Here's how to determine point values:

0–5 or 5–0: One of the statements totally reflects your attitude while the other does not.
1–4 or 4–1: One of the statements usually reflects your attitude while the other does not.
2–3 or 3–2: Both statements reflect your attitude, though one more than the other.

1. _____ People enjoy working.
   _____ People do not like to work.
2. _____ Employees don't have to be closely watched in order to do their jobs well.
   _____ Employees won't do good jobs unless they're closely supervised.
3. _____ Employees will do tasks well if you ask them to.
   _____ If you want something done right, do it yourself.
4. _____ Employees want to be involved in decision making.
   _____ Employees want managers to make decisions.
5. _____ Employees will do their best work when you allow them to do their jobs in their own ways.
   _____ Employees do their best work when they're taught the one best way of doing a job.
6. _____ Managers should give employees all information that's not confidential.
   _____ Managers should give employees only the information they need to do their jobs.
7. _____ Employees work just as hard when managers aren't around as they do when managers are around.
   _____ Employees will take things easier when managers aren't around than they will when managers are around.
8. _____ Managers should share managerial responsibilities with members of employee groups.
   _____ Managers should perform managerial functions for employee groups.

Now you can determine your attitude about how people regard work and behave in the workplace. Simply do the following:

- Add up the numbers (0–5) for the first statement in each pair (ignore the numbers for the second statements). Your score should fall somewhere between 0 and 40.
- Place your score on the following continuum:
  Theory X 0_____5_____10_____15_____20_____
  25_____30_____35_____40 *Theory* Y

Generally speaking, the higher your score, the greater your leaning toward Theory Y; the lower your score, the greater your leaning toward Theory X.

Adapted from Robert N. Lussier and Christopher F. Achua, *Leadership: Theory, Application, and Skill Development*, 4th ed. (Mason, OH: South-Western Cengage Learning, 2010), p. 48.

Chapter 3: Building Effective Time-Management Skills

Exercise Overview

Time-management skills refer to the ability to prioritize tasks, to work efficiently, and to delegate appropriately. This exercise gives you an opportunity to apply your time-management skills to your understanding of the tasks that managers typically perform.

Exercise Background

A key problem faced by all managers is the fact that time is a finite resource: There are only so many hours in a day and only so many tasks that you can take on in a given period of time. As a result, managers are constantly making choices about how they spend their time. Obviously, they must use it wisely, and as any veteran manager will tell you, spending time on trivial matters and neglecting more pressing concerns is not only a mistake but a surprisingly easy trap to fall into. Using your time wisely means dividing it appropriately among the various tasks that you have to perform on a daily basis.

Many time-management experts suggest that managers begin each day by listing what they need to accomplish before the workday is done. After they've compiled this list, they can then sort their daily tasks into three groups: (1) those that must be addressed today, (2) those that should be addressed today but can be postponed if necessary, and (3) those that can easily be postponed. The next step is a matter of common sense: Perform the tasks in order of priority.

You can use the organization of the material in Chapter 3 to get a better understanding of managerial tasks and how to prioritize them. As we saw in Chapter 3, for example, both managers and organizations must be sensitive to a variety of forces at work in a firm's *external* and *internal* environments. We then divided the external environment into two categories—the *general* and *task* environments. For the purpose of this exercise, you can focus on the *task environment*, which includes competitors, customers, suppliers, strategic partners, and regulators. You also need to remember that the *internal environment* consists of a firm's owners, board of directors, employees, physical work environment, and organization culture.

Exercise Task

This exercise consists of the following steps:
1. Across the top of a sheet of paper, write the three priority levels that we described above (tasks that need to be done today, etc.).
2. Down the left side of the same sheet of paper, list the elements of the *task environment* plus the elements of a firm's *internal environment*.
3. At the intersection of each row and column, provide an appropriate example of a task that a manager might face:

When you come to *Customers*, for example, think of three hypothetical tasks—one that's of high priority (do today), one that's of moderate priority (postpone if necessary), and one that's of lower priority (postpone).
4. When you've finished, your instructor will divide the class into small groups of three or four people. Once your group is assembled, share the examples that you came up with. Focus on whether the group agrees or disagrees about the way that each person has prioritized his or her tasks.

Chapter 3: Building Effective Communication Skills

Exercise Overview

Communication skills refer to the ability not only to convey information and ideas to others but also to handle information and ideas received from them. This exercise will help you develop your skills in conveying certain information that you've received during your study of business—namely, information about customer segments as an element in an organization's task environment.

Exercise Background

You're a newly hired middle manager in the marketing department of a large food manufacturer. Having just completed your formal study of marketing management, you're excited about the opportunity to apply some of the theories that you've read about to real situations faced by a real business. As luck would have it, you haven't been on the job very long when you're confronted by an intriguing problem. Your boss, the VP for marketing, has developed a survey to solicit customer feedback about the company's products. Unfortunately, the feedback varies considerably, with responses typically ranging from 2 to 5 on a scale of 1 to 5. Even you can see that such a wide range of data isn't very helpful in drawing conclusions about customer opinions. Moreover, sales have been slowly but steadily declining over time, and upper management has been putting pressure on the marketing department to figure out why.

Suspecting that the survey results are so broad because they reflect a broad range of customers, you make a suggestion to

your boss: "To get a better idea of what their needs are, why don't we gather some information about our customers themselves? For example, our customers include individual consumers, schools, restaurants, and other organizations. Maybe each type of customer wants something different from our products." Your boss gives you a patronizing look and says, "Our products have been best-sellers for years, and do you want to know why? Because good quality is good quality—always has been and always will be. Show me a 'customer' and I'll show you somebody who just wants good quality."

Exercise Task

1. Go back to your office (or your dorm room, the library, or your kitchen table) and compose a written proposal for your boss in which you outline your position on developing a customer-needs survey. Be sure that your proposal accomplishes two goals: (1) It emphasizes your fundamental concern—namely, that in order to provide products that meet customer needs, the marketing department must better understand what those needs are. (2) It communicates some good reasons why

the marketing department should follow through on your proposal. (*Hint:* Telling your boss bluntly that he's wrong probably won't get the job done.)

2. Now review what you've written. Do you think that your boss will change his mind? If yes, which of your reasons is most likely to persuade him? If no, what might be your next move in trying to get your proposal a fair hearing from management?

Chapter 4: Building Effective Diagnostic and Decision-Making Skills

Exercise Overview

Diagnostic and decision-making skills are closely related. Diagnostic skills enable a manager to visualize the most appropriate response to a situation, thereby providing a foundation for effective decision making. Decision-making skills refer to the ability to recognize and define problems and opportunities

correctly and then to select an appropriate course of action for solving problems or capitalizing on opportunities. This exercise will help you develop your diagnostic and decision-making skills by applying them to the kind of ethical dilemma with which you might be confronted during your business career.

Exercise Background

As businesses, industries, and technologies—not to mention societies—become more complex, ethical dilemmas also tend to become more complicated. Consider, for example, the business of publishing music online, in which a variety of factors—the advent of split-second cyber connections, the

desire of many businesses to bypass intermediaries, new definitions of *theft*—conspire to contribute to a number of potential ethical dilemmas. In this exercise, we'll use the Internet to collect some up-to-date information about online music publishing and then answer a few ethics-oriented questions.

Exercise Task

1. Start by considering each of the stakeholders in the online music publishing industry—recording artists, recording companies, online file-sharing companies such as Napster, and consumers. Consider the kinds of ethical problems faced by the industry and explain how each stakeholder is affected by each problem.

2. For each problem, determine the best outcome for each stakeholder.

3. For each problem, do you see any way to satisfy the needs of every stakeholder? If yes, explain how this outcome can be brought about. If no, explain why no mutually beneficial solution is possible.

4. In what ways did your own code of ethics influence your various answers to question 2 and your reasoning in question 3?

Chapter 4: Building Effective Interpersonal Skills

Exercise Overview

Interpersonal skills refer to the ability to communicate with, understand, and motivate individuals and groups. Because they may prove especially important in situations involving issues of ethics and social responsibility, we'll use this exercise to help you apply interpersonal skills to a situation in which you're called upon to make an ethical decision.

Exercise Background

You're a department manager in a large retail store, and your work group has had a brush with allegations of sexual harassment. Specifically, one of your female employees reported that a male colleague was in the habit of telling off-color jokes and making mildly suggestive comments. When you asked the accused employee about the charges, he didn't deny them but rather attributed them to a misunderstanding.

You passed along the allegations to the HR department, which suspended the male employee, with pay, pending an investigation. When the process was completed, the HR manager who interviewed both parties and other employees concluded that the male employee should be placed on six months' probation. Any further substantiated charges during this period would be cause for immediate dismissal.

HR's decision was based on the following factors: (1) The employee had worked in the store for over ten years, with a good performance record and without any previous problems. (2) The female who made the charges believed that he was guilty of general insensitivity and hadn't targeted her directly. (3) She didn't think that his behaviors were sufficient to warrant dismissal but simply wanted him to stop them.

Tomorrow will be the accused employee's first day back at work since the HR decision was handed down. You're satisfied with the ruling, but you're a bit worried about potential tension in your work group. You intend to meet with the female today and the male tomorrow morning and try to head off as much tension as possible.

Exercise Task

In preparing for these two meetings, do the following:
1. Jot down some general notes for your conversation with the male employee.
2. Jot down some general notes for your conversation with the female employee.
3. Make sure that you have a handle on the ethical issues in this situation. Precisely what are they?
4. Consider the options of having the two employees work closely together or keeping them separated. Which will you choose? Why?

Chapter 5: Building Effective Technical Skills

Exercise Overview

Technical skills are necessary to understand or perform the specific kind of work that an organization does. At some companies, the work involves analyzing data in order to develop effective international strategies. This exercise will help you develop certain technical skills related to the tasks of collecting information and determining its possible effects on a firm's activities.

Exercise Background

As of 2002, the five largest countries in the world, in terms of population, were China, India, the United States, Indonesia, and Brazil. As the manager of a large U.S.-based multinational firm, you need some information about trade and population in each of these countries. You can isolate the information that you need by reviewing the six items that constitute the Exercise Task below. Here are a few helpful hints for using the Internet to find the information that you need. You can get import/export data from the U.S. Census Bureau; go to **www.census.gov/foreign-trade/aip/index .html#profile** and, working from this main page, locate the most recent figures. You can also get estimates of future population from the Census Bureau at **www.census.gov/ ipc/www/idb/rank.php**. You can gather the rest of the data you need from the *World Factbook*, which is published by the U.S. Central Intelligence Agency at **www.cia.gov/cia/ publications/factbook/index.html**.

Exercise Task

To compile the information you need, do the following:

1. List the five countries in the world projected to have the largest populations in 2050. Explain how the list will have changed since 2002.
2. List the five countries that currently export the most products to the United States.
3. List the five countries that currently import the most products from the United States.
4. Life span is a measure of individual prosperity in a country. What is the average life span in each of the five largest countries in the world? In each of the five largest exporters to the United States? In each of the five largest importers from the United States?
5. Gross domestic product (GDP) per capita is a measure of a country's economic health. What is the GDP per capita, in U.S. dollars, of each of the world's five largest countries? Of each of the five largest exporters to the United States? Of each of the five largest importers from the United States?
6. What are the implications for your firm? What, for example, do the data suggest about the desirability of various countries as current trading partners? What do the data suggest about the desirability of the same countries as future trading partners?

Chapter 5: Building Effective Communication Skills

Exercise Overview

Communication skills refer not only to the ability to convey information and ideas to others but to handle information and ideas received from them. Obviously, differences in language and a whole array of cultural differences mean that international managers face additional communication adjustments. This exercise focuses on communication skills in a context to which you probably haven't given much thought—differences in time zones.

Exercise Background

You're a manager in a large multinational firm headquartered in San Francisco. You need to arrange a conference call with several other managers to discuss an upcoming strategic change. The other managers are located in New York, London, Rome, Moscow, Tokyo, Singapore, and Sydney.

Exercise Task

To arrange your conference call, do the following:

1. Determine the time zone differences in each of the cities involved.
2. Assuming that people in each city have a typical workday of 8:00 A.M. to 5:00 P.M., determine the optimal time for your conference call. At what time, in other words, can you schedule the call so that the fewest people are inconvenienced?
3. Now assume that, as a result of the call, you need to visit each office in person, spending one full day in each office. Using the Internet, review airline schedules and develop an efficient itinerary.

Chapter 6: Building Effective Technical Skills

Exercise Overview

Technical skills are necessary to understand or perform the specific kind of work that an organization does. At some organizations, the work involves gathering and analyzing data in order to develop effective policies for dealing with issues of diversity and multiculturalism. This exercise asks you to gather such data from the Internet and then to transform it into information that managers can use to assess diversity-related issues.

Exercise Background

You're the dean in charge of diversity-related issues at a college that's committed to maintaining an appropriate level of diversity within the student body. You're assigned to prepare a report to the president's special committee on diversity-related policies, in which you will describe the school's current level of diversity and identify any areas of concern. As you begin, you remind yourself that the way an organization defines and measures *diversity* is crucial in determining its approach to diversity-related issues.

Exercise Task

1. Use the Internet to gather information about the gender and ethnic diversity of your school's student body. Next, gather similar information about your school's workforce, both faculty and staff. (*Hint:* You might consult the school's website for pages related to admissions and human resources.)
2. Use the Internet to gather information about the diversity of the state and local communities in which your school operates. Then gather similar information about the United States as a whole. (*Hint:* Demographic data at all three levels are available on the U.S. Census Bureau's Census 2000 website; go to **www. census.gov.**)
3. Based on the information that you've gathered, would you say that your school's student body is at an appropriate level of diversity? Explain why or why not.
4. Identify a few areas in which the student-body population could reflect a greater degree of diversity.

Chapter 6: Building Effective Time-Management Skills

Exercise Overview

Time-management skills refer to the ability to prioritize tasks, to work efficiently, and to delegate appropriately. In this exercise, you'll explore your personal values and some of the ways in which they influence the importance that you attach to various tasks.

Exercise Background

Because each of us has unique characteristics, backgrounds, relationships, and experiences, we're all unique. Not surprisingly, our uniqueness extends to our *values*. Each of us, for example, places more or less importance—or value—on different aspects of our lives. For some of us, religion or education are primary motivators, whereas for others, occupation or past experience are extremely important factors in determining the way we go about things.

In other words, values play a key role in the way we assign priorities to the tasks that we perform in daily life. In an ideal world, of course, we'd be able to spend more time on tasks of greater importance to us and less time on relatively unimportant tasks. For most of us, however, the mundane demands of everyday living tend to take precedence. This in-class exercise is designed to show that we can clarify our values and actually use them to manage our time.

Exercise Task

Listen as your instructor provides a demonstration to the class. Then respond to each of the following items:

1. What are your "rocks"? What are your "pebbles"? What are your "grains of sand"?
2. Using this classification scheme, determine your most important personal values.
3. Having prioritized your values, determine whether you typically spend enough time on tasks that support your most important values. If you do manage to allocate your time to things that are important to you, explain how you do it. If you *don't* manage to allocate your time to things that are important to you, explain what the problem is.
4. Discuss some steps that you could take to ensure that more of your time is spent on tasks related to your most important values.

Chapter 6: Building Effective Decision-Making Skills

Exercise Overview

Decision-making skills refer to the ability to recognize and define problems and opportunities correctly and then to select an appropriate course of action for solving problems or capitalizing on opportunities. This exercise focuses on decision making about issues related to diversity and multiculturalism.

Exercise Background

For years, the 1,000-member workforce at the factory where you're general manager had been almost exclusively white and male. In recent years, however, you've succeeded in increasing diversity substantially. Today, nearly one-third of your employees are female and over 40 percent are Latino or African American.

Unfortunately, you've been hit with some financial setbacks. You've crunched the numbers and arrived at the conclusion that you have no choice but to lay off about 300 employees for a period of at least six months. On the upside, if everything goes well, you'll be able to bring back the same number of employees after six months.

Exercise Task

Basing your decision on the above conclusions, do the following:

1. Develop a layoff plan that won't substantially affect the level of your firm's diversity.
2. Decide how best to communicate your decision to your workforce.
3. Make a list of the potential obstacles to implementing your plan.

Chapter 7: Building Effective Decision-Making Skills

Exercise Overview

Decision-making skills refer to the ability to recognize and define problems and opportunities correctly and then to select an appropriate course of action for solving problems or capitalizing on opportunities. In this exercise, you're asked to apply your decision-making skills to a situation calling for both good business sense and a sense of personal values.

Exercise Background

You're the owner of a company that makes dress and casual shoes at two small factories, each with a workforce of 40 people. One is located in Smallville, Illinois, and the other in Modesto, Texas, both small towns. You've been in business for 40 years, and both factories have long been profitable. Unfortunately, however, competitive conditions in the industry have changed in recent years. In particular, you're now facing stiff competition from Italian firms whose shoes not only sell for less money but boast higher quality.

You're confident that you can close the quality gap with new high-tech equipment, but your overhead is still 30 percent higher than that of your Italian competitors. At the moment, you feel that your best option is to close the Smallville factory and lay off the workers, but you're a little reluctant to do so. You're the major employer in Smallville, which is dependent on your factory and has just spent a good deal of money to improve utility service and highway access. In addition, most of your employees are older people who have lived most of their lives in Smallville.

Exercise Task

1. Your instructor will divide the class into groups of three or four people each. Each group will meet as a management team responsible for deciding the fate of the Smallville plant.
2. The team may decide to close the plant or to keep it open, but the goal of the decision-making process is twofold: (1) to keep the company viable and (2) to reflect the team's individual and group values.

3. If the team decides to close the plant, it must draw up a list of the factors on which it based its decision and be prepared to justify it.
4. If the team decides to keep the plant open, it must draw up a plan explaining how the company can still remain competitive.

5. Each member of each team should be prepared to explain the choices that he or she made in helping the group reach its decision.

Chapter 7: Building Effective Time-Management Skills

Exercise Overview

Time-management skills refer to the ability to prioritize tasks, to work efficiently, and to delegate appropriately. This exercise asks you to apply your time-management skills to the process of goal optimization.

Exercise Background

All managers face a variety of goals, challenges, opportunities, and, of course, demands on their time. Juggling all these demands successfully requires a clear understanding of priorities, scheduling, and a number of related factors. You're about to learn just how difficult this task is because you're about to open your own business—a retail store in a local shopping mall. You're starting from scratch, with no prior business connections, but you do have a strong business plan and you're sure that it will work.

In getting ready to open your business, you know that you need to meet and draw up plans with each of the following parties:

1. The mall manager, to negotiate a lease
2. A local banker, to arrange partial financing
3. An attorney, to incorporate your business
4. An accountant, to set up a bookkeeping system
5. Suppliers, to arrange credit terms and delivery schedules
6. An advertising agency, to start promoting your business
7. A staffing agency, to hire employees
8. A design firm, to plan the physical layout of the store

Exercise Task

Review all the information above and then do the following:
1. Develop a schedule listing the sequence in which you need to meet with the eight parties that you've listed above. Do the best that you can to minimize backtracking (seeing one party and then having to see him again after seeing someone else).

2. Compare your schedule with that of a classmate and discuss the differences.
3. Do you find that it's possible to draw up different schedules which are nevertheless equally valid? If so, why? If not, why not?

Chapter 8: Building Effective Decision-Making Skills

Exercise Overview

Decision-making skills refer to the ability to recognize and define problems and opportunities correctly and then to select an appropriate course of action for solving problems or capitalizing on opportunities. As we noted in Chapter 8, many organizations use SWOT analysis as part of the strategy-formulation process. This exercise will help you better understand both how managers obtain the information they need to perform such an analysis and how they use it as a framework for making decisions.

Exercise Background

SWOT is an acronym for *Strengths, Weaknesses, Opportunities,* and *Threats*. The idea behind SWOT is that a good strategy exploits an organization's opportunities and strengths while neutralizing threats and avoiding or correcting weaknesses.

You've just been hired to run a medium-size company that manufactures electric motors, circuit breakers, and similar electronic components for industrial use. In recent years, the firm's financial performance has gradually eroded, and your job is to turn things around.

At one time, the firm was successful in part because it was able to charge premium prices for top-quality products. In recent years, however, management has tried cutting costs as a means of bringing prices in line with those of new competitors in the market. Unfortunately, the strategy hasn't worked very well, with the effect of cost cutting being primarily a fall-off in product quality. Convinced that a new strategy is called for, you've decided to begin with a SWOT analysis.

Exercise Task

Reviewing the situation, you take the following steps:
1. List the sources that you'll use to gather information about the firm's strengths, weaknesses, opportunities, and threats.
2. Then ask yourself: For what types of information are data readily available on the Internet? What categories of data are difficult or impossible to find on the Internet?

(*Note*: When using the Internet, be sure to provide specific websites or URLs.)
3. Next, rate each source that you consult in terms of probable reliability.
4. Finally, ask yourself how confident you'd be in basing decisions on the information that you've obtained.

Chapter 8: Building Effective Conceptual Skills

Exercise Overview

Conceptual skills require you to think in the abstract, and they're particularly important to top managers who are responsible for managing a firm's strategy. Because strategic management is a process of pursuing goals in a competitive environment, it naturally invites metaphors involving war or sports. And that's one reason why people tend to forget that cooperation is often a viable strategic alternative to competition. Indeed, cooperation has been a popular business strategy in many countries for years, and the choice of cooperative alternatives—such as strategic alliances and joint ventures—is also on the rise in the United States. The game that we'll play in this exercise is designed to illustrate the advantages of cooperative strategy as an alternative to competitive strategy.

Exercise Background

Needless to say, both competitive and cooperative strategies can be quite complex when you're trying to implement them in an organizational context. Perhaps, however, we can simplify matters by playing a simple game.

The game we have in mind reflects a classic situation that has proved quite useful in demonstrating some basic concepts in game theory. Here's the original "Prisoner's Dilemma" scenario:

Authorities suspect two criminals of a crime but don't have enough evidence to convict either of them. So they separate the two and offer each prisoner a deal:

- *If one rats on the other and the other refuses to rat, the rat goes free and the other prisoner gets a full ten-year sentence.*
- *If both refuse to rat, then both get lesser six-month sentences.*
- *If each rats on the other, both get reduced five-year sentences.*

The prisoners must choose one of the two options—to rat or not to rat.

Assuming that the lowest possible sentence is of optimal value to the prisoners, what's the optimal outcome—that is, the outcome that's most beneficial to both prisoners?

The optimal outcome for *both* prisoners occurs when they cooperate and neither rats on the other: Each gets the lowest possible sentence (six months). The most common outcome, however, is mutual ratting: Both rat and both get five-year sentences.

Game theorists use the "Prisoner's Dilemma" scenario as a hypothetical situation in which people are obliged to make a decision about whether to act cooperatively or competitively. Although real life presents us with many "competitive" situations in which cooperation would be more beneficial for both parties, people often gravitate toward competition—an option that often leads to less-than-optimal outcomes. The game that you're about to play should be a good illustration of the point.

Exercise Task

1. Break into small groups and play the board game according to the instructions you receive from your professor.
2. Present your group's results to the class.

3. Analyze the results reported by every group and be prepared to share your thoughts about the outcomes.

Chapter 9: Building Effective Conceptual Skills

Exercise Overview

Conceptual skills require you to think in the abstract—an area that's fraught with the risk of error (or at least mistakes in judgment). This exercise is designed to show you how certain pitfalls in abstract thinking—namely, nonrational biases and risk propensity—can lead to faulty decision making.

Exercise Background

Psychologists Amos Tversky and Daniel Kahneman conducted much of the research contributing to the current state of our knowledge about decision-making biases. Tversky and Kahneman tested tendencies in people's real-life choices by presenting experimental subjects with laboratory-simulated decision-making situations. From the results they developed a set of principles called *prospect theory* to explain why people tend to be nonrational in making economic decisions.

Tversky and Kahneman's most important finding was that an individual's *perception* of gain or loss in a situation is more important than an objective measure of gain or loss. In this respect, they're being *nonrational*—that is, they aren't making decisions based purely on rational criteria. Similarly, they found that different people think differently about gains and losses—a phenomenon they call *framing*. Not surprisingly, people also tend to allow their perceptions to be skewed (positively or negatively) by the information they receive about a situation. Unfortunately, when new information later becomes available, they have a hard time letting go of their initial perceptions, even if the new information contradicts their original impressions. Tversky and Kahneman refer to this process as *anchoring and adjustment.*

In this exercise, we're going to ask you to answer a few questions. To answer them, however, you must know how to calculate an *expected value*. To do this, you multiply each possible outcome value of a situation by the probability of its occurrence and then sum all the results. Here's a simple example: Let's say you have a 50 percent chance of earning 80 points on an exam and a 50 percent chance of earning 70 points. You can calculate the expected value as

$$(.5 + 80) + (.5 \times 70) = 75$$

In other words, a .5 chance of 80 points equals 40 points and a .5 chance of 70 points equals 35 points. Therefore, the expected value of your exam is $40 + 35 = 75$ points.

Exercise Task

1. Respond to the list of brief questions that your professor provides to you. Remember: No answer is correct or incorrect; simply choose *your most likely response.* Then, when your instructor tells you to, share your answers with the class.

2. Discuss the answers given by the class. Why do students' answers differ?
3. What have you learned from this exercise about decision-making biases and risk propensity?

Chapter 9: Building Effective Decision-Making Skills

Exercise Overview

Decision-making skills refer to the ability to recognize and define problems and opportunities correctly and then to select an appropriate course of action for solving problems or capitalizing on opportunities. This exercise allows you to compare the results of individual decision making with the results of decision making conducted by nominal groups.

Exercise Background

Individual decision making, of course, has its advantages—speed, simplicity, lack of conflict. At times, however, these advantages are outweighed by other considerations. In particular, solitary decision making isn't conducive to innovation. Groups are better at innovating because they benefit from the input of diverse individuals, which, in turn, generates greater variety in alternative courses of action.

Exercise Task

Listen as your professor describes a problem situation and then do the following:

1. Write down as many creative responses to the problem as you can. Don't worry about whether or not they're practical. In fact, try to come up with as many unexpected—even "far-out"—responses as you can.
2. When your instructor calls on you, share your list with the class.
3. Query other students about their suggestions for clarification only. *Do not, under any circumstances, reveal whether you think any idea is "good" or "bad."*
4. After all individual ideas have been listed and clarified, add to the list any other ideas that you've

Nominal groups—so called because they exist *in name only*—are especially well suited for fostering creativity. They allow individuals the freedom to develop as many creative options as they can without having to worry about criticism or political pressure. Nominal groups also pool input from many individuals and encourage creative responses to the pooled input. In short, nominal groups foster creativity because they combine techniques for improving both individual and group creativity.

developed while participating in the in-class part of the exercise.

5. Vote on the list, focusing on the "creativity" of individual items: Which suggestion does the class regard as the "best" solution to the problem at hand?
6. Did the nominal-group technique generate more creative alternatives than those that you generated on your own?
7. In your opinion, is the alternative voted "best" by the class a "better" solution than anything you thought of on your own? Explain your answer.
8. Give some suggestions about the types of organizational decisions that could be more effective if made by nominal groups. When should nominal groups *not* be used?

Chapter 10: Building Effective Interpersonal Skills

Exercise Overview

Interpersonal skills refer to your ability to communicate with, understand, and motivate both individuals and groups. Needless to say, such skills are extremely important to the manager of a new or small business who wants to improve his or her chances of survival and success through the process of

networking—getting together with other managers to discuss common problems and opportunities. This exercise asks you to take stock of your networking skills, whether well developed already or likely to be developed as you embark on your work life.

Exercise Task

Consider each of the following statements. How accurately does each describe your current attitudes or behavior? Rate each item on a scale of 1–5 according to how well it describes you: If it describes you very well, give it a 5; if it doesn't describe you, rate it *1*.

1. ___ When I start something (taking on a new project, making a major purchase, making a career move), I seek help from people whom I know and look for new contacts who may be helpful.
2. ___ I view networking as a way to create win–win situations.

3. ___ I like meeting new people; I don't have trouble striking up conversations with people whom I don't know.
4. ___ I can quickly explain two or three of my most significant accomplishments.
5. ___ Before contacting businesspeople who may be of help to me in my career (say, by providing me with career information), I set goals that I want to achieve through the interaction.
6. ___ Before contacting businesspeople who may be of help to me, I plan out a short opening statement.

7. ___ Before contacting businesspeople who may be of help to me, I draw up a set of questions to ask.

8. ___ When I contact businesspeople who may be of help to me, I make sure to praise their accomplishments.

9. ___ I have contact information for at least ten people who may be of help to me.

10. ___ I maintain a file or database of people who may be of help to me; I keep it updated and continually add new names.

11. ___ During communications with people who may be of help to me, I ask them for the names of other people whom I can contact for further information.

12. ___ When seeking help from other people, I ask them how I might be of help to them.

13. ___ When people help me, I thank them at the time, and when someone does me an especially important favor, I follow up with thanks.

14. ___ I keep in touch with people who have helped me or may help me at least once a year and update them on my career progress.

15. ___ I maintain regular communications with people who work in other organizations related to my line of business, such as members of trade or professional organizations.

16. ___ I attend trade, professional, and career meetings in order to maintain relationships and make new contacts.

Now add up your total score and place it on the following continuum:

Effective networking   80—70—60—50—40—30—16   *Ineffective networking*

Adapted from Robert N. Lussier and Christopher F. Achua, *Leadership: Theory, Application, and Skill Development,* 4th ed. (Mason, OH: South-Western Cengage Learning, 2010), pp. 127–128.

Chapter 10: Building Effective Conceptual Skills

Exercise Overview

Conceptual skills require you to think in the abstract. This exercise will help you apply your conceptual skills to an analysis of certain criteria for successful entrepreneurship.

Exercise Background

Now that you're about to graduate, you've decided to open a small business in the local community where you've been attending college. We won't ask where you got them, but we'll assume that you have enough funds to start a business without having to worry about finding investors.

Based solely on your personal interests, list five businesses that you might want to open and operate. For the moment, forget about such technicalities as market potential or profitability. If, for example, you like riding your bicycle, think about opening a shop that caters to cyclists.

Next, *without regard to any personal interest you might have in them,* list five businesses that you might want to open and operate. In this case, your only criteria are market opportunity and profitability. What types of businesses might be profitable in your chosen community? Use the Internet to gather information on such factors as population, local economic conditions, local competition, franchising opportunities, and so on.

Finally, evaluate the prospects for success of each of the ten businesses that you've listed and jot down some notes to summarize your conclusions.

Exercise Task

Reviewing your lists, the information that you've gathered, and the conclusions that you've drawn, do the following:

1. Form a small group of four or five classmates and discuss your respective lists. Look for instances in which the same type of business appears either on (1) both of your lists or (2) on one of your lists and one of a classmate's lists. Also look for cases in which the same business appears on more than one list with either similar or dissimilar prospects for success.

2. At this point, how important do you regard personal interest as a factor in small-business success?

3. How important do you regard market potential as a factor in small-business success?

Chapter 11: Building Effective Time-Management Skills

Exercise Overview

Not surprisingly, time-management skills—which refer to the ability to prioritize tasks, to work efficiently, and to delegate appropriately—play a major role in performing the control function: Managers can use time-management skills to control their own work activities more effectively. The purpose of this exercise is to demonstrate the relationship between time-management skills and the process of controlling workplace activities.

Exercise Background

You're a middle manager in a small manufacturing plant. Today is Monday, and you've just returned from a week's vacation. The first thing you discover is that your assistant won't be in today (his aunt died, and he's out of town at the funeral). He did, however, leave you the following note:

Dear Boss:
Sorry about not being here today. I will be back tomorrow. In the meantime, here are some things you need to know:
Ms. Glinski [your boss] wants to see you today at 4:00.
The shop steward wants to see you as soon as possible about a labor problem.
Mr. Bateman [one of your big customers] has a complaint about a recent shipment.

Ms. Ferris [one of your major suppliers] wants to discuss a change in delivery schedules.
Mr. Prescott from the Chamber of Commerce wants you to attend a breakfast meeting on Wednesday to discuss our expansion plans.
The legal office wants to discuss our upcoming OSHA inspection.
Human resources wants to know when you can interview someone for the new supervisor's position.
Jack Williams, the machinist you fired last month, has been hanging around the parking lot, and his presence is making some employees uncomfortable.

Exercise Task

Review the information above and then do the following:
1. Prioritize the work that needs to be done by sorting the information into three categories: *very timely*, *moderately timely*, and *less timely*. Then address the following questions.
2. Are *importance* and *timeliness* the same thing?
3. What additional information do you need before you can begin to prioritize all of these demands on your time?
4. How would your approach differ if your assistant were in the office?

Chapter 11: Building Effective Technical Skills

Exercise Overview

Technical skills are necessary to understand or perform the specific kind of work that an organization does. This exercise allows you to develop the technical skills needed to construct and evaluate the effectiveness of a budget.

Exercise Background

Although corporate budgets are obviously much more complicated, the basic processes of creating a corporate budget on the one hand and a personal budget on the other share a few important features. Both, for instance, begin with estimations of inflow and outflow. In addition, both compare actual results with estimated results, and both culminate in plans for corrective action.

Exercise Task

1. Prepare lists of your *estimated* expenditures and income for one month. Remember: You're dealing with budgeted amounts, not the amounts that you actually spend and take in. You're also dealing with figures that represent a typical month or a reasonable minimum. If, for example, you estimate that you spend $200 a month on groceries, you need to ask yourself whether that's a reasonable amount to spend on groceries for a month. If it's not, perhaps a more typical or reasonable figure is, say, $125.

    First, estimate your necessary monthly expenses for tuition, rent, car payments, childcare, food, utilities, and so on. Then estimate your income from all sources, such as wages, allowance, loans, and funds borrowed on credit cards. Calculate both totals.

2. Now write down all of your *actual* expenses and all your *actual* income over the last month. If you don't have exact figures, estimate as closely as you can. Calculate both totals.

3. Compare your *estimates* to your *actual* expenses and actual income. Are there any discrepancies? If so, what caused them?

4. Did you expect to have a surplus or a deficit for the month? Did you actually have a surplus or a deficit? What can you do to make up any deficit or manage any surplus?

5. Do you regularly use a personal budget? If yes, how is it helpful? If no, how might it be helpful?

Chapter 12: Building Effective Communication Skills

Exercise Overview

Communication skills refer not only to the ability to convey information and ideas to others but to handle information and ideas received from them. This exercise shows how you can use your communication skills in addressing issues of quality.

Exercise Background

You're the customer-service manager of a large auto parts distributor. The general manager of a large auto dealer, one of your best customers, has sent the following letter, and it's your job to write a letter in response.

Dear Customer Service Manager:

On the first of last month, ABC Autos submitted a purchase order to your firm. Attached to this letter is a copy of the order. Unfortunately, the parts shipment that we received from you did not contain every item on the order. Further, that fact was not noted on the packing slip that accompanied your shipment, and

ABC was charged for the full amount of the order. To resolve the problem, please send the missing items immediately. If you are unable to do so by the end of the week, please cancel the remaining items and refund the overpayment. In the future, if you ship a partial order, please notify us at that time and do not bill for items not shipped.

I look forward to your reply and a resolution to my problem.

Sincerely,
A. N. Owner, ABC Autos
Attachment: Purchase Order 00001

Exercise Task

1. Write an answer to the customer's letter which assumes that you now have the parts available.

2. How would your answer differ if ABC Autos were not a valued customer?

3. How would your answer differ if you found out that the parts were in the original shipment but had been stolen by one of your delivery personnel?

4. How would your answer differ if you found out that the owner of ABC Autos made a mistake and that the order had been filled correctly?

5. Now review your answers to the previous questions. What are the important components of an effective response to a customer quality complaint (setting the tone, expressing an apology, suggesting a solution, and so on)? How did you use these components in your various responses?

Chapter 12: Building Effective Diagnostic Skills

Exercise Overview

As we noted in Chapter 12, the quality of a product or service is relative to price and customer expectations. This exercise is designed to show that a manager's diagnostic skills—his or her ability to visualize the most appropriate response to a situation—can be useful in positioning a product's quality relative to price and customer expectations.

Exercise Background

Think of a recent occasion when you purchased a tangible product—say, clothing, electronic equipment, luggage, or professional supplies—which you subsequently came to feel was of especially high quality. Now think of another product that you regarded as being of appropriate or adequate quality, and then a third product that you judged to be of low or poor quality. (You should now have three separate products in mind.) Next, recall three parallel experiences involving purchases of services. Examples might include an airline, train, or bus trip; a restaurant meal; a haircut; or an oil change for your car. (Again, you should have three examples total.)

Finally, recall three experiences involving both products and services. Perhaps you got some information about a product that you were buying or you returned a defective or broken product for a refund or warranty repair. Were there any instances in which there was an apparent disparity between product and service quality? Did a poor-quality product, for instance, receive surprisingly good service or a high-quality product receive mediocre service?

Exercise Task

Review your list of nine purchase experiences and then do the following:

1. Assess the extent to which the quality that you associated with each was a function of price and your expectations.
2. Could the quality of each product or service be improved without greatly affecting its price? If so, how?
3. Can high-quality customer service offset adequate or even poor product quality? Can outstanding product quality offset adequate or even poor customer service?

Chapter 13: Building Effective Technical Skills

Exercise Overview

Technical skills are necessary to understand or perform the specific kind of work that an organization does. This exercise asks you to consider the potential costs and benefits of automating a manual process.

Exercise Background

There's no shortage of innovative information-technology products, both hardware and software, available to today's business. Many firms, however, continue to use manual processes for much of the work they do. Why? Are they unaware of or indifferent to the benefits of technology? Do they regard the technology as too expensive? Or are there other sound reasons—reasons other than budgetary—that limit the application of IT to their business processes?

Exercise Task

1. Observe a business that currently relies on a manual process to perform some information function—say, a hospital that maintains patient records on paper or a receptionist who answers and routes calls.
2. Use the Internet to find an example of a company that uses information technology to perform a comparable process. (*Hint:* Look for organizations of the same type, such as another hospital. Or explore the websites of companies that provide IT; many of them post sections about successful projects, usually as "Case Studies" or "Success Stories.")
3. Explain how the business that you first observed—the one still operating manually—could switch to an IT-based operation.
4. Explain the benefits that the business would realize if it automated the process currently being performed manually. Then explain the costs, limitations, or potential problems that it might encounter in making the switch.
5. Make a recommendation: Should the business automate? Why or why not?

Chapter 13: Building Effective Time-Management Skills

Exercise Overview

Time-management skills refer to the ability to prioritize tasks, to work efficiently, and to delegate appropriately. This exercise studies some ways in which you can use information technology to improve those skills.

Exercise Background

In theory, one of the greatest boons of modern information technology is time savings: Modern IT, we're told, will make us all more productive and more efficient by making it easier to manage all the information that we need to manage our lives. Often, however, it seems that, thanks to modern IT, we have more information at our disposal than we have time to manage.

This exercise can be approached in two different ways: (1) by reviewing your use of information technology over the past week or (2) by tracking your use of information technology during the coming week. In either case, consider all the IT tools that you had or have occasion to use — cell phones, e-mail, the Internet, instant messaging, handheld devices such as PalmPilots, and so on. You're interested in the ways in which each of these tools can both save and waste time.

Exercise Task

Now do the following:
1. List every form of technology that you used or do use over the course of the week. Note how frequently you used or do use it and for how long.
2. Which form did you use most often? Least often? Which did you use for the longest total amount of time? For the shortest total amount of time? Which did you use to perform "critically important" functions for you? Less important functions? Explain your answers.
3. For each device, list alternative, less technologically sophisticated ways of performing the same function — say, picking up a newspaper instead of checking out the news on the Internet, or simply calling someone on the phone rather than sending an e-mail.
4. Decide whether each form of technology was in fact a time saver: Did it actually perform its function more efficiently than the "lower-tech" alternative? Did any form of IT at your disposal actually contribute to wasting time?
5. In general, what recommendations can you now offer when it comes to genuinely time-efficient use of information technology?

Chapter 14: Building Effective Conceptual Skills

Exercise Overview

Conceptual skills require you to think in the abstract. This exercise calls on your conceptual skills to address questions about span of management.

Exercise Background

Finding an optimal span of management is as important as it's always been in trying to ensure a level of supervision that provides adequate control but which doesn't stifle workplace flexibility. The process of finding the right level, however, has changed fairly dramatically. Early management scholars, for instance, believed that there was one optimal span of management or that, at the very least, analysts could determine an optimal span by examining just one or a very few variables. Today, however, most experts agree that identifying an optimal span of management depends on the answers to a number of complex questions.

Exercise Task

With this change in expert opinion in mind, do the following:
1. First, survey ten workers and managers about the span of management in their respective workplaces.
2. Now choose one of these individuals for further investigation. Interview this person to get a better idea about the type of work that he or she does, the amount of required interaction with supervisors, the skill levels expected of workers, and other factors that may enter into the determination of optimal span of management. (See Table 14.1 for guidance.)

3. Given the information that you gathered in performing task 2, does the span of management in the workplace make sense? Why or why not?

4. If the span of management seems to be appropriate, what are some of the likely outcomes that the organization can expect? What are some likely outcomes if it seems inappropriate?

Chapter 14: Building Effective Diagnostic Skills

Exercise Overview

Diagnostic skills enable a manager to visualize the most appropriate response to a situation. In this exercise, you're asked to apply your diagnostic skills to the question of centralization versus decentralization in an organization.

Exercise Background

Managers often find it necessary to change an organization's degree of centralization or decentralization. Begin this exercise by reflecting on two very different scenarios in which this issue has arisen:

Scenario A. You're the top manager in a large organization with a long and successful history of centralized operations.

For valid reasons beyond the scope of this exercise, however, you've decided to make the firm much more decentralized.

Scenario B. Assume the exact opposite of the situation in Scenario A: You still occupy the top spot in your firm, but this time you're going to centralize operations in an organization that's always been decentralized.

Exercise Task

Now do the following:

1. For Scenario A, list the major barriers to decentralization that you foresee.
2. For Scenario B, list the major barriers to centralization that you foresee.
3. In your opinion, which scenario would be easier to implement in reality? In other words, is it probably easier to move from centralization to decentralization or vice versa? Whatever your opinion in the matter, be ready to explain it.
4. Given a choice of starting your career in a firm that's either highly centralized or highly decentralized, which would you prefer? Why?

Chapter 15: Building Effective Conceptual Skills

Exercise Overview

Conceptual skills require you to think in the abstract. In this exercise, you'll use you conceptual skills in analyzing organizational structure.

Exercise Background

Looking at its organization chart allows you to understand a company's structure, including its distribution of authority, its divisional breakdown, its levels of hierarchy, and its reporting relationships. The reverse is also true: When you understand the elements of a company's structure, you can draw up an organization chart to reflect it. In this exercise, that's just what you'll do: You'll use the Internet to research a firm's structure and then draw an appropriate organization chart.

Exercise Task

1. Alone or with a partner, go online to research a publicly traded U.S. firm in which you're interested. Focus on information that will help you understand the company's structure. If you research Ford Motor Company, for example, you should look for information about different types of vehicles, different regions in which Ford products

are sold, and different functions that the company performs. (*Hint*: The firm's annual report is usually available online and typically contains a great deal of helpful information. In particular, take a look at the section containing an editorial message from the chairman or CEO and the section summarizing financial information.

Note: In many cases, "segment" data reveal a lot about divisional structure.)

2. Draw an organization chart based on your research.
3. Share your results with another group or with the class as a whole. Be prepared to explain and justify the decisions that you made in determining the firm's structure.

Chapter 15: Building Effective Technical Skills

Exercise Overview

Technical skills are necessary to understand or perform the specific kind of work that an organization does. This exercise asks you to use your technical skills to understand the impact of an organization's strategy on its structure.

Exercise Background

You're a manager in a firm that's developed an innovative new system of personal transportation, much like the Segway HT but different enough to get you a patent. (If you're not familiar with Segway products, go to the website at **www.segway.com**.)

Exercise Task

Each of the following items provides you with a hypothetical direction for your firm's corporate-level strategy. Combining this information about your strategy with your knowledge of your Segway-like product, choose an appropriate form of organization structure for your company.

1. Your corporate-level strategy calls for continued production of a limited line of similar products for sale in the United States. What would be the most appropriate organization structure for your firm?
2. Your corporate-level strategy calls for continued production of your core product only, but you intend to sell it in Asia and Europe as well as North America. What would be the most appropriate organization structure for your firm?
3. Your corporate-level strategy calls for you to move into areas related to your core product, integrating the design innovations that you developed for that product into several other products. What would be the most appropriate organization structure for your firm?

4. Your corporate-level strategy calls for you to exploit your expertise in personal ground transportation in order to move into other areas, such as personal air or personal water transport. What would be the most appropriate organization structure for your firm?
5. Your corporate-level strategy calls for you to invest the revenue generated by core-product sales in industries unrelated to that product. What would be the most appropriate organization structure for your firm?
6. Review your responses to each of the five strategies listed above. Explain precisely how a given strategy influenced your choice of a given organizational design.

Chapter 16: Building Effective Decision-Making Skills

Exercise Overview

Decision-making skills include the ability to recognize and define problems or opportunities and then select the proper course of action. This exercise provides a format for analyzing the phases in a decision-making process. As you'll see, the condition prompting the decision can be characterized as either a problem or an opportunity.

Exercise Task

At the risk of oversimplifying, let's begin by supplementing our discussion of "Force Field Analysis" on page 395 by dividing the process of change making—both personal and organizational—into three broad phases:

1. *Unfreezing:* Recognizing the need for change—identifying the problem(s) that make change necessary
2. *Changing:* Making the change—designing and implementing a plan for a new way of doing things
3. *Refreezing:* Locking in the change—replacing old attitudes and behaviors with new ones that become just as habitual

Step 1: Individual Preparation

This step should be done in writing. Think of a change at work or in your personal life that you would like to make. Now develop a plan for making it, using the three phases of the change process:

1. *Unfreezing:* Briefly describe the change and explain why you think it's needed.
2. *Changing:* Decide upon a date on which you intend to initiate the change and a date by which you want to feel that you've accomplished your goal. Describe your plan for making the change.
3. *Refreezing:* Describe your plans for *maintaining* the change.

Step 2: In-Class Exercise (10–30 minutes)

Your instructor will choose an in-class procedure from among these two options:

- *Option A:* Break the class into three to six groups in which members share their plans and offer suggestions for improvement.
- *Option B:* Break the class into three to six groups in which members share their plans. The group selects its best plan to be shared with the class. Each group shares its best plan with the class.

Your instructor may offer some concluding remarks.

Step 3: Application (2–4 minutes)

This step should be done in writing. Respond to the following questions:

- What did I learn from this experience?
- How will I use the knowledge that I gained in the future?

You may also want to restate the dates in your original plan.

Adapted from Robert N. Lussier and Christopher F. Achua, *Leadership: Theory, Application, and Skill Development*, 4th ed. (Mason, OH: South-Western Cengage Learning, 2010), pp. 435–438, 448.

Chapter 16: Building Effective Diagnostic Skills

Exercise Overview

Diagnostic skills, which enable a manager to visualize the most appropriate response to a situation, are especially important during periods of organizational change.

Exercise Background

You're the general manager of a hotel situated along a beautiful stretch of beach on a tropical island. One of the oldest of six large resorts in the immediate area, your hotel is owned by a group of foreign investors. For several years, it's been operated as a franchise unit of a large international hotel chain, as have all the other hotels on the island.

For the past few years, the hotel's franchisee-owners have been taking most of the profits for themselves and putting relatively little back into the hotel. They've also let you know that their business is not in good financial health and that the revenue from the hotel is being used to offset losses incurred elsewhere. In contrast, most of the other hotels on the island have recently been refurbished, and plans for two brand-new hotels have been announced for the near future.

A team of executives from franchise headquarters has just visited your hotel. They're quite disappointed in the property,

particularly because it's failed to keep pace with other resorts on the island. They've informed you that if the property isn't brought up to standards, the franchise agreement, which is up for review in a year, will be revoked. You realize that this move would be a potential disaster because you can ill afford to lose the franchisor's brand name, access to its reservation system, or any other benefits of the franchise arrangement.

Sitting alone in your office, you've identified several seemingly viable courses of action:

1. Convince the franchisee-owners to remodel the hotel. You estimate that it will take $5 million to meet the franchisor's minimum standards and another $5 million to bring the hotel up to the standards of the island's top resort.
2. Convince the franchisor to give you more time and more options for upgrading the facility.

3. Allow the franchise agreement to terminate and try to succeed as an independent hotel.
4. Assume that the hotel will fail and start looking for another job. You have a pretty good reputation, but you're not terribly happy about the possibility of having to accept a lower-level position (say, as an assistant manager) with another firm.

Exercise Task

Having mulled over your options, do the following:
1. Rank-order your four alternatives in terms of probable success. Make any necessary assumptions.
2. Identify alternatives other than the four that you identified above.
3. Can more than one alternative be pursued simultaneously? Which ones?
4. Develop an overall strategy for trying to save the hotel while protecting your own interests.

Chapter 17: Building Effective Decision-Making Skills

Exercise Overview

Decision-making skills refer to the ability to recognize and define problems and opportunities correctly and then to select an appropriate course of action for solving problems or capitalizing on opportunities. For obvious reasons, these skills should be important to you in making career choices.

Exercise Background

If you're in the process of making a career choice, you need to have a firm grip on your own abilities, preferences, and limitations. This is particularly true for recent college graduates, who are often preparing to enter career fields that are largely unknown to them. Fortunately, there are many sources of helpful information out there. The Bureau of Labor Statistics, for example, maintains data about occupations, employment prospects, compensation, working conditions, and many other issues of interest to job seekers. Information is available by industry, occupation, employer type, and region.

Exercise Task

1. Access a summary of the Department of Labor's *National Compensation Survey* at **http://stats.bls.gov/ncs/ocs/sp/ncbl0449.pdf**. (If the page has moved, search by the survey title.) Find detailed data related to the occupation that you regard as your most likely career choice when you graduate. Then locate detailed data about two other occupations that you might consider—one with a salary that's higher than that of your number-one career choice and one with a salary that's lower.
2. Next, record the hourly salary data for each of your three choices, and then use the hourly salary to project an expected annual income. (*Hint:* Full-time jobs require about 2,000 hours annually.)
3. Based *purely on salary information*, which occupation would be "best" for you?
4. Now go to **www.bls.gov/oco** and access job descriptions for various occupations. Review the description for each of the three career choices that you've already investigated.
5. Based *purely on job characteristics*, which occupation would be "best" for you?
6. Is there any conflict between your answers to questions 3 and 5? If so, how do you plan to resolve it?
7. Are there any job characteristics that you desire strongly enough to sacrifice compensation in order to get them? What are they? What are the limits, if any, on your willingness to sacrifice pay for these job characteristics?

Chapter 17: Building Effective Technical Skills

Exercise Overview

Technical skills are necessary to understand or perform the specific kind of work that an organization does. In many organizations, this work includes hiring appropriate people to fill positions. This exercise will help you apply certain technical skills to the process of employee selection.

Exercise Background

You may choose either of the exercise variations below. We tend to favor Variation 1 because the exercise is usually more useful if you can relate to real job requirements on a personal level.

Variation 1. If you currently work or have worked in the past, select two jobs with which you have some familiarity. Try to select one job that entails relatively low levels of skill, responsibility, education, and pay and one job that entails relatively high levels in the same categories.

Variation 2. If you've never worked or you're not personally familiar with an array of jobs, assume that you're a manager of a small manufacturing plant. You need to hire people to fill two jobs. One job is for a plant custodian to sweep floors, clean bathrooms, empty trash cans, and so forth. The other job is for an office manager who will supervise a staff of three clerks and secretaries, administer the plant payroll, and coordinate the administrative operations of the plant.

Exercise Task

Keeping in mind what you've done so far, do the following:
1. Identify the most basic skills needed to perform each of the two jobs effectively.
2. Identify the general indicators or predictors of whether a given individual can perform each job.
3. Develop a brief set of interview questions that you might use to determine whether an applicant has the qualifications for each job.

4. How important is it for you, as a manager hiring an employee to perform a job, to possess the technical skills needed to perform the job that you're trying to fill?

Chapter 18: Building Effective Interpersonal Skills

Exercise Overview

Interpersonal skills refer to the ability to communicate with, understand, and motivate individuals and groups. This exercise introduces you to a widely used tool for personality assessment and shows how an understanding of personality can be of use in developing effective interpersonal relationships within organizations.

Exercise Background

Of the many different ways of interpreting personality, the widely used Myers–Briggs Type Indicator categorizes individual personality types along four dimensions:

1. *Extraversion (E) Versus Introversion (I).* Extraverts get their energy from being around other people, whereas introverts are worn out by others and need solitude to recharge their energy.
2. *Sensing (S) Versus Intuition (N).* The sensing type prefers concrete things, whereas the intuitivist prefers abstract concepts.
3. *Thinking (T) Versus Feeling (F).* Thinking individuals base their decisions more on logic and reason, whereas feeling individuals base their decisions more on feelings and emotions.
4. *Judging (J) Versus Perceiving (P).* Judging types enjoy completion or being finished, whereas perceiving types enjoy process and open-ended situations.

Using the Myers–Briggs Type Indicator, researchers use survey answers to classify individuals into 16 personality types—all the possible combinations of the four Myers–Briggs dimensions. The resulting personality type is then expressed as a four-character code, such as *ESTP* for *Extravert-Sensing-Thinking-Perceiving*. These four-character codes are then used to describe an individual's preferred way of interacting with others.

Exercise Task

1. Use a Myers–Briggs assessment form to determine your own personality type. You can find a form at **www.keirsey.com/scripts/newkts.cgi**, a website that also contains additional information about personality type. (*Note:* There are no fees for taking the Temperament Sorter, nor must you agree to receive e-mail.)

2. When you've determined the four-letter code for your personality type, you can get a handout from your instructor which will explain how your personality type affects not only your preferred style of working but your leadership style as well.

3. Conclude by responding to the following questions:

   - How easy is it to measure personality?
   - Do you feel that the online test accurately assessed your personality?
   - Why or why not? Share your assessment results and your responses with the class.

Chapter 18: Building Effective Time-Management Skills

Exercise Overview

Time-management skills refer to the ability to prioritize tasks, to work efficiently, and to delegate appropriately. Among other reasons, they're important because poor time-management skills may result in stress. This exercise shows you how effective time-management skills can help reduce stress.

Exercise Background

List several of the major events or expectations that tend to be stressful for you. Common stressors include school (classes, exams), work (finances, schedules), and personal circumstances (friends, romance, family). Try to be as specific as possible and try to identify at least ten different stressors.

Exercise Task

Using your list, do each of the following:
1. Evaluate the extent to which poor time-management skills on your part play a role in the way each stressor affects you. Do exams cause stress, for example, because you tend to put off studying?
2. For each stressor that's affected by your time-management habits, develop a strategy for using your time more efficiently.
3. Note the interrelationships among different kinds of stressors to see if they revolve around time-related problems. For example, financial pressures may cause you to work, and work may interfere with school. Can you manage any of these interrelationships more effectively by managing your time more effectively?
4. How do you typically manage the stress in your life? Can you manage stress in a more time-effective manner?

Chapter 19: Building Effective Interpersonal Skills

Exercise Overview

Interpersonal skills refer to your ability to communicate with, understand, and motivate both individuals and groups. This exercise gives you a chance to see whether the factors that motivate you come primarily from you and your work itself or from factors that are external to you and the nature of your work.

Exercise Task

Below is a list of 12 factors that contribute to job satisfaction. To find out how important each factor is to you, select a number from 1 to 5 according to the following scale:

5	4	3	2	1
Very Important		Somewhat Important		Not Important

1. ___ An interesting job that I enjoy doing
2. ___ A boss who treats everyone the same regardless of the circumstances
3. ___ Getting praise and other recognition and appreciation for my work
4. ___ A job that's routine without much change from day to day
5. ___ Opportunity for advancement
6. ___ A nice title regardless of pay
7. ___ Job responsibility that gives me the freedom to do things my way
8. ___ Good working conditions (e.g., safe environment, convenient cafeteria, etc.)
9. ___ Opportunity to learn new things
10. ___ Emphasis on following rules, regulations, procedures, and policies

11. ___ A job that I can do well and succeed at
12. ___ Job security; a job with one company

Scoring

Below, the 12 factors are divided into 2 lists. For each factor, record the number (from 1 to 5) that you put in the blank before it. Then add up each column (each column score should be from 6 to 30 points):

Motivating factor	Maintenance factor
1. ___	2. ___
3. ___	4. ___
5. ___	6. ___
7. ___	8. ___
9. ___	10. ___
11. ___	12. ___
Totals ___	___

Which factors tend to be more important to you—internal (motivating) or external (maintenance)? *The closer your column score to a total of 30, the more important that factor is to you.*

Adapted from Robert N. Lussier and Christopher F. Achua, *Leadership: Theory, Application, and Skill Development*, 4th ed. (Mason, OH: South-Western Cengage Learning, 2010), pp. 82–84.

Chapter 19: Building Effective Decision-Making Skills

Exercise Overview

Decision-making skills refer to the ability to recognize and define problems and opportunities correctly and then to select an appropriate course of action for solving problems or capitalizing on opportunities. This exercise allows you to build your decision-making skills while applying goal-setting theory to the task of planning your career.

Exercise Background

Lee Iacocca started his career at Ford in 1946 in an entry-level engineering job. By 1960 he was a vice president and in charge of the group that designed the Mustang, and ten years later he was a president of the firm. After being fired from Ford in 1978, he then became president at Chrysler and eventually rose to the CEO spot, a job he held until he retired in 1992. What's really remarkable about Iacocca's career arc—at least the upward trajectory—is the fact that he apparently had it all planned out, even before he finished college.

The story goes that, while he was still an undergraduate, Iacocca wrote out a list of all the positions that he'd like to hold during his career. Number one was "engineer at an auto maker," followed by all the career steps that he planned to take until he was a CEO. He also included a timetable for his climb up the corporate ladder. Then he put his list on a three-by-five-inch card that he folded and stowed in his wallet, and we're told that every time he took out that card and looked at it, he gained fresh confidence and drive. He apparently reached the top several years ahead of schedule, but otherwise he followed his career path and timetable faithfully.

As you can see, Iacocca used goal-setting theory to motivate himself, and there's no reason why you can't do the same.

Exercise Task

1. Consider the position that you'd like to hold at the peak of your career. It may be CEO, owner of a chain of clothing stores, partner in a law or accounting firm, or president of a university. Then again, it may be something less lofty. Whatever it is, write it down.
2. Now describe a career path that will lead you toward that goal. It may help to work "backwards"—that is, starting with your final position and working backwards in time to some entry-level job. If you aren't sure about the career path that will lead to your ultimate goal, do some research. Talk to someone in your selected career field, ask an instructor who teaches in it, or go online. The website of the American Institute of Certified Public Accountants, for example, has a section on "Career Resources," which includes information about career paths and position descriptions for accounting.
3. Write down each step in your path on a card or a sheet of paper.
4. If, like Lee Iacocca, you were to carry this piece of paper with you and refer to it often as you pursued your career goals, do you think it would help you achieve them? Why or why not?

Chapter 20: Building Effective Interpersonal Skills

Exercise Overview

Interpersonal skills refer to your ability to communicate with, understand, and motivate both individuals and groups. This exercise asks you to examine the ways in your attitudes toward work relationships reflect your political behavior in the workplace.

Exercise Task

Below is a series of 20 statements. To what extent does each statement describe your use—actual or planned—of the described behavior when you're on the job? To address this question, rate your response to each statement according to the following scale:

1	2	3	4	5
Rarely		Occasionally		Usually

1. ___ I use personal contacts to get jobs and promotions.
2. ___ I try to find out what's going on in every organizational department.
3. ___ I dress the same way as the people in power and develop the same interests (e.g., watch or play sports, join the same clubs, etc.).
4. ___ I purposely seek contacts and network with higher-level managers.
5. ___ If upper management offered me a raise and promotion requiring me to move to a new location, I'd say yes even if I didn't want to move.
6. ___ I get along with everyone, even people regarded as difficult to get along with.
7. ___ I try to make people feel important by complimenting them.
8. ___ I do favors for other people and ask favors in return, and I thank people, often sending thank-you notes.
9. ___ I work at developing a good working relationship with my supervisor.
10. ___ I ask my supervisor and other people for advice.
11. ___ When someone opposes me, I still work to maintain a positive working relationship with that person.
12. ___ I'm courteous, positive, and pleasant in my relationships with other people.
13. ___ When my supervisor makes a mistake, I never point it out publicly.
14. ___ I'm more cooperative (I compromise) than competitive (I try to get my own way).
15. ___ I tell the truth.
16. ___ I avoid saying negative things about my supervisor or other people behind their backs.
17. ___ I work at getting people to know me by name and face by continually introducing myself.
18. ___ I ask satisfied customers and other people familiar with my work to let my supervisor know how good a job I'm doing.

19. ___ I try to win contests and get prizes, pins, and other awards.
20. ___ I send notices of my accomplishments to higher-level managers and such outlets as company newsletters.

Scoring

1. Add up the 20 numbers in the blanks before all the questions. Your total will range between 20 and 100. This number reflects your overall political behavior: *The higher your score, the greater your political behavior.*
2. Record your score here ___ and on the scale below:

   20——30——40——50——60——70——80——90——100

   Nonpolitical   *Political*

3. Now you want to determine your use of political power in *four different areas* (e.g., learning organizational culture, being a team player, etc.). To do this, add up your numbers for each of the following *sets of questions* and then divide by 5. You will then have your average score for each area:

   A. *Learning the organizational culture and getting to know the power players:*
      Questions 1–5 total ___ divided by 5 = ___

   B. *Developing good working relationships, especially with your boss:*
      Questions 6–12 total ___ divided by 5 = ___

   C. *Being a loyal, honest team player:*
      Questions 13–16 total ___ divided by 5 = ___

   D. *Gaining recognition:*
      Questions 17–20 total ___ divided by 5 = ___

The higher your average score for each set of questions, the greater your use of political power in that area. Do you rate about the same in each area, or do you rate more highly in some areas more than others?

Adapted from Robert N. Lussier and Christopher F. Achua, *Leadership: Theory, Application, and Skill Development,* 4th ed. (Mason, OH: South-Western Cengage Learning, 2010), pp. 120–121.

Chapter 20: Building Effective Conceptual Skills

Exercise Overview

Conceptual skills require you to think in the abstract. This exercise introduces you to one approach to assessing leadership skills and relating leadership theory to practice.

Exercise Background

At any given time, there's no shortage of publications offering practical advice on management and leadership. Most business bestseller lists in 2008 included such titles as *Good to Great*, by Jim Collins; *First, Break All the Rules*, by Marcus Buckingham; and *The 21 Irrefutable Laws of Leadership*, by John C. Maxwell. Some of these books, such as *Winning*, by former General Electric CEO Jack Welch, are written by managers with years of experience. Others are written by consultants, professors, or reporters.

Granted, a lot of these books—okay, most of them—don't have much theoretical foundation, and many are basically compendiums of opinions and suggestions unsupported by scientific evidence. Even so, many touch upon ideas that may well be worth the time it takes a busy manager to read them. Thus a real issue for contemporary managers is knowing how to analyze what they read in the popular press and how to separate the practical wheat from the pop-culture chaff. This exercise gives you a little practice in doing just that.

Exercise Task

1. Visit the *Fortune* magazine website at **www.fortune .com/fortune/quizzes/careers/boss_quiz.html**. Take the leadership-assessment quiz devised by management expert Stephen Covey. Then look at Covey's scoring and comments.
2. Review carefully each question and each suggested answer. Do you see any correlation between Covey's questions and the theoretical models of leadership discussed in Chapter 20? Which model or models do you think Covey is using? What details in his questions, answers, or both led you to that conclusion?
3. Use the Internet to investigate Covey's background, training, and experience. Does the information that you've gathered give you any clues to Covey's attitudes and opinions about leadership? Do you see any connection between Covey's attitudes and the items on his quiz? Explain.
4. Based on what you've learned from this exercise, how confident are you that Covey's quiz is an accurate measure of leadership ability? Explain.

Chapter 21: Building Effective Technical Skills

Exercise Overview

Technical skills are necessary to understand or perform the specific kind of work that an organization does. This exercise will help you develop and apply technical skills in using the Internet to gather information for making important decisions.

Exercise Background

The management of a large retailer wants to leverage the company's enormous purchasing power to buy products in bulk quantities at relatively low prices. The plan calls for individual stores to order specific quantities from a single warehouse and distribution center, and as the company's operations manager, it's your job to identify potential locations for the new facility.

First, you know that you'll need quite a lot of land; the warehouse itself will occupy more than four acres. In addition, because incoming shipments will arrive by both rail and truck, you'll need to be close to railroads and major highways. Land price is important, of course, and the cost of living should be relatively low. Finally, you want relatively mild weather conditions so that shipping disruptions are minimal.

Experience has shown that small to midsize communities work best. Moreover, because the company already maintains warehouses in the West and East, the new one will probably be located in the central or south-central area of the country. Your boss wants you to identify three or four possible sites.

Exercise Task

With all of this information in mind, do the following:

1. Use the Internet to identify as many as ten possible locations.
2. Using additional information gathered from the Internet, narrow your set of ten locations to three or four.
3. Continuing to use the Internet, find out as much as you can about each of the three of four finalists on your list and be ready to discuss the pros and cons of each as they relate to your selection criteria.

Chapter 21: Building Effective Interpersonal Skills

Exercise Overview

Interpersonal skills refer to the ability to communicate with, understand, and motivate individuals and groups. This in-class demonstration gives you some practice in understanding the roles played by verbal and nonverbal elements in the interaction between two people.

Exercise Background

Because more than half the information in any face-to-face exchange is conveyed by nonverbal means, body language is a significant factor in any interpersonal communication. Consider, for example, the impact of a yawn or a frown (never mind a shaken fist). At the same time, however, most people pay relatively little conscious attention to the nonverbal elements of an exchange, especially the more subtle ones. And if you misread the complete set of signals that someone is sending you, you're not likely to receive that person's message in the way that's intended.

In this exercise, you'll examine some interactions between two people from which we've eliminated sound; in other words, you'll have only visual clues to help you decipher the meaning of the messages being sent and received. Then you'll be asked to examine those same interactions with both visual and verbal clues intact.

Exercise Task

1. Observe the silent video segments that your professor shows to the class. For each segment, describe the nature of the relationship and interaction between the two individuals. What nonverbal clues did you rely on in reaching your conclusions?
2. Next, observe the same video segments with audio included. Describe the interaction again, this time indicating any verbal clues that you relied on.
3. How accurate were your assessments when you had only visual information? Explain why you were or were not accurate in your assessment of the situation.
4. What does this exercise show you about the role of nonverbal factors in interpersonal communication? What advice would you now give managers about the importance of these factors?

Chapter 22: Building Effective Conceptual Skills

Exercise Overview

Conceptual skills require you to think in the abstract. This exercise will allow you to practice your conceptual skills as they apply to the activities of work teams in organizations.

Exercise Background

Business organizations, of course, don't have a monopoly on effective groups. Basketball teams and military squadrons are teams, as is a government policy group such as the president's cabinet, the leadership of a church or civic organization, or even a student committee.

Exercise Task

1. Use the Internet to identify an example of a real-life team. Be sure to choose one that meets two criteria: (i) it's not part of a for-profit business and (ii) you can argue that it's highly effective.
2. Determine the reasons for the team's effectiveness. (*Hint:* You might look for websites sponsored by the group itself, review online news sources for current articles about it, or enter the group name in a search engine.) Consider team characteristics and activities, such as role structures, norms, cohesiveness, and conflict management.
3. What can a manager learn from the characteristics and activities of this particular team? How might the factors that contribute to this team's success be adopted in a business setting?

Chapter 22: Building Effective Communication Skills

Exercise Overview

Communication skills refer not only to the ability to convey information and ideas to others but to handle information and ideas received from them. They're essential to effective teamwork because teams depend on the ability of members to send and receive information that's accurate. This exercise invites you to play a game designed to demonstrate how good communication skills can lead to improved teamwork and team performance.

Exercise Background

You'll play this game in three separate rounds. In round 1, you're own your own. In round 2, you'll work in a small group and share information. You'll also work in a small group in round 3, but this time, you'll have the additional benefit of some suggestions for improving the group's performance. Typically, students find that performance improves over the course of the three rounds. In particular, they find that creativity is enhanced when information is shared.

Exercise Task

1. Play the "Name Game" that your professor will explain to you. In round 1, work out your answers individually and then report your individual score to the class.
2. For round 2, you'll join a group of three to five students. Work out your answers together and write your group answers on a single sheet of paper. Now allow each group member to look at the answer sheet. If you can do so without being overheard by other groups, have each group member whisper the answers on the sheet to the group. Report your group score to the class.
3. Your professor will then ask the highest-performing individuals and groups to share their methods with the class.

   At this point, your professor will make some suggestions. Be sure to consider at least two strategies for improving your score.
4. Now play round 3, working together in the same small groups in which you participated in round 2. Report your group scores to the class.
5. Did average group scores improve upon average individual scores? Why or why not?
6. Did average group scores improve after methods for improvement were discussed at the end of round 2? Why or why not?
7. What has this game taught you about teamwork and effectiveness? Share your thoughts with the class.

Management at Work

Chapter 1: Management at Work

Jumpin' Jack Flash

Jack Armstrong doesn't have the cutest little baby face, but he has other qualifications for getting ahead despite the fact that he's still relatively young. He's smart and creative, and he combines a high-energy approach to getting things done with aggressive marketing instincts.

He's just 36 now, but Jack can already boast a wealth of management experience, largely because he's been quite adept at moving around in order to move up. He started out in sales for a technology company, outsold his colleagues by wide margins for two years, and was promoted to regional sales director. After a year, he began angling for a position as marketing manager, but when the job went to a senior sales director, Jack left for a job as a marketing manager with a company specializing in travel products. Though a little impatient with the tedious process of sifting through market-research data, he devoted his considerable energy and creativity to planning new products. His very first pet project—a super-lightweight compact folding chair—outstripped all sales projections and provided just the impetus he needed to ask for a promotion to vice president of marketing.

When the company took too much time to make a decision, Jack moved on again, having found a suitable vice presidency at a consumer-products firm. Here, his ability to spot promising items in the company's new-product pipeline—notably a combination oral-hygiene and teeth-whitening rinse for dogs—brought him to the attention of upper management. Jack expected to go to the top of the list of candidates for president of some division within the company, but instead the president of overseas operations called Jack into his office and offered him a yearlong special assignment: How would Jack like to head up a team to develop strategies for adapting existing company products as new products for sales in developing countries? It was the perfect opportunity, he suggested, for Jack to broaden his skills by working with managers from every area of the company. Moreover, there'd be a significant bonus if he succeeded, and promotion to a divisional presidency would be next. It was certainly an interesting opportunity, but it would sidetrack Jack's projected ascent to CEO status before the age of 40. He asked for a little time to think over the offer, which, as he well knew, would also be a stretch for him. As luck would have it, however, he didn't have to make the troublesome decision, because it was then that he was offered his current job as divisional president at a rising consumer-electronics firm.

And that's where we find Jack now—with his job on the line. What happened? Jack had been in his new corner office for about six months when his marketing department came to him with an idea for a sleek high-fashion combination cellphone–music and video player. It was just the kind of product that Jack had been looking for, and he ordered his marketing people to draw up some performance specs and get them to the design department. His VP for marketing suggested that Jack assemble a project team to shepherd the product from marketing through the design, engineering, and production stages, but Jack had heard too many stories about projects getting bogged down in the endless process of team decision making, and if there was one thing that he knew from his own experience, it was that the key to a successful new product was getting it to market as quickly as possible. Besides, he had a reputation for aggressiveness to uphold.

Determined to take the bull by the horns, he put the project on an accelerated eight-month schedule from design to rollout. He himself took charge of marketing and launched an aggressive promotional campaign designed to capture the attention not only of the market but of the company's investors. Everything went according to plan until the middle of month seven, when Jack got some bad news from the production facility in Malaysia. Tests on preliminary versions of the product revealed that the placement of the cellphone antenna inside the mouthpiece was producing a weak cellular signal. The only solutions, it seems, were either to redesign for an external antenna or to provide a kit containing an antenna and adapter. In either case, the product design would be compromised and the rollout delayed by months. Electronics engineers had warned mechanical engineers of the potential glitch at an early stage of the project, but when news of the problem got back to marketing, managers had decided to proceed because the project was such a high priority with Jack.

As it turns out, thousands of orders were delayed, customers got mad, and when the news got out, the company's stock price began to slip.

Case Questions

1. What *management skills* did Jack demonstrate as a marketing manager at the travel-products company? What management skills did he demonstrate as a VP at the consumer-products firm?
2. Should Jack have taken the special assignment offered him by the consumer-products firm? What kinds of skills

was the president of overseas operations thinking about when he offered the assignment to Jack?

3. What management skills would have helped Jack avoid the catastrophe that befell his project at the consumer-electronics firm?

Case References

Kerry A. Bunker, Kathy E. Kram, and Sharon Ting, "The Young and the Clueless: How to Manage Your Bad Boys," *Harvard Business School Working Knowledge*, January 20, 2003, http://hbswk.hbs.edu on January 25, 2011; Kirk Shinkle, "Young Managers Take Bigger Risks," *U.S. News &*

World Report, June 30, 2008, http://money.usnews.com on January 25, 2011; Nitin Gupta, "A Young Manager's Guide to Taking Charge of Her Own Career," *Wall Street Journal*, October 26, 2009, http://online.wsj .com on January 25, 2011.

Chapter 2: Management at Work

How GE Manages to Do It

Founded by Thomas Edison in 1878, GE is the only one of the original Dow Jones Industrial Average 12—the dozen firms that made up the first DJIA in 1896—that's still on that venerable list. In fact, while all the other original firms have been acquired or gone out of business, GE is still one of the most consistently profitable companies in the world. It doesn't boast the fastest growth or the highest market value, but it's consistently among the world's most highly regarded firms, garnering high marks year after year in surveys of the world's "most admired" and "most innovative" companies.

Indeed, from its earliest days, GE has been a leader in developing not only new products and manufacturing processes, but new management techniques and practices as well. Many of these have been duplicated by other firms, but rarely does a firm beat GE to a new development or surpass GE's skill in implementation. The company's first organizational innovation was the creation of a corporate research and development lab, established in 1900, and in the 1930s, GE was the first U.S. firm to offer pension and profit-sharing plans.

GE also centralized decision making in the 1950s, producing the unique "Blue Books" that governed managers' every move until the 1980s. In the 1960s, the company pioneered the application of *strategic management* as an approach to handling business opportunities and challenges, and today the principles of strategic management are so thoroughly ingrained in management thinking and practice that they're often the capstone course for undergraduate degrees in business. At about the same time, the company lent its name to the *GE Business Screen*—a process, developed jointly with the consulting firm McKinsey, for identifying a corporation's optimal portfolio of business units. By the 1980s and 1990s, GE was building an effective global culture

while pioneering such programs as Six Sigma quality initiatives and Work Out, a reengineering program designed to simplify work and empower employees.

GE also has a reputation for reconfiguring or even abandoning long-standing programs when they no longer serve their original purposes. "Most people inside GE," says current CEO Jeff Immelt, "learn from the past but have a healthy disrespect for history. They have an ability to live in the moment and not be burdened by the past." Since taking over in 2001, for example, Immelt has pushed hard for innovation to complement the tendency of Six Sigma to promote efficiency over creativity. He's also worked to give the company's traditional internal orientation a sharper "external focus" on its customers.

In 2008, GE Research was awarded the INFORMS prize, which is given annually to a firm that effectively uses the techniques of *management science*—mathematical modeling and other analytical methods—to make better management decisions. Management science is important to GE, says VP for Global Research Mark Little, "because it's so relevant to how we perform for our customers"; at GE, he adds, the ultimate aim of management science technology is "to create more customer value at lower risk."

Today, GE is also focusing on innovations in environmental technology. Launched in 2005, its "Ecomagination" initiative, according to Immelt, reflects the company's "commitment to address challenges such as the need for cleaner, more efficient sources of energy, reduced emissions, and abundant sources of clean water." In July 2010, for example, GE announced a $200 million "Ecomagination Challenge"—a contest to fund promising ideas for improving America's electricity infrastructure. In November, round one ended with 12 start-up companies receiving a total of $55 million in investments, plus the prospect of accelerated product development and promotion from GE's army of engineers and marketers. According to Immelt, the contest and other initiatives demonstrate GE's willingness to seek innovation outside the company: "A lot of these energy ideas," he explains, "are never going to see the light of day because [startups] don't have the muscle to commercialize them. . . . [I]t's kind of win-win," he adds. "Selfishly for GE, we can be the go-to player to get more good ideas faster."

Finally, GE works hard to develop leaders. Every year, for instance, about 9,000 GE employees take classes at the company's legendary in-house management school in Crotonville,

New York. The current curriculum at Crotonville revolves around what Immelt characterizes as "a whole new set of leadership traits," including "external focus" and "imagination and courage"—traits, according to Immelt, that lay "the foundation of how you become innovative. . . . What I tell people is that we have to develop new leaders for growth—people who are passionate about customers and innovation, [people] who really know markets and products. [Traditional] professional management isn't going to give you the kind of growth you need in a slow-growth world. . . . You have to change," Immelt concludes, "or else you don't have a great future with this company."

Case Questions

1. Does the pattern of management developments at GE over the last century seem to reflect the pattern suggested by management theory? Explain your answer.

2. Which of GE's management innovations seem to draw on a *classical management perspective*? Which seem to draw on a *behavioral management perspective*? How does the *contingency perspective* explain the management

changes that GE has made over the years? Explain each of your responses.

3. Why, in your opinion, has GE been so successful in integrating the *management science approach* with less quantitative approaches?

4. In what ways does the change in GE's approach to leadership reflect the same conditions as those that influence its current approach to management?

Case References

Geoffrey Colvin, "What Makes GE Great?" *Fortune*, March 6, 2006, http://money.cnn.com on January 27, 2011; Betsy Morris, "The GE Mystique," *Fortune*, March 6, 2006, http://money.cnn.com on January 27, 2011; Bill Lane, "Management Secrets from Inside GE," *U.S. News & World Report*, January 25, 2008, http://money.usnews.com on January 27, 2011; "GE Research Named Winner of 2008 INFORMS Prize," *FirstScience News*, April 15, 2008, www.firstscience.com on January 27, 2011; Ryan McCarthy, "GE Launches $200 Million Innovation Contest for Smart Grid Technologies," *Huffington Post*, July 13, 2010, www.huffingtonpost.com on January 27, 2011; Adam Aston, "GE's Innovation Avalanche," *GreenBiz.com*, November 17, 2010, www.greenbiz.com on January 27, 2011.

Chapter 3: Management at Work

Goldman Sachs Banks on Cultural Capital

The investment bank Goldman Sachs went public in 1999, but to many people on Wall Street, it's still "The Partnership." Goldman partners—currently about 470 of the firm's roughly 35,000 employees—get a share of the profits and what the *New York Times* identifies as "investment opportunities not offered to other employees." They remain among the firm's chief owners, and they still make up its highest-level management teams. They reap the biggest rewards when the company is managed at the highest level of profitability, and they stand to lose the most when it falters. As a rule, they tend to invest their own money in Goldman for decades, and, not surprisingly, they manage the company's assets for the long term. Goldman Sachs has always epitomized a high-risk, high-return culture, but its history shows that heavily vested senior executives tend to

value the difference between high-risk investing and overly risky adventuring.

Since the mid-1970s, says Lisa Endlich, a former trader and VP at Goldman, there has been "no greater prize on Wall Street" than a Goldman Sachs partnership. She adds, however, that "rising through the ranks at Goldman Sachs is one of the steepest and most challenging corporate climbs," and getting to the top means mastering a culture "which on its face is rife with contradictions. . . . You'll be immersed," she promises, "in one of the world's most competitive environments. . . . Doing a good job will get you nowhere. Doing a superb job will get you noticed," but you won't make much progress at all unless you're willing to demonstrate a resolute commitment to upward mobility. You have to win every head-to-head contest with everybody else in the company who wants what you want, but—and here's one of those troublesome contradictions—"nothing will derail you faster than not being a team player."

Charles D. Ellis, a business-strategy consultant who's worked with Goldman executives for 30 years, attributes the company's "decisive advantage in management" to "the speed, accuracy, and extent of communication inside the company. . . . Goldman Sachs culture works," concludes Ellis, because it thoroughly integrates two of the firm's core strengths: the loyalty of its employees and its approach to recruiting.

Liz Beshel, the firm's global treasurer, agrees with Ellis: "You constantly feel there's more you can do at work," she says, "because that's the kind of people Goldman hires—we're all perfectionists." Ellis observes that Goldman recruits only the top 5 percent of job candidates in the industry and typically lands most of them, mainly because the company's top executives get involved in the process. "By and large," adds Ellis, "Goldman Sachs people . . . do not come with silver spoons. . . . They are upwardly mobile with a drive to succeed." The firm's strategy, he suggests, is based on the theory that if you come from a working-class background, you'll be hungrier for the kind of success that a job at Goldman makes possible.

Unfortunately, Goldman has recently been forced to cut more than 3,000 of its coveted jobs, or about 10 percent of its workforce. What happened? Ultimately, Goldman got caught in the undertow of the global financial crisis, and although executives tried to reassure stakeholders that it was in no danger of going under, nervous investors began selling off shares until the company's stock price had fallen about 50 percent from a peak of $247.92. In September 2008, Goldman succumbed to the pressure and announced that it was transforming itself from an investment bank into a holding-company bank. It's now able to take deposits and buy other banks, but it's also subject to much stricter federal regulation. It isn't nearly as profitable, and it no longer enjoys the agility and creativity that fostered a high-risk, high-return culture. "No matter how good it was," muses a Wall Street executive, Goldman "was not impervious to the fortunes of fate." One analyst, however, sees Goldman's self-engineered transformation as another sign of the agility that has helped it to survive seven decades of ups and downs in financial markets: "They change to fit their environment," he observes. "When it was good to go public, they went public. . . . Now that it's good to be a bank, they became a bank."*

* In April 2010, the Securities and Exchange Commission charged Goldman with creating and selling a mortgage-based investment that was secretly designed to fail. Three months later, the bank agreed to pay a penalty of $550 million—the largest ever assessed by the SEC against a financial services firm.

Case Questions

1. Which forces in Goldman Sachs's *external environment* have accounted most for "the fortunes of fate" that the company—indeed, the investment banking industry—has experienced since 2008?

2. Explain the roles of Goldman's partners, both as *owners* and as *employees*, in forming and managing its *internal environment*.

3. Which *models of organizational effectiveness* are evident in Goldman's approach to management?

4. In 2008, citing Goldman as one of the "Top 20 Most Admired Companies" in the United States, *Fortune* magazine characterized the firm's culture as "an impossible-to-replicate mix of extreme aggression, deep paranoia, individual ambition, and robot-like teamwork."† Judging from our case, how valid do you regard this characterization? If you were a top manager at Goldman, how would you deal with the apparent conflict between "individual ambition" and "robot-like teamwork"?

† Bethany McLean, "Top 20 Most Admired Companies: Goldman Sachs Group," *Fortune*, March 3, 2008, http://money.cnn.com on February 2, 2011.

Case References

Liz Rappaport, "Goldman Sachs Names 110 Partners," *Wall Street Journal*, November 18, 2010, http://online.wsj.com on February 2, 2011; Jessica Pressler, "The Mysteries of the Goldman Sachs Partnering Process, Revealed," *New York*, September 13, 2010, http://nymag.com on February 3, 2011; Lisa Endlich, *Goldman Sachs: The Culture of Success* (New York: Alfred A. Knopf, 1999); Julie Creswell and Ben White, "Wall Street, R.I.P.: The End of an Era, Even at Goldman," *New York Times*, September 28, 2008, www.nytimes.com on February 2, 2011; Ben White and Louise Story, "Last Two Big Investment Banks Reinvent Their Businesses," *New York Times*, September 23, 2008, www.nytimes.com on February 2, 2011; Louise Story and Gretchen Morgenson, "S.E.C. Accuses Goldman of Fraud in Housing Deal," *New York Times*, April 16, 2010, www.nytimes.com on February 2, 2011; Securities and Exchange Commission, "Goldman Sachs to Pay Record $550 Million to Settle SEC Charges Related to Subprime Mortgage CDO," press release, July 15, 2010, www.sec.gov on February 2, 2011.

Chapter 4: Management at Work

Sex, Drugs, and Reckless Controls

In late 2008, Interior Department Inspector General Earl E. Devaney launched an investigation into accusations of wrongdoing by employees of the department's Minerals Management Service (MMS), which collected the royalties paid by companies to extract oil and gas from public lands. Through its royalty-in-kind program, the agency also accepted oil and gas as royalty payments and then sold them on the open market. Among other things, Devaney discovered that program officials had allowed buyers of agency-sold gas and oil to revise their bids downward after they'd been awarded purchase contracts. The cost to taxpayers amounted to about $4.4 million.

Perhaps much more interesting—at least in this day and age, when we like to take our hard news with a hint of the unsavory and all-too-human—was Devaney's revelation of "a culture of substance abuse and promiscuity" within MMS. The nature of their jobs, observed the *New York Times*, exposed agency employees to "the expense-account-fueled world of oil and gas executives," but the newspaper also cited Devaney's depiction of MMS as "a dysfunctional organization that has been riddled with conflicts of interest, unprofessional behavior, and a free-for-all atmosphere for much of the Bush administration's watch."

Devaney's report concluded that MMS officials "frequently consumed alcohol at industry functions, had used cocaine and marijuana, and had sexual relationships with oil and gas company representatives." In the process of developing cozy professional relationships, employees of the royalty-in-kind program had also taken inappropriate gifts from industry contacts. The employees explained that socializing with industry representatives was simply a function of their involvement in industry culture, and they assured investigators that such relationships had no effect on the performance of their official duties. Skeptical investigators, however, replied that "sexual relationships with prohibited sources cannot, by definition, be arms-length" and concluded that the whole agency "appeared to be devoid of both ethical standards and internal controls sufficient to protect the integrity of [a] vital revenue-producing program."

In February 2010, during his first month in office, the Obama administration's new Interior Secretary, Ken Salazar, announced his intention "to restore the public's trust, to enact meaningful reform . . . to uphold the law, and to ensure that all of us—career public servants and political appointees—do our jobs with the highest level of integrity."

Two months later, MMS, which also regulated offshore oil-drilling activities, received a plan for drilling in the Gulf of Mexico submitted by the petroleum giant BP, which assured the agency that environmental damage from any spill would be "minimal or nonexistent." The company's worst-case scenario predicted spillage of 1,500 to 4,600 barrels, and escaping oil, according to BP, would dissipate before reaching land. BP also asked MMS to approve a plan for setting a cement plug for temporary closures of the well at 3,300 feet below sea level—more than three times the depth required by regulations. The request was approved during a 90-minute phone conversation between MMS and BP officials. Normally, drilling applications would undergo detailed environmental review, but MMS declared BP's application "categorically excluded" from evironmental analysis and gave the oil company a green light in early April.

On April 20, a giant oil rig exploded at the newly approved BP facility, killing 11 workers and pouring oil into the Gulf of Mexico. By the time the leak was finally capped (87 days later), it had discharged nearly 5 *million* barrels—206 million gallons—of oil into the Gulf, creating an oil slick that affected 4,200 miles of coastline (about five times the length of California).

Critics of the Interior Department were quick to point out that the oil and gas industry had spent $169 million to lobby government officials in 2009—$15.9 of it by BP—and MMS, not surprisingly, was back in the news. "Secretary Salazar," charged Kierán Suckling, executive director of the Center for Biological Diversity,

> has utterly failed to reform the Mineral Management Service. Instead of protecting the public interest by conducting environmental reviews, his agency rubber-stamped BP's drilling plan, just as it does hundreds of others every year. . . . The Minerals Management Service has gotten worse, not better, under Salazar's watch.

"My favorite agency," mused Senator Bill Nelson of Florida. "Remember in the Bush administration, these were the guys having sex orgies and pot parties and weren't showing up for work."

In May 2010, Secretary Salazar dissolved MMS. Responsibility for offshore drilling is now in the hands of the Bureau of Ocean Management, and the rest of MMS's former functions have been delegated to other agencies.

Case Questions

1. The section on "Managerial Ethics" highlights three sets of relationships involved in the exercise of *managerial ethics*—the relationships of the organization to its employees, of its employees to the firm, and of the firm to other economic agents. Explain how each of these relationships was a factor in the ethical failings of the Minerals Management Service. In your opinion, which of the three was the biggest factor? Explain your answer.

2. It's too late now, but if you had been drafted to fix MMS in the wake of the BP oil spill, how would you have applied the approaches to "Managing Ethical Behavior" discussed in the text? On which of these approaches would you have focused the most time and energy? Is it likely that you'd have been successful? Why or why not?

3. According to Earthjustice, a nonprofit environmental law firm, the BP disaster happened because "managers weren't managing, oil companies and regulators were colluding, and high risk was acceptable risk."* Obviously, problems like those that led up to the BP spill can be extremely complex. In light of this fact, what, in your opinion, should be the primary responsibilities of managers at regulatory agencies such as MMS? Of managers at oil companies such as BP?

*Terry Winckler, "Commission Blames Entire Oil Industry for Gulf Oil Spill," *Earthjustice*, January 7, 2011, http://earthjustice.org on February 6, 2011.

Case References

Charlie Savage, "Sex, Drug Use and Graft Cited in Interior Department," *New York Times*, September 11, 2008, www.nytimes.com on February 6, 2011; Center for Biological Diversity, "Interior Department Exempted BP Drilling from Environmental Review," press release, May 5, 2010, www.biological diversity.org on February 6, 2011; Juliet Eilperin, "U.S. Exempted BP's Gulf of Mexico Drilling from Environmental Impact Study," *Washington Post*, May 5, 2010, www.washingtonpost.com on February 6, 2011; Alan Fram and Sharon Theimer, "BP Spends Big in Washington, but Will That Help It Survive during Gulf Oil Spill Crisis?" *Los Angeles Times*, May 10, 2010, http://m.startribune.com on February 6, 2011; Jim Efstathiou Jr. and Katarzyna Klimasinska, "BP Spill Shows Industry Needs to Change, Panel Says," *BusinessWeek*, January 6, 2011, www.businessweek.com on February 6, 2011.

Chapter 5: Management at Work

Shifting Gears in the Auto Industry

In November 2008, U.S. automaker Chrysler announced that it was cutting 25 percent of its workforce and acknowledged that domestic sales had dropped 35 percent in 12 months. CEO Robert Nardelli also admitted that the company could survive only by means of an alliance with another automaker and an infusion of government cash. In December, Chrysler announced that it would shut down all production through January 2009, that it planned to file for bankruptcy, and that it ultimately expected to cease production permanently. Federal aid to both Chrysler and General Motors was authorized in the same month and had topped $17 billion by March 2009, when the Obama administration gave Chrysler 30 days to finalize a previously announced merger agreement with the Italian carmaker Fiat or face the loss of another $6 billion in government subsidies.

Fiat? Things, it seems, had changed since the days when, for many American car buyers, *Fiat* stood for "Fix it again, Tony." As recently as 2005, GM had been only too happy to pay $2 billion to bail out of a joint venture with Fiat, which was wallowing in debt after accumulated losses of $14 billion. A year later, however, Fiat had actually shown a profit—its first since 2000—and its stock price had doubled. By 2009, it was on *Fortune* magazine's list of the "World's Most Admired Companies." It's now Europe's third-largest car company, behind only Volkswagen and Peugeot Citroën and ahead of Renault, Daimler (Mercedes-Benz), and BMW, and number 9 in the world, producing more cars than Hyundai, Mitsubishi, or Chrysler.

The credit for this remarkable turnaround goes to CEO Sergio Marchionne, an accountant and industry outsider who, in 2004, became Fiat's fifth CEO in two years. Billie Blair, a consultant specializing in corporate change management, reports that Marchionne brought an "unconventional approach" to the task of managing a car company in the twenty-first century. In the process, she says—citing Marchionne's own explanation of his success at Fiat—he "revolutionized the [Fiat] culture in a way that will keep the company competitive in the long term." Adds David Johnston, whose Atlanta-based marketing company has worked with Chrysler, Marchionne "has been able to garner respect for Fiat again after its down years and reestablish it as a business leader."

What was Marchionne's "unconventional approach"? It's the same approach that he plans to take at Chrysler. Taking over Fiat after nearly 15 years of continuously poor performance, Marchionne was forced to lay off employees, but he focused his job-cutting strategy on longer-term goals: He cut 10 percent of the company's white-collar workforce of about 20,000, stripping away layers of management and making room for a younger generation of managers with experience in brand marketing rather than engineering. Refocusing the company on market-driven imperatives, he cut the design-to-market process from four years to 18 months, and, even more importantly, he spurred the introduction of a slew of new products. The Grande Punto, which was launched in mid-2005, was the best-selling subcompact in Western Europe a year later and spearheaded the firm's resurgence. The Fiat Nuova 500, a subcompact with a distinctive retro look (think Volkswagen New Beetle), was first introduced in 2007. Both the car and its marketing launch were designed with heavy customer involvement, and the 500, like the Grande Punto, was an immediate success, with first-year sales outstripping Fiat's original target by 160 percent.

Under the merger agreement reached with Fiat in June 2009, the 500 is one of at least seven Fiat vehicles that Chrysler will begin building and selling in the United States by 2014. Produced in four versions—hatchback, sporty hatchback, convertible, and station wagon—the U.S. adaptation of the 500 went to market in 2011, and Marchionne is convinced that, with a full range of body styles, "the 500 . . .

will be a smash if we do it right." Strategically, Marchionne knows that he has to reposition Chrysler from a maker of clunky gas-guzzlers to a marketer of stylish, energy-efficient technology, and the 500, which one marketing association in Japan has declared "the sexiest car in the world," has been designated the flagship of Fiat Chrysler's new North American fleet.

Many analysts, however, remain skeptical about Marchionne's prospects for turning Chrysler around even if the 500 turns out to be "a smash." A big issue, they say, is time: Can "New Chrysler" (officially Chrysler Group LLC) hang on financially until projected new-product revenues start filling the company coffers? Completely new and improved Chryslers won't hit showrooms until 2013, but the new management has managed to roll out some new products, including a revamped Jeep Compass and an all-new Chrysler 300 sedan. "We've attacked the bulk of the product portfolio," says Marchionne. "What we've got now is a commercially viable set of products in the marketplace." He also points out that Chrysler sales are ahead of internal targets and claims that he's more confident now about the prospects for a turnaround than he had been when the merger plans were being drawn up. "We've been sticking to our guns," he says, "and it's worked well so far."

Case Questions

1. According to a major economics consulting firm, Fiat's "South American operations are the jewel in the Italian company's global operations."* Fiat has plants in Brazil and Argentina, and Brazil is its biggest market, well ahead of its home-country market. In 2011, with the Chrysler venture taking up more and more of the firm's attention—and as European sales suffered a steep decline—rumors began to circulate that Marchionne might move Fiat headquarters from Italy to the United States. Discuss Fiat's takeover of Chrysler as part of a strategy to transform itself from an *international business* into a *multinational* or *global business*.

2. What benefits does Fiat hope to gain from its arrangement with Chrysler? What potential drawbacks does it

face? Judging from your analysis of benefits and drawbacks, explain why the Fiat–Chrysler arrangement might best characterized as a *strategic alliance*? In what sense is it best characterized as a *direct investment*?

3. What challenges in the U.S. *cultural environment* do you expect Fiat to face as it uses its Chrysler connection to compete in the American car market? What *management challenges* will Marchionne face in the areas of *planning and decision making*, *organizing*, and *leading*?

*"Fiat to Shift Model to Argentina to Free Up Brazilian Capacity; Hires 1,700 New Workers in Brazil," IHS Global Insight, May 31, 2007, www.ihsglobalinsight.com on February 11, 2011.

Case References

Dale Buss, "Fiat CEO Marchionne Has Led Unlikely Turnaround," *Edmunds Auto Observer*, January 21, 2009, www.autoobserver.com on February 10, 2011; Leslie Wayne, "Sergio Marchionne," *New York Times*, May 1, 2009, http://topics.nytimes.com on February 10, 2011; Joann Muller, "Obama Takes the Wheel in Detroit," *Forbes.com*, March 30, 2009, www.forbes.com on February 10, 2011; James R. Healey, "7 New Fiat Models Bound for U.S.; 9 Chryslers to Go Abroad," *USA Today*, April 21, 2010, www.usatoday.com on February 10, 2011; Soyoung Kim, "Chrysler Rescue under Fiat Still Uncertain," Reuters, April 20, 2010, www.reuters.com on February 10, 2011; "Fiat Plays Double or Quits with Chrysler," *The Economist*, November 25, 2010, www.economist.com on February 10, 2011; Deepa Seetharaman, "Fiat Raises Chrysler Stake, Readies for IPO," Reuters, January 10, 2011, www.reuters.com on February 10, 2011.

Chapter 6: Management at Work

BET Bets It Can Be Better

When founder Robert L. Johnson stepped down as CEO of Black Entertainment Television (BET) in 2005, Debra L. Lee, who'd served as the company's chief operating officer for more than a decade, took over the top spot at the network, which specializes in programming for African American audiences. Lee had already pioneered BET's expansion into original movies, concerts, talk shows, and public-policy programming—all the while delivering record-setting ratings during a time when the cable market as a whole was experiencing slow growth.

Just as she was settling into her new job, her bosses at parent company Viacom charged Lee with developing a strategy for growth through expanded content. As it happened, Lee had already taken a first step in meeting her bosses' goals by hiring Reginald Hudlin to fill the newly created position of President of Entertainment. At a time when "original programming is a strategic priority for BET," announced Lee, Hudlin, a veteran film producer, would take over programming development and acquisition for BET's music, entertainment, specials, sports, public-affairs, and home-entertainment units.

Lee also put Hudlin on the front line of the network's efforts to combat growing criticism of its current content. For several years, critics within the African American community had been chastising BET for its increasing reliance on music videos and other programs that perpetuated demeaning stereotypes of its own African American audience. For many African Americans, BET had forsaken its original promise as the first black-owned network, having abandoned its original family-oriented programming in favor of youth-oriented shows with a harder edge, including and especially programming that seemed to celebrate the ethos of gangsta rap. "People always ask me what's wrong with BET," says activist and writer Kevin Powell, a frequent contributor to BET news programs, who immediately offered an answer to his own question: "We have to stop participating in the one-dimensional portrayals of ourselves."

"I don't like everything that's on [BET] now," admitted Lee when she introduced Hudlin. "But it's all about how young people express themselves. . . . We are not PBS, and we'll never be PBS," she added, indicating that BET executives did not intend to abandon their core (largely male) audience of 18- to 34-year-old viewers. Hudlin soon announced a forthcoming lineup of no fewer than 16 original shows, but most of them either failed to materialize or died untimely deaths. Among those that did hit the airwaves, *Hot Ghetto Mess* featured video clips in which young African Americans in Washington, D.C., displayed cultural ignorance and a penchant for stupid behavior.

The program quickly inspired a petition from more than 5,000 African Americans protesting BET's habit of "mak[ing] black people look like buffoons." Two major advertisers—State Farm Insurance and Home Depot—requested that their ads not be shown during or in conjunction with the show. Meanwhile, an anti-BET group calling itself "Enough Is Enough" was formed, and in September 2007, in the first of a series of demonstrations that lasted through the following April, members camped outside Lee's Washington, D.C., home, brandishing signs reading "We Are NOT Gangsters and Pimps" and chanting, "BET—Be better! Do better!" "The purpose of this campaign," stated organizer Delman Coates, a D.C.-area pastor, "is to protest the commercialization, marketing, and distribution of content that degrades black men and women and portrays negative stereotypes of black men . . . as pimps, players, hustlers, and thugs."

In April 2008, Enough Is Enough and the Parents Television Council released the results of a study, called "The Rap on Rap," which focused on the content of three music video programs, one airing on MTV and two on BET. It found that viewers were presented with adult content—references to drugs, sex, or violence—an average of once every 38 seconds. Only the MTV program was rated TV-14, and 40 percent of the total viewership was under the age of 18. Lee responded by pointing out that music videos made up only 20 percent of BET's programming, down from 70 percent just three years earlier, but it was clear to most observers that BET had drifted a long way from Robert Johnson's vision of a network that "should be for black media what Disney is to the general media." One of those critics was cofounder Sheila Johnson, Robert's former wife. "Don't even get me started," she told an interviewer in 2010. "When we started BET . . . we had public-affairs programming. We had news. . . . [W]e had a large variety of programming, but the problem is that then the video revolution started up. . . . I just really wish . . . that they'd stop lowering the bar so far just so they can get eyeballs to the screen."

Rex Hudlin had resigned in 2008, the result of what Lee called "a mutual decision," but after two years on the job, he had at least identified what many people still regard as BET's key challenge—changing people's perception of the network. That problem, however, appears to go deeper than matters of mere perception: It may in fact be rooted in the network's culture and marketing infrastructure, both of which revolve around the 18-to-34 demographic on which its success has long depended. "The folks who run BET really have to be honest about the demographic of their audience," says Mark Anthony Neal, a professor of black studies at Duke

University. "If we're talking about African Americans over 35, that's not their audience. Older audiences are turned off by a lot of stuff they do," concludes Neal, who suggests that the task still facing Lee and her team is more complicated than simply adding blocs of less controversial programs designed to satisfy an "older audience" that BET isn't going to attract anyway. Any new programming on BET, says Neal, must deflect increasingly energetic criticism while continuing to hold the attention of the network's current audience of younger African American viewers.

Case Questions

1. In general, do you think that a member of its target ethnic group makes the most effective leader at an ethnically oriented business like BET? Why or why not?
2. Among the six arguments for organizational diversity as a contributor to competitive advantage, focus on the following: *marketing*, *creativity*, and *flexibility*. Apply each of these arguments to show how BET might approach its programming problems by reflecting greater diversity in its management decisions.
3. You're an intern in the program-development department at BET and you've been asked to participate in a meeting to brainstorm new programming ideas. What sort of programs might you suggest as possibilities for the network? What sort of programs would probably be successful? What sort of new programs do you think BET should avoid?
4. BET, says Sheila Johnson, got off to a good start, "but the problem is that then the video revolution started up." What does she mean by "the video revolution"? Do you agree or disagree with her assessment of its impact? In what ways does that impact reflect *multiculturalism* among U.S. consumers? In what ways does it transcend multiculturalism?

Case References

Teresa Wiltz, "Channel Changer," *Washington Post*, May 4, 2008, www .washingtonpost.com on February 22, 2011; Todd M. Pree, "Over 500 People Demonstrate at Home of BET Networks CEO Debra Lee," *MMD-Newswire.com*, September 18, 2007, www.mmdnewswire.com on February 22, 2011; Greg Braxton, "BET Shaky, Even in Its Sunday Best," *Los Angeles Times*, December 4, 2007, http://articles.latimes.com on February 22, 2011; Marybeth Hicks, "Sheltered from Bad TV, Poor Influences," *Washington Times*, April 27, 2008, www.washingtontimes.com on February 22, 2011; Teresa Wiltz and Paul Fahri, "BET President Resigns," *Washington Post*, September 12, 2008, www.washingtonpost.com on February 22, 2011; Lloyd Grove, "Sheila Johnson Slams BET," *The Daily Beast*, April 29, 2010, www .thedailybeast.com on February 22, 2011.

Chapter 7: Management at Work

How to Succeed in Business

How important is Steve Jobs to Apple Computer, the company that he co-founded in 1976 and which he has twice served as CEO?* Apple's remarkable success in marketing a steady stream of new-product innovations depends in part on its ability to project a certain mystique and generate buzz, and Jobs has been crucial to that strategy. "He's really the face of the company," says Kendall Whitehouse of the University of Pennsylvania's Wharton School of business. "Jobs [has been] the centerpiece for refocusing the company and brand."

In January 2009, however, Jobs disclosed that he was suffering from a "hormone imbalance" and announced that he was taking a medical leave of absence during which chief operating officer Tim Cook would assume the bulk of his responsibilities. Jobs hastened to add that he was receiving treatment and promised that "I will be the first one to step up and tell our board of directors that I can no longer continue to fulfill my duties as Apple's CEO." For some analysts, however, this personal reassurance wasn't enough to resolve questions about the company's future. Apple, they felt, had done little to quell long-standing rumors about Jobs's health and had revealed even less about its plans for carrying on in his absence, whether short or long term.

It's not an unusual reaction. "Investors get worried," says Wharton's Peter Capelli, "if they think the future of an entire company depends on a couple of key individuals." Capelli hastens to add, however, that "in fact, that's almost never the case. This bias—attributing the success of organizations to individuals—is pretty common. [But] all the studies show that . . . companies don't collapse when the leader departs and there's some time to fill the job."

Filling the job, especially at large organizations, is usually a matter of *succession planning*—the process of managing the transition from one CEO (or, indeed, just about any manager) to another. Having such a plan is obviously a good idea—if, as Capelli and other experts emphasize, it's approached in the right way. "Succession planning per se," says Capelli, "is a waste of time. . . . Because [a firm's] needs change so frequently . . .

---

*This case went to print before Jobs announced, in August 2011, that he was resigning as CEO of Apple. He died in October 2011.

there's no real ability to plan. [Formal succession plans] . . . almost always get tossed aside because they're out of date."

So what's the right approach to filling an organization's top jobs? Jim Moore, former chief learning officer at Sun Microsystems, suggests that executives and experts alike start thinking in terms of succession *development* instead of succession *planning*. "Plans," he contends, "do not develop anyone—only development experiences develop people." In fact, he adds, "succession-planning processes . . . sometimes create a false sense that the planning process is an end in itself rather than a precursor to real development."

And what constitutes "real development"? According to Robert M. Fulmer of Pepperdine University's Graziado School of Business and Management, it includes "leadership development, tracking, and developmental opportunities. The real key," says Fulmer, who prefers the term "succession *management*," "is to create a match between the organization's needs and the aspirations of individuals" within the organization. As such, the process involves human resource directors as well as strategic planners: Succession management, says Fulmer, a member of a team commissioned by the American Productivity and Quality Center (APQC) to study best practices in succession management among U.S. companies, "identifies and monitors various talent pools within the organization to match the future needs of the organization with the bench strength of available talent." Capelli agrees: "It's important for any company to be developing talent internally," he says. "And it's also important to

be promoting people from within." The APQC study found that best-practice firms spend a lot of time creating developmental activities that are in line with their organizational needs.

Another tricky issue is the extent to which the succession-development process should be transparent. Experts agree that when a company is in the process of putting a succession plan into action, it needs to let stakeholders—investors, customers, partners, employees—know what's going on. But *how much* should the company make known about the process and its ongoing status? As we've already seen, Apple's reluctance to reveal details about Steve Jobs's health and its plans for functioning without him as CEO caused some concern among investment analysts when he stepped down in January 2009. Jobs was back at work six months later, but the issue arose again in January of 2011, when Jobs announced that he was taking another leave of absence in a terse e-mail that Apple released publicly.

Jobs's brief statement, said Charles Elson, an expert in corporate governance at the University of Delaware, "leaves a lot to the imagination—and that was the problem last time. . . . It does leave a lot for investors to worry about." And once again, some analysts were dissatisfied with Apple's handling of the situation. Said Kim Caughey Forrest of Fort Pitt Capital, an investment fund: "I'm not sure that the company, and the board of directors in particular, have answered the question about succession planning. We had this issue [before], and the board was supposed to learn from it, but they haven't."

Case Questions

1. In what ways can succession planning be regarded as a type of *contingency planning*? Under what circumstances might it be necessary for a company to treat its succession-planning process as a *crisis management* process?

2. How might a company use the process of *goal setting* to help it implement its succession plan? Be sure to consider the barriers to successful implementation that it might encounter.

3. When asked if Apple would provide more details about Jobs's second leave of absence, a company spokeswoman responded: "We've said all we're going to say."

Is Apple obligated to offer any more details, particularly about the health of its CEO? One lawyer who advises corporate boards on such questions says that such details are material to investment decisions only "if you're asking shareholders to make decision based on [that] information. . . . You can't expect the company," he adds, "to give a blow-by-blow account of Steve Jobs's health." What do you think? If you were an Apple investor, what information would you regard as "material" to your decisions? What would you want to know in deciding whether to keep or sell your shares of Apple?

Case References

"Job-Less: Steve Jobs's Succession Plan Should Be a Top Priority for Apple," *Knowledge@Wharton*, January 7, 2009, http://knowledge.wharton.upenn.edu on February 23, 2011; Robert M. Fulmer, "Choose Tomorrow's Leaders Today: Succession Planning Grooms Firms for Success," *Graziado Business Report*, Vol. 5, No. 1, 2002, http://gbr.pepperdine.edu on February 23, 2011; Marshall Goldsmith, "Four Tips for Efficient Succession Planning,"

HarvardBusiness.org, May 12, 2009, http://blogs.hbr.org on February 23, 2011; Yukari Iwatani Kane and Joann S. Lublin, "Jobs Had Liver Transplant," *WSJ.com*, June 20, 2009, http://macdailynews.com on February 23, 2011; Kane and Lublin, "Apple Chief to Take Leave," *Wall Street Journal*, January 18, 2011, http://online.wsj.com on February 23, 2011.

Chapter 8: Management at Work

Acting on a Strategic Vision

Established as Amazin' Software in 1982 by an ex-Apple marketing executive named Trip Hawkins, Electronic Arts (EA) was a pioneer in the home-computer–games industry. From the outset, EA published games created by outside developers—a strategy that offered higher profit margins and forced the new company to stay in close contact with its market. By 1984, having built the largest sales force in the industry, EA had generated revenue of $18 million. Crediting its developers as "software artists," EA regularly gave game creators photo credits on packaging and advertising spreads and, what's more important, developed a generous profit-sharing policy that helped it to attract some of the industry's best development talent.

By 1986, the company had become the country's largest supplier of entertainment software. It went public in 1989, and net revenue took off in the early 1990s, climbing from $113 million in 1991 to $298 million in 1993. In the next 13 years, the company continued to grow by developing two key strategies:

- Acquiring independent game makers (at the rate of 1.2 studios per year between 1995 and 2006).
- Rolling out products in series, such as *John Madden Football, Harry Potter*, and *Need for Speed*.

Activision's path to success in the industry wasn't quite as smooth as EA's. Activision was founded in 1979 as a haven for game developers unhappy with prevailing industry policy. At the time, systems providers like Atari hired developers to create games only for their own systems; in-house developers were paid straight salaries and denied credit for individual contributions, and there was no channel at all for would-be independents. Positioning itself as the industry's first third-party developer, Activision began promoting creators as well as games. The company went public in 1983 and successfully rode the crest of a booming market until the mid-1980s. Between 1986 and 1990, however, Activision's growth strategies—acquisitions and commitment to a broader product line—fizzled, and it had become, as *Forbes* magazine put it, "a company with a sorry balance sheet but a storied history."

Enter Robert Kotick, a serial entrepreneur with no particular passion for video games, who bought one-fourth of the firm in December 1990 and became CEO two months later. Kotick looked immediately to Electronic Arts for a survey of best practices in the industry. What he discovered was a company whose culture was disrupted by internal conflict—namely, between managers motivated by productivity and profit and developers driven by independence and imagination. It seems that EA's strategy for acquiring and managing a burgeoning portfolio of studios had slipped into a counterproductive pattern: Identify an extremely popular game, buy the developer, delegate the original creative team to churn out sequels until either the team burned out or the franchise fizzled, and then close down or absorb what was left.

On the other hand, EA still sold a lot of video games, and to Kotick, the basic tension in EA culture wasn't entirely surprising: Clearly the business of making and marketing video games succeeded when the creative side of the enterprise was supported by financing and distribution muscle, but it was equally true that a steady stream of successful games came from a company's creative people. The key to getting Activision back in the game, Kotick decided, was managing this complex of essential resources better than his competition did.

So the next year Kotick moved the company to Los Angeles and began to recruit the people who could furnish the resources that he needed most—creative expertise and a connection with the passion that its customers brought to the video-game industry. Activision, he promised prospective developers, would not manage its human resources the way that EA did: EA, he argued, "has commoditized development. We won't absorb you into a big Death Star culture."

Between 1997 and 2003, Kotick proceeded to buy no fewer than nine studios, but his concept of a video-game studio system was quite different from that of EA, which was determined to make production more efficient by centralizing groups of designers and programmers into regional offices. Kotick allows his studios to keep their own names, often lets them stay where they are, and further encourages autonomy by providing seed money for Activision alumni who want to launch out on their own. Each studio draws up its own financial statements and draws on its own bonus pool, and the paychecks of studio heads reflect company-wide profits and losses.

The strategy paid off big time. For calendar year 2007, the company, now known as Activision Blizzard, estimated compiled revenues of $3.8 billion—just enough to squeeze past EA's $3.7 billion and sneak into the top spot as the best-selling video-game publisher in the world not affiliated with a maker of game consoles (such as Nintendo and Microsoft). Revenues for calendar year 2010 were $4.4 billion, up more than 20 percent over 2009, making Activision Blizzard the number one video-game publisher in North America and Europe. Today, its market capitalization of $13.3 billion is nearly twice that of EA.

Kotick attributes the firm's success to a "focus on a select number of proven franchises and genres where we have proven development expertise. . . . We look for ways to broaden the footprints of our franchises, and where appropriate, we develop innovative business models like subscription-based online gaming."

Case Questions

1. How might a *SWOT analysis* have helped Electronic Arts assess its slippage in the video-game market?
2. How might *Porter's generic strategies* theory help to explain why Electronic Arts lost its leadership in the video-game market to Activision Blizzard?
3. How would you use the *Miles and Snow typology* theory to advise Activision Blizzard on the best way to maintain its leadership in the video-game market?
4. If you ran a small video-game start-up, what would be your strategy for competing with EA and Activision Blizzard?
5. If you're a video-game player, what aspects of Activision's strategy have led to your playing more (or fewer) of its games? If you're not a video-game player, what aspects of Activision Blizzard's strategy might induce you to try a few of its games?

Case References

Eric-Jon Rossel Waugh, "A Short History of Electronic Arts," *Business-Week*, August 25, 2006, www.businessweek.com on March 1, 2011; Peter C. Beller, "Activision's Unlikely Hero," *Forbes*, February 2, 2009, www.forbes.com on March 1, 2011; "Activision Beats EA as Top Third Party Publisher in U.S.," *Gamasutra*, July 24, 2007, www.gamasutra.com on March 1, 2011; "Activision Posts 92% Revenue Increase in Record Year," *Gamasutra*, May 8, 2008, www.gamasutra.com on March 1, 2011; "Activision Blizzard Reports December Quarter and Calendar Year 2010 Financial Results," *PRNewswire*, February 9, 2011, http://investor.activision.com on March 1, 2011.

Chapter 9: Management at Work

The Verdict on Groupthink

In the 1957 movie *Twelve Angry Men*, Henry Fonda plays a mild-mannered architect who's been selected to serve on a jury with 11 other white, middle-class, middle-aged men. Within the confines of the claustrophobic jury room, attitudes and preconceptions gradually begin to harden and the group's decision seems increasingly like a foregone conclusion—guilty in a case of capital murder. Fonda, however, has his doubts and starts to suggest alternative interpretations of the case until, by movie's end, he has steered the group to a more cogently considered decision. "My favorite part of a trial," reports one Texas attorney, "is when the judge . . . tells the jurors that deliberations should involve discussions, the questioning of their beliefs, and a willingness to change their minds. I really want jurors to do that," he says, but "I don't think they do." Like many lawyers, he doubts very seriously if the kind of deliberative decision making extolled in *Twelve Angry Men* goes on in many real jury rooms.

David A. Mitchell and Daniel Eckstein, authors of "Jury Dynamics and Decision-Making: A Prescription for Groupthink," aren't so sure either. They characterize a jury as "a unique variety of an autonomous work group"—"one in which group members are chosen, essentially at random, to perform a function of great importance for which they generally have no direct training." It's a prescription, they suggest, for "group dynamics that are not conducive to quality decision making." The problem, they argue, is *groupthink*, and they agree with Irving Janis, who conducted early studies on the phenomenon, that it infects groups whose members let their "strivings for unanimity override their motivation to realistically appraise alternative courses of action."

Mitchell (a clinical psychologist) and Eckstein (a psychologist and consultant on leadership development) focus on Janis's seven "antecedent conditions" for groupthink—factors that make groupthink more likely—in order to show how "the conditions under which juries operate" add up to "a substantial risk of jury decisions being tainted by groupthink":

- *Cohesiveness.* A number of factors combine to ensure that the jury is a cohesive group. From the moment that jurors are selected, for example, they're "treated as a unit [and] their individual identities become submerged in the group identity." They eat together and often spend a great deal of time together prior to deliberations, and because they're not supposed to discuss the case during the trial itself, they often talk about such topics as the shared experience of being on a jury.
- *Insulation.* Once it's impaneled, the jury is isolated from other individuals and groups; jurors are physically separated from other people in the courthouse and sometimes even kept under guard to ensure their isolation.
- *Lack of a tradition of impartial leadership.* The only leadership in the group comes from the foreperson, who typically has an opinion on the case and therefore can't really be impartial in relating to other members.
- *Lack of norms requiring methodical procedures.* Juries have no set rules for how to proceed in arriving at a decision. In fact, the only specific requirement—to reach a unanimous decision—increases the likelihood of faulty decision making.

- *Homogeneity of social background and ideology.* Juries are rarely valid cross sections of the community. Desirable jury members, for example, share certain qualities that lawyers look for, and because lawyers try to seat jurors who share qualities favorable to their cases, juries often tend toward homogeneity on those qualities.
- *High stress from external threats/low hope of a solution better than the leader's.* This factor basically underscores the fact that stress—and the desire to avoid it—contribute to groupthink, and it reflects two hypotheses: (1) Jurors find that having to choose among unpleasant or complicated alternatives increases stress, especially if the group leader is authoritarian or tends to promote a particular decision. (2) Jurors are more likely to agree with the leader's decision if they feel that opposing it will increase stress among group members.
- *Temporarily low self-esteem induced by situational factors.* The more difficult it becomes to sort out alternatives and reach a decision, the lower a juror's sense of *self-efficacy*

may become (see Chapter 18); in other words, as jurors lose their confidence in their ability to perform the task at hand, they may try to alleviate the feeling by taking refuge in conformity and consensus.

Mitchell and Eckstein acknowledge that none of these seven conditions by itself "is sufficient to cause . . . groupthink," but they hasten to point out that "the greater the number of these conditions that exist, the greater the propensity toward" groupthink. They also admit that any group is susceptible to groupthink but emphasize that "the structure of the jury system places juries at particularly high risk. . . . Considering the regularity with which many of the above antecedent conditions occur in juries," they argue, "the structure of the jury system may not only be conducive but often helps create the occurrence of groupthink." Finally, they observe that different types of groups make different types of errors, but caution that groupthink "increases the risk that all types of decision-making errors will occur."

Case Questions

1. In your experience, have you found that decision-making groups tend toward *groupthink*? If so, what factors contributed to this tendency? If not, what factors helped to prevent it?
2. Review the steps in the *rational decision-making* model (especially steps 1–4). This model, of course, applies to individuals and might be difficult to apply to group decision-making situations. If, however, you were a juror, how might you apply these steps to your own deliberations? In what ways might they give you some useful guidance? In what ways would you have to make

adjustments because of the context (a trial) and situation (a group process)?
3. In what ways might *bounded rationality* affect a juror's approach to a decision? How about *satisficing? Intuition? Ethics?*
4. A recent study found that racially mixed juries "deliberated longer, raised more facts, and conducted broader and more wide-ranging deliberations" than either all-white or all-black juries. Why do you think this was so? Do you think that "mixed" juries are more likely to avoid groupthink than racially homogeneous juries? Explain your reasoning.

Case References

Twelve Angry Men (United Artists, 1957); David H. Mitchell and Daniel Eckstein, "Jury Dynamics and Decision-Making: A Prescription for Groupthink," *International Journal of Academic Research*, Vol. 1 (September 2009), www.ijar.lit.az on March 5, 2011; Irving L. Janis, *Groupthink*, 2nd ed. (Boston: Houghton Mifflin, 1972); Michael P. Maslanka, "The Dirty Realities

of Group-Think," *Texas Lawyer*, December 23, 2009, http://texaslawyer .typepad.com on March 5, 2011; Samuel R. Sommers, "On Racial Diversity and Group Decision Making: Identifying Multiple Effects of Racial Composition on Jury Deliberations," *Journal of Personality and Social Psychology*, Vol. 90, No. 4 (2006), http://ase.tufts.edu on March 5, 2011.

Chapter 10: Management at Work

Facebook Takes Credits Where Credits Are Due

Do you *facebook*? About 600 million people do—a particularly impressive number when you consider that Facebook began the year 2010 with a mere 350 million users. If you saw the movie *The Social Network*,

you know that the immensely popular social-networking website was started by Harvard sophomore Mark Zuckerberg in February 2004. Today, Facebook.com is the second most visited site on the Internet, behind only Google. Worldwide, users spend more than 700 billion minutes a month on Facebook, uploading 3 billion photos and 2 billion videos and sharing 30 billion pieces of content (news stories, blog posts, photo albums, etc.) every month.

Its growth in value has been as spectacular as the growth of its user base. From $100 million in 2005, its valuation jumped to $15 billion in late 2007, to $33 billion in mid-2010, to $50 billion by the end of the year. In January 2011, when its valuation hit $82.9 billion, it surpassed Amazon as the number-two U.S. Internet company (again, behind only Google). Zuckerberg has announced that Facebook, which is currently a privately held company, will begin reporting its financial results in April 2012—a move suggesting that a plan to take the company public is in the works.*

That announcement, of course, shouldn't be surprising: Facebook is, after all, a business, and money is an issue with any business—especially one that's growing at the rate of Facebook. Exactly how does Facebook make money? In 2009, according to Inside Facebook, an independent news source, about 98 percent of the company's total revenue came from advertising—$625 million out of $635 million (though both figures may be higher, the latter as high as $700 million). Facebook advertising for the year fell into three classes:

- *Performance advertising*: Branded ads that ask users to click through to an advertising message on a destination site ($350 million)
- *Brand advertising*: Advertising placed through agencies by large companies ($225 million)
- *Microsoft advertising*: Banner ads and sponsor links targeted mainly at college students ($50 million—the result of a revenue-sharing agreement in effect from 2007 to 2009)

About 2 percent ($10 million) of Facebook's 2009 revenue resulted from the sale of *virtual goods* and *direct Credits*—from the sale of *virtual gifts* (those little icons that pop up in certain Facebook programs and which users can exchange for about $1) and from Facebook's percentage of the *Credits* that many online developers who use the Facebook platform accept as payment from their customers.

Inside Facebook estimates that the company's revenues roughly doubled each year from 2007 to 2009—from $150 million in 2007, to $280–$300 million in 2008, to more than $600 million in 2009. Revenues for 2010 ballooned to $2 billion, and early projections for 2011 have gone as high as $4 billion. And what about profits? The business-news site Business Insider reports 2010 profits of $600 million, and projections for 2011 have ranged from $1 billion to $2 billion.

Obviously these are impressive numbers, but there are still some people—including a number of analysts—who remain skeptical about Facebook's prospects as a premier investment opportunity. Why? They're not sure that Facebook can ultimately increase profitability to a level that will justify its market valuation—and thus its eventual price per share once it goes public.

Such skepticism often boils down to a comparison of Facebook with Google, the world's number-one Internet company. As we've seen, for example, Facebook's valuation has skyrocketed in the past five years, but even at $82.9 billion, it's dwarfed by Google, whose value, as of January 2011, stood at a whopping $192 billion. Likewise, Facebook's $2 billion in 2010 revenues included $1.86 billion in ad revenue—a healthy figure, to say the least, but it pales in comparison with Google ad revenues of $2 billion *a month*. (Ironically, Google is Facebook's fifth-largest advertiser.) Finally, as Business Insider points out, although Facebook has enjoyed spectacular growth over its first seven years, it hasn't grown nearly as fast as Google did over its first seven years (indeed, over its first ten years).

Thus, in order to make his company's valuation look good to potential investors, Zuckerberg probably needs to show that it can emulate the epic growth of Google. It may seem like a daunting task, but on the upside, says Business Insider's Nicholas Carlson, Google is "a one-trick pony. It makes almost all of its money from one business—search." Facebook, on the other hand, already enjoys a diversified revenue base. Consider, for example, Zynga, a maker of online games that use the platforms of social networking sites, particularly Facebook. First of all, gamemakers like Zynga buy about one-third of all performance advertising on Facebook. Second, gamemakers like Zynga allow players to pay with "Facebook Credits"—a virtual currency with which users can pay for goods and services from Facebook apps. Facebook collects a 30 percent "tax" from all these Credits, and combined with advertising revenues, Facebook's take from gamemakers in 2010 was about $400 million.

Zynga, says Carlson, is a good example of Facebook's revenue base, not only because it exemplifies a relatively new type of company—it's a maker of multiplayer browser-based games founded in 2007—but because its own growth has been so explosive: Zynga is already worth $5 billion and its own 2010 revenues topped $500 million. For Carlson, the Facebook–Zynga synergy suggests that Facebook will continue to grow at an investment-worthy rate because its real business "is taxing other businesses that figure out ways to make money off of social networking." It's a formula for success that Zuckerberg is well aware of: "In gaming," he remarked in the fall of 2010, "we get some percentage of the value of those companies

---

*In 2010, *Time* magazine gave its prestigious Person of the Year award to Zuckerberg. "In less than seven years," explained the editors, Facebook "has changed the way human beings relate to one another on a species-wide scale. We are now running our social lives through a for-profit network that . . . has made Zuckerberg a billionaire six times over."

through ads and credits. But that's all because we're helping them. . . . Over the next five years," he added,

> most industries are going to get rethought [as] social. . . . A social version of anything can almost always . . . outperform a non-social version. There are

going to be some really good businesses built. . . . Our view is that we should play a role in helping to reform and rethink all those industries and . . . get value proportional to what we put in. . . . If we're helpful to other industries in building what would be a good solution, then there will be some way we get value from that.

Case Questions

1. If you use Facebook (or any other social networking site), which of its features are most attractive to you? If you don't use any social networking site, what features are most likely to cause you to try one?
2. Explain Facebook's *distinctive competencies* in as much detail as you can. If you use Facebook, you can obviously draw on your own experience. If you don't use the site, talk to a few people who do.
3. Its *click-through rate* measures the number of visitors to a website who actually click on the ads. Industrywide, it's not good, and in 2010, Facebook's click-through rate

was below the industry average. What about you—do you *click through*? What does it take for you to venture away—even temporarily—from a host site when you're online? What can a company like Facebook do to improve its click-through rate—and its advertising revenue?
4. According to one popular technology blog, its current policy on users' privacy means that "your name, profile picture, gender, current city, networks, Friends List, and all the pages you subscribe to are now publicly available information on Facebook. This means everyone on the web can see it; it is searchable." Is this okay with you? Why or why not?

Case References

Facebook, "Statistics," "Company Timeline," 2011, www.facebook.com on March 8, 2011; Nick Bilton, "2010 Online, by the Numbers," *New York Times*, January 14, 2011, http://bits.blogs.nytimes.com on March 8, 2011; Eric Eldon, "Facebook Revenues Up to $700 Million in 2009, on Track Towards $1.1 Billion in 2010, *Inside Facebook*, March 2, 2010, www.insidefacebook.com on March 8, 2011; Lev Grossman, "Person of the Year 2010," *Time*, December 15, 2010, www.time.com on March 11, 2011; Leslie Horn, "How Facebook Earned $1.86 Billion Ad Revenue in 2010," *PCMag.com*, January 18, 2011, www.pcmag.com on March 9, 2011; Nicholas Carlson, "Facebook's Plan to Make a $50 Billion Valuation Look Cheap," *Business Insider*, January 7, 2011, www.businessinsider.com on March 9, 2011; Nicholas Carlson, "Facebook Earned $250 Million in Q4, Profits Growing at an Astounding Rate," *Business Insider*, February 10, 2011, www.businessinsider.com on March 8, 2011; Mike Taylor, "Facebook Click-Through Rates Are Below Average and Sinking," *New York Observer*, February 1, 2011, www.observer.com on March 11, 2011; Marshall Kirkpatrick, "Facebook's Zuckerberg Says the Age of Privacy Is Over," *ReadWriteWeb*, January 9, 2010, www.readwriteweb.com on March 12, 2011.

Chapter 11: Management at Work

How Indiana Lost Control of Its Welfare System

By the time she was six months pregnant, Stacie Kelly had been trying long and hard to see a doctor. "It's just really hard to be excited about having a baby," she said, "when you're worried all the time. There are all kinds of medical tests that I should have had run." Kelly, 27, had no medical insurance and depended on Indiana's Family and Social Services Administration (FSSA) to process her application for Medicaid coverage. "I just wanted to go to the doctor. That's all," explained Kelly, who said that she'd submitted the required Medicaid application to FSSA two months earlier. "And then," she reports, "basically, they dropped off the face of the planet. . . . I haven't heard anything since then, and so I called my caseworker and left numerous messages. They don't return your calls."

"We don't call back because we're not getting paid for it," said George Thompson, a former employee at an FSSA call center. As an FSSA agent, Thompson worked not for the state of Indiana, but for Affiliated Computer Services (ACS),

which had been contracted to handle calls from residents seeking such welfare benefits as food stamps and Medicaid coverage. "It [was] just about ACS making money," says Thompson, who adds that training for call center employees "was very substandard." Angie Kennaugh, another ex-ACS employee, agrees: "Your job," she told a local reporter, was "to get people off the phone. The people running the call centers came from Sprint and Taco Bell. They had absolutely no experience whatsoever." Scott Severns, an attorney representing thousands of Indiana residents in a class-action lawsuit against ACS, was just as harsh in assessing the company's approach to making a profit in the contract call-center business: "It's like a company that produces a whole lot of junk," he said. "They can be proud of how fast they get it out, but it really doesn't matter if it isn't right."

ACS, a Dallas-based provider of business-process outsourcing, had been hired by IBM to handle calls from social-services applicants when IBM contracted with the state to manage approximately one-third of its welfare caseload. The $1.3 billion contract had been signed in December 2007, with Governor Mitch Daniels promising that privatizing the state's welfare and food stamp programs would save taxpayers $1 billion over the next decade. Serious problems, however, surfaced and multiplied over the next 18 months concerning the performance not only of ACS but that of IBM itself. Both companies came under mounting scrutiny from state officials and criticism from welfare-rights organizations, and in July 2009, both were put on notice by the Daniels administration that their contract with the state might be in jeopardy.

In August, IBM announced plans to fix such problems as "inaccurate and incomplete data gathering" and "incorrect communications to clients"—problems that critics boiled down to lengthy call center hold times and too many errors in processing applications (including loss of documents). "Too many seniors, people with disabilities, and other of our most vulnerable citizens," charged an official of AARP Indiana, "have endured monstrous challenges [to efforts] to address their basic healthcare, nutritional, and other daily necessities." A lawsuit filed by the American Civil Liberties Union cited the case of a mother of two who'd lost her food stamps and healthcare for her children because her tax form was missing one document.

"There are a thousand of these stories," said ACLU attorney Gavin Rose, who explained that all of the parties to the lawsuit had been denied benefits because FSSA was missing some document—a document which each applicant had, like Stacie Kelly, duly submitted. According to Rose, every applicant received a letter citing "failure to cooperate" as the reason for denial of services. "You cannot deny someone for 'failing to cooperate,'" says Rose, who points out that Medicaid and other federal rules bar failure to cooperate as a reason for dismissing claims. "[People] get this letter, and they have absolutely no idea what they did wrong. . . . I'm sure

there are cases out there where people are quite literally facing a life-or-death situation." One woman told a panel of state legislators that her husband had died of a heart ailment within a year of being denied Medicaid benefits by FSSA. "It's not right," said Nanceen Alexander. "He did his part, and now it's time for the system to do its part."

Many critics blamed the failure of the system, at least in part, on the elimination of individual caseworkers. Prior to privatization, each household was assigned a caseworker who monitored its eligibility for benefits and, when problems arose, intervened to make sure that applications were properly submitted and assessed. Under the privatized system, a household's welfare records were stored electronically for access by caseworkers located across the state.

Testifying before a state administrative committee in September 2009, FSSA Secretary Anne Murphy admitted that greater personal contact between the agency and its clients might be beneficial but reaffirmed that individual caseworkers were a thing of the past. "If [clients] wish to stay at home and apply online," said Murphy, "they can do that. If they wish to apply by telephone, they can do that. I'm not saying there haven't been problems," she added, promising that IBM was in the process of fixing them.

The fix, however, did not come fast enough to suit exasperated state officials. In October, just 22 months after he'd authorized Indiana's privatized welfare system, Gov. Daniels fired IBM as its primary contractor. "The intended service improvements," explained the governor, "have not been delivered, and that's not acceptable." In place of the failed system, Daniels announced a new "hybrid system" that would retain some of the best features of the privatized process while restoring some of the best elements of the traditional state-operated system. IBM would no longer be involved, but workers hired by certain contractors—including ACS—would stay on under state supervision.

Case Questions

1. For what *purposes of control* was Indiana's privatized social-services system created in the first place?
2. In what *areas of control* was the new system supposed to improve the operations of the Family and Social Services Administration (FSSA)? In what ways did the new system affect the following *levels of control* at FSSA—(a) *financial*, (b) *structural*, and (c) *strategic*? Then focus on *operations control*: In what ways did IBM and ACS act to

exercise *preliminary control*? *Screening control*? *Postaction control*?
3. In your opinion, how did the approach of IBM and ACS to *bureaucratic control* contribute to the collapse of the privatized system? In what ways might *decentralization* have improved its operations?
4. Refer to each of the *characteristics of effective control* in order to explain why the privatized social-services system proved to be ineffective.

Case References

"Pregnant Woman Frustrated by FSSA Slowness," *TheIndyChannel.com*, July 8, 2009, www.theindychannel.com on May 1, 2011; Sandra Chapman, "Former ACS Workers Highlight Call Center Problems," wthr.com, August 10, 2009, www.wthr.com on May 1, 2011; "Advocates for Seniors, Disabled Take Aim at IBM," *TheIndyChannel.com*, September 25, 2009, www .theindychannel.com on May 1, 2011; "ACLU Lawsuit Targets Indiana Welfare Changes," *Chesterton* (Indiana) *Tribune*, May 20, 2008, http://

chestertontribune.com on May 1, 2011; "Face-to-Face Help, Less [*sic*] Phones Part of FSSA Plan," *TheIndyChannel.com*, September 25, 2009, www .theindychannel.com on May 1, 2011; Rick Callahan, "Ind. Panel Approves Ending Welfare Privatization," *The Street*, December 14, 2009, www .thestreet.com on May 1, 2011; Leonard Gilroy, "Indiana Cancels IBM Welfare Modernization Contract," Reason Foundation, October 16, 2009, http://reason.org on May 1, 2011.

Chapter 12: Management at Work

Amazon Rekindles Its Flair for Technology

As you probably know, selling things online—online retailing or *e-tailing*—is the only thing that Amazon .com does. Unlike such online rivals as, say, Barnes & Noble.com or Walmart.com, Amazon has no roof over its head—no bricks-and-mortar presence to anchor its online presence. The seller and its customers interact by website, e-mail, or phone. Behind the website, however, is one of the largest direct-to-consumer distribution operations in the world.

Founded in 1995 as a bookseller, Amazon does pretty well these days—$32.4 billion in sales for 2010—but it's had its ups and downs. Early investors believed that the promise of online business outweighed the risks associated with the new type of enterprise, but it wasn't long before giddy expectation gave way to more sober assessment, as soaring costs kept pace with expanding sales and wiped out profits. That's when Amazon diversified its range of product offerings, adding toys, music, electronics and software, and household goods. Expansion continued to eat into profits, and the company had to make huge investments in infrastructure and IT before it finally went into the black in 2002.

Though fairly commonplace among today's online enterprises, Amazon's business model was revolutionary for its time. There was no need to open stores in high-rent shopping areas, and the company was free to choose locations for distribution centers based on cost and convenience to transportation facilities. Amazon's seven distribution centers stock thousands of popular items, but many of the goods that end consumers buy through Amazon are in fact "drop-shipped" directly from manufacturers. Amazon, therefore, can offer a multitude of products without incurring high inventory expenses, and because the middleman has been eliminated, delivery times are faster.

In addition, much of the work at Amazon facilities is automated. Workers use simple, menu-driven computer programs to access and monitor customer orders. Goods are then picked from the shelves and placed in a vast system of automated chutes and bins that bundles them appropriately. At one point, Amazon had tried to minimize shipping costs by bundling all items for shipment to a single address into one package. Now, however, the system relies on a more effective sorting algorithm that calculates optimal package size, both to protect items and to reduce costs. Automated scanners track the progress of every order, and automated boxers and labelers prepare goods for shipping.

Software, of course, is an important part of Amazon's operations because better systems hold down labor costs, increase accuracy and speed, enhance the customer experience, and support effective planning. Supply-chain software, for example, uses a complex formula to choose which goods should be carried in distribution centers and which should be drop-shipped. Yet another algorithm constantly recalculates item popularity ratings to choose which goods to store in the most highly frequented sections of warehouses.

Amazon is also a pioneer in the development of several operations technologies:

- "One-click" buying allows customers to make final purchases with a single mouse click. (The process is patented and licensed to other companies.)
- Amazon was one of the first online retailers to let customers post online product reviews, which not only boost sales but contribute to a sense of community among users.
- Customers can review their order histories, create wish and favorites lists, share information with friends, receive personalized recommendations and gift-giving reminders, and tag items with customized category data.

Amazon's operations software is so popular with other firms that the company has launched a feature called Amazon Web Services, which allows independent programmers and merchants to access Amazon's library of software and adapt it for their own use. The library is free unless the "borrower" intends to sell through Amazon, in which case there's a 15 percent commission on each sale. The service has proven so popular that 30 percent of Amazon's sales are now conducted by other merchants. In February 2009, as part of Amazon Web Services, Amazon launched Amazon SimpleDB, a system that allows businesses to store and quickly retrieve simple data. Some companies already rely on Amazon's expertise to manage their websites. Target and Office Depot, for instance, contract their online presence to Amazon.

And now—for consumers—there's Kindle, which, ironically, hearkens back to Amazon's origins as a bookseller. Developed by an Amazon subsidiary called Lab126, Kindle is a software–hardware platform for reading electronic print material. The first-generation Kindle device came out at the very end of 2007 and was aimed primarily at readers of books, which Amazon founder and CEO Jeff Bezos promptly labeled "the last bastion of analog. . . . The vision [of Kindle]," he hastened to add, "is that you should be able to get any book—not just any book in print, but any book that's *ever* been in print—on this device in less than a minute."

Amazon now has 900,000 titles available for download, but Kindle is designed to handle much more than books. With this device, which doesn't require a computer, Amazon allows you not only to download 630,000 books, but even to subscribe to newspapers and magazines, which will automatically be downloaded as soon as new issues go to press. You can search for material through Google, follow links from blogs and other web pages, jot down notes on the page you're reading, and even capture selected passages with the equivalent of an electric highlighter. Kindle 2 and Kindle DX, each with larger displays and other new and improved features, arrived in early 2009, and there's also a Kindle for the iPhone.

Eight months after its release, Amazon had sold nearly $100 million worth of Kindles, and by the end of the year,

amid speculation that it was the iPod of the book world, the Kindle had sold double its projected sales figure (and equaled sales of the iPod in its first year of release). Amazon does not disclose sales of Kindle and Kindle-related content, but reports indicate that it sold 8 million Kindles in 2010—a staggering 60 percent over analysts' predictions. In July 2010, the company did announce that it was selling 180 Kindles for every 100 hardback books, and in January 2011, it announced that Kindle sales had overtaken paperback sales as well, with U.S. customers buying 115 Kindles for every 100 paperback books.

Case Questions

1. Describe Amazon's *product-service mix*. Which areas of Amazon's operations are characteristic of a *manufacturing* organization? Which areas are characteristic of a *service organization*? How do both areas relate to the marketing of Kindle and Kindle-related products?

2. Describe the role of *technology* in both Amazon's manufacturing and service operations.

3. Discuss the nature of Amazon's *supply chain* in terms of *control, purchasing management*, and *inventory management*. At what points in the supply chain does Amazon outsource or contract activities to outside parties? How does Amazon's *supply chain management* affect its revenues and costs?

4. Log on to Amazon.com and select an item that comes from Amazon itself rather than from a drop-shipper. What kind of *purchasing* decisions were necessary to make this product available at Amazon's price? What kind of *inventory-control* decisions were necessary?

5. What facets of Amazon's operations allow it to create and control *quality*, both as a manufacturing organization and as a service organization? What facets of its operations allow Amazon to control *productivity* (again, both as a manufacturing organization and as a service organization)? Give two or three examples of ways in which Amazon's operations contribute to high productivity.

Case References

Mark Brohan, "Amazon Sales and Profits Boom in 2010," *Internet Retailer*, January 27, 2011, www.internet.retailer on May 3, 2011; Robert Hof, "Amazon's Brighter Horizon?" *BusinessWeek*, April 26, 2006, www.businessweek.com on May 3, 2011; Jeff Cogswell, "Amazon Simple DB a Solid Choice for Simple Web-Based Data Storage," *eweek*, February 5, 2009, www.eweek.com on May 3, 2011; Steven Levy, "The Future of Reading," *Newsweek*, November 26, 2007, www.newsweek.com on May 3, 2011; Amy Martinez,

"Amazon Says Kindle Sales Top Its 'Most Optimistic' Projections," *Seattle Times*, April 17, 2009, http://seattletimes.nwsource.com on May 3, 2011; Joseph Galante and Peter Burrows, "Amazon.com Kindle Sales Are Said to Exceed Estimates," *Bloomberg*, December 21, 2010, www.bloomberg.com on May 3, 2011; Claire Cain Miller, "E-Books Top Hardcovers at Amazon," *New York Times*, July 19, 2010, www.nytimes.com on May 3, 2011.

Chapter 13: Management at Work

The Wiki World of Jimmy Wales

As you probably know, Wikipedia is a nonprofit online encyclopedia written entirely by volunteers. According to a reliable source (Wikipedia), *wiki* derives from the Hawaiian phrase *wiki wiki*, meaning "quick." A wiki, writes the anonymous author of the article, is "a type of website that allows users to add, remove, or otherwise edit all content very quickly and easily, sometimes without the need for registration. This ease of interaction and operation makes a wiki an effective tool for collaborative writing."

Developed principally by Jimmy Wales, a former options trader, and Larry Sanger, a graduate student whom Wales

had originally hired as an editor, Wikipedia was launched in January 2001. By the middle of February, the site had posted its 1,000th article, and just nine months later, it posted its 10,000th entry. For a while, Wikipedia grew at a rate of 1,500 articles a month, topping 40,000 in August 2002. Two years later, there were more than a million articles in 105 languages.

Wikipedia now exists in more than 240 languages and features more than 3.6 million articles in English alone. If it were printed and bound on book form, it would run to more than 1,500 volumes. Almost all technical staff and

30,000 writers are unpaid volunteers, although Wales reports that the organization pays about 35 people to handle its legal, accounting, fund-raising, and software-development operations.

The Wikipedia philosophy, at once radical and simple, is summarized by the Wikipedia Foundation, a nonprofit organization that manages the portfolio of Wiki sites (e.g., Wiktionary, Wikiquote, Wikibooks, Wikinews, Wikiversity, and Meta-Wiki): "Imagine a world in which every single person is given free access to the sum of all human knowledge." Users are invited to edit content, and articles, which grow and change over time with the input of many contributors, are never "finished."

Wales thinks he knows why Wiki is so popular: "The main thing about Wikipedia," he explains, "is that it's fun and addictive." At the same time, however, he also believes that Wikipedia reflects a significant change in an information-driven society—namely, a shift from dependence on authoritarian experts toward a more democratic and collaborative spirit of knowledge sharing. In the future, he predicts, distrust for traditional encyclopedias will eventually render them obsolete: "People will say, 'This was written by one person? Then looked at by only two or three other people? How can I trust that process?'" According to *Time* magazine, Wales' image is that of "a champion of Internet-enabled egalitarianism." American novelist Nicholson Baker calls Wikipedia a "point of convergence for the self-taught and the expensively educated" and credits its popularity to its success in "tapp[ing] into the heretofore unmarshaled energies of the uncredentialed."

Wales himself likes the term "anticredentialist." "Not to be too dramatic about," he says, "but 'to create and distribute a free encyclopedia of the highest possible quality to every single person on the planet in their own language'—that's who I am. That's what I'm doing. That's my life goal."

Not surprisingly, a lot of people, especially academics and librarians, aren't so sure that anticredentialism is such a good thing. They argue that the reliability of information on Wikipedia varies widely and that no one can be held responsible for unsigned contributions. Other critics worry that Wikipedia can be too easily corrupted by a few users with biased points of view, that it doesn't provide an adequate format for presenting divergent perspectives, and that a lot of the information that appears there reflects popular opinion rather than researched conclusions.

Wikipedians, however, are quick to cite a survey of "'relevant' field experts" by the journal *Nature* which showed that a selection of Wikipedia articles contained no more "serious errors" than a comparable selection from the *Encyclopedia Britannica*. Other research reported that experts tended to regard Wikipedia articles more highly than non-experts. A study conducted at the University of Minnesota revealed that a significant portion of the most authoritative and durable edits made to articles on the site are the work of a relatively small group of perhaps 1,200 contributors. John Broughton, for example, author of *How Wikipedia Works* and *Wikipedia: The Missing Manual* (a how-to guide for would-be contributors), has made more than 15,000 edits.

In an interesting twist on the subject of authorial responsibility, Wales himself was accused in early 2008 of tinkering with the Wikipedia article on TV commentator Rachel Marsden, with whom he became romantically involved, and then added a little more fuel to the critical fire by updating his own page to inform inquiring readers (and Ms. Marsden) that the relationship had ended. Wales admitted forwarding edits suggested by Marsden to a team of Wikipedia editors responsible for handling complaints but wasn't entirely forthright about the source of the edits. "I care deeply about the integrity of Wikipedia," he said on his own post, "and take very seriously my responsibilities as a Member of the Board and as a member of the Wikipedia community. I would never knowingly do anything to compromise that trust."

Perhaps more troublesome are questions about Wikipedia's financial structure. "A surprising number of people," says Sue Gardner, executive director of the Wikipedia Foundation, "don't even know it's a nonprofit. They say, 'How do they make their money, anyway?' They assumed there were ads or some other way." There are no ads on any of the Wiki sites, which are in fact financed by professional fund raisers who seek donations. A fund-raising campaign, for example, might bring in an average of $30 from 45,000 individuals. The issue of whether or not to accept advertising arises periodically, but the seven-member board of trustees, which includes both Wales and Gardner, continues to reject the idea. Among Wikipedians, the organization's commitment to noncommercial operations goes hand in hand with its decentralized management process to ensure its democratic principles and the integrity of the content on its various sites. Nor will there be any investment in Wikipedia, adds Wales. "Wikipedia is a nonprofit and always will be."

At the same time, however, Wales admits that "existing on donations keeps us on a shoestring budget," and he's open to the idea of leveraging the Wikipedia brand as long as doing so doesn't compromise the organization's civic-minded values. While would-be investors, including venture-capital firms, have regularly been turned away from Wikipedia's core operations, Wales regards such sources of funding as a viable option for other brand-related activities. "We do not want to touch the core," he explains, but "there are some kinds of ways of using our brand name—a trivia game, a branded home-edition trivia game. That kind of thing seems to fit. . . . [Investors] could be involved in that kind of stuff."

Case Questions

1. Do you use Wikipedia? Why or why not? Do you think Wikipedia will ultimately eliminate the need for traditional reference sources? Why or why not?
2. Think of three topics that interest you. Locate the articles on these topics on Wikipedia and comment on their usefulness and accuracy. Which article is the most reliable? Which is the least reliable?
3. Because they support collaboration so conveniently, wikis are becoming increasingly common in business.

Think of two potential applications of wiki sites in a business context and describe the way each would work.

4. Why is integrity of content so important to services like those offered by Wikipedia? What sort of factors can render information unreliable? Can you think of an example in which unreliable information could affect someone using it for business purposes? How about for your own purposes as a student?

Case References

Nathan C. Kaiser, "Interview with Jimmy Wales, CEO of Wikipedia," *nPost*, November 1, 2005, www.npost.com on May 4, 2011; Wikipedia Foundation Inc., "Wikipedia: Statistics," 2011, http://en.wkipedia.org on May 4, 2011; Noam Cohen, "Wikipedia's Foundation Plans Expansion," *New York Times*, July 9, 2010, http://bits.blogs.nytimes.com on May 4, 2011;

"What Do Wikipedia's Sole 35 Employees Do?" *SFGate.com*, May 21, 2010, www.sfgate.com on May 4, 2011; Nicholson Baker, "The Charms of Wikipedia," *New York Review of Books*, March 20, 2008, www.nybooks.com on May 4, 2011; Chris Anderson, "Jimmy Wales," *Time*, April 30, 2006, www.time.com on May 4, 2011.

Chapter 14: Management at Work

Who Governs the Governing Authority?

The position of "ethics officer" first became popular in both for-profit and nonprofit organizations because other members of the executive hierarchy wanted to stay out of jail.

Okay, that's not *exactly* true. The position did, however, begin appearing on organization charts in the early 1990s in response to the establishment, in 1984, of the U.S. Sentencing Commission. The Commission was authorized by Congress to establish the U.S. Sentencing Guidelines for Organizations and the U.S. Sentencing Guidelines for Individuals in order to ensure uniformity in the sentencing of parties convicted of violating federal law.

In order to recommend good corporate citizenship as a means of complying with the law, the Commission's Guidelines for Organizations (issued in 1991) took into consideration not only the relative seriousness of an organization's crime but also the degree of its culpability. The Guidelines present the elements of an "Effective Compliance and Ethics Program"—a set of principles by which organizations can deal proactively with the factors that courts will consider in assessing culpability and handing down sentences for violations. They include promoting an ethical culture, communicating ethical standards and procedures, and preventing and detecting criminal conduct.

The Guidelines also define the main activities for which the organization's "ethics officer" or "compliance and ethics officer" is responsible. A survey conducted by the Ethics Resource Center (ERC), a Washington, D.C.-based nonprofit dedicated to research on organizational ethics, reveals that the position tends to feature certain core responsibilities:

- Overseeing the ethics requirements of organizational activities
- Collecting and analyzing ethics-related data
- Developing and interpreting ethics-related policy
- Developing and administering ethics education and training
- Overseeing ethics investigations

Ethics officers, according to the Ethics and Compliance Officer Association (ECOA), a nonprofit organization serving practitioners in the field, are responsible for "integrating their organizations' ethics and values initiatives, compliance activities, and business-conduct practices into the decision-making processes at all levels of the organization."

Organizations such as the ERC and the ECOA agree that while ethics and compliance standards and procedures must be institutionalized in organization-wide efforts, all levels of an organization are not equal when it comes to ensuring that programs are effective. They emphasize that effectiveness depends on a close working relationship between the ethics officer and *high-level* management. As the ERC points out, the federal Sentencing Guidelines, as revised in 2002 and 2004, encourage organizations to take a closer look at the clause that makes an organization's "governing authority" and "high-level personnel" responsible for its ethics and compliance program. At a large corporation, the "governing authority" is the board of directors, but the term "high-level personnel" must be interpreted much more broadly: It includes not only directors, but also executives, any individuals in charge of business or functional units, and even individuals with substantial ownership interests. All of these people are responsible for seeing that the organization's program is effective, and one or more of these individuals must be assigned ultimate and overall responsibility.

Although they must report to appropriate "high-level personnel," ethics officers themselves don't have to be among an organization's high-level personnel. As a practical matter, however, many organizations have found that the key function of an ethics program—effectiveness—is better served when the head of the program is in fact a high-level executive. For one thing, the presence of a high-level ethics officer underscores the organization's commitment to the program. For another, it makes much more sense to empower an ethics officer with the authority of high-level management if he or she is actually a high-level manager. At the American Arbitration Association, for example, the

post of ethics officer has been a senior-level job since its inception. Current ethics officer Jennifer Coffman reports directly to the CEO and makes regular presentations to the board of directors. Coffman reports that both the CEO and the board insist that she be included in "critical and key decision-making discussions" of all organizational activities at the highest level.

"We believe," states the ERC, "that an ethics officer who has direct and unfettered access to the highest authorities within an organization can most effectively impact an ethical culture and contribute substantively to the ethical integrity of an organization." Unfortunately, adds the ERC, "ethics officers in many companies have become removed from top-level managers and directors, severing a critical link between senior management and line supervisors."

Case Questions

1. Explain the role of an ethics officer as a specialized managerial position. In your opinion, what are the benefits to an organization of *specialization* in performing the job of an ethics officer? What are the limitations?
2. In a traditional setting, is an ethics officer more likely to hold a *line position* or a *staff position*? Could the position be *either* a line position or a staff position? How about *both*? In all of your answers, be sure to consider the nature of the *authority* that is—or ought to be—attached to the position.
3. Who's the ethics officer for student affairs at your school? At the University of Vermont (UVM), for example, it's

the Dean of Students, who can hand out various "sanctions," such as warnings, probation, or dismissal. What kind of *authority* does the comparable officer have at your school? UVM also publishes a *Code of Student Rights and Responsibilities*, which "reaffirms the principle of student freedom coupled with personal responsibility and accountability for individual action." Does your school have a student ethics code? If so, what does it have to say about your "responsibility and accountability" as a student?

Case References

United States Sentencing Commission, *2005 Federal Sentencing Guideline Manual*, November 1, 2005, http://ftp.ussc.gov on March 14, 2011; Ethics Resource Center, "What Is an Ethics Officer?" *Ethics Today Online*, October 2004, www.ethics.org on March 8, 2009; American Society of Association Executives, "Should You Hire an Ethics Officer?" *Executive Update Magazine*, 2008, www.asaecenter.org on March 14, 2011; Wyche Burgess Freeman and Parham, *U.S. Sentencing Commission Amends Guidelines for Corporate Compliance and Ethics Programs*, August 4, 2004, http://apps.americanbar.org on March 14, 2011; University of Vermont, *Code of Student Rights and Responsibilities*, July 1, 2009, www.uvm.edu on March 14, 2011.

Chapter 15: Management at Work

Codesharing the Wealth

Let's say you're a businessperson in New York who needs to fly to Hong Kong. Logging on to Orbitz, you find that American Airlines (AMR) offers a nonstop round-trip flight for $2,692. Because Orbitz recommends that you "Act Fast! Only 1 ticket left at this price!" you buy your ticket online. On your departure date, you arrive at the American Airlines ticket desk, only to be referred to the Cathay Pacific Airways counter. Your flight, the ticket agent informs you, is actually operated by Cathay, and she points to the four-digit "codeshare number" on your ticket. Bewildered but hoping that you're still booked on a flight to Hong Kong, you hustle to the Cathay counter, where your ticket

is in fact processed. Settled into your seat a few hours later, you decide to get on your laptop to see if you can figure out why you are and aren't on the flight that you booked. Going back to Orbitz, you find that, like American, Cathay does indeed offer a nonstop round-trip flight to and from its home city of Hong Kong—for $1,738. It dawns on you that if you'd bought your ticket directly from Cathay, you'd be sitting in the same seat on the same airplane for almost $1,000 less.

If this scenario sounds confusing, that's because it is, even to veteran flyers. What's confusing about it is the practice of *codesharing*, which works like this: You buy a ticket from Airline A for a flight operated by Airline B on a route that

Airline A doesn't otherwise serve. This practice is possible if both airlines, like AMR and Cathay, belong to the same *airline alliance* (in this case, Oneworld).

On the surface, the advantages to the airlines may seem mostly a matter of perception: An airline *seems* to be serving certain markets that it doesn't actually serve and flying certain routes more frequently than it actually does. The networks formed by codesharing agreements, however, are real, and the breadth of an airline's network is a real factor in attracting high-margin corporate travelers. In fact, the spread of codesharing has led directly to the formation of much larger "alliances" of carriers who cooperate on a substantial level, including codesharing and shared frequent-flyer programs. The three largest airline alliances are the Star Alliance, which includes United Airlines, US Airways, Air Canada, Air China, and Scandinavian Airlines; SkyTeam, which includes Delta, Air France, Alitalia, and Dutch-based KLM; and Oneworld, which includes AMR, Cathay, Qantas, British Airways, and Japan's JAL.

An airline alliance is one form of a *virtual organization*—in this case, a temporary alliance formed by two or more organizations to pursue a specific venture or to exploit a specific opportunity. Although each member remains an independently owned and managed organization, alliance members can save money by sharing sales, maintenance, and operational facilities and staff (such as check-in, boarding, and other on-the-ground personnel), and they can also cut costs on purchases and investments by negotiating volume discounts. The chief advantages, however, are breadth of service and geographical reach—in short, size (both perceived and real). Star Alliance, for example, operates 21,000 daily flights to 1,160 airports in 181 countries. According to the most recent data, its members carried 603.8 million passengers for a total of nearly 1 trillion *revenue passenger kilometers* (1 *rpk* means that 1 paying passenger was flown 1 kilometer). Based on rpk (which is really a measure of sales volume), Star commands 29.8 percent of global market share in the airline industry—greater than the combined market share of all airlines that don't belong to any of the three major alliances.

Note that our definition of a *virtual organization* indicates a "*temporary* alliance," and shifts by members of airline alliances are not unheard of. In January 2009, for example, a few months after merger talks had broken down with United Airlines, Continental Airlines, a member of SkyTeam since 2004, announced that it was joining United

in the Star Alliance. According to one analyst, the move, which took effect in October 2009, "was obviously a precursor to a full-blown merger," and, sure enough, Continental and United merged in May 2010 under a parent company called United Continental Holdings. The new airline remains a member of the Star Alliance.

The Continental–United merger was particularly bad news for both AMR, a member of Oneworld and the country's largest stand-alone airline, and US Airways Group, a member of SkyTeam and the fifth-largest U.S. carrier. With the merger of Continental and United, says Vaughn Cordle, chief analyst at Airline Forecasts, a specialist in industry investment research, "the odds of . . . bankruptcy for US Airways and American increase because it will be too difficult, if not impossible, for them to remain viable as stand-alone businesses. . . . [W]ithout a new strategic direction and significant changes in the industry's structure," Cordle predicts, AMR and US Airways "will continue on the slow . . . path to failure."

Cordle recommends consolidation, and many analysts say that AMR management had begun considering its options even before the Continental–United merger. The best strategy, adds George Van Horn, an analyst at the research firm IBISWorld, needn't be a merger but could involve some kind of looser alliance. Who is the likely partner if AMR decides to consolidate? John Kasarda, an aviation expert at the University of North Carolina's Kenan-Flagler Business School, thinks that an AMR–US Airways merger isn't out of the question: "It would be more out of necessity," he admits, but both airlines have been "asleep at the switch" and can expect their respective shareholders to demand some kind of action. A merger, however, would require US Airways to leave the Star Alliance, and US Airways says that "we highly value our membership in Star and maintain that it's the strongest alliance."

In any case, observers agree that AMR needs to make some kind of strategic move. Once the world's largest airline, it's now number three, behind the new Continental–United and Delta Airlines. Among U.S. airlines, AMR has the lowest margins and highest costs, and it's also the only U.S. airline that lost money in 2010. IBISWorld's Van Horn points out, however, that AMR has considerable experience at the kind of deal making in question: American, he reminds potential investors, "helped originate the whole idea of alliances and partnerships. If somebody should be good at it, you could make the argument they should be."

Case Questions

1. Take a *situational view of organization design*: What roles have *technology* and *environment* played in the development of alliances and virtual organizations in the airline industry? In what ways does the *corporate-level strategy* of joining an alliance affect an airline's *organizational functions*?

2. In what ways might the *divisional (m-form) designs* of most airlines lend themselves to the requirements of alliance membership? In what ways might they be compatible with the organizational needs of the alliances themselves?

3. According to one industry analyst, "in a scale business . . . size does matter." What does he mean by "a scale business"? Why is the airline industry "a scale business"? Once you've thought about these two questions, how would you describe the "specific opportunity" which, as *virtual organizations*, airline alliances are designed to exploit?

4. Have you ever been on a flight that involved a *codesharing* arrangement? Did you notice then—or do you realize now—that there were advantages to the practice of codesharing? Based on what you know about airline travel, list a few of the possible advantages of codesharing for passengers.

Case References

"Orbitz: Flights," *Orbitz.com*, May 3, 2010, www.orbitz.com on May 3, 2010; David Grossman, "The Anomalies of Code Share," *USA Today*, June 23, 2006, www.usatoday.com on March 22, 2011; Star Alliance, "Star Alliance Statistics," July 2010, www.staralliance.com on March 22, 2011; Ben Mutzabaugh, "Continental: SkyTeam Membership Ends Oct. 24," *USA Today*, January 30, 2009, http://travel.usatoday.com on March 22, 2011; Andrew Clark, "United and Continental Merge to Create World's Biggest Airline," *The Guardian*, September 17, 2010, www.guardian.co.uk on March 22, 2011; Susanna Ray, "AMR May Seek Alliances as Mergers Erase Lead in Size," *Bloomberg Businessweek*, May 3, 2010, www.businessweek.com on March 22, 2011; Robert Herbst, "Airlines Will Report Big Profits for 2010," *Seeking Alpha*, January 17, 2011, http://seekingalpha.com on March 22, 2011.

Chapter 16: Management at Work

Cultivating Innovation at IKEA

According to *BusinessWeek* magazine, IKEA "is the quintessential cult brand," and its customers belong to "a like-minded cost/design/environmentally-sensitive global tribe." The founder of this global "cult" is a Swedish entrepreneur named Ingvar Kamprad, who started the company in his rural hometown in 1943, at the age of 17. Kamprad has always referred to his targeted customers as "the many," and at least from the late 1950s, his plan has been to bring affordable, well-designed furniture to this target market. "The many," then, is hardly a "mass" market: In reality, it's a profitable niche consisting primarily of consumers who want stylish furniture at a low cost. Its goal, says the company, is to offer "affordable solutions for better living," with "better living" referring to a range of well-designed furniture and furnishings and "affordable" referring to the price range of consumers who are starting up their own homes and/or expanding their families.

IKEA's marketing strategy depends on constant innovation, and the company's ability to innovate successfully depends in part on an organizational structure that encourages creativity and communication. In order to understand how it's all designed to work, however, we first need to break down the elements of "the IKEA way"—the factors which, *taken in combination*, have made the IKEA approach so successful. The *target market* that we've just described is the first of these factors, and we can identify four others in terms that any marketer would recognize:

- *Product.* With nearly 12,000 items, the IKEA product line is quite large, and because smaller products complement larger products, customers can experiment with ensembles that satisfy their own needs and tastes while calculating total costs as they proceed through the store or catalog. The company didn't pay much attention to product design until the early 1990s, but today, admits one expert, "you will always find some pieces which are good designs and very reasonable in pricing." IKEA also wants consumers—especially Americans—to stop thinking of furniture as durable goods. Older Americans, says one company marketing manager, "keep a sofa longer than a car" because they believe that it's going to be the long-term "icon of the living room." IKEA wants to appeal to the willingness of younger consumers to experiment with changes, and its price structure makes it possible for them to do it.

- *Price.* "Designing beautiful-but-expensive products is easy," says one IKEA executive. "Designing beautiful products that are inexpensive and functional is a huge challenge." Nevertheless, IKEA prices are typically from 20 percent to 50 percent below those of stores selling fully assembled furniture. "When we decide about a product, we always start with the price," reports one product developer, and after starting with an original competitive price, IKEA then proceeds to drive it even lower. The company maintains price leadership not only by purchasing in large quantities but by constantly looking for cheaper suppliers; nearly 50 percent of IKEA's outsourcing partners are located in developing economies.

- *Distribution.* In addition to a global network of thousands of manufacturers and nearly 1,400 suppliers in

54 countries, IKEA maintains a system of 27 distribution centers (which ship products to stores) and 11 customer-distribution centers (which ship goods to consumers) in 16 countries. Its stores, too, are an important facet of IKEA's distribution strategy. A key innovation is the way they're laid out. Unlike the traditional furniture outlet, which directs customers to separate sections to view multiple versions of one product (e.g., beds) or one room (e.g., bedrooms), IKEA stores are laid out around a wide one-way path—the "natural path," according to the company—that carries customers directly from one section to the next. The "natural path" not only exposes them to the whole range of IKEA offerings but also encourages them to extend their in-store visits.

- *Promotion.* Promotion at IKEA revolves around the near-legendary annual catalog, a 300-page compendium of color photos and blurbs for about 12,000 products. Boasting a circulation of 175 million copies worldwide, the catalog covers the whole range of the company's new products, focuses on ideas for innovations in the customer's home, and relies on word-of-mouth publicity among the faithful. Not surprisingly, IKEA stores are arranged to accomplish essentially the same goals. Like the IKEA catalog, for example, they're designed to encourage repeat visits by showcasing the company's regular turnover in new products (about one-third per year).

The IKEA store is also the company's most obvious and most important process innovation. Averaging around 300,000 square feet, most boxlike blue-and-yellow stores feature both the series of showrooms arranged along the "natural path" and an in-store self-serve warehouse. After choosing items from the Showroom, customers collect trolleys for transporting their purchases and pass into the Market Hall, where they can pick up smaller items, such as linen, lighting, glassware, and rugs. Next along the path is the Self Serve Warehouse,

where they collect their furniture purchases in flat-pack form and then proceed to the rows of cashier's stations to pay for everything. Once they've paid for their purchases, customers can arrange for delivery or roll them to the loading dock, pack them in or on their vehicles, and take them home.

As important as process innovation has been to the company's success, the IKEA engine is powered by the introduction of new products and a constant stream of product innovations. Finding new products from outside sources, however, isn't the same thing as innovating within the company. At IKEA, innovation from within signals the company's commitment not only to respond to changes in the needs of customers all around the world, but to maintain a global brand identity and to convey an ongoing sense of excitement among the brand-loyal faithful.

At any given time, about 50 designers at the company's Swedish workshop are busy creating five to ten new products, but designers aren't the only people in the organization who are responsible for innovative ideas. "[E]veryone contributes," says Bill Agee, head of marketing at IKEA U.S. "Whoever you are within the IKEA organization, you're expected to contribute your ideas—your new ideas, your old ideas or whatever it may be—and every idea is welcome." The concept works, explains Agee, because "we're a very process-oriented company. . . . [W]e have three basic processes: creating, communicating, and selling the home-furnishings offer. Each of these processes," he adds, "has a matrix structure": Working as members of what amounts to a companywide team, designers design products, marketers like Agee communicate the product message, and "coworkers" in the company's warehouses and stores deliver the product to the customer. "Our independence," Agee thinks, "has a lot to do with our innovation because we don't know any better. . . . We feel that we are, to a certain extent, operating outside of standard operating procedures."

Case Questions

1. You're an IKEA store manager, and corporate headquarters has instructed you to change the layout of your store. The change must be "dramatic," but the details are up to you. Wanting to make the most of the opportunity, you intend to manage the project as *planned change.* What steps will you take to ensure that you'll be successful?

2. There's an IKEA TV ad that features a discarded lamp, forsaken on a rainy night in some American city. A man looks at the camera and says in a sympathetic Swedish accent, "Many of you feel bad for this lamp," and then, after a well-timed pause, "That's because you're crazy." What's the message of the commercial?

3. One IKEA executive says that the current global economic situation has "pushed innovation" at the company. In fact, he says, "This is a great time to be more innovative." Explain what he means.

4. Would you want to manage an IKEA store? Why or why not?

Case References

Zachary Lewis, "IKEA Has Inspired a Cult of Devoted Fans," *NJ.com*, May 14, 2008, www.nj.com on March 30, 2011; Kerry Capell, "Understanding IKEA: How the Swedish Company Turned into a Global Obsession," *BusinessWeek*, November 8, 2005, www.msnbc.msn.com on March 30, 2011; Colin White, "Strategic Management: The IKEA Way," *Business Innovation*, December 22, 2008, www.unitedbit.com on March 23, 2009; "Key of IKEA," *Hub*, January 1, 2009, www.hubmagazine.com on March 30, 2011; IKEA, "IKEA History: How It All Began," "The IKEA Concept," "Facts & Figures," 2010–2011, www.ikea.com on March 30, 2011; "Bill Agee: IKEA, the Recession and Innovation," *Hub*, January 9, 2009, www.ikeafans.com on March 30, 2010.

Chapter 17: Management at Work

The Temptations of Temping

Back in 2002, New Yorker Diana Bloom logged on to Craigslist, an online network that posts free classified ads, and offered her services as a tutor, editor, and translator. She's been making a living on the short-term jobs that come her way from the website ever since. A former English professor who couldn't find secure long-term employment, Bloom works out of her home in order to take care of a young son. Temp work is also appealing, she says, because "I'm not very outgoing, and getting my foot in the door to companies would have been hard."

Craigslist works in the other direction, too, with employers posting openings for jobs both permanent and temporary. Another New Yorker, Simone Sneed, scours the Craigslist "Gigs" section for jobs that last for perhaps a day, often for just a few hours. Whether as a backup singer or a grants writer, she's turned the strategy of patching together "gigs" into a convenient way to supplement the income from her full-time job. "I'll use the extra money to pay off my school loan," she says. "Every little bit helps."

In the current economic climate, unfortunately, overall job postings are down on Craigslist and everywhere else, except for short-term jobs—gigs that usually include no health benefits, sick days, or paid vacations. If you're employed short term or part time for economic reasons (probably because you got laid off), the Bureau of Labor Statistics (BLS) classifies you as "underemployed."

Naturally, most people who are "underemployed" are, by definition, "overqualified." In fact, they often have years of professional experience but are willing to take jobs that don't call for their levels of training or experience. Take the case of Gloria Christ. As national project manager for an information-technology company in the Chicago area, Christ used to coordinate the installation of WiFi hotspots all over the country. She has nearly 20 years of managerial experience, but today she's willing to put it to use as a temporary office manager. Of course, she'd like something with a little more long-term promise: "At this point in time," she says, "I think even if there was something that was temporary it could become full time later on. . . . Sometimes," she explains, "you can go in at a low level to interview just to get your foot in the door."

It may be small compensation (so to speak), but during the current recession, although many companies are reluctant to add costly permanent jobs, they are increasingly willing to open up temporary positions to tide them over. Often, of course, you'll have to take a job that isn't exactly what you've trained for or set your sights on, but as one employment-services manager observes, job seekers today "are more than willing to try new occupations—much more willing than they were even a year ago."

Interestingly, for a lot of people, the adjustment to current labor-market conditions isn't necessarily as traumatic as you might think. A recent survey conducted by the temporary-staffing agency Kelly Services found that as many as 26 percent of employed American adults regard themselves as "free agents" when it comes to the type of job that they're willing to take (up from 19 percent in 2006). Of all those polled, only 10 percent said that they're doing temporary work because they've been laid off from permanent jobs; 90 percent said that they're doing it because they like the variety and flexibility that temping affords them.

Kelly client Jaime Gacharna's first assignment was packaging products for a light-industrial wholesaler—"putting doorknobs into little bags," he recalls. Since then, he's worked for eight different employers, working at a job for a few days, a few weeks, or a few months. He doesn't mind the constant adjustments because the variety in his work life compensates for the drawbacks. "If I want to try something out, and I like it," says Gacharna, "I can stay with [the company]. If I don't, I can always just call up Kelly and say I want something different."

In fact, temping offers several advantages. It can, for example, provide income during career transitions, and it's a good way to exercise a little control over the balance between your work and the rest of your life. In 1995, for example, when she was seven months pregnant with her first child, veteran retail manager Stacey Schick accepted a two-week data-entry job with the Orange County (New York) Association of Realtors. "I didn't know how to turn on a computer," she remembers, but "they needed bodies." Now the mother of two, Schick is still with the Association as its education coordinator. "I would never have considered it," she says, if a job in her field had come up, but the job she landed in has turned out to be a much better fit with her lifestyle: "It's afforded me the opportunity to have a family and be able to have time with them."

The path taken by Schick is called "temp-to-perm," and it offers employers several advantages as well. Companies that are hesitant to make commitments to untested employees can try before they buy—they get a chance to see employees in action before finalizing hiring decisions. Because there are no fees to pay when an employee goes from temp to perm, trying out temps is also cheaper than paying an agency outright to find a hire. The big savings, of course, come from benefits, which can amount to one-third of the total cost of compensating a permanent position.

And then there's the recession. While many employers are laying off full-time workers, many are also trying to compensate by turning over some of the work to temp staff. Ironically, of course, many of those who've been laid off are highly qualified, and as they hit the job market willing to accept lower-level positions, the ranks of job hunters are being joined by a substantial number of highly qualified (which is to say, overqualified) workers. "The quality of candidates," says Laura Long of Banner Personnel, a Chicago-area staffing agency, "is tremendous. . . . As an employer, you can get great employees for a great price."

As a matter of fact, if you're a U.S. employer, you've always been able to get temp workers at a relatively good price. As of December 2010, according to the BLS, the average cost of a full-time worker in private industry was $22.26 per hour in wages plus $9.75 in benefits, for a total of $32.01 in compensation. By contrast, the average wages for a temp were $12.14 and the average benefits were $3.42, for total compensation of $15.56. One of the results of this cost differential has been a long-term increase in the number of temp workers which, over the last 20 years, has far outstripped the increase in jobs occupied by full-time workers.

Case Questions

1. You're a senior manager at a growing business and you're ready to add employees. Your HR manager has recommended a temp-to-perm policy. You know the advantages of this approach, but what might be some of the disadvantages?
2. Assume that you're a prospective job seeker (which you may very well be). What do you personally see as the advantages and disadvantages of taking a temp-to-perm position? Under what circumstances are you most likely to take a temp-to-perm position?
3. What sort of challenges are likely to confront a manager who supervises a mix of temporary and permanent employees? In what ways might these challenges differ if the temporary workers have been hired on a temp-to-perm basis rather than on a strictly temporary basis?

Case References

"For Some, a Patchwork of Jobs Pays the Bills," *Boston.com*, March 27, 2009, www.boston.com on April 15, 2011; Kristin Kridel, "Overqualified Applying for Temporary Work," *Spokesman.com*, March 4, 2009, www.spokesman.com on April 15, 2011; Anne Fisher, "Be a Manager and a Temp?" *CNNMoney.com*, March 16, 2009, www.cmfassociates.com on April 15, 2011; Sital Patel, "Skill Level of Temp Workers Rises amid Recession," *Fox Business*, February 27, 2009, www.jobs-work-employment.com on April 15, 2011; U.S. Bureau of Labor Statistics (BLS), "Employer Costs for Employee Compensation," news release, December 2010, www.bls.gov on March 31, 2009; BLS, "Table 12. Private Industry, by Industry Group and Full-Time and Part-Time Status," news release, December 2010, www.bls.gov on April 15, 2011.

Chapter 18: Management at Work

Is Anybody in Control Here?

The media called it the "Miracle on the Hudson." On the wintry afternoon of January 15, 2009, just minutes after takeoff from New York's LaGuardia Airport, US Airways Flight 1549 struck a flock of birds. Both engines were knocked out, and pilot Chesley "Sully" Sullenberger had no choice but to land his 81-ton Airbus A320 in the frigid Hudson River on the west side of Manhattan. It was the first crash-landing of a major aircraft in the water in some 50 years, but all of the 155 people on board survived. "It was intense," said one passenger. "You've got to give it to the pilot." Fortunately, Sullenberger had 40 years of flying experience, and at least one other US Airways pilot wasn't all that surprised at his extraordinary feat. "He held his cool," said Rick Kurner, who'd flown with Sullenberger for more than 20 years.

As for Sullenberger, he remembered "the worst sickening, pit-of-your stomach, falling-through-the-floor feeling" that he'd ever experienced. For weeks after the crash, he suffered symptoms of posttraumatic stress, including sleeplessness and flashbacks, but acknowledged that his condition had improved after a month or two. No wonder Sullenberger experienced some repercussion from the stress, says Patrick Harten, the LaGuardia air traffic controller who was on the other end of the line when Sullenberger radioed his intention to put down in the river. "I thought it was his own death sentence," recalled Harten. "I believed at that moment I was going to be the last person to talk to anyone on that plane alive. . . . I felt like I'd been hit by a bus." For his own part, says Harten, "the trauma of working an airplane that crash-landed" didn't begin to subside until about a year later.

Interestingly, if Sullenberger, who was 57 at the time of the crash, had been an air traffic controller instead of a pilot, he would probably have been required to retire a year before

Flight 1549 took off. Both jobs, of course, are extremely stressful, and the Federal Aviation Administration (FAA) mandates retirement ages for both. Pilots, however, can stay on the job until they're 65, while controllers must in most cases call it quits at age 56. Why? Because being an air traffic controller, it seems, is *more* stressful than being a pilot.

At any given moment, there are about 5,000 airplanes in the skies over the United States. The National Air Traffic Controllers Association (NATCA) reports that, on an average day, controllers handle 87,000 flights. In a year, they manage 64 million takeoffs and landings. And that's just sheer volume of traffic. Needless to say, all that traffic is also very complex. "Air traffic control is like playing chess at high speed," says Pete Rogers, who helps manage 52,000 flights a year to and from (and over) Martha's Vineyard, Massachusetts. Melvin Davis, who's been directing air traffic in southern California for more than 20 years, agrees: "My daily routine," he reports, "is dealing with aircraft that have anywhere between two and four hundred people on board and are traveling at about 600 miles an hour."

In addition, not all aircraft are traveling at the same speed or at the same altitude, and very few of them are traveling at a steady perpendicular to the ground. Once they learn to "see traffic," according to New York controller Christopher Tucker, controllers "have to learn how to solve the conflicts, preferably in the simplest . . . manner. It can be as simple as stopping someone's climb/descent to pass below/above converging traffic or issuing speed assignments to ensure constant spacing." Often, of course, it's not that simple. For example, explains Tucker, "newer aircraft with highly efficient wings cannot descend quickly while going slow, so that has to be taken into account when setting up an intrail operation where arrivals must be descended as well as slowed down."

And then there's the weather. Controllers record weather data every hour and have to be constantly aware of changing conditions. "We have to make sure we don't launch somebody into a thunderstorm," says Rogers. Moreover, because storm systems often appear on radar with little or no notice,

controllers must also be able to make quick decisions. According to Tucker, "the ability to run through possible solutions and quickly choose the best one" is a necessary skill for any controller, and so is "being able to make a bad situation work after having made a poor decision."

At present, there are about 11,000 fully trained air traffic controllers in the United States—the lowest number in 17 years. The total number of positions is slated to increase by 13 percent between now and 2018, but that rate won't keep pace with the projected increase in the number of aircraft that will be in the skies—not to mention vying for air and runway space at the nation's airports. At lower-traffic airports, cost considerations already require controllers to work eight-hour shifts by themselves, performing the jobs of all tower positions, communicating with aircraft in the sky and on the ground, and coordinating the activities of perhaps three separate facilities.

"And so we have a rise in operational errors," both at regional and national airports, admits Melvin Davis. In 2007, for instance, there were 370 *runway incursions* at U.S. airports—incidents in which planes invaded one another's ground space—and according to the FAA's risk/severity matrix, the potential for catastrophic accident at that rate was "unacceptable." The next year, however, there were 951 such incidents, and the total rose to 1,009 in 2009. This alarming increase, charges Davis, can be traced to the kind of working conditions that have made air traffic control more stressful than ever, especially the policy of assigning controllers to long shifts during which many of them work alone. "It's a business decision," he says, arguing that the current situation at the nation's airports is

> clearly the result of a reduction in staffing, a decline in experience, and an increase in the use of employee overtime, which leads to increased fatigue. The result is a 300 percent to 400 percent increase in operational errors . . . which results in two bullet trains coming together at 600 miles an hour.

Case Questions

1. What about you? Do you think that you could handle the kind of stress that air traffic controllers face on the job? Why or why not?
2. In your opinion, which causes of work stress, or *organizational stressors*, are likely to be among the most common experienced by air traffic controllers? Explain your reasoning.
3. Controller Pete Rogers says that any gathering of air traffic controllers is "almost like a mini-convention of Type A personalities." Does this assessment surprise you or make sense to you? In what ways is it perhaps a good thing? A not-so-good thing?

4. "This business of people saying they 'thrive on stress'? It's nuts," says one eminent psychiatrist who goes so far as to say that such people are in danger of slipping into a pathological state. Nevertheless, some people say that they like getting into chaotic situations and putting them back in order. What about you? Are there times when you seem to be motivated and satisfied by circumstances that most people would call stressful? If your answer is yes, what kinds of circumstances are they, and why do you think you react the way you do? If your answer is no, what do you normally do when faced with such circumstances?

Case References

"'Miracle on the Hudson': All Safe in Jet Crash," *MSNBC.com*, January 15, 2009, www.msnbc.msn.com on April 14, 2011; Phil Derner Jr., "One Year after the 'Miracle on the Hudson,' an Exclusive Interview with Air Traffic Controller Patrick Harten," *NYCAviation.com*, January 18, 2010, http://nycaviation.com on April 14, 2011; Steve Myrick, "Air Traffic Control—'Chess at High Speed,'" *Martha's Vineyard Times*, December 24, 2009, www.mvtimes.com on April 14, 2011; Alex Altman and Tiffany Sharples, "Air Traffic Controller Sounds Alarm," *Time*, April 26, 2008, www.time.com on April 14, 2011; Christopher Tucker, "I Am an Air Traffic Controller," *Daily Speculations*, March 15, 2009, www.dailyspeculations.com on April 14, 2011; Mary Carmichael, "Who Says Stress Is Bad for You?" *Newsweek*, February 14, 2009, www.newsweek.com on April 14, 2011.

Chapter 19: Management at Work

The Law of Diminishing Motivation

The enrollment of women in U.S. law schools took off after 1970, and women have been graduating at the same rate as men for more than 25 years. Today, however, the census of American law firms still counts relatively few women *partners*—typically, the veteran lawyers who are joint owners and directors. Currently, for example, 32.4 percent of all lawyers are women, yet only 19.2 percent of law-firm partners are women. Most female lawyers are *associates*—paid employees with the prospect of becoming partners. Moreover, the further up the law-firm ladder you look, the greater the disparity. According to the National Association of Women Lawyers, 92 percent of all managing partners (partners who run the business end of a firm) are men; men occupy 85 percent of the seats on the governing committees that control a firm's policies, and they hold 84 percent of all equity partnerships (which come with ownership and profit sharing). At this rate, women will achieve parity with their male colleagues in approximately 2088.

So what happens between the time women get job offers and the time firms hand out partnerships and promotions? Bettina B. Plevan, an employment-law specialist and partner in the Manhattan firm of Proskauer Rose, believes that, somewhere along the way, female lawyers lose the kind of motivation necessary to get ahead in a law office. "You have a given population of people," she observes, "who were significantly motivated to go through law school with a certain career goal in mind. What de-motivates them," she asks, "to want to continue working in the law?"

The problem, says Karen M. Lockwood, a partner in the Washington, D.C., firm Howrey, is neither discrimination nor lack of opportunity. "Law firms," she says, "are way beyond discrimination. Problems with advancement and retention are grounded in biases, not discrimination." In part, these biases issue from institutional inertia. Lauren Stiller Rikleen, a partner in the Worcester, Massachusetts, firm of Bowditch & Dewey, points out that most law firms are "running on an institutional model that's about 200 years old." And most of them, she adds, "do a horrible job of managing their personnel, in terms of training them and communicating with them." Such problems, of course, affect men as well as women, but because of lingering preconceptions about women's attitudes, values, and goals, women bear the brunt of the workplace burden. In practical terms, they face less adequate mentoring, poorer networking opportunities, lower-grade case assignments, and unequal access to positions of committee control.

To all of these barriers to success Lockwood adds the effect of what she calls the "maternal wall": Male partners, she says, assume that women who return to the firm after having children will be less willing to work hard and less capable of dedicating themselves to their jobs. As a result, men get the choice assignments and senior positions. Jane DiRenzo Pigott, a onetime law-firm partner who now owns a consultancy firm, agrees but thinks the issues run deeper than maternity leave. "People explain it simply as the fact that women have children," she explains,

> but so many other factors play into it. Women self-promote in a different way than men, and because women don't get their success acknowledged in the same way as men who more aggressively self-promote, it creates a high level of professional dissatisfaction for women. Saying these two words "I want" is not something women are used to doing. They're not saying, "I want the top bonus" or "I want that position.". . . [W]omen need to learn how to be comfortable saying "I want" and how to say it effectively.

The fact remains that, according to a study of "Women in Law" conducted by Catalyst, a New York research firm, 1 in 8 female lawyers work only part time, compared to just 1 in 50 males. Why? According to Plevan, most female attorneys would prefer to work and raise children at the same time but find that they can't do both effectively. "I organized my personal life so I was able to move toward my goals," she says, but admits that it helped to have a gainfully employed spouse (also a lawyer), dual incomes sufficient to hire household help, and nearby relatives to pick up the slack in home-life responsibilities. In most cases, of course, although dual incomes are an advantage to a household, it's difficult for either spouse to devote time to child rearing when they're both working. The Catalyst study shows that 44 percent of male lawyers have spouses who are employed full time—and are thus unavailable for such household duties as attending to children. Among women, nearly twice as many—84 percent—have spouses with full-time jobs.

Like firms in many other industries, law firms have experimented with such options as flexible scheduling and parental leave. More and more, however, they report that such measures have not been as effective as they'd hoped. Says

Edith R. Matthai, founder with her husband of the Los Angeles firm Robie & Matthai: "We're very accommodating with leaves and flexible schedules, and even with that we still lose women. . . . [The] pressures on women from spouses, family, peers, schools, and others is huge," she adds. The situation has improved over the last 30 years, but "we have a long way to go. . . . I think the real solution is a reassessment of the role that women play in the family. One thing we need is a sense of shared responsibilities for the household and, most importantly, shared responsibilities for taking care of the kids."

Case Questions

1. Among the various approaches to enhancing workplace satisfaction and productivity discussed in Chapter 19, which ones might you take under the circumstances described in the case? Why are some of the other approaches less likely to be effective (or even relevant)?
2. You're the managing partner in a law firm with 55 male associates and 45 female associates, and you agree with the argument that women lawyers need to "self-promote" more effectively. Which approach to motivation would you apply in order to encourage female associates in your firm to "self-promote" more actively? Explain your choice of approach.

3. What about your own values when it comes to balancing your home and work life? Assume that you're about to graduate from law school and about to get married to a fiancé(e) who's also about to graduate from law school. When you sit down with your future husband/wife to discuss your plans for married life ever after, what do you want to do about raising a family? What kind of adjustments will you propose if it turns out that your fiancé(e)'s ideas on the matter are more or less the opposite of your own? Be sure to consider such factors as the debt you've racked up while in law school and the standard of living that you'd like to achieve.

Case References

Patricia Gillette, "Lack of Self-Promotion Hurts Women in Large Firms," *Law.com*, July 9, 2009, http://amlawdaily.typepad.com on April 18, 2011; Lizz O'Donnell, "Women in Law Firms: Stuck in the Middle," *The Glass Hammer*, July 23, 2009, www.theglasshammer.com on April 18, 2011; Timothy L. O'Brien, "Why Do So Few Women Reach the Top of Big Law Firms?" *New York Times*, March 19, 2006, www.nytimes.com on April 18, 2011; Catalyst, "Women in Law," May 3, 2010, www.catalyst.org on April 18, 2011; Lynne Marek, "Women Lawyers Find Their Own Paths as Law Firms Struggle to Keep Them," *Law.com*, June 25, 2007, www.law.com on April 18, 2011.

Chapter 20: Management at Work

Inside Leadership at Intel

Intel is the largest maker of semiconductor chips in the world. It dominates its industry, producing twice as many chips as its nearest competitor and selling almost $100 million worth of them every day. For over 40 years now, one of the company's most valuable resources has been its leadership. Intel has had five CEOs since it was founded in 1969, and although each has naturally brought different strengths and taken different approaches to the job, each has contributed to Intel's remarkable record of continuous success.

Bob Noyce, a physicist with an aptitude for technology, started Intel in 1969 with chemist-physicist Gordon Moore and served as its CEO until 1975. As a leader, Noyce was known as a loyal and charismatic risk taker who had a knack for knowing when his people knew what they were doing: He was general

manager at Fairchild Semiconductor when its scientists invented the integrated chip in 1959, and as head of Intel, he oversaw the development of the microprocessor by researcher Ted Hoff in the late 1960s. "The people that are supervising [a project]," he once said, "are more dependent on their ability to judge people than they are dependent on their ability to judge the work that's going on." Known affectionately as the "Mayor of Silicon Valley," Noyce also epitomized the image of the casual California high-tech executive. He had no use for corporate jets, gaudy offices, or even reserved parking spaces and preferred a relaxed working environment in which bright employees were given the freedom to do what they were hired to do. Under his leadership, Intel developed a culture that emphasized technical proficiency over fiscal performance.

When Noyce stepped down in 1975, Gordon Moore took over as CEO and held the post until 1987, when he became chairman of the board. Back in 1965, Moore had set forth the now classic Moore's Law—the observation that the number of transistors on a microchip will double every two years—and when the new company was founded, he naturally assumed the role of chief technology innovator. From the start, Intel scientists were committed to proving the validity of Moore's Law, and they've always been fairly successful at maintaining the pace, delivering next-generation silicon technology and new processor architecture on an almost yearly basis. Today, Moore's Law is institutionalized as Intel's "tick-tock model," which is designed to put technology innovation on a reliable and predictable timetable.

Moore's leadership style was quite similar to Noyce's but—if possible—even more committed to hands-off management and the primacy of technology. According to his successor, Andy Grove, "Gordon is rational, technically based, [and] minimalist in terms of intervention. When he has something to say, it's usually worth listening to." Much of what Gordon had to say, he said to Grove, whom he promoted to president in 1979 and who actually ran the company along with Moore until the latter's retirement. "Much of [my success] is due to standing on his shoulders," says Grove, who has always extolled the value of the mentoring relationship. "If he hadn't been there," Grove admits, "I would have been a happy, productive engineer . . . but I don't think I would have ended up running the company."

At the same time, however, Grove acknowledges the conspicuous differences in leadership styles—he himself is decisive and sometimes arrogant—and makes it clear that he thinks his was the style the company needed when he took over as CEO in 1987. He likes to refer to management theorist Peter Drucker's idea that CEOs can be identified by one of three chief roles: According to Grove, Noyce was Intel's public face or "front man" and Moore its "thought man"; he himself is a "man of action." "If I had relied on [Gordon's] leadership style," he says, "I would have been in deep trouble because [Gordon was] not an activist. My role was to be exactly the opposite [of Gordon]."

In 1985, Grove announced that Intel was staking its future on a product which, ironically, it had itself introduced back in 1971—the microprocessor, which had been biding its time in such applications as timing traffic lights. When IBM selected the Intel processor for its PC line, the company was set to begin an extremely profitable ten-year run. In 1992, profits topped $1 billion for the first time, and for Grove's 11-year tenure as CEO, Intel grew at a compounded annual rate of 30 percent. By the time he stepped down in 1998, Grove had overseen an increase in Intel's market capitalization from $18 billion to $197 billion—a gain of 4,500 percent.

When Craig Barrett succeeded Grove as CEO, Intel was the most valuable company in the world. A specialist in materials science, Barrett joined Intel in 1974 as a technology development manager, and in successive positions at the VP level, he headed the company's manufacturing operations. In the 1980s, as Intel faced increasingly stiff competition from Japanese chipmakers, Barrett developed a manufacturing strategy called "copy exactly," which called for the perfection of engineering processes at a single plant before rolling out the same method in another facility. The strategy allowed Intel to avoid costly flaws in the production process. "It wasn't until we got the Japanese competition in the mid-1980s," Barrett recalls, that "we figured out how to combine technology with manufacturing and exist as a manufacturing company, not just a technology company." When he retired as chairman in January 2009, his successor as CEO, Paul Otellini, remarked that Barrett's "legacy spans the creation of the best semiconductor manufacturing machine in the world."

How had Barrett risen through the ranks to become CEO? "Just luck," he quips, though he's quick to add that "we were able to turn manufacturing around. That caught the eye of Andy [Grove] and Gordon Moore." As chief operating officer from 1993 and the company's fourth president from 1997, Barrett had also developed a working relationship with Grove, who remained with the company as chairman and senior advisor, much like the one that Grove had enjoyed earlier with Gordon Moore. And like Grove, Barrett credits the difference in leadership styles as a critical factor in his success in the top spot: "Andy and I," says Barrett, "are very different in style. . . . Andy has a pretty instantaneous opinion. . . . I'm more of a classic engineer and a data-driven guy. Faced with a problem, I wait for the data and analyze the problem. Andy probably gets frustrated with that approach because he wants to take action. That drove me to do my part of the equation a bit faster. It was very complementary."

Barrett turned over the CEO job to Paul Otellini in 2005. With a background in finance, Otellini is the first nonengineer to lead Intel, but he's had a lot of experience in computer hardware: From 1993 to 1996, as general manager of the Peripheral Components Operation and then of the Intel Architecture Group, he was responsible for chipset operations, microprocessor and chipset business strategies, and giving technical advice to Andy Grove. He served as COO from 2002 to May 2005, when he became CEO. He announced that he would "restructure, repurpose, and resize" the company and has since moved to eliminate redundant jobs, to simplify operations by reducing the total number of products, and to sell off non-core and unprofitable businesses. He's also initiated strategies designed to bring new products to market more quickly.

Case Questions

1. What roles have referent power and expert power played in leadership at Intel? Which Intel CEOs seem to have inclined toward job-centered leader behavior? Toward employee-centered leader behavior? Toward initiation-structure behavior? Toward consideration behavior?

2. Apply the *path–goal theory of leadership* to Intel's succession of CEOs: Which kind of leader behavior best applies to each CEO—*directive, supportive, participative, achievement-oriented*?

3. Intel appears to rely heavily on mentoring and long-term leadership development from within. In your opinion, what are the pros and cons of such an approach? Intel also seems to have thrived on a pattern of alternating leadership styles. What are the pros and cons of this approach?

4. Of the five profiled Intel CEOs, whose leadership style most closely resembles your own? Which of the five profiled CEOs would you most like to work for? Which would you least like to work for?

Case References

Leslie Berlin, *The Man Behind the Microchip: Robert Noyce and the Invention of Silicon Valley* (New York: Oxford University Press, 2005), http://books.google.com on April 24, 2011; Cliff Edwards, "Inside Intel," *BusinessWeek*, January 9, 2006, www.businessweek.com on April 24, 2011; Intel Corp., "Corporate Timeline: Our History of Innovation," "Moore's Law," "Intel's Tick-Tock Model," 2011, www.intel.com on April 24, 2011; Richard S. Tedlow, "The Education of Andy Grove," *Fortune*, December 12, 2005, http:// money.cnn.com on April 24, 2011; Dean Takahashi, "Exit Interview: Retiring Intel Chairman Craig Barrett on the Industry's Unfinished Business," *VentureBeat*, May 8, 2009, http://venturebeat.com on April 24, 2011; Cliff Edwards, "Craig Barrett's Mixed Record at Intel," *BusinessWeek*, January 23, 2009, www.businessweek.com on April 24, 2011; Adam Lashinsky, "Is This the Right Man for Intel?" *Fortune*, April 18, 2005, http://money.cnn.com on April 24, 2011.

Chapter 21: Management at Work

¿Qué Pasa in the Ad Agency?

- *A recent Toyota television ad:* A father is explaining Toyota's hybrid engine to his son. "[The car] runs on gas and electricity," he says. "Mira. Mira aquí. [Look. Look here.] It uses both." The son replies, "Like you, with English and Spanish." "Sí," replies the father.

As the makeup of U.S. society changes, organizations have realized that they need to change the ways in which they communicate with diverse customer bases. It might come as something of a surprise, but this Toyota TV spot reflects a virtually revolutionary change in the way American companies address potential buyers from different cultures. Once, for example, they assumed that Hispanics living in the United States were immigrants, spoke no English, and clung to old-world values. Today, however, they're well aware of the fact that over half of the country's 50 million Hispanics were born in this country. Like the father and son in Toyota's depiction of Hispanic life, most Spanish speakers know English and mix elements not only of both languages but of both U.S. and Latino culture. "This group is not about nostalgia for the home country," says Jaime Fortuño, managing partner of Azafrán, a New York–based ad agency.

There was also a time when advertisers relied on mainstream ads—ads aimed at the center of the market where they expected to find the "typical" consumer. But as the purchasing power of minorities has increased, companies have put more energy into developing targeted ads—ads aimed at specific groups of consumers and often delivered through language-targeted media. Today, for example, a corporation thinks nothing of budgeting $100 million a year for Hispanic-themed ads. Since 2004, about one-third of ads targeted to Hispanics have been presented in Spanish, and that proportion is growing—for good reason. The buying power of Hispanics grew from $490 billion in 2000 to $1 trillion in 2010—a rate of 108 percent over the decade (compared to a 49 percent rate for the majority market). By 2015, Hispanic buying power will hit $1.5 trillion and will account for 11 percent of the national total.

Although advertising slumped across the board in 2008 and 2009, the decline in Spanish-language media was more moderate than in the industry as a whole. And although Spanish-language advertising in 2009 was down from in 2008, the Association of Hispanic Advertising Agencies (AHAA) reports a rebound in 2010, especially among its "best-in-class" Spanish-language advertisers—those that allocate more than 11.8 percent of their ad budgets to Hispanic audiences. "Our 2009 report," says AHAA chair Gisela Girard, "revealed that many corporations 'don't get it,' [but] our 2010 . . . findings indicate that it's the current best-in-class companies that are spending more in the Hispanic market in an effort to turn around those businesses."

- *An ad for Southwest Airlines:* A virile young Hispanic rollerblades up to a parked car to admire his image in the tinted window. The window unexpectedly rolls down to reveal two men inside the car who are also admiring him. "Want to get away?" reads the punchline, which is followed by a low airfare price.

"In advertising," observes Juan Pablo Oubiña, art director at Grupo Gallegos, an L.A.-area agency, "it's not easy to be different. It takes ten times as much work." And getting the language right isn't really the hardest part of making Spanish-language ads. Like this Southwest ad from the Hispanic-owned agency Dieste Harmel & Partners, many of the latest-vintage Spanish-language ads have succeeded in appealing to Hispanic audiences by playing with and against stereotypes, but as one Hispanic marketing consultant observes, it's a tricky balancing act. "Not only are Americans comfortable with positive stereotypes as a means to be politically correct," says Jennifer Woodard, "but so are many Hispanics." The problem of stereotyping, she reminds us, is usually twofold: Advertisers tend to rely on stereotypes because they assume that they're somehow reflective of the mainstream, and the consumers being stereotyped tend to settle for stereotypes because they dominate the images of themselves that are available to them in the media.

- *An ad for Fox Sports Net:* Returning home from a shopping trip, a Hispanic woman detects an unpleasant odor in the house. The camera pursues her as she follows her nose from room to room until she reaches the living room, where she realizes that her husband is so thoroughly immersed in a televised soccer game that he's been watching through the open door of a nearby toilet.

This ad—a Grupo Gallegos creation—does a good job of playing *with and against* stereotypes because it bounces off the stereotype of the soccer-obsessed Latino in what Woodard describes as "a great example of taking a slice of life from a husband and wife, no matter the culture, and pushing the ad into entertainment." Contrast this ad, however, with the far more common appropriation of the same stereotype in TV advertising aimed at Hispanics. "[W]atch a few hours," suggests agency executive Tommy Thompson, ". . . and count how many soccer-themed spots you see. And I'm not talking about World Cup season or during the airing of soccer matches where contextually it makes sense. It almost seems that soccer is the only way to connect with [Hispanic viewers]. What does soccer have to do with life insurance, for example? Are there really no other insights as relates to Hispanics' need for life insurance that can be communicated without soccer?"

Thompson, founder and president of Dallas-based iNSPIRE!, argues that advertisers should focus on "what makes the target [market] tick as it relates to [a] particular brand or category." It's advice that Gallegos put to good use in an ad for Energizer batteries. Gallegos was originally given the task of making the brand "iconic" for Hispanic consumers—giving it immediately familiar symbolic value so that Spanish speakers would think of perpetual motion and say *"como el conejito Energizer"* the same way that English speakers think of perpetual motion and say "like the Energizer bunny." At Grupo Gallegos, however, brainstorming on a new account always starts with "Okay, *aquí está el problema que tenemos* when we really start looking at the brand," and the Gallegos team realized early on that most Hispanics don't associate batteries with perpetual motion (or anything else): For them, a battery is a battery. So Gallegos came up with an ad in which a Mexican man walks down the street and shares his realization that he's immortal—whereupon a two-story commercial sign falls on his head. Among other things, he observes, being immortal means that you need a very long-lasting battery for your camera.

Case Questions

1. You're assistant director of marketing for a maker of upscale furniture, and your company is preparing to enter new markets in California and the Southwest. Entering new markets, especially one of this size, is expensive, and your boss has decided to forgo Spanish-language advertising as part of the firm's market-entry strategy. You're inclined to disagree. What might you say to your boss to change her mind?

2. You're a top manager in a large factory whose workforce is approximately 40 percent Hispanic. Business is down because of the recession, and you've learned that there's a rumor about layoffs circulating in the grapevine. In particular, a lot of Hispanic-speaking employees seem to think that they'll be laid off first. How should you deal with the rumor?

3. Arnold Schwarzenegger, the Austrian-born ex-governor of California, which is home to 13.6 million Hispanics, advised Latino immigrants that if they wanted to learn English more quickly, "You've got to turn off Spanish[-language] television. . . . I know that when I came to this country, I very rarely spoke German to anyone." Do you agree with Schwarzenegger's advice to immigrants on learning English in the United States? Why or why not?

Case References

Cynthia Gorney, "How Do You Say 'Got Milk' en Español?" *New York Times*, September 23, 2007, www.nytimes.com on April 25, 2011; Sam Fahmy, "Despite Recession, Hispanic and Asian Buying Power Expected to Surge in U.S., According to Annual UGA Selig Center Multicultural Economy Study," University of Georgia, Terry College of Business, November 4, 2010, www.terry.uga.edu on April 25, 2011; Aimee Valentine, "The State of Spanish Language Media Industries: A Summary of Spanish Language Advertising 2010," *The State of Spanish Language Media: 2010 Annual Report* (The Center for Spanish Language Media, University of North Texas), January 2011, www.spanishmedia.unt.edu on April 25, 2011; Mark Maier, "Breaking Down Hispanic Stereotypes," Luce Performance Group, January 11, 2009, www.luceperformancegroup.com on April 25, 2011; Tommy Thompson, "The Problem with 'Hispanic Insights,' " *Advertising Age*, August 14, 2008, http://adage.com on April 25, 2011.

Chapter 22: Management at Work

Tracking Carbon Footprints Across Scientific Borders

If you're one of the world's 700 million richest people, you're probably a "high emitter" living a "carbon-intensive" lifestyle (at least statistically speaking). In plain English, because your lifestyle probably includes air travel, the use of a car, and a house to heat and cool, you're probably responsible for releasing more than your share of CO_2—carbon dioxide—into the earth's atmosphere.

"We estimate that . . . half the world's emissions come from just 700 million people," explains Shoibal Chakravarty, lead author of a 2009 study conducted by researchers at Princeton University. "It's mischievous," admits coauthor Robert Socolow, "but it's meant to be a logjam-breaking concept," and the proposals for cutting CO_2 emissions offered by the Princeton team have been widely praised for the fairness that they inject into a debate that's been stalemated for nearly 20 years.

The research team's report, entitled "Sharing Global CO_2 Emission Reductions among One Billion High Emitters," appeared in the July 2009 *Proceedings of the National Academy of Sciences* under the names of six coauthors. Shoibal Chakravarty, a physicist specializing in CO_2 emissions, is a research associate at the Princeton Environmental Institute (PEI), an interdisciplinary center for environmental research and education. Also associated with PEI is Massimo Tavoni, an economist who studies international policies on climate change. Stephen Pacala, who's the director of PEI, is a professor of ecology and evolutionary biology who focuses on the interactions of climate and the global biosphere. Robert Socolow, a professor of mechanical and aerospace engineering, studies global carbon management. Ananth Chikkatur, of Harvard's Belfer Center for Science and International Affairs, is a physicist who specializes in energy policy and technology innovation. Heleen de Coninck, a chemist, works on international climate policy and technology at the Energy Research Centre of the Netherlands.

Needless to say, the carbon footprint team was a diverse group in terms of academic discipline (not to mention nationality). Its innovative approach to the problem of CO_2 emissions—one

which shows that it's possible to cut emissions and reduce poverty at the same time—resulted from an approach to high-level scientific problem solving that's typically called *interdisciplinary* or *multidisciplinary research*. The global footprint study, says Pacala, "represents a collaboration among young people from disparate disciplines—physics, economics, political science. . . . The team," he stresses, "worked together to formulate a novel approach to a longstanding and intractable problem," and its interdisciplinary approach to that problem reflects the prevailing model for the study of today's most complex and daunting issues, such as AIDS, terrorism, and global climate change.

To determine the extent to which team-based research has supplanted individual research among academics, a group at Northwestern University examined nearly 20 million papers published over a period of five decades. They found that

> teams increasingly dominate solo authors in the production of knowledge. Research is increasingly done in teams across virtually all fields. Teams typically produce more highly cited research than individuals do, and this advantage is increasing over time. Teams now also produce the exceptionally high-impact research, even where that distinction was once the domain of solo authors.

Not surprisingly, the shift from the individual to the team-based model of research has been most significant in the sciences, where there's been, says the Northwestern study, "a substantial shift toward collective research." One reason for the shift, suggest the authors, may be "the increasing capital intensity of research" in laboratory sciences, where the growth of collaboration has been particularly striking. The increasing tendency toward specialization may be another reason. As knowledge grows in a discipline, scientists tend to devote themselves to specialty areas, the discipline itself becomes fragmented into "finer divisions of labor," and studies of larger issues in the discipline thus require greater collaboration.

And what about collaboration that extends beyond the confines of academia? As it happens, Robert Socolow and Stephen

Pacala, in addition to working on the carbon footprint team, are codirectors of the Carbon Mitigation Initiative (CMI), a partnership among Princeton, Ford, and BP, the world's third-largest oil company. BP picks up 75 percent of the tab for research whose goal, according to CMI's mission statement, is "a compelling and sustainable solution of the carbon and climate change problem." CMI seeks "a novel synergy across fundamental science, technological development, and business principles that accelerates the pace of discovery," and collaboration is essential to its work because it crosses the borders between scientific, technological, and business interests.

It's also crucial because CMI's research is geared toward what Socolow calls a "whole system" approach to the problem of reducing carbon emissions. "If BP takes a whole system view of the problem," explains Socolow, "and as a

supplier pays attention to the use of its products and finds ways of improving their efficiency during the use phase, that may be the most important thing this company can do over the next 10 years to save carbon." A whole system approach, for example, may include research into a process called CCS, for *carbon capture and storage*, which involves capturing CO_2 emissions from a major source, such as a power plant, and storing it somewhere away from the atmosphere, perhaps in a deep geological formation, such as an oil field or a seam of coal. Accordingly, CMI is divided into research groups, including the Capture Group, which works on technologies for capturing emissions from fossil fuels, and the Storage Group, which investigates the potential risks of injecting CO_2 underground. Working through CMI, BP has been able to launch a CCS trial at a gas-development facility in Algeria.

Case Questions

1. In what sense was the carbon footprint team a *task group*? As a task group, in what ways was it a *team*? As a team, in what ways was it a *virtual team*?
2. Consider both the carbon footprint team and the Carbon Mitigation Initiative (CMI). In what ways must such groups work to achieve *cohesiveness*? What factors are likely to make this effort difficult?
3. What's your experience with teamwork? Have you ever undertaken a solo project which, in retrospect, would

have benefited from a team-based approach? If you've ever been part of a team, either permanent or formed to tackle a specific set of problems, explain why, in your opinion, it succeeded (or failed) at its appointed task(s).
4. Some researchers are wary about collaborations between academic and industry organizations, such as CMI. Why do you suppose this is so? What potential problems do you see? How can they best be avoided?

Case References

Douglas Fischer, "Solving the Climate Dilemma One Billion Emitters at a Time," *Daily Climate*, July 6, 2009, www.thedailygreen.org on April 30, 2011; Kitta McPherson, "New Princeton Method May Help Allocate Carbon Emissions Responsibility among Nations," *News at Princeton*, July 6, 2009, www.princeton.edu on April 30, 2011; Shoibal Chakravarty et al., "Sharing Global CO_2 Emission Reductions among One Billion High Emitters,"

Proceedings of the National Academy of Sciences, Vol. 106 (July 2009), www.pnas.org on April 30, 2011; Stefan Wuchty et al., "The Increasing Dominance of Teams in Production of Knowledge," *Sciencexpress*, April 12, 2009, www.kellogg.northwestern.edu on April 30, 2011; Carbon Mitigation Initiative, "About the Carbon Mitigation Initiative," Princeton University, February 24, 2011, http://cmi.princeton.edu on April 30, 2011.

You Make the Call

CHAPTER 1: YOU MAKE THE CALL What Reed Hastings Has to Say for Himself

1. Which of Reed Hastings' *managerial roles* are most prominent in the case? Rank the roles discussed in the text—*interpersonal, informational,* and *decisional*—according to their importance in the case and explain your ranking. Do the same thing in considering Hastings' *managerial skills*. Which of his roles and skills will he probably need to rely on most because of the events of 2011?

2. Consider the Hastings quote at the beginning of the case—"Don't be afraid to change the model." What sort of "model" is Hastings talking about? Which Netflix models are described in the case? What does this attitude toward "the model" have to do with Hastings and Netflix as "disruptive innovators"? Can you think of any other businesses and business leaders who've successfully practiced *disruptive innovation*?

3. When asked to explain how he "botched" the changes announced by Netflix in 2011, Hastings said:

   Over the last couple of years . . . we simply moved too quickly, and that's where you get those missed execution details. . . . We need to take a few deep breaths

   and not move quite as quickly. But we also don't want to overcorrect and start moving stodgily.

   What did he mean? In what ways did Hastings' performance of his *management functions—planning and decision making, organizing, leading,* and *controlling*—contribute to the situation in which he found himself? What roles will they play in his efforts to recover from the debacle?

4. When asked, "Have you considered stepping down?" Hastings replied:

   No, not for a second. I founded Netflix. I've built it steadily over 12 years now, first with DVD becoming profitable in 2002, a head-to-head ferocious battle with Blockbuster and evolving the company toward streaming. This is the first time there have been material missteps. If you look at the cumulative track record, it's extremely positive.

   What do you think of this answer?

CHAPTER 2: YOU MAKE THE CALL Some Keys to Making a Steinway

1. Explain the process by which a Steinway grand piano is constructed as a *subsystem* of a larger *system*. From what the vignette tells you, give some examples of how the production subsystem is affected by the management, financial, and marketing subsystems. (*Note:* Recall the discussion of *areas of management* in Chapter 1.)

2. Discuss the Steinway process in terms of the *systems perspective* of organizations summarized in Figure 2.3.

Explain the role of each of the three elements highlighted by the figure—*inputs from the environment,* the *transformation process,* and *outputs into the environment.*

3. Discuss some of the ways in which the principles of *behavioral management* and *operations management* can throw light on the Steinway process. How about the *contingency perspective*? In what ways does the Steinway process reflect a *universal perspective* and in what ways does it reflect a *contingency perspective*?

CHAPTER 3: YOU MAKE THE CALL   The NetApp Approach to Net Satisfaction

1. Analyze the NetApp *culture*. Begin by visiting the NetApp website at **www.netapp.com/nl/company/careers/culture**, where you'll find a brief statement of the company's six "living values." Judging from this statement, make a list of three or four items that are "important" to NetApp. Explain each item on your list and show how it's reflected in our opening story. Judging from the story, address each of the following questions as best you can: What does NetApp "stand for"? How does NetApp "do things"?

2. In what ways does the *culture* at NetApp reflect the influence of the *sociocultural dimension* of its *general environment*?

3. In what ways does the presence of *competitors* in its *task environment* influence NetApp's *culture*? In what ways might the *systems resource* and *internal process approaches* help explain NetApp's *organizational effectiveness*?

4. According to NetApp CFO Steve Como, a major question facing the company's managers is: "What is an effective way to manage people who have [the] freedom" that NetApp employees do? He also observes that "most of the jobs we do require a lot of social interaction." In what *practical* ways might the need to encourage "social interaction" affect the company's policy to permit as much workplace freedom as possible?*

* "NetApp's Social Culture," *Forbes.com Video Network: CIO Network*, 2010, http://video.forbes.com on January 31, 2011.

CHAPTER 4: YOU MAKE THE CALL   Is Fair Trade a Fair Trade-off?

1. What are the trade-offs in the fair-trade process? Do you think that fair trade promotes fair trade-offs? Why or why not?

2. Do you pay attention to fair-trade products in your own purchasing behavior? For what kind of products might you be willing to pay premium prices?

3. Under what circumstances could unethical parties abuse the fair-trade concept?

4. Under what circumstances might fair trade actually cause harm? To whom? At what point would fair-trade trade-offs no longer be acceptable?

5. In what ways does fair trade meet the ethical norm of *utility*? The ethical norm of *justice*? The ethical norm of *caring*?

CHAPTER 5: YOU MAKE THE CALL   The Embargo Grinds On

1. In your opinion, is Thanksgiving Coffee's Paul Katzeff doing the right thing in working against the U.S. embargo? Explain your opinion. If your answer is yes, can you think of any additional steps that Katzeff might take?

2. How have changes in the *structure of the global economy* affected the U.S. embargo, which has been in effect for nearly 50 years? More specifically, how can U.S. companies deal with changing *environmental challenges*—*economic, political and legal*, and *cultural*—in their relations not only with Cuba but with other countries in Latin America?

3. The Cuban exile community in the United States has traditionally supported the embargo against Cuba because they believe that it's a crucial factor in U.S. pressure to topple dictator Fidel Castro. Half a century and ten U.S. presidents later, the Castro government is still in power, and even anti-Castro groups within Cuba admit that the embargo actually works to *strengthen* Castro's position. What's your opinion? Should the United States lift the embargo against Cuba? Whether your answer is yes or no, give both the strongest arguments for your conclusion and a few of your key reservations.

CHAPTER 6: YOU MAKE THE CALL   Are Minorities Subprime Citizens?

1. Explain the role of *ethnicity* in the organizational behavior described in the case. What assumptions did lenders such as Countrywide make about certain ethnic groups? Which of those assumptions were accurate? Which were inaccurate?

2. Think back to Chapter 3, on organizational culture and environment, for a moment. In what ways might a home lender use its understanding of diversity and multiculturalism in the *economic* and *customer dimensions* of its external environment to build a legitimate competitive advantage?

3. Now think back to Chapter 4, on ethics and social responsibility. Explain the relationship between Countrywide management and minority borrowers as a relationship between an organization and "other economic agents." In what way can the actions of the organization's managers be characterized as *unethical behavior*?

4. Prior to reading this case, what was your opinion on the role of minority borrowers in the so-called "subprime meltdown" and the avalanche of home foreclosures that resulted? Has your opinion changed? In what ways? What about your opinion on measures that might be taken to avoid another such crisis? In what ways, if any, has that opinion changed?

CHAPTER 7: YOU MAKE THE CALL   Did AIG Ensure Risky Decisions?

1. Consider the range of activities and decisions attributed to AIG and AIGFP in the story. Which ones probably resulted from the pursuit of *strategic goals*? Which ones probably resulted from the pursuit of *operational goals*? Which ones probably resulted from the pursuit of *long-range plans*? Which ones probably resulted from the pursuit of *intermediate plans*?

2. In what sense can Cassano's actions be seen as an effort to *optimize* conflicting goals? In what sense can they be seen as a reflection of *contingency planning*? Of *crisis management*?

3. Explain how the following *barriers to goal setting and planning* may have played a role in the failure of the decisions made by AIG and AIGFP: *inappropriate goals*, an *improper reward system*, a *dynamic and complex environment*, *constraints*.

4. Have you ever been in a situation in which you asked (or worried) about the legality of a decision that you had to make? If so, how did you handle the situation? Would you handle it differently today? If you've never been in such a situation, explain how you'd handle it if it did arise. What factors would you consider in coming to a decision?

CHAPTER 8: YOU MAKE THE CALL   The Hype about Hybrids

1. Explain how each of its strategic *components—distinctive competence*, *scope*, and *resource deployment*—plays a role in Toyota's strategy for competing in the U.S. market. Be as specific as you can.

2. In what ways is Toyota's strategy designed to respond to both *organizational opportunities* and *organizational threats* in the U.S. market?

3. How can *Porter's generic strategies* approach help to explain Toyota's U.S. strategy? How about the *Miles and Snow typology*? Don't expect either model to explain everything: Focus on the factors on which each model sheds some light.

4. A statement issued by the Union of Concerned Scientists in 2007 called Toyota "the poster child for an auto industry with an identity crisis. . . . At the same time that Toyota is producing ads with hybrids driving through green fields, it's making less fuel-efficient vehicles [especially trucks] and its lobbyists are pushing for a watered-down fuel economy law." Does this seem to be a reasonable (and fair) assessment of the automaker's strategy as it's described in the case? Whether you say yes or no, explain your answer.*

* David Friedman, "Preliminary Government MPG Numbers Show CAFE Success, Toyota Faltering" (Union of Concerned Scientists, August 31, 2007), press release, www.ucsusa.org on February 28, 2011.

CHAPTER 9: YOU MAKE THE CALL   Citi ODs on CDOs

1. Summarize the *state of risk* as it stood at Citigroup in the years 2005 to 2008. What were the payoffs and costs that should have been considered in making risk-assessment estimates?
2. Identify the specific decisions made at Citi by Charles Prince. In your opinion, which single decision contributed most to the breakdown in risk management at the bank?
3. Sometimes ambiguity complicates the task of making a good decision under conditions of risk. How did ambiguity affect some of the factors that the Citi management team needed to consider?
4. To what extent was the Citi management team operating under a *state of uncertainty*?
5. Take advantage of hindsight: What should the Citi management team have done, and when? What might have been the outcome had Prince and his managers followed this course of action?

CHAPTER 10: YOU MAKE THE CALL   The Creative Imprint at Bigfoot

1. In what ways is Bigfoot *innovative*? In what ways does it deal with *big business*? In what *industries* does it operate?
2. Which *niches* does Bigfoot serve in established markets? What *new markets* does it target? Can you think of any other niches or new markets that it should consider in the future?
3. Does Bigfoot have any *first-mover advantages*? If so, what are these advantages, and how important do you think they are now and will be in the future?
4. In what ways does Bigfoot rely on *distinctive competencies*? In what ways is experience in *international management* among these competencies? In what ways do you expect this particular competency to become even more important in the future?

CHAPTER 11: YOU MAKE THE CALL   Facets of Jamie Dimon's Strategy at JPMorgan

1. In what ways is Jamie Dimon's approach to management pretty much what you'd expect of a top-level manager in the financial industry? In what ways is it different from what you'd expect?
2. Under what circumstances might Dimon need to change his approach to organizational control?
3. Explain how Dimon has practiced each of the following *levels of control* at JPMorgan Chase: (a) *financial*; (b) *structural*; (c) *strategic*. Then focus on *operations control*: What steps has Dimon taken to exercise each form of operations control—*preliminary*, *screening*, and *postaction*?
4. What aspects of Dimon's approach to control were important in steering JPMorgan Chase through the subprime crisis that crippled or toppled other financial institutions?
5. Under what circumstances might Dimon need to change his approach to organizational control?

CHAPTER 12: YOU MAKE THE CALL   Orchestrating Outcomes

1. Explain the "Orpheus Process" as a system of *operations management*. In what ways is it important to the orchestra's productivity, competitiveness, and overall organizational performance?
2. How would you explain "quality" in an orchestral performance? In what ways are the *eight dimensions of quality* in Table 12.2 useful in explaining the quality of a concert? In what ways are they not useful (or at least difficult to apply)?
3. Discuss the *importance of quality* in Orpheus's operations in terms of *competition*, *productivity*, and *costs*.
4. In what ways does the "Orpheus Process" reflect the basic elements of *total quality management*, particularly *strategic commitment*, *employee involvement*, and *methods*?

CHAPTER 13: YOU MAKE THE CALL   You Can't Make This Stuff Up

1. What aspects of the *Internet* make it such a useful tool in circulating misinformation, whether intentionally or unintentionally? What is it about the attitudes of many Internet users that makes them susceptible to misinformation?

2. Watch an evening newscast (national or local) or tune in to one of the major TV news channels, such as CNN, Fox News Channel, BBC World News, or MSNBC. Select one news story. How did the *way* it was presented contribute to your accepting it as factual and accurate? Aside from your own biases, why might you call some aspects of the story into question?

3. Concoct a simple bit of misinformation as if you intend to post it online (strictly as an experiment, of course). Develop your message by ensuring that it possesses (or seems to possess) the *characteristics of useful information* — *accuracy, timeliness, completeness,* and *relevance.*

4. You've just read the following story on an Internet site that you're not familiar with:

In July 2006, a teenager in Colorado received serious injuries when lightning struck a nearby tree as he was listening to Metallica on his iPod while mowing the lawn. He suffered burns on the side of his face from the earphone wires, a nasty burn on the hip where he was carrying the iPod in his pants pocket, and "a bad line up the side of [his] body," even though the iPod cord was outside his shirt.

Is the story true? Is it possible that having an electronic device on your body can make lightning-strike injuries more severe? How would you go about investigating the accuracy of the story and the answer to the question?

CHAPTER 14: YOU MAKE THE CALL   Delayering as a Defense Mechanism

1. Based on what you can tell from the case, make a quick chart of Anglo's organization prior to Cynthia Carroll's changes. Then make a similar chart of its organization after those changes. Be prepared to explain the key differences highlighted by your two charts, as well as the advantages that Carroll sees in her changes.

2. Describe the results of Anglo's changes to its *organization structure* in terms of *departmentalization, reporting relationships,* and *decentralization/centralization.*

3. In addition to seven business units, Anglo's restructuring creates five *functional departments* — Finance,

Mining & Technology, Business Performance & Projects, HR & Communications, and Strategy & Business Development. Describe some of the ways in which these new functional groups will interact with the company's new business units, which are, in effect, *product departments.*

4. A manager's *responsibility* refers to his or her obligation to achieve something. In what ways has Carroll balanced her responsibility with her *authority*? In your opinion, what does she have to do in order to sustain or improve that balance and to ensure that her strategy is successful?

CHAPTER 15: YOU MAKE THE CALL   Authority & Function at A&F

1. If you were hired to advise Michael Jeffries on A&F's current organizational design, what weaknesses and potential threats would you identify? What strengths and opportunities?

2. What kind of organizational design do you think would be best suited to Jeffries' managerial style?

3. What's the current status of A&F in the organizational life cycle? In what ways is it typical of its current stage? In which ways does it appear to be atypical?

4. It seems that mergers, acquisitions, and divestitures are currently business as usual in the retailing sector.

Following such an event, does it make more sense to retain the current organizational design for a while or to modify it right away? Why?

5. What differences might you expect to see between the organizational designs of such traditional retailers as A&F and American Eagle and those at online retailers such as Amazon.com and eBay?

6. Assuming that you wanted a career in retailing, would you want to work for A&F? Why or why not?

CHAPTER 16: YOU MAKE THE CALL The Science of the Deal

1. You're an up-and-coming assistant to a mid-level manager at Roche Group. Your boss is being transferred to the company's recently acquired research facilities at the former Genentech headquarters in San Francisco. She's asked you to compile a brief report on Genentech's overall approach to product innovation. What will you say in your report? *Hint:* Structure your report according to the three *forms of innovation* discussed in the text: *radical versus incremental, technical versus managerial,* and *product versus process.*

2. Ex-Roche Chairman Franz Humer committed the parent company to sustaining Genentech's "innovative culture," and his successor, Severin Schwan, has stated that he intends to "keep the two respective research and early development organizations as independent units"; merging the two R&D units, he says, "would kill innovation" at Genentech. Schwan needs suggestions on how best to follow through on both Humer's commitment and his own. Not surprisingly, your boss has asked you to furnish her with two or three ideas that she might pass on to the CEO. What will your suggestions be?

3. Despite the commitments made by its CEOs, Roche Group is an immense company: It employs more than 80,000 people in 150 countries and posted revenues of $47 billion in 2010. There will undoubtedly be changes at Genentech. Generally speaking, what sort of changes might you expect in the following areas—*organization structure and design, technology and operations,* and *people, attitudes, and behaviors?*

CHAPTER 17: YOU MAKE THE CALL No Company for Old-Fashioned Management

1. If you were an HR executive at Wegmans, would you focus more on *internal recruiting* or on *external recruiting?* Would your strategy for higher-level positions differ from your strategy for lower-level positions? How would current economic conditions influence your strategy?

2. As an HR executive at Wegmans, you need to hire a group of new employees as part of your management-trainee program—people who will be put on a track leading, ultimately, to positions as store managers. Briefly outline your program for developing these employees.

3. If you were an employee at Wegmans, how would you expect your annual performance appraisal to be conducted? Given the company's customer-relations strategy, which appraisal methods do you think would be most appropriate?

CHAPTER 18: YOU MAKE THE CALL The Psychopath in the Executive Suite

1. Have you ever worked with or for someone who exhibited psychopathic or narcissistic behavior? If so, describe that behavior and explain why it indicates a diagnosis of psychopathy or narcissism.

2. You're a top manager at a large company, and you're about to be promoted. You've come to realize that the fast-track manager who's in line for your job has psychopathic tendencies. What will you do?

3. Once again, you're in the situation described in question 2. This time, however, the fast-track manager in question is a narcissist. Would you handle the case of the narcissist differently from the case of the psychopath? Be specific in explaining your answer.

4. Your unit works directly under an executive VP of the company. She clearly exhibits narcissistic tendencies, but you just got another handsome year-end bonus. You wonder: Are narcissistic managers occasionally beneficial to organizations? On what grounds would you argue that they can be? On what grounds would you argue that they can't be?

CHAPTER 19: YOU MAKE THE CALL   Are You Happily Productive or Productively Happy?

1. How might the relationship between happiness and productivity be approached by each of the following motivational theories—ERG, *two-factor, expectancy, equity,* and *goal-setting theory?*
2. What factors help to engage you in a task? What factors tend to contribute to "positivity" when you're working on a task? What factors tend to make your attitude negative?
3. Paul Larson says that "people tend to join a company but leave their supervisor." Do you agree or disagree? Explain your answer.

4. According to Alexander Kjerulf, there are two things that you can do to enhance happiness in your work life: (1) get happy in the job you have or (2) get another job. In your opinion, which of these options is most likely to be successful? Personally, which option appeals to you more? If you must accept option number 1, what steps would you take to make yourself happier in a job?

CHAPTER 20: YOU MAKE THE CALL   When to Stand on Your Head and Other Tips from the Top

1. Studies indicate that good leaders are typically positive and enthusiastic. In what ways do the tips cited in the vignette suggest the possession of these qualities by the various leaders who offer them? Based on their suggestions for managing stress and information flow, what other qualities might you assign, in general, to the leaders cited in the vignette?
2. Recall our discussion, in Chapter 18, of *locus of control,* which we defined as the degree to which an individual believes that his or her behavior has a direct impact on the consequences of that behavior. In what ways do the attitudes

expressed or implied in the vignette suggest the degree of locus control possessed by the leaders who are cited?
3. We discussed *delegation*—the process by which managers assign work to subordinates—in Chapter 14. Not surprisingly, effective delegation eases the stress on managers. Judging from their advice on managing information flow, what sort of tasks do you think these managers delegate to others? What sort of tasks do they *not* delegate? As a result of your efforts to address these questions, can you think of a good rule of thumb for what a successful leader should and should not delegate?

CHAPTER 21: YOU MAKE THE CALL   The Converse of In-Person Communication

1. Experts suggest that you dress professionally for a telephone interview even though the interviewer can't see you. Do you agree that this is important? Why or why not?
2. In getting ready for a telephone interview for a new job, what are the three or four things for which you most want to be prepared? If you were getting ready to interview someone else for a job, what are the three or four major things that you'd expect that person to be prepared for?
3. Matt Aberham warns against simply trying to "sell yourself" during a phone interview. You agree, but you also believe that selling yourself is one of the things that you have to do as a job seeker. What sort of strategies do you

regard as legitimate and effective in trying to sell yourself to a phone interviewer (or an in-person interviewer, for that matter)?
4. Think of one or two experiences from your own life that you'd particularly like to come up in a job interview. What sort of questions might allow you to "take the initiative" in making sure that they didn't fall through the cracks? How much time do you think each incident would be worth in a 30–45-minute interview?
5. Linking video cameras to computers has become quite popular in setting up the complete online conversation. How might this technology be used in conjunction with telephone interviews? How about other forms of communication, such as text messaging?

1. Explain a surgical team as a kind of *functional group*. What features does it share with most functional groups? What features distinguish it from most functional groups?

2. Explain a surgical team in terms of its *role structures*. What factors might lead to *role ambiguity*? To *role conflict*? To *role overload*?

3. Explain a surgical team in terms of its *behavioral norms*. How might *norm variation* and *norm conformity* contribute to either effective or ineffective communications?

4. How do various strategies for improving surgical-team communications reflect a desire to achieve *cohesiveness*? Is increased cohesiveness always a desirable goal? Why or why not?

Notes

Chapter 1

1 "How Netflix Got Started," *CNNMoney.com*, January 28, 2009, http://money .cnn.com on October 25, 2011; Reed Hastings, "How I Did It: Reed Hastings, Netflix," *Inc.com*, December 1, 2005, www.inc.com on October 25, 2011; Craig Tomashoff, "You Are What You Queue," *New York Times*, March 2, 2003, www .nytimes.com on October 25, 2011; Sally Aaron, "Netflix Script Spells Disruption," *Harvard Business School Working Knowledge*, March 22, 2004, http://hbswk .hbs.edu on October 25, 2011; Beth Snyder Bulik, "How Netflix Stays Ahead of Shifting Consumer Behavior," *Advertising Age*, February 22, 2010, http://adage .com on October 25, 2011; John M. Caddell, "Frontiers of Innovation–Netflix Demolishes Its Own Business Model," *PennLive.com*, February 11, 2009, http:// blog.pennlive.com on June 21, 2010; Larry Dignan, "Netflix's Saga: The Dark Side of Creative Destruction," *CBSNews.com*, October 25, 2011, www.cbsnews .com on October 25, 2011; "Netflix Subscriber Loss Triggers Panic Selling," *CBSNews.com*, October 24, 2011, www.cbsnews.com on October 25, 2011; Andrew Goldman, "Reed Hastings Knows He Messed Up," *New York Times*, October 20, 2011, www.nytimes.com on October 25, 2011.

2 Fred Luthans, "Successful vs. Effective Real Managers," *Academy of Management Executive*, May 1988, pp. 127–132. See also "The Best Performers," *BusinessWeek*, Spring 2011 Special Issue, pp. 57–95.

3 See "The Best (& Worst) Managers of the Year," *BusinessWeek*, January 22, 2011, pp. 50–72.

4 Sumantsa Ghospal and Christopher A. Bartlett, "Changing the Role of Top Management: Beyond Structure to Process," *Harvard Business Review*, January– February 1995, pp. 86–96.

5 "Ford's Savior?" *BusinessWeek*, March 16, 2009, pp. 31–34.

6 *BusinessWeek*, March 16, 2009, pp. 31–32.

7 "Fastener Woes to Delay Flight of First Boeing 787 Jets," *Wall Street Journal*, November 5, 2008, p. B1.

8 See "Executive Pay," *BusinessWeek*, April 15, 2002, pp. 80–100. See also Jim Collins, "The Ten Greatest CEO's of All Times," *Fortune*, July 21, 2003, pp. 54–68.

9 "Executive Compensation for 50 of the Largest U.S. Companies," *USA Today*, May 4, 2010, p. 3B.

10 Rosemary Stewart, "Middle Managers: Their Jobs and Behaviors," in Jay W. Lorsch (ed.), *Handbook of Organizational Behavior* (Englewood Cliffs, NJ: Prentice-Hall, 1987), pp. 385–391. See also Bill Woolridge, Torsten Schmid, and Steven W. Floyd, "The Middle Management Perspective on Strategy Process: Contributions, Synthesis, and Future Research," *Journal of Management*, 2008, Vol. 34, No. 6, pp. 1190–1221; and Anneloes Raes, Mrielle Heijltjes, Ursula Glunk, and Robert Row, "The Interface of the Top Management Team and Middle Managers: A Process Model," *Academy of Management Review*, January 2011, pp. 102–126.

11 John P. Kotter, "What Effective General Managers Really Do," *Harvard Business Review*, March–April 1999, pp. 145–155. See also Peter Drucker, "What Makes an Effective Executive," *Harvard Business Review*, June 2004, pp. 58–68.

12 Henry Mintzberg, *The Nature of Managerial Work* (Englewood Cliffs, NJ: 1973).

13 See Robert L. Katz, "The Skills of an Effective Administrator," *Harvard Business Review*, September–October 1974, pp. 90–102, for a classic discussion of several of these skills. For a recent perspective, see J. Brian Atwater, Vijay R. Kannan, and Alan A. Stephens, "Cultivating Systemic Thinking in the Next Generation of Business Leaders," *Academy of Management Learning & Education*, 2008, Vol. 7, No. 1, pp. 9–25.

14 See Mark Gottfredson, Steve Schaubert, and Hernan Saenz, "The New Leader's Guide to Diagnosing the Business," *Harvard Business Review*, February 2008, pp. 63–72, for an interesting application.

15 See "The Real Reasons You're Working so Hard . . . And What You Can Do about It," *BusinessWeek*, October 3, 2005, pp. 60–68; "I'm Late, I'm Late, I'm Late," *USA Today*, November 26, 2002, pp. 1B–2B.

16 For a thorough discussion of the importance of time-management skills, see David Barry, Catherine Durnell Cramton, and Stephen J. Carroll, "Navigating the Garbage Can: How Agendas Help Managers Cope with Job Realities," *Academy of Management Executive*, May 1997, pp. 26–42.

17 "Taming the Out-of-Control In-Box," *Wall Street Journal*, February 4, 2000, pp. B1, B4.

18 See Michael A. Hitt, "Transformation of Management for the New Millennium," *Organizational Dynamics*, Winter 2000, pp. 7–17.

19 James H. Davis, F. David Schoorman, and Lex Donaldson, "Toward a Stewardship Theory of Management," *Academy of Management Review*, January 1997, pp. 20–47.

20 *Forbes*, February 14, 2005, p. 110.

21 Gary Hamel and C. K. Prahalad, "Competing for the Future," *Harvard Business Review*, July–August 1994, pp. 122–128; see also Joseph M. Hall and M. Eric Johnson, "When Should a Process Be Art, Not Science?" *Harvard Business Review*," March 2009, pp. 58–65.

22 James Waldroop and Timothy Butler, "The Executive as Coach," *Harvard Business Review*, November–December 1996, pp. 111–117.

23 *Biz Ed*, May/June 2010, p. 23.

24 See Steven J. Armstrong and Anis Mahmud, "Experiential Learning and the Acquisition of Managerial Tacit Knowledge," *Academy of Management Learning & Education*, 2008, Vol. 7, No. 2, pp. 189–208.

25 "The Executive MBA Your Way," *BusinessWeek*, October 18, 1999, pp. 88–92.

26 "Despite Cutbacks, Firms Invest in Developing Leaders," *Wall Street Journal*, February 9, 2009, p. B4.

27 "Turning B-School into E-School," *BusinessWeek*, October 18, 1999, p. 94.

28 See "Reunion at P&G University," *Wall Street Journal*, June 7, 2000, pp. B1, B4, for a discussion of Procter & Gamble's training programs.

29 For an interesting discussion of these issues, see Rakesh Khurana, "The Curse of the Superstar CEO," *Harvard Business Review*, September 2002, pp. 60–70.

30 James L. Perry and Hal G. Rainey, "The Public-Private Distinction in Organization Theory: A Critique and Research Strategy," *Academy of Management Review*, April 1988, pp. 182–201. See also Ran Lachman, "Public and Private Sector Differences: CEOs' Perceptions of Their Role Environments," *Academy of Management Journal*, September 1985, pp. 671–680.

31 "The Way We'll Work," *Time*, May 25, 2009, pp. 39–51.

32 Patricia L. Nemetz and Sandra L. Christensen, "The Challenge of Cultural Diversity: Harnessing a Diversity of Views to Understand Multiculturalism," *Academy of Management Review*, 1996, Vol. 21, No. 2, pp. 434–462; Frances J. Milliken and Luis L. Martins, "Searching for Common Threads: Understanding the Multiple Effects of Diversity in Organizational Groups," *Academy of Management Review*, 1996, Vol. 21, No. 2, pp. 402–433.

33 "When Gen X Runs the Show," *Time*, May 25, 2009, p. 48.

34 Craig L. Pearce and Charles P. Osmond, "Metaphors for Change: The ALPS Model of Change Management," *Organizational Dynamics*, Winter 1996, pp. 23–35.

Chapter 2

1 Steinway & Sons, "The Steinway Restoration Center," 2011, www.steinway.com on January 29, 2011; Steinway & Sons, "Online Factory Tour," 2009, http://archive.steinway.com on January 29, 2011; WGBH (Boston), "Note by Note: The Making of Steinway L1037," 2010, www.wgbh.org on January 29, 2011; Maya Roney, "Steinway: Worth Much More Than a Song," *BusinessWeek*, March 6, 2007, www.businessweek.com on January 29, 2011; James Barron, "88 Keys, Many Languages, One Proud Name," *New York Times*, October 6, 2003, www.nytimes.com on January 29, 2011; Michael Lenehen, "K 2571: The Making of a Steinway Grand," *Atlantic Monthly*, August 1982, www.sherwinbeach.com on January 29, 2011; Rick Rogers, "Steinway Builds a Legacy with Distinctive Pianos," *Daily Oklahoman* (Oklahoma City), December 2000, www.richardhuggins.com on January 29, 2011.

2 Terence Mitchell and Lawrence James, "Building Better Theory: Time and the Specification of When Things Happen," *Academy of Management Review*, 2001, Vol. 26, No. 4, pp. 530–547.

3 Peter F. Drucker, "The Theory of the Business," *Harvard Business Review*, September–October 1994, pp. 95–104.

4 "Why Business History?" *Audacity*, Fall 1992, pp. 7–15. See also Alan L. Wilkins and Nigel J. Bristow, "For Successful Organization Culture, Honor Your Past," *Academy of Management Executive*, August 1987, pp. 221–227.

5 Daniel Wren, *The Evolution of Management Thought*, 5th ed. (New York: Wiley, 2005); Page Smith, *The Rise of Industrial America* (New York: McGraw-Hill, 1984).

6 Martha I. Finney, "Books That Changed Careers," *HR Magazine*, June 1997, pp. 141–145. See also "Leadership in Literature," *Harvard Business Review*, March 2006, pp. 47–55.

7 See Harriet Rubin, *The Princessa: Machiavelli for Women* (New York: Doubleday/Currency, 1997). See also Nanette Fondas, "Feminization Unveiled: Management Qualities in Contemporary Writings," *Academy of Management Review*, January 1997, pp. 257–282.

8 Alan M. Kantrow (ed.), "Why History Matters to Managers," *Harvard Business Review*, January–February 1986, pp. 81–88.

9 *Audacity*, Fall 1992, p. 15.

10 Wren, *The Evolution of Management Theory*.

11 Charles Babbage, *On the Economy of Machinery and Manufactures* (London: Charles Knight, 1832).

12 Wren, *The Evolution of Management Theory*.

13 Frederick W. Taylor, *Principles of Scientific Management* (New York: Harper and Brothers, 1911).

14 Charles D. Wrege and Amedeo G. Perroni, "Taylor's Pig-Tale: A Historical Analysis of Frederick W. Taylor's Pig-Iron Experiment," *Academy of Management Journal*, March 1974, pp. 6–27; Charles D. Wrege and Ann Marie Stoka, "Cooke Creates a Classic: The Story Behind Taylor's Principles of Scientific Management," *Academy of Management Review*, October 1978, pp. 736–749.

15 Robert Kanigel, *The One Best Way* (New York: Viking, 1997); Oliver E. Allen, "'This Great Mental Revolution,'" *Audacity*, Summer 1996, pp. 52–61; Jill Hough and Margaret White, "Using Stories to Create Change: The Object Lesson of Frederick Taylor's 'Pig-Tale,'" *Journal of Management*, 2001, Vol. 27, pp. 585–601.

16 Henri Fayol, *General and Industrial Management*, trans. J. A. Coubrough (Geneva: International Management Institute, 1930).

17 Max Weber, *Theory of Social and Economic Organizations*, trans. T. Parsons (New York: Free Press, 1947); Richard M. Weis, "Weber on Bureaucracy: Management Consultant or Political Theorist?" *Academy of Management Review*, April 1983, pp. 242–248.

18 Chester Barnard, *The Functions of the Executive* (Cambridge, MA: Harvard University Press, 1938).

19 "The Line Starts Here," *Wall Street Journal*, January 11, 1999, pp. R1, R25.

20 Hugo Munsterberg, *Psychology and Industrial Efficiency* (Boston: Houghton Mifflin, 1913).

21 Wren, *The Evolution of Management Theory*, pp. 255–264.

22 Elton Mayo, *The Human Problems of an Industrial Civilization* (New York: Macmillan, 1933); Fritz J. Roethlisberger and William J. Dickson, *Management and the Worker* (Cambridge, MA: Harvard University Press, 1939).

23 Abraham Maslow, "A Theory of Human Motivation," *Psychological Review*, July 1943, pp. 370–396.

24 Douglas McGregor, *The Human Side of Enterprise* (New York: McGraw-Hill, 1960).

25 Sara L. Rynes and Christine Quinn Trank, "Behavioral Science in the Business School Curriculum: Teaching in a Changing Institutional Environment," *Academy of Management Review*, 1999, Vol. 24, No. 4, pp. 808–824.

26 See Ricky W. Griffin and Gregory Moorhead, *Organizational Behavior*, 10th ed. (Cincinnati: Cengage, 2012), for a recent review of current developments in the field of organizational behavior.

27 Wren, *The Evolution of Management Thought*, Chapter 21.

28 "Math Will Rock Your World," *BusinessWeek*, January 23, 2006, pp. 54–61.

29 "Quantitative Analysis Offers Tools to Predict Likely Terrorist Moves," *Wall Street Journal*, February 17, 2006, p. B1.

30 *BusinessWeek*, January 23, 2006, p. 57.

31 For more information on systems theory in general, see Ludwig von Bertalanffy, C. G. Hempel, R. E. Bass, and H. Jonas, "General Systems Theory: A New Approach to Unity of Science," *Human Biology*, Vol. 23, 1951, pp. 302–361. For systems theory as applied to organizations, see Fremont E. Kast and James E. Rosenzweig, "General Systems Theory: Applications for Organizations and Management," *Academy of Management Journal*, December 1972, pp. 447–465. For a recent update, see Donde P. Ashmos and George P. Huber, "The Systems Paradigm in Organization Theory: Correcting the Record and Suggesting the Future," *Academy of Management Review*, October 1987, pp. 607–621.

32 *USA Today*, June 16, 2011, p. 1B.

33 See Robert S. Kaplan and David P. Norton, "Mastering the Management System," *Harvard Business Review*, January 2008, pp. 63–72.

34 "United, Continental Merger to Create Synergies, Cut Costs," *International Business Times*, May 3, 2010, pp. 17–19.

35 Fremont E. Kast and James E. Rosenzweig, *Contingency Views of Organization and Management* (Chicago: Science Research Associates, 1973).

36 "There Is No More Normal," *BusinessWeek*, March 23, 2009, pp. 30–34.

37 *BusinessWeek*, March 23, 2009, p. 30.

38 "Welch Memoirs Fetch $7.1M," *USA Today*, July 14, 2000, p. 1B.

39 *HR Magazine*, June 1997, p. 141.

40 "The BusinessWeek Best-Seller List," *BusinessWeek*, November 4, 2002, p. 26.

41 See Phanish Puranam and Bart S. Vanneste, "Trust and Governance: Untangling a Tangled Web," *Academy of Management Review*, Vol. 34, No. 1, January 2009, pp. 11–31.

42 "Yes, We'll Still Make Stuff," *Time*, May 25, 2009, p. 49.

43 "Despite China's Might, U.S. Factories Maintain Edge," *MSNBC*, February 1, 2011.

Chapter 3

1 "100 Best Companies to Work For," *Fortune*, February 7, 2011, http://money.cnn.com on January 26, 2011; "NetApp Ranked #5 on the 'Best Companies to Work For' List by Fortune Magazine," *PR-USA.Net*, January 26, 2011, http://pr-usa.net on January 26, 2011; "25 Top-Paying Companies," *Fortune*, January 26, 2010, http://money.cnn.com on January 26, 2011; Amy Lyman, *NetApp: Culture—Values—Leadership* (San Francisco: Great Place to Work® Institute, 2009), http://resources.greatplacetowork.com on January 26, 2011; George Brymer, "NetApp: A Great Place to Work," *Vital Integrities*, April 2009, http://allsquareinc.blogspot.com on January 26, 2011; J. P. Gallagher, "I Work for One of the 10 Best Companies," *Fortune*, January 21, 2010, http://money.cnn.com on January 26, 2011; NetApp, "NetApp Is a Great Place to Work Worldwide!" 2011, www.netapp.com on January 26, 2011.

2 Arie de Geus, *The Living Company—Habits for Surviving in a Turbulent Business Environment* (Boston: Harvard Business School Press, 1997). See also John G.

Sifonis and Beverly Goldberg, *Corporation on a Tightrope* (New York: Oxford University Press, 1996), for an interesting discussion of how organizations must navigate through the environment.

3 Eric D. Beinhocker, "Robust Adaptive Strategies," *Sloan Management Review*, Spring 1999, pp. 95–105; see also John Crotts, Duncan Dickson, and Robert Ford, "Aligning Organizational Processes with Mission: The Case of Service Excellence," *Academy of Management Executive*, Vol. 19, No. 3, 2005, pp. 54–63; Sebastian Raisch and Julian Birkinshaw, "Organizational Ambidexterity: Antecedents, Outcomes, and Moderators," *Journal of Management*, 2008, Vol. 34, No. 3, pp. 375–409.

4 *Fortune*, March 16, 2009, p. 111.

5 See Jay B. Barney and William G. Ouchi (eds.), *Organizational Economics* (San Francisco: Jossey-Bass, 1986), for a detailed analysis of linkages between economics and organizations.

6 See, for example, "Political Pendulum Swings Toward Stricter Regulation," *Wall Street Journal*, March 24, 2008, pp. A1, A11; see also "Changing Safety Rules Perplex and Polarize," *USA Today*, February 5, 2009, pp. 1B, 2B; Nina Easton and Telis Demos, "The Business Guide to Congress," *Fortune*, May 11, 2009, pp. 72–75.

7 *Wall Street Journal*, March 24, 2009, p. A1.

8 See Ricky Griffin and Michael Pustay, *International Business: A Managerial Perspective*, 7th ed. (Upper Saddle River, NJ: Prentice Hall, 2013), for an overview.

9 For example, see Susanne G. Scott and Vicki R. Lane, "A Stakeholder Approach to Organizational Identity," *Academy of Management Review*, 2000, Vol. 25, No. 1, pp. 43–62.

10 "Rising Retailer Threat: Liquidations," *Wall Street Journal*, December 12, 2008, p. B1.

11 Richard N. Osborn and John Hagedoorn, "The Institutionalization and Evolutionary Dynamics of Interorganizational Alliances and Networks," *Academy of Management Journal*, April 1997, pp. 261–278. See also "More Companies Cut Risk by Collaborating with Their 'Enemies,'" *Wall Street Journal*, January 31, 2000, pp. A1, A10.

12 "Disney, Spielberg to Team Up," *Wall Street Journal*, January 10, 2009, p. B7.

13 "Behind Sony-Samsung Rivalry, An Unlikely Alliance Develops," *Wall Street Journal*, January 13, 2006, p. A1.

14 "Watchdogs Hound E-Waste Exports," *USA Today*, December 30, 2008, pp. 1B, 2B.

15 "Group Urges Caramel Coloring in Colas be Banned," *USA Today*, February 21, 2011, p. 1B.

16 *USA Today*, December 30, 2008, p. 2B.

17 "The Best & Worst Boards," *BusinessWeek*, October 7, 2002, pp. 104–114. See also Amy Hillman and Thomas Dalziel, "Boards of Directors and Firm Performance: Integrating Agency and Resource Dependence Perspectives," *Academy of Management Review*, 2003, Vol. 23, No. 3, pp. 383–396.

18 "The Wild New Workforce," *BusinessWeek*, December 6, 1999, pp. 38–44.

19 "Temporary Workers Getting Short Shrift," *USA Today*, April 11, 1997, pp. 1B, 2B.

20 Terrence E. Deal and Allan A. Kennedy, *Corporate Cultures: The Rights and Rituals of Corporate Life* (Reading, MA: Addison-Wesley, 1982).

21 Jay B. Barney, "Organizational Culture: Can It Be a Source of Sustained Competitive Advantage?" *Academy of Management Review*, July 1986, pp. 656–665.

22 For example, see Carol J. Loomis, "Sam Would Be Proud," *Fortune*, April 17, 2000, pp. 131–144. See also Yair Berson, Shaul Oreg, and Taly Dvir, "CEO Values, Organizational Culture, and Firm Outcomes," *Journal of Organizational Behavior*, 2008, Vol. 29, pp. 615–633.

23 "United Continental: How the Mega-Carrier Works," *Fortune*, May 2, 2011, pp. 50–57.

24 "Taking the Hill Less Climbed," *The Economist*, October 29, 2010.

25 See Tomothy Galpin, "Connecting Culture to Organizational Change," *HR Magazine*, March 1996, pp. 84–94.

26 For a recent review, see Allen C. Bluedorn, "Pilgrim's Progress: Trends and Convergence in Research on Organizational Size and Environments," *Journal of Management*, 1993, Vol. 19, No. 2, pp. 163–191.

27 James D. Thompson, *Organizations in Action* (New York: McGraw-Hill, 1967).

28 *Fortune*, April 18, 2005, p. 88.

29 Michael E. Porter, *Competitive Strategy: Techniques for Analyzing Industries and Competitors* (New York: Free Press, 1980). See also Joel A. C. Baum and Helaine J. Korn, "Competitive Dynamics of Interfirm Rivalry," *Academy of Management Journal*, April 1996, pp. 255–291.

30 "United Plans Huge Jet Order," *Wall Street Journal*, June 4, 2009, pp. A1, A10.

31 "Starting Over," *Fortune*, January 21, 2002, pp. 50–68.

32 "Toyota Rations Japanese Parts; Honda to Cut Hours," *USA Today*, March 30, 2011, p. 1B.

33 Bala Chakravarthy, "A New Strategy Framework for Coping with Turbulence," *Sloan Management Review*, Winter 1997, pp. 69–82.

34 "Companies Devise Strategies for Flu Interruptions," *Wall Street Journal*, May 4, 2009, p. B4.

35 "G.M. Pieces Together Japanese Supply Chain," *New York Times*, May 13, 2011, p. 5.

36 See Magali A. Delmas and Michael W. Toffel, "Organizational Responses to Environmental Demands: Opening the Black Box," *Strategic Management Journal*, 2008, Vol. 29, pp. 1027–1055.

37 "In Wooing AT&T, SBC Has Eye on Business Customers," *Wall Street Journal*, January 28, 2005, pp. A1, A2.

38 Sean Lux, T. Russell Crook, and David Woehr, "Mixing Business with Politics: A Meta-Analysis of the Antecedents and Outcomes of Corporate Political Activity," *Journal of Management*, January 2011, pp. 223–247.

39 Gareth Jones, *Organizational Theory, Design, and Change*, 5th ed. (Upper Saddle River, NJ: Prentice Hall, 2007).

40 E. Yuchtman and S. Seashore, "A Systems Resource Approach to Organizational Effectiveness," *American Sociological Review*, 1967, Vol. 32, pp. 891–903.

41 B. S. Georgopoules and A. S. Tannenbaum, "The Study of Organizational Effectiveness," *American Sociological Review*, 1957, Vol. 22, pp. 534–540.

42 Anthony A. Atkinson, John H. Waterhouse, and Robert B. Wells, "A Stakeholder Approach to Strategic Performance Measurement," *Sloan Management Review*, Spring 1997, pp. 25–37.

Chapter 4

1 Rodney North, "V-Day's Dark Side," Equal Exchange, February 2010, www.equalexchange.com on February 5, 2011; "Cocoa's Bitter Child Labour Ties," *BBC News*, February 24, 2010, http://newsvote.bbc.co on February 5, 2011; Bill Baue, "Abolishing Child Labor on West African Cocoa Farms," *Social Funds*, April 24, 2008, www.socialfunds.com on February 5, 2011; Fairtrade International, "Our Vision," "Aims of Fairtrade Standards," "Cocoa," 2010, www.fairtrade.net on February 5, 2011; TransFair USA, "What Is Fair Trade?" "Cocoa," 2010, www.transfairusa.org on February 5, 2011; Leslie Josephs, "Selling Candy with a Conscience," *Wall Street Journal*, December 24, 2010, http://online.wsj.com on February 5, 2011; Jennifer Alsever, "Fair Prices for Farmers: Simple Idea, Complex Reality," *New York Times*, March 19, 2006, www.nytimes.com on February 5, 2011.

2 See Norman Barry, *Business Ethics* (West Lafayette, IN: Purdue University Press, 1999).

3 Thomas Donaldson and Thomas W. Dunfee, "Toward a Unified Conception of Business Ethics: An Integrative Social Contracts Theory," *Academy of Management Review*, 1994, Vol. 19, No. 2, pp. 252–284.

4 *Wall Street Journal*, April 22, 2009, p. B1.

5 "CareerBuilder Releases Annual List of the Most Unusual Excuses for Calling in Sick, According to U.S. Employers," *CareerBuilder*, October 27, 2010.

6 "Chains' Ties Run Deep on Pharmacy Boards," *USA Today*, December 31, 2008, pp. 1B, 2B.

7 Jeremy Kahn, "Presto Chango! Sales Are Huge," *Fortune*, March 20, 2000, pp. 90–96; "More Firms Falsify Revenue to Boost Stocks," *USA Today*, March 29, 2000, p. 1B.

8 "U.S. Probes Hilton Over Theft Claims," *Wall Street Journal*, April 22, 2009, pp. B1, B4.

9 "How U.S. Concerns Compete in Countries Where Bribes Flourish," *Wall Street Journal*, September 29, 1995, pp. A1, A14; Patricia Digh, "Shades of Gray in the Global Marketplace," *HR Magazine*, April 1997, pp. 90–98.

10 "Alcoa Faces Allegation by Bahrain of Bribery," *Wall Street Journal*, February 28, 2009, p. A2.

11 *USA Today*, April 11, 2006, p. 1B.

12 Patricia H. Werhane, *Moral Imagination and Management Decision Making* (New York: Oxford University Press, 1999).

13 "Bad Boys," *Forbes*, July 22, 2002, pp. 99–104.

14 "Training Managers to Behave," *Time*, May 25, 2009, p. 41.

15 William Dill, "Beyond Codes and Courses," *Selections*, Fall 2002, pp. 21–23.

16 See Donald Lange, "A Multidimensional Conceptualization of Organizational Corruption Control," *Academy of Management Review*, 2008, Vol. 33, No. 3, pp. 710–729, for a recent discussion of these perspectives.

17 Gerald F. Cavanagh, *American Business Values*, 2nd ed. (Upper Saddle River, NJ: Prentice-Hall, 1998).

18 See Jerald Greenberg and Jason Colquitt, *Handbook of Organizational Justice* (Mahwah, NJ: Lawrence Erlbaum Associates, 2004) for a comprehensive discussion and review of the literature on justice in organization. See also James Lavelle, Deborah Rupp, and Joel Brockner, "Taking a Multifoci Approach to the Study of Justice, Social Exchange, and Citizenship Behavior," *Journal of Management*, 2007, Vol. 33, No. 6, pp. 841–866; and Russell Cropanzano, David Bowen, and Stephen Gilliland, "The Management of Organizational Justice," *Academy of Management Perspectives*, November 2008, pp. 34–44, for recent updates.

19 "U.S. Announces Settlement in Global Bribery Scandal," *Washington Times*, November 4, 2010.

20 "How to Fix Corporate Governance," *BusinessWeek*, May 6, 2002, pp. 68–78. See also Catherine Daily, Dan Dalton, and Albert Cannella, "Corporate Governance: Decades of Dialogue and Data," *Academy of Management Review*, 2003, Vol. 28, No. 3, pp. 371–382; "CEOs Report Stricter Rules," *USA Today*, March 20, 2006, p. 1B.

21 *USA Today*, March 20, 2006, p. 1B.

22 "Hello, Big Brother: Digital Sensors Are Watching Us," *USA Today*, January 26, 2011, p. 1A, 2A.

23 Ibid, p. 2A.

24 Dirk Matten and Jeremy Moon, "'Implicit' and 'Explicit' CSR: A Conceptual Framework for a Comparative Understanding of Corporate Social Responsibility," *Academy of Management Review*, 2008, Vol. 33, No. 2, pp. 404–424.

25 Thomas Donaldson and Lee E. Preston, "The Stakeholder Theory of the Corporation: Concepts, Evidence, and Implications," *Academy of Management Review*, 1995, Vol. 20, No. 1, pp. 65–91. See also Jeffrey S. Harrison and R. Edward Freeman, "Stakeholders, Social Responsibility, and Performance: Empirical Evidence and Theoretical Perspectives," *Academy of Management Journal*, 1999, Vol. 42, No. 5, pp. 479–495; André O. Laplume, Karan Sonpar, and Reginald A. Litz, "Stakeholder Theory: Reviewing a Theory That Moves Us," *Journal of Management*, 2008, Vol. 34, No. 6, pp. 1152–1189.

26 See Douglas A. Bosse, Robert A. Phillips, and Jeffrey S. Harrison, "Stakeholders, Reciprocity, and Firm Performance," *Strategic Management Journal*, 2009, Vol. 30, pp. 447–456.

27 Aseem Prakash, *Greening the Firm* (Cambridge, UK: Cambridge University Press, 2000); Forest L. Reinhardt, *Down to Earth* (Cambridge, MA: Harvard Business School Press, 2000).

28 "Oil Companies Strive to Turn a New Leaf to Save Rain Forest," *Wall Street Journal*, July 17, 1997, pp. A1, A8.

29 See J. Alberto Aragon-Correa and Sanjay Sharma, "A Contingent Resource-Based View of Proactive Corporate Environmental Strategy," *Academy of Management Review*, 2003, Vol. 28, No. 1, pp. 71–88.

30 Linda Grant, "There's Gold in Going Green," *Fortune*, April 14, 1997, pp. 116–118.

31 "Ford to Reveal Plans for Think Brand," *USA Today*, January 10, 2000, p. 1B. See also "Lean Green Machine," *Forbes*, February 3, 2003, p. 44.

32 Christine Y. Chen and Greg Lindsay, "Will Amazon(.com) Save the Amazon?" *Fortune*, March 20, 2000, pp. 224–226.

33 "Ashland Just Can't Seem to Leave Its Checkered Past Behind," *BusinessWeek*, October 31, 1988, pp. 122–126.

34 For discussions of this debate, see Jean B. McGuire, Alison Sundgren, and Thomas Schneeweis, "Corporate Social Responsibility and Firm Financial Performance," *Academy of Management Journal*, December 1988, pp. 854–872; Margaret A. Stroup, Ralph L. Neubert, and Jerry W. Anderson, Jr., "Doing Good, Doing Better: Two Views of Social Responsibility," *Business Horizons*, March–April 1987, pp. 22–25.

35 "Is It Rainforest Crunch Time?" *BusinessWeek*, July 15, 1996, pp. 70–71; "Yo, Ben! Yo, Jerry! It's Just Ice Cream," *Fortune*, April 28, 1997, p. 374.

36 Andrew Singer, "Can a Company Be Too Ethical?" *Across the Board*, April 1993, pp. 17–22.

37 "Peanut Plant's Practices Not 'Rampant,'" *USA Today*, February 6, 2009, p. 4B.

38 "UBS Admits to Helping U.S. Tax Evaders," *USA Today*, February 10, 2009, p. 1B.

39 "Former Glaxo Lawyer Indicted," *New York Times*, November 9, 2010.

40 "Rent-a-Car Companies Putting Recalled Autos on the Road," *ABC News*, July 7, 2010.

41 *USA Today*, February 12, 2009, p.1B.

42 "Philip Morris Unbound," *BusinessWeek*, May 4, 2009, pp. 38–42.

43 *BusinessWeek*, May 4, 2009, p. 41.

44 *USA Today*, March 27, 2006, p. 1B.

45 "How Barbie Is Making Business a Little Better," *USA Today*, March 27, 2006, pp. 1B, 2B.

46 "L'Occitane Leading the Blind," *Fortune*, November 13, 2006, p. 55.

47 "Into Africa: Capitalism From the Ground Up," *BusinessWeek*, May 4, 2009, pp. 60–61.

48 "Over 70 Pfizer Drugs Could Be Free for Laid-Off Workers," *USA Today*, May 15, 2009, p. 6B.

49 "Subway Reduces Sodium Content in Sandwiches," *USA Today*, April 18, 2011, p. 1B.

50 "Nestle's Palm Oil Woes," *Green Living Tips*, March 21, 2010.

51 Nina Easton and Telis Demos, "The Business Guide to Congress," *Fortune*, May 11, 2009, pp. 72–75.

52 "Siemens to Pay Huge Fine in Bribery Inquiry," *Wall Street Journal*, December 15, 2008, pp. B1, B5.

53 "Daimler Pleads Guilty to Bribing Foreign Governments," *Business Pundit*, April 5, 2010; "Daimler Charged with Bribing Government Officials," *Motor Trend*, March 23, 2010.

54 Nina Easton and Telis Demos, "The Business Guide to Congress," *Fortune*, May 11, 2009, pp. 72–75.

55 Peter A. Heslin and Jenna Ochoa, "Understanding and Developing Strategic Corporate Social Responsibility," *Organizational Dynamics*, 2008, Vol. 37, No. 2, pp. 125–144.

56 "Legal—But Lousy," *Fortune*, September 2, 2002, p. 192.

57 Lynn Sharp Paine, "Managing for Organizational Integrity," *Harvard Business Review*, March–April 1994, pp. 106–115.

58 "To Give, or Not to Give," *Time*, May 11, 2009, p. 10.

59 "Battling 'Donor Dropsy,'" *Wall Street Journal*, July 19, 2002, pp. B1, B4.

60 "A New Way of Giving," *Time*, July 24, 2000, pp. 48–51. See also Michael Porter and Mark Kramwe, "The Competitive Advantage of Corporate Philanthropy," *Harvard Business Review*, December 2002, pp. 57–66.

61 "To Give, or Not to Give," *Time*, May 11, 2009, p. 10.

62 *Time*, May 11, 2009, p. 10.

63 David M. Messick and Max H. Bazerman, "Ethical Leadership and the Psychology of Decision Making," *Sloan Management Review*, Winter 1996, pp. 9–22; see also Muel Kaptein, "Developing and Testing a Measure for the Ethical Culture of Organizations," *Journal of Organizational Behavior*, 2008, Vol. 29, pp. 923–947.

64 "Ethics in Action: Getting It Right," *Selections*, Fall 2002, pp. 24–27.

65 For a thorough review of the literature on whistle-blowing, see Janet P. Near and Marcia P. Miceli, "Whistle-Blowing: Myth and Reality," *Journal of Management*, 1996, Vol. 22, No. 3, pp. 507–526. See also Michael Gundlach, Scott Douglas, and Mark Martinko, "The Decision to Blow the Whistle: A Social Information Processing Framework," *Academy of Management Review*, 2003, Vol. 28, No.1, pp. 107–123.

66 For instance, see "The Complex Goals and Unseen Costs of Whistle-Blowing," *Wall Street Journal*, November 25, 2002, pp. A1, A10.

67 "A Whistle-Blower Rocks an Industry," *BusinessWeek*, June 24, 2002, pp. 126–130.

68 "Lockheed to Pay $2 Million to Settle Lawsuit," *Washington Post*, January 25, 2011; "Feds Intervening in Mississippi Bid-Rigging Lawsuit at Stennis Space Center," *Associated Press*, July 3, 2009.

69 "He Blew a Whistle for 9 Years," *USA Today*, February 13, 2009, pp. 1B, 2B.

70 "SEC Announces a Whistle-Blower Overhaul Plan," *USA Today*, March 6, 2009, p. 1B.

Chapter 5

1 Merchants of Green Coffee, "About the Merchants," 2006, www
.merchantsofgreencoffee.com on February 8, 2011; "Cuban Organic
Shade-Grown Coffee from Merchants of Green Coffee," *TreeHugger.com*, May 19,
2005, www.treehugger.com on February 8, 2011; Thanksgiving Coffee
Co., "End the Embargo on Cuba," 2005, www.endtheembargo.com on
February 8, 2011; Larry Luxner, "Coffee with a Cause," *Tea & Coffee Trade
Journal*, October 2002, www.teaandcoffee.net on February 8, 2011;
Carol J. Williams, "Some Cuban Exiles Hope Obama Can Help," *Los Angeles
Times*, November 10, 2008, http://articles.latimes.com on February 8, 2011;
Doug Palmer, "Business Urges Obama to Loosen Cuba Embargo," December 4,
2008, *Reuters*, www.reuters.com on February 8, 2011; "Cuba Embargo Benefits
European, Canadian Firms," *Reuters*, March 20, 2008, www.reuters.com on
February 8, 2011; Paul Katzeff, "Cooperatives," Thanksgiving Coffee Co., 2005,
www.thanksgivingcoffee.com on February 8, 2011.

2 See Ricky W. Griffin and Michael Pustay, *International Business*, 7th ed. (Upper
Saddle River, NJ: Prentice-Hall, 2013), for an overview of international business.

3 See Thomas Begley and David Boyd, "The Need for a Global Mind-Set," *Sloan
Management Review*, Winter 2003, pp. 25–36.

4 For a more complete discussion of forms of international business, see Griffin and
Pustay, *International Business*.

5 *Hoover's Handbook of American Business 2011* (Austin, TX: Hoover's Business
Press, 2011), pp. 726–727.

6 See "Coke Bets on Russia for Sales Even as Economy Falls Flat," *Wall Street
Journal*, January 28, 2009, pp. A1, A12.

7 John H. Dunning, *Multinational Enterprises and the Global Economy*
(Wokingham, UK: Addison-Wesley, 1993); Christopher Bartlett and Sumantra
Ghoshal, *Transnational Management* (Homewood, IL: Irwin, 1992).

8 "A Company Without a Country?" *BusinessWeek*, May 5, 1997, p. 40.

9 "Philip Morris Unbound," *BusinessWeek*, May 4, 2009, pp. 38–42.

10 *Wall Street Journal*, November 19, 2008, p. B1.

11 "The Fortune Global 500—World's Largest Corporations," *Fortune*, July 25, 2011.

12 "Taco Bell Parent Yum Brands to Continue Global Growth," *Los Angeles Business*,
January 11, 2011.

13 "GE to Increase Focus on Chinese Market," *China Daily*, March 15, 2011.

14 "Going Global—Lessons from Late Movers," *Harvard Business Review*, March–
April 2000, pp. 132–142.

15 Kenichi Ohmae, "The Global Logic of Strategic Alliances," *Harvard Business
Review*, March–April 1989, pp. 143–154.

16 "Global Logistics: FedEx Trade Networks Forms Strategic Alliance with Fritz
Companies Israel," *Logistics Management*, July 7, 2010.

17 "A Starbucks Venture in Tea-Drinking India," *The New York Times*, January 13,
2011.

18 See Balaji R. Koka and John E. Prescott, "Designing Alliance Networks: The
Influence of Network Position, Environmental Change, and Strategy on Firm
Performance," *Strategic Management Journal*, 2008, Vol. 29, pp. 639–661.

19 Dovev Lavie, "Capturing Value from Alliance Portfolios," *Organizational
Dynamics*, January–March 2009, pp. 26–36; see also Paul Beamish and Nathaniel
Lupton, "Managing Joint Ventures," *Academy of Management Perspectives*, 2009,
Vol. 23, No. 2, pp. 75–84.

20 Hans Mjoen and Stephen Tallman, "Control and Performance in International
Joint Ventures," *Organization Science*, May–June 1997, pp. 257–274; see
also Hemant Merchant, "International Joint Venture Configurations in
Big Emerging Markets," *The Multinational Business Review*, Vol. 16,
No. 3, 2008, pp. 93–120.

21 "Misreading the Kremlin Costs BP Control in Russia Venture," *Wall Street
Journal*, December 16, 2008, pp. A1, A6.

22 See "Corporate Culture Shock is a Big Deal," *Financial Times*, July 31, 2008, p. 9.

23 "Harley-Davidson to Build Bikes in India," CNN, November 4, 2010.

24 Mike Westfall, "Maquiladoras—American Industry Creates Modern-Day Mexican
Slaves," *The Cutting Edge*, June 8, 2009.

25 Arindam K. Bhattacharya and David C. Michael, "How Local Companies Keep
Multinationals at Bay," *Harvard Business Review*, March 2008, pp. 85–94.

26 Griffin and Pustay, *International Business*.

27 "Background Note: Mexico," Bureau of Western Hemisphere Affairs, U.S.
Department of State, April 15, 2011.

28 Eileen P. Gunn, "Emerging Markets," *Fortune*, August 18, 1997, pp. 168–173;
see also Tarun Khanna, "China + India—The Power of Two," *Harvard Business
Review*, December 2007, pp. 60–70.

29 "In Many Ways, Return of Hong Kong to China Has Already Happened,"
Wall Street Journal, June 9, 1997, pp. A1, A2; "How You Can Win in China,"
BusinessWeek, May 26, 1997, pp. 66–68.

30 "Cartoon Characters Get a Big Makeover for Overseas Fans," *Wall Street Journal*,
October 16, 2007, p. A1.

31 "Wal-Mart Exports Bog-Box Concept to India," *Wall Street Journal*, May 28, 2009,
p. B1.

32 "Argentina Cries Foul as Choice Employers Beat a Path Next Door," *Wall Street
Journal*, May 2, 2000, pp. A1, A8.

33 "GM Is Building Plants in Developing Nations to Woo New Markets," *Wall Street
Journal*, August 4, 1997, pp. A1, A4.

34 For example, see "China Weighs Lifting Curbs on Foreign Firms," *Wall Street
Journal*, January 1, 2000, p. A17.

35 *BusinessWeek*, March 23/30, 2009, p. 38.

36 Griffin and Pustay, *International Business*.

37 "Oil Companies Strive to Turn a New Leaf to Save Rain Forest," *Wall Street
Journal*, July 17, 1997, pp. A1, A8.

38 *Fortune*, June 27, 2010, p. 160.

39 *Wall Street Journal*, February 6, 2009, p. A1.

40 "Nations Rush to Establish New Barriers to Trade," *Wall Street Journal*, February
6, 2009, pp. A1, A6.

41 "Host of Companies Pocket Windfalls from Tariff Law," *Wall Street Journal*,
December 5, 2002, pp. A1, A14.

42 "Main Street, H.K.—Disney Localizes Mickey to Boost Its Hong Kong Theme
Park," *Wall Street Journal*, January 23, 2008, pp. B1, B2.

43 "What if There Weren't Any Clocks to Watch?" *Newsweek*, June 30, 1997, p. 14.

44 Geert Hofstede, *Culture's Consequences: International Differences in Work-Related
Values* (Beverly Hills, CA: Sage, 1980).

45 I have taken the liberty of changing the actual labels applied to each dimension
for several reasons. The terms I have chosen are more descriptive, simpler, and
more self-evident in their meanings.

46 Geert Hofstede, "The Business of International Business Is Culture," *International
Business Review*, 1994, Vol. 3, No. 1, pp. 1–14.

47 "Crazy Crunches: U.S. Companies Cash in on a Fitness Craze," *Newsweek*, April
28, 1997, p. 49.

48 Stratford Sherman, "Are You as Good as the Best in the World?" *Fortune*,
December 13, 1993, pp. 95–96.

49 Riki Takeuchi, Jeffrey P. Shay, and Jiatao Li, "When Does Decision Autonomy
Increase Expatriate Managers' Adjustment? An Empirical Test," *Academy of
Management Journal*, 2008, Vol. 51, No. 1, pp. 45–60.

Chapter 6

1 Sue Kirchhoff and Judy Keen, "Minorities Hit Hard by Rising Costs of
Subprime Loans," *USA Today*, April 25, 2007, www.usatoday.com on February
22, 2011; Bob Tedeschi, "Subprime Loans' Wide Reach," *New York Times*,
August 3, 2008, www.nytimes.com on February 22, 2011; Kimberly Blanton,
"A 'Smoking Gun' on Race, Subprime Loans," *Boston Globe*, March 16,
2007, www.boston.com on February 22, 2011; "Brown Sues Countrywide for
Mortgage Deception," *Home Loan News*, June 26, 2008, http://loanworkout
.org on February 22, 2011; Bowdeya Tweh, "Analysis: Minorities Had a Greater
Share of 2008 Subprime Loans," *nwi.com*, March 9, 2010, www.nwitimes
.com on February 22, 2011; Nick Carey, "Racial Predatory Loans Fueled
U.S. Housing Crisis: Study," *Reuters*, October 4, 2010, www.reuters.com on
February 22, 2011.

2   "Employment and Earnings, 2010 Annual Averages and the Monthly Labor Review," U.S. Department of Labor, Bureau of Labor Statistics, April 2011.

3   Gail Robinson and Kathleen Dechant, "Building a Business Case for Diversity," *Academy of Management Executive*, August 1997, pp. 21–31. See also Orlando C. Richard, "Racial Diversity, Business Strategy, and Firm Performance: A Resource-Based View," *Academy of Management Journal*, 2000, Vol. 43, No. 2, pp. 164–177.

4   "The Coming Job Bottleneck," *BusinessWeek*, March 24, 1997, pp. 184–185; Linda Thornburg, "The Age Wave Hits," *HR Magazine*, February 1995, pp. 40–46; "How to Manage an Aging Workforce," *The Economist*, February 18, 2006, p. 11.

5   *HR Magazine*, May 2011, pp. 24–25.

6   "Gender Workforce Equality Grows," United Federation of Teachers, January 11, 2010; "Female Power," *The Economist*, December 30, 2009.

7   Gary Powell and D. Anthony Butterfield, "Investigating the 'Glass Ceiling' Phenomenon: An Empirical Study of Actual Promotions to Top Management," *Academy of Management Journal*, 1994, Vol. 37, No. 1, pp. 68–86.

8   "Number of Women Managers Barely Grows," *CNN Money*, September 28, 2010.

9   Karen S. Lyness and Donna E. Thompson, "Above the Glass Ceiling? A Comparison of Matched Samples of Female and Male Executives," *Journal of Applied Psychology*, 1997, Vol. 82, No. 3, pp. 359–375.

10 "What Glass Ceiling?" *USA Today*, July 20, 1999, pp. 1B, 2B; see also Patricia Sellers, "The 50 Most Powerful Women in Business," *Fortune*, November 14, 2005, pp. 125–170.

11 *Occupational Outlook Handbook* (Washington, DC: U.S. Bureau of Labor Statistics, 1990–1991).

12 "Hispanic Nation," *BusinessWeek*, March 15, 2004, pp. 58–70.

13 "The Power of Diversity: Who's Got the Clout?" *Fortune*, August 22, 2005, special issue.

14 "In a Factory Schedule, Where Does Religion Fit In?" *Wall Street Journal*, March 4, 1999, pp. B1, B12.

15 Jane Easter Bahls, "Make Room for Diverse Beliefs," *HR Magazine*, August 1997, pp. 89–95; see also Cliff Edwards, "Coming Out in Corporate America," *BusinessWeek*, December 15, 2003, pp. 64–72.

16 "Immigrants in the United States, 2007," Center for Immigration Studies, November 2007.

17 Based on Taylor H. Cox and Stacy Blake, "Managing Cultural Diversity: Implications for Organizational Competitiveness," *Academy of Management Executive*, August 1991, pp. 45–56. See also Jacqueline A. Gilbert and John M. Ivancevich, "Valuing Diversity: A Tale of Two Organizations," *Academy of Management Executive*, 2000, Vol. 14, No. 1, pp. 93–103.

18 Michelle Neely Martinez, "Work-Life Programs Reap Business Benefits," *HR Magazine*, June 1997, pp. 110–119. See also Cox and Blake, "Managing Cultural Diversity: Implications for Organizational Competitiveness."

19 Jonathan Hickman, "America's 50 Best Companies for Minorities," *Fortune*, July 8, 2002, pp. 110–120.

20 "100 Best Companies to Work for in the United States," *Fortune*, February 7, 2011.

21 For an example, see "A Female Executive Tells Furniture Maker What Women Want," *Wall Street Journal*, June 25, 1999, pp. A1, A11.

22 "Target Makes a Play for Minority Group Sears Has Cultivated," *Wall Street Journal*, April 12, 1999, pp. A1, A8.

23 For example, see Tony Simons, Lisa Hope Pelled, and Ken A. Smith, "Making Use of Difference: Diversity, Debate, and Decision Comprehensiveness in Top Management Teams," *Academy of Management Journal*, 2000, Vol. 42, No. 6, pp. 662–673.

24 C. Marlene Fiol, "Consensus, Diversity, and Learning in Organizations," *Organization Science*, August 1994, pp. 403–415; see also Eric Kearney, Diether Gebert, and Sven C. Voelpel, "When and How Diversity Benefits Teams: The Importance of Team Members' Need for Cognition," *Academy of Management Journal*, 2009, Vol. 52, No. 3, 581–598.

25 Patrick Reinmoeller and Nicole van Baardwijk, "The Link Between Diversity and Resilience," *MIT Sloan Management Review*, Summer 2005, pp. 61–70.

26 *Wall Street Journal*, October 31, 2005, p. B1.

27 Patricia L. Nemetz and Sandra L. Christensen, "The Challenge of Cultural Diversity: Harnessing a Diversity of Views to Understand Multiculturalism," *Academy of Management Review*, 1996, Vol. 21, No. 2, pp. 434–462. See also "Generational Warfare," *Forbes*, March 22, 1999, pp. 62–66; "Do Women Compete in Unhealthy Ways at Work?" *USA Today*, December 30, 2005, p. 1B.

28 Christine M. Riordan and Lynn McFarlane Shores, "Demographic Diversity and Employee Attitudes: An Empirical Examination of Relational Demography Within Work Units," *Journal of Applied Psychology*, 1997, Vol. 82, No. 3, pp. 342–358.

29 "Groupon, Tencent's Co-ops at Odds," *Global Times*, February 17, 2011.

30 Cora Daniels, "Women vs. Wal-Mart," *Fortune*, July 21, 2003, pp. 78–82; "How Shoney's, Belted by a Lawsuit, Found the Path to Diversity," *Wall Street Journal*, April 16, 1996, pp. A1, A6; Fay Rice, "Denny's Changes Its Spots," *Fortune*, May 13, 1996, pp. 133–142; "The Ugly Talk on the Texaco Tape," *BusinessWeek*, November 18, 1996, p. 58; "Smith Barney's Woman Problem," *BusinessWeek*, June 3, 1996, pp. 102–106.

31 Jonathan Hickman, "America's 50 Best Companies for Minorities," *Fortune*, July 7, 2003, pp. 103–120.

32 "Firms Address Workers' Cultural Variety," *Wall Street Journal*, February 10, 1989, p. B1.

33 Sara Rynes and Benson Rosen, "What Makes Diversity Programs Work?" *HR Magazine*, October 1994, pp. 67–75.

34 Karen Hildebrand, "Use Leadership Training to Increase Diversity," *HR Magazine*, August 1996, pp. 53–59.

35 "Learning to Accept Cultural Diversity," *Wall Street Journal*, September 12, 1990, pp. B1, B9.

36 "Firms Address Workers' Cultural Variety."

37 Anthony Carneville and Susan Stone, "Diversity—Beyond the Golden Rule," *Training and Development*, October 1994, pp. 22–27.

38 Janice R. W. Joplin and Catherine S. Daus, "Challenges of Leading a Diverse Workforce," *Academy of Management Executive*, August 1997, pp. 32–47.

39 This discussion derives heavily from Taylor H. Cox, "The Multicultural Organization," *Academy of Management Executive*, May 1991, pp. 34–47.

Chapter 7

1   Tim Rayment, "Joseph Cassano: The Man with the Trillion-Dollar Price on His Head," *The Sunday Times* (London), May 17, 2009, http://business .timesonline.co.uk on February 25, 2011; "AIG's Fall: Bad Business or Criminal Acts?" *CBSNews*, April 27, 2009, www.cbsnews.com on February 25, 2011; Amir Efrati and Susan Pulliam, "Prosecutors Are Poised to Impanel AIG Grand Jury," *Reuters*, September 11, 2009, http://online.reuters.com on February 25, 2011; Gretchen Morgenson, "Behind Insurer's Crisis, Blind Eye to a Web of Risk," *New York Times*, September 28, 2009, www.nytimes.com on February 25, 2011; Matthew Goldstein, "AIG Filing Casts Doubt on 'Limited Exposure' Claim," *Reuters*, January 29, 2010, www.reuters.com on February 25, 2011; Richard Wray, "Joseph Cassano Unlikely to Face Charges over AIG Crisis," *The Guardian*, April 4, 2010, www.guardian.co.uk on February 25, 2011; Shahien Nasiripou, "Joseph Cassano, Ex-AIG Exec, Is Unapologetic, Blames Auditors for Losses," *Huffington Post*, June 30, 2010, www.huffingtonpost.com on February 25, 2011.

2   "IBM Execs Tout Success of Roadmap, Reiterate 2015 Targets," *Wall Street Journal*, March 8, 2011.

3   Patrick R. Rogers, Alex Miller, and William Q. Judge, "Using Information-Processing Theory to Understand Planning/Performance Relationships in the Context of Strategy," *Strategic Management Journal*, 1999, Vol. 20, pp. 567–577.

4   See Peter J. Brews and Michelle R. Hunt, "Learning to Plan and Planning to Learn: Resolving the Planning School/Learning School Debate," *Strategic Management Journal*, 1999, Vol. 20, pp. 889–913.

5   Max D. Richards, *Setting Strategic Goals and Objectives*, 2nd ed. (St. Paul, MN: West, 1986).

6   Jim Collins, "Turning Goals into Results: The Power of Catalytic Mechanisms," *Harvard Business Review*, July–August 1999, pp. 71–81.

7   "GE, No. 2 in Appliances, Is Agitating to Grab Share from Whirlpool," *Wall Street Journal*, July 2, 1997, pp. A1, A6. See also "A Talk with Jeff Immelt," *BusinessWeek*, January 28, 2002, pp. 102–104.

8 Kenneth R. Thompson, Wayne A. Hochwarter, and Nicholas J. Mathys, "Stretch Targets: What Makes Them Effective?" *Academy of Management Executive*, August 1997, pp. 48–58.

9 "A Methodical Man," *Forbes*, August 11, 1997, pp. 70–72.

10 *USA Today*, May 7, 2009, p. 1B.

11 "FDA Not Meeting Its Audit Goals," *USA Today*, May 7, 2009, p. 1B.

12 See Thomas Bateman, Hugh O'Neill, and Amy Kenworthy-U'Ren, "A Hierarchical Taxonomy of Top Managers' Goals," *Journal of Applied Psychology*, 2002, Vol. 87, No. 6, pp. 1134–1148.

13 John A. Pearce II and Fred David, "Corporate Mission Statements: The Bottom Line," *Academy of Management Executive*, May 1987, p. 109.

14 "Starbucks Mission Statement," Starbucks website, www.starbucks.com/aboutus/environment.asp on May 20, 2011.

15 "Renovating Home Depot," *BusinessWeek*, March 6, 2006, pp. 50–58; see also Ram Charan, "Home Depot's Blueprint for Culture Change," *Harvard Business Review*, April 2006, pp. 60–71.

16 "Lowe's Is Sprucing Up Its House," *BusinessWeek*, June 3, 2002, pp. 56–58.

17 "Airlines Try Cutting Business Fares, Find They Don't Lose Revenue," *Wall Street Journal*, November 22, 2002, pp. A1, A6.

18 *Business Week*, June 13, 2011, p. 23.

19 *Hoover's Handbook of World Business 2011* (Austin, TX: Hoover's Business Press, 2011), pp. 356–357.

20 *Fortune*, December 6, 2010, p. 104.

21 See "Disney Cuts Strategic-Planning Unit," *Wall Street Journal*, March 28, 2005, pp. A1, A12.

22 See Jeffrey L. Kerr and William B. Werther Jr., "Engaging the Board in Strategy," *Organizational Dynamics*, 2008, Vol. 37, No. 2, pp. 112–124.

23 K. A. Froot, D. S. Scharfstein, and J. C. Stein, "A Framework for Risk Management," *Harvard Business Review*, November–December 1994, pp. 91–102.

24 "How the Fixers Fended off Big Disasters," *Wall Street Journal*, December 23, 1999, pp. B1, B4.

25 "At Wal-Mart, Emergence Plan Has Big Payoff," *Wall Street Journal*, September 12, 2005, pp. B1, B3.

26 "Next Time," *USA Today*, October 4, 2005, pp. 1B, 2B; see also Judith A. Clair and Ronald L. Dufresne, "How Companies Can Experience Positive Transformation from a Crisis," *Organizational Dynamics*, 2007, Vol. 36, No. 1, pp. 63–77.

27 "Lacking Parts, G.M. Will Close Plant," *New York Times*, March 17, 2011.

28 "G.M. Pieces Together Japanese Supply Chain," *New York Times*, May 13, 2011, p. 5.

29 Michael Watkins and Max Bazerman, "Predictable Surprises: The Disasters You Should Have Seen Coming," *Harvard Business Review*, March 2003, pp. 72–81.

30 James Brian Quinn, Henry Mintzberg, and Robert M. James, *The Strategy Process* (Englewood Cliffs, NJ: Prentice-Hall, 1988).

31 Vasudevan Ramanujam and N. Venkatraman, "Planning System Characteristics and Planning Effectiveness," *Strategic Management Journal*, 1987, Vol. 8, No. 2, pp. 453–468.

32 "Coca-Cola May Need to Slash Its Growth Targets," *Wall Street Journal*, January 28, 2000, p. B2. See also "Pepsi and Coke Roll Out Flavors to Boost Sales," *Wall Street Journal*, May 7, 2002, pp. B1, B4.

33 "Finally, Coke Gets It Right," *BusinessWeek*, February 10, 2003, p. 47.

34 "Disney, Revisited," *USA Today*, December 14, 1999, pp. 1B, 2B.

35 "At Starbucks, a Tall Order for New Cuts, Store Closures," *Wall Street Journal*, January 29, 2009, pp. B1, B4.

36 Quoted in *Fortune*, June 27, 2005, p. 98.

37 Andrew Campbell, "Tailored, Not Benchmarked," *Harvard Business Review*, March–April 1999, pp. 41–48.

38 For a review of the strengths and weaknesses of MBO, see Jack N. Kondrasuk, "Studies in MBO Effectiveness," *Academy of Management Review*, July 1981, pp. 419–430.

Chapter 8

1 Alex Taylor III, "The Birth of the Prius," *Fortune*, March 6, 2006, www.money.cnn.com on February 28, 2011; Chrissie Thompson, "Hybrid Sales in U.S. Slip 9.9% in 2008," *Automotive News*, January 23, 2009, www.autoweek.com on February 28, 2011; "Worldwide Toyota Prius Sales Crack 2-Million Mark, 10-Year Anniversary Celebration Planned," *Autoblog*, October 8, 2010, www.autoblog.com on February 28, 2011; Pablo Päster, "Ask Pablo: Should I Buy a Hybrid?" *Triple Pundit*, December 3, 2007, www.triplepundit.com on February 16, 2009; Irv Miller, "Irv's Sheet: Once More—We at Toyota Want New CAFE Standards!" *Toyota: Open Road Blog*, October 3, 2007, http://blog.toyota.com on February 16, 2009; Union of Concerned Scientists, "Toyota Campaign to Scuttle Stronger Fuel Economy Measures in Energy Bill Undermines Its Green Reputation," press release, October 5, 2007, www.ucsusa.org on February 28, 2011; Juliet Eilperin, "Emissions Limits, Greater Fuel Efficiency for Cars, Trucks Made Official," *Washington Post*, April 2, 2010, www.washingtonpost.com on February 28, 2010.

2 For early discussions of strategic management, see Kenneth Andrews, *The Concept of Corporate Strategy*, rev. ed. (Homewood, IL: Dow Jones–Irwin, 1980); and Igor Ansoff, *Corporate Strategy* (New York: McGraw-Hill, 1965). For more recent perspectives, see Michael E. Porter, "What Is Strategy?" *Harvard Business Review*, November–December 1996, pp. 61–78; Kathleen M. Eisenhardt, "Strategy as Strategic Decision Making," *Sloan Management Review*, Spring 1999, pp. 65–74; Sarah Kaplan and Eric Beinhocker, "The Real Value of Strategic Planning," *Sloan Management Review*, Winter 2003, pp. 71–80.

3 *Hoover's Handbook of American Business 2011* (Austin, TX: Hoover's Business Press, 2011), pp. 29–30.

4 "Abercrombie & Fitch Improves Supply Chain with Management Dynamics," *Retail Technology Review*, April 13, 2010.

5 See Gary Hamel, "Strategy as Revolution," *Harvard Business Review*, July–August 1996, pp. 69–82.

6 See Henry Mintzberg, "Patterns in Strategy Formulation," *Management Science*, October 1978, pp. 934–948; Henry Mintzberg, "Strategy Making in Three Modes," *California Management Review*, 1973, pp. 44–53.

7 T. R. Holcomb, R. M. Holmes Jr., and B. L. Connelly, "Making the Most of What You Have: Managerial Ability as a Source of Resource Value Creation," *Strategic Management Journal*, Vol. 32, No. 5, 2011, pp. 457–486.

8 Jay Barney, "Firm Resources and Sustained Competitive Advantage," *Journal of Management*, June 1991, pp. 99–120; see also T. Russell Crook, David J. Ketchen Jr., James G. Combs, and Samuel Y. Todd, "Strategic Resources and Performance: A Meta-Analysis," *Strategic Management Journal*, 2008, Vol. 29, pp. 1141–1154.

9 Jay Barney, "Strategic Factor Markets," *Management Science*, December 1986, pp. 1231–1241. See also Constantinos C. Markides, "A Dynamic View of Strategy," *Sloan Management Review*, Spring 1999, pp. 55–64.

10 See Michael Porter, *Competitive Strategy* (New York: Free Press, 1980).

11 Porter, *Competitive Strategy*. See also Colin Campbell-Hunt, "What Have We Learned about Generic Competitive Strategy? A Meta-Analysis," *Strategic Management Journal*, 2000, Vol. 21, pp. 127–154. See also Michael E. Porter, "The Five Competitive Forces That Shape Strategy," *Harvard Business Review*, January 2008, pp. 79–90 for a recent update.

12 Ian C. MacMillan and Rita Gunther McGrath, "Discovering New Points of Differentiation," *Harvard Business Review*, July–August 1997, pp. 133–136.

13 "In a Water Fight, Coke and Pepsi Try Opposite Tacks," *Wall Street Journal*, April 18, 2009, pp. A1, A8.

14 "Abercrombie Fights Discount Tide," *Wall Street Journal*, December 8, 2008, p. B1.

15 "When Service Means Survival," *BusinessWeek*, March 2, 2010, pp. 26–40.

16 "Recession Puts Hershey in Sweet Spot," *Wall Street Journal*, January 28, 2009, p. B1.

17 "P&G, Colgate Hit by Consumer Thrift," *Wall Street Journal*, May 1, 2009, pp. B1, B8.

18 "It Ain't the Bellagio. . ." *Business Week*, June 20–26, 2011, pp. 84–85.

19 Raymond E. Miles and Charles C. Snow, *Organizational Strategy, Structure, and Process* (New York: McGraw-Hill, 1978); see also Wayne DeSarbo, C. Anthony Benedetto, Michael Song, and Indrajit Sinha, "Revisiting the Miles and Snow Strategic Framework: Uncovering the Interrelationships Between Strategic Types, Capabilities, Environmental Uncertainty, and Firm Performance," *Strategic Management Journal*, 2005, Vol. 26, pp. 47–74.

20 See Donald L. Laurie, Yves L. Doz, and Claude P. Sheer, "Creating New Growth Platforms," *Harvard Business Review*, May 2006, pp. 80–91.

21 See Lawrence G. Hrebiniak, "Obstacles to Effective Strategy Implementation," *Organizational Dynamics*, February 2006, pp. 12–21.

22 Robert Kaplan and David Norton, "How to Implement a New Strategy Without Disrupting Your Organization," *Harvard Business Review*, March 2006, pp. 100–109.

23 *Fortune*, February 21, 2005, p. 100.

24 Suzanne Kapner, "The Almighty Dollar," *Fortune*, April 27, 2009, pp. 64–66.

25 See Scott D. Anthony, Matt Eyring, and Lib Gibson, "Mapping Your Innovation Strategy," *Harvard Business Review*, May 2011, pp. 104–113.

26 Larry Huston and Nabil Sakkab, "Connect and Develop: Inside Procter & Gamble's New Model for Innovation," *Harvard Business Review*, March 2006, pp. 58–67.

27 Alfred Chandler, *Strategy and Structure: Chapters in the History of the American Industrial Enterprise* (Cambridge, Mass.: MIT Press, 1962); Richard Rumelt, *Strategy, Structure, and Economic Performance* (Cambridge, Mass.: Division of Research, Graduate School of Business Administration, Harvard University, 1974); Oliver Williamson, *Markets and Hierarchies* (New York: Free Press, 1975).

28 "Mars's Takeover of Wrigley Creates a Global Powerhouse," *Wall Street Journal*, April 29, 2010, p. 1A.

29 K. L. Stimpert and Irene M. Duhaime, "Seeing the Big Picture: The Influence of Industry, Diversification, and Business Strategy on Performance," *Academy of Management Journal*, 1997, Vol. 40, No. 3, pp. 560–583.

30 See Chandler, *Strategy and Structure*; Yakov Amihud and Baruch Lev, "Risk Reduction as a Managerial Motive for Conglomerate Mergers," *Bell Journal of Economics*, 1981, pp. 605–617.

31 Chandler, *Strategy and Structure*; Williamson, *Markets and Hierarchies*.

32 *USA Today*, February 11, 2005, p. 1B.

33 For a discussion of the limitations of unrelated diversification, see Jay Barney and William G. Ouchi, *Organizational Economics* (San Francisco: Jossey-Bass, 1986).

34 See Belen Villalonga and Anita McGahan, "The Choice among Acquisitions, Alliances, and Divestitures," *Strategic Management Journal*, 2005, Vol. 26, pp. 1183–1208; see also Xiaoli Yin and Mark Shanley, "Industry Determinants of the 'Merger Versus Alliance' Decision," *Academy of Management Review*, 2008, Vol. 33, No. 2, pp. 473–491.

35 "Latest Merger Boom Is Happening in China, and Bears Watching," *Wall Street Journal*, July 30, 1997, pp. A1, A9; "A Breakthrough in Bavaria," *BusinessWeek*, August 4, 1997, p. 54.

36 Kathleen M. Eisenhardt and D. Charles Galunic, "Coevolving—At Last: A Way to Make Synergies Work," *Harvard Business Review*, January–February 2000, pp. 91–100; see also Harry G. Barkema and Mario Schijven, "How Do Firms Learn to Make Acquisitions? A Review of Past Research and an Agenda for the Future," *Journal of Management*, 2008, Vol. 34, No. 3, pp. 594–634.

37 *BusinessWeek*, April 13, 2010, p. 45.

38 "Mr. Clean Takes Car-Wash Gig," *Wall Street Journal*, February 5, 2011, p. B1.

39 See Constantinoes C. Markides and Peter J. Williamson, "Corporate Diversification and Organizational Structure: A Resource-Based View," *Academy of Management Journal*, April 1996, pp. 340–367; see also Harry Bowen and Margarethe Wiersema, "Foreign-Based Competition and Corporate Diversification Strategy," *Strategic Management Journal*, 2005, Vol. 26, pp. 1153–1171.

40 See Barry Hedley, "A Fundamental Approach to Strategy Development," *Long Range Planning*, December 1976, pp. 2–11; Bruce Henderson, "The Experience Curve—Reviewed. IV: The Growth Share Matrix of the Product Portfolio," *Perspectives*, No. 135 (Boston: Boston Consulting Group, 1973).

41 "Yum Brands Will Sell A&W, Long John Silver's," *USA Today*, January 18, 2011, p. B3.

42 Michael G. Allen, "Diagramming G.E.'s Planning for What's WATT," in Robert J. Allio and Malcolm W. Pennington (eds.), *Corporate Planning: Techniques and Applications* (New York: AMACOM, 1979). Limits of this approach are discussed in R. A. Bettis and W. K. Hall, "The Business Portfolio Approach: Where It Falls Down in Practice," *Long Range Planning*, March 1983, pp. 95–105.

43 "Unilever to Sell Specialty-Chemical Unit to ICI of the U.K. for About $8 Billion," *Wall Street Journal*, May 7, 1997, pp. A3, A12; "For Unilever, It's Sweetness and Light," *Wall Street Journal*, April 13, 2000, pp. B1, B4.

44 "Unprofitable Businesses Getting Axed More Often," *Wall Street Journal*, February 17, 2010, pp. B1, B2.

45 Howard Thomas, Timothy Pollock, and Philip Gorman, "Global Strategic Analyses: Frameworks and Approaches," *Academy of Management Executive*, 1999, Vol. 13, No. 1, pp. 70–80.

46 Kasra Ferdows, "Making the Most of Foreign Factories," *Harvard Business Review*, March–April 1997, pp. 73–88.

47 "Russia Bans U.S. Chicken Shipments, Inspiring Fears of Tough Trade Battle," *Wall Street Journal*, February 23, 1996, p. A2.

48 Anil K. Gupta and Vijay Govindarajan, "Knowledge Flows Within Multinational Corporations," *Strategic Management Journal*, 2000, Vol. 21, No. 4, pp. 473–496; see also Jane Lu and Paul Beamish, "International Diversification and Firm Performance: The S-Curve Hypothesis," *Academy of Management Journal*, 2004, Vol. 47, pp. 598–609.

49 Christopher A. Bartlett and Sumantra Ghoshal, *Transnational Management*, 2nd ed. (Chicago: Irwin, 1995), pp. 237–242. See also Tatiana Kostova, "Transnational Transfer of Strategic Organizational Practices: A Contextual Perspective," *Academy of Management Review*, 1999, Vol. 24, No. 2, pp. 308–324.

50 *BizEd*, July/August 2005, p. 22.

51 "At Nokia, a Comeback—And Then Some," *BusinessWeek*, December 2, 1996, p. 106.

Chapter 9

1 Eric Dash and Julie Creswell, "Citigroup Saw No Red Flags Even as It Made Bolder Bets," *New York Times*, November 23, 2008, www.nytimes.com on March 3, 2011; Susanne Craig and Ben Protess, "New Details Emerge about Morgan Stanley and Citi in the Crisis," *New York Times*, February 10, 2011, http://dealbook.nytimes.com on March 3, 2011; Jenny Anderson and Eric Dash, "Citigroup Loss Raises Anxiety over Economy," *New York Times*, January 16, 2008, www.nytimes.com on March 3, 2011; Floyd Norris, "An Effort to Stem Losses at Citigroup Produces a Renewed Focus on Risk," *New York Times*, January 16, 2008, www.nytimes.com on March 3, 2011; Eric Dash, "Citigroup Reports Big Loss and a Breakup Plan," *New York Times*, January 17, 2009, www.nytimes.com on March 3, 2011; Carrick Mollenkamp, "Citigroup's Risk Chief Learned the Hard Way," *Wall Street Journal*, July 24, 2010, http://online.wsj.com on March 3, 2011.

2 Richard Priem, "Executive Judgment, Organizational Congruence, and Firm Performance," *Organization Science*, August 1994, pp. 421–432. See also R. Duane Ireland and C. Chet Miller, "Decision-Making and Firm Success," *Academy of Management Executive*, 2004, Vol. 18, No. 4, pp. 8–12.

3 Paul Nutt, "The Formulation Processes and Tactics Used in Organizational Decision Making," *Organization Science*, May 1993, pp. 226–240.

4 For a review of decision making, see E. Frank Harrison, *The Managerial Decision Making Process*, 5th ed. (Boston: Houghton Mifflin, 1999). See also Elke U. Weber and Eric J. Johnson, "Mindful Judgment and Decision Making," in Susan T. Fiske, Daniel L. Schacter, and Robert Sternberg (eds.), *Annual Review of Psychology 2009* (Palo Alto, CA: Annual Reviews, 2009), pp. 53–86; Gerd Gigerenzer and Wolfgang Gaissmaier, "Heuristic Decision Making," in Susan T. Fiske, Daniel L. Schacter, and Shelley Taylor (eds.), *Annual Review of Psychology 2011* (Palo Alto, CA: Annual Reviews, 2011), pp. 451–482.

5 "Companies Cope with Too Much Cash," *USA Today*, March 2, 2004, p. 1B.

6 George P. Huber, *Managerial Decision Making* (Glenview, IL: Scott, Foresman, 1980).

7 For an example, see Paul D. Collins, Lori V. Ryan, and Sharon F. Matusik, "Programmable Automation and the Locus of Decision-Making Power," *Journal of Management*, 1999, Vol. 25, pp. 29–53.

8 Huber, *Managerial Decision Making*. See also David W. Miller and Martin K. Starr, *The Structure of Human Decisions* (Englewood Cliffs, NJ: Prentice-Hall, 1976); Alvar Elbing, *Behavioral Decisions in Organizations*, 2nd ed. (Glenview, IL: Scott, Foresman, 1978).

9 Rene M. Stulz, "Six Ways Companies Mismanage Risk," *Harvard Business Review*, March 2009, pp. 86–94.

10 "Ford Lays Bet on New Truck by Rehiring 1,000 Workers," *Wall Street Journal*, October 31, 2008, pp. B1, B2.

11 Gerard P. Hodgkinson, Nicola J. Bown, A. John Maule, Keith W. Glaister, and Alan D. Pearman, "Breaking the Frame: An Analysis of Strategic Cognition and Decision Making under Uncertainty," *Strategic Management Journal*, 1999, Vol. 20, pp. 977–985.

12 "Using Intuition in Your Business Plan," *Forbes*, September 20, 2010.

13 Glen Whyte, "Decision Failures: Why They Occur and How to Prevent Them," *Academy of Management Executive*, August 1991, pp. 23–31. See also Jerry Useem, "Decisions, Decisions," *Fortune*, June 27, 2005, pp. 55–154.

14 Jerry Useem, "Boeing vs. Boeing," *Fortune*, October 2, 2000, pp. 148–160; "Airbus Prepares to 'Bet the Company' as It Builds a Huge New Jet," *Wall Street Journal*, November 3, 1999, pp. A1, A10.

15 Robert C. Litchfield, "Brainstorming Reconsidered: A Goal-Based View," *Academy of Management Review*, 2008, Vol. 33, No. 3, pp. 649–668.

16 Paul Nutt, "Expanding the Search for Alternatives During Strategic Decision-Making," *Academy of Management Executive*, 2004, Vol. 18, No. 4, pp. 13–22.

17 "Queens-Based JetBlue Is Seeking New Corporate Office Site," *New York Daily News*, April 8, 2009; "JetBlue Headquarters to Stay in New York," *The New York Times*, March 22, 2010.

18 *Wall Street Journal*, May 27, 2005, p. A1.

19 See Paul J. H. Schoemaker and Robert E. Gunther, "The Wisdom of Deliberate Mistakes," *Harvard Business Review*, June 2006, pp. 108–115.

20 "Airbus Clips Superjumbo Production," *Wall Street Journal*, May 7, 2009, p. B1.

21 "Accommodating the A380," *Wall Street Journal*, November 29, 2005, p. B1; "Boeing Roars Ahead," *BusinessWeek*, November 7, 2005, pp. 44–45; "Boeing's New Tailwind," *Newsweek*, December 5, 2005, p. 45.

22 "The Wisdom of Solomon," *Newsweek*, August 17, 1987, pp. 62–63.

23 "Making Decisions in Real Time," *Fortune*, June 26, 2000, pp. 332–334. See also Eugene Sadler-Smith and Erella Shefy, "The Intuitive Executive: Understanding and Applying 'Gut Feel' in Decision-Making," *Academy of Management Executive*, 2004, Vol. 18, No. 4, pp. 76–91; Don A. Moore and Francis J. Flynn, "The Case of Behavioral Decision Research in Organizational Behavior," in James P. Walsh and Arthur P. Brief, *The Academy of Management Annals*, Vol. 2 (London: Routledge, 2008), pp. 399–432.

24 "Hard Choices," *Business Week*, November 22–28, 2010, p. 92.

25 Herbert A. Simon, *Administrative Behavior* (New York: Free Press, 1945). Simon's ideas have been refined and updated in Herbert A. Simon, *Administrative Behavior*, 3rd ed. (New York: Free Press, 1976), and Herbert A. Simon, "Making Management Decisions: The Role of Intuition and Emotion," *Academy of Management Executive*, February 1987, pp. 57–63.

26 Patricia Corner, Angelo Kinicki, and Barbara Keats, "Integrating Organizational and Individual Information Processing Perspectives on Choice," *Organization Science*, August 1994, pp. 294–302.

27 "Lessons from Saturn's Fall," *BusinessWeek*, March 2, 2009, p. 25.

28 Kimberly D. Elsbach and Greg Elofson, "How the Packaging of Decision Explanations Affects Perceptions of Trustworthiness," *Academy of Management Journal*, 2000, Vol. 43, pp. 80–89.

29 Kenneth Brousseau, Michael Driver, Gary Hourihan, and Rikard Larsson, "The Seasoned Executive's Decision-Making Style," *Harvard Business Review*, February 2006, pp. 111–112; see also Erik Dane and Michael G. Pratt, "Exploring Intuition

and Its Role in Managerial Decision Making," *Academy of Management Review*, 2007, Vol. 32, No. 1, pp. 33–54.

30 "Three Good Hires? He'll Pay More for One Who's Great," *New York Times*, March 13, 2010.

31 Quoted in *Fortune*, June 27, 2005, p. 55.

32 Barry M. Staw and Jerry Ross, "Good Money after Bad," *Psychology Today*, February 1988, pp. 30–33; D. Ramona Bobocel and John Meyer, "Escalating Commitment to a Failing Course of Action: Separating the Roles of Choice and Justification," *Journal of Applied Psychology*, 1994, Vol. 79, pp. 360–363.

33 Mark Keil and Ramiro Montealegre, "Cutting Your Losses: Extricating Your Organization When a Big Project Goes Awry," *Sloan Management Review*, Spring 2000, pp. 55–64.

34 "Closing Time for a Rock Theme Park," *Wall Street Journal*, January 7, 2009, p. B1.

35 Gerry McNamara and Philip Bromiley, "Risk and Return in Organizational Decision Making," *Academy of Management Journal*, 1999, Vol. 42, pp. 330–339.

36 For an example, see Brian O'Reilly, "What It Takes to Start a Startup," *Fortune*, June 7, 1999, pp. 135–140.

37 Martha I. Finney, "The Catbert Dilemma—The Human Side of Tough Decisions," *HR Magazine*, February 1997, pp. 70–78.

38 See Ann E. Tenbrunsel and Kristen Smith-Crowe, "Ethical Decision Making: Where We've Been and Where We're Going," in James P. Walsh and Arthur P. Brief, *The Academy of Management Annals*, Vol. 2 (London: Routledge, 2008), pp. 545–607.

39 Edwin A. Locke, David M. Schweiger, and Gary P. Latham, "Participation in Decision Making: When Should It Be Used?" *Organizational Dynamics*, Winter 1986, pp. 65–79; Nicholas Baloff and Elizabeth M. Doherty, "Potential Pitfalls in Employee Participation," *Organizational Dynamics*, Winter 1989, pp. 51–62.

40 "The Art of Brainstorming," *BusinessWeek*, August 26, 2002, pp. 168–169.

41 Andre L. Delbecq, Andrew H. Van de Ven, and David H. Gustafson, *Group Techniques for Program Planning* (Glenview, IL: Scott, Foresman, 1975); Michael J. Prietula and Herbert A. Simon, "The Experts in Your Midst," *Harvard Business Review*, January–February 1989, pp. 120–124.

42 See Kevin P. Coyne, Patricia Gorman Clifford, and Renee Dye, "Breakthrough Thinking from Inside the Box," *Harvard Business Review*, December 2007, pp. 71–80, for an extension of the nominal group method.

43 Norman P. R. Maier, "Assets and Liabilities in Group Problem Solving: The Need for an Integrative Function," in J. Richard Hackman, Edward E. Lawler III, and Lyman W. Porter (eds.), *Perspectives on Business in Organizations*, 2nd ed. (New York: McGraw-Hill, 1983), pp. 385–392.

44 Anthony L. Iaquinto and James W. Fredrickson, "Top Management Team Agreement about the Strategic Decision Process: A Test of Some of Its Determinants and Consequences," *Strategic Management Journal*, 1997, Vol. 18, pp. 63–75.

45 Richard A. Cosier and Charles R. Schwenk, "Agreement and Thinking Alike: Ingredients for Poor Decisions," *Academy of Management Executive*, February 1990, pp. 69–78.

46 Irving L. Janis, *Groupthink*, 2nd ed. (Boston: Houghton Mifflin, 1982).

47 Ibid.

Chapter 10

1 Kellen Merrill, "The Big Imprint in the Film Industry," *inmag.com*, 2010, www.inmag.com on March 9, 2011; Stephanie N. Mehta, "Hollywood, South Pacific-Style," *CNNMoney.com*, June 8, 2006, http://money.cnn.com on March 9, 2011; Marlene Rodriguez, "Bigfoot Entertainment's International Academy of Film and Television in Mactan Island, Cebu," *NEDA Knowledge Emporium*, November 5, 2007, www.neda.gov.ph on March 9, 2011; Josh Elmets with Rebecca Pahle, "International Academy of Film and TV Flourishes in the Philippines," *MovieMaker*, January 29, 2010, www.moviemaker.com on March 9, 2011; Jonathan Landreth, "Bigfoot Entertainment Expands, Launches Distribution Company," *Hollywood Reporter*, November 2, 2010, www.hollywoodreporter.com on March 9, 2010; Richard Verrier, "Indie Filmmaker Bigfoot Has an Insider Track to Theater," *Los Angeles Times*, October 6, 2010, http://articles.latimes.com on March 9, 2011.

2 Bro Uttal, "Inside the Deal That Made Bill Gates $350,000,000," *Fortune*, July 21, 1986, pp. 23–33.

3 "The World's Billionaires," *Forbes*, March 10, 2011.

4 Murray B. Low and Ian MacMillan, "Entrepreneurship: Past Research and Future Challenges," *Journal of Management*, June 1988, pp. 139–159.

5 U.S. Bureau of the Census, *Statistical Abstract of the United States*, 2009 (Washington, DC: Government Printing Office, 2009).

6 "Small Business 'Vital Statistics,'" www.sba.gov/aboutsba on May 24, 2009.

7 "Small Business 'Vital Statistics.'"

8 "Small Business 'Vital Statistics.'"

9 "A World That's All a-Twitter," *USA Today*, May 26, 2009, pp. 1B, 2B.

10 *USA Today*, May 26, 2009, p. 1B.

11 "Heaven on Wheels," *Forbes*, April 13, 2009, pp. 74–75.

12 Amar Bhide, "How Entrepreneurs Craft Strategies That Work," *Harvard Business Review*, March–April 1994, pp. 150–163.

13 *USA Today*, April 7, 2004, p. 8B.

14 "Three Men and a Baby Bell," *Forbes*, March 6, 2000, pp. 134–135.

15 *Hoover's Handbook of American Business 2011* (Austin, TX: Hoover's Business Press, 2011), pp. 896–897; "Whole Foods Market 2010 Annual Report," Wholefoodsmarket.com.

16 Nancy J. Lyons, "Moonlight over Indiana," *Inc.*, January 2000, pp. 71–74.

17 F. M. Scherer, *Industrial Market Structure and Economic Performance*, 2nd ed. (Boston: Houghton Mifflin, 1980).

18 "Three Biker-Entrepreneurs Take on Mighty Harley," *New York Times*, August 20, 1999, p. F1.

19 The importance of discovering niches is emphasized in Charles Hill and Gareth Jones, *Strategic Management: An Integrative Approach*, 7th ed. (Boston: Houghton Mifflin, 2007).

20 "A Startup's New Prescription for Eyewear," *Business Week*, July 4–10, 2011, pp. 49–51.

21 D. Kirsch, B. Goldfarb, and A. Gera, "Form or Substance: The Role of Business Plans in Venture Capital Decision Making," *Strategic Management Journal*, Vol. 30, No. 5, 2009, pp. 487–516.

22 *Forbes*, April 13, 2009, p. 75.

23 "Cheap Tricks," *Forbes*, February 21, 2000, p. 116.

24 U.S. Bureau of the Census, *Statistical Abstract of the United States*, 2009.

25 "This Recession Isn't Being Kind to Entrepreneurs," *USA Today*, June 8, 2009, p. 1B.

26 James Combs, David Ketchen, Christopher Shook, and Jeremy Short, "Antecedents and Consequences of Franchising: Past Accomplishments and Future Challenges," *Journal of Management*, January 2011, pp. 99–126.

27 "Up-and-Comers," *BusinessWeek*, May 15, 2000, pp. EB70–EB72.

28 "High-Tech Advances Push C.I.A. into New Company," *New York Times*, September 29, 1999, p. A14.

29 "BET: African-Americans Grow in Numbers, Buying Power," *Multichannel News*, January 26, 2010.

30 AP wire story, January 29, 2006.

31 Norman M. Scarborough and Thomas W. Zimmerer, *Effective Small Business Management: An Entrepreneurial Approach*, 6th ed. (Upper Saddle River, NJ: Prentice Hall, 2000), pp. 412–413.

32 See Robert A. Baron, "The Role of Affect in the Entrepreneurial Process," *Academy of Management Review*, 2008, Vol. 33, No. 2, pp. 328–340; see also Keith M. Hmieleski and Robert A. Baron, "Entrepreneurs' Optimism and New Venture Performance: A Social Cognition Perspective," *Academy of Management Journal*, 2009, Vol. 52, No. 3, pp. 540–572.

33 "Expert Entrepreneur Got Her Show on the Road at an Early Age," *USA Today*, May 24, 2000, p. 5B.

34 "Flush Times for Liquidators," *Wall Street Journal*, January 20, 2009, p. B1.

Chapter 11

1 Roger Lowenstein, "Jamie Dimon: America's Least-Hated Banker," *New York Times*, December 1, 2010, www.nytimes.com on May 1, 2011; Felix Salmon, "Dimon in the Rough: How JPMorgan's CEO Manages Risk," *Seeking Alpha*, September 3, 2008, www.seekingalpha.com on May 1, 2011; Duff McDonald, "The Banker Who Saved Wall Street," *Newsweek*, September 11, 2009, www .newsweek.com on May 1, 2011; Shawn Tully, "How J.P. Morgan Steered Clear of the Credit Crunch," *CNNMoney.com*, September 2, 2008, http://money.cnn.com on May 1, 2011; Jamie Dimon, "No More 'Too Big to Fail,'" *Washington Post*, November 13, 2009, www.washingtonpost.com on May 1, 2011; Mike Taylor, "Hardest-Hitting Jamie Dimon Profile Ever Still Concludes He's Pretty Great," *The New York Observer*, November 2, 2010, www.observer.com on March 2, 2011.

2 For a complete discussion of how FedEx uses control in its operations, see "The FedEx Edge," *Fortune*, April 3, 2006, pp. 77–84.

3 Thomas A. Stewart, "Welcome to the Revolution," *Fortune*, December 13, 1993, pp. 66–77.

4 William Taylor, "Control in an Age of Chaos," *Harvard Business Review*, November–December 1994, pp. 64–70.

5 "Fastener Woes to Delay Flight of First Boeing 787 Jets," *Wall Street Journal*, November 5, 2008, p. B1.

6 "Starbucks Brews Up New Cost Cuts By Putting Lid on Afternoon Decaf," *Wall Street Journal*, January 28, 2009, p. B1.

7 "Cadbury Factory Cuts Energy 605, Costs 50% with Dehumidifier," *Environmental Leader*, April 5, 2011.

8 "An Apple a Day," *BusinessWeek*, October 14, 2002, pp. 122–125; "More Business People Say: Let's Not Do Lunch," *USA Today*, December 24, 2002, p. 1B; David Stires, "The Breaking Point," *Fortune*, March 3, 2003, pp. 107–114.

9 Mark Kroll, Peter Wright, Leslie Toombs, and Hadley Leavell, "Form of Control: A Critical Determinant of Acquisition Performance and CEO Rewards," *Strategic Management Journal*, 1997, Vol. 18, No. 2, pp. 85–96.

10 See Donald Lange, "A Multidimensional Conceptualization of Organizational Corruption Control," *Academy of Management Review*, 2008, Vol. 33, No. 3, pp. 710–729 for an example.

11 See Karynne Turner and Mona Makhija, "The Role of Organizational Controls in Managing Knowledge," *Academy of Management Review*, 2006, Vol. 31, No. 1, pp. 197–217.

12 "It's Showtime for the Airlines," *BusinessWeek*, September 2, 2002, pp. 36–37.

13 "United's Bid to Cut Labor Costs Could Force Rivals to Follow," *Wall Street Journal*, February 25, 2003, pp. A1, A6.

14 Sim Sitkin, Kathleen Sutcliffe, and Roger Schroeder, "Distinguishing Control from Learning in Total Quality Management: A Contingency Perspective," *Academy of Management Review*, 1994, Vol. 19, No. 3, pp. 537–564.

15 Robert Lusch and Michael Harvey, "The Case for an Off-Balance-Sheet Controller," *Sloan Management Review*, Winter 1994, pp. 101–110.

16 Edward E. Lawler III and John G. Rhode, *Information and Control in Organizations* (Pacific Palisades, CA: Goodyear, 1976).

17 Charles W. L. Hill, "Establishing a Standard: Competitive Strategy and Technological Standards in Winner-Take-All Industries," *Academy of Management Executive*, 1997, Vol. 11, No. 2, pp. 7–16.

18 "Airbus Clips Superjumbo Production," *Wall Street Journal*, May 7, 2009, p. B1.

19 "Shifting Burden Helps Employers Cut Health Costs," *Wall Street Journal*, December 8, 2005, pp. B1, B2.

20 *USA Today*, April 13, 2009, p. 3B.

21 "Toyota Plans to Reduce Production for 6 Weeks," *New York Times*, April 19, 2011.

22 "An Efficiency Guru Refits Honda to Fight Auto Giants," *Wall Street Journal*, September 15, 1999, p. B1.

23 See "To Shed Idled Workers, Ford Offers to Foot Bill for College," *Wall Street Journal*, January 18, 2006, pp. B1, B3; "GM's Employees Buyout Offer," *Fast Company*, May 2006, p. 58.

24 See Belverd E. Needles, Jr., Henry R. Anderson, and James C. Caldwell, *Principles of Accounting*, 2002 ed. (Boston: Houghton Mifflin, 2002).

25 "At Disney, String of Weak Cartoons Leads to Cost Cuts," *Wall Street Journal*, June 18, 2002, pp. A1, A6.

26 Needles, Anderson, and Caldwell, *Principles of Accounting*.

27 "Mickey Mouse, CPA," *Forbes*, March 10, 1997, pp. 42–43.

28 Needles, Anderson, and Caldwell, *Principles of Accounting*.

29 Jeremy Kahn, "Do Accountants Have a Future?" *Fortune*, March 3, 2003, pp. 115–117.

30 "Indian Accounting Firm Is Fined $7.5 Million over Fraud at Satyam," *The New York Times*, April 5, 2011.

31 William G. Ouchi, "The Transmission of Control Through Organizational Hierarchy," *Academy of Management Journal*, June 1978, pp. 173–192; Richard E. Walton, "From Control to Commitment in the Workplace," *Harvard Business Review*, March–April 1985, pp. 76–84.

32 "Nordstrom Cleans Out Its Closets," *BusinessWeek*, May 22, 2000, pp. 105–108.

33 "Best Managed Companies in America," *Forbes*, January 9, 2006, p. 118.

34 See "In Bow to Retailers New Clout, Levi Strauss Makes Alterations," *Wall Street Journal*, June 17, 2005, pp. A1, A15.

35 Peter Lorange, Michael F. Scott Morton, and Sumantra Ghoshal, *Strategic Control* (St. Paul, MN: West, 1986). See also Joseph C. Picken and Gregory G. Dess, "Out of (Strategic) Control," *Organizational Dynamics*, Summer 1997, pp. 35–45.

36 "Pfizer Plans Layoffs in Research," *Wall Street Journal*, January 14, 2009, p. B1.
37 "Kohl's Works to Refill Consumers' Bags," *USA Today*, April 8, 2005, pp. B1, B1.
38 *USA Today*, April 8, 2005, p. B1.
39 See Hans Mjoen and Stephen Tallman, "Control and Performance in International Joint Ventures," *Organization Science*, May–June 1997, pp. 257–265.
40 For a recent study of effective control, see Diana Robertson and Erin Anderson, "Control System and Task Environment Effects on Ethical Judgment: An Exploratory Study of Industrial Salespeople," *Organization Science*, November 1993, pp. 617–629.
41 "Workers, Surf at Your Own Risk," *BusinessWeek*, June 12, 2000, pp. 105–106.
42 "Enterprise Takes Idea of Dressed for Success to a New Extreme," *Wall Street Journal*, November 20, 2002, p. B1.
43 "UBS Relaxing Dress Code, Which Set Underwear Standards," *USA Today*, January 25, 2011, p. 1B.
44 Ibid.

Chapter 12

1 Vivien Schweitzer, "Players with No Conductor and, Increasingly, with No Fear," *New York Times*, May 7, 2007, www.nytimes.com on May 3, 2011; Jennifer Higgs, "Orpheus Chamber Orchestra Embodies Democratic Principles," *Axiom News*, October 28, 2008, www.yourbrandplan.com on May 3, 2011; Amanda Gordon, "Self-Governing Orpheus Chamber Orchestra Has Broader Lessons to Offer, Says Banking and Civic Leader John Whitehead," *New York Sun*, April 25, 2009, www.nysun.com on May 3, 2011; Harvey Seifter, "The Conductor-Less Orchestra," *Leader to Leader Journal*, No. 21 (Summer 2001), www.pfdf.org on May 3, 2011; J. Richard Hackman, *Leading Teams: Setting the Stage for Great Performances* (Cambridge: Harvard Business School Press, 2002), http://books.google.com on May 3, 2011.
2 Paul M. Swamidass, "Empirical Science: New Frontier in Operations Management Research," *Academy of Management Review*, October 1991, pp. 793–814.
3 See Anil Khurana, "Managing Complex Production Processes," *Sloan Management Review*, Winter 1999, pp. 85–98.
4 Office of Services, International Trade Administration, ita.doc.gov/td/sif on June 12, 2011.
5 For an example, see Robin Cooper and Regine Slagmulder, "Develop Profitable New Products with Target Costing," *Sloan Management Review*, Summer 1999, pp. 23–34.
6 Joan Woodward, *Industrial Organization: Theory and Practice* (London: Oxford University Press, 1965).
7 See "Tight Labor? Tech to the Rescue," *BusinessWeek*, March 20, 2000, pp. 36–37.
8 "New Plant Gets Jaguar in Gear," *USA Today*, November 27, 2000, p. 4B.
9 "Ford Focuses on Flexibility," *USA Today*, February 28, 2011, pp. 1B, 3B.
10 Ibid.
11 "Thinking Machines," *BusinessWeek*, August 7, 2000, pp. 78–86.
12 *Newsweek*, June 12, 2006, p. 56.
13 James Brian Quinn and Martin Neil Baily, "Information Technology: Increasing Productivity in Services," *Academy of Management Executive*, 1994, Vol. 8, No. 3, pp. 28–37.
14 See Charles J. Corbett, Joseph D. Blackburn, and Luk N. Van Wassenhove, "Partnerships to Improve Supply Chains," *Sloan Management Review*, Summer 1999, pp. 71–82; and Jeffrey K. Liker and Yen-Chun Wu, "Japanese Automakers, U.S. Suppliers, and Supply-Chain Superiority," *Sloan Management Review*, Fall 2000, pp. 81–93. See also Mark Pagell and Zhaohui Wu, "Building a More Complete Theory of Sustainable Supply Chain Management Using Case Studies of 10 Exemplars," *Journal of Supply Chain Management*, 2009, Vol. 45, No. 2, pp. 37–56.
15 "Fastener Woes to Delay Flight of First Boeing 787 Jets," *Wall Street Journal*, November 5, 2008.
16 "G.M. Pieces Together Japanese Supply Chain," *New York Times*, May 13, 2011, p. 5.
17 See "Siemens Climbs Back," *BusinessWeek*, June 5, 2000, pp. 79–82.
18 See M. Bensaou, "Portfolios of Buyer-Supplier Relationships," *Sloan Management Review*, Summer 1999, pp. 35–44.
19 "Just-in-Time Manufacturing Is Working Overtime," *BusinessWeek*, November 8, 1999, pp. 36–37.
20 Rhonda Reger, Loren Gustafson, Samuel DeMarie, and John Mullane, "Reframing the Organization: Why Implementing Total Quality Is Easier Said Than Done," *Academy of Management Review*, 1994, Vol. 19, No. 3, pp. 565–584.
21 Ross Johnson and William O. Winchell, *Management and Quality* (Milwaukee, WI: American Society for Quality Control, 1989). See also Carol Reeves and David Bednar, "Defining Quality: Alternatives and Implications," *Academy of Management Review*, 1994, Vol. 19, No. 3, pp. 419–445; and C. K. Prahalad and M. S. Krishnan, "The New Meaning of Quality in the Information Age," *Harvard Business Review*, September–October 1999, pp. 109–120.
22 *USA Today*, June 28, 2006, p. B4.
23 "Quality Isn't Just for Widgets," *BusinessWeek*, July 22, 2002, pp. 72–73.
24 W. Edwards Deming, *Out of the Crisis* (Cambridge, MA: MIT Press, 1986).
25 "When Service Means Survival," *BusinessWeek*, March 2, 2009, pp. 26–40.
26 *BusinessWeek*, March 2, 2009, p. 29.
27 Joel Dreyfuss, "Victories in the Quality Crusade," *Fortune*, October 10, 1988, pp. 80–88.
28 Thomas Y. Choi and Orlando C. Behling, "Top Managers and TQM Success: One More Look After All These Years," *Academy of Management Executive*, 1997, Vol. 11, No. 1, pp. 37–48.
29 James Dean and David Bowen, "Management Theory and Total Quality: Improving Research and Practice Through Theory Development," *Academy of Management Review*, 1994, Vol. 19, No. 3, pp. 392–418.
30 See "Porsche Figures Out What Americans Want," *USA Today*, June 28, 2006, p. 4B.
31 Edward E. Lawler, "Total Quality Management and Employee Involvement: Are They Compatible?" *Academy of Management Executive*, 1994, Vol. 8, No. 1, pp. 68–79.
32 Jeremy Main, "How to Steal the Best Ideas Around," *Fortune*, October 19, 1992, pp. 102–106.
33 See James Brian Quinn, "Strategic Outsourcing: Leveraging Knowledge Capabilities," *Sloan Management Review*, Summer 1999, pp. 8–22.
34 "Global Gamble," *Forbes*, April 17, 2006, pp. 78–82.
35 *Forbes*, April 17, 2006, p. 82.
36 Thomas Robertson, "How to Reduce Market Penetration Cycle Times," *Sloan Management Review*, Fall 1993, pp. 87–96.
37 "Speed Demons," *BusinessWeek*, March 27, 2006, pp. 68–76.
38 "Ford Does Fast Update of Taurus," *USA Today*, April 20, 2011, p. 1B.
39 Ronald Henkoff, "The Hot New Seal of Quality," *Fortune*, June 28, 1993, pp. 116–120. See also Mustafa V. Uzumeri, "ISO 9000 and Other Metastandards: Principles for Management Practice?" *Academy of Management Executive*, 1997, Vol. 11, No. 1, pp. 21–28.
40 Paula C. Morrow, "The Measurement of TQM Principles and Work-Related Outcomes," *Journal of Organizational Behavior*, July 1997, pp. 363–376.
41 John W. Kendrick, *Understanding Productivity: An Introduction to the Dynamics of Productivity Change* (Baltimore, MD: Johns Hopkins University Press, 1977).
42 "Study: USA Losing Competitive Edge," *USA Today*, April 25, 1997, p. 9D.
43 "Why the Productivity Revolution Will Spread," *BusinessWeek*, February 14, 2000, pp. 112–118. See also "Productivity Grows in Spite of Recession," *USA Today*, July 29, 2002, pp. 1B, 2B; and "Productivity's Second Wind," *BusinessWeek*, February 17, 2003, pp. 36–37.
44 Michael van Biema and Bruce Greenwald, "Managing Our Way to Higher Service-Sector Productivity," *Harvard Business Review*, July–August 1997, pp. 87–98.

Chapter 13

1 "Oeuf the Wall," *Snopes.com*, March 17, 2009, www.snopes.com on May 4, 2011; "Weekend Eating: Mobile Cooking," *Wymsey Weekend*, 2008, www.wymsey.co.uk on May 4, 2011; David Hochman, "Rumor Detectives: True Story or Online Hoax?" *Reader's Digest*, April 2009, www.rd.com on May 4, 2011; "For Snopes .com, Debunking the Bambi Hoax Was All in a Day's Work," *Online Journalism Review*, July 31, 2003, www.ojr.org on May 4, 2011; David Pogue, "Tech Tips for the Basic Computer User," *New York Times*, October 2, 2008, www.nytimes.com on May 4, 2011; Viveca Novak, "Snopes.com," *FactCheck.org*, April 10, 2009, www.factcheck.org on May 4, 2011.

2 See Charlie Feld and Donna Stoddard, "Getting IT Right," *Harvard Business Review*, February 2005, pp. 72–80.

3 See Michael H. Zack, "Managing Codified Knowledge," *Sloan Management Review*, Summer 1999, pp. 45–58.

4 Donald A. Marchand, William J. Kettinger, and John D. Rollins, "Information Orientation: People, Technology, and the Bottom Line," *Sloan Management Review*, Summer 2000, pp. 69–79.

5 Justin Fox, "Inside the New Earnings Game," *Fortune*, March 3, 2003, pp. 97–103.

6 "Investigation to Delay Porsche-Volkswagen Merger," *ABC News/Money*, February 24, 2011.

7 "UAL Shares Dive as Old News Surfaces on Net," *Wall Street Journal*, September 2008, pp. B1, B10.

8 William J. Burns, Jr., and F. Warren McFarlin, "Information Technology Puts Power in Control Systems," *Harvard Business Review*, September–October 1987, pp. 89–94.

9 N. Venkatraman, "IT-Enabled Business Transformation: From Automation to Business Scope Redefinition," *Sloan Management Review*, Winter 1994, pp. 73–84.

10 *Houston Chronicle*, January 30, 2006, p. D1.

11 "America's Best Leaders: John Chambers," *U.S. News and World Reports*, October 22, 2009.

12 Kenneth C. Laudon and Jane P. Laudon, *Essentials of Management Information Systems*, 3rd ed. (Upper Saddle River, NJ: Prentice Hall, 1999), p. 267.

13 "Internet Usage Statistics," internetworldstats.com on June 30, 2010; "United States of America: Internet Usage and Broadband Usage Report," internetworldstats.com in June 2010.

14 Laudon and Laudon, *Essentials of Management Information Systems*, p. 270.

15 *Newsweek*, June 12, 2006, p. 57.

16 See "The Killer Ad Machine," *Forbes*, December 11, 2000, pp. 168–178.

17 Mary Cronin, "Ford's Intranet Success," *Fortune*, March 30, 1998, p. 158.

18 "The Messy Business of Culling Company Files," *Wall Street Journal*, May 22, 1997, pp. B1, B2.

19 "Software That Plows Through Possibilities," *BusinessWeek*, August 7, 2000, p. 84.

20 See "Do One Thing, and Do It Well," *BusinessWeek*, June 19, 2000, pp. 94–100.

21 "On the Job, You're Never Alone," *Houston Chronicle*, January 30, 2006, pp. D1, D4.

22 For example, see "Swamped Workers Switch to 'Unlisted' E-Mails," *USA Today*, September 7, 1999, p. 1A. See also Nicholas Varchaver, "The Perils of E-Mail," *Fortune*, February 17, 2003, pp. 96–103.

23 Robert Kraut, Charles Steinfield, Alice P. Chan, Brian Butler, and Anne Hoag, "Coordination and Virtualization: The Role of Electronic Networks and Personal Relationships," *Organization Science*, 1999, Vol. 10, No. 6, pp. 722–740.

24 See Mahmoud M. Watad and Frank J. DiSanzo, "The Synergism of Telecommuting and Office Automation," *Sloan Management Review*, Winter 2000, pp. 85–96.

25 Manju K. Ahuja and Kathleen M. Carley, "Network Structure in Virtual Organizations," *Organization Science*, 1999, Vol. 10, No. 6, pp. 741–757.

26 "Worksite Face-Off: Techie vs. User," *USA Today*, June 17, 1997, pp. B1, B2.

Chapter 14

1 Jeffrey Sparshott, "Miner Anglo to Sell Assets in Shake-Up," *Wall Street Journal*, October 22, 2009, http://www.dailytenders.co.za on March 14, 2011; Kate Holton et al., "Xstrata Seeks $68 Billion Merger with Anglo," *Reuters*, June 21, 2009, www.reuters.com on March 14, 2011; Julia Werdigier, "Xstrata Makes a New Move for Merger with Anglo," *New York Times*, June 25, 2009, www.nytimes .com on March 14, 2011; Martin Waller and David Robinson, "Business Big Shot: Cynthia Carroll of Anglo American," *Times* (London) *Online*, August 1, 2009, http://business.timesonline.co.uk on March 14, 2011; Andrew Cave, "Cynthia Carroll Digs Deep for Anglo," *Telegraph*, August 1, 2009, www.telegraph.co.uk on March 14, 2011; Julia Werdigier, "Xstrata Ends Bid for Rival in London," *New York Times*, October 16, 2009, www.nytimes.com on March 14, 2011.

2 See David Lei and John Slocum, "Organization Designs to Renew Competitive Advantage," *Organizational Dynamics*, 2002, Vol. 31, No. 1, pp. 1–18.

3 For a related discussion, see Kathleen M. Eisenhardt and Shona L. Brown, "Patching—Restitching Business Portfolios in Dynamic Markets," *Harvard Business Review*, May–June 1999, pp. 106–115.

4 David A. Nadler and Michael L. Tushman, *Competing by Design: The Power of Organizational Architecture* (New York: Oxford University Press, 1997).

5 Ricky W. Griffin and Gary McMahan, "Motivation Through Job Design," in Jerald Greenberg (ed.), *Organizational Behavior: The State of the Science* (Hillsdale, NJ: Lawrence Erlbaum Associates, 1994), pp. 23–44. See also Adam M. Grant, Yitzhak Fried, and Tina Juillerat, "Work Matters: Job Design in Classic and Contemporary Perspectives," in Sheldon Zedeck (ed.), *Handbook of Industrial and Organizational Psychology* (Washington, DC: American Psychological Association, 2010), pp. 190–225.

6 Adam Smith, *Wealth of Nations* (New York: Modern Library, 1937; originally published in 1776).

7 Andrea Gabor, *The Capitalist Philosophers* (New York: Times Business, 2000).

8 Ricky W. Griffin, *Task Design* (Glenview, IL: Scott Foresman, 1982).

9 Anne S. Miner, "Idiosyncratic Jobs in Formal Organizations," *Administrative Science Quarterly*, September 1987, pp. 327–351.

10 M. D. Kilbridge, "Reduced Costs Through Job Enlargement: A Case," *Journal of Business*, Vol. 33, 1960, pp. 357–362.

11 *Fortune*, June 12, 2006, p. 150.

12 Griffin and McMahan, "Motivation Through Job Enrichment."

13 "Jacks of All Trades, and Masters of All," *USA Today*, July 6, 2011, p. 1B.

14 Kilbridge, "Reduced Costs Through Job Enrichment: A Case."

15 Frederick Herzberg, *Work and the Nature of Man* (Cleveland: World Press, 1966).

16 Robert Ford, "Job Enrichment Lessons from AT&T," *Harvard Business Review*, January–February 1973, pp. 96–106.

17 "Companies Do More with Fewer Workers," *USA Today*, February 23, 2011, p. 1B.

18 J. Richard Hackman and Greg R. Oldham, *Work Redesign* (Reading, MA: Addison-Wesley, 1980).

19 Jerry Useem, "What's That Spell? Teamwork!" *Fortune*, June 12, 2006, pp. 64–66.

20 For a related discussion, see Etienne C. Wenger and William M. Snyder, "Communities of Practice: The Organizational Frontier," *Harvard Business Review*, January–February 2000, pp. 139–148.

21 George P. Huber, "Organizations: Theory, Design, Future," in Sheldon Zedeck (ed.), *Handbook of Industrial and Organizational Psychology* (Washington, DC: American Psychological Association, 2010), pp. 80–105.

22 A. V. Graicunas, "Relationships in Organizations," *Bulletin of the International Management Institute*, March 7, 1933, pp. 39–42.

23 Ralph C. Davis, *Fundamentals of Top Management* (New York: Harper & Row, 1951); Lyndall F. Urwick, *Scientific Principles and Organization* (New York: American Management Association, 1938), p. 8; Ian Hamilton, *The Soul and Body of an Army* (London: Edward Arnold, 1921), pp. 229–230.

24 David D. Van Fleet and Arthur G. Bedeian, "A History of the Span of Management," *Academy of Management Review*, 1977, pp. 356–372.

25 James C. Worthy, "Factors Influencing Employee Morale," *Harvard Business Review*, January 1950, pp. 61–73.

26 Dan R. Dalton, William D. Todor, Michael J. Spendolini, Gordon J. Fielding, and Lyman W. Porter, "Organization Structure and Performance: A Critical Review," *Academy of Management Review*, January 1980, pp. 49–64.

27 "Allergan Board of Directors Announces Departure of President F. Michael Ball; Chairman of the Board and Chief Executive Officer David E. I. Pyott Resumes Role as President," *CNBC*, March 7, 2011.

28 "Cadbury Gives Its CEO More Control," *Wall Street Journal*, October 15, 2008, p. B2.

29 See Jerry Useem, "Welcome to the New Company Town," *Fortune*, January 10, 2000, pp. 62–70, for a related discussion. See also "Wherever You Go, You're on the Job," *BusinessWeek*, June 20, 2005, pp. 87–90.

30 David Van Fleet, "Span of Management Research and Issues," *Academy of Management Journal*, September 1983, pp. 546–552.

31 Philip Siekman, "Where 'Build to Order' Works Best," *Fortune*, April 26, 1999, pp. 160C–160V.

32 See Daft, *Organization Theory and Design*.

33 William Kahn and Kathy Kram, "Authority at Work: Internal Models and Their Organizational Consequences," *Academy of Management Review*, 1994, Vol. 19, No. 1, pp. 17–50.

34 Carrie R. Leana, "Predictors and Consequences of Delegation," *Academy of Management Journal*, December 1986, pp. 754–774.

35 Jerry Useem, "In Corporate America It's Cleanup Time," *Fortune*, September 16, 2002, pp. 62–70.

36 "Delegate, Step Back, and Let Go," *livemint.com*, March 8, 2011.

37 "Remote Control," *HR Magazine*, August 1997, pp. 82–90.

38 "Toppling the Pyramids," *Canadian Business*, May 1993, pp. 61–65.

39 "New Shell CEO Begins Shake-Up," *Wall Street Journal*, May 28, 2009, p. B4.

40 "Yahoo CEO to Install Top-Down Management," *Wall Street Journal*, February 23, 2009, p. B1.

41 *BusinessWeek*, March 23/30, 2009, p. 33.

42 Kevin Crowston, "A Coordination Theory Approach to Organizational Process Design," *Organization Science*, March–April 1997, pp. 157–166.

43 James Thompson, *Organizations in Action* (New York: McGraw-Hill, 1967). For a recent discussion, see Bart Victor and Richard S. Blackburn, "Interdependence: An Alternative Conceptualization," *Academy of Management Review*, July 1987, pp. 486–498.

44 Jay R. Galbraith, *Designing Complex Organizations* (Reading, MA: Addison-Wesley, 1973) and *Organizational Design* (Reading, MA: Addison-Wesley, 1977).

45 Paul R. Lawrence and Jay W. Lorsch, "Differentiation and Integration in Complex Organizations," *Administrative Science Quarterly*, March 1967, pp. 1–47.

Chapter 15

1 Robert Berner, "Flip-Flops, Torn Jeans—And Control," *BusinessWeek*, May 30, 2005, www.businessweek.com on April 20, 2010; Jess Cartner-Morley, "History of Abercrombie & Fitch: Tracing a Line from JFK's Blazer," *The Guardian*, June 24, 2009, www.guardian.com on April 20, 2010; Benoit Denizet-Lewis, "The Man Behind Abercrombie & Fitch," *Salon.com*, January 24, 2006, www.salon.com on April 20, 2010; Andria Cheng, "Abercrombie & Fitch Clothed in Green," *MarketWatch*, February 13, 2009, www.marketwatch.com on March 17, 2009.

2 See George P. Huber, "Organizations: Theory, Design, Future," in Sheldon Zedeck (ed.), *Handbook of Industrial and Organizational Psychology*, Vol. 1: *Building and Developing the Organization* (Washington, DC: American Psychological Association, 2010), pp. 117–160.

3 Royston Greenwood and Danny Miller, "Tackling Design Anew: Getting Back to the Heart of Organizational theory," *Academy of Management Perspectives*, November 2010, pp. 78–88.

4 Max Weber, *Theory of Social and Economic Organizations*, trans. T. Parsons (New York: Free Press, 1947).

5 Paul Jarley, Jack Fiorito, and John Thomas Delany, "A Structural Contingency Approach to Bureaucracy and Democracy in U.S. National Unions," *Academy of Management Journal*, 1997, Vol. 40, No. 4, pp. 831–861.

6 Rensis Likert, *New Patterns in Management* (New York: McGraw-Hill, 1961), and *The Human Organization* (New York: McGraw-Hill, 1967).

7 William F. Dowling, "At General Motors: System 4 Builds Performance and Profits," *Organizational Dynamics*, Winter 1975, pp. 23–28.

8 Gareth Jones, *Organizational Theory, Design, and Change*, 6th ed. (Upper Saddle River, NJ: Prentice Hall, 2009). See also "The Great Transformation," *BusinessWeek*, August 28, 2000, pp. 84–99.

9 See N. Anand and Richard L. Daft, "What Is the Right Organization Design?" *Organizational Dynamics*, 2007, Vol. 36, No. 4, pp. 329–344 for a recent review.

10 Joan Woodward, *Industrial Organization: Theory and Practice* (London: Oxford University Press, 1965).

11 Joan Woodward, *Management and Technology, Problems of Progress Industry*, No. 3 (London: Her Majesty's Stationery Office, 1958).

12 William Bridges, "The End of the Job," *Fortune*, September 19, 1994, pp. 62–74.

13 For example, see Michael Russo and Niran Harrison, "Organizational Design and Environmental Performance: Clues from the Electronics Industry," *Academy of Management Journal*, 2005, Vol. 48, No. 4, pp. 582–593; see also Sebastian Raisch and Julian Birkinshaw, "Organizational Ambidexterity: Antecedents, Outcomes, and Moderators," *Journal of Management*, 2008, Vol. 34, No. 3, pp. 375–409.

14 Tom Burns and G. M. Stalker, *The Management of Innovation* (London: Tavistock, 1961).

15 *BusinessWeek*, June 20, 2005, p. 81.

16 Paul R. Lawrence and Jay W. Lorsch, *Organization and Environment* (Homewood, IL: Irwin, 1967).

17 Edward E. Lawler III, "Rethinking Organization Size," *Organizational Dynamics*, Autumn 1997, pp. 24–33. See also Henrich R. Greve, "A Behavioral Theory of Firm Growth: Sequential Attention to Size and Performance Goals," *Academy of Management Journal*, 2008, Vol. 51, No. 3, pp. 476–494.

18 Derek S. Pugh and David J. Hickson, *Organization Structure in Its Context: The Aston Program I* (Lexington, MA: D. C. Heath, 1976).

19 "Can Wal-Mart Get Any Bigger?" *Time*, January 13, 2003, pp. 38–43.

20 "Marathon Oil to Split in Two," *New York Times*, January 13, 2011.

21 Robert H. Miles and Associates, *The Organizational Life Cycle* (San Francisco: Jossey-Bass, 1980). See also "Is Your Company Too Big?" *BusinessWeek*, March 27, 1989, pp. 84–94.

22 Douglas Baker and John Cullen, "Administrative Reorganization and Configurational Context: The Contingent Effects of Age, Size, and Change in Size," *Academy of Management Journal*, 1993, Vol. 36, No. 6, pp. 1251–1277. See also Kevin Crowston, "A Coordination Theory Approach to Organizational Process Design," *Organization Science*, March–April 1997, pp. 157–168.

23 See "The Corporate Ecosystem," *BusinessWeek*, August 28, 2000, pp. 166–197.

24 Richard D'Aveni and David Ravenscraft, "Economies of Integration Versus Bureaucratic Costs: Does Vertical Integration Improve Performance?" *Academy of Management Journal*, 1994, Vol. 37, No. 5, pp. 1167–1206.

25 Gerardine DeSanctis, Jeffrey Glass, and Ingrid Morris Ensing, "Organizational Designs for R&D," *Academy of Management Executive*, 2002, Vol. 16, No. 2, pp. 55–64.

26 Oliver E. Williamson, *Markets and Hierarchies* (New York: Free Press, 1975).

27 Ibid.

28 Michael E. Porter, "From Competitive Advantage to Corporate Strategy," *Harvard Business Review*, May–June 1987, pp. 43–59.

29 Williamson, *Markets and Hierarchies*.

30 Jay B. Barney and William G. Ouchi (eds.), *Organizational Economics* (San Francisco: Jossey-Bass, 1986); Robert E. Hoskisson, "Multidivisional Structure and Performance: The Contingency of Diversification Strategy," *Academy of Management Journal*, December 1987, pp. 625–644. See also Bruce Lamont, Robert Williams, and James Hoffman, "Performance During 'M-Form' Reorganization and Recovery Time: The Effects of Prior Strategy and Implementation Speed," *Academy of Management Journal*, 1994, Vol. 37, No. 1, pp. 153–166.

31 Stanley M. Davis and Paul R. Lawrence, *Matrix* (Reading, MA: Addison-Wesley, 1977).

32 "Martha, Inc.," *BusinessWeek*, January 17, 2000, pp. 63–72.

33 Davis and Lawrence, *Matrix*.

34 See Lawton Burns and Douglas Wholey, "Adoption and Abandonment of Matrix Management Programs: Effects of Organizational Characteristics and Interorganizational Networks," *Academy of Management Journal*, 1993, Vol. 36, No. 1, pp. 106–138.

35 See Michael Hammer and Steven Stanton, "How Process Enterprises Really Work," *Harvard Business Review*, November–December 1999, pp. 108–118.

36 Raymond E. Miles, Charles C. Snow, John A. Mathews, Grant Miles, and Henry J. Coleman, Jr., "Organizing in the Knowledge Age: Anticipating the Cellular Form," *Academy of Management Executive*, November 1997, pp. 7–24.

37 John Mathieu, M. Travis Maynard, Tammy Rapp, and Lucy Gibson, "Team Effectiveness 1997–2007: A Review of Recent Advancements and a Glimpse into the Future," *Journal of Management*, 2008, Vol. 34, No. 3, pp. 410–476.

38 "Management by Web," *BusinessWeek*, August 28, 2000, pp. 84–96.

39 *Fortune*, June 12, 2006, p. 136.

40 Peter Senge, *The Fifth Discipline* (New York: Free Press, 1993). See also David Lei, John W. Slocum, and Robert A. Pitts, "Designing Organizations for Competitive Advantage: The Power of Unlearning and Learning," *Organizational Dynamics*, Winter 1999, pp. 24–35.

41 Amy C. Edmondson, "The Competitive Imperative of Learning," *Harvard Business Review*, July–August 2008, pp. 60–70.

42 See William G. Egelhoff, "Strategy and Structure in Multinational Corporations: A Revision of the Stopford and Wells Model," *Strategic Management Journal*, 1988, Vol. 9, pp. 1–14, for a recent discussion of these issues. See also Ricky W. Griffin and Michael Pustay, *International Business: A Managerial Perspective*, 7th ed. (Upper Saddle River, NJ: Prentice-Hall, 2012).

43 Riki Takeuchi, Jeffrey P. Shay, and Jiatao Li, "When Does Decision Autonomy Increase Expatriate Managers' Adjustment? An Empirical Test," *Academy of Management Journal*, 2008, Vol. 51, No. 1, pp. 45–60.

Chapter 16

1 "Genentech's Joe McCracken Is on the Hunt," *The Burrill Report*, May 7, 2007, www.burrillreport.com on March 28, 2011; Querida Anderson, "OSI Pharma Needs to Expand Pipeline," *Genetic Engineering & Biotechnology News*, June 15, 2007, www.genengnews.com on March 28, 2011; "Seattle Genetics Reports Final SGN-40 Phase I Non-Hodgkin Lymphoma Data at International Conference on Malignant Lymphoma," *Drugs.com*, February 3, 2011, www.drugs.com on March 28, 2011; Genentech Inc., "Genentech Announces Voluntary Withdrawal of Raptiva from the U.S. Market," press release, April 8, 2009, www.gene.com on March 28, 2011; Maureen Martino, "CEO: Roche, Genentech R&D Won't Merge," *Fierce Biotech*, September 15, 2010, www.fiercebiotech.com on March 28, 2011; "Business Development at Roche and Genentech: An Interview with Joe McCracken and Dan Zabrowski," *BioPharma Today*, July 28, 2009, www.biopharmatoday.com on March 28, 2011.

2 For an excellent review of this area, see Achilles A. Armenakis and Arthur G. Bedeian, "Organizational Change: A Review of Theory and Research in the 1990s," *Journal of Management*, 1999, Vol. 25, No. 3, pp. 293–315. For a more recent review, see Luis L. Martins, "Organizational Change and Development," in Sheldon Zedeck (ed.), *Handbook of Industrial and Organizational Psychology*, Vol. 3: *Maintaining, Expanding, and Contracting the Organization* (Washington, DC: American Psychological Association, 2010), pp. 691–728.

3 For additional insights into how technological change affects other parts of the organization, see P. Robert Duimering, Frank Safayeni, and Lyn Purdy, "Integrated Manufacturing: Redesign the Organization Before Implementing Flexible Technology," *Sloan Management Review*, Summer 1993, pp. 47–56.

4 Joel Cutcher-Gershenfeld, Ellen Ernst Kossek, and Heidi Sandling, "Managing Concurrent Change Initiatives," *Organizational Dynamics*, Winter 1997, pp. 21–38.

5 Michael A. Hitt, "The New Frontier: Transformation of Management for the New Millennium," *Organizational Dynamics*, Winter 2000, pp. 7–15. See also Michael Beer and Nitin Nohria, "Cracking the Code of Change," *Harvard Business Review*, May–June 2000, pp. 133–144; Clark Gilbert, "The Disruption Opportunity," *MIT Sloan Management Review*, Summer 2003, pp. 27–32.

6 *BusinessWeek*, March 23/30, 2009, p. 33.

7 See Warren Boeker, "Strategic Change: The Influence of Managerial Characteristics and Organizational Growth," *Academy of Management Journal*, 1997, Vol. 40, No. 1, pp. 152–170.

8 Alan L. Frohman, "Igniting Organizational Change from Below: The Power of Personal Initiative," *Organizational Dynamics*, Winter 1997, pp. 39–53.

9 Nandini Rajagopalan and Gretchen M. Spreitzer, "Toward a Theory of Strategic Change: A Multi-Lens Perspective and Integrative Framework," *Academy of Management Review*, 1997, Vol. 22, No. 1, pp. 48–79.

10 Anne Fisher, "Danger Zone," *Fortune*, September 8, 1997, pp. 165–167.

11 "Kodak to Cut Staff up to 21% amid Digital Push," *Wall Street Journal*, January 22, 2005, pp. A1, A7.

12 John P. Kotter and Leonard A. Schlesinger, "Choosing Strategies for Change," *Harvard Business Review*, March–April 1979, p. 106.

13 Clayton M. Christensen and Michael Overdorf, "Meeting the Challenge of Disruptive Change," *Harvard Business Review*, March–April 2000, pp. 67–77.

14 "To Maintain Success, Managers Must Learn How to Direct Change," *Wall Street Journal*, August 13, 2002, p. B1. See also Andrew Van de Ven and Kangyong Sun, "Breakdowns in Implementing Models of Organization Change," *Academy of Management Perspectives*, August 2011, pp. 58–68.

15 See Eric Abrahamson, "Change Without Pain," *Harvard Business Review*, July–August 2000, pp. 75–85. See also Gib Akin and Ian Palmer, "Putting Metaphors to Work for Change in Organizations," *Organizational Dynamics*, Winter 2000, pp. 67–76.

16 Erik Brynjolfsson, Amy Austin Renshaw, and Marshall Van Alstyne, "The Matrix of Change," *Sloan Management Review*, Winter 1997, pp. 37–54.

17 Kurt Lewin, "Frontiers in Group Dynamics: Concept, Method, and Reality in Social Science," *Human Relations*, June 1947, pp. 5–41.

18 Michael Roberto and Lynne Levesque, "The Art of Making Change Initiatives Stick," *MIT Sloan Management Review*, Summer 2005, pp. 53–62.

19 "Time for a Turnaround," *Fast Company*, January 2003, pp. 55–61.

20 See Connie J. G. Gersick, "Revolutionary Change Theories: A Multilevel Exploration of the Punctuated Equilibrium Paradigm," *Academy of Management Review*, January 1991, pp. 10–36; see also John P. Kotter and Leonard A. Schlesinger, "Choosing Strategies for Change," *Harvard Business Review*, July–August 2008, pp. 130–141.

21 See Mel Fugate, Angelo J. Kinicki, and Gregory E. Prussia, "Employee Coping with Organizational Change: An Examination of Alternative Theoretical Perspectives and Models," *Personnel Psychology*, 2008, Vol. 61, pp. 1–36. See also Jeffrey D. Ford and Laurie W. Ford, "Decoding Resistance to Change," *Harvard Business Review*," April 2009, pp. 99–104.

22 See Clark Gilbert and Joseph Bower, "Disruptive Change," *Harvard Business Review*, May 2002, pp. 95–104.

23 "RJR Employees Fight Distraction amid Buy-Out Talks," *Wall Street Journal*, November 1, 1988, p. A8.

24 "Flight Chaos Looms as BA Staff Vow to Strike," *Sydney Morning Herald*, December 16, 2010.

25 Arnon E. Reichers, John P. Wanous, and James T. Austin, "Understanding and Managing Cynicism about Organizational Change," *Academy of Management Executive*, February 1997, pp. 48–59.

26 For a classic discussion, see Paul R. Lawrence, "How to Deal with Resistance to Change," *Harvard Business Review*, January–February 1969, pp. 4–12, 166–176; for a more recent discussion, see Jeffrey D. Ford, Laurie W. Ford, and Angelo D'Amelio, "Resistance to Change: The Rest of the Story," *Academy of Management Review*, 2008, Vol. 33, No. 2, pp. 362–377.

27 Lester Coch and John R. P. French, Jr., "Overcoming Resistance to Change," *Human Relations*, August 1948, pp. 512–532.

28 "9 Keys to Driving Cultural Change," *Business Insider*, April 19, 2011.

29 Benjamin Schneider, Arthur P. Brief, and Richard A. Guzzo, "Creating a Climate and Culture for Sustainable Organizational Change," *Organizational Dynamics*, Spring 1996, pp. 7–19.

30 "Troubled GM Plans Major Tuneup," *USA Today*, June 6, 2005, pp. 1B, 2B.

31 Paul Bate, Raza Khan, and Annie Pye, "Towards a Culturally Sensitive Approach to Organization Structuring: Where Organization Design Meets Organization Development," *Organization Science*, March–April 2000, pp. 197–211.

32 David Kirkpatrick, "The New Player," *Fortune*, April 17, 2000, pp. 162–168.

33 Jeffrey A. Alexander, "Adaptive Change in Corporate Control Practices," *Academy of Management Journal*, March 1991, pp. 162–193.

34 "Microsoft to Boost Cash Pay for Employees," *Wall Street Journal*, April 22, 2011.

35 "CIO Innovator on Creative Destruction: Getting Out of the Comfort Zone," *SearchCIO.com*, April 21, 2011.

36 Gerd Bohner and Nina Dickel, "Attitudes and Attitude Change," in Susan T. Fiske, Daniel L. Schacter, and Shelley Taylor (eds.), *Annual Review of Psychology 2011* (Palo Alto, CA: Annual Reviews, 2011), pp. 391–418.

37 Thomas A. Stewart, "Reengineering—The Hot New Managing Tool," *Fortune*, August 23, 1993, pp. 41–48.

38 "Old Company Learns New Tricks," *USA Today*, April 10, 2000, pp. 1B, 2B.

39 "10 Practices of Fortune's 2010 Top 10 Business People," *Brian Dodd on Leadership*, December 25, 2010.

40 Paul Nunes and Tim Breen, "Reinvent Your Business Before It's Too Late," *Harvard Business Review*, January–February 2011, pp. 80–87.

41 Richard Beckhard, *Organization Development: Strategies and Models* (Reading, MA: Addison-Wesley, 1969), p. 9.

42 W. Warner Burke, "The New Agenda for Organization Development," *Organizational Dynamics*, Summer 1997, pp. 7–20.

43 Wendell L. French and Cecil H. Bell, Jr., *Organization Development: Behavioral Science Interventions for Organization Improvement*, 2nd ed. (Englewood Cliffs, NJ: Prentice-Hall, 1978).

44 "Memo to the Team: This Needs Salt!" *Wall Street Journal*, April 4, 2000, pp. B1, B14.

45 Raymond A. Noe, Michael J. Tews, and Alison McConnell Dachner, "Learner Engagement: A New Perspective for Enhancing Our Understanding of Learner Motivation and Workplace Learning," in James P. Walsh and Arthur P. Brief (eds.), *The Academy of Management Annals 2010* (Philadelphia: Taylor and Francis, 2010), pp. 279–316.

46 Roger J. Hower, Mark G. Mindell, and Donna L. Simmons, "Introducing Innovation Through OD," *Management Review*, February 1978, pp. 52–56.

47 "Is Organization Development Catching On? A Personnel Symposium," *Personnel*, November–December 1977, pp. 10–22.

48 For a recent discussion on the effectiveness of various OD techniques in different organizations, see John M. Nicholas, "The Comparative Impact of Organization Development Interventions on Hard Criteria Measures," *Academy of Management Review*, October 1982, pp. 531–542.

49 Constantinos Markides, "Strategic Innovation," *Sloan Management Review*, Spring 1997, pp. 9–24. See also James Brian Quinn, "Outsourcing Innovation: The New Engine of Growth," *Sloan Management Review*, Summer 2000, pp. 13–21.

50 L. B. Mohr, "Determinants of Innovation in Organizations," *American Political Science Review*, 1969, pp. 111–126; G. A. Steiner, *The Creative Organization* (Chicago: University of Chicago Press, 1965); R. Duncan and A. Weiss, "Organizational Learning: Implications for Organizational Design," in B. M. Staw (ed.), *Research in Organizational Behavior*, Vol. 1 (Greenwich, CT: JAI

Press, 1979), pp. 75–123; J. E. Ettlie, "Adequacy of Stage Models for Decisions on Adoption of Innovation," *Psychological Reports*, 1980, pp. 991–995.

51 See Alan Patz, "Managing Innovation in High Technology Industries," *New Management*, September 1986, pp. 54–59.

52 "Apple Can't Keep Up with Demand for Newest iMac," *USA Today*, August 26, 2002, p. 3B.

53 See Willow A. Sheremata, "Centrifugal and Centripetal Forces in Radical New Product Development under Time Pressure," *Academy of Management Review*, 2000, Vol. 25, No. 2, pp. 389–408. See also Richard Leifer, Gina Colarelli O'Connor, and Mark Rice, "Implementing Radical Innovation in Mature Firms: The Role of Hobs," *Academy of Management Executive*, 2001, Vol. 15, No. 3, pp. 102–113.

54 See Julian Birkinshaw, Gary Hamel, and Michael J. Mol, "Management Innovation," *Academy of Management Review*, 2008, Vol. 33, No. 4, pp. 825–845.

55 See "Amid Japan's Gloom, Corporate Overhauls Offer Hints of Revival," *Wall Street Journal*, February 21, 2002, pp. A1, A11.

56 See Clayton M. Christensen, Stephen P. Kaufman, and Willy C. Shih, "Innovation Killers," *Harvard Business Review*, January 2008, pp. 98–107.

57 Dorothy Leonard and Jeffrey F. Rayport, "Spark Innovation Through Empathic Design," *Harvard Business Review*, November–December 1997, pp. 102–115.

58 "The 25 Most Innovative Companies," *BusinessWeek*, April 20, 2009, pp. 46–47.

59 Geoffrey Moore, "Innovating Within Established Enterprises," *Harvard Business Review*, July–August 2004, pp. 87–96. See also David A. Garvin and Lynne C. Levesque, "Meeting the Challenge of Corporate Entrepreneurship," *Harvard Business Review*, October 2006, pp. 102–113.

60 See Gifford Pinchot III, *Intrapreneuring* (New York: Harper & Row, 1985).

61 "What Is Intrapreneurship?" *Entrepreneurship*, June 3, 2009.

Chapter 17

1 Jon Springer, "Danny Wegman," *Supermarket News*, July 14, 2009, http://supermarketnews.com on April 15, 2011; Michael A. Prospero, "Employee Innovator: Wegmans," *Fast Company*, October 2004, www.fastcompany.com on April 15, 2011; Dan Mitchell, "Wegmans Price War Against Itself," *The Big Money*, November 2, 2009, www.thebigmoney.com on April 15, 2011; "100 Best Companies to Work For," *Fortune*, 2011, http://money.cnn.com on April 15, 2011; Business Civic Leadership Center, "Wegmans," *2009 Corporate Citizenship Awards* (U.S. Chamber of Commerce, 2009), www.bclc.uschamber.com on April 15, 2011; "In 2010, Wegmans Announces Largest Group of Employee Scholarship Recipients Yet," press release, June 16, 2010, www.wegmans.com on April 15, 2011.

2 For a complete review of human resource management, see Angelo S. DeNisi and Ricky W. Griffin, *Human Resource Management* (Cincinnati: Cengage, 2011).

3 Patrick Wright and Gary McMahan, "Strategic Human Resources Management: A Review of the Literature," *Journal of Management*, June 1992, pp. 280–319; see also Peter Cappelli, "Talent Management for the Twenty-First Century," *Harvard Business Review*, March 2008, pp. 74–84; and Edward E. Lawler III, "Making Human Capital a Source of Competitive Advantage," *Organizational Dynamics*, January–March 2009, pp. 1–7.

4 "From the Ashes, New Tech Start-Ups Can Bloom," *USA Today*, February 17, 2009, p. 1B.

5 Augustine Lado and Mary Wilson, "Human Resource Systems and Sustained Competitive Advantage: A Competency-Based Perspective," *Academy of Management Review*, 1994, Vol. 19, No. 4, pp. 699–727.

6 David Lepak and Scott Snell, "Examining the Human Resource Architecture: The Relationships among Human Capital, Employment, and Human Resource Configurations," *Journal of Management*, 2002, Vol. 28, No. 4, pp. 517–543. See also Wayne F. Cascio and Herman Aguinis, "Staffing Twenty-First Century Organizations," in James P. Walsh and Arthur P. Brief, *The Academy of Management Annals*, Vol. 2 (London: Routledge, 2008), pp. 133–166.

7 "Maryland First to OK 'Wal-Mart Bill,' " *USA Today*, January 13, 2006, p. 1B.

8 "OSHA Claims Company Knowingly Overexposed Workers to Lead," *Advanced Safety and Health*, January 21, 2011.

9 "The Hidden Perils of Layoffs," *BusinessWeek*, March 2, 2009, pp. 52–53.

10 *USA Today*, March 28, 2006, p. 2B.

11 "While Hiring at Most Firms Chills, Wal-Mart's Heats Up," *USA Today*, August 26, 2002, p. 1B.

12 Peter Cappelli, "A Supply Chain Approach to Workforce Planning," *Organizational Dynamics*, January–March 2009, pp. 8–15.

13 "The New Workforce," *BusinessWeek*, March 20, 2000, pp. 64–70.

14 John Beeson, "Succession Planning," *Across the Board*, February 2000, pp. 38–41.

15 "Xerox Names Burns Chief as Mulcahy Retires Early," *Wall Street Journal*, May 22, 2009, pp. B1, B2.

16 "Star Search," *BusinessWeek*, October 10, 2005, pp. 66–78. See also Claudio Fernandez-Aráoz, Boris Groysberg, and Nitin Nohria, "The Definitive Guide to Recruiting in Good Times and Bad," *Harvard Business Review*, May 2009, pp. 74–85; and Brian R. Dineen and Scott M. Soltis, "Recruitment: A Review of Research and Emerging Directions," in Sheldon Zedeck (ed.), *Handbook of Industrial and Organizational Psychology*, Vol. 2: *Selecting and Developing Members for the Organization* (Washington, DC: American Psychological Association, 2010), pp. 43–66.

17 Robert Gatewood, Mary Gowan, and Gary Lautenschlager, "Corporate Image, Recruitment Image, and Initial Job Choice Decisions," *Academy of Management Journal*, 1993, Vol. 36, No. 2, pp. 414–427; see also Karen Holcombe Ehrhart and Jonathan Ziegert, "Why Are Individuals Attracted to Organizations?" *Journal of Management*, 2005, Vol. 31, No. 6, pp. 901–919; and Donald M. Truxillo and Talya N. Bauer, "Applicant Reactions to Organizations and Selection Systems," in Sheldon Zedeck (ed.), *Handbook of Industrial and Organizational Psychology*, Vol. 2: *Selecting and Developing Members for the Organization* (Washington, DC: American Psychological Association, 2010), pp. 379–398.

18 *Wall Street Journal*, October 15, 2008, p. B1.

19 "Firms Cook Up New Ways to Keep Workers," *USA Today*, January 18, 2000, p. 1B.

20 "Lean Times Swell Avon's Sales Force," *Wall Street Journal*, October 15, 2008, p. B1.

21 James A. Breaugh and Mary Starke, "Research on Employee Recruiting: So Many Studies, So Many Remaining Questions," *Journal of Management*, 2000, Vol. 26, No. 3, pp. 405–434.

22 See Paul R. Sackett and Filip Lievens, "Personnel Selection," in Susan T. Fiske, Daniel L. Schacter, and Robert Sternberg (eds.), *Annual Review of Psychology 2008* (Palo Alto, CA: Annual Reviews, 2008), pp. 419–450.

23 "Pumping Up Your Past," *Time*, June 10, 2002, p. 96.

24 Frank L. Schmidt and John E. Hunter, "Employment Testing: Old Theories and New Research Findings," *American Psychologist*, October 1981, pp. 1128–1137.

25 Robert Liden, Christopher Martin, and Charles Parsons, "Interviewer and Applicant Behaviors in Employment Interviews," *Academy of Management Journal*, 1993, Vol. 36, No. 2, pp. 372–386.

26 Allen I. Huffcutt and Satoris S. Culbertson, "Interviews," in Sheldon Zedeck (ed.), *Handbook of Industrial and Organizational Psychology*, Vol. 2: *Selecting*

and Developing Members for the Organization (Washington, DC: American Psychological Association, 2010), pp. 185–204.

27 Winfred Arthur Jr. and Eric Anthony Day, "Assessment Centers," in Sheldon Zedeck (ed.), *Handbook of Industrial and Organizational Psychology*, Vol. 2: *Selecting and Developing Members for the Organization* (Washington, DC: American Psychological Association), pp. 205–236.

28 Paul R. Sackett, "Assessment Centers and Content Validity: Some Neglected Issues," *Personnel Psychology*, 1987, Vol. 40, pp. 13–25.

29 Kenneth B. Brown and Traci Sitzmann, "Training and Employee Development for Improved Performance," in Sheldon Zedeck (ed.), *Handbook of Industrial and Organizational Psychology*, Vol. 2: *Selecting and Developing Members for the Organization* (Washington, DC: American Psychological Association), pp. 469–504.

30 "2010 Training Industry Report," *Training Magazine*, November 19, 2010.

31 Renee DeRouin, Barbara Fritzsche, and Eduardo Salas, "E-Learning in Organizations," *Journal of Management*, 2005, Vol. 31, No. 6, pp. 920–940. See Fred Luthans, James B. Avey, and Jaime L. Patera, "Experimental Analysis of a Web-Based Training Intervention to Develop Positive Psychological Capital," *Academy of Management Learning & Education*, 2008, Vol. 7, No. 2, pp. 209–221 for a recent illustration.

32 "'Boeing U': Flying by the Book," *USA Today*, October 6, 1997, pp. 1B, 2B. See also "Is Your Airline Pilot Ready for Surprises?" *Time*, October 14, 2002, p. 72.

33 "The Secret Sauce at In-N-Out Burger," *BusinessWeek*, April 20, 2009, pp. 68–69; "Despite Cutbacks, Firms Invest in Developing Leaders," *Wall Street Journal*, February 9, 2009, p. B4.

34 *Wall Street Journal*, February 9, 2009, p. B4.

35 Jessica L. Wildman, Wendy L. Bedwell, Eduardo Salas, and Kimberly A. Smith-Jentsch, "Performance Measurement at Work: A Multilevel Perspective," in Sheldon Zedeck (ed.), *Handbook of Industrial and Organizational Psychology*, Vol. 1: *Building and Developing the Organization* (Washington, DC: American Psychological Association, 2010), pp. 303–341.

36 See Paul Levy and Jane Williams, "The Social Context of Performance Appraisal: A Review and Framework for the Future," *Journal of Management*, 2004, Vol. 30, No. 6, pp. 881–905.

37 See Michael Hammer, "The 7 Deadly Sins of Performance Measurement (and How to Avoid Them)," *MIT Sloan Management Review*, Spring 2007, pp. 19–30.

38 See Angelo S. DeNisi and Avraham N. Kluger, "Feedback Effectiveness: Can 360-Degree Appraisals Be Improved?" *Academy of Management Executive*, 2000, Vol. 14, No. 1, pp. 129–139.

39 Barry R. Nathan, Allan Mohrman, and John Milliman, "Interpersonal Relations as a Context for the Effects of Appraisal Interviews on Performance and Satisfaction: A Longitudinal Study," *Academy of Management Journal*, June 1991, pp. 352–369.

40 "Goodyear to Stop Labeling 10% of Its Workers as Worst," *USA Today*, September 12, 2002, p. 1B.

41 Joseph J. Martocchio, "Strategic Reward and Compensation Plans," in Sheldon Zedeck (ed.), *Handbook of Industrial and Organizational Psychology*, Vol. 1: *Building and Developing the Organization* (Washington, DC: American Psychological Association, 2010), pp. 343–372.

42 Jaclyn Fierman, "The Perilous New World of Fair Pay," *Fortune*, June 13, 1994, pp. 57–64. See also "The Best vs. the Rest," *Wall Street Journal*, January 30, 2006, pp. B1, B3.

43 "Pay Cuts Made Palatable," *BusinessWeek*, May 4, 2009, p. 67. See also "The Right Way to Pay," *Forbes*, May 11, 2009, pp. 78–80; and "Do Pay Cuts Pay Off?" *Time*, April 27, 2009, p. 6.

44 Stephanie Armour, "Show Me the Money, More Workers Say," *USA Today*, June 6, 2000, p. 1B.

45 "To Each According to His Needs: Flexible Benefits Plans Gain Favor," *Wall Street Journal*, September 16, 1986, p. 29.

46 "The Future Look of Employee Benefits," *Wall Street Journal*, September 7, 1988, p. 21.

47 See "Companies Chisel Away at Workers' Benefits," *USA Today*, November 18, 2002, pp. 1B, 2B. See also "The Benefits Trap," *BusinessWeek*, July 19, 2004, pp. 64–72.

48 "More Companies Freeze Pensions," *USA Today*, May 11, 2009, p. 1A.

49 "Prudential Report: Stabilizing Outlook for Corporate Defined Benefit Plans," *Prudential*, April 14, 2011.

50 "Financially Pinched Companies Snip Employee Benefits," *USA Today*, April 7, 2011.

51 See Sherry E. Sullivan, "The Changing Nature of Careers: A Review and Research Agenda," *Journal of Management*, 1999, Vol. 25, No. 3, pp. 457–484.

52 Barbara Presley Nobel, "Reinventing Labor," *Harvard Business Review*, July–August 1993, pp. 115–125.

53 "Big Gains for Unions," *New York Times*, January 29, 2009, p. C1.

54 John A. Fossum, "Labor Relations: Research and Practice in Transition," *Journal of Management*, Summer 1987, pp. 281–300.

55 "How Wal-Mart Keeps Unions at Bay," *BusinessWeek*, October 28, 2002, pp. 94–96.

56 "Outsourcing at Crux of Boeing Strike," *Wall Street Journal*, September 8, 2008, pp. B1, B4.

57 "Was the Mott's Strike 'Victory' Really a Victory?" *Huffington Post*, September 14, 2010. "Mott's Strike Comes to an End," *New York Daily News*, September 13, 2010.

58 "UAW Gives Concessions to Big Three," *Wall Street Journal*, December 4, 2008, pp. B1, B2.

59 Max Boisot, *Knowledge Assets* (Oxford, UK: Oxford University Press, 1998).

60 *USA Today*, March 28, 2006, p. 2B.

61 Thomas Stewart, "In Search of Elusive Tech Workers," *Fortune*, February 16, 1998, pp. 171–172.

62 Elizabeth George and Carmen Kaman Ng, "Nonstandard Workers: Work Arrangements and Outcomes," in Sheldon Zedeck (ed.), *Handbook of Industrial and Organizational Psychology*, Vol. 1: *Building and Developing the Organization* (Washington, DC: American Psychological Association, 2010), pp. 573–596.

63 "FBI Taps Retiree Experience for Temporary Jobs," *USA Today*, October 3, 2002, p. 1A.

64 "Special Report on Contingent Staffing," *Workforce Management*, October 19, 2009.

65 "When Is a Temp Not a Temp?" *BusinessWeek*, December 7, 1998, pp. 90–92.

66 "Drivers Deliver Trouble to FedEx by Seeking Employee Benefits," *Wall Street Journal*, January 7, 2005, pp. A1, A8; "FedEx Wins Ruling That Contract Drivers Seeking Benefits Aren't Employees," *Bloomberg*, December 14, 2010.

Chapter 18

1 Julie Creswell and Landon Thomas Jr., "The Talented Mr. Madoff," *New York Times*, January 25, 2009, www.nytimes.com on April 1, 2011; Jeffrey Kluger, "Putting Bernie Madoff on the Couch," *Time*, December 31, 2008, www.time.com on April 1, 2011; Henry Blodget, "Madoff: The Ted Bundy of Money," *The Business Insider*, January 24, 2009, www.businessinsider.com on April 1, 2011; Andy Serwer, " 'Financial Psychopaths' Wreak Havoc," *CNNMoney.com*, http://money.cnn.com on April 1, 2011; Paul Babiak and Robert D. Hare, *Snakes in Suits: When Psychopaths Go to Work* (New York: Regan, 2006), http://books.google.com on April 1, 2011; Steve Fishman, "The Madoff Tapes," *New York*, February 27, 2011, http://nymag.com on April 1, 2011; Alan Deutschman, "Is Your Boss a Psychopath?" *Fast Company*, July 2005, www.fastcompany.com on April 1, 2011.

2 Lynn McGarlane Shore and Lois Tetrick, "The Psychological Contract as an Explanatory Framework in the Employment Relationship," in C. L. Cooper and D. M. Rousseau (eds.), *Trends in Organizational Behavior* (London: Wiley, 1994). See also Denise M. Rousseau, "The Individual–Organization Relationship: The Psychological Contract," in Sheldon Zedeck (ed.), *Handbook*

of Industrial and Organizational Psychology*, Vol. 3: *Maintaining, Expanding, and Contracting the Organization* (Washington, DC: American Psychological Association, 2010), pp. 191–220.

3 For an illustration see Zhen Xiong Chen, Anne Tsui, and Lifeng Zhong, "Reactions to Psychological Contract Breach: A Dual Perspective," *Journal of Organizational Behavior*, 2008, Vol. 29, pp. 527–548.

4 Elizabeth Wolfe Morrison and Sandra L. Robinson, "When Employees Feel Betrayed: A Model of How Psychological Contract Violation Develops," *Academy of Management Review*, January 1997, pp. 226–256.

5 *USA Today*, March 28, 2006, p. 2B.

6 *Fortune*, November 15, 2010.

7 See Arne Kalleberg, "The Mismatched Worker: When People Don't Fit Their Jobs," *Academy of Management Perspectives*, 2008, Vol. 22, No. 1, pp. 24–40.

8 Oleksandr S. Chernyshenko, Stephen Stark, and Fritz Drasgow, "Individual Differences: Their Measurement and Validity," in Sheldon Zedeck (ed.), *Handbook of Industrial and Organizational Psychology*, Vol. 2: *Selecting*

and Developing Members for the Organization (Washington, DC: American Psychological Association, 2010), pp. 117–151.

9 Lawrence Pervin, "Personality" in Mark Rosenzweig and Lyman Porter (eds.), *Annual Review of Psychology*, Vol. 36 (Palo Alto, CA: Annual Reviews, 1985), pp. 83–114; S. R. Maddi, *Personality Theories: A Comparative Analysis*, 4th ed. (Homewood, IL: Dorsey, 1980); see also Dan P. McAdams and Bradley D. Olson, "Personality Development: Continuity and Change Over the Life Course," in Susan T. Fiske, Daniel L. Schacter, and Robert J. Sternberg (eds.), *Annual Review of Psychology 2010* (Palo Alto, CA: Annual Reviews, 2010), pp. 517–542.

10 L. R. Goldberg, "An Alternative 'Description of Personality': The Big Five Factor Structure," *Journal of Personality and Social Psychology*, 1990, Vol. 59, pp. 1216–1229.

11 Michael K. Mount, Murray R. Barrick, and J. Perkins Strauss, "Validity of Observer Ratings of the Big Five Personality Factors," *Journal of Applied Psychology*, 1994, Vol. 79, no. 2, pp. 272–280; Timothy A. Judge, Joseph J. Martocchio, and Carl J. Thoreson, "Five-Factor Model of Personality and Employee Absence," *Journal of Applied Psychology*, 1997, Vol. 82, No. 5, pp. 745–755.

12 See Robert Renn, David Allen, and Tobias Huning, "Empirical Examination of the Individual-Level Personality-Based Theory of Self-Management Failure," *Journal of Organizational Behavior*, January 2011, pp. 25–43 for a recent extension of the Big Five framework.

13 J. B. Rotter, "Generalized Expectancies for Internal vs. External Control of Reinforcement," *Psychological Monographs*, 1966, Vol. 80, pp. 1–28. See also Simon S. K. Lam and John Schaubroeck, "The Role of Locus of Control in Reactions to Being Promoted and to Being Passed Over: A Quasi Experiment," *Academy of Management Journal*, 2000, Vol. 43, No. 1, pp. 66–78.

14 Marilyn E. Gist and Terence R. Mitchell, "Self-Efficacy: A Theoretical Analysis of Its Determinants and Malleability," *Academy of Management Review*, April 1992, pp. 183–211.

15 T. W. Adorno, E. Frenkel-Brunswick, D. J. Levinson, and R. N. Sanford, *The Authoritarian Personality* (New York: Harper & Row, 1950).

16 "The Rise and Fall of Dennis Kozlowski," *BusinessWeek*, December 23, 2002, pp. 64–77.

17 Jon L. Pierce, Donald G. Gardner, and Larry L. Cummings, "Organization-Based Self-Esteem: Construct Definition, Measurement, and Validation," *Academy of Management Journal*, 1989, Vol. 32, pp. 622–648.

18 Michael Harris Bond and Peter B. Smith, "Cross-Cultural Social and Organizational Psychology," in Janet Spence (ed.), *Annual Review of Psychology*, Vol. 47 (Palo Alto, CA: Annual Reviews, 1996), pp. 205–235.

19 See Daniel Goleman, *Emotional Intelligence: Why It Can Matter More Than IQ* (New York: Bantam, 1995).

20 Daniel Goleman, "Leadership That Gets Results," *Harvard Business Review*, March–April 2000, pp. 78–90. See also Kenneth Law, Chi-Sum Wong, and Lynda Song, "The Construct and Criterion Validity of Emotional Intelligence and Its Potential Utility for Management Studies," *Journal of Applied Psychology*, 2004, Vol. 87, No. 3, pp. 483–496; Joseph C. Rode, Christine H. Mooney, Marne L. Arthaud-Day, Janet P. Near, Timothy T. Baldwin, Robert S. Rubin, and William H. Bommer, "Emotional Intelligence and Individual Performance: Evidence of Direct and Indirect Effects," *Journal of Organizational Behavior*, 2007, Vol. 28, pp. 399–421; and John D. Mayer, Richard D. Roberts, and Sigal G. Barsade, "Human Abilities: Emotional Intelligence," in Susan T. Fiske, Daniel L. Schacter, and Robert Sternberg (eds.), *Annual Review of Psychology 2008* (Palo Alto, CA: Annual Reviews, 2008), pp. 507–536.

21 For a recent review see Gerd Bohner and Nina Dickel, "Attitudes and Attitude Change," in Susan T. Fiske, Daniel L. Schacter, and Shelley Taylor (eds.), *Annual Review of Psychology 2011* (Palo Alto, CA: Annual Reviews, 2011), pp. 391–418.

22 Leon Festinger, *A Theory of Cognitive Dissonance* (Palo Alto, CA: Stanford University Press, 1957).

23 See John J. Clancy, "Is Loyalty Really Dead?" *Across the Board*, June 1999, pp. 15–19.

24 Patricia C. Smith, L. M. Kendall, and Charles Hulin, *The Measurement of Satisfaction in Work and Behavior* (Chicago: Rand-McNally, 1969). See also Steven Currall, Annette Towler, Tomothy Judge, and Laura Kohn, "Pay Satisfaction and Organizational Outcomes," *Personnel Psychology*, 2005, Vol. 58, pp. 613–640.

25 "Companies Are Finding Real Payoffs in Aiding Employee Satisfaction," *Wall Street Journal*, October 11, 2000, p. B1.

26 James R. Lincoln, "Employee Work Attitudes and Management Practice in the U.S. and Japan: Evidence from a Large Comparative Study," *California Management Review*, Fall 1989, pp. 89–106.

27 *USA Today*, November 30, 2004, p. 1B.

28 Ibid.

29 Richard M. Steers, "Antecedents and Outcomes of Organizational Commitment," *Administrative Science Quarterly*, 1977, Vol. 22, pp. 46–56.

30 See Timothy R. Clark, "Engaging the Disengaged," *HR Magazine*, April 2008, pp. 109–115.

31 Omar N. Solinger, Woody van Olffen, and Robert A. Roe, "Beyond the Three-Component Model of Organizational Commitment," *Journal of Applied Psychology*, 2008, Vol. 93, No. 1, pp. 70–83; see also Steven M. Elias, "Employee Commitment in Times of Change: Assessing the Importance of Attitudes Toward Organizational Change," *Journal of Management*, 2009, Vol. 35, No. 1, pp. 37–55.

32 For research work in this area, see Jennifer M. George and Gareth R. Jones, "The Experience of Mood and Turnover Intentions: Interactive Effects of Value Attainment, Job Satisfaction, and Positive Mood," *Journal of Applied Psychology*, 1996, Vol. 81, no. 3, pp. 318–325; Larry J. Williams, Mark B. Gavin, and Margaret Williams, "Measurement and Nonmeasurement Processes with Negative Affectivity and Employee Attitudes," *Journal of Applied Psychology*, 1996, Vol. 81, No. 1, pp. 88–101.

33 See Robert A. Baron, "The Role of Affect in the Entrepreneurial Process," *Academy of Management Review*, 2008, Vol. 33, No. 2, pp. 328–340.

34 Kathleen Sutcliffe, "What Executives Notice: Accurate Perceptions in Top Management Teams," *Academy of Management Journal*, 1994, Vol. 37, No. 5, pp. 1360–1378.

35 Richard A. Posthuma and Michael A. Campion, "Age Stereotypes in the Workplace: Common Stereotypes, Moderators, and Future Research Directions," *Journal of Management*, 2009, Vol. 35, No. 1, pp. 158–188.

36 For a classic treatment of attribution, see H. H. Kelley, *Attribution in Social Interaction* (Morristown, NJ: General Learning Press, 1971). For a recent application, see Edward C. Tomlinson and Roger C. Mayer, "The Role of Causal Attribution Dimensions in Trust Repair," *Academy of Management Review*, Vol. 34, No. 1, January 2009, pp. 85–104.

37 For an overview of the stress literature, see Frank Landy, James Campbell Quick, and Stanislav Kasl, "Work, Stress, and Well-Being," *International Journal of Stress Management*, 1994, Vol. 1, No. 1, pp. 33–73; see also Mark A. Griffin and Sharon Clarke, "Stress and Well-Being at Work," in Sheldon Zedeck (ed.), *Handbook of Industrial and Organizational Psychology*, Vol. 3: *Maintaining, Expanding, and Contracting the Organization* (Washington, DC: American Psychological Association: Washington, D.C., 2010), pp. 359–397.

38 Hans Selye, *The Stress of Life* (New York: McGraw-Hill, 1976).

39 M. Friedman and R. H. Rosenman, *Type A Behavior and Your Heart* (New York: Knopf, 1974).

40 "Work & Family," *BusinessWeek*, June 28, 1993, pp. 80–88.

41 Quoted in *USA Today*, December 13, 2007, p. 2B.

42 Richard S. DeFrank, Robert Konopaske, and John M. Ivancevich, "Executive Travel Stress: Perils of the Road Warrior," *Academy of Management Executive*, 2000, Vol. 14, No. 2, pp. 58–67.

43 Steven Rogelberg, Desmond Leach, Peter Warr, and Jennifer Burnfield, "'Not Another Meeting!' Are Meeting Time Demands Related to Employee Well Being?" *Journal of Applied Psychology*, 2006, Vol. 91, No. 1, pp. 86–96.

44 "Those Doing Layoffs Can Feel the Pain," *USA Today*, April 23, 2009, p. 5D.

45 Remus Ilies, Michael Johnson, Timothy Judge, and Jessica Keeney, "A Within-Individual Study of Interpersonal Conflict as a Work Stressor: Dispositional and Situational Moderators," *Journal of Organizational Behavior*, January 2011, pp. 44–64.

46 *USA Today*, April 23, 2009, p. 5D.

47 Michael R. Frone, "Are Work Stressors Related to Employee Substance Abuse? The Importance of Temporal Context in Assessments of Alcohol and Illicit Drug Use," *Journal of Applied Psychology*, 2008, Vol. 93, No. 1, pp. 199–296.

48 "Breaking Point," *Newsweek*, March 6, 1995, pp. 56–62. See also "Rising Job Stress Could Affect Bottom Line," *USA Today*, July 28, 2003, p. 18.

49 See Christopher M. Barnes and John R. Hollenbeck, "Sleep Deprivation and Decision-Making Teams: Burning the Midnight Oil or Playing with Fire?" *Academy of Management Review*, Vol. 34, No. 1, January 2009, pp. 56–66.

50 John M. Kelly, "Get a Grip on Stress," *HR Magazine*, February 1997, pp. 51–58; see also Marilyn Macik-Frey, James Campbell Quick, and Debra Nelson, "Advances in Occupational Health: From a Stressful Beginning to a Positive Future," *Journal of Management*, 2007, Vol. 33, No. 6, pp. 809–840.

51 Charlotte Fritz, Sabine Sonnentag, Paul Spector, and Jennifer McInroe, "The Weekend Matters: Relationships Between Stress Recovery and Affective Experiences," *Journal of Organizational Behavior*, November 2010, pp. 1137–1162.

52 "Work Stress: What Are Companies Doing About It?" *AOL Jobs*, August 10, 2010.

53 "Nice Work if You Can Get It," *BusinessWeek*, January 9, 2006, pp. 56–57; see also "Wellness," *Time*, February 23, 2009, pp. 78–79.

54 See Richard W. Woodman, John E. Sawyer, and Ricky W. Griffin, "Toward a Theory of Organizational Creativity," *Academy of Management Review*, April 1993, pp. 293–321. See also Beth A. Hennessey and Teresa M. Amabile,

"Creativity," in Susan T. Fiske, Daniel L. Schacter, and Robert J. Sternberg (eds.), *Annual Review of Psychology 2010* (Palo Alto, CA: Annual Reviews, 2010), pp. 569–598; and Jing Zhou and Christina E. Shalley, "Deepening Our Understanding of Creativity in the Workplace: A Review of Different Approaches to Creativity Research," in Sheldon Zedeck (ed.), *Handbook of Industrial and Organizational Psychology*, Vol. 1: *Building and Developing the Organization* (Washington, DC: American Psychological Association, 2010), pp. 275–302.

55 Emily Thornton, "Japan's Struggle to Be Creative," *Fortune*, April 19, 1993, pp. 129–134.

56 "In Secret Hideaway, Bill Gates Ponders Microsoft's Future," *Wall Street Journal*, March 28, 2005, pp. A1, A13.

57 Christina E. Shalley, Lucy L. Gilson, and Terry C. Blum, "Matching Creativity Requirements and the Work Environment: Effects on Satisfaction and Intentions to Leave," *Academy of Management Journal*, 2000, Vol. 43, No. 2, pp. 215–223. See also Filiz Tabak, "Employee Creative Performance: What Makes It Happen?" *Academy of Management Executive*, 1997, Vol. 11, No. 1, pp. 119–122; and Giles Hirst, Daan van Knippenberg, and Jing Zhou, "A Cross-Level Perspective on Employee Creativity: Goal Orientation, Team Learning Behavior, and Individual Creativity," *Academy of Management Journal*, Vol. 52, No. 2, 2009, pp. 280–293.

58 "Real Life Imitates *Real World*," *BusinessWeek*, March 23/30, 2009, p. 42.

59 "Apple's Startup Culture," *Bloomberg Businessweek*, June 14, 2010, pp. 45–46.

60 See Ryan D. Zimmerman, "Understanding the Impact of Personality Traits on Individuals' Turnover Decisions: A Meta-Analytic Path Model," *Personnel Psychology*, 2008, Vol. 61, pp. 309–348.

61 For recent findings regarding this behavior, see Philip M. Podsakoff, Scott B. MacKenzie, Julie Beth Paine, and Daniel G. G. Bacharah, "Organizational Citizenship Behaviors: A Critical Review of the Theoretical and Empirical Literature and Suggestions for Future Research," *Journal of Management*, 2000,

Vol. 26, No. 3, pp. 513–563; see also Dennis W. Organ, Philip M. Podsakoff, and Nathan P. Podsakoff, "Expanding the Criterion Domain to Include Organizational Citizenship Behavior: Implications for Employee Selection," in Sheldon Zedeck (ed.), *Handbook of Industrial and Organizational Psychology*, Vol. 2: *Selecting and Developing Members for the Organization* (Washington, DC: American Psychological Association, 2010), pp. 281–323.

62 Dennis W. Organ, "Personality and Organizational Citizenship Behavior," *Journal of Management*, 1994, Vol. 20, No. 2, pp. 465–478; Mary Konovsky and S. Douglas Pugh, "Citizenship Behavior and Social Exchange," *Academy of Management Journal*, 1994, Vol. 37, No. 3, pp. 656–669; and Jacqueline A.-M. Coyle-Shapiro, "A Psychological Contract Perspective on Organizational Citizenship," *Journal of Organizational Behavior*, 2002, Vol. 23, pp. 927–946.

63 Ricky Griffin and Yvette Lopez, "'Bad Behavior' in Organization: A Review and Typology for Future Research," *Journal of Management*, 2005, Vol. 31, No. 6, pp. 988–1005.

64 For an illustration, see Sandy Lim, Lilia M. Cortina, and Vicki J. Magley, "Personal and Workgroup Incivility: Impact on Work and Health Outcomes," *Journal of Applied Psychology*, 2008, Vol. 93, No. 1, pp. 95–107.

65 See Anne O'Leary-Kelly, Ricky W. Griffin, and David J. Glew, "Organization-Motivated Aggression: A Research Framework," *Academy of Management Review*, January 1996, pp. 225–253. See also Scott C. Douglas, Christian Kiewitz, Mark J. Martinko, Paul Harvey, Younhee Kim, and Jae Uk Chun, "Cognitions, Emotions, and Evaluations: An Elaboration Likelihood Model for Workplace Aggression, "*Academy of Management Review*, 2008, Vol. 33, No. 2, p. 425–451; and Laurie J. Barclay and Karl Aquino, "Workplace Aggression and Violence," in Sheldon Zedeck (ed.), *Handbook of Industrial and Organizational Psychology*, Vol. 3: *Maintaining, Expanding, and Contracting the Organization* (Washington, DC: American Psychological Association, 2010), pp. 615–640.

Chapter 19

1 Sara Caputo, "Which Comes First: Happiness or Productivity?" *Toolbox for HR*, April 15, 2009, http://hr.toolbox.com on April 18, 2011; Alexander Kjerulf, "Top 10 Reasons Why Happiness at Work Is the Ultimate Productivity Booster," *PositiveSharing.com*, March 27, 2007, http://positivesharing.com on April 18, 2011; Paul Larson, "Do Happy Employees Make Productive Employees?" *Suite101.com*, May 4, 2009, www.suite101.com on April 18, 2011; Charles Kerns, "Putting Performance and Happiness Together in the Workplace," *Graziado Business Report*, Vol. 11 (2008), http://gbr.pepperdine.edu on April 18, 2011.

2 Richard M. Steers, Gregory A. Bigley, and Lyman W. Porter, *Motivation and Leadership at Work*, 6th ed. (New York: McGraw-Hill, 1996). See also Maureen L. Ambrose and Carol T. Kulik, "Old Friends, New Faces: Motivation Research in the 1990s," *Journal of Management*, 1999, Vol. 25, No. 3, pp. 231–292; and Edwin Locke and Gary Lartham, "What Should We Do about Motivation Theory? Six Recommendations for the Twenty-First Century," *Academy of Management Review*, 2004, Vol. 29, No. 3, pp. 388–403.

3 See Nigel Nicholson, "How to Motivate Your Problem People," *Harvard Business Review*, January 2003, pp. 57–67. See also Hugo Kehr, "Integrating Implicit Motives, Explicit Motives, and Perceived Abilities: The Compensatory Model of Work Motivation and Volition," *Academy of Management Review*, 2004, Vol. 29, No. 3, pp. 479–499; and James M. Diefendorff and Megan M. Chandler, "Motivating Employees," in Sheldon Zedeck (ed.), *Handbook of Industrial and Organizational Psychology*, Vol. 3: *Maintaining, Expanding, and Contracting the Organization* (Washington, DC: American Psychological Association, 2010), pp. 635–135.

4 See Jeffrey Pfeffer, *The Human Equation* (Cambridge, MA: Harvard Business School Press, 1998); see also Nitin Nohria, Boris Groysberg, and Linda-Eling Lee, "Employee Motivation—A Powerful New Model," *Harvard Business Review*, July–August 2008, pp. 78–89.

5 See Craig Pinder, *Work Motivation in Organizational Behavior* (Upper Saddle River, NJ: Prentice-Hall, 1998).

6 Frederick W. Taylor, *Principles of Scientific Management* (New York: Harper & Brothers, 1911).

7 Elton Mayo, *The Social Problems of an Industrial Civilization* (Cambridge, MA: Harvard University Press, 1945); Fritz J. Rothlisberger and W. J. Dickson, *Management and the Worker* (Cambridge, MA: Harvard University Press, 1939).

8 For a recent discussion of these questions, see Eryn Brown, "So Rich So Young—But Are They Really Happy?" *Fortune*, September 18, 2000, pp. 99–110.

9 Abraham H. Maslow, "A Theory of Human Motivation," *Psychological Review*, 1943, Vol. 50, pp. 370–396; Abraham H. Maslow, *Motivation and Personality* (New York: Harper & Row, 1954). Maslow's most recent work is Abraham H. Maslow and Richard Lowry, *Toward a Psychology of Being* (New York: Wiley, 1999).

10 *USA Today*, August 16, 2004, p. 2B.

11 For a review, see Pinder, *Work Motivation in Organizational Behavior*.

12 Clayton P. Alderfer, *Existence, Relatedness, and Growth* (New York: Free Press, 1972).

13 Frederick Herzberg, Bernard Mausner, and Barbara Snyderman, *The Motivation to Work* (New York: Wiley, 1959); Frederick Herzberg, "One More Time: How Do You Motivate Employees?" *Harvard Business Review*, January–February 1987, pp. 109–120 (reprinted in *Harvard Business Review*, January 2003, pp. 87–98).

14 Robert J. House and Lawrence A. Wigdor, "Herzberg's Dual-Factor Theory of Job Satisfaction and Motivation: A Review of the Evidence and a Criticism," *Personnel Psychology*, Winter 1967, pp. 369–389; Victor H. Vroom, *Work and Motivation* (New York: Wiley, 1964). See also Pinder, *Work Motivation in Organizational Behavior*.

15 David C. McClelland, *The Achieving Society* (Princeton, NJ: Van Nostrand, 1961); David C. McClelland, *Power: The Inner Experience* (New York: Irvington, 1975).

16 "Best Friends Good for Business," *USA Today*, December 1, 2004, pp. 1B, 2B.

17 David McClelland and David H. Burnham, "Power Is the Great Motivator," *Harvard Business Review*, March–April 1976, pp. 100–110 (reprinted in *Harvard Business Review*, January 2003, pp. 117–127).

18 See "The Rise and Fall of Dennis Kozlowski," *BusinessWeek*, December 23, 2002, pp. 64–77.

19 "HP Chief Executive Hurd Resigns after Sexual Harrassment Probe," *Bloomberg Businessweek*, August 7, 2010.

20 Victor H. Vroom, *Work and Motivation* (New York: Wiley, 1964).

21 "Starbucks' Secret Weapon," *Fortune*, September 29, 1997, p. 268.

22 *Harvard Business Review*, May 2009, p. 101.

23 Lyman W. Porter and Edward E. Lawler III, *Managerial Attitudes and Performance* (Homewood, IL: Dorsey, 1968).

24 J. Stacy Adams, "Towards an Understanding of Inequity," *Journal of Abnormal and Social Psychology*, November 1963, pp. 422–436.

25 "The Best vs. the Rest," *Wall Street Journal*, January 30, 2006, pp. B1, B3.

26 Mark C. Bolino and William H. Turnley, "Old Faces, New Places: Equity Theory in Cross-Cultural Contexts," *Journal of Organizational Behavior*, 2008, Vol. 29, pp. 29–50.

27 *BusinessWeek*, June 8, 2009, p. 48.

28 See Edwin A. Locke, "Toward a Theory of Task Performance and Incentives," *Organizational Behavior and Human Performance*, 1968, Vol. 3, pp. 157–189.

29 Gary P. Latham and J. J. Baldes, "The Practical Significance of Locke's Theory of Goal Setting," *Journal of Applied Psychology*, 1975, Vol. 60, pp. 187–191.

30 For a recent extension of goal-setting theory, see Yitzhak Fried and Linda Haynes Slowik, "Enriching Goal-Setting Theory with Time: An Integrated Approach," *Academy of Management Review*, 2004, Vol. 29, No. 3, pp. 404–422.

31 B. F. Skinner, *Beyond Freedom and Dignity* (New York: Knopf, 1971). See also Raymond A. Noe, Michael J. Tews, and Alison McConnell Dachner, "Learner Engagement: A New Perspective for Enhancing Our Understanding of Learner Motivation and Workplace Learning," in James P. Walsh and Arthur P. Brief (eds.), *The Academy of Management Annals 2010* (Philadelphia: Taylor and Francis, 2010), pp. 279–316.

32 Fred Luthans and Robert Kreitner, *Organizational Behavior Modification and Beyond: An Operant and Social Learning Approach* (Glenview, IL: Scott, Foresman, 1985).

33 Ibid.; W. Clay Hamner and Ellen P. Hamner, "Behavior Modification on the Bottom Line," *Organizational Dynamics*, Spring 1976, pp. 2–21.

34 "At Emery Air Freight: Positive Reinforcement Boosts Performance," *Organizational Dynamics*, Winter 1973, pp. 41–50; for a recent update, see Alexander D. Stajkovic and Fred Luthans, "A Meta-Analysis of the Effects of Organizational Behavior Modification on Task Performance, 1975–95," *Academy of Management Journal*, 1997, Vol. 40, No. 5, pp. 1122–1149.

35 David J. Glew, Anne M. O'Leary-Kelly, Ricky W. Griffin, and David D. Van Fleet, "Participation in Organizations: A Preview of the Issues and Proposed Framework for Future Analysis," *Journal of Management*, 1995, Vol. 21, No. 3, pp. 395–421.

36 Robert E. Quinn and Gretchen M. Spreitzer, "The Road to Empowerment: Seven Questions Every Leader Should Consider," *Organizational Dynamics*, Autumn 1997, pp. 37–47.

37 "On Factory Floors, Top Workers Hide Secrets to Success," *Wall Street Journal*, July 1, 2002, pp. A1, A10.

38 Russ Forrester, "Empowerment: Rejuvenating a Potent Idea," *Academy of Management Executive*, 2000, Vol. 14, No. 3, pp. 67–77.

39 Baxter W. Graham, "The Business Argument for Flexibility," *HR Magazine*, May 1996, pp. 104–110.

40 A. R. Cohen and H. Gadon, *Alternative Work Schedules: Integrating Individual and Organizational Needs* (Reading, MA: Addison Wesley, 1978). See also Ellen Ernst Kossek and Jesse S. Michel, "Flexible Work Schedules," in Sheldon Zedeck (ed.), *Handbook of Industrial and Organizational Psychology*, Vol. 1: *Building and Developing the Organization* (Washington, DC: American Psychological Association, 2010), pp. 535–572.

41 *BusinessWeek*, December 12, 2005, p. 79.

42 "How Telecommuting Lets Workers Mobilize for Sustainability," *GreenBiz.com*, February 17, 2011; "Study: Telecommuting can Save American Households $1.7 Billion per Year," *SmartPlanet.com*, March 16, 2011.

43 Barry Gerhart, Sara L. Rynes, Ingrid Smithey Fulmer, "Pay and Performance: Individuals, Groups, and Executives," in James P. Walsh and Arthur P. Brief (eds.), *The Academy of Management Annals 2009* (Philadelphia: Taylor and Francis, 2009), pp. 251–316. See also Joseph J. Martocchio, "Strategic Reward and Compensation Plans," in Sheldon Zedeck (ed.), *Handbook of Industrial and Organizational Psychology*, Vol. 1: *Building and Developing the Organization* (Washington, DC: American Psychological Association, 2010), pp. 343–372.

44 Daniel Wren, *The Evolution of Management Theory*, 4th ed. (New York: Wiley, 1994).

45 Eric Krell, "All for Incentives, Incentives for All," *HR Magazine*, January 2011, pp. 34–38.

46 C. Wiley, "Incentive Plan Pushes Production," *Personnel Journal*, August 1993, p. 91.

47 "When Money Isn't Enough," *Forbes*, November 18, 1996, pp. 164–169.

48 Jacquelyn DeMatteo, Lillian Eby, and Eric Sundstrom, "Team-Based Rewards: Current Empirical Evidence and Directions for Future Research," in L. L. Cummings and Barry Staw (eds.), *Research in Organizational Behavior*, Vol. 20 (Greenwich, CT: JAI, 1998), pp. 141–183.

49 Theresa M. Welbourne and Luis R. Gomez-Mejia, "Gainsharing: A Critical Review and a Future Research Agenda," *Journal of Management*, 1995, Vol. 21, No. 3, pp. 559–609.

50 National Center for Employee Ownership, "A Statistical Profile of Employee Ownership," March 2010.

51 "2010 Compensation for 25 of the Most Highly Paid CEOs," *USA Today*, April 1, 2011, p. 2B.

52 Ibid.

53 Ibid.

54 Ibid.

55 Harry Barkema and Luis Gomez-Mejia, "Managerial Compensation and Firm Performance: A General Research Framework," *Academy of Management Journal*, 1998, Vol. 41, No. 2, pp. 135–145.

56 Rajiv D. Banker, Seok-Young Lee, Gordon Potter, and Dhinu Srinivasan, "Contextual Analysis of Performance Impacts of Outcome-Based Incentive Compensation," *Academy of Management Journal*, 1996, Vol. 39, No. 4, pp. 920–948.

57 "GE Defends CEO's Pay Package," *The Ledger*, April 11, 2011.

58 "Not Exactly 'Pay for Performance' for These Big Pharma CEOs," *DailyFinance.com*, March 3, 2011.

59 "Average Japanese CEO Earns One-Sixth as Much as American CEOS," *thinkprogress.org*, July 8, 2010.

60 Steve Kerr, "The Best-Laid Incentive Plans," *Harvard Business Review*, January 2003, pp. 27–40.

61 "Now It's Getting Personal," *BusinessWeek*, December 16, 2002, pp. 90–92.

Chapter 20

1 Geoffrey Colvin, "Catch a Rising Star," *Fortune*, February 6, 2006, http://money.cnn.com on April 23, 2011; Klaus Kneale, "Stress Management for the CEO," *Forbes.com*, April 17, 2009, www.forbes.com on April 23, 2011; Susan Berfield, "The Real Effects of Workplace Anxiety," *BusinessWeek*, July 24, 2009, www.businessweek.com on April 23, 2011; Susan Berfield, "How Executives Manage Stress," *BusinessWeek*, July 24, 2009, http://images.businessweek.com on April 23, 2011; Jerry Useem, "Making Your Work Work for You," *Fortune*, March 15, 2006, http://money.cnn.com on April 23, 2011; Bill Gates, "How I Work," *Fortune*, April 7, 2006, http://money.cnn.com on April 23, 2011.

2 See Ronald A. Heifetz and Donald L. Laurie, "The Work of Leadership," *Harvard Business Review*, January–February 1997, pp. 124–134. See also Arthur G. Jago, "Leadership: Perspectives in Theory and Research," *Management Science*, March 1982, pp. 315–336; and "The New Leadership," *BusinessWeek*, August 28, 2000, pp. 100–187.

3 Gary A. Yukl, *Leadership in Organizations*, 7th ed. (Upper Saddle River, NJ: Pearson, 2010), p. 5. See also Bruce J. Avolio, Fred O. Walumbwa, and Todd J. Weber, "Leadership: Current Theories, Research, and Future Decisions," in Susan T. Fiske, Daniel L. Schacter, and Robert J. Sternberg (eds.), *Annual Review of Psychology 2009* (Palo Alto, CA: Annual Reviews, 2009), pp. 421–450; and Julian Barling, Amy Christie, and Colette Hoption, "Leadership," in Sheldon Zedeck (ed.), *Handbook of Industrial and Organizational Psychology*, Vol. 1: *Building and Developing the Organization* (Washington, DC: American Psychological Association, 2010), pp. 183–240.

4 John P. Kotter, "What Leaders Really Do," *Harvard Business Review*, May–June 1990, pp. 103–111 (reprinted in *Harvard Business Review*, December 2001,

pp. 85–93). See also Daniel Goleman, "Leadership That Gets Results," *Harvard Business Review*, March–April 2000, pp. 78–88; and Keith Grints, *The Arts of Leadership* (Oxford, UK: Oxford University Press, 2000).

5 John R. P. French and Bertram Raven, "The Bases of Social Power," in Dorwin Cartwright (ed.), *Studies in Social Power* (Ann Arbor, MI: University of Michigan Press, 1959), pp. 150–167.

6 Hugh D. Menzies, "The Ten Toughest Bosses," *Fortune*, April 21, 1980, pp. 62–73.

7 Bennett J. Tepper, "Consequences of Abusive Supervision," *Academy of Management Journal*, 2000, Vol. 43, No. 2, pp. 178–190; see also Bennett J. Tepper, "Abusive Supervision in Work Organizations: Review, Synthesis, and Research Agenda," *Journal of Management*, 2007, Vol. 33, No. 3, pp. 261–289.

8 *Time*, July 21, 2008, p. 46.

9 Thomas A. Stewart, "Get with the New Power Game," *Fortune*, January 13, 1997, pp. 58–62.

10 For more information on the bases and uses of power, see Philip M. Podsakoff and Chester A. Schriesheim, "Field Studies of French and Raven's Bases of Power: Critique, Reanalysis, and Suggestions for Future Research," *Psychological Bulletin*, 1985, Vol. 97, pp. 387–411; Robert C. Benfari, Harry E. Wilkinson, and Charles D. Orth, "The Effective Use of Power," *Business Horizons*, May–June 1986, pp. 12–16; and Yukl, *Leadership in Organizations*.

11 Bernard M. Bass, *Bass & Stogdill's Handbook of Leadership*, 3rd ed. (Riverside, NJ: Free Press, 1990).

12 Shelley A. Kirkpatrick and Edwin A. Locke, "Leadership: Do Traits Matter?" *Academy of Management Executive*, May 1991, pp. 48–60. See also Robert J. Sternberg, "Managerial Intelligence: Why IQ Isn't Enough," *Journal of Management*, 1997, Vol. 23, No. 3, pp. 475–493.

13 Timothy Judge, Amy Colbert, and Remus Ilies, "Intelligence and Leadership: A Quantitative Review and Test of Theoretical Propositions," *Journal of Applied Psychology*, 2004, Vol. 89, No. 3, pp. 542–552.

14 Rensis Likert, *New Patterns of Management* (New York: McGraw-Hill, 1961); Rensis Likert, *The Human Organization* (New York: McGraw-Hill, 1967).

15 The Ohio State studies stimulated many articles, monographs, and books. A good overall reference is Ralph M. Stogdill and A. E. Coons (eds.), *Leader Behavior: Its Description and Measurement* (Columbus, OH: Bureau of Business Research, Ohio State University, 1957).

16 Edwin A. Fleishman, E. F. Harris, and H. E. Burt, *Leadership and Supervision in Industry* (Columbus, OH: Bureau of Business Research, Ohio State University, 1955).

17 See Timothy Judge, Ronald Piccolo, and Remus Ilies, "The Forgotten One? The Validity of Consideration and Initiating Structure in Leadership Research," *Journal of Applied Psychology*, 2004, Vol. 89, No. 1, pp. 36–51.

18 Robert R. Blake and Jane S. Mouton, *The Managerial Grid* (Houston: Gulf Publishing, 1964); Robert R. Blake and Jane S. Mouton, *The Versatile Manager: A Grid Profile* (Homewood, IL: Dow Jones-Irwin, 1981).

19 Robert Tannenbaum and Warren H. Schmidt, "How to Choose a Leadership Pattern," *Harvard Business Review*, March–April 1958, pp. 95–101.

20 Fred E. Fiedler, *A Theory of Leadership Effectiveness* (New York: McGraw-Hill, 1967).

21 Chester A. Schriesheim, Bennett J. Tepper, and Linda A. Tetrault, "Least Preferred Co-Worker Score, Situational Control, and Leadership Effectiveness: A Meta-Analysis of Contingency Model Performance Predictions," *Journal of Applied Psychology*, 1994, Vol. 79, No. 4, pp. 561–573.

22 Fiedler, *A Theory of Leadership Effectiveness*; Fred E. Fiedler and M. M. Chemers, *Leadership and Effective Management* (Glenview, IL: Scott, Foresman, 1974).

23 For recent reviews and updates, see Lawrence H. Peters, Darrell D. Hartke, and John T. Pohlmann, "Fiedler's Contingency Theory of Leadership: An Application of the Meta-Analysis Procedures of Schmidt and Hunter," *Psychological Bulletin*, Vol. 97, pp. 274–285; and Fred E. Fiedler, "When to Lead, When to Stand Back," *Psychology Today*, September 1987, pp. 26–27.

24 Martin G. Evans, "The Effects of Supervisory Behavior on the Path-Goal Relationship," *Organizational Behavior and Human Performance*, May 1970, pp. 277–298; Robert J. House and Terence R. Mitchell, "Path-Goal Theory of Leadership," *Journal of Contemporary Business*, Autumn 1974, pp. 81–98. See also Yukl, *Leadership in Organizations*.

25 For a recent review, see J. C. Wofford and Laurie Z. Liska, "Path-Goal Theories of Leadership: A Meta-Analysis," *Journal of Management*, 1993, vol. 19, no. 4, pp. 857–876.

26 See Victor H. Vroom and Philip H. Yetton, *Leadership and Decision Making* (Pittsburgh: University of Pittsburgh Press, 1973); and Victor H. Vroom and Arthur G. Jago, *The New Leadership* (Englewood Cliffs, NJ: Prentice-Hall, 1988).

27 Victor Vroom, "Leadership and the Decision-Making Process," *Organizational Dynamics*, 2000, Vol. 28, No. 4, pp. 82–94.

28 Vroom and Jago, *The New Leadership*.

29 Ibid.

30 See Madeline E. Heilman, Harvey A. Hornstein, Jack H. Cage, and Judith K. Herschlag, "Reaction to Prescribed Leader Behavior as a Function of Role Perspective: The Case of the Vroom-Yetton Model," *Journal of Applied Psychology*, February 1984, pp. 50–60; R. H. George Field, "A Test of the Vroom-Yetton Normative Model of Leadership," *Journal of Applied Psychology*, February 1982, pp. 523–532.

31 George Graen and J. F. Cashman, "A Role-Making Model of Leadership in Formal Organizations: A Developmental Approach," in J. G. Hunt and L. L. Larson (eds.), *Leadership Frontiers* (Kent, OH: Kent State University Press, 1975), pp. 143–165; Fred Dansereau, George Graen, and W. J. Haga, "A Vertical Dyad Linkage Approach to Leadership Within Formal Organizations: A Longitudinal Investigation of the Role-Making Process," *Organizational Behavior and Human Performance*, 1975, Vol. 15, pp. 46–78.

32 See Kathryn Sherony and Stephen Green, "Coworker Exchange: Relationships Between Coworkers, Leader-Member Exchange, and Work Attitudes," *Journal of Applied Psychology*, 2002, Vol. 87, No. 3, pp. 542–548.

33 See Bruce J. Avolio, Fred O. Walumbwa, and Todd J. Weber, "Leadership: Current Theories, Research, and Future Directions," in Susan T. Fiske, Daniel L. Schacter, and Robert Sternberg (eds.), *Annual Review of Psychology 2009* (Palo Alto, CA: Annual Reviews, 2009), pp. 421–450.

34 Steven Kerr and John M. Jermier, "Substitutes for Leadership: Their Meaning and Measurement," *Organizational Behavior and Human Performance*, December 1978, pp. 375–403.

35 See Charles C. Manz and Henry P. Sims, Jr., "Leading Workers to Lead Themselves: The External Leadership of Self-Managing Work Teams,"

Administrative Science Quarterly, March 1987, pp. 106–129. See also "Living Without a Leader," *Fortune*, March 20, 2000, pp. 218–219.

36 See Robert J. House, "A 1976 Theory of Charismatic Leadership," in J. G. Hunt and L. L. Larson (eds.), *Leadership: The Cutting Edge* (Carbondale, IL: Southern Illinois University Press, 1977), pp. 189–207. See also Jay A. Conger and Rabindra N. Kanungo, "Toward a Behavioral Theory of Charismatic Leadership in Organizational Settings," *Academy of Management Review*, October 1987, pp. 637–647.

37 David A. Nadler and Michael L. Tushman, "Beyond the Charismatic Leader: Leadership and Organizational Change," *California Management Review*, Winter 1990, pp. 77–97.

38 Jane Howell and Boas Shamir, "The Role of Followers in the Charismatic Leadership Process: Relationships and Their Consequences," *Academy of Management Review*, 2005, Vol. 30, No. 1, pp. 96–112.

39 James MacGregor Burns, *Leadership* (New York: Harper & Row, 1978). See also Rajnandini Pillai, Chester A. Schriesheim, and Eric J. Williams, "Fairness Perceptions and Trust as Mediators for Transformational and Transactional Leadership: A Two-Sample Study," *Journal of Management*, 1999, Vol. 25, No. 6, pp. 897–933.

40 Robert Rubin, David Munz, and William Bommer, "Leading from Within: The Effects of Emotion Recognition and Personality on Transformational Leadership Behaviors," *Academy of Management Journal*, 2005, Vol. 48, No. 5, pp. 845–858.

41 Kenneth Labich, "The Seven Keys to Business Leadership," *Fortune*, October 24, 1998, pp. 55–61.

42 Jerry Useem, "Tape + Light Bulbs = ?" *Fortune*, August 12, 2002, pp. 127–132.

43 *BusinessWeek*, January 10, 2005, p. 62.

44 Dusya Vera and Mary Crossan, "Strategic Leadership and Organizational Learning," *Academy of Management Review*, 2004, Vol. 29, No. 2, pp. 222–240; see also Cynthia A. Montgomery, "Putting Leadership Back into Strategy," *Harvard Business Review*, January 2008, pp. 54–63.

45 "The Best Performing CEOs in the World," *Harvard Business Review*, January–February 2010.

46 "Which of These 9 Grossly Overpaid CEOs Are Worth It?" *seekingalpha.com*, April 20, 2011; "CEO Mike Jeffries Overvalues His Own Brand and Loses His Cool," *About.com*, September 7, 2009.

47 "3M's Buckley Lifts Spending, Fights 'Zombie' Products," *BusinessWeek*, December 22, 2009, pp. 46–47.

48 See Kurt Dirks and Donald Ferrin, "Trust in Leadership," *Journal of Applied Psychology*, 2002, Vol. 87, No. 4, pp. 611–628. See also Russell A. Eisenstat, Michael Beer, Nathanial Foote, Tobias Fredberg, and Flemming Norrgren, "The Uncompromising Leader," *Harvard Business Review*, July–August 2008, pp. 51–59.

49 *USA Today*, April 25, 2005, p. 1B.

50 Jeffrey Pfeffer, *Power in Organizations* (Marshfield, MA: Pitman, 1981), p. 7.

51 Gerald R. Ferris and Wayne A. Hochwarter, "Organizational Politics," in Sheldon Zedeck (ed.), *Handbook of Industrial and Organizational Psychology*, Vol. 3: *Maintaining, Expanding, and Contracting the Organization* (Washington, DC: American Psychological Association, 2010), pp. 435–459.

52 Victor Murray and Jeffrey Gandz, "Games Executives Play: Politics at Work," *Business Horizons*, December 1980, pp. 11–23; Jeffrey Gandz and Victor Murray, "The Experience of Workplace Politics," *Academy of Management Journal*, June 1980, pp. 237–251.

53 Don R. Beeman and Thomas W. Sharkey, "The Use and Abuse of Corporate Power," *Business Horizons*, March–April 1987, pp. 26–30.

54 "How Ebbers Kept the Board in His Pocket," *BusinessWeek*, October 14, 2002, pp. 138–139.

55 See William L. Gardner, "Lessons in Organizational Dramaturgy: The Art of Impression Management," *Organizational Dynamics*, Summer 1992, pp. 51–63; Elizabeth Wolf Morrison and Robert J. Bies, "Impression Management in the Feedback-Seeking Process: A Literature Review and Research Agenda," *Academy of Management Review*, July 1991, pp. 522–541; Mark C. Bolino, K. Michele Kacmar, William H. Turnley, and J. Bruce Gilstrap, "A Multi-Level Review of Impression Management Motives and Behaviors," *Journal of Management*, 2008, Vol. 34, No. 6, pp. 1080–1109.

56 *BusinessWeek*, April 13, 2009, p. 54.

57 See Chad Higgins, Timothy Judge, and Gerald Ferris, "Influence Tactics and Work Outcomes: A Meta-Analysis," *Journal of Organizational Behavior*, 2003, Vol. 24, pp. 89–106; and Gerald R. Ferris, Darren C. Treadway, Pamela L. Perrewe, Robyn L. Brour, Ceasar Douglas, and Sean Lux, "Political Skill in Organizations," *Journal of Management*, 2007, Vol. 33, No. 3, pp. 290–320.

58 Murray and Gandz, "Games Executives Play."

59 Beeman and Sharkey, "The Use and Abuse of Corporate Power."

60 Stefanie Ann Lenway and Kathleen Rehbein, "Leaders, Followers, and Free Riders: An Empirical Test of Variation in Corporate Political Involvement," *Academy of Management Journal*, December 1991, pp. 893–905.

Chapter 21

1 Hugh Anderson, "Phone-Interview Tips for Savvy Candidates," *BNet*, 2010, http://jobfunctions.bnet.com on April 25, 2011; Anne Fisher, "Fear of Phoning," *Fortune*, September 6, 2005, http://money.cnn.com on April 25, 2011; Fisher, "How Can I Survive a Phone Interview?" *Fortune*, April 19, 2004, http://money.cnn.com on April 25, 2011; "Phone Interview Success," *CollegeGrad.com*, May 2, 2006, www.collegegrad.com on April 25, 2011; "Need Some Phone Interview Help? Score Big with Our 11 Top Tips," *BNet*, 2009, http://jobfunctions.bnet.com on April 25, 2011; Matt Aberham, "JobsBlog Rewind: Five Ways to Fail My Phone Interview," *The JobsBlog*, April 14, 2010, http://microsoftjobsblog.com on April 25, 2011.

2 See John J. Gabarro, "The Development of Working Relationships," in Jay W. Lorsch (ed.), *Handbook of Organizational Behavior* (Englewood Cliffs, NJ: Prentice-Hall, 1987), pp. 172–189. See also "Team Efforts, Technology, Add New Reasons to Meet," *USA Today*, December 8, 1997, pp. 1A, 2A.

3 Tara C. Reich and M. Sandy Hershcovis, "Interpersonal Relationships at Work," in Sheldon Zedeck (ed.), *Handbook of Industrial and Organizational Psychology*, Vol. 3: *Maintaining, Expanding, and Contracting the Organization* (Washington, DC: American Psychological Association, 2010), pp. 223–248.

4 *BusinessWeek*, November 29, 2010, p. 18.

5 Martin Kilduff and Daniel J. Brass, "Organizational Social Network Research: Core Ideas and Key Debates," in James P. Walsh and Arthur P. Brief (eds.), *The Academy of Management Annals 2010* (Philadelphia: Taylor and Francis, 2010), pp. 317–358.

6 See C. Gopinath and Thomas E. Becker, "Communication, Procedural Justice, and Employee Attitudes: Relationships under Conditions of Divestiture," *Journal of Management*, 2000, Vol. 26, No. 1, pp. 63–83.

7 Henry Mintzberg, *The Nature of Managerial Work* (New York: Harper & Row, 1973).

8 Marshall Scott Poole, "Communication," in Sheldon Zedeck (ed.), *Handbook of Industrial and Organizational Psychology*, Vol. 3: *Maintaining, Expanding, and Contracting the Organization* (Washington, DC: American Psychological Association, 2010), pp. 249–270.

9 Ibid.

10 See Batia M. Wiesenfeld, Sumita Charan, and Raghu Garud, "Communication Patterns as Determinants of Organizational Identification in a Virtual Organization," *Organization Science*, 1999, Vol. 10, No. 6, pp. 777–790.

11 Bruce Barry and Ingrid Fulmer, "The Medium and the Message: The Adaptive Use of Communication Media in Dyadic Influence," *Academy of Management Review*, 2004, Vol. 29, No. 2, pp. 272–292.

12 Mintzberg, *The Nature of Managerial Work*.

13 Reid Buckley, "When You Have to Put It to Them," *Across the Board*, October 1999, pp. 44–48.

14 "'Did I Just Say That?!' How to Recover from Foot-in-Mouth," *Wall Street Journal*, June 19, 2002, p. B1.

15 "Executives Who Dread Public Speaking Learn to Keep Their Cool in the Spotlight," *Wall Street Journal*, May 4, 1990, pp. B1, B6.

16 Mintzberg, *The Nature of Managerial Work*.

17 Buckley, "When You Have to Put It to Them."

18 See "Watch What You Put in That Office Email," *BusinessWeek*, September 30, 2002, pp. 114–115.

19 Nicholas Varchaver, "The Perils of E-mail," *Fortune*, February 17, 2003, pp. 96–102; "How a String of E-Mail Came to Haunt CSFB and Star Banker," *Wall Street Journal*, February 28, 2003, pp. A1, A6; "How Morgan Stanley Botched a Big Case by Fumbling Emails," *Wall Street Journal*, May 16, 2005, pp. A1, A10.

20 *Fortune*, December 12, 2005, leadership insert.

21 A. Vavelas, "Communication Patterns in Task-Oriented Groups," *Journal of the Acoustical Society of America*, 1950, Vol. 22, pp. 725–730; Jerry Wofford, Edwin Gerloff, and Robert Cummins, *Organizational Communication* (New York: McGraw-Hill, 1977).

22 Nelson Phillips and John Brown, "Analyzing Communications in and Around Organizations: A Critical Hermeneutic Approach," *Academy of Management Journal*, 1993, Vol. 36, No. 6, pp. 1547–1576.

23 Walter Kiechel III, "Breaking Bad News to the Boss," *Fortune*, April 9, 1990, pp. 111–112.

24 Mary Young and James Post, "How Leading Companies Communicate with Employees," *Organizational Dynamics*, Summer 1993, pp. 31–43.

25 For one example, see Kimberly D. Elsbach and Greg Elofson, "How the Packaging of Decision Explanations Affects Perceptions of Trustworthiness," *Academy of Management Journal*, 2000, Vol. 43, No. 1, pp. 80–89.

26 Kristin Byron, "Carrying Too Heavy a Load? The Communication and Miscommunication of Emotion by Email," *Academy of Management Review*, 2008, Vol. 33, No. 2, pp. 309–327.

27 "Those Bawdy E-Mails Were Good for a Laugh—Until the Ax Fell," *Wall Street Journal*, February 4, 2000, pp. A1, A8.

28 Keith Davis, "Management Communication and the Grapevine," *Harvard Business Review*, September–October 1953, pp. 43–49.

29 "Spread the Word: Gossip Is Good," *Wall Street Journal*, October 4, 1988, p. B1.

30 See David M. Schweiger and Angelo S. DeNisi, "Communication with Employees Following a Merger: A Longitudinal Field Experiment," *Academy of Management Journal*, March 1991, pp. 110–135.

31 "Job Fears Make Offices All Fears," *Wall Street Journal*, January 20, 2009, p. B7.

32 Institute of Leadership and Management, "32% of People Making Inappropriate Use of Work Emails," April 20, 2011.

33 *Wall Street Journal*, January 20, 2009, p. B7.

34 Nancy B. Kurland and Lisa Hope Pelled, "Passing the Word: Toward a Model of Gossip and Power in the Workplace," *Academy of Management Review*, 2000, Vol. 25, No. 2, pp. 428–438.

35 See Tom Peters and Nancy Austin, *A Passion for Excellence* (New York: Random House, 1985).

36 Albert Mehrabian, *Non-Verbal Communication* (Chicago: Aldine, 1972).

37 Michael B. McCaskey, "The Hidden Messages Managers Send," *Harvard Business Review*, November–December 1979, pp. 135–148.

38 Suzanne Kapner, "Changing of the Guard at Wal-Mart," *Fortune*, March 2, 2009, pp. 68–76.

39 *Fortune*, March 2, 2009, p. 72.

40 David Givens, "What Body Language Can Tell You That Words Cannot," *U.S. News & World Report*, November 19, 1984, p. 100.

41 Edward J. Hall, *The Hidden Dimension* (New York: Doubleday, 1966).

42 For a detailed discussion of improving communication effectiveness, see Courtland L. Bovee, John V. Thill, and Barbara E. Schatzman, *Business Communication Today*, 7th ed. (Upper Saddle River, NJ: Prentice Hall, 2003).

43 See Otis W. Baskin and Craig E. Aronoff, *Interpersonal Communication in Organizations* (Glenview, IL: Scott, Foresman, 1980).

44 *BusinessWeek*, December 22, 2008, p. 15.

45 See "You Have (Too Much) E-Mail," *USA Today*, March 12, 1999, p. 3B.

46 Justin Fox, "The Triumph of English," *Fortune*, September 18, 2000, pp. 209–212.

47 Joseph Allen and Bennett P. Lientz, *Effective Business Communication* (Santa Monica, CA: Goodyear, 1979).

48 See "Making Silence Your Ally," *Across the Board*, October 1999, p. 11.

49 Boyd A. Vander Houwen, "Less Talking, More Listening," *HR Magazine*, April 1997, pp. 53–58.

50 *Fortune*, January 24, 2005, p. 112.

51 For a discussion of these and related issues, see Eric M. Eisenberg and Marsha G. Witten, "Reconsidering Openness in Organizational Communication," *Academy of Management Review*, July 1987, pp. 418–426.

52 For a recent illustration, see Barbara Kellerman, "When Should a Leader Apologize—And When Not?" *Harvard Business Review*, April 2006, pp. 72–81.

Chapter 22

1 Felice J. Freyer, "Another Wrong-Site Surgery at R.I. Hospital," *Providence* (RI) *Journal*, October 28, 2009, www.projo.com on April 30, 2011; "Wrong-Site Surgery Problems Common: Study," *Philadelphia Business Journal*, June 26, 2007, www.bizjournals.com on April 30, 2011; Steven Reinberg, "Errors in Surgical Procedure Persist," *HealthDay*, November 19, 2009, http://health.usnews.com on April 30, 2011; Peter Mills, Julia Neily, and Ed Dunn, "Teamwork and Communication in Surgical Teams: Implications for Patient Safety," *Journal of the American College of Surgeons*, Vol. 206 (January 2008), www.surgicalpatientsafety.facs.org on April 30, 2011; Johns Hopkins Medicine, "RX for Wrong-Site Surgery: Two Minutes of Conversation," press release, January 23, 2007, www.hopkinsmedicine.org on April 30, 2011.

2   For a review of definitions of groups, see Gregory Moorhead and Ricky W. Griffin, *Organizational Behavior*, 10th ed. (Cincinnati, OH: Cengage, 2012).

3   Dorwin Cartwright and Alvin Zander (eds.), *Group Dynamics: Research and Theory*, 3rd ed. (New York: Harper & Row, 1968).

4   See Willem Verbeke and Stefan Wuyts, "Moving in Social Circles—Social Circle Membership and Performance Implications," *Journal of Organizational Behavior*, 2007, Vol. 28, pp. 357–379 for an interesting extension of these ideas.

5   Rob Cross, Nitin Nohria, and Andrew Parker, "Six Myths about Informal Networks—And How to Overcome Them," *Sloan Management Review*, Spring 2002, pp. 67–77.

6   Robert Schrank, *Ten Thousand Working Days* (Cambridge, MA: MIT Press, 1978); Bill Watson, "Counter Planning on the Shop Floor," in Peter Frost, Vance Mitchell, and Walter Nord (eds.), *Organizational Reality*, 2nd ed. (Glenview, IL: Scott, Foresman, 1982), pp. 286–294.

7   "After Layoffs, More Workers Band Together," *Wall Street Journal*, February 26, 2002, p. B1.

8   Bradley L. Kirkman and Benson Rosen, "Powering Up Teams," *Organizational Dynamics*, Winter 2000, pp. 48–58.

9   John Mathieu, M. Travis Maynard, Tammy Rapp, and Lucy Gibson, "Team Effectiveness 1997–2007: A Review of Recent Advancements and a Glimpse into the Future," *Journal of Management*, 2008, Vol. 34, No. 3, p. 410–476.

10 Arvind Malhotra, Ann Majchrzak, and Benson Rosen, "Leading Virtual Teams," *Academy of Management Perspectives*, 2007, Vol. 21, No. 1, pp. 60–70.

11 "Why Teams Fail," *USA Today*, February 25, 1997, pp. 1B, 2B.

12 Brian Dumaine, "The Trouble with Teams," *Fortune*, September 5, 1994, pp. 86–92. See also Susan G. Cohen and Diane E. Bailey, "What Makes Teams Work: Group Effectiveness Research from the Shop Floor to the Executive Suite," *Journal of Management*, 1997, Vol. 23, No. 3, pp. 239–290; and John Mathieu, Lucy Gilson, and Thomas Ruddy, "Empowerment and Team Effectiveness: An Empirical Test of an Integrated Model," *Journal of Applied Psychology*, 2006, Vol. 91, No. 1, pp. 97–108.

13 *Fortune*, June 12, 2006, p. 122.

14 Marvin E. Shaw, *Group Dynamics: The Psychology of Small Group Behavior*, 4th ed. (New York: McGraw-Hill, 1985).

15 "How to Avoid Hiring the Prima Donnas Who Hate Teamwork," *Wall Street Journal*, February 15, 2000, p. B1.

16 *Fortune*, June 12, 2006, p. 88.

17 See Connie Gersick, "Marking Time: Predictable Transitions in Task Groups," *Academy of Management Journal*, June 1989, pp. 274–309. See also Janis A. Cannon-Bowers and Clint Bowers, "Team Development and Functioning," in Sheldon Zedeck (ed.), *Handbook of Industrial and Organizational Psychology*, Vol. 1: *Building and Developing the Organization* (Washington, DC: American Psychological Association, 2010), pp. 597–650.

18 See Gilad Chen, "Newcomer Adaptation in Teams: Multilevel Antecedents and Outcomes," *Academy of Management Journal*, 2005, Vol. 48, No. 1, pp. 101–116.

19 For a review of other team characteristics, see Michael Campion, Gina Medsker, and A. Catherine Higgs, "Relations Between Work Group Characteristics and Effectiveness: Implications for Designing Effective Work Groups," *Personnel Psychology*, Winter 1993, pp. 823–850.

20 David Katz and Robert L. Kahn, *The Social Psychology of Organizations*, 2nd ed. (New York: Wiley, 1978), pp. 187–221. See also David M. Sluss, Rolf van Dick, and Bryant S. Thompson, "Role Theory in Organizations: A Relational Perspective," in Sheldon Zedeck (ed.), *Handbook of Industrial and Organizational Psychology*, Vol. 1: *Building and Developing the Organization* (Washington, DC: American Psychological Association, 2010), pp. 503–534.

21 See Travis C. Tubre and Judith M. Collins, "Jackson and Schuler (1985) Revisited: A Meta-Analysis of the Relationships Between Role Ambiguity, Role Conflict, and Job Performance," *Journal of Management*, 2000, Vol. 26, No. 1, pp. 155–169.

22 Robert L. Kahn, D. M. Wolfe, R. P. Quinn, J. D. Snoek, and R. A. Rosenthal, *Organizational Stress: Studies in Role Conflict and Role Ambiguity* (New York: Wiley, 1964).

23 *Fortune*, June 12, 2006, p. 88.

24 Daniel C. Feldman, "The Development and Enforcement of Group Norms," *Academy of Management Review*, January 1984, pp. 47–53.

25 "Companies Turn to Peer Pressure to Cut Injuries as Psychologists Join the Battle," *Wall Street Journal*, March 29, 1991, pp. B1, B3.

26 James Wallace Bishop and K. Dow Scott, "How Commitment Affects Team Performance," *HR Magazine*, February 1997, pp. 107–115.

27 Anne O'Leary-Kelly, Joseph Martocchio, and Dwight Frink, "A Review of the Influence of Group Goals on Group Performance," *Academy of Management Journal*, 1994, Vol. 37, No. 5, pp. 1285–1301.

28 See Anat Drach-Zahavy and Anat Freund, "Team Effectiveness Under Stress: A Structural Contingency Approach," *Journal of Organizational Behavior*, 2007, Vol. 28, pp. 423–450 for an interesting application of these ideas.

29 Philip M. Podsakoff, Michael Ahearne, and Scott B. MacKenzie, "Organizational Citizenship Behavior and the Quantity and Quality of Work Group Performance," *Journal of Applied Psychology*, 1997, Vol. 82, No. 2, pp. 262–270.

30 Suzy Wetlaufer, "Common Sense and Conflict," *Harvard Business Review*, January–February 2000, pp. 115–125.

31 Kathleen M. Eisenhardt, Jean L. Kahwajy, and L. J. Bourgeois III, "How Management Teams Can Have a Good Fight," *Harvard Business Review*, July–August 1997, pp. 77–89.

32 Thomas Bergmann and Roger Volkema, "Issues, Behavioral Responses and Consequences in Interpersonal Conflicts," *Journal of Organizational Behavior*, 1994, Vol. 15, pp. 467–471; see also Carsten K. W. De Dreu, "The Virtue and Vice of Workplace Conflict: Food for (Pessimistic) Thought," *Journal of Organizational Behavior*, 2008, Vol. 29, pp. 5–18.

33 Robin Pinkley and Gregory Northcraft, "Conflict Frames of Reference: Implications for Dispute Processes and Outcomes," *Academy of Management Journal*, 1994, Vol. 37, No. 1, pp. 193–205.

34 "How 2 Computer Nuts Transformed Industry before Messy Breakup," *Wall Street Journal*, August 27, 1996, pp. A1, A10.

35 Bruce Barry and Greg L. Stewart, "Composition, Process, and Performance in Self-Managed Groups: The Role of Personality," *Journal of Applied Psychology*, 1997, Vol. 82, No. 1, pp. 62–78.

36 "Acer CEO Resigns Suddenly amid Conflict with Board," *Gadget News Today*, March 31, 2011.

37 "Hilton and Starwood Settle Dispute," *New York Times*, December 22, 2010.

38 See Patrick Nugent, "Managing Conflict: Third-Party Interventions for Managers," *Academy of Management Executive*, 2002, Vol. 16, No. 1, pp. 139–148.

39 Gerardo A. Okhuysen and Beth A. Bechky, "Coordination in Organizations: An Integrative Perspective," in James P. Walsh and Arthur P. Brief (eds.), *The Academy of Management Annals 2009* (Philadelphia: Taylor and Francis, 2009), pp. 463–502.

40 See Kristin J. Behfar, Randall S. Peterson, Elizabeth A. Mannix, and William M. K. Trochim, "The Critical Role of Conflict Resolution in Teams: A Close Look at the Links Between Conflict, Conflict Management Strategies, and Team Outcomes," *Journal of Applied Psychology*, 2008, Vol. 93, No. 1, pp. 170–188.

41 "Solving Conflicts in the Workplace Without Making Losers," *Wall Street Journal*, May 27, 1997, p. B1.

42 "Teaching Business How to Cope with Workplace Conflicts," *BusinessWeek*, February 18, 1990, pp. 136, 139.

43 See Kimberly Wade-Benzoni, Andrew Hoffman, Leigh Thompson, Don Moore, James Gillespie, and Max Bazerman, "Barriers to Resolution in Ideologically Based Negotiations: The Role of Values and Institutions," *Academy of Management Review*, 2002, Vol. 27, No. 1, pp. 41–57.

44 J. Z. Rubin and B. R. Brown, *The Social Psychology of Bargaining and Negotiation* (New York: Academic Press, 1975).

45 R. J. Lewicki and J. A. Litterer, *Negotiation* (Homewood, IL: Irwin, 1985).

46 Howard Raiffa, *The Art and Science of Negotiation* (Cambridge, MA: Belknap, 1982).

47 K. H. Bazerman and M. A. Neale, *Negotiating Rationally* (New York: Free Press, 1992).

Name Index

A

Aaron, Sally, 3
Aberham, Matt, 530–531
Aboulafia, Richard, 305
Agee, Bill, 634
Agon, Jean-Paul, 204
Alexander, Nanceen, 626
Anderson, Paul, 144
Armstrong, Jack, 611–612

B

Babbage, Charles, 30
Babiak, Paul, 445
Baesler, Randy, 218
Baker, Nicholson, 629
Baldridge, Malcolm, 302
Barnard, Charles, 32
Barnard, Kurt, 276
Barnes, Richard, 158
Barrett, Craig, 640
Benedict XVI, 4
Berman, Francine, 326
Bezos, Jeff, 15, 560, 627
Bhargava, Swati, 460
Bich, Marcel, 243
Biden, Joe, 302
Blake, Robert R., 509
Blanchard, Ken, 394
Bloom, Diana, 635
Blumenthal, Neil, 243
Bonaparte, Napoleon, 223
Booth, Lewis, 161
Branson, Richard, 355
Brin, Sergey, 6, 10, 13, 18
Brooks, Carl, 523
Brooks, Rodney, 295
Brown, Debra, 297
Brown, Jerry, 135
Brudney, James, 419
Brymer, George, 52

Budwig, Darin, 184
Buffett, Warren, 45
Burke, Diana, 141
Burke, Joseph, 572
Burns, Tom, 373
Burns, Ursula, 4, 423
Bush, George W., 521
Bushnell, David C., 211
Byrd, Robert, 122

C

Caddell, John M., 3
Camilleri, Louis, 95
Capelli, Peter, 619–620
Caputo, Sara, 472
Carabetta, Michael, 350
Carey, Dennis, 518
Carnegie, Andrew, 28
Carroll, Cynthia, 340
Carter, Rob, 277
Cassano, Joseph, 154–155
Cavanagh, Gerald F., 86
Cavanaugh, Teresa, 252
Chaifetz, Richard, 454
Chakravarty, Shoibal, 643
Challenger, John, 438
Chambers, John, 42, 251, 356, 522
Chandler, Alfred, 29
Chao, Natasha, 297
Chassin, Mark R., 557
Chenault, Ken, 524
Chikkatur, Ananth, 643
Christ, Gloria, 635
Churchill, Winston, 28
Clinton, Bill, 521
Coates, Delman, 618
Coffman, Jennifer, 631
Cole, David, 295
Collins, Jim, 45
Conaty, William, 483
Correll, A.D., 391

Covey, Stephen, 45, 581
Cox, Taylor H., 150

D

Daniels, Mitch, 626
Dansereau, Fred, 519
Davis, Melvin, 637
Davis, Ralph C., 351
Davis, Ray, 391
Dell, Michael, 18, 522, 547
Devaney, Earl E., 615–616
DeWitt, Lyle, 326
Dimon, Jamie, 258–259
Disney, Walt, 65, 343
Donald, Jim, 518
Dougherty, Debbie, 421
Drucker, Peter, 640
Dunn, Brian, 13
Dutt, James, 506

E

Ebbers, Bernard, 88, 524–525
Eckert, Scott, 277
Eckstein, Daniel, 622–623
Edison, Thomas, 612
Edmond, Kathleen, 360
Edmunds, Gladys, 253–254
Egidi, Gabriel, 561
Ellis, Charles D., 614
Ellis-Lamkins, Phaedra, 145
Ellison, Larry, 445
Ellison, Lawrence, 174
Elson, Charles, 620
Emerson, Harrington, 30–32
Endlich, Lisa, 614
Engardio, Peter, 370
English, Paul, 292
Espinoza, Luis, 241
Evans, Martin, 513

Organization and Product Index

A

Abercrombie & Fitch, 182, 187, 225, 280, 364–366, 373, 522
Accenture, 236 fig. 10.2
Ace Hardware, 302
Acer, 571
ACS, 625–626
Active Corps of Executives (ACE), 248
Activision, 621–622
Adidas, 60, 160, 224, 563–564
Advanced Micro Devices, 522
Aetna, 22, 236 fig. 10.2
Aflac, 143
AIG, 154–155, 272, 320
Air Canada, 632
Air China, 632
Air France, 632
Airbus, 68, 217–218, 221, 264–265
Albertson's, 60
Alcoa, 100, 176
Alitalia, 632
Allergan, 351
Alliance Entertainment Corporation, 246
Allkauf, 62
Allstate, 394
Amazon.com, 15, 89, 189, 238, 251–252, 302, 627–628
America Online, 326
American Airlines, 216, 289, 302, 325, 402, 632
American Cyanamid, 344, 380
American Eagle Outfitters, 187
American Express, 68, 108, 143, 281
American Productivity and Quality Center (APQC), 620
AMF-Head, 195 table 8.3
AMR, 631–632
Anderen Bank, 344–345
Anglo American, 340–341
Anheuser-Busch, 434
Ann Taylor, 265–266

Apple Computer, 21, 67, 74, 243, 247, 302, 404–405, 409, 562, 571, 619–620
Aramark, 88
Asda, 114
Ask.com, 328
AT&T, 28, 71, 344, 426, 461, 489
AutoZone, 355
Avis, 289
Avon Products, 172
A&W, 199
AXA, 128 table 5.2

B

Ball Corporation, 67
Bang & Olufsen, 110
Bank of America, 64, 128 table 5.2, 522
Basel Action Network (BAN), 62
Bath & Body Works, 160
Beatrice Company, 506
Bed, Bath, and Beyond, 60
Beecham Group, 575
Ben & Jerry's Homemade Holdings, 94, 200, 432
Benetton, 291
Berkshire Hathaway, 128 table 5.2
Best Buy, 13, 28, 60, 236, 360, 464
BET, 618–619
Bethlehem Steel, 31, 289, 344
BFGoodrich, 402
BIC, 188 table 8.1, 192
Bigfoot Entertainment, 232–233
Bigstep, 251
Black & Decker, 28, 169, 176
Black Entertainment Television, 618
Blockbuster, 3, 249
Bloomingdale's, 191
BMW, 18, 199, 203
Boeing, 18, 56, 58, 68, 164, 176, 194, 195 table 8.3, 217, 219, 221, 243, 261, 291, 299, 305, 436, 550

Boise Cascade, 434
Borland International, 517
Boston Consulting Group, 198 fig. 8.3, 199
Bowditch & Dewey, 638
BP, 112, 128 table 5.2, 277, 644
BP Amoco, 101, 489
BP Exploration, 438
British Airways, 68, 216, 394
British Telecom, 305
Burger King, 60
Burlington Industries, 542
Burlington Northern, 359

C

Cadbury PLC, 262, 351
Cadbury Schweppes, 168
Calvin Klein, 191
Campbell Soup Company, 72, 197, 241
Canon, 406, 427, 536
CarMax, 143
Carnation Company, 112, 127
Carnett's Car Wash, 198
Carnival Cruise Line, 60
Case Corporation, 353
Caterpillar, 18, 108, 164, 176, 186, 236 fig. 10.2, 309, 391–392, 395
Cathway, 632
CBS, 18, 164, 359
Celebrity Cruise Lines, 71
Center for the Study of Responsive Law, 62
Century 21 Real Estate, 18
Cereal Partners Worldwide, 111
Challenger, Gray, & Christmas, 438
Champion Spark Plug Company, 278–279
Chanel, 191
Chaparral Steel, 432
Charles Wells Brewery, 111
Chase Manhattan Bank, 380
Chevrolet, 281
Chevron, 94, 108, 128 table 5.2, 374

Subject Index